Visual C++® 2008

How to Program

SECOND EDITION

Deitel® Ser

How To Program Series

Internet & World Wide Web How to Program, 4/E

Java How to Program, 7/E

C++ How to Program, 6/E

C How to Program, 5/E

Visual Basic® 2005 How to Program, 3/E

Visual C#® 2005 How to Program, 2/E

Small Java™ How to Program, 6/E

Small C++ How to Program, 5/E

Advanced Java™ 2 Platform How to Program

XML How to Program

Visual C++® 2008 How to Program, 2/E

Perl How to Program

Python How to Program

Simply Series

Simply C++: An Application-Driven
Tutorial Approach

Simply C#: An Application-Driven
Tutorial Approach

Simply Java™ Programming: An
Application-Driven Tutorial
Approach

Simply Visual Basic® 2005, 2/E: An
Application-Driven Tutorial
Approach

ies Page

SafariX Web Books

www.deitel.com/books/SafariX.html

C++ How to Program, 5/E & 6/E

Java How to Program, 6/E & 7/E

Simply C++: An Application-Driven
  Tutorial Approach

Simply Visual Basic 2005: An Application-
  Driven Tutorial Approach, 2/E

Small C++ How to Program, 5/E

Small Java How to Program, 6/E

Visual Basic 2005 How to Program, 3/E

Visual C# 2005 How to Program, 2/E

To follow the Deitel publishing program, please register for the free *Deitel® Buzz Online* e-mail newsletter at:

> www.deitel.com/newsletter/subscribe.html

To communicate with the authors, send e-mail to:

> deitel@deitel.com

For information on corporate on-site seminars offered by Deitel & Associates, Inc. worldwide, visit:

> www.deitel.com/training/

or write to

> deitel@deitel.com

For continuing updates on Prentice Hall/Deitel publications visit:

> www.deitel.com
> www.prenhall.com/deitel

Check out our Resource Centers for valuable web resources that will help you master C++, other important programming languages, software and Web 2.0 topics:

> www.deitel.com/ResourceCenters.html

Library of Congress Cataloging-in-Publication Data
On file

Vice President and Editorial Director, ECS: *Marcia J. Horton*
Associate Editor: *Carole Snyder*
Supervisor/Editorial Assistant: *Dolores Mars*
Director of Team-Based Project Management: *Vince O'Brien*
Senior Managing Editor: *Scott Disanno*
Managing Editor: *Robert Engelhardt*
Production Editor: *Marta Samsel*
A/V Production Editor: *Greg Dulles*
Art Studio: *Artworks, York, PA*
Art Director: *Kristine Carney*
Cover Design: *Abbey S. Deitel, Harvey M. Deitel, Francesco Santalucia, Kristine Carney*
Interior Design: *Harvey M. Deitel, Kristine Carney*
Manufacturing Manager: *Alexis Heydt-Long*
Manufacturing Buyer: *Lisa McDowell*
Director of Marketing: *Margaret Waples*

© 2008 by Pearson Education, Inc.
Upper Saddle River, New Jersey 07458

Printed in the United States of America

10 9 8 7 6 5 4 3 2 1

ISBN 0-13-615157-4

Pearson Education Ltd., *London*
Pearson Education Australia Pty. Ltd., *Sydney*
Pearson Education Singapore, Pte. Ltd.
Pearson Education North Asia Ltd., *Hong Kong*
Pearson Education Canada, Inc., *Toronto*
Pearson Educación de Mexico, S.A. de C.V.
Pearson Education–Japan, *Tokyo*
Pearson Education Malaysia, Pte. Ltd.
Pearson Education, Inc., *Upper Saddle River, New Jersey*

Visual C++® 2008
HOW TO PROGRAM

SECOND EDITION

P. J. Deitel

Deitel & Associates, Inc.

H. M. Deitel

Deitel & Associates, Inc.

D. T. Quirk

Upper Saddle River, New Jersey 07458

Trademarks

In memory of John Backus:

For your vision of a language that would simplify programming and for realizing that vision by leading the IBM team that created Fortran, the world's first widely used high-level programming language, in 1957. We owe our careers as programming-language book authors and educators to your foresight.

Paul and Harvey Deitel

To Mom and Dad:

For all your love and support through the years.

Dan

Deitel Resource Centers

Our Resource Centers focus on the vast amounts of free content available online. Find resources, downloads, tutorials, documentation, books, e-books, journals, articles, blogs, RSS feeds and more on many of today's hottest programming and technology topics. For the most up-to-date list of our Resource Centers, visit:

www.deitel.com/ResourceCenters.html

Let us know what other Resource Centers you'd like to see! Also, please register for the free *Deitel®Buzz Online* e-mail newsletter at:

www.deitel.com/newsletter/subscribe.html

Computer Science
Regular Expressions

Programming
ASP.NET 3.5
Adobe Flex
Ajax
Apex
ASP.NET Ajax
ASP.NET
C
C++
C++ Boost Libraries
C++ Game Programming
C#
Code Search Engines and Code Sites
Computer Game Programming
CSS 2.1
Dojo
Facebook Developer Platform
Flash 9
Java
Java Certification and Assessment Testing
Java Design Patterns
Java EE 5
Java SE 6
Java SE 7 (Dolphin) Resource Center
JavaFX
JavaScript
JSON
Microsoft LINQ
Microsoft Popfly
.NET
.NET 3.0
.NET 3.5
OpenGL
Perl
PHP
Programming Projects
Python
Regular Expressions
Ruby
Ruby on Rails
Silverlight

Visual Basic
Visual C++
Visual Studio Team System
Web 3D Technologies
Web Services
Windows Presentation Foundation
XHTML
XML

Games and Game Programming
Computer Game Programming
Computer Games
Mobile Gaming
Sudoku

Internet Business
Affiliate Programs
Competitive Analysis
Facebook Social Ads
Google AdSense
Google Analytics
Google Services
Internet Advertising
Internet Business Initiative
Internet Public Relations
Link Building
Location-Based Services
Online Lead Generation
Podcasting
Search Engine Optimization
Selling Digital Content
Sitemaps
Web Analytics
Website Monetization
YouTube and AdSense

Java
Java
Java Certification and Assessment Testing
Java Design Patterns
Java EE 5
Java SE 6

Java SE 7 (Dolphin) Resource Center
JavaFX

Microsoft
ASP.NET
ASP.NET 3.5
ASP.NET Ajax
C#
DotNetNuke (DNN)
Internet Explorer 7 (IE7)
Microsoft LINQ
.NET
.NET 3.0
.NET 3.5
SharePoint
Silverlight
Visual Basic
Visual C++
Visual Studio Team System
Windows Presentation Foundation
Windows Vista
Microsoft Popfly

Open Source & LAMP Stack
Apache
DotNetNuke (DNN)
Eclipse
Firefox
Linux
MySQL
Open Source
Perl
PHP
Python
Ruby

Software
Apache
DotNetNuke (DNN)
Eclipse
Firefox
Internet Explorer 7 (IE7)
Linux
MySQL
Open Source

Search Engines
SharePoint
Skype
Web Servers
Wikis
Windows Vista

Web 2.0
Alert Services
Attention Economy
Blogging
Building Web Communities
Community Generated Content
Facebook Developer Platform
Facebook Social Ads
Google Base
Google Video
Google Web Toolkit (GWT)
Internet Video
Joost
Location-Based Services
Mashups
Microformats
Recommender Systems
RSS
Social Graph
Social Media
Social Networking
Software as a Service (SaaS)
Virtural Worlds
Web 2.0
Web 3.0
Widgets

Dive Into Web 2.0 eBook
Web 2 eBook

Other Topics
Computer Games
Computing Jobs
Gadgets and Gizmos
Ring Tones
Sudoku

Contents

10 Classes: A Deeper Look, Part I 541

11 Classes: A Deeper Look, Part 2 586

18   Files and Streams in .NET   975

19   Class `string` and String Stream Processing   1004

20 Searching and Sorting   1060

21 Data Structures   1083

22 Bits, Characters, C Strings and `structs`   1142

23 Standard Template Library (STL)   1195

Preface

"The chief merit of language is clearness ..."
—Galen

Welcome to Visual C++ 2008 and *Visual C++ 2008 How to Program, Second Edition*! At Deitel & Associates, we write programming language textbooks and professional books for Prentice Hall, deliver corporate training courses worldwide and develop Web 2.0 Internet businesses. This book reflects significant changes to the Visual C++ language and to the preferred ways of teaching and learning programming. The book is based on our C++-standard-compliant textbook *C++ How to Program, Sixth Edition* and is intended for courses that offer a Microsoft-specific C++ programming focus.

Since the first edition of *Visual C++ How to Program*, Microsoft has changed the way C++ interacts with the .NET Framework—the Managed Extensions to C++ have been replaced by the cleaner C++/CLI. Deitel has also refined the pedagogy used in its books since the first edition of *Visual C++ How to Program*. Consequently, all the chapters have undergone significant updates and tuning. If you're interested in learning Visual C++ using Microsoft's Visual Studio Integrated Development Environment (IDE) and the .NET Framework, then this book is for you.

New and Updated Features

Here's the updates we've made to the second edition of *Visual C++ 2008 How to Program*:

- **Early Classes and Objects Approach.** Students are introduced to the basic concepts and terminology of object technology in Chapter 1 and begin developing customized, reusable classes and objects in Chapter 4, using native C++ and managed code with C++/CLI. This book presents object-oriented programming, where appropriate, from the start and throughout the text. The early discussion of objects and classes gets students "thinking about objects" immediately and mastering these concepts more completely. Object-oriented programming is not trivial by any means, but it's fun to write object-oriented programs, and students can see immediate results.

- **New Native-Code Approach.** Microsoft has determined that most Visual C++ developers do the majority of their programming in native C++. As a result, this edition of the book represents a major overhaul in approach from the first edition. We now introduce new programming concepts first with native C++ followed by managed code sections with C++/CLI, where appropriate. We worked closely with members of Microsoft's Visual C++ team and determined that this was the best approach for this new edition.

- **Major Content Revisions and Updates for the .NET Framework.** All the chapters have been significantly updated and upgraded. We added sections and chapters introducing managed code concepts with C++/CLI. We tuned the writing for clarity and precision and adjusted our use of Visual C++ terminology in accordance with the ISO/IEC standard document that defines the C++ language.

- **Introduction to the Visual C++ 2008 Express IDE and the Visual Studio Debugger.** Chapter 2 provides a detailed tutorial on using the Visual C++ Express 2008 Integrated Development Environment to create and run native C++ and .NET projects. Appendix H, explains the basics of debugging programs using Visual C++ Express 2008. You can download Visual C++ 2008 Express from www.microsoft.com/express/vc/.

- **The Managed Heap and CLR Garbage Collector.** Chapters 9 and 11 include new sections on the managed heap, the CLR garbage collector, and memory management in .NET. We introduce handles and tracking references for using managed objects with C++/CLI.

- **New Content on the .NET Framework Class Library (FCL).** New sections introducing managed code concepts with C++/CLI use numerous classes from the .NET Framework Class Library. Chapter 18 teaches file processing in .NET using the File and Directory classes. Chapter 19 provides an in-depth look at classes String, StringBuilder and Char. Chapter 25 focuses exclusively on collections in the .NET Framework using FCL classes.

- **Exception Handling in .NET.** After introducing exception handling in native C++, Chapter 16 introduces the .NET Exception class hierarchy. We demonstrate the use of finally and stack semantics for writing safer C++/CLI code.

- **Templates and Generics.** New sections in Chapter 15 introduce managed templates in C++/CLI as well as .NET generics. We compare and contrast the strengths and weaknesses of both types of generic programming.

- **Integrated Case Studies.** We provide several case studies spanning multiple sections and chapters that often build on a class introduced earlier in the book to demonstrate new programming concepts later in the book. These case studies include the development of a GradeBook class in Chapters 4–8, a Time class in several sections of Chapters 10–11, an Employee class in Chapters 13–14, and the optional OOD/UML ATM case study in Chapters 1, 3–8, 10, 14 and Appendix F.

- **Integrated GradeBook Case Study.** The GradeBook case study reinforces our early classes presentation. It uses classes and objects in Chapters 4–8 to incrementally build a GradeBook class that represents an instructor's grade book and performs various calculations based on a set of student grades, such as calculating the average grade, finding the maximum and minimum, and printing a bar chart.

- **Unified Modeling Language™ 2 (UML 2).** The Unified Modeling Language (UML) has become the preferred graphical modeling language for designers of object-oriented systems. All the UML diagrams in the book comply with the UML 2 specification. We use UML class diagrams to visually represent classes and their inheritance relationships, and we use UML activity diagrams to demonstrate the flow of control in each of Visual C++'s control statements. We use the UML extensively in the optional OOD/UML ATM case study.

- **Optional OOD/UML ATM Case Study.** The optional OOD/UML automated teller machine (ATM) case study in the Software Engineering Case Study sections of Chapters 1, 3–8, 10 and 14 is appropriate for first and second programming courses. The case study sections present a carefully paced introduction to object-oriented design using the UML. We introduce a concise, simplified subset of the UML 2, then guide you through a first design experience intended for the novice object-oriented designer/programmer. Our goal in this case study is to help students develop an object-oriented design to complement the object-oriented programming concepts they begin learning in Chapter 1 and implementing in Chapter 4. The case study was reviewed by a distinguished team of OOD/UML academic and industry professionals. The case study is not an exercise; rather, it is a fully developed end-to-end learning experience that concludes with a detailed walkthrough of the complete 877-line C++ code implementation. We take a detailed tour of the case study later in the Preface.

- **Compilation and Linking Process for Multiple-Source-File Programs.** Chapter 4 includes a detailed diagram and discussion of the compilation and linking process that produces an executable application.

- **Function Call Stack Explanation.** In Chapter 7, we provide a detailed discussion (with illustrations) of the function-call stack and activation records to explain how Visual C++ is able to keep track of which function is currently executing, how automatic variables of functions are maintained in memory, and how a function knows where to return after it completes execution.

- **C++ Standard Library `string` and `vector` Classes.** The `string` and `vector` classes are used to make earlier examples more object-oriented.

- **Class `string`.** We use class `string` instead of C-like pointer-based `char *` strings for most string manipulations throughout the book. We continue to include discussions of `char *` strings in Chapters 9, 11, 12 and 22 to give students practice with pointer manipulations, to illustrate dynamic memory allocation with `new` and `delete`, to build our own `String` class, and to prepare students for working with `char *` strings in C and C++ legacy code.

- **Class Template `vector`.** We use class template `vector` instead of C-like pointer-based array manipulations throughout the book. However, we begin by discussing C-like pointer-based arrays in Chapter 8 to prepare students for working with C and C++ legacy code and to establish a basis for building our own customized `Array` class in Chapter 12.

- **Tuned Treatment of Inheritance and Polymorphism.** Chapters 13–14 have been carefully tuned using an `Employee` class hierarchy to make the treatment of inheritance and polymorphism clearer, more natural and more accessible for students who are new to OOP.

- **Discussion and Illustration of How Polymorphism Works "Under the Hood."** Chapter 14 contains a detailed diagram and explanation of how Visual C++ can implement polymorphism, `virtual` functions and dynamic binding internally. This gives students a solid understanding of how these capabilities really work. More importantly, it helps students appreciate the overhead of polymorphism—in terms of additional memory consumption and processor time. This helps students determine when to use polymorphism and when to avoid it.

- **Standard Template Library (STL).** This might be one of the most important topics in the book in terms of your appreciation of software reuse. The STL defines powerful, template-based, reusable components that implement many common data structures and algorithms used to process those data structures. Chapter 23 introduces the STL and discusses its three key components—containers, iterators and algorithms. We show that using STL components provides tremendous expressive power, often reducing many lines of code to a single statement. We also introduce the STL/CLR, a new Microsoft library enabling managed code with C++/CLI to leverage the power of STL containers and algorithms.

- **ISO/IEC C++ Standard Compliance.** We have audited our presentation against the most recent ISO/IEC C++ standard document for completeness and accuracy. [*Note:* A PDF copy of the C++ standard (document number INCITS/ISO/IEC 14882-2003) can be purchased at `webstore.ansi.org/ansidocstore/default.asp`.]

All of this has been carefully reviewed by distinguished academics and industry developers who worked with us on *C++ How to Program, Sixth Edition* and *Visual C++ 2008 How to Program*.

We believe that this book and its support materials will provide students and professionals with an informative, interesting, challenging and entertaining Visual C++ educational experience. We also provide a suite of ancillary materials that help instructors maximize their students' learning experience.

As you read the book, if you have questions, send an e-mail to `deitel@deitel.com`; we'll respond promptly. For updates on this book and the status of all supporting Visual C++ software, and for the latest news on all Deitel publications and services, visit `www.deitel.com`. Sign up at `www.deitel.com/newsletter/subscribe.html` for the free *Deitel*® *Buzz Online* e-mail newsletter and check out our growing list of Visual C++ and related Resource Centers at `www.deitel.com/ResourceCenters.html`. Each week we announce our latest Resource Centers in the newsletter. Please let us know of other Resource Centers you'd like to see.

Dependency Chart

Figure 1 illustrates the dependencies that exist between chapters in the book. An arrow pointing into a chapter indicates that the chapter depends on the content of the chapter from which the arrow points. We recommend that you study all of a given chapter's dependencies before studying that chapter, though other orders are possible. Some of the dependencies apply only to sections of chapters, so we advise readers to browse the material before designing a course of study. We've also commented on some additional dependencies in the diagram's footnotes. This book is intended for courses that prefer a more Microsoft-specific C++ focus and that mix and match some native C++ and some managed C++.

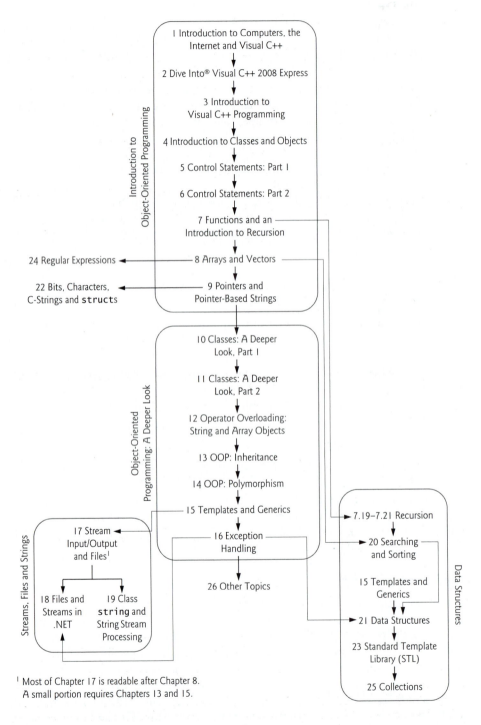

Fig. 1 | *Visual C++ 2008 How to Program, 2/e* chapter dependency chart.

Teaching Approach

Visual C++ 2008 How to Program, 2/e contains a rich collection of examples. The book concentrates on the principles of good software engineering and stresses program clarity. We teach by example. We are educators who teach leading-edge topics in industry classrooms worldwide. Dr. Harvey M. Deitel has 20 years of college teaching experience and 18 years of industry teaching experience. Paul Deitel has 16 years of industry teaching experience. The Deitels have taught courses at all levels to government, industry, military and academic clients of Deitel & Associates.

Live-Code Approach. Visual C++ 2008 How to Program, 2/e is loaded with "live-code" examples—by this we mean that each new concept is presented in the context of a complete working Visual C++ program that is immediately followed by one or more actual executions showing the program's inputs and outputs. This style exemplifies the way we teach and write about programming; we call this the "live-code approach."

Syntax Shading. We syntax shade all the Visual C++ code, similar to the way Visual Studio syntax colors code. This improves code readability—an important goal, given that the book contains about 19,000 lines of code in complete, working Visual C++ programs. Our syntax-shading conventions are as follows:

```
comments appear in italic
keywords appear in bold italic
errors appear in bold black
constants and literal values appear in bold, gray
all other code appears in plain black
```

Code Highlighting. We place gray rectangles around the key code segments in each program.

Programming Tips. We include programming tips to help you focus on important aspects of program development. These tips and practices represent the best we have gleaned from a combined six decades of programming and teaching experience. One of our students—a mathematics major—told us that she feels this approach is like the highlighting of axioms, theorems and corollaries in mathematics books; it provides a basis on which to build good software.

Good Programming Practice

Good Programming Practices *call attention to techniques that will help you produce programs that are clearer, more understandable and more maintainable.*

Common Programming Error

Students tend to make certain kinds of errors frequently. Pointing out these Common Programming Errors *reduces the likelihood that you'll make the same mistakes.*

Error-Prevention Tip

These tips contain suggestions for exposing bugs and removing them from your programs; many describe aspects of Visual C++ that prevent bugs from getting into programs in the first place.

Performance Tip

Students like to "turbo charge" their programs. These tips highlight opportunities for making your programs run faster or minimizing the amount of memory that they occupy.

Portability Tip

We include Portability Tips *to help you write code that will run on a variety of platforms and to explain how Visual C++ achieves its high degree of portability.*

Software Engineering Observation

The Software Engineering Observations *highlight architectural and design issues that affect the construction of software systems, especially large-scale systems.*

Using Fonts and Colors for Emphasis. We place the key terms and the index's page reference for each defining occurrence in *bold italic* text for easier reference. We emphasize on-screen components in the **bold Helvetica** font (e.g., the **File** menu) and emphasize Visual C++ program text in the Lucida font (e.g., int x = 5).

Web Access. All of the source-code examples for *Visual C++ 2008 How to Program, 2/e* are available for download from:

www.deitel.com/books/vcpphtp2/

Site registration is quick and easy. Download all the examples, then run each program as you read the corresponding text discussions. Making changes to the examples and seeing the effects of those changes is a great way to enhance your Visual C++ learning experience.

Objectives. Each chapter begins with a statement of objectives. This lets you know what to expect and gives you an opportunity, after reading the chapter, to determine if you have met the objectives.

Quotations. The learning objectives are followed by quotations. Some are humorous; some are philosophical; others offer interesting insights. We hope that you enjoy relating the quotations to the chapter material.

Outline. The chapter outline helps you approach the material in a top-down fashion, so you can anticipate what is to come and set a comfortable and effective learning pace.

Illustrations/Figures. Abundant charts, tables, line drawings, programs and program output are included. We model the flow of control in control statements with UML activity diagrams. UML class diagrams model the fields, constructors and methods of classes. We make extensive use of six major UML diagram types in the optional OOD/UML 2 ATM case study.

Wrap-Up Section. Each of the chapters ends with a brief "wrap-up" section that recaps the chapter content and transitions to the next chapter.

Summary Bullets. Each chapter ends with additional pedagogical features. We present a thorough, bullet-list-style summary of the chapter, section by section.

Terminology. We include an alphabetized list of the important terms defined in each chapter. Each term also appears in the index, with its defining occurrence highlighted with a *bold, italic* page number.

Self-Review Exercises and Answers. Extensive self-review exercises and answers are included for self-study.

Exercises. Each chapter concludes with a set of exercises including simple recall of important terminology and concepts; identifying the errors in code samples; writing individual Visual C++ statements; writing small portions of functions and classes; writing complete Visual C++ functions, classes and programs; and writing major term projects. The large number of exercises enables instructors to tailor their courses to the unique needs of their students and to vary course assignments each semester. Instructors can use these exercises to form homework assignments, short quizzes, major examinations and term projects. See our Programming Projects Resource Center (www.deitel.com/ProgrammingProjects/) for many additional exercise and project possibilities.

[*NOTE:* **Please do not write to us requesting access to the Prentice Hall Instructor's Resource Center, which contains the exercise solutions and the book's ancillaries. Access is limited strictly to college instructors teaching from the book. Instructors may obtain access only through their Prentice Hall representatives.**]

Thousands of Index Entries. We have included an extensive index which is especially useful when you use the book as a reference.

"Double Indexing" of Visual C++ Live-Code Examples. For every source-code program in the book, we index the figure caption both alphabetically and as a subindex item under "Examples." This makes it easier to find examples using particular features.

Object-Oriented Design of an ATM with the UML: A Tour of the Optional Software Engineering Case Study

In this section, we tour the book's optional case study of object-oriented design with the UML. This tour previews the contents of the ten Software Engineering Case Study sections (in Chapters 1, 3–8, 10, 14 and Appendix F). After completing this case study, you'll be thoroughly familiar with a carefully reviewed object-oriented design and implementation for a significant C++ application.

The design presented in the ATM case study was developed at Deitel & Associates, Inc. and scrutinized by a distinguished developmental review team of industry professionals and academics. We crafted this design to meet the requirements of introductory course sequences. Real ATM systems used by banks and their customers worldwide are based on more sophisticated designs that take into consideration many more issues than we have addressed here. Our primary goal throughout the design process was to create a simple design that would be clear to OOD and UML novices, while still demonstrating key OOD concepts and the related UML modeling techniques. We worked hard to keep the design and the code relatively small so that it would work well in the introductory course sequence.

Section 1.21, (Only Required Section of the Case Study) Software Engineering Case Study: Introduction to Object Technology and the UML—introduces the object-oriented design case study with the UML. The section introduces the basic object technology concepts and terminology, including classes, objects, encapsulation, inheritance and polymorphism. We discuss the history of the UML. This is the case study's only required section.

Section 3.8, (Optional) Software Engineering Case Study: Examining the ATM Requirements Specification—discusses a *requirements specification* that specifies the requirements for a system that we'll design and implement—the software for a simple automated teller machine (ATM). We investigate the structure and behavior of object-oriented systems in general. We discuss how the UML will facilitate the design process in subsequent Software Engineering Case Study sections by providing several additional types of diagrams to model our system. We include a list of URLs and book references on object-oriented design with the UML. We discuss the interaction between the ATM system specified by the requirements specification and its user. Specifically, we investigate the scenarios that may occur between the user and the system itself—these are called *use cases*. We model these interactions, using *use case diagrams* of the UML.

Section 4.13, (Optional) Software Engineering Case Study: Identifying the Classes in the ATM Requirements Specification—begins to design the ATM system. We identify its classes, or "building blocks," by extracting the nouns and noun phrases from the requirements specification. We arrange these classes into a UML class diagram that describes the class structure of our simulation. The class diagram also describes relationships, known as *associations*, among classes.

Section 5.13, (Optional) Software Engineering Case Study: Identifying Class Attributes in the ATM System—focuses on the attributes of the classes discussed in Section 4.13. A class contains both *attributes* (data) and *operations* (behaviors). As we'll see in later sections, changes in an object's attributes often affect the object's behavior. To determine the attributes for the classes in our case study, we extract the adjectives describing the nouns and noun phrases (which defined our classes) from the requirements specification, then place the attributes in the class diagram we created in Section 4.13.

Section 6.11, (Optional) Software Engineering Case Study: Identifying Objects' States and Activities in the ATM System—discusses how an object, at any given time, occupies a specific condition called a *state*. A *state transition* occurs when that object receives a message to change state. The UML provides the *state machine diagram*, which identifies the set of possible states that an object may occupy and models that object's state transitions. An object also has an *activity*—the work it performs in its lifetime. The UML provides the *activity diagram*—a flowchart that models an object's activity. In this section, we use both types of diagrams to begin modeling specific behavioral aspects of our ATM system, such as how the ATM carries out a withdrawal transaction and how the ATM responds when the user is authenticated.

Section 7.23, (Optional) Software Engineering Case Study: Identifying Class Operations in the ATM System—identifies the operations, or services, of our classes. We extract from the requirements specification the verbs and verb phrases that specify the operations for each class. We then modify the class diagram of Section 4.13 to include each operation with its associated class. At this point in the case study, we will have gathered all information possible from the requirements specification. However, as future chapters introduce such topics as inheritance, we'll modify our classes and diagrams.

Section 8.15, (Optional) Software Engineering Case Study: Collaboration Among Objects in the ATM System—provides a "rough sketch" of the model for our ATM system. In this section, we see how it works. We investigate the behavior of the simulation by discussing *collaborations*—messages that objects send to each other to communicate. The class operations that we discovered in Section 7.23 turn out to be the collaborations among the objects in our system. We determine the collaborations, then collect them into a *communication diagram*—the UML diagram for modeling collaborations. This diagram reveals which objects collaborate and when. We present a communication diagram of the collaborations among objects to perform an ATM balance inquiry. We then present the

UML *sequence diagram* for modeling interactions in a system. This diagram emphasizes the chronological ordering of messages. A sequence diagram models how objects in the system interact to carry out withdrawal and deposit transactions.

Section 10.12, (Optional) Software Engineering Case Study: Starting to Program the Classes of the ATM System—takes a break from designing the system's behavior. We begin the implementation process to emphasize the material discussed in Chapter 10. Using the UML class diagram of Section 4.13 and the attributes and operations discussed in Section 5.13 and Section 7.23, we show how to implement a class in C++ from a design. We do not implement all classes—because we have not completed the design process. Working from our UML diagrams, we create code for the Withdrawal class.

Section 14.11, (Optional) Software Engineering Case Study: Incorporating Inheritance into the ATM System—continues our discussion of object-oriented programming. We consider inheritance—classes sharing common characteristics may inherit attributes and operations from a "base" class. In this section, we investigate how our ATM system can benefit from using inheritance. We document our discoveries in a class diagram that models inheritance relationships—the UML refers to these relationships as *generalizations*. We modify the class diagram of Section 4.13 by using inheritance to group classes with similar characteristics. This section concludes the design of the model portion of our simulation. We fully implement this model in 877 lines of C++ code in Appendix F.

Appendix F, ATM Case Study Code—The majority of the case study involves designing the model (i.e., the data and logic) of the ATM system. In this appendix, we implement that model in C++. Using all the UML diagrams we created, we present the C++ classes necessary to implement the model. We apply the concepts of object-oriented design with the UML and object-oriented programming in C++ that you learned in the chapters. By the end of this appendix, students will have completed the design and implementation of a real-world system, and should feel confident tackling larger systems, such as those that professional software engineers build.

Appendix G, UML 2: Additional Diagram Types—Overviews the UML 2 diagram types that are not found in the OOD/UML Case Study.

Instructor Resources for *Visual C++ 2008 How to Program, 2/e*

Visual C++ 2008 How to Program, 2/e has extensive instructor resources. The Prentice Hall *Instructor's Resource Center* contains the *Solutions Manual* with solutions to the vast majority of the end-of-chapter exercises, a *Test Item File* of multiple-choice questions (approximately two per book section) and PowerPoint® slides containing the code and figures in the text, plus bulleted items that summarize the key points in the text. Instructors can customize the slides. If you are not already a registered faculty member, contact your Prentice Hall representative or visit vig.prenhall.com/replocator/.

[*NOTE:* Please do not write to us requesting access to the Prentice Hall Instructor's Resource Center, which contains the exercise solutions and the book's ancillaries. Access is limited strictly to college instructors teaching from the book. Instructors may obtain access only through their Prentice Hall representatives.]

Ordering Option for the Education Market

Instructors can order this book packaged with Microsoft Visual C++ 2008 Express for their students. The ISBN for this value pack is 0-13-712940-8.

Deitel® Buzz Online Free E-mail Newsletter

Each week, the *Deitel® Buzz Online* newsletter announces our latest Resource Center(s) and includes commentary on industry trends and developments, links to free articles and resources from our published books and upcoming publications, product-release schedules, errata, challenges, anecdotes, information on our corporate instructor-led training courses and more. It's also a good way for you to keep posted about issues related to *Visual C++ 2008 How to Program, 2/e.* To subscribe, visit

> www.deitel.com/newsletter/subscribe.html

The Deitel Online Resource Centers

Our website www.deitel.com provides Resource Centers on various topics including programming languages, software, Web 2.0, Internet business and open source projects. (You can see the complete list of Resource Centers in the first few pages of this book.) The Resource Centers evolved out of the research we've done for our books and business endeavors. We've found many exceptional resources online including tutorials, documentation, software downloads, articles, blogs, videos, code samples, books, e-books and more. Most of them are free. In the spirit of Web 2.0, we share these resources with the worldwide community. The Deitel Resource Centers are a starting point for your own research. We help you wade through the vast amount of content on the Internet by providing links to the most valuable resources. Each week we announce our latest Resource Centers in our newsletter, the *Deitel® Buzz Online* (www.deitel.com/newsletter/subscribe.html). The following Resource Centers may be of interest to you as you study *Visual C++ 2008 How to Program, 2/e*:

- Visual C++
- Visual Studio Team System
- C++
- C++ Boost Libraries
- C++ Game Programming
- Code Search Engines and Code Sites
- Computer Game Programming
- Computing Jobs
- Open Source
- Programming Projects
- Eclipse
- .NET
- .NET 3.0
- .NET 3.5
- Windows Vista

Acknowledgments

It is a pleasure to acknowledge the efforts of many people whose names may not appear on the cover, but whose hard work, cooperation, friendship and understanding were crucial to the production of the book. Many people at Deitel & Associates, Inc. devoted long hours to this project—thanks especially to Abbey Deitel and Barbara Deitel.

We'd also like to thank one of the participants in our Honors Internship program who made significant contributions to this publication—Greg Ayer, a computer science major at Northeastern University. Greg worked on the Collections chapter and the discussion of .NET generics in the Templates and Generics chapter. He also significantly updated the Regular Expressions chapter.

We are fortunate to have worked on this project with the talented and dedicated team of publishing professionals at Prentice Hall. We appreciate the extraordinary efforts of Marcia Horton, Editorial Director of Prentice Hall's Engineering and Computer Science Division. Carole Snyder and Dolores Mars did an extraordinary job recruiting the book's review team and managing the review process. Francesco Santalucia (an independent artist) and Kristine Carney of Prentice Hall did a wonderful job designing the book's cover—we provided the concept, and they made it happen. Bob Engelhardt and Marta Samsel did a marvelous job managing the book's production.

We wish to acknowledge the efforts of our reviewers. Adhering to a tight time schedule, they scrutinized the text and the programs, providing countless suggestions for improving the accuracy and completeness of the presentation.

We sincerely appreciate the efforts of our reviewers:

Visual C++ 2008 How to Program 2/e Reviewers
Microsoft Reviewers: Alvin Chardon, Mykola Dudar, Gordon Hogenson (author of *C++/ CLI: The Visual C++ Language for .NET*; Apress), Vytautas Leonavicius and April Reagan. **Academic Reviewers:** Ronald DiNapoli (Cornell University) and Tim H. Lin (California State Polytechnic University, Pomona).

These reviewers scrutinized every aspect of the text and made countless suggestions for improving the accuracy and completeness of the presentation.

This book is heavily based on *C++ How to Program, 6/e*. We'd like to thank the reviewers of the 5th and 6th editions of that book:

C++ How to Program 6/e Reviewers
Academic and Industry Reviewers: Dr. Richard Albright (Goldey-Beacom College), William B. Higdon (University of Indianapolis), Howard Hinnant (Apple), Anne B. Horton (Lockheed Martin), Terrell Hull (Logicalis Integration Solutions), Rex Jaeschke (Independent Consultant), Maria Jump (The University of Texas at Austin), Geoffrey S. Knauth (GNU), Don Kostuch (Independent Consultant), Colin Laplace (Freelance Software Consultant), Stephan T. Lavavej (Microsoft), Amar Raheja (California State Polytechnic University, Pomona), G. Anthony Reina (University of Maryland University College, Europe), Daveed Vandevoorde (C++ Standards Committee), Jeffrey Wiener (DEKA Research & Development Corporation, New Hampshire Community Technical College), and Chad Willwerth (University of Washington, Tacoma). **Ogre Reviewers:** Casey Borders (Sensis Corp.), Gregory Junker (Author of *Pro OGRE3D Programming*, Apress Books), Mark Pope (THQ, Inc.), and Steve Streeting (Torus Knot Software, Ltd.). **Boost/ C++0X Reviewers:** Edward Brey (Kohler Co.), Jeff Garland (Boost.org), Douglas Gregor (Indiana University), and Björn Karlsson (Author of *Beyond the C++ Standard Library: An Introduction to Boost*, Addison-Wesley/Readsoft, Inc.).

C++ How to Program 5/e Reviewers

Academic Reviewers: Richard Albright (Goldey-Beacom College), Karen Arlien (Bismarck State College), David Branigan (DeVry University, Illinois), Jimmy Chen (Salt Lake Community College), Martin Dulberg (North Carolina State University), Ric Heishman (Northern Virginia Community College), Richard Holladay (San Diego Mesa College), William Honig (Loyola University), Earl LaBatt (OPNET Technologies, Inc./ University of New Hampshire), Brian Larson (Modesto Junior College), Robert Myers (Florida State University), Gavin Osborne (Saskatchewan Institute of Applied Science and Technology), Wolfgang Pelz (The University of Akron), and Donna Reese (Mississippi State University). **Industry Reviewers:** Curtis Green (Boeing Integrated Defense Systems), Mahesh Hariharan (Microsoft), James Huddleston (Independent Consultant), Ed James-Beckham (Borland Software Corporation), Don Kostuch (Independent Consultant), Meng Lee (Hewlett-Packard), Kriang Lerdsuwanakij (Siemens Limited), William Mike Miller (Edison Design Group, Inc.), Mark Schimmel (Borland International), Vicki Scott (Metrowerks), James Snell (Boeing Integrated Defense Systems), and Raymond Stephenson (Microsoft). **OOD/UML Optional Software Engineering Case Study Reviewers:** Sinan Si Alhir (Independent Consultant), Karen Arlien (Bismarck State College), David Branigan (DeVry University, Illinois), Martin Dulberg (North Carolina State University), Ric Heishman (Northern Virginia Community College), Richard Holladay (San Diego Mesa College), Earl LaBatt (OPNET Technologies, Inc./University of New Hampshire), Brian Larson (Modesto Junior College), Gavin Osborne (Saskatchewan Institute of Applied Science and Technology), Praveen Sadhu (Infodat International, Inc.), Cameron Skinner (Embarcadero Technologies, Inc./OMG), and Steve Tockey (Construx Software).

Well, there you have it! Welcome to the exciting world of Visual C++ and object-oriented programming. We hope you enjoy this look at contemporary computer programming. Good luck!

As you read the book, we would sincerely appreciate your comments, criticisms, corrections and suggestions for improving the text. Please address all correspondence to:

deitel@deitel.com

We'll respond promptly, and post corrections and clarifications on:

www.deitel.com/books/vcpphtp2/

We hope you enjoy reading *Visual C++ 2008 How to Program, Second Edition* as much as we enjoyed writing it!

Paul J. Deitel
Dr. Harvey M. Deitel
Dan T. Quirk
Maynard, Massachusetts
December 2007

About the Authors

Paul J. Deitel, CEO and Chief Technical Officer of Deitel & Associates, Inc., is a graduate of MIT's Sloan School of Management, where he studied Information Technology. He holds the Java Certified Programmer and Java Certified Developer certifications, and has been designated by Sun Microsystems as a Java Champion. Through Deitel & Associates, Inc., he has delivered C++, C#, VB, C and Java courses to industry clients, including Cisco, IBM, Sun Microsystems, Dell, Lucent Technologies, Fidelity, NASA at the Kennedy Space Center, the National Severe Storm Laboratory, White Sands Missile Range, Rogue Wave Software, Boeing, Stratus, Cambridge Technology Partners, Open Environment Corporation, One Wave, Hyperion Software, Adra Systems, Entergy, CableData Systems, Nortel Networks, Puma, iRobot, Invensys and many more. He has also lectured on Java and C++ for the Boston Chapter of the Association for Computing Machinery. He and his father, Dr. Harvey M. Deitel, are the world's best-selling programming language textbook authors.

Dr. Harvey M. Deitel, Chairman and Chief Strategy Officer of Deitel & Associates, Inc., has 46 years of academic and industry experience in the computer field. Dr. Deitel earned B.S. and M.S. degrees from MIT and a Ph.D. from Boston University. He has 20 years of college teaching experience, including earning tenure and serving as the Chairman of the Computer Science Department at Boston College before founding Deitel & Associates, Inc., with his son, Paul J. Deitel. He and Paul are the co-authors of several dozen books and multimedia packages and they are writing many more. The Deitels' texts have earned international recognition with translations published in Japanese, German, Russian, Spanish, Traditional Chinese, Simplified Chinese, Korean, French, Polish, Italian, Portuguese, Greek, Urdu and Turkish. Dr. Deitel has delivered hundreds of professional seminars to major corporations, academic institutions, government organizations and the military.

Dan T. Quirk is a senior at the University of Rochester completing a B.S. in Computer Science. His industry experience includes web application development, database development and networking. His course work includes artificial intelligence, systems programming, computational theory, operating systems and various programming languages.

About Deitel & Associates, Inc.

Deitel & Associates, Inc., is an internationally recognized corporate training and content-creation organization specializing in computer programming languages, Internet and World Wide Web software technology, object technology education and Internet business development through its Web 2.0 Internet Business Initiative. The company provides instructor-led courses on major programming languages and platforms, such as C++, Java, C, C#, Visual C++, Visual Basic, XML, Perl, object technology and Internet and World Wide Web programming. The founders of Deitel & Associates, Inc., are Dr. Harvey M. Deitel and Paul J. Deitel. The company's clients include many of the world's largest companies, government agencies, branches of the military, and academic institutions. Through its 31-year publishing partnership with Prentice Hall, Deitel & Associates, Inc. publishes leading-edge programming textbooks, professional books, interactive multimedia *Cyber Classrooms*, *LiveLessons* video courses, web-based training courses and e-content for the popular course management systems WebCT, Blackboard and Pearson's Course-Compass. Deitel & Associates, Inc., and the authors can be reached via e-mail at:

> deitel@deitel.com

To learn more about Deitel & Associates, Inc., its publications and its worldwide *Dive Into*® Series Corporate Training curriculum, visit:

> www.deitel.com

and subscribe to the free *Deitel*® *Buzz Online* e-mail newsletter at:

> www.deitel.com/newsletter/subscribe.html

Check out the growing list of online Deitel Resource Centers at:

> www.deitel.com/resourcecenters.html

Individuals wishing to purchase Deitel publications can do so through:

> www.deitel.com

Bulk orders by corporations, the government, the military and academic institutions should be placed directly with Prentice Hall. For more information, visit

> www.prenhall.com/mischtm/support.html#order

Before You Begin

Please follow these instructions to download Visual C++ 2008 Express Edition and the book's examples before you begin using this book.

Download Microsoft Visual C++® 2008 Express

We wrote *Visual C++ 2008 How to Program, 2/e* using Microsoft's free Visual C++ 2008 Express Edition. You can learn more about Visual C++ 2008 Express and download it at:

> www.microsoft.com/express/vc/

Additional resources and software downloads are available in our Visual C++ Resource Center:

> www.deitel.com/visualcplusplus/

and at the website for this book:

> www.deitel.com/books/vcpphtp2/

Download the *Visual C++ 2008 How to Program, 2/e* Source Code

The source code in *Visual C++ 2008 How to Program, 2/e* can be downloaded as a ZIP archive file from www.deitel.com/books/vcpphtp2/. After you register and log in, click the link for the examples under **Download Code Examples and Other Premium Content for Registered Users**. Extract the example files to your hard disk using a ZIP file extractor program, such as WinZip (www.winzip.com). We suggest that you extract the files to a folder such as C:\vcpphtp2_examples. [*Note:* If you are working in a computer lab, ask your instructor where you can save the example code.]

You are now ready to begin your Visual C++ programming studies with *Visual C++ 2008 How to Program, 2/e*. We hope you enjoy the book! If you have any questions, please feel free to email us at deitel@deitel.com. We'll respond promptly.

1

Introduction to Computers, the Internet and Visual C++

OBJECTIVES

In this chapter you will learn:

- Basic hardware and software concepts.
- The different types of programming languages.
- Which programming languages are most widely used.
- The history of the Visual C++ programming language.
- Some basics of object technology.
- The history of the UML—the industry-standard object-oriented system modeling language.
- The history of the Internet and the World Wide Web.
- The motivation behind and an overview of Microsoft's .NET initiative, which involves the Internet in developing and using software systems.
- To test-drive a Visual C++ 2008 application.

1.1 Introduction

Welcome to Visual C++ 2008! We have worked hard to provide you with accurate and complete information regarding this powerful computer programming language. Visual C++ is appropriate for technically oriented people with little or no programming experience and for experienced programmers for use in building substantial information systems. *Visual C++ 2008 How to Program, Second Edition* is an effective learning tool for each of these audiences. We hope that working with this book will be an informative, challenging and entertaining learning experience for you.

How can one book appeal to both novices and skilled programmers? The core of this book emphasizes achieving program clarity through the proven techniques of object-oriented programming (OOP). Nonprogrammers learn basic skills that underlie good programming; experienced developers receive a rigorous explanation of the language and may improve their programming styles. Perhaps most important, the book presents hundreds of complete, working Visual C++ programs and depicts their inputs and outputs. We call this the *live-code approach.* All of the book's examples may be downloaded from `www.deitel.com/books/vcpphtp2/index.html` and `www.prenhall.com/deitel`.

The early chapters introduce the fundamentals of computers, computer programming and the Visual C++ computer programming language, providing a solid foundation for the deeper treatment of Visual C++ in the later chapters. Experienced programmers tend to read the early chapters quickly, then find the treatment of Visual C++ in the remainder of the book both rigorous and challenging.

Computer use is increasing in almost every field of endeavor. Computing costs have been decreasing dramatically due to rapid developments in both hardware and software technologies. Computers that might have filled large rooms and cost millions of dollars a few decades ago can now be inscribed on silicon chips smaller than a fingernail, costing a few dollars each. Fortunately, silicon is one of the most abundant materials on earth—it's an ingredient in common sand. Silicon-chip technology has made computing so economical that about a billion general-purpose computers are in use worldwide, helping people in business, industry and government, and in their personal lives.

We hope that you will enjoy learning with *Visual C++ 2008 How to Program, Second Edition.* You are embarking on a challenging and rewarding path. If you have any questions as you proceed, please send e-mail to

```
deitel@deitel.com
```

To keep current with Visual C++ developments at Deitel & Associates and to receive updates to this book, please register for our free e-mail newsletter, the *Deitel® Buzz Online,* at

```
www.deitel.com/newsletter/subscribe.html
```

1.2 What Is a Computer?

A *computer* is an electronic device capable of performing computations and making logical decisions at speeds millions, billions and even trillions of times faster than a human being. For example, many of today's personal computers can perform a billion additions per second. A person operating a desk calculator could spend an entire lifetime performing calculations and still not complete as many calculations as even today's more modest personal computers can perform in one second. (Points to ponder: How would you know whether the person added the numbers correctly? How would you know whether the computer added the numbers correctly?) The most powerful computers are called *supercomputers*; some of these are already performing trillions of additions per second!

Computers process *data* under the control of sets of instructions called *computer programs.* These programs guide computers through orderly sets of actions that are specified by people known as *computer programmers.*

A computer consists of various devices referred to as *hardware* (e.g., the keyboard, screen, mouse, hard drive, memory, DVDs and processing units). The programs that run on a computer are referred to as *software* (e.g., word-processing programs, e-mail and games). Hardware costs have been declining dramatically in recent years, to the point that personal computers have become a commodity. Historically, however, software development costs have risen steadily as programmers develop ever more powerful and complex applications without being able to significantly improve the software development process. In this book, you will learn object-oriented programming—a technology that is dramatically reducing software development costs.

1.3 Computer Organization

Regardless of differences in physical appearance, virtually every computer may be envisioned as being divided into six *logical units* or sections:

1. *Input unit.* This is the "receiving" section of the computer. It obtains information (data and computer programs) from *input devices* (e.g., the keyboard and the mouse) and places this information at the disposal of the other units so that it can be processed. Information also can be entered in many other ways, including by speaking to your computer, scanning images and having your computer receive information from a network, such as the Internet.

2. *Output unit.* This is the "shipping" section of the computer. It takes information that the computer has processed and places it on various *output devices* to make the information available for use outside the computer. Most information output from computers today is displayed on screens, printed on paper or used to control other devices. Computers also can output their information to networks, such as the Internet.

3. *Memory unit.* This is the rapid-access, relatively low-capacity "warehouse" section of the computer. The memory unit retains information entered through the input unit so that it will be immediately available for processing when needed. The memory unit also retains processed information until it can be placed on output devices by the output unit. Information in the memory unit is typically lost when the computer's power is turned off. The memory unit is often called either *memory* or *primary memory.* (Historically, this unit has been called "core memory," but that term is fading from use today.)

4. *Arithmetic and logic unit (ALU).* This is the "manufacturing" section of the computer. It is responsible for performing calculations, such as addition, subtraction, multiplication and division. It contains the decision mechanisms that allow the computer, for example, to compare two items from the memory unit to determine whether they are equal.

5. *Central processing unit (CPU).* This is the "administrative" section of the computer. It coordinates and supervises the operation of the other sections. The CPU tells the input unit when information should be read into the memory unit, tells the ALU when information from the memory unit should be used in calculations and tells the output unit when to send information from the memory unit to certain output devices. Many of today's computers have multiple CPUs and thus can perform many operations simultaneously—such computers are called *multiprocessors.*

6. *Secondary storage unit.* This is the long-term, high-capacity "warehousing" section of the computer. Programs or data not actively being used by the other units normally are placed on secondary storage devices, such as your hard drive, until they are needed, hours, days, months or even years later. Information in secondary storage takes much longer to access than information in primary memory, but the cost per unit of secondary storage is much less than that of primary memory. Other secondary storage devices include CDs and DVDs, which can hold up to hundreds of millions of characters and billions of characters, respectively.

1.4 Early Operating Systems

Computers of the 1950s could perform only one *job* or *task* at a time. This mode of operation is often called single-user *batch processing*. The computer runs one program at a time while processing data in groups or batches. In these early systems, users generally submitted their jobs to a computer center on decks of punched cards and often had to wait hours or even days before printouts were returned to their desks. Computers were very large (often filling entire rooms) and expensive (often costing millions of dollars). Personal computers did not exist; people did not have computers at their desks and in their homes.

Software systems called *operating systems* were developed to make using computers more convenient. Early operating systems smoothed and speeded up the transition between jobs, increasing the amount of work, or *throughput*, computers could process.

As computers became more powerful, it became evident that single-user batch processing was inefficient, because so much time was spent waiting for slow input/output devices to complete their tasks. It was thought that many jobs or tasks could share the resources of the computer to achieve better utilization. This is achieved by *multiprogramming*—the simultaneous operation of many jobs that are competing to share the computer's resources. With early multiprogramming operating systems, users still submitted jobs on decks of punched cards and waited hours or days for results.

In the 1960s, several groups in industry and the universities pioneered *timesharing* operating systems. Timesharing is a special case of multiprogramming in which users access the computer through terminals, typically devices with keyboards and screens. Dozens, or even hundreds, of users share the computer at once. The computer actually does not run the users' jobs simultaneously. Rather, it runs a small portion of one user's job, then moves on to service the next user, perhaps providing service to each user several times per second. Thus, the users' programs *appear* to be running simultaneously. An advantage of timesharing is that user requests receive almost immediate responses.

1.5 Personal Computing, Distributed Computing and Client/Server Computing

In the early years of computing, computer systems were too large and expensive for individuals to own. In the 1970s, silicon-chip technology appeared, making it possible for computers to be much smaller and so economical that individuals and small organizations could own the machines. In 1977, Apple Computer—creator of today's popular Mac personal computers and iPod digital music players—popularized *personal computing*. In 1981, IBM, the world's largest computer vendor, introduced the IBM Personal Computer (PC), legitimizing personal computing in business, industry and government organizations.

These PCs were "stand-alone" units—people transported disks between computers to share information (often called "sneakernet"). Although early PCs were not powerful enough to timeshare several users, they could be linked together in computer networks, via over telephone lines or *local area networks* (*LANs*) within an organization. This led to the phenomenon of *distributed computing*, in which an organization's computing, instead of being performed only at some central computer installation, is distributed over networks to the geographically dispersed sites where the organization's work is performed. PCs were powerful enough to handle the computing requirements of individuals as well as the basic communications tasks of passing information between computers electronically.

Today's personal computers are as powerful as the million-dollar machines of just a few decades ago; complete personal computer systems often sell for as little as $500–$1000. The most powerful desktop machines provide individual users with enormous capabilities. Information is shared easily across computer networks, where computers called *file servers* offer a common data store that may be used by *client* computers distributed throughout the network—hence the term *client/server computing*. Visual C++ has become widely used for writing software for operating systems, for computer networking and for distributed client/server applications. Today's popular operating systems, such as UNIX, Linux, Mac OS X and Microsoft's Windows-based systemsn provide the kinds of capabilities discussed in this section.

1.6 The Internet and the World Wide Web

The *Internet*—a global network of computers—was initiated almost four decades ago with funding supplied by the U.S. Department of Defense. Originally designed to connect the main computer systems of about a dozen universities and research organizations, its chief benefit proved early on to be the capability for quick and easy communication via what came to be known as *electronic mail* (*e-mail*). This is true even on today's Internet, with e-mail, instant messaging and file transfer facilitating communications among hundreds of millions of people worldwide. The Internet has exploded into one of the world's premier communication mechanisms and continues to grow rapidly.

The *World Wide Web* allows computer users to locate and view multimedia-based documents on almost any subject over the Internet. Even though the Internet was developed decades ago, the introduction of the web was a relatively recent event. In 1989, Tim Berners-Lee of CERN (the European Organization for Nuclear Research) began to develop a technology for sharing information via hyperlinked text documents. Berners-Lee called his invention the *HyperText Markup Language* (*HTML*). He also wrote communication protocols to form the backbone of his new information system, which he referred to as the World Wide Web.

In the past, most computer applications ran on computers that were not connected to one another. Today's applications can be written to communicate among the world's computers. The Internet mixes computing and communications technologies, making our work easier. It makes information instantly and conveniently accessible worldwide, and enables individuals and small businesses to get worldwide exposure. It is changing the way business is done. People can search for the best prices on virtually any product or service, while special-interest communities can stay in touch with one another, and researchers can be made instantly aware of the latest breakthroughs. The Internet and the World Wide Web are surely among humankind's most profound creations.

1.7 Hardware Trends

Every year, people generally expect to pay at least a little more for most products and services. The opposite has been the case in the computer and communications fields, especially with regard to the costs of the hardware supporting these technologies. For many decades, hardware costs have fallen rapidly, if not precipitously. Every year or two, the capacities of computers have approximately doubled without any increase in price. This often is called *Moore's Law*, named after the person who first identified and explained the trend, Gordon Moore, co-founder of Intel—the company that manufactures the vast majority of the processors in today's personal computers. Moore's Law is especially true in relation to the amount of memory that computers have for programs, the amount of secondary storage (such as disk storage) they have to hold programs and data over longer periods of time, and their processor speeds—the speeds at which computers execute their programs (i.e., do their work). Similar growth has occurred in the communications field, in which costs have plummeted as enormous demand for communications bandwidth has attracted intense competition. We know of no other fields in which technology improves so quickly and costs fall so rapidly. Such phenomenal improvement in the computing and communications fields is truly fostering the so-called Information Revolution.

When computer use exploded in the 1960s and 1970s, many people discussed the dramatic improvements in human productivity that computing and communications would cause, but these improvements did not materialize. Organizations were spending vast sums of money on these technologies, but without realizing the expected productivity gains. The invention of microprocessor chip technology and its wide deployment in the late 1970s and 1980s laid the groundwork for the productivity improvements that individuals and businesses have achieved in recent years.

1.8 Microsoft's Windows® Operating System

Microsoft Corporation became the dominant software company in the 1980s and 1990s. In 1981, Microsoft released the first version of its DOS operating system for the IBM personal computer. In the mid-1980s, Microsoft developed the *Windows operating system*, a graphical user interface built on top of DOS. Microsoft released Windows 3.0 in 1990; this new version featured a user-friendly interface and rich functionality. The Windows operating system became incredibly popular after the 1992 release of Windows 3.1, whose successors, Windows 95 and Windows 98, virtually cornered the desktop operating systems market by the late 1990s. These operating systems, which borrowed many concepts (such as icons, menus and windows) popularized by early Apple Macintosh operating systems, enabled users to navigate multiple applications simultaneously. Microsoft entered the corporate operating systems market with the 1993 release of Windows NT®. Windows XP, which is based on the Windows NT operating system, was released in 2001 and combines Microsoft's corporate and consumer operating system lines. Windows Vista, released in 2007, is Microsoft's newest operating system designed to build on the features of Windows XP by adding a better security model and a more user-friendly interface. Windows is by far the world's most widely used operating system.

The biggest competitor to the Windows operating system is Linux. The name Linux derives from Linus (after Linus Torvalds, who developed Linux) and UNIX—the operating system upon which Linux is based; UNIX was developed at Bell Laboratories and was written in the C programming language. Linux is a free, *open source* operating system, unlike Windows, which is proprietary (owned and controlled by Microsoft)—the source code for Linux is freely available to users, and they can modify it to fit their needs.

1.9 Machine Languages, Assembly Languages and High-Level Languages

Programmers write instructions in various programming languages, some directly understandable by computers and others requiring intermediate *translation* steps. Hundreds of computer languages are in use today. These may be divided into three general types:

1. Machine languages

2. Assembly languages

3. High-level languages

Machine Languages

Any computer can directly understand only its own *machine language*—the "natural language" of a computer that is defined by its hardware design. Machine languages generally consist of strings of numbers (ultimately reduced to 1s and 0s) that instruct computers to perform their most elementary operations. Machine languages are *machine dependent* (i.e., any given machine language can be used on only one type of computer). Such languages are cumbersome for humans, as illustrated by the following section of an early machine-language program that adds overtime pay to base pay and stores the result in gross pay:

```
+1300042774
+1400593419
+1200274027
```

Assembly Languages

Machine-language programming was simply too slow and tedious for most programmers. Instead of using the strings of numbers that computers could directly understand, programmers began using English-like abbreviations to represent the elementary machine operations. These abbreviations formed the basis of *assembly languages*. *Translator programs* called *assemblers* were developed to convert early assembly-language programs to machine language at computer speeds. The following section of an assembly-language program also adds overtime pay to base pay and stores the result in gross pay:

```
load    basepay
add     overpay
store   grosspay
```

Although such code is clearer to humans, it is incomprehensible to computers until translated to machine language.

High-Level Languages

Computer usage increased rapidly with the advent of assembly languages, but programmers still had to use many instructions to accomplish even the simplest tasks. To speed the programming process, *high-level languages* were developed in which single statements could be written to accomplish substantial tasks. Translator programs called *compilers* convert high-level language programs into machine language. High-level languages allow programmers to write instructions that look almost like everyday English and contain commonly used mathematical notations. A payroll program written in a high-level language might contain a statement such as

```
grossPay = basePay + overTimePay
```

From the programmer's standpoint, obviously, high-level languages are preferable to machine and assembly languages. Microsoft's Visual Studio languages (e.g., Visual C++, Visual C# and Visual Basic) and other languages such as C and Java are among the most widely used high-level programming languages. Figure 1.1 compares machine, assembly and high-level languages.

The process of compiling a high-level language program into machine language can take a considerable amount of computer time. *Interpreter* programs were developed to execute high-level language programs directly, although much more slowly. Interpreters are popular in program development environments in which new features are being added and errors corrected. Once a program is fully developed, a compiled version can be produced to run most efficiently. Interpreters are also popular with so-called scripting languages (such as JavaScript, PHP, Perl, Python and Ruby) on the web.

	Sample code	Translator	From the programmer's perspective	From the computer's perspective
Machine language	+1300042774 +1400593419 +1200274027	None	Slow, tedious, error prone	Natural language of a computer; the only language the computer can understand directly
Assembly language	LOAD BASEPAY ADD OVERPAY STORE GROSSPAY	Assembler	English-like abbreviations, easier to understand	Assemblers convert assembly language into machine language so the computer can understand
High-level language	grossPay = basePay + overTimePay	Compiler	Instructions resemble everyday English; single statements accomplish substantial tasks	Compilers convert high-level languages into machine language so the computer can understand

Fig. 1.1 | Comparing machine, assembly and high-level languages.

1.10 Visual C++

Standard C++ evolved from C, which was developed from two previous programming languages, BCPL and B. BCPL was developed in 1967 by Martin Richards as a language for writing operating systems software and compilers. Ken Thompson modeled many features in his B language after their counterparts in BCPL and used B in 1970 to create early versions of the UNIX operating system at Bell Laboratories on a DEC PDP-7 computer. Both BCPL and B were "typeless" languages—every data item occupied one "word" in memory and the burden of typing variables fell on the shoulders of the programmer.

The C language was evolved from B by Dennis Ritchie at Bell Laboratories and was originally implemented on a DEC PDP-11 computer in 1972. C uses many important concepts of BCPL and B while adding data typing and other powerful features. C initially became widely known as the development language of the UNIX operating system. Today, virtually all new major operating systems are written in C and/or C++ (with some portions in assembly language). C is available for most computers. C is also hardware independent. With careful design, it is possible to write C programs that are *portable* to most computers.

By the late 1970s, C had evolved into what now is referred to as "traditional C." The publication in 1978 of Kernighan and Ritchie's book, *The C Programming Language,* brought attention to the language. This publication became one of the most successful computer science books of all time.

The rapid expansion of C over various types of computers (sometimes called *hardware platforms*) led to many variations that were similar but often incompatible. This was a serious problem for program developers, who needed to develop code that would run on several platforms. It became clear that a standard version of C was needed. In 1983, the X3J11 technical committee was created under the American National Standards Committee on Computers and Information Processing (X3) to "provide an unambiguous and machine-independent definition of the language." In 1989, the standard was approved; this standard was updated in 1999. The standards document is referred to as *INCITS/ ISO/IEC 9899-1999.* Copies of this document may be ordered from the American National Standards Institute (www.ansi.org) at webstore.ansi.org/ansidocstore.

 Portability Tip 1.1

C is a standardized, hardware-independent, widely available language. Applications written in C often can be run with little or no modification on a wide range of different computer systems.

C++ is an evolution of C developed by Bjarne Stroustrup in the early 1980s at Bell Laboratories. C++ provides a number of features that "spruce up" the C language, but more importantly, it provides capabilities for *object-oriented programming.*

Developed in the early 1990s, Visual C++ is a Microsoft implementation of C++ that includes Microsoft's proprietary extensions to the language. Over the past decade, Microsoft has released several versions of Visual C++ and introduced C++/CLI. Visual C++ is known as a *visual programming language*—the developer can use graphical tools, such as Visual Studio 2008, to create applications that have *graphical user interfaces* (*GUIs*). We discuss Visual Studio 2008 later in this section.

Early graphics and *graphical user interface* (*GUI*) programming with Visual C++ was implemented using the *Microsoft Foundation Classes* (*MFC*). The *MFC library* is a collection of classes that help Visual C++ programmers create powerful Windows-based applications. Now, with the introduction of .NET, Microsoft provides an additional library (.NET's FCL, discussed in Section 1.15) for implementing GUI, graphics, networking, multithreading and other functionality. This library is available to .NET-compliant languages such as Visual C++, Visual Basic .NET and Visual C#. However, developers still can use MFC—Microsoft is upgrading MFC to MFC 9, which will include new classes and documentation that can be accessed using Visual Studio. In fact, using Visual Studio 2008, developers can recompile existing MFC applications and the compiler will update them to the new Windows Vista look and feel without any extra coding required. MFC often is used to develop *unmanaged code* (also called *native code*), or code that does not make use of the .NET Framework. In 2007, Microsoft unveiled Windows Presentation Foundation, the next-generation GUI and graphics platform for Windows development using managed code. It is primarily aimed at C# and Visual Basic .NET applications. This means Visual C++ will not be the language of choice for GUI programming in the future but will continue to be used when performance matters most.

The .NET platform offers a new software development model that allows applications created in disparate programming languages to communicate with each other. C++/CLI was designed specifically for the .NET platform so that Visual C++ programmers could easily create applications for .NET. However, Microsoft also designed Visual C++ to support existing Visual C++ developers, and has continued to emphasize and enhance compliance with the ANSI/ISO standard for C++.

Microsoft's first attempt to combine Visual C++ and the .NET Framework, upon which the previous edition of this book was based, is called *Managed Extensions for C++* (*MC++*). While it did enable using Visual C++ with .NET, the syntax was complex, confusing and not well received by the development community. Microsoft realized its mistake, and with Visual Studio 2005 came the newest version of Visual C++, which introduced *C++/CLI*. This addition to the language provides the functionality of MC++ and more, but uses a new syntax which is far more natural and elegant for experienced C++ developers. In fact, the Visual C++ 2008 compiler issues a warning that MC++ syntax is deprecated and will not be supported in future versions. Programmers can use C++/CLI with the .NET Framework to create objects subject to automatic memory management and capable of language interoperability. Such objects are known as *managed objects*; the code that defines them is known as *managed code*. [*Note*: The different implementations of C++ and Visual C++ have yielded several industry terms. For the remainder of this book, we use the terms "Visual C++", "native C++" or just "C++" when referring to standard C++. We use the term "C++/CLI" when referring to features of managed C++ or code that uses these features. Finally, we use the term "Visual Studio 2008" or "Visual C++ 2008" when referring to the Microsoft product/compiler, which can be used to write both managed and unmanaged code.]

C++/CLI gives the programmer access to new data types provided by the .NET Framework. These new data types aid in standardization across different platforms and .NET programming languages. In C++/CLI, standard C++ data types are mapped to .NET Framework types.

The true power of Visual C++ lies in its interoperability between managed and unmanaged code. An enormous amount of existing code is written in native C++. Rather than forcing developers to discard large amounts of existing code, Visual C++ enables programmers to mix managed (C++/CLI) and unmanaged (native C++) code across programs, within projects, and even within the same file.

In Visual C++, programs are created using Visual Studio 2008, an *Integrated Development Environment* (*IDE*). With the IDE, a programmer can create, run, test and debug programs conveniently, producing a working program in a fraction of the time it would have taken without using the IDE. This process typically is referred to as *Rapid Application Development* (*RAD*). For fast Windows application programming, Visual Studio 2008 provides a *Windows Form Designer*, a visual programming tool that simplifies GUI and database programming. With the Windows Form Designer, Visual Studio 2008 generates program code from various programmer *actions* (such as using the mouse for pointing, clicking, dragging and dropping).

Visual C++ enables a new degree of language interoperability: Software components from different languages can interact as never before. Developers can package even old software to work with new Visual C++ programs. In addition, Visual C++ applications can interact via the Internet, using industry standards such as the Simple Object Access Protocol (SOAP) and XML. The programming advances embodied in .NET and Visual C++ will lead to a new style of programming, in which applications are created from building blocks available over the Internet.

Building software quickly, correctly and economically remains an elusive goal, and this at a time when the demand for new and more powerful software is soaring. *Objects* are essentially reusable software components that model items in the real world. Software developers have discovered that using a modular, object-oriented design and implementation approach making them much more productive than they were with older programming techniques. Object-oriented programs are easier to understand, correct and modify.

For this reason, we've adopted an early classes and objects pedagogy. You'll be introduced to the basic concepts and terminology of object technology in Section 1.16. You'll begin developing customized, reusable classes and objects in Chapter 4. This new edition is object oriented, where appropriate, from the start and throughout the text. Moving the discussion of objects and classes to earlier chapters gets you "thinking about objects" immediately and mastering these concepts more completely. Object-oriented programming is not trivial by any means, but it's fun to write object-oriented programs, and students can see immediate results.

We also provide an optional automated teller machine (ATM) case study in the Software Engineering Case Study sections of Chapters 1, 3–8, 10 and 14, and Appendix F, which contains a complete Visual C++ implementation. The nine case-study sections present a carefully paced introduction to object-oriented design using the UML—an industry-standard graphical modeling language for developing object-oriented systems. We guide you through a first design experience intended for the novice object-oriented designer/programmer. Our goal is to help you develop an object-oriented design to complement the object-oriented programming concepts you learn in this chapter and begin implementing in Chapter 4.

1.11 C++ Standard Library

Visual C++ programs consist of pieces called *classes* and *functions*. You can program each piece that you may need to form a Visual C++ program. However, most Visual C++ programmers take advantage of the rich collections of existing classes and functions in the *C++ Standard Library*. Thus, there are really two parts to learning the Visual C++ "world." The first is learning the Visual C++ language itself; the second is learning how to use the classes and functions in the C++ Standard Library. Throughout the book, we discuss many of these classes and functions. P. J. Plauger's book, *The Standard C Library* (Upper Saddle River, NJ: Prentice Hall PTR, 1992), is a must read for programmers who need a deep understanding of the ANSI C library functions that are included in Visual C++, how to implement them and how to use them to write portable code. The standard class libraries generally are provided by compiler vendors. Many special-purpose class libraries are supplied by independent software vendors.

Software Engineering Observation 1.1

*Use a "building-block" approach to create programs. Avoid reinventing the wheel. Use existing pieces wherever possible. Called **software reuse**, this practice is central to object-oriented programming.*

Software Engineering Observation 1.2

When programming in Visual C++, you typically will use the following building blocks: classes and functions from the C++ Standard Library, classes and functions you and your colleagues create and classes and functions from various popular third-party libraries.

We include many *Software Engineering Observations* throughout the book to explain concepts that affect and improve the overall architecture and quality of software systems. We also highlight other kinds of tips, including *Good Programming Practices* (to help you write programs that are clearer, more understandable, more maintainable and easier to test and *debug*—or remove programming errors), *Common Programming Errors* (problems to watch out for and avoid), *Performance Tips* (techniques for writing programs that run faster and use less memory), *Portability Tips* (techniques to help you write programs that can run, with little or no modification, on a variety of computers— these tips also include general observations about how Visual C++ achieves its high degree of portability) and *Error-Prevention Tips* (techniques for removing bugs from your programs and, more important, techniques for writing bug-free programs in the first place). Many of these tips and observations are only guidelines. You'll, no doubt, develop your own preferred programming style or follow a company's coding standards.

The advantage of creating your own functions and classes is that you'll know exactly how they work. You'll be able to examine the Visual C++ code. The disadvantage is the time-consuming and complex effort that goes into designing, developing and maintaining new functions and classes that are correct and that operate efficiently.

Many of the features in the C++ Standard Library have analogous libraries in .NET. In Visual Studio 2008 Microsoft is introducing STL/CLR, an implementation of the C++ Standard Library for .NET and managed types. This allows C++ developers who invested time learning the C++ Standard Library to use their existing knowledge with Visual C++ and managed types.

Performance Tip 1.1

Using C++ Standard Library functions and classes instead of writing your own versions can improve program performance, because they are written carefully to perform efficiently. This technique also shortens program development time.

Portability Tip 1.2

Using C++ Standard Library functions and classes instead of writing your own improves program portability, because they are included in every C++ implementation.

1.12 Java, C# and Visual Basic

Java

Microprocessors are having a profound impact in intelligent consumer electronic devices. Recognizing this, Sun Microsystems in 1991 funded an internal corporate research project that resulted in the development of a C++-based language. When a group of Sun people visited a local coffee shop, the name *Java* was suggested and it stuck. As the World Wide Web exploded in popularity in 1993, Sun saw the possibility of using Java to add *dynamic content* (e.g., interactivity, animations and the like) to web pages. Sun formally announced the language in 1995. This generated immediate interest in the business community because of the commercial potential of the web. Java is now used to develop large-scale enterprise applications, to enhance the functionality of web servers (the computers that provide the content we see in our web browsers), to provide applications for consumer devices (such as cell phones, pagers and personal digital assistants) and for many other purposes. Visual C++ is similar in capability to Java.

Visual C#
In 2000, Microsoft announced the *C#* (pronounced "C-Sharp") programming language—created specifically for the .NET platform (which is discussed in Section 1.14). C# has roots in C, C++ and Java, adapting the best features of each. Like Visual C++, C# is object oriented and contains a powerful *class library* of prebuilt components, enabling programmers to develop applications quickly—Visual C++ and C# share the Framework Class Library (FCL); the FCL is discussed in Section 1.14.

Visual Basic
Visual Basic evolved from BASIC (Beginner's All-Purpose Symbolic Instruction Code), developed in the mid-1960s by Professors John Kemeny and Thomas Kurtz of Dartmouth College as a language for writing simple programs. BASIC's primary purpose was to familiarize novices with programming techniques.

The widespread use of BASIC on various types of computers (sometimes called hardware platforms) led to many language enhancements. When Bill Gates co-founded Microsoft, he implemented BASIC on several early PCs. With the development of the Microsoft Windows graphical user interface (GUI) in the late 1980s and early 1990s, the natural evolution of BASIC was Visual Basic, introduced by Microsoft in 1991.

Until the first version of Visual Basic appeared in 1991, developing Microsoft Windows-based applications was a difficult and cumbersome process. Visual Basic makes it convenient. Although Visual Basic is derived from the BASIC programming language, it is a distinctly different language that offers such powerful features as graphical user interfaces, event handling, object-oriented programming, and exception handling. Visual Basic is an event-driven language (i.e., the programs respond to user-initiated events such as mouse clicks and keystrokes) and a visual programming language in which programs are created using an Integrated Development Environment (IDE).

1.13 Other High-Level Languages
Although hundreds of high-level languages have been developed, only a few, other than those we've discussed, have achieved broad acceptance.

Fortran
IBM Corporation developed *Fortran* (FORmula TRANslator) in the mid-1950s to create scientific and engineering applications that require complex mathematical computations. Fortran is still widely used.

COBOL
COBOL (COmmon Business Oriented Language) was developed in 1959 by a group of computer manufacturers in conjunction with government and industrial computer users. COBOL is used primarily for commercial applications that require the precise and effi-

cient manipulation of large amounts of data. Much of today's business software is still programmed in COBOL.

Pascal

During the 1960s, many large software development efforts encountered severe difficulties. People began to realize that software development was a far more complex activity than they had imagined. Research activity resulted in the evolution of *structured programming*—a disciplined approach to creating programs that are clear, demonstrably correct and easy to modify. One result of this research was the development of the *Pascal* programming language by Professor Niklaus Wirth in 1971. Pascal, named after the mathematician and philosopher Blaise Pascal, was designed for teaching structured programming in academic environments and rapidly became the preferred introductory programming language in most colleges. Unfortunately, the language lacked many features needed to make it useful in commercial, industrial and government applications. By contrast, C, which also arose from research on structured programming, did not have the limitations of Pascal, and programmers quickly adopted it instead.

Ada

The *Ada* programming language was developed under the sponsorship of the U.S. Department of Defense (DOD) through the early 1980s. DOD wanted a single language that would meet its needs. The language was named after Lady Ada Lovelace, daughter of the poet Lord Byron. Lady Lovelace is generally credited with having written, in the early 1800s, the world's first computer program (for the Analytical Engine mechanical computing device designed by Charles Babbage). An important capability of Ada is *multitasking*, which allows programmers to specify that many activities are to occur in parallel.

1.14 Microsoft's .NET

In 2000, Microsoft announced its *.NET initiative* (www.microsoft.com/net). It includes a variety of key technologies to enable programmers to develop new applications faster and more easily. One key aspect of .NET is its independence from a specific language or platform. Rather than being forced to use a single programming language, developers can create a .NET application in any .NET-compatible language. Programmers can contribute to the same software project, writing code in the .NET languages (such as Microsoft's Visual C++, Visual C#, Visual Basic and many others) in which they are most competent. Any .NET language can also take advantage of the huge class library Microsoft has created as well enjoy the benefits of automatic memory management, type safety and safe exception handling.

The .NET architecture can exist on multiple platforms—not just Microsoft Windows–based systems—further extending the portability of .NET programs. One example is Mono (www.mono-project.com/Main_Page), an open source project by Novell. Another is DotGNU Portable .NET (www.dotgnu.org). However, these projects do not include all the features of the .NET architecture, and developers should not assume their .NET applications will necessarily work outside Windows.

A key component of the .NET architecture is *web services*, which are reusable application software components that can be used over the Internet. Clients and other applications can use web services as reusable building blocks. One example of a web service is Dollar Rent A Car's reservation system (www.microsoft.com/resources/casestudies/

CaseStudy.asp?CaseStudyID=11626). An airline partner wanted to enable customers to make rental-car reservations from the airline's website. To do so, the airline needed to access Dollar's reservation system. In response, Dollar created a web service that allowed the airline to access Dollar's database and make reservations. Web services enable computers at the two companies to communicate over the web, even though the airline uses UNIX systems and Dollar uses Microsoft Windows. Dollar could have created a one-time solution for that particular airline, but it would not have been able to reuse such a customized system. Dollar's web service enables many airlines, hotels and travel companies to use its reservation system without creating a custom program for each relationship.

The .NET strategy extends the concept of software reuse to the Internet, allowing programmers and companies to concentrate on their specialties without having to implement every component of every application. Instead, companies can use existing web services and devote their resources to developing their own products. For example, a single application using web services from various companies could manage bill payments, tax refunds, loans and investments. An online merchant could buy web services for online credit-card payments, user authentication, network security and inventory databases to create an e-commerce website.

1.15 The .NET Framework and the Common Language Runtime

The Microsoft *.NET Framework* is at the heart of the .NET strategy. This framework manages and executes applications and web services, contains a class library (called the *.NET Framework Class Library,* or *FCL*), enforces security and provides many other programming capabilities. The details of the .NET Framework are found in the *Common Language Infrastructure* (*CLI*), which contains information about the storage of data types (i.e., data that has predefined characteristics such as a date, percentage or currency amount), objects and so on. The CLI has been standardized by Ecma International (originally known as the European Computer Manufacturers Association), making it easier to create the .NET Framework for other platforms. This is like publishing the blueprints of the framework—anyone can build it by following the specifications. Microsoft's C++/CLI was given its name because it combines native C++ with the CLI.

The *Common Language Runtime (CLR)* is another central part of the .NET Framework—it is Microsoft's implementation of the CLI standard and it is responsible for executing .NET programs. Programs are compiled into machine-specific instructions in two steps. First, the program is compiled into *Microsoft Intermediate Language* (*MSIL*), which defines instructions for the CLR. Code converted into MSIL from other languages and sources can be woven together by the CLR. The MSIL for an application's components is placed into the application's executable file (known as an *assembly*). When the application executes, another compiler (known as the *just-in-time compiler* or *JIT compiler*) in the CLR translates the MSIL in the executable file into machine-language code (for a particular platform); then the machine-language code executes on that platform.

If the .NET Framework exists (and is installed) for a platform, that platform can run any .NET program. The ability of a program to run (without modification) across multiple platforms is known as *platform independence*. Code written once can be used on another type of computer without modification, saving both time and money. In addition, software can target a wider audience—previously, companies had to decide whether converting their programs to different platforms (sometimes called *porting*) was worth the cost. With .NET, porting programs is no longer an issue (once .NET itself has been made available on the platforms).

The .NET Framework also provides a high level of *language interoperability*. Programs written in different languages are all compiled into MSIL—the different parts can be combined to create a single unified program. MSIL allows the .NET Framework to be *language independent*, because .NET programs are not tied to a particular programming language. Any language that can be compiled into MSIL is called a *.NET-compliant language*. Figure 1.2 lists many of the programming languages for the .NET platform (msdn2.microsoft.com/en-us/netframework/Aa497336.aspx). Not all .NET languages interoperate easily with other .NET languages. This is one of C++/CLI's strengths.

Another benefit of the .NET Framework is the CLR's execution-management features. The CLR manages memory, security and other features, relieving the programmer of these responsibilities. With languages like native C++, programmers must manage their own memory. This leads to problems if programmers request memory and never release it—programs could consume all available memory, which would prevent applications from running. By managing the program's memory with a *garbage collector*, the .NET Framework allows programmers to concentrate on program logic.

Language interoperability offers many benefits to software companies. For example, Visual C++, Visual Basic and Visual C# developers can work side by side on the same project without having to learn another programming language—all of their code compiles into MSIL and links together to form one program.

The .NET Framework Class Library (FCL) can be used by any .NET language. The FCL contains many reusable components, saving programmers the trouble of creating new components. This book explains how to develop .NET software with Visual C++.

.NET programming languages			
APL	Forth	Mondrian	RPG
C#	Fortran	Oberon	Scheme
COBOL	Haskell	Oz	Smalltalk
Component Pascal	Java	Pascal	Standard ML
Curriculum	JScript	Perl	Visual Basic
Eiffel	Mercury	Python	Visual C++

Fig. 1.2 | .NET programming languages.

1.16 Key Software Trend: Object Technology

One of the authors, Harvey Deitel, remembers the great frustration that was felt in the 1960s by software development organizations, especially those working on large-scale projects. During his undergraduate years, he had the privilege of working summers at a leading computer vendor on the teams developing timesharing, virtual-memory operating systems. This was a great experience for a college student. But, in the summer of 1967, reality set in when the company "decommitted" from producing as a commercial product the particular system on which hundreds of people had been working for many years. It was difficult to get this software right—software is "complex stuff."

Improvements to software technology did emerge with the benefits of structured programming (and the related disciplines of *structured systems analysis and design)* being realized in the 1970s. Not until the technology of object-oriented programming became widely used in the 1990s, though, did software developers feel they had the necessary tools for making major strides in the software development process.

Actually, object technology dates back to the mid 1960s. The C++ programming language, developed at AT&T by Bjarne Stroustrup in the early 1980s, is based on two languages—C, which initially was developed at AT&T to implement the UNIX operating system in the early 1970s, and Simula 67, a simulation programming language developed in Europe and released in 1967. C++ absorbed the features of C and added Simula's capabilities for creating and manipulating objects. Neither C nor C++ was originally intended for wide use beyond the AT&T research laboratories. But grass-roots support rapidly developed for each.

What are objects and why are they special? Actually, object technology is a packaging scheme that helps us create meaningful software units. These can be large and are highly focused on particular applications areas. There are date objects, time objects, paycheck objects, invoice objects, audio objects, video objects, file objects, record objects and so on. In fact, almost any noun can be reasonably represented as an object.

We live in a world of objects. Just look around you. There are cars, planes, people, animals, buildings, traffic lights, elevators and the like. Before object-oriented languages appeared, procedural programming languages (such as Fortran, COBOL, Pascal, BASIC and C) were focused on actions (verbs) rather than on things or objects (nouns). Programmers living in a world of objects programmed primarily using verbs. This made it awkward to write programs. Now, with the availability of popular object-oriented languages such as C++ and Java, programmers continue to live in an object-oriented world and can program in an object-oriented manner. This is a more natural process than procedural programming and has resulted in significant productivity gains.

A key problem with procedural programming is that the program units do not effectively mirror real-world entities, so these units are not particularly reusable. It's not unusual for programmers to "start fresh" on each new project and have to write similar software "from scratch." This wastes time and money, as people repeatedly "reinvent the wheel." With object technology, the software entities created (called *classes*), if properly designed, tend to be reusable on future projects. Using libraries of reusable components can greatly reduce the effort required to implement certain kinds of systems (compared to the effort that would be required to reinvent these capabilities on new projects).

Software Engineering Observation 1.3

Extensive class libraries of reusable software components are available on the Internet. Many of these libraries are free.

Some organizations report that the key benefit object-oriented programming gives them is not software reuse, but a tendency to produce software that is more understandable, better organized and easier to maintain, modify and debug. This can be significant, because it an estimated 80 percent of software costs are associated not with the original efforts to develop the software, but with the continued evolution and maintenance of that software throughout its lifetime.

Whatever its perceived benefits may be, it's clear that object-oriented programming will be the key programming methodology for the next several decades.

1.17 Typical Visual C++ Development Life Cycle

Let's consider the steps in creating and executing a Visual C++ application using Visual Studio 2008. Visual C++ systems consist of three parts: a program development environment, the language and the libraries. Visual C++ programs typically go through six phases: *edit, preprocess, compile, link, load* and *execute* (Fig. 1.3). Visual Studio streamlines this process for you and does much of it behind the scenes so you can focus on writing your programs. The following discussion explains a typical Visual C++ program development life cycle.

Phase 1: Creating a Program

Phase 1 consists of editing a file with an *editor program* (normally known simply as an *editor*). We will use Visual Studio 2008 to edit Visual C++ files. You type a Visual C++ program (typically referred to as *source code*) using the editor, make any necessary corrections and save the program on a secondary storage device, such as your hard drive. C++ source code filenames typically end with the .cpp.

Phases 2 and 3: Preprocessing and Compiling a C++ Program

In phase 2, you give the command to *compile* the program. In a Visual C++ system, a *preprocessor* program executes automatically before the compiler's translation phase begins (so we call preprocessing phase 2 and compiling phase 3). The Visual C++ preprocessor obeys commands called *preprocessor directives,* which indicate that certain manipulations are to be performed on the source code before compilation. These manipulations usually insert other text files into source code, and perform various text replacements. The most common preprocessor directives are discussed in the early chapters; a detailed discussion of preprocessor features appears in Chapter E, Preprocessor. The details of phase 3 differ, depending on whether or not our program is intended to be run on the .NET Framework. If it is, then in phase 3 the compiler translates the Visual C++ program into Microsoft Intermediate Language (MSIL), which is ready to be compiled into machine-language code at runtime. If, instead, we have written native C++ code that we don't want to require the .NET Framework, then in phase 3 the compiler simply translates the C++ program into machine-language code (also referred to as object code).

Phase 4: Linking

Phase 4 is called *linking*. Visual C++ programs typically contain references to functions and data defined elsewhere, such as in the standard libraries or in the private libraries of groups of programmers working on a particular project. The object code produced by the Visual C++ compiler typically contains "holes" due to these missing parts. A *linker* fills in these holes with the code for the missing functions (from the libraries and other object files). The result is an an *executable image*, which represents a complete version of the application. If the program compiles and links correctly, an executable image is producedn in a format that is suitable for a particular operating system or for the .NET framework.

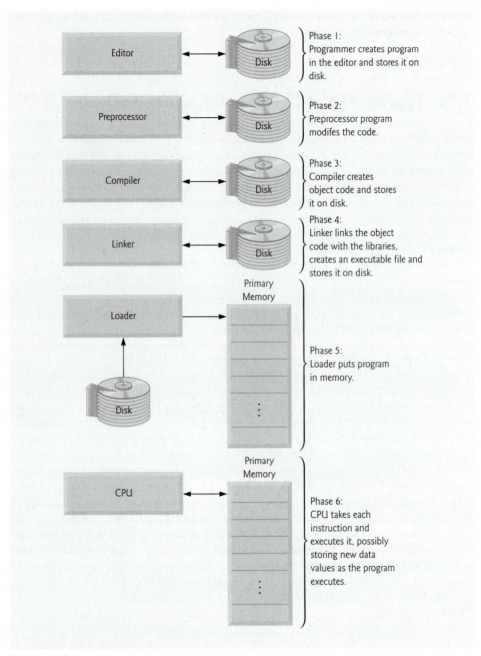

Fig. 1.3 | Typical C++ environment.

Phase 5: Loading

Phase 5 is called *loading*. Before a program can be executed, it must first be placed in memory. This is done by the operating system's *loader,* which takes the executable image from disk and transfers it to memory. Additional components from shared libraries that support the program are also loaded.

Phase 6: Execution
If the program uses the .NET Framework, then at runtime the .NET just-in-time compiler converts the MSIL code from phase 3 into machine-language code that is ready to be executed. Finally, the computer, under the control of its CPU, *executes* the program.

Problems That May Occur at Execution Time
Programs do not always work on the first try. Each of the preceding phases can fail because of various errors that we discuss throughout the book. For example, an executing program might attempt to divide by zero (an illegal operation for whole-number arithmetic in Visual C++). This would cause the Visual C++ program to display an error message. If this occurred, you would have to return to the edit phase, make the necessary corrections and proceed through the remaining phases again to determine that the corrections fixed the problem(s).

Most programs in Visual C++ input and/or output data. Certain Visual C++ functions take their input from cin (the *standard input stream* object; pronounced "see-in"), which is normally the keyboard, but cin can be redirected to another device. Data is often output to cout (the *standard output stream* object; pronounced "see-out"), which is normally the computer screen, but cout can be redirected to another device. When we say that a program prints a result, we normally mean that the result is displayed on a screen. Data may be output to other devices, such as disks and hardcopy printers. There is also a *standard error stream* object referred to as **cerr**. The cerr stream (normally connected to the screen) is used for displaying error messages. It is common for users to assign cout to a device other than the screen while keeping cerr assigned to the screen, so that normal outputs are separated from errors. The .NET Framework provides other classes that we can use for input and output when writing managed code. These classes will be discussed later in the book.

Common Programming Error 1.1

Errors such as division by zero occur as a program runs, so they are called **runtime errors** *or* **execution-time errors**. *Fatal runtime errors cause programs to terminate immediately without having successfully performed their jobs.* **Nonfatal runtime errors** *allow programs to run to completion, often producing incorrect results. [Note: On some systems, divide-by-zero is not a fatal error. Please see your system documentation.]*

1.18 Test-Driving a Visual C++ Application
In this section, you'll run your first Visual C++ application. You'll begin by running an entertaining guess-the-number game, which picks a number from 1 to 1000 and prompts you to guess the number. If your guess is correct, the game ends. If your guess is not correct, the application indicates whether your guess is higher or lower than the correct number. There is no limit on the number of guesses you can make. [*Note:* For this test drive only, we have modified this application from the exercise you'll be asked to create in Chapter 7, Functions and an Introduction to Recursion. Normally, this application randomly selects the correct answer as you execute the program. The modified application uses the same correct answer every time the program executes (though this may vary by

compiler), so you can use the same guesses we use in this section and see the same results as we walk you through interacting with your first Visual C++ application.]

We'll demonstrate running a Visual C++ application in Windows Vista from the **Command Prompt**. In the steps that follow, you'll run the application and enter various numbers to guess the correct number. The elements and functionality that you see in this application are typical of those you'll learn to program in this book. Throughout the book, we use fonts to distinguish between features you see on the screen (e.g., the **Command Prompt**) and elements that are not directly related to the screen. Our convention is to emphasize screen features like titles and menus (e.g., the **File** menu) in a semibold **sans-serif Helvetica** font and to emphasize file names, text displayed by an application and values you should enter into an application (e.g., GuessNumber or 500) in a sans-serif Lucida font. As you have noticed, the *defining occurrence* of each term is set in bold italic. For the figures in this section, we highlight the user input required by each step and point out significant parts of the application. To make these features more visible, we have modified the background color of the **Command Prompt** window. To modify the **Command Prompt** colors on your system, open a **Command Prompt**, then right click the title bar and select **Properties**. In the **Command Prompt Properties** dialog box that appears, click the **Colors** tab, and select your preferred text and background colors.

Running a Visual C++ Application from the Command Prompt

1. *Checking your setup.* Read the *Before You Begin* section at the beginning of this textbook to make sure that you have copied the book's examples to your hard drive correctly.

2. *Locating the completed application.* Open Windows Explorer and navigate to the C:\examples\Ch01\GuessNumber directory.

3. *Running the GuessNumber application.* Now that you are in the directory that contains the **GuessNumber** application, double click the file GuessNumber to run the application. [*Note*: GuessNumber.exe is the actual name of the application; however, Windows hides the file extension by default.]

4. *Entering your first guess.* The application displays "Please type your first guess.", then displays a question mark (?) as a prompt on the next line (Fig. 1.4). At the prompt, enter **500** (Fig. 1.5). [*Note:* This program assumes that you enter only whole number values.]

5. *Entering another guess.* The application displays "Too high. Try again.", meaning that the value you entered is greater than the number the application chose as the correct guess. So, you should enter a lower number for your next guess. At the prompt, enter **250** (Fig. 1.6). The application again displays "Too high. Try again.", because the value you entered is still greater than the number that the application chose.

6. *Entering additional guesses.* Continue to play the game by entering values until you guess the correct number. Once you guess the answer, the application will display "Excellent! You guessed the number!" (Fig. 1.7).

7. *Playing the game again or exiting the application.* After you've guessed the correct number, the application asks if you would like to play another game

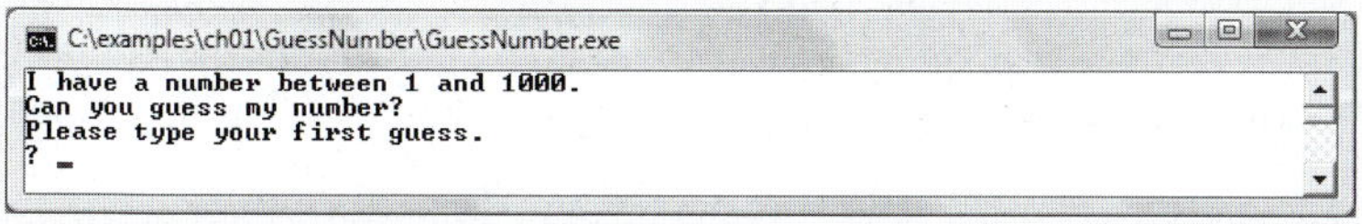

Fig. 1.4 | Running the **GuessNumber** application.

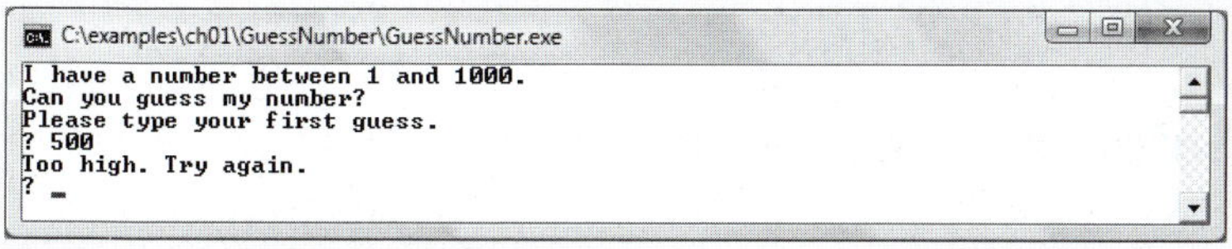

Fig. 1.5 | Entering your first guess.

Fig. 1.6 | Entering a second guess and receiving feedback.

(Fig. 1.7). At the "Would you like to play again (y or n)?" prompt, entering the one character **y** causes the application to choose a new number and displays the message "Please type your first guess." followed by a question-mark prompt (Fig. 1.8), so that you can make your first guess in the new game. Entering the character **n** ends the application and returns you to the application's directory at the **Command Prompt**. Each time you execute this application from the beginning (i.e., *Step 3*), it will choose the same numbers for you to guess.

8. *Close the **Command Prompt** window.*

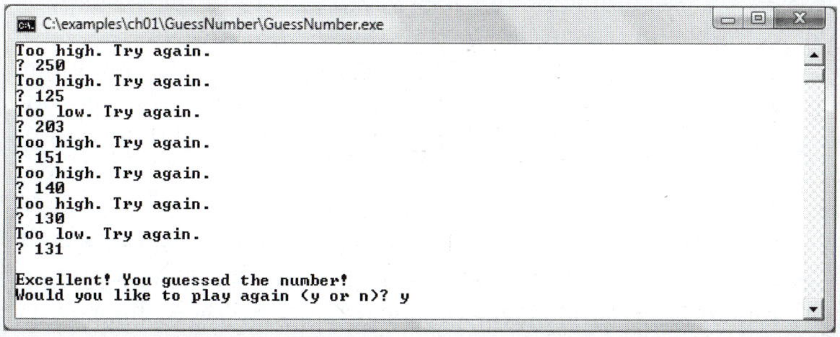

Fig. 1.7 | Entering additional guesses and guessing the correct number.

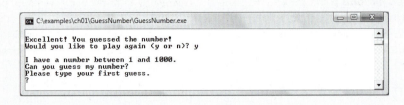

Fig. 1.8 | Playing the game again.

1.19 Software Technologies

In this section, we discuss a number of software engineering buzzwords that you'll hear in the software development community. We've created Resource Centers on most of these topics, with many more on the way.

Agile Software Development is a set of methodologies that try to get software implemented quickly with fewer resources than previous methodologies. Check out the Agile Alliance (www.agilealliance.org) and the Agile Manifesto (www.agilemanifesto.org).

Refactoring involves reworking code to make it clearer and easier to maintain while preserving its functionality. It's widely employed with agile development methodologies. Many refactoring tools are available to do major portions of the reworking automatically.

Design patterns are proven architectures for constructing flexible and maintainable object-oriented software. The field of design patterns tries to enumerate those recurring patterns, and encourages software designers to reuse them to develop better-quality software with less time, money and effort.

Game programming. The computer game business is larger than the first-run movie business. College courses and even majors are now devoted to the sophisticated software techniques used in game programming. Check out our Game Programming, C++ Game Programming and Programming Projects Resource Centers.

Open source software is developed in a style unlike the proprietary development that dominated software's early years. Individuals and companies contribute their efforts in developing, maintaining and evolving software in exchange for the right to use that software for their own purposes, typically at no charge. Open source code generally gets scrutinized by a much larger audience than proprietary software, so bugs get removed faster. Open source also encourages more innovation. Sun recently announced that it is open sourcing Java. Some organizations you'll hear a lot about in the open source community are the Eclipse Foundation (the Eclipse IDE is popular for C++ and Java software development), the Mozilla Foundation (creators of the Firefox browser), the Apache Software Foundation (creators of the Apache web server) and SourceForge (which provides the tools for managing open source projects and currently has over 150,000 open source projects under development).

Linux is an open source operating system and one of the greatest successes of the open source movement. *MySQL* is an open source database management system. *PHP* is the most popular open source server-side "scripting" language for developing Internet-based applications. *LAMP* is an acronym for the set of open source technologies that many developers used to build web applications—it stands for Linux, Apache, MySQL and PHP (or Perl or Python—two other languages used for similar purposes).

Ruby on Rails combines the scripting language Ruby with the Rails web application framework developed by the company 37Signals. Their book, *Getting Real*, is a must read for today's web application developers; read it free at `gettingreal.37signals.com/toc.php`. Many Ruby on Rails developers have reported significant productivity gains over using other languages when developing database-intensive web applications.

Software has generally been viewed as a product; most software still is offered this way. If you want to run an application, you buy a software package from a software vendor. You then install that software on your computer and run it as needed. As new versions of the software appear you upgrade your software, often at significant expense. This process can become cumbersome for organizations with tens of thousands of systems that must be maintained on a diverse array of computer equipment. With *Software as a Service (SaaS)* the software runs on servers elsewhere on the Internet. When those servers are updated, all clients worldwide see the new capabilities; no local installation is needed. You access the service through a browser—these are quite portable so you can run the same applications on different kinds of computers from anywhere in the world. Salesforce.com, Google, and Microsoft's Office Live and Windows Live all offer SaaS.

1.20 Future of Visual C++: Open Source Boost Libraries, TR1 and C++0x

Bjarne Stroustrup, the creator of C++, has expressed his vision for the future of C++—the main goals for the new standard are to make C++ easier to learn, improve library-building capabilities, and increase compatibility with the C programming language.

The *Boost C++ Libraries* are free, open source libraries created by members of the C++ community. Boost has grown to over 70 libraries, with more being added regularly. Today there are thousands of programmers in the Boost open source community. Boost provides C++ programmers with useful, well-designed libraries that work well with the existing C++ Standard Library. The Boost libraries can be used by C++ programmers working on a wide variety of platforms with many different compilers.

Regular expressions are used to match specific character patterns in text. They can be used to validate data to ensure that it is in a particular format, to replace parts of one string with another, or to split a string.

Many common bugs in C and C++ code are related to pointers, a powerful programming capability you'll study in Chapter 9. *Smart pointers* help you avoid errors by providing additional functionality to standard pointers. This functionality typically strengthens the process of memory allocation and deallocation.

Technical Report 1 describes the proposed changes to the C++ Standard Library, many of which are based on current Boost libraries. These libraries add useful functionality to C++. The C++ Standards Committee is currently revising the C++ Standard. The last standard was published in 1998. Work on the new standard, currently referred to as *C++0x*, began in 2003. The new standard is likely to be released in 2009. It will include changes to the core language and, most likely, many of the libraries in TR1.

Note that many of the features provided for native C++ with the Boost libraries are already available in the .NET FCL for managed code developers. You will see an example in Chapter 24 when we use the .NET FCL classes to teach regular expressions. In the future, Visual C++ will comply with the new standards in C++0x, once they are approved.

It will also focus more heavily on native C++ than in the past and strengthen C++/CLI's power as a tool for interoperability between languages.

1.21 (Only Required Section of the Case Study) Software Engineering Case Study: Introduction to Object Technology and the UML

Now we begin our early introduction to object orientation, a natural way of thinking about the world and writing computer programs. Chapters 1, 3–8, 10 and 14 each end with a brief Software Engineering Case Study section in which we present a carefully paced introduction to object orientation. Our goal here is to help you develop an object-oriented way of thinking and to introduce you to the *Unified Modeling Language*™ (*UML*™)—a graphical language that allows people who design object-oriented software systems to use an industry-standard notation to represent them.

In this, the only required section of the case study, we introduce basic object-oriented concepts and terminology. The optional sections in Chapters 3–8, 10 and 14 present an object-oriented design and implementation of the software for a simple automated teller machine (ATM) system. The Software Engineering Case Study sections at the ends of Chapters 3–8:

- analyze a typical requirements document that describes a software system (the ATM) to be built.

- determine the objects required to implement the system.

- determine the attributes the objects will have.

- determine the behaviors the objects will exhibit.

- specify how the objects will interact with one another to meet the system requirements.

The Software Engineering Case Study sections at the ends of Chapters 10 and 14 modify and enhance the design presented in Chapters 3–8. Appendix F contains a complete, working Visual C++ implementation of the object-oriented ATM system.

Although our case study is a scaled-down version of an industry-level problem, we nevertheless cover many common industry practices. You will experience a solid introduction to object-oriented design with the UML. Also, you will sharpen your code-reading skills by touring a complete, straightforward and well-documented Visual C++ implementation of the ATM.

Basic Object Technology Concepts

We begin our introduction to object orientation with some key terminology. Everywhere you look in the real world you see *objects*—people, animals, plants, cars, planes, buildings, computers and so on. Humans think in terms of objects. Telephones, houses, traffic lights, microwave ovens and water coolers are just a few more objects we see around us every day.

We sometimes divide objects into two categories: animate and inanimate. Animate objects are "alive" in some sense—they move around and do things. Inanimate objects do not move on their own. Objects of both types, however, have some things in common. They all have *attributes* (e.g., size, shape, color and weight), and they all exhibit *behaviors* (e.g., a ball rolls, bounces, inflates and deflates; a baby cries, sleeps, crawls, walks and blinks; a car accelerates, brakes and turns; a towel absorbs water). We will study the kinds of attributes and behaviors that software objects have.

Humans learn about objects by studying their attributes and observing their behaviors. Different objects can have similar attributes and can exhibit similar behaviors. Comparisons can be made, for example, between babies and adults and between humans and chimpanzees.

Object-oriented design (*OOD*) models software in terms similar to those that people use to describe real-world objects. It takes advantage of class relationships, where objects of a certain class, such as a class of vehicles, have the same characteristics—cars, trucks, little red wagons and roller skates have much in common. OOD takes advantage of *inheritance* relationships, where new classes of objects are derived by absorbing characteristics of existing classes and adding unique characteristics of their own. An object of "convertible" class certainly has the characteristics of the more general class "automobile," but more specifically, the roof goes up and down.

Object-oriented design provides a natural and intuitive way to view the software design process—namely, modeling objects by their attributes, behaviors and interrelationships, just as we describe real-world objects. OOD also models communication between objects. Just as people send messages to one another (e.g., a sergeant commands a soldier to stand at attention, or a teenager text-messages a friend to meet at the movies), objects also communicate via messages. A bank account object may receive a message to decrease its balance by a certain amount because the customer has withdrawn that amount of money.

OOD *encapsulates* (i.e., wraps) attributes and *operations* (behaviors) into objects—an object's attributes and operations are intimately tied together. Objects have the property of *information hiding*. This means that objects may know how to communicate with one another across well-defined *interfaces*, but normally they are not allowed to know how other objects are implemented—implementation details are hidden within the objects themselves. You can drive a car effectively, for instance, without knowing the details of how engines, transmissions, brakes and exhaust systems work internally—as long as you know how to use the accelerator pedal, the brake pedal, the steering wheel and so on. Information hiding, as you will see, is crucial to good software engineering.

Languages like Visual C++ are *object oriented*. Programming in such a language is called *object-oriented programming* (*OOP*), and it allows computer programmers to conveniently implement an object-oriented design as a working software system. Languages like C, on the other hand, are *procedural*, so programming tends to be *action oriented*. In C, the unit of programming is the *function*. In Visual C++, the unit of programming is the *class*, from which objects are eventually *instantiated* (an OOP term for "created"). Visual C++ classes contain *member functions* that implement operations, and data that implements attributes.

Classes, Data Members and Functions

Visual C++ programmers concentrate on creating their own *user-defined types* called classes. Each class contains data as well as the set of functions (called methods in some other languages) that manipulate the data and provide services to *clients* (i.e., other classes that use the class). The data components of a class are called attributes, or *fields*. For example, a bank account class might include an account number and a balance. The operation components of a class are called functions. For example, a bank account class might include functions to make a deposit (increase the balance), make a withdrawal (decrease the balance) and inquire what the current balance is. The programmer uses built-in types (and other user-defined types) as the "building blocks" for constructing new user-defined types (classes). The *nouns in a system specification* help the Visual C++ programmer determine the set of classes from which objects are created that work together to implement the system.

Classes are to objects as blueprints are to houses—a class is a "plan" for building objects of the class. Just as we can build many houses from one blueprint, we can instantiate (create) many objects from one class. You cannot cook meals in the kitchen of a blueprint, but you can cook meals in the kitchen of a house. You cannot sleep in the bedroom of a blueprint, but you can sleep in the bedroom of a house.

Classes can have relationships with other classes. For example, in an object-oriented design of a bank, the "bank teller" class needs to relate to other classes, such as the "customer" class, the "cash drawer" class, the "safe" class and so on. These relationships are called *associations*.

Packaging software as classes makes it possible for future software systems to *reuse* the classes. Groups of related classes often are packaged as reusable *components*. Just as realtors often say that the three most important factors affecting the price of real estate are "location, location and location," some people in the software development community often say that the three most important factors affecting the future of software development are "reuse, reuse and reuse."

Software Engineering Observation 1.4

Reuse of existing classes when building new classes and programs saves time, money and effort. Reuse also helps programmers build more reliable and effective systems, because existing classes and components often have gone through extensive testing, debugging and performance tuning.

Indeed, with object technology, you can build much of the new software you will need by combining existing classes, just as automobile manufacturers combine interchangeable parts. Each new class you create will have the potential to become a valuable software asset that you and other programmers can reuse to speed and enhance the quality of future software development efforts.

Introduction to Object-Oriented Analysis and Design (OOAD)

Soon you will be writing programs in Visual C++. How will you create the code for your programs? Perhaps, like many beginning programmers, you will simply turn on your computer and start typing. This approach may work for small programs (like the ones we present in the early chapters of the book), but what if you were asked to create a software system to control thousands of automated teller machines for a major bank? Or what if you were asked to work as part of a team of 1000 software developers building the next generation of the U.S. air traffic control system? For projects so large and complex, you could not simply sit down and start writing programs.

To create the best solutions, you should follow a detailed process for *analyzing* your project's *requirements* (i.e., determining *what* your system is supposed to do) and developing a *design* that satisfies them (i.e., deciding *how* your system should do it). Ideally, you would go through this process and carefully review the design (and have your design reviewed by other software professionals) before writing any code. If this process involves analyzing and designing your system from an object-oriented point of view, it is called *object-oriented analysis and design* (*OOAD*). Experienced programmers know that proper analysis and design can save many hours by helping avoid an ill-planned system development approach that has to be abandoned partway through its implementation, possibly wasting considerable time, money and effort.

OOAD is the generic term for the process of analyzing a problem and developing an approach for solving it. Small problems like the ones discussed in the first few chapters of this book do not require an exhaustive OOAD process. It may be sufficient, before we begin writing Visual C++ code, to write *pseudocode*—an informal natural language based means of expressing program logic. It is not actually a programming language, but you can use it as an outline to guide you as you write your code. We introduce pseudocode in Chapter 6.

As problems and the groups of people solving them increase in size, OOAD quickly becomes more appropriate than pseudocode. Ideally, a group should agree on a strictly defined process for solving its problem and a uniform way of communicating the results of that process to one another. Although many different OOAD processes exist, a single graphical language for communicating the results of *any* OOAD process has come into wide use. This language, known as the Unified Modeling Language (UML), was developed in the mid-1990s under the initial direction of three software methodologists: Grady Booch, James Rumbaugh and Ivar Jacobson.

History of the UML

In the 1980s, increasing numbers of organizations began using OOP to build their applications, and a need developed for a standard OOAD process. Many methodologists—including Grady Booch, James Rumbaugh and Ivar Jacobson—individually produced and promoted separate processes to satisfy this need. Each process had its own notation, or "language" (in the form of graphical diagrams), to convey the results of analysis (i.e., determining *what* a proposed system is supposed to do) and design (i.e., determining *how* a proposed system should be implemented to do what it is supposed to do).

By the early 1990s, different organizations were using their own unique processes and notations. At the same time, these organizations also wanted to use software tools that would support their particular processes. Software vendors found it difficult to provide tools for so many processes. A standard notation and standard process were needed.

In 1994, James Rumbaugh joined Grady Booch at Rational Software Corporation (now a division of IBM), and the two began working to unify their popular processes. They soon were joined by Ivar Jacobson. In 1996, the group released early versions of the UML to the software engineering community and requested feedback. Around the same time, an organization known as the Object Management Group™ (OMG™) invited submissions for a common modeling language. The OMG (www.omg.org) is a nonprofit organization that promotes the standardization of object-oriented technologies by issuing guidelines and specifications, such as the UML. Several corporations—among them HP, IBM, Microsoft, Oracle and Rational Software—had already recognized the need for a common modeling language. In response to the OMG's request for proposals, these companies formed the UML Partners—the consortium that developed the UML version 1.1 and submitted it to the OMG. The OMG accepted the proposal and, in 1997, assumed responsibility for the continuing maintenance and revision of the UML. We present the recently adopted UML 2 terminology and notation throughout this book.

What is the UML?

The *Unified Modeling Language* (*UML*) is the most widely used graphical representation scheme for modeling object-oriented systems. It has indeed unified the various popular notational schemes. Those who design systems use the language (in the form of diagrams, many of which we discuss throughout our ATM case study) to model their systems. We use several popular types of UML diagrams in this book.

An attractive feature of the UML is its flexibility. The UML is *extensible* (i.e., capable of being enhanced with new features) and is independent of any particular OOAD process. UML modelers are free to use various processes in designing systems, but all developers can now express their designs with one standard set of graphical notations.

The UML is a feature-rich graphical language. In our subsequent (and optional) Software Engineering Case Study sections on developing the software for an automated teller machine (ATM), we present a simple, concise subset of these features. We then use this subset to guide you through a first design experience with the UML. We will use some Visual C++ notations in our UML diagrams to avoid confusion and improve clarity. In industry practice, especially with UML tools that automatically generate code (a nice feature of many UML tools), you would probably adhere more closely to UML keywords and UML naming conventions for attributes and operations.

This case study was carefully developed under the guidance of distinguished academic and professional reviewers. We sincerely hope you enjoy working through it. If you have any questions, please communicate with us at `deitel@deitel.com`. We'll respond promptly.

Internet and Web UML Resources

For more information about the UML, refer to the following websites. For additional UML sites, please refer to the Internet and web resources listed at the end of Section 4.13.

`www.uml.org`
This UML resource site from the Object Management Group (OMG) provides specification documents for the UML and other object-oriented technologies.

`www.ibm.com/software/rational/uml`
This is the UML resource page for IBM Rational—the successor to the Rational Software Corporation (the company that created the UML).

Recommended Readings

Many books on the UML have been published. The following recommended books provide information about object-oriented design with the UML.

- Arlow, J., and I. Neustadt. *UML and the Unified Process: Practical Object-Oriented Analysis and Design, Second Edition*. London: Addison-Wesley, 2005.

- Fowler, M. *UML Distilled, Third Edition: Applying the Standard Object Modeling Language*. Boston: Addison-Wesley, 2004.

- Rumbaugh, J., I. Jacobson, and G. Booch. *The Unified Modeling Language User Guide, Second Edition*. Upper Saddle River, NJ: Addison-Wesley, 2005.

For additional books on the UML, please refer to the recommended readings listed at the end of Section 4.13, or visit `www.amazon.com`, `www.bn.com` and `www.informIT.com`. IBM Rational, formerly Rational Software Corporation, also provides a recommended-readings list for UML books at `www.ibm.com/software/rational/info/technical/books.jsp`.

Section 1.21 Self-Review Exercises

1.1 List three examples of real-world objects that we did not mention. For each object, list several attributes and behaviors.

1.2 Pseudocode is _____.
  a) another term for OOAD
  b) a programming language used to display UML diagrams
  c) an informal means of expressing program logic
  d) a graphical representation scheme for modeling object-oriented systems

1.3 The UML is used primarily to _____.
  a) test object-oriented systems
  b) design object-oriented systems
  c) implement object-oriented systems
  d) Both a and b

Answers to Section 1.21 Self-Review Exercises

1.1 [*Note:* Answers may vary.] a) A television's attributes include the size of the screen, the number of colors it can display, and its current channel and volume. A television turns on and off, changes channels, displays video and plays sounds. b) A coffee maker's attributes include the maximum volume of water it can hold, the time required to brew a pot of coffee and the temperature of the heating plate under the coffee pot. A coffee maker turns on and off, brews coffee and heats coffee. c) A turtle's attributes include its age, the size of its shell and its weight. A turtle crawls, retreats into its shell, emerges from its shell and eats vegetation.

1.2 c.

1.3 b.

1.22 Wrap-Up

This chapter introduced basic hardware and software concepts and basic object-technology concepts, including classes, objects, attributes and behaviors. We discussed the history of the Internet and the World Wide Web. We presented a brief history of operating systems, including Microsoft's Windows operating system.

We presented the history of C++ and Microsoft's .NET initiative, which provides platform independence and great language interoperability with Visual C++. You learned the basics about the C++ Standard Library and the future of C++. We discussed the different types of programming languages and which languages are most widely used. You learned the steps for executing a Visual C++ application. You test-drove a sample Visual C++ application similar to the types of applications you will learn to program in this book.

You learned about the history and purpose of the UML—the industry-standard graphical language for modeling software systems. We launched our early objects and classes presentation with the first of our Software Engineering Case Study sections (and the only one which is required). The remaining (all optional) sections of the case study use object-oriented design and the UML to design the software for our simplified automated teller machine system. We present the complete Visual C++ code implementation of the ATM system in Appendix F.

In the next chapter, you will use the Visual Studio 2008 IDE (Integrated Development Environment) to create your first Visual C++ application. You will also learn about Visual Studio's help features.

Summary

Section 1.1 Introduction
- Computers that might have filled large rooms and cost millions of dollars a few decades ago can now be inscribed on silicon chips smaller than a fingernail, costing a few dollars each.
- Silicon-chip technology has made computing so economical that about a billion general-purpose computers are in use worldwide, helping people in business, industry and government, and in their personal lives.

Section 1.2 What Is a Computer?
- Computers process data under the control of sets of instructions called computer programs. These programs guide the computer through sets of actions specified by computer programmers.
- A computer consists of various devices referred to as hardware (e.g., the keyboard, screen, disk drives, memory and processing units).
- The computer programs that run on a computer are referred to as software.
- A computer is a device capable of performing computations and making logical decisions at speeds millions, billions and even trillions of times faster than humans.

Section 1.3 Computer Organization
- The input unit is the "receiving" section of the computer. It obtains information from input devices and places it at the disposal of the other units for processing.
- The output unit is the "shipping" section of the computer. It takes information processed by the computer and places it on output devices to make it available for use outside the computer.
- The memory unit is the rapid-access, relatively low-capacity "warehouse" section of the computer. It retains information that has been entered through the input unit, making it immediately available for processing when needed, and retains information that has already been processed until it can be placed on output devices by the output unit.
- The arithmetic and logic unit (ALU) is the "manufacturing" section of the computer. It is responsible for performing calculations and making decisions.
- The central processing unit (CPU) is the "administrative" section of the computer. It coordinates and supervises the operation of the other sections.
- The secondary storage unit is the long-term, high-capacity "warehousing" section of the computer. Programs or data not being used by the other units are normally placed on secondary storage devices (e.g., disks) until they are needed, hours, days, months or even years later.

Section 1.4 Early Operating Systems
- Software systems called operating systems were developed to help make using computers more convenient.
- Multiprogramming involves the simultaneous operation of many jobs that are competing to share the computer's resources.

Section 1.5 Personal Computing, Distributed Computing and Client/Server Computing
- With distributed computing, an organization's computing is distributed over networks to the sites where the work of the organization is performed.
- The most powerful desktop machines provide individual users with enormous capabilities. Information is shared easily across computer networks, where computers called file servers offer a common data store that may be used by client computers distributed throughout the network—hence the term client/server computing.

Section 1.6 The Internet and the World Wide Web
- The Internet—a global network of computers—was initiated almost four decades ago with funding supplied by the U.S. Department of Defense. Originally designed to connect the main computer systems of about a dozen universities and research organizations, the Internet today is accessible by hundreds of millions of computers worldwide.
- The World Wide Web allows computer users to locate and view multimedia-based documents on almost any subject over the Internet.
- In 1989, Tim Berners-Lee of CERN (the European Organization for Nuclear Research) began to develop a technology for sharing information via hyperlinked text documents. Berners-Lee called his invention the HyperText Markup Language (HTML).

Section 1.7 Hardware Trends
- Every year or two, computers' capacities approximately double while their prices remain relatively constant. This trend often is called Moore's Law, named after the person who first observed it, Gordon Moore, co-founder of Intel.
- The invention of microprocessor chip technology and its wide deployment in the late 1970s and 1980s laid the groundwork for the productivity improvements that individuals and businesses have achieved in recent years.

Section 1.8 Microsoft's Windows® Operating System
- In the mid-1980s, Microsoft developed the Windows operating system, a graphical user interface built on top of the DOS operating system.
- The Windows operating system became incredibly popular after the 1993 release of Windows 3.1, whose successors, Windows 95 and Windows 98, virtually cornered the desktop operating systems market by the late 1990s.
- These operating systems, which borrowed many concepts (such as icons, menus and windows) popularized by early Apple Macintosh operating systems, enabled users to navigate multiple applications simultaneously.
- Windows XP, which is based on the Windows NT operating system, was released in 2001 and combines Microsoft's corporate and consumer operating system lines. Windows Vista was released in 2007 to provide a better user experience and security model than Windows XP. Windows is by far the most widely used operating system.
- The biggest competitor to the Windows operating system is Linux. Linux is a free, open source operating system.

Section 1.9 Machine Languages, Assembly Languages and High-Level Languages
- Any computer can directly understand only its own machine language. Machine languages generally consist of strings of numbers (ultimately reduced to 1s and 0s) that instruct computers to perform their most elementary operations one at a time.
- English-like abbreviations form the basis of assembly languages. Translator programs called assemblers convert assembly-language programs to machine language.
- Compilers translate high-level language programs into machine-language programs. High-level languages (like Visual C++) contain English words and conventional mathematical notations.
- Interpreter programs execute high-level language programs directly, although much more slowly. Once a program is fully developed, a compiled version can be produced to run efficiently.

Section 1.10 Visual C++
- The C programming language was developed by Dennis Ritchie at Bell Laboratories in 1973. C first gained widespread recognition as the development language of the UNIX operating system.

- Objects are reusable software components that model items in the real world. A modular, object-oriented approach to design and implementation can make software development groups much more productive than they can be possible using only earlier programming techniques, such as structured programming. Object-oriented programs are often easier to understand, correct and modify.

- C++ was developed by Bjarne Stroustrup in the early 1980s at Bell Laboratories. C++ provides a number of features that "spruce up" the C language, but more important, it provides capabilities for object-oriented programming (OOP).

- Visual C++ is object oriented and contains a powerful class library of prebuilt components, enabling programmers to develop applications quickly—Visual C++ shares the Framework Class Library (FCL) with the other .NET languages.

- The .NET platform is one over which web-based applications can be distributed to a great variety of devices (even cell phones) and to desktop computers.

- C++/CLI is an extension of C++ that allows developers to program C++ programs that target the .NET Framework. Its most powerful feature is the ability to easily create programs that mix or bridge managed and unmanaged code.

- C++/CLI is an event-driven, fully object-oriented, visual programming language in which programs are created using an Integrated Development Environment (IDE).

Section 1.12 Java, C# and Visual Basic

- The C# programming language, developed at Microsoft, was designed specifically for the .NET platform as a language combining features from C++, Java, and other languages in a way that would enable programmers to migrate easily to .NET.

- Java is now used to develop large-scale enterprise applications, to enhance the functionality of web servers, to provide applications for consumer devices and for many other purposes.

- Visual Basic offers powerful features including graphical user interfaces, event handling, object-oriented programming and exception handling.

- Visual Basic is an event-driven language (i.e., the programs respond to user-initiated events such as mouse clicks and keystrokes) and a visual programming language in which programs are created using an Integrated Development Environment (IDE).

Section 1.13 Other High-Level Languages

- Fortran (FORmula TRANslator) was developed by IBM Corporation in the mid-1950s for scientific and engineering applications that require complex mathematical computations.

- Pascal, named after the mathematician and philosopher Blaise Pascal, was designed for teaching structured programming in academic environments.

- COBOL (COmmon Business Oriented Language) was developed in the late 1950s. COBOL is used primarily for commercial applications that require precise and efficient data manipulation.

- Ada was developed under the sponsorship of the U.S. Department of Defense through the early 1980s. An important capability of Ada is multitasking, which allows programmers to specify that many activities are to occur in parallel. The language was named after Lady Ada Lovelace, daughter of the poet Lord Byron. She is generally credited with having written the world's first computer program, in the early 1800s.

Section 1.14 Microsoft's .NET

- In 2000, Microsoft announced its .NET initiative, a new vision for embracing the Internet and the web in the development and use of software. One key aspect of .NET is its independence from a specific language or platform. Rather than being forced to use a single programming language, developers can create a .NET application in any .NET-compatible language.

- A key component of the .NET architecture is web services, which are reusable application components that can be used over the Internet. Clients and other applications can use these web services as reusable building blocks.

- The .NET strategy extends the concept of software reuse to the Internet, allowing programmers and companies to concentrate on their specialties without having to implement every component of every application. Instead, companies can buy web services and devote their resources to developing their own products.

Section 1.15 The .NET Framework and the Common Language Runtime

- Microsoft's .NET Framework manages and executes applications and web services, contains a class library called the Framework Class Library (FCL), enforces security and provides many other programming capabilities.

- The details of the .NET Framework are found in the Common Language Infrastructure (CLI), which contains information about the storage of data types, objects and so on.

- The Common Language Runtime (CLR) executes .NET programs.

- Programs are compiled into machine-specific instructions in two steps. First, the program is compiled into Microsoft Intermediate Language (MSIL), which defines instructions for the CLR. When an application executes, another compiler (known as the just-in-time compiler or JIT compiler) in the CLR translates the MSIL in the executable file into machine-language code (for a particular platform); then the machine-language code executes on that platform. This second compilation phase is known as just-in-time compilation.

- The Framework Class Library (FCL) can be used by any .NET language. It contains reusable components, saving programmers the trouble of creating new components.

Section 1.16 Key Software Trend: Object Technology

- Improvements to software technology emerged with the benefits of structured programming (and the related disciplines of structured systems analysis and design) being realized in the 1970s.

- Not until the technology of object-oriented programming became widely used in the 1990s did software developers feel they had the necessary tools for making major strides in the software development process.

- Object technology dates back to the mid 1960s.

- The C++ programming language, developed at AT&T by Bjarne Stroustrup in the early 1980s, is based on two languages—C, which initially was developed at AT&T to implement the UNIX operating system in the early 1970s, and Simula 67, a simulation programming language developed in Europe and released in 1967.

- C++ absorbed the features of C and added Simula's capabilities for creating and manipulating objects. Neither C nor C++ was originally intended for wide use beyond the AT&T research laboratories. But grass-roots support rapidly developed for each.

- Object technology is a packaging scheme that helps us create meaningful software units.

- A key problem with procedural programming is that the program units do not effectively mirror real-world entities, so these units are not particularly reusable.

- With object technology, the software entities created (called classes), if properly designed, tend to be reusable on future projects. Using libraries of reusable components can greatly reduce the effort required to implement certain kinds of system.

- Some organizations report that the key benefit object-oriented programming gives them is not software reuse, but a tendency to produce software that is more understandable, better organized and easier to maintain, modify and debug.

Section 1.17 Typical Visual C++ Development Life Cycle

- Visual C++ systems generally consist of three parts: a program development environment, the language and the libraries.
- Visual C++ programs typically go through six phases: edit, preprocess, compile, link, load and execute. Visual Studio streamlines this process for you and does much of it behind the scenes so you can focus on writing your programs.
- C++ source code filenames typically end with the .cpp.
- A preprocessor program executes automatically before the compiler's translation phase begins. The Visual C++ preprocessor obeys commands called preprocessor directives, which indicate that certain manipulations are to be performed on the source code before compilation. These manipulations usually insert other text files into source code, and perform various text replacements.
- The compiler translates the Visual C++ program into Microsoft Intermediate Language (MSIL), which is ready to be compiled into machine-language code at runtime. For native C++ code that does not require the .NET Framework, the compiler simply translates the C++ program into machine-language code (also referred to as object code).
- Visual C++ programs typically contain references to functions and data defined elsewhere, such as in the standard libraries or in the private libraries of groups of programmers working on a particular project. The object code produced by the Visual C++ compiler typically contains "holes" due to these missing parts. A linker fills in these holes with the code for the missing functions to produce an executable image, which represents a complete version of the application.
- Before a program can be executed, it must first be placed in memory. This is done by the operating system's loader.
- If the program uses the .NET Framework, then at runtime the .NET just-in-time compiler converts the MSIL code into machine-language code that is ready to be executed.

Section 1.20 Future of Visual C++: Open Source Boost Libraries, TR1 and C++0x

- The Boost C++ Libraries are free, open source libraries created by members of the C++ community. Boost provides C++ programmers with useful, well-designed libraries that work well with the existing C++ Standard Library. The Boost libraries can be used by C++ programmers working on a wide variety of platforms with many different compilers.
- Technical Report 1 describes the proposed changes to the C++ Standard Library, many of which are based on current Boost libraries. These libraries add useful functionality to C++.
- The C++ Standards Committee is currently revising the C++ Standard. The last standard was published in 1998. Work on the new standard, currently referred to as C++0x, began in 2003. The new standard is likely to be released in 2009. It will include changes to the core language and, most likely, many of the libraries in TR1.
- Note that many of the features provided for native C++ with the Boost libraries are already available in the .NET FCL for managed code developers.

Section 1.21 (Only Required Section of the Case Study) Software Engineering Case Study: Introduction to Object Technology and the UML

- The Unified Modeling Language (UML) is a graphical language that allows people who build systems to represent their object-oriented designs in a common notation.

- Object-oriented design (OOD) models software components in terms of real-world objects. It takes advantage of class relationships, where objects of a certain class have the same characteristics. It also takes advantage of inheritance relationships, where newly created classes of objects are derived by absorbing characteristics of existing classes and adding unique characteristics of their own. OOD encapsulates data (attributes) and functions (behavior) into objects—the data and functions of an object are intimately tied together.

- Objects have the property of information hiding—objects of one class are normally not allowed to know how objects of other classes are implemented.

- Object-oriented programming (OOP) allows programmers to implement object-oriented designs as working systems.

- Visual C++ programmers concentrate on creating their own user-defined types called classes. Each class contains data as well as the set of functions that manipulate that data and provide services to clients (i.e., other classes or functions that use the class).

- The data components of a class are called attributes or fields. The operation components of a class are called functions.

- Classes can have relationships with other classes. These relationships are called associations.

- Packaging software as classes makes it possible for future software systems to reuse the classes. Groups of related classes are often packaged as reusable components.

- An instance of a class is called an object.

- With object technology, programmers can build much of the software they will need by combining standardized, interchangeable parts called classes.

- The process of analyzing and designing a system from an object-oriented point of view is called object-oriented analysis and design (OOAD).

Terminology

action	COBOL programming language
action oriented	Common Language Infrastructure (CLI)
Ada programming language	Common Language Runtime (CLR)
"administrative" section of the computer	compiler
arithmetic and logic unit (ALU)	component
assembler	computer
assembly language	computer program
association	computer programmer
attribute of an object	control
batch processing	data
behavior of an object	data independence
C programming language	design
C# programming language	distributed computing
C++ programming language	dynamic content
C++/CLI programming language	e-mail (electronic mail)
central processing unit (CPU)	encapsulate
class	extensible
class library	field of a class
client	file server
client of a class	Fortran programming language
client/server computing	Framework Class Library (FCL)
close box	function

garbage collector
hardware
hardware platform
high-level language
HTML (HyperText Markup Language)
information hiding
inheritance
input device
input unit
instantiate an object of a class
Integrated Development Environment (IDE)
interface
Internet
interpreter
Java programming language
job
just-in-time (JIT) compiler
language independence
language interoperability in .NET
live-code approach
local area network (LAN)
logical unit
machine dependent
machine language
"manufacturing" section of the computer
member function
memory
memory unit
Microsoft .NET
Microsoft Intermediate Language (MSIL)
Moore's Law
multiprocessor
multiprogramming
multitasking
multithreading
.NET Framework
.NET initiative
.NET-compliant language
nouns in a system specification
object
object oriented

object-oriented analysis and design (OOAD)
object-oriented design (OOD)
object-oriented programming (OOP)
operating system
operation of an object
output device
output unit
Pascal programming language
personal computer
personal computing
platform independence
portability
primary memory
procedural programming
pseudocode
"receiving" section of the computer
reusable software component
secondary storage unit
"shipping" section of the computer
SOAP (Simple Object Access Protocol)
software
software reuse
standard error stream
standard input stream
standard output stream
structured programming
supercomputer
task
throughput
timesharing
translation
translator program
UML (Unified Modeling Language)
user-defined type
Visual Basic programming language
Visual C# programming language
visual programming
web service
Windows operating system
World Wide Web (WWW)

Self-Review Exercises

1.1 Fill in the blanks in each of the following statements:

a) Computers can directly understand only their native _____ language, which is composed only of 1s and 0s.

b) Computers process data under the control of sets of instructions called computer _____.

c) The _____ is the long-term, high-capacity "warehousing" section of the computer.

d) The three types of languages discussed in the chapter are machine languages, _____ and _____.

e) Programs that translate high-level language programs into machine language are called _____.

f) Visual Studio is a(n) _____ in which Visual C++ programs are developed.

g) C is widely known as the development language of the _____ operating system.

h) Microsoft's _____ provides a large programming library for the .NET languages.

i) The Department of Defense developed the Ada language with a capability called _____, which allows programmers to specify activities that can proceed in parallel. Visual C++ offers a similar capability called multithreading.

j) Web services use _____ and _____ to mark up and send information over the Internet, respectively.

1.2 State whether each of the following is *true* or *false*. If *false*, explain why.

a) The UML is used primarily to implement object-oriented systems.

b) Visual C++ is an object-oriented language.

c) Visual C++ is the only language available for programming .NET applications.

d) Procedural programming models the world more naturally than object-oriented programming.

e) Computers can directly understand high-level languages.

f) MSIL is the common intermediate format to which all .NET programs compile, regardless of their original .NET language.

g) The .NET Framework is portable to non-Windows platforms.

h) Compiled programs run faster than their corresponding interpreted programs.

i) Multiprogramming involves the simultaneous operation of many jobs that are competing to share the computer's resources.

Answers to Self-Review Exercises

1.1 a) machine. b) programs. c) secondary storage unit. d) assembly languages, high-level languages. e) compilers. f) Integrated Development Environment (IDE). g) UNIX. h) Framework Class Library (FCL). i) multitasking. j) XML, SOAP.

1.2 a) False. The UML is used primarily to design object-oriented systems. b) True. c) False. Visual C++ is one of many .NET languages (others are Visual Basic and C#). d) False. Object-oriented programming (because it focuses on *things*) is a more natural way to model the world than procedural programming. e) False. Computers can directly understand only their own machine languages. f) True. g) True. h) True. i) True.

Exercises

1.3 Categorize each of the following items as either hardware or software:

a) CPU.

b) Compiler.

c) Keyboard.

d) A word-processor program.

e) A Visual C++ program.

1.4 Translator programs, such as assemblers and compilers, convert programs from one language (referred to as the source language) to another language (referred to as the target language). Determine which of the following statements are *true* and which are *false*:

a) A compiler translates high-level language programs into target-language programs.

b) An assembler translates source-language programs into machine-language programs.

    c) A compiler converts source-language programs into target-language programs.
    d) High-level languages are generally machine dependent.
    e) A machine-language program requires translation before it can be run on a computer.
    f) The Visual C++ compiler translates high-level language programs into MSIL.

1.5 What are the basic requirements of a .NET language? What is needed to run a .NET program on a new type of computer (machine)?

1.6 Expand each of the following acronyms:
    a) SOAP.
    b) OOP.
    c) CLR.
    d) CLI.
    e) FCL.
    f) MSIL.
    g) UML.
    h) OMG.
    i) IDE.

1.7 What are the key benefits of the .NET Framework and the CLR? What are the drawbacks?

1.8 What are the advantages to using object-oriented techniques?

1.9 You are probably wearing on your wrist one of the world's most common types of objects—a watch. Discuss how each of the following terms and concepts applies to the notion of a watch: object, attributes and behaviors.

1.10 What was the key reason that Visual C++ was developed?

1.11 What is the key accomplishment of the UML?

1.12 What did the chief benefit of the early Internet prove to be?

1.13 What is the key capability of the web?

1.14 What is the key vision of Microsoft's .NET initiative?

1.15 How does the FCL facilitate the development of .NET applications?

1.16 What are web services and why are they so crucial to Microsoft's .NET strategy?

1.17 What is the key advantage of standardizing .NET's CLI (Common Language Infrastructure) with Ecma?

1.18 Why is programming in an object-oriented language such as Visual C++ more "natural" than programming in a procedural programming language such as C?

1.19 Despite the obvious benefits of reuse made possible by OOP, what do many organizations report as the key benefit of OOP?

2

Dive Into® Visual C++® 2008 Express

Seeing is believing.
—Proverb

Form ever follows function.
—Louis Henri Sullivan

Intelligence … is the faculty of making artificial objects, especially tools to make tools.
—Henri-Louis Bergson

OBJECTIVES

In this chapter, you will learn:

- The basics of the Visual Studio Integrated Development Environment (IDE) that assists you in writing, running and debugging your Visual C++ programs.

- Visual Studio's help features.

- Key commands contained in the IDE's menus and toolbars.

- The purpose of the various kinds of windows in the Visual Studio 2008 IDE.

- What visual programming is and how it simplifies and speeds program development.

- To create, compile and execute a simple Visual C++ program that displays text and an image using the Visual Studio IDE and the technique of visual programming.

2.1 Introduction

Visual Studio® 2008 is Microsoft's Integrated Development Environment (IDE) for creating, running and debugging programs (also called *applications*) written in a variety of programming languages. In this chapter, we provide an overview of the Visual Studio 2008 IDE and demonstrate how to create a simple Visual C++ program. This chapter is specific to Visual C++—Microsoft's implementation of Ecma standard C++. Throughout this book we use Visual Studio 2008 for creating native C++ and C++/CLI applications.

2.2 Overview of the Visual Studio 2008 IDE

Many versions of Visual Studio are available. For this book, we used the *Microsoft Visual C++ 2008 Express Edition*, which supports only native C++ and C++/CLI. The Express Edition is available from www.microsoft.com/express/. Microsoft also offers a full version of Visual Studio 2008, which includes support for other languages in addition to Visual C++, such as Visual Basic and Visual C#. Our screen captures and discussions focus on the IDE of the Visual C++ 2008 Express Edition. We assume that you have some familiarity with Windows.

Again, we use fonts to distinguish between IDE features (such as menu names and menu items) and other elements that appear in the IDE. We emphasize IDE features in a sans-serif bold **Helvetica** font (e.g., **File** menu) and emphasize other elements, such as filenames (e.g., main.cpp) and property names (discussed in Section 2.4), in a sans-serif Lucida font.

Introduction to Microsoft Visual C++ 2008 Express Edition
To start Microsoft Visual C++ 2008 Express Edition in Windows Vista or Windows XP, select **Start > All Programs > Visual C++ 9.0 Express Edition > Visual C++ 2008 Express Edition**. Once the Express Edition begins execution, the ***Start Page*** displays (Fig. 2.1). Depending on your version of Visual Studio, your **Start Page** may look different. For new programmers unfamiliar with Visual C++, the **Start Page** contains a list of links to resources in the Visual Studio 2008 IDE and on the Internet. From this point forward, we refer to the Visual Studio 2008 IDE simply as "Visual Studio" or "the IDE." For experienced developers, the **Start Page** provides links to the latest developments in Visual C++ (such as updates and bug fixes) and to information on advanced programming topics. Once you start exploring the IDE, you can return to the **Start Page** by selecting **View > Other Windows >**

New Project button   Start Page tab

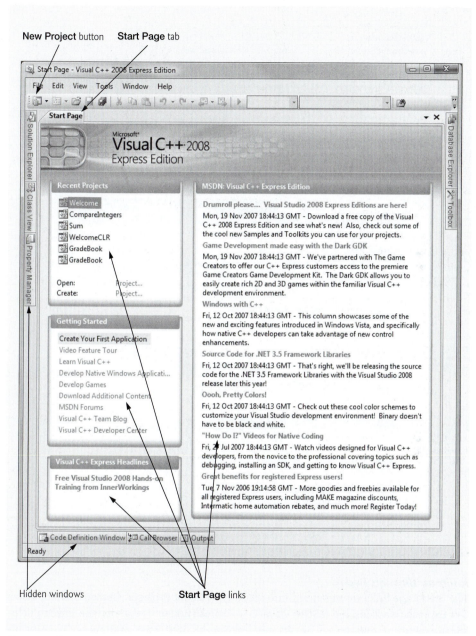

Fig. 2.1 | **Start Page** in Visual C++ 2008 Express Edition.

Hidden windows   Start Page links

Start Page or by clicking the Start Page icon ( ) from the IDE's Toolbar. We discuss the Toolbar and its various icons in Section 2.3. We use the > character to indicate the selection of a menu command from a menu. For example, we use the notation File > Open File to indicate that you should select the Open File command from the File menu.

Request web page
(URL in location bar
drop-down menu)

Selected tab for requested web page

Fig. 2.2 | Displaying a web page in Visual Studio

Links on the Start Page

The **Start Page** links are organized into sections—**Recent Projects, Getting Started, Visual C++ Express Headlines** and **MSDN: Visual C++ Express Edition**—that contain links to helpful programming resources. Clicking any link on the **Start Page** displays the relevant information associated with the specific link. We refer to *single clicking* with the left mouse button as *selecting* or *clicking*; we refer to double clicking with the left mouse button simply as *double clicking*.

The **Recent Projects** section contains information on projects you have recently created or modified. You can also open existing projects or create new ones by clicking the links in the section. The **Getting Started** section focuses on using the IDE to create programs, learning Visual C++, connecting to the Visual C++ developer community (i.e., other software developers with whom you can communicate through newsgroups and websites) and providing various development tools.

The **Visual C++ Express Headlines** and **MSDN: Visual C++ Express Edition** sections provide links to information about programming in Visual C++, including a tour of the language, new Visual C++ 2008 features and online courses. To access more extensive information on Visual Studio, you can browse the *MSDN* (*Microsoft Developer Network*) online library at msdn.microsoft.com. The MSDN site contains articles, downloads and tutorials on technologies of interest to Visual Studio developers. You can also browse the web from the IDE using Internet Explorer. To request a web page, type its URL into the location bar (Fig. 2.2) and press the *Enter* key—your computer, of course, must be connected to the Internet. (If the location bar is not already present in the IDE, select **View > Other Windows > Web Browser**.) The web page that you wish to view will appear as another *tab*, which you can select, inside the Visual Studio IDE (Fig. 2.2).

Creating a New Project

To begin programming in Visual C++, you must create a new project or open an existing one. There are two ways to proceed. You can select either **File > New Project...** or **File > Open Project...** from the **File** menu, which creates a new project or opens an existing project, respectively. From the **Start Page**, under the **Recent Projects** section, you can also click the links **Create: Project...** or **Open: Project....** A *project* is a group of related files, such as the Visual C++ source code and any other resources that might make up a program. Visual Studio organizes programs into projects and *solutions*, which contain one or more projects. Multiple-project solutions are used to create large-scale programs. Each of the solutions we create in this book contains one project.

Select **File > New Project...** or the **Create: Project...** link on the **Start Page** to display the ***New Project*** *dialog* (Fig. 2.3). *Dialogs* are windows that facilitate user/computer communication. We will discuss the detailed process of creating new projects momentarily.

This book discusses two types of projects, native C++ projects and C++/CLI projects. The differences between the two will be discussed throughout the book. For now, you need to know how to create a project of each type. Visual Studio provides templates for several project types (Fig. 2.3). *Templates* are the project types users can create in Visual C++—Windows applications, console applications and others (you will use console applications in this textbook). Users can also use or create custom application templates.

In this chapter, we teach you how to create a native C++ console application and a C++/CLI console application. We begin by discussing how to create a native C++ console application.

Creating a New C++ Project

From the **New Project dialog** we must select the project type. Visual Studio allows you to choose from one of several project types. Click the **Visual C++** node in the **Project Types:** pane (Fig. 2.3) to display the list of Visual C++ project types in the **Templates:** pane. [*Note: Depending on your version of Visual Studio, the names and number of items shown in the* **Project Types:** *and* **Templates:** *panes could differ.*] For a native C++ project we select ***Win32 Console Application***, which you will use to create a project that does not include any source code. We have provided you with the source code, which you will add to your project once it has been created.

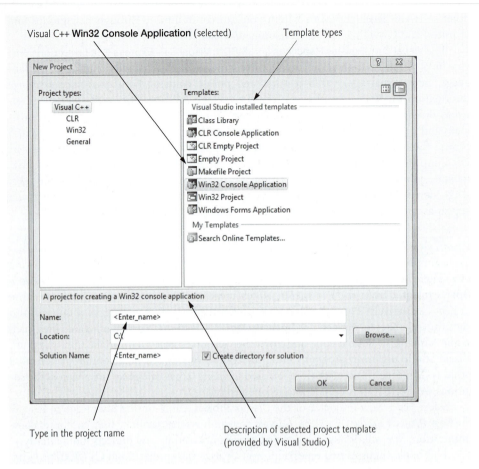

Visual C++ **Win32 Console Application** (selected)   Template types

Type in the project name

Description of selected project template
(provided by Visual Studio)

Fig. 2.3 | **New Project** dialog.

By default, Visual Studio displays the text <Enter_name> in the **Name:** field (Fig. 2.3). To rename the project, type Welcome in the **Name:** field. Save this project to the C:\vcpphtp2e directory. To change the project's location, click the **Browse...** button (Fig. 2.3) to display the **Project Location** dialog. In this dialog, locate the directory, then click **Open**. After providing the project's name and location, click **OK**.

The **Win32 Application Wizard** dialog appears (Fig. 2.4). Click **Next** to customize the project settings. In the **Win32 Application Wizard Application Settings** dialog, the **Console Application** radio button is selected by default (Fig. 2.4). To indicate that you want to create an empty project, click the **Empty Project** checkbox. Notice that a black check mark appears inside the box, indicating that it has been selected. This will also disable the **Precompiled Header** checkbox that was selected by default. Finally, click the **Finish** button to complete the **Win32 Application Wizard**. This creates a new solution named **Welcome** and a new project named **Welcome**. The **Solution Explorer** (Fig. 2.5) window displays the currently open solution and project and the files in your C++ project. If the **Solution Explorer** window does not appear, select **View > Solution Explorer**. We discuss the **Solution Explorer** in Section 2.4.1.

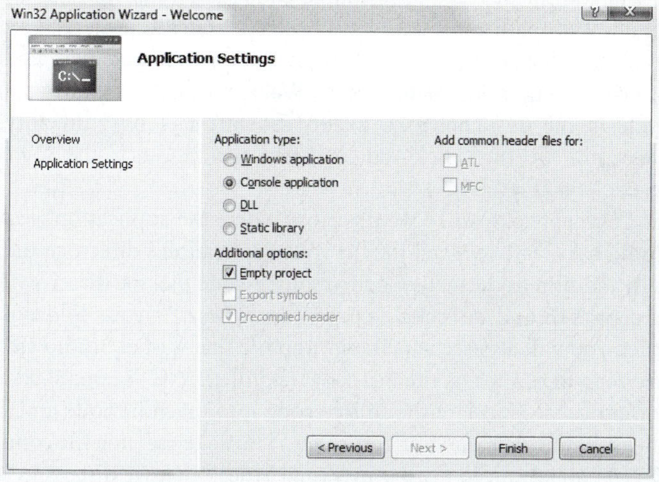

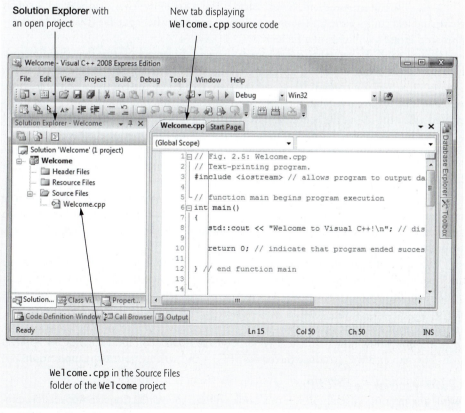

Fig. 2.4 | Win32 Application Wizard Application Settings dialog.

Solution Explorer with an open project

New tab displaying `Welcome.cpp` source code

`Welcome.cpp` in the Source Files folder of the `Welcome` project

Fig. 2.5 | Solution Explorer.

Now you will add the `Welcome.cpp` source-code file to your project. Before you can compile the application, you must add its source code to the project. To add the `Welcome.cpp` source-code file to your project, right click the **Source Files** folder and select **Add > Existing Item…**. The **Add Existing Item - Welcome** dialog should appear. Find the `Welcome.cpp` file in the `C:\vcpphtp2e\examples\ch02\Welcome` directory. Click `Welcome.cpp` to select the file, then click **Add**. `Welcome.cpp` appears in the **Source Files** folder in the **Solution Explorer** (Fig. 2.5).

Locate the `C:\vcpphtp2e\Welcome` directory where the application is saved. Observe that Visual Studio has created several files in your application's directory and its subdirectory `Welcome`. In addition to the `Welcome.cpp` source-code file, the directory contains `Welcome.ncb`, `Welcome.sln` and `Welcome.vcproj` files. [*Note:* If your folder is set to show hidden files, then you will also see a `Welcome.suo` file that Visual Studio created.]

Recall that `.cpp` files, such as the `Welcome.cpp` file, are C++ source-code files. These files must be compiled to translate the source code into machine code and linked so that you can run the machine code on your computer. The `Welcome.ncb` file contains information for *IntelliSense*, an advanced feature in Visual Studio that we discuss in later tutorials. `Welcome.sln` is a solution file (a file with the `.sln` extension), which stores information about your solution. Similarly, `Welcome.vcproj` is a Visual C++ project file (a file with the `.vcproj` extension), which stores information regarding your project.

Now compile the program. Select **Build > Build Solution**. The **Build > Build Solution** command will compile the C++ source-code file (and any other code files that are in a solution) and create a `Welcome.exe` file.

Return to the `C:\vcpphtp2e\Welcome\Welcome` directory. Notice that the directory now contains a `Debug` directory. Double click the `Debug` directory to display its contents. The `Welcome.obj` file contains the machine code created by the compiler before linking. `Welcome.exe` is the executable file that you will use to run your application. This file is created when the object file is linked. The remaining files in the directory are files created by Visual Studio to store information, such as debugging information, related to the compiled application. We introduce debugging in Appendix H.

In Visual Studio, select **Debug > Start Without Debugging** to run your application. At this point, the application prints a single line of output `"Welcome to Visual C++!"`. The C++ applications you create will display text to the user and often retrieve input from the user before exiting. When the application terminates, the **Press any key to continue** prompt appears. This prompt is generated by Visual Studio. Close the **Command Prompt** window by pressing any key or by clicking its close button

The name of each open document is listed on a tab—in Fig. 2.5, the open documents are **Welcome.cpp** and **Start Page**. To view a document, click its tab. Tabs facilitate easy access to multiple open documents. The *active tab* (the tab of the document currently displayed in the IDE) is displayed in bold text (e.g., **Welcome.cpp** in Fig. 2.5) and is positioned in front of all the other tabs.

You now know how to create a **Win32 Console Application** for a native C++ application. In Chapter 3 we introduce the basics of C++ and writing your own applications.

Creating a New C++/CLI Project

While the majority of examples in this book will use the **Win32 Console Application** template, certain chapters will introduce managed code in C++/CLI that requires a different project template. The process is quite similar to creating a **Win32 Console Application**.

Select **File > New Project...** as before. From the **New Project dialog** again click the **Visual C++** directory in the **Project Types:** pane. This time, instead of a **Win32 Console Application**, select **_CLR Console Application_**. Using the same technique as before, change the project name to WelcomeCLR and change the project's location to C:\vcpphtp2\ WelcomeCLR. Now click **OK**.

With a **CLR Console Application** no **Application Wizard** appears. Instead, you've already created a new solution named **WelcomeCLR** and a new project named **WelcomeCLR**. The **Solution Explorer** should display the currently open solution just as it did with a **Win32 Console Application**. We didn't specify an empty project, and Visual Studio has generated a WelcomeCLR.cpp file with some default code. Right click on this file in the **Solution Explorer** and select **Remove**. In the subsequent dialog, when asked whether to delete the file, select **Delete**. Now use the same technique as above to add an existing file to the project. We have provided a version of WelcomeCLR.cpp for you to use.

If you browse to the C:\vcpphtp2e\WelcomeCLR directory, you'll see a set of files similar to those described for a **Win32 Console Application**. You can build and compile a **CLR Console Application** the same way as a **Win32 Console Application**. Select **Build > Build Solution** to create a WelcomeCLR.exe in the C:\vcpphtp2e\WelcomeCLR\WelcomeCLR\Debug directory. Now, as before, select **Debug > Start Without Debugging** to run your C++/CLI application. You will see that the program outputs the same sentence as our **Win32 Console Application**. Although the output is the same, things are done quite differently underneath. You've just created your first **CLR Console Application** that can be used to develop C++/ CLI using managed code. We introduce our first C++/CLI application in Chapter 4.

2.3 Menu Bar and Toolbars

Commands for managing the IDE and for developing, maintaining and executing programs are contained in *menus*, which are located on the *menu bar* of the IDE (Fig. 2.6). Note that the set of menus displayed in Fig. 2.6 changes, based on what you are currently doing in the IDE.

Menus contain groups of related commands (also called *menu items*) that, when selected, cause the IDE to perform specific actions (e.g., open a window, save a file, print a file and execute a program). For example, new projects can be created by selecting **File > New Project...**. The menus depicted in Fig. 2.6 are summarized in Fig. 2.7.

| File | Edit | View | Project | Build | Debug | Tools | Window | Help |

Fig. 2.6 | Visual Studio menu bar.

Menu	Description
File	Contains commands for opening, closing, adding and saving projects, as well as printing project data and exiting Visual Studio.
Edit	Contains commands for editing programs, such as cut, copy, paste, undo, redo, delete, find and select.

Fig. 2.7 | Summary of Visual Studio 2008 IDE menus. (Part 1 of 2.)

Menu	Description
View	Contains commands for displaying windows (e.g., **Solution Explorer**, **Properties** window) and for adding toolbars to the IDE.
Project	Contains commands for managing projects and their files.
Build	Contains commands for compiling a program.
Debug	Contains commands for debugging (i.e., identifying and correcting problems in a program) and running a program. Debugging is discussed in detail in Appendix 2, Dive Into® Visual C++® 2008 Express.
Data	Contains commands for interacting with databases (i.e., organized collections of data stored on computers).
Tools	Contains commands for accessing additional IDE tools and options that enable you to customize the IDE.
Window	Contains commands for arranging and displaying windows.
Help	Contains commands for accessing the IDE's help features.

Fig. 2.7 | Summary of Visual Studio 2008 IDE menus. (Part 2 of 2.)

Rather than navigating the menus from the menu bar, you can access many of the more common commands from the *toolbar* (Fig. 2.8), which contains graphics, called *icons*, that graphically represent commands. [*Note:* Figure 2.8 divides the toolbar into two parts so that we can illustrate the graphics more clearly—the toolbar appears on one line inside the IDE.] By default, the standard toolbar is displayed when you run Visual Studio

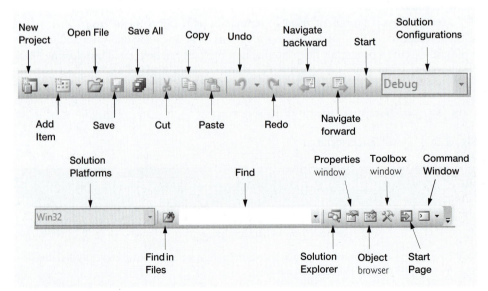

Fig. 2.8 | Standard toolbar in Visual Studio.

for the first time; it contains icons for the most commonly used commands, such as opening a file, adding an item to a project, saving and running (Fig. 2.8). Some commands are initially disabled (i.e., unavailable to use). These commands, which are initially grayed out, are enabled by Visual Studio only when they are necessary. For example, Visual Studio enables the command for saving a file once you begin editing the file.

You can customize the IDE by adding more toolbars. Select **View > Toolbars** (Fig. 2.9). Each toolbar you select will be displayed with the other toolbars at the top of the Visual Studio window (Fig. 2.9). Another way (which we do not show in this chapter) in which you can add toolbars to your IDE is by selecting **Tools > Customize**. Then, under the **Toolbars** tab, select the additional toolbars you would like to have appear in the IDE.

To execute a command via the toolbar, click its icon. Some icons contain a down arrow that, when clicked, displays a related command or commands, as shown in Fig. 2.10.

It's difficult to remember what each of the icons on the toolbar represents. Positioning the mouse pointer over an icon highlights it and, after a brief delay, displays a description of the icon called a ***tool tip*** (Fig. 2.11). Tool tips help novice programmers become familiar with the IDE's features and serve as useful reminders of each toolbar icon's functionality.

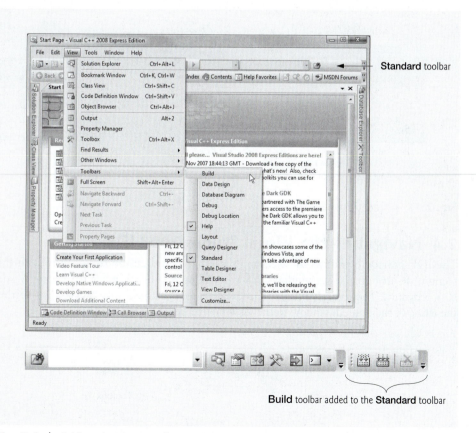

Fig. 2.9 | Adding the **Build** toolbar to the IDE.

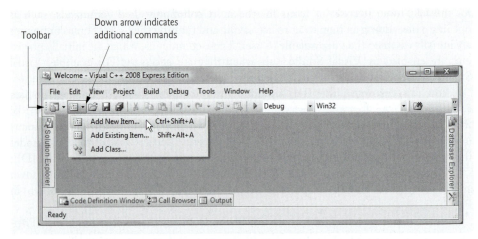

Fig. 2.10 | IDE toolbar icon showing additional commands.

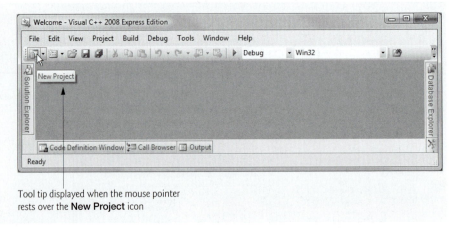

Fig. 2.11 | Tool tip demonstration.

2.4 Navigating the Visual Studio 2008 IDE

The IDE provides windows for accessing project files and customizing controls. In this section, we introduce some windows that you will use frequently when developing Visual C++ programs. These windows can be accessed via toolbar icons (Fig. 2.12) or by selecting the name of the desired window in the **View** menu.

Fig. 2.12 | Toolbar icons for four Visual Studio windows.

Visual Studio provides a space-saving feature called ***auto-hide***. When auto-hide is enabled, a tab appears along the edge of the IDE window (Fig. 2.13). This tab contains one or more icons, each of which identifies a hidden window.

Placing the mouse pointer over one of these icons displays that window (Fig. 2.13). The window is hidden again when the mouse pointer is moved outside of the window's area. To "pin down" a window (i.e., to disable auto-hide and keep the window open), click the pin icon. Note that when auto-hide is enabled, the pin icon is horizontal (Fig. 2.13), whereas when a window is "pinned down," the pin icon is vertical (Fig. 2.14). The next few sections overview two of the main windows used in Visual Studio—the **Solution Explorer** and the **Properties** window.

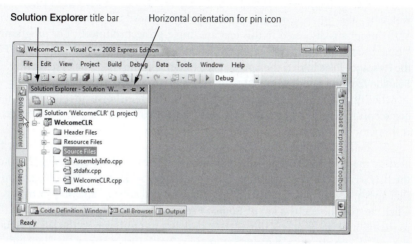

Fig. 2.13 | Displaying a hidden window when auto-hide is enabled.

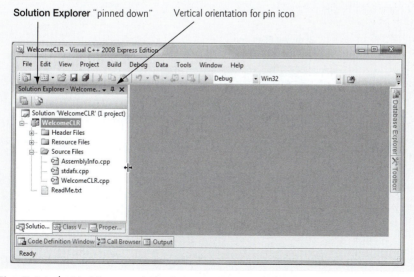

Fig. 2.14 | Disabling auto-hide ("pinning down" a window).

2.4.1 Solution Explorer

The **Solution Explorer** window (Fig. 2.15) provides access to all of the files in a solution. If the **Solution Explorer** window is not shown in the IDE, select **View > Solution Explorer** or click the **Solution Explorer** icon (Fig. 2.12). When you first open Visual Studio, the **Solution Explorer** is empty; there are no files to display. Once you open a solution, the **Solution Explorer** displays the contents of the solution and its projects, or when you create a new project, its contents are displayed.

The solution's *startup project* is the project that runs when the program executes. If you have multiple projects in a given solution, you can specify the startup project by right-clicking the project name in the **Solution Explorer** window, then selecting **Set as StartUp Project**. For a single-project solution, the startup project is the only project (in this case, **Welcome**) and the project name appears in bold text in the **Solution Explorer** window. All of the programs discussed in this text are single-project solutions. For programmers using Visual Studio for the first time, the **Solution Explorer** window lists the **Header Files** folder, the **Resource Files** folder, the **Source Files** folder and the **Welcome.cpp** file (Fig. 2.15). The **Solution Explorer** window includes a toolbar that contains several icons.

The Visual C++ file that corresponds to the file shown in Fig. 2.5 is named **Welcome.cpp** (selected in Fig. 2.15). (Visual C++ files use the *.cpp filename extension*, which is short for "C Plus Plus.")

By default, the IDE displays only files that you may need to edit—other files generated by the IDE are hidden. When clicked, the **Show All Files** *icon* (Fig. 2.15) displays all the files in the solution, including those generated by the IDE. The plus and minus boxes that appear (Fig. 2.15) can be clicked to expand and collapse the project tree, respectively. Click the plus box to the left of **Source Files** to display items grouped under the heading to the right of the plus box (Fig. 2.15); click the minus boxes to the left of **Source Files** to collapse the tree from its expanded state (Fig. 2.16). Other Visual Studio windows also use this plus-box/minus-box convention.

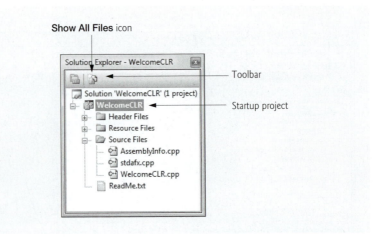

Fig. 2.15 | **Solution Explorer** with an open project, expanding the **Source Files** folder after clicking its plus box.

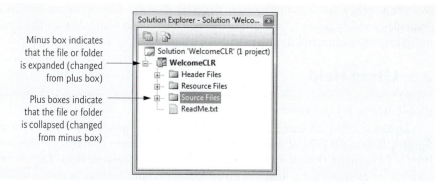

Minus box indicates that the file or folder is expanded (changed from plus box)

Plus boxes indicate that the file or folder is collapsed (changed from minus box)

Fig. 2.16 | **Solution Explorer** collapsing all files after clicking a minus box.

2.4.2 Properties Window

To display the **Properties** window if it's not visible, you can select **View > Other Windows > Properties Window**, click the **Properties** window icon shown in Fig. 2.12 or press *Alt + Enter*. The *Properties window* displays the properties for the currently selected code file, control or file in design view. *Properties* specify information about files or certain pieces of code. Each file and piece of code has its own set of properties; a property's description is displayed at the bottom of the **Properties** window whenever that property is selected.

Figure 2.17 shows the **Properties** window for the source-code file. The left column lists the file properties; the right column displays the current value of each property. Icons on the toolbar sort the properties either alphabetically the *Alphabetical* icon or categorically when you click the *Categorized* icon. You can sort the properties alphabetically in ascending or descending order—clicking the **Alphabetical** icon repeatedly toggles between sorting the properties from A–Z and from Z–A. Sorting by category groups the properties

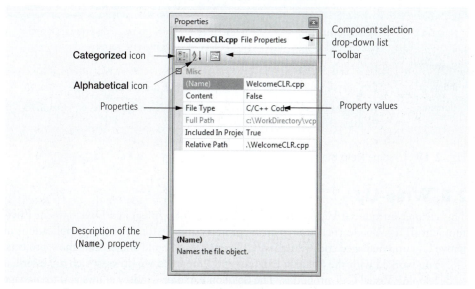

Categorized icon

Alphabetical icon

Properties

Description of the (Name) property

Component selection drop-down list

Toolbar

Property values

Fig. 2.17 | **Properties** window displaying the **Name** property of `Welcome.cpp`.

according to their use (i.e., **Appearance**, **Behavior**, **Design**). Depending on the size of the **Properties** window, some of the properties may be hidden from view on the screen, in which case users can scroll through the list of properties.

2.5 Using Help

Visual Studio provides extensive help features. Some of the *Help menu* commands are summarized in Fig. 2.18.

Dynamic help is an excellent way to get information quickly about the IDE and its features. It provides a list of articles pertaining to the "current content" (i.e., the selected items). To open the *Dynamic Help window*, select **Help > Dynamic Help**. Then, when you click a word or component, links to help articles appear in the **Dynamic Help** window. The window lists help topics, code samples and other relevant information. There is also a toolbar that provides access to the **How Do I**, **Search**, **Index** and **Contents** help features. (Some of these may be be hidden due to image size constraints).

Visual Studio also provides *context-sensitive help*, which is similar to dynamic help, except that it immediately displays a relevant help article rather than presenting a list. To use context-sensitive help, click an item or code segment and press the *F1* key. If there are multiple entries in the help for the term you selected, a list of articles will be displayed.

The **Help** options can be set in the **Options** dialog (accessed by selecting **Tools > Options...**) in Fig. 2.19. To change whether the **Help** is displayed internally or externally, select **Help** on the left, then locate the **Show Help using:** drop-down list on the right. Depending on your preference, selecting **External Help Viewer** displays a relevant help article in a separate window outside the IDE (some programmers like to view web pages separately from the project on which they are working on in the IDE). Selecting **Integrated Help Viewer** displays a help article as a tabbed window inside the IDE.

Command	Description
How Do I	Contains links to relevant topics, including how to upgrade programs, architecture and design, files and I/O, data, debugging and more.
Search	Finds help articles based on search keywords.
Index	Displays an alphabetized list of terms you can browse like a book's index.
Contents	Displays a categorized table of contents in which help articles are organized by topic.

Fig. 2.18 | Some **Help** menu commands.

2.6 Wrap-Up

This chapter introduced key features of the Visual Studio Integrated Development Environment (IDE). You learned how to create projects suitable for developing applications in native C++ and managed code with C++/CLI, and how to build and execute those projects.

You worked with the **Solution Explorer** and **Properties** windows, which are essential to developing Visual C++ programs. The **Solution Explorer** window allows you to manage your solution's files visually.

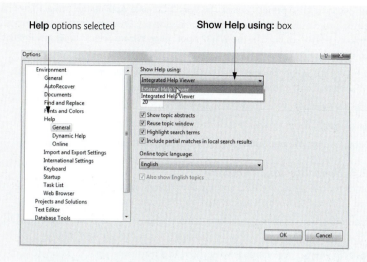

Help options selected

Show Help using: box

Fig. 2.19 | **Options** dialog displaying **Help** settings.

You explored Visual Studio's help features, including the **Dynamic Help** window and the **Help** menu. The **Dynamic Help** window displays links related to the item that you click with the mouse. You learned how to set **Help** options to display and use help resources. We also demonstrated how to use context-sensitive help.

In the next chapter, we begin programming—you will create your first programs that contain Visual C++ code that you write, instead of having Visual Studio write the code. You will study console applications (programs that display text to the screen without using a GUI). You will also learn memory concepts, arithmetic, decision making and how to use a dialog to display a message.

Summary

Section 2.1 Introduction
- Visual Studio is Microsoft's Integrated Development Environment (IDE) for creating, running and debugging programs written in a variety of .NET programming languages.

Section 2.2 Overview of the Visual Studio 2008 IDE
- The **Start Page** contains a list of links to resources either within the Visual Studio 2005 IDE or on the Internet.
- The Visual Studio 2008 IDE organizes programs into projects and solutions; a solution may contain one or more projects.
- A project is a group of related files, such as the Visual C++ code and any resources that might make up a program.
- Dialogs are windows that facilitate user-computer communication.
- Visual Studio provides templates for the project types available for users to create in Visual C++, including Windows applications and console applications for both the Win32 and CLR platforms.

- To create a native C++ project, select the **Win32 Console Application** project template. Enter a name for the project and select a location by clicking the **Browse...** button and choosing a folder in the **Project Location** dialog. In the **Win32 Application Wizard** select the **Empty Project** radio button, then click the **Finish** button.
- Create a C++/CLI project by selecting the **CLR Console Application** project template. After entering a project name and choosing a location, click **OK**.
- Use the **Add > Existing Item...** menu item to add existing files to a project.
- Compile a Visual Studio project by selecting **Build > Build Solution**.
- Select **Debug > Start Without Debugging** to run an application from Visual Studio.

Section 2.3 Menu Bar and Toolbars
- Commands for managing the IDE and for developing, maintaining and executing programs are contained in the menus, which are located on the menu bar.
- Menus contain groups of commands (menu items) that, when selected, cause the IDE to perform actions (e.g., open a window, save a file, print a file and execute a program).
- Tool tips help you become familiar with the IDE's features.

Section 2.4 Navigating the Visual Studio 2008 IDE
- The **Solution Explorer** window lists all the files in the solution.
- Moving the mouse pointer over a hidden window's icon opens that window. When the mouse pointer leaves the area of the window, the window is hidden. This feature is known as auto-hide. To "pin down" a window (i.e., to disable auto-hide), click the pin icon into the vertical position.
- The **Properties** window displays the properties for project items or code segments. The **Properties** window allows you to modify controls visually, without writing code.

Section 2.5 Using Help
- The **Help** menu contains a variety of options: The **How Do I** menu provides specific resources to help users accomplish a given task, such as converting programs and participating in community discussions. The **Contents** menu displays a categorized table of contents; the **Index** menu displays an alphabetical index that you can browse; the **Search** menu allows you to find particular help articles by entering search keywords.
- **Dynamic Help** provides a list of articles based on the current content.
- Context-sensitive help is similar to dynamic help, except that it immediately brings up a relevant help article instead of a list. To use context-sensitive help, click an item and press the *F1* key.

Terminology

active tab
Alphabetical icon
application
auto-hide
Categorized icon
clicking
close a project
collapse a tree
context-sensitive help
.cpp filename extension

debug a program
Debug menu
dialog
double clicking
down arrow
dragging
dynamic help
Dynamic Help window
Edit menu
ellipsis button

expand a tree
external help
F1 help key
File menu
GUI (graphical user interface)
Help menu
icon
IDE (Integrated Development Environment)
input
integrated help
menu
menu item
menu bar in Visual Studio
Microsoft Visual C++ 2008 Express Edition
mouse pointer
MSDN (Microsoft Developers Network)
New Project dialog
opening a project
output
pin a window
project
Project menu
Project Location dialog
Properties window

property of an item or code segment
run mode
Save Project dialog
selecting
Show all files icon
single clicking
solution
Solution Explorer in Visual Studio
Start Page
startup project
tabbed window
template
title bar
tool tip
toolbar
toolbar icon
Toolbox
Tools menu
View menu
visual programming
Visual Studio
Windows application
Windows menu

Self-Review Exercises

2.1 Fill in the blanks in each of the following statements:
a) A(n) _____ is a group of one or more projects that collectively form a Visual C++ program.
b) The _____ feature hides a window when the mouse pointer is moved outside the window's area.
c) A(n) _____ appears when the mouse pointer hovers over an icon.
d) The _____ window allows you to browse solution files.
e) A plus box indicates that the tree in the **Solution Explorer** can _____.
f) The properties in the **Properties** window's can be sorted _____ or _____.
g) Using _____ displays relevant help articles, based on the current context.

2.2 State whether each of the following is *true* or *false*. If *false*, explain why.
a) The title bar displays the IDE's mode.
b) The **X** box toggles auto-hide.
c) The toolbar icons represent various menu commands.
d) Visual C++ files use the filename extension .cpp.

Answers to Self-Review Exercises

2.1   a) solution. b) auto-hide. c) tool tip. d) **Solution Explorer**. e) expand. f) alphabetically, categorically. g) **Dynamic Help**.

2.2   a) True. b) False. The pin icon toggles auto-hide. The **X** box closes a window. c) True. h) True.

Exercises

2.3   Fill in the blanks in each of the following statements:
a) To save every file in a solution, select _____.
b) Using _____help immediately displays a relevant help article. It can be accessed using the _____ key.
c) GUI is an acronym for _____.

2.4   Some features that appear throughout Visual Studio perform similar actions in different contexts. Explain and give examples of how the plus and minus boxes, ellipsis buttons, down-arrow buttons and tool tips act in this manner. Why do you think the Visual Studio 2005 IDE was designed this way?

2.5   Briefly describe each of the following terms:
a) toolbar
b) menu bar
c) solution

3

Introduction to Visual C++ Programming

What's in a name?
that which we call a rose
By any other name
would smell as sweet.

—William Shakespeare

When faced with a decision,
I always ask, "What would
be the most fun?"

—Peggy Walker

"Take some more tea," the
March Hare said to Alice,
very earnestly. "I've had
nothing yet," Alice replied
in an offended tone: "so I
can't take more." "You mean
you can't take less," said the
Hatter: "it's very easy to take
more than nothing."

—Lewis Carroll

OBJECTIVES

In this chapter you'll learn:

- To write simple computer programs in Visual C++.
- To write simple input and output statements.
- To use fundamental types.
- Basic computer memory concepts.
- To use arithmetic operators.
- The precedence of arithmetic operators.
- To write simple decision-making statements.

3.1 Introduction

We now introduce Visual C++ programming with native code, which facilitates a disciplined approach to program design. Most of the Visual C++ programs you'll study in this book use native C++ to process information and display results. Later chapters will introduce new C++/CLI syntax and examples of programs written in managed C++ code. Be aware that unless otherwise noted, any native C++ concepts are equally applicable to C++/CLI. Generally any differences between native and managed C++ will be explained in specific C++/CLI sections at the end of chapters. In this chapter, we present five examples in native C++ that demonstrate how your programs can display messages and obtain information from the user for processing. The first three examples simply display messages on the screen. The next obtains two numbers from a user, calculates their sum and displays the result. The accompanying discussion shows you how to perform various arithmetic calculations and save their results for later use. The fifth example demonstrates decision-making fundamentals by showing you how to compare two numbers, then display messages based on the comparison results. We analyze each program one line at a time to help you ease your way into Visual C++ programming. To help you apply the skills you learn here, we provide many programming problems in the chapter's exercises.

3.2 First Program in Visual C++: Printing a Line of Text

Visual C++ uses notations that may appear strange to nonprogrammers. We now consider a simple program that prints a line of text (Fig. 3.1). This program illustrates several important features of the Visual C++ language. We consider each line in detail.

Lines 1 and 2

```
// Fig. 3.1: Welcome.cpp
// Text-printing program.
```

each begin with **//**, indicating that the remainder of each line is a *comment*. You insert comments to document your programs and to help other people read and understand them. Comments do not cause the computer to perform any action when the program is run—they are ignored by the Visual C++ compiler and do not cause any machine-lan-

```
 1   // Fig. 3.1: Welcome.cpp
 2   // Text-printing program.
 3   #include <iostream> // allows program to output data to the screen
 4
 5   // function main begins program execution
 6   int main()
 7   {
 8      std::cout << "Welcome to Visual C++!\n"; // display message
 9
10      return 0; // indicate that program ended successfully
11
12   } // end function main
```

```
Welcome to Visual C++!
```

Fig. 3.1 | Text-printing program.

guage object code to be generated. The comment `Text-printing program` describes the purpose of the program. A comment beginning with `//` is called a ***single-line comment*** because it terminates at the end of the current line. [*Note:* You also may use C's style in which a comment—possibly containing many lines—begins with `/*` and ends with `*/`.] Every program should begin with a comment that describes the purpose of the program, author, date and time. (We are not showing the author, date and time in this book's programs because this information would be redundant.)

Line 3

```
#include <iostream> // allows program to output data to the screen
```

is a ***preprocessor directive***, which is a message to the Visual C++ preprocessor (introduced in Section 1.17). Lines that begin with `#` are processed by the preprocessor before the program is compiled. This line notifies the preprocessor to include in the program the contents of the ***input/output stream header file `<iostream>`***. This file must be included for any program that outputs data to the screen or inputs data from the keyboard using native C++-style stream input/output. The program in Fig. 3.1 outputs data to the screen, as we'll soon see. We discuss header files in more detail in Chapter 8, Arrays and Vectors and explain the contents of `<iostream>` in Chapter 17, Stream Input/Output and Files.

Common Programming Error 3.1

Forgetting to include the `<iostream>` header file in a program that inputs data from the keyboard or outputs data to the screen causes the compiler to issue an error message, because the compiler cannot recognize references to the stream components (e.g., `cout`).

Line 4 is simply a blank line. You use blank lines, space characters and tab characters (i.e., "tabs") to make programs easier to read. Together, these characters are known as ***white space***. White-space characters are normally ignored by the compiler. In this chapter and several that follow, we discuss conventions for using white-space characters to enhance program readability.

Good Programming Practice 3.1

Use blank lines, space characters and tabs to enhance program readability.

Line 5

```
// function main begins program execution
```

is another single-line comment indicating that program execution begins at the next line.
Line 6

```
int main()
```

is a part of every Visual C++ program you'll see in this book. The parentheses after main
indicate that main is a program building block called a *function*. Visual C++ programs typically consist of one or more functions and classes (as you'll learn in Chapter 4, Introduction to Classes and Objects). Exactly one function in every program must be main (also
known as the program's entry point; other entry point names are possible depending on
the type of application you create). Figure 3.1 contains only one function. Visual C++ programs begin executing at function main, even if main is not the first function in the program. The keyword int to the left of main indicates that main "returns" an integer (whole-
number) value. A *keyword* is a word in code that is reserved by Visual C++ for a specific
use. The complete list of Visual C++ keywords can be found in Fig. 5.3. We'll explain
what it means for a function to "return a value" when we demonstrate how to create your
own functions in Section 4.5 and when we study functions in greater depth in Chapter 7.
For now, simply include the keyword int to the left of main in each of your programs.

The *left brace*, {, (line 7) must begin the *body* of every function. A corresponding
right brace, }, (line 12) must end each function's body. Line 8

```
std::cout << "Welcome to Visual C++!\n"; // display message
```

instructs the computer to *perform an action*—namely, to print the *string* of characters
contained between the double quotation marks. A string is sometimes called a *character
string*, a *message* or a *string literal*. We refer to characters between double quotation
marks simply as *strings*. White-space characters in strings are not ignored by the compiler.

The entire line 8, including std::cout, the << *operator*, the string "Welcome to
Visual C++!\n" and the *semicolon* (;), is called a *statement*. Every Visual C++ statement
must end with a semicolon (also known as the *statement terminator*). Preprocessor directives (like #include) do not end with a semicolon. Output and input in Visual C++ are
accomplished with *streams* of characters. Thus, when the preceding statement is executed,
it sends the stream of characters Welcome to Visual C++!\n to the *standard output stream
object*—*std::cout*—which is normally "connected" to the screen. We discuss
std::cout's many features in detail in Chapter 17.

Notice that we placed std:: before cout. This is required when we use names that
we've brought into the program by the preprocessor directive #include <iostream>. The
notation std::cout specifies that we are using a name, in this case cout, that belongs to
"namespace" std. The names cin (the standard input stream) and cerr (the standard error
stream)—introduced in Chapter 1—also belong to namespace std. Namespaces are an
advanced Visual C++ feature that we discuss in depth in Chapter 26, Other Topics. For
now, you should simply remember to include std:: before each mention of cout, cin and
cerr in a program. This can be cumbersome—in Fig. 3.13, we introduce the using declaration, which will enable us to omit std:: before each use of a name in the std
namespace.

The << operator is referred to as the ***stream insertion operator***. When this program executes, the value to the operator's right, the right ***operand***, is inserted in the output stream. Notice that the operator points in the direction of where the data goes. The right operand's characters normally print exactly as they appear between the double quotes. However, the characters \n are not printed on the screen (Fig. 3.1). The backslash (\) is called an ***escape character***. It indicates that a "special" character is to be output. When a backslash is encountered in a string of characters, the next character is combined with the backslash to form an ***escape sequence***. The escape sequence \n means ***newline***. It causes the ***cursor*** (i.e., the current screen-position indicator) to move to the beginning of the next line on the screen. Some common escape sequences are listed in Fig. 3.2.

Common Programming Error 3.2

*Omitting the semicolon at the end of a Visual C++ statement is a syntax error. (Again, preprocessor directives do not end in a semicolon.) The **syntax** of a programming language specifies the rules for creating proper programs in that language. A **syntax error** occurs when the compiler encounters code that violates Visual C++'s language rules (i.e., its syntax). The compiler normally issues an error message to help you locate and fix the incorrect code. Syntax errors are also called **compiler errors**, **compile-time errors** or **compilation errors**, because the compiler detects them during the compilation phase. You cannot execute your program until you correct all the syntax errors in it. As you'll see, some compilation errors are not syntax errors.*

Line 10

```
return 0; // indicate that program ended successfully
```

is one of several means we'll use to ***exit a function***. When the return statement is used at the end of main, as shown here, the value 0 indicates that the program has terminated successfully. In Chapter 7 we discuss functions in detail, and the reasons for including this statement will become clear. For now, simply include this statement in each program. The right brace, }, (line 12) indicates the end of function main.

Escape sequence	Description
\n	Newline. Position the screen cursor to the beginning of the next line.
\t	Horizontal tab. Move the screen cursor to the next tab stop.
\r	Carriage return. Position the screen cursor to the beginning of the current line; do not advance to the next line.
\a	Alert. Sound the system bell.
\\	Backslash. Used to print a backslash character.
\'	Single quote. Use to print a single-quote character.
\"	Double quote. Used to print a double-quote character.

Fig. 3.2 | Escape sequences.

Good Programming Practice 3.2

Many programmers make the last character printed by a function a newline (\n). This ensures that the function will leave the screen cursor positioned at the beginning of a new line. Conventions of this nature encourage software reusability—a key goal in software development.

Good Programming Practice 3.3

Indent the entire body of each function one level within the braces that delimit the body of the function. This makes a program's functional structure stand out and makes the program easier to read.

Good Programming Practice 3.4

Set a convention for the size of indent you prefer, then apply it uniformly. The tab key may be used to create indents, but tab stops may vary. We recommend using either 1/4-inch tab stops or (preferably) three spaces to form a level of indent.

3.3 Modifying Our First Visual C++ Program

This section continues our introduction to Visual C++ programming with two examples, showing how to modify the program in Fig. 3.1 to print text on one line by using multiple statements, and to print text on several lines by using a single statement.

Printing a Single Line of Text with Multiple Statements

Welcome to Visual C++! can be printed several ways. For example, Fig. 3.3 performs stream insertion in multiple statements (lines 8–9), yet produces the same output as the program of Fig. 3.1. [*Note:* From this point forward, we use a darker shade of gray than the code table background to highlight the key features each program introduces.] Each stream insertion resumes printing where the previous one stopped. The first stream insertion (line 8) prints Welcome followed by a space, and the second stream insertion (line 9) begins printing on the same line immediately following the space. In general, Visual C++ allows you to express statements in a variety of ways.

```
 1   // Fig. 3.3: Welcome2.cpp
 2   // Printing a line of text with multiple statements.
 3   #include <iostream> // allows program to output data to the screen
 4
 5   // function main begins program execution
 6   int main()
 7   {
 8      std::cout << "Welcome ";
 9      std::cout << "to  Visual C++!\n";
10
11      return 0; // indicate that program ended successfully
12
13   } // end function main
```

```
Welcome to Visual C++!
```

Fig. 3.3 | Printing a line of text with multiple statements.

Printing Multiple Lines of Text with a Single Statement

A single statement can print multiple lines by using newline characters, as in line 8 of Fig. 3.4. Each time the \n (newline) escape sequence is encountered in the output stream, the screen cursor is positioned to the beginning of the next line. To get a blank line in your output, place two newline characters back to back, as in line 8.

```
 1   // Fig. 3.4: Welcome3.cpp
 2   // Printing multiple lines of text with a single statement.
 3   #include <iostream> // allows program to output data to the screen
 4
 5   // function main begins program execution
 6   int main()
 7   {
 8      std::cout << "Welcome\nto\n\nVisual C++!\n";
 9
10      return 0; // indicate that program ended successfully
11
12   } // end function main
```

```
Welcome
to

Visual C++!
```

Fig. 3.4 | Printing multiple lines of text with a single statement.

3.4 Another Visual C++ Program: Adding Integers

Our next program uses the input stream object **std::cin** and the *stream extraction operator*, **>>**, to obtain two integers typed by a user at the keyboard, computes the sum of these values and outputs the result using std::cout. Figure 3.5 shows the program and sample inputs and outputs. Note that we highlight the user's input in bold.

```
 1   // Fig. 3.5: Sum.cpp
 2   // Addition program that displays the sum of two integers.
 3   #include <iostream> // allows program to perform input and output
 4
 5   // function main begins program execution
 6   int main()
 7   {
 8      // variable declarations
 9      int number1; // first integer to add
10      int number2; // second integer to add
11      int sum; // sum of number1 and number2
12
13      std::cout << "Enter first integer: "; // prompt user for data
14      std::cin >> number1; // read first integer from user into number1
```

Fig. 3.5 | Addition program that displays the sum of two integers entered at the keyboard. (Part I of 2.)

```
15
16       std::cout << "Enter second integer: "; // prompt user for data
17       std::cin >> number2; // read second integer from user into number2
18
19       sum = number1 + number2; // add the numbers; store result in sum
20
21       std::cout << "Sum is " << sum << std::endl; // display sum; end line
22
23       return 0; // indicate that program ended successfully
24
25     } // end function main
```

```
Enter first integer: 45
Enter second integer: 72
Sum is 117
```

Fig. 3.5 | Addition program that displays the sum of two integers entered at the keyboard. (Part 2 of 2.)

The comments in lines 1 and 2

```
// Fig. 3.5: Sum.cpp
// Addition program that displays the sum of two numbers.
```

state the name of the file and the purpose of the program. The Visual C++ preprocessor directive

```
#include <iostream> // allows program to perform input and output
```

in line 3 includes the contents of the <iostream> header file in the program.

The program begins execution with function main (line 6). The left brace (line 7) marks the beginning of main's body and the corresponding right brace (line 25) marks the end of main.

Lines 9–11

```
int number1; // first integer to add
int number2; // second integer to add
int sum; // sum of number1 and number2
```

are *declarations*. The identifiers number1, number2 and sum are the names of *variables*. A variable is a location in the computer's memory where a value can be stored for use by a program. These declarations specify that the variables number1, number2 and sum are data of type *int*, meaning that these variables will hold *integer* values, i.e., whole numbers such as 7, –11, 0 and 31914. All variables must be declared with a name and a data type before they can be used in a program. Several variables of the same type may be declared in one declaration or in multiple declarations. We could have declared all three variables in one declaration as follows:

```
int number1, number2, sum;
```

This makes the program less readable and prevents us from providing comments that describe each variable's purpose. If more than one name is declared in a declaration (as shown here), the names are separated by commas (,); this is referred to as a *comma-separated list*.

Good Programming Practice 3.5

Place a space after each comma (,) to make programs more readable.

Good Programming Practice 3.6

Some programmers prefer to declare each variable on a separate line. This format allows for easy insertion of a descriptive comment next to each declaration.

We'll soon discuss the data type `double` for specifying real numbers, and the data type `char` for specifying character data. Real numbers are numbers with decimal points, such as 3.4, 0.0 and −11.19. A `char` variable may hold only a single lowercase letter, a single uppercase letter, a single digit or a single special character (e.g., $ or *). Types such as `int`, `double` and `char` are often called *fundamental types*, *primitive types* or *built-in types*. Fundamental-type names are keywords and therefore must appear in all lowercase letters. Appendix C, Fundamental Types contains the complete list of fundamental types.

A variable name (such as `number1`) is any valid *identifier* that is not a keyword. An identifier is a series of characters consisting of letters, digits, underscores (_) and dollar signs ($) that does not begin with a digit. Visual C++ is *case sensitive*—uppercase and lowercase letters are different, so `a1` and `A1` are different identifiers.

Good Programming Practice 3.7

*Choosing meaningful identifiers makes a program more **self-documenting**—a person can understand the program simply by reading it rather than having to refer to manuals or comments.*

Good Programming Practice 3.8

Avoid using abbreviations in identifiers. This promotes program readability.

Good Programming Practice 3.9

Avoid identifiers that begin with underscores and double underscores, because Visual C++ compilers may use names like that for their own purposes internally. This will prevent names you choose from being confused with names the compilers choose.

Error-Prevention Tip 3.1

Languages like Visual C++ are "moving targets." As they evolve, more keywords could be added to the language. Avoid using "loaded" words like "object" as identifiers. Even though "object" is not currently a keyword in Visual C++, it could become one; therefore, future compiling with new compilers could break existing code.

Declarations of variables can be placed almost anywhere in a program, but they must appear before their corresponding variables are used in the program. For example, in the program of Fig. 3.5, the declaration in line 9

```
int number1; // first integer to add
```

could have been placed immediately before line 14

```
std::cin >> number1; // read first integer from user into number1
```

the declaration in line 10

```
int number2; // second integer to add
```

could have been placed immediately before line 17

```
std::cin >> number2; // read second integer from user into number2
```

and the declaration in line 11

```
int sum; // sum of number1 and number2
```

could have been placed immediately before line 19

```
sum = number1 + number2; // add the numbers; store result in sum
```

Good Programming Practice 3.10

Always place a blank line between a declaration and adjacent executable statements. This makes the declarations stand out in the program and contributes to program clarity.

Good Programming Practice 3.11

If you prefer to place declarations at the beginning of a function, separate them from the executable statements in that function with one blank line to highlight where the declarations end and the executable statements begin.

Line 13

```
std::cout << "Enter first integer: "; // prompt user for data
```

prints the string Enter first integer: on the screen. This message is called a *prompt* because it directs the user to take a specific action. We like to pronounce the preceding statement as "std::cout *gets* the character string "Enter first integer: "." Line 14

```
std::cin >> number1; // read first integer from user into number1
```

uses the *input stream object cin* (of namespace std) and the *stream extraction operator*, >>, to obtain a value from the keyboard. Using the stream extraction operator with std::cin takes character input from the standard input stream, which is usually the keyboard. We like to pronounce the preceding statement as, "std::cin *gives* a value to number1" or simply "std::cin *gives* number1."

Error-Prevention Tip 3.2

Programs should validate the correctness of all input values to prevent erroneous information from affecting a program's calculations.

When the computer executes the preceding statement, it waits for the user to enter a value for variable number1. The user responds by typing an integer (as characters), then pressing the *Enter* key (sometimes called the *Return* key) to send the characters to the computer. The computer converts the character representation of the number to an integer and assigns (i.e., copies) this number (or *value*) to the variable number1. Any subsequent references to number1 in this program will use this same value.

The `std::cout` and `std::cin` stream objects facilitate interaction between the user and the computer. Because this interaction resembles a dialog, it is often called ***conversational computing*** or ***interactive computing.***

Line 16

```
std::cout << "Enter second integer: "; // prompt user for data
```

prints `Enter second integer:` on the screen, prompting the user to take action. Line 17

```
std::cin >> number2; // read second integer from user into number2
```

obtains a value for variable `number2` from the user.

The assignment statement in line 19

```
sum = number1 + number2; // add the numbers; store result in sum
```

calculates the sum of the variables `number1` and `number2` and assigns the result to variable `sum` using the ***assignment operator*** *=*. The statement is read as, "sum *gets* the value of `number1 + number2`." Most calculations are performed in assignment statements. The = operator and the + operator are called ***binary operators*** because each has two operands. In the case of the + operator, the two operands are `number1` and `number2`. In the case of the preceding = operator, the two operands are `sum` and the value of the expression `number1 + number2`.

Good Programming Practice 3.12

Place spaces on either side of a binary operator. This makes the operator stand out and makes the program more readable.

Line 21

```
std::cout << "Sum is " << sum << std::endl; // display sum; end line
```

displays the character string `Sum is` followed by the numerical value of variable `sum` followed by `std::endl`—a so-called ***stream manipulator.*** The name `endl` is an abbreviation for "end line" and belongs to namespace `std`. The `std::endl` stream manipulator outputs a newline, then "flushes the output buffer." This simply means that, on some systems where outputs accumulate in the machine until there are enough to "make it worthwhile" to display them on the screen, `std::endl` forces any accumulated outputs to be displayed at that moment. This can be important when the outputs are prompting the user for an action, such as entering data.

Note that the preceding statement outputs multiple values of different types. The stream insertion operator "knows" how to output each type of data. Using multiple stream insertion operators (<<) in a single statement is referred to as ***concatenating, chaining*** or ***cascading stream insertion operations.*** It is unnecessary to have multiple statements to output multiple pieces of data.

Calculations can also be performed in output statements. We could have combined the statements in lines 19 and 21 into the statement

```
std::cout << "Sum is " << number1 + number2 << std::endl;
```

thus eliminating the need for the variable `sum`.

A powerful feature of Visual C++ is that users can create their own data types called classes (we introduce this capability in Chapter 4 and explore it in depth in Chapters 10 and 11). Users can then "teach" Visual C++ how to input and output values of these new data types using the >> and << operators (this is called *operator overloading*—a topic we explore in Appendix 12, Operator Overloading; String and Array Objects).

3.5 Memory Concepts

Variable names such as number1, number2 and sum actually correspond to *locations* in the computer's memory. Every variable has a name, a type, a size and a value.

In the addition program of Fig. 3.5, when the statement

```
std::cin >> number1; // read first integer from user into number1
```

in line 14 is executed, the characters typed by the user are converted to an integer that is placed into a memory location to which the name number1 has been assigned by the Visual C++ compiler. Suppose the user enters the number 45 as the value for number1. The computer will place 45 into location number1, as shown in Fig. 3.6.

Whenever a value is placed in a memory location, the value overwrites the previous value in that location; thus, placing a new value into a memory location is said to be *destructive*.

Returning to our addition program, when the statement

```
std::cin >> number2; // read second integer from user into number2
```

in line 17 is executed, suppose the user enters the value 72. This value is placed into location number2, and memory appears as in Fig. 3.7. Note that these locations are not necessarily adjacent in memory.

Once the program has obtained values for number1 and number2, it adds these values and places the sum into variable sum. The statement

```
sum = number1 + number2; // add the numbers; store result in sum
```

that performs the addition also replaces whatever value was stored in sum. This occurs when the calculated sum of number1 and number2 is placed into location sum (without

number1	45

Fig. 3.6 | Memory location showing the name and value of variable number1.

number1	45
number2	72

Fig. 3.7 | Memory locations after storing values for number1 and number2.

regard to what value may already be in sum; that value is lost). After sum is calculated, memory appears as in Fig. 3.8. Note that the values of number1 and number2 appear exactly as they did before they were used in the calculation of sum. These values were used, but not destroyed, as the computer performed the calculation. Thus, when a value is read out of a memory location, the process is *nondestructive*.

number1	45
number2	72
sum	117

Fig. 3.8 | Memory locations after calculating and storing the sum of number1 and number2.

3.6 Arithmetic

Most programs perform arithmetic calculations. Figure 3.9 summarizes the Visual C++ *arithmetic operators*. Note the use of various special symbols not used in algebra. The *asterisk* (*) indicates multiplication, and the *percent sign* (%) is the *modulus* operator that will be discussed shortly. The arithmetic operators in Fig. 3.9 are all binary operators, i.e., operators that take two operands. For example, the expression number1 + number2 contains the binary operator + and the two operands number1 and number2.

Integer division (i.e., where both the numerator and the denominator are integers) yields an integer quotient; for example, the expression 7 / 4 evaluates to 1 and the expression 17 / 5 evaluates to 3. Note that any fractional part in integer division is discarded (i.e., *truncated*)—no rounding occurs.

Visual C++ provides the *modulus operator*, %, that yields the remainder after integer division. The modulus operator can be used only with integer operands. The expression x % y yields the remainder after x is divided by y. Thus, 7 % 4 yields 3 and 17 % 5 yields 2. In

Operation	Arithmetic operator	Algebraic expression	Visual C++ expression
Addition	+	$f + 7$	f + 7
Subtraction	-	$p - c$	p - c
Multiplication	*	bm or $b \cdot m$	b * m
Division	/	x / y or $\frac{x}{y}$ or $x \div y$	x / y
Modulus	%	$r \bmod s$	r % s

Fig. 3.9 | Arithmetic operators.

later chapters, we discuss many interesting applications of the modulus operator, such as determining whether one number is a multiple of another (a special case of this is determining whether a number is odd or even).

Common Programming Error 3.3

Attempting to use the modulus operator (%) with noninteger operands is a compilation error.

Arithmetic Expressions in Straight-Line Form

Arithmetic expressions in Visual C++ must be entered into the computer in *straight-line form*. Thus, expressions such as "a divided by b" must be written as a / b, so that all constants, variables and operators appear in a straight line. The algebraic notation

$$\frac{a}{b}$$

is generally not acceptable to compilers, although some special-purpose software packages do support more natural notation for complex mathematical expressions.

Parentheses for Grouping Subexpressions

Parentheses are used in Visual C++ expressions in the same manner as in algebraic expressions. For example, to multiply a times the quantity b + c we write a * (b + c).

Rules of Operator Precedence

Visual C++ applies the operators in arithmetic expressions in a precise sequence determined by the following *rules of operator precedence*, which are generally the same as those followed in algebra:

1. Operators in expressions contained within pairs of parentheses are evaluated first. Parentheses are said to be at the "highest level of precedence." In cases of *nested*, or *embedded*, *parentheses*, such as

   ((a + b) + c)

   the operators in the innermost pair of parentheses are applied first.

2. Multiplication, division and modulus operations are applied next. If an expression contains several multiplication, division and modulus operations, operators are applied from left to right. Multiplication, division and modulus are said to be on the same level of precedence.

3. Addition and subtraction operations are applied last. If an expression contains several addition and subtraction operations, operators are applied from left to right. Addition and subtraction also have the same level of precedence.

The set of rules of operator precedence defines the order in which Visual C++ applies operators. When we say that certain operators are applied from left to right, we are referring to the *associativity* of the operators. For example, in the expression

    a + b + c

the addition operators (+) associate from left to right, so a + b is calculated first, then c is added to that sum to determine the value of the whole expression. We'll see that some operators associate from right to left. Figure 3.10 summarizes these rules of operator precedence. This table will be expanded as additional Visual C++ operators are introduced. A complete precedence chart is included in Appendix A, Operator Precedence and Associativity Chart.

Operator(s)	Operation(s)	Order of evaluation (precedence)
( )	Parentheses	Evaluated first. If the parentheses are nested, the expression in the innermost pair is evaluated first. If there are several pairs of parentheses "on the same level" (i.e., not nested), they are evaluated left to right.
* / %	Multiplication, Division, Modulus	Evaluated second. If there are several, they are evaluated left to right.
+ -	Addition Subtraction	Evaluated last. If there are several, they are evaluated left to right.

Fig. 3.10 | Precedence of arithmetic operators.

Sample Algebraic and Visual C++ Expressions

Now consider several expressions in light of the rules of operator precedence. Each example lists an algebraic expression and its Visual C++ equivalent. The following is an example of an arithmetic mean (average) of five terms:

Algebra: $\quad m = \dfrac{a + b + c + d + e}{5}$

Visual C++: $\quad$ m = (a + b + c + d + e) / 5;

The parentheses are required because division has higher precedence than addition. The entire quantity (a + b + c + d + e) is to be divided by 5. If the parentheses are erroneously omitted, we obtain a + b + c + d + e / 5, which evaluates incorrectly as

$$a + b + c + d + \frac{e}{5}$$

The following is an example of the equation of a straight line:

Algebra: $\quad y = mx + b$

Visual C++: $\quad$ y = m * x + b;

No parentheses are required. The multiplication is applied first because multiplication has a higher precedence than addition.

The following example contains modulus (%), multiplication, division, addition, subtraction and assignment operations:

Algebra: $\quad z = pr\,\%q + w/x - y$

C++: $\quad$ z = p * r % q + w / x - y;

⑥ ① ② ④ ③ ⑤

The circled numbers under the statement indicate the order in which Visual C++ applies the operators. The multiplication, modulus and division are evaluated first in left-to-right order (i.e., they associate from left to right) because they have higher precedence than addition and subtraction. The addition and subtraction are applied next. These are also applied left to right. Then the assignment operator is applied.

Evaluation of a Second-Degree Polynomial

To develop a better understanding of the rules of operator precedence, consider the evaluation of a second-degree polynomial ($y = ax^2 + bx + c$):

The circled numbers under the statement indicate the order in which Visual C++ applies the operators. There is no arithmetic operator for exponentiation in Visual C++, so we have represented x^2 as x * x. We'll soon discuss the standard library function pow ("power") that performs exponentiation. Because of some subtle issues related to the data types required by pow, we defer a detailed explanation of pow until Chapter 7.

 Common Programming Error 3.4

*Some programming languages use operators ** or ^ to represent exponentiation. Visual C++ does not support these exponentiation operators; using them for exponentiation results in errors.*

Suppose variables a, b, c and x in the preceding second-degree polynomial are initialized as follows: a = 2, b = 3, c = 7 and x = 5. Figure 3.11 illustrates the order in which the operators are applied.

As in algebra, it is acceptable to place unnecessary parentheses in an expression to make the expression clearer. These are called *redundant parentheses*. For example, the preceding assignment statement could be parenthesized as follows:

```
y = ( a * x * x ) + ( b * x ) + c;
```

 Good Programming Practice 3.13

Using redundant parentheses in complex arithmetic expressions can make the expressions clearer.

3.7 Decision Making: Equality and Relational Operators

This section introduces a simple version of Visual C++'s *if statement* that allows a program to take alternative action based on the truth or falsity of some *condition*. If the condition is met, i.e., the condition is true, the statement in the body of the if statement is executed. If the condition is not met, i.e., the condition is false, the body statement is not executed. We'll see an example shortly.

Conditions in if statements can be formed by using the *equality operators* and *relational operators* summarized in Fig. 3.12. The relational operators all have the same level of precedence and associate left to right. The equality operators both have the same level of precedence, which is lower than that of the relational operators, and associate left to right.

Step 1.   y = 2 * 5 * 5 + 3 * 5 + 7;   (*Leftmost multiplication*)

2 * 5 is 10

Step 2.   y = 10 * 5 + 3 * 5 + 7;   (*Leftmost multiplication*)

10 * 5 is 50

Step 3.   y = 50 + 3 * 5 + 7;   (*Multiplication before addition*)

3 * 5 is 15

Step 4.   y = 50 + 15 + 7;   (*Leftmost addition*)

50 + 15 is 65

Step 5.   y = 65 + 7;   (*Last addition*)

65 + 7 is 72

Step 6.   y = 72   (*Last operation—place* 72 *in* y)

Fig. 3.11 | Order in which a second-degree polynomial is evaluated.

Standard algebraic equality or relational operator	Visual C++ equality or relational operator	Sample Visual C++ condition	Meaning of Visual C++ condition
Relational operators			
>	>	x > y	x is greater than y
<	<	x < y	x is less than y
≥	>=	x >= y	x is greater than or equal to y
≤	<=	x <= y	x is less than or equal to y
Equality operators			
=	==	x == y	x is equal to y
≠	!=	x != y	x is not equal to y

Fig. 3.12 | Equality and relational operators.

Common Programming Error 3.5

A syntax error will occur if any of the operators ==, !=, >= *and* <= *appears with spaces between its pair of symbols.*

Common Programming Error 3.6

*Reversing the order of the pair of symbols in any of the operators !=, >= and <= (by writing them as =!, => and =<, respectively) is normally a syntax error. In some cases, writing != as =! will not be a syntax error but almost certainly will be a **logic error** that has an effect at execution time. You'll understand why when you learn about logical operators in Chapter 6. A **fatal logic error** causes a program to fail and terminate prematurely. A **nonfatal logic error** allows a program to continue executing, but usually produces incorrect results.*

Common Programming Error 3.7

Confusing the equality operator == with the assignment operator = results in logic errors. The equality operator should be read "is equal to," and the assignment operator should be read "gets" or "gets the value of" or "is assigned the value of." Some people prefer to read the equality operator as "double equals." As we discuss in Section 6.9, confusing these operators may not necessarily cause an easy-to-recognize syntax error, but may cause extremely subtle logic errors.

The following example uses six if statements to compare two numbers input by the user. If the condition in any of these if statements is satisfied, the output statement associated with that if statement is executed. Figure 3.13 shows the program and the input/output dialogs of three sample executions.

```
1   // Fig. 3.13: CompareIntegers.cpp
2   // Comparing integers using if statements, relational operators
3   // and equality operators.
4   #include <iostream> // allows program to perform input and output
5
6   using std::cout; // program uses cout
7   using std::cin; // program uses cin
8   using std::endl; // program uses endl
9
10  // function main begins program execution
11  int main()
12  {
13     int number1; // first integer to compare
14     int number2; // second integer to compare
15
16     cout << "Enter two integers to compare: "; // prompt user for data
17     cin >> number1 >> number2; // read two integers from user
18
19     if ( number1 == number2 )
20        cout << number1 << " == " << number2 << endl;
21
22     if ( number1 != number2 )
23        cout << number1 << " != " << number2 << endl;
24
25     if ( number1 < number2 )
26        cout << number1 << " < " << number2 << endl;
27
28     if ( number1 > number2 )
29        cout << number1 << " > " << number2 << endl;
```

Fig. 3.13 | Comparing integers using if statements, relational operators and equality operators. (Part 1 of 2.)

```
30
31      if ( number1 <= number2 )
32         cout << number1 << " <= " << number2 << endl;
33
34      if ( number1 >= number2 )
35         cout << number1 << " >= " << number2 << endl;
36
37      return 0; // indicate that program ended successfully
38
39   } // end function main
```

```
Enter two integers to compare: 3 7
3 != 7
3 < 7
3 <= 7
```

```
Enter two integers to compare: 22 12
22 != 12
22 > 12
22 >= 12
```

```
Enter two integers to compare: 7 7
7 == 7
7 <= 7
7 >= 7
```

Fig. 3.13 | Comparing integers using if statements, relational operators and equality operators. (Part 2 of 2.)

Lines 6–8

```
using std::cout; // program uses cout
using std::cin; // program uses cin
using std::endl; // program uses endl
```

are *using declarations* that eliminate the need to repeat the std:: prefix as we did in earlier programs. Once we insert these using declarations, we can write cout instead of std::cout, cin instead of std::cin and endl instead of std::endl, respectively, in the remainder of the program. [*Note:* From this point forward in the book, each example contains one or more using declarations.]

Good Programming Practice 3.14

Place using declarations immediately after the #include to which they refer.

Lines 13–14

```
int number1; // first integer to compare
int number2; // second integer to compare
```

declare the variables used in the program. Remember that variables may be declared in one declaration or in separate declarations.

The program uses cascaded stream extraction operations (line 17) to input two integers. Remember that we are allowed to write `cin` (instead of `std::cin`) because of line 7. First a value is read into variable `number1`, then a value is read into variable `number2`.

The `if` statement in lines 19–20

```
if ( number1 == number2 )
    cout << number1 << " == " << number2 << endl;
```

compares the values of variables `number1` and `number2` to test for equality. If the values are equal, the statement in line 20 displays a line of text indicating that the numbers are equal. If the conditions are `true` in one or more of the `if` statements starting in lines 22, 25, 28, 31 and 34, the corresponding body statement displays an appropriate line of text.

Notice that each `if` statement in Fig. 3.13 has a single statement in its body and that each body statement is indented. In Chapter 5, Control Statements: Part 1 we show how to specify `if` statements with multiple-statement bodies (by enclosing the body statements in a pair of braces, { }, creating what is called a *compound statement* or a *block*).

Good Programming Practice 3.15

Indent the statement(s) in the body of an `if` statement to enhance readability.

Good Programming Practice 3.16

For readability, there should be no more than one statement per line in a program.

Common Programming Error 3.8

Placing a semicolon immediately after the right parenthesis after the condition in an `if` statement is often a logic error (although not a syntax error). The semicolon causes the body of the `if` statement to be empty, so the `if` statement performs no action, regardless of whether or not its condition is true. Worse yet, the original body statement of the `if` statement now becomes a statement in sequence with the `if` statement and always executes, often causing the program to produce incorrect results.

Note the use of white space in Fig. 3.13. Recall that white-space characters, such as tabs, newlines and spaces, are normally ignored by the compiler. So, statements may be split over several lines and may be spaced according to your preferences. It is a syntax error to split identifiers, strings (such as `"hello"`) and constants (such as the number 1000) over several lines.

Common Programming Error 3.9

It is a syntax error to split an identifier by inserting white-space characters (e.g., writing `main` as `ma in`).

Good Programming Practice 3.17

A lengthy statement may be spread over several lines. If a single statement must be split across lines, choose meaningful breaking points, such as after a comma in a comma-separated list, or after an operator in a lengthy expression. If a statement is split across two or more lines, indent all subsequent lines and left-align the group of indented lines.

Figure 3.14 shows the precedence and associativity of the operators introduced in this chapter. The operators are shown top to bottom in decreasing order of precedence. Notice that all these operators, with the exception of the assignment operator =, associate from left to right. Addition is left associative, so an expression such as x + y + z is evaluated as if it had been written (x + y) + z. The assignment operator = associates from right to left, so an expression such as x = y = 0 is evaluated as if it had been written x = (y = 0), which, as we'll soon see, first assigns 0 to y, then assigns the result of that assignment, 0, to x.

Good Programming Practice 3.18

Refer to the operator precedence and associativity chart when writing expressions containing many operators. Confirm that the operators in the expression are performed in the order you expect. If you are uncertain about the order of evaluation in a complex expression, break the expression into smaller statements or use parentheses to force the order of evaluation, exactly as you would do in an algebraic expression. Be sure to observe that some operators such as assignment (=) associate right to left rather than left to right.

Operators				Associativity	Type
()				left to right	parentheses
*	/	%		left to right	multiplicative
+	-			left to right	additive
<<	>>			left to right	stream insertion/extraction
<	<=	>	>=	left to right	relational
==	!=			left to right	equality
=				right to left	assignment

Fig. 3.14 | Precedence and associativity of the operators discussed so far.

3.8 (Optional) Software Engineering Case Study: Examining the ATM Requirements Specification

Now we begin our optional object-oriented design and implementation case study. The Software Engineering Case Study sections at the ends of this and the next several chapters will ease you into object orientation. We'll develop software for a simple automated teller machine (ATM) system, providing you with a concise, carefully paced, complete design and implementation experience. In Chapters 4–8, 10 and 14, we'll perform the various steps of an object-oriented design (OOD) process using the UML, while relating these steps to the object-oriented concepts discussed in the chapters. Appendix F implements the ATM using the techniques of object-oriented programming (OOP) in Visual C++. We present the complete case study solution. This is not an exercise; rather, it is an end-to-end learning experience that concludes with a detailed walkthrough of the Visual C++ code that implements our design. It will acquaint you with the kinds of substantial problems encountered in industry and their potential solutions.

We begin our design process by presenting a ***requirements specification*** that specifies the overall purpose of the ATM system and *what* it must do. Throughout the case study, we refer to the requirements specification to determine precisely what functionality the system must include.

Requirements Specification

A local bank intends to install a new automated teller machine (ATM) to allow users (i.e., bank customers) to perform basic financial transactions (Fig. 3.15). Each user can have only one account at the bank. ATM users should be able to view their account balance, withdraw cash (i.e., take money out of an account) and deposit funds (i.e., place money into an account).

The user interface of the automated teller machine contains the following hardware components:

- a screen that displays messages to the user
- a keypad that receives numeric input from the user
- a cash dispenser that dispenses cash to the user and
- a deposit slot that receives deposit envelopes from the user.

The cash dispenser begins each day loaded with 500 $20 bills. [*Note:* Owing to the limited scope of this case study, certain elements of the ATM described here do not accurately mimic those of a real ATM. For example, a real ATM typically contains a device that reads a user's account number from an ATM card, whereas this ATM asks the user to type an account number using the keypad. A real ATM also usually prints a receipt at the end of a session, but all output from this ATM appears on the screen.]

The bank wants you to develop software to perform the financial transactions initiated by bank customers through the ATM. The bank will integrate the software with the

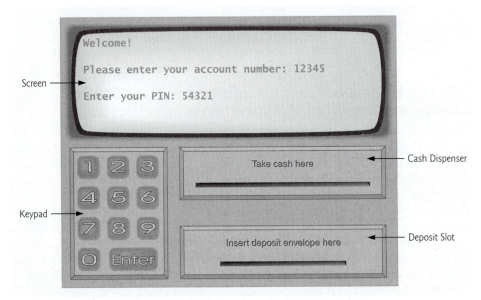

Fig. 3.15 | Automated teller machine user interface.

ATM's hardware at a later time. The software should encapsulate the functionality of the hardware devices (e.g., cash dispenser, deposit slot) within software components, but it need not concern itself with how these devices perform their duties. The ATM hardware has not been developed yet, so instead of writing your software to run on the ATM, you should develop a first version of the software to run on a personal computer. This version should use the computer's monitor to simulate the ATM's screen, and the computer's keyboard to simulate the ATM's keypad.

An ATM session consists of authenticating a user (i.e., proving the user's identity) based on an account number and personal identification number (PIN), followed by creating and executing financial transactions. To authenticate a user and perform transactions, the ATM must interact with the bank's account information database. [*Note:* A database is an organized collection of data stored on a computer.] For each bank account, the database stores an account number, a PIN and a balance indicating the amount of money in the account. [*Note:* For simplicity, we assume that the bank plans to build only one ATM, so we do not need to worry about multiple ATMs accessing this database at the same time. Furthermore, we assume that the bank does not make any changes to the information in the database while a user is accessing the ATM. Also, any business system like an ATM faces reasonably complicated security issues that go well beyond the scope of a first- or second-semester computer science course. We make the simplifying assumption, however, that the bank trusts the ATM to access and manipulate the information in the database without significant security measures.]

Upon first approaching the ATM, the user should experience the following sequence of events (shown in Fig. 3.15):

1. The screen displays a welcome message and prompts the user to enter an account number.

2. The user enters a five-digit account number, using the keypad.

3. The screen prompts the user to enter the PIN (personal identification number) associated with the specified account number.

4. The user enters a five-digit PIN, using the keypad.

5. If the user enters a valid account number and the correct PIN for that account, the screen displays the main menu (Fig. 3.16). If the user enters an invalid account number or an incorrect PIN, the screen displays an appropriate message, then the ATM returns to *Step 1* to restart the authentication process.

After the ATM authenticates the user, the main menu (Fig. 3.16) displays a numbered option for each of the three types of transactions: balance inquiry (option 1), withdrawal (option 2) and deposit (option 3). The main menu also displays an option that allows the user to exit the system (option 4). The user then chooses either to perform a transaction (by entering 1, 2 or 3) or to exit the system (by entering 4). If the user enters an invalid option, the screen displays an error message, then redisplays to the main menu.

If the user enters 1 to make a balance inquiry, the screen displays the user's account balance. To do so, the ATM must retrieve the balance from the bank's database.

The following actions occur when the user enters 2 to make a withdrawal:

1. The screen displays a menu (shown in Fig. 3.17) containing standard withdrawal amounts: $20 (option 1), $40 (option 2), $60 (option 3), $100 (option 4) and

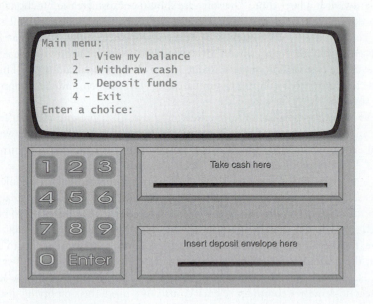

Fig. 3.16 | ATM main menu.

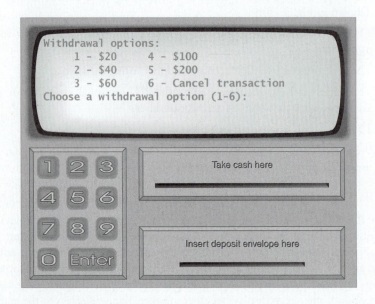

Fig. 3.17 | ATM withdrawal menu.

$200 (option 5). The menu also contains an option to allow the user to cancel the transaction (option 6).

2. The user enters a menu selection (1–6) using the keypad.

3. If the withdrawal amount chosen is greater than the user's account balance, the screen displays a message stating this and telling the user to choose a smaller amount. The ATM then returns to *Step 1*. If the withdrawal amount chosen is less than or equal to the user's account balance (i.e., an acceptable withdrawal amount), the ATM proceeds to *Step 4*. If the user chooses to cancel the transaction (option 6), the ATM displays the main menu (Fig. 3.16) and waits for user input.

4. If the cash dispenser contains enough cash to satisfy the request, the ATM proceeds to *Step 5*. Otherwise, the screen displays a message indicating the problem and telling the user to choose a smaller withdrawal amount. The ATM then returns to *Step 1*.

5. The ATM debits (i.e., subtracts) the withdrawal amount from the user's account balance in the bank's database.

6. The cash dispenser dispenses the desired amount of money to the user.

7. The screen displays a message reminding the user to take the money.

The following actions occur when the user enters 3 (while the main menu is displayed) to make a deposit:

1. The screen prompts the user to enter a deposit amount or to type 0 (zero) to cancel the transaction.

2. The user enters a deposit amount or 0, using the keypad. [*Note:* The keypad does not contain a decimal point or a dollar sign, so the user cannot type a real dollar amount (e.g., $1.25). Instead, the user must enter a deposit amount as a number of cents (e.g., 125). The ATM then divides this number by 100 to obtain a number representing a dollar amount (e.g., 125 ÷ 100 = 1.25).]

3. If the user specifies a deposit amount, the ATM proceeds to *Step 4*. If the user chooses to cancel the transaction (by entering 0), the ATM displays the main menu (Fig. 3.16) and waits for user input.

4. The screen displays a message telling the user to insert a deposit envelope into the deposit slot.

5. If the deposit slot receives a deposit envelope within two minutes, the ATM credits (i.e., adds) the deposit amount to the user's account balance in the bank's database. [*Note:* This money is not immediately available for withdrawal. The bank first must physically verify the amount of cash in the deposit envelope, and any checks in the envelope must clear (i.e., money must be transferred from the check writer's account to the check recipient's account). When either of these events occurs, the bank appropriately updates the user's balance stored in its database. This occurs independently of the ATM system.] If the deposit slot does not receive a deposit envelope within this time period, the screen displays a message that the system has canceled the transaction due to inactivity. The ATM then displays the main menu and waits for user input.

After the system successfully executes a transaction, the system should redisplay the main menu (Fig. 3.16) so that the user can perform additional transactions. If the user chooses to exit the system (option 4), the screen should display a thank-you message, then display the welcome message for the next user.

Analyzing the ATM System

The preceding statement is a simplified example of a requirements specification. Typically, such a document is the result of a detailed process of *requirements gathering* that might include interviews with potential users of the system and specialists in fields related to the system. For example, a systems analyst who is hired to prepare a requirements specification for banking software (e.g., the ATM system described here) might interview financial experts to gain a better understanding of *what* the software must do. The analyst would use the information gained to compile a list of *system requirements* to guide systems designers.

The process of requirements gathering is a key task of the first stage of the software life cycle. The *software life cycle* specifies the stages through which software evolves from the time it is first conceived to the time it is retired from use. These stages typically include: analysis, design, implementation, testing and debugging, deployment, maintenance and retirement. Several software life-cycle models exist, each with its own preferences and specifications for when and how often software engineers should perform each of these stages. *Waterfall models* perform each stage once in succession, whereas *iterative models* may repeat one or more stages several times throughout a product's life cycle.

The analysis stage of the software life cycle focuses on defining the problem to be solved. When designing any system, one must certainly *solve the problem right*, but of equal importance, one must *solve the right problem*. Systems analysts collect the requirements that indicate the specific problem to solve. Our requirements specification describes our ATM system in sufficient detail that you do not need to go through an extensive analysis stage—it has been done for you.

To capture what a proposed system should do, developers often employ a technique known as *use case modeling*. This process identifies the *use cases* of the system, each of which represents a different capability that the system provides to its clients. For example, ATMs typically have several use cases, such as "View Account Balance," "Withdraw Cash," "Deposit Funds," "Transfer Funds Between Accounts" and "Buy Postage Stamps." The simplified ATM system we build in this case study allows only the first three of these use cases (Fig. 3.18).

Each use case describes a typical scenario in which the user uses the system. You have already read descriptions of the ATM system's use cases in the requirements specification; the lists of steps required to perform each type of transaction (i.e., balance inquiry, withdrawal and deposit) actually described the three use cases of our ATM—"View Account Balance," "Withdraw Cash" and "Deposit Funds."

Use Case Diagrams

We now introduce the first of several UML diagrams in our ATM case study. We create a *use case diagram* to model the interactions between a system's clients (in this case study, bank customers) and the system. The goal is to show the kinds of interactions users have with a system without providing the details—these are provided in other UML diagrams (which we present throughout the case study). Use case diagrams are often accompanied by informal text that describes the use cases in more detail—like the text that appears in the requirements specification. Use case diagrams are produced during the analysis stage of the software life cycle. In larger systems, use case diagrams are simple but indispensable tools that help system designers remain focused on satisfying the users' needs.

Figure 3.18 shows the use case diagram for our ATM system. The stick figure represents an *actor*, which defines the roles that an external entity—such as a person or another system—plays when interacting with the system. For our automated teller machine, the actor is a User who can view an account balance, withdraw cash and deposit funds from the ATM. The User is not an actual person, but instead comprises the roles that a real person—when playing the part of a User—can play while interacting with the ATM. Note that a use case diagram can include multiple actors. For example, the use case diagram for a real bank's ATM system might also include an actor named Administrator who refills the cash dispenser each day.

We identify the actor in our system by examining the requirements specification, which states, "ATM users should be able to view their account balance, withdraw cash and deposit funds." Therefore, the actor in each of the three use cases is the User who interacts with the ATM. An external entity—a real person—plays the part of the User to perform financial transactions. Figure 3.18 shows one actor, whose name, User, appears below the actor in the diagram. The UML models each use case as an oval connected to an actor with a solid line.

Software engineers (more precisely, systems analysts) must analyze the requirements specification or a set of use cases and design the system before programmers implement it. During the analysis stage, systems analysts focus on understanding the requirements specification to produce a high-level specification that describes *what* the system is supposed to do. The output of the design stage—a *design specification*—should specify clearly *how* the system should be constructed to satisfy these requirements. In the next several Software Engineering Case Study sections, we perform the steps of a simple object-oriented design (OOD) process on the ATM system to produce a design specification containing a collection of UML diagrams and supporting text. Recall that the UML is designed for use with any OOD process. Many such processes exist, the best known of which is the Rational Unified Process™ (RUP) developed by Rational Software Corporation (now a division of IBM). RUP is a rich process intended for designing "industrial strength" applications. For this case study, we present our own simplified design process.

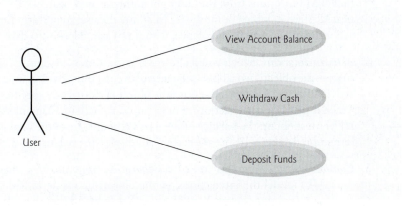

Fig. 3.18 | Use case diagram for the ATM system from the User's perspective.

Designing the ATM System

We now begin the design stage of our ATM system. A *system* is a set of components that interact to solve a problem. For example, to perform the ATM system's designated tasks, our ATM system has a user interface (Fig. 3.15), contains software that executes financial transactions and interacts with a database of bank-account information. *System structure* describes the system's objects and their interrelationships. *System behavior* describes how the system changes as its objects interact with one another. Every system has both structure and behavior—designers must specify both. There are several distinct types of system structures and behaviors. For example, the interactions among objects in the system differ from those between the user and the system, yet both constitute a portion of the system behavior.

The UML 2 specifies 13 diagram types for documenting the models of systems. Each models a distinct characteristic of a system's structure or behavior—six diagrams relate to system structure; the remaining seven relate to system behavior. We list here only the six types of diagrams used in our case study—one of these (class diagrams) models system structure—the remaining five model system behavior. We overview the remaining seven UML diagram types in Chapter G, UML 2: Additional Diagram Types.

1. *Use case diagrams*, such as the one in Fig. 3.18, model the interactions between a system and its external entities (actors) in terms of use cases (system capabilities, such as "View Account Balance," "Withdraw Cash" and "Deposit Funds").

2. *Class diagrams*, which you'll study in Section 4.13, model the classes, or "building blocks," used in a system. Each noun or "thing" described in the requirements specification is a candidate to be a class in the system (e.g., "account," "keypad"). Class diagrams help us specify the structural relationships between parts of the system. For example, the ATM system class diagram will specify that the ATM is physically composed of a screen, a keypad, a cash dispenser and a deposit slot.

3. *State machine diagrams*, which you'll study in Section 4.13, model the ways in which an object changes state. An object's *state* is indicated by the values of all the object's attributes at a given time. When an object changes state, that object may behave differently in the system. For example, after validating a user's PIN, the ATM transitions from the "user not authenticated" state to the "user authenticated" state, at which point the ATM allows the user to perform financial transactions (e.g., view account balance, withdraw cash, deposit funds).

4. *Activity diagrams*, which you'll also study in Section 6.11, model an object's *activity*—the object's workflow (sequence of events) during program execution. An activity diagram models the actions the object performs and specifies the order in which it performs these actions. For example, an activity diagram shows that the ATM must obtain the balance of the user's account (from the bank's account information database) before the screen can display the balance to the user.

5. *Communication diagrams* (called *collaboration diagrams* in earlier versions of the UML) model the interactions among objects in a system, with an emphasis on *what* interactions occur. You'll learn in Section 8.15 that these diagrams show which objects must interact to perform an ATM transaction. For example, the

ATM must communicate with the bank's account-information database to retrieve an account balance.

6. *Sequence diagrams* also model the interactions among the objects in a system, but unlike communication diagrams, they emphasize *when* interactions occur. You'll learn in Section 8.15 that these diagrams help show the order in which interactions occur in executing a financial transaction. For example, the screen prompts the user to enter a withdrawal amount before cash is dispensed.

In Section 4.13, we continue designing our ATM system by identifying the classes from the requirements specification. We accomplish this by extracting key nouns and noun phrases from the requirements specification. Using these classes, we develop our first draft of the class diagram that models the structure of our ATM system.

Internet and Web Resources

The following URLs provide information on object-oriented design with the UML.

`www-306.ibm.com/software/rational/uml/`
Lists frequently asked questions (FAQs) about the UML, provided by IBM Rational.

`www.douglass.co.uk/documents/softdocwiz.com.UML.htm`
Hosts the Unified Modeling Language Dictionary. Lists and defines all terms used in the UML.

`www-306.ibm.com/software/rational/offerings/design.html`
Provides information about IBM Rational software available for designing systems. Provides downloads of 30-day trial versions of several products, such as IBM Rational Rose® XDE Developer.

`www.borland.com/us/products/together/index.html`
Provides a free 30-day license to download a trial version of Borland® Together® ControlCenter™—a software-development tool that supports the UML.

`www.ilogix.com/sublevel.aspx?id=53`
Provides a free 30-day license to download a trial version of I-Logix Rhapsody®—a UML 2 based model-driven development environment.

`argouml.tigris.org`
Contains information and downloads for ArgoUML, a free open source UML tool written in Java.

`www.objectsbydesign.com/books/booklist.html`
Lists books on the UML and object-oriented design.

`www.objectsbydesign.com/tools/umltools_byCompany.html`
Lists software tools that use the UML, such as IBM Rational Rose, Embarcadero Describe, Sparx Systems Enterprise Architect, I-Logix Rhapsody and Gentleware Poseidon for UML.

`www.ootips.org/ood-principles.html`
Provides answers to the question, "What Makes a Good Object-Oriented Design?"

`parlezuml.com/tutorials/umlforjava.htm`
Provides a UML tutorial for Java developers that presents UML diagrams side by side with the Java code that implements them.

`www.cetus-links.org/oo_uml.html`
Introduces the UML and provides links to numerous UML resources.

`www.agilemodeling.com/essays/umlDiagrams.htm`
Provides in-depth descriptions and tutorials on each of the 13 UML 2 diagram types.

Recommended Readings

The following books provide information on object-oriented design with the UML.

Booch, G. *Object-Oriented Analysis and Design with Applications*. 3rd ed. Boston: Addison-Wesley, 2004.

Eriksson, H., et al. *UML 2 Toolkit*. New York: John Wiley, 2003.

Fowler, M. *UML Distilled*. 3rd ed. Boston: Addison-Wesley Professional, 2004.

Kruchten, P. *The Rational Unified Process: An Introduction*. Boston: Addison-Wesley, 2004.

Larman, C. *Applying UML and Patterns: An Introduction to Object-Oriented Analysis and Design*. 2nd ed. Upper Saddle River, NJ: Prentice Hall, 2002.

Roques, P. *UML in Practice: The Art of Modeling Software Systems Demonstrated Through Worked Examples and Solutions*. Hoboken, NJ: John Wiley, 2004.

Rosenberg, D., and K. Scott. *Applying Use Case Driven Object Modeling with UML: An Annotated e-Commerce Example*. Reading, MA: Addison-Wesley, 2001.

Rumbaugh, J., I. Jacobson and G. Booch. *The Complete UML Training Course*. Upper Saddle River, NJ: Prentice Hall, 2000.

Rumbaugh, J., I. Jacobson and G. Booch. *The Unified Modeling Language Reference Manual*. Reading, MA: Addison-Wesley, 1999.

Rumbaugh, J., I. Jacobson and G. Booch. *The Unified Software Development Process*. Reading, MA: Addison-Wesley, 1999.

Schneider, G. and J. Winters. *Applying Use Cases: A Practical Guide*. 2nd ed. Boston: Addison-Wesley Professional, 2002.

Software Engineering Case Study Self-Review Exercises

3.1   Suppose we enabled a user of our ATM system to transfer money between two bank accounts. Modify the use case diagram of Fig. 3.18 to reflect this change.

3.2   _____ model the interactions among objects in a system with an emphasis on *when* these interactions occur.
  a) Class diagrams
  b) Sequence diagrams
  c) Communication diagrams
  d) Activity diagrams

3.3   Which of the following choices lists stages of a typical software life cycle in sequential order?
  a) design, analysis, implementation, testing
  b) design, analysis, testing, implementation
  c) analysis, design, testing, implementation
  d) analysis, design, implementation, testing

Answers to Software Engineering Case Study Self-Review Exercises

3.1   Figure 3.19 shows a use case diagram for a modified version of our ATM system that also allows users to transfer money between accounts.

3.2   b.

3.3   d.

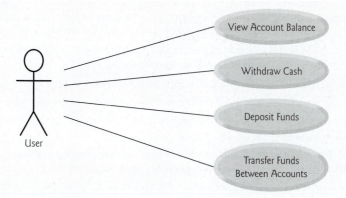

Fig. 3.19 | Use case diagram for a modified version of our ATM system that also allows users to transfer money between accounts.

3.9 Wrap-Up

You learned many important basic features of Visual C++ in this chapter, including displaying data on the screen, inputting data from the keyboard and declaring variables of fundamental types. In particular, you learned to use the output stream object cout and the input stream object cin to build simple interactive programs. We explained how variables are stored in and retrieved from memory. You also learned how to use arithmetic operators to perform calculations. We discussed the order in which Visual C++ applies operators (i.e., the rules of operator precedence), as well as the associativity of the operators. You also learned how Visual C++'s if statement allows a program to make decisions. Finally, we introduced the equality and relational operators, which you use to form conditions in if statements. All of these concepts can be used when writing native or managed C++.

The non-object-oriented applications presented here introduced you to basic programming concepts. As you'll see in Chapter 4, Visual C++ applications typically contain just a few lines of code in function main—these statements normally create the objects that perform the work of the application, then the objects "take over from there." In Chapter 4, you'll learn how to implement your own classes and use objects of those classes in applications.

Summary

Section 3.2 First Program in Visual C++: Printing a Line of Text
- Single-line comments begin with //. You insert comments to document your programs and improve their readability.
- Comments do not cause the computer to perform any action when the program is run—they are ignored by the Visual C++ compiler and do not cause any machine-language object code to be generated.
- A preprocessor directive begins with # and is a message to the Visual C++ preprocessor. Preprocessor directives are processed by the preprocessor before the program is compiled and don't end with a semicolon as Visual C++ statements do.

- The line #include <iostream> tells the Visual C++ preprocessor to include the contents of the input/output stream header file in the program. This file contains information necessary to compile programs that use std::cin and std::cout and operators << and >>.

- White space (i.e., blank lines, space characters and tab characters) makes programs easier to read. White-space characters outside of literals are ignored by the compiler.

- Visual C++ programs begin executing at main, even if main does not appear first in the program.

- The keyword int to the left of main indicates that main "returns" an integer value.

- A left brace, {, must begin the body of every function. A corresponding right brace, }, must end each function's body.

- A string in double quotes is sometimes referred to as a character string, message or string literal. White-space characters in strings are not ignored by the compiler.

- Every statement must end with a semicolon (also known as the statement terminator).

- Output and input in Visual C++ are accomplished with streams of characters.

- The output stream object std::cout—normally connected to the screen—is used to output data. Multiple data items can be output by concatenating stream insertion (<<) operators.

- The input stream object std::cin—normally connected to the keyboard—is used to input data. Multiple data items can be input by concatenating stream extraction (>>) operators.

- The std::cout and std::cin stream objects facilitate interaction between the user and the computer. Because this interaction resembles a dialog, it is often called conversational computing or interactive computing.

- The notation std::cout specifies that we are using a name, in this case cout, that belongs to "namespace" std.

- When a backslash (i.e., an escape character) is encountered in a string of characters, the next character is combined with the backslash to form an escape sequence.

- The escape sequence \n means newline. It causes the cursor (i.e., the current screen-position indicator) to move to the beginning of the next line on the screen.

- A message that directs the user to take a specific action is known as a prompt.

- Visual C++ keyword return is one of several means to exit a function.

Section 3.3 Modifying Our First Visual C++ Program
- Each stream insertion resumes printing where the previous one stopped. To print on a new line use the \n escape sequence inside a string or send std::endl to the stream.

Section 3.4 Another Visual C++ Program: Adding Integers
- All variables in a Visual C++ program must be declared before they can be used.

- A variable name in Visual C++ is any valid identifier that is not a keyword. An identifier is a series of characters consisting of letters, digits and underscores (_). Identifiers cannot start with a digit. Visual C++ identifiers can be any length; however, some systems and/or Visual C++ implementations may impose some restrictions on the length of identifiers.

- Visual C++ is case sensitive.

- Most calculations are performed in assignment statements.

- A variable is a location in the computer's memory where a value can be stored for use by a program.

- Variables of type int hold integer values, i.e., whole numbers such as 7, –11, 0, 31914.

Section 3.5 Memory Concepts

- Every variable stored in the computer's memory has a name, a value, a type and a size.

- Whenever a new value is placed in a memory location, the process is destructive; i.e., the new value replaces the previous value in that location. The previous value is lost.

- When a value is read from memory, the process is nondestructive; i.e., a copy of the value is read, leaving the original value undisturbed in the memory location.

- The `std::endl` stream manipulator outputs a newline, then "flushes the output buffer."

Section 3.6 Arithmetic

- Visual C++ evaluates arithmetic expressions in a precise sequence determined by the rules of operator precedence and associativity.

- Parentheses may be used to group expressions.

- Integer division (i.e., both the numerator and the denominator are integers) yields an integer quotient. Any fractional part in integer division is truncated—no rounding occurs.

- The modulus operator, `%`, yields the remainder after integer division. The modulus operator can be used only with integer operands.

Section 3.7 Decision Making: Equality and Relational Operators

- The `if` statement allows a program to take alternative action based on whether a condition is met. The format for an `if` statement is

      if (condition)
          statement;

  If the condition is true, the statement in the body of the `if` is executed. If the condition is not met, i.e., the condition is false, the body statement is skipped.

- Conditions in `if` statements are commonly formed by using equality operators and relational operators. The result of using these operators is always the value true or false.

- The declaration

      using std::cout;

  is a `using` declaration that informs the compiler where to find `cout` (namespace `std`) and eliminates the need to repeat the `std::` prefix. Once we include this `using` declaration, we can, for example, write `cout` instead of `std::cout` in the remainder of a program.

Terminology

/* ... */ comment (C-style comment)
// comment
arithmetic operator
assignment operator (=)
associativity of operators
binary operator
block
body of a function
cascading stream insertion operations
case sensitive
chaining stream insertion operations
character string
cin object

comma-separated list
comment (//)
compilation error
compiler error
compile-time error
compound statement
concatenating stream insertion operations
condition
cout object
cursor
data type
decision
declaration

destructive write
equality operators
    == "is equal to"
    != "is not equal to"
escape character (\)
escape sequence
exit a function
fatal error
function
identifier
if statement
input/output stream header file <iostream>
int data type
integer (int)
integer division
left-to-right associativity
literal
logic error
main function
memory
memory location
message
modulus operator (%)
multiplication operator (*)
nested parentheses
newline character (\n)
nondestructive read
nonfatal logic error
operand
operator

operator associativity
parentheses ()
perform an action
precedence
preprocessor directive
prompt
redundant parentheses
relational operators
    < "is less than"
    <= "is less than or equal to"
    > "is greater than"
    >= "is greater than or equal to"
return statement
rules of operator precedence
self-documenting program
semicolon (;) statement terminator
standard input stream object (cin)
standard output stream object (cout)
statement
statement terminator (;)
stream
stream extraction operator (>>)
stream insertion operator (<<)
stream manipulator
string
string literal
syntax error
using declaration
variable
white space

Self-Review Exercises

3.1 Fill in the blanks in each of the following.
    a) Every Visual C++ program begins execution at the function _____.
    b) A(n) _____ begins the body of every function and a _____ ends the body.
    c) Every Visual C++ statement ends with a(n) _____.
    d) The escape sequence \n represents the _____ character, which causes the cursor to position to the beginning of the next line on the screen.
    e) The _____ statement is used to make decisions.

3.2 State whether each of the following is *true* or *false*. If *false*, explain why. Assume the statement using std::cout; is used.
    a) Comments cause the computer to print the text after the // on the screen when the program is executed.
    b) The escape sequence \n, when output with cout and the stream insertion operator, causes the cursor to position to the beginning of the next line on the screen.
    c) All variables must be declared before they are used.
    d) All variables must be given a type when they are declared.
    e) Visual C++ considers the variables number and NuMbEr to be identical.
    f) Declarations can appear almost anywhere in the body of a Visual C++ function.
    g) The modulus operator (%) can be used only with integer operands.

h) The arithmetic operators *, /, %, + and – all have the same level of precedence.

i) A Visual C++ program that prints three lines of output must contain three statements using cout and the stream insertion operator.

3.3 Write a single Visual C++ statement to accomplish each of the following (assume that us-ing declarations have not been used):

a) Declare the variables c, thisIsAVariable, q76354 and number to be of type int.

b) Prompt the user to enter an integer. End your prompting message with a colon (:) fol-lowed by a space and leave the cursor positioned after the space.

c) Read an integer from the user at the keyboard and store it in integer variable age.

d) If the variable number is not equal to 7, print "The variable number is not equal to 7".

e) Print the message "This is a Visual C++ program" on one line.

f) Print the message "This is a Visual C++ program" on two lines. End the first line with C++.

g) Print the message "This is a Visual C++ program" with each word on a separate line.

h) Print the message "This is a Visual C++ program". Separate each word from the next by a tab.

3.4 Write a statement (or comment) to accomplish each of the following (assume that using declarations have been used for cin, cout and endl):

a) State that a program calculates the product of three integers.

b) Declare the variables x, y, z and result to be of type int (in separate statements).

c) Prompt the user to enter three integers.

d) Read three integers from the keyboard and store them in the variables x, y and z.

e) Compute the product of the three integers contained in variables x, y and z, and assign the result to the variable result.

f) Print "The product is " followed by the value of the variable result.

g) Return a value from main indicating that the program terminated successfully.

3.5 Using the statements you wrote in Exercise 3.4, write a complete program that calculates and displays the product of three integers. Add comments to the code where appropriate. [*Note:* You'll need to write the necessary using declarations.]

3.6 Identify and correct the errors in each of the following statements (assume that the state-ment using std::cout; is used):

a) *if* (c < 7);
      cout << "c is less than 7\n";

b) *if* (c => 7)
      cout << "c is equal to or greater than 7\n";

Answers to Self-Review Exercises

3.1 a) main. b) left brace ({), right brace (}). c) semicolon. d) newline. e) if.

3.2 a) False. Comments do not cause any action to be performed when the program is exe-cuted. They are used to document programs and improve their readability.

b) True.

c) True.

d) True.

e) False. Visual C++ is case sensitive, so these variables are unique.

f) True.

g) True.

h) False. The operators *, / and % have the same precedence, and the operators + and – have a lower precedence.

i) False. One statement with cout and multiple \n escape sequences can print several lines.

3.3 a) *int* c, thisIsAVariable, q76354, number;

b) std::cout << "Enter an integer: ";

c) std::cin >> age;

d) *if* (number != 7)
std::cout << "The variable number is not equal to 7\n";

e) std::cout << "This is a Visual C++ program\n";

f) std::cout << "This is a Visual C++\nprogram\n";

g) std::cout << "This\nis\na\nVisual C++\nprogram\n";

h) std::cout << "This\tis\ta\tVisual C++\tprogram\n";

3.4 a) *// Calculate the product of three integers*

b) *int* x;
int y;
int z;
int result;

c) cout << "Enter three integers: ";

d) cin >> x >> y >> z;

e) result = x * y * z;

f) cout << "The product is " << result << endl;

g) *return* 0;

3.5 (See program below.)

```
1    // Calculate the product of three integers
2    #include <iostream> // allows program to perform input and output
3
4    using std::cout; // program uses cout
5    using std::cin; // program uses cin
6    using std::endl; // program uses endl
7
8    // function main begins program execution
9    int main()
10   {
11       int x; // first integer to multiply
12       int y; // second integer to multiply
13       int z; // third integer to multiply
14       int result; // the product of the three integers
15
16       cout << "Enter three integers: "; // prompt user for data
17       cin >> x >> y >> z; // read three integers from user
18       result = x * y * z; // multiply the three integers; store result
19       cout << "The product is " << result << endl; // print result; end line
20
21       return 0; // indicate program executed successfully
22   } // end function main
```

3.6 a) *Error:* Semicolon after the right parenthesis of the condition in the if statement.
Correction: Remove the semicolon after the right parenthesis. [*Note:* The result of this error is that the output statement will be executed whether or not the condition in the if statement is true.] The semicolon after the right parenthesis is a null (or empty) statement—a statement that does nothing. We'll learn more about the null statement in the next chapter.

b) *Error:* The relational operator =>.
   Correction: Change => to >=, and you may want to change "equal to or greater than" to "greater than or equal to" as well.

Exercises

3.7   Discuss the meaning of each of the following objects:
   a) `std::cin`
   b) `std::cout`

3.8   Fill in the blanks in each of the following:
   a) _____ are used to document a program and improve its readability.
   b) The object used to print information on the screen is _____.
   c) A Visual C++ statement that makes a decision is _____.
   d) Most calculations are normally performed by _____ statements.
   e) The _____ object inputs values from the keyboard.

3.9   Write a single Visual C++ statement or line that accomplishes each of the following:
   a) Print the message `"Enter two numbers"`.
   b) Assign the product of variables `b` and `c` to variable `a`.
   c) State that a program performs a payroll calculation (i.e., use text that helps to document a program).
   d) Input three integer values from the keyboard into integer variables a, b and c.

3.10   State which of the following are *true* and which are *false*. If false, explain your answers.
   a) Visual C++ operators are evaluated from left to right.
   b) The following are all valid variable names: `_under_bar_`, `m928134`, `t5`, `j7`, `her_sales`, `his_account_total`, `a`, `b`, `c`, `z`, `z2`.
   c) The statement `cout << "a = 5;";` is a typical example of an assignment statement.
   d) A valid Visual C++ arithmetic expression with no parentheses is evaluated from left to right.
   e) The following are all invalid variable names: `3g`, `87`, `67h2`, `h22`, `2h`.

3.11   Fill in the blanks in each of the following:
   a) What arithmetic operations are on the same level of precedence as multiplication? _____.
   b) When parentheses are nested, which set of parentheses is evaluated first in an arithmetic expression? _____.
   c) A location in the computer's memory that may contain different values at various times throughout the execution of a program is called a _____.

3.12   What, if anything, prints when each of the following Visual C++ statements is performed? If nothing prints, then answer "nothing." Assume x = 2 and y = 3.
   a) `cout << x;`
   b) `cout << x + x;`
   c) `cout << "x=";`
   d) `cout << "x = " << x;`
   e) `cout << x + y << " = " << y + x;`
   f) `z = x + y;`
   g) `cin >> x >> y;`
   h) `// cout << "x + y = " << x + y;`
   i) `cout << "\n";`

3.13   Which of the following Visual C++ statements contain variables whose values are replaced?
   a) `cin >> b >> c >> d >> e >> f;`

b) `p = i + j + k + 7;`
c) `cout << "variables whose values are replaced";`
d) `cout << "a = 5";`

3.14   Given the algebraic equation $y = ax^3 + 7$, which of the following, if any, are correct Visual C++ statements for this equation?

a) `y = a * x * x * x + 7;`
b) `y = a * x * x * ( x + 7 );`
c) `y = ( a * x ) * x * ( x + 7 );`
d) `y = (a * x) * x * x + 7;`
e) `y = a * ( x * x * x ) + 7;`
f) `y = a * x * ( x * x + 7 );`

3.15   State the order of evaluation of the operators in each of the following Visual C++ statements and show the value of x after each statement is performed.

a) `x = 7 + 3 * 6 / 2 - 1;`
b) `x = 2 % 2 + 2 * 2 - 2 / 2;`
c) `x = ( 3 * 9 * ( 3 + ( 9 * 3 / ( 3 ) ) ) );`

3.16   Write a program that asks the user to enter two numbers, obtains the two numbers from the user and prints the sum, product, difference, and quotient of the two numbers.

3.17   Write a program that prints the numbers 1 to 4 on the same line with each pair of adjacent numbers separated by one space. Do this several ways:

a) Using one statement with one stream insertion operator.
b) Using one statement with four stream insertion operators.
c) Using four statements.

3.18   Write a program that asks the user to enter two integers, obtains the numbers from the user, then prints the larger number followed by the words `"is larger."` If the numbers are equal, print the message `"These numbers are equal."`

3.19   Write a program that inputs three integers from the keyboard and prints the sum, average, product, smallest and largest of these numbers. The screen dialog should appear as follows:

```
Input three different integers: 13 27 14
Sum is 54
Average is 18
Product is 4914
Smallest is 13
Largest is 27
```

3.20   Write a program that reads in the radius of a circle as an integer and prints the circle's diameter, circumference and area. Use the constant value 3.14159 for π. Do all calculations in output statements. [*Note:* In this chapter, we have discussed only integer constants and variables. In Chapter 5 we discuss floating-point numbers, i.e., values that can have decimal points.]

3.21   Write a program that prints a box, an oval, an arrow and a diamond as follows:

```
*********           ***              *                 *
*       *         *     *           ***               * *
*       *        *       *         *****             *   *
*       *        *       *           *              *     *
*       *        *       *           *             *       *
*       *        *       *           *              *     *
*       *        *       *           *               *   *
*       *         *     *            *                * *
*********           ***              *                 *
```

3.22 What does the following code print?

```
cout << "*\n**\n***\n****\n*****" << endl;
```

3.23 Write a program that reads in five integers and determines and prints the largest and the smallest integers in the group. Use only the programming techniques you learned in this chapter.

3.24 Write a program that reads an integer and determines and prints whether it is odd or even. [*Hint:* Use the modulus operator. An even number is a multiple of two. Any multiple of two leaves a remainder of zero when divided by 2.]

3.25 Write a program that reads in two integers and determines and prints whether the first is a multiple of the second. [*Hint:* Use the modulus operator.]

3.26 Display the following checkerboard pattern with eight output statements, then display the same pattern using as few statements as possible.

```
* * * * * * * *
 * * * * * * * *
* * * * * * * *
 * * * * * * * *
* * * * * * * *
 * * * * * * * *
* * * * * * * *
 * * * * * * * *
```

3.27 Here is a peek ahead. In this chapter you learned about integers and the type `int`. Visual C++ can also represent uppercase letters, lowercase letters and a considerable variety of special symbols. Visual C++ uses small integers internally to represent each different character. The set of characters a computer uses and the corresponding integer representations for those characters are called that computer's *character set*. You can print a character by enclosing that character in single quotes, as with

```
cout << 'A'; // print an uppercase A
```

You can print the integer equivalent of a character using `static_cast` as follows:

```
cout << static_cast< int >( 'A' ); // print 'A' as an integer
```

This is called a *cast* operation (we formally introduce casts in Chapter 5). When the preceding statement executes, it prints the value 65 (on systems that use the *ASCII character set*). Write a program that prints the integer equivalent of a character typed at the keyboard. Store the input in a variable of type `char`. Test your program several times using uppercase letters, lowercase letters, digits and special characters (like $).

3.28 Write a program that inputs a five-digit integer, separates the integer into its individual digits and prints the digits separated from one another by three spaces each. [*Hint:* Use the integer division and modulus operators.] For example, if the user types in 42339, the program should print:

```
4   2   3   3   9
```

3.29 Using only the techniques you learned in this chapter, write a program that calculates the squares and cubes of the integers from 0 to 10 and uses tabs to print the following neatly formatted table of values:

```
integer square   cube
0        0        0
1        1        1
2        4        8
3        9        27
4        16       64
5        25       125
6        36       216
7        49       343
8        64       512
9        81       729
10       100      1000
```

4

Introduction to Classes and Objects

OBJECTIVES

In this chapter you'll learn:

- What classes, objects, member functions and data members are.
- How to define classes and use them to create objects.
- How to define member functions in a class to implement the class's behaviors.
- How to declare data members in a class to implement the class's attributes.
- How to call a member function of an object to make that member function perform its task.
- The differences between data members of a class and local variables of a function.
- How to use a constructor to ensure that an object's data is initialized when the object is created.
- How to engineer a class to separate its interface from its implementation and encourage reuse.

4.1 Introduction

In Chapter 3, you created simple programs that displayed messages to the user, obtained information from the user, performed calculations and made decisions. In this chapter, you'll begin writing programs that employ the basic concepts of object-oriented programming that we introduced in Section 1.21. One common feature of every program in Chapter 3 was that all the statements that performed tasks were located in function main. Typically, the programs you develop in this book will consist of function main and one or more classes, each containing data members and member functions. If you become part of a development team in industry, you might work on software systems that contain hundreds, or even thousands, of classes. In this chapter, we develop a simple, well-engineered framework for organizing object-oriented programs in Visual C++.

First, we motivate the notion of classes with a real-world example. Then we present a carefully paced sequence of seven complete working programs to demonstrate creating and using your own classes. These examples begin our integrated case study on developing a grade-book class that instructors can use to maintain student test scores. This case study is enhanced over the next several chapters, culminating with the version presented in Chapter 8, Arrays and Vectors. We also introduce the C++ standard library class string in this chapter. Finally, we present a first look at C++/CLI syntax for creating classes with managed code.

4.2 Classes, Objects, Member Functions and Data Members

Let's begin with a simple analogy to help you reinforce your understanding from Section 1.21 of classes and their contents. Suppose you want to drive a car and make it go faster by pressing down on its accelerator pedal. What must happen before you can do this? Well, before you can drive a car, someone has to design it and build it. A car typically begins as engineering drawings, similar to the blueprints used to design a house. These drawings include the design for an accelerator pedal that the driver will use to make the car go faster. In a sense, the pedal "hides" the complex mechanisms that actually make the car go faster, just as the brake pedal "hides" the mechanisms that slow the car, the steering wheel "hides" the mechanisms that turn the car and so on. This enables people with little or no knowledge of how cars are engineered to drive a car easily, simply by using the accelerator pedal, the brake pedal, the steering wheel, the transmission shifting mechanism and other such simple and user-friendly "interfaces" to the car's complex internal mechanisms.

Unfortunately, you cannot drive the engineering drawings of a car—before you can drive a car, it must be built from the engineering drawings that describe it. A completed car will have an actual accelerator pedal to make the car go faster. But even that's not enough—the car will not accelerate on its own, so the driver must press the accelerator pedal to tell the car to go faster.

Now let's use our car example to introduce the key object-oriented programming concepts of this section. Performing a task in a program requires a function (such as main, as described in Chapter 3). The function describes the mechanisms that actually perform its tasks. The function hides from its user the complex tasks that it performs, just as the accelerator pedal of a car hides from the driver the complex mechanisms of making the car go faster. In Visual C++, we begin by creating a program unit called a class to house a function, just as a car's engineering drawings house the design of an accelerator pedal. Recall from Section 1.21 that a function belonging to a class is called a member function. In a class, you provide one or more member functions that are designed to perform the class's tasks. For example, a class that represents a bank account might contain one member function to deposit money into the account, another to withdraw money from the account and a third to inquire what the current account balance is.

Just as you cannot drive an engineering drawing of a car, you cannot "drive" a class. Just as someone has to build a car from its engineering drawings before you can actually drive the car, you must create an object of a class before you can get a program to perform the tasks the class describes. That is one reason Visual C++ is known as an object-oriented programming language. Note also that just as *many* cars can be built from the same engineering drawing, *many* objects can be built from the same class.

When you drive a car, pressing its gas pedal sends a message to the car to perform a task—that is, make the car go faster. Similarly, you send *messages* to an object—each message is known as a *member-function call* and tells a member function of the object to perform its task. This is often called *requesting a service from an object*.

Thus far, we have used the car analogy to introduce classes, objects and member functions. In addition to the capabilities a car provides, it also has many attributes, such as its color, the number of doors, the amount of gas in its tank, its current speed and its total miles driven (i.e., its odometer reading). Like the car's capabilities, these attributes are represented as part of a car's design in its engineering diagrams. As you drive a car, these attributes are always associated with the car. Every car maintains its own attributes. For example, each car knows how much gas is in its own gas tank, but not how much is in the tanks of other cars. Similarly, an object has attributes that are carried with it as it is used in a program. These attributes are specified as part of the object's class. For example, a bank-account object has a balance attribute that represents the amount of money in the account. Each bank-account object knows the balance in the account it represents, but not the balances of the other accounts in the bank. Attributes are specified by the class's data members.

4.3 Overview of the Chapter Examples

The remainder of this chapter presents nine simple examples that demonstrate the concepts we introduced in the context of the car analogy. These examples, summarized below, incrementally build a GradeBook class to demonstrate these concepts:

1. The first example presents a GradeBook class with one member function that simply displays a welcome message when it is called. We show how to create an object of that class and call the member function so that it displays the welcome message.

2. The second example modifies the first by allowing the member function to receive a course name as a so-called argument. Then, the member function displays the course name as part of the welcome message.

3. The third example shows how to store the course name in a GradeBook object. For this version of the class, we also show how to use member functions to set the course name in the object and get the course name from the object.

4. The fourth example demonstrates how the data in a GradeBook object can be initialized when the object is created—the initialization is performed by a special member function called the class's constructor. This example also demonstrates that each GradeBook object maintains its own course-name data member.

5. The fifth example modifies the fourth by demonstrating how to place class GradeBook into a separate file to enable software reusability.

6. The sixth example modifies the fifth by demonstrating the good software engineering principle of separating the interface of the class from its implementation. This makes the class easier to modify without affecting any *clients of the class's objects*—that is, any classes or functions that call the member functions of the class's objects from outside the objects.

7. The seventh, and last, native C++ example enhances class GradeBook by introducing data validation, which ensures that data in an object adheres to a particular format or is in a proper value range. For example, a Date object would require a month value in the range 1–12. In this GradeBook example, the member function that sets the course name for a GradeBook object ensures that the course name is 25 characters or fewer. If not, the member function uses only the first 25 characters of the course name and displays a warning message.

8. The eighth example presents a first look at C++/CLI by rewriting the second example using .NET classes and managed code.

9. The final example uses C++/CLI properties to create a simpler version of the sixth example that doesn't require *set* and *get* functions.

Note that the GradeBook examples in this chapter do not actually process or store grades. We begin processing grades with class GradeBook in Chapter 5 and we store grades in a GradeBook object in Chapter 8, .

4.4 Defining a Class with a Member Function

We begin with an example (Fig. 4.1) that consists of class GradeBook (lines 9–17), which represents a grade book that an instructor can use to maintain student test scores, and a main function (lines 20–25) that creates a GradeBook object. Function main uses this object and its member function to display a message on the screen welcoming the instructor to the grade-book program.

First we describe how to define a class and a member function. Then we explain how an object is created and how to call a member function of an object. The first few examples contain function main and the GradeBook class it uses in the same file. Later in the chapter, we introduce more sophisticated ways to structure your programs to achieve better software engineering.

```
1   // Fig. 4.1: GradeBook.cpp
2   // Define class GradeBook with a member function displayMessage,
3   // create a GradeBook object, and call its displayMessage function.
4   #include <iostream>
5   using std::cout;
6   using std::endl;
7
8   // GradeBook class definition
9   class GradeBook
10  {
11  public:
12     // function that displays a welcome message to the GradeBook user
13     void displayMessage()
14     {
15        cout << "Welcome to the Grade Book!" << endl;
16     } // end function displayMessage
17  }; // end class GradeBook
18
19  // function main begins program execution
20  int main()
21  {
22     GradeBook myGradeBook; // create a GradeBook object named myGradeBook
23     myGradeBook.displayMessage(); // call object's displayMessage function
24     return 0; // indicate successful termination
25  } // end main
```

```
Welcome to the Grade Book!
```

Fig. 4.1 | Define class GradeBook with a member function displayMessage, create a GradeBook object, and call its displayMessage function.

Class GradeBook

Before function main (lines 20–25) can create an object of class GradeBook, we must tell the compiler what member functions and data members belong to the class. This is known as *defining a class*. The GradeBook *class definition* (lines 9–17) contains a member function called displayMessage (lines 13–16) that displays a message on the screen (line 15). Recall that a class is like a blueprint—so we need to make an object of class GradeBook (line 22) and call its `displayMessage` member function (line 23) to get line 15 to execute and display the welcome message. We'll soon explain lines 22–23 in detail.

The class definition begins in line 9 with the keyword `class` followed by the class name `GradeBook`. By convention, the name of a user-defined class begins with a capital letter, and for readability, each subsequent word in the class name begins with a capital letter. This capitalization style is often referred to as *camel case*, because the pattern of uppercase and lowercase letters resembles the silhouette of a camel.

Every class's *body* is enclosed in a pair of left and right braces ({ and }), as in lines 10 and 17. The class definition terminates with a semicolon (line 17).

Common Programming Error 4.1

Forgetting the semicolon at the end of a class definition is a syntax error.

Recall that the function `main` is always called automatically when you execute a program. Most functions do not get called automatically. As you'll soon see, you must call member function `displayMessage` explicitly to tell it to perform its task.

Line 11 contains the *access-specifier label* `public:`. The keyword **public** is an *access specifier*. Lines 13–16 define member function `displayMessage`, which appears after access specifier `public:` to indicate that the function is "available to the public"—that is, it can be called by other functions in the program (such as `main`), and by member functions of other classes (if there are any). Access specifiers are always followed by a colon (:). For the remainder of the text, when we refer to the access specifier `public`, we'll omit the colon as we did in this sentence. Section 4.6 introduces a second access specifier, `private`.

Each function in a program performs a task and may return a value when it completes its task—for example, a function might perform a calculation, then return the result of that calculation. When you define a function, you must specify a *return type* to indicate the type of the value returned by the function when it completes its task. In line 13, keyword **void** to the left of the function name `displayMessage` is the function's return type. Return type `void` indicates that `displayMessage` will not return (i.e., give back) any data to its *calling function* (in this example, `main`, as we'll see in a moment) when it completes its task. In Fig. 4.5, you'll see an example of a function that returns a value.

The name of the member function, `displayMessage`, follows the return type. By convention, function names begin with a lowercase first letter and all subsequent words in the name begin with a capital letter. The parentheses after the member function name indicate that this is a function. An empty set of parentheses, as shown in line 13, indicates that this member function does not require additional data to perform its task. You'll see an example of a member function that does require additional data in Section 4.5. Line 13 is commonly referred to as the *function header*. Every function's body is delimited by left and right braces ({ and }), as in lines 14 and 16.

The body of a function contains statements that perform the function's task. In this case, member function `displayMessage` contains one statement (line 15) that displays the message `"Welcome to the Grade Book!"`. After this statement executes, the function has completed its task.

Common Programming Error 4.2

Returning a value from a function whose return type has been declared `void` is a compilation error.

Common Programming Error 4.3

Defining a function inside another function is a syntax error.

Testing Class GradeBook

Next, we'd like to use class GradeBook in a program. As you learned in Chapter 3, function main (lines 20–25) begins the execution of every program.

In this program, we'd like to call class GradeBook's displayMessage member function to display the welcome message. Typically, you cannot call a member function of a class until you create an object of that class. (As you'll learn in Section 11.7, static member functions are an exception.) Line 22 creates an object of class GradeBook called myGrade-Book. Note that the variable's type is GradeBook—the class we defined in lines 9–17. When we declare variables of type int, as we did in Chapter 3, the compiler knows what int is—it's a fundamental type. In line 22, however, the compiler does not automatically know what type GradeBook is—it's a *user-defined type*. We tell the compiler what Grade-Book is by including the class definition (lines 9–17). If we omitted these lines, the compiler would issue an error message: "'GradeBook': undeclared identifier." Each class you create becomes a new type that can be used to create objects. You can define new class types as needed; this is one reason why Visual C++ is known as an *extensible language*.

Line 23 calls the member function displayMessage (defined in lines 13–16) using variable myGradeBook followed by the *dot operator* (.), the function name displayMessage and an empty set of parentheses. This call causes the displayMessage function to perform its task. At the beginning of line 23, "myGradeBook." indicates that main should use the GradeBook object that was created in line 22. The empty parentheses in line 13 indicate that displayMessage does not require additional data to perform its task. (In Section 4.5, you'll see how to pass data to a function.) When displayMessage completes its task, function main continues executing in line 24, which indicates that main performed its tasks successfully. This is the end of main, so the program terminates.

UML Class Diagram for Class GradeBook

Recall from Section 1.21 that the UML is a standardized graphical language used by programmers to represent their object-oriented systems. In the UML, each class is modeled in a *UML class diagram* as a rectangle with three compartments. Figure 4.2 presents a class diagram for class GradeBook (Fig. 4.1). The top compartment contains the class's name centered horizontally and in boldface type. The middle compartment contains the class's attributes, which correspond to data members in Visual C++. This compartment is currently empty, because class GradeBook does not have any attributes. (Section 4.6 presents a version of class GradeBook with an attribute.) The bottom compartment contains the class's operations, which correspond to member functions in Visual C++. The UML models operations by listing the operation name followed by a set of parentheses. Class GradeBook has only one member function, displayMessage, so the bottom compartment of Fig. 4.2 lists one operation with this name. Member function displayMessage does not require additional information to perform its tasks, so the parentheses following displayMessage in the class diagram are empty, just as they are in the member function's header in line 13 of Fig. 4.1. The plus sign (+) in front of the operation name indicates that displayMessage is a public operation in the UML (i.e., a public member function in Visual C++).

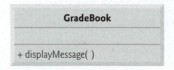

Fig. 4.2 | UML class diagram indicating that class GradeBook has a public displayMessage operation.

4.5 Defining a Member Function with a Parameter

In our car analogy from Section 4.2, we mentioned that pressing a car's gas pedal sends a message to the car to perform a task—make the car go faster. But how fast should the car accelerate? As you know, the farther down you press the pedal, the faster the car accelerates. So the message to the car includes both the task to perform and additional information that helps the car perform the task. This additional information is known as a *parameter*—the value of the parameter helps the car determine how fast to accelerate. Similarly, a member function can require one or more parameters that represent additional data it needs to perform its task. A function call supplies values—called *arguments*—for each of the function's parameters. For example, to make a deposit into a bank account, suppose a deposit member function of an Account class specifies a parameter that represents the deposit amount. When the deposit member function is called, an argument value representing the deposit amount is copied to the member function's parameter. The member function then adds that amount to the account balance.

Defining and Testing Class GradeBook

Our next example (Fig. 4.3) redefines class GradeBook (lines 14–23) with a display-Message member function (lines 18–22) that displays the course name as part of the welcome message. The new version of displayMessage requires a parameter (courseName in line 18) that represents the course name to output.

```
 1   // Fig. 4.3: GradeBook.cpp
 2   // Define class GradeBook with a member function that takes a parameter;
 3   // Create a GradeBook object and call its displayMessage function.
 4   #include <iostream>
 5   using std::cout;
 6   using std::cin;
 7   using std::endl;
 8
 9   #include <string> // program uses C++ standard string class
10   using std::string;
11   using std::getline;
12
13   // GradeBook class definition
14   class GradeBook
15   {
```

Fig. 4.3 | Define class GradeBook with a member function that takes a parameter, create a GradeBook object and call its displayMessage function. (Part 1 of 2.)

```
16    public:
17       // function that displays a welcome message to the GradeBook user
18       void displayMessage( string courseName )
19       {
20          cout << "Welcome to the grade book for\n" << courseName << "!"
21             << endl;
22       } // end function displayMessage
23    }; // end class GradeBook
24
25    // function main begins program execution
26    int main()
27    {
28       string nameOfCourse; // string of characters to store the course name
29       GradeBook myGradeBook; // create a GradeBook object named myGradeBook
30
31       // prompt for and input course name
32       cout << "Please enter the course name:" << endl;
33       getline( cin, nameOfCourse ); // read a course name with blanks
34       cout << endl; // output a blank line
35
36       // call myGradeBook's displayMessage function
37       // and pass nameOfCourse as an argument
38       myGradeBook.displayMessage( nameOfCourse );
39       return 0; // indicate successful termination
40    } // end main
```

```
Please enter the course name:
CS101 Introduction to Visual C++ Programming

Welcome to the grade book for
CS101 Introduction to Visual C++ Programming!
```

Fig. 4.3 | Define class GradeBook with a member function that takes a parameter, create a GradeBook object and call its displayMessage function. (Part 2 of 2.)

Before discussing the new features of class GradeBook, let's see how the new class is used in main (lines 26–40). Line 28 creates a variable of type *string* called nameOfCourse that will be used to store the course name entered by the user. A variable of type string represents a string of characters such as "CS101 Introduction to Visual C++ Programming". A string is actually an object of the C++ Standard Library class string. This class is defined in *header file <string>*, and the name string, like cout, belongs to namespace std. To enable line 28 to compile, line 9 includes the <string> header file. Note that the using declaration in line 10 allows us to simply write string in line 28 rather than std::string. For now, you can think of string variables like variables of other types such as int. You'll learn additional string capabilities in Section 4.10.

Line 29 creates an object of class GradeBook named myGradeBook. Line 32 prompts the user to enter a course name. Line 33 reads the name from the user and assigns it to the nameOfCourse variable, using the library function *getline* to perform the input. Before we explain this line of code, let's explain why we cannot simply write

```
cin >> nameOfCourse;
```

to obtain the course name. In our sample program execution, we use the course name "CS101 Introduction to Visual C++ Programming," which contains multiple words. (Recall that we highlight user-supplied input in bold.) When `cin` is used with the stream extraction operator, it reads characters until the first white-space character is reached. Thus, only "CS101" would be read by the preceding statement. The rest of the course name would have to be read by subsequent input operations.

In this example, we'd like the user to type the complete course name and press *Enter* to submit it to the program, and we'd like to store the entire course name in the `string` variable `nameOfCourse`. The function call `getline( cin, nameOfCourse )` in line 33 reads characters (including the space characters that separate the words in the input) from the standard input stream object `cin` (i.e., the keyboard) until the newline character is encountered, places the characters in the `string` variable `nameOfCourse` and discards the newline character. Note that when you press *Enter* while typing program input, a newline is inserted in the input stream. Also the `<string>` header file must be included in the program to use function `getline` and that the name `getline` belongs to namespace `std`.

Line 38 calls `myGradeBook`'s `displayMessage` member function. The `nameOfCourse` variable in parentheses is the argument that is passed to member function `displayMessage` so that it can perform its task. The value of variable `nameOfCourse` in `main` becomes the value of member function `displayMessage`'s parameter `courseName` in line 18. When you execute this program, notice that member function `displayMessage` outputs as part of the welcome message the course name you type (in our sample execution, CS101 Introduction to Visual C++ Programming).

More on Arguments and Parameters

To specify that a function requires data to perform its task, you place additional information in the function's *parameter list*, which is located in the parentheses following the function name. The parameter list may contain any number of parameters, including none at all (represented by empty parentheses as in Fig. 4.1, line 13) to indicate that a function does not require any parameters. Member function `displayMessage`'s parameter list (Fig. 4.3, line 18) declares that the function requires one parameter. Each parameter must specify a type and an identifier. In this case, the type `string` and the identifier `courseName` indicate that member function `displayMessage` requires a `string` to perform its task. The member-function body uses the parameter `courseName` to access the value that is passed to the function in the function call (line 38 in main). Lines 20–21 display parameter `courseName`'s value as part of the welcome message. Note that the parameter variable's name (line 18) can be the same as or different from the argument variable's name (line 38)—you'll learn why in Chapter 7, Functions and an Introduction to Recursion.

A function can specify multiple parameters by separating each parameter from the next with a comma (we'll see an example in Figs. 7.4–7.5). The number and order of arguments in a function call must match the number and order of parameters in the parameter list of the called member function's header. Also, the argument types in the function call must be consistent with the types of the corresponding parameters in the function header. (As you'll learn in subsequent chapters, an argument's type and its corresponding parameter's type need not always be identical, but they must be "consistent.") In our example, the one `string` argument in the function call (i.e., `nameOfCourse`) exactly matches the one `string` parameter in the member-function definition (i.e., `courseName`).

Common Programming Error 4.4

Placing a semicolon after the right parenthesis enclosing the parameter list of a function definition is a syntax error.

Common Programming Error 4.5

Defining a function parameter again as a local variable in the function is a compilation error.

Good Programming Practice 4.1

To avoid ambiguity, do not use the same names for the arguments passed to a function and the corresponding parameters in the function definition.

Good Programming Practice 4.2

Choosing meaningful function names and meaningful parameter names makes programs more readable and helps avoid excessive use of comments.

Updated UML Class Diagram for Class GradeBook

The UML class diagram of Fig. 4.4 models class GradeBook of Fig. 4.3. Like the class GradeBook defined in Fig. 4.1, this GradeBook class contains public member function displayMessage. However, this version of displayMessage has a parameter. The UML models a parameter by listing the parameter name, followed by a colon and the parameter type in the parentheses following the operation name. The UML has its own data types similar to those of Visual C++. The UML is language independent—it is used with many different programming languages—so its terminology does not exactly match that of Visual C++. For example, the UML type String corresponds to the native C++ type string. Member function displayMessage of class GradeBook (Fig. 4.3, lines 18–22) has a string parameter named courseName, so Fig. 4.4 lists courseName : String between the parentheses following the operation name displayMessage. Note that this version of the GradeBook class still does not have any data members.

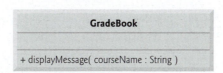

Fig. 4.4 | UML class diagram indicating that class GradeBook has a displayMessage operation with a courseName parameter of UML type String.

4.6 Data Members, *set* Functions and *get* Functions

In Chapter 3, we declared all of a program's variables in its main function. Variables declared in a function definition's body are known as *local variables* and can be used only from the line of their declaration in the function to the immediately closing right brace (}) of the block enclosing the variable's declaration. A local variable must be declared before it can be used in a function. A local variable cannot be accessed outside the function in which it is declared. When a function terminates, the values of its local variables are lost. (You'll see an exception to this in Chapter 7 when we discuss static local variables.) Recall from Section 4.2 that an object has attributes that are carried with it as it is used in a program. Such attributes exist throughout the life of the object.

A class normally consists of one or more member functions that manipulate the attributes that belong to a particular object of the class. Attributes are represented as variables in a class definition. Such variables are called *data members* and are declared inside a class definition but outside the bodies of the class's member-function definitions. Each object of a class maintains its own copy of its attributes in memory. The example in this section demonstrates a GradeBook class that contains a courseName data member to represent a particular GradeBook object's course name.

GradeBook Class with a Data Member, a set Function and a get Function

In our next example, class GradeBook (Fig. 4.5) maintains the course name as a data member so that it can be used or modified at any time during a program's execution. The class contains member functions setCourseName, getCourseName and displayMessage. Member function setCourseName stores a course name in a GradeBook data member. Member function getCourseName obtains the course name from that data member. Member function displayMessage—which now specifies no parameters—still displays a welcome message that includes the course name. However, as you'll see, the function now obtains the course name by calling another function in the same class—getCourseName.

```cpp
1   // Fig. 4.5: GradeBook.cpp
2   // Define class GradeBook that contains a courseName data member
3   // and member functions to set and get its value;
4   // Create and manipulate a GradeBook object with these functions.
5   #include <iostream>
6   using std::cout;
7   using std::cin;
8   using std::endl;
9
10  #include <string> // program uses C++ standard string class
11  using std::string;
12  using std::getline;
13
14  // GradeBook class definition
15  class GradeBook
16  {
17  public:
18     // function that sets the course name
19     void setCourseName( string name )
20     {
21        courseName = name; // store the course name in the object
22     } // end function setCourseName
23
24     // function that gets the course name
25     string getCourseName()
26     {
27        return courseName; // return the object's courseName
28     } // end function getCourseName
```

Fig. 4.5 | Defining and testing class GradeBook with a data member and *set* and *get* functions. (Part 1 of 2.)

```
29
30      // function that displays a welcome message
31      void displayMessage()
32      {
33          // this statement calls getCourseName to get the
34          // name of the course this GradeBook represents
35          cout << "Welcome to the grade book for\n" << getCourseName() << "!"
36              << endl;
37      } // end function displayMessage
38  private:
39      string courseName; // course name for this GradeBook
40  }; // end class GradeBook
41
42  // function main begins program execution
43  int main()
44  {
45      string nameOfCourse; // string of characters to store the course name
46      GradeBook myGradeBook; // create a GradeBook object named myGradeBook
47
48      // display initial value of courseName
49      cout << "Initial course name is: " << myGradeBook.getCourseName()
50          << endl;
51
52      // prompt for, input and set course name
53      cout << "\nPlease enter the course name:" << endl;
54      getline( cin, nameOfCourse ); // read a course name with blanks
55      myGradeBook.setCourseName( nameOfCourse ); // set the course name
56
57      cout << endl; // outputs a blank line
58      myGradeBook.displayMessage(); // display message with new course name
59      return 0; // indicate successful termination
60  } // end main
```

```
Initial course name is:

Please enter the course name:
CS101 Introduction to Visual C++ Programming

Welcome to the grade book for
CS101 Introduction to Visual C++ Programming!
```

Fig. 4.5 | Defining and testing class GradeBook with a data member and *set* and *get* functions. (Part 2 of 2.)

Good Programming Practice 4.3

Place a blank line between member-function definitions to enhance program readability.

A typical instructor teaches multiple courses, each with its own course name. Line 39 declares that courseName is a variable of type string. Because the variable is declared in the class definition (lines 15–40) but outside the bodies of the class's member-function definitions (lines 19–22, 25–28 and 31–37), the variable is a data member. Every instance (i.e., object) of class GradeBook contains one copy of each of the class's data members—if there are two `GradeBook` objects, each has its own copy of `courseName` (one per object), as you'll see in the example of Fig. 4.7. A benefit of making `courseName` a data member is that all the member functions of the class (in this case, class `GradeBook`) can manipulate any data members that appear in the class definition (in this case, `courseName`).

Access Specifiers `public` and `private`

Most data-member declarations appear after the access-specifier label ***private:*** (line 38). Like `public`, keyword `private` is an access specifier. Variables or functions declared after access specifier `private` (and before the next access specifier) are accessible only to member functions of the class for which they are declared. Thus, data member `courseName` can be used only in member functions `setCourseName`, `getCourseName` and `displayMessage` of (every object of) class `GradeBook`. Data member `courseName`, because it is `private`, cannot be accessed by functions outside the class (such as `main`) or by member functions of other classes in the program. Attempting to access data member `courseName` in one of these program locations with an expression such as `myGradeBook.courseName` would result in Visual Studio's issuing a compilation error

```
error C2248: 'GradeBook::courseName' : cannot access private member
declared in class 'GradeBook'
```

Software Engineering Observation 4.1

In general, data members should be declared `private` and member functions should be declared `public`. (We'll see that it is appropriate to declare certain member functions `private`, if they are to be accessed only by other member functions of the class.)

Common Programming Error 4.6

An attempt by a function that is not a member of a particular class (or a friend of that class, as we'll see in Chapter 11, Classes: A Deeper Look, Part 2) to access a `private` member of that class is a compilation error.

The default access for class members is `private`, so all members after the class header and before the first access specifier are `private`. The access specifiers `public` and `private` may be repeated, but this is unnecessary and can be confusing.

Good Programming Practice 4.4

Despite the fact that the `public` and `private` access specifiers may be repeated and intermixed, list all the `public` members of a class first in one group and then list all the `private` members in another group. This focuses the client's attention on the class's `public` interface, rather than on the class's implementation.

Good Programming Practice 4.5

If you list the `private` members first in a class definition, explicitly use the `private` access specifier despite the fact that `private` is assumed by default. This improves program clarity.

Declaring data members with access specifier `private` is known as ***data hiding***. When a program creates (instantiates) a `GradeBook` object, data member `courseName` is encapsulated (hidden) in the object and can be accessed only by member functions of the object's class. In class `GradeBook`, member functions `setCourseName` and `getCourseName` manipulate the data member `courseName` directly (and `displayMessage` could do so as well).

Software Engineering Observation 4.2

You'll learn in Chapter 11 that functions and classes declared by a class to be friends can access the `private` *members of the class.*

Error-Prevention Tip 4.1

Making the data members of a class `private` *and the member functions of the class* `public` *facilitates debugging, because problems with data manipulations are localized to either the class's member functions or the friends of the class.*

Member Functions setCourseName and getCourseName

Member function `setCourseName` (defined in lines 19–22) does not return any data when it completes its task, so its return type is `void`. The member function receives one parameter—`name`—which represents the course name that will be passed to it as an argument (as we'll see in line 55 of `main`). Line 21 assigns `name` to data member `courseName`. In this example, `setCourseName` does not attempt to validate the course name—i.e., the function does not check that the course name adheres to any particular format or follows any other rules regarding what a "valid" course name looks like. Suppose, for instance, that a university can print student transcripts containing course names of only 25 characters or fewer. In this case, we might want class `GradeBook` to ensure that its data member `courseName` never contains more than 25 characters. We discuss basic validation techniques in Section 4.10.

Member function `getCourseName` (defined in lines 25–28) returns a particular `GradeBook` object's `courseName`. The member function has an empty parameter list, so it does not require additional data to perform its task. The function specifies that it returns a `string`. When a function that specifies a return type other than `void` is called and completes its task, the function returns a result to its calling function. For example, when you go to an automated teller machine (ATM) and request your account balance, you expect the ATM to give you back a value that represents your balance. Similarly, when a statement calls member function `getCourseName` on a `GradeBook` object, the statement expects to receive the `GradeBook`'s course name (in this case, a `string`, as specified by the function's return type). If you have a function `square` that returns the square of its argument, the statement

```
result = square( 2 );
```

returns 4 from function `square` and assigns to variable `result` the value 4. If you have a function `maximum` that returns the largest of three integer arguments, the statement

```
biggest = maximum( 27, 114, 51 );
```

returns 114 from function `maximum` and assigns to variable `biggest` the value 114.

Common Programming Error 4.7

Forgetting to return a value from a function that is supposed to return a value is a compilation error.

Note that the statements in lines 21 and 27 each use variable `courseName` (line 39) even though it was not declared in any of the member functions. We can use `courseName` in the member functions of class `GradeBook` because `courseName` is a data member of the class. Also note that the order in which member functions are defined does not determine when they are called at execution time. So member function getCourseName could be defined before member function setCourseName.

Member Function displayMessage

Member function displayMessage (lines 31–37) does not return any data when it completes its task, so its return type is void. The function does not receive parameters, so its parameter list is empty. Lines 35–36 output a welcome message that includes the value of data member courseName. Line 35 calls member function getCourseName to obtain the value of courseName. Note that member function displayMessage could also access data member courseName directly, just as member functions setCourseName and getCourse-Name do. We explain shortly why we choose to call member function getCourseName to obtain the value of courseName.

Testing Class GradeBook

The main function (lines 43–60) creates one object of class GradeBook and uses each of its member functions. Line 46 creates a GradeBook object named myGradeBook. Lines 49–50 display the initial course name by calling the object's getCourseName member function. Note that the first line of the output does not show a course name, because the object's courseName data member (i.e., a string) is initially empty—by default, the initial value of a string is the so-called *empty string*, i.e., a string that does not contain any characters. Nothing appears on the screen when an empty string is displayed.

Line 53 prompts the user to enter a course name. Local string variable nameOfCourse (declared in line 45) is set to the course name entered by the user, which is obtained by the call to the getline function (line 54). Line 55 calls object myGradeBook's setCourseName member function and supplies nameOfCourse as the function's argument. When the function is called, the argument's value is copied to parameter name (line 19) of member function setCourseName (lines 19–22). Then the parameter's value is assigned to data member courseName (line 21). Line 57 skips a line in the output; then line 58 calls object myGrade-Book's displayMessage member function to display the welcome message containing the course name.

Software Engineering with set and get Functions

A class's private data members can be manipulated only by member functions of that class (and by "friends" of the class, as we'll see in Chapter 11). So a client of an object—that is, any class or function that calls the object's member functions from outside the object—calls the class's public member functions to request the class's services for particular objects of the class. This is why the statements in function main (Fig. 4.5, lines 43–60) call member functions setCourseName, getCourseName and displayMessage on a GradeBook object. Classes often provide public member functions to allow clients of the class to *set* (i.e., assign values to) or *get* (i.e., obtain the values of) private data members. The names of these member functions need not begin with set or get, but this naming convention is common. In this example, the member function that *sets* the courseName data member is called setCourseName, and the member function that *gets* the value of the courseName data member is called getCourseName. Note that *set* functions are also sometimes called *mutators* (because they mutate, or change, values), and *get* functions are also sometimes called *accessors* (because they access values).

Recall that declaring data members with access specifier `private` enforces data hiding. Providing `public` *set* and *get* functions allows clients of a class to access the hidden data, but only *indirectly*. The client knows that it is attempting to modify or obtain an object's data, but the client does not know how the object performs these operations. In some cases, a class may internally represent a piece of data one way, but expose that data to clients in a different way. For example, suppose a `Clock` class represents the time of day as a `private int` data member `time` that stores the number of seconds since midnight. However, when a client calls a `Clock` object's `getTime` member function, the object could return the time with hours, minutes and seconds in a `string` in the format `"HH:MM:SS"`. Similarly, suppose the `Clock` class provides a *set* function named `setTime` that takes a `string` parameter in the `"HH:MM:SS"` format. Using `string` capabilities presented in Chapter 19, the `setTime` function could convert this `string` to a number of seconds, which the function stores in its `private` data member. The *set* function could also check that the value it receives represents a valid time (e.g., `"12:30:45"` is valid but `"42:85:70"` is not). The *set* and *get* functions allow a client to interact with an object, but the object's `private` data remains safely encapsulated (i.e., hidden) in the object itself.

The *set* and *get* functions of a class also should be used by other member functions within the class to manipulate the class's `private` data, although these member functions *can* access the `private` data directly. In Fig. 4.5, member functions `setCourseName` and `getCourseName` are `public` member functions, so they are accessible to clients of the class, as well as to the class itself. Member function `displayMessage` calls member function `getCourseName` to obtain the value of data member `courseName` for display purposes, even though `displayMessage` can access `courseName` directly—accessing a data member via its *get* function creates a better, more robust class (i.e., a class that is easier to maintain and less likely to stop working). If we decide to change the data member `courseName` in some way, the `displayMessage` definition will not require modification—only the bodies of the *get* and *set* functions that directly manipulate the data member will need to change. For example, suppose we decide that we want to represent the course name as two separate data members—`courseNumber` (e.g., `"CS101"`) and `courseTitle` (e.g., `"Introduction to Visual C++ Programming"`). Member function `displayMessage` can still issue a single call to member function `getCourseName` to obtain the full course name to display as part of the welcome message. In this case, `getCourseName` would need to build and return a `string` containing the `courseNumber` followed by the `courseTitle`. Member function `displayMessage` would continue to display the complete course title "CS101 Introduction to Visual C++ Programming," because it is unaffected by the change to the class's data members. The benefits of calling a *set* function from another member function of a class will become clear when we discuss validation in Section 4.10.

Good Programming Practice 4.6

Always try to localize the effects of changes to a class's data members by accessing and manipulating the data members through their get *and* set *functions. Changes to the name of a data member or the data type used to store a data member then affect only the corresponding* get *and* set *functions, but not the callers of those functions.*

Software Engineering Observation 4.3

It is important to write programs that are understandable and easy to maintain. Change is the rule rather than the exception. You should anticipate that your code will be modified.

Software Engineering Observation 4.4

The class designer need not provide set *or* get *functions for each* private *data item; these capabilities should be provided only when appropriate. If a service is useful to the client code, that service should typically be provided in the class's* public *interface.*

GradeBook's UML Class Diagram with a Data Member and* set *and* get *Functions
Figure 4.6 contains an updated UML class diagram for the version of class GradeBook in Fig. 4.5. This diagram models GradeBook's data member courseName as an attribute in the middle compartment. The UML represents data members as attributes by listing the attribute name, followed by a colon and the attribute type. The UML type of attribute courseName is String, which corresponds to string in Visual C++. Data member courseName is private in Visual C++, so the class diagram lists a minus sign (-) in front of the corresponding attribute's name. The minus sign in the UML is equivalent to the private access specifier in Visual C++. Class GradeBook contains three public member functions, so the class diagram lists three operations in the third compartment. Recall that the plus (+) sign before each operation name indicates that the operation is public in Visual C++. Operation setCourseName has a String parameter called name. The UML indicates the return type of an operation by placing a colon and the return type after the parentheses following the operation name. Member function getCourseName of class GradeBook (Fig. 4.5) has a string return type in Visual C++, so the class diagram shows a String return type in the UML. Note that operations setCourseName and displayMessage do not return values (i.e., they return void), so the UML class diagram does not specify a return type after the parentheses of these operations. The UML does not use void as Visual C++ does when a function does not return a value.

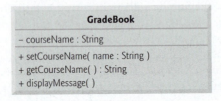

Fig. 4.6 | UML class diagram for class GradeBook with a private courseName attribute and public operations setCourseName, getCourseName and displayMessage.

4.7 Initializing Objects with Constructors

As mentioned in Section 4.6, when an object of class GradeBook (Fig. 4.5) is created, its data member courseName is initialized to the empty string by default. What if you want to provide a course name when you create a GradeBook object? Each class you declare can provide a *constructor* that can be used to initialize an object of the class when the object is created. A constructor is a special member function that must be defined with the same name as the class, so that the compiler can distinguish it from the class's other member functions. An important difference between constructors and other functions is that constructors cannot return values, so they cannot specify a return type (not even void). Normally, constructors are declared public. The term "constructor" is often abbreviated as "ctor" in the literature—we generally avoid abbreviations.

Visual C++ requires a constructor call for each object that is created, which helps ensure that each object is initialized before it is used in a program. The constructor call occurs implicitly when the object is created. If a class does not explicitly include a constructor, the compiler provides a *default constructor*—that is, a constructor with no parameters. For example, when line 46 of Fig. 4.5 creates a GradeBook object, the default constructor is called. The default constructor provided by the compiler creates a Grade-Book object without giving any initial values to the object's fundamental type data members. [*Note:* For data members that are objects of other classes, the default constructor implicitly calls each data member's default constructor to ensure that the data member is initialized properly. This is why the string data member courseName (in Fig. 4.5) was initialized to the empty string—the default constructor for class string sets the string's value to the empty string. You'll learn more about initializing data members that are objects of other classes in Section 11.3.]

In the example of Fig. 4.7, we specify a course name for a GradeBook object when the object is created (line 49). In this case, the argument "CS101 Introduction to Visual C++ Programming" is passed to the GradeBook object's constructor (lines 17–20) and used to initialize the courseName. Figure 4.7 defines a modified GradeBook class containing a constructor with a string parameter that receives the initial course name.

```cpp
1   // Fig. 4.7: GradeBook.cpp
2   // Instantiating multiple objects of the GradeBook class and using
3   // the GradeBook constructor to specify the course name
4   // when each GradeBook object is created.
5   #include <iostream>
6   using std::cout;
7   using std::endl;
8
9   #include <string> // program uses C++ standard string class
10  using std::string;
11
12  // GradeBook class definition
13  class GradeBook
14  {
15  public:
16     // constructor initializes courseName with string supplied as argument
17     GradeBook( string name )
18     {
19        setCourseName( name ); // call set function to initialize courseName
20     } // end GradeBook constructor
21
22     // function to set the course name
23     void setCourseName( string name )
24     {
25        courseName = name; // store the course name in the object
26     } // end function setCourseName
27
```

Fig. 4.7 | Instantiating multiple objects of the GradeBook class and using the GradeBook constructor to specify the course name when each GradeBook object is created. (Part 1 of 2.)

```
28        // function to get the course name
29        string getCourseName()
30        {
31           return courseName; // return object's courseName
32        } // end function getCourseName
33
34        // display a welcome message to the GradeBook user
35        void displayMessage()
36        {
37           // call getCourseName to get the courseName
38           cout << "Welcome to the grade book for\n" << getCourseName()
39              << "!" << endl;
40        } // end function displayMessage
41     private:
42        string courseName; // course name for this GradeBook
43     }; // end class GradeBook
44
45     // function main begins program execution
46     int main()
47     {
48        // create two GradeBook objects
49        GradeBook gradeBook1( "CS101 Introduction to Visual C++ Programming" );
50        GradeBook gradeBook2( "CS102 Data Structures in Visual C++" );
51
52        // display initial value of courseName for each GradeBook
53        cout << "gradeBook1 created for course: "
54           << gradeBook1.getCourseName()
55           << "\ngradeBook2 created for course: "
56           << gradeBook2.getCourseName()
57           << endl;
58        return 0; // indicate successful termination
59     } // end main
```

```
gradeBook1 created for course: CS101 Introduction to Visual C++ Programming
gradeBook2 created for course: CS102 Data Structures in Visual C++
```

Fig. 4.7 | Instantiating multiple objects of the GradeBook class and using the GradeBook constructor to specify the course name when each GradeBook object is created. (Part 2 of 2.)

Defining a Constructor

Lines 17–20 of Fig. 4.7 define a constructor for class GradeBook. Notice that the constructor has the same name as its class, GradeBook. A constructor specifies in its parameter list the data it requires to perform its task. When you create a new object, you place this data in the parentheses that follow the object name (as we did in lines 49–50). Line 17 indicates that class GradeBook's constructor has a string parameter called name. Note that line 17 does not specify a return type, because constructors cannot return values (or even void).

Line 19 in the constructor's body passes the constructor's parameter name to member function setCourseName, which assigns a value to data member courseName. The setCourseName member function (lines 23–26) simply assigns its parameter name to the data member courseName, so you might be wondering why we bother making the call to setCourseName in line 19—the constructor certainly could perform the assignment courseName = name. In Section 4.10, we modify setCourseName to perform validation (ensuring that, in this case, the courseName is 25 or fewer characters in length). At that point the benefits of calling setCourseName from the constructor will become clear. Note that both the constructor (line 17) and the setCourseName function (line 23) use a parameter called name. You can use the same parameter names in different functions because the parameters are local to each function; they do not interfere with one another.

Testing Class *GradeBook*

Lines 46–57 of Fig. 4.7 define the main function that tests class GradeBook and demonstrates initializing GradeBook objects using a constructor. Line 49 in function main creates and initializes a GradeBook object called gradeBook1. When this line executes, the GradeBook constructor (lines 17–20) is called (implicitly by Visual C++) with the argument "CS101 Introduction to Visual C++ Programming" to initialize gradeBook1's course name. Line 50 repeats this process for the GradeBook object called gradeBook2, this time passing the argument "CS102 Data Structures in Visual C++" to initialize gradeBook2's course name. Lines 54 and 56 each use the object's getCourseName member function to obtain the course names and show that they were indeed initialized when the objects were created. The output confirms that each GradeBook object maintains its own copy of data member courseName.

Two Ways to Provide a Default Constructor for a Class

Any constructor that takes no arguments is called a default constructor. A class gets a default constructor in one of two ways:

1. The compiler implicitly creates a default constructor in a class that does not define a constructor. Such a default constructor does not initialize the class's data members, but does call the default constructor for each data member that is an object of another class. [*Note:* An uninitialized variable typically contains a "garbage" value (e.g., an uninitialized int variable might contain -858993460, which is likely to be an incorrect value for that variable in most programs).]

2. You explicitly define a constructor that takes no arguments. Such a default constructor will perform the initialization specified by you and will call the default constructor for each data member that is an object of another class.

If you define a constructor with arguments, Visual C++ will not implicitly create a default constructor for that class. Note that for each version of class GradeBook in Fig. 4.1, Fig. 4.3 and Fig. 4.5 the compiler implicitly defined a default constructor.

Error-Prevention Tip 4.2

Unless no initialization of your class's data members is necessary (almost never), provide a constructor to ensure that your class's data members are initialized with meaningful values when each new object of your class is created.

Software Engineering Observation 4.5

Data members can be initialized in a constructor of the class, or their values may be set later after the object is created. However, it is a good software engineering practice to ensure that an object is fully initialized before the client code invokes the object's member functions. In general, you should not rely on the client code to ensure that an object gets initialized properly.

Adding the Constructor to Class GradeBook's UML Class Diagram

The UML class diagram of Fig. 4.8 models class GradeBook of Fig. 4.7, which has a constructor with a name parameter of type string (represented by type String in the UML). Like operations, the UML models constructors in the third compartment of a class in a class diagram. To distinguish a constructor from a class's operations, the UML places the word "constructor" between guillemets (« and ») before the constructor's name. It is customary to list the class's constructor before other operations in the third compartment.

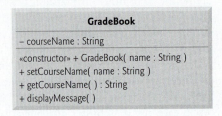

Fig. 4.8 | UML class diagram indicating that class GradeBook has a constructor with a name parameter of UML type String.

4.8 Placing a Class in a Separate File for Reusability

We have developed class GradeBook as far as we need to for now from a programming perspective, so let's consider some software engineering issues. One of the benefits of creating class definitions is that, when packaged properly, our classes can be reused by programmers—potentially worldwide. For example, we can reuse C++ Standard Library type string in any Visual C++ program by including the header file <string> in the program (and, as we'll see, by being able to link to the library's object code).

Unfortunately, programmers who wish to use our GradeBook class cannot simply include the file from Fig. 4.7 in another program. As you learned in Chapter 3, function main begins the execution of every program, and every program must have exactly one main function. If other programmers include the code from Fig. 4.7, they get extra baggage—our main function—and their programs will then have two main functions. When they attempt to compile their programs, the compiler will indicate an error. Attempting to compile a program with two main functions in Visual Studio 2008 produces the error

```
error C2084: function 'int main(void)' already has a body
```

when the compiler tries to compile the second main function it encounters. This error indicates that a program already has a main function. So, placing main in the same file with a class definition prevents that class from being reused by other programs. In this section, we demonstrate how to make class GradeBook reusable by separating it into another file from the main function.

Header Files

Each of the previous examples in the chapter consists of a single .cpp file, also known as a *source-code file*, that contains a GradeBook class definition and a main function. When building an object-oriented Visual C++ program, it is customary to define reusable source code (such as a class) in a file that by convention ends with the .h filename extension—

known as a *header file*. Programs use #include preprocessor directives to include header files and take advantage of reusable software components, such as type string provided in the C++ Standard Library and user-defined types such as class GradeBook.

In our next example, we separate the code from Fig. 4.7 into two files—GradeBook.h (Fig. 4.9) and GradeBookTest.cpp (Fig. 4.10). As you look at the header file in Fig. 4.9, notice that it contains only the GradeBook class definition (lines 11–41) and lines 3–8, which allow class GradeBook to use cout, endl and type string. The main function that uses class GradeBook is defined in the source-code file GradeBookTest.cpp (Fig. 4.10) in lines 10–21. To help you prepare for the larger programs you'll encounter later in this book and in industry, we often use a separate source-code file containing function main to test our classes (this is called a *driver program*). You'll soon learn how a source-code file with main can use the class definition found in a header file to create objects of a class.

Including a Header File That Contains a User-Defined Class

A header file such as GradeBook.h (Fig. 4.9) cannot be used to begin program execution, because it does not contain a main function. If you try to compile and link GradeBook.h by itself to create an executable application, Visual Studio produces the linker error message:

```
error LNK2019: unresolved external symbol _main referenced in
function _tmainCRTStartup
```

This error indicates that the linker could not locate the program's main function. To test class GradeBook (defined in Fig. 4.9), you must write a separate source-code file containing a main function (such as Fig. 4.10) that instantiates and uses objects of the class.

```cpp
 1   // Fig. 4.9: GradeBook.h
 2   // GradeBook class definition in a separate file from main.
 3   #include <iostream>
 4   using std::cout;
 5   using std::endl;
 6
 7   #include <string> // class GradeBook uses C++ standard string class
 8   using std::string;
 9
10   // GradeBook class definition
11   class GradeBook
12   {
13   public:
14      // constructor initializes courseName with string supplied as argument
15      GradeBook( string name )
16      {
17         setCourseName( name ); // call set function to initialize courseName
18      } // end GradeBook constructor
19
20      // function to set the course name
21      void setCourseName( string name )
22      {
23         courseName = name; // store the course name in the object
24      } // end function setCourseName
```

Fig. 4.9 | GradeBook class definition. (Part 1 of 2.)

```
25
26      // function to get the course name
27      string getCourseName()
28      {
29          return courseName; // return object's courseName
30      } // end function getCourseName
31
32      // display a welcome message to the GradeBook user
33      void displayMessage()
34      {
35          // call getCourseName to get the courseName
36          cout << "Welcome to the grade book for\n" << getCourseName()
37              << "!" << endl;
38      } // end function displayMessage
39   private:
40      string courseName; // course name for this GradeBook
41   }; // end class GradeBook
```

Fig. 4.9 | GradeBook class definition. (Part 2 of 2.)

```
1    // Fig. 4.10: GradeBookTest.cpp
2    // Including class GradeBook from file GradeBook.h for use in main.
3    #include <iostream>
4    using std::cout;
5    using std::endl;
6
7    #include "GradeBook.h" // include definition of class GradeBook
8
9    // function main begins program execution
10   int main()
11   {
12      // create two GradeBook objects
13      GradeBook gradeBook1( "CS101 Introduction to Visual C++ Programming" );
14      GradeBook gradeBook2( "CS102 Data Structures in Visual C++" );
15
16      // display initial value of courseName for each GradeBook
17      cout << "gradeBook1 created for course: " << gradeBook1.getCourseName()
18          << "\ngradeBook2 created for course: " << gradeBook2.getCourseName()
19          << endl;
20      return 0; // indicate successful termination
21   } // end main
```

```
gradeBook1 created for course: CS101 Introduction to Visual C++ Programming
gradeBook2 created for course: CS102 Data Structures in Visual C++
```

Fig. 4.10 | Including class GradeBook from file GradeBook.h for use in main.

Recall from Section 4.4 that, while the compiler knows what fundamental data types like int are, the compiler does not know what a GradeBook is because it is a user-defined type. In fact, the compiler does not even know the classes in the C++ Standard Library. To help it understand how to use a class, we must explicitly provide the compiler with the class's definition—that's why, for example, to use type string, a program must include the `<string>` header file. This enables the compiler to determine the amount of memory that it must reserve for each object of the class and ensure that a program calls the class's member functions correctly.

To create `GradeBook` objects `gradeBook1` and `gradeBook2` in lines 13–14 of Fig. 4.10, the compiler must know the size of a `GradeBook` object. While objects conceptually contain data members and member functions, Visual C++ objects contain only data. The compiler creates only one copy of the class's member functions and shares that copy among all the class's objects. Each object, of course, needs its own copy of the class's data members, because their contents can vary among objects (such as two different `Bank-Account` objects having two different `balance` data members). The member-function code, however, is not modifiable, so it can be shared among all objects of the class. Therefore, the size of an object depends on the amount of memory required to store the class's data members. By including `GradeBook.h` in line 7, we give the compiler access to the information it needs (Fig. 4.9, line 40) to determine the size of a `GradeBook` object and to determine whether objects of the class are used correctly (in lines 13–14 and 17–18 of Fig. 4.10).

Line 7 instructs the Visual C++ preprocessor to replace the directive with a copy of the contents of `GradeBook.h` (i.e., the `GradeBook` class definition) *before* the program is compiled. When the source-code file `GradeBookTest.cpp` is compiled, it now contains the `GradeBook` class definition (because of the `#include`), and the compiler is able to determine how to create `GradeBook` objects and see that their member functions are called correctly. Now that the class definition is in a header file (without a `main` function), we can include that header in *any* program that needs to reuse our `GradeBook` class.

How Header Files Are Located

Notice that the name of the `GradeBook.h` header file in line 7 of Fig. 4.10 is enclosed in quotes (" ") rather than angle brackets (< >). Normally, a program's source-code files and user-defined header files are placed in the same directory. When the preprocessor encounters a header file name in quotes (e.g., `"GradeBook.h"`), the preprocessor attempts to locate the header file in the same directory as the file in which the `#include` directive appears. If the preprocessor cannot find the header file in that directory, it searches for it in the same location(s) as the C++ Standard Library header files and other operating system header files. When the preprocessor encounters a header file name in angle brackets (e.g., `<iostream>`), it assumes that the header is part of the C++ Standard Library or an operating system library and does not look in the directory of the program that is being preprocessed.

Error-Prevention Tip 4.3

To ensure that the preprocessor can locate header files correctly, `#include` preprocessor directives should place the names of user-defined header files in quotes (e.g., `"GradeBook.h"`) and place the names of C++ Standard Library header files in angle brackets (e.g., `<iostream>`).

Additional Software Engineering Issues

Now that class `GradeBook` is defined in a header file, the class is reusable. Unfortunately, placing a class definition in a header file as in Fig. 4.9 still reveals the entire implementation of the class to the class's clients—`GradeBook.h` is simply a text file that anyone can open and read. Conventional software engineering wisdom says that to use an object of a class, the client code needs to know only what member functions to call, what arguments to provide to each member function and what return type to expect from each member function. The client code does not need to know how those functions are implemented.

If client code does know how a class is implemented, the client-code programmer might write client code based on the class's implementation details. Ideally, if that implementation changes, the class's clients should not have to change. Hiding the class's implementation details makes it easier to change the class's implementation while minimizing, and hopefully eliminating, changes to client code.

In Section 4.9, we show how to break up the GradeBook class into two files so that

1. the class is reusable

2. the clients of the class know what member functions the class provides, how to call them and what return types to expect

3. the clients do not know how the class's member functions are implemented.

4.9 Separating Interface from Implementation

In the preceding section, we showed how to promote software reusability by separating a class definition from the client code (e.g., function main) that uses the class. We now introduce another fundamental principle of good software engineering—*separating interface from implementation*.

Interface of a Class

Interfaces define and standardize the ways in which things such as people and systems interact with one another. For example, a radio's controls serve as an interface between the radio's users and its internal components. The controls allow users to perform a limited set of operations (such as changing the station, adjusting the volume, and choosing between AM and FM stations). Various radios may implement these operations differently—some provide push buttons, some provide dials and some support voice commands. The interface specifies *what* operations a radio permits users to perform but does not specify *how* the operations are implemented inside the radio.

Similarly, the *interface of a class* describes *what* services a class's clients can use and how to *request* those services, but not *how* the class carries out the services. A class's interface consists of the class's public member functions (also known as the class's **public** *services*). For example, class GradeBook's interface (Fig. 4.9) contains a constructor and member functions setCourseName, getCourseName and displayMessage. GradeBook's clients (e.g., main in Fig. 4.10) use these functions to request the class's services. As you'll soon see, you can specify a class's interface by writing a class declaration that lists only the member-function names, return types and parameter types.

Separating the Interface from the Implementation

In our prior examples, each class definition contained the complete definitions of the class's public member functions and the declarations of its private data members. However, it is better software engineering to define member functions outside the class definition, so that their implementation details can be hidden from the client code. This practice ensures that programmers do not write client code that depends on the class's implementation details. If they were to do so, the client code would be more likely to "break" if the class's implementation changed.

The program of Figs. 4.11–4.13 separates class GradeBook's interface from its implementation by splitting the class definition of Fig. 4.9 into two files—the header file GradeBook.h (Fig. 4.11) in which class GradeBook is defined, and the source-code file GradeBook.cpp (Fig. 4.12) in which GradeBook's member functions are defined. By convention, member-function definitions are placed in a source-code file of the same base name (e.g., GradeBook) as the class's header file but with a .cpp filename extension. The source-code file GradeBookTest.cpp (Fig. 4.13) defines function main (the client code). The code and output of Fig. 4.13 are identical to those of Fig. 4.10. Figure 4.14 shows how this three-file program is compiled from the perspectives of the GradeBook class programmer and the client-code programmer—we'll explain this figure in detail.

GradeBook.h: Defining a Class's Interface with Function Prototypes

Header file GradeBook.h (Fig. 4.11) contains another version of GradeBook's class definition (lines 9–18). This version is similar to the one in Fig. 4.9, but the function definitions in Fig. 4.9 are replaced here with *function prototypes* (lines 12–15) that describe the class's public interface without revealing the class's member-function implementations. A function prototype is a declaration of a function that tells the compiler the function's name, its return type and the types of its parameters. Note that the header file still specifies the class's private data member (line 17) as well. Again, the compiler must know the data members of the class to determine how much memory to reserve for each object of the class. Including the header file GradeBook.h in the client code (line 8 of Fig. 4.13) provides the compiler with the information it needs to ensure that the client code calls the member functions of class GradeBook correctly.

The function prototype in line 12 (Fig. 4.11) indicates that the constructor requires one string parameter. Recall that constructors do not have return types, so no return type appears in the function prototype. Member function setCourseName's function prototype (line 13) indicates that setCourseName requires a string parameter and does not return a

```
 1   // Fig. 4.11: GradeBook.h
 2   // GradeBook class definition. This file presents GradeBook's public
 3   // interface without revealing the implementations of GradeBook's member
 4   // functions, which are defined in GradeBook.cpp.
 5   #include <string> // class GradeBook uses C++ standard string class
 6   using std::string;
 7
 8   // GradeBook class definition
 9   class GradeBook
10   {
11   public:
12      GradeBook( string ); // constructor that initializes courseName
13      void setCourseName( string ); // function that sets the course name
14      string getCourseName(); // function that gets the course name
15      void displayMessage(); // function that displays a welcome message
16   private:
17      string courseName; // course name for this GradeBook
18   }; // end class GradeBook
```

Fig. 4.11 | GradeBook class definition containing function prototypes that specify the interface of the class.

value (i.e., its return type is void). Member function getCourseName's function prototype (line 14) indicates that the function does not require parameters and returns a string. Finally, member function displayMessage's function prototype (line 15) specifies that displayMessage does not require parameters and does not return a value. These function prototypes are the same as the corresponding function headers in Fig. 4.9, except that the parameter names (which are optional in prototypes) are not included and each function prototype must end with a semicolon.

Common Programming Error 4.8

Forgetting the semicolon at the end of a function prototype is a syntax error.

Good Programming Practice 4.7

Although parameter names in function prototypes are optional (they are ignored by the compiler), many programmers use these names for documentation purposes.

Error-Prevention Tip 4.4

Parameter names in a function prototype (which, again, are ignored by the compiler) can be misleading if wrong or confusing names are used. For this reason, many programmers create function prototypes by copying the first line of the corresponding function definitions (when the source code for the functions is available), then appending a semicolon to the end of each prototype.

GradeBook.cpp: Defining Member Functions in a Separate Source-Code File

Source-code file GradeBook.cpp (Fig. 4.12) defines class GradeBook's member functions, which were declared in lines 12–15 of Fig. 4.11. The member-function definitions appear in lines 11–34 and are nearly identical to the member-function definitions in lines 15–38 of Fig. 4.9.

```cpp
1   // Fig. 4.12: GradeBook.cpp
2   // GradeBook member-function definitions. This file contains
3   // implementations of the member functions prototyped in GradeBook.h.
4   #include <iostream>
5   using std::cout;
6   using std::endl;
7
8   #include "GradeBook.h" // include definition of class GradeBook
9
10  // constructor initializes courseName with string supplied as argument
11  GradeBook::GradeBook( string name )
12  {
13     setCourseName( name ); // call set function to initialize courseName
14  } // end GradeBook constructor
15
16  // function to set the course name
17  void GradeBook::setCourseName( string name )
18  {
19     courseName = name; // store the course name in the object
20  } // end function setCourseName
```

Fig. 4.12 | GradeBook member-function definitions represent the implementation of class GradeBook. (Part 1 of 2.)

```
21
22   // function to get the course name
23   string GradeBook::getCourseName()
24   {
25      return courseName; // return object's courseName
26   } // end function getCourseName
27
28   // display a welcome message to the GradeBook user
29   void GradeBook::displayMessage()
30   {
31      // call getCourseName to get the courseName
32      cout << "Welcome to the grade book for\n" << getCourseName()
33         << "!" << endl;
34   } // end function displayMessage
```

Fig. 4.12 | GradeBook member-function definitions represent the implementation of class GradeBook. (Part 2 of 2.)

Notice that each member-function name in the function headers (lines 11, 17, 23 and 29) is preceded by the class name and ::, which is known as the *binary scope resolution operator.* This "ties" each member function to the (now separate) GradeBook class definition (Fig. 4.11), which declares the class's member functions and data members. Without "GradeBook::" preceding each function name, these functions would not be recognized by the compiler as member functions of class GradeBook—the compiler would consider them "free" or "loose" functions (also called *global functions*), like main. Such functions cannot access GradeBook's private data or call the class's member functions without specifying an object. So, the compiler would not be able to compile these functions. For example, lines 19 and 25 that access variable courseName would cause compilation errors because courseName is not declared as a local variable in each function—the compiler would not know that courseName is already declared as a data member of class GradeBook.

 Common Programming Error 4.9

When defining a class's member functions outside that class, omitting the class name and binary scope resolution operator (::) preceding the function names causes compilation or linker errors.

To indicate that the member functions in GradeBook.cpp are part of class GradeBook, we must first include the GradeBook.h header file (line 8 of Fig. 4.12). This allows us to access the class name GradeBook in the GradeBook.cpp file. When compiling Grade-Book.cpp, the compiler uses the information in GradeBook.h to ensure that

1. the first line of each member function (lines 11, 17, 23 and 29) matches its prototype in the GradeBook.h file—for example, the compiler ensures that get-CourseName accepts no parameters and returns a string.

2. each member function knows about the class's data members and other member functions—for example, lines 19 and 25 can access variable courseName because it is declared in GradeBook.h as a data member of class GradeBook, and lines 13 and 32 can call functions setCourseName and getCourseName, respectively, because each is declared as a member function of the class in GradeBook.h (and because these calls conform with the corresponding prototypes).

Testing Class GradeBook

Figure 4.13 performs the same GradeBook object manipulations as Fig. 4.10. Separating GradeBook's interface from the implementation of its member functions does not affect the way that this client code uses the class. It affects only how the program is compiled and linked, which we discuss in detail shortly.

As in Fig. 4.10, line 8 of Fig. 4.13 includes the GradeBook.h header file so that the compiler can ensure that GradeBook objects are created and manipulated correctly in the client code. Before executing this program, the source-code files in Fig. 4.12 and Fig. 4.13 must both be compiled, then linked together—that is, the member-function calls in the client code need to be tied to the implementations of the class's member functions—a job performed by the linker.

```cpp
 1   // Fig. 4.13: GradeBookTest.cpp
 2   // GradeBook class demonstration after separating
 3   // its interface from its implementation.
 4   #include <iostream>
 5   using std::cout;
 6   using std::endl;
 7
 8   #include "GradeBook.h" // include definition of class GradeBook
 9
10   // function main begins program execution
11   int main()
12   {
13      // create two GradeBook objects
14      GradeBook gradeBook1( "CS101 Introduction to Visual C++ Programming" );
15      GradeBook gradeBook2( "CS102 Data Structures in Visual C++" );
16
17      // display initial value of courseName for each GradeBook
18      cout << "gradeBook1 created for course: " << gradeBook1.getCourseName()
19         << "\ngradeBook2 created for course: " << gradeBook2.getCourseName()
20         << endl;
21      return 0; // indicate successful termination
22   } // end main
```

```
gradeBook1 created for course: CS101 Introduction to Visual C++ Programming
gradeBook2 created for course: CS102 Data Structures in Visual C++
```

Fig. 4.13 | GradeBook class demonstration after separating its interface from its implementation.

The Compilation and Linking Process

The diagram in Fig. 4.14 shows the compilation and linking process that results in an executable GradeBook application that can be used by instructors. Often a class's interface and implementation will be created and compiled by one programmer and used by a separate programmer who implements the client code that uses the class. So, the diagram shows what is required by both the class-implementation programmer and the client-code programmer. The dashed lines in the diagram show the pieces required by the class-imple-

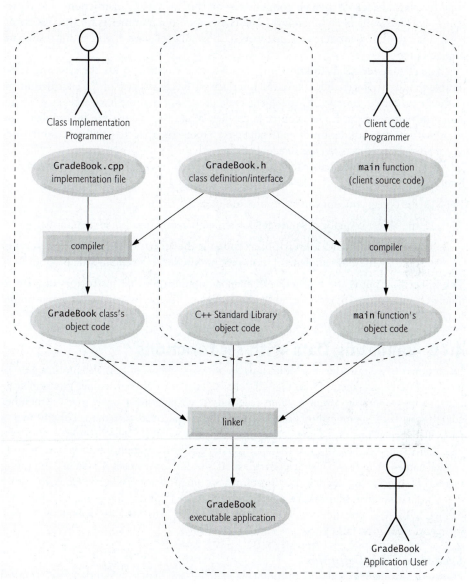

Fig. 4.14 | Compilation and linking process that produces an executable application.

mentation programmer, the client-code programmer and the GradeBook application user, respectively. [*Note:* Figure 4.14 is not a UML diagram.]

A class-implementation programmer responsible for creating a reusable GradeBook class creates the header file GradeBook.h and the source-code file GradeBook.cpp that #includes the header file, then compiles the source-code file to create GradeBook's object code. To hide class GradeBook's member-function implementation details, the class-implementation programmer would provide the client-code programmer with the header file GradeBook.h (which specifies the class's interface and data members) and the object code for class GradeBook (which contains the machine-language instructions that represent GradeBook's member functions). The client-code programmer is not given GradeBook.cpp, so the client remains unaware of how GradeBook's member functions are implemented.

The client code needs to know only GradeBook's interface to use the class and must be able to link its object code. Since the interface of the class is part of the class definition in the GradeBook.h header file, the client-code programmer must have access to this file and #include it in the client's source-code file. When the client code is compiled, the compiler uses the class definition in GradeBook.h to ensure that the main function creates and manipulates objects of class GradeBook correctly.

To create the executable GradeBook application to be used by instructors, the last step is to link

1. the object code for the main function (i.e., the client code)

2. the object code for class GradeBook's member-function implementations

3. the C++ Standard Library object code for the Visual C++ classes (e.g., string) used by the class-implementation programmer and the client-code programmer.

The linker's output is the executable GradeBook application that instructors can use to manage their students' grades. Visual Studio 2008 handles this for you and makes it simple to compile and link projects with one or many source files into an executable.

4.10 Validating Data with *set* Functions

In Section 4.6, we introduced *set* functions for allowing clients of a class to modify the value of a private data member. In Fig. 4.5, class GradeBook defines member function setCourseName to simply assign a value received in its parameter name to data member courseName. This member function does not ensure that the course name adheres to any particular format or follows any other rules regarding what a "valid" course name looks like. As we stated earlier, suppose that a university can print student transcripts containing course names of only 25 characters or less. If the university uses a system containing GradeBook objects to generate the transcripts, we might want class GradeBook to ensure that its data member courseName never contains more than 25 characters. The program of Figs. 4.15–4.17 enhances class GradeBook's member function setCourseName to perform this *validation* (also known as *validity checking*).

GradeBook Class Definition
Notice that GradeBook's class definition (Fig. 4.15)—and hence, its interface—is identical to that of Fig. 4.11. Since the interface remains unchanged, clients of this class need not be changed when the definition of member function setCourseName is modified. This enables clients to take advantage of the improved GradeBook class simply by linking the client code to the updated GradeBook's object code.

```
1   // Fig. 4.15: GradeBook.h
2   // GradeBook class definition presents the public interface of
3   // the class. Member-function definitions appear in GradeBook.cpp.
```

Fig. 4.15 | GradeBook class definition. (Part 1 of 2.)

```
4   #include <string> // program uses C++ standard string class
5   using std::string;
6
7   // GradeBook class definition
8   class GradeBook
9   {
10  public:
11     GradeBook( string ); // constructor that initializes a GradeBook object
12     void setCourseName( string ); // function that sets the course name
13     string getCourseName(); // function that gets the course name
14     void displayMessage(); // function that displays a welcome message
15  private:
16     string courseName; // course name for this GradeBook
17  }; // end class GradeBook
```

Fig. 4.15 | GradeBook class definition. (Part 2 of 2.)

Validating the Course Name with GradeBook Member Function setCourseName

The enhancement to class GradeBook is in the definition of setCourseName (Fig. 4.16, lines 18–31). The if statement in lines 20–21 determines whether parameter name contains a valid course name (i.e., a string of 25 or fewer characters). If the course name is valid, line 21 stores the course name in data member courseName. Note the expression name.length() (line 20). This is a member-function call just like myGradeBook.displayMessage(). The C++ Standard Library's string class defines a member function **length** that returns the number of characters in a string object. Parameter name is a string object, so the call name.length() returns the number of characters in name. If this value is less than or equal to 25, name is valid and line 21 executes.

The if statement in lines 23–30 handles the case in which setCourseName receives an invalid course name (i.e., a name that is more than 25 characters long). Even if parameter name is too long, we still want to leave the GradeBook object in a *consistent state*—that is, a state in which the object's data member courseName contains a valid value (i.e., a string of 25 characters or less). Thus, we truncate (i.e., shorten) the specified course name and assign the first 25 characters of name to the courseName data member (unfortunately, this could truncate the course name awkwardly). Standard class string provides member function **substr** (short for "substring") that returns a new string object created by copying part of an existing string object. The call in line 26 (i.e., name.substr(0, 25)) passes two integers (0 and 25) to name's member function substr. These arguments indicate the portion of the string name that substr should return. The first argument specifies the starting position in the original string from which characters are copied—the first character in every string is considered to be at position 0. The second argument specifies the number of characters to copy. Therefore, the call in line 26 returns a 25-character substring of name starting at position 0 (i.e., the first 25 characters in name). For example, if name holds the value "CS101 Introduction to Programming in Visual C++", substr returns "CS101 Introduction to Pro". After the call to substr, line 26 assigns the substring returned by substr to data member courseName. In this way, member function setCourseName ensures that courseName is always assigned a string containing 25 or fewer characters. If the member function has to truncate the course name to make it valid, lines 28–29 display a warning message.

```
1    // Fig. 4.16: GradeBook.cpp
2    // Implementations of the GradeBook member-function definitions.
3    // The setCourseName function performs validation.
4    #include <iostream>
5    using std::cout;
6    using std::endl;
7
8    #include "GradeBook.h" // include definition of class GradeBook
9
10   // constructor initializes courseName with string supplied as argument
11   GradeBook::GradeBook( string name )
12   {
13       setCourseName( name ); // validate and store courseName
14   } // end GradeBook constructor
15
16   // function that sets the course name;
17   // ensures that the course name has at most 25 characters
18   void GradeBook::setCourseName( string name )
19   {
20       if ( name.length() <= 25 ) // if name has 25 or fewer characters
21           courseName = name; // store the course name in the object
22
23       if ( name.length() > 25 ) // if name has more than 25 characters
24       {
25           // set courseName to first 25 characters of parameter name
26           courseName = name.substr( 0, 25 ); // start at 0, length of 25
27
28           cout << "Name \"" << name << "\" exceeds maximum length (25).\n"
29               << "Limiting courseName to first 25 characters.\n" << endl;
30       } // end if
31   } // end function setCourseName
32
33   // function to get the course name
34   string GradeBook::getCourseName()
35   {
36       return courseName; // return object's courseName
37   } // end function getCourseName
38
39   // display a welcome message to the GradeBook user
40   void GradeBook::displayMessage()
41   {
42       // call getCourseName to get the courseName
43       cout << "Welcome to the grade book for\n" << getCourseName()
44           << "!" << endl;
45   } // end function displayMessage
```

Fig. 4.16 | Member-function definitions for class GradeBook with a *set* function that validates the length of data member courseName.

Note that the if statement in lines 23–30 contains two body statements—one to set the courseName to the first 25 characters of parameter name and one to print an accompanying message to the user. We want both of these statements to execute when name is too long, so we place them in a pair of braces, { }. Recall from Chapter 3 that this creates a block. You'll learn more about placing multiple statements in the body of a control statement in Chapter 5.

Note that the statement in lines 28–29 could also appear without a stream insertion operator at the start of the second line of the statement, as in:

```
cout << "Name \"" << name << "\" exceeds maximum length (25).\n"
       "Limiting courseName to first 25 characters.\n" << endl;
```

The compiler combines adjacent string literals, even if they appear on separate lines of a program. Thus, in the statement above, the compiler would combine the string literals "\" exceeds maximum length (25).\n" and "Limiting courseName to first 25 characters.\n" into a single string literal that produces output identical to that of lines 28–29 in Fig. 4.16. This behavior allows you to print lengthy strings by breaking them across lines in your program without including additional stream insertion operations.

Testing Class GradeBook

Figure 4.17 demonstrates the modified version of class GradeBook (Figs. 4.15–4.16) featuring validation. Line 14 creates a GradeBook object named gradeBook1. Recall that the GradeBook constructor calls setCourseName to initialize data member courseName. In previous versions of the class, the benefit of calling setCourseName in the constructor was not evident. Now, however, the constructor takes advantage of the validation provided by set-CourseName. The constructor simply calls setCourseName, rather than duplicating its validation code. When line 14 of Fig. 4.17 passes the initial course name "CS101 Introduction to Programming in Visual C++" to the GradeBook constructor, the constructor passes this value to setCourseName, where the actual initialization occurs. Because this course name contains more than 25 characters, the body of the second if statement executes, causing courseName to be initialized to the truncated 25-character course name "CS101 Introduction to Vis" (the truncated part is highlighted in bold black text in line 14). Notice that the output in Fig. 4.17 contains the warning message output by lines 28–29 of Fig. 4.16 in member function setCourseName. Line 15 creates another GradeBook object called gradeBook2—the valid course name passed to the constructor is exactly 25 characters.

```
1   // Fig. 4.17: GradeBookTest.cpp
2   // Create and manipulate a GradeBook object; illustrate validation.
3   #include <iostream>
4   using std::cout;
5   using std::endl;
6
7   #include "GradeBook.h" // include definition of class GradeBook
8
9   // function main begins program execution
10  int main()
11  {
12     // create two GradeBook objects;
13     // initial course name of gradeBook1 is too long
14     GradeBook gradeBook1( "CS101 Introduction to Visual C++ Programming" );
15     GradeBook gradeBook2( "CS102 Data Structures" );
```

Fig. 4.17 | Creating and manipulating a GradeBook object in which the course name is limited to 25 characters in length. (Part 1 of 2.)

```
16
17     // display each GradeBook's courseName
18     cout << "gradeBook1's initial course name is: "
19        << gradeBook1.getCourseName()
20        << "\ngradeBook2's initial course name is: "
21        << gradeBook2.getCourseName() << endl;
22
23     // modify myGradeBook's courseName (with a valid-length string)
24     gradeBook1.setCourseName( "CS101 Visual C++" );
25
26     // display each GradeBook's courseName
27     cout << "\ngradeBook1's course name is: "
28        << gradeBook1.getCourseName()
29        << "\ngradeBook2's course name is: "
30        << gradeBook2.getCourseName() << endl;
31     return 0; // indicate successful termination
32  } // end main
```

```
Name "CS101 Introduction to Visual C++ Programming" exceeds maximum length
(25).

Limiting courseName to first 25 characters.

gradeBook1's initial course name is: CS101 Introduction to Vis
gradeBook2's initial course name is: CS102 Data Structures

gradeBook1's course name is: CS101 Visual C++
gradeBook2's course name is: CS102 Data Structures
```

Fig. 4.17 | Creating and manipulating a GradeBook object in which the course name is limited to 25 characters. (Part 2 of 2.)

Lines 18–21 of Fig. 4.17 display the truncated course name for gradeBook1 (we highlight this in bold black text in the program output) and the course name for gradeBook2. Line 24 calls gradeBook1's setCourseName member function directly, to change the course name in the GradeBook object to a shorter name that does not need to be truncated. Then, lines 27– 30 output the course names for the GradeBook objects again.

Additional Notes on Set Functions
A public *set* function such as setCourseName should carefully scrutinize any attempt to modify the value of a data member (e.g., courseName) to ensure that the new value is appropriate for that data item. For example, an attempt to *set* the day of the month to 37 should be rejected, an attempt to *set* a person's weight to zero or a negative value should be rejected, an attempt to *set* a grade on an exam to 185 (when the proper range is zero to 100) should be rejected, and so on

Software Engineering Observation 4.6
Making data members private and controlling access, especially write access, to those data members through public member functions helps ensure data integrity.

Error-Prevention Tip 4.5

The benefits of data integrity are not automatic simply because data members are made private—you must provide appropriate validity checking and report the errors.

Software Engineering Observation 4.7

Member functions that set the values of private data should verify that the intended new values are proper; if they are not, the set functions should place the private data members into an appropriate state.

A class's *set* functions can return values to the class's clients indicating that attempts were made to assign invalid data to objects of the class. A client of the class can test the return value of a *set* function to determine whether the client's attempt to modify the object was successful and to take appropriate action. In Chapter 16, we demonstrate how clients of a class can be notified via the exception-handling mechanism when an attempt is made to modify an object with an inappropriate value. To keep the program of Figs. 4.15–4.17 simple at this early point in the book, setCourseName in Fig. 4.16 just prints an appropriate message on the screen.

4.11 Defining a Managed Class with Member Functions in C++/CLI

Now we demonstrate how to use the concepts from above and apply them in managed code using *C++/CLI*. Unlike Managed Extensions for C++, Microsoft's previous attempt to combine C++ and .NET, C++/CLI syntax is clean, simple, and much closer to native C++ syntax. For the following examples you will need to create a **CLR Console Application** as described in Section 2.2.

To define a *managed class* in C++/CLI you must use one of C++/CLI's *spaced keywords*. Native C++ does not allow white space in keywords, so spaced keywords were created for C++/CLI so that the language designers could introduce new keywords without breaking existing C++ applications.

Declare a managed class in C++/CLI with **ref class** followed by the class name. By declaring a class using ref class instead of class you have defined a managed C++/CLI class. Now when you create instances of this class they will be *managed objects* instead of native objects. We refer to all objects instantiated from ref classes to be managed objects. When you define a class with ref class, the compiler tells the Common Language Runtime (CLR) that it is a managed, reference class whose instances should be created in the managed memory. As the name implies, managed memory is managed entirely for you by the CLR. Unmanaged objects in native C++ may require that you manually allocate and deallocate the memory they use (explained in Chapter 11). This is a common source of programming errors. By declaring a class to be a managed type using the ref class declaration you don't have to worry about memory management nearly as much. This automatic memory management is an attractive feature of C++/CLI and other .NET languages. We discuss memory management in more detail in later chapters.

We begin by rewriting the example in Fig. 4.3 using managed code with C++/CLI. Some new concepts are only explained briefly now but clarified in later chapters. Figure 4.18 is a good first look at managed code with C++/CLI. Note that this example doesn't separate the interface from the implementation as you learned how to do earlier.

The aim is simply to provide a more direct comparison to the earlier example in native C++. The final example of the chapter using C++/CLI properly separates the interface from the implementation.

```
1   // Fig. 4.18: ManagedGradeBook.cpp
2   // Managed class GradeBook with a member function that takes a parameter.
3   // Create a GradeBook object and call its displayMessage function
4
5   // include the default precompiled header required by Visual Studio
6   #include "stdafx.h"
7
8   // this class will use classes from the .NET System namespace
9   using namespace System;
10
11  // GradeBook class definition
12  ref class GradeBook
13  {
14  public:
15     // function that displays a welcome message to the GradeBook user
16     void displayMessage( String ^courseName )
17     {
18        Console::WriteLine( "Welcome to the grade book for\n{0}!",
19           courseName );
20     } // end function displayMessage
21  }; // end managed class GradeBook
22
23  // function main begins program execution
24  int main( array< System::String ^ > ^args )
25  {
26     String ^nameOfCourse; // string of characters to store the course name
27     GradeBook myGradeBook; // create a GradeBook object named myGradeBook
28
29     // prompt for and input course name
30     Console::WriteLine( "Please enter the course name:" );
31     // read a line of user input and store it in string nameOfCourse
32     nameOfCourse = Console::ReadLine();
33     Console::WriteLine(); // output a blank line
34
35     // call myGradeBook's displayMessage function
36     // and pass nameOfCourse as an argument
37     myGradeBook.displayMessage( nameOfCourse );
38     return 0; // indicate successful termination
39  } // end main
```

```
Please enter the course name:
CS101 Introduction to Visual C++ Programming

Welcome to the grade book for
CS101 Introduction to Visual C++ Programming!
```

Fig. 4.18 | Define a managed class GradeBook with a member function that takes a parameter, create a managed GradeBook object and call its displayMessage function.

The first difference you'll notice from Fig. 4.3 is line 6. The file `stdafx.h` is a special header file that is automatically created in Visual C++ applications. In large projects, you can place your common `#include` directives in that file, rather than in each separate source-code file. This enables Visual C++ to speed up the compilation process. Also, we removed the `#include` statements of lines 5–11 because in managed code with C++/CLI we don't use the C++ `string` class from `<string>`, nor do we use the contents of `<iostream>`. Line 9

```
using namespace System;
```

is a *using* directive that helps the compiler locate .NET classes used in this application. This lets us use .NET classes with similar functionality to `<string>` and `<iostream>`. A great strength of the .NET Framework is its rich set of predefined classes that you can reuse rather than "reinventing the wheel." Like the C++ Standard Library, .NET classes are organized in "namespaces". Collectively, .NET's namespaces are referred to as the *Framework Class Library (FCL)*. Each `using` directive identifies classes that a C++/CLI application should be able to use. The `using` directive in line 9 indicates that this example uses classes from the `System` namespace, which contains the `Console` class (discussed shortly) and many other useful classes. Namespaces are explained further in Chapter 26.

Next we define our new managed class at line 12 using the `ref class` spaced keyword. This tells the Visual C++ compiler that `GradeBook` is a managed class and any instances of it will be created in managed memory. At line 16 we define the `displayMessage` member function of class `GradeBook` just as we did in native C++, but the parameter is slightly different. Rather than use the native `string` class from `<string>` we use the .NET `System::String` class with managed code. Note that we only have to write `String` and not the fully qualified `System::String` because of the `using` directive in line 9. This tells the compiler to automatically look in the `System` namespace for types that are not defined directly in the program. Variables of class `System::String` must be declared using the ^ (pronounced "hat") notation, which indicates that the parameter name `coursName` is a managed-code *handle*. Using handles is an advanced topic that is explained in detail in Chapter 9. For now just remember that the ^ is always necessary when using instances of the .NET `System::String` class. Line 18 calls the *WriteLine* function of the .NET Console class to print output to the console. We use the `Console` class for console input and output with managed code instead of `cout` and `cin`. The format item `{0}` is a placeholder for the first argument after the format string. Other than the `{0}` format item, the remaining characters in the format string are all fixed text. Function `WriteLine` displays `"Welcome to the grade book for"`, followed by the value of `courseName` (printed in the position of the `{0}` format item) and a newline.

Line 23 declares function `main`. Don't worry about the complicated argument; it's automatically created by Visual Studio when you make a new Visual C++ project. For now just leave it alone in your C++/CLI programs. To test our new managed class `GradeBook` we create a reference to a .NET `System::String` object (instead of a C++ Standard Library class `string` object) to hold the course name entered by the user (line 25). We also create an object of class `GradeBook` called `myGradeBook` (lines 26). Notice the syntax for creating the `GradeBook` object is the same as native C++. Line 32

```
nameOfCourse = Console::ReadLine();
```

uses `Console`'s *ReadLine* function to accomplish what we did in native C++ with `getline`. This function waits for the user to type a string of characters at the keyboard and press the

Enter key to submit the string to the application. Once submitted, the value is stored in the nameOfCourse variable. Note that ReadLine captures the entire line of input, whether it be a single word or multiple words separated by white space. Finally, in line 36 we call myGradeBook's displayMessage member function and pass it the courseName string as a parameter exactly the same way as in native C++.

Note that, as in native C++, if you do not define a constructor for a managed class the compiler generates a default one for you. And, as in native C++, if you do define a constructor for a managed class, then the compiler won't generate a default constructor. Unlike a default constructor in native code, a managed object will have its default constructor automatically initialize all data members to a default value. For instance, any integer data member will be initialized to 0, rather than a "garbage value." This is actually true for any variable in managed code, not just data members of a class. This will be explained in more detail in later chapters.

4.12 Instance Variables and Properties in C++/CLI

In Section 4.6 you learned about local variables, data members of classes, and how to use *set* and *get* functions to access those private data members. Some classes may have many private data members, requiring you to write separate *set* and *get* functions for each one. This can be tedious and requires writing many similar functions for each class you define. C++/CLI provides convenient **syntactic sugar** for accessing or modifying data members of a class in the form of the **property** keyword. Syntactic sugar refers to language features which do not provide additional expressiveness but allow for simpler, easier ways of coding an existing concept. In this case, properties are a shorter, cleaner way to accomplish what *set* and *get* functions do. We'll now look at a C++/CLI version of the example in Figs. 4.11–4.13, using properties instead of *set* and *get* functions. Pay attention to the **property declaration** in lines 16–26 of Fig. 4.19. Also notice that the interface has been separated from the implementation; this is a good programming practice whether in native or managed C++. However, unlike *set* and *get* functions, we place the property definitions inside the header file. While they can be placed in the .cpp file, it is often syntactically easier to write them in the header.

```
1   // Fig. 4.19: ManagedGradeBook.h
2   // Managed GradeBook class definition. This file presents GradeBook's
3   // public interface without revealing the implementations of GradeBook's
4   // member functions, which are defined in GradeBook.cpp.
5
6   // this class will use classes from the .NET System namespace
7   using namespace System;
8
9   // managed GradeBook class definition
10  ref class GradeBook
11  {
12  public:
13     GradeBook( String ^ ); // constructor that initializes courseName
14
```

Fig. 4.19 | Managed GradeBook class definition containing function prototypes that specify the interface of the class. (Part 1 of 2.)

```
15        // property to get and set the private data member courseName
16        property String^ CourseName
17        {
18           String^ get()
19           {
20              return courseName;
21           } // end get
22           void set( String ^value )
23           {
24              courseName = value;
25           } // end set
26        } // end property CourseName
27        void displayMessage(); // function that displays a welcome message
28     private:
29        String ^courseName; // course name for this GradeBook
30  }; // end class GradeBook
```

Fig. 4.19 | Managed `GradeBook` class definition containing function prototypes that specify the interface of the class. (Part 2 of 2.)

The property declaration begins with the keyword `property` followed by the type the property accesses (`String^`) and the property's name (`CourseName`). A property name is normally the name of the data member it represents but with the first character capitalized. Notice that we place the ^ symbol next to the return type without a space. This is simply a convention, but you can place a space after the type name before the ^ symbol and the program functions no differently. Properties contain accessors that handle the details of returning and modifying data. A property declaration can contain a `get` accessor, a `set` accessor or both. The `get` accessor (lines 18–21) enables a client to read the value of private instance variable `courseName`; the `set` accessor (lines 22–25) enables a client to modify `courseName`. Formally we say that data member `courseName` has been defined as the *backing store* for the `CourseName` property. Note that, like a normal function, each accessor must specify its own return type and parameter list in the declaration. These are functionally equivalent to the `getCourseName` and `setCourseName` functions you wrote in native C++.

After defining a property, you can use it syntactically like a data member in your code. For example, you can assign a value to a property using the = (assignment) operator (line 14 in Fig. 4.20). This executes the code in the property's `set` accessor to set the value of the corresponding instance variable. Similarly, accessing the property to use its value (for example, to display it on the screen) executes the code in the property's `get` accessor to obtain the corresponding instance variable's value. You can see examples of this in lines 21–22 in Figure 4.20 and lines 16–19 in Figure 4.21.

```
1   // Fig. 4.20: ManagedGradeBook.cpp
2   // GradeBook member-function definitions. This file contains
3   // implementations of the member functions prototyped in GradeBook.h.
4
```

Fig. 4.20 | Managed `GradeBook` member-function definitions represent the implementation of class `GradeBook`. (Part 1 of 2.)

```
 5    // include the default precompiled header required by Visual Studio
 6    #include "stdafx.h"
 7    #include "ManagedGradeBook.h" // include definition of class GradeBook
 8
 9    using namespace System;
10
11    // constructor initializes courseName with string supplied as argument
12    GradeBook::GradeBook( String ^name )
13    {
14       CourseName = name;
15    } // end managed GradeBook constructor
16
17    // display a welcome message to the GradeBook user
18    void GradeBook::displayMessage()
19    {
20       // use CourseName property to get the courseName
21       Console::WriteLine( "Welcome to the grade book for\n{0}!",
22          CourseName );
23    } // end function displayMessage
```

Fig. 4.20 | Managed GradeBook member-function definitions represent the implementation of class GradeBook. (Part 2 of 2.)

```
 1    // Fig. 4.21: ManagedGradeBookTest.cpp
 2    // Managed GradeBook class demonstration after separating
 3    // its interface from its implementation.
 4
 5    #include "stdafx.h"
 6    #include "ManagedGradeBook.h" // include definition of class GradeBook
 7
 8    // function main begins program execution
 9    int main( array< System::String ^ > ^args )
10    {
11       // create two managed GradeBook objects
12       GradeBook gradeBook1( "CS101 Introduction to Visual C++ Programming" );
13       GradeBook gradeBook2( "CS102 Data Structures in Visual C++" );
14
15       // print initial value of courseName for each GradeBook via properties
16       Console::WriteLine(
17          "gradeBook1 created for course: {0}", gradeBook1.CourseName);
18       Console::WriteLine(
19          "gradeBook2 created for course: {0}", gradeBook2.CourseName);
20
21       return 0; // indicate successful termination
22    } // end main
```

Fig. 4.21 | Managed GradeBook class demonstration after separating its interface from its implementation.

Sometimes we might choose to define only the get accessor which makes the private data member *read-only*. Now a client can read the value but never change it. Conversely, if you define only the set accessor, then the client is not able to read the data but can set it to a new value. Another way to control data hiding is by changing the access specifier for one or both of the accessors. You could write a private set accessor by doing the following:

```
private: void set( String ^value )
{
    courseName = value;
}
```

You can preface the set or get accessor declarations with a different access specifier just as you would with any function. Note that, just like the setCourseName function in lines 20–30 of Figure 4.16, you can put validation code inside the set or get accessors of a property; they do not need to be as simple as the one in Fig. 4.19. Note that since we are not using the string class from the C++ Standard Library, we would not use substr for validation; we would use a .NET class that provides similar functionality for Sys-tem::String objects (see Chapter 19, Class **string** and String Stream Processing).

If you are writing a property as we did in Fig. 4.19 with no validation, then C++/CLI provides further syntactic sugar in the form of *trivial properties*. Instead of lines 16–26 and 29 of Figure 4.19 we could have simply written the following statement:

```
property String^ CourseName;
```

The compiler generates almost exactly the same *get* and *set* code that we wrote in lines 16–26. The difference lies in what data member the property uses as a backing store. With a trivial property we cannot explicitly declare the backing-store data member as courseName. Instead, the compiler generates a backing store that contains the same name as the property. So, using the trivial property definition, the managed GradeBook class has a private CourseName data member (not to be confused with the previously defined data member courseName) to serve as the property's backing store. This is why we no longer need line 29 if we use a trivial property. A trivial property declaration ends in a semicolon unlike when you write explicit set and get accessors. If you need a property which has both set and get accessors and doesn't require validation, then you can save yourself time by using trivial properties. Then, if you decide to add validation or other code to the property later, the code that uses the property does not need to change. Properties provide simple, clean syntax for enforcing data hiding without having to use explicit set and get functions. We call an explicitly written property declaration like that in Figure 4.19 a nontrivial property.

Error-Prevention Tip 4.6

When you write a property declaration, the Visual C++ compiler generates hidden set *and* get *functions that get called when you use the property. For an instance variable x these functions are named* set_X *and* get_X. *For example, in Fig. 4.19 the compiler would generate functions* set_CourseName *and* get_CourseName. *You cannot call these functions yourself, and defining functions with those names (even if the return type or parameter differs) results in a compilation error, because the function name is reserved by the compiler.*

4.13 (Optional) Software Engineering Case Study: Identifying the Classes in the ATM Requirements Specification

Now we begin designing the ATM system that we introduced in Chapter 3. In this section, we identify the classes that are needed to build the ATM system by analyzing the nouns and noun phrases that appear in the requirements specification. We introduce UML class diagrams to model the relationships between these classes. This is an important first step in defining the structure of our system.

Identifying the Classes in a System

We begin our OOD process by identifying the classes required to build the ATM system. We'll eventually describe these classes using UML class diagrams and implement these classes in Visual C++. First, we review the requirements specification of Section 3.8 and find key nouns and noun phrases to help us identify classes that comprise the ATM system. We may decide that some of these nouns and noun phrases are attributes of other classes in the system. We may also conclude that some of the nouns do not correspond to parts of the system and thus should not be modeled at all. Additional classes may become apparent to us as we proceed through the design process.

Figure 4.22 lists the nouns and noun phrases in the requirements specification. We list them from left to right in the order in which they appear in the requirements specification. We list only the singular form of each noun or noun phrase.

We create classes only for the nouns and noun phrases that have significance in the ATM system. We do not need to model "bank" as a class, because the bank is not a part of the ATM system—the bank simply wants us to build the ATM. "Customer" and "user" also represent entities outside of the system—they are important because they interact with our ATM system, but we do not need to model them as classes in the ATM software. Recall that we modeled an ATM user (i.e., a bank customer) as the actor in the use case diagram of Fig. 3.18.

We do not model "$20 bill" or "deposit envelope" as classes. These are physical objects in the real world, but they are not part of what is being automated. We can adequately represent the presence of bills in the system using an attribute of the class that models the cash dispenser. (We assign attributes to classes in Section 5.13.) For example, the cash dispenser maintains a count of the number of bills it contains. The requirements specification doesn't say anything about what the system should do with deposit envelopes after it receives them. We can assume that acknowledging the receipt of an envelope—an operation performed by the class that models the deposit slot—is sufficient to represent

Nouns and noun phrases in the requirements specification		
bank	money / fund	account number
ATM	screen	PIN
user	keypad	bank database
customer	cash dispenser	balance inquiry
transaction	$20 bill / cash	withdrawal
account	deposit slot	deposit
balance	deposit envelope	

Fig. 4.22 | Nouns and noun phrases in the requirements specification.

the presence of an envelope in the system. (We assign operations to classes in Section 7.23.)

In our simplified ATM system, representing various amounts of "money," including an account's "balance," as attributes of other classes seems most appropriate. Likewise, the nouns "account number" and "PIN" represent significant information in the ATM system. They are important attributes of a bank account. They do not, however, exhibit behaviors. Thus, we can most appropriately model them as attributes of an account class.

Though the requirements specification frequently describes a "transaction" in a general sense, we do not model the broad notion of a financial transaction at this time. Instead, we model the three types of transactions (i.e., "balance inquiry," "withdrawal" and "deposit") as individual classes. These classes possess specific attributes needed for executing the transactions they represent. For example, a withdrawal needs to know the amount of money the user wants to withdraw. A balance inquiry, however, does not require any additional data. Furthermore, the three transaction classes exhibit unique behaviors. A withdrawal includes dispensing cash to the user, whereas a deposit involves receiving deposit envelopes from the user. [*Note:* In Section 14.11, we "factor out" common features of all transactions into a general "transaction" class using the object-oriented concepts of abstract classes and inheritance.]

We determine the classes for our system based on the remaining nouns and noun phrases from Fig. 4.22. Each of these refers to one or more of the following:

- ATM
- screen
- keypad
- cash dispenser
- deposit slot
- account
- bank database
- balance inquiry
- withdrawal
- deposit

The elements of this list are likely to be classes we'll need to implement our system.

We can now model the classes in our system based on the list we have created. We capitalize class names in the design process—a UML convention—as we'll do when we write the actual Visual C++ code that implements our design. If the name of a class contains more than one word, we run the words together and capitalize the first letter of each word (e.g., `MultipleWordName`). Using this convention, we create classes `ATM`, `Screen`, `Keypad`, `CashDispenser`, `DepositSlot`, `Account`, `BankDatabase`, `BalanceInquiry`, `Withdrawal` and `Deposit`. We construct our system using all of these classes as building blocks. Before we begin building the system, however, we must gain a better understanding of how the classes relate to one another.

Modeling Classes

The UML enables us to model, via *class diagrams*, the classes in the ATM system and their interrelationships. Figure 4.23 represents class `ATM`. In the UML, each class is modeled as

Fig. 4.23 | Representing a class in the UML using a class diagram.

a rectangle with three compartments. The top compartment contains the name of the class, centered horizontally and in boldface. The middle compartment contains the class's attributes. (We discuss attributes in Section 5.13 and Section 6.11.) The bottom compartment contains the class's operations (discussed in Section 7.23). In Fig. 4.23 the middle and bottom compartments are empty, because we have not yet determined this class's attributes and operations.

Class diagrams also show the relationships among the classes of the system. Figure 4.24 shows how our classes ATM and Withdrawal relate to one another. For the moment, we choose to model only this subset of classes for simplicity; we present a more complete class diagram later in this section. Notice that the rectangles representing classes in this diagram are not subdivided into compartments. The UML allows the suppression of class attributes and operations in this manner, when appropriate, to create more readable diagrams. Such a diagram is said to be an *elided diagram*—one in which some information, such as the contents of the second and third compartments, is not modeled. We'll place information in these compartments in Section 5.13 and Section 7.23.

In Fig. 4.24, the solid line that connects the two classes represents an *association*—a relationship between classes. The numbers near each end of the line are *multiplicity* values, which indicate how many objects of each class participate in the association. In this case, following the line from one end to the other reveals that, at any given moment, one ATM object participates in an association with either zero or one Withdrawal objects—zero if the current user is not currently performing a transaction or has requested a different type of transaction, and one if the user has requested a withdrawal. The UML can model many types of multiplicity. Figure 4.25 lists and explains the multiplicity types.

An association can be named. For example, the word Executes above the line connecting classes ATM and Withdrawal in Fig. 4.24 indicates the name of that association. This part of the diagram reads "one object of class ATM executes zero or one objects of class Withdrawal." Note that association names are directional, as indicated by the filled arrowhead—so it would be improper, for example, to read the preceding association from right to left as "zero or one objects of class Withdrawal execute one object of class ATM."

The word currentTransaction at the Withdrawal end of the association line in Fig. 4.24 is a *role name*, which identifies the role the Withdrawal object plays in its relationship with the ATM. A role name adds meaning to an association between classes by identifying the role a class plays in the context of an association. A class can play several roles

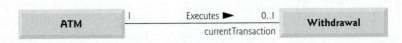

Fig. 4.24 | Class diagram showing an association among classes.

Symbol	Meaning
0	None
1	One
m	An integer value
0..1	Zero or one
m, n	m or n
$m..n$	At least m, but not more than n
*	Any nonnegative integer (zero or more)
0..*	Zero or more (identical to *)
1..*	One or more

Fig. 4.25 | Multiplicity types.

in the same system. For example, in a school personnel system, a person may play the role of "professor" when relating to students. The same person may take on the role of "colleague" when participating in a relationship with another professor, and "coach" when coaching student athletes. In Fig. 4.24, the role name currentTransaction indicates that the Withdrawal object participating in the Executes association with an object of class ATM represents the transaction currently being processed by the ATM. In other contexts, a Withdrawal object may take on other roles (e.g., the previous transaction). Notice that we do not specify a role name for the ATM end of the Executes association. Role names in class diagrams are often omitted when the meaning of an association is clear without them.

In addition to indicating simple relationships, associations can specify more complex relationships, such as objects of one class being composed of objects of other classes. Consider a real-world automated teller machine. What "pieces" does a manufacturer put together to build a working ATM? Our requirements specification tells us that the ATM is composed of a screen, a keypad, a cash dispenser and a deposit slot.

In Fig. 4.26, the ***solid diamonds*** attached to the association lines of class ATM indicate that class ATM has a ***composition*** relationship with classes Screen, Keypad, CashDispenser and DepositSlot. Composition implies a whole/part relationship. The class that has the composition symbol (the solid diamond) on its end of the association line is the whole (in this case, ATM), and the classes on the other end of the association lines are the parts—in this case, classes Screen, Keypad, CashDispenser and DepositSlot. The compositions in Fig. 4.26 indicate that an object of class ATM is formed from one object of class Screen, one object of class CashDispenser, one object of class Keypad and one object of class DepositSlot. The ATM *has a* screen, a keypad, a cash dispenser and a deposit slot. The *has-a relationship* defines composition. (We'll see in the Software Engineering Case Study section in Chapter 14 that the *is-a* relationship defines inheritance.)

According to the UML specification, composition relationships have the following properties:

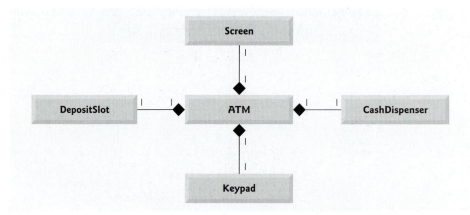

Fig. 4.26 | Class diagram showing composition relationships.

1. Only one class in the relationship can represent the whole (i.e., the diamond can be placed on only one end of the association line). For example, either the screen is part of the ATM or the ATM is part of the screen, but the screen and the ATM cannot both represent the whole in the relationship.

2. The parts in the composition relationship exist only as long as the whole, and the whole is responsible for creating and destructing its parts. For example, the act of constructing an ATM includes manufacturing its parts. Furthermore, if the ATM is destroyed, its screen, keypad, cash dispenser and deposit slot are also destroyed.

3. A part may belong to only one whole at a time, although the part may be removed and attached to another whole, which then assumes responsibility for the part.

The solid diamonds in our class diagrams indicate composition relationships that fulfill these three properties. If a *has-a* relationship does not satisfy one or more of these criteria, the UML specifies that hollow diamonds be attached to the ends of association lines to indicate *aggregation*—a weaker form of composition. For example, a personal computer and a computer monitor participate in an aggregation relationship—the computer *has a* monitor, but the two parts can exist independently, and the same monitor can be attached to multiple computers at once, thus violating the second and third properties of composition.

Figure 4.27 shows a class diagram for the ATM system. This diagram models most of the classes that we identified earlier in this section, as well as the associations between them that we can infer from the requirements specification. [*Note:* Classes BalanceInquiry and Deposit participate in associations similar to those of class Withdrawal, so we have chosen to omit them from this diagram to keep it simple. In Chapter 14, we expand our class diagram to include all the classes in the ATM system.]

Figure 4.27 presents a graphical model of the structure of the ATM system. This class diagram includes classes BankDatabase and Account and several associations that were not present in either Fig. 4.24 or Fig. 4.26. The class diagram shows that class ATM has a *one-to-one relationship* with class BankDatabase—one ATM object authenticates users against one BankDatabase object. In Fig. 4.27, we also model the fact that the bank's database contains information about many accounts—one object of class BankDatabase partici-

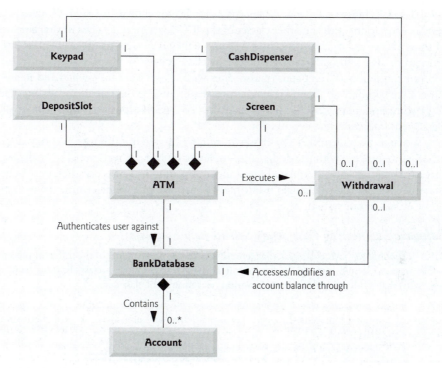

Fig. 4.27 | Class diagram for the ATM system model.

pates in a composition relationship with zero or more objects of class Account. Recall from Fig. 4.25 that the multiplicity value 0..* at the Account end of the association between class BankDatabase and class Account indicates that zero or more objects of class Account take part in the association. Class BankDatabase has a ***one-to-many relationship*** with class Account—the BankDatabase contains many Accounts. Similarly, class Account has a ***many-to-one relationship*** with class BankDatabase—many Accounts can be contained in the BankDatabase. [*Note:* Recall from Fig. 4.25 that the multiplicity value * is identical to 0..*. We include 0..* in our class diagrams for clarity.]

Figure 4.27 also indicates that if the user is performing a withdrawal, "one object of class Withdrawal accesses/modifies an account balance through one object of class Bank-Database." We could have created an association directly between class Withdrawal and class Account. The requirements specification, however, states that the "ATM must interact with the bank's account-information database" to perform transactions. A bank account contains sensitive information, and systems engineers must always consider the security of personal data when designing a system. Thus, only the BankDatabase can access and manipulate an account directly. All other parts of the system must interact with the database to retrieve or update account information (e.g., an account balance).

The class diagram in Fig. 4.27 also models associations between class Withdrawal and classes Screen, CashDispenser and Keypad. A withdrawal transaction includes prompting the user to choose a withdrawal amount and receiving numeric input. These actions require the use of the screen and the keypad, respectively. Furthermore, dispensing cash to the user requires access to the cash dispenser.

Classes `BalanceInquiry` and `Deposit`, though not shown in Fig. 4.27, take part in several associations with the other classes of the ATM system. Like class `Withdrawal`, each of these classes associates with classes `ATM` and `BankDatabase`. An object of class `BalanceInquiry` also associates with an object of class `Screen` to display the balance of an account to the user. Class `Deposit` associates with classes `Screen`, `Keypad` and `DepositSlot`. Like withdrawals, deposit transactions require use of the screen and the keypad to display prompts and receive input, respectively. To receive deposit envelopes, an object of class `Deposit` accesses the deposit slot.

We have now identified the classes in our ATM system (although we may discover others as we proceed with the design and implementation). In Section 5.13, we determine the attributes for each of these classes, and in Section 6.11, we use these attributes to examine how the system changes over time. In Section 7.23, we determine the operations of the classes in our system.

Software Engineering Case Study Self-Review Exercises

4.1 Suppose we have a class `Car` that represents a car. Think of some of the different pieces that a manufacturer would put together to produce a whole car. Create a class diagram (similar to Fig. 4.26) that models some of the composition relationships of class `Car`.

4.2 Suppose we have a class `File` that represents an electronic document in a stand-alone, non-networked computer represented by class `Computer`. What sort of association exists between class `Computer` and class `File`?

    a) Class `Computer` has a one-to-one relationship with class `File`.
    b) Class `Computer` has a many-to-one relationship with class `File`.
    c) Class `Computer` has a one-to-many relationship with class `File`.
    d) Class `Computer` has a many-to-many relationship with class `File`.

4.3 State whether the following statement is *true* or *false*; if *false*, explain why: A UML diagram in which a class's second and third compartments are not modeled is said to be an elided diagram.

4.4 Modify the class diagram of Fig. 4.27 to include class `Deposit` instead of class `Withdrawal`.

Answers to Software Engineering Case Study Self-Review Exercises

4.1 [*Note:* Student answers may vary.] Figure 4.28 presents a class diagram that shows some of the composition relationships of a class `Car`.

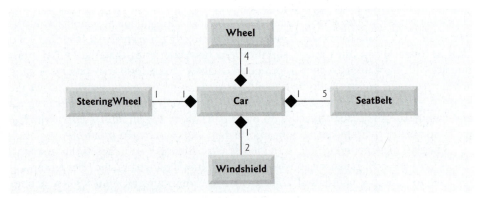

Fig. 4.28 | Class diagram showing composition relationships of a class `Car`.

4.2   c. [*Note:* In a computer network, this relationship could be many-to-many.]

4.3   True.

4.4   Figure 4.29 presents a class diagram for the ATM including class Deposit instead of class Withdrawal (as in Fig. 4.27). Note that Deposit does not access CashDispenser, but does access DepositSlot.

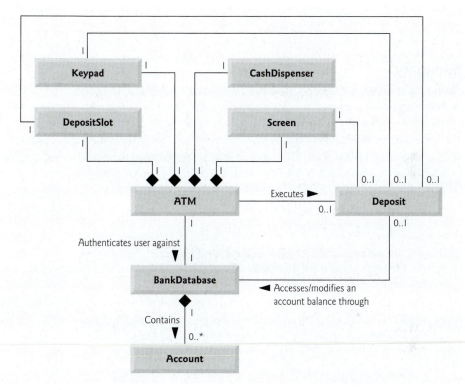

Fig. 4.29 | Class diagram for the ATM system model including class Deposit.

4.14 Wrap-Up

In this chapter, you learned how to create user-defined classes, and how to create and use objects of those classes. We declared data members of a class to maintain data for each object of the class. We also defined member functions that operate on that data. You learned how to call an object's member functions to request the services the object provides and how to pass data to those member functions as arguments. We discussed the difference between a local variable of a member function and a data member of a class. We also showed how to use a constructor to specify initial values for an object's data members. You learned how to separate the interface of a class from its implementation to promote good software engineering. We presented a diagram that shows the files that class-implementation programmers and client-code programmers need to compile the code they write. We demonstrated how *set* functions can be used to validate an object's data and ensure that objects are maintained in a consistent state.

We presented a first look at C++/CLI and how to create managed classes using the .NET Framework. We also discussed how to use the `property` keyword instead of writing explicit *set* and *get* functions.

In addition, UML class diagrams were used to model classes and their constructors, member functions and data members. In the next chapter, we begin our introduction to control statements, which specify the order in which a function's actions are performed.

Summary

Section 4.2 Classes, Objects, Member Functions and Data Members

- Performing a task in a program requires a function. The function hides from its user the complex tasks that it performs.
- A function in a class is known as a member function and performs one of the class's tasks.
- You must create an object of a class before a program can perform the tasks the class describes. That is one reason Visual C++ is known as an object-oriented programming language.
- Each message sent to an object is a member-function call that tells the object to perform a task.
- An object has attributes that are carried with the object as it is used in a program. These attributes are specified as data members in the object's class.

Section 4.4 Defining a Class with a Member Function

- A class definition contains the data members and member functions that define the class's attributes and behaviors, respectively.
- A native class definition begins with the keyword `class` followed immediately by the class name.
- By convention, the name of a user-defined class begins with a capital letter, and, for readability, each subsequent word in the class name begins with a capital letter.
- Every class's body is enclosed in a pair of braces (`{` and `}`) and ends with a semicolon.
- Member functions that appear after access specifier `public` can be called by other functions in a program and by member functions of other classes.
- Access specifiers are always followed by a colon (`:`).
- Keyword `void` is a special return type which indicates that a function will perform a task but will not return any data to its calling function when it completes its task.
- By convention, function names begin with a lowercase first letter and all subsequent words in the name begin with a capital letter.
- An empty set of parentheses after a function name indicates that the function does not require additional data to perform its task.
- Every function's body is delimited by left and right braces (`{` and `}`).
- Typically, you cannot call a member function until you create an object of its class.
- Each new class you create becomes a new type in Visual C++ that can be used to declare variables and create objects. This is one reason why Visual C++ is known as an extensible language.
- In the UML, each class is modeled in a class diagram as a rectangle with three compartments. The top compartment contains the class name, centered horizontally in boldface. The middle compartment contains the class's attributes (data members in Visual C++). The bottom compartment contains the class's operations (member functions and constructors in Visual C++).

- The UML models operations by listing the operation name followed by a set of parentheses. A plus sign (+) preceding the operation name indicates a `public` operation in the UML (i.e., a `public` member function in Visual C++).

Section 4.5 Defining a Member Function with a Parameter
- A member function can require one or more parameters that represent additional data it needs to perform its task. A function call supplies arguments for each of the function's parameters.
- A member function is called by following the object name with a dot operator (`.`), the function name and a set of parentheses containing the function's arguments.
- A variable of C++ Standard Library class `string` represents a string of characters. This class is defined in header file `<string>`, and the name `string` belongs to namespace `std`.
- Function `getline` (from header `<string>`) reads characters from its first argument until a newline character is encountered, then places the characters (not including the newline) in the `string` variable specified as its second argument. The newline character is discarded.
- A parameter list may contain any number of parameters, including none at all (represented by empty parentheses) to indicate that a function does not require any parameters.
- The number of arguments in a function call must match the number of parameters in the parameter list of the called member function's header. Also, the argument types in the function call must be consistent with the types of the corresponding parameters in the function header.
- The UML models a parameter of an operation by listing the parameter name, followed by a colon and the parameter type between the parentheses following the operation name.
- The UML has its own data types. Not all the UML data types have the same names as the corresponding Visual C++ types. The UML type `String` corresponds to the Visual C++ type `string`.

Section 4.6 Data Members, set Functions and get Functions
- Variables declared in a function's body are local variables and can be used only from the point of their declaration to the closing right brace (`}`) of the block in which they are declared. When a function terminates, the values of its local variables are lost.
- A local variable must be declared before it can be used in a function. A local variable cannot be accessed outside the function in which it is declared.
- Data members normally are `private`. Variables or functions declared `private` are accessible only to member functions of the class in which they are declared, or to friends of the class, as you'll see in Chapter 11.
- When a program creates (instantiates) an object of a class, its `private` data members are encapsulated (hidden) in the object and can be accessed only by member functions of the object's class.
- When a function that specifies a return type other than `void` is called and completes its task, the function returns a result to its calling function.
- By default, the initial value of a `string` is the empty string—i.e., a string that does not contain any characters. Nothing appears on the screen when an empty string is displayed.
- Classes often provide `public` member functions to allow clients of the class to *set* or *get* `private` data members. The names of these member functions normally begin with *set* or *get*.
- *Set* and *get* functions allow clients of a class to indirectly access the hidden data. The client does not know how the object performs these operations.
- A class's *set* and *get* functions should be used by other member functions of the class to manipulate the class's `private` data. If the class's data representation is changed, member functions that access the data only via the *set* and *get* functions will not require modification.

- A public *set* function should carefully scrutinize any attempt to modify the value of a data member to ensure that the new value is appropriate for that data item.
- The UML represents data members as attributes by listing the attribute name, followed by a colon and the attribute type. Private attributes are preceded by a minus sign (-) in the UML.
- The UML indicates the return type of an operation by placing a colon and the return type after the parentheses following the operation name.
- UML class diagrams do not specify return types for operations that do not return values.

Section 4.7 Initializing Objects with Constructors
- Each class should provide a constructor to initialize an object of the class when the object is created. A constructor must be defined with the same name as the class.
- A difference between constructors and functions is that constructors cannot return values, so they cannot specify a return type (not even void). Normally, constructors are declared public.
- Visual C++ requires a constructor call at the time each object is created, which helps ensure that every object is initialized before it is used in a program.
- A constructor with no parameters is a default constructor. If you do not provide a constructor, the compiler provides a default constructor. You can also define a default constructor explicitly. If you define a constructor for a class, Visual C++ will not create a default constructor.
- The UML models constructors as operations in a class diagram's third compartment. To distinguish a constructor from a class's operations, the UML places the word "constructor" between guillemets (« and ») before the constructor's name.

Section 4.8 Placing a Class in a Separate File for Reusability
- Class definitions, when packaged properly, can be reused by programmers worldwide.
- It is customary to define a class in a header file that ends with the .h filename extension.
- If the class's implementation changes, the class's clients should not be required to change.
- Interfaces define and standardize the ways in which things such as people and systems interact.
- A class's interface describes the public member functions that are made available to the class's clients. The interface describes *what* services clients can use and how to *request* those services, but does not specify *how* the class carries out the services.

Section 4.9 Separating Interface from Implementation
- Separating interface from implementation makes programs easier to modify. Changes in the class's implementation do not affect the client as long as the class's interface remains unchanged.
- A function prototype contains a function's name, its return type and the number, types and order of the parameters the function expects to receive.
- Once a class is defined and its member functions are declared (via function prototypes), the member functions should be defined in a separate source-code file
- For each member function defined outside of its corresponding class definition, the function name must be preceded by the class name and the binary scope resolution operator (::).

Section 4.10 Validating Data with *set* Functions
- Class string's length member function returns the number of characters in a string object.
- Class string's member function substr returns a new string object containing a copy of part of an existing string object. The first argument specifies the starting position in the original string. The second argument specifies the number of characters to copy.

Section 4.11 Defining a Managed Class with Member Functions in C++/CLI

- A managed class definition begins with the spaced keyword ref class followed immediately by the class name. The rest of the class definition follows the same rules as native C++.

- The memory and resources used by an object of a managed type are managed by the CLR.

- The .NET Framework Class Library's namespaces (like System) enable you to use existing .NET classes in your programs. To use these classes in your program you need a using directive.

- In C++/CLI use the .NET functions Console::WriteLine and Console::ReadLine to write lines to and read lines from the console (respectively) instead of cout and cin.

Section 4.12 Instance Variables and Properties in C++/CLI

- Properties use easier syntax to provide the same power of data hiding and data validation that *set* and *get* functions do.

- A property declaration starts with the context-sensitive keyword property followed by the type of variable the property accesses and the property's name.

- The property declaration can contain a set accessor, a get accessor, or both. Each accessor must specify its own return type and parameter, and optionally its own access specifier.

- If you aren't going to add validation code to your accessors, you can use a trivial property. The compiler generates a backing-store data member that the compiler-generated set and get accessors use. A trivial property doesn't use an existing class data member as a backing store.

Terminology

access specifier
accessor
argument
attribute (UML)
backing store of a property
binary scope resolution operator (::)
body of a class definition
C++/CLI
calling function (caller)
camel case
class definition
class diagram (UML)
class-implementation programmer
client-code programmer
client of an object or class
compartment in a class diagram (UML)
consistent state
Console::ReadLine function
Console::WriteLine function
constructor
data hiding
data member
default constructor
defining a class
dot operator (.)
driver program
empty string
extensible language

fixed text in a format string
Framework Class Library (FCL)
function call
function header
function prototype
get function
getline function of <string> library
guillemets, « and » (UML)
.h filename extension
header file
implementation of a class
instance of a class
interface of a class
invoke a member function
length member function of class string
local variable
managed class
managed object
member function
member-function call
message (send to an object)
minus (-) sign (UML)
mutator
nontrivial property
object code
operation (UML)
operation parameter (UML)
parameter

parameter list	source-code file
plus (+) sign (UML)	spaced keyword
`private` access specifier	`string` class
property	`<string>` header file
property declaration	`substr` member function of class `string`
`public` access specifier	syntactic sugar
`public` services of a class	trivial property
read-only	UML class diagram
`ref class`	using directive
request a service from an object	user-defined type
return type	validation
separate interface from implementation	validity checking
set function	void return type
software engineering	

Self-Review Exercises

4.1 Fill in the blanks in each of the following:

a) A house is to a blueprint as a(n) _____ is to a class.

b) Every class definition contains the keyword _____ followed immediately by the class's name.

c) A class definition is typically stored in a file with the _____ filename extension.

d) Each parameter in a function header must specify both a(n) _____ and a(n) _____.

e) When each object of a class maintains its own copy of an attribute, the variable that represents the attribute is also known as a(n) _____.

f) Keyword `public` is a(n) _____.

g) Return type _____ indicates that a function will perform a task but will not return any information when it completes its task.

h) Function _____ from the `<string>` library reads characters until a newline character is encountered, then copies those characters into the specified `string`.

i) When a member function is defined outside the class definition, the function header must include the class name and the _____, followed by the function name to "tie" the member function to the class definition.

j) The source-code file and any other files that use a class can include the class's header file via a(n) _____ preprocessor directive.

4.2 State whether each of the following is *true* or *false*. If *false*, explain why.

a) By convention, function names begin with a capital letter and all subsequent words in the name begin with a capital letter.

b) Empty parentheses following a function name in a function prototype indicate that the function does not require any parameters to perform its task.

c) Data members or member functions declared with access specifier `private` are accessible to member functions of the class in which they are declared.

d) Variables declared in the body of a particular member function are known as data members and can be used in all member functions of the class.

e) Every function's body is delimited by left and right braces (`{` and `}`).

f) A source-code file that contains `int main()` can be used to execute a program.

g) The types of arguments in a function call must be consistent with the types of the corresponding parameters in the function prototype's parameter list.

4.3 What is the difference between a local variable and a data member?

4.4   Explain the purpose of a function parameter. What is the difference between a parameter and an argument?

4.5   What syntax is required to declare a managed class?

4.6   What is the difference in the way compiler-generated default constructors work in native classes compared to managed classes?

4.7   What class data member can be accessed when you declare a nontrivial property? What about when you declare a trivial property?

Answers to Self-Review Exercises

4.1   a) object. b) `class`. c) `.h` d) type, name. e) data member. f) access specifier. g) `void`. h) `getline`. i) binary scope resolution operator (`::`). j) `#include`.

4.2   a) False. Function names begin with a lowercase letter, and all subsequent words in the name begin with a capital letter. b) True. c) True. d) False. Such variables are local variables and can be used only in the member function in which they are declared. e) True. f) True. g) True.

4.3   A local variable is declared in the body of a function and can be used only from the point at which it is declared to the closing brace of the block in which the variable is declared. A data member is declared in a class, but not in the body of any of the class's member functions. Every object of a class has a separate copy of the class's data members. Data members are accessible to all member functions of the class.

4.4   A parameter represents additional information that a function requires to perform its task. Each parameter required by a function is specified in the function header. An argument is the value supplied in the function call. When the function is called, the argument value is passed into the function parameter so that the function can perform its task.

4.5   Declare the class with `ref class` followed by the class name.

4.6   A compiler-generated default constructor for a managed class will initialize data members to default values according to their type instead of leaving them as "garbage values" as a native default constructor does.

4.7   A nontrivial property can be declared to use any class data member of your choice. A nontrivial property should be named according to the data member it accesses. A trivial property doesn't access an existing data member. The compiler generates a data member that contains the name of the trivial property to use as the backing store for the `set` and `get` accessors.

Exercises

4.8   Explain the difference between a function prototype and a function definition.

4.9   What is a default constructor? How are an object's data members initialized if a class has only an implicitly defined default constructor?

4.10   Explain the purpose of a data member.

4.11   What is a header file? What is a source-code file? Discuss the purpose of each.

4.12   Explain how a program could use class `string` without inserting a `using` declaration.

4.13   Explain why a class might provide a *set* function and a *get* function for a data member.

4.14   *(Modifying Class `GradeBook`)* Modify class `GradeBook` (Figs. 4.11–4.12) as follows:
   a)   Include a second `string` data member that represents the course instructor's name.
   b)   Provide a *set* function to change the instructor's name and a *get* function to retrieve it.
   c)   Modify the constructor to specify course-name and instructor-name parameters.

d) Modify function `displayMessage` to output the welcome message and course name, then the `string` "This course is presented by: " followed by the instructor's name.

Use your modified class in a test program that demonstrates the class's new capabilities.

4.15 *(Account Class)* Create an `Account` class that a bank might use to represent customers' bank accounts. Include a data member of type `int` to represent the account balance. [*Note:* In subsequent chapters, we'll use numbers that contain decimal points (e.g., 2.75)—called floating-point values— to represent dollar amounts.] Provide a constructor that receives an initial balance and uses it to initialize the data member. The constructor should validate the initial balance to ensure that it is greater than or equal to 0. If not, set the balance to 0 and display an error message indicating that the initial balance was invalid. Provide three member functions. Member function `credit` should add an amount to the current balance. Member function `debit` should withdraw money from the `Account` and ensure that the debit amount does not exceed the `Account`'s balance. If it does, the balance should be left unchanged and the function should print a message indicating "Debit amount exceeded account balance." Member function `getBalance` should return the current balance. Create a program that creates two `Account` objects and tests the member functions of class `Account`.

4.16 *(Invoice Class)* Create a class called `Invoice` that a hardware store might use to represent an invoice for an item sold at the store. An `Invoice` should include four data members—a part number (type `string`), a part description (type `string`), a quantity of the item being purchased (type `int`) and a price per item (type `int`). [*Note:* In subsequent chapters, we'll use numbers that contain decimal points (e.g., 2.75)—called floating-point values—to represent dollar amounts.] Your class should have a constructor that initializes the four data members. Provide a *set* and a *get* function for each data member. In addition, provide a member function named `getInvoiceAmount` that calculates the invoice amount (i.e., multiplies the quantity by the price per item), then returns the amount as an `int` value. If the quantity is not positive, it should be set to 0. If the price per item is not positive, it should be set to 0. Write a test program that demonstrates class `Invoice`'s capabilities.

4.17 *(Employee Class)* Create a class called `Employee` that includes three pieces of information as data members—a first name (type `string`), a last name (type `string`) and a monthly salary (type `int`). [*Note:* In subsequent chapters, we'll use numbers that contain decimal points (e.g., 2.75)— called floating-point values—to represent dollar amounts.] Your class should have a constructor that initializes the three data members. Provide a *set* and a *get* function for each data member. If the monthly salary is not positive, set it to 0. Write a test program that demonstrates class `Employee`'s capabilities. Create two `Employee` objects and display each object's *yearly* salary. Then give each Employee a 10 percent raise and display each `Employee`'s yearly salary again.

4.18 *(Date Class)* Create a class called `Date` that includes three pieces of information as data members—a month (type `int`), a day (type `int`) and a year (type `int`). Your class should have a constructor with three parameters that uses the parameters to initialize the three data members. For the purpose of this exercise, assume that the values provided for the year and day are correct, but ensure that the month value is in the range 1–12; if it is not, set the month to 1. Provide a *set* and a *get* function for each data member. Provide a member function `displayDate` that displays the month, day and year separated by forward slashes (/). Write a test program that demonstrates class `Date`'s capabilities.

4.19 *(Managed Date Class)* Create a managed class called `Date` similar to the one in the previous exercise. The class should include three pieces of information as data members—a month (type `int`), a day (type `int`) and a year (type `int`). Your class should have a constructor with three parameters that uses the parameters to initialize the three data members. For the purpose of this exercise, assume that the values provided for the year and day are correct, but ensure that the month value is in the range 1–12; if it is not, set the month to 1. Use nontrivial properties rather than *set* and *get* functions for each data member. Provide a member function `displayDate` that displays the month, day and year separated by forward slashes (/). Write a test program that demonstrates class `Date`'s capabilities.

5

Control Statements: Part 1

Let's all move one place on.
—Lewis Carroll

The wheel is come full circle.
—William Shakespeare

How many apples fell on Newton's head before he took the hint!
—Robert Frost

All the evolution we know of proceeds from the vague to the definite.
—Charles Sanders Peirce

OBJECTIVES

In this chapter you'll learn:

- Basic problem-solving techniques.

- To develop algorithms through the process of top-down, stepwise refinement.

- To use the if and if...else selection statements to choose among alternative actions.

- To use the while repetition statement to execute statements in a program repeatedly.

- Counter-controlled repetition and sentinel-controlled repetition.

- To use the increment, decrement and assignment operators.

5.1 Introduction

Before writing a program to solve a problem, we must have a thorough understanding of the problem and a carefully planned approach to solving it. When writing a program, we must also understand the types of building blocks that are available and employ proven program construction techniques. In this chapter and in Chapter 6, Control Statements: Part 2, we discuss these issues as we present the theory and principles of structured programming. The concepts presented here are crucial to building effective classes and manipulating objects.

In this chapter, we introduce Visual C++'s `if`, `if...else` and `while` statements, three of the building blocks that allow you to specify the logic required for member functions to perform their tasks. We devote a portion of this chapter (and Chapters 6 and 8) to further developing the `GradeBook` class introduced in Chapter 4. In particular, we add a member function to the `GradeBook` class that uses control statements to calculate the average of a set of student grades. Another example demonstrates additional ways to combine control statements to solve a similar problem. We introduce Visual C++'s assignment operators and explore Visual C++'s increment and decrement operators. These additional operators abbreviate and simplify many program statements. Unlike the last chapter, this chapter does not include any sections specific to C++/CLI syntax, because C++/CLI uses these control statements in exactly the same way as native C++.

5.2 Algorithms

Any solvable computing problem can be solved by the execution of a series of actions in a specific order. A *procedure* for solving a problem in terms of

1. the *actions* to execute and
2. the *order* in which the actions execute

is called an *algorithm*. The following example demonstrates that correctly specifying the order in which the actions execute is important.

Consider the "rise-and-shine algorithm" followed by one junior executive for getting out of bed and going to work: (1) Get out of bed, (2) take off pajamas, (3) take a shower, (4) get dressed, (5) eat breakfast, (6) carpool to work. This routine gets the executive to work well prepared to make critical decisions. Suppose that the same steps are performed in a slightly different order: (1) Get out of bed, (2) take off pajamas, (3) get dressed, (4) take a shower, (5) eat breakfast, (6) carpool to work. In this case, our junior executive shows up for work soaking wet. Specifying the order in which statements (actions) execute in a computer program is called *program control*. This chapter investigates program control using Visual C++'s *control statements*.

5.3 Pseudocode

Pseudocode (or "fake" code) is an artificial and informal language that helps you develop algorithms without having to worry about the strict details of Visual C++ language syntax. The pseudocode we present here is particularly useful for developing algorithms that will be converted to structured portions of Visual C++ programs. Pseudocode is similar to everyday English; it is convenient and user friendly, although it is not an actual computer programming language.

Pseudocode does not execute on computers. Rather, it helps you "think out" a program before attempting to write it in a programming language, such as Visual C++. This chapter provides several examples of how to use pseudocode to develop Visual C++ programs.

The style of pseudocode we present consists purely of characters, so you can type pseudocode conveniently, using any editor program. The computer can produce a freshly printed copy of a pseudocode program on demand. A carefully prepared pseudocode program can easily be converted to a corresponding Visual C++ program. In many cases, this simply requires replacing pseudocode statements with Visual C++ equivalents.

Pseudocode normally describes only *executable statements*, which cause specific actions to occur after a programmer converts a program from pseudocode to Visual C++ and the program is run on a computer. Declarations (that do not have initializers or do not involve constructor calls) are not executable statements. For example, the declaration

```
int i;
```

tells the compiler variable i's type and instructs the compiler to reserve space in memory for the variable. This declaration does not cause any action—such as input, output or a calculation—to occur when the program executes. We typically do not include variable declarations in our pseudocode. However, some programmers choose to list variables and mention their purposes at the beginning of pseudocode programs.

Let's look at an example of pseudocode that may be written to help a programmer create the addition program of Fig. 3.5. This pseudocode (Fig. 5.1) corresponds to the algorithm that inputs two integers from the user, adds these integers and displays their sum. Although we show the complete pseudocode listing here, we'll show how to create pseudocode from a problem statement later in the chapter.

Lines 1–2 correspond to the statements in lines 13–14 of Fig. 3.5. Notice that the pseudocode statements are simply English statements that convey what task is to be per-

1	*Prompt the user to enter the first integer*
2	*Input the first integer*
3	
4	*Prompt the user to enter the second integer*
5	*Input the second integer*
6	
7	*Add first integer and second integer, store result*
8	*Display result*

Fig. 5.1 | Pseudocode for the addition program of Fig. 3.5.

formed in Visual C++. Likewise, lines 4–5 correspond to the statements in lines 16–17 of Fig. 3.5 and lines 7–8 correspond to the statements in lines 19 and 21 of Fig. 3.5.

There are several important aspects of the pseudocode in Fig. 5.1. Notice that the pseudocode corresponds to code only in function main. This occurs because pseudocode is normally used for algorithms, not complete programs. In this case, the pseudocode represents the algorithm. The function in which this code is placed is not important to the algorithm itself. For the same reason, line 23 of Fig. 3.5 (the return statement) is not included in the pseudocode—this return statement is placed at the end of every main function and is not important to the algorithm. Finally, lines 9–11 of Fig. 3.5 are not included in the pseudocode because these variable declarations are not executable statements.

5.4 Control Structures

Normally, statements in a program execute one after the other in the order in which they are written. This is called *sequential execution*. Various Visual C++ statements we'll soon discuss enable you to specify that the next statement to execute may be other than the next one in sequence. This is called *transfer of control*.

During the 1960s, it became clear that the indiscriminate use of transfers of control was the root of much difficulty experienced by software development groups. The finger of blame was pointed at the *goto statement*, which allows you to specify a transfer of control to one of a wide range of possible destinations in a program (creating what is often called "spaghetti code"). The notion of so-called *structured programming* became almost synonymous with "*goto elimination*."

The research of Böhm and Jacopini[1] demonstrated that programs could be written without any goto statements. It became the challenge of the era for programmers to shift their styles to "goto-less programming." It was not until the 1970s that programmers started taking structured programming seriously. The results have been impressive, as software development groups have reported reduced development times, more frequent on-time delivery of systems and more frequent within-budget completion of software projects. The key to these successes is that structured programs are clearer, are easier to debug, test and modify and are more likely to be bug free in the first place.

Böhm and Jacopini's work demonstrated that all programs could be written in terms of only three *control structures*, namely, the *sequence structure*, the *selection structure*

---

1. C. Böhm and G. Jacopini, "Flow Diagrams, Turing Machines, and Languages with Only Two Formation Rules," *Communications of the ACM*, Vol. 9, No. 5, May 1966, pp. 366–371.

and the ***repetition structure***. The term "control structures" comes from the field of computer science. When we introduce Visual C++'s implementations of control structures, we'll refer to them in the terminology of the C++ standard document[2] as "control statements."

Sequence Structure in Visual C++

The sequence structure is built into Visual C++. Unless directed otherwise, the computer executes Visual C++ statements one after the other in the order in which they are written—that is, in sequence. The Unified Modeling Language (UML) ***activity diagram*** of Fig. 5.2 illustrates a typical sequence structure in which two calculations are performed in order. Visual C++ allows us to have as many actions as we want in a sequence structure. As we'll soon see, anywhere a single action may be placed, we may place several actions in sequence.

In this figure, the two statements involve adding a grade to a `total` variable and adding the value 1 to a `counter` variable. Such statements might appear in a program that takes the average of several student grades. To calculate an average, the total of the grades being averaged is divided by the number of grades. A counter variable would be used to keep track of the number of values being averaged. You'll see similar statements in the program of Section 5.8.

Activity diagrams are part of the UML. An activity diagram models the ***workflow*** (also called the ***activity***) of a portion of a software system. Such workflows may include a portion of an algorithm, such as the sequence structure in Fig. 5.2. Activity diagrams are composed of special-purpose symbols, such as ***action state symbols*** (a rectangle with its left and right sides replaced with arcs curving outward), ***diamonds*** and ***small circles***; these symbols are connected by ***transition arrows***, which represent the flow of the activity.

Like pseudocode, activity diagrams help you develop and represent algorithms, although many programmers prefer pseudocode. Activity diagrams clearly show how control structures operate.

Consider the sequence-structure activity diagram of Fig. 5.2. It contains two ***action states*** that represent actions to perform. Each action state contains an ***action expression***—e.g., "add grade to total" or "add 1 to counter"—that specifies a particular action to

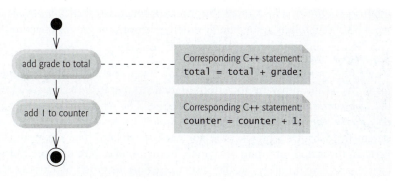

Fig. 5.2 | Sequence-structure activity diagram.

---

2. This document is more specifically known as *INCITS/ISO/IEC 14882-2003 Programming languages—C++* and is available for download (for a fee) at: `webstore.ansi.org/ansidocstore/product.asp?sku=INCITS%2FISO%2FIEC+14882%2D2003`.

perform. Other actions might include calculations or input/output operations. The arrows in the activity diagram are called transition arrows. These arrows represent *transitions*, which indicate the order in which the actions represented by the action states occur—the program that implements the activities illustrated by the activity diagram in Fig. 5.2 first adds grade to total, then adds 1 to counter.

The *solid circle* located at the top of the activity diagram represents the activity's *initial state*—the beginning of the workflow before the program performs the modeled activities. The solid circle surrounded by a hollow circle that appears at the bottom of the activity diagram represents the *final state*—the end of the workflow after the program performs its activities.

Figure 5.2 also includes rectangles with the upper-right corners folded over. These are called *notes* in the UML. Notes are explanatory remarks that describe the purpose of symbols in the diagram. Notes can be used in any UML diagram—not just activity diagrams. Figure 5.2 uses UML notes to show the Visual C++ code associated with each action state in the activity diagram. A *dotted line* connects each note with the element that the note describes. Activity diagrams normally do not show the Visual C++ code that implements the activity. We use notes for this purpose here to illustrate how the diagram relates to Visual C++ code. For more information on the UML, see our optional case study, which appears in the Software Engineering Case Study sections at the ends of Chapters 1, 3–8, 10, 13 and 14, or visit www.uml.org.

Selection Statements in Visual C++

Visual C++ provides three types of selection statements (discussed in this chapter and Chapter 6). The if selection statement either performs (selects) an action if a condition (predicate) is true or skips the action if the condition is false. The if...else selection statement performs an action if a condition is true or performs a different action if the condition is false. The switch selection statement (Chapter 6) performs one of many different actions, depending on the value of an integral expression.

The if selection statement is a *single-selection statement* because it selects or ignores a single action (or, as we'll soon see, a single group of actions). The if...else statement is called a *double-selection statement* because it selects between two different actions (or groups of actions). The switch selection statement is called a *multiple-selection statement* because it selects among many different actions (or groups of actions).

Repetition Statements in Visual C++

Visual C++ provides four types of repetition statements (also called *looping statements* or *loops*) that enable programs to perform statements repeatedly as long as a condition (called the *loop-continuation condition*) remains true. The repetition statements are the *while*, *do...while*, *for* statements and *for each... in*. (Chapter 6 presents the do...while and for statements; Chapter 8 presents the for each statement.) The while and for statements perform the action (or group of actions) in their bodies zero or more times—if the loop-continuation condition is initially false, the action (or group of actions) will not execute. The do...while statement performs the action (or group of actions) in its body at least once.

Each of the words if, else, switch, while, do, for and each is a Visual C++ keyword. These words are reserved by the Visual C++ programming language to implement various features, such as Visual C++'s control statements. Keywords must not be used as identifiers, such as variable names. Figure 5.3 provides a complete list of Visual C++ keywords.

Visual C++ Keywords

Keywords common to the C, C++ and Visual C++ programming languages

auto	break	case	char	const
continue	default	do	double	else
enum	extern	float	for	goto
if	int	long	register	return
short	signed	sizeof	static	struct
switch	typedef	union	unsigned	void
volatile	while			

Keywords common to the C++ and Visual C++ programming languages

and	and_eq	asm	bitand	bitor
bool	catch	class	compl	const_cast
delete	dynamic_cast	explicit	export	false
friend	inline	mutable	namespace	new
not	not_eq	nothrow	operator	or
or_eq	private	protected	public	reinterpret_cast
static_cast	template	this	throw	true
try	typeid	typename	using	virtual
wchar_t	xor	xor_eq		

Visual C++-only keywords

__abstract	abstract	__alignof	array	__asm
__assume	__based	__box	__cdecl	__declspec
__delegate	delegate	deprecated	dllexport	dllimport
enum class	enum struct	event	__event	__except
__fastcall	__finally	finally	for each/in	__forceinline
friend_as	__gc	gcnew	generic	__hook
__identifier	__if_exists	__if_not_exists	initonly	__inline
__int8	__int16	__int32	__int64	__interface
interface class	interface struct	interior_ptr	__leave	literal
__m64	__m128	__m128d	__m128i	
__multiple_inheritance		naked	__nogc	noinline
__noop	noreturn	novtable	nullptr	__pin
__property	property	__raise	ref struct	ref class
safecast	__sealed	sealed	selectany	thread
__single_inheritance		__stdcall	__super	
__try/__except	__try/__finally	__try_cast	__unaligned	__unhook
__uuidof	value struct	value class	__value	
__virtual_inheritance		__w64	__wchar_t	

Fig. 5.3 | Visual C++ keywords.

Common Programming Error 5.1

Using a keyword as an identifier is a syntax error.

Common Programming Error 5.2

Spelling a keyword with any uppercase letters is a syntax error. All of Visual C++'s keywords contain only lowercase letters.

Summary of Control Statements in Visual C++

Visual C++ has only three kinds of control structures, which from this point forward we refer to as control statements: the sequence statement, selection statements (three types—`if`, `if...else` and `switch`) and repetition statements (four types—`while`, `for`, `do...while` and `for each...in`). Each Visual C++ program combines as many of these control statements as is appropriate for the algorithm the program implements. As with the sequence statement of Fig. 5.2, we can model each control statement as an activity diagram. Each diagram contains an initial state and a final state, which represent a control statement's entry point and exit point, respectively. These *single-entry/single-exit control statements* make it easy to build programs—the control statements are attached to one another by connecting the exit point of one to the entry point of the next. This is similar to the way a child stacks building blocks, so we call this *control-statement stacking*. We'll learn shortly that there is only one other way to connect control statements—called *control-statement nesting*, in which one control statement is contained inside another. Thus, algorithms in Visual C++ programs are constructed from only three kinds of control statements, combined in only two ways.

Software Engineering Observation 5.1

Any Visual C++ program we'll ever build can be constructed from only seven different types of control statements (sequence, `if`, `if...else`, `switch`, `while`, `do...while` and `for`) combined in only two ways (control-statement stacking and control-statement nesting).

5.5 if Selection Statement

Programs use selection statements to choose among alternative courses of action. For example, suppose the passing grade on an exam is 60. The pseudocode statement

> *If student's grade is greater than or equal to 60*
> *Print "Passed"*

determines whether the condition "student's grade is greater than or equal to 60" is `true` or `false`. If the condition is `true`, then "Passed" is printed and the next pseudocode statement in order is "performed" (remember that pseudocode is not a real programming language). If the condition is `false`, the *Print* statement is ignored and the next pseudocode statement in order is performed. Note that the second line of this selection statement is indented. Such indentation is optional, but it is recommended because it emphasizes the inherent structure of structured programs. When you convert your pseudocode into Visual C++ code, the Visual C++ compiler ignores white-space characters (like blanks, tabs and newlines) used for indentation and vertical spacing.

Good Programming Practice 5.1

Consistently applying reasonable indentation conventions throughout your programs greatly improves program readability. We suggest three blanks per indent. Some people prefer using tabs, but these can vary across editors, causing a program written on one editor to align differently when used with another.

The preceding pseudocode *If* statement can be written in Visual C++ as

```
if ( grade >= 60 )
    cout << "Passed";
```

Notice that the Visual C++ code corresponds closely to the pseudocode. This is one of the properties of pseudocode that make it such a useful program development tool.

Figure 5.4 illustrates the single-selection if statement. It contains what is perhaps the most important symbol in an activity diagram—the diamond or *decision symbol*, which indicates that a decision is to be made. A decision symbol indicates that the workflow will continue along a path determined by the symbol's associated *guard conditions*, which can be true or false. Each transition arrow emerging from a decision symbol has a guard condition (specified in square brackets above or next to the transition arrow). If a particular guard condition is true, the workflow enters the action state to which that transition arrow points. In Fig. 5.4, if the grade is greater than or equal to 60, the program prints "Passed" to the screen, then transitions to the final state of this activity. If the grade is less than 60, the program immediately transitions to the final state without displaying a message.

We learned in Chapter 1 that decisions can be based on conditions containing relational or equality operators. Actually, in Visual C++, a decision can be based on any expression—if the expression evaluates to zero, it is treated as false; if the expression evaluates to nonzero, it is treated as true. Visual C++ provides the data type *bool* for variables that can hold only the values *true* and *false*—each of these is a Visual C++ keyword.

Portability Tip 5.1

For compatibility with earlier versions of C, which used integers for Boolean values, the bool *value* true *also can be represented by any nonzero value (compilers typically use 1) and the* bool *value* false *also can be represented as the value zero.*

Note that the if statement is a single-entry/single-exit statement. We'll see that the activity diagrams for the remaining control statements also contain initial states, transition arrows, action states that indicate actions to perform, decision symbols (with associated guard conditions) that indicate decisions to be made and final states. This is consistent with the *action/decision model of programming* we have been emphasizing.

We can envision eight bins, each containing only empty UML activity diagrams of one of the eight types of control statements. Your task, then, is assembling a program from

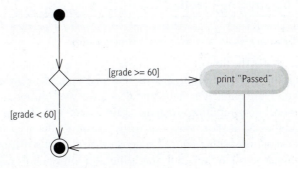

Fig. 5.4 | if single-selection statement activity diagram.

the activity diagrams of as many of each type of control statement as the algorithm demands, combining the activity diagrams in only two possible ways (stacking or nesting), then filling in the action states and decisions with action expressions and guard conditions in a manner appropriate to form a structured implementation for the algorithm. We'll discuss the variety of ways in which actions and decisions may be written.

5.6 `if...else` Double-Selection Statement

The `if` single-selection statement performs an indicated action only when the condition is `true`; otherwise the action is skipped. The `if...else` double-selection statement allows you to specify an action to perform when the condition is true and a different action to perform when the condition is `false`. For example, the pseudocode statement

> *If student's grade is greater than or equal to 60*
> > *Print "Passed"*
> *Else*
> > *Print "Failed"*

prints "Passed" if the student's grade is greater than or equal to 60, but prints "Failed" if the student's grade is less than 60. In either case, after printing occurs, the next pseudocode statement in sequence is "performed."

The preceding pseudocode *If...Else* statement can be written in Visual C++ as

```
if ( grade >= 60 )
    cout << "Passed";
else
    cout << "Failed";
```

Note that the body of the `else` is also indented.

Good Programming Practice 5.2

Whatever indentation convention you choose should be applied consistently throughout your programs. It is difficult to read programs that do not obey uniform spacing conventions.

Good Programming Practice 5.3

Indent both body statements of an `if...else` statement.

Good Programming Practice 5.4

If there are several levels of indentation, each level should be indented the same additional amount of space to promote readability and maintainability.

Figure 5.5 illustrates the flow of control in the `if...else` statement. Once again, note that (besides the initial state, transition arrows and final state) the only other symbols in the activity diagram represent action states and decisions. We continue to emphasize this action/decision model of computing. Imagine again a deep bin of empty UML activity diagrams of double-selection statements—as many as you might need to stack and nest with the activity diagrams of other control statements to form a structured implementation of an algorithm. You fill in the action states and decision symbols with action expressions and guard conditions appropriate to the algorithm.

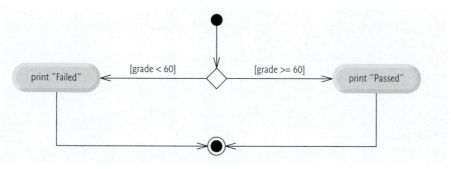

Fig. 5.5 | if...else double-selection statement activity diagram.

Conditional Operator (?:)

Visual C++ provides the ***conditional operator*** (**?:**), which is closely related to the if...else statement. The conditional operator is Visual C++'s only ***ternary operator***—it takes three operands. The operands, together with the conditional operator, form a ***conditional expression***. The first operand is a condition, the second operand is the value for the entire conditional expression if the condition is `true` and the third operand is the value for the entire conditional expression if the condition is `false`. For example, the output statement

```
cout << ( grade >= 60 ? "Passed" : "Failed" );
```

contains a conditional expression, `grade >= 60 ? "Passed" : "Failed"`, that evaluates to the string `"Passed"` if the condition `grade >= 60` is `true`, but evaluates to the string `"Failed"` if the condition is `false`. Thus, the statement with the conditional operator performs essentially the same as the preceding if...else statement. As we'll see, the precedence of the conditional operator is low, so the parentheses in the preceding expression are required.

Error-Prevention Tip 5.1

To avoid precedence problems (and for clarity), place conditional expressions (that appear in larger expressions) in parentheses.

The values in a conditional expression also can be actions to execute. For example, the following conditional expression also prints `"Passed"` or `"Failed"`:

```
grade >= 60 ? cout << "Passed" : cout << "Failed";
```

The preceding conditional expression is read, "If `grade` is greater than or equal to 60, then `cout << "Passed"`; otherwise, `cout << "Failed"`." This, too, is comparable to the preceding if...else statement. Conditional expressions can appear in some program locations where if...else statements cannot.

Nested if...else Statements

*Nested **if...else** statements* test for multiple cases by placing if...else selection statements inside other if...else selection statements. For example, the following pseudocode if...else statement prints A for exam grades greater than or equal to 90, B for grades in the range 80 to 89, C for grades in the range 70 to 79, D for grades in the range 60 to 69 and F for all other grades:

> *If student's grade is greater than or equal to 90*
> > *Print "A"*
> *Else*
> > *If student's grade is greater than or equal to 80*
> > > *Print "B"*
> > *Else*
> > > *If student's grade is greater than or equal to 70*
> > > > *Print "C"*
> > > *Else*
> > > > *If student's grade is greater than or equal to 60*
> > > > > *Print "D"*
> > > > *Else*
> > > > > *Print "F"*

This pseudocode can be written in Visual C++ as

```
if ( studentGrade >= 90 ) // 90 and above gets "A"
   cout << "A";
else
   if ( studentGrade >= 80 ) // 80-89 gets "B"
      cout << "B";
   else
      if ( studentGrade >= 70 ) // 70-79 gets "C"
         cout << "C";
      else
         if ( studentGrade >= 60 ) // 60-69 gets "D"
            cout << "D";
         else // less than 60 gets "F"
            cout << "F";
```

If studentGrade is greater than or equal to 90, the first four conditions will be true, but only the output statement after the first test will execute. After that statement executes, the program skips the else part of the "outermost" if...else statement. Most Visual C++ programmers prefer to write the preceding if...else statement as

```
if ( studentGrade >= 90 ) // 90 and above gets "A"
   cout << "A";
else if ( studentGrade >= 80 ) // 80-89 gets "B"
   cout << "B";
else if ( studentGrade >= 70 ) // 70-79 gets "C"
   cout << "C";
else if ( studentGrade >= 60 ) // 60-69 gets "D"
   cout << "D";
else // less than 60 gets "F"
   cout << "F";
```

The two forms are identical except for the spacing and indentation, which the compiler ignores. The latter form is popular because it avoids deep indentation of the code to the right. Such indentation can leave little room on a line, forcing the line to be split and decreasing program readability.

Performance Tip 5.1

A nested if...else statement can perform much faster than a series of single-selection if state-ments because of the possibility of early exit after one of the conditions is satisfied.

Performance Tip 5.2

In a nested if...else statement, test the conditions that are more likely to be true at the begin-ning of the nested if...else statement. This will enable the nested if...else statement to run faster by exiting earlier than it would if infrequently occurring cases were tested first.

Dangling-else Problem

The Visual C++ compiler always associates an else with the immediately preceding if un-less told to do otherwise by the placement of braces ({ and }). This behavior can lead to what is referred to as the *dangling-else problem*. For example,

```
if ( x > 5 )
   if ( y > 5 )
      cout << "x and y are > 5";
else
   cout << "x is <= 5";
```

appears to indicate that if x is greater than 5, the nested if statement determines whether y is also greater than 5. If so, "x and y are > 5" is output. Otherwise, it appears that if x is not greater than 5, the else part of the if...else outputs "x is <= 5".

Beware! This nested if...else statement does not execute as it appears. The compiler actually interprets the statement as

```
if ( x > 5 )
   if ( y > 5 )
      cout << "x and y are > 5";
   else
      cout << "x is <= 5";
```

in which the body of the first if is a nested if...else. The outer if statement tests wheth-er x is greater than 5. If so, execution continues by testing whether y is also greater than 5. If the second condition is true, the proper string—"x and y are > 5"—is displayed. How-ever, if the second condition is false, the string "x is <= 5" is displayed, even though we know that x is greater than 5.

To force the nested if...else statement to execute as originally intended, we can write it as follows:

```
if ( x > 5 )
{
   if ( y > 5 )
      cout << "x and y are > 5";
}
else
   cout << "x is <= 5";
```

The braces ({}) indicate to the compiler that the second if statement is in the body of the first if and that the else is associated with the first if. Exercises 5.23–5.24 further inves-tigate the dangling-else problem.

Blocks

The if selection statement expects only one statement in its body. Similarly, the if and else parts of an if...else statement each expect only one body statement. To include several statements in the body of an if or in either part of an if...else, enclose the statements in braces ({ and }). A set of statements contained within a pair of braces is called a *compound statement* or a *block*. We use the term "block" from this point forward.

Software Engineering Observation 5.2

A block can be placed anywhere in a program that a single statement can be placed.

The following example includes a block in the else part of an if...else statement.

```
if ( studentGrade >= 60 )
   cout << "Passed.\n";
else
{
   cout << "Failed.\n";
   cout << "You must take this course again.\n";
}
```

In this case, if studentGrade is less than 60, the program executes both statements in the body of the else and prints

```
Failed.
You must take this course again.
```

Notice the braces surrounding the two statements in the else clause. These braces are important. Without the braces, the statement

```
cout << "You must take this course again.\n";
```

would be outside the body of the else part of the if and would execute regardless of whether the grade was less than 60. This is an example of a logic error.

Common Programming Error 5.3

Forgetting one or both of the braces that delimit a block can lead to syntax errors or logic errors in a program.

Good Programming Practice 5.5

Always putting the braces in an if...else statement (or any control statement) helps prevent their accidental omission, especially when adding statements to an if or else clause at a later time. To avoid omitting one or both of the braces, some programmers prefer to type the beginning and ending braces of blocks even before typing the individual statements within the braces.

Just as a block can be placed anywhere a single statement can be placed, it is also possible to have no statement at all—called a *null statement* (or an *empty statement*). The null statement is represented by placing a semicolon (;) where a statement would normally be.

Common Programming Error 5.4

Placing a semicolon after the condition in an if statement leads to a logic error in single-selection if statements and a syntax error in double-selection if...else statements (when the if part contains an actual body statement).

5.7 while Repetition Statement

A *repetition statement* (also called a *looping statement* or a *loop*) allows you to specify that a program should repeat an action while some condition remains true. The pseudocode statement

> *While there are more items on my shopping list*
> *Purchase next item and cross it off my list*

describes the repetition that occurs during a shopping trip. The condition, "there are more items on my shopping list" is either true or false. If it is true, then the action, "Purchase next item and cross it off my list" is performed. This action will be performed repeatedly while the condition remains true. The statement contained in the *While* repetition statement constitutes the body of the *While*, which can be a single statement or a block. Eventually, the condition will become false (when the last item on the shopping list has been purchased and crossed off the list). At this point, the repetition terminates, and the first pseudocode statement after the repetition statement executes.

As an example of Visual C++'s while repetition statement, consider a program segment designed to find the first power of 3 larger than 100. Suppose the integer variable product has been initialized to 3. When the following while repetition statement finishes executing, product contains the result:

```
int product = 3;

while ( product <= 100 )
    product = 3 * product;
```

When the while statement begins execution, the value of product is 3. Each repetition of the while statement multiplies product by 3, so product takes on the values 9, 27, 81 and 243 successively. When product becomes 243, the while statement condition—product <= 100—becomes false. This terminates the repetition, so the final value of product is 243. At this point, program execution continues with the next statement after the while statement.

Common Programming Error 5.5

Not providing, in the body of a while statement, an action that eventually causes the condition in the while to become false normally results in a logic error called an infinite loop, *in which the repetition statement never terminates. This can make a program appear to "hang" or "freeze" if the loop body does not contain statements that interact with the user.*

The UML activity diagram of Fig. 5.6 illustrates the flow of control that corresponds to the preceding while statement. Once again, the symbols in the diagram (besides the initial state, transition arrows, a final state and three notes) represent an action state and a decision. This diagram also introduces the UML's *merge symbol*, which joins two flows of activity into one flow of activity. The UML represents both the merge symbol and the decision symbol as diamonds. In this diagram, the merge symbol joins the transitions from the initial state and from the action state, so they both flow into the decision that determines whether the loop should begin (or continue) executing. The decision and merge symbols can be distinguished by the number of "incoming" and "outgoing" transition arrows. A decision symbol has one transition arrow pointing to the diamond and two or more transition arrows pointing out from the diamond to indicate possible transitions from that point. In addition, each transition arrow pointing out of a decision symbol has a guard condition next to it. A merge symbol has two or more transition arrows pointing to the diamond and only one transition arrow pointing from the diamond, to indicate multiple activity flows merging to continue the activity. Note that, unlike the decision symbol, the merge symbol does not have a counterpart in Visual C++ code. None of the transition arrows associated with a merge symbol have guard conditions.

The diagram of Fig. 5.6 clearly shows the repetition of the while statement discussed earlier in this section. The transition arrow emerging from the action state points to the merge, which transitions back to the decision that is tested each time through the loop until the guard condition product > 100 becomes true. Then the while statement exits (reaches its final state) and control passes to the next statement in sequence in the program.

Imagine a deep bin of empty UML while repetition statement activity diagrams—as many as you might need to stack and nest with the activity diagrams of other control statements to form a structured implementation of an algorithm. You fill in the action states and decision symbols with action expressions and guard conditions appropriate to the algorithm.

Performance Tip 5.3

Many of the performance tips we mention in this text result in only small improvements, so you might be tempted to ignore them. However, a small performance improvement for code that executes many times in a loop can result in substantial overall performance improvement.

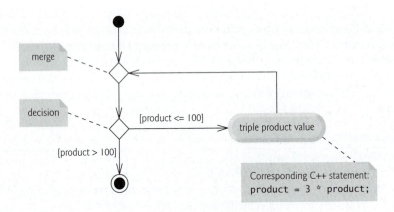

Fig. 5.6 | while repetition statement UML activity diagram.

5.8 Formulating Algorithms: Counter-Controlled Repetition

To illustrate how programmers develop algorithms, this section and Section 5.9 solve two variations of a class-average problem. Consider the following problem statement:

A class of ten students took a quiz. The grades (integers in the range 0 to 100) for this quiz are available to you. Calculate and display the total of all student grades and the class average on the quiz.

The class average is equal to the sum of the grades divided by the number of students. The algorithm for solving this problem on a computer must input each of the grades, calculate the average and print the result.

Pseudocode Algorithm with Counter-Controlled Repetition

Let's use pseudocode to list the actions to execute and specify the order in which these actions should occur. We use *counter-controlled repetition* to input the grades one at a time. This technique uses a variable called a *counter* to control the number of times a group of statements will execute (also known as the number of *iterations* of the loop).

Counter-controlled repetition is often called *definite repetition* because the number of repetitions is known before the loop begins executing. In this example, repetition terminates when the counter exceeds 10. This section presents a fully developed pseudocode algorithm (Fig. 5.7) and a version of class GradeBook (Figs. 5.8–5.9) that implements the algorithm in a Visual C++ member function. The section then presents an application (Fig. 5.10) that demonstrates the algorithm in action. In Section 5.9 we demonstrate how to use pseudocode to develop such an algorithm from scratch.

Software Engineering Observation 5.3

Experience has shown that the most difficult part of solving a problem on a computer is developing the algorithm for the solution. Once a correct algorithm has been specified, the process of producing a working Visual C++ program from the algorithm is normally straightforward.

```
 I   Set total to zero
 2   Set grade counter to one
 3
 4   While grade counter is less than or equal to ten
 5       Prompt the user to enter the next grade
 6       Input the next grade
 7       Add the grade into the total
 8       Add one to the grade counter
 9
10   Set the class average to the total divided by ten
11   Print the total of the grades for all students in the class
12   Print the class average
```

Fig. 5.7 | Pseudocode algorithm that uses counter-controlled repetition to solve the class-average problem.

```
I   // Fig. 5.8: GradeBook.h
2   // Definition of class GradeBook that determines a class average.
3   // Member functions are defined in GradeBook.cpp
4   #include <string> // program uses C++ standard string class
5   using std::string;
6
```

Fig. 5.8 | Definition of class GradeBook that determines a class average. (Part 1 of 2.)

```
 7   // GradeBook class definition
 8   class GradeBook
 9   {
10   public:
11      GradeBook( string ); // constructor initializes cours=e name
12      void setCourseName( string ); // function to set the course name
13      string getCourseName(); // function to retrieve the course name
14      void displayMessage(); // display a welcome message
15      void determineClassAverage(); // averages grades entered by the user
16   private:
17      string courseName; // course name for this GradeBook
18   }; // end class GradeBook
```

Fig. 5.8 | Definition of class `GradeBook` that determines a class average. (Part 2 of 2.)

```
 1   // Fig. 5.9: GradeBook.cpp
 2   // Member-function definitions for class GradeBook that solves the
 3   // class average program with counter-controlled repetition.
 4   #include <iostream>
 5   using std::cout;
 6   using std::cin;
 7   using std::endl;
 8
 9   #include "GradeBook.h" // include definition of class GradeBook
10
11   // constructor initializes courseName with string supplied as argument
12   GradeBook::GradeBook( string name )
13   {
14      setCourseName( name ); // validate and store courseName
15   } // end GradeBook constructor
16
17   // function to set the course name;
18   // ensures that the course name has at most 30 characters
19   void GradeBook::setCourseName( string name )
20   {
21      if ( name.length() <= 30 ) // if name has 30 or fewer characters
22         courseName = name; // store the course name in the object
23      else // if name is longer than 30 characters
24      { // set courseName to first 30 characters of parameter name
25         courseName = name.substr( 0, 30 ); // select first 30 characters
26         cout << "Name \"" << name << "\" exceeds maximum length (30).\n"
27            << "Limiting courseName to first 30 characters.\n" << endl;
28      } // end if...else
29   } // end function setCourseName
30
31   // function to retrieve the course name
32   string GradeBook::getCourseName()
33   {
34      return courseName;
35   } // end function getCourseName
```

Fig. 5.9 | Class-average problem using counter-controlled repetition: `GradeBook` source-code file. (Part I of 2.)

```
36
37    // display a welcome message to the GradeBook user
38    void GradeBook::displayMessage()
39    {
40       cout << "Welcome to the grade book for\n" << getCourseName() << "!\n"
41          << endl;
42    } // end function displayMessage
43
44    // determine class average based on 10 grades entered by user
45    void GradeBook::determineClassAverage()
46    {
47       int total; // sum of grades entered by user
48       int gradeCounter; // number of the grade to be entered next
49       int grade; // grade value entered by user
50       int average; // average of grades
51
52       // initialization phase
53       total = 0; // initialize total
54       gradeCounter = 1; // initialize loop counter
55
56       // processing phase
57       while ( gradeCounter <= 10 ) // loop 10 times
58       {
59          cout << "Enter grade: "; // prompt for input
60          cin >> grade; // input next grade
61          total = total + grade; // add grade to total
62          gradeCounter = gradeCounter + 1; // increment counter by 1
63       } // end while
64
65       // termination phase
66       average = total / 10; // integer division yields integer result
67
68       // display total and average of grades
69       cout << "\nTotal of all 10 grades is " << total << endl;
70       cout << "Class average is " << average << endl;
71    } // end function determineClassAverage
```

Fig. 5.9 | Class-average problem using counter-controlled repetition: GradeBook source-code file. (Part 2 of 2.)

Note the references in the pseudocode algorithm of Fig. 5.7 to a total and a counter. A *total* is a variable used to accumulate the sum of several values. A *counter* is a variable used to count—in this case, the grade counter indicates which of the 10 grades is about to be entered by the user. Variables used to store totals are normally initialized to zero before being used in a program; otherwise, the sum would include the previous value stored in the total's memory location.

Enhancing GradeBook Validation

Before we discuss the class-average algorithm's implementation, let's consider an enhancement we made to our GradeBook class. In Fig. 4.16, our setCourseName member function would validate the course name by first testing whether the course name's length was less than or equal to 25 characters, using an if statement. If this was true, the course name would be set. This code was then followed by another if statement that tested whether the course name's length was larger than 25 characters (in which case the course name would be shortened). Notice that the second if statement's condition is the exact opposite of the first if statement's condition. If one condition evaluates to true, the other must evaluate to false. Such a situation is ideal for an if...else statement, so we have modified our code, replacing the two if statements with one if...else statement (lines 21–28 of Fig. 5.9). Note that there is also a purely cosmetic change in the new version of the set-CourseName member function, where we now allow names up to 30 characters instead of 25. This is only so we can use more descriptive names.

Implementing Counter-Controlled Repetition in Class GradeBook

Class GradeBook (Figs. 5.8–5.9) contains a constructor (declared in line 11 of Fig. 5.8 and defined in lines 12–15 of Fig. 5.9) that assigns a value to the class's instance variable courseName (declared in line 17 of Fig. 5.8). Lines 19–29, 32–35 and 38–42 of Fig. 5.9 define member functions setCourseName, getCourseName and displayMessage, respectively. Lines 45–71 define member function determineClassAverage, which implements the class-average algorithm described by the pseudocode in Fig. 5.7.

Lines 47–50 declare local variables total, gradeCounter, grade and average to be of type int. Variable grade stores the user input. Notice that the preceding declarations appear in the body of member function determineClassAverage.

In this chapter's versions of class GradeBook, we simply read and process a set of grades. The averaging calculation is performed in member function determineClassAverage using local variables—we do not preserve any information about student grades in the class's instance variables. In Chapter 8, we modify class GradeBook to maintain the grades in memory using an instance variable that refers to a data structure known as an array. This allows a GradeBook object to perform various calculations on the same set of grades without requiring the user to enter the grades multiple times.

Good Programming Practice 5.6

Separate declarations from other statements in functions with a blank line for readability.

Lines 53–54 initialize total to 0 and gradeCounter to 1. Note that variables total and gradeCounter are initialized before they are used in a calculation. Counter variables normally are initialized to zero or one, depending on their use (we'll present examples showing each possibility). An uninitialized variable contains a *"garbage" value* (also called an *undefined value*)—the value last stored in the memory location reserved for that variable. Variables grade and average (for the user input and calculated average, respectively) need not be initialized here—their values will be assigned as they are input or calculated later in the function.

Common Programming Error 5.6

Not initializing counters and totals can lead to logic errors.

Error-Prevention Tip 5.2

Initialize each counter and total, either in its declaration or in an assignment statement. Totals are normally initialized to 0. Counters are normally initialized to 0 or 1, depending on how they are used (we'll show examples of when to use 0 and when to use 1).

Good Programming Practice 5.7

Declare each variable on a separate line with its own comment to make programs more readable.

Line 57 indicates that the while statement should continue looping (also called *iterating*) as long as gradeCounter's value is less than or equal to 10. While this condition remains true, the while statement repeatedly executes the statements between the braces that delimit its body (lines 58–63).

Line 59 displays the prompt "Enter grade: ". This line corresponds to the pseudocode statement *"Prompt the user to enter the next grade."* Line 60 reads the grade entered by the user and assigns it to variable grade. This line corresponds to the pseudocode statement *"Input the next grade."* Recall that variable grade was not initialized earlier in the program, because the program obtains the value for grade from the user during each iteration of the loop. Line 61 adds the new grade entered by the user to the total and assigns the result to total, which replaces its previous value.

Line 62 adds 1 to gradeCounter to indicate that the program has processed a grade and is ready to input the next grade from the user. Incrementing gradeCounter eventually causes gradeCounter to exceed 10. At that point the while loop terminates because its condition (line 57) becomes false.

When the loop terminates, line 66 performs the averaging calculation and assigns its result to the variable average. Line 69 displays the text "Total of all 10 grades is " followed by variable total's value. Line 70 then displays the text "Class average is " followed by variable average's value. Member function determineClassAverage then returns control to the calling function (i.e., main in Fig. 5.10).

Demonstrating Class GradeBook

Figure 5.10 contains this application's main function, which creates an object of class GradeBook and demonstrates its capabilities. Line 9 of Fig. 5.10 creates a new GradeBook object called myGradeBook. The string in line 9 is passed to the GradeBook constructor (lines 12–15 of Fig. 5.9). Line 11 of Fig. 5.10 calls myGradeBook's displayMessage member function to display a welcome message to the user. Line 12 then calls myGradeBook's determineClassAverage member function to allow the user to enter 10 grades, for which the member function then calculates and prints the average—the member function performs the algorithm shown in the pseudocode of Fig. 5.7.

```cpp
1   // Fig. 5.10: GradeBookTest.cpp
2   // Create GradeBook object and invoke its determineClassAverage function.
3   #include "GradeBook.h" // include definition of class GradeBook
4
5   int main()
6   {
7      // create GradeBook object myGradeBook and
8      // pass course name to constructor
9      GradeBook myGradeBook( "CS101 Visual C++ Programming" );
10
```

Fig. 5.10 | Class-average problem using counter-controlled repetition: Creating an object of class GradeBook (Figs. 5.8–5.9) and invoking its determineClassAverage member function. (Part 1 of 2.)

```
11      myGradeBook.displayMessage(); // display welcome message
12      myGradeBook.determineClassAverage(); // find average of 10 grades
13      return 0; // indicate successful termination
14   } // end main
```

```
Welcome to the grade book for
CS101 Visual C++ Programming

Enter grade: 67
Enter grade: 78
Enter grade: 89
Enter grade: 67
Enter grade: 87
Enter grade: 98
Enter grade: 93
Enter grade: 85
Enter grade: 82
Enter grade: 100

Total of all 10 grades is 846
Class average is 84
```

Fig. 5.10 | Class-average problem using counter-controlled repetition: Creating an object of class `GradeBook` (Figs. 5.8–5.9) and invoking its `determineClassAverage` member function. (Part 2 of 2.)

Notes on Integer Division and Truncation

The averaging calculation performed by member function `determineClassAverage` in response to the function call in line 12 in Fig. 5.10 produces an integer result. The program's output indicates that the sum of the grade values in the sample execution is 846, which, when divided by 10, should yield 84.6—a number with a decimal point. However, the result of the calculation `total / 10` (line 66 of Fig. 5.9) is the integer 84, because `total` and 10 are both integers. Dividing two integers results in integer division—any fractional part of the calculation is lost (i.e., *truncated*). We'll see how to obtain a result that includes a decimal point from the averaging calculation in the next section.

Common Programming Error 5.7

Assuming that integer division rounds (rather than truncates) can lead to incorrect results. For example, 7 ÷ 4, which yields 1.75 in conventional arithmetic, truncates to 1 in integer arithmetic, rather than rounding to 2.

In Fig. 5.9, if line 66 used `gradeCounter` rather than 10 for the calculation, the output for this program would display an incorrect value, 76. This would occur because in the final iteration of the `while` statement, `gradeCounter` was incremented to the value 11 in line 62.

Common Programming Error 5.8

*Using a loop's counter-control variable in a calculation after the loop often causes a common logic error called an **off-by-one error**. In a counter-controlled loop that counts up by one each time through the loop, the loop terminates when the counter's value is one higher than its last legitimate value (i.e., 11 in the case of counting from 1 to 10).*

5.9 Formulating Algorithms: Sentinel-Controlled Repetition

Let us generalize the class-average problem. Consider the following problem:

> *Develop a class-average program that processes grades for an arbitrary number of students each time it is run.*

In the previous class-average example, the problem statement specified the number of students, so the number of grades (10) was known in advance. In this example, no indication is given of how many grades the user will enter during the program's execution. The program must process an arbitrary number of grades. How can the program determine when to stop the input of grades? How will it know when to calculate and print the class average?

One way to solve this problem is to use a special value called a *sentinel value* (also called a *signal value*, a *dummy value* or a *flag value*) to indicate "end of data entry." The user types grades in until all legitimate grades have been entered. The user then types the sentinel value to indicate that the last grade has been entered. Sentinel-controlled repetition is often called *indefinite repetition* because the number of repetitions is not known before the loop begins executing.

Clearly, the sentinel value must be chosen so that it cannot be confused with an acceptable input value. Grades on a quiz are normally nonnegative integers, so −1 is an acceptable sentinel value for this problem. Thus, a run of the class-average program might process a stream of inputs such as 95, 96, 75, 74, 89 and −1. The program would then compute and print the class average for the grades 95, 96, 75, 74 and 89. Since −1 is the sentinel value, it should not enter into the averaging calculation.

 Common Programming Error 5.9

Choosing a sentinel value that is also a legitimate data value is a logic error.

Developing the Pseudocode Algorithm with Top-Down, Stepwise Refinement: The Top and First Refinement

We approach the class-average program with a technique called *top-down, stepwise refinement*, a technique that is essential to the development of well-structured programs. We begin with a pseudocode representation of the *top*—a single statement that conveys the overall function of the program:

> *Determine the class average for the quiz for an arbitrary number of students*

The top is, in effect, a *complete* representation of a program. Unfortunately, the top (as in this case) rarely conveys sufficient detail from which to write a program. So we now begin the refinement process. We divide the top into a series of smaller tasks and list these in the order in which they need to be performed. This results in the following *first refinement*.

> *Initialize variables*
> *Input, sum and count the quiz grades*
> *Calculate and print the total of all student grades and the class average*

This refinement uses only the sequence structure—the steps listed should execute in order, one after the other.

Software Engineering Observation 5.4

Each refinement, as well as the top itself, is a complete specification of the algorithm; only the level of detail varies.

Software Engineering Observation 5.5

Many programs can be divided logically into three phases: an initialization phase that initializes the program variables; a processing phase that inputs data values and adjusts program variables (such as counters and totals) accordingly; and a termination phase that calculates and outputs the final results.

Proceeding to the Second Refinement

The preceding *Software Engineering Observation* is often all you need for the first refinement in the top-down process. To proceed to the next level of refinement, i.e., the ***second refinement***, we commit to specific variables. In this example, we need a running total of the numbers, a count of how many numbers have been processed, a variable to receive the value of each grade as it is input by the user and a variable to hold the calculated average. The pseudocode statement

> *Initialize variables*

can be refined as follows:

> *Initialize total to zero*
> *Initialize counter to zero*

Only the variables *total* and *counter* need to be initialized before they are used. The variables *average* and *grade* (for the calculated average and the user input, respectively) need not be initialized, because their values will be replaced as they are calculated or input.

The pseudocode statement

> *Input, sum and count the quiz grades*

requires a repetition statement (i.e., a loop) that successively inputs each grade. We don't know in advance how many grades are to be processed, so we'll use sentinel-controlled repetition. The user enters legitimate grades one at a time. After entering the last legitimate grade, the user enters the sentinel value. The program tests for the sentinel value after each grade is input and terminates the loop when the user enters the sentinel value. The second refinement of the preceding pseudocode statement is then

> *Prompt the user to enter the first grade*
> *Input the first grade (possibly the sentinel)*
>
> *While the user has not yet entered the sentinel*
> > *Add this grade into the running total*
> > *Add one to the grade counter*
> > *Prompt the user to enter the next grade*
> > *Input the next grade (possibly the sentinel)*

In pseudocode, we do not use braces around the statements that form the body of the *While* structure. We simply indent the statements under the *While* to show that they belong to the *While*. Again, pseudocode is only an informal program development aid.

The pseudocode statement

Calculate and print the total of all student grades and the class average

can be refined as follows:

If the counter is not equal to zero
    Set the average to the total divided by the counter
    Print the total of the grades for all students in the class
    Print the class average
Else
    Print "No grades were entered"

We are careful here to test for the possibility of division by zero—normally a *fatal logic error* that, if undetected, would cause the program to fail (often called *"bombing"* or *"crashing"*). The complete second refinement of the pseudocode for the class-average problem is shown in Fig. 5.11.

Common Programming Error 5.10

An attempt to divide by zero normally causes a fatal runtime error.

Error-Prevention Tip 5.3

When performing division by an expression whose value could be zero, explicitly test for this possibility and handle it appropriately in your program (such as by printing an error message) rather than allowing the fatal error to occur.

In Fig. 5.7 and Fig. 5.11, we include some blank lines and indentation in the pseudocode to make it more readable. The blank lines separate the pseudocode algorithms into their various phases, and the indentation emphasizes the control-statement bodies.

1	*Initialize total to zero*
2	*Initialize counter to zero*
3	
4	*Prompt the user to enter the first grade*
5	*Input the first grade (possibly the sentinel)*
6	
7	*While the user has not yet entered the sentinel*
8	*Add this grade into the running total*
9	*Add one to the grade counter*
10	*Prompt the user to enter the next grade*
11	*Input the next grade (possibly the sentinel)*
12	
13	*If the counter is not equal to zero*
14	*Set the average to the total divided by the counter*
15	*Print the total of the grades for all students in the class*
16	*Print the class average*
17	*Else*
18	*Print "No grades were entered"*

Fig. 5.11 | Class-average problem pseudocode algorithm with sentinel-controlled repetition.

The pseudocode algorithm in Fig. 5.11 solves the more general class-average problem. This algorithm was developed after only two levels of refinement. Sometimes more levels are necessary.

Software Engineering Observation 5.6

Terminate the top-down, stepwise refinement process when the pseudocode algorithm is specified in sufficient detail for you to be able to convert the pseudocode to Visual C++. Normally, implementing the Visual C++ program is then straightforward.

Software Engineering Observation 5.7

Many experienced programmers write programs without ever using program development tools like pseudocode. These programmers feel that their ultimate goal is to solve the problem on a computer and that writing pseudocode merely delays the production of final outputs. Although this method might work for simple and familiar problems, it can lead to serious difficulties in large, complex projects.

Implementing Sentinel-Controlled Repetition in Class *GradeBook*

Figures 5.12 and 5.13 show class GradeBook containing member function determineClassAverage that implements the pseudocode algorithm of Fig. 5.11 (this class is demonstrated in Fig. 5.14). Although each grade entered is an integer, the averaging calculation is likely to produce a number with a decimal point—i.e., a real number or *floating-point number* (e.g., 7.33, 0.0975 or 1000.12345). The type int cannot represent such a number, so this class must use another type to do so. There are several data types for storing floating-point numbers in memory, including *float* and *double*. The primary difference between these types is that, compared to float variables, double variables can typically store numbers with larger magnitude and finer detail (i.e., more digits to the right of the decimal point—also known as the number's *precision*). This program introduces a special operator called a *cast operator* to force the averaging calculation to produce a floating-point numeric result. These features are explained in detail as we discuss the program.

```
 1   // Fig. 5.12: GradeBook.h
 2   // Definition of class GradeBook that determines a class average.
 3   // Member functions are defined in GradeBook.cpp
 4   #include <string> // program uses C++ standard string class
 5   using std::string;
 6
 7   // GradeBook class definition
 8   class GradeBook
 9   {
10   public:
11      GradeBook( string ); // constructor initializes course name
12      void setCourseName( string ); // function to set the course name
13      string getCourseName(); // function to retrieve the course name
14      void displayMessage(); // display a welcome message
15      void determineClassAverage(); // averages grades entered by the user
16   private:
17      string courseName; // course name for this GradeBook
18   }; // end class GradeBook
```

Fig. 5.12 | Class-average problem using sentinel-controlled repetition: GradeBook header file.

```cpp
1   // Fig. 5.13: GradeBook.cpp
2   // Member-function definitions for class GradeBook that solves the
3   // class average program with sentinel-controlled repetition.
4   #include <iostream>
5   using std::cout;
6   using std::cin;
7   using std::endl;
8   using std::fixed; // ensures that decimal point is displayed
9
10  #include <iomanip> // parameterized stream manipulators
11  using std::setprecision; // sets numeric output precision
12
13  // include definition of class GradeBook from GradeBook.h
14  #include "GradeBook.h"
15
16  // constructor initializes courseName with string supplied as argument
17  GradeBook::GradeBook( string name )
18  {
19     setCourseName( name ); // validate and store courseName
20  } // end GradeBook constructor
21
22  // function to set the course name;
23  // ensures that the course name has at most 30 characters
24  void GradeBook::setCourseName( string name )
25  {
26     if ( name.length() <= 30 ) // if name has 30 or fewer characters
27        courseName = name; // store the course name in the object
28     else // if name is longer than 30 characters
29     { // set courseName to first 30 characters of parameter name
30        courseName = name.substr( 0, 30 ); // select first 30 characters
31        cout << "Name \"" << name << "\" exceeds maximum length (30).\n"
32           << "Limiting courseName to first 30 characters.\n" << endl;
33     } // end if...else
34  } // end function setCourseName
35
36  // function to retrieve the course name
37  string GradeBook::getCourseName()
38  {
39     return courseName;
40  } // end function getCourseName
41
42  // display a welcome message to the GradeBook user
43  void GradeBook::displayMessage()
44  {
45     cout << "Welcome to the grade book for\n" << getCourseName() << "!\n"
46        << endl;
47  } // end function displayMessage
48
49  // determine class average based on 10 grades entered by user
50  void GradeBook::determineClassAverage()
51  {
```

Fig. 5.13 | Class-average problem using sentinel-controlled repetition: GradeBook source-code file. (Part 1 of 2.)

```
52    int total; // sum of grades entered by user
53    int gradeCounter; // number of grades entered
54    int grade; // grade value
55    double average; // number with decimal point for average
56
57    // initialization phase
58    total = 0; // initialize total
59    gradeCounter = 0; // initialize loop counter
60
61    // processing phase
62    // prompt for input and read grade from user
63    cout << "Enter grade or -1 to quit: ";
64    cin >> grade; // input grade or sentinel value
65
66    // loop until sentinel value read from user
67    while ( grade != -1 ) // while grade is not -1
68    {
69        total = total + grade; // add grade to total
70        gradeCounter = gradeCounter + 1; // increment counter
71
72        // prompt for input and read next grade from user
73        cout << "Enter grade or -1 to quit: ";
74        cin >> grade; // input grade or sentinel value
75    } // end while
76
77    // termination phase
78    if ( gradeCounter != 0 ) // if user entered at least one grade...
79    {
80        // calculate average of all grades entered
81        average = static_cast< double >( total ) / gradeCounter;
82
83        // display total and average (with two digits of precision)
84        cout << "\nTotal of all " << gradeCounter << " grades entered is "
85            << total << endl;
86        cout << "Class average is " << setprecision( 2 ) << fixed << average
87            << endl;
88    } // end if
89    else // no grades were entered, so output appropriate message
90        cout << "No grades were entered" << endl;
91 } // end function determineClassAverage
```

Fig. 5.13 | Class-average problem using sentinel-controlled repetition: GradeBook source-code file. (Part 2 of 2.)

In this example, we see that control statements can be stacked on top of one another (in sequence) just as a child stacks building blocks. The while statement (lines 67–75 of Fig. 5.13) is immediately followed by an if...else statement (lines 78–90) in sequence. Much of the code in this program is identical to the code in Fig. 5.9, so we concentrate on the new features and issues.

Line 55 declares the double variable average. Recall that we used an int variable in the preceding example to store the class average. Using type double in the current example

```
1   // Fig. 5.14: GradeBookTest.cpp
2   // Create GradeBook object and invoke its determineClassAverage function.
3
4   // include definition of class GradeBook from GradeBook.h
5   #include "GradeBook.h"
6
7   int main()
8   {
9      // create GradeBook object myGradeBook and
10     // pass course name to constructor
11     GradeBook myGradeBook( "CS101 Visual C++ Programming" );
12
13     myGradeBook.displayMessage(); // display welcome message
14     myGradeBook.determineClassAverage(); // find average of 10 grades
15     return 0; // indicate successful termination
16  } // end main
```

```
Welcome to the grade book for
CS101 Visual C++ Programming

Enter grade or -1 to quit: 97
Enter grade or -1 to quit: 88
Enter grade or -1 to quit: 72
Enter grade or -1 to quit: -1

Total of all 3 grades entered is 257
Class average is 85.67
```

Fig. 5.14 | Class-average problem using sentinel-controlled repetition: Creating an object of class GradeBook (Figs. 5.12–5.13) and invoking its determineClassAverage member function.

allows us to store the class-average calculation's result as a floating-point number. Line 59 initializes the variable gradeCounter to 0, because no grades have been entered yet. Remember that this program uses sentinel-controlled repetition. To keep an accurate record of the number of grades entered, the program increments variable gradeCounter only when the user enters a valid grade value (i.e., not the sentinel value) and the program completes the processing of the grade. Finally, notice that both input statements (lines 64 and 74) are preceded by an output statement that prompts the user for input.

Good Programming Practice 5.8

Prompt the user for each keyboard input. The prompt should indicate the form of the input and any special input values. For example, in a sentinel-controlled loop, the prompts requesting data entry should explicitly remind the user what the sentinel value is.

Program Logic for Sentinel-Controlled Repetition vs. Counter-Controlled Repetition

Compare the program logic for sentinel-controlled repetition in this application with that for counter-controlled repetition in Fig. 5.9. In counter-controlled repetition, each iteration of the while statement (lines 57–63 of Fig. 5.9) reads a value from the user, for the specified number of iterations. In sentinel-controlled repetition, the program reads the first value (lines 63–64 of Fig. 5.13) before reaching the `while`. This value determines whether the program's flow of control should enter the body of the `while`. If the condition of the `while` is false, the user entered the sentinel value, so the body of the `while` does not execute (i.e., no grades were entered). If, on the other hand, the condition is true, the body begins execution, and the loop adds the `grade` value to the `total` (line 69). Then lines 73–74 in the loop's body prompt for and input the next value from the user. Next, program control reaches the closing right brace (}) of the body in line 75, so execution continues with the test of the `while`'s condition (line 67). The condition uses the most recent `grade` input by the user to determine whether the loop's body should execute again. Note that the value of variable `grade` is always input from the user immediately before the program tests the `while` condition. This allows the program to determine whether the value just input is the sentinel value *before* the program processes that value (i.e., adds it to the `total` and increments `gradeCounter`). If the sentinel value is input, the loop terminates, and the program does not add –1 to the `total`.

After the loop terminates, the `if...else` statement in lines 78–90 executes. The condition in line 78 determines whether any grades were entered. If none were, the `else` part (lines 89–90) of the `if...else` statement executes and displays the message "No grades were entered" and the member function returns control to the calling function.

Notice the block in the `while` loop in Fig. 5.13. Without the braces, the last three statements in the body of the loop would fall outside the loop, causing the computer to interpret this code incorrectly, as follows:

```
// loop until sentinel value read from user
while ( grade != -1 )
   total = total + grade; // add grade to total
gradeCounter = gradeCounter + 1; // increment counter

// prompt for input and read next grade from user
cout << "Enter grade or -1 to quit: ";
cin >> grade;
```

This would cause an infinite loop in the program if the user did not input –1 for the first grade (in line 64).

Common Programming Error 5.11

Omitting the braces that delimit a block can lead to logic errors, such as infinite loops. To prevent this problem, some programmers enclose the body of every control statement in braces, even if the body contains only a single statement.

Floating-Point Number Precision and Memory Requirements

Variables of type `float` represent *single-precision floating-point numbers* and have seven significant digits on most 32-bit systems. Variables of type `double` represent *double-precision floating-point numbers*. These require twice as much memory as `float` variables and provide 15 significant digits on most 32-bit systems—approximately double the precision of `float` variables. For the range of values required by most programs, variables of type `float` should suffice, but you can use `double` to "play it safe." In some programs, even variables of type `double` will be inadequate—such programs are beyond the scope of this book. Most programmers represent floating-point numbers with type `double`. In fact, Visual C++ treats all floating-point numbers you type in a program's source code (such as

7.33 and 0.0975) as double values by default. Such values in the source code are known as *floating-point constants*. See Appendix C, Fundamental Types, for the ranges of values for floats and doubles.

Floating-point numbers often arise as a result of division. In conventional arithmetic, when we divide 10 by 3, the result is 3.3333333..., with the sequence of 3s repeating infinitely. The computer allocates only a fixed amount of space to hold such a value, so clearly the stored floating-point value can be only an approximation.

Common Programming Error 5.12

Using floating-point numbers in a manner that assumes they are represented exactly (e.g., using them in comparisons for equality) can lead to incorrect results. Floating-point numbers are represented only approximately by most computers.

Although floating-point numbers are not always 100 percent precise, they have numerous applications. For example, when we speak of a "normal" body temperature of 98.6, we do not need to be precise to a large number of digits. When we read the temperature on a thermometer as 98.6, it may actually be 98.5999473210643. Calling this number simply 98.6 is fine for most applications involving body temperatures. Due to the imprecise nature of floating-point numbers, type double is preferred over type float, because double variables can represent floating-point numbers more accurately. For this reason, we use type double throughout the book.

Converting Between Fundamental Types Explicitly and Implicitly
The variable average is declared to be of type double (line 55 of Fig. 5.13) to capture the fractional result of our calculation. However, total and gradeCounter are both integer variables. Recall that dividing two integers results in integer division, in which any fractional part of the calculation is lost (i.e., *truncated*). In the following statement:

```
average = total / gradeCounter;
```

the division calculation is performed first, so the fractional part of the result is lost before it is assigned to average. To perform a floating-point calculation with integer values, we must create temporary values that are floating-point numbers for the calculation. Visual C++ provides the *unary cast operator* to accomplish this task. Line 81 uses the cast operator static_cast< double >(total) to create a *temporary* floating-point copy of its operand in parentheses—total. Using a cast operator in this manner is called *explicit conversion*. The value stored in total is still an integer.

The calculation now consists of a floating-point value (the temporary double version of total) divided by the integer gradeCounter. The Visual C++ compiler knows how to evaluate only expressions in which the data types of the operands are identical. To ensure that the operands are of the same type, the compiler performs an operation called *promotion* (also called *implicit conversion*) on selected operands. For example, in an expression containing values of data types int and double, Visual C++ *promotes* int operands to double values. In our example, we are treating total as a double (by using the unary cast operator), so the compiler promotes gradeCounter to double, allowing the calculation to be performed—the result of the floating-point division is assigned to average. In Chapter 7, Functions and an Introduction to Recursion, we discuss all the fundamental data types and their order of promotion.

Common Programming Error 5.13

The cast operator can be used to convert between fundamental numeric types, such as int *and* double, *and between related class types (as we discuss in Chapter 14, Object-Oriented Programming: Polymorphism). Casting to the wrong type may cause compilation errors or runtime errors.*

Cast operators are available for use with every data type and with class types as well. The static_cast operator is formed by following keyword static_cast with angle brackets (< and >) around a data-type name. The cast operator is a *unary operator*—an operator that takes only one operand. In Chapter 3, we studied the binary arithmetic operators. Visual C++ also supports unary versions of the plus (+) and minus (-) operators, so that you can write such expressions as -7 or +5. Cast operators have higher precedence than other unary operators, such as unary + and unary -. This precedence is higher than that of the *multiplicative operators* *, / and %, and lower than that of parentheses. We indicate the cast operator with the notation static_cast< *type* >() in our precedence charts (see, for example, Fig. 5.22).

Formatting for Floating-Point Numbers

The formatting capabilities in Fig. 5.13 are discussed here briefly and explained in depth in Chapter 17, Stream Input/Output and Files. The call to *setprecision* in line 86 (with an argument of 2) indicates that double variable average should be printed with two digits of *precision* to the right of the decimal point (e.g., 92.37). This call is referred to as a *parameterized stream manipulator* (because of the 2 in parentheses). Programs that use these calls must contain the preprocessor directive (line 10)

    #include <iomanip>

Line 11 specifies the name from the <iomanip> header file that is used in this program. Note that endl is a *nonparameterized stream manipulator* (because it is not followed by a value or expression in parentheses) and does not require the <iomanip> header file. If the precision is not specified, floating-point values are normally output with six digits of precision (i.e., the *default precision* on most 32-bit systems today), although we'll see an exception to this in a moment.

The stream manipulator *fixed* (line 86) indicates that floating-point values should be output in so-called *fixed-point format*, as opposed to *scientific notation*. Scientific notation is a way of displaying a number as a floating-point number between the values of 1.0 and 10.0, multiplied by a power of 10. For instance, the value 3,100.0 would be displayed in scientific notation as 3.100000 E+003. Scientific notation is useful when displaying values that are very large or very small. Formatting using scientific notation is discussed further in Chapter 17. Fixed-point formatting, on the other hand, is used to force a floating-point number to display a specific number of digits. Specifying fixed-point formatting also forces the decimal point and trailing zeros to print, even if the value is a whole-number amount, such as 88.00. Without the fixed-point formatting option, such a value prints in Visual C++ as 88 without the trailing zeros and without the decimal point. When the stream manipulators fixed and setprecision are used in a program, the printed value is *rounded* to the number of decimal positions indicated by the value passed to setprecision (e.g., the value 2 in line 86), although the value in memory remains unaltered. For example, the values 87.946 and 67.543 are output as 87.95 and 67.54, respectively. Note that it also is possible to force a decimal point to appear by using stream manipulator *showpoint*. If showpoint is specified without fixed, then trailing zeros will not print. Like endl, stream manipulators fixed and showpoint are nonparameterized and do not require the <iomanip> header file. Both can be found in header <iostream>.

Lines 86 and 87 of Fig. 5.13 output the class average. In this example, we display the class average rounded to the nearest hundredth and output it with exactly two digits to the right of the decimal point. The parameterized stream manipulator (line 86) indicates that variable average's value should be displayed with two digits of precision to the right of the decimal point—indicated by setprecision(2). The three grades entered during the sample execution of the program in Fig. 5.14 total 257, which yields the average 85.666666.... The parameterized stream manipulator setprecision causes the value to be rounded to the specified number of digits. In this program, the average is rounded to the hundredths position and displayed as 85.67.

5.10 Formulating Algorithms: Nested Control Statements

For the next example, we once again formulate an algorithm by using pseudocode and top-down, stepwise refinement, and write a corresponding Visual C++ program. We have seen that control statements can be stacked on top of one another (in sequence) just as a child stacks building blocks. In this case study, we examine the only other structured way control statements can be connected, namely, by *nesting* one control statement within another.

Consider the following problem statement:

> *A college offers a course that prepares students for the state licensing exam for real estate brokers. Last year, ten of the students who completed this course took the exam. The college wants to know how well its students did on the exam. You have been asked to write a program to summarize the results. You have been given a list of these 10 students. Next to each name is written a 1 if the student passed the exam or a 2 if the student failed.*
>
> *Your program should analyze the results of the exam as follows:*
>
> 1. *Input each test result (i.e., a 1 or a 2). Display the prompting message "Enter result" each time the program requests another test result.*
>
> 2. *Count the number of test results of each type.*
>
> 3. *Display a summary of the test results indicating the number of students who passed and the number who failed.*
>
> 4. *If more than eight students passed the exam, print the message "Raise tuition."*

After reading the problem statement carefully, we make the following observations:

1. The program must process test results for 10 students. A counter-controlled loop can be used because the number of test results is known in advance.

2. Each test result is a number—either a 1 or a 2. Each time the program reads a test result, the program must determine whether the number is a 1 or a 2. We test for a 1 in our algorithm. If the number is not a 1, we assume that it is a 2. (Exercise 5.20 considers the consequences of this assumption.)

3. Two counters are used to keep track of the exam results—one to count the number of students who passed the exam and one to count the number of students who failed the exam.

4. After the program has processed all the results, it must decide whether more than eight students passed the exam.

Let us proceed with top-down, stepwise refinement. We begin with a pseudocode representation of the top:

Analyze exam results and decide whether tuition should be raised

Once again, it is important to emphasize that the top is a *complete* representation of the program, but several refinements are likely to be needed before the pseudocode evolves naturally into a Visual C++ program.

Our first refinement is

Initialize variables
Input the 10 exam results, and count passes and failures
Print a summary of the exam results and decide if tuition should be raised

Here, too, even though we have a complete representation of the entire program, further refinement is necessary. We now commit to specific variables. Counters are needed to record the passes and failures, a counter will be used to control the looping process and a variable is needed to store the user input. The last variable is not initialized, because its value is read from the user during each iteration of the loop.

The pseudocode statement

Initialize variables

can be refined as follows:

Initialize passes to zero
Initialize failures to zero
Initialize student counter to one

Notice that only the counters are initialized at the start of the algorithm.

The pseudocode statement

Input the 10 exam results, and count passes and failures

requires a loop that successively inputs the result of each exam. Here it is known in advance that there are precisely 10 exam results, so counter-controlled looping is appropriate. Inside the loop (i.e., *nested* within the loop), an `if...else` statement will determine whether each exam result is a pass or a failure and will increment the appropriate counter. The refinement of the preceding pseudocode statement is then

While student counter is less than or equal to 10
    Prompt the user to enter the next exam result
    Input the next exam result

    If the student passed
        Add one to passes
    Else
        Add one to failures

    Add one to student counter

We use blank lines to isolate the *If...Else* control structure, which improves readability.

The pseudocode statement

Print a summary of the exam results and decide whether tuition should be raised

can be refined as follows:

Print the number of passes
Print the number of failures

If more than eight students passed
Print "Raise tuition"

The complete second refinement appears in Fig. 5.15. Notice that blank lines are also used to set off the *While* structure for program readability. This pseudocode is now sufficiently refined for conversion to Visual C++.

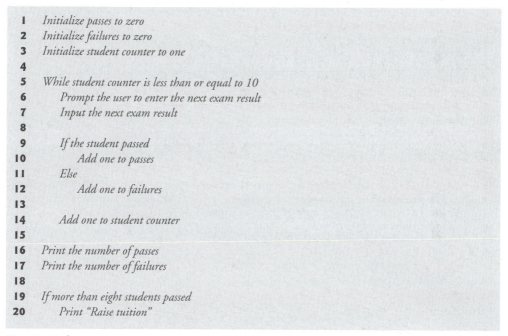

1	*Initialize passes to zero*
2	*Initialize failures to zero*
3	*Initialize student counter to one*
4	
5	*While student counter is less than or equal to 10*
6	*Prompt the user to enter the next exam result*
7	*Input the next exam result*
8	
9	*If the student passed*
10	*Add one to passes*
11	*Else*
12	*Add one to failures*
13	
14	*Add one to student counter*
15	
16	*Print the number of passes*
17	*Print the number of failures*
18	
19	*If more than eight students passed*
20	*Print "Raise tuition"*

Fig. 5.15 | Pseudocode for examination-results problem.

Conversion to Class Analysis

The Visual C++ class, Analysis, that implements the pseudocode algorithm is shown in Figs. 5.16–5.17, and two sample executions appear in Fig. 5.18.

Lines 16–18 of Fig. 5.17 declare the variables that member function processExamResults of class Analysis uses to process the examination results. Note that we have taken advantage of a feature of Visual C++ that allows variable initialization to be incorporated into declarations (passes is initialized to 0, failures is initialized to 0 and studentCounter is initialized to 1). Looping programs may require initialization at the beginning of each repetition; such reinitialization normally would be performed by assignment statements rather than in declarations or by moving the declarations inside the loop bodies.

```
1   // Fig. 5.16: Analysis.h
2   // Definition of class Analysis that analyzes examination results.
3   // Member function is defined in Analysis.cpp
4
5   // Analysis class definition
6   class Analysis
7   {
8   public:
9      void processExamResults(); // process 10 students' examination results
10  }; // end class Analysis
```

Fig. 5.16 | Examination-results problem: `Analysis` header file.

```
1   // Fig. 5.17: Analysis.cpp
2   // Member-function definitions for class Analysis that
3   // analyzes examination results.
4   #include <iostream>
5   using std::cout;
6   using std::cin;
7   using std::endl;
8
9   // include definition of class Analysis from Analysis.h
10  #include "Analysis.h"
11
12  // process the examination results of 10 students
13  void Analysis::processExamResults()
14  {
15     // initializing variables in declarations
16     int passes = 0; // number of passes
17     int failures = 0; // number of failures
18     int studentCounter = 1; // student counter
19     int result; // one exam result (1 = pass, 2 = fail)
20
21     // process 10 students using counter-controlled loop
22     while ( studentCounter <= 10 )
23     {
24        // prompt user for input and obtain value from user
25        cout << "Enter result (1 = pass, 2 = fail): ";
26        cin >> result; // input result
27
28        // if...else nested in while
29        if ( result == 1 )            // if result is 1,
30           passes = passes + 1;       // increment passes;
31        else                          // else result is not 1, so
32           failures = failures + 1;   // increment failures
33
34        // increment studentCounter so loop eventually terminates
35        studentCounter = studentCounter + 1;
36     } // end while
37
```

Fig. 5.17 | Examination-results problem: Nested control statements in `Analysis` source-code file. (Part 1 of 2.)

```
38      // termination phase; display number of passes and failures
39      cout << "Passed " << passes << "\nFailed " << failures << endl;
40
41      // determine whether more than eight students passed
42      if ( passes > 8 )
43         cout << "Raise tuition " << endl;
44   } // end function processExamResults
```

Fig. 5.17 | Examination-results problem: Nested control statements in `Analysis` source-code file. (Part 2 of 2.)

```
1    // Fig. 5.18: AnalysisTest.cpp
2    // Test program for class Analysis.
3    #include "Analysis.h" // include definition of class Analysis
4
5    int main()
6    {
7       Analysis application; // create Analysis object
8       application.processExamResults(); // call function to process results
9       return 0; // indicate successful termination
10   } // end main
```

```
Enter result (1 = pass, 2 = fail): 1
Enter result (1 = pass, 2 = fail): 1
Enter result (1 = pass, 2 = fail): 1
Enter result (1 = pass, 2 = fail): 1
Enter result (1 = pass, 2 = fail): 2
Enter result (1 = pass, 2 = fail): 1
Enter result (1 = pass, 2 = fail): 1
Enter result (1 = pass, 2 = fail): 1
Enter result (1 = pass, 2 = fail): 1
Enter result (1 = pass, 2 = fail): 1
Passed 9
Failed 1
Raise tuition
```

```
Enter result (1 = pass, 2 = fail): 1
Enter result (1 = pass, 2 = fail): 2
Enter result (1 = pass, 2 = fail): 2
Enter result (1 = pass, 2 = fail): 1
Enter result (1 = pass, 2 = fail): 1
Enter result (1 = pass, 2 = fail): 1
Enter result (1 = pass, 2 = fail): 2
Enter result (1 = pass, 2 = fail): 1
Enter result (1 = pass, 2 = fail): 1
Enter result (1 = pass, 2 = fail): 2
Passed 6
Failed 4
```

Fig. 5.18 | Test program for class `Analysis`.

The `while` statement (lines 22–36) loops 10 times. During each iteration, the loop inputs and processes one exam result. Notice that the `if...else` statement (lines 29–32) for processing each result is nested in the `while` statement. If the `result` is 1, the `if...else` statement increments `passes`; otherwise, it assumes the `result` is 2 and increments `failures`. Line 35 increments `studentCounter` before the loop condition is tested again in line 22. After 10 values have been input, the loop terminates and line 39 displays the number of `passes` and the number of `failures`. The `if` statement in lines 42–43 determines whether more than eight students passed the exam and, if so, outputs the message `"Raise Tuition"`.

Demonstrating Class `Analysis`

Figure 5.18 creates an `Analysis` object (line 7) and invokes the object's `processExamResults` member function (line 8) to process a set of exam results entered by the user. Figure 5.18 shows the input and output from two sample executions of the program. At the end of the first sample execution, the condition in line 42 of member function `processExamResults` in Fig. 5.17 is true—more than eight students passed the exam, so the program outputs a message indicating that the tuition should be raised.

5.11 Assignment Operators

Visual C++ provides several *assignment operators* for abbreviating assignment expressions. For example, the statement

        c = c + 3;

can be abbreviated with the *addition assignment operator* += as

        c += 3;

The += operator adds the value of the expression on the right of the operator to the value of the variable on the left of the operator and stores the result in the variable on the left of the operator. Any statement of the form

        variable = variable operator expression;

in which the same *variable* appears on both sides of the assignment operator and *operator* is one of the binary operators +, -, *, /, or % (or others we'll discuss later in the text), can be written in the form

        variable operator= expression;

Thus the assignment c += 3 adds 3 to c. Figure 5.19 shows the arithmetic assignment operators, sample expressions using these operators and explanations.

Assignment operator	Sample expression	Explanation	Assigns
Assume: **int** c = 3, d = 5, e = 4, f = 6, g = 12;			
+=	c += 7	c = c + 7	10 to c
-=	d -= 4	d = d - 4	1 to d
*=	e *= 5	e = e * 5	20 to e

Fig. 5.19 | Arithmetic assignment operators. (Part 1 of 2.)

Assignment operator	Sample expression	Explanation	Assigns
/=	f /= 3	f = f / 3	2 to f
%=	g %= 9	g = g % 9	3 to g

Fig. 5.19 | Arithmetic assignment operators. (Part 2 of 2.)

5.12 Increment and Decrement Operators

In addition to the arithmetic assignment operators, Visual C++ also provides two unary operators for adding 1 to or subtracting 1 from the value of a numeric variable. These are the unary *increment operator*, ++, and the unary *decrement operator*, --, which are summarized in Fig. 5.20. A program can increment by 1 the value of a variable called c using the increment operator, ++, rather than the expression c = c + 1 or c += 1. An increment or decrement operator that is prefixed to (placed before) a variable is referred to as the *prefix increment* or *prefix decrement operator*, respectively. An increment or decrement operator that is postfixed to (placed after) a variable is referred to as the *postfix increment* or *postfix decrement operator*, respectively.

Using the prefix increment (or decrement) operator to add (or subtract) 1 from a variable is known as *preincrementing* (or *predecrementing*) the variable. Preincrementing (or predecrementing) causes the variable to be incremented (decremented) by 1, then the new value of the variable is used in the expression in which it appears. Using the postfix increment (or decrement) operator to add (or subtract) 1 from a variable is known as *postincrementing* (or *postdecrementing*) the variable. Postincrementing (or postdecrementing) causes the current value of the variable to be used in the expression in which it appears; then the variable's value is incremented (decremented) by 1.

 Good Programming Practice 5.9

Unlike binary operators, the unary increment and decrement operators should be placed next to their operands, with no intervening spaces.

Operator	Called	Sample expression	Explanation
++	preincrement	++a	Increment a by 1, then use the new value of a in the expression in which a resides.
++	postincrement	a++	Use the current value of a in the expression in which a resides, then increment a by 1.
--	predecrement	--b	Decrement b by 1, then use the new value of b in the expression in which b resides.
--	postdecrement	b--	Use the current value of b in the expression in which b resides, then decrement b by 1.

Fig. 5.20 | Increment and decrement operators.

Figure 5.21 demonstrates the difference between the prefix increment and postfix increment versions of the ++ increment operator. The decrement operator (--) works similarly. Note that this example does not contain a class, but just a source-code file with function main performing all the application's work. In this chapter and in Chapter 4, you have seen examples consisting of one class (including the header and source-code files for this class), as well as another source-code file testing the class. This source-code file contained function main, which created an object of the class and called its member functions. In this example, we simply want to show the mechanics of the ++ operator, so we use only one source-code file with function main. Occasionally, when it does not make sense to try to create a reusable class to demonstrate a simple concept, we'll use a mechanical example contained entirely within the main function of a single source-code file.

Line 12 initializes the variable c to 5, and line 13 outputs c's initial value. Line 14 outputs the value of the expression c++. This expression postincrements the variable c, so c's original value (5) is output, then c's value is incremented. Thus, line 14 outputs c's initial value (5) again. Line 15 outputs c's new value (6) to prove that the variable's value was indeed incremented in line 14.

```cpp
1   // Fig. 5.21: IncrementOperators.cpp
2   // Preincrementing and postincrementing.
3   #include <iostream>
4   using std::cout;
5   using std::endl;
6
7   int main()
8   {
9      int c;
10
11     // demonstrate postincrement
12     c = 5; // assign 5 to c
13     cout << c << endl; // print 5
14     cout << c++ << endl; // print 5 then postincrement
15     cout << c << endl; // print 6
16
17     cout << endl; // skip a line
18
19     // demonstrate preincrement
20     c = 5; // assign 5 to c
21     cout << c << endl; // print 5
22     cout << ++c << endl; // preincrement then print 6
23     cout << c << endl; // print 6
24     return 0; // indicate successful termination
25  } // end main
```

```
5
5
6

5
6
6
```

Fig. 5.21 | Preincrementing and postincrementing.

Line 20 resets c's value to 5, and line 21 outputs that value. Line 22 outputs the value of the expression ++c. This expression preincrements c, so its value is incremented, then the new value (6) is output. Line 23 outputs c's value again to show that the value of c is still 6 after line 22 executes.

The arithmetic assignment operators and the increment and decrement operators can be used to simplify program statements. The three assignment statements in Fig. 5.17

```
passes = passes + 1;
failures = failures + 1;
studentCounter = studentCounter + 1;
```

can be written more concisely with assignment operators as

```
passes += 1;
failures += 1;
studentCounter += 1;
```

with prefix increment operators as

```
++passes;
++failures;
++studentCounter;
```

or with postfix increment operators as

```
passes++;
failures++;
studentCounter++;
```

Note that, when incrementing (++) or decrementing (--) of a variable occurs in a statement by itself, the preincrement and postincrement forms have the same effect, and the predecrement and postdecrement forms have the same effect. It is only when a variable appears in the context of a larger expression that preincrementing the variable and postincrementing the variable have different effects (and similarly for predecrementing and postdecrementing).

Common Programming Error 5.14

Attempting to use the increment or decrement operator on an expression other than a modifiable variable name or reference, e.g., writing ++(x + 1), is a syntax error.

Figure 5.22 shows the precedence and associativity of the operators introduced to this point. The operators are shown top-to-bottom in decreasing order of precedence. The

Operators			Associativity	Type
::			left to right	scope resolution
()			left to right	parentheses
++	--	static_cast< *type* >()	left to right	unary (postfix)
++	--	+ -	right to left	unary (prefix)

Fig. 5.22 | Operator precedence for the operators encountered so far in the text. (Part 1 of 2.)

Operators						Associativity	Type
*	/	%				left to right	multiplicative
+	-					left to right	additive
<<	>>					left to right	insertion/extraction
<	<=	>	>=			left to right	relational
==	!=					left to right	equality
?:						right to left	conditional
=	+=	-=	*=	/=	%=	right to left	assignment

Fig. 5.22 | Operator precedence for the operators encountered so far in the text. (Part 2 of 2.)

second column indicates the associativity of the operators at each level of precedence. Notice that the conditional operator (?:), the unary operators preincrement (++), predecrement (--), plus (+) and minus (-), and the assignment operators =, +=, -=, *=, /= and %= associate from right to left. All other operators in the operator precedence chart of Fig. 5.22 associate from left to right. The third column names the various groups of operators.

5.13 (Optional) Software Engineering Case Study: Identifying Class Attributes in the ATM System

In Section 4.13, we began the first stage of an object-oriented design (OOD) for our ATM system—analyzing the requirements specification and identifying the classes needed to implement the system. We listed the nouns and noun phrases in the requirements specification and identified a separate class for each one that plays a significant role in the ATM system. We then modeled the classes and their relationships in a UML class diagram (Fig. 4.27). Classes have attributes (data) and operations (behaviors). Class attributes are implemented in Visual C++ programs as data members, and class operations are implemented as member functions. In this section, we determine many of the attributes needed in the ATM system. In Chapter 6, we examine how these attributes represent an object's state. In Chapter 7, we determine class operations.

Identifying Attributes
Consider the attributes of some real-world objects: A person's attributes include height, weight and whether the person is left-handed, right-handed or ambidextrous. A radio's attributes include its station setting, its volume setting and its AM or FM setting. A car's attributes include its speedometer and odometer readings, the amount of gas in its tank and what gear it is in. A personal computer's attributes include its manufacturer (e.g., Dell, Sun, Apple or IBM), type of screen (e.g., LCD or CRT), main memory size and hard disk size.

We can identify many attributes of the classes in our system by looking for descriptive words and phrases in the requirements specification. For each one we find that plays a significant role in the ATM system, we create an attribute and assign it to one or more of the classes identified in Section 4.13. We also create attributes to represent any additional data that a class may need, as such needs become apparent throughout the design process.

Figure 5.23 lists the words or phrases from the requirements specification that describe each class. We formed this list by reading the requirements specification and identifying any words or phrases that refer to characteristics of the classes in the system. For example, the requirements specification describes the steps taken to obtain a "withdrawal amount," so we list "amount" next to class Withdrawal.

Figure 5.23 leads us to create one attribute of class ATM. Class ATM maintains information about the state of the ATM. The phrase "user is authenticated" describes a state of the ATM (we introduce states in Section 6.11), so we include userAuthenticated as a Boolean *attribute* (i.e., an attribute that has a value of either true or false). The UML Boolean type is equivalent to the bool type in Visual C++. This attribute indicates whether the ATM has successfully authenticated the current user—userAuthenticated must be true for the system to allow the user to perform transactions and access account information. This attribute helps ensure the security of the data in the system.

Classes BalanceInquiry, Withdrawal and Deposit share one attribute. Each transaction involves an "account number" that corresponds to the account of the user making the transaction. We assign an integer attribute accountNumber to each transaction class to identify the account to which an object of the class applies.

Descriptive words and phrases in the requirements specification also suggest some differences in the attributes required by each transaction class. The requirements specification indicates that to withdraw cash or deposit funds, users must enter a specific "amount" of money to be withdrawn or deposited, respectively. Thus, we assign to classes Withdrawal and Deposit an attribute amount to store the value supplied by the user. The

Class	Descriptive words and phrases
ATM	user is authenticated
BalanceInquiry	account number
Withdrawal	account number amount
Deposit	account number amount
BankDatabase	[no descriptive words or phrases]
Account	account number PIN balance
Screen	[no descriptive words or phrases]
Keypad	[no descriptive words or phrases]
CashDispenser	begins each day loaded with 500 $20 bills
DepositSlot	[no descriptive words or phrases]

Fig. 5.23 | Descriptive words and phrases from the ATM requirements.

amounts of money related to a withdrawal and a deposit are defining characteristics of these transactions that the system requires for them to take place. Class `BalanceInquiry`, however, needs no additional data to perform its task—it requires only an account number to indicate the account whose balance should be retrieved.

Class `Account` has several attributes. The requirements specification states that each bank account has an "account number" and "PIN," which the system uses for identifying accounts and authenticating users. We assign to class `Account` two integer attributes: `accountNumber` and `pin`. The requirements specification also specifies that an account maintains a "balance" of the amount of money in the account and that money the user deposits does not become available for a withdrawal until the bank verifies the amount of cash in the deposit envelope, and any checks in the envelope clear. An account must still record the amount of money that a user deposits, however. Therefore, we decide that an account should represent a balance using two attributes of UML type `Double`: `availableBalance` and `totalBalance`. Attribute `availableBalance` tracks the amount of money that a user can withdraw from the account. Attribute `totalBalance` refers to the total amount of money that the user has "on deposit" (i.e., the amount of money available, plus the amount waiting to be verified or cleared). For example, suppose an ATM user deposits $50.00 into an empty account. The `totalBalance` attribute would increase to $50.00 to record the deposit, but the `availableBalance` would remain at $0. [*Note:* We assume that the bank updates the `availableBalance` attribute of an `Account` soon after the ATM transaction occurs, in response to confirming that $50 worth of cash or checks was found in the deposit envelope. We assume that this update occurs through a transaction that a bank employee performs using some piece of bank software other than the ATM. Thus, we do not discuss this transaction in our case study.]

Class `CashDispenser` has one attribute. The requirements specification states that the cash dispenser "begins each day loaded with 500 $20 bills." The cash dispenser must keep track of the number of bills it contains to determine whether enough cash is on hand to satisfy withdrawal requests. We assign to class `CashDispenser` an integer attribute `count`, which is initially set to 500.

For real problems in industry, there is no guarantee that requirements specifications will be rich enough and precise enough for the object-oriented systems designer to determine all the attributes or even all the classes. The need for additional (or fewer) classes, attributes and behaviors may become clear as the design process proceeds. As we progress through this case study, we too will continue to add, modify and delete information about the classes in our system.

Modeling Attributes

The class diagram in Fig. 5.24 lists some of the attributes for the classes in our system—the descriptive words and phrases in Fig. 5.23 helped us identify these attributes. For simplicity, Fig. 5.24 does not show the associations among classes—we showed these in Fig. 4.27. This is a common practice of systems designers when designs are being developed. Recall from Section 4.13 that in the UML, a class's attributes are placed in the middle compartment of the class's rectangle. We list each attribute's name and type separated by a colon (:), followed in some cases by an equal sign (=) and an initial value.

Consider the `userAuthenticated` attribute of class `ATM`:

```
userAuthenticated : Boolean = false
```

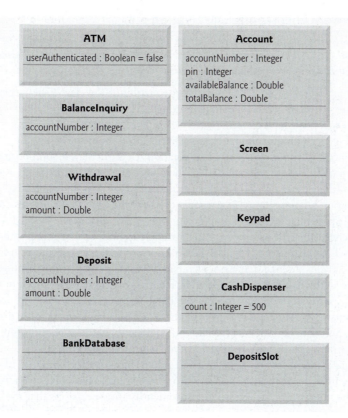

Fig. 5.24 | Classes with attributes.

This attribute declaration contains three pieces of information. The ***attribute name*** is userAuthenticated. The ***attribute type*** is Boolean. In Visual C++, an attribute can be represented by a fundamental type, such as bool, int or double, or a class type—as discussed in Chapter 4. We modeled only primitive-type attributes in Fig. 5.24—we discuss the reasoning behind this decision shortly. [*Note:* Figure 5.24 lists UML data types for the attributes. When we implement the system, we'll associate the UML types Boolean, Integer and Double with the Visual C++ fundamental types bool, int and double, respectively.]

We can also indicate an initial value for an attribute. The userAuthenticated attribute in class ATM has an initial value of false. This indicates that the system initially does not consider the user to be authenticated. If an attribute has no initial value specified, only its name and type (separated by a colon) are shown. For example, the accountNumber attribute of class BalanceInquiry is an Integer. Here we show no initial value, because the value of this attribute is a number that we do not yet know—it will be determined at execution time based on the account number entered by the current ATM user.

Figure 5.24 does not include any attributes for classes Screen, Keypad and DepositSlot. These are important components of our system, for which our design process simply has not yet revealed any attributes. We may still discover some, however, in the remaining design phases or when we implement these classes in Visual C++. This is perfectly normal for the iterative process of software engineering.

Software Engineering Observation 5.8

At early stages in the design process, classes often lack attributes (and operations). Such classes should not be eliminated, however, because attributes (and operations) may become evident in the later phases of design and implementation.

Note that Fig. 5.24 also does not include attributes for class BankDatabase. Recall from Chapter 4 that in Visual C++, attributes can be represented by either fundamental types or class types. We have chosen to include only fundamental-type attributes in the class diagram in Fig. 5.24 (and in similar class diagrams throughout the case study). A class-type attribute is modeled more clearly as an association (in particular, a composition) between the class with the attribute and the class of the object of which the attribute is an instance. For example, the class diagram in Fig. 4.27 indicates that class BankDatabase participates in a composition relationship with zero or more Account objects. From this composition, we can determine that when we implement the ATM system in Visual C++, we'll be required to create an attribute of class BankDatabase to hold zero or more Account objects. Similarly, we'll assign attributes to class ATM that correspond to its composition relationships with classes Screen, Keypad, CashDispenser and DepositSlot. These composition-based attributes would be redundant if modeled in Fig. 5.24, because the compositions modeled in Fig. 4.27 already convey the fact that the database contains information about zero or more accounts and that an ATM is composed of a screen, keypad, cash dispenser and deposit slot. Software developers typically model these whole/part relationships as compositions rather than as attributes required to implement the relationships.

The class diagram in Fig. 5.24 provides a solid basis for the structure of our model, but the diagram is not complete. In Section 6.11 we identify the states and activities of the objects in the model, and in Section 7.23 we identify the operations that the objects perform. As we present more of the UML and object-oriented design, we'll continue to strengthen the structure of our model.

Software Engineering Case Study Self-Review Exercises

5.1 We typically identify the attributes of the classes in our system by analyzing the _____ in the requirements specification.
a) nouns and noun phrases
b) descriptive words and phrases
c) verbs and verb phrases
d) All of the above.

5.2 Which of the following is not an attribute of an airplane?
a) length
b) wingspan
c) fly
d) number of seats

5.3 Describe the meaning of the following attribute declaration of class CashDispenser in the class diagram in Fig. 5.24:

```
count : Integer = 500
```

Answers to Software Engineering Case Study Self-Review Exercises

5.1 b.

5.2 c. Fly is an operation or behavior of an airplane, not an attribute.

5.3   This indicates that `count` is an `Integer` with an initial value of 500. This attribute keeps track of the number of bills available in the `CashDispenser` at any given time.

5.14 Wrap-Up

This chapter presented basic problem-solving techniques that you use in building native or managed classes and developing member functions for these classes. We demonstrated how to construct an algorithm (i.e., an approach to solving a problem) in pseudocode, then how to refine the algorithm through several phases of pseudocode development, resulting in Visual C++ code that can be executed as part of a function. You learned how to use top-down, stepwise refinement to plan out the specific actions that a function must perform and the order in which the function must perform them.

You learned that only three types of control structures—sequence, selection and repetition—are needed to develop any algorithm. We demonstrated two of Visual C++'s selection statements—the `if` single-selection statement and the `if...else` double-selection statement. The `if` statement is used to execute a set of statements based on a condition—if the condition is true, the statements execute; if it is not, the statements are skipped. The `if...else` double-selection statement is used to execute one set of statements if a condition is true, and another set of statements if the condition is false. We then discussed the `while` repetition statement, where a set of statements are executed repeatedly as long as a condition is true. We used control-statement stacking to total and compute the average of a set of student grades with counter- and sentinel-controlled repetition, and we used control-statement nesting to analyze and make decisions based on a set of exam results. We introduced assignment operators, which can be used for abbreviating statements. We presented the increment and decrement operators, which can be used to add or subtract the value 1 from a variable. In Chapter 6, Control Statements: Part 2, we continue our discussion of control statements, introducing the `for`, `do...while` and `switch` statements.

Summary

Section 5.2 Algorithms
- An algorithm is a procedure for solving a problem in terms of the actions to execute and the order in which to execute them.
- Specifying the order in which statements (actions) execute in a program is called program control.

Section 5.3 Pseudocode
- Pseudocode helps a programmer think out a program before attempting to write it in a programming language.
- Activity diagrams are part of the Unified Modeling Language (UML)—an industry standard for modeling software systems.

Section 5.4 Control Structures
- An activity diagram models the workflow (also called the activity) of a software system.
- Activity diagrams are composed of special-purpose symbols, such as action-state symbols, diamonds and small circles. These symbols are connected by transition arrows that represent the flow of the activity.

- Like pseudocode, activity diagrams help you develop and represent algorithms.
- An action state is represented as a rectangle with its left and right sides replaced with arcs curving outward. The action expression appears inside the action state.
- The arrows in an activity diagram represent transitions, which indicate the order in which the actions represented by action states occur.
- The solid circle located at the top of an activity diagram represents the initial state—the beginning of the workflow before the program performs the modeled actions.
- The solid circle surrounded by a hollow circle that appears at the bottom of the activity diagram represents the final state—the end of the workflow after the program performs its actions.
- Rectangles with the upper-right corners folded over are called notes in the UML. Notes are explanatory remarks that describe the purpose of symbols in the diagram. A dotted line connects each note with the element that the note describes.
- A diamond or decision symbol in an activity diagram indicates that a decision is to be made. The workflow will continue along a path determined by the symbol's associated guard conditions, which can be true or false. Each transition arrow emerging from a decision symbol has a guard condition (specified in square brackets next to the transition arrow). If a guard condition is true, the workflow enters the action state to which the transition arrow points.
- A diamond in an activity diagram also represents the merge symbol, which joins two flows of activity into one. A merge symbol has two or more transition arrows pointing to the diamond and only one transition arrow pointing from the diamond, to indicate multiple activity flows merging to continue the activity.
- Top-down, stepwise refinement is a process for refining pseudocode by maintaining a complete representation of the program during each refinement.
- There are three types of control structures—sequence, selection and repetition.
- The sequence structure is built in—by default, statements execute in the order they appear.
- A selection structure chooses among alternative courses of action.

Section 5.5 if Selection Statement
- The if single-selection statement either performs (selects) an action if a condition is true, or skips the action if the condition is false.

Section 5.6 if...else Double-Selection Statement
- The if...else double-selection statement performs (selects) an action if a condition is true and performs a different action if the condition is false.
- To include several statements in an if's body (or the body of an else for an if...else statement), enclose the statements in braces ({ and }). A set of statements contained in a pair of braces is called a block. A block can be placed anywhere in a program that a single statement can be placed.
- A null statement, indicating that no action is to be taken, is indicated by a semicolon (;).

Section 5.7 while Repetition Statement
- A repetition statement repeats an action while some condition remains true.
- A value that contains a fractional part is referred to as a floating-point number and is represented approximately by data types such as float and double.

Section 5.8 Formulating Algorithms: Counter-Controlled Repetition
- Counter-controlled repetition is used when the number of repetitions is known before a loop begins executing, i.e., when there is definite repetition.

- The unary cast operator static_cast can be used to create a temporary floating-point copy of its operand.
- Unary operators take only one operand; binary operators take two.
- The parameterized stream manipulator setprecision indicates the number of digits of precision that should be displayed to the right of the decimal point.
- The stream manipulator fixed indicates that floating-point values should be output in so-called fixed-point format, as opposed to scientific notation.

Section 5.9 Formulating Algorithms: Sentinel-Controlled Repetition
- Sentinel-controlled repetition is used when the number of repetitions is not known before a loop begins executing, i.e., when there is indefinite repetition.

Section 5.10 Formulating Algorithms: Nested Control Statements
- A nested control statement appears in the body of another control statement.

Section 5.11 Assignment Operators
- Visual C++ provides the arithmetic assignment operators +=, -=, *=, /= and %= for abbreviating assignment expressions.

Section 5.12 Increment and Decrement Operators
- The increment operator, ++, and the decrement operator, --, increment or decrement a variable by 1, respectively. If the operator is prefixed to the variable, the variable is incremented or decremented by 1 first, then its new value is used in the expression in which it appears. If the operator is postfixed to the variable, the variable is first used in the expression in which it appears, then the variable's value is incremented or decremented by 1.

Terminology

action
action expression
action state
action-state symbol
action/decision model of programming
activity diagram
addition assignment operator (+=)
algorithm
approximation of floating-point numbers
arithmetic assignment operators
arrow symbol
assignment operators
associate from left to right
associate from right to left
averaging calculation
binary arithmetic operator
block
"bombing"
bool fundamental type
cast operator
compound statement
conditional expression
conditional operator (?:)

control statement
control-statement nesting
control-statement stacking
counter
counter-controlled repetition
"crashing"
dangling-else problem
decision symbol
decrement operator (--)
default precision
definite repetition
diamond symbol
divide by zero
dotted line
double data type
double-precision floating-point number
double-selection statement
dummy value
empty statement
executable statement
explicit conversion
fatal logic error
final state

first refinement

fixed-point format

`fixed` stream manipulator

flag value

`float` data type

floating-point constant

floating-point number

"garbage" value

goto elimination

goto statement

`if...else` double-selection statement

implicit conversion

increment operator (++)

indefinite repetition

initial state

integer division

integer promotion

iterating

iterations of a loop

keywords

loop

loop-continuation condition

loop iterations

loop nested within a loop

looping statement

merge symbol

multiple-selection statement

nested control statement

nonparameterized stream manipulator

note in the UML

null statement

object-oriented design (OOD)

off-by-one error

operand

operator precedence

order in which actions should execute

parameterized stream manipulator

postdecrement

postfix decrement operator

postfix increment operator

postincrement

precision

predecrement

prefix decrement operator

prefix increment operator

preincrement

procedure

program control

promotion

pseudocode

repetition statement

rounding

scientific notation

second refinement

selection statement

sentinel-controlled repetition

sentinel value

sequence statement

sequence-statement activity diagram

sequential execution

`setprecision` stream manipulator

`showpoint` stream manipulator

signal value

single-entry/single-exit control statement

single-selection `if` statement

single-precision floating-point number

small circle symbol

solid circle symbol

`static_cast` operator

stream manipulator

structured programming

ternary operator

top

top-down, stepwise refinement

total

transfer of control

transition

transition arrow symbol

truncate

unary cast operator

unary minus (-) operator

unary operator

unary plus (+) operator

undefined value

`while` repetition statement

workflow of a portion of a software system

Self-Review Exercises

5.1   Answer each of the following questions.

a) All programs can be written in terms of three types of control structures: _____, _____ and _____.

b) The _____ selection statement is used to execute one action when a condition is `true` or a different action when that condition is `false`.

c) Repeating a set of instructions a specific number of times is called _____ repetition.

d) When it is not known in advance how many times a set of statements will be repeated, a(n)_____value can be used to terminate the repetition.

5.2   Write four different Visual C++ statements that each add 1 to integer variable x.

5.3   Write Visual C++ statements to accomplish each of the following:

a) In one statement, assign the sum of the current value of x and y to z and postincrement the value of x.

b) Determine whether the value of the variable count is greater than 10. If it is, print "Count is greater than 10."

c) Predecrement the variable x by 1, then subtract it from the variable total.

d) Calculate the remainder after q is divided by divisor and assign the result to q. Write this statement two different ways.

5.4   Write C++ statements to accomplish each of the following tasks.

a) Declare variables sum and x to be of type int.

b) Set variable x to 1.

c) Set variable sum to 0.

d) Add variable x to variable sum and assign the result to variable sum.

e) Print "The sum is: " followed by the value of variable sum.

5.5   Combine the statements that you wrote in Exercise 5.4 into a program that calculates and prints the sum of the integers from 1 to 10. Use the while statement to loop through the calculation and increment statements. The loop should terminate when the value of x becomes 11.

5.6   State the values of each variable after the calculation is performed. Assume that, when each statement begins executing, all variables have the integer value 5.

a) product *= x++;

b) quotient /= ++x;

5.7   Write single Visual C++ statements or portions of statements that do the following:

a) Input integer variable x with cin and >>.

b) Input integer variable y with cin and >>.

c) Set integer variable i to 1.

d) Set integer variable power to 1.

e) Multiply variable power by x and assign the result to power.

f) Preincrement variable i by 1.

g) Determine whether i is less than or equal to y.

h) Output integer variable power with cout and <<.

5.8   Write a Visual C++ program that uses the statements in Exercise 5.7 to calculate x raised to the y power. The program should have a while repetition statement.

5.9   Identify and correct the errors in each of the following:

a) *while* (c <= 5)
```
   {
       product *= c;
       ++c;
```

b) cin << value;

c) *if* (gender == 1)
```
       cout << "Woman" << endl;
```
   else;
```
       cout << "Man" << endl;
```

5.10 What is wrong with the following `while` repetition statement?

```
while ( z >= 0 )
    sum += z;
```

Answers to Self-Review Exercises

5.1 a) Sequence, selection and repetition. b) `if...else`. c) Counter-controlled or definite. d) Sentinel, signal, flag or dummy.

5.2
```
x = x + 1;
x += 1;
++x;
x++;
```

5.3 a) `z = x++ + y;`
b)
```
if ( count > 10 )
    cout << "Count is greater than 10" << endl;
```
c) `total -= --x;`
d)
```
q %= divisor;
q = q % divisor;
```

5.4 a)
```
int sum;
int x;
```
b) `x = 1;`
c) `sum = 0;`
d)
```
sum += x;
```
or
```
sum = sum + x;
```
e) `cout << "The sum is: " << sum << endl;`

5.5 See the following code:

```cpp
1   // Exercise 5.5 Solution: ex05_05.cpp
2   // Calculate the sum of the integers from 1 to 10.
3   #include <iostream>
4   using std::cout;
5   using std::endl;
6
7   int main()
8   {
9      int sum; // stores sum of integers 1 to 10
10     int x; // counter
11
12     x = 1; // count from 1
13     sum = 0; // initialize sum
14
15     while ( x <= 10 ) // loop 10 times
16     {
17        sum += x; // add x to sum
18        ++x; // increment x
19     } // end while
20
21     cout << "The sum is: " << sum << endl;
22     return 0; // indicate successful termination
23  } // end main
```

```
The sum is: 55
```

5.6   a) product = 25, x = 6;
       b) quotient = 0, x = 6;

```cpp
1   // Exercise 5.6 Solution: ex05_06.cpp
2   // Calculate the value of product and quotient.
3   #include <iostream>
4   using std::cout;
5   using std::endl;
6
7   int main()
8   {
9      int x = 5;
10     int product = 5;
11     int quotient = 5;
12
13     // part a
14     product *= x++; // part a statement
15     cout << "Value of product after calculation: " << product << endl;
16     cout << "Value of x after calculation: " << x << endl << endl;
17
18     // part b
19     x = 5; // reset value of x
20     quotient /= ++x; // part b statement
21     cout << "Value of quotient after calculation: " << quotient << endl;
22     cout << "Value of x after calculation: " << x << endl << endl;
23     return 0; // indicate successful termination
24  } // end main
```

```
Value of product after calculation: 25
Value of x after calculation: 6

Value of quotient after calculation: 0
Value of x after calculation: 6
```

5.7   a) cin >> x;
       b) cin >> y;
       c) i = 1;
       d) power = 1;
       e) power *= x;
            or
            power = power * x;
       f) ++i;
       g) if (i <= y)
       h) cout << power << endl;

5.8   See the following code:

```cpp
1   // Exercise 5.8 Solution: ex05_08.cpp
2   // Raise x to the y power.
3   #include <iostream>
4   using std::cout;
5   using std::cin;
6   using std::endl;
7
```

```
 8    int main()
 9    {
10       int x; // base
11       int y; // exponent
12       int i; // counts from 1 to y
13       int power; // used to calculate x raised to power y
14
15       i = 1; // initialize i to begin counting from 1
16       power = 1; // initialize power
17
18       cout << "Enter base as an integer: ";  // prompt for base
19       cin >> x; // input base
20
21       cout << "Enter exponent as an integer: "; // prompt for exponent
22       cin >> y; // input exponent
23
24       // count from 1 to y and multiply power by x each time
25       while ( i <= y )
26       {
27          power *= x;
28          ++i;
29       } // end while
30
31       cout << power << endl; // display result
32       return 0; // indicate successful termination
33    } // end main
```

```
Enter base as an integer: 2
Enter exponent as an integer: 3
8
```

5.9   a) Error: Missing the closing right brace of the while body.
Correction: Add closing right brace after the statement c++;.
    b) Error: Used stream insertion instead of stream extraction.
Correction: Change << to >>.
    c) Error: Semicolon after else results in a logic error. The second output statement will always be executed.
Correction: Remove the semicolon after else.

5.10   The value of the variable z is never changed in the while statement. Therefore, if the loop-continuation condition (z >= 0) is initially true, an infinite loop is created. To prevent the infinite loop, z must be decremented so that it eventually becomes less than 0.

Exercises

5.11   Identify and correct the error(s) in each of the following:
    a) `if ( age >= 65 );`
`        cout << "Age is greater than or equal to 65" << endl;`
`    else`
`        cout << "Age is less than 65 << endl";`
    b) `if ( age >= 65 )`
`        cout << "Age is greater than or equal to 65" << endl;`
`    else;`
`        cout << "Age is less than 65 << endl";`

c) `int x = 1, total;`

```
while ( x <= 10 )
{
  total += x;
  ++x;
}
```

d) `While ( x <= 100 )`
```
  total += x;
  ++x;
```

e) `while ( y > 0 )`
```
{
  cout << y << endl;
  ++y;
}
```

5.12 What does the following program print?

```cpp
// Exercise 5.12: ex05_12.cpp
// What does this program print?
#include <iostream>
using std::cout;
using std::endl;

int main()
{
  int y; // declare y
  int x = 1; // initialize x
  int total = 0; // initialize total

  while ( x <= 10 ) // loop 10 times
  {
    y = x * x; // perform calculation
    cout << y << endl; // output result
    total += y; // add y to total
    x++; // increment counter x
  } // end while

  cout << "Total is " << total << endl; // display result
  return 0; // indicate successful termination
} // end main
```

For Exercises 5.13–5.16, perform each of these steps:

a) Read the problem statement.
b) Formulate the algorithm using pseudocode and top-down, stepwise refinement.
c) Write a Visual C++ program.
d) Test, debug and execute the Visual C++ program.

5.13 Drivers are concerned with the mileage obtained by their automobiles. One driver has kept track of several tankfuls of gasoline by recording miles driven and gallons used for each tankful. Develop a C++ program that uses a `while` statement to input the miles driven and gallons used for each tankful. The program should calculate and display the miles per gallon obtained for each tankful and print the combined miles per gallon obtained for all tankfuls up to this point.

```
Enter the miles driven (-1 to quit): 287
Enter gallons used: 13
MPG this tankful: 22.076923
Total MPG: 22.076923

Enter the miles driven (-1 to quit): 200
Enter gallons used: 10
MPG this tankful: 20.000000
Total MPG: 21.173913

Enter the miles driven (-1 to quit): 120
Enter gallons used: 5
MPG this tankful: 24.000000
Total MPG: 21.678571

Enter the miles driven (-1 to quit): -1
```

5.14   Develop a Visual C++ program that will determine whether a department-store customer has exceeded the credit limit on a charge account. For each customer, the following facts are available:

    a) Account number (an integer)
    b) Balance at the beginning of the month
    c) Total of all items charged by this customer this month
    d) Total of all credits applied to this customer's account this month
    e) Allowed credit limit

    The program should use a `while` statement to input each of these facts, calculate the new balance (= beginning balance + charges – credits) and determine whether the new balance exceeds the customer's credit limit. For those customers whose credit limit is exceeded, the program should display the customer's account number, credit limit, new balance and the message "Credit Limit Exceeded."

```
Enter account number (or -1 to quit): 100
Enter beginning balance: 5394.78
Enter total charges: 1000.00
Enter total credits: 500.00
Enter credit limit: 5500.00
New balance is 5894.78
Account:      100
Credit limit: 5500.00
Balance:      5894.78
Credit Limit Exceeded.

Enter account number (or -1 to quit): 200
Enter beginning balance: 1000.00
Enter total charges: 123.45
Enter total credits: 321.00
Enter credit limit: 1500.00
New balance is 802.45

Enter account number (or -1 to quit): 300
Enter beginning balance: 500.00
Enter total charges: 274.73
Enter total credits: 100.00
Enter credit limit: 800.00
New balance is 674.73

Enter account number (or -1 to quit): -1
```

5.15   A large chemical company pays its salespeople on a commission basis. The salespeople each receive $200 per week plus 9 percent of their gross sales for that week. For example, a salesperson who sells $5000 worth of chemicals in a week receives $200 plus 9 percent of $5000, or a total of $650. Develop a program that uses a `while` statement to input each salesperson's gross sales for last week and calculates and displays that salesperson's earnings. Process one salesperson's figures at a time.

```
Enter sales in dollars (-1 to end): 5000.00
Salary is: $650.00

Enter sales in dollars (-1 to end): 6000.00
Salary is: $740.00

Enter sales in dollars (-1 to end): 7000.00
Salary is: $830.00

Enter sales in dollars (-1 to end): -1
```

5.16   Develop a Visual C++ program that uses a `while` statement to determine the gross pay for each of several employees. The company pays "straight time" for the first 40 hours worked by each employee and pays "time-and-a-half" for all hours worked in excess of 40 hours. You are given a list of the employees of the company, the number of hours each employee worked last week and the hourly rate of each employee. Your program should input this information for each employee and should determine and display the employee's gross pay.

```
Enter hours worked (-1 to end): 39
Enter hourly rate of the employee ($00.00): 10.00
Salary is $390.00

Enter hours worked (-1 to end): 40
Enter hourly rate of the employee ($00.00): 10.00
Salary is $400.00

Enter hours worked (-1 to end): 41
Enter hourly rate of the employee ($00.00): 10.00
Salary is $415.00

Enter hours worked (-1 to end): -1
```

5.17   The process of finding the largest number (i.e., the maximum of a group of numbers) is used frequently in computer applications. For example, a program that determines the winner of a sales contest inputs the number of units sold by each salesperson. The salesperson who sells the most units wins the contest. Write a pseudocode program, then a Visual C++ program that uses a `while` statement to determine and print the largest number of 10 numbers input by the user. Your program should use three variables, as follows:

counter:	A counter to count to 10 (i.e., to keep track of how many numbers have been input and to determine when all 10 numbers have been processed).
number:	The current number input to the program.
largest:	The largest number found so far.

5.18   Write a Visual C++ program that uses a `while` statement and the tab escape sequence \t to print the following table of values:

```
N       10*N    100*N   1000*N

1       10      100     1000
2       20      200     2000
3       30      300     3000
4       40      400     4000
5       50      500     5000
```

5.19 Using an approach similar to that in Exercise 5.17, find the *two* largest values among the 10 numbers. [*Note:* You must input each number only once.]

5.20 The examination-results program of Fig. 5.16–Fig. 5.18 assumes that any value input by the user that is not a 1 must be a 2. Modify the application to validate its inputs. On any input, if the value entered is other than 1 or 2, keep looping until the user enters a correct value.

5.21 What does the following program print?

```cpp
1  // Exercise 5.21: ex05_21.cpp
2  // What does this program print?
3  #include <iostream>
4  using std::cout;
5  using std::endl;
6
7  int main()
8  {
9     int count = 1; // initialize count
10
11    while ( count <= 10 ) // loop 10 times
12    {
13       // output line of text
14       cout << ( count % 2 ? "****" : "++++++++" ) << endl;
15       ++count; // increment count
16    } // end while
17
18    return 0; // indicate successful termination
19 } // end main
```

5.22 What does the following program print?

```cpp
1  // Exercise 5.22: ex05_22.cpp
2  // What does this program print?
3  #include <iostream>
4  using std::cout;
5  using std::endl;
6
7  int main()
8  {
9     int row = 10; // initialize row
10    int column; // declare column
11
12    while ( row >= 1 ) // loop until row < 1
13    {
14       column = 1; // set column to 1 as iteration begins
15
16       while ( column <= 10 ) // loop 10 times
17       {
18          cout << ( row % 2 ? "<" : ">" ); // output
19          ++column; // increment column
20       } // end inner while
21
22       --row; // decrement row
23       cout << endl; // begin new output line
24    } // end outer while
25
26    return 0; // indicate successful termination
27 } // end main
```

5.23   *(Dangling-else Problem)* State the output for each of the following when x is 9 and y is 11 and when x is 11 and y is 9. Note that the compiler ignores the indentation in a Visual C++ program. The Visual C++ compiler always associates an else with the previous if unless told to do otherwise by the placement of braces {}. On first glance, you may not be sure which if and else match, so this is referred to as the "dangling-else" problem. We eliminated the indentation from the following code to make the problem more challenging. [*Hint:* Apply indentation conventions you have learned.]

a)
```
if ( x < 10 )
if ( y > 10 )
cout << "*****" << endl;
else
cout << "#####" << endl;
cout << "$$$$$" << endl;
```

b)
```
if ( x < 10 )
{
if ( y > 10 )
cout << "*****" << endl;
}
else
{
cout << "#####" << endl;
cout << "$$$$$" << endl;
}
```

5.24   *(Another Dangling-else Problem)* Modify the following code to produce the output shown. Use proper indentation techniques. You must not make any changes other than inserting braces. The compiler ignores indentation in a Visual C++ program. We eliminated the indentation from the following code to make the problem more challenging. [*Note:* It is possible that no modification is necessary.]

```
if ( y == 8 )
if ( x == 5 )
cout << "@@@@@" << endl;
else
cout << "#####" << endl;
cout << "$$$$$" << endl;
cout << "&&&&&" << endl;
```

a) Assuming x = 5 and y = 8, the following output is produced.

```
@@@@@
$$$$$
&&&&&
```

b) Assuming x = 5 and y = 8, the following output is produced.

```
@@@@@
```

c) Assuming x = 5 and y = 8, the following output is produced.

```
@@@@@
&&&&&
```

d) Assuming x = 5 and y = 7, the following output is produced. [*Note:* The last three output statements after the else are all part of a block.]

```
#####
$$$$$
&&&&&
```

5.25 Write a program that reads in the size of the side of a square, then prints a hollow square of that size using asterisks and blanks. Your program should work for squares of all side sizes between 1 and 20. For example, if your program reads a size of 5, it should print

```
*****
*   *
*   *
*   *
*****
```

5.26 A palindrome is a number or a text phrase that reads the same backward as forward. For example, each of the following five-digit integers is a palindrome: 12321, 55555, 45554 and 11611. Write a program that reads in a five-digit integer and determines whether it is a palindrome. [*Hint:* Use the division and modulus operators to separate the number into its individual digits.]

5.27 Input an integer containing only 0s and 1s (i.e., a "binary" integer) and print its decimal equivalent. Use the modulus and division operators to pick off the "binary" number's digits one at a time from right to left. Much as in the decimal number system, where the rightmost digit has a positional value of 1, the next digit left has a positional value of 10, then 100, then 1000, and so on, in the binary number system the rightmost digit has a positional value of 1, the next digit left has a positional value of 2, then 4, then 8, and so on. Thus the decimal number 234 can be interpreted as 2 * 100 + 3 * 10 + 4 * 1. The decimal equivalent of binary 1101 is 1 * 1 + 0 * 2 + 1 * 4 + 1 * 8 or 1 + 0 + 4 + 8, or 13. [*Note:* To learn more about binary numbers, refer to Appendix D.]

5.28 Write a program that displays the checkerboard pattern shown below. Your program must use only three output statements, one of each of the following forms:

```
cout << "* ";
cout << ' ';
cout << endl;
```

```
* * * * * * * *
 * * * * * * * *
* * * * * * * *
 * * * * * * * *
* * * * * * * *
 * * * * * * * *
* * * * * * * *
 * * * * * * * *
```

5.29 Write a program that prints the powers of the integer 2, namely 2, 4, 8, 16, 32, 64, etc. Your while loop should not terminate (i.e., you should create an infinite loop). To do this, simply use the keyword true as the expression for the while statement. What happens when you run this program?

5.30 Write a program that reads the radius of a circle (as a double value) and computes and prints the diameter, the circumference and the area. Use the value 3.14159 for π.

5.31   What is wrong with the following statement? Provide the correct statement to accomplish what the programmer was probably trying to do.

```
cout << ++( x + y );
```

5.32   Write a program that reads three nonzero `double` values and determines and prints whether they could represent the sides of a triangle.

5.33   Write a program that reads three nonzero integers and determines and prints whether they could be the sides of a right triangle.

5.34   *(Cryptography)* A company wants to transmit data over the telephone but is concerned that its phones could be tapped. All of the data is transmitted as four-digit integers. The company has asked you to write a program that encrypts the data so that it can be transmitted more securely. Your program should read a four-digit integer and encrypt it as follows: Replace each digit by *(the sum of that digit plus 7) modulus 10*. Then, swap the first digit with the third, swap the second digit with the fourth and print the encrypted integer. Write a separate program that inputs an encrypted four-digit integer and decrypts it to form the original number.

5.35   The factorial of a nonnegative integer *n* is written *n*! (pronounced "*n* factorial") and is defined as follows:

$$n! = n \cdot (n-1) \cdot (n-2) \cdot \ldots \cdot 1 \quad \text{(for values of } n \text{ greater than 1)}$$

and

$$n! = 1 \quad \text{(for } n = 0 \text{ or } n = 1)$$

For example, 5! = 5 · 4 · 3 · 2 · 1, which is 120. Use `while` statements in each of the following:

    a) Write a program that reads a nonnegative integer and computes and prints its factorial.

    b) Write a program that estimates the value of the mathematical constant *e* by using the formula:

$$e = 1 + \frac{1}{1!} + \frac{1}{2!} + \frac{1}{3!} + \ldots$$

Prompt the user for the desired accuracy of *e* (i.e., the number of terms in the summation).

    c) Write a program that computes the value of e^x by using the formula

$$e^x = 1 + \frac{x}{1!} + \frac{x^2}{2!} + \frac{x^3}{3!} + \ldots$$

Prompt the user for the desired accuracy of *e* (i.e., the number of terms in the summation).

5.36   [*Note:* This exercise corresponds to Section 5.13, a portion of our Software Engineering Case Study.] Describe in 200 words or fewer what an automobile is and does. List the nouns and verbs separately. In the text, we stated that each noun might correspond to an object that will need to be built to implement a system, in this case a car. Pick five of the objects you listed, and, for each, list several attributes and several behaviors. Describe briefly how these objects interact with one another and other objects in your description. You have just performed several of the key steps in a typical object-oriented design.

6

Control Statements: Part 2

OBJECTIVES

In this chapter you'll learn:

- The essentials of counter-controlled repetition.

- To use the `for` and `do...while` repetition statements to execute statements in a program repeatedly.

- To implement multiple selection using the `switch` selection statement.

- To use the `break` and `continue` program control statements to alter the flow of control.

- To use the logical operators to form complex conditional expressions in control statements.

- To avoid the consequences of confusing the equality and assignment operators.

6.1 Introduction

Chapter 5 began our introduction to the types of building blocks that are available for problem solving. We used those building blocks to employ proven program construction techniques. In this chapter, we continue our presentation of the theory and principles of structured programming by introducing Visual C++'s remaining control statements. The control statements we study here and in Chapter 5 will help us in building and manipulating objects. We continue our early emphasis on object-oriented programming that began with a discussion of basic concepts in Chapter 1 and extensive object-oriented code examples and exercises in Chapters 4–5.

In this chapter, we demonstrate the `for`, `do...while` and `switch` statements. Through a series of short examples using `while` and `for`, we explore the essentials of counter-controlled repetition. We devote a portion of the chapter to expanding the `GradeBook` class presented in Chapters 4–5. In particular, we create a version of class `GradeBook` that uses a `switch` statement to count the number of A, B, C, D and F grades in a set of letter grades entered by the user. We introduce the `break` and `continue` program control statements. We discuss the logical operators, which enable you to use more powerful conditional expressions in control statements. We also examine the common error of confusing the equality (==) and assignment (=) operators, and how to avoid it. Finally, we summarize Visual C++'s control statements and the proven problem-solving techniques presented in this chapter and Chapter 5. Like Chapter 5, this chapter doesn't require any C++/CLI-specific information, as the concepts it presents are all equally applicable to native and managed C++.

6.2 Essentials of Counter-Controlled Repetition

This section uses the `while` repetition statement introduced in Chapter 5 to formalize the elements required to perform counter-controlled repetition. Counter-controlled repetition requires

1. the *name of a control variable* (or loop counter)

2. the *initial value* of the control variable

3. the *loop-continuation condition* that tests for the *final value* of the control variable (i.e., whether looping should continue)

4. the *increment* (or *decrement*) by which the control variable is modified each time through the loop.

Consider the simple program in Fig. 6.1, which prints the numbers from 1 to 10. The declaration in line 9 *names* the control variable (`counter`), declares it to be an integer, reserves space for it in memory and sets it to an *initial value* of 1. Declarations that require initialization are, in effect, executable statements. In Visual C++, it is more precise to call a declaration that also reserves memory—as the preceding declaration does—a *definition*. Because definitions are declarations, too, we'll use the term "declaration" except when the distinction is important.

The declaration and initialization of `counter` (line 9) also could have been accomplished with the statements

```
int counter; // declare control variable
counter = 1; // initialize control variable to 1
```

We use both methods of initializing variables.

Line 14 *increments* the loop counter by 1 each time the loop's body is performed. The loop-continuation condition (line 11) in the `while` statement determines whether the value of the control variable is less than or equal to 10 (the final value for which the condition is `true`). Note that the body of this `while` executes even when the control variable is 10. The loop terminates when the control variable is greater than 10 (i.e., when `counter` becomes 11).

```
 1    // Fig. 6.1: WhileTest.cpp
 2    // Counter-controlled repetition.
 3    #include <iostream>
 4    using std::cout;
 5    using std::endl;
 6
 7    int main()
 8    {
 9        int counter = 1; // declare and initialize control variable
10
11        while ( counter <= 10 ) // loop-continuation condition
12        {
13            cout << counter << " ";
14            counter++; // increment control variable by 1
15        } // end while
16
17        cout << endl; // output a newline
18        return 0; // successful termination
19    } // end main
```

Fig. 6.1 | Counter-controlled repetition. (Part 1 of 2.)

```
1 2 3 4 5 6 7 8 9 10
```

Fig. 6.1 | Counter-controlled repetition. (Part 2 of 2.)

Figure 6.1 can be made more concise by initializing `counter` to 0 and by replacing the `while` statement with

```
while ( ++counter <= 10 ) // loop-continuation condition
    cout << counter << " ";
```

This code saves a statement, because the incrementing is done directly in the `while` condition before the condition is tested. Also, the code eliminates the braces around the body of the `while`, because the `while` now contains only one statement. Coding in such a condensed fashion takes some practice and can lead to programs that are more difficult to read, debug, modify and maintain.

Common Programming Error 6.1

Floating-point values are approximate, so controlling counting loops with floating-point variables can result in imprecise counter values and inaccurate tests for termination.

Error-Prevention Tip 6.1

Control counting loops with integer values.

Good Programming Practice 6.1

Put a blank line before and after each control statement to make it stand out in the program.

Good Programming Practice 6.2

Too many levels of nesting can make a program difficult to understand. As a rule, try to avoid using more than three levels of indentation.

Good Programming Practice 6.3

Vertical spacing above and below control statements and indentation of the bodies of control statements within the control-statement headers give programs a two-dimensional appearance that greatly improves readability.

6.3 for Repetition Statement

Section 6.2 presented the essentials of counter-controlled repetition. The `while` statement can be used to implement any counter-controlled loop. Visual C++ also provides the *for repetition statement*, which specifies the counter-controlled repetition details in a single line of code. To illustrate the power of `for`, let us rewrite the program of Fig. 6.1. The result is shown in Fig. 6.2.

When the `for` statement (lines 11–12) begins executing, the control variable `counter` is declared and initialized to 1. Then, the loop-continuation condition (line 11 between the semicolons) `counter <= 10` is checked. The initial value of `counter` is 1, so the condition is satisfied and the body statement (line 12) prints the value of `counter`, namely 1.

```
1   // Fig. 6.2: ForTest.cpp
2   // Counter-controlled repetition with the for statement.
3   #include <iostream>
4   using std::cout;
5   using std::endl;
6
7   int main()
8   {
9       // for statement header includes initialization,
10      // loop-continuation condition and increment.
11      for ( int counter = 1; counter <= 10; counter++ )
12          cout << counter << " ";
13
14      cout << endl; // output a newline
15      return 0; // indicate successful termination
16  } // end main
```

```
1 2 3 4 5 6 7 8 9 10
```

Fig. 6.2 | Counter-controlled repetition with the `for` statement.

Then, the expression `counter++` increments control variable `counter` and the loop begins again with the loop-continuation test. The control variable is now equal to 2, so the final value is not exceeded and the program performs the body statement again. This process continues until the loop body has executed 10 times and the control variable `counter` is incremented to 11—this causes the loop-continuation test to fail and repetition to terminate. The program continues by performing the first statement after the `for` statement (in this case, the output statement in line 14).

for-Statement Header Components
Figure 6.3 takes a closer look at the `for`-statement header (line 11) of Fig. 6.2. Notice that the `for`-statement header "does it all"—it specifies each of the items needed for counter-controlled repetition with a control variable. If there is more than one statement in the body of the `for`, braces are required to enclose the body of the loop.

Notice that Fig. 6.2 uses the loop-continuation condition `counter <= 10`. If you incorrectly wrote `counter < 10`, then the loop would execute only 9 times. This is a common *off-by-one error*.

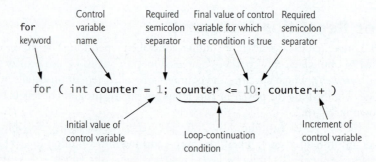

Fig. 6.3 | for-statement header components.

Common Programming Error 6.2

Using an incorrect relational operator or using an incorrect final value of a loop counter in the condition of a while *or* for *statement can cause off-by-one errors.*

Good Programming Practice 6.4

Using the final value in the condition of a while *or* for *statement and using the* <= *relational operator will help avoid off-by-one errors. For a loop used to print the values 1 to 10, for example, the loop-continuation condition should be* counter <= 10 *rather than* counter < 10 *(which is an off-by-one error) or* counter < 11 *(which is nevertheless correct). Many programmers prefer so-called **zero-based counting**, in which, to count 10 times through the loop,* counter *would be initialized to zero and the loop-continuation test would be* counter < 10.*

The general form of the for statement is

> **for** (*initialization*; *loopContinuationCondition*; *increment*)
>   *statement*

where the *initialization* expression initializes the loop's control variable, *loopContinuation-Condition* determines whether the loop should continue executing (this condition typically contains the final value of the control variable for which the condition is true) and *increment* increments the control variable. In most cases, the for statement can be represented by an equivalent while statement, as follows:

> *initialization*;
>
> **while** (*loopContinuationCondition*)
> {
>   *statement*
>   *increment*;
> }

There is an exception to this rule, which we'll discuss in Section 6.7.

If the *initialization* expression in the for statement header declares the control variable (i.e., the control variable's type is specified before the variable name), the control variable can be used only in the body of the for statement—the control variable will be unknown outside the for statement. This restricted use of the control-variable name is known as the variable's *scope*. The scope of a variable specifies where it can be used in a program. Scope is discussed in detail in Chapter 7, Functions and an Introduction to Recursion.

Common Programming Error 6.3

When the control variable of a for *statement is declared in the initialization section of the for-statement header, using the control variable after the body of the statement is a compilation error.*

Portability Tip 6.1

In the C++ Standard, the scope of the control variable declared in the initialization section of a for *statement differs from the scope in older C++ compilers. In prestandard compilers, the scope of the control variable does not terminate at the end of the block defining the body of the* for *statement; rather, the scope terminates at the end of the block that encloses the* for *statement.*

C++ code created with prestandard C++ compilers can break when compiled on standard-compliant compilers. If you are working with prestandard compilers and you want to be sure your code will work with standard-compliant compilers, there are two defensive programming strategies you can use: either declare control variables with different names in every for *statement, or, if you prefer to use the same name for the control variable in several* for *statements, declare the control variable before the first* for *statement.*

As we'll see, the *initialization* and *increment* expressions can be comma-separated lists of expressions. The commas, as used in these expressions, are **comma operators**, which guarantee that lists of expressions evaluate from left to right. The comma operator has the lowest precedence of all Visual C++ operators. The value and type of a comma-separated list of expressions are the value and type of the rightmost expression in the list. The comma operator is most often used in for statements. Its primary application is to enable you to use multiple initialization expressions and/or multiple increment expressions. For example, there may be several control variables in a single for statement that must be initialized and incremented.

Good Programming Practice 6.5

Place only expressions involving the control variables in the initialization and increment sections of a for *statement. Manipulations of other variables should appear either before the loop (if they should execute only once, like initialization statements) or in the loop body (if they should execute once per repetition, like incrementing or decrementing statements).*

The three expressions in the for-statement header are optional (but the two semi-colon separators are required). If the *loopContinuationCondition* is omitted, Visual C++ assumes that the condition is true, thus creating an infinite loop. One might omit the *initialization* expression if the control variable is initialized earlier in the program. One might omit the *increment* expression if the increment is calculated by statements in the body of the for or if no increment is needed. The increment expression in the for statement acts as a stand-alone statement at the end of the body of the for. Therefore, the expressions

```
counter = counter + 1
counter += 1
++counter
counter++
```

are all equivalent in the incrementing portion of the for statement (when no other code appears there). Many programmers prefer the form counter++, because for loops evaluate the increment expression after the loop body executes. The postincrementing form therefore seems more natural. The variable being incremented here does not appear in a larger expression, so both preincrementing and postincrementing actually have the same effect.

Common Programming Error 6.4

Using commas instead of the two required semicolons in a for *header is a syntax error.*

Common Programming Error 6.5

Placing a semicolon immediately to the right of the right parenthesis of a for *header makes the body of that* for *statement an empty statement. This is usually a logic error.*

The initialization, loop-continuation condition and increment expressions of a for statement can contain arithmetic expressions. For example, if x = 2 and y = 10, and x and y are not modified in the loop body, the for header

```
for ( int j = x; j <= 4 * x * y; j += y / x )
```

is equivalent to

```
for ( int j = 2; j <= 80; j += 5 )
```

The "increment" of a for statement can be negative, in which case it is really a decrement and the loop actually counts downward (as shown in Section 6.4).

If the loop-continuation condition is initially false, the body of the for statement is not performed. Instead, execution proceeds with the statement following the for.

Frequently, the control variable is printed or used in calculations in the body of a for statement, but this is not required. It is common to use the control variable for controlling repetition while never mentioning it in the body of the for statement.

Error-Prevention Tip 6.2

Although the value of the control variable can be changed in the body of a for statement, avoid doing so, because this practice can lead to subtle logic errors.

for-Statement UML Activity Diagram

The for statement's UML activity diagram is similar to that of the while statement (Fig. 5.6). Figure 6.4 shows the activity diagram of the for statement in Fig. 6.2. The di-

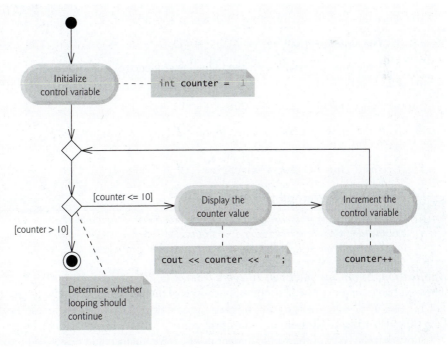

Fig. 6.4 | UML activity diagram for the for statement in Fig. 6.2.

agram makes it clear that initialization occurs once before the loop-continuation test is evaluated the first time, and that incrementing occurs each time through the loop *after* the body statement executes. Note that (besides an initial state, transition arrows, a merge, a final state and several notes) the diagram contains only action states and a decision. Imagine, again, that you have a bin of empty for-statement UML activity diagrams—as many as you might need to stack and nest with the activity-diagrams of other control statements to form a structured implementation of an algorithm. You fill in the action states and decision symbols with action expressions and guard conditions appropriate to the algorithm.

6.4 Examples Using the for Statement

The following examples show methods of varying the control variable in a for statement. In each case, we write the appropriate for-statement header. Note the change in the relational operator for loops that decrement the control variable.

a)   Vary the control variable from 1 to 100 in increments of 1.

```
for ( int i = 1; i <= 100; i++ )
```

b)   Vary the control variable from 100 down to 1 in increments of -1 (that is, decrements of 1).

```
for ( int i = 100; i >= 1; i-- )
```

c)   Vary the control variable from 7 to 77 in steps of 7.

```
for ( int i = 7; i <= 77; i += 7 )
```

d)   Vary the control variable from 20 down to 2 in steps of -2.

```
for ( int i = 20; i >= 2; i -= 2 )
```

e)   Vary the control variable over the following sequence of values: 2, 5, 8, 11, 14, 17, 20.

```
for ( int i = 2; i <= 20; i += 3 )
```

f)   Vary the control variable over the following sequence of values: 99, 88, 77, 66, 55, 44, 33, 22, 11, 0.

```
for ( int i = 99; i >= 0; i -= 11 )
```

 Common Programming Error 6.6

Not using the proper relational operator in the loop-continuation condition of a loop that counts downward (such as incorrectly using i <= 1 instead of i >= 1 in a loop counting down to 1) is usually a logic error that yields incorrect results when the program runs.

Application: Summing the Even Integers from 2 to 20

The next two examples provide simple applications of the for statement. The program of Fig. 6.5 uses a for statement to sum the even integers from 2 to 20. Each iteration of the loop (lines 12–13) adds the current value of the control variable number to variable total.

Note that the body of the for statement in Fig. 6.5 actually could be merged into the increment portion of the for header by using the comma operator as follows:

```
 1   // Fig. 6.5: ForTest.cpp
 2   // Summing integers with the for statement.
 3   #include <iostream>
 4   using std::cout;
 5   using std::endl;
 6
 7   int main()
 8   {
 9      int total = 0; // initialize total
10
11      // total even integers from 2 through 20
12      for ( int number = 2; number <= 20; number += 2 )
13         total += number;
14
15      cout << "Sum is " << total << endl; // display results
16      return 0; // successful termination
17   } // end main
```

```
Sum is 110
```

Fig. 6.5 | Summing integers with the **for** statement.

```
for ( int number = 2; // initialization
        number <= 20; // loop-continuation condition
        total += number, number += 2 ) // total and increment
   ; // empty body
```

Good Programming Practice 6.6

Although statements preceding a for *and statements in the body of a* for *often can be merged into the* for *header, doing so can make the program more difficult to read, maintain, modify and debug.*

Good Programming Practice 6.7

Limit the size of control-statement headers to a single line, if possible.

Application: Compound Interest Calculations

The next example computes compound interest using a for statement. Consider the following problem statement:

> *A person invests $1000.00 in a savings account yielding 5 percent interest. Assuming that all interest is left on deposit in the account, calculate and print the amount of money in the account at the end of each year for 10 years. Use the following formula for determining these amounts:*
>
> $$a = p(1 + r)^n$$
>
> *where*
>> *p is the original amount invested (i.e., the principal),*
>> *r is the annual interest rate,*
>> *n is the number of years and*
>> *a is the amount on deposit at the end of the nth year.*

This problem involves a loop that performs the indicated calculation for each of the 10 years the money remains on deposit. The solution is shown in Fig. 6.6.

The for statement (lines 28–35) executes its body 10 times, varying a control variable from 1 to 10 in increments of 1. Visual C++ does not include an exponentiation operator, so we use the *Standard library function pow* (line 31) for this purpose. The function pow(x, y) calculates the value of x raised to the yth power. In this example, the algebraic expression $(1 + r)^n$ is written as pow(1.0 + rate, year), where variable rate represents r and variable year represents n. Function pow takes two arguments of type double and returns a double value.

This program will not compile without including header file <cmath> (line 12). Function pow requires two double arguments. Note that year is an integer. Header <cmath>

```
1    // Fig. 6.6: ForTest.cpp
2    // Compound interest calculations with for.
3    #include <iostream>
4    using std::cout;
5    using std::endl;
6    using std::fixed;
7
8    #include <iomanip>
9    using std::setw; // enables program to set a field width
10   using std::setprecision;
11
12   #include <cmath> // standard C++ math library
13   using std::pow; // enables program to use function pow
14
15   int main()
16   {
17      double amount; // amount on deposit at end of each year
18      double principal = 1000.0; // initial amount before interest
19      double rate = .05; // interest rate
20
21      // display headers
22      cout << "Year" << setw( 21 ) << "Amount on deposit" << endl;
23
24      // set floating-point number format
25      cout << fixed << setprecision( 2 );
26
27      // calculate amount on deposit for each of ten years
28      for ( int year = 1; year <= 10; year++ )
29      {
30         // calculate new amount for specified year
31         amount = principal * pow( 1.0 + rate, year );
32
33         // display the year and the amount
34         cout << setw( 4 ) << year << setw( 21 ) << amount << endl;
35      } // end for
36
37      return 0; // indicate successful termination
38   } // end main
```

Fig. 6.6 | Compound interest calculations with for. (Part 1 of 2.)

```
Year    Amount on deposit
 1               1050.00
 2               1102.50
 3               1157.63
 4               1215.51
 5               1276.28
 6               1340.10
 7               1407.10
 8               1477.46
 9               1551.33
10               1628.89
```

Fig. 6.6 | Compound interest calculations with for. (Part 2 of 2.)

includes information that tells the compiler to convert the value of year to a temporary double representation before calling the function. This information is contained in pow's function prototype. Chapter 7 summarizes other math library functions.

Common Programming Error 6.7

In general, forgetting to include the appropriate header file when using standard library functions (e.g., <cmath> in a program that uses math library functions) is a compilation error.

A Caution about Using Type float or double for Monetary Amounts

Notice that lines 17–19 declare the double variables amount, principal and rate. We did this for simplicity because we're dealing with fractional parts of dollars, and we need a type that allows decimal points in its values. Unfortunately, this can cause trouble. Here is a simple explanation of what can go wrong when using float or double to represent dollar amounts (assuming setprecision(2) is used to specify two digits of precision when printing): Two dollar amounts stored in the machine could be 14.234 (which prints as 14.23) and 18.673 (which prints as 18.67). When these amounts are added, they produce the internal sum 32.907, which prints as 32.91. Thus your printout could appear as

```
  14.23
+ 18.67
-------
  32.91
```

but a person adding the individual numbers as printed would expect the sum 32.90! You have been warned!

Good Programming Practice 6.8

Do not use variables of type float or double to perform monetary calculations. The imprecision of floating-point numbers can cause errors that result in incorrect monetary values. In the exercises, we explore the use of integers to perform monetary calculations. [Note: Some third-party vendors sell Visual C++ class libraries that perform precise monetary calculations.]

Using Stream Manipulators to Format Numeric Output

The output statement in line 25 before the for loop and the output statement in line 34 in the for loop combine to print the values of the variables year and amount with the formatting specified by the parameterized stream manipulators setprecision and *setw* and the nonparameterized stream manipulator fixed. The stream manipulator setw(4) specifies that the next value output should appear in a *field width* of 4—i.e., cout prints the value with at least 4 character positions. If the value to be output is less than 4 character positions wide, the value is *right justified* in the field by default. If the value to be output is more than 4 character positions wide, the field width is extended to accommodate the entire value. To indicate that values should be output *left justified*, simply output nonparameterized stream manipulator **left** (found in header <iostream>). Right justification can be restored by outputting nonparameterized stream manipulator **right**.

The other formatting in the output statements indicates that variable amount is printed as a fixed-point value with a decimal point (specified in line 25 with the stream manipulator fixed) right justified in a field of 21 character positions (specified in line 34 with setw(21)) and two digits of precision to the right of the decimal point (specified in line 25 with manipulator setprecision(2)). We applied the stream manipulators fixed and setprecision to the output stream (i.e., cout) before the for loop because these format settings remain in effect until they are changed—such settings are called *sticky settings* and they do not need to be applied during each iteration of the loop. However, the field width specified with setw applies only to the next value output. We discuss Visual C++'s powerful input/output formatting capabilities in detail in Chapter 17.

Note that the calculation 1.0 + rate, which appears as an argument to the pow function, is contained in the body of the for statement. In fact, this calculation produces the same result during each iteration of the loop, so repeating it is wasteful—it should be performed once before the loop.

Performance Tip 6.1

Avoid placing expressions whose values do not change inside loops—but, even if you do, many of today's sophisticated optimizing compilers will automatically place such expressions outside the loops in the generated machine-language code.

Performance Tip 6.2

Many compilers contain optimization features that improve the performance of the code you write, but it is still better to write good code from the start.

Be sure to try our Peter Minuit problem in Exercise 6.29. This problem demonstrates the wonders of compound interest.

6.5 do...while Repetition Statement

The do...while repetition statement is similar to the while statement. In the while statement, the loop-continuation condition test occurs at the beginning of the loop before the body of the loop executes. The do...while statement tests the loop-continuation condition *after* the loop body executes; therefore, the loop body always executes at least once. When a do...while terminates, execution continues with the statement after the while clause. Note that it is not necessary to use braces in the do...while statement if there is only one statement in the body; however, most programmers include the braces to avoid confusion between the while and do...while statements. For example,

while (*condition*)

normally is regarded as the header of a while statement. A do...while with no braces around the single statement body appears as

```
do
    statement
while ( condition );
```

which can be confusing. You might misinterpret the last line—while (*condition*);—as a while statement containing as its body an empty statement. Thus, the do...while with one statement often is written as follows to avoid confusion:

```
do
{
    statement
} while ( condition );
```

Good Programming Practice 6.9

Always including braces in a do...while statement helps eliminate ambiguity between the while statement and the do...while statement containing one statement.

Figure 6.7 uses a do...while statement to print the numbers 1–10. Upon entering the do...while statement, line 13 outputs counter's value and line 14 increments counter. Then the program evaluates the loop-continuation test at the bottom of the loop (line 15). If the condition is true, the loop continues from the first body statement in the do...while (line 13). If the condition is false, the loop terminates and the program continues with the next statement after the loop (line 17).

```cpp
1   // Fig. 6.7: DoWhileTest.cpp
2   // do...while repetition statement.
3   #include <iostream>
4   using std::cout;
5   using std::endl;
6
7   int main()
8   {
9       int counter = 1; // initialize counter
10
11      do
12      {
13          cout << counter << " "; // display counter
14          counter++; // increment counter
15      } while ( counter <= 10 ); // end do...while
16
17      cout << endl; // output a newline
18      return 0; // indicate successful termination
19  } // end main
```

```
1 2 3 4 5 6 7 8 9 10
```

Fig. 6.7 | do...while repetition statement.

***do...while* Statement UML Activity Diagram**

Figure 6.8 contains the UML activity diagram for the do...while statement. This diagram makes it clear that the loop-continuation condition is not evaluated until after the loop performs the loop-body action states at least once. Compare this activity diagram with that of the while statement (Fig. 5.6). Again, note that (besides an initial state, transition arrows, a merge, a final state and several notes) the diagram contains only action states and a decision. Imagine, again, that you have access to a bin of empty do...while-statement UML activity diagrams—as many as you might need to stack and nest with the activity diagrams of other control statements to form a structured implementation of an algorithm. You fill in the action states and decision symbols with action expressions and guard conditions appropriate to the algorithm.

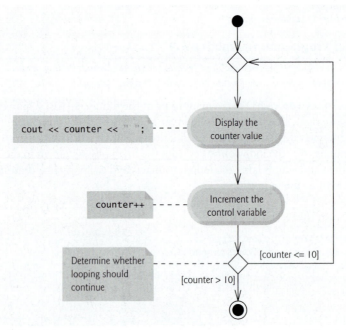

Fig. 6.8 | UML activity diagram for the do...while repetition statement of Fig. 6.7.

6.6 switch Multiple-Selection Statement

We discussed the if single-selection statement and the if...else double-selection statement in Chapter 5. Visual C++ provides the ***switch multiple-selection*** statement to perform many different actions based on the possible values of a variable or expression. Each action is associated with the value of a ***constant integral expression*** (i.e., any combination of character constants and integer constants that evaluates to a constant integer value) to which the variable or expression may evaluate.

GradeBook Class with switch Statement to Count A, B, C, D and F Grades

We now present an enhanced version of the GradeBook class introduced in Chapter 4 and further developed in Chapter 5. The new version of the class asks the user to enter a set of letter grades, then displays a summary of the number of students who received each grade.

The class uses a switch to determine whether each grade entered is an A, B, C, D or F and to increment the appropriate grade counter. Class GradeBook is defined in Fig. 6.9, and its member-function definitions appear in Fig. 6.10. Figure 6.11 shows sample inputs and outputs of the main program that uses class GradeBook to process a set of grades.

Like earlier versions of the class definition, the GradeBook class definition (Fig. 6.9) contains function prototypes for member functions setCourseName (line 13), getCourseName (line 14) and displayMessage (line 15), as well as the class's constructor (line 12). The class definition also declares private data member courseName (line 19).

Class GradeBook (Fig. 6.9) now contains five additional private data members (lines 20–24)—counter variables for each grade category (i.e., A, B, C, D and F). The class also contains two additional public member functions—inputGrades and displayGradeReport. Member function inputGrades (declared in line 16) reads an arbitrary number of letter grades from the user using sentinel-controlled repetition and updates the appropriate grade counter for each grade entered. Member function displayGradeReport (declared in line 17) outputs a report containing the number of students who received each letter grade.

Source-code file GradeBook.cpp (Fig. 6.10) contains the member-function definitions for class GradeBook. Notice that lines 16–20 in the constructor initialize the five grade counters to 0—when a GradeBook object is first created, no grades have been entered yet. As you'll soon see, these counters are incremented in member function inputGrades as the user enters grades. The definitions of member functions setCourseName, getCourseName and displayMessage are identical to those found in the earlier versions of class GradeBook. Let's consider the new GradeBook member functions in detail.

```
1   // Fig. 6.9: GradeBook.h
2   // Definition of class GradeBook that counts A, B, C, D and F grades.
3   // Member functions are defined in GradeBook.cpp
4
5   #include <string> // program uses C++ Standard string class
6   using std::string;
7
8   // GradeBook class definition
9   class GradeBook
10  {
11  public:
12     GradeBook( string ); // constructor initializes course name
13     void setCourseName( string ); // function to set the course name
14     string getCourseName(); // function to retrieve the course name
15     void displayMessage(); // display a welcome message
16     void inputGrades(); // input arbitrary number of grades from user
17     void displayGradeReport(); // display a report based on the grades
18  private:
19     string courseName; // course name for this GradeBook
20     int aCount; // count of A grades
21     int bCount; // count of B grades
22     int cCount; // count of C grades
23     int dCount; // count of D grades
24     int fCount; // count of F grades
25  }; // end class GradeBook
```

Fig. 6.9 | GradeBook class definition.

```cpp
1   // Fig. 6.10: GradeBook.cpp
2   // Member-function definitions for class GradeBook that
3   // uses a switch statement to count A, B, C, D and F grades.
4   #include <iostream>
5   using std::cout;
6   using std::cin;
7   using std::endl;
8
9   #include "GradeBook.h" // include definition of class GradeBook
10
11  // constructor initializes courseName with string supplied as argument;
12  // initializes counter data members to 0
13  GradeBook::GradeBook( string name )
14  {
15     setCourseName( name ); // validate and store courseName
16     aCount = 0; // initialize count of A grades to 0
17     bCount = 0; // initialize count of B grades to 0
18     cCount = 0; // initialize count of C grades to 0
19     dCount = 0; // initialize count of D grades to 0
20     fCount = 0; // initialize count of F grades to 0
21  } // end GradeBook constructor
22
23  // function to set the course name; limits name to 30 or fewer characters
24  void GradeBook::setCourseName( string name )
25  {
26     if ( name.length() <= 30 ) // if name has 30 or fewer characters
27        courseName = name; // store the course name in the object
28     else // if name is longer than 30 characters
29     { // set courseName to first 30 characters of parameter name
30        courseName = name.substr( 0, 30 ); // select first 30 characters
31        cout << "Name \"" << name << "\" exceeds maximum length (30).\n"
32           << "Limiting courseName to first 30 characters.\n" << endl;
33     } // end if...else
34  } // end function setCourseName
35
36  // function to retrieve the course name
37  string GradeBook::getCourseName()
38  {
39     return courseName;
40  } // end function getCourseName
41
42  // display a welcome message to the GradeBook user
43  void GradeBook::displayMessage()
44  {
45     // this statement calls getCourseName to get the
46     // name of the course this GradeBook represents
47     cout << "Welcome to the grade book for\n" << getCourseName() << "!\n"
48        << endl;
49  } // end function displayMessage
50
```

Fig. 6.10 | GradeBook class uses `switch` statement to count letter grades A, B, C, D and F. (Part 1 of 3.)

```
51   // input arbitrary number of grades from user; update grade counter
52   void GradeBook::inputGrades()
53   {
54      int grade; // grade entered by user
55
56      cout << "Enter the letter grades." << endl
57         << "Enter the EOF character to end input." << endl;
58
59      // loop until user types end-of-file key sequence
60      while ( ( grade = cin.get() ) != EOF )
61      {
62         // determine which grade was entered
63         switch ( grade ) // switch statement nested in while
64         {
65            case 'A': // grade was uppercase A
66            case 'a': // or lowercase a
67               aCount++; // increment aCount
68               break; // necessary to exit switch
69
70            case 'B': // grade was uppercase B
71            case 'b': // or lowercase b
72               bCount++; // increment bCount
73               break; // exit switch
74
75            case 'C': // grade was uppercase C
76            case 'c': // or lowercase c
77               cCount++; // increment cCount
78               break; // exit switch
79
80            case 'D': // grade was uppercase D
81            case 'd': // or lowercase d
82               dCount++; // increment dCount
83               break; // exit switch
84
85            case 'F': // grade was uppercase F
86            case 'f': // or lowercase f
87               fCount++; // increment fCount
88               break; // exit switch
89
90            case '\n': // ignore newlines,
91            case '\t': // tabs,
92            case ' ': // and spaces in input
93               break; // exit switch
94
95            default: // catch all other characters
96               cout << "Incorrect letter grade entered."
97                  << " Enter a new grade." << endl;
98               break; // optional; will exit switch anyway
99         } // end switch
100     } // end while
101  } // end function inputGrades
```

Fig. 6.10 | GradeBook class uses switch statement to count letter grades A, B, C, D and F. (Part 2 of 3.)

```
102
103     // display a report based on the grades entered by user
104     void GradeBook::displayGradeReport()
105     {
106        // output summary of results
107        cout << "\n\nNumber of students who received each letter grade:"
108           << "\nA: " << aCount // display number of A grades
109           << "\nB: " << bCount // display number of B grades
110           << "\nC: " << cCount // display number of C grades
111           << "\nD: " << dCount // display number of D grades
112           << "\nF: " << fCount // display number of F grades
113           << endl;
114     } // end function displayGradeReport
```

Fig. 6.10 | GradeBook class uses switch statement to count letter grades A, B, C, D and F. (Part 3 of 3.)

Reading Character Input

The user enters letter grades for a course in member function inputGrades (lines 52–101). Inside the while header, in line 60, the parenthesized assignment (grade = cin.get()) executes first. The cin.get() function reads one character from the keyboard and stores that character in integer variable grade (declared in line 54). Characters normally are stored in variables of type *char*; however, characters can be stored in any integer data type, because types short, int and long are guaranteed to be at least as big as type char. Thus, we can treat a character either as an integer or as a character, depending on its use. For example, the statement

```
cout << "The character (" << 'a' << ") has the value "
   << static_cast< int > ( 'a' ) << endl;
```

prints the character a and its integer value as follows:

```
The character (a) has the value 97
```

The integer 97 is the character's numerical representation in the computer. Most computers today use the *ASCII (American Standard Code for Information Interchange) character set*, in which 97 represents the lowercase letter 'a'. A table of the ASCII characters and their decimal equivalents is presented in Appendix B.

Assignment statements as a whole have the value that is assigned to the variable on the left side of the =. Thus, the value of the assignment expression grade = cin.get() is the same as the value returned by cin.get() and assigned to the variable grade.

The fact that assignment expressions have values can be useful for assigning the same value to several variables. For example,

```
a = b = c = 0;
```

first evaluates the assignment c = 0 (because the = operator associates from right to left). The variable b is then assigned the value of the assignment c = 0 (which is 0). Then, the variable a is assigned the value of the assignment b = (c = 0) (which is also 0). In the program, the value of the assignment grade = cin.get() is compared with the value of EOF (a symbol whose acronym stands for "end-of-file"). We use EOF (which normally has the value –1) as the sentinel value. *However, you do not type the value –1, nor do you type the letters EOF as the sentinel value.* Rather, you type a system-dependent keystroke combination that means "end-of-file" to indicate that you have no more data to enter. EOF is a symbolic integer constant defined in the <iostream> header file. If the value assigned to grade is equal to EOF, the while loop (lines 60–100) terminates. We have chosen to represent the characters entered into this program as ints, because EOF has type int.

On Microsoft Windows, end-of-file can be entered by typing

    <Ctrl> z

on a line by itself. This notation means to press and hold down the *Ctrl* key, then press the z key. [*Note:* In some cases, you must press *Enter* after the preceding key sequence. Also, the characters ^Z sometimes appear on the screen to represent end-of-file, as shown in Fig. 6.11.]

Portability Tip 6.2

The keystroke combinations for entering end-of-file are system dependent. Use <Ctrl> z on Windows systems.

Portability Tip 6.3

Testing for the symbolic constant EOF rather than –1 makes programs more portable. The ANSI/ISO C Standard, from which Visual C++ adopts the definition of EOF, states that EOF is a negative integral value (but not necessarily –1), so EOF could have different values on different systems.

In this program, the user enters grades at the keyboard. When the user presses the *Enter* (or *Return*) key, the characters are read by the cin.get() function, one character at a time. If the character entered is not end-of-file, the flow of control enters the switch statement (lines 63–99), which increments the appropriate letter-grade counter based on the grade entered.

switch-Statement Details

The switch statement consists of a series of **case** *labels* and an optional **default** *case*. These are used in this example to determine which counter to increment, based on a grade. When the flow of control reaches the switch, the program evaluates the expression in the parentheses (i.e., grade) following keyword switch (line 63). This is called the *controlling expression*. The switch statement compares the value of the controlling expression with each case label. Assume the user enters the letter C as a grade. The program compares C to each case in the switch. If a match occurs (case 'C': in line 75), the program executes the statements for that case. For the letter C, line 77 increments cCount by 1. The break statement (line 78) causes program control to proceed with the first statement after the switch—in this program, control transfers to line 100. This line marks the end of the body of the while loop that inputs grades (lines 60–100), so control flows to the while's condition (line 60) to determine whether the loop should continue executing.

The cases in our switch explicitly test for the lowercase and uppercase versions of the letters A, B, C, D and F. Note the cases in lines 65–66 that test for the values 'A' and 'a' (both of which represent the grade A). Listing cases consecutively in this manner with no statements between them enables the cases to perform the same set of statements—when the controlling expression evaluates to either 'A' or 'a', the statements in lines 67–68 will execute. Note that each case can have multiple statements. The switch selection statement differs from other control statements in that it does not require braces around multiple statements in each case.

Without break statements, each time a match occurs in the switch, the statements for that case and subsequent cases execute until a break statement or the end of the switch is encountered. This is often referred to as "falling through" to the statements in subsequent cases. (This feature is perfect for writing a concise program that displays the iterative song "The Twelve Days of Christmas" in Exercise 6.28.)

Common Programming Error 6.8

Forgetting a break statement when one is needed in a switch statement is a logic error.

Common Programming Error 6.9

Omitting the space between the word case and the integral value being tested in a switch statement can cause a logic error. For example, writing case3: instead of case 3: simply creates an unused label. In this situation, the switch statement will not perform the appropriate actions when the switch's controlling expression has a value of 3.

Providing a default *Case*

If no match occurs between the controlling expression's value and a case label, the default case (lines 95–98) executes. We use the default case in this example to process all controlling-expression values that are neither valid grades nor newline, tab or space characters (we discuss how the program handles these white-space characters shortly). If no match occurs, the default case executes, and lines 96–97 print an error message indicating that an incorrect letter grade was entered. If no match occurs in a switch statement that does not contain a default case, program control simply continues with the first statement after the switch.

Good Programming Practice 6.10

Provide a default case in switch statements. Cases not explicitly tested in a switch statement without a default case are ignored. Including a default case focuses you on the need to process exceptional conditions. There are situations in which no default processing is needed. Although the case clauses and the default case clause in a switch statement can occur in any order, it is common practice to place the default clause last.

Good Programming Practice 6.11

The last case in a switch statement does not require a break statement. Some programmers include this break for clarity and for symmetry with other cases.

Ignoring Newline, Tab and Blank Characters in Input

Note that lines 90–93 in the switch statement of Fig. 6.10 cause the program to skip newline, tab and blank characters. Reading characters one at a time can cause some problems. To have the program read the characters, we must send them to the computer by pressing the *Enter* key on the keyboard. This places a newline character in the input after the character we wish to process. Often, this newline character must be specially processed to make the program work correctly. By including the preceding cases in our switch statement, we prevent the error message in the default case from being printed each time a newline, tab or space is encountered in the input.

Common Programming Error 6.10

Not processing newline and other white-space characters in the input when reading characters one at a time can cause logic errors.

Testing Class *GradeBook*

Figure 6.11 creates a GradeBook object (line 9). Line 11 invokes its displayMessage member function to output a welcome message to the user. Line 12 invokes member function inputGrades to read a set of grades from the user and keep track of how many students received each grade. Note that the output window in Fig. 6.11 shows an error message displayed in response to entering an invalid grade (i.e., E). Line 13 invokes GradeBook member function displayGradeReport (defined in lines 104–114 of Fig. 6.10), which outputs a report based on the grades entered (as in the output in Fig. 6.11).

```cpp
1   // Fig. 6.11: GradeBookTest.cpp
2   // Create GradeBook object, input grades and display grade report.
3
4   #include "GradeBook.h" // include definition of class GradeBook
5
6   int main()
7   {
8      // create GradeBook object
9      GradeBook myGradeBook( "CS101 Visual C++ Programming" );
10
11     myGradeBook.displayMessage(); // display welcome message
12     myGradeBook.inputGrades(); // read grades from user
13     myGradeBook.displayGradeReport(); // display report based on grades
14     return 0; // indicate successful termination
15  } // end main
```

```
Welcome to the grade book for
CS101 Visual C++ Programming!

Enter the letter grades.
Enter the EOF character to end input.
a
B
c
C
A
d
f
C
E
Incorrect letter grade entered. Enter a new grade.
```

Fig. 6.11 | Creating a GradeBook object and calling its member functions. (Part 1 of 2.)

```
D
A
b
^Z

Number of students who received each letter grade:
A: 3
B: 2
C: 3
D: 2
F: 1
```

Fig. 6.11 | Creating a `GradeBook` object and calling its member functions. (Part 2 of 2.)

switch-Statement UML Activity Diagram

Figure 6.12 shows the UML activity diagram for the general `switch` multiple-selection statement. Most `switch` statements use a `break` in each `case` to terminate the `switch` statement after processing the `case`. Figure 6.12 emphasizes this by including `break` statements

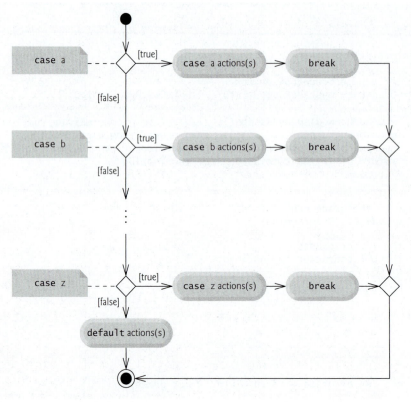

Fig. 6.12 | `switch` multiple-selection statement UML activity diagram with `break` statements.

in the activity diagram. Without the break statement, control would not transfer to the first statement after the switch statement after a case is processed. Instead, control would transfer to the next case's actions.

The diagram makes it clear that the break statement at the end of a case causes control to exit the switch statement immediately. Again, note that (besides an initial state, transition arrows, a final state and several notes) the diagram contains action states and decisions. Also, note that the diagram uses merge symbols to merge the transitions from the break statements to the final state.

Imagine, again, that you have a bin of empty switch-statement UML activity diagrams—as many as you might need to stack and nest with the activity diagrams of other control statements to form a structured implementation of an algorithm. You fill in the action states and decision symbols with action expressions and guard conditions appropriate to the algorithm. Note that, although nested control statements are common, it is rare to find nested switch statements in a program.

When using the switch statement, remember that each case can be used to test only a *constant* integral expression—any combination of character constants and integer constants that evaluates to a constant integer value. A character constant is represented as the specific character in single quotes, such as 'A'. An integer constant is simply an integer value. Also, each case label can specify only one constant integral expression.

Common Programming Error 6.11

Specifying a nonconstant integral expression in a switch statement's case label is a syntax error.

Common Programming Error 6.12

Providing identical case labels in a switch statement is a compilation error. Providing case labels containing different expressions that evaluate to the same value also is a compilation error. For example, placing case 4 + 1: and case 3 + 2: in the same switch statement is a compilation error, because these are both equivalent to case 5:.

In Chapter 14, we present a more elegant way to implement switch logic. We'll use a technique called polymorphism to create programs that are often clearer, more concise, easier to maintain and easier to extend than programs that use switch logic.

Notes on Data Types

Visual C++ has flexible data type sizes (see Appendix C, Fundamental Types). Different applications, for example, might need integers of different sizes. Visual C++ provides several data types to represent integers. The range of integer values for each type depends on the particular computer's hardware. In addition to the types int and char, Visual C++ provides the types short (an abbreviation of short int) and long (an abbreviation of long int). The minimum range of values for short integers is −32,768 to 32,767. For the vast majority of integer calculations, long integers are sufficient. The minimum range of values for long integers is −2,147,483,648 to 2,147,483,647. On most computers, ints are equivalent either to short or to long. The range of values for an int is at least the same as that for short integers and no larger than that for long integers. The data type char can be used to represent any of the characters in the computer's character set. It also can be used to represent small integers.

Portability Tip 6.4

Because ints *can vary in size between systems, use* long *integers if you expect to process integers outside the range −32,768 to 32,767 and you would like to run the program on several different computer systems.*

Performance Tip 6.3

If memory is at a premium, it might be desirable to use smaller integer sizes.

Performance Tip 6.4

Using smaller integer sizes can result in a slower program if the machine's instructions for manipulating them are not as efficient as those for the natural-size integers—i.e., integers whose size equals the machine's word size (e.g., 32 bits on a 32-bit machine, 64 bits on a 64-bit machine). Always test proposed efficiency "upgrades" to be sure they really improve performance.

6.7 break and continue Statements

In addition to the selection and repetition statements, Visual C++ provides statements break and continue to alter the flow of control. The preceding section showed how break can be used to terminate a switch statement's execution. This section discusses how to use break in a repetition statement.

break *Statement*

The **break** *statement*, when executed in a while, for, do...while or switch statement, causes immediate exit from that statement. Program execution continues with the next statement. Common uses of the break statement are to escape early from a loop or to skip the remainder of a switch statement (as in Fig. 6.10). Figure 6.13 demonstrates the break statement (line 14) exiting a for repetition statement.

```cpp
1   // Fig. 6.13: BreakTest.cpp
2   // break statement exiting a for statement.
3   #include <iostream>
4   using std::cout;
5   using std::endl;
6
7   int main()
8   {
9      int count; // control variable also used after loop terminates
10
11     for ( count = 1; count <= 10; count++ ) // loop 10 times
12     {
13        if ( count == 5 )
14           break; // break loop only if x is 5
15
16        cout << count << " ";
17     } // end for
18
19     cout << "\nBroke out of loop at count = " << count << endl;
```

Fig. 6.13 | break statement exiting a for statement. (Part 1 of 2.)

```
20        return 0; // indicate successful termination
21  } // end main
```

```
1 2 3 4
Broke out of loop at count = 5
```

Fig. 6.13 | break statement exiting a for statement. (Part 2 of 2.)

When the if statement detects that count is 5, the break statement executes. This terminates the for statement, and the program proceeds to line 19 (immediately after the for statement), which displays a message indicating the control-variable value that terminated the loop. The for statement fully executes its body only four times instead of 10. Note that the control-variable count is defined outside the for-statement header, so that we can use the control variable both in the loop's body and after the loop completes its execution.

continue *Statement*

The continue statement, when executed in a while, for or do...while statement, skips the remaining statements in the body of that statement and proceeds with the next iteration of the loop. In while and do...while statements, the loop-continuation test evaluates immediately after the continue statement executes. In the for statement, the increment expression executes, then the loop-continuation test evaluates.

Figure 6.14 uses the continue statement (line 12) in a for statement to skip the output statement (line 14) when the nested if (lines 11–12) determines that the value of count is 5. When the continue statement executes, program control continues with the increment of the control variable in the for header (line 9) and loops five more times.

In Section 6.3, we stated that the while statement could be used in most cases to represent the for statement. The one exception occurs when the increment expression in the while statement follows the continue statement. In this case, the increment does not execute before the program tests the loop-continuation condition, and the while does not execute in the same manner as the for.

Good Programming Practice 6.12

Some programmers feel that break and continue violate structured programming. The effects of these statements can be achieved by structured programming techniques we soon will learn, so these programmers do not use break and continue. Most programmers consider the use of break in switch statements acceptable.

Performance Tip 6.5

The break and continue statements, when used properly, perform faster than do the corresponding structured techniques.

Software Engineering Observation 6.1

There is a tension between achieving quality software engineering and achieving the best-performing software. Often, one of these goals is achieved at the expense of the other. For all but the most performance-intensive situations, apply the following guidelines: First, make your code simple and correct; then make it fast and small, but only if necessary.

```
 1   // Fig. 6.14: ContinueTest.cpp
 2   // continue statement terminating an iteration of a for statement.
 3   #include <iostream>
 4   using std::cout;
 5   using std::endl;
 6
 7   int main()
 8   {
 9      for ( int count = 1; count <= 10; count++ ) // loop 10 times
10      {
11         if ( count == 5 ) // if count is 5,
12            continue;        // skip remaining code in loop
13
14         cout << count << " ";
15      } // end for
16
17      cout << "\nUsed continue to skip printing 5" << endl;
18      return 0; // indicate successful termination
19   } // end main
```

```
1 2 3 4 6 7 8 9 10
Used continue to skip printing 5
```

Fig. 6.14 | continue statement terminating a single iteration of a for statement.

6.8 Logical Operators

So far we have studied only *simple conditions*, such as counter <= 10, total > 1000 and number != sentinelValue. We expressed these conditions in terms of the relational operators >, <, >= and <=, and the equality operators == and !=. Each decision tested precisely one condition. To test multiple conditions while making a decision, we performed these tests in separate statements or in nested if or if...else statements.

Visual C++ provides *logical operators* that are used to form more complex conditions by combining simple conditions. The logical operators are && (logical AND), || (logical OR) and ! (logical NOT, also called logical negation).

Logical AND (&&) Operator

Suppose that we wish to ensure that two conditions are *both* true before we choose a certain path of execution. In this case, we can use the **&&** (*logical AND*) operator, as follows:

```
if ( gender == 1 && age >= 65 )
    seniorFemales++;
```

This if statement contains two simple conditions. The condition gender == 1 is used here to determine whether a person is a female. The condition age >= 65 determines whether a person is a senior citizen. The simple condition to the left of the && operator evaluates first. If necessary, the simple condition to the right of the && operator evaluates next. As we'll discuss shortly, the right side of a logical AND expression is evaluated only if the left side is true. The if statement then considers the combined condition

```
gender == 1 && age >= 65
```

This condition is true if and only if both of the simple conditions are true. Finally, if this combined condition is indeed true, the statement in the if statement's body increments the count of seniorFemales. If either of the simple conditions is false (or both are), then the program skips the incrementing and proceeds to the statement following the if. The preceding combined condition can be made more readable by adding redundant parentheses:

```
( gender == 1 ) && ( age >= 65 )
```

 Common Programming Error 6.13

Although 3 < x < 7 is a mathematically correct condition, it does not evaluate as you might expect in Visual C++. Use (3 < x && x < 7) to get the proper evaluation in Visual C++.

Figure 6.15 summarizes the && operator. The table shows all four possible combinations of false and true values for *expression1* and *expression2*. Such tables are often called *truth tables*. Visual C++ evaluates to false or true all expressions that include relational operators, equality operators and/or logical operators.

expression1	expression2	expression1 && expression2
false	false	false
false	true	false
true	false	false
true	true	true

Fig. 6.15 | && (logical AND) operator truth table.

Logical OR (||) Operator

Now let us consider the || (*logical OR*) operator. Suppose we wish to ensure at some point in a program that either *or* both of two conditions are true before we choose a certain path of execution. In this case, we use the || operator, as in the following program segment:

```
if ( ( semesterAverage >= 90 ) || ( finalExam >= 90 ) )
   cout << "Student grade is A" << endl;
```

This preceding condition also contains two simple conditions. The simple condition semesterAverage >= 90 evaluates to determine whether the student deserves an "A" in the course because of a solid performance throughout the semester. The simple condition finalExam >= 90 evaluates to determine whether the student deserves an "A" in the course because of an outstanding performance on the final exam. The if statement then considers the combined condition

```
( semesterAverage >= 90 ) || ( finalExam >= 90 )
```

and awards the student an "A" if either or both of the simple conditions are true. Note that the message "Student grade is A" prints unless both of the simple conditions are false. Figure 6.16 is a truth table for the logical OR operator (||).

The && operator has a higher precedence than the || operator. Both operators associate from left to right. An expression containing && or || operators evaluates only until the truth or falsehood of the expression is known. Thus, evaluation of the expression

```
( gender == 1 ) && ( age >= 65 )
```

stops immediately if gender is not equal to 1 (i.e., the entire expression is false) and continues if gender is equal to 1 (i.e., the entire expression could still be true if the condition age >= 65 is true). This performance feature for the evaluation of logical AND and logical OR expressions is called *short-circuit evaluation*.

Performance Tip 6.6

In expressions using operator && , if the separate conditions are independent of one another, make the condition most likely to be false the leftmost condition. In expressions using operator || , make the condition most likely to be true the leftmost condition. This use of short-circuit evaluation can reduce a program's execution time.

expression1	expression2	expression1 || expression2
false	false	false
false	true	true
true	false	true
true	true	true

Fig. 6.16 | || (logical OR) operator truth table.

Logical Negation (!) Operator

Visual C++ provides the *!* (*logical NOT*, also called *logical negation*) operator to enable a programmer to "reverse" the meaning of a condition. Unlike the && and || binary operators, which combine two conditions, the unary logical negation operator has only a single condition as an operand. The unary logical negation operator is placed before a condition when we are interested in choosing a path of execution if the original condition (without the logical negation operator) is false, such as in the following program segment:

```
if ( !( grade == sentinelValue ) )
   cout << "The next grade is " << grade << endl;
```

The parentheses around the condition grade == sentinelValue are needed because the logical negation operator has a higher precedence than the equality operator.

In most cases, you can avoid using logical negation by expressing the condition with an appropriate relational or equality operator. For example, the preceding if statement also can be written as follows:

```
if ( grade != sentinelValue )
   cout << "The next grade is " << grade << endl;
```

This flexibility often can help a programmer express a condition in a more "natural" or convenient manner. Figure 6.17 is a truth table for the logical negation operator (!).

expression	!expression
false	true
true	false

Fig. 6.17 | ! (logical negation) operator truth table.

Logical Operators Example

Figure 6.18 demonstrates the logical operators by producing their truth tables. The output shows each expression that is evaluated and its bool result. By default, bool values true and false are displayed by cout and the stream insertion operator as 1 and 0, respectively. We use *stream manipulator boolalpha* (a sticky manipulator) in line 11 to specify that the value of each bool expression should be displayed as either the word "true" or the word "false." For example, the result of the expression false && false in line 12 is false, so the second line of output includes the word "false." Lines 11–15 produce the truth table for &&. Lines 18–22 produce the truth table for ||. Lines 25–27 produce the truth table for !.

```cpp
1   // Fig. 6.18: LogicalOperators.cpp
2   // Logical operators.
3   #include <iostream>
4   using std::cout;
5   using std::endl;
6   using std::boolalpha; // causes bool values to print as "true" or "false"
7
8   int main()
9   {
10      // create truth table for && (logical AND) operator
11      cout << boolalpha << "Logical AND (&&)"
12         << "\nfalse && false: " << ( false && false )
13         << "\nfalse && true: " << ( false && true )
14         << "\ntrue && false: " << ( true && false )
15         << "\ntrue && true: " << ( true && true ) << "\n\n";
16
17      // create truth table for || (logical OR) operator
18      cout << "Logical OR (||)"
19         << "\nfalse || false: " << ( false || false )
20         << "\nfalse || true: " << ( false || true )
21         << "\ntrue || false: " << ( true || false )
22         << "\ntrue || true: " << ( true || true ) << "\n\n";
23
24      // create truth table for ! (logical negation) operator
25      cout << "Logical NOT (!)"
26         << "\n!false: " << ( !false )
27         << "\n!true: " << ( !true ) << endl;
28      return 0; // indicate successful termination
29   } // end main
```

Fig. 6.18 | Logical operators. (Part 1 of 2.)

```
Logical AND (&&)
false && false: false
false && true: false
true && false: false
true && true: true

Logical OR (||)
false || false: false
false || true: true
true || false: true
true || true: true

Logical NOT (!)
!false: true
!true: false
```

Fig. 6.18 | Logical operators. (Part 2 of 2.)

Summary of Operator Precedence and Associativity

Figure 6.19 adds the logical operators to the operator precedence and associativity chart. The operators are shown from top to bottom, in decreasing order of precedence.

Operators						Associativity	Type
::						left to right	scope resolution
()						left to right	parentheses
++	--	static_cast< *type* >()				left to right	unary (postfix)
++	--	+	-	!		right to left	unary (prefix)
*	/	%				left to right	multiplicative
+	-					left to right	additive
<<	>>					left to right	insertion/extraction
<	<=	>	>=			left to right	relational
==	!=					left to right	equality
&&						left to right	logical AND
||						left to right	logical OR
?:						right to left	conditional
=	+=	-=	*=	/=	%=	right to left	assignment
,						left to right	comma

Fig. 6.19 | Operator precedence and associativity.

6.9 Confusing the Equality (==) and Assignment (=) Operators

There is one type of error that Visual C++ programmers, no matter how experienced, tend to make so frequently that we feel it requires a separate section. That error is accidentally swapping the operators == (equality) and = (assignment). What makes these swaps so damaging is the fact that they ordinarily do not cause syntax errors. Rather, statements with these errors tend to compile correctly and the programs run to completion, often generating incorrect results through runtime logic errors. [*Note:* Some compilers issue a warning when = is used in a context where == normally is expected.]

Two aspects of Visual C++ contribute to these problems. One is that any expression that produces a value can be used in the decision portion of any control statement. If the value of the expression is zero, it is treated as false, and if the value is nonzero, it is treated as true. The second is that assignments produce a value—namely, the value assigned to the variable on the left side of the assignment operator. For example, suppose we intend to write

```
if ( payCode == 4 )
    cout << "You get a bonus!" << endl;
```

but we accidentally write

```
if ( payCode = 4 )
    cout << "You get a bonus!" << endl;
```

The first if statement properly awards a bonus to the person whose payCode is equal to 4. The second if statement—the one with the error—evaluates the assignment expression in the if condition to the constant 4. Any nonzero value is interpreted as true, so the condition in this if statement is always true and the person always receives a bonus regardless of what the actual paycode is! Even worse, the paycode has been modified when it was only supposed to be examined!

Common Programming Error 6.14

Using operator == for assignment and using operator = for equality are logic errors.

Error-Prevention Tip 6.3

Programmers normally write conditions such as x == 7 with the variable name on the left and the constant on the right. By reversing these so that the constant is on the left and the variable name is on the right, as in 7 == x, you'll be protected by the compiler if you accidentally replace the == operator with =. The compiler treats this as a compilation error, because you cannot change the value of a constant. This will prevent the potential devastation of a runtime logic error.

Variable names are said to be *lvalues* (for "left values") because they can be used on the left side of an assignment operator. Constants are said to be *rvalues* (for "right values") because they can be used on only the right side of an assignment operator. Note that *lvalues* can also be used as *rvalues*, but not vice versa.

There is another equally unpleasant situation. Suppose you want to assign a value to a variable with a simple statement like

```
x = 1;
```

but instead write

```
x == 1;
```

Here, too, this is not a syntax error. Rather, the compiler simply evaluates the conditional expression. If x is equal to 1, the condition is `true` and the expression evaluates to the value `true`. If x is not equal to 1, the condition is `false` and the expression evaluates to the value `false`. Regardless of the expression's value, there is no assignment operator, so the value simply is lost. The value of x remains unaltered, probably causing an execution-time logic error. Unfortunately, we do not have a handy trick available to help you with this problem!

Error-Prevention Tip 6.4

Use your text editor to search for all occurrences of = in your program and check that you have the correct assignment operator or logical operator in each place.

6.10 Structured Programming Summary

Just as architects design buildings by employing the collective wisdom of their profession, so should programmers design programs. Our field is younger than architecture is, and our collective wisdom is considerably sparser. We have learned that structured programming produces programs that are easier than unstructured programs to understand, test, debug, modify, and even prove correct in a mathematical sense.

Figure 6.20 uses activity diagrams to summarize Visual C++'s control statements. The initial and final states indicate the single entry point and the single exit point of each control statement. Arbitrarily connecting individual symbols in an activity diagram can lead to unstructured programs. Therefore, the programming profession uses only a limited set of control statements that can be combined in only two simple ways to build structured programs.

For simplicity, only single-entry/single-exit control statements are used—there is only one way to enter and only one way to exit each control statement. Connecting control statements in sequence to form structured programs is simple—the final state of one control statement is connected to the initial state of the next—that is, they are placed one after another in a program. We have called this "control-statement stacking." The rules for forming structured programs also allow for control statements to be nested.

Figure 6.21 shows the rules for forming structured programs. The rules assume that action states may be used to indicate any action. The rules also assume that we begin with the so-called simplest activity diagram (Fig. 6.22), consisting of only an initial state, an action state, a final state and transition arrows.

Applying the rules of Fig. 6.21 always results in an activity diagram with a neat, building-block appearance. For example, repeatedly applying Rule 2 to the simplest activity diagram results in an activity diagram containing many action states in sequence (Fig. 6.23). Rule 2 generates a stack of control statements, so let us call Rule 2 the *stacking rule*. [*Note:* The vertical dashed lines in Fig. 6.23 are not part of the UML. We use them to separate the four activity diagrams that demonstrate Rule 2 of Fig. 6.21 being applied.]

Rule 3 is the *nesting rule*. Repeatedly applying Rule 3 to the simplest activity diagram results in one with neatly nested control statements. For example, in Fig. 6.24, the action

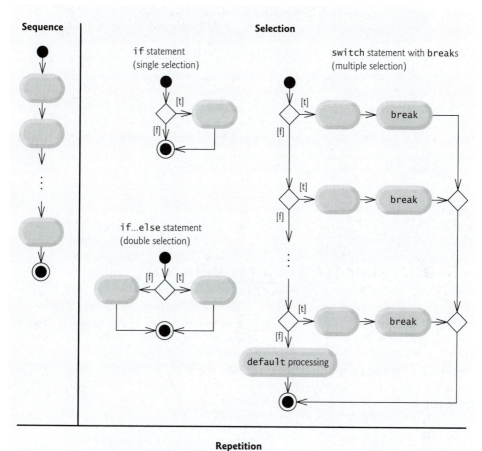

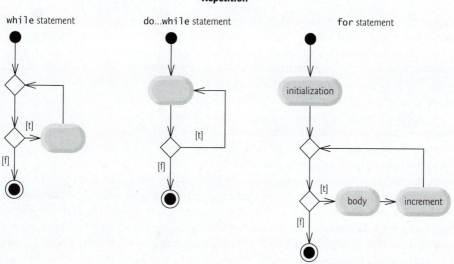

Fig. 6.20 | Single-entry/single-exit sequence, selection and repetition statements.

Rules for forming structured programs
1) Begin with the "simplest activity diagram" (Fig. 6.22).
2) Any action state can be replaced by two action states in sequence.
3) Any action state can be replaced by any control statement (sequence, `if`, `if...else`, `switch`, `while`, `do...while` or `for`).
4) Rules 2 and 3 can be applied as often as you like and in any order.

Fig. 6.21 | Rules for forming structured programs.

Fig. 6.22 | Simplest activity diagram.

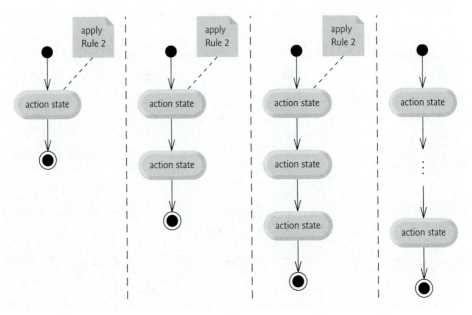

Fig. 6.23 | Repeatedly applying Rule 2 of Fig. 6.21 to the simplest activity diagram.

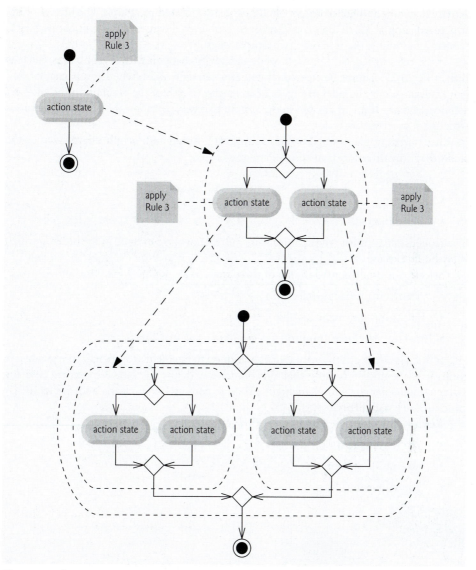

Fig. 6.24 | Applying Rule 3 of Fig. 6.21 to the simplest activity diagram several times.

state in the simplest activity diagram is replaced with a double-selection (if...else) statement. Then Rule 3 is applied again to the action states in the double-selection statement, replacing each with a double-selection statement. The dashed action-state symbols around each of the double-selection statements represent an action state that was replaced in the preceding activity diagram. [*Note:* The dashed arrows and dashed action-state symbols shown in Fig. 6.24 are not part of the UML. They are used here as pedagogic devices to illustrate that any action state may be replaced with a control statement.]

Rule 4 generates larger, more involved and more deeply nested statements. The diagrams that emerge from applying the rules in Fig. 6.21 constitute the set of all possible activity diagrams and hence the set of all possible structured programs. The beauty of the structured approach is that we use only seven simple single-entry/single-exit control statements and assemble them in only two simple ways.

If the rules in Fig. 6.21 are followed, an activity diagram with illegal syntax (such as that in Fig. 6.25) cannot be created. If you are uncertain about whether a particular diagram is legal, apply the rules of Fig. 6.21 in reverse to reduce the diagram to the simplest activity diagram. If it is reducible to the simplest activity diagram, the original diagram is structured; otherwise, it is not.

Structured programming promotes simplicity. Böhm and Jacopini have given us the result that only three forms of control are needed:

- Sequence
- Selection
- Repetition

The sequence structure is trivial. Simply list the statements to execute in the order in which they should execute.

Selection is implemented in one of three ways:

- `if` statement (single selection)
- `if...else` statement (double selection)
- `switch` statement (multiple selection)

It is straightforward to prove that the simple `if` statement is sufficient to provide any form of selection—everything that can be done with the `if...else` statement and the `switch` statement can be implemented (although perhaps not as clearly and efficiently) by combining `if` statements.

Repetition is implemented in one of three ways:

- `while` statement
- `do...while` statement
- `for` statement

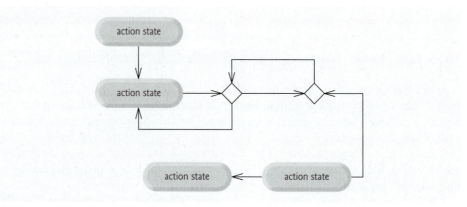

Fig. 6.25 | Activity diagram with illegal syntax.

It is straightforward to prove that the `while` statement is sufficient to provide any form of repetition. Everything that can be done with the `do...while` statement and the `for` statement can be done (although perhaps not as smoothly) with the `while` statement.

Combining these results illustrates that any form of control ever needed in a Visual C++ program can be expressed in terms of the following:

- sequence
- `if` statement (selection)
- `while` statement (repetition)

and that these control statements can be combined in only two ways—stacking and nesting. Indeed, structured programming promotes simplicity.

6.11 (Optional) Software Engineering Case Study: Identifying Objects' States and Activities in the ATM System

In Section 5.13, we identified many of the class attributes needed to implement the ATM system and added them to the class diagram in Fig. 5.24. In this section, we show how these attributes represent an object's state. We identify some key states that our objects may occupy and discuss how objects change state in response to various events occurring in the system. We also discuss the workflow, or *activities*, that objects perform in the ATM system. We present the activities of `BalanceInquiry` and `Withdrawal` transaction objects in this section, as they represent two of the key activities in the ATM system.

State Machine Diagrams

Each object in a system goes through a series of discrete states. An object's current state is indicated by the values of the object's attributes at a given time. *State machine diagrams* (commonly called *state diagrams*) model key states of an object and show under what circumstances the object changes state. Unlike the class diagrams presented in earlier case study sections, which focused primarily on the structure of the system, state diagrams model some of the behavior of the system.

Figure 6.26 is a simple state diagram that models some of the states of an object of class ATM. The UML represents each state in a state diagram as a *rounded rectangle* with the name of the state placed inside it. A *solid circle* with an attached stick arrowhead designates the *initial state*. Recall that we modeled this state information as the `Boolean` attribute `userAuthenticated` in the class diagram of Fig. 5.24. This attribute is initialized to `false`, or the "User not authenticated" state, according to the state diagram.

The arrows with stick arrowheads indicate *transitions* between states. An object can transition from one state to another in response to various events that occur in the system.

Fig. 6.26 | State diagram for the ATM object.

The name or description of the event that causes a transition is written near the line that corresponds to the transition. For example, the ATM object changes from the "User not authenticated" state to the "User authenticated" state after the database authenticates the user. Recall from the requirements specification that the database authenticates a user by comparing the account number and PIN entered by the user with those of the corresponding account in the database. If the database indicates that the user has entered a valid account number and the correct PIN, the ATM object transitions to the "User authenticated" state and changes its userAuthenticated attribute to a value of true. When the user exits the system by choosing the "exit" option from the main menu, the ATM object returns to the "User not authenticated" state in preparation for the next ATM user.

Software Engineering Observation 6.2

Software designers do not generally create state diagrams showing every possible state and state transition for all attributes—there are simply too many of them. State diagrams typically show only the most important or complex states and state transitions.

Activity Diagrams

Like a state diagram, an activity diagram models aspects of system behavior. Unlike a state diagram, an activity diagram models an object's workflow (sequence of events) during program execution. An activity diagram models the actions the object will perform and in what order. Recall that we used UML activity diagrams to illustrate the flow of control for the control statements presented in Chapter 5 and this chapter.

The activity diagram in Fig. 6.27 models the actions involved in executing a Balance-Inquiry transaction. We assume that a BalanceInquiry object has already been initialized and assigned a valid account number (that of the current user), so the object knows which balance to retrieve. The diagram includes the actions that occur after the user selects a balance inquiry from the main menu and before the ATM returns the user to the main menu—a BalanceInquiry object does not perform or initiate these actions, so we do not model them here. The diagram begins with retrieving the available balance of the user's account from the database. Next, the BalanceInquiry retrieves the total balance of the

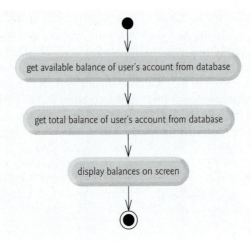

Fig. 6.27 | Activity diagram for a BalanceInquiry transaction.

account. Finally, the transaction displays the balances on the screen. This action completes the execution of the transaction.

The UML represents an action in an activity diagram as an action state modeled by a rectangle with its left and right sides replaced by arcs curving outward. Each action state contains an action expression—for example, "get available balance of user's account from database"—that specifies an action to be performed. An arrow with a stick arrowhead connects two action states, indicating the order in which the actions represented by the action states occur. The solid circle (at the top of Fig. 6.27) represents the activity's initial state—the beginning of the workflow before the object performs the modeled actions. In this case, the transaction first executes the "get available balance of user's account from database" action expression. Second, the transaction retrieves the total balance. Finally, the transaction displays both balances on the screen. The solid circle enclosed in an open circle (at the bottom of Fig. 6.27) represents the final state—the end of the workflow after the object performs the modeled actions.

Figure 6.28 shows an activity diagram for a Withdrawal transaction. We assume that a Withdrawal object has been assigned a valid account number. We do not model the user selecting a withdrawal from the main menu or the ATM returning the user to the main menu because these are not actions performed by a Withdrawal object. The transaction first displays a menu of standard withdrawal amounts (Fig. 3.17) and an option to cancel the transaction. The transaction then inputs a menu selection from the user. The activity flow now arrives at a decision symbol. This point determines the next action based on the associated guard conditions. If the user cancels the transaction, the system displays an appropriate message. Next, the cancellation flow reaches a merge symbol, where this activity flow joins the transaction's other possible activity flows (which we discuss shortly). Note that a merge can have any number of incoming transition arrows, but only one outgoing transition arrow. The decision at the bottom of the diagram determines whether the transaction should repeat from the beginning. When the user has canceled the transaction, the guard condition "cash dispensed or user canceled transaction" is true, so control transitions to the activity's final state.

If the user selects a withdrawal amount from the menu, the transaction sets amount (an attribute of class Withdrawal originally modeled in Fig. 5.24) to the value chosen by the user. The transaction next gets the available balance of the user's account (i.e., the availableBalance attribute of the user's Account object) from the database. The activity flow then arrives at another decision. If the requested withdrawal amount exceeds the user's available balance, the system displays an appropriate error message informing the user of the problem. Control then merges with the other activity flows before reaching the decision at the bottom of the diagram. The guard decision "cash not dispensed and user did not cancel" is true, so the activity flow returns to the top of the diagram, and the transaction prompts the user to input a new amount.

If the requested withdrawal amount is less than or equal to the user's available balance, the transaction tests whether the cash dispenser has enough cash to satisfy the withdrawal request. If it does not, the transaction displays an appropriate error message and passes through the merge before reaching the final decision. Cash was not dispensed, so the activity flow returns to the beginning of the activity diagram, and the transaction prompts the user to choose a new amount. If sufficient cash is available, the transaction interacts with the database to debit the withdrawal amount from the user's account (i.e., subtract

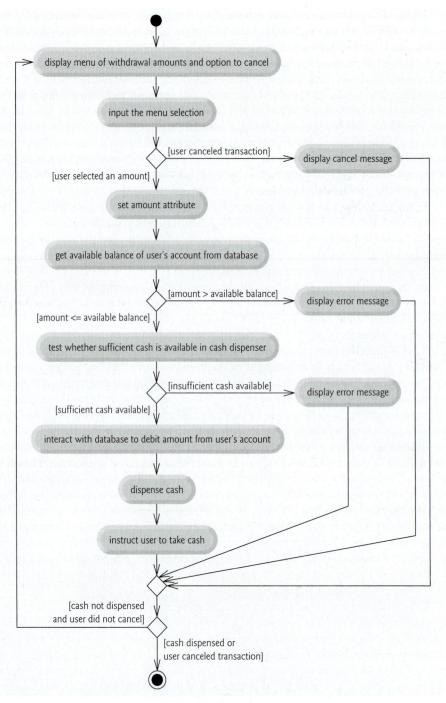

Fig. 6.28 | Activity diagram for a `Withdrawal` transaction.

the amount from both the availableBalance and totalBalance attributes of the user's Account object). The transaction then dispenses the desired amount of cash and instructs the user to take the cash that is dispensed. The main flow of activity next merges with the two error flows and the cancellation flow. In this case, cash was dispensed, so the activity flow reaches the final state.

We have taken the first steps in modeling the behavior of the ATM system and have shown how an object's attributes participate in the object's activities. In Section 7.23, we investigate the operations of our classes to create a more complete model of the system's behavior.

Software Engineering Case Study Self-Review Exercises

6.1 State whether the following statement is *true* or *false*, and if *false*, explain why: State diagrams model structural aspects of a system.

6.2 An activity diagram models the _____ that an object performs and the order in which it performs them.
  a) actions
  b) attributes
  c) states
  d) state transitions

6.3 Based on the requirements specification, create an activity diagram for a deposit transaction.

Answers to Software Engineering Case Study Self-Review Exercises

6.1 False. State diagrams model some of the behavior of a system.

6.2 a.

6.3 Figure 6.29 presents an activity diagram for a deposit transaction. The diagram models the actions that occur after the user chooses the deposit option from the main menu and before the ATM returns the user to the main menu. Recall that part of receiving a deposit amount from the user involves converting an integer number of cents to a dollar amount. Also recall that crediting a deposit amount to an account involves increasing only the totalBalance attribute of the user's Account object. The bank updates the availableBalance attribute of the user's Account object only after confirming the amount of cash in the deposit envelope and after the enclosed checks clear—this occurs independently of the ATM system.

6.12 Wrap-Up

In this chapter, we completed our introduction to Visual C++'s control statements, which enable you to control the flow of execution in functions. Chapter 5 discussed the if, if...else and while statements. The current chapter demonstrated Visual C++'s remaining control statements—for, do...while and switch. We have shown that any algorithm can be developed using combinations of the sequence structure (i.e., statements listed in the order in which they should execute), the three types of selection statements—if, if...else and switch, and the three types of repetition statements—while, do...while and for. In this chapter and Chapter 5, we have discussed how you can combine these building blocks to utilize proven program construction and problem-solving techniques.

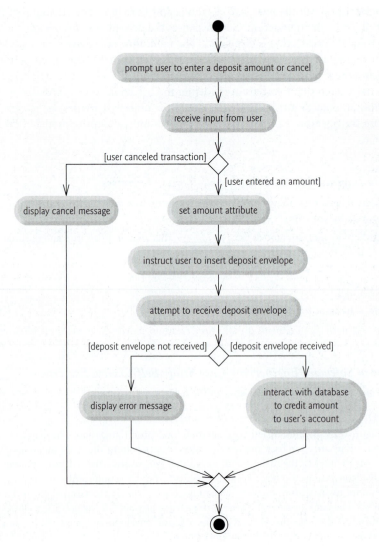

Fig. 6.29 | Activity diagram for a `Deposit` transaction.

This chapter also introduced Visual C++'s logical operators, which enable you to use more complex conditional expressions in control statements. Finally, we examined the common errors of confusing the equality and assignment operators and provided suggestions for avoiding these errors.

In Chapter 4, we introduced Visual C++ programming with the basic concepts of classes, objects and member functions. Chapter 5 and this chapter provided a thorough introduction to the control statements that you typically use to specify program logic in functions. In Chapter 7, we examine functions in greater depth.

Summary

Section 6.2 Essentials of Counter-Controlled Repetition

- In Visual C++, it is more precise to call a declaration that also reserves memory a definition.
- The `for` repetition statement handles all the details of counter-controlled repetition. The general format of the `for` statement is

  > `for` (*initialization*; *loopContinuationCondition*; *increment*)
  >   *statement*

  where *initialization* initializes the loop's control variable, *loopContinuationCondition* is the condition that determines whether the loop should continue executing and *increment* increments the control variable.

Section 6.3 for Repetition Statement

- Typically, `for` statements are used for counter-controlled repetition and `while` statements are used for sentinel-controlled repetition.
- The scope of a variable specifies where it can be used in a program. For example, a control variable declared in the header of a `for` statement can be used only in the body of the `for` statement—the control variable will be unknown outside the `for` statement.
- The initialization and increment expressions in a `for` statement header can be comma-separated lists of expressions. The commas, as used in these expressions, are comma operators, which guarantee that lists of expressions evaluate from left to right. The comma operator has the lowest precedence of all Visual C++ operators. The value and type of a comma-separated list of expressions is the value and type of the rightmost expression in the list.
- The initialization, loop-continuation condition and increment expressions of a `for` statement can contain arithmetic expressions. Also, the increment of a `for` statement can be negative, in which case it is really a decrement and the loop counts downward.
- If the loop-continuation condition in a `for` header is initially `false`, the body of the `for` statement is not performed. Instead, execution proceeds with the statement following the `for`.

Section 6.4 Examples Using the for Statement

- Standard library function pow(x, y) (from header `<cmath>`) calculates the value of x raised to the yth power. Function pow takes two arguments of type `double` and returns a `double` value.
- Parameterized stream manipulator `setw` specifies the field width in which the next value output should appear. The value is right justified in the field by default. If the value to be output is larger than the field width, the field width is extended to accommodate the entire value. Nonparameterized stream manipulator `left` (found in header `<iostream>`) can be used to cause a value to be left justified in a field and `right` can be used to restore right justification.
- Sticky settings are those output-formatting settings that remain in effect until they are changed.

Section 6.5 do...while Repetition Statement

- The do...while repetition statement tests the loop-continuation condition at the end of the loop, so the body of the loop will be executed at least once. The format for the do...while statement is

  > `do`
  > `{`
  >   *statement*
  > `}` `while` (*condition*);

Section 6.6 `switch` *Multiple-Selection Statement*

- The `switch` multiple-selection statement performs different actions based on the possible values of a variable or expression. Each action is associated with the value of a constant integral expression (i.e., any combination of character constants and integer constants that evaluates to a constant integer value) that the variable or expression on which the `switch` is based may assume.

- The `switch` statement consists of a series of `case` labels and an optional `default` case.

- The `cin.get()` function reads one character from the keyboard. Characters normally are stored in variables of type `char`; however, characters can be stored in any integer data type, because types `short`, `int` and `long` are guaranteed to be at least as big as type `char`. Thus, a character can be treated either as an integer or as a character, depending on its use.

- The end-of-file indicator is a system-dependent keystroke combination that specifies that there is no more data to input. `EOF` is a symbolic integer constant defined in the `<iostream>` header file that indicates "end-of-file."

- The expression in the parentheses following keyword `switch` is called the controlling expression of the `switch`. The `switch` statement compares the value of the controlling expression with each `case` label.

- Listing cases consecutively with no statements between them enables the `cases` to perform the same set of statements.

- Each `case` can have multiple statements. The `switch` selection statement differs from other control statements in that it does not require braces around multiple statements in each `case`.

- Each `case` can be used only to test only a constant integral expression. A character constant is represented as the specific character in single quotes, such as `'A'`. An integer constant is simply an integer value. Also, each `case` label can specify only one constant integral expression.

- Visual C++ provides several data types to represent integers—`int`, `char`, `short` and `long`. The range of integer values for each type depends on the particular computer's hardware.

Section 6.7 `break` and `continue` *Statements*

- The `break` statement, when executed in one of the repetition statements (`for`, `while` and `do...while`), causes immediate exit from the statement.

- The `continue` statement, when executed in one of the repetition statements (`for`, `while` and `do...while`), skips any remaining statements in the body of the repetition statement and proceeds with the next iteration of the loop. In a `while` or `do...while` statement, execution continues with the next evaluation of the condition. In a `for` statement, execution continues with the increment expression in the `for` statement header.

Section 6.8 *Logical Operators*

- Logical operators enable you to form complex conditions by combining simple conditions. The logical operators are `&&` (logical AND), `||` (logical OR) and `!` (logical negation).

- The `&&` (logical AND) operator ensures that two conditions are *both* `true` before choosing a certain path of execution.

- The `||` (logical OR) operator ensures that either *or* both of two conditions are `true` before choosing a certain path of execution.

- An expression containing `&&` or `||` operators evaluates only until the truth or falsehood of the expression is known. This performance feature for the evaluation of logical AND and logical OR expressions is called short-circuit evaluation.

- The `!` (logical NOT, also called logical negation) operator enables a programmer to "reverse" the meaning of a condition. The unary logical negation operator is placed before a condition to choose a path of execution if the original condition (without the logical negation operator) is `false`. In most cases, you can avoid using logical negation by expressing the condition with an appropriate relational or equality operator.

- When used as a condition, any nonzero value implicitly converts to `true`; 0 (zero) implicitly converts to `false`.
- By default, `bool` values `true` and `false` are displayed by `cout` as 1 and 0, respectively. Stream manipulator `boolalpha` (a sticky manipulator) specifies that the value of each `bool` expression should be displayed as either the word "true" or the word "false."

Section 6.9 Confusing the Equality (==) and Assignment (=) Operators
- Any expression that produces a value can be used in the decision portion of any control statement. If the value of the expression is zero, it is treated as `false`, and if the value is nonzero, it is treated as `true`.
- An assignment produces a value—namely, the value assigned to the variable on the left side of the assignment operator.

Section 6.10 Structured Programming Summary
- Any form of control ever needed in a Visual C++ program can be expressed in terms of sequence, selection and repetition statements, and these can be combined in only two ways—stacking and nesting.

Terminology

!, logical NOT operator	logical AND (&&)
&&, logical AND operator	logical negation (!)
||, logical OR operator	logical NOT (!)
ASCII character set	logical operator
`boolalpha` stream manipulator	logical OR (||)
`break` statement	loop-continuation condition
`case` label	*lvalue* ("left value")
char fundamental type	name of a control variable
comma operator	nesting rule
constant integral expression	off-by-one error
`continue` statement	right justification
controlling expression of a `switch`	`right` stream manipulator
decrement a control variable	*rvalue* ("right value")
`default` case in `switch`	scope of a variable
definition	`setw` stream manipulator
field width	short-circuit evaluation
final value of a control variable	simple condition
`for` repetition statement	stacking rule
`for` header	Standard library function `pow`
increment a control variable	sticky setting
initial value of a control variable	`switch` multiple-selection statement
left justification	truth table
`left` stream manipulator	zero-based counting

Self-Review Exercises

6.1 State whether the following are *true* or *false*. If the answer is *false*, explain why.

  a) The `default` case is required in the `switch` selection statement.

b) The break statement is required in the default case of a switch selection statement to exit the switch properly.

c) The expression (x > y && a < b) is true if either the expression x > y is true or the expression a < b is true.

d) An expression containing operator || is true if either or both of its operands are true.

6.2 Write a Visual C++ statement or a set of Visual C++ statements to accomplish each of the following:

a) Sum the odd integers between 1 and 99, inclusive, using a for statement. Assume the integer variables sum and count have been declared.

b) Print the value 333.546372 in a field width of 15 characters with precisions of 1, 2 and 3. Print each number on the same line. Left-justify each number in its field. What three values print?

c) Calculate the value of 2.5 raised to the power 3 using function pow. Print the result with a precision of 2 in a field width of 10 positions. What prints?

d) Print the integers from 1 to 20 using a while loop and the counter variable x. Assume that the variable x has been declared, but not initialized. Print only 5 integers per line. [*Hint:* Use the calculation x % 5. When the value of this is 0, print a newline character; otherwise, print a tab character.]

e) Repeat Exercise 6.2(d) using a for statement.

6.3 Find the error(s), if any, in each of the following code segments and explain how to correct it (them).

a)
```
x = 1;
while ( x <= 10 );
    x++;
}
```

b)
```
for ( y = .1; y != 1.0; y += .1 )
    cout << y << endl;
```

c)
```
switch ( n )
{
    case 1:
        cout << "The number is 1" << endl;
    case 2:
        cout << "The number is 2" << endl;
        break;
    default:
        cout << "The number is not 1 or 2" << endl;
        break;
}
```

d) The following code should print the values 1 to 10.
```
n = 1;
while ( n < 10 )
    cout << n++ << endl;
```

Answers to Self-Review Exercises

6.1
a) False. The default case is optional. Nevertheless, it is considered good software engineering to always provide a default case.

b) False. The break statement is used to exit the switch statement. The break statement is not required when the default case is the last case. Nor will the break statement be required if having control proceed with the next case makes sense.

c) False. When using the && operator, both of the relational expressions must be true for the entire expression to be true.

d) True.

6.2 a) ```
sum = 0;
for (count = 1; count <= 99; count += 2)
   sum += count;
```

b)  ```
cout << fixed << left
     << setprecision( 1 ) << setw( 15 ) << 333.546372
     << setprecision( 2 ) << setw( 15 ) << 333.546372
     << setprecision( 3 ) << setw( 15 ) << 333.546372
     << endl;
```
Output is:

333.5   333.55   333.546

c) ```
cout << fixed << setprecision(2)
     << setw(10) << pow(2.5, 3)
     << endl;
```
Output is:

    15.63

d)  ```
x = 1;

while ( x <= 20 )
{
   cout << x;

   if ( x % 5 == 0 )
      cout << endl;
   else
      cout << '\t';

   x++;
}
```

e) ```
for (x = 1; x <= 20; x++)
{
   cout << x;

   if (x % 5 == 0)
      cout << endl;
   else
      cout << '\t';
}
```

or

```
for (x = 1; x <= 20; x++)
{
   if (x % 5 == 0)
      cout << x << endl;
   else
      cout << x << '\t';
}
```
```

6.3 a) Error: The semicolon after the while header causes an infinite loop.
    Correction: Replace the semicolon by a {, or remove both the ; and the }.
  b) Error: Using a floating-point number to control a for repetition statement.
    Correction: Use an integer and perform the proper calculation in order to get the values
    you desire.

```
for ( y = 1; y != 10; y++ )
    cout << ( static_cast< double >( y ) / 10 ) << endl;
```

  c) Error: Missing break statement in the first case.
    Correction: Add a break statement at the end of the statements for the first case. Note
    that this is not an error if you want the statement of case 2: to execute every time the
    case 1: statement executes.
  d) Error: Improper relational operator used in the while repetition-continuation condi-
    tion.
    Correction: Use <= rather than <, or change 10 to 11.

Exercises

6.4 Find the error(s), if any, in each of the following:
  a) ```For (x = 100, x >= 1, x++)
        cout << x << endl;```
  b) The following code should print whether integer value is odd or even:

```
switch ( value % 2 )
{
    case 0:
        cout << "Even integer" << endl;
    case 1:
        cout << "Odd integer" << endl;
}
```

  c) The following code should output the odd integers from 19 to 1:

```
for ( x = 19; x >= 1; x += 2 )
    cout << x << endl;
```

  d) The following code should output the even integers from 2 to 100:

```
counter = 2;

do
{
    cout << counter << endl;
    counter += 2;
} While ( counter < 100 );
```

6.5 Write a program that uses a for statement to sum a sequence of integers. Assume that the
first integer read specifies the number of values remaining to be entered. Your program should read
only one value per input statement. A typical input sequence might be

```
5 100 200 300 400 500
```

where the 5 indicates that the subsequent 5 values are to be summed.

6.6 Write a program that uses a for statement to calculate and print the average of several integers. Assume the last value read is the sentinel 9999. A typical input sequence might be

```
10 8 11 7 9 9999
```

indicating that the program should calculate the average of all the values preceding 9999.

6.7 What does the following program do?

```cpp
 1   // Exercise 6.7: ex06_07.cpp
 2   // What does this program print?
 3   #include <iostream>
 4   using std::cout;
 5   using std::cin;
 6   using std::endl;
 7
 8   int main()
 9   {
10      int x; // declare x
11      int y; // declare y
12
13      // prompt user for input
14      cout << "Enter two integers in the range 1-20: ";
15      cin >> x >> y;   // read values for x and y
16
17      for ( int i = 1; i <= y; i++ ) // count from 1 to y
18      {
19         for ( int j = 1; j <= x; j++ ) // count from 1 to x
20            cout << '@'; // output @
21
22         cout << endl; // begin new line
23      } // end outer for
24
25      return 0; // indicate successful termination
26   } // end main
```

6.8 Write a program that uses a for statement to find the smallest of several integers. Assume that the first value read specifies the number of values remaining.

6.9 Write a program that uses a for statement to calculate and print the product of the odd integers from 1 to 15.

6.10 The factorial function is used frequently in probability problems. Using the definition of factorial in Exercise 5.35, write a program that uses a for statement to evaluate the factorials of the integers from 1 to 5. Print the results in tabular format. What difficulty might prevent you from calculating the factorial of 20?

6.11 Modify the compound interest program of Section 6.4 to repeat its steps for the interest rates 5 percent, 6 percent, 7 percent, 8 percent, 9 percent and 10 percent. Use a for statement to vary the interest rate.

6.12 Write a program that uses for statements to print the following patterns separately, one below the other. Use for loops to generate the patterns. All asterisks (*) should be printed by a single statement of the form cout << '*'; (this causes the asterisks to print side by side). [*Hint:* The last two patterns require that each line begin with an appropriate number of blanks. *Extra credit:* Combine your code from the four separate problems into a single program that prints all four patterns side by side by making clever use of nested for loops.]

(a)	(b)	(c)	(d)
*	**********	**********	*
**	*********	*********	**
***	********	********	***
****	*******	*******	****
*****	******	******	*****
******	*****	*****	******
*******	****	****	*******
********	***	***	********
*********	**	**	*********
**********	*	*	**********

6.13 One interesting application of computers is drawing graphs and bar charts. Write a program that reads five numbers (each between 1 and 30). Assume that the user enters only valid values. For each number that is read, your program should print a line containing that number of adjacent asterisks. For example, if your program reads the number 7, it should print *******.

6.14 A mail-order house sells five different products whose retail prices are: product 1 — $2.98, product 2—$4.50, product 3—$9.98, product 4—$4.49 and product 5—$6.87. Write a program that reads a series of pairs of numbers as follows:
   a) product number
   b) quantity sold

Your program should use a switch statement to determine the retail price for each product. Your program should calculate and display the total retail value of all products sold. Use a sentinel-controlled loop to determine when the program should stop looping and display the final results.

6.15 Modify the GradeBook program of Fig. 6.9–Fig. 6.11 so that it calculates the grade-point average for the set of grades. A grade of A is worth 4 points, B is worth 3 points, and so on.

6.16 Modify the program in Fig. 6.6 so it uses only integers to calculate the compound interest. [*Hint:* Treat all monetary amounts as integral numbers of pennies. Then "break" the result into its dollars portion and cents portion by using the division and modulus operations. Insert a period.]

6.17 Assume i = 1, j = 2, k = 3 and m = 2. What does each of the following statements print? Are the parentheses necessary in each case?
   a) cout << (i == 1) << endl;
   b) cout << (j == 3) << endl;
   c) cout << (i >= 1 && j < 4) << endl;
   d) cout << (m <= 99 && k < m) << endl;
   e) cout << (j >= i || k == m) << endl;
   f) cout << (k + m < j || 3 - j >= k) << endl;
   g) cout << (!m) << endl;
   h) cout << (!(j - m)) << endl;
   i) cout << (!(k > m)) << endl;

6.18 Write a program that prints a table of the binary, octal and hexadecimal equivalents of the decimal numbers in the range 1 through 256. If you are not familiar with these number systems, read Appendix D, Number Systems, first.

6.19 Calculate the value of π from the infinite series

$$\pi = 4 - \frac{4}{3} + \frac{4}{5} - \frac{4}{7} + \frac{4}{9} - \frac{4}{11} + \cdots$$

Print a table that shows the approximate value of π after each of the first 1000 terms of this series.

6.20 *(Pythagorean Triples)* A right triangle can have sides that are all integers. A set of three integer values for the sides of a right triangle is called a Pythagorean triple. These three sides must satisfy the relationship that the sum of the squares of two of the sides is equal to the square of the hypotenuse. Find all Pythagorean triples for side1, side2 and hypotenuse all no larger than 500. Use a triple-nested for loop that tries all possibilities. This is an example of **brute force** computing. You'll learn in more advanced computer science courses that there are many interesting problems for which there is no known algorithmic approach other than sheer brute force.

6.21 A company pays its employees as managers (who receive a fixed weekly salary), hourly workers (who receive a fixed hourly wage for up to the first 40 hours they work and "time-and-a-half"— 1.5 times their hourly wage—for overtime hours worked), commission workers (who receive $250 plus 5.7 percent of their gross weekly sales), or pieceworkers (who receive a fixed amount of money per item for each of the items they produce—each pieceworker in this company works on only one type of item). Write a program to compute the weekly pay for each employee. You do not know the number of employees in advance. Each type of employee has its own pay code: Managers have code 1, hourly workers have code 2, commission workers have code 3 and pieceworkers have code 4. Use a switch to compute each employee's pay according to that employee's paycode. Within the switch, prompt the user (i.e., the payroll clerk) to enter the appropriate facts your program needs to calculate each employee's pay according to that employee's paycode.

6.22 *(De Morgan's Laws)* In this chapter, we discussed the logical operators &&, || and !. De Morgan's laws can sometimes make it more convenient for us to express a logical expression. These laws state that the expression !(*condition1* && *condition2*) is logically equivalent to the expression (!*condition1* || !*condition2*). Also, the expression !(*condition1* || *condition2*) is logically equivalent to the expression (!*condition1* && !*condition2*). Use De Morgan's laws to write equivalent expressions for each of the following, then write a program to show that the original expression and the new expression in each case are equivalent:

a) !(x < 5) && !(y >= 7)
b) !(a == b) || !(g != 5)
c) !((x <= 8) && (y > 4))
d) !((i > 4) || (j <= 6))

6.23 Write a program that prints the following diamond shape. You may use output statements that print either a single asterisk (*) or a single blank. Maximize your use of repetition (with nested for statements) and minimize the number of output statements.

```
       *
      ***
     *****
    *******
   *********
    *******
     *****
      ***
       *
```

6.24 Modify the program you wrote in Exercise 6.23 to read an odd number in the range 1 to 19 to specify the number of rows in the diamond, then display a diamond of the appropriate size.

6.25 A criticism of the break and continue statements is that each is unstructured. Actually these statements can always be replaced by structured statements, although doing so can be awkward. Describe in general how you would remove any break statement from a loop in a program and replace it with some structured equivalent. [*Hint:* The break statement leaves a loop from within the body of the loop. Another way to leave is by failing the loop-continuation test. Consider using in the loop-continuation test a second test that indicates "early exit because of a 'break' condition."] Use the technique you developed here to remove the break statement from the program of Fig. 6.13.

6.26 What does the following program segment do?

```
 1   for ( int i = 1; i <= 5; i++ )
 2   {
 3      for ( int j = 1; j <= 3; j++ )
 4      {
 5         for ( int k = 1; k <= 4; k++ )
 6            cout << '*';
 7
 8         cout << endl;
 9      } // end inner for
10
11      cout << endl;
12   } // end outer for
```

6.27 Describe in general how you would remove any continue statement from a loop in a program and replace it with some structured equivalent. Use the technique you developed here to remove the continue statement from the program of Fig. 6.14.

6.28 *("The Twelve Days of Christmas" Song)* Write a program that uses repetition and switch statements to print the song "The Twelve Days of Christmas." One switch statement should be used to print the day (i.e., "First," "Second," etc.). A separate switch statement should be used to print the remainder of each verse. Visit the website www.12days.com/library/carols/12daysofxmas.htm for the complete lyrics to the song.

6.29 *(Peter Minuit Problem)* Legend has it that, in 1626, Peter Minuit purchased Manhattan Island for $24.00 in barter. Did he make a good investment? To answer this question, modify the compound interest program of Fig. 6.6 to begin with a principal of $24.00 and to calculate the amount of interest on deposit if that money had been kept on deposit until this year (e.g., 382 years through 2008). Place the for loop that performs the compound interest calculation in an outer for loop that varies the interest rate from 5 percent to 10 percent to observe the wonders of compound interest.

7

Functions and an Introduction to Recursion

Form ever follows function.
—Louis Henri Sullivan

E pluribus unum.
(One composed of many.)
—Virgil

O! call back yesterday, bid time return.
—William Shakespeare

Call me Ishmael.
—Herman Melville

When you call me that, smile!
—Owen Wister

Answer me in one word.
—William Shakespeare

There is a point at which methods devour themselves.
—Frantz Fanon

Life can only be understood backwards; but it must be lived forwards.
—Soren Kierkegaard

OBJECTIVES

In this chapter you'll learn:

- To construct programs modularly from functions.

- To use common math functions available in the C++ Standard Library.

- To create functions with multiple parameters.

- The mechanisms for passing information between functions and returning results.

- How the function call/return mechanism is supported by the function-call stack and activation records.

- To use random number generation to implement game-playing applications.

- How the visibility of identifiers is limited to specific regions of programs.

- To write and use recursive functions, i.e., functions that call themselves.

7.1 Introduction

Most computer programs that solve real-world problems are much larger than the programs presented in the first few chapters of this book. Experience has shown that the best way to develop and maintain a large program is to construct it from small, simple pieces, or components. This technique is called *divide and conquer*. We introduced functions (as program pieces) in Chapter 4. In this chapter, we study functions in more depth. We emphasize how to declare and use functions to facilitate the design, implementation, operation and maintenance of large programs.

We'll overview a portion of the C++ Standard Library's math functions, showing several that require more than one parameter. Next, you'll learn how to declare a function with more than one parameter. We'll also present additional information about function prototypes and how the compiler uses them to convert the type of an argument in a function call to the type specified in a function's parameter list, if necessary.

Next, we'll take a brief diversion into simulation techniques with random number generation, and we'll develop a version of the casino dice game called craps that uses most of the programming techniques you have learned to this point in the book.

We then present Visual C++'s storage classes and scope rules. These determine the period during which an object exists in memory and the place where its identifier can be referenced in a program. You'll also learn how Visual C++ is able to keep track of which function is currently executing, how parameters and other local variables of functions are maintained in memory and how a function knows where to return after it completes execution. We discuss two topics that help improve program performance—inline functions that can eliminate the overhead of a function call and reference parameters that can be used to pass large data items to functions efficiently.

Many of the applications you develop will have more than one function of the same name. This technique, called function overloading, is used by programmers to implement functions that perform similar tasks for arguments of different types or possibly for different numbers of arguments. We consider function templates—a mechanism for defining a family of overloaded functions. The chapter concludes with a discussion of functions that call themselves, either directly, or indirectly (through another function)—a topic called recursion that is discussed at length in upper-level computer science courses. Note that all the topics in this chapter except for Section 7.14, References and Reference Parameters and Section 7.15, Default Arguments are equally applicable to writing managed code with C++/CLI (C++ Standard Library functions notwithstanding). References in C++/ CLI are explained in later chapters and managed code doesn't allow default arguments.

7.2 Program Components in Visual C++

Visual C++ programs are typically written by combining new functions and classes you write with "prepackaged" functions and classes available in the C++ Standard Library and other libraries. In this chapter, we concentrate on functions.

The C++ Standard Library provides a rich collection of functions for performing common mathematical calculations, string manipulations, character manipulations, input/output, error checking and many other useful operations for native code. Managed code with C++/CLI uses the Framework Class Library to perform these same sorts of functions. This makes your job easier, because these functions provide many of the capabilities programmers need. The C++ Standard Library functions are provided as part of the Visual C++ programming environment.

> **Software Engineering Observation 7.1**
>
> *Read the documentation from Visual Studio 2008 to familiarize yourself with the functions and classes in the C++ Standard Library.*

Functions (called *methods* or *procedures* in other programming languages) allow you to modularize a program by separating its tasks into self-contained units. You have used functions in every program you have written. These are sometimes referred to as *user-defined functions* or *programmer-defined functions*. The statements in the function bodies are written only once, are reused from perhaps several locations in a program and are hidden from other functions.

There are several motivations for modularizing a program with functions. One is the *divide-and-conquer* approach, which makes program development more manageable by constructing programs from small, simple pieces. Another is software reuse—using existing functions as building blocks to create new programs. For example, in earlier programs, we did not have to define how to read a line of text from the keyboard—Visual C++ provides this capability via the `getline` function of the `<string>` header file. A third motivation is to avoid repeating code. Also, dividing a program into meaningful functions makes the program easier to debug and maintain.

Software Engineering Observation 7.2

To promote software reusability, every function should be limited to performing a single, well-defined task, and the name of the function should express that task effectively. Such functions make programs easier to write, test, debug and maintain.

Error-Prevention Tip 7.1

A small function that performs one task is easier to test and debug than a larger function that performs many tasks.

Software Engineering Observation 7.3

If you cannot choose a concise name that expresses a function's task, your function might be attempting to perform too many diverse tasks. It is usually best to break such a function into several smaller functions.

As you know, a function is invoked by a function call, and when the called function completes its task, it either returns a result or simply returns control to the caller. An analogy to this program structure is the hierarchical form of management (Figure 7.1). A boss (similar to the calling function) asks a worker (similar to the called function) to perform a task and report back (i.e., return) the results after completing the task. The boss function does not know how the worker function performs its designated tasks. The worker may also call other worker functions, unbeknown to the boss. This hiding of implementation details promotes good software engineering. Figure 7.1 shows the `boss` function communicating with several worker functions in a hierarchical manner. The `boss` function divides the responsibilities among the various `worker` functions. Note that `worker1` acts as a "boss function" to `worker4` and `worker5`.

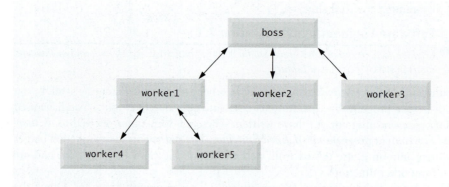

Fig. 7.1 | Hierarchical boss function/worker function relationship.

7.3 Math Library Functions

As you know, a class can provide member functions that perform the services of the class. For example, in Chapters 4–6, you have called the member functions of various versions of a GradeBook object to display the GradeBook's welcome message, to set its course name, to obtain a set of grades and to calculate the average of those grades.

Sometimes functions are not members of a class. Such functions are called *global functions*. Like a class's member functions, the function prototypes for global functions are placed in header files, so that the global functions can be reused in any program that includes the header file and that can link to the function's object code. For example, recall that we used function pow of the <cmath> header file to raise a value to a power in Figure 6.6. We introduce various functions from the <cmath> header file here to present the concept of global functions that do not belong to a particular class. In this chapter and in subsequent chapters, we use a combination of global functions (such as main) and classes with member functions to implement our example programs.

The <cmath> header file provides a collection of functions that enable you to perform common mathematical calculations. For example, you can calculate the square root of 900.0 with the function call

```
sqrt( 900.0 )
```

The preceding expression evaluates to 30.0. Function sqrt takes an argument of type double and returns a double result. Note that there is no need to create any objects before calling function sqrt. Also note that *all* functions in the <cmath> header file are global functions—therefore, each is called simply by specifying the name of the function followed by parentheses containing the function's arguments.

Function arguments may be constants, variables or more complex expressions. If c = 13.0, d = 3.0 and f = 4.0, then the statement

```
cout << sqrt( c + d * f ) << endl;
```

calculates and prints the square root of 13.0 + 3.0 * 4.0 = 25.0—namely, 5.0. Some math library functions are summarized in Fig. 7.2. In the figure, the variables x and y are of type double.

Function	Description	Example
ceil(x)	rounds x to the smallest integer not less than x	ceil(9.2) is 10.0 ceil(-9.8) is -9.0
cos(x)	trigonometric cosine of x (x in radians)	cos(0.0) is 1.0
exp(x)	exponential function e^x	exp(1.0) is 2.71828 exp(2.0) is 7.38906
fabs(x)	absolute value of x	fabs(5.1) is 5.1 fabs(0.0) is 0.0 fabs(-8.76) is 8.76

Fig. 7.2 | Math library functions. (Part 1 of 2.)

Function	Description	Example
floor(x)	rounds *x* to the largest integer not greater than *x*	floor(9.2) is 9.0 floor(-9.8) is -10.0
fmod(x, y)	remainder of *x*/*y* as a floating-point number	fmod(2.6, 1.2) is 0.2
log(x)	natural logarithm of *x* (base *e*)	log(2.718282) is 1.0 log(7.389056) is 2.0
log10(x)	logarithm of *x* (base 10)	log10(10.0) is 1.0 log10(100.0) is 2.0
pow(x, y)	*x* raised to power *y* (x^y)	pow(2, 7) is 128 pow(9.0, .5) is 3
sin(x)	trigonometric sine of *x* (*x* in radians)	sin(0.0) is 0
sqrt(x)	square root of *x* (where *x* is a nonnegative value)	sqrt(9.0) is 3.0
tan(x)	trigonometric tangent of *x* (*x* in radians)	tan(0.0) is 0

Fig. 7.2 | Math library functions. (Part 2 of 2.)

7.4 Function Definitions with Multiple Parameters

Chapters 4–6 presented classes containing simple functions that had at most one parameter. Functions often require more than one piece of information to perform their tasks. We now consider functions with multiple parameters.

The program in Figs. 7.3–7.5 modifies our GradeBook class by including a user-defined function called maximum that determines and returns the largest of three int values. When the application begins execution, the main function (lines 5–14 of Fig. 7.5) creates one object of class GradeBook (line 8) and calls the object's inputGrades member function (line 11) to read three integer grades from the user. In class GradeBook's implementation file (Fig. 7.4), lines 54–55 of member function inputGrades prompt the user to enter three integer values and read them from the user. Line 58 calls member function maximum (defined in lines 62–75). Function maximum determines the largest value, then the return statement (line 74) returns that value to the point at which function inputGrades invoked maximum (line 58). Member function inputGrades then stores maximum's return value in data member maximumGrade. This value is then output by calling function displayGradeReport (line 12 of Fig. 7.5). [*Note:* We named this function displayGradeReport because subsequent versions of class GradeBook will use it to display a complete grade report, including the maximum and minimum grades.] In Chapter 8, Arrays and Vectors, we'll enhance the GradeBook to process an arbitrary number of grades.

```
I   // Fig. 7.3: GradeBook.h
2   // Definition of class GradeBook that finds the maximum of three grades.
3   // Member functions are defined in GradeBook.cpp
4   #include <string> // program uses C++ standard string class
5   using std::string;
6
7   // GradeBook class definition
8   class GradeBook
9   {
10  public:
11     GradeBook( string ); // constructor initializes course name
12     void setCourseName( string ); // function to set the course name
13     string getCourseName(); // function to retrieve the course name
14     void displayMessage(); // display a welcome message
15     void inputGrades(); // input three grades from user
16     void displayGradeReport(); // display a report based on the grades
17     int maximum( int, int, int ); // determine max of 3 values
18  private:
19     string courseName; // course name for this GradeBook
20     int maximumGrade; // maximum of three grades
21  }; // end class GradeBook
```

Fig. 7.3 | GradeBook header file.

```
I   // Fig. 7.4: GradeBook.cpp
2   // Member-function definitions for class GradeBook that
3   // determines the maximum of three grades.
4   #include <iostream>
5   using std::cout;
6   using std::cin;
7   using std::endl;
8
9   #include "GradeBook.h" // include definition of class GradeBook
10
11  // constructor initializes courseName with string supplied as argument;
12  // initializes maximumGrade to 0
13  GradeBook::GradeBook( string name )
14  {
15     setCourseName( name ); // validate and store courseName
16     maximumGrade = 0; // this value will be replaced by the maximum grade
17  } // end GradeBook constructor
18
19  // function to set the course name; limits name to 30 or fewer characters
20  void GradeBook::setCourseName( string name )
21  {
22     if ( name.length() <= 30 ) // if name has 30 or fewer characters
23        courseName = name; // store the course name in the object
24     else // if name is longer than 30 characters
25     { // set courseName to first 30 characters of parameter name
26        courseName = name.substr( 0, 30 ); // select first 30 characters
```

Fig. 7.4 | GradeBook class defines function maximum. (Part 1 of 3.)

```
27          cout << "Name \"" << name << "\" exceeds maximum length (30).\n"
28             << "Limiting courseName to first 30 characters.\n" << endl;
29       } // end if...else
30    } // end function setCourseName
31
32    // function to retrieve the course name
33    string GradeBook::getCourseName()
34    {
35       return courseName;
36    } // end function getCourseName
37
38    // display a welcome message to the GradeBook user
39    void GradeBook::displayMessage()
40    {
41       // this statement calls getCourseName to get the
42       // name of the course this GradeBook represents
43       cout << "Welcome to the grade book for\n" << getCourseName() << "!\n"
44          << endl;
45    } // end function displayMessage
46
47    // input three grades from user; determine maximum
48    void GradeBook::inputGrades()
49    {
50       int grade1; // first grade entered by user
51       int grade2; // second grade entered by user
52       int grade3; // third grade entered by user
53
54       cout << "Enter three integer grades: ";
55       cin >> grade1 >> grade2 >> grade3;
56
57       // store maximum in member maximumGrade
58       maximumGrade = maximum( grade1, grade2, grade3 );
59    } // end function inputGrades
60
61    // returns the maximum of its three integer parameters
62    int GradeBook::maximum( int x, int y, int z )
63    {
64       int maximumValue = x; // assume x is the largest to start
65
66       // determine whether y is greater than maximumValue
67       if ( y > maximumValue )
68          maximumValue = y; // make y the new maximumValue
69
70       // determine whether z is greater than maximumValue
71       if ( z > maximumValue )
72          maximumValue = z; // make z the new maximumValue
73
74       return maximumValue;
75    } // end function maximum
76
77    // display a report based on the grades entered by user
78    void GradeBook::displayGradeReport()
79    {
```

Fig. 7.4 | GradeBook class defines function maximum. (Part 2 of 3.)

```
80      // output maximum of grades entered
81      cout << "Maximum of grades entered: " << maximumGrade << endl;
82   } // end function displayGradeReport
```

Fig. 7.4 | GradeBook class defines function `maximum`. (Part 3 of 3.)

```
1    // Fig. 7.5: GradeBookTest.cpp
2    // Create GradeBook object, input grades and display grade report.
3    #include "GradeBook.h" // include definition of class GradeBook
4
5    int main()
6    {
7       // create GradeBook object
8       GradeBook myGradeBook( "CS101 Visual C++ Programming" );
9
10      myGradeBook.displayMessage(); // display welcome message
11      myGradeBook.inputGrades(); // read grades from user
12      myGradeBook.displayGradeReport(); // display report based on grades
13      return 0; // indicate successful termination
14   } // end main
```

```
Welcome to the grade book for
CS101 Visual C++ Programming!

Enter three integer grades: 86 67 75
Maximum of grades entered: 86
```

```
Welcome to the grade book for
CS101 Visual C++ Programming!

Enter three integer grades: 67 86 75
Maximum of grades entered: 86
```

```
Welcome to the grade book for
CS101 Visual C++ Programming!

Enter three integer grades: 67 75 86
Maximum of grades entered: 86
```

Fig. 7.5 | Demonstrating function `maximum`.

Software Engineering Observation 7.4

The commas used in line 58 of Fig. 7.4 to separate the arguments to function maximum are not comma operators as discussed in Section 6.3. The comma operator guarantees that its operands are evaluated left to right. The order of evaluation of a function's arguments, however, is not specified by the C++ standard. Thus, different compilers can evaluate function arguments in different orders. The C++ standard does guarantee that all arguments in a function call are evaluated before the called function executes.

Portability Tip 7.1

Sometimes when a function's arguments are more involved expressions, such as those with calls to other functions, the order in which the compiler evaluates the arguments could affect the values of one or more of the arguments. If the evaluation order changes between compilers, the argument values passed to the function could vary, causing subtle logic errors.

Error-Prevention Tip 7.2

If you have doubts about the order of evaluation of a function's arguments and whether the order would affect the values passed to the function, evaluate the arguments in separate assignment statements before the function call, assign the result of each expression to a local variable, then pass those variables as arguments to the function.

The prototype of member function `maximum` (Fig. 7.3, line 17) indicates that the function returns an integer value, that the function's name is `maximum` and that the function requires three integer parameters to accomplish its task. Function `maximum`'s header (Fig. 7.4, line 62) matches the function prototype and indicates that the parameter names are x, y and z. When `maximum` is called (Fig. 7.4, line 58), the parameter x is initialized with the value of the argument `grade1`, the parameter y is initialized with the value of the argument `grade2` and the parameter z is initialized with the value of the argument `grade3`. There must be one argument in the function call for each parameter (also called a *formal parameter*) in the function definition.

Notice that multiple parameters are specified in both the function prototype and the function header as a comma-separated list. The compiler refers to the function prototype to check that calls to `maximum` contain the correct number and types of arguments and that the types of the arguments are in the correct order. In addition, the compiler uses the prototype to ensure that the value returned by the function can be used correctly in the expression that called the function (e.g., a function call that returns `void` cannot be used as the right side of an assignment statement). Each argument must be consistent with the type of the corresponding parameter. For example, a parameter of type `double` can receive values like 7.35, 22 or –0.03456, but not a string like `"hello"`. If the arguments passed to a function do not match the types specified in the function's prototype, the compiler attempts to convert the arguments to those types. Section 7.5 discusses this conversion.

Common Programming Error 7.1

Declaring method parameters of the same type as `double x, y` *instead of* `double x, double y` *is a syntax error—an explicit type is required for each parameter in the parameter list.*

Common Programming Error 7.2

Compilation errors occur if the function prototype, function header and function calls do not all agree in the number, type and order of arguments and parameters, and in the return type.

Software Engineering Observation 7.5

A function that has many parameters may be performing too many tasks. Consider dividing the function into smaller functions that perform the separate tasks. Limit the function header to one line if possible.

To determine the maximum value (lines 62–75 of Fig. 7.4), we begin with the assumption that parameter x contains the largest value, so line 64 of function `maximum` declares local variable `maximumValue` and initializes it with the value of parameter x. Of course, it is possible that parameter y or z contains the actual largest value, so we must compare each of these values with `maximumValue`. The `if` statement in lines 67–68 determines whether y is greater than `maximumValue` and, if so, assigns y to `maximumValue`. The `if` statement in lines 71–72 determines whether z is greater than `maximumValue` and, if so, assigns z to `maximumValue`. At this point the largest of the three values is in `maximumValue`, so line 74 returns that value to the call in line 58. When program control returns to the point in the program where `maximum` was called, `maximum`'s parameters x, y and z are no longer accessible to the program. We'll see why in the next section.

There are three ways to return control to the point at which a function was invoked. If the function does not return a result (i.e., the function has a `void` return type), control returns when the program reaches the function-ending right brace, or by execution of the statement

> ***return***;

If the function does return a result, the statement

> ***return*** *expression;*

evaluates *expression* and returns the value of *expression* to the caller.

7.5 Function Prototypes and Argument Coercion

A function prototype (also called a ***function declaration***) tells the compiler the name of a function, the type of data returned by the function, the number of parameters the function expects to receive, the types of those parameters and the order in which the parameters of those types are expected.

Software Engineering Observation 7.6

Function prototypes are required in Visual C++. Use #include preprocessor directives to obtain function prototypes for the C++ Standard Library functions from the header files for the appropriate libraries (e.g., the prototype for math function sqrt is in header file <cmath>; a partial list of C++ Standard Library header files appears in Section 7.6). Also use #include to obtain header files containing function prototypes written by you or your group members.

Common Programming Error 7.3

If a function is defined before it is invoked, then the function's definition also serves as the function's prototype, so a separate prototype is unnecessary. If a function is invoked before it is defined, and that function does not have a function prototype, a compilation error occurs.

Software Engineering Observation 7.7

Always provide function prototypes, even though it is possible to omit them when functions are defined before they are used (in which case the function header acts as the function prototype as well). Providing the prototypes avoids tying the code to the order in which functions are defined (which can easily change as a program evolves).

Function Signatures

The portion of a function prototype that includes the name of the function and the types of its arguments is called the ***function signature*** or simply the ***signature***. The function signature does not specify the function's return type. Functions in the same scope must have unique signatures. The scope of a function is the region of a program in which the function is known and accessible. We'll say more about scope in Section 7.10.

Common Programming Error 7.4

It is a compilation error if two functions in the same scope have the same signature but different return types.

In Fig. 7.3, if the function prototype in line 17 had been written

```
void maximum( int, int, int );
```

the compiler would report an error, because the void return type in the function prototype would differ from the int return type in the function header. Similarly, such a prototype would cause the statement

```
cout << maximum( 6, 7, 0 );
```

to generate a compilation error, because that statement depends on maximum to return a value to be displayed.

Argument Coercion

An important feature of function prototypes is *argument coercion*—i.e., forcing arguments to the appropriate types specified by the parameter declarations. For example, a program can call a function with an integer argument, even though the function prototype specifies a double argument—the function will still work correctly.

Argument Promotion Rules

Sometimes, argument values that do not correspond precisely to the parameter types in the function prototype can be converted by the compiler to the proper type before the function is called. These conversions occur as specified by Visual C++'s *promotion rules*. The promotion rules indicate how to convert between types without losing data. An int can be converted to a double without changing its value. However, a double converted to an int truncates the fractional part of the double value. Keep in mind that double variables can hold numbers of much greater magnitude than int variables, so the loss of data may be considerable. Values may also be modified when converting large integer types to small integer types (e.g., long to short), signed to unsigned or unsigned to signed.

The promotion rules apply to expressions containing values of two or more data types; such expressions are also referred to as *mixed-type expressions*. The type of each value in a mixed-type expression is promoted to the "highest" type in the expression (actually a temporary version of each value is created and used for the expression—the original values remain unchanged). Promotion also occurs when the type of a function argument does not match the parameter type specified in the function definition or prototype. Figure 7.6 lists the fundamental data types in order from "highest type" to "lowest type."

Converting values to lower fundamental types can result in incorrect values. Therefore, a value can be converted to a lower fundamental type only by explicitly assigning the value to a variable of lower type (some compilers will issue a warning in this case) or by using a cast operator (see Section 5.9). Function argument values are converted to the parameter types in a function prototype as if they were being assigned directly to variables

Data types	
long double	
double	
float	
unsigned long int	(synonymous with *unsigned long*)
long int	(synonymous with *long*)
unsigned int	(synonymous with *unsigned*)
int	
unsigned short int	(synonymous with *unsigned short*)
short int	(synonymous with *short*)
unsigned char	
char	
bool	

Fig. 7.6 | Promotion hierarchy for fundamental data types.

of those types. If a square function that uses an integer parameter is called with a floating-point argument, the argument is converted to int (a lower type), and square could return an incorrect value. For example, square(4.5) returns 16, not 20.25.

Common Programming Error 7.5

Converting from a higher data type in the promotion hierarchy to a lower type, or between signed and unsigned, can corrupt the data value, causing a loss of information.

Common Programming Error 7.6

It is a compilation error if the arguments in a function call do not match the number and types of the parameters declared in the corresponding function prototype; or if the number of arguments in the call matches, but the arguments cannot be implicitly converted to the expected types.

7.6 C++ Standard Library Header Files

The C++ Standard Library is divided into many portions, each with its own header file. The header files contain the function prototypes for the related functions that form each portion of the library. The header files also contain definitions of various class types and functions, as well as constants needed by those functions. A header file "instructs" the compiler on how to interface with library and user-written components.

Figure 7.7 lists some common C++ Standard Library header files, most of which are discussed later in the book. The term "macro" that is used several times in Fig. 7.7 is discussed in detail in Appendix E, Preprocessor.

Header file	Explanation
<iostream>	Contains classes and objects for the C++ standard input and standard output capabilities, introduced in Chapter 3, and is covered in more detail in Chapter 17, Stream Input/Output and Files.

Fig. 7.7 | C++ Standard Library header files. (Part I of 3.)

Header file	Explanation
`<iomanip>`	Contains function prototypes for stream manipulators that format streams of data. This header file is first used in Section 5.9 and is discussed in more detail in Chapter 17, Stream Input/Output and Files.
`<cmath>`	Contains function prototypes for math library functions (discussed in Section 7.3).
`<cstdlib>`	Contains function prototypes for conversions of numbers to text, text to numbers, memory allocation, random numbers and various other utility functions. Portions of the header file are covered in Section 7.7; Chapter 12, Operator Overloading; String and Array Objects; Chapter 16, Exception Handling; and Chapter 22, Bits, Characters, C Strings and `structs`.
`<ctime>`	Contains function prototypes and types for manipulating the time and date. This header file is used in Section 7.7.
`<vector>`, `<list>`, `<deque>`, `<queue>`, `<stack>`, `<map>`, `<set>`, `<bitset>`	These header files contain classes that implement the C++ Standard Library containers. Containers store data during a program's execution. The `<vector>` header is first introduced in Chapter 8, Arrays and Vectors. We discuss all these header files in Chapter 23, Standard Template Library (STL).
`<cctype>`	Contains function prototypes for functions that test characters for certain properties (such as whether the character is a digit or a punctuation), and function prototypes for functions that can be used to convert lowercase letters to uppercase letters and vice versa. These topics are discussed in Chapter 9, Pointers and Pointer-Based Strings, and Chapter 22, Bits, Characters, C Strings and `structs`.
`<cstring>`	Contains classes and function prototypes for C-style string-processing functions. This header file is used in Chapter 12, Operator Overloading; String and Array Objects.
`<typeinfo>`	Contains classes for runtime type identification (determining data types at execution time). This header file is discussed in Section 14.8.
`<exception>`, `<stdexcept>`	These header files contain classes that are used for exception handling (discussed in Chapter 16, Exception Handling).
`<memory>`	Contains classes and functions used by the C++ Standard Library to allocate memory to the C++ Standard Library containers. This header is used in Chapter 16, Exception Handling.
`<fstream>`	Contains function prototypes for functions that perform input from files on disk and output to files on disk (discussed in Chapter 17, Stream Input/Output and Files).

Fig. 7.7 | C++ Standard Library header files. (Part 2 of 3.)

Header file	Explanation
`<string>`	Contains the definition of class `string` from the C++ Standard Library (discussed in Chapter 19, Class `string` and String Stream Processing).
`<sstream>`	Contains function prototypes for functions that perform input from strings in memory and output to strings in memory (discussed in Chapter 19, Class `string` and String Stream Processing).
`<functional>`	Contains classes and functions used by C++ Standard Library algorithms. This header file is used in Chapter 23.
`<iterator>`	Contains classes for accessing data in the C++ Standard Library containers. This header file is used in Chapter 23, Standard Template Library (STL).
`<algorithm>`	Contains functions for manipulating data in C++ Standard Library containers. This header file is used in Chapter 23.
`<cassert>`	Contains macros for adding diagnostics that aid program debugging. This replaces header file `<assert.h>` from prestandard C++. This header file is used in Appendix E, Preprocessor.
`<cfloat>`	Contains the floating-point size limits of the system. This header file replaces header file `<float.h>`.
`<climits>`	Contains the integral size limits of the system.
`<cstdio>`	Contains function prototypes for the C-style standard input/output library functions and information used by them.
`<locale>`	Contains classes and functions normally used by stream processing to process data in the natural form for different languages (e.g., monetary formats, sorting strings, character presentation, etc.).
`<limits>`	Contains classes for defining the numerical data type limits on each computer platform.
`<utility>`	Contains classes and functions that are used by many C++ Standard Library header files.

Fig. 7.7 | C++ Standard Library header files. (Part 3 of 3.)

7.7 Case Study: Random Number Generation

We now take a brief and hopefully entertaining diversion into a popular programming application, namely simulation and game playing. In this and the next section, we develop a game-playing program that includes multiple functions. The program uses many of the control statements and concepts discussed to this point.

The element of chance can be introduced into computer applications by using the C++ Standard Library function rand.

Consider the following statement:

```
i = rand();
```

The function rand generates an unsigned integer between 0 and RAND_MAX (a symbolic constant defined in the <cstdlib> header file). The value of RAND_MAX must be at least 32767—the maximum positive value for a two-byte (16-bit) integer. For Visual Studio, the value of RAND_MAX is 32767. If rand truly produces integers at random, every number between 0 and RAND_MAX has an equal *chance* (or *probability*) of being chosen each time rand is called.

The range of values produced directly by the function rand often is different than what a specific application requires. For example, a program that simulates coin tossing might require only 0 for "heads" and 1 for "tails." A program that simulates rolling a six-sided die would require random integers in the range 1 to 6. A program that randomly predicts the next type of spaceship (out of four possibilities) that will fly across the horizon in a video game might require random integers in the range 1 through 4.

Rolling a Six-Sided Die

To demonstrate rand, let us develop a program (Fig. 7.8) to simulate 20 rolls of a six-sided die and print the value of each roll. The function prototype for the rand function is in <cstdlib>. To produce integers in the range 0 to 5, we use the modulus operator (%) with rand as follows:

```
rand() % 6
```

This is called *scaling*. The number 6 is called the *scaling factor*. We then *shift* the range of numbers produced by adding 1 to our previous result. Figure 7.8 confirms that the results are in the range 1 to 6.

```cpp
1   // Fig. 7.8: RandomNumberTest.cpp
2   // Shifted and scaled random integers.
3   #include <iostream>
4   using std::cout;
5   using std::endl;
6
7   #include <iomanip>
8   using std::setw;
9
10  #include <cstdlib> // contains function prototype for rand
11  using std::rand;
12
13  int main()
14  {
15     // loop 20 times
16     for ( int counter = 1; counter <= 20; counter++ )
17     {
18        // pick random number from 1 to 6 and output it
19        cout << setw( 10 ) << ( 1 + rand() % 6 );
20
21        // if counter is divisible by 5, start a new line of output
22        if ( counter % 5 == 0 )
23           cout << endl;
24     } // end for
```

Fig. 7.8 | Shifted, scaled integers produced by 1 + rand() % 6. (Part 1 of 2.)

```
25
26       return 0; // indicates successful termination
27   } // end main
```

6	6	5	5	6
5	1	1	5	3
6	6	2	4	2
6	2	3	4	1

Fig. 7.8 | Shifted, scaled integers produced by `1 + rand() % 6`. (Part 2 of 2.)

Rolling a Six-Sided Die 6,000,000 Times

To show that the numbers produced by function `rand` occur with approximately equal likelihood, Fig. 7.9 simulates 6,000,000 rolls of a die. Each integer in the range 1 to 6 should appear approximately 1,000,000 times, which is confirmed in the output window.

```cpp
1    // Fig. 7.9: RollDie.cpp
2    // Roll a six-sided die 6,000,000 times.
3    #include <iostream>
4    using std::cout;
5    using std::endl;
6
7    #include <iomanip>
8    using std::setw;
9
10   #include <cstdlib> // contains function prototype for rand
11   using std::rand;
12
13   int main()
14   {
15      int frequency1 = 0; // count of 1s rolled
16      int frequency2 = 0; // count of 2s rolled
17      int frequency3 = 0; // count of 3s rolled
18      int frequency4 = 0; // count of 4s rolled
19      int frequency5 = 0; // count of 5s rolled
20      int frequency6 = 0; // count of 6s rolled
21
22      int face; // stores most recently rolled value
23
24      // summarize results of 6,000,000 rolls of a die
25      for ( int roll = 1; roll <= 6000000; roll++ )
26      {
27         face = 1 + rand() % 6; // random number from 1 to 6
28
29         // determine roll value 1-6 and increment appropriate counter
30         switch ( face )
31         {
32            case 1:
33               ++frequency1; // increment the 1s counter
34               break;
```

Fig. 7.9 | Rolling a six-sided die 6,000,000 times. (Part 1 of 2.)

```
35              case 2:
36                  ++frequency2; // increment the 2s counter
37                  break;
38              case 3:
39                  ++frequency3; // increment the 3s counter
40                  break;
41              case 4:
42                  ++frequency4; // increment the 4s counter
43                  break;
44              case 5:
45                  ++frequency5; // increment the 5s counter
46                  break;
47              case 6:
48                  ++frequency6; // increment the 6s counter
49                  break;
50              default: // invalid value
51                  cout << "Program should never get here!";
52          } // end switch
53      } // end for
54
55      cout << "Face" << setw( 13 ) << "Frequency" << endl; // output headers
56      cout << "   1" << setw( 13 ) << frequency1
57          << "\n   2" << setw( 13 ) << frequency2
58          << "\n   3" << setw( 13 ) << frequency3
59          << "\n   4" << setw( 13 ) << frequency4
60          << "\n   5" << setw( 13 ) << frequency5
61          << "\n   6" << setw( 13 ) << frequency6 << endl;
62      return 0; // indicates successful termination
63  } // end main
```

Face	Frequency
1	999702
2	1000823
3	999378
4	998898
5	1000777
6	1000422

Fig. 7.9 | Rolling a six-sided die 6,000,000 times. (Part 2 of 2.)

As the output shows, we can simulate the rolling of a six-sided die by scaling and shifting the values rand produces. Note that the program should never get to the `default` case (lines 50–51) provided in the `switch` statement, because the `switch`'s controlling expression (face) always has values in the range 1–6; however, we provide the `default` case as a matter of good practice. After we study arrays in Chapter 8, we show how to replace the entire `switch` statement in Fig. 7.9 elegantly with a single-line statement.

Error-Prevention Tip 7.3

Provide a `default` *case in a* `switch` *to catch errors even if you are absolutely, positively certain that you have no bugs!*

Randomizing the Random Number Generator

Executing the program of Fig. 7.8 again produces

6	6	5	5	6
5	1	1	5	3
6	6	2	4	2
6	2	3	4	1

Notice that the program prints exactly the same sequence of values shown in Fig. 7.8. How can these be random numbers? Ironically, this repeatability is an important characteristic of function rand. When debugging a simulation program, this repeatability is essential for proving that corrections to the program work properly.

Function rand actually generates *pseudorandom numbers*. Repeatedly calling rand produces a sequence of numbers that appears to be random. However, the sequence repeats itself each time the program executes. Once a program has been thoroughly debugged, it can be conditioned to produce a different sequence of random numbers for each execution. This is called *randomizing* and is accomplished with the C++ Standard Library function srand. Function srand takes an unsigned integer argument and *seeds* the rand function to produce a different sequence of random numbers for each execution of the program.

Figure 7.10 demonstrates function srand. The program uses the data type unsigned, which is short for unsigned int. An int is stored in at least two bytes of memory (typically four bytes of memory on today's popular 32-bit systems) and can have positive and negative values. A variable of type unsigned int is also stored in at least two bytes of memory. A two-byte unsigned int can have only nonnegative values in the range 0–65535. A four-byte unsigned int can have only nonnegative values in the range 0–4294967295. Function srand takes an unsigned int value as an argument. The function prototype for the srand function is in header file <cstdlib>.

```
 1    // Fig. 7.10: RandomDieRoll.cpp
 2    // Randomizing die-rolling program.
 3    #include <iostream>
 4    using std::cout;
 5    using std::cin;
 6    using std::endl;
 7
 8    #include <iomanip>
 9    using std::setw;
10
11    #include <cstdlib> // contains prototypes for functions srand and rand
12    using std::rand;
13    using std::srand;
14
15    int main()
16    {
17       unsigned seed; // stores the seed entered by the user
```

Fig. 7.10 | Randomizing the die-rolling program. (Part 1 of 2.)

```
18
19     cout << "Enter seed: ";
20     cin >> seed;
21     srand( seed ); // seed random number generator
22
23     // loop 10 times
24     for ( int counter = 1; counter <= 10; counter++ )
25     {
26         // pick random number from 1 to 6 and output it
27         cout << setw( 10 ) << ( 1 + rand() % 6 );
28
29         // if counter is divisible by 5, start a new line of output
30         if ( counter % 5 == 0 )
31             cout << endl;
32     } // end for
33
34     return 0; // indicates successful termination
35 } // end main
```

```
Enter seed: 67
         6         1         4         6         2
         1         6         1         6         4
```

```
Enter seed: 432
         4         6         3         1         6
         3         1         5         4         2
```

```
Enter seed: 67
         6         1         4         6         2
         1         6         1         6         4
```

Fig. 7.10 | Randomizing the die-rolling program. (Part 2 of 2.)

Let us run the program several times and observe the results. Notice that the program produces a *different* sequence of random numbers each time it executes, provided that the user enters a different seed. We used the same seed in the first and third sample outputs, so the same series of 10 numbers is displayed in each of those outputs.

To randomize without having to enter a seed each time, we may use a statement like

```
srand( time( 0 ) );
```

This causes the computer to read its clock to obtain the value for the seed. Function `time` (with the argument 0 as written in the preceding statement) returns the current time as the number of seconds since January 1, 1970, at midnight Greenwich Mean Time (GMT). This value is converted to an `unsigned` integer and used as the seed to the random number generator. The function prototype for `time` is in `<ctime>`.

Common Programming Error 7.7

Calling function `srand` more than once in a program restarts the pseudorandom number sequence and can affect the randomness of the numbers produced by `rand`.

Generalized Scaling and Shifting of Random Numbers

Previously, we demonstrated how to write a single statement to simulate the rolling of a six-sided die with the statement

```
face = 1 + rand() % 6;
```

which always assigns an integer (at random) to variable face in the range 1 ≤face ≤6. Note that the width of this range (i.e., the number of consecutive integers in the range) is 6 and the starting number in the range is 1. Referring to the preceding statement, we see that the width of the range is determined by the number used to scale rand with the modulus operator (i.e., 6), and the starting number of the range is equal to the number (i.e., 1) that is added to the expression rand % 6. We can generalize this result as

number = *shiftingValue* + rand() % *scalingFactor*;

where *shiftingValue* is equal to the first number in the desired range of consecutive integers and *scalingFactor* is equal to the width of the desired range of consecutive integers. The exercises show that it is possible to choose integers at random from sets of values other than ranges of consecutive integers.

Common Programming Error 7.8

Using srand in place of rand to attempt to generate random numbers is a compilation error— function srand does not return a value.

7.8 Case Study: Game of Chance; Introducing enum

One of the most popular games of chance is a dice game known as "craps," which is played in casinos and back alleys worldwide. The rules of the game are straightforward:

> *A player rolls two dice. Each die has six faces. These faces contain 1, 2, 3, 4, 5 and 6 spots. After the dice have come to rest, the sum of the spots on the two upward faces is calculated. If the sum is 7 or 11 on the first roll, the player wins. If the sum is 2, 3 or 12 on the first roll (called "craps"), the player loses (i.e., the "house" wins). If the sum is 4, 5, 6, 8, 9 or 10 on the first roll, then that sum becomes the player's "point." To win, you must continue rolling the dice until you "make your point." The player loses by rolling a 7 before making the point.*

The program in Fig. 7.11 simulates the game of craps.

```
1   // Fig. 7.11: CrapsSimulation.cpp
2   // Craps simulation.
3   #include <iostream>
4   using std::cout;
5   using std::endl;
6
7   #include <cstdlib> // contains prototypes for functions srand and rand
8   using std::rand;
9   using std::srand;
10
```

Fig. 7.11 | Craps simulation. (Part 1 of 3.)

```
11    #include <ctime> // contains prototype for function time
12    using std::time;
13
14    int rollDice(); // rolls dice, calculates and displays sum
15
16    int main()
17    {
18       // enumeration with constants that represent the game status
19       enum Status { CONTINUE, WON, LOST }; // all caps in constants
20
21       int myPoint; // point if no win or loss on first roll
22       Status gameStatus; // can contain CONTINUE, WON or LOST
23
24       // randomize random number generator using current time
25       srand( static_cast< unsigned >( time( 0 ) ) );
26
27       int sumOfDice = rollDice(); // first roll of the dice
28
29       // determine game status and point (if needed) based on first roll
30       switch ( sumOfDice )
31       {
32          case 7: // win with 7 on first roll
33          case 11: // win with 11 on first roll
34             gameStatus = WON;
35             break;
36          case 2: // lose with 2 on first roll
37          case 3: // lose with 3 on first roll
38          case 12: // lose with 12 on first roll
39             gameStatus = LOST;
40             break;
41          default: // did not win or lose, so remember point
42             gameStatus = CONTINUE; // game is not over
43             myPoint = sumOfDice; // remember the point
44             cout << "Point is " << myPoint << endl;
45             break; // optional at end of switch
46       } // end switch
47
48       // while game is not complete
49       while ( gameStatus == CONTINUE ) // not WON or LOST
50       {
51          sumOfDice = rollDice(); // roll dice again
52
53          // determine game status
54          if ( sumOfDice == myPoint ) // win by making point
55             gameStatus = WON;
56          else
57             if ( sumOfDice == 7 ) // lose by rolling 7 before point
58                gameStatus = LOST;
59       } // end while
60
61       // display won or lost message
62       if ( gameStatus == WON )
63          cout << "Player wins" << endl;
```

Fig. 7.11 | Craps simulation. (Part 2 of 3.)

```
64      else
65         cout << "Player loses" << endl;
66
67      return 0; // indicates successful termination
68   } // end main
69
70   // roll dice, calculate sum and display results
71   int rollDice()
72   {
73      // pick random die values
74      int die1 = 1 + rand() % 6; // first die roll
75      int die2 = 1 + rand() % 6; // second die roll
76
77      int sum = die1 + die2; // compute sum of die values
78
79      // display results of this roll
80      cout << "Player rolled " << die1 << " + " << die2
81         << " = " << sum << endl;
82      return sum; // end function rollDice
83   } // end function rollDice
```

```
Player rolled 2 + 5 = 7
Player wins
```

```
Player rolled 6 + 6 = 12
Player loses
```

```
Player rolled 3 + 3 = 6
Point is 6
Player rolled 5 + 3 = 8
Player rolled 4 + 5 = 9
Player rolled 2 + 1 = 3
Player rolled 1 + 5 = 6
Player wins
```

```
Player rolled 1 + 3 = 4
Point is 4
Player rolled 4 + 6 = 10
Player rolled 2 + 4 = 6
Player rolled 6 + 4 = 10
Player rolled 2 + 3 = 5
Player rolled 2 + 4 = 6
Player rolled 1 + 1 = 2
Player rolled 4 + 4 = 8
Player rolled 4 + 3 = 7
Player loses
```

Fig. 7.11 | Craps simulation. (Part 3 of 3.)

In the rules of the game, notice that the player must roll two dice on the first roll and on all subsequent rolls. We define function `rollDice` (lines 71–83) to roll the dice and compute and print their sum. Function `rollDice` is defined once, but it is called from two places (lines 27 and 51) in the program. Interestingly, `rollDice` takes no arguments, so we have indicated an empty parameter list in the prototype (line 14) and in the function header (line 71). Function `rollDice` does return the sum of the two dice, so return type `int` is indicated in the function prototype and function header.

The game is reasonably involved. The player may win or lose on the first roll or on any subsequent roll. The program uses variable `gameStatus` to keep track of this. Variable `gameStatus` is declared to be of new type `Status`. Line 19 declares a user-defined type called an *enumeration*. An enumeration, introduced by the keyword `enum` and followed by a *type name* (in this case, `Status`), is a set of integer constants represented by identifiers. The values of these *enumeration constants* start at 0, unless specified otherwise, and increment by 1. In the preceding enumeration, the constant `CONTINUE` has the value 0, `WON` has the value 1 and `LOST` has the value 2. The identifiers in an `enum` must be unique, but separate enumeration constants can have the same integer value (we show how to accomplish this momentarily).

Good Programming Practice 7.1

Capitalize the first letter of an identifier used as a user-defined type name.

Good Programming Practice 7.2

Use only uppercase letters in the names of enumeration constants. This makes these constants stand out in a program and reminds you that enumeration constants are not variables.

Variables of user-defined type `Status` can be assigned only one of the three values declared in the enumeration unless a cast to that type is used on an integer value (such as `static_cast< Status >( 1 )`). When the game is won, the program sets variable `gameStatus` to `WON` (lines 34 and 55). When the game is lost, the program sets variable `gameStatus` to `LOST` (lines 39 and 58). Otherwise, the program sets variable `gameStatus` to `CONTINUE` (line 42) to indicate that the dice must be rolled again.

Another popular enumeration is

```
enum Months { JAN = 1, FEB, MAR, APR, MAY, JUN, JUL, AUG,
   SEP, OCT, NOV, DEC };
```

which creates user-defined type `Months` with enumeration constants representing the months of the year. The first value in the preceding enumeration is explicitly set to 1, so the remaining values increment from 1, resulting in the values 1 through 12. Any enumeration constant can be assigned an integer value in the enumeration definition, and subsequent enumeration constants each have a value 1 higher than the preceding constant in the list until the next explicit setting.

After the first roll, if the game is won or lost, the program skips the body of the `while` statement (lines 49–59) because `gameStatus` is not equal to `CONTINUE`. The program proceeds to the `if...else` statement in lines 62–65, which prints `"Player wins"` if `gameStatus` is equal to `WON` and `"Player loses"` if `gameStatus` is equal to `LOST`.

After the first roll, if the game is not over, the program saves the sum in `myPoint` (line 43). Execution proceeds with the `while` statement, because `gameStatus` is equal to CON-

TINUE. During each iteration of the `while`, the program calls `rollDice` to produce a new sum. If sum matches `myPoint`, the program sets `gameStatus` to `WON` (line 55), the `while`-test fails, the `if...else` statement prints `"Player wins"` and execution terminates. If sum is equal to 7, the program sets `gameStatus` to `LOST` (line 58), the `while`-test fails, the `if...else` statement prints `"Player loses"` and execution terminates.

Note the interesting use of the various program control mechanisms we have discussed. The craps program uses two functions—`main` and `rollDice`—and the `switch`, `while`, `if...else`, nested `if...else` and nested `if` statements. In the exercises, we investigate various interesting characteristics of the game of craps.

Good Programming Practice 7.3

Using enumerations rather than integer constants can make programs clearer and more maintainable. You can set the value of an enumeration constant once in the enumeration declaration.

Common Programming Error 7.9

Assigning the integer equivalent of an enumeration constant (rather than the enumeration constant, itself) to a variable of the enumeration type is a compilation error unless a cast is used.

Common Programming Error 7.10

After an enumeration constant has been defined, attempting to assign another value to the enumeration constant is a compilation error.

7.9 Storage Classes

The programs you have seen so far use identifiers for variable names. The attributes of variables include name, type, size and value. This chapter also uses identifiers as names for user-defined functions. Actually, each identifier in a program has other attributes, including *storage class*, scope and *linkage*.

Visual C++ provides five *storage-class specifiers*: **auto**, **register**, **extern**, **mutable** and **static**. This section discusses storage-class specifiers `auto`, `register`, and `static`. Storage-class specifier `mutable` (discussed in detail in Chapter 26) is used exclusively with classes. Visual C++ does not support `extern` though it is part of the C++ Standard.

Storage Class, Scope and Linkage

An identifier's storage class determines the period during which that identifier exists in memory. Some exist briefly, some are repeatedly created and destroyed and others exist for the entire execution of a program. First we discuss the storage classes *static* and *automatic*.

An identifier's scope is where the identifier can be referenced in a program. Some identifiers can be referenced throughout a program; others can be referenced from only limited portions of a program. Section 7.10 discusses the scope of identifiers.

An identifier's linkage determines whether it is known only in the source file where it is declared or across multiple files that are compiled, then linked together. An identifier's storage-class specifier helps determine its storage class and linkage.

Storage Class Categories

The storage-class specifiers can be split into two storage classes: automatic storage class and static storage class. Keywords `auto` and `register` are used to declare variables of the automatic storage class. Such variables are created when program execution enters the block in which they are defined, they exist while the block is active and they are destroyed when the program exits the block.

Local Variables

Only local variables of a function can be of automatic storage class. A function's local variables and parameters normally are of automatic storage class. The storage-class specifier `auto` explicitly declares variables of automatic storage class. For example, the following declaration indicates that `double` variable x is a local variable of automatic storage class— it exists only in the nearest enclosing pair of curly braces within the body of the function in which the definition appears:

> *auto double* x;

Local variables are of automatic storage class by default, so keyword `auto` rarely is used. For the remainder of the text, we refer to variables of automatic storage class simply as automatic variables.

Performance Tip 7.1

Automatic storage is a means of conserving memory, because automatic storage-class variables exist in memory only when the block in which they are defined is executing.

Software Engineering Observation 7.8

*Automatic storage is an example of the **principle of least privilege**, which is fundamental to good software engineering. The principle states that code should be granted only the amount of privilege and access that it needs to accomplish its designated task, but no more. Why should we have variables stored in memory and accessible when they are not needed?*

Register Variables

Data in the machine-language version of a program is normally loaded into registers for calculations and other processing.

Performance Tip 7.2

The storage-class specifier `register` can be placed before an automatic variable declaration to suggest that the compiler maintain the variable in one of the computer's high-speed hardware registers rather than in memory. If intensely used variables such as counters or totals are maintained in hardware registers, the overhead of repeatedly loading the variables from memory into the registers and storing the results back into memory is eliminated.

Common Programming Error 7.11

Using multiple storage-class specifiers for an identifier is a syntax error. For example, if you include `register`, do not also include `auto`.

The compiler might ignore `register` declarations. For example, there might not be a sufficient number of registers available for the compiler to use. The following definition *suggests* that the integer variable `counter` be placed in one of the computer's registers; regardless of whether the compiler does this, `counter` is initialized to 1:

> *register int* counter = 1;

The `register` keyword can be used only with local variables and function parameters.

Performance Tip 7.3

Often, register *is unnecessary. Optimizing compilers can recognize frequently used variables and may place them in registers without needing a* register *declaration.*

Static Storage Class

Keyword static declares identifiers for variables of the static storage class and for functions. Static-storage-class variables exist from the point at which the program begins execution and last for the duration of the program. A static-storage-class variable's storage is allocated when the program begins execution. Such a variable is initialized once when its declaration is encountered. For functions, the name of the function exists when the program begins execution, just as for all other functions. However, even though the variables and the function names exist from the start of program execution, this does not mean that these identifiers can be used throughout the program. Storage class and scope (where a name can be used) are separate issues, as we'll see in Section 7.10.

Identifiers with Static Storage Class

There are two types of identifiers with static storage class—external identifiers (such as *global variables* and global function names) and local variables declared with the storage-class specifier static. Global variables are created by placing variable declarations outside any class or function definition. Global variables retain their values throughout the execution of the program. Global variables and global functions can be referenced by any function that follows their declarations or definitions in the source file.

Software Engineering Observation 7.9

Declaring a variable as global rather than local allows unintended side effects to occur when a function that does not need access to the variable accidentally or maliciously modifies it. This is another example of the principle of least privilege. In general, except for truly global resources such as cin *and* cout, *the use of global variables should be avoided except in certain situations with unique performance requirements.*

Software Engineering Observation 7.10

Variables used only in a particular function should be declared as local variables in that function rather than as global variables.

Local variables declared with the keyword static are still known only in the function in which they are declared, but, unlike automatic variables, static local variables retain their values when the function returns to its caller. The next time the function is called, the static local variables contain the values they had when the function last completed execution. The following statement declares local variable count to be static and to be initialized to 1:

```
static int count = 1;
```

All numeric variables of the static storage class are initialized to zero if they are not explicitly initialized by you, but it is nevertheless a good practice to explicitly initialize all variables.

7.10 Scope Rules

The portion of the program where an identifier can be used is known as its scope. For example, when we declare a local variable in a block, it can be referenced only in that block and in blocks nested within that block. This section discusses four scopes for an identifier—*function scope*, *file scope*, *block scope* and *function-prototype scope*. Later we'll see two other scopes—*class scope* (Chapter 9) and *namespace scope* (Chapter 26).

An identifier declared outside any function or class has file scope. Such an identifier is "known" in all functions from the point at which it is declared until the end of the file. Global variables, function definitions and function prototypes placed outside a function all have file scope.

Labels (identifiers followed by a colon such as start:) are the only identifiers with function scope. Labels can be used anywhere in the function in which they appear, but cannot be referenced outside the function body. Labels are used in goto statements. Labels are implementation details that functions hide from one another.

Identifiers declared inside a block have block scope. Block scope begins at the identifier's declaration and ends at the terminating right brace (}) of the block in which the identifier is declared. Local variables have block scope, as do function parameters, which are also local variables of the function. Any block can contain variable declarations. When blocks are nested and an identifier in an outer block has the same name as an identifier in an inner block, the identifier in the outer block is "hidden" until the inner block terminates. While executing in the inner block, the inner block sees the value of its own local identifier and not the value of the identically named identifier in the enclosing block. Local variables declared static still have block scope, even though they exist from the time the program begins execution. Storage duration does not affect the scope of an identifier.

The only identifiers with function prototype scope are those used in the parameter list of a function prototype. As mentioned previously, function prototypes do not require names in the parameter list—only types are required. Names appearing in the parameter list of a function prototype are ignored by the compiler. Identifiers used in a function prototype can be reused elsewhere in the program without ambiguity. In a single prototype, a particular identifier can be used only once.

Common Programming Error 7.12

Accidentally using the same name for an identifier in an inner block that is used for an identifier in an outer block, when in fact you want the identifier in the outer block to be active for the duration of the inner block, is normally a logic error.

Good Programming Practice 7.4

Avoid variable names that hide names in outer scopes. This can be accomplished by avoiding the use of duplicate identifiers in a program.

The program of Fig. 7.12 demonstrates scoping issues with global variables, automatic local variables and static local variables.

Line 11 declares and initializes global variable x to 1. This global variable is hidden in any block (or function) that declares a variable named x. In main, line 15 displays the value of global variable x. Line 17 declares a local variable x and initializes it to 5. Line 19 outputs this variable to show that the global x is hidden in main. Next, lines 21–25 define a new block in main in which another local variable x is initialized to 7 (line 22). Line 24 outputs this variable to show that it hides x in the outer block of main. When the block exits, the variable x with value 7 is destroyed automatically. Next, line 27 outputs the local variable x in the outer block of main to show that it is no longer hidden.

```cpp
1   // Fig. 7.12: ScopeExample.cpp
2   // A scoping example.
3   #include <iostream>
4   using std::cout;
5   using std::endl;
6
7   void useLocal(); // function prototype
8   void useStaticLocal(); // function prototype
9   void useGlobal(); // function prototype
10
11  int x = 1; // global variable
12
13  int main()
14  {
15     cout << "global x in main is " << x << endl;
16
17     int x = 5; // local variable to main
18
19     cout << "local x in main's outer scope is " << x << endl;
20
21     { // start new scope
22        int x = 7; // hides both x in outer scope and global x
23
24        cout << "local x in main's inner scope is " << x << endl;
25     } // end new scope
26
27     cout << "local x in main's outer scope is " << x << endl;
28
29     useLocal(); // useLocal has local x
30     useStaticLocal(); // useStaticLocal has static local x
31     useGlobal(); // useGlobal uses global x
32     useLocal(); // useLocal reinitializes its local x
33     useStaticLocal(); // static local x retains its prior value
34     useGlobal(); // global x also retains its prior value
35
36     cout << "\nlocal x in main is " << x << endl;
37     return 0; // indicates successful termination
38  } // end main
39
40  // useLocal reinitializes local variable x during each call
41  void useLocal()
42  {
43     int x = 25; // initialized each time useLocal is called
44
45     cout << "\nlocal x is " << x << " on entering useLocal" << endl;
46     x++;
47     cout << "local x is " << x << " on exiting useLocal" << endl;
48  } // end function useLocal
49
50  // useStaticLocal initializes static local variable x only the
51  // first time the function is called; value of x is saved
52  // between calls to this function
```

Fig. 7.12 | Scoping example. (Part 1 of 2.)

```
53   void useStaticLocal()
54   {
55       static int x = 50; // initialized first time useStaticLocal is called
56
57       cout << "\nlocal static x is " << x << " on entering useStaticLocal"
58          << endl;
59       x++;
60       cout << "local static x is " << x << " on exiting useStaticLocal"
61          << endl;
62   } // end function useStaticLocal
63
64   // useGlobal modifies global variable x during each call
65   void useGlobal()
66   {
67       cout << "\nglobal x is " << x << " on entering useGlobal" << endl;
68       x *= 10;
69       cout << "global x is " << x << " on exiting useGlobal" << endl;
70   } // end function useGlobal
```

```
global x in main is 1
local x in main's outer scope is 5
local x in main's inner scope is 7
local x in main's outer scope is 5

local x is 25 on entering useLocal
local x is 26 on exiting useLocal

local static x is 50 on entering useStaticLocal
local static x is 51 on exiting useStaticLocal

global x is 1 on entering useGlobal
global x is 10 on exiting useGlobal

local x is 25 on entering useLocal
local x is 26 on exiting useLocal

local static x is 51 on entering useStaticLocal
local static x is 52 on exiting useStaticLocal

global x is 10 on entering useGlobal
global x is 100 on exiting useGlobal

local x in main is 5
```

Fig. 7.12 | Scoping example. (Part 2 of 2.)

To demonstrate other scopes, the program defines three functions, each of which takes no arguments and returns nothing. Function useLocal (lines 41–48) declares automatic variable x (line 43) and initializes it to 25. When the program calls useLocal, the function prints the variable, increments it and prints it again before the function returns program control to its caller. Each time the program calls this function, the function recreates automatic variable x and reinitializes it to 25.

Function useStaticLocal (lines 53–62) declares static variable x and initializes it to 50. Local variables declared as static retain their values even when they are out of scope (i.e., the function in which they are declared is not executing). When the program calls useStaticLocal, the function prints x, increments it and prints it again before the function returns program control to its caller. In the next call to this function, static local variable x contains the value 51. The initialization in line 55 occurs only once—the first time useStaticLocal is called.

Function useGlobal (lines 65–70) does not declare any variables. Therefore, when it refers to variable x, the global x (line 11, preceding main) is used. When the program calls useGlobal, the function prints the global variable x, multiplies it by 10 and prints it again before the function returns program control to its caller. The next time the program calls useGlobal, the global variable has its modified value, 10. After executing functions use-Local, useStaticLocal and useGlobal twice each, the program prints the local variable x in main again to show that none of the function calls modified the value of x in main, because the functions all referred to variables in other scopes. Note that you can use the symbolic constant __FUNCTION__ to return the name of the current function rather than explicitly writing the function name with a string.

7.11 Function-Call Stack and Activation Records

To understand how Visual C++ performs function calls, we first need to consider a data structure (i.e., collection of related data items) known as a *stack*. Think of a stack as analogous to a pile of dishes. When a dish is placed on the pile, it is normally placed at the top (referred to as *pushing* the dish onto the stack). Similarly, when a dish is removed from the pile, it is normally removed from the top (referred to as *popping* the dish off the stack). Stacks are known as *last-in, first-out (LIFO) data structures*—the last item pushed (inserted) on the stack is the first item popped (removed) from the stack.

One of the most important mechanisms for computer science students to understand is the *function-call stack* (sometimes referred to as the *program execution stack*). This data structure—working "behind the scenes"—supports the function-call/return mechanism. It also supports the creation, maintenance and destruction of each called function's automatic variables. We explained the last-in, first-out (LIFO) behavior of stacks with our dish-stacking example. As we'll see later in this section, this LIFO behavior is exactly what a function does when returning to the function that called it.

As each function is called, it may, in turn, call other functions, which may, in turn, call other functions—all before any of the functions returns. Each function eventually must return control to the function that called it. So, somehow, we must keep track of the return addresses that each function needs to return control to the function that called it. The function-call stack is the perfect data structure for handling this information. Each time a function calls another function, an entry is pushed onto the stack. This entry, called a *stack frame* or an *activation record*, contains the return address that the called function needs in order to return to the calling function. It also contains some additional information we'll soon discuss. If the called function returns, instead of calling another function before returning, the stack frame for the function call is popped, and control transfers to the return address in the popped stack frame.

The beauty of the call stack is that each called function always finds the information it needs to return to its caller at the top of the call stack. And, if a function makes a call to another function, a stack frame for the new function call is simply pushed onto the call stack. Thus, the return address required by the newly called function to return to its caller is now located at the top of the stack.

The stack frames have another important responsibility. Most functions have automatic variables—parameters and any local variables the function declares. Automatic variables need to exist while a function is executing. They need to remain active if the function makes calls to other functions. But when a called function returns to its caller, the called function's automatic variables need to "go away." The called function's stack frame is a perfect place to reserve the memory for the called function's automatic variables. That stack frame exists as long as the called function is active. When that function returns—and no longer needs its local automatic variables—its stack frame is popped from the stack, and those local automatic variables are no longer known to the program.

Of course, the amount of memory in a computer is finite, so only a certain amount of memory can be used to store activation records on the function-call stack. If more function calls occur than can have their activation records stored on the function-call stack, an error known as *stack overflow* occurs.

Function-Call Stack in Action

So, as we have seen, the call stack and activation records support the function-call/return mechanism and the creation and destruction of automatic variables. Now let's consider how the call stack supports the operation of a square function called by main (lines 11–17 of Fig. 7.13). First the operating system calls main—this pushes an activation record onto the stack (shown in Fig. 7.14). The activation record tells main how to return to the

```cpp
1   // Fig. 7.13: CallStack.cpp
2   // square function used to demonstrate the function-
3   // call stack and activation records.
4   #include <iostream>
5   using std::cin;
6   using std::cout;
7   using std::endl;
8
9   int square( int ); // prototype for function square
10
11  int main()
12  {
13     int a = 10; // value to square (local automatic variable in main)
14
15     cout << a << " squared: " << square( a ) << endl; // display a squared
16     return 0; // indicate successful termination
17  } // end main
18
19  // returns the square of an integer
20  int square( int x ) // x is a local variable
21  {
22     return x * x; // calculate square and return result
23  } // end function square
```

Fig. 7.13 | square function used to demonstrate the function-call stack and activation records. (Part 1 of 2.)

```
10 squared: 100
```

Fig. 7.13 | `square` function used to demonstrate the function-call stack and activation records. (Part 2 of 2.)

operating system (i.e., transfer to return address R1) and contains the space for `main`'s automatic variable (i.e., a, which is initialized to 10).

Function `main`—before returning to the operating system—now calls function `square` in line 15 of Fig. 7.13. This causes a stack frame for `square` (lines 20–23) to be pushed onto the function-call stack (Fig. 7.15). This stack frame contains the return address that `square` needs to return to `main` (i.e., R2) and the memory for `square`'s automatic variable (i.e., x).

After `square` calculates the square of its argument, it needs to return to `main`—and no longer needs the memory for its automatic variable x. So the stack is popped—giving `square` the return location in `main` (i.e., R2) and losing `square`'s automatic variable. Figure 7.16 shows the function-call stack after `square`'s activation record has been popped.

Function `main` displays the result of calling `square` (line 15), then executes the `return` statement (line 16). This causes the activation record for `main` to be popped from the stack. This gives `main` the address it needs to return to the operating system (i.e., R1 in Fig. 7.14) and causes the memory for `main`'s automatic variable (i.e., a) to become unavailable.

You have now seen how valuable the notion of the stack data structure is in implementing a key mechanism that supports program execution. Data structures have many important applications in computer science. We discuss stacks, queues, lists, trees and other data structures in Chapter 21, Data Structures, and Chapter 23, Standard Template Library (STL).

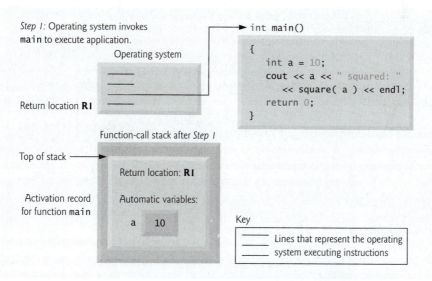

Fig. 7.14 | Function-call stack after the operating system invokes `main` to execute the application.

Step 2: main invokes function square to perform calculation.

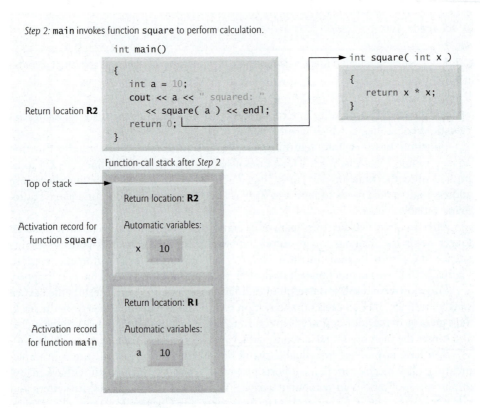

Fig. 7.15 | Function-call stack after main invokes function square.

Step 3: square returns its result to main.

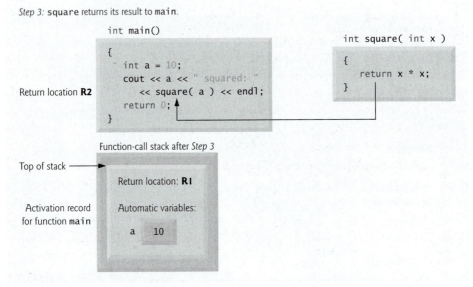

Fig. 7.16 | Function-call stack after function square returns to main.

7.12 Functions with Empty Parameter Lists

In Visual C++, an empty parameter list is specified by writing either void or nothing at all in parentheses. The prototype

```
void print();
```

specifies that print does not take arguments and does not return a value. Figure 7.17 demonstrates both ways to declare and use functions with empty parameter lists.

Portability Tip 7.2

The meaning of an empty function parameter list in Visual C++ is dramatically different than in C. In C, it means all argument checking is disabled (i.e., the function call can pass any arguments it wants). In Visual C++, it means that the function explicitly takes no arguments. Thus, C programs using this feature might cause compilation errors when compiled in Visual C++.

Common Programming Error 7.13

Visual C++ programs do not compile unless function prototypes are provided for every function or each function is defined before it is called.

```cpp
 1   // Fig. 7.17: NoArguments.cpp
 2   // Functions that take no arguments.
 3   #include <iostream>
 4   using std::cout;
 5   using std::endl;
 6
 7   void function1(); // function that takes no arguments
 8   void function2( void ); // function that takes no arguments
 9
10   int main()
11   {
12      function1(); // call function1 with no arguments
13      function2(); // call function2 with no arguments
14      return 0; // indicates successful termination
15   } // end main
16
17   // function1 uses an empty parameter list to specify that
18   // the function receives no arguments
19   void function1()
20   {
21      cout << "function1 takes no arguments" << endl;
22   } // end function1
23
24   // function2 uses a void parameter list to specify that
25   // the function receives no arguments
26   void function2( void )
27   {
28      cout << "function2 also takes no arguments" << endl;
29   } // end function2
```

```
function1 takes no arguments
function2 also takes no arguments
```

Fig. 7.17 | Functions that take no arguments.

7.13 Inline Functions

Implementing a program as a set of functions is good from a software engineering standpoint, but function calls involve execution-time overhead. Visual C++ provides *inline functions* to help reduce function-call overhead—especially for small functions. Placing the qualifier *inline* before a function's return type in the function definition "advises" the compiler to generate a copy of the function's code in place (when appropriate) to avoid a function call. The trade-off is that multiple copies of the function code are inserted in the program (often making the program larger) rather than there being a single copy of the function to which control is passed each time the function is called. The compiler can ignore the inline qualifier and typically does so for all but the smallest functions.

Software Engineering Observation 7.11

Any change to an inline function requires all clients of the function to be recompiled. This can be significant in some program development and maintenance situations.

Good Programming Practice 7.5

The inline qualifier should be used only with small, frequently used functions.

Performance Tip 7.4

Using inline functions can reduce execution time but may increase program size.

Figure 7.18 uses inline function cube (lines 11–14) to calculate the volume of a cube of side side. Keyword const in the parameter list of function cube (line 11) tells the compiler that the function does not modify variable side. This ensures that the value of side is not changed by the function when the calculation is performed. (Keyword const is discussed in detail in Chapters 8, 9 and 11.) Notice that the complete definition of function cube appears before it is used in the program. This is required so that the compiler knows how to expand a cube function call into its inlined code. For this reason, reusable inline functions are typically placed in header files, so that their definitions can be included in each source file that uses them.

Software Engineering Observation 7.12

The const qualifier should be used to enforce the principle of least privilege. Using the principle of least privilege to properly design software can greatly reduce debugging time and improper side effects and can make a program easier to modify and maintain.

```
1   // Fig. 7.18: InlineFunction.cpp
2   // Using an inline function to calculate the volume of a cube.
3   #include <iostream>
4   using std::cout;
5   using std::cin;
6   using std::endl;
7
8   // Definition of inline function cube. Definition of function appears
9   // before function is called, so a function prototype is not required.
10  // First line of function definition acts as the prototype.
```

Fig. 7.18 | inline function that calculates the volume of a cube. (Part 1 of 2.)

```
11   inline double cube( const double side )
12   {
13      return side * side * side; // calculate cube
14   } // end function cube
15
16   int main()
17   {
18      double sideValue; // stores value entered by user
19      cout << "Enter the side length of your cube: ";
20      cin >> sideValue; // read value from user
21
22      // calculate cube of sideValue and display result
23      cout << "Volume of cube with side "
24         << sideValue << " is " << cube( sideValue ) << endl;
25      return 0; // indicates successful termination
26   } // end main
```

```
Enter the side length of your cube: 3.5
Volume of cube with side 3.5 is 42.875
```

Fig. 7.18 | `inline` function that calculates the volume of a cube. (Part 2 of 2.)

7.14 References and Reference Parameters

Two ways to pass arguments to functions in many programming languages are *pass-by-value* and *pass-by-reference*. When an argument is passed by value, a *copy* of the argument's value is made and passed (on the function-call stack) to the called function. Changes to the copy do not affect the original variable's value in the caller. This prevents the accidental side effects that so greatly hinder the development of correct and reliable software systems. Each argument that has been passed in the programs in this chapter so far has been passed by value. Note that the following concepts are specific to native C++. Refer to Section 9.16 for C++/CLI-specific information related to references and reference parameters.

Performance Tip 7.5

One disadvantage of pass-by-value is that, if a large data item is being passed, copying that data can take a considerable amount of execution time and memory space.

Reference Parameters

This section introduces *reference parameters*—the first of the two means Visual C++ provides for performing pass-by-reference. With pass-by-reference, the caller gives the called function the ability to access the caller's data directly, and to modify that data if the called function chooses to do so.

Performance Tip 7.6

Pass-by-reference is good for performance reasons, because it can eliminate the pass-by-value overhead of copying large amounts of data.

Software Engineering Observation 7.13

Pass-by-reference can weaken security, because the called function can corrupt the caller's data.

Later, we'll show how to achieve the performance advantage of pass-by-reference while simultaneously achieving the software engineering advantage of protecting the caller's data from corruption.

A reference parameter is an alias for its corresponding argument in a function call. To indicate that a function parameter is passed by reference, simply follow the parameter's type in the function prototype by an ampersand (&); use the same convention when listing the parameter's type in the function header. For example, the following declaration in a function header

```
int &count
```

when read from right to left is pronounced "count is a reference to an int." In the function call, simply mention the variable by name to pass it by reference. Then, mentioning the variable by its parameter name in the body of the called function actually refers to the original variable in the calling function, and the original variable can be modified directly by the called function. As always, the function prototype and header must agree.

Passing Arguments by Value and by Reference
Figure 7.19 compares pass-by-value and pass-by-reference with reference parameters. The "styles" of the arguments in the calls to function squareByValue and function squareByReference are identical—both variables are simply mentioned by name in the function calls. Without checking the function prototypes or function definitions, it is not possible to tell from the calls alone whether either function can modify its arguments. Because function prototypes are mandatory, the compiler has no trouble resolving the ambiguity.

```cpp
1   // Fig. 7.19: References.cpp
2   // Comparing pass-by-value and pass-by-reference with references.
3   #include <iostream>
4   using std::cout;
5   using std::endl;
6
7   int squareByValue( int ); // function prototype (value pass)
8   void squareByReference( int & ); // function prototype (reference pass)
9
10  int main()
11  {
12     int x = 2; // value to square using squareByValue
13     int z = 4; // value to square using squareByReference
14
15     // demonstrate squareByValue
16     cout << "x = " << x << " before squareByValue\n";
17     cout << "Value returned by squareByValue: "
18        << squareByValue( x ) << endl;
19     cout << "x = " << x << " after squareByValue\n" << endl;
20
21     // demonstrate squareByReference
22     cout << "z = " << z << " before squareByReference" << endl;
23     squareByReference( z );
24     cout << "z = " << z << " after squareByReference" << endl;
```

Fig. 7.19 | Passing arguments by value and by reference. (Part 1 of 2.)

```
25        return 0; // indicates successful termination
26    } // end main
27
28    // squareByValue multiplies number by itself, stores the
29    // result in number and returns the new value of number
30    int squareByValue( int number )
31    {
32        return number *= number; // caller's argument not modified
33    } // end function squareByValue
34
35    // squareByReference multiplies numberRef by itself and stores the result
36    // in the variable to which numberRef refers in function main
37    void squareByReference( int &numberRef )
38    {
39        numberRef *= numberRef; // caller's argument modified
40    } // end function squareByReference
```

```
x = 2 before squareByValue
Value returned by squareByValue: 4
x = 2 after squareByValue

z = 4 before squareByReference
z = 16 after squareByReference
```

Fig. 7.19 | Passing arguments by value and by reference. (Part 2 of 2.)

Common Programming Error 7.14

Because reference parameters are mentioned only by name in the body of the called function, you might inadvertently treat reference parameters as pass-by-value parameters. This can cause unexpected side effects if the original copies of the variables are changed by the function.

Chapter 9 discusses pointers; pointers enable an alternate form of pass-by-reference in which the style of the call clearly indicates pass-by-reference (and the potential for modifying the caller's arguments).

Performance Tip 7.7

For passing large objects, use a constant reference parameter to simulate the appearance and security of pass-by-value and avoid the overhead of passing a copy of the large object.

Software Engineering Observation 7.14

Many programmers do not bother to declare parameters passed by value as const, even though the called function should not be modifying the passed argument. Keyword const in this context would protect only a copy of the original argument, not the original argument itself, which when passed by value is safe from modification by the called function.

To specify a reference to a constant, place the const qualifier before the type specifier in the parameter declaration.

Note the placement of & in function squareByReference's parameter list (line 37, Fig. 7.19). Some Visual C++ programmers prefer to write the equivalent form int& numberRef.

Software Engineering Observation 7.15

For the combined reasons of clarity and performance, many Visual C++ programmers prefer that modifiable arguments be passed to functions by using pointers (which we study in Chapter 9), small nonmodifiable arguments be passed by value and large nonmodifiable arguments be passed to functions by using references to constants.

References as Aliases within a Function

References can also be used as aliases for other variables within a function (although they typically are used with functions, as shown in Fig. 7.19). For example, the code

```
int count = 1; // declare integer variable count
int &cRef = count; // create cRef as an alias for count
cRef++; // increment count (using its alias cRef)
```

increments variable count by using its alias cRef. Reference variables must be initialized in their declarations (see Fig. 7.20 and Fig. 7.21) and cannot be reassigned as aliases to other variables. Once a reference is declared as an alias for another variable, all operations supposedly performed on the alias (i.e., the reference) are actually performed on the original variable. The alias is simply another name for the original variable. Unless it is a reference to a constant, a reference argument must be an *lvalue* (e.g., a variable name), not a constant or expression that returns an *rvalue* (e.g., the result of a calculation). See Section 6.9 for definitions of the terms *lvalue* and *rvalue*.

```
1  // Fig. 7.20: References.cpp
2  // References must be initialized.
3  #include <iostream>
4  using std::cout;
5  using std::endl;
6
7  int main()
8  {
9     int x = 3;
10    int &y = x; // y refers to (is an alias for) x
11
12    cout << "x = " << x << endl << "y = " << y << endl;
13    y = 7; // actually modifies x
14    cout << "x = " << x << endl << "y = " << y << endl;
15    return 0; // indicates successful termination
16 } // end main
```

```
x = 3
y = 3
x = 7
y = 7
```

Fig. 7.20 | Initializing and using a reference.

```
1  // Fig. 7.21: References.cpp
2  // References must be initialized.
3  #include <iostream>
```

Fig. 7.21 | Uninitialized reference causes a syntax error. (Part 1 of 2.)

```
 4   using std::cout;
 5   using std::endl;
 6
 7   int main()
 8   {
 9      int x = 3;
10      int &y; // Error: y must be initialized
11
12      cout << "x = " << x << endl << "y = " << y << endl;
13      y = 7;
14      cout << "x = " << x << endl << "y = " << y << endl;
15      return 0; // indicates successful termination
16   } // end main
```

```
C:\examples\ch07\fig07_21\References.cpp(10) : error C2530: 'y' :
   references must be initialized
```

Fig. 7.21 | Uninitialized reference causes a syntax error. (Part 2 of 2.)

Returning a Reference from a Function

Functions can return references, but this can be dangerous. When returning a reference to a variable declared in the called function, the variable should be declared static within that function. Otherwise, the reference refers to an automatic variable that is discarded when the function terminates; such a variable is said to be "undefined," and the program's behavior is unpredictable. We will see in Chapter 11 that there are valid reasons for returning references from a function. References to undefined variables are sometimes called *dangling references*.

Common Programming Error 7.15

Not initializing a reference variable when it is declared is a compilation error, unless the declaration is part of a function's parameter list. Reference parameters are initialized when the function in which they are declared is called.

Common Programming Error 7.16

Attempting to reassign a previously declared reference to be an alias to another variable is a logic error. The value of the other variable is simply assigned to the variable for which the reference is already an alias.

Common Programming Error 7.17

Returning a reference to an automatic variable in a called function is a logic error. Some compilers issue a warning when this occurs.

7.15 Default Arguments

It is not uncommon for a program to invoke a function repeatedly with the same argument value for a particular parameter. In such cases, you can specify that such a parameter has a *default argument*, i.e., a default value to be passed to that parameter. When a program omits an argument for a parameter with a default argument in a function call, the compiler rewrites the function call and inserts the default value of that argument. Note that managed code in C++/CLI does not support default arguments.

Default arguments must be the rightmost (trailing) arguments in a function's parameter list. When calling a function with two or more default arguments, if an omitted argument is not the rightmost argument in the argument list, then all arguments to the right of that argument also must be omitted. Default arguments must be specified with the first occurrence of the function name—typically, in the function prototype. If the function prototype is omitted because the function definition also serves as the prototype, then the default arguments should be specified in the function header. Default values can be any expression, including constants, global variables or function calls. Default arguments also can be used with `inline` functions.

Figure 7.22 demonstrates using default arguments in calculating the volume of a box. The function prototype for `boxVolume` (line 8) specifies that all three parameters have been given default values of 1. Note that we provided variable names in the function prototype for readability. As always, variable names are not required in function prototypes.

 Common Programming Error 7.18

It is a compilation error to specify default arguments in both a function's prototype and header.

```cpp
1  // Fig. 7.22: DefaultArguments.cpp
2  // Using default arguments.
3  #include <iostream>
4  using std::cout;
5  using std::endl;
6
7  // function prototype that specifies default arguments
8  int boxVolume( int length = 1, int width = 1, int height = 1 );
9
10 int main()
11 {
12    // no arguments--use default values for all dimensions
13    cout << "The default box volume is: " << boxVolume();
14
15    // specify length; default width and height
16    cout << "\n\nThe volume of a box with length 10,\n"
17       << "width 1 and height 1 is: " << boxVolume( 10 );
18
19    // specify length and width; default height
20    cout << "\n\nThe volume of a box with length 10,\n"
21       << "width 5 and height 1 is: " << boxVolume( 10, 5 );
22
23    // specify all arguments
24    cout << "\n\nThe volume of a box with length 10,\n"
25       << "width 5 and height 2 is: " << boxVolume( 10, 5, 2 )
26       << endl;
27    return 0; // indicates successful termination
28 } // end main
29
30 // function boxVolume calculates the volume of a box
31 int boxVolume( int length, int width, int height )
32 {
```

Fig. 7.22 | Default arguments to a function. (Part 1 of 2.)

```
33      return length * width * height;
34   } // end function boxVolume
```

```
The default box volume is: 1

The volume of a box with length 10,
width 1 and height 1 is: 10

The volume of a box with length 10,
width 5 and height 1 is: 50

The volume of a box with length 10,
width 5 and height 2 is: 100
```

Fig. 7.22 | Default arguments to a function. (Part 2 of 2.)

The first call to boxVolume (line 13) specifies no arguments, thus using all three default values of 1. The second call (line 17) passes only a length argument, thus using default values of 1 for the width and height arguments. The third call (line 21) passes arguments for only length and width, thus using a default value of 1 for the height argument. The last call (line 25) passes arguments for length, width and height, thus using no default values. Note that any arguments passed to the function explicitly are assigned to the function's parameters from left to right. Therefore, when boxVolume receives one argument, the function assigns the value of that argument to its length parameter (i.e., the leftmost parameter in the parameter list). When boxVolume receives two arguments, the function assigns the values of those arguments to its length and width parameters in that order. Finally, when boxVolume receives all three arguments, the function assigns the values of those arguments to its length, width and height parameters, respectively.

Good Programming Practice 7.6

Using default arguments can simplify writing function calls. However, some programmers feel that explicitly specifying all arguments is clearer.

Software Engineering Observation 7.16

If the default values for a function change, all client code using the function must be recompiled.

Common Programming Error 7.19

Specifying and attempting to use a default argument that is not a rightmost (trailing) argument (while not simultaneously defaulting all the rightmost arguments) is a syntax error.

7.16 Unary Scope Resolution Operator

It is possible to declare local and global variables of the same name. Visual C++ provides the *unary scope resolution operator* (::) to access a global variable when a local variable of the same name is in scope. The unary scope resolution operator cannot be used to access a local variable of the same name in an outer block. A global variable can be accessed directly without the unary scope resolution operator if the name of the global variable is not the same as that of a local variable in scope.

Figure 7.23 demonstrates the unary scope resolution operator with local and global variables of the same name (lines 7 and 11). To emphasize that the local and global versions of variable number are distinct, the program declares one variable of type int and the other double.

Using the unary scope resolution operator (::) with a given variable name is optional when the only variable with that name is a global variable.

Common Programming Error 7.20

It is an error to attempt to use the unary scope resolution operator (::) to access a nonglobal variable in an outer block. If no global variable with that name exists, a compilation error occurs. If a global variable with that name exists, this is a logic error, because the program will refer to the global variable when you intended to access the nonglobal variable in the outer block.

Good Programming Practice 7.7

Always using the unary scope resolution operator (::) to refer to global variables makes programs easier to read and understand, because it makes it clear that you are intending to access a global variable rather than a nonglobal variable.

Software Engineering Observation 7.17

Always using the unary scope resolution operator (::) to refer to global variables makes programs easier to modify by reducing the risk of name collisions with nonglobal variables.

Error-Prevention Tip 7.4

Always using the unary scope resolution operator (::) to refer to a global variable eliminates possible logic errors that might occur if a nonglobal variable hides the global variable.

Error-Prevention Tip 7.5

Avoid using variables of the same name for different purposes in a program. Although this is allowed in various circumstances, it can lead to errors.

```cpp
1   // Fig. 7.23: ScopeResolutionOperator.cpp
2   // Using the unary scope resolution operator.
3   #include <iostream>
4   using std::cout;
5   using std::endl;
6
7   int number = 7; // global variable named number
8
9   int main()
10  {
11     double number = 10.5; // local variable named number
12
13     // display values of local and global variables
14     cout << "Local double value of number = " << number
15        << "\nGlobal int value of number = " << ::number << endl;
16     return 0; // indicates successful termination
17  } // end main
```

Fig. 7.23 | Unary scope resolution operator. (Part 1 of 2.)

```
Local double value of number = 10.5
Global int value of number = 7
```

Fig. 7.23 | Unary scope resolution operator. (Part 2 of 2.)

7.17 Function Overloading

Visual C++ enables several functions of the same name to be defined, as long as these functions have different signatures. This capability is called *function overloading*. When an overloaded function is called, the Visual C++ compiler selects the proper function by examining the number, types and order of the arguments in the call. Function overloading is commonly used to create several functions of the same name that perform similar tasks, but on different data types. For example, many functions in the math library are overloaded for different numeric data types—the C++ standard requires float, double and long double overloaded versions of the math library functions discussed in Section 7.3.

Good Programming Practice 7.8

Overloading functions that perform closely related tasks can make programs more readable and understandable.

Overloaded square Functions

Figure 7.24 uses overloaded square functions to calculate the square of an int (lines 8–12) and the square of a double (lines 15–19). Line 23 invokes the int version of function square by passing the literal value 7. Visual C++ treats whole-number literal values as type int by default. Similarly, line 25 invokes the double version of function square by passing the literal value 7.5, which Visual C++ treats as a double value by default. In each case the compiler chooses the proper function to call, based on the type of the argument. The last two lines of the output window confirm that the proper function was called in each case.

```cpp
1   // Fig. 7.24: OverloadedFunctions.cpp
2   // Overloaded functions.
3   #include <iostream>
4   using std::cout;
5   using std::endl;
6
7   // function square for int values
8   int square( int x )
9   {
10     cout << "square of integer " << x << " is ";
11     return x * x;
12  } // end function square with int argument
13
14  // function square for double values
15  double square( double y )
16  {
17     cout << "square of double " << y << " is ";
18     return y * y;
19  } // end function square with double argument
```

Fig. 7.24 | Overloaded square functions. (Part 1 of 2.)

```
20
21   int main()
22   {
23      cout << square( 7 ); // calls int version
24      cout << endl;
25      cout << square( 7.5 ); // calls double version
26      cout << endl;
27      return 0; // indicates successful termination
28   } // end main
```

```
square of integer 7 is 49
square of double 7.5 is 56.25
```

Fig. 7.24 | Overloaded square functions. (Part 2 of 2.)

How the Compiler Differentiates Overloaded Functions

Overloaded functions are distinguished by their signatures. A signature is a combination of a function's name and its parameter types (in order). The compiler encodes each function identifier with the number and types of its parameters (sometimes referred to as *name mangling* or *name decoration*) to enable *type-safe linkage.* Type-safe linkage ensures that the proper overloaded function is called and that the types of the arguments conform to the types of the parameters.

Common Programming Error 7.21

Creating overloaded functions with identical parameter lists and different return types is a compilation error.

The compiler uses only the parameter lists to distinguish between functions of the same name. Overloaded functions need not have the same number of parameters. You should use caution when overloading functions with default parameters, because this may cause ambiguity.

Common Programming Error 7.22

A function with default arguments omitted might be called identically to another overloaded function; this is a compilation error. For example, having in a program both a function that explicitly takes no arguments and a function of the same name that contains all default arguments results in a compilation error when an attempt is made to use that function name in a call passing no arguments. The compiler does not know which version of the function to choose.

Overloaded Operators

In Chapter 12, we discuss how to overload operators to define how they should operate on objects of user-defined data types. (In fact, we have been using many overloaded operators to this point, including the stream insertion operator << and the stream extraction operator >>, each of which is overloaded to be able to display data of all the fundamental types. We say more about overloading << and >> to be able to handle objects of user-defined types in Chapter 12.) Section 7.18 introduces function templates for automatically generating overloaded functions that perform identical tasks on different data types.

7.18 Function Templates

Overloaded functions are normally used to perform similar operations that involve different program logic on different data types. If the program logic and operations are identical for each data type, overloading may be performed more compactly and conveniently by using *function templates*. You write a single function-template definition. Given the argument types provided in calls to this function, Visual C++ automatically generates separate *function-template specializations* to handle each type of call appropriately. Thus, defining a single function template essentially defines a whole family of overloaded functions.

Figure 7.25 contains the definition of a function template (lines 4–18) for a maximum function that determines the largest of three values. All function-template definitions begin with the template keyword (line 4) followed by a *template parameter list* to the function template enclosed in angle brackets (< and >). Every parameter in the template parameter list (often referred to as a *formal type parameter*) is preceded by keyword typename or keyword class (which are synonyms in this context). The formal type parameters are placeholders for fundamental types or user-defined types. These placeholders are used to specify the types of the function's parameters (line 5), to specify the function's return type (line 5) and to declare variables within the body of the function definition (line 7). A function template is defined like any other function, but uses the formal type parameters as placeholders for actual data types.

The function template in Fig. 7.25 declares a single formal type parameter T (line 4) as a placeholder for the type of the data to be tested by function maximum. The name of a type parameter must be unique in the template parameter list for a particular template definition. When the compiler detects a maximum invocation in the program source code, the type of the data passed to maximum is substituted for T throughout the template definition, and C++ creates a complete function for determining the maximum of three values of the specified data type. Then the newly created function is compiled. Thus, templates are a means of code generation.

```
1   // Fig. 7.25: maximum.h
2   // Definition of function template maximum.
3
4   template < class T >   // or template< typename T >
5   T maximum( T value1, T value2, T value3 )
6   {
7      T maximumValue = value1; // assume value1 is maximum
8
9      // determine whether value2 is greater than maximumValue
10     if ( value2 > maximumValue )
11        maximumValue = value2;
12
13     // determine whether value3 is greater than maximumValue
14     if ( value3 > maximumValue )
15        maximumValue = value3;
16
17     return maximumValue;
18  } // end function template maximum
```

Fig. 7.25 | Function template maximum header file.

Common Programming Error 7.23

Not placing keyword class *or keyword* typename *before every formal type parameter of a function template (e.g., writing < class S, T > instead of < class S, class T >) is a syntax error.*

Figure 7.26 uses the maximum function template (lines 20, 30 and 40) to determine the largest of three int values, three double values and three char values, respectively.

In Fig. 7.26, three functions are created as a result of the calls in lines 20, 30 and 40—expecting three int values, three double values and three char values, respectively. The

```cpp
1   // Fig. 7.26: MaximumTest.cpp
2   // Function template maximum test program.
3   #include <iostream>
4   using std::cout;
5   using std::cin;
6   using std::endl;
7
8   #include "maximum.h" // include definition of function template maximum
9
10  int main()
11  {
12     // demonstrate maximum with int values
13     int int1, int2, int3;
14
15     cout << "Input three integer values: ";
16     cin >> int1 >> int2 >> int3;
17
18     // invoke int version of maximum
19     cout << "The maximum integer value is: "
20        << maximum( int1, int2, int3 );
21
22     // demonstrate maximum with double values
23     double double1, double2, double3;
24
25     cout << "\n\nInput three double values: ";
26     cin >> double1 >> double2 >> double3;
27
28     // invoke double version of maximum
29     cout << "The maximum double value is: "
30        << maximum( double1, double2, double3 );
31
32     // demonstrate maximum with char values
33     char char1, char2, char3;
34
35     cout << "\n\nInput three characters: ";
36     cin >> char1 >> char2 >> char3;
37
38     // invoke char version of maximum
39     cout << "The maximum character value is: "
40        << maximum( char1, char2, char3 ) << endl;
41     return 0; // indicates successful termination
42  } // end main
```

Fig. 7.26 | Demonstrating function template maximum. (Part 1 of 2.)

```
Input three integer values: 1 2 3
The maximum integer value is: 3

Input three double values: 3.3 2.2 1.1
The maximum double value is: 3.3

Input three characters: A C B
The maximum character value is: C
```

Fig. 7.26 | Demonstrating function template `maximum`. (Part 2 of 2.)

function-template specialization created for type `int` replaces each occurrence of T with
int as follows:

```
int maximum( int value1, int value2, int value3 )
{
    int maximumValue = value1;

    // determine whether value2 is greater than maximumValue
    if ( value2 > maximumValue )
       maximumValue = value2;

    // determine whether value3 is greater than maximumValue
    if ( value3 > maximumValue )
       maximumValue = value3;

    return maximumValue;
} // end function template maximum
```

7.19 Recursion

The programs we have discussed are generally structured as functions that call one another
in a disciplined, hierarchical manner. For some problems, it is useful to have functions call
themselves. A *recursive function* is a function that calls itself, either directly, or indirectly
(through another function). [*Note:* Although many compilers allow function `main` to call
itself, Section 3.6.1, paragraph 3, and Section 5.2.2, paragraph 9, of the C++ standard document indicate that `main` should not be called within a program or recursively. Its sole purpose is to be the starting point for program execution.] Recursion is an important topic
discussed at length in upper-level computer science courses. This section and the next
present simple examples of recursion. This book contains an extensive treatment of recursion. Figure 7.32 (at the end of Section 7.21) summarizes the recursion examples and exercises in the book.

　　We first consider recursion conceptually, then examine two programs containing
recursive functions. Recursive problem-solving approaches have a number of elements in
common. A recursive function is called to solve a problem. The function actually knows
how to solve only the simplest case(s), or so-called *base case(s)*. If the function is called
with a base case, the function simply returns a result. If the function is called with a more
complex problem, it typically divides the problem into two conceptual pieces—a piece
that the function knows how to do and a piece that it does not know how to do. To make
recursion feasible, the latter piece must resemble the original problem, but be a slightly

simpler or slightly smaller version. This new problem looks like the original problem, so the function launches (calls) a fresh copy of itself to work on the smaller problem—this is referred to as a *recursive call* and is also called the *recursion step*. The recursion step often includes the keyword `return`, because its result will be combined with the portion of the problem the function knew how to solve to form a result that will be passed back to the original caller, possibly `main`.

The recursion step executes while the original call to the function is still "open," i.e., it has not yet finished executing. The recursion step can result in many more such recursive calls, as the function keeps dividing each new subproblem with which the function is called into two conceptual pieces. In order for the recursion to eventually terminate, each time the function calls itself with a slightly simpler version of the original problem, this sequence of smaller and smaller problems must eventually converge on the base case. At that point, the function recognizes the base case and returns a result to the previous copy of the function, and a sequence of returns ensues all the way up the line until the original function call eventually returns the final result to `main`. All of this sounds quite exotic compared to the kind of "conventional" problem solving we have been using to this point. As an example of these concepts at work, let us write a recursive program to perform a popular mathematical calculation.

The factorial of a nonnegative integer n, written $n!$ (and pronounced "n factorial"), is the product

$$n \cdot (n-1) \cdot (n-2) \cdot \ldots \cdot 1$$

with $1!$ equal to 1, and $0!$ defined to be 1. For example, $5!$ is the product $5 \cdot 4 \cdot 3 \cdot 2 \cdot 1$, which is equal to 120.

The factorial of an integer, `number`, greater than or equal to 0, can be calculated *iteratively* (nonrecursively) by using a `for` statement as follows:

```
factorial = 1;

for ( int counter = number; counter >= 1; counter-- )
    factorial *= counter;
```

A recursive definition of the factorial function is arrived at by observing the following algebraic relationship:

$$n! = n \cdot (n-1)!$$

For example, $5!$ is clearly equal to $5 * 4!$, as is shown by the following:

$$5! = 5 \cdot 4 \cdot 3 \cdot 2 \cdot 1$$
$$5! = 5 \cdot (4 \cdot 3 \cdot 2 \cdot 1)$$
$$5! = 5 \cdot (4!)$$

The evaluation of $5!$ would proceed as shown in Fig. 7.27. Figure 7.27(a) shows how the succession of recursive calls proceeds until $1!$ is evaluated to be 1, which terminates the recursion. Figure 7.27(b) shows the values returned from each recursive call to its caller until the final value is calculated and returned.

The program of Fig. 7.28 uses recursion to calculate and print the factorials of the integers 0–10. (The choice of the data type `unsigned long` is explained momentarily.) The

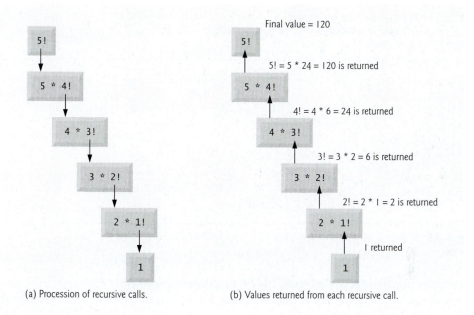

(a) Procession of recursive calls.   (b) Values returned from each recursive call.

Fig. 7.27 | Recursive evaluation of 5!.

```
1    // Fig. 7.28: Factorial.cpp
2    // Demonstrating the recursive function factorial.
3    #include <iostream>
4    using std::cout;
5    using std::endl;
6
7    #include <iomanip>
8    using std::setw;
9
10   unsigned long factorial( unsigned long ); // function prototype
11
12   int main()
13   {
14      // calculate the factorials of 0 through 10
15      for ( int counter = 0; counter <= 10; counter++ )
16         cout << setw( 2 ) << counter << "! = " << factorial( counter )
17            << endl;
18
19      return 0; // indicates successful termination
20   } // end main
21
22   // recursive definition of function factorial
23   unsigned long factorial( unsigned long number )
24   {
25      if ( number <= 1 ) // test for base case
26         return 1; // base cases: 0! = 1 and 1! = 1
```

Fig. 7.28 | Demonstrating the recursive function `factorial`. (Part 1 of 2.)

```
27          else // recursion step
28              return number * factorial( number - 1 );
29      } // end function factorial
```

```
 0! = 1
 1! = 1
 2! = 2
 3! = 6
 4! = 24
 5! = 120
 6! = 720
 7! = 5040
 8! = 40320
 9! = 362880
10! = 3628800
```

Fig. 7.28 | Demonstrating the recursive function `factorial`. (Part 2 of 2.)

recursive function `factorial` (lines 23–29) first determines whether the terminating condition `number <= 1` (line 25) is true. If `number` is less than or equal to 1, the `factorial` function returns 1 (line 26), no further recursion is necessary and the function terminates. If `number` is greater than 1, line 28 expresses the problem as the product of `number` and a recursive call to `factorial` evaluating the factorial of `number - 1`. Note that `factorial( number - 1 )` is a slightly simpler problem than the original calculation `factorial( number )`.

Function `factorial` has been declared to receive a parameter of type `unsigned long` and return a result of type `unsigned long`. This is shorthand notation for `unsigned long int`. The C++ standard requires that a variable of type `unsigned long int` be at least as big as an `int`. Typically, an `unsigned long int` is stored in at least four bytes (32 bits); such a variable can hold a value in the range 0 to at least 4294967295. (The data type `long int` is also stored in at least four bytes and can hold a value at least in the range –2147483648 to 2147483647.) As can be seen in Fig. 7.28, factorial values become large quickly. We chose the data type `unsigned long` so that the program can calculate factorials greater than 7! on computers with small (such as two-byte) integers. Unfortunately, the function `factorial` produces large values so quickly that even `unsigned long` does not help us compute many factorial values before even the size of an `unsigned long` variable is exceeded.

The exercises explore using variables of data type `double` to calculate factorials of larger numbers. This points to a weakness in most programming languages, namely, that the languages are not easily extended to handle the unique requirements of various applications. As we'll see when we discuss object-oriented programming in more depth, Visual C++ is an extensible language that allows us to create classes that can represent arbitrarily large integers if we wish. Such classes already are available in popular class libraries,[1] and we work on similar classes of our own in Exercise 10.14 and Exercise 12.14.

---

1.   Such classes can be found at `shoup.net/ntl`, `cliodhna.cop.uop.edu/~hetrick/c-sources.html` and `www.trumphurst.com/cpplibs/datapage.phtml?category='intro'`.

Common Programming Error 7.24

Either omitting the base case, or writing the recursion step incorrectly so that it does not converge on the base case, causes "infinite" recursion, eventually exhausting memory. This is analogous to the problem of an infinite loop in an iterative (nonrecursive) solution.

7.20 Example Using Recursion: Fibonacci Series

The Fibonacci series

0, 1, 1, 2, 3, 5, 8, 13, 21, ...

begins with 0 and 1 and has the property that each subsequent Fibonacci number is the sum of the previous two Fibonacci numbers.

The series occurs in nature and, in particular, describes a form of spiral. The ratio of successive Fibonacci numbers converges on a constant value of 1.618.... This number, too, frequently occurs in nature and has been called the *golden ratio* or the *golden mean.* Humans tend to find the golden mean aesthetically pleasing. Architects often design windows, rooms and buildings whose length and width are in the ratio of the golden mean. Postcards are often designed with a golden mean length/width ratio.

The Fibonacci series can be defined recursively as follows:

fibonacci(0) = 0
fibonacci(1) = 1
fibonacci(n) = fibonacci($n - 1$) + fibonacci($n - 2$)

The program of Fig. 7.29 calculates the nth Fibonacci number recursively by using function `fibonacci`. Notice that Fibonacci numbers also tend to become large quickly, although slower than factorials do. Therefore, we chose the data type `unsigned long` for the parameter type and the return type in function `fibonacci`. Figure 7.29 shows the execution of the program, which displays the Fibonacci values for several numbers.

```cpp
1   // Fig. 7.29: Fibonacci.cpp
2   // Testing the recursive fibonacci function.
3   #include <iostream>
4   using std::cout;
5   using std::cin;
6   using std::endl;
7
8   unsigned long fibonacci( unsigned long ); // function prototype
9
10  int main()
11  {
12     // calculate the fibonacci values of 0 through 10
13     for ( int counter = 0; counter <= 10; counter++ )
14        cout << "fibonacci( " << counter << " ) = "
15           << fibonacci( counter ) << endl;
16
17     // display higher fibonacci values
18     cout << "fibonacci( 20 ) = " << fibonacci( 20 ) << endl;
```

Fig. 7.29 | Demonstrating recursive function `fibonacci`. (Part 1 of 2.)

```
19          cout << "fibonacci( 30 ) = " << fibonacci( 30 ) << endl;
20          cout << "fibonacci( 35 ) = " << fibonacci( 35 ) << endl;
21          return 0; // indicates successful termination
22       } // end main
23
24       // recursive method fibonacci
25       unsigned long fibonacci( unsigned long number )
26       {
27          if ( ( number == 0 ) || ( number == 1 ) ) // base cases
28             return number;
29          else // recursion step
30             return fibonacci( number - 1 ) + fibonacci( number - 2 );
31       } // end function fibonacci
```

```
fibonacci( 0 ) = 0
fibonacci( 1 ) = 1
fibonacci( 2 ) = 1
fibonacci( 3 ) = 2
fibonacci( 4 ) = 3
fibonacci( 5 ) = 5
fibonacci( 6 ) = 8
fibonacci( 7 ) = 13
fibonacci( 8 ) = 21
fibonacci( 9 ) = 34
fibonacci( 10 ) = 55
fibonacci( 20 ) = 6765
fibonacci( 30 ) = 832040
fibonacci( 35 ) = 9227465
```

Fig. 7.29 | Demonstrating recursive function `fibonacci`. (Part 2 of 2.)

The application begins with a `for` statement that calculates and displays the Fibonacci values for the integers 0–10 and is followed by three calls to calculate the Fibonacci values of the integers 20, 30 and 35 (lines 18–20). The calls to `fibonacci` (lines 15, 18, 19 and 20) from `main` are not recursive calls, but the calls from line 30 of `fibonacci` are recursive. Each time the program invokes `fibonacci` (lines 25–31), the function immediately tests the base case to determine whether `number` is equal to 0 or 1 (line 27). If this is true, line 28 returns `number`. Interestingly, if `number` is greater than 1, the recursion step (line 30) generates *two* recursive calls, each for a slightly smaller problem than the original call to `fibonacci`. Figure 7.30 shows how function `fibonacci` would evaluate `fibonacci( 3 )`.

This figure raises some interesting issues about the order in which the Visual C++ compiler will evaluate the operands of operators. This is a separate issue from the order in which operators are applied to their operands, namely, the order dictated by the rules of operator precedence and associativity. Figure 7.30 shows that evaluating `fibonacci( 3 )` causes two recursive calls, `fibonacci( 2 )` and `fibonacci( 1 )`. But in what order are these calls made?

Most programmers simply assume that the operands are evaluated left to right. Visual C++ does not specify the order in which the operands of most operators (including +) are to be evaluated. Therefore, you must make no assumption about the order in which these calls execute. The calls could in fact execute `fibonacci( 2 )` first, then `fibonacci( 1 )`, or

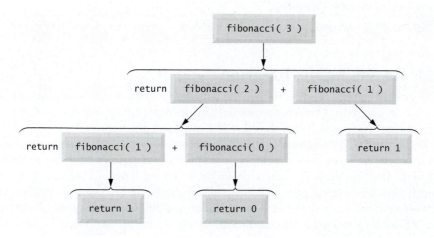

Fig. 7.30 | Set of recursive calls to function `fibonacci`.

they could execute in the reverse order: `fibonacci( 1 )`, then `fibonacci( 2 )`. In this program and in most others, it turns out that the final result would be the same. However, in some programs the evaluation of an operand can have *side effects* (changes to data values) that could affect the final result of the expression.

Visual C++ specifies the order of evaluation of the operands of only four operators—namely, &&, ||, the comma (,) operator and ?:. The first three are binary operators whose two operands are guaranteed to be evaluated left to right. The last operator is Visual C++'s only ternary operator. Its leftmost operand is always evaluated first; if it evaluates to nonzero (true), the middle operand evaluates next and the last operand is ignored; if the leftmost operand evaluates to zero (false), the third operand evaluates next and the middle operand is ignored.

Common Programming Error 7.25

Writing programs that depend on the order of evaluation of the operands of operators other than && , || , ?: and the comma (,) operator can lead to logic errors.

Portability Tip 7.3

Programs that depend on the order of evaluation of the operands of operators other than && , || , ?: and the comma (,) operator can function differently on systems with different compilers.

A word of caution is in order about recursive programs like the one we use here to generate Fibonacci numbers. Each level of recursion in function `fibonacci` has a doubling effect on the number of function calls; i.e., the number of recursive calls that are required to calculate the nth Fibonacci number is on the order of 2^n. This rapidly gets out of hand. Calculating only the 20th Fibonacci number would require on the order of 2^{20} or about a million calls, calculating the 30th Fibonacci number would require on the order of 2^{30} or about a billion calls, and so on. Computer scientists refer to this as *exponential complexity*. Problems of this nature humble even the world's most powerful computers! Complexity issues in general, and exponential complexity in particular, are discussed in detail in the upper-level computer science course generally called "Algorithms."

Performance Tip 7.8

Avoid Fibonacci-style recursive programs that result in an exponential "explosion" of calls.

7.21 Recursion vs. Iteration

In the two previous sections, we studied two functions that easily can be implemented recursively or iteratively. This section compares the two approaches and discusses why you might choose one approach over the other in a particular situation.

Both iteration and recursion are based on a control statement: Iteration uses a repetition structure; recursion uses a selection structure. Both iteration and recursion involve repetition: Iteration explicitly uses a repetition structure; recursion achieves repetition through repeated function calls. Iteration and recursion both involve a termination test: Iteration terminates when the loop-continuation condition fails; recursion terminates when a base case is recognized. Iteration with counter-controlled repetition and recursion both gradually approach termination: Iteration modifies a counter until the counter assumes a value that makes the loop-continuation condition fail; recursion produces simpler versions of the original problem until the base case is reached. Both iteration and recursion can occur infinitely: An infinite loop occurs with iteration if the loop-continuation test never becomes false; infinite recursion occurs if the recursion step does not reduce the problem during each recursive call in a manner that converges on the base case.

To illustrate the differences between iteration and recursion, let us examine an iterative solution to the factorial problem (Fig. 7.31). Note that a repetition statement is used

```cpp
 1  // Fig. 7.31: IterativeFactorial.cpp
 2  // Testing the iterative factorial function.
 3  #include <iostream>
 4  using std::cout;
 5  using std::endl;
 6
 7  #include <iomanip>
 8  using std::setw;
 9
10  unsigned long factorial( unsigned long ); // function prototype
11
12  int main()
13  {
14     // calculate the factorials of 0 through 10
15     for ( int counter = 0; counter <= 10; counter++ )
16        cout << setw( 2 ) << counter << "! = " << factorial( counter )
17           << endl;
18
19     return 0;
20  } // end main
21
22  // iterative function factorial
23  unsigned long factorial( unsigned long number )
24  {
```

Fig. 7.31 | Iterative factorial solution. (Part 1 of 2.)

```
25      unsigned long result = 1;
26
27      // iterative factorial calculation
28      for ( unsigned long i = number; i >= 1; i-- )
29          result *= i;
30
31      return result;
32  } // end function factorial
```

```
0!  = 1
1!  = 1
2!  = 2
3!  = 6
4!  = 24
5!  = 120
6!  = 720
7!  = 5040
8!  = 40320
9!  = 362880
10! = 3628800
```

Fig. 7.31 | Iterative factorial solution. (Part 2 of 2.)

(lines 28–29 of Fig. 7.31) rather than the selection statement of the recursive solution (lines 25–28 of Fig. 7.28). Note that both solutions use a termination test. In the recursive solution, line 24 tests for the base case. In the iterative solution, line 28 tests the loop-continuation condition—if the test fails, the loop terminates. Finally, note that instead of producing simpler versions of the original problem, the iterative solution uses a counter that is modified until the loop-continuation condition becomes false.

Recursion has many negatives. It repeatedly invokes the mechanism, and consequently the overhead, of function calls. This can be expensive in both processor time and memory space. Each recursive call causes another copy of the function (actually only the function's variables) to be created; this can consume considerable memory. Iteration normally occurs within a function, so the overhead of repeated function calls and extra memory assignment is omitted. So why choose recursion?

Software Engineering Observation 7.18

Any problem that can be solved recursively can also be solved iteratively (nonrecursively). A recursive approach is normally chosen in preference to an iterative approach when the recursive approach more naturally mirrors the problem and results in a program that is easier to understand and debug. Another reason to choose a recursive solution is that an iterative solution is not apparent.

Performance Tip 7.9

Avoid using recursion in performance situations. Recursive calls take time and consume additional memory.

Common Programming Error 7.26

Accidentally having a nonrecursive function call itself, either directly or indirectly (through another function), is a logic error.

Most programming textbooks introduce recursion later than we have done here. We feel that recursion is a sufficiently rich and complex topic that it is better to introduce it earlier and spread the examples over the remainder of the text. Figure 7.32 summarizes the recursion examples and exercises in the text.

Location in text	Recursion examples and exercises
Chapter 7	
Section 7.19, Fig. 7.28	Factorial function
Section 7.19, Fig. 7.29	Fibonacci function
Exercise 7.7	Sum of two integers
Exercise 7.40	Raising an integer to an integer power
Exercise 7.42	Towers of Hanoi
Exercise 7.44	Visualizing recursion
Exercise 7.45	Greatest common divisor
Exercise 7.50, Exercise 7.51	Mystery "What does this program do?" exercise
Chapter 8	
Exercise 8.20	Mystery "What does this program do?" exercise
Exercise 8.23	Mystery "What does this program do?" exercise
Exercise 8.33	Selection sort
Exercise 8.34	Determine whether a string is a palindrome
Exercise 8.35	Linear search
Exercise 8.36	Eight Queens
Exercise 8.37	Print an array
Exercise 8.38	Print a string backward
Exercise 8.39	Minimum value in an array
Chapter 9	
Exercise 9.26	Quicksort
Exercise 9.27	Maze traversal
Exercise 9.28	Generating mazes randomly
Exercise 9.29	Mazes of any size
Chapter 20	
Section 20.3.3, Figs. 20.5–20.7	Mergesort
Exercise 20.8	Linear search

Fig. 7.32 | Summary of recursion examples and exercises in the text. (Part 1 of 2.)

Location in text	Recursion examples and exercises
Exercise 20.9	Binary search
Exercise 20.10	Quicksort
Chapter 21	
Section 21.7, Figs. 21.20–21.22	Binary tree insert
Section 21.7, Figs. 21.20–21.22	Preorder traversal of a binary tree
Section 21.7, Figs. 21.20–21.22	Inorder traversal of a binary tree
Section 21.7, Figs. 21.20–21.22	Postorder traversal of a binary tree
Exercise 21.20	Print a linked list backward
Exercise 21.21	Search a linked list
Exercise 21.22	Binary tree delete
Exercise 21.23	Binary tree search
Exercise 21.24	Level order binary search
Exercise 21.25	Printing tree

Fig. 7.32 | Summary of recursion examples and exercises in the text. (Part 2 of 2.)

7.22 Enumerations in C++/CLI

All the previous concepts in this chapter relating to functions are equally applicable to native and managed code. The only concept different in C++/CLI is the way enumerations are declared and accessed. First, to declare an enum in C++/CLI you use a new spaced-keyword *enum class* as follows

```
enum class Status { CONTINUE, WON, LOST };
```

This declares an enum analogous to the one used in line 19 of Figure 7.11 but of a managed type Status. As a result, you cannot compare an enum type directly to an integer or other simple type without an explicit cast. Also, when using a C++/CLI enum you must use the scope resolution operator and the enum name to access enum values. The scope resolution operator is explained in this context in detail in Chapter 10. For now just mimic the syntax shown here when using enumerations in C++/CLI. For example, line 34 of Figure 7.11 uses the statement

```
gameStatus = WON;
```

to set the gameStatus variable to the enum value WON (equivalent to the integer value 1). If we were using the C++/CLI Status enum defined above, then the equivalent of line 34 in managed code would be

```
gameStatus = Status::WON;
```

You must precede the value of the enum with the enum name and the scope resolution operator or else the Visual Studio compiler will issue a compilation error.

7.23 (Optional) Software Engineering Case Study: Identifying Class Operations in the ATM System

In the Software Engineering Case Study sections at the ends of Chapters 4, 5 and 6, we performed the first few steps in the object-oriented design of our ATM system. In Chapter 4, we identified the classes that we'll need to implement and we created our first class diagram. In Chapter 5, we described some attributes of our classes. In Chapter 6, we examined object states and modeled object-state transitions and activities. Now, we determine some of the class operations (or behaviors) needed to implement the ATM system.

Identifying Operations

An operation is a service that objects of a class provide to clients of the class. Consider the operations of some real-world objects. A radio's operations include setting its station and volume (typically invoked by a person adjusting the radio's controls). A car's operations include accelerating (invoked by the driver pressing the accelerator pedal), decelerating (invoked by the driver pressing the brake pedal or releasing the gas pedal), turning and shifting gears. Software objects can offer operations as well—for example, a software graphics object might offer operations for drawing a circle, drawing a line, drawing a square and the like. A spreadsheet software object might offer operations like printing the spreadsheet, totaling the elements in a row or column and graphing information in the spreadsheet as a bar chart or pie chart.

We can derive many of the operations of each class by examining the key verbs and verb phrases in the requirements specification. We then relate each of these to particular classes in our system (Fig. 7.33). The verb phrases in Fig. 7.33 help us determine the operations of each class.

Modeling Operations

To identify operations, we examine the verb phrases listed for each class in Fig. 7.33. The "executes financial transactions" phrase associated with class ATM implies that class ATM instructs transactions to execute. Therefore, classes BalanceInquiry, Withdrawal and Deposit each need an operation to provide this service to the ATM. We place this operation (which we have named execute) in the third compartment of the three transaction classes

Class	Verbs and verb phrases
ATM	executes financial transactions
BalanceInquiry	[none in the requirements specification]
Withdrawal	[none in the requirements specification]
Deposit	[none in the requirements specification]
BankDatabase	authenticates a user, retrieves an account balance, credits a deposit amount to an account, debits a withdrawal amount from an account
Account	retrieves an account balance, credits a deposit amount to an account, debits a withdrawal amount from an account

Fig. 7.33 | Verbs and verb phrases for each class in the ATM system. (Part 1 of 2.)

Class	Verbs and verb phrases
Screen	displays a message to the user
Keypad	receives numeric input from the user
CashDispenser	dispenses cash, indicates whether it contains enough cash to satisfy a withdrawal request
DepositSlot	receives a deposit envelope

Fig. 7.33 | Verbs and verb phrases for each class in the ATM system. (Part 2 of 2.)

in the updated class diagram of Fig. 7.34. During an ATM session, the ATM object will invoke the execute operation of each transaction object to tell it to execute.

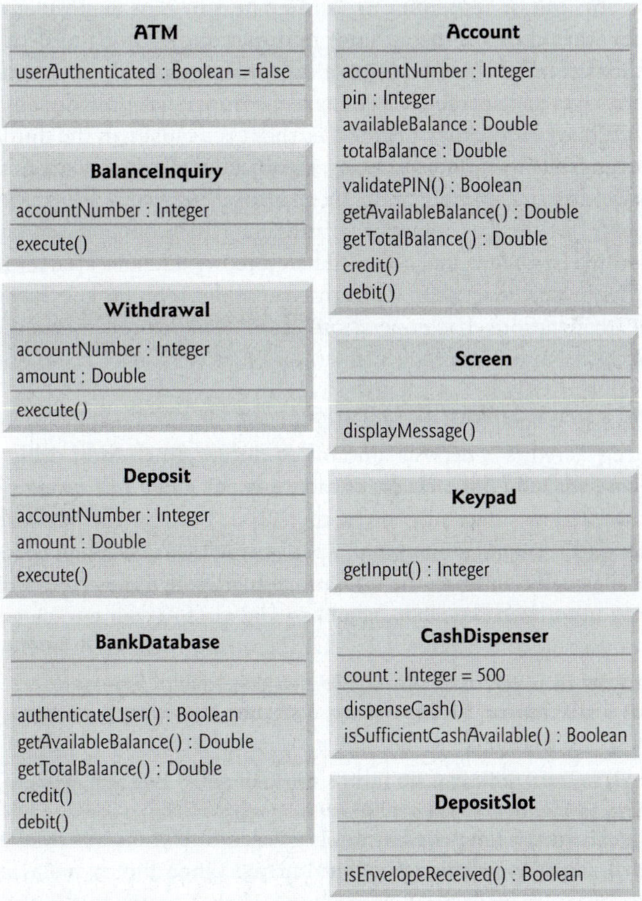

Fig. 7.34 | Classes in the ATM system with attributes and operations.

The UML represents operations (which are implemented as member functions in Visual C++) by listing the operation name, followed by a comma-separated list of parameters in parentheses, a colon and the return type:

operationName(*parameter1*, *parameter2*, ..., *parameterN*) : *return type*

Each parameter in the comma-separated parameter list consists of a parameter name, followed by a colon and the parameter type:

parameterName : *parameterType*

For the moment, we do not list the parameters of our operations—we'll identify and model some of them shortly. For some, we do not yet know the return types, so we also omit them from the diagram. These omissions are perfectly normal at this point. As our design and implementation proceed, we'll add the remaining return types.

Operations of Class BankDatabase *and Class* Account

Figure 7.33 lists the phrase "authenticates a user" next to class BankDatabase—the database is the object that contains the account information necessary to determine whether the account number and PIN entered by a user match those of an account held at the bank. Therefore, class BankDatabase needs an operation that provides an authentication service to the ATM. We place the operation authenticateUser in the third compartment of class BankDatabase (Fig. 7.34). However, an object of class Account, not class BankDatabase, stores the account number and PIN that must be accessed to authenticate a user, so class Account must provide a service to validate a PIN obtained through user input against a PIN stored in an Account object. Therefore, we add a validatePIN operation to class Account. Note that we specify a return type of Boolean for the authenticateUser and validatePIN operations. Each operation returns a value indicating either that the operation was successful in performing its task (i.e., a return value of true) or that it was not (i.e., a return value of false).

Figure 7.33 lists several additional verb phrases for class BankDatabase: "retrieves an account balance," "credits a deposit amount to an account" and "debits a withdrawal amount from an account." Like "authenticates a user," these remaining phrases refer to services that the database must provide to the ATM, because the database holds all the account data used to authenticate a user and perform ATM transactions. However, objects of class Account actually perform the operations to which these phrases refer. Thus, we assign an operation to both class BankDatabase and class Account to correspond to each of these phrases. Recall from Section 4.13 that, because a bank account contains sensitive information, we do not allow the ATM to access accounts directly. The database acts as an intermediary between the ATM and the account data, thus preventing unauthorized access. As we'll see in Section 8.15, class ATM invokes the operations of class BankDatabase, each of which in turn invokes the operation with the same name in class Account.

The phrase "retrieves an account balance" suggests that classes BankDatabase and Account each need a getBalance operation. However, recall that we created two attributes in class Account to represent a balance—availableBalance and totalBalance. A balance inquiry requires access to both balance attributes so that it can display them to the user, but a withdrawal needs to check only the value of availableBalance. To allow objects in the system to obtain each balance attribute individually, we add operations getAvailableBalance and getTotalBalance to the third compartment of classes Bank-Database and Account (Fig. 7.34). We specify a return type of Double for each of these operations, because the balance attributes which they retrieve are of type Double.

The phrases "credits a deposit amount to an account" and "debits a withdrawal amount from an account" indicate that classes BankDatabase and Account must perform operations to update an account during a deposit and withdrawal, respectively. We therefore assign credit and debit operations to classes BankDatabase and Account. You may recall that crediting an account (as in a deposit) adds an amount only to the totalBalance attribute. Debiting an account (as in a withdrawal), on the other hand, subtracts the amount from both balance attributes. We hide these implementation details inside class Account. This is a good example of encapsulation and information hiding.

If this were a real ATM system, classes BankDatabase and Account would also provide a set of operations to allow another banking system to update a user's account balance after either confirming or rejecting all or part of a deposit. Operation confirmDepositAmount, for example, would add an amount to the availableBalance attribute, thus making deposited funds available for withdrawal. Operation rejectDepositAmount would subtract an amount from the totalBalance attribute to indicate that a specified amount, which had recently been deposited through the ATM and added to the totalBalance, was not found in the deposit envelope. The bank would invoke this operation after determining either that the user failed to include the correct amount of cash or that any checks did not clear (i.e., they "bounced"). While adding these operations would make our system more complete, we do not include them in our class diagrams or our implementation because they are beyond the scope of the case study.

Operations of Class Screen

Class Screen "displays a message to the user" at various times in an ATM session. All visual output occurs through the screen of the ATM. The requirements specification describes many types of messages (e.g., a welcome message, an error message, a thank-you message) that the screen displays to the user. The requirements specification also indicates that the screen displays prompts and menus to the user. However, a prompt is really just a message describing what the user should input next, and a menu is essentially a type of prompt consisting of a series of messages (i.e., menu options) displayed consecutively. Therefore, rather than assign class Screen an individual operation to display each type of message, prompt and menu, we simply create one operation that can display any message specified by a parameter. We place this operation (displayMessage) in the third compartment of class Screen in our class diagram (Fig. 7.34). Note that we do not worry about the parameter of this operation at this time—we model the parameter later in this section.

Operations of Class Keypad

From the phrase "receives numeric input from the user" listed by class Keypad in Fig. 7.33, we conclude that class Keypad should perform a getInput operation. Because the ATM's keypad, unlike a computer keyboard, contains only the numbers 0–9, we specify that this operation returns an integer value. Recall from the requirements specification that in different situations the user may be required to enter a different type of number (e.g., an account number, a PIN, the number of a menu option, a deposit amount as a number of cents). Class Keypad simply obtains a numeric value for a client of the class—it does not determine whether the value meets any specific criteria. Any class that uses this operation must verify that the user enters appropriate numbers, and if not, display error messages via class Screen). [*Note:* When we implement the system, we simulate the ATM's keypad with a computer keyboard, and for simplicity we assume that the user does not enter nonnumeric input using keys on the computer keyboard that do not appear on the ATM's keypad. Later in the book, you'll learn how to examine inputs to determine if they are of particular types.]

Operations of Class CashDispenser and Class DepositSlot

Figure 7.33 lists "dispenses cash" for class CashDispenser. Therefore, we create operation dispenseCash and list it under class CashDispenser in Fig. 7.34. Class CashDispenser also "indicates whether it contains enough cash to satisfy a withdrawal request." Thus, we include isSufficientCashAvailable, an operation that returns a value of UML type Boolean, in class CashDispenser. Figure 7.33 also lists "receives a deposit envelope" for class DepositSlot. The deposit slot must indicate whether it received an envelope, so we place an operation isEnvelopeReceived, which returns a Boolean value, in the third compartment of class DepositSlot. [*Note:* A real hardware deposit slot would most likely send the ATM a signal to indicate that an envelope was received. We simulate this behavior, however, with an operation in class DepositSlot that class ATM can invoke to find out whether the deposit slot received an envelope.]

Operations of Class ATM

We do not list any operations for class ATM at this time. We are not yet aware of any services that class ATM provides to other classes in the system. When we implement the system with Visual C++ code, however, operations of this class, and additional operations of the other classes in the system, may emerge.

Identifying and Modeling Operation Parameters

So far, we have not been concerned with the parameters of our operations—we have attempted to gain only a basic understanding of the operations of each class. Let's now take a closer look at some operation parameters. We identify an operation's parameters by examining what data the operation requires to perform its assigned task.

Consider the authenticateUser operation of class BankDatabase. To authenticate a user, this operation must know the account number and PIN supplied by the user. Thus we specify that operation authenticateUser takes integer parameters userAccountNumber and userPIN, which the operation must compare to the account number and PIN of an Account object in the database. We prefix these parameter names with "user" to avoid confusion between the operation's parameter names and the attribute names that belong to class Account. We list these parameters in the class diagram in Fig. 7.35 that models only class BankDatabase. [*Note:* It is perfectly normal to model only one class in a class diagram. In this case, we are most concerned with examining the parameters of this one class in particular, so we omit the other classes. In class diagrams later in the case study, in which parameters are no longer the focus of our attention, we omit the parameters to save space. Remember, however, that the operations listed in these diagrams still have parameters.]

Recall that the UML models each parameter in an operation's comma-separated parameter list by listing the parameter name, followed by a colon and the parameter type (in UML notation). Figure 7.35 thus specifies that operation authenticateUser takes two

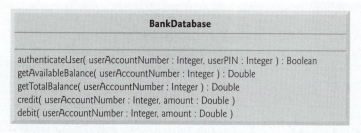

Fig. 7.35 | Class `BankDatabase` with operation parameters.

parameters—userAccountNumber and userPIN, both of type Integer. When we implement the system in Visual C++, we'll represent these parameters with int values.

Class BankDatabase operations getAvailableBalance, getTotalBalance, credit and debit also each require a userAccountNumber parameter to identify the account to which the database must apply the operations, so we include these parameters in the class diagram of Fig. 7.35. In addition, operations credit and debit each require a Double parameter amount to specify the amount of money to be credited or debited, respectively.

The class diagram in Fig. 7.36 models the parameters of class Account's operations. Operation validatePIN requires only a userPIN parameter, which contains the user-specified PIN to be compared with the PIN associated with the account. Like their counterparts in class BankDatabase, operations credit and debit in class Account each require a Double parameter amount that indicates the amount of money involved in the operation. Operations getAvailableBalance and getTotalBalance in class Account require no additional data to perform their tasks. Note that class Account's operations do not require an account-number parameter—each of these operations can be invoked only on a specific Account object, so including a parameter to specify an Account is unnecessary.

Figure 7.37 models class Screen with a parameter specified for operation display-Message. This operation requires only a String parameter message that indicates the text to be displayed. Recall that the parameter types listed in our class diagrams are in UML notation, so the String type listed in Fig. 7.37 refers to the UML type. When we implement the system in Visual C++, we'll in fact use a Visual C++ string object to represent this parameter.

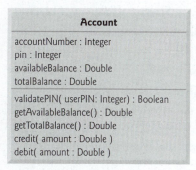

Fig. 7.36 | Class `Account` with operation parameters.

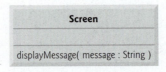

Screen
displayMessage(message : String)

Fig. 7.37 | Class Screen with operation parameters.

The class diagram in Fig. 7.38 specifies that operation dispenseCash of class CashDispenser takes a Double parameter amount to indicate the amount of cash (in dollars) to be dispensed. Operation isSufficientCashAvailable also takes a Double parameter amount to indicate the amount of cash in question.

Note that we do not discuss parameters for operation execute of classes BalanceInquiry, Withdrawal and Deposit, operation getInput of class Keypad and operation isEnvelopeReceived of class DepositSlot. At this point in our design process, we cannot determine whether these operations require additional data to perform their tasks, so we leave their parameter lists empty. As we progress through the case study, we may decide to add parameters to these operations.

In this section, we have determined many of the operations performed by the classes in the ATM system. We have identified the parameters and return types of some of the operations. As we continue our design process, the number of operations belonging to each class may vary—we might find that new operations are needed or that some current operations are unnecessary—and we might determine that some of our class operations need additional parameters and different return types.

CashDispenser
count : Integer = 500
dispenseCash(amount : Double) isSufficientCashAvailable(amount : Double) : Boolean

Fig. 7.38 | Class CashDispenser with operation parameters.

Software Engineering Case Study Self-Review Exercises

7.1 Which of the following is not a behavior?
a) reading data from a file
b) printing output
c) text output
d) obtaining input from the user

7.2 If you were to add to the ATM system an operation that returns the amount attribute of class Withdrawal, how and where would you specify this operation in the class diagram of Fig. 7.34?

7.3 Describe the meaning of the following operation listing that might appear in a class diagram for an object-oriented design of a calculator:

```
add( x : Integer, y : Integer ) : Integer
```

Answers to Software Engineering Case Study Self-Review Exercises

7.1   c.

7.2   To specify an operation that retrieves the amount attribute of class Withdrawal, the following operation would be placed in the operation (i.e., third) compartment of class Withdrawal:

```
getAmount( ) : Double
```

7.3   This is an operation named add that takes integers x and y as parameters and returns an integer value.

7.24 Wrap-Up

In this chapter, you learned more details of function declarations. Functions have different pieces, such as the function prototype, function signature, function header and function body. You learned about argument coercion, or the forcing of arguments to the appropriate types specified by a function's parameter declarations. We demonstrated how to use functions rand and srand to generate sets of random numbers that can be used for simulations. You also learned about the scope of variables, or the portion of a program where an identifier can be used. Two different ways to pass arguments to functions were covered—pass-by-value and pass-by-reference. For pass-by-reference, references are used as an alias to a variable. You learned that multiple functions in one class can be overloaded by providing functions with the same name and different signatures. Such functions can be used to perform the same or similar tasks, using different types or different numbers of parameters. We then demonstrated a simpler way of overloading functions using function templates, where a function is defined once but can be used for several different types. You were then introduced to the concept of recursion, where a function calls itself to solve a problem.

In Chapter 8, you'll learn how to maintain lists and tables of data in arrays. You'll see a more elegant array-based implementation of the dice-rolling application and two enhanced versions of our GradeBook case study that you studied in Chapters 4–6 that will use arrays to store the actual grades entered.

Summary

Section 7.1 Introduction
- Experience has shown that the best way to develop and maintain a large program is to construct it from small, simple pieces, or components. This technique is called divide and conquer.

Section 7.2 Program Components in Visual C++
- Visual C++ programs are typically written by combining new functions and classes you write with "prepackaged" functions and classes available in the C++ Standard Library and other libraries.
- Functions allow you to modularize a program by separating its tasks into self-contained units.
- The statements in the function bodies are written only once, are reused from perhaps several locations in a program and are hidden from other functions.

Section 7.3 Math Library Functions
- Sometimes functions are not members of a class. Such functions are called global functions.

- The function prototypes for global functions are placed in header files, so that the global functions can be reused in any program that includes the header file and that can link to the function's object code.

Section 7.4 Function Definitions with Multiple Parameters

- The compiler refers to the function prototype to check that calls to a method contain the correct number and types of arguments, that the types of the arguments are in the correct order and that the value returned by the function can be used correctly in the expression that called the function.

- There are three ways to return control to the point at which a function was invoked. If the function does not return a result, control returns when the program reaches the function-ending right brace, or by execution of the statement

    `return`;

    If the function does return a result, the statement

    `return` *expression*;

evaluates *expression* and returns the value of *expression* to the caller.

Section 7.5 Function Prototypes and Argument Coercion

- A function prototype tells the compiler the name of a function, the type of data returned by that function, the number of parameters the function expects to receive, the types of those parameters and the order in which the parameters of those types are expected.

- The portion of a function prototype that includes the name of the function and the types of its arguments is called the function signature or simply the signature.

- An important feature of function prototypes is argument coercion—i.e., forcing arguments to the appropriate types specified by the parameter declarations.

- Argument values that do not correspond precisely to the parameter types in the function prototype can be converted by the compiler to the proper type as specified by Visual C++'s promotion rules. The promotion rules indicate how to convert between types without losing data.

Section 7.6 C++ Standard Library Header Files

- The C++ Standard Library is divided into many portions, each with its own header file. The header files also contain definitions of various class types, functions and constants.

- A header file "instructs" the compiler on how to interface with library and user-written components.

Section 7.7 Case Study: Random Number Generation

- The element of chance can be introduced into computer applications by using the C++ Standard Library function `rand`.

- Function `rand` actually generates pseudorandom numbers. Calling `rand` repeatedly produces a sequence of numbers that appears to be random. However, the sequence repeats itself each time the program executes.

- Once a program has been thoroughly debugged, it can be conditioned to produce a different sequence of random numbers for each execution. This is called randomizing and is accomplished with the C++ Standard Library function `srand`.

- Function `srand` takes an `unsigned` integer argument and seeds the `rand` function to produce a different sequence of random numbers for each execution of the program.

- Random numbers in a range can be generated with

  number = *shiftingValue* + rand() % *scalingFactor*;

  where *shiftingValue* is equal to the first number in the desired range of consecutive integers and *scalingFactor* is equal to the width of the desired range of consecutive integers.

Section 7.8 Case Study: Game of Chance; Introducing enum
- An enumeration, introduced by the keyword enum and followed by a type name, is a set of integer constants represented by identifiers. The values of these enumeration constants start at 0, unless specified otherwise, and increment by 1.

Section 7.9 Storage Classes
- An identifier's storage class determines the period during which that identifier exists in memory.
- An identifier's scope is where the identifier can be referenced in a program.
- An identifier's linkage determines whether an identifier is known only in the source file where it is declared or across multiple files that are compiled, then linked together.
- Keywords auto and register are used to declare variables of the automatic storage class. Such variables are created when program execution enters the block in which they are defined, they exist while the block is active and they are destroyed when the program exits the block.
- Only local variables of a function can be of automatic storage class.
- The storage-class specifier auto explicitly declares variables of automatic storage class. Local variables are of automatic storage class by default, so keyword auto is rarely used.
- Keyword static declares identifiers for variables of the static storage class and for functions. Static-storage-class variables exist from the point at which the program begins execution and last for the duration of the program.
- A static-storage-class variable's storage is allocated when the program begins execution. Such a variable is initialized once when its declaration is encountered. For functions, the name of the function exists when the program begins execution, just as for all other functions.
- There are two types of identifiers with static storage class—external identifiers (such as global variables and global function names) and local variables declared with the storage-class specifier static.
- Global variables are created by placing variable declarations outside any class or function definition. Global variables retain their values throughout the execution of the program. Global variables and global functions can be referenced by any function that follows their declarations or definitions in the source file.

Section 7.10 Scope Rules
- Local variables declared with the keyword static are still known only in the function in which they are declared, but, unlike automatic variables, static local variables retain their values when the function returns to its caller. The next time the function is called, the static local variables contain the values they had when the function last completed execution.
- An identifier declared outside any function or class has file scope.
- Labels are the only identifiers with function scope. Labels can be used anywhere in the function in which they appear, but cannot be referenced outside the function body.
- Identifiers declared inside a block have block scope. Block scope begins at the identifier's declaration and ends at the terminating right brace (}) of the block in which the identifier is declared.

- The only identifiers with function-prototype scope are those used in the parameter list of a function prototype.

Section 7.11 Function-Call Stack and Activation Records
- Stacks are known as last-in, first-out (LIFO) data structures—the last item pushed (inserted) on the stack is the first item popped (removed) from the stack.
- One of the most important mechanisms for computer science students to understand is the function-call stack (sometimes referred to as the program execution stack). This data structure supports the function-call/return mechanism.
- The function-call stack also supports the creation, maintenance and destruction of each called function's automatic variables.
- Each time a function calls another function, an entry is pushed onto the stack. This entry, called a stack frame or an activation record, contains the return address that the called function needs to return to the calling function, and the function call's automatic variables and parameters.
- The stack frame exists as long as the called function is active. When the called function returns—and no longer needs its local automatic variables—its stack frame is popped from the stack, and those local automatic variables are no longer known to the program.

Section 7.12 Functions with Empty Parameter Lists
- An empty parameter list is specified by writing either void or nothing in parentheses.

Section 7.13 Inline Functions
- Visual C++ provides inline functions to help reduce function-call overhead—especially for small functions. Placing the qualifier inline before a function's return type in the function definition "advises" the compiler to generate a copy of the function's code in place to avoid a function call.

Section 7.14 References and Reference Parameters
- Two ways to pass arguments to functions in many programming languages are pass-by-value and pass-by-reference.
- When an argument is passed by value, a *copy* of the argument's value is made and passed (on the function-call stack) to the called function. Changes to the copy do not affect the original variable's value in the caller.
- With pass-by-reference, the caller gives the called function the ability to access the caller's data directly and to modify it if the called function chooses to do so.
- A reference parameter is an alias for its corresponding argument in a function call.
- To indicate that a function parameter is passed by reference, simply follow the parameter's type in the function prototype by an ampersand (&); use the same convention when listing the parameter's type in the function header.
- Once a reference is declared as an alias for another variable, all operations supposedly performed on the alias (i.e., the reference) are actually performed on the original variable. The alias is simply another name for the original variable.

Section 7.15 Default Arguments
- It is not uncommon for a program to invoke a function repeatedly with the same argument value for a particular parameter. In such cases, you can specify that such a parameter has a default argument, i.e., a default value to be passed to that parameter.
- When a program omits an argument for a parameter with a default argument, the compiler rewrites the function call and inserts the default value of that argument to be passed to the function call.

- Default arguments must be the rightmost (trailing) arguments in a function's parameter list.
- Default arguments should be specified with the first occurrence of the function name—typically, in the function prototype.

Section 7.16 Unary Scope Resolution Operator
- Visual C++ provides the unary scope resolution operator (::) to access a global variable when a local variable of the same name is in scope.

Section 7.17 Function Overloading
- Visual C++ enables several functions of the same name to be defined, as long as these functions have different sets of parameters. This capability is called function overloading.
- When an overloaded function is called, the Visual C++ compiler selects the proper function by examining the number, types and order of the arguments in the call.
- Overloaded functions are distinguished by their signatures.
- The compiler encodes each function identifier with the number and types of its parameters to enable type-safe linkage. Type-safe linkage ensures that the proper overloaded function is called and that the types of the arguments conform to the types of the parameters.

Section 7.18 Function Templates
- Overloaded functions are normally used to perform similar operations that involve different program logic on different data types. If the program logic and operations are identical for each data type, overloading may be performed more compactly and conveniently using function templates.
- You write a single function-template definition. Given the argument types provided in calls to this function, Visual C++ automatically generates separate function-template specializations to handle each type of call appropriately. Thus, defining a single function template essentially defines a family of overloaded functions.
- All function-template definitions begin with the `template` keyword followed by a template parameter list to the function template enclosed in angle brackets (< and >).
- The formal type parameters are placeholders for fundamental types or user-defined types. These placeholders are used to specify the types of the function's parameters, to specify the function's return type and to declare variables within the body of the function definition.

Section 7.19 Recursion
- A recursive function is a function that calls itself, either directly or indirectly.
- A recursive function knows how to solve only the simplest case(s), or so-called base case(s). If the function is called with a base case, the function simply returns a result.
- If the function is called with a more complex problem, the function typically divides the problem into two conceptual pieces—a piece that the function knows how to do and a piece that it does not know how to do. To make recursion feasible, the latter piece must resemble the original problem, but be a slightly simpler or slightly smaller version of it.
- In order for the recursion to eventually terminate, each time the function calls itself with a slightly simpler version of the original problem, this sequence of smaller and smaller problems must eventually converge on the base case.

Section 7.20 Example Using Recursion: Fibonacci Series
- Visual C++ does not specify the order in which the operands of most operators (including +) are to be evaluated. Therefore, you must make no assumption about the order in which these calls

execute. In some programs the evaluation of an operand can have side effects (changes to data values) that could affect the final result of the expression.

Section 7.21 Recursion vs. Iteration

- Iteration and recursion have many similarities: both are based on a control statement, involve repetition, involve a termination test, gradually approach termination and can occur infinitely.

- Recursion has many negatives. It repeatedly invokes the mechanism, and consequently the overhead, of function calls. This can be expensive in both processor time and memory space. Each recursive call causes another copy of the function (actually only the function's variables) to be created; this can consume considerable memory.

Section 7.22 Enumerations in C++/CLI

- Introduce a managed enumeration in C++/CLI with `enum class` followed by the type name.

- When using a value of a managed enumeration make, sure to have the enum name and scope resolution operator preceding the `enum` value.

- C++/CLI enumerations are their own type that cannot be compared to other types without an appropriate cast.

Terminology

& to declare reference
activation record
alias
argument coercion
`auto` storage-class specifier
automatic local variable
automatic storage class
base case(s)
block scope
class scope
`class enum` keyword
converge on a base case
dangling reference
default argument
divide-and-conquer approach
`enum` keyword
enumeration
enumeration constant
exponential complexity
`extern` storage-class specifier
factorial
Fibonacci series
file scope
formal parameter
formal type parameter
function-call overhead
function-call stack
function declaration
function definition
function name

function overloading
function prototype
function-prototype scope
function scope
function signature
function template
function-template specialization
global function
global variable
golden mean
golden ratio
"highest" type
infinite loop
infinite recursion
initializing a reference
inline function
`inline` keyword
inner block
integral size limits
invoke a method
iteration
iterative solution
label
LIFO (last-in, first-out)
linkage
"lowest type"
mandatory function prototypes
mangled function name
mixed-type expression
modularizing a program with functions

`mutable` storage-class specifier	rightmost (trailing) arguments
name decoration	scaling
name mangling	scaling factor
name of a variable	scope of an identifier
namespace scope	seed
nested blocks	sequence of random numbers
numerical data type limits	shift a range of numbers
optimizing compiler	shifted, scaled integers
out of scope	shifting value
outer block	side effect of an expression
overloading	signature
parameter	software reuse
pass-by-reference	`srand` function
pass-by-value	stack
pop off a stack	stack frame
"prepackaged" functions	stack overflow
principle of least privilege	`static` keyword
procedure	`static` local variable
program execution stack	static storage class
programmer-defined function	`static` storage-class specifier
promotion rules	storage class
pseudorandom numbers	storage-class specifiers
push onto a stack	template definition
rand function	template function
`RAND_MAX` symbolic constant	`template` keyword
random number	template parameter list
randomizing	terminating condition
recursion	terminating right brace (}) of a block
recursion overhead	termination test
recursion step	truncate fractional part of a `double`
recursive call	type name (enumerations)
recursive evaluation	type of a variable
recursive function	type parameter
recursive solution	type-safe linkage
reference parameter	unary scope resolution operator (::)
reference to a constant	user-defined function
reference to an automatic variable	user-defined type
`register` storage-class specifier	validate a function call
repeatability of function `rand`	`void` return type
returning a reference from a function	width of random number range

Self-Review Exercises

7.1   Answer each of the following:

     a)   Program components in Visual C++ are called _____ and_____.

     b)   A function is invoked with a(n) _____.

     c)   A variable that is known only within the function in which it is defined is called a(n) _____.

     d)   The _____ statement in a called function passes the value of an expression back to the calling function.

e) The keyword _____ is used in a function header to indicate that a function does not return a value or to indicate that a function contains no parameters.

f) The _____ of an identifier is the portion of the program in which the identifier can be used.

g) The three ways to return control from a called function to a caller are _____, _____ and _____.

h) A(n) _____ allows the compiler to check the number, types and order of the arguments passed to a function.

i) Function _____ is used to produce random numbers.

j) Function _____ is used to set the random number seed to randomize a program.

k) The storage-class specifiers are `mutable`, `extern`, _____, _____ and _____.

l) Variables declared in a block or in the parameter list of a function are assumed to be of storage class _____ unless specified otherwise.

m) Storage-class specifier _____ is a recommendation to the compiler to store a variable in one of the computer's registers.

n) A variable declared outside any block or function is a(n) _____ variable.

o) For a local variable in a function to retain its value between calls to the function, it must be declared with the _____ storage-class specifier.

p) The six possible scopes of an identifier are _____, _____, _____, _____, _____ and _____.

q) A function that calls itself either directly or indirectly is a(n) _____ function.

r) A recursive function typically has two components—one that provides a means for the recursion to terminate by testing for a(n) _____ case and one that expresses the problem as a recursive call for a slightly simpler problem than the original call.

s) It is possible to have various functions with the same name that operate on different types or numbers of arguments. This is called function _____.

t) The _____ enables access to a global variable with the same name as a variable in the current scope.

u) The _____ qualifier is used to declare read-only variables.

v) A function _____ enables a single function to be defined to perform a task on many different data types.

7.2 For the program in Fig. 7.39, state the scope (either function scope, file scope, block scope or function-prototype scope) of each of the following elements:

a) The variable x in `main`.

b) The variable y in `cube`.

c) The function `cube`.

d) The function `main`.

e) The function prototype for `cube`.

f) The identifier y in the function prototype for `cube`.

7.3 Write a program that tests whether the examples of the math library function calls shown in Fig. 7.2 actually produce the indicated results.

7.4 Give the function header for each of the following functions:

a) Function `hypotenuse` that takes two double-precision, floating-point arguments, `side1` and `side2`, and returns a double-precision, floating-point result.

b) Function `smallest` that takes three integers, x, y and z, and returns an integer.

c) Function `instructions` that does not receive any arguments and does not return a value. [*Note:* Such functions are commonly used to display instructions to a user.]

d) Function `intToDouble` that takes an integer argument, `number`, and returns a double-precision, floating-point result.

```
 1    // Exercise 7.2: Ex07_02.cpp
 2    #include <iostream>
 3    using std::cout;
 4    using std::endl;
 5
 6    int cube( int y ); // function prototype
 7
 8    int main()
 9    {
10       int x;
11
12       for ( x = 1; x <= 10; x++ ) // loop 10 times
13          cout << cube( x ) << endl; // calculate cube of x and output results
14
15       return 0; // indicates successful termination
16    } // end main
17
18    // definition of function cube
19    int cube( int y )
20    {
21       return y * y * y;
22    } // end function cube
```

Fig. 7.39 | Program for Exercise 7.2.

7.5   Give the function prototype (without parameter names) for each of the following:
a) The function described in Exercise 7.4(a).
b) The function described in Exercise 7.4(b).
c) The function described in Exercise 7.4(c).
d) The function described in Exercise 7.4(d).

7.6   Write a declaration for each of the following:
a) Integer count that should be maintained in a register. Initialize count to 0.
b) Double-precision, floating-point variable lastVal that is to retain its value between calls to the function in which it is defined.

7.7   Find the error(s) in each of the following program segments, and explain how the error(s) can be corrected (see also Exercise 7.53):
a)
```
int g()
{
   cout << "Inside function g" << endl;
   int h()
   {
      cout << "Inside function h" << endl;
   }
}
```
b)
```
int sum( int x, int y )
{
   int result;
   result = x + y;
}
```
c)
```
int sum( int n )
{
   if ( n == 0 )
      return 0;
```

```
            else
                n + sum( n - 1 );
        }
    d)  void f( double a );
        {
            float a;
            cout << a << endl;
        }
    e)  void product()
        {
            int a;
            int b;
            int c;
            int result;
            cout << "Enter three integers: ";
            cin >> a >> b >> c;
            result = a * b * c;
            cout << "Result is " << result;
            return result;
        }
```

7.8 Why would a function prototype contain a parameter type declaration such as `double &`?

7.9 (True/False) All arguments to function calls in Visual C++ are passed by value.

7.10 Write a complete program that prompts the user for the radius of a sphere, and calculates and prints the volume of that sphere. Use an `inline` function `sphereVolume` that returns the result of the following expression: `( 4.0 / 3.0 ) * 3.14159 * pow( radius, 3 )`.

Answers to Self-Review Exercises

7.1 a) functions, classes. b) function call. c) local variable. d) return. e) void. f) scope. g) return;, return *expression*; or encounter the closing right brace of a function. h) function prototype. i) rand. j) srand. k) auto, register, static. l) auto. m) register. n) global. o) static. p) function scope, file scope, block scope, function-prototype scope, class scope, namespace scope. q) recursive. r) base. s) overloading. t) unary scope resolution operator (::). u) const. v) template.

7.2 a) block scope. b) block scope. c) file scope. d) file scope. e) file scope. f) function-prototype scope.

7.3 See the following program:

```
1   // Exercise 7.3: Ex07_03.cpp
2   // Testing the math library functions.
3   #include <iostream>
4   using std::cout;
5   using std::endl;
6   using std::fixed;
7
8   #include <iomanip>
9   using std::setprecision;
10
11  #include <cmath>
12  using namespace std;
13
```

```
14  int main()
15  {
16     cout << fixed << setprecision( 1 );
17
18     cout << "sqrt(" << 900.0 << ") = " << sqrt( 900.0 )
19        << "\nsqrt(" << 9.0 << ") = " << sqrt( 9.0 );
20     cout << "\nexp(" << 1.0 << ") = " << setprecision( 6 )
21        << exp( 1.0 ) << "\nexp(" << setprecision( 1 ) << 2.0
22        << ") = " << setprecision( 6 ) << exp( 2.0 );
23     cout << "\nlog(" << 2.718282 << ") = " << setprecision( 1 )
24        << log( 2.718282 )
25        << "\nlog(" << setprecision( 6 ) << 7.389056 << ") = "
26        << setprecision( 1 ) << log( 7.389056 );
27     cout << "\nlog10(" << 1.0 << ") = " << log10( 1.0 )
28        << "\nlog10(" << 10.0 << ") = " << log10( 10.0 )
29        << "\nlog10(" << 100.0 << ") = " << log10( 100.0 ) ;
30     cout << "\nfabs(" << 13.5 << ") = " << fabs( 13.5 )
31        << "\nfabs(" << 0.0 << ") = " << fabs( 0.0 )
32        << "\nfabs(" << -13.5 << ") = " << fabs( -13.5 );
33     cout << "\nceil(" << 9.2 << ") = " << ceil( 9.2 )
34        << "\nceil(" << -9.8 << ") = " << ceil( -9.8 );
35     cout << "\nfloor(" << 9.2 << ") = " << floor( 9.2 )
36        << "\nfloor(" << -9.8 << ") = " << floor( -9.8 );
37     cout << "\npow(" << 2.0 << ", " << 7.0 << ") = "
38        << pow( 2.0, 7.0 ) << "\npow(" << 9.0 << ", "
39        << 0.5 << ") = " << pow( 9.0, 0.5 );
40     cout << setprecision(1) << "\nfmod("
41        << 2.6 << ", " << 1.2 << ") = "
42        << fmod( 2.6, 1.2 )
43     cout << "\nsin(" << 0.0 << ") = " << sin( 0.0 );
44     cout << "\ncos(" << 0.0 << ") = " << cos( 0.0 );
45     cout << "\ntan(" << 0.0 << ") = " << tan( 0.0 ) << endl;
46     return 0; // indicates successful termination
47  } // end main
```

```
sqrt(900.0) = 30.0
sqrt(9.0) = 3.0
exp(1.0) = 2.718282
exp(2.0) = 7.389056
log(2.718282) = 1.0
log(7.389056) = 2.0
log10(1.0) = 0.0
log10(10.0) = 1.0
log10(100.0) = 2.0
fabs(13.5) = 13.5
fabs(0.0) = 0.0
fabs(-13.5) = 13.5
ceil(9.2) = 10.0
ceil(-9.8) = -9.0
floor(9.2) = 9.0
floor(-9.8) = -10.0
pow(2.0, 7.0) = 128.0
pow(9.0, 0.5) = 3.0
fmod(13.675, 2.333) = 2.010
sin(0.0) = 0.0
cos(0.0) = 1.0
tan(0.0) = 0.0
```

7.4 a) *double* hypotenuse(*double* side1, *double* side2)
  b) *int* smallest(*int* x, *int* y, *int* z)
  c) *void* instructions()
  d) *double* intToDouble(*int* number)

7.5 a) *double* hypotenuse(*double*, *double*);
 b) *int* smallest(*int*, *int*, *int*);
 c) *void* instructions();
 d) *double* intToDouble(*int*);

7.6 a) *register int* count = 0;
 b) *static double* lastVal;

7.7 a) Error: Function h is defined in function g.
 Correction: Move the definition of h out of the definition of g.
 b) Error: The function is supposed to return an integer, but does not.
 Correction: Delete variable result and place the following statement in the function:

  return x + y;

 c) Error: The result of n + sum(n - 1) is not returned; sum returns an improper result.
 Correction: Rewrite the statement in the else clause as

  return n + sum(n - 1);

 d) Errors: Semicolon after the right parenthesis that encloses the parameter list, and re-defining the parameter a in the function definition.
 Corrections: Delete the semicolon after the right parenthesis of the parameter list, and delete the declaration float a;.
 e) Error: The function returns a value when it is not supposed to.
 Correction: Eliminate the return statement.

7.8 This creates a reference parameter of type "reference to double" that enables the function to modify the original variable in the calling function.

7.9 False. Visual C++ enables pass-by-reference using reference parameters (and pointers, as we discuss in Chapter 9).

7.10 See the following program:

```cpp
// Exercise 7.10 Solution: Ex07_10.cpp
// Inline function that calculates the volume of a sphere.
#include <iostream>
using std::cin;
using std::cout;
using std::endl;

#include <cmath>
using std::pow;

const double PI = 3.14159; // define global constant PI

// calculates volume of a sphere
inline double sphereVolume( const double radius )
{
   return 4.0 / 3.0 * PI * pow( radius, 3 );
} // end inline function sphereVolume

int main()
{
   double radiusValue;
```

```
23        // prompt user for radius
24        cout << "Enter the length of the radius of your sphere: ";
25        cin >> radiusValue; // input radius
26
27        // use radiusValue to calculate volume of sphere and display result
28        cout << "Volume of sphere with radius " << radiusValue
29           << " is " << sphereVolume( radiusValue ) << endl;
30        return 0; // indicates successful termination
31    } // end main
```

Exercises

7.11 Show the value of x after each of the following statements is performed:

a) x = fabs(7.5)
b) x = floor(7.5)
c) x = fabs(0.0)
d) x = ceil(0.0)
e) x = fabs(-6.4)
f) x = ceil(-6.4)
g) x = ceil(-fabs(-8 + floor(-5.5)))

7.12 A parking garage charges a $2.00 minimum fee to park for up to three hours. The garage charges an additional $0.50 per hour for each hour *or part thereof* in excess of three hours. The maximum charge for any given 24-hour period is $10.00. Assume that no car parks for longer than 24 hours at a time. Write a program that calculates and prints the parking charges for each of three customers who parked their cars in this garage yesterday. You should enter the hours parked for each customer. Your program should print the results in a neat tabular format and should calculate and print the total of yesterday's receipts. The program should use the function calculateCharges to determine the charge for each customer. Your outputs should appear in the following format:

```
Car       Hours       Charge
1          1.5         2.00
2          4.0         2.50
3         24.0        10.00
TOTAL     29.5        14.50
```

7.13 An application of function floor is rounding a value to the nearest integer. The statement

```
y = floor( x + .5 );
```

rounds the number x to the nearest integer and assigns the result to y. Write a program that reads several numbers and uses the preceding statement to round each of these numbers to the nearest integer. For each number processed, print both the original number and the rounded number.

7.14 Function floor can be used to round a number to a specific decimal place. The statement

```
y = floor( x * 10 + .5 ) / 10;
```

rounds x to the tenths position (the first position to the right of the decimal point). The statement

```
y = floor( x * 100 + .5 ) / 100;
```

rounds x to the hundredths position (the second position to the right of the decimal point). Write a program that defines four functions to round a number x in various ways:

    a) `roundToInteger( number )`
    b) `roundToTenths( number )`
    c) `roundToHundredths( number )`
    d) `roundToThousandths( number )`

For each value read, your program should print the original value, the number rounded to the nearest integer, the number rounded to the nearest tenth, the number rounded to the nearest hundredth and the number rounded to the nearest thousandth.

7.15 Answer each of the following questions:
    a) What does it mean to choose numbers "at random?"
    b) Why is the `rand` function useful for simulating games of chance?
    c) Why would you randomize a program by using `srand`? Under what circumstances is it desirable not to randomize?
    d) Why is it often necessary to scale or shift the values produced by `rand`?
    e) Why is computerized simulation of real-world situations a useful technique?

7.16 Write statements that assign random integers to the variable n in the following ranges:
    a) $1 \le n \le 2$
    b) $1 \le n \le 100$
    c) $0 \le n \le 9$
    d) $1000 \le n \le 1112$
    e) $-1 \le n \le 1$
    f) $-3 \le n \le 11$

7.17 For each of the following sets of integers, write a single statement that prints a number at random from the set:
    a) 2, 4, 6, 8, 10.
    b) 3, 5, 7, 9, 11.
    c) 6, 10, 14, 18, 22.

7.18 Write a function `integerPower( base, exponent )` that returns the value of

$$base^{\,exponent}$$

For example, `integerPower( 3, 4 )` = 3 * 3 * 3 * 3. Assume that *exponent* is a positive, non-zero integer and that *base* is an integer. The function `integerPower` should use `for` or `while` to control the calculation. Do not use any math library functions.

7.19 *(Hypotenuse)* Define a function `hypotenuse` that calculates the length of the hypotenuse of a right triangle when the other two sides are given. Use this function in a program to determine the length of the hypotenuse for each of the triangles shown below. The function should take two `double` arguments and return the hypotenuse as a `double`.

Triangle	Side 1	Side 2
1	3.0	4.0
2	5.0	12.0
3	8.0	15.0

7.20 Write a function `multiple` that determines for a pair of integers whether the second is a multiple of the first. The function should take two integer arguments and return `true` if the second is a multiple of the first, `false` otherwise. Use this function in a program that inputs a series of pairs of integers.

7.21 Write a program that inputs a series of integers and passes them one at a time to function even, which uses the modulus operator to determine whether an integer is even. The function should take an integer argument and return `true` if the integer is even and `false` otherwise.

7.22 Write a function that displays at the left margin of the screen a solid square of asterisks whose side is specified in integer parameter `side`. For example, if `side` is 4, the function displays the following:

```
****
****
****
****
```

7.23 Modify the function created in Exercise 7.22 to form the square using whatever character is contained in character parameter `fillCharacter`. Thus, if `side` is 5 and `fillCharacter` is #, then this function should print the following:

```
#####
#####
#####
#####
#####
```

7.24 Use techniques similar to those developed in Exercise 7.22 and Exercise 7.23 to produce a program that graphs a wide range of shapes.

7.25 Write program segments that accomplish each of the following:
   a) Calculate the integer part of the quotient when integer a is divided by integer b.
   b) Calculate the integer remainder when integer a is divided by integer b.
   c) Use the program pieces developed in (a) and (b) to write a function that inputs an integer between 1 and 32767 and prints it as a series of digits, each pair of which is separated by two spaces. For example, the integer 4562 should print as follows:

```
4   5   6   2
```

7.26 Write a function that takes the time as three integer arguments (hours, minutes and seconds) and returns the number of seconds since the last time the clock "struck 12." Use this function to calculate the amount of time in seconds between two times, both of which are within one 12-hour cycle of the clock.

7.27 *(Celsius and Fahrenheit Temperatures)* Implement the following integer functions:
   a) Function `celsius` returns the Celsius equivalent of a Fahrenheit temperature.
   b) Function `fahrenheit` returns the Fahrenheit equivalent of a Celsius temperature.
   c) Use these functions to write a program that prints charts showing the Fahrenheit equivalents of all Celsius temperatures from 0 to 100 degrees, and the Celsius equivalents of all Fahrenheit temperatures from 32 to 212 degrees. Print the outputs in a neat tabular format that minimizes the number of lines of output while remaining readable.

7.28 Write a program that inputs three double-precision, floating-point numbers and passes them to a function that returns the smallest number.

7.29 *(Perfect Numbers)* An integer is said to be a *perfect number* if the sum of its divisors, including 1 (but not the number itself), is equal to the number. For example, 6 is a perfect number, because

6 = 1 + 2 + 3. Write a function perfect that determines whether parameter number is a perfect number. Use this function in a program that determines and prints all the perfect numbers between 1 and 1000. Print the divisors of each perfect number to confirm that the number is indeed perfect. Challenge the power of your computer by testing numbers much larger than 1000.

7.30   (*Prime Numbers*) An integer is said to be *prime* if it is divisible by only 1 and itself. For example, 2, 3, 5 and 7 are prime, but 4, 6, 8 and 9 are not.

    a) Write a function that determines whether a number is prime.

    b) Use this function in a program that determines and prints all the prime numbers between 2 and 10,000. How many of these numbers do you really have to test before being sure that you have found all the primes?

    c) Initially, you might think that $n/2$ is the upper limit for which you must test to see whether a number is prime, but you need only go as high as the square root of n. Why? Rewrite the program, and run it both ways. Estimate the performance improvement.

7.31   (*Reverse Digits*) Write a function that takes an integer value and returns the number with its digits reversed. For example, given the number 7631, the function should return 1367.

7.32   The *greatest common divisor (GCD)* of two integers is the largest integer that evenly divides each of the numbers. Write a function gcd that returns the greatest common divisor of two integers.

7.33   Write a function qualityPoints that inputs a student's average and returns 4 if a student's average is 90–100, 3 if the average is 80–89, 2 if the average is 70–79, 1 if the average is 60–69 and 0 if the average is lower than 60.

7.34   Write a program that simulates coin tossing. For each toss of the coin, the program should print Heads or Tails. Let the program toss the coin 100 times and count the number of times each side of the coin appears. Print the results. The program should call a separate function flip that takes no arguments and returns 0 for tails and 1 for heads. [*Note:* If the program realistically simulates the coin tossing, then each side of the coin should appear approximately half the time.]

7.35   (*Computers in Education*) Computers are playing an increasing role in education. Write a program that helps an elementary-school student learn multiplication. Use rand to produce two positive one-digit integers. It should then type a question such as

```
How much is 6 times 7?
```

The student then types the answer. Your program checks the student's answer. If it is correct, print "Very good!", then ask another multiplication question. If the answer is wrong, print "No. Please try again.", then let the student try the same question repeatedly until the student finally gets it right.

7.36   (*Computer-Assisted Instruction*) The use of computers in education is referred to as *computer-assisted instruction* (CAI). One problem that develops in CAI environments is student fatigue. This can be eliminated by varying the computer's dialogue to hold the student's attention. Modify the program of Exercise 7.35 so the various comments are printed for each correct answer and each incorrect answer as follows:

Responses to a correct answer

```
Very good!
Excellent!
Nice work!
Keep up the good work!
```

Responses to an incorrect answer

```
No. Please try again.
Wrong. Try once more.
Don't give up!
No. Keep trying.
```

Use the random number generator to choose a number from 1 to 4 to select an appropriate response to each answer. Use a `switch` statement to issue the responses.

7.37   More sophisticated computer-aided instruction systems monitor the student's performance over a period of time. The decision to begin a new topic often is based on the student's success with previous topics. Modify the program of Exercise 7.36 to count the number of correct and incorrect responses typed by the student. After the student types 10 answers, your program should calculate the percentage of correct responses. If the percentage is lower than 75 percent, your program should print "Please ask your instructor for extra help" and terminate.

7.38   *(Guess-the-Number Game)* Write a program that plays the game of "guess the number" as follows: Your program chooses the number to be guessed by selecting an integer at random in the range 1 to 1000. The program then displays the following:

```
I have a number between 1 and 1000.
Can you guess my number?
Please type your first guess.
```

The player then types a first guess. The program responds with one of the following:

```
1. Excellent! You guessed the number!
   Would you like to play again (y or n)?
2. Too low. Try again.
3. Too high. Try again.
```

If the player's guess is incorrect, your program should loop until the player finally gets the number right. Your program should keep telling the player Too high or Too low to help the player "zero in" on the correct answer.

7.39   Modify the program of Exercise 7.38 to count the number of guesses the player makes. If the number is 10 or fewer, print "Either you know the secret or you got lucky!" If the player guesses the number in 10 tries, then print "Ahah! You know the secret!" If the player makes more than 10 guesses, then print "You should be able to do better!" Why should it take no more than 10 guesses? Well, with each "good guess" the player should be able to eliminate half of the numbers. Now show why any number from 1 to 1000 can be guessed in 10 or fewer tries.

7.40   Write a recursive function power(base, exponent) that, when invoked, returns

$$base^{\,exponent}$$

For example, power(3, 4) = 3 * 3 * 3 * 3. Assume that exponent is an integer greater than or equal to 1. *Hint:* The recursion step would use the relationship

$$base^{\,exponent} = base \cdot base^{\,exponent - 1}$$

and the terminating condition occurs when exponent is equal to 1, because

$$base^1 = base$$

7.41   *(Fibonacci Series)* The Fibonacci series

$$0, 1, 1, 2, 3, 5, 8, 13, 21, \ldots$$

begins with the terms 0 and 1 and has the property that each succeeding term is the sum of the two preceding terms. (a) Write a *nonrecursive* function fibonacci(n) that calculates the *n*th Fibonacci number. (b) Determine the largest int Fibonacci number that can be printed on your system. Modify the program of part (a) to use double instead of int to calculate and return Fibonacci numbers, and use this modified program to repeat part (b).

7.42 *(Towers of Hanoi)* In this chapter, you studied functions that can be easily implemented both recursively and iteratively. In this exercise, we present a problem whose recursive solution demonstrates the elegance of recursion, and whose iterative solution may not be as apparent.

The **Towers of Hanoi** is one of the most famous classic problems every budding computer scientist must grapple with. Legend has it that in a temple in the Far East, priests are attempting to move a stack of golden disks from one diamond peg to another (Fig. 7.40). The initial stack has 64 disks threaded onto one peg and arranged from bottom to top by decreasing size. The priests are attempting to move the stack from one peg to another under the constraints that exactly one disk is moved at a time and at no time may a larger disk be placed above a smaller disk. Three pegs are provided, one being used for temporarily holding disks. Supposedly, the world will end when the priests complete their task, so there is little incentive for us to facilitate their efforts.

Let us assume that the priests are attempting to move the disks from peg 1 to peg 3. We wish to develop an algorithm that prints the precise sequence of peg-to-peg disk transfers.

If we were to approach this problem with conventional methods, we would rapidly find ourselves hopelessly knotted up in managing the disks. Instead, attacking this problem with recursion in mind allows the steps to be simple. Moving n disks can be viewed in terms of moving only $n - 1$ disks (hence, the recursion), as follows:

a) Move $n - 1$ disks from peg 1 to peg 2, using peg 3 as a temporary holding area.
b) Move the last disk (the largest) from peg 1 to peg 3.
c) Move the $n - 1$ disks from peg 2 to peg 3, using peg 1 as a temporary holding area.

The process ends when the last task involves moving $n = 1$ disk (i.e., the base case). This task is accomplished by simply moving the disk, without the need for a temporary holding area.

Write a program to solve the Towers of Hanoi problem. Use a recursive function with four parameters:

a) The number of disks to be moved
b) The peg on which these disks are initially threaded
c) The peg to which this stack of disks is to be moved
d) The peg to be used as a temporary holding area

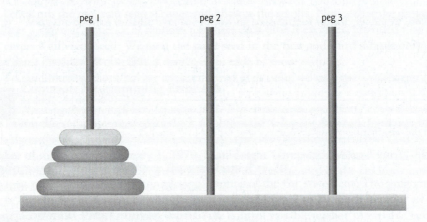

Fig. 7.40 | Towers of Hanoi for the case with four disks.

Your program should print the precise instructions it will take to move the disks from the starting peg to the destination peg. For example, to move a stack of three disks from peg 1 to peg 3, your program should print the following series of moves:

1 → 3 (This means move one disk from peg 1 to peg 3.)
1 → 2
3 → 2
1 → 3
2 → 1
2 → 3
1 → 3

7.43   Any program that can be implemented recursively can be implemented iteratively, although sometimes with more difficulty and less clarity. Try writing an iterative version of the Towers of Hanoi. If you succeed, compare your iterative version with the recursive version developed in Exercise 7.42. Investigate issues of performance, clarity and your ability to demonstrate the correctness of the programs.

7.44   *(Visualizing Recursion)* It is interesting to watch recursion "in action." Modify the factorial function of Fig. 7.28 to print its local variable and recursive call parameter. For each recursive call, display the outputs on a separate line and add a level of indentation. Do your utmost to make the outputs clear, interesting and meaningful. Your goal here is to design and implement an output format that helps a person understand recursion better. You may want to add such display capabilities to the many other recursion examples and exercises throughout the text.

7.45   *(Recursive Greatest Common Divisor)* The greatest common divisor of integers x and y is the largest integer that evenly divides both x and y. Write a recursive function gcd that returns the greatest common divisor of x and y, defined recursively as follows: If y is equal to 0, then gcd(x, y) is x; otherwise, gcd(x, y) is gcd(y, x % y), where % is the modulus operator. [*Note:* For this algorithm, x must be larger than y.]

7.46   Can main be called recursively on your system? Write a program containing a function main. Include static local variable count and initialize it to 1. Postincrement and print the value of count each time main is called. Compile your program. What happens?

7.47   Exercises 7.35–7.37 developed a computer-assisted instruction program to teach an elementary-school student multiplication. This exercise suggests enhancements to that program.

a) Modify the program to allow the user to enter a grade-level capability. A grade level of 1 means to use only single-digit numbers in the problems, a grade level of 2 means to use numbers as large as two digits, etc.

b) Modify the program to allow the user to pick the type of arithmetic problems he or she wishes to study. An option of 1 means addition problems only, 2 means subtraction problems only, 3 means multiplication problems only, 4 means division problems only and 5 means a random mix of problems of all these types.

7.48   Write function distance that calculates the distance between two points *(x1, y1)* and *(x2, y2)*. All numbers and return values should be of type double.

7.49   What is wrong with the following program?

```
1   // Exercise 7.49: ex07_49.cpp
2   // What is wrong with this program?
3   #include <iostream>
4   using std::cin;
5   using std::cout;
6
```

```
7    int main()
8    {
9       int c;
10
11      if ( ( c = cin.get() ) != EOF )
12      {
13         main();
14         cout << c;
15      } // end if
16
17      return 0; // indicates successful termination
18   } // end main
```

7.50   What does the following program do?

```
1    // Exercise 7.50: ex07_50.cpp
2    // What does this program do?
3    #include <iostream>
4    using std::cout;
5    using std::cin;
6    using std::endl;
7
8    int mystery( int, int ); // function prototype
9
10   int main()
11   {
12      int x, y;
13
14      cout << "Enter two integers: ";
15      cin >> x >> y;
16      cout << "The result is " << mystery( x, y ) << endl;
17
18      return 0; // indicates successful termination
19   } // end main
20
21   // Parameter b must be a positive integer to prevent infinite recursion
22   int mystery( int a, int b )
23   {
24      if ( b == 1 ) // base case
25         return a;
26      else // recursion step
27         return a + mystery( a, b - 1 );
28   } // end function mystery
```

7.51   After you determine what the program of Exercise 7.50 does, modify the program to function properly after removing the restriction that the second argument be nonnegative.

7.52   Write a program that tests as many of the math library functions in Fig. 7.2 as you can. Exercise each of these functions by having your program print out tables of return values for a diversity of argument values.

7.53   Find the error in each of the following program segments and explain how to correct it:

a) ```
    float cube(float); // function prototype
    cube(float number) // function definition
    {
       return number * number * number;
    }
    ```
    ```

b) *register auto int* x = 7;
c) *int* randomNumber = srand();
d) *float* y = 123.45678;
   int x;
   x = y;
   cout << *static_cast*< *float* >(x) << endl;
e) *double* square(*double* number)
   {
       double number;
       return number * number;
   }
f) *int* sum(*int* n)
   {
       if (n == 0)
           return 0;
       else
           return n + sum(n);
   }

7.54   Modify the craps program of Fig. 7.11 to allow wagering. Package as a function the portion of the program that runs one game of craps. Initialize variable bankBalance to 1000 dollars. Prompt the player to enter a wager. Use a while loop to check that wager is less than or equal to bankBalance and, if not, prompt the user to reenter wager until a valid wager is entered. After a correct wager is entered, run one game of craps. If the player wins, increase bankBalance by wager and print the new bankBalance. If the player loses, decrease bankBalance by wager, print the new bankBalance, check whether bankBalance has become zero and, if so, print the message "Sorry. You busted!" As the game progresses, print messages to create some "chatter" such as "Oh, you're going for broke, huh?", "Aw cmon, take a chance!" or "You're up big. Now's the time to cash in your chips!".

7.55   Write a Visual C++ program that prompts the user for the radius of a circle, then calls inline function circleArea to calculate the area of that circle.

7.56   Write a complete Visual C++ program with the two alternate functions specified below, of which each simply triples the variable count defined in main. Then compare and contrast the two approaches. These two functions are
   a) function tripleByValue that passes a copy of count by value, triples the copy and returns the new value and
   a) function tripleByReference that passes count by reference via a reference parameter and triples the original value of count through its alias (i.e., the reference parameter).

7.57   What is the purpose of the unary scope resolution operator?

7.58   Write a program that uses a function template called min to determine the smaller of two arguments. Test the program using integer, character and floating-point number arguments.

7.59   Write a program that uses a function template called max to determine the larger of two arguments. Test the program using integer, character and floating-point number arguments.

7.60   Determine whether the following program segments contain errors. For each error, explain how it can be corrected. [*Note:* For a particular program segment, there may be no errors.]
   a) *template* < *class* A >
      int sum(*int* num1, *int* num2, *int* num3)
      {
          return num1 + num2 + num3;
      }

b)
```cpp
void printResults( int x, int y )
{
    cout << "The sum is " << x + y << '\n';
    return x + y;
}
```
c)
```cpp
template < A >
A product( A num1, A num2, A num3 )
{
    return num1 * num2 * num3;
}
```
d)
```cpp
double cube( int );
int cube( int );
```

Arrays and Vectors

*Now go, write it
before them in a table,
and note it in a book.*

—Isaiah 30:8

*Begin at the beginning, …
and go on till you come to
the end: then stop.*

—Lewis Carroll

*To go beyond is as
wrong as to fall short.*

—Confucius

OBJECTIVES

In this chapter you'll learn:

- To use the array data structure to represent a set of related data items.

- To use arrays to store, sort and search lists and tables of values.

- To declare arrays, initialize arrays and refer to the individual elements of arrays.

- To pass arrays to functions.

- Basic searching and sorting techniques.

- To declare and manipulate multidimensional arrays.

- To use C++ Standard Library class template `vector`.

- To create and use managed arrays with C++/CLI.

8.1 Introduction

This chapter introduces the important topic of *data structures*—collections of related data items. *Arrays* are data structures consisting of related data items of the same type. You learned about classes in Chapter 4. In Chapter 22, we discuss the notion of *structures*. Structures and classes can each hold related data items of possibly different types. Arrays, structures and classes are "static" entities in that they remain the same size throughout program execution. (They may, of course, be of automatic storage class and hence be created and destroyed each time the blocks in which they are defined are entered and exited.)

After discussing how arrays are declared, created and initialized, we present a series of practical examples that demonstrate several common array manipulations. We present an example of searching arrays to find particular elements. The chapter also introduces one of the most important computing applications—sorting data (i.e., putting the data in some particular order). Two sections of the chapter enhance the case study of class Grade-Book in Chapters 4–7. In particular, we use arrays to enable the class to maintain a set of grades in memory and analyze student grades from multiple exams in a semester—two capabilities that were absent from previous versions of the GradeBook class. These and other chapter examples demonstrate the ways in which arrays allow programmers to organize and manipulate data.

The style of arrays we use throughout most of this chapter are C-style, pointer-based arrays. (We'll study pointers in Chapter 9.) In Section 8.11, and in Chapter 23, Standard Template Library (STL), we'll cover arrays as full-fledged objects called vectors. We'll discover that these object-based arrays are safer and more versatile than the C-style, pointer-based arrays we discuss in the early part of this chapter.

The last part of the chapter is devoted to demonstrating the use of managed arrays with C++/CLI. You will see how to declare, initialize, and manipulate managed arrays as well as how to use the for each control statement with them. Finally, we demonstrate the use of managed multidimensional arrays in C++/CLI.

8.2 Arrays

An array is a consecutive group of memory locations that all have the same type. To refer to a particular location or element in the array, we specify the name of the array and the *position number* of the particular element in the array.

Figure 8.1 shows an integer array called c. This array contains 12 *elements*. A program refers to any one of these elements by giving the name of the array followed by the position number of the particular element in square brackets ([]). The position number is more formally called a *subscript* or *index* (this number specifies the number of elements from the beginning of the array). The first element in every array has *subscript 0* (*zero*) and is sometimes called the *zeroth element*. Thus, the elements of array c are c[0] (pro-

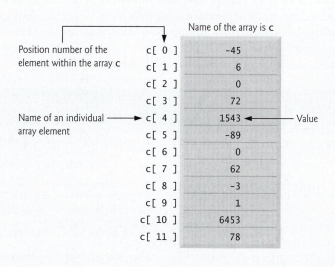

Fig. 8.1 | Array of 12 elements

nounced "c sub zero"), c[1], c[2] and so on. The highest subscript in array c is 11, which is 1 less than the number of elements in the array (12). Array names follow the same conventions as other variable names, i.e., they must be identifiers.

A subscript must be an integer or integer expression (using any integral type). If a program uses an expression as a subscript, then the program evaluates the expression to determine the subscript. For example, if we assume that variable a is equal to 5 and that variable b is equal to 6, then the statement

```
c[ a + b ] += 2;
```

adds 2 to array element c[11]. Note that a subscripted array name is an *lvalue*—it can be used on the left side of an assignment, just as nonarray variable names can.

Let us examine array c in Fig. 8.1 more closely. The ***name*** of the entire array is c. Its 12 elements are referred to as c[0] to c[11]. The ***value*** of c[0] is -45, the value of c[1] is 6, the value of c[2] is 0, the value of c[7] is 62, and the value of c[11] is 78. To print the sum of the values contained in the first three elements of array c, we'd write

```
cout << c[ 0 ] + c[ 1 ] + c[ 2 ] << endl;
```

To divide the value of c[6] by 2 and assign the result to the variable x, we would write

```
x = c[ 6 ] / 2;
```

Common Programming Error 8.1

Note the difference between the "seventh element of the array" and "array element 7." Array subscripts begin at 0, so the "seventh element of the array" has a subscript of 6, while "array element 7" has a subscript of 7 and is actually the eighth element of the array. Unfortunately, this distinction frequently is a source of off-by-one errors. To avoid such errors, we refer to specific array elements explicitly by their array name and subscript number (e.g., c[6] or c[7]).

The brackets used to enclose the subscript of an array are actually an operator. Brackets have the same level of precedence as parentheses. Figure 8.2 shows the precedence and associativity of the operators introduced so far. Note that brackets ([]) have been added to the second row of Fig. 8.2. The operators are shown top to bottom in decreasing order of precedence with their associativity and type.

Operators			Associativity	Type
::			left to right	scope resolution
()	[]		left to right	highest
++	--	***static_cast***< *type* >(*operand*)	left to right	unary (postfix)
++	--	+ - !	right to left	unary (prefix)
*	/	%	left to right	multiplicative
+	-		left to right	additive

Fig. 8.2 | Operator precedence and associativity. (Part 1 of 2.)

Operators	Associativity	Type
<< >>	left to right	insertion/extraction
< <= > >=	left to right	relational
== !=	left to right	equality
&&	left to right	logical AND
||	left to right	logical OR
?:	right to left	conditional
= += -= *= /= %=	right to left	assignment
,	left to right	comma

Fig. 8.2 | Operator precedence and associativity. (Part 2 of 2.)

8.3 Declaring Arrays

Arrays occupy space in memory. To specify the type of the elements and the number of elements required by an array use a declaration of the form:

>   *type arrayName*[*arraySize*];

The compiler reserves the appropriate amount of memory. (Recall that a declaration which reserves memory is more properly known as a definition in Visual C++.) The *array-Size* must be an integer constant greater than zero. For example, to tell the compiler to reserve 12 elements for integer array c, use the declaration

```
int c[ 12 ]; // c is an array of 12 integers
```

Memory can be reserved for several arrays with a single declaration. The following declaration reserves 100 elements for the integer array b and 27 elements for the integer array x.

```
int b[ 100 ], // b is an array of 100 integers
    x[ 27 ]; // x is an array of 27 integers
```

Good Programming Practice 8.1

Declare one array per declaration for readability, modifiability and ease of commenting.

Arrays can hold values of any nonreference data type. For example, an array of type char can be used to store a character string. Until now, we have used string objects to store character strings. Character strings and their similarity to arrays (a relationship Visual C++ inherited from C), and the relationship between pointers and arrays, are discussed in Chapter 9.

8.4 Examples Using Arrays

This section presents many examples that demonstrate how to declare arrays, how to initialize arrays and how to perform common array manipulations.

8.4.1 Declaring an Array and Using a Loop to Initialize the Array's Elements

The program in Fig. 8.3 declares 10-element integer array n (line 12). Lines 15–16 use a for statement to initialize the array elements to zeros. Like other automatic variables, automatic arrays are not implicitly initialized to zero, although static arrays are. The first output statement (line 18) displays the column headings for the columns printed in the subsequent for statement (lines 21–22), which prints the array in tabular format. Remember that setw specifies the field width in which only the *next* value is to be output.

```cpp
1   // Fig. 8.3: InitializeArray.cpp
2   // Initializing an array.
3   #include <iostream>
4   using std::cout;
5   using std::endl;
6
7   #include <iomanip>
8   using std::setw;
9
10  int main()
11  {
12     int n[ 10 ]; // n is an array of 10 integers
13
14     // initialize elements of array n to 0
15     for ( int i = 0; i < 10; i++ )
16        n[ i ] = 0; // set element at location i to 0
17
18     cout << "Element" << setw( 13 ) << "Value" << endl;
19
20     // output each array element's value
21     for ( int j = 0; j < 10; j++ )
22        cout << setw( 7 ) << j << setw( 13 ) << n[ j ] << endl;
23
24     return 0; // indicates successful termination
25  } // end main
```

```
Element        Value
      0            0
      1            0
      2            0
      3            0
      4            0
      5            0
      6            0
      7            0
      8            0
      9            0
```

Fig. 8.3 | Initializing an array's elements to zeros and printing the array.

8.4.2 Initializing an Array in a Declaration with an Initializer List

The elements of an array also can be initialized in the array declaration by following the array name with an equals sign and a brace-delimited comma-separated list of *initializers*.

The program in Fig. 8.4 uses an *initializer list* to initialize an integer array with 10 values (line 13) and prints the array in tabular format (lines 15–19).

If there are fewer initializers than elements in the array, the remaining array elements are initialized to zero. For example, the elements of array n in Fig. 8.3 could have been initialized to zero with the declaration

```
int n[ 10 ] = {}; // initialize elements of array n to 0
```

The declaration implicitly initializes the elements to zero, because there are fewer initializers (none in this case) than elements in the array. This technique can be used only in the array's declaration, whereas the initialization technique shown in Fig. 8.3 can be used repeatedly during program execution to "reinitialize" an array's elements.

If the array size is omitted from a declaration with an initializer list, the compiler determines the number of elements in the array by counting the number of elements in the initializer list. For example,

```
1   // Fig. 8.4: InitializeArray.cpp
2   // Initializing an array in a declaration.
3   #include <iostream>
4   using std::cout;
5   using std::endl;
6
7   #include <iomanip>
8   using std::setw;
9
10  int main()
11  {
12     // use initializer list to initialize array n
13     int n[ 10 ] = { 32, 27, 64, 18, 95, 14, 90, 70, 60, 37 };
14
15     cout << "Element" << setw( 13 ) << "Value" << endl;
16
17     // output each array element's value
18     for ( int i = 0; i < 10; i++ )
19        cout << setw( 7 ) << i << setw( 13 ) << n[ i ] << endl;
20
21     return 0; // indicates successful termination
22  } // end main
```

```
Element        Value
      0           32
      1           27
      2           64
      3           18
      4           95
      5           14
      6           90
      7           70
      8           60
      9           37
```

Fig. 8.4 | Initializing the elements of an array in its declaration.

```
int n[] = { 1, 2, 3, 4, 5 };
```

creates a five-element array.

If the array size and an initializer list are specified in an array declaration, the number of initializers must be less than or equal to the array size. The array declaration

```
int n[ 5 ] = { 32, 27, 64, 18, 95, 14 };
```

causes a compilation error, because there are six initializers and only five array elements.

Common Programming Error 8.2

Providing more initializers in an array initializer list than there are elements in the array is a compilation error.

Common Programming Error 8.3

Forgetting to initialize the elements of an array whose elements should be initialized is a logic error.

8.4.3 Specifying an Array's Size with a Constant Variable and Setting Array Elements with Calculations

Figure 8.5 sets the elements of a 10-element array s to the even integers 2, 4, 6, ..., 20 (lines 17–18) and prints the array in tabular format (lines 20–24). These numbers are generated (line 18) by multiplying each successive value of the loop counter by 2 and adding 2.

```
1   // Fig. 8.5: SetArrayElements.cpp
2   // Set array s to the even integers from 2 to 20.
3   #include <iostream>
4   using std::cout;
5   using std::endl;
6
7   #include <iomanip>
8   using std::setw;
9
10  int main()
11  {
12     // constant variable can be used to specify array size
13     const int arraySize = 10;
14
15     int s[ arraySize ]; // array s has 10 elements
16
17     for ( int i = 0; i < arraySize; i++ ) // set the values
18        s[ i ] = 2 + 2 * i;
19
20     cout << "Element" << setw( 13 ) << "Value" << endl;
21
22     // output contents of array s in tabular format
23     for ( int j = 0; j < arraySize; j++ )
24        cout << setw( 7 ) << j << setw( 13 ) << s[ j ] << endl;
25
```

Fig. 8.5 | Generating values to be placed into elements of an array. (Part 1 of 2.)

```
26        return 0; // indicates successful termination
27    } // end main
```

```
Element        Value
       0            2
       1            4
       2            6
       3            8
       4           10
       5           12
       6           14
       7           16
       8           18
       9           20
```

Fig. 8.5 | Generating values to be placed into elements of an array. (Part 2 of 2.)

Line 13 uses the **const *qualifier*** to declare a so-called *constant variable* arraySize with the value 10. Constant variables must be initialized with a constant expression when they are declared and cannot be modified thereafter (as shown in Fig. 8.6 and Fig. 8.7). Constant variables are also called *named constants* or *read-only variables*.

Common Programming Error 8.4

Not assigning a value to a constant variable when it is declared is a compilation error.

```
 1    // Fig. 8.6: ConstantVariable.cpp
 2    // Using a properly initialized constant variable.
 3    #include <iostream>
 4    using std::cout;
 5    using std::endl;
 6
 7    int main()
 8    {
 9       const int x = 7; // initialized constant variable
10
11       cout << "The value of constant variable x is: " << x << endl;
12
13       return 0; // indicates successful termination
14    } // end main
```

```
The value of constant variable x is: 7
```

Fig. 8.6 | Initializing and using a constant variable.

```
 1    // Fig. 8.7: ConstVariable.cpp
 2    // A const variable must be initialized.
 3
```

Fig. 8.7 | const variables must be initialized. (Part 1 of 2.)

```
 4    int main()
 5    {
 6       const int x; // Error: x must be initialized
 7
 8       x = 7; // Error: cannot modify a const variable
 9
10       return 0; // indicates successful termination
11    } // end main
```

```
C:\examples\ch08\fig08_07\ConstTest.cpp(6) : error C2734: 'x' : const
   object must be initialized if not extern
C:\examples\ch08\fig08_07\ConstTest.cpp(8) : error C3892: 'x' : you
   cannot assign to a variable that is const
```

Fig. 8.7 | const variables must be initialized. (Part 2 of 2.)

Common Programming Error 8.5

Assigning a value to a constant variable in an executable statement is a compilation error.

In Fig. 8.7, note that the compilation errors produced by Visual Studio 2008 refer to the int variable x as a "const object." The ISO/IEC C++ standard defines an "object" as any "region of storage." Like objects of classes, fundamental-type variables also occupy space in memory, so they are often referred to as "objects."

Constant variables can be placed anywhere a constant expression is expected. In Fig. 8.5, constant variable arraySize specifies the size of array s in line 15.

Common Programming Error 8.6

Only constants can be used to declare the size of automatic and static arrays. Not using a constant for this purpose is a compilation error.

Using constant variables to specify array sizes makes programs more *scalable*. In Fig. 8.5, the first for statement could fill a 1000-element array by simply changing the value of arraySize in its declaration from 10 to 1000. If the constant variable arraySize had not been used, we would have to change lines 15, 17 and 23 of the program to scale the program to handle 1000 array elements. As programs get larger, this technique becomes more useful for writing clearer, easier-to-modify programs.

Software Engineering Observation 8.1

Defining the size of each array as a constant variable instead of a literal constant can make programs more scalable.

Good Programming Practice 8.2

*Defining the size of an array as a constant variable instead of a literal constant makes programs clearer. This technique eliminates so-called **magic numbers**. For example, repeatedly mentioning the size 10 in array-processing code for a 10-element array gives the number 10 an artificial significance and can be confusing when the program includes other 10s that have nothing to do with the array size.*

8.4.4 Summing the Elements of an Array

Often, the elements of an array represent a series of values to be used in a calculation. For example, if the elements of an array represent exam grades, a professor may wish to total the elements of the array and use that sum to calculate the class average for the exam. The examples using class GradeBook later in the chapter, namely Figs. 8.15–8.16 and Figs. 8.22–8.23, use this technique.

The program in Fig. 8.8 sums the values contained in the 10-element integer array a. The program declares, creates and initializes the array in line 10. The for statement (lines 14–15) performs the calculations. The values being supplied as initializers for array a also could be read into the program from the user at the keyboard, or from a file on disk (see Chapter 17, Stream Input/Output and Files). For example, the for statement

```
for ( int j = 0; j < arraySize; j++ )
   cin >> a[ j ];
```

reads one value at a time from the keyboard and stores the value in element a[j].

```cpp
 1   // Fig. 8.8: SumElements.cpp
 2   // Compute the sum of the elements of the array.
 3   #include <iostream>
 4   using std::cout;
 5   using std::endl;
 6
 7   int main()
 8   {
 9      const int arraySize = 10; // constant variable indicating size of array
10      int a[ arraySize ] = { 87, 68, 94, 100, 83, 78, 85, 91, 76, 87 };
11      int total = 0;
12
13      // sum contents of array a
14      for ( int i = 0; i < arraySize; i++ )
15         total += a[ i ];
16
17      cout << "Total of array elements: " << total << endl;
18
19      return 0; // indicates successful termination
20   } // end main
```

```
Total of array elements: 849
```

Fig. 8.8 | Computing the sum of the elements of an array.

8.4.5 Using Bar Charts to Display Array Data Graphically

Many programs present data to users in a graphical manner. For example, numeric values are often displayed as bars in a bar chart. In such a chart, longer bars represent proportionally larger numeric values. One simple way to display numeric data graphically is with a bar chart that shows each numeric value as a bar of asterisks (*).

Professors often like to examine the distribution of grades on an exam. A professor might graph the number of grades in each of several categories to visualize the grade distribution. Suppose the grades were 87, 68, 94, 100, 83, 78, 85, 91, 76 and 87. Note that there was one grade of 100, two grades in the 90s, four grades in the 80s, two grades in the 70s, one grade in the 60s and no grades below 60. Our next program (Fig. 8.9) stores this grade-distribution data in an array of 11 elements, each corresponding to a category of grades. For example, n[0] indicates the number of grades in the range 0–9, n[7] indicates the number of grades in the range 70–79 and n[10] indicates the number of grades of 100. The two versions of class GradeBook later in the chapter (Figs. 8.15–8.16 and Figs. 8.22–8.23) contain code that calculates these grade frequencies based on a set of grades. For now, we manually create the array by looking at the set of grades.

The program reads the numbers from the array and graphs the information as a bar chart, displaying each grade range followed by a bar of asterisks indicating the number of grades in that range. To label each bar, lines 20–25 output a grade range (e.g., "70-79: ") based on the current value of counter variable i. The nested for statement (lines 28–29)

```cpp
1  // Fig. 8.9: BarChart.cpp
2  // Bar chart printing program.
3  #include <iostream>
4  using std::cout;
5  using std::endl;
6
7  #include <iomanip>
8
9  int main()
10 {
11    const int arraySize = 11;
12    int n[ arraySize ] = { 0, 0, 0, 0, 0, 0, 1, 2, 4, 2, 1 };
13
14    cout << "Grade distribution:" << endl;
15
16    // for each element of array n, output a bar of the chart
17    for ( int i = 0; i < arraySize; i++ )
18    {
19       // output bar labels ("0-9:", ..., "90-99:", "100:" )
20       if ( i == 0 )
21          cout << "  0-9: ";
22       else if ( i == 10 )
23          cout << "  100: ";
24       else
25          cout << i * 10 << "-" << ( i * 10 ) + 9 << ": ";
26
27       // print bar of asterisks
28       for ( int stars = 0; stars < n[ i ]; stars++ )
29          cout << '*';
30
31       cout << endl; // start a new line of output
32    } // end outer for
33
34    return 0; // indicates successful termination
35 } // end main
```

Fig. 8.9 | Bar chart printing program. (Part 1 of 2.)

```
Grade distribution:
   0-9:
  10-19:
  20-29:
  30-39:
  40-49:
  50-59:
  60-69: *
  70-79: **
  80-89: ****
  90-99: **
   100: *
```

Fig. 8.9 | Bar chart printing program. (Part 2 of 2.)

outputs the bars. Note the loop-continuation condition in line 28 (stars < n[i]). Each time the program reaches the inner for, the loop counts from 0 up to n[i], thus using a value in array n to determine the number of asterisks to display. In this example, n[0]–n[5] contain zeros because no students received a grade below 60. Thus, the program displays no asterisks next to the first six grade ranges.

Common Programming Error 8.7

Although it is possible to use the same control variable in a for statement and in a second for statement nested inside, this is confusing and can lead to logic errors.

8.4.6 Using the Elements of an Array as Counters

Sometimes, programs use counter variables to summarize data, such as the results of a survey. In Fig. 7.9, we used separate counters in our die-rolling program to track the number of occurrences of each side of a die as the program rolled the die 6,000,000 times. An array version of this program is shown in Fig. 8.10.

Figure 8.10 uses the array frequency (line 20) to count the occurrences of each side of the die. In line 23 we use time(0) to create a seed value for the random number generator. This call returns a time_t variable so we use a static_cast to unsigned to pass srand the type it requires. *The single statement in line 27 of this program replaces the switch statement in lines 30–52 of Fig. 7.9.* Line 27 uses a random value to determine which frequency element to increment during each iteration of the loop. The calculation in line 27 produces a random subscript from 1 to 6, so array frequency must be large enough to store six counters. However, we use a seven-element array in which we ignore frequency[0]—it is more logical to have the die face value 1 increment frequency[1] than frequency[0]. Thus, each face value is used as a subscript for array frequency. We also replace lines 56–61 of Fig. 7.9 by looping through array frequency to output the results (lines 32–34).

```
1   // Fig. 8.10: RollDie.cpp
2   // Roll a six-sided die 6,000,000 times.
3   #include <iostream>
4   using std::cout;
5   using std::endl;
```

Fig. 8.10 | Die-rolling program using an array instead of switch. (Part 1 of 2.)

```
 6
 7   #include <iomanip>
 8   using std::setw;
 9
10   #include <cstdlib>
11   using std::rand;
12   using std::srand;
13
14   #include <ctime>
15   using std::time;
16
17   int main()
18   {
19      const int arraySize = 7; // ignore element zero
20      int frequency[ arraySize ] = {}; // initialize elements to 0
21
22      // seed random number generator
23      srand( static_cast< unsigned >( time( 0 ) ) );
24
25      // roll die 6,000,000 times; use die value as frequency index
26      for ( int roll = 1; roll <= 6000000; roll++ )
27         frequency[ 1 + rand() % 6 ]++;
28
29      cout << "Face" << setw( 13 ) << "Frequency" << endl;
30
31      // output each array element's value
32      for ( int face = 1; face < arraySize; face++ )
33         cout << setw( 4 ) << face << setw( 13 ) << frequency[ face ]
34            << endl;
35
36      return 0; // indicates successful termination
37   } // end main
```

Face	Frequency
1	1000167
2	1000149
3	1000152
4	998748
5	999626
6	1001158

Fig. 8.10 | Die-rolling program using an array instead of `switch`. (Part 2 of 2.)

8.4.7 Using Arrays to Summarize Survey Results

Our next example (Fig. 8.11) uses arrays to summarize the results of data collected in a survey. Consider the following problem statement:

> *Forty students were asked to rate the quality of the food in the student cafeteria on a scale of 1 to 10 (1 meaning awful and 10 meaning excellent). Place the 40 responses in an integer array and summarize the results of the poll.*

This is a typical array-processing application. We wish to summarize the number of responses of each type (i.e., 1 through 10). The array `responses` (lines 17–19) is a 40-element integer array of the students' responses to the survey. Note that array `responses` is

```
 1   // Fig. 8.11: StudentPoll.cpp
 2   // Student poll program.
 3   #include <iostream>
 4   using std::cout;
 5   using std::endl;
 6
 7   #include <iomanip>
 8   using std::setw;
 9
10   int main()
11   {
12      // define array sizes
13      const int responseSize = 40; // size of array responses
14      const int frequencySize = 11; // size of array frequency
15
16      // place survey responses in array responses
17      const int responses[ responseSize ] = { 1, 2, 6, 4, 8, 5, 9, 7, 8,
18         10, 1, 6, 3, 8, 6, 10, 3, 8, 2, 7, 6, 5, 7, 6, 8, 6, 7,
19         5, 6, 6, 5, 6, 7, 5, 6, 4, 8, 6, 8, 10 };
20
21      // initialize frequency counters to 0
22      int frequency[ frequencySize ] = {};
23
24      // for each answer, select value from responses and use it
25      // as frequency subscript to determine element to increment
26      for ( int answer = 0; answer < responseSize; answer++ )
27         frequency[ responses[ answer ] ]++;
28
29      cout << "Rating" << setw( 17 ) << "Frequency" << endl;
30
31      // output each array element's value
32      for ( int rating = 1; rating < frequencySize; rating++ )
33         cout << setw( 6 ) << rating << setw( 17 ) << frequency[ rating ]
34            << endl;
35
36      return 0; // indicates successful termination
37   } // end main
```

Rating	Frequency
1	2
2	2
3	2
4	2
5	5
6	11
7	5
8	7
9	1
10	3

Fig. 8.11 | Poll analysis program.

declared const, as its values do not (and should not) change. We use an 11-element array frequency (line 22) to count the number of occurrences of each response. Each element of the array is used as a counter for one of the survey responses and is initialized to zero. As in Fig. 8.10, we ignore frequency[0].

Software Engineering Observation 8.2

The const qualifier should be used to enforce the principle of least privilege. Using the principle of least privilege to properly design software can greatly reduce debugging time and improper side effects and can make a program easier to modify and maintain.

Good Programming Practice 8.3

Strive for program clarity. It is sometimes worthwhile to trade off the most efficient use of memory or processor time in favor of writing clearer programs.

Performance Tip 8.1

Sometimes performance considerations far outweigh clarity considerations.

The first for statement (lines 26–27) takes the responses one at a time from the array responses and increments one of the 10 counters in the frequency array (frequency[1] to frequency[10]). The key statement in the loop is line 27, which increments the appropriate frequency counter, depending on the value of responses[answer].

Let's consider several iterations of the for loop. When control variable answer is 0, the value of responses[answer] is the value of responses[0] (i.e., 1 in line 17), so the program interprets frequency[responses[answer]]++ as

```
frequency[ 1 ]++
```

which increments the value in array element 1. To evaluate the expression, start with the value in the innermost set of square brackets (answer). Once you know answer's value (which is the value of the loop control variable in line 26), plug it into the expression and evaluate the next outer set of square brackets (i.e., responses[answer], which is a value selected from the responses array in lines 17–19). Then use the resulting value as the subscript for the frequency array to specify which counter to increment.

When answer is 1, responses[answer] is the value of responses[1], which is 2, so the program interprets frequency[responses[answer]]++ as

```
frequency[ 2 ]++
```

which increments array element 2.

When answer is 2, responses[answer] is the value of responses[2], which is 6, so the program interprets frequency[responses[answer]]++ as

```
frequency[ 6 ]++
```

which increments array element 6, and so on. Regardless of the number of responses processed in the survey, the program requires only an 11-element array (ignoring element zero) to summarize the results, because all the response values are between 1 and 10 and the subscript values for an 11-element array are 0 through 10.

If the data in the responses array had contained an invalid value, such as 13, the program would have attempted to add 1 to frequency[13], which is outside the bounds of the array. *Visual C++ has no array bounds checking to prevent the computer from referring to an element that does not exist.* Thus, an executing program can "walk off" either end of an array without warning. You should ensure that all array references remain within the bounds of the array.

Common Programming Error 8.8

Referring to an element outside the array bounds is an execution-time logic error. It is not a syntax error.

Error-Prevention Tip 8.1

When looping through an array, the array subscript should never go below 0 and should always be less than the total number of elements in the array (one less than the size of the array). Make sure that the loop-termination condition prevents accessing elements outside this range.

Portability Tip 8.1

The (normally serious) effects of referencing elements outside the array bounds are system dependent. Often this results in changes to the value of an unrelated variable or a fatal error that terminates program execution.

Visual C++ is an extensible language. Section 8.11 presents C++ Standard Library class template `vector`, which enables programmers to perform many operations that are not available for Visual C++'s built-in arrays. For example, we'll be able to compare `vector`s directly and assign one `vector` to another. In Chapter 12, we extend Visual C++ further by implementing an array as a user-defined class of our own. This new array definition will enable us to input and output entire arrays with `cin` and `cout`, initialize arrays when they are created, prevent access to out-of-range array elements and change the range of subscripts (and even their subscript type) so that the first element of an array is not required to be element 0. We'll even be able to use noninteger subscripts.

Error-Prevention Tip 8.2

In Chapter 12, we'll see how to develop a class representing a "smart array," which checks that all subscript references are in bounds at runtime. Using such smart data types helps eliminate bugs.

8.4.8 Static Local Arrays and Automatic Local Arrays

Chapter 7 discussed the storage-class specifier `static`. A `static` local variable in a function definition exists for the program's duration but is visible only in the function's body.

Performance Tip 8.2

We can apply `static` to a local array declaration so that the array is not created and initialized each time the program calls the function and is not destroyed each time the function terminates in the program. This can improve performance, especially when using large arrays.

A program initializes `static` local arrays when their declarations are first encountered. If a `static` array is not initialized explicitly by you, each element of that array is initialized to zero by the compiler when the array is created. Recall that Visual C++ does not perform such default initialization for automatic variables.

Figure 8.12 demonstrates function `staticArrayInit` (lines 25–41) with a `static` local array (line 28) and function `automaticArrayInit` (lines 44–60) with an automatic local array (line 47).

```
1   // Fig. 8.12: StaticArray.cpp
2   // Static arrays are initialized to zero.
3   #include <iostream>
4   using std::cout;
5   using std::endl;
6
7   void staticArrayInit( void ); // function prototype
8   void automaticArrayInit( void ); // function prototype
9
10  int main()
11  {
12     cout << "First call to each function:\n";
13     staticArrayInit();
14     automaticArrayInit();
15
16     cout << "\n\nSecond call to each function:\n";
17     staticArrayInit();
18     automaticArrayInit();
19     cout << endl;
20
21     return 0; // indicates successful termination
22  } // end main
23
24  // function to demonstrate a static local array
25  void staticArrayInit( void )
26  {
27     // initializes elements to 0 first time function is called
28     static int array1[ 3 ]; // static local array
29
30     cout << "\nValues on entering staticArrayInit:\n";
31
32     // output contents of array1
33     for ( int i = 0; i < 3; i++ )
34        cout << "array1[" << i << "] = " << array1[ i ] << "  ";
35
36     cout << "\nValues on exiting staticArrayInit:\n";
37
38     // modify and output contents of array1
39     for ( int j = 0; j < 3; j++ )
40        cout << "array1[" << j << "] = " << ( array1[ j ] += 5 ) << "  ";
41  } // end function staticArrayInit
42
43  // function to demonstrate an automatic local array
44  void automaticArrayInit( void )
45  {
46     // initializes elements each time function is called
47     int array2[ 3 ] = { 1, 2, 3 }; // automatic local array
48
49     cout << "\n\nValues on entering automaticArrayInit:\n";
50
51     // output contents of array2
52     for ( int i = 0; i < 3; i++ )
53        cout << "array2[" << i << "] = " << array2[ i ] << "  ";
```

Fig. 8.12 | static array initialization and automatic array initialization. (Part I of 2.)

```
54
55       cout << "\nValues on exiting automaticArrayInit:\n";
56
57       // modify and output contents of array2
58       for ( int j = 0; j < 3; j++ )
59          cout << "array2[" << j << "] = " << ( array2[ j ] += 5 ) << "  ";
60    } // end function automaticArrayInit
```

```
First call to each function:

Values on entering staticArrayInit:
array1[0] = 0  array1[1] = 0  array1[2] = 0
Values on exiting staticArrayInit:
array1[0] = 5  array1[1] = 5  array1[2] = 5

Values on entering automaticArrayInit:
array2[0] = 1  array2[1] = 2  array2[2] = 3
Values on exiting automaticArrayInit:
array2[0] = 6  array2[1] = 7  array2[2] = 8

Second call to each function:

Values on entering staticArrayInit:
array1[0] = 5  array1[1] = 5  array1[2] = 5
Values on exiting staticArrayInit:
array1[0] = 10  array1[1] = 10  array1[2] = 10

Values on entering automaticArrayInit:
array2[0] = 1  array2[1] = 2  array2[2] = 3
Values on exiting automaticArrayInit:
array2[0] = 6  array2[1] = 7  array2[2] = 8
```

Fig. 8.12 | static array initialization and automatic array initialization. (Part 2 of 2.)

Function staticArrayInit is called twice (lines 13 and 17). The static local array is initialized to zero by the compiler the first time the function is called. The function prints the array, adds 5 to each element and prints the array again. The second time the function is called, the static array contains the modified values stored during the first function call. Function automaticArrayInit also is called twice (lines 14 and 18). The elements of the automatic local array are initialized (line 47) with the values 1, 2 and 3. The function prints the array, adds 5 to each element and prints the array again. The second time the function is called, the array elements are reinitialized to 1, 2 and 3. The array has automatic storage class, so the array is recreated and reinitialized during each call to automaticArrayInit.

 Common Programming Error 8.9

Assuming that elements of a function's local static array are initialized every time the function is called can lead to logic errors in a program.

8.5 Passing Arrays to Functions

To pass an array argument to a function, specify the name of the array without any brackets. For example, if array hourlyTemperatures has been declared as

```
int hourlyTemperatures[ 24 ];
```

the function call

```
modifyArray( hourlyTemperatures, 24 );
```

passes array `hourlyTemperatures` and its size to function `modifyArray`. When passing an array to a function, the array size is normally passed as well, so the function can process the specific number of elements in the array. Otherwise, we would need to build this knowledge into the called function itself or, worse yet, place the array size in a global variable. In Section 8.11, when we present C++ Standard Library class template `vector` to represent a more robust type of array, you'll see that the size of a `vector` is built in—every `vector` object "knows" its own size, which can be obtained by invoking the `vector` object's `size` member function. Thus, when we pass a `vector` *object* into a function, we will not have to pass the size of the `vector` as an argument.

Visual C++ passes arrays to functions by reference—the called functions can modify the element values in the callers' original arrays. The value of the name of the array is the address in the computer's memory of the first element of the array. Because the starting address of the array is passed, the called function knows precisely where the array is stored in memory. Therefore, when the called function modifies array elements in its function body, it is modifying the actual elements of the array in their original memory locations.

Performance Tip 8.3

Passing arrays by reference makes sense for performance reasons. If arrays were passed by value, a copy of each element would be passed. For large, frequently passed arrays, this would be time consuming and would require considerable storage for the copies of the array elements.

Software Engineering Observation 8.3

It is possible to pass an array by value (by using a simple trick we explain in Chapter 22)— however, this is rarely done.

Although entire arrays are passed by reference, individual array elements are passed by value exactly as simple variables are. Such simple single pieces of data are called ***scalars*** or ***scalar quantities***. To pass an element of an array to a function, use the subscripted name of the array element as an argument in the function call. In Chapter 7, we showed how to pass scalars (i.e., individual variables and array elements) by reference with references. In Chapter 9, we show how to pass scalars by reference with pointers.

For a function to receive an array through a function call, the function's parameter list must specify that the function expects to receive an array. For example, the function header for function `modifyArray` might be written as

```
void modifyArray( int b[], int arraySize )
```

indicating that `modifyArray` expects to receive the address of an array of integers in parameter `b` and the number of array elements in parameter `arraySize`. The array's size is not required in the array brackets. If it is included, the compiler ignores it; thus, arrays of any size can be passed to the function. Visual C++ passes arrays to functions by reference— when the called function uses the array name `b`, it refers to the actual array in the caller (i.e., array `hourlyTemperatures` discussed at the beginning of this section).

Note the strange appearance of the function prototype for `modifyArray`

```
void modifyArray( int [], int );
```

This prototype could have been written

```
void modifyArray( int anyArrayName[], int anyVariableName );
```

but, as we learned in Chapter 4, Visual C++ compilers ignore variable names in prototypes. Remember, the prototype tells the compiler the number of arguments and the type of each argument (in the order in which the arguments are expected to appear).

The program in Fig. 8.13 demonstrates the difference between passing an entire array and passing an array element. Lines 22–23 print the five original elements of integer array a. Line 28 passes a and its size to function modifyArray (lines 45–50), which multiplies each of a's elements by 2 (through parameter b). Then, lines 32–33 print array a again in main. As the output shows, the elements of a are indeed modified by modifyArray. Next, line 36 prints the value of scalar a[3], then line 38 passes element a[3] to function modifyElement (lines 54–58), which multiplies its parameter by 2 and prints the new value. Note that when line 39 again prints a[3] in main, the value has not been modified, because individual array elements are passed by value.

```cpp
 1   // Fig. 8.13: PassingArray.cpp
 2   // Passing arrays and individual array elements to functions.
 3   #include <iostream>
 4   using std::cout;
 5   using std::endl;
 6
 7   #include <iomanip>
 8   using std::setw;
 9
10   void modifyArray( int [], int ); // appears strange; array and size
11   void modifyElement( int ); // receive array element value
12
13   int main()
14   {
15      const int arraySize = 5; // size of array a
16      int a[ arraySize ] = { 0, 1, 2, 3, 4 }; // initialize array a
17
18      cout << "Effects of passing entire array by reference:"
19         << "\n\nThe values of the original array are:\n";
20
21      // output original array elements
22      for ( int i = 0; i < arraySize; i++ )
23         cout << setw( 3 ) << a[ i ];
24
25      cout << endl;
26
27      // pass array a to modifyArray by reference
28      modifyArray( a, arraySize );
29      cout << "The values of the modified array are:\n";
30
31      // output modified array elements
32      for ( int j = 0; j < arraySize; j++ )
33         cout << setw( 3 ) << a[ j ];
```

Fig. 8.13 | Passing arrays and individual array elements to functions. (Part 1 of 2.)

```
34
35        cout << "\n\n\nEffects of passing array element by value:"
36           << "\n\na[3] before modifyElement: " << a[ 3 ] << endl;
37
38        modifyElement( a[ 3 ] ); // pass array element a[ 3 ] by value
39        cout << "a[3] after modifyElement: " << a[ 3 ] << endl;
40
41        return 0; // indicates successful termination
42     } // end main
43
44     // in function modifyArray, "b" points to the original array "a" in memory
45     void modifyArray( int b[], int sizeOfArray )
46     {
47        // multiply each array element by 2
48        for ( int k = 0; k < sizeOfArray; k++ )
49           b[ k ] *= 2;
50     } // end function modifyArray
51
52     // in function modifyElement, "e" is a local copy of
53     // array element a[ 3 ] passed from main
54     void modifyElement( int e )
55     {
56        // multiply parameter by 2
57        cout << "Value of element in modifyElement: " << ( e *= 2 ) << endl;
58     } // end function modifyElement
```

```
Effects of passing entire array by reference:

The values of the original array are:
   0   1   2   3   4
The values of the modified array are:
   0   2   4   6   8


Effects of passing array element by value:

a[3] before modifyElement: 6
Value of element in modifyElement: 12
a[3] after modifyElement: 6
```

Fig. 8.13 | Passing arrays and individual array elements to functions. (Part 2 of 2.)

There may be situations in your programs in which a function should not be allowed to modify array elements. Visual C++ provides the type qualifier const that can be used to prevent modification of array values in the caller by code in a called function. When a function specifies an array parameter that is preceded by the const qualifier, the elements of the array become constant in the function body, and any attempt to modify an element of the array in the function body results in a compilation error. This enables you to prevent accidental modification of array elements in the function's body.

Figure 8.14 demonstrates the const qualifier. Function tryToModifyArray (lines 21–26) is defined with parameter const int b[], which specifies that array b is constant and cannot be modified. Each of the three attempts by the function to modify array b's elements (lines 23–25) results in a compilation error. The Visual Studio 2008 compiler pro-

```
 1   // Fig. 8.14: ConstTest.cpp
 2   // Demonstrating the const type qualifier.
 3   #include <iostream>
 4   using std::cout;
 5   using std::endl;
 6
 7   void tryToModifyArray( const int [] ); // function prototype
 8
 9   int main()
10   {
11      int a[] = { 10, 20, 30 };
12
13      tryToModifyArray( a );
14      cout << a[ 0 ] << ' ' << a[ 1 ] << ' ' << a[ 2 ] << '\n';
15
16      return 0; // indicates successful termination
17   } // end main
18
19   // In function tryToModifyArray, "b" cannot be used
20   // to modify the original array "a" in main.
21   void tryToModifyArray( const int b[] )
22   {
23      b[ 0 ] /= 2; // compilation error
24      b[ 1 ] /= 2; // compilation error
25      b[ 2 ] /= 2; // compilation error
26   } // end function tryToModifyArray
```

```
c:\examples\ch08\fig08_14\ConstTest.cpp(23) : error C3892: 'b' : you
   cannot assign to a variable that is const
c:\examples\ch08\fig08_14\ConstTest.cpp(24) : error C3892: 'b' : you
   cannot assign to a variable that is const
c:\examples\ch08\fig08_14\ConstTest.cpp(25) : error C3892: 'b' : you
   cannot assign to a variable that is const
```

Fig. 8.14 | const type qualifier applied to an array parameter.

duces the error error C3892: 'b' : you cannot assign to a variable that is const.
This message indicates that using a const object (e.g., b[0]) as an *lvalue* is an error—you
cannot assign a new value to a const object by placing it on the left of an assignment operator. Note that compiler error messages vary between compilers (as shown in Fig. 8.14).
The const qualifier will be discussed again in Chapter 11.

Common Programming Error 8.10

*Forgetting that arrays in the caller are passed by reference, and hence can be modified in called
functions, may result in logic errors.*

Software Engineering Observation 8.4

*Applying the const type qualifier to an array parameter in a function definition to prevent the
original array from being modified in the function body is another example of the principle of
least privilege. Functions should not be given the capability to modify an array unless it is
absolutely necessary.*

8.6 Case Study: Class GradeBook Using an Array to Store Grades

This section further evolves class GradeBook, introduced in Chapter 4 and expanded in Chapters 5–7. Recall that this class represents a grade book used by a professor to store and analyze student grades. Previous versions of the class process grades entered by the user, but do not maintain the individual grade values in the class's data members. Thus, repeat calculations require the user to reenter the grades. One way to solve this problem would be to store each grade entered in an individual data member of the class. For example, we could create data members grade1, grade2, ..., grade10 in class GradeBook to store 10 student grades. However, the code to total the grades and determine the class average would be cumbersome. In this section, we solve this problem by storing grades in an array.

Storing Student Grades in an Array in Class GradeBook

The version of class GradeBook (Figs. 8.15–8.16) presented here uses an array of integers to store the grades of several students on a single exam. This eliminates the need to repeatedly input the same set of grades. Array grades is declared as a data member in line 29 of Fig. 8.15—therefore, each GradeBook object maintains its own set of grades.

```cpp
1   // Fig. 8.15: GradeBook.h
2   // Definition of class GradeBook that uses an array to store test grades.
3   // Member functions are defined in GradeBook.cpp
4
5   #include <string> // program uses C++ Standard Library string class
6   using std::string;
7
8   // GradeBook class definition
9   class GradeBook
10  {
11  public:
12     // constant -- number of students who took the test
13     const static int students = 10; // note public data
14
15     // constructor initializes course name and array of grades
16     GradeBook( string, const int [] );
17
18     void setCourseName( string ); // function to set the course name
19     string getCourseName(); // function to retrieve the course name
20     void displayMessage(); // display a welcome message
21     void processGrades(); // perform various operations on the grade data
22     int getMinimum(); // find the minimum grade for the test
23     int getMaximum(); // find the maximum grade for the test
24     double getAverage(); // determine the average grade for the test
25     void outputBarChart(); // output bar chart of grade distribution
26     void outputGrades(); // output the contents of the grades array
27  private:
28     string courseName; // course name for this grade book
29     int grades[ students ]; // array of student grades
30  }; // end class GradeBook
```

Fig. 8.15 | Definition of class GradeBook using an array to store test grades.

```cpp
1   // Fig. 8.16: GradeBook.cpp
2   // Member-function definitions for class GradeBook that
3   // uses an array to store test grades.
4   #include <iostream>
5   using std::cout;
6   using std::cin;
7   using std::endl;
8   using std::fixed;
9
10  #include <iomanip>
11  using std::setprecision;
12  using std::setw;
13
14  #include "GradeBook.h" // GradeBook class definition
15
16  // constructor initializes courseName and grades array
17  GradeBook::GradeBook( string name, const int gradesArray[] )
18  {
19     setCourseName( name ); // initialize courseName
20
21     // copy grades from gradesArray to grades data member
22     for ( int grade = 0; grade < students; grade++ )
23        grades[ grade ] = gradesArray[ grade ];
24  } // end GradeBook constructor
25
26  // function to set the course name
27  void GradeBook::setCourseName( string name )
28  {
29     courseName = name; // store the course name
30  } // end function setCourseName
31
32  // function to retrieve the course name
33  string GradeBook::getCourseName()
34  {
35     return courseName;
36  } // end function getCourseName
37
38  // display a welcome message to the GradeBook user
39  void GradeBook::displayMessage()
40  {
41     // this statement calls getCourseName to get the
42     // name of the course this GradeBook represents
43     cout << "Welcome to the grade book for\n" << getCourseName() << "!"
44        << endl;
45  } // end function displayMessage
46
47  // perform various operations on the data
48  void GradeBook::processGrades()
49  {
50     // output grades array
51     outputGrades();
52
```

Fig. 8.16 | GradeBook class member functions manipulating an array of grades. (Part 1 of 3.)

```
53      // call function getAverage to calculate the average grade
54      cout << "\nClass average is " << setprecision( 2 ) << fixed <<
55         getAverage() << endl;
56
57      // call functions getMinimum and getMaximum
58      cout << "Lowest grade is " << getMinimum() << "\nHighest grade is "
59         << getMaximum() << endl;
60
61      // call function outputBarChart to print grade distribution chart
62      outputBarChart();
63   } // end function processGrades
64
65   // find minimum grade
66   int GradeBook::getMinimum()
67   {
68      int lowGrade = 100; // assume lowest grade is 100
69
70      // loop through grades array
71      for ( int grade = 0; grade < students; grade++ )
72      {
73         // if current grade lower than lowGrade, assign it to lowGrade
74         if ( grades[ grade ] < lowGrade )
75            lowGrade = grades[ grade ]; // new lowest grade
76      } // end for
77
78      return lowGrade; // return lowest grade
79   } // end function getMinimum
80
81   // find maximum grade
82   int GradeBook::getMaximum()
83   {
84      int highGrade = 0; // assume highest grade is 0
85
86      // loop through grades array
87      for ( int grade = 0; grade < students; grade++ )
88      {
89         // if current grade higher than highGrade, assign it to highGrade
90         if ( grades[ grade ] > highGrade )
91            highGrade = grades[ grade ]; // new highest grade
92      } // end for
93
94      return highGrade; // return highest grade
95   } // end function getMaximum
96
97   // determine average grade for test
98   double GradeBook::getAverage()
99   {
100     int total = 0; // initialize total
101
102     // sum grades in array
103     for ( int grade = 0; grade < students; grade++ )
104        total += grades[ grade ];
105
```

Fig. 8.16 | GradeBook class member functions manipulating an array of grades. (Part 2 of 3.)

```
106    // return average of grades
107    return static_cast< double >( total ) / students;
108 } // end function getAverage
109
110 // output bar chart displaying grade distribution
111 void GradeBook::outputBarChart()
112 {
113    cout << "\nGrade distribution:" << endl;
114
115    // stores frequency of grades in each range of 10 grades
116    const int frequencySize = 11;
117    int frequency[ frequencySize ] = {}; // initialize elements to 0
118
119    // for each grade, increment the appropriate frequency
120    for ( int grade = 0; grade < students; grade++ )
121       frequency[ grades[ grade ] / 10 ]++;
122
123    // for each grade frequency, print bar in chart
124    for ( int count = 0; count < frequencySize; count++ )
125    {
126       // output bar labels ("0-9:", ..., "90-99:", "100:" )
127       if ( count == 0 )
128          cout << "  0-9: ";
129       else if ( count == 10 )
130          cout << "  100: ";
131       else
132          cout << count * 10 << "-" << ( count * 10 ) + 9 << ": ";
133
134       // print bar of asterisks
135       for ( int stars = 0; stars < frequency[ count ]; stars++ )
136          cout << '*';
137
138       cout << endl; // start a new line of output
139    } // end outer for
140 } // end function outputBarChart
141
142 // output the contents of the grades array
143 void GradeBook::outputGrades()
144 {
145    cout << "\nThe grades are:\n\n";
146
147    // output each student's grade
148    for ( int student = 0; student < students; student++ )
149       cout << "Student " << setw( 2 ) << student + 1 << ": " << setw( 3 )
150          << grades[ student ] << endl;
151 } // end function outputGrades
```

Fig. 8.16 | GradeBook class member functions manipulating an array of grades. (Part 3 of 3.)

Note that the size of the array in line 29 of Fig. 8.15 is specified by public const static data member students (declared in line 13). This data member is public so that it is accessible to the clients of the class. We'll soon see an example of a client program using this constant. Declaring students with the const qualifier indicates that this data member is constant—its value cannot be changed after being initialized. Keyword static in this variable declaration indicates that the data member is shared by all objects of the class—all GradeBook objects store grades for the same number of students. Recall from Section 4.6 that when each object of a class maintains its own copy of an attribute, the variable that represents the attribute is known as a data member—each object (instance) of the class has a separate copy of the variable in memory. There are variables for which each object of a class does not have a separate copy. That is the case with static data members, which are also known as *class variables*. When objects of a class containing static data members are created, all the objects share one copy of the class's static data members. A static data member can be accessed within the class definition and the member-function definitions like any other data member. As you'll soon see, a public static data member can also be accessed outside of the class, even when no objects of the class exist, using the class name followed by the binary scope resolution operator (::) and the name of the data member. You'll learn more about static data members in Chapter 11.

The class's constructor (declared in line 16 of Fig. 8.15 and defined in lines 17–24 of Fig. 8.16) has two parameters—the course name and an array of grades. When a program creates a GradeBook object (e.g., line 13 of GradeBookTest.cpp), the program passes an existing int array to the constructor, which copies the array's values into the data member grades (lines 22–23 of Fig. 8.16). The grade values in the passed array could have been input from a user or read from a file on disk (as discussed in Chapter 17). In our test program, we simply initialize an array with a set of grade values (Fig. 8.17, lines 10–11). Once the grades are stored in data member grades of class GradeBook, all the class's member functions can access the grades array as needed to perform various calculations.

Member function processGrades (declared in line 21 of Fig. 8.15 and defined in lines 48–63 of Fig. 8.16) contains a series of member-function calls that output a report summarizing the grades. Line 51 calls member function outputGrades to print the con-

```
1   // Fig. 8.17: GradeBookTest.cpp
2   // Creates GradeBook object using an array of grades.
3
4   #include "GradeBook.h" // GradeBook class definition
5
6   // function main begins program execution
7   int main()
8   {
9      // array of student grades
10     int gradesArray[ GradeBook::students ] =
11        { 87, 68, 94, 100, 83, 78, 85, 91, 76, 87 };
12
13     GradeBook myGradeBook(
14        "CS101 Introduction to Visual C++ Programming", gradesArray );
15     myGradeBook.displayMessage();
16     myGradeBook.processGrades();
17     return 0;
18  } // end main
```

Fig. 8.17 | Creating a GradeBook object using an array of grades, then invoking member function processGrades to analyze them. (Part 1 of 2.)

```
Welcome to the grade book for
CS101 Introduction to Visual C++ Programming!

The grades are:

Student  1:  87
Student  2:  68
Student  3:  94
Student  4: 100
Student  5:  83
Student  6:  78
Student  7:  85
Student  8:  91
Student  9:  76
Student 10:  87

Class average is 84.90
Lowest grade is 68
Highest grade is 100

Grade distribution:
  0-9:
 10-19:
 20-29:
 30-39:
 40-49:
 50-59:
 60-69: *
 70-79: **
 80-89: ****
 90-99: **
   100: *
```

Fig. 8.17 | Creating a GradeBook object using an array of grades, then invoking member function processGrades to analyze them. (Part 2 of 2.)

tents of the array grades. Lines 148–150 in member function outputGrades use a for statement to output each student's grade. Although array indices start at 0, a professor would typically number students at 1. Thus, lines 149–150 output student + 1 as the student number to produce grade labels "Student 1: ", "Student 2: ", and so on.

Member function processGrades next calls member function getAverage (lines 54–55) to obtain the average of the grades in the array. Member function getAverage (declared in line 24 of Fig. 8.15 and defined in lines 98–108 of Fig. 8.16) uses a for statement to total the values in array grades before calculating the average. Note that the averaging calculation in line 107 uses const static data member students to determine the number of grades being averaged.

Lines 58–59 in member function processGrades call member functions getMinimum and getMaximum to determine the lowest and highest grades of any student on the exam, respectively. Let's examine how member function getMinimum finds the *lowest* grade. Because the highest grade allowed is 100, we begin by assuming that 100 is the lowest grade (line 68). Then, we compare each of the elements in the array to the lowest grade, looking for smaller values. Lines 71–76 in member function getMinimum loop through the array, and lines 74–75 compare each grade to lowGrade. If a grade is less than lowGrade, lowGrade is set to that grade. When line 78 executes, lowGrade contains the lowest grade in the array. Member function getMaximum (lines 82–95) works similarly to member function getMinimum.

Finally, line 62 in member function processGrades calls member function output-BarChart to print a distribution chart of the grade data using a technique similar to that in Fig. 8.9. In that example, we manually calculated the number of grades in each category (i.e., 0–9, 10–19, …, 90–99 and 100) by simply looking at a set of grades. In this example, lines 120–121 use a technique similar to that in Fig. 8.10 and Fig. 8.11 to calculate the frequency of grades in each category. Line 117 declares and creates array frequency of 11 ints to store the frequency of grades in each grade category. For each grade in array grades, lines 120–121 increment the appropriate element of the frequency array. To determine which element to increment, line 121 divides the current grade by 10 using integer division. For example, if grade is 85, line 121 increments frequency[8] to update the count of grades in the range 80–89. Lines 124–139 next print the bar chart (see Fig. 8.17) based on the values in array frequency. Like lines 29–30 of Fig. 8.9, lines 135–136 of Fig. 8.16 use a value in array frequency to determine the number of asterisks to display in each bar.

Testing Class GradeBook
The program of Fig. 8.17 creates an object of class GradeBook (Figs. 8.15–8.16) using the int array gradesArray (declared and initialized in lines 10–11). Note that we use the binary scope resolution operator (::) in the expression "GradeBook::students" (line 10) to access class GradeBook's static constant students. We use this constant here to create an array that is the same size as array grades stored as a data member in class GradeBook. Lines 13–14 pass a course name and gradesArray to the GradeBook constructor. Line 15 displays a welcome message, and line 16 invokes the GradeBook object's processGrades member function. The output reveals the summary of the 10 grades in myGradeBook.

8.7 Searching Arrays with Linear Search

Often a programmer will be working with large amounts of data stored in arrays. It may be necessary to determine whether an array contains a value that matches a certain *key value*. The process of finding a particular element of an array is called *searching*. In this section we discuss the simple linear search. Exercise 8.35 at the end of this chapter asks you to implement a recursive version of the linear search. In Chapter 20, Searching and Sorting, we present the more complex, yet more efficient, binary search.

Linear Search
The *linear search* (Fig. 8.18, lines 37–44) compares each element of an array with a *search key* (line 40). Because the array is not in any particular order, it is just as likely that the value will be found in the first element as the last. On average, therefore, the program must compare the search key with half the elements of the array. To determine that a value is not in the array, the program must compare the search key to every element of the array.

The linear searching method works well for small arrays or for unsorted arrays (i.e., arrays whose elements are in no particular order). However, for large arrays, linear searching is inefficient. If the array is sorted (e.g., its elements are in ascending order), you can use the high-speed binary search technique that you'll learn about in Chapter 20, Searching and Sorting.

```cpp
 1   // Fig. 8.18: LinearSearch.cpp
 2   // Linear search of an array.
 3   #include <iostream>
 4   using std::cout;
 5   using std::cin;
 6   using std::endl;
 7
 8   int linearSearch( const int [], int, int ); // prototype
 9
10   int main()
11   {
12      const int arraySize = 100; // size of array a
13      int a[ arraySize ]; // create array a
14      int searchKey; // value to locate in array a
15
16      for ( int i = 0; i < arraySize; i++ )
17         a[ i ] = 2 * i; // create some data
18
19      cout << "Enter integer search key: ";
20      cin >> searchKey;
21
22      // attempt to locate searchKey in array a
23      int element = linearSearch( a, searchKey, arraySize );
24
25      // display results
26      if ( element != -1 )
27         cout << "Found value in element " << element << endl;
28      else
29         cout << "Value not found" << endl;
30
31      return 0; // indicates successful termination
32   } // end main
33
34   // compare key to every element of array until location is
35   // found or until end of array is reached; return subscript of
36   // element if key or -1 if key not found
37   int linearSearch( const int array[], int key, int sizeOfArray )
38   {
39      for ( int j = 0; j < sizeOfArray; j++ )
40         if ( array[ j ] == key ) // if found,
41            return j; // return location of key
42
43      return -1; // key not found
44   } // end function linearSearch
```

```
Enter integer search key: 36
Found value in element 18
```

```
Enter integer search key: 37
Value not found
```

Fig. 8.18 | Linear search of an array.

8.8 Sorting Arrays with Insertion Sort

Sorting data (i.e., placing the data into some particular order such as ascending or descending) is one of the most important computing applications. A bank sorts all checks by account number so that it can prepare individual bank statements at the end of each month. Telephone companies sort their phone directories by last name and, within that, by first name to make it easy to find phone numbers. Virtually every organization must sort some data and, in many cases, massive amounts of it. Sorting data is an intriguing problem that has attracted some of the most intense research efforts in the field of computer science. In this chapter, we discuss a simple sorting scheme. In the exercises and Chapter 20, we investigate more complex schemes that yield superior performance, and we introduce Big O (pronounced "Big Oh") notation for characterizing how hard each scheme must work to accomplish its task.

Performance Tip 8.4

Sometimes, simple algorithms perform poorly. Their virtue is that they are easy to write, test and debug. More complex algorithms are sometimes needed to realize optimal performance.

Insertion Sort

The program in Fig. 8.19 sorts the values of the 10-element array `data` into ascending order. The technique we use is called *insertion sort*—a simple, but inefficient, sorting algorithm. The first iteration of this algorithm takes the second element and, if it is less than the first element, swaps it with the first element (i.e., the program *inserts* the second element in front of the first element). The second iteration looks at the third element and inserts it into the correct position with respect to the first two elements, so all three elements are in order. At the ith iteration of this algorithm, the first i elements in the original array will be sorted.

```cpp
1   // Fig. 8.19: AscendingSort.cpp
2   // This program sorts an array's values into ascending order.
3   #include <iostream>
4   using std::cout;
5   using std::endl;
6
7   #include <iomanip>
8   using std::setw;
9
10  int main()
11  {
12     const int arraySize = 10; // size of array a
13     int data[ arraySize ] = { 34, 56, 4, 10, 77, 51, 93, 30, 5, 52 };
14     int insert; // temporary variable to hold element to insert
15
16     cout << "Unsorted array:\n";
17
18     // output original array
19     for ( int i = 0; i < arraySize; i++ )
20        cout << setw( 4 ) << data[ i ];
```

Fig. 8.19 | Sorting an array with insertion sort. (Part 1 of 2.)

```
21
22      // insertion sort
23      // loop over the elements of the array
24      for ( int next = 1; next < arraySize; next++ )
25      {
26         insert = data[ next ]; // store the value in the current element
27
28         int moveItem = next; // initialize location to place element
29
30         // search for the location in which to put the current element
31         while ( ( moveItem > 0 ) && ( data[ moveItem - 1 ] > insert ) )
32         {
33            // shift element one slot to the right
34            data[ moveItem ] = data[ moveItem - 1 ];
35            moveItem--;
36         } // end while
37
38         data[ moveItem ] = insert; // place inserted element into the array
39      } // end for
40
41      cout << "\nSorted array:\n";
42
43      // output sorted array
44      for ( int i = 0; i < arraySize; i++ )
45         cout << setw( 4 ) << data[ i ];
46
47      cout << endl;
48      return 0; // indicates successful termination
49   } // end main
```

```
Unsorted array:
  34  56   4  10  77  51  93  30   5  52
Sorted array:
   4   5  10  30  34  51  52  56  77  93
```

Fig. 8.19 | Sorting an array with insertion sort. (Part 2 of 2.)

Line 13 of Fig. 8.19 declares and initializes array data with the following values:

    34   56   4   10   77   51   93   30   5   52

The program first looks at data[0] and data[1], whose values are 34 and 56, respectively. These two elements are already in order, so the program continues—if they were out of order, the program would swap them.

In the second iteration, the program looks at the value of data[2], 4. This value is less than 56, so the program stores 4 in a temporary variable and moves 56 one element to the right. The program then checks and determines that 4 is less than 34, so it moves 34 one element to the right. The program has now reached the beginning of the array, so it places 4 in data[0]. The array now is

    4   34   56   10   77   51   93   30   5   52

In the third iteration, the program stores the value of data[3], 10, in a temporary variable. Then the program compares 10 to 56 and moves 56 one element to the right because it is larger than 10. The program then compares 10 to 34, moving 34 right one element. When the program compares 10 to 4, it observes that 10 is larger than 4 and places 10 in data[1]. The array now is

4   10   34   56   77   51   93   30   5   52

Using this algorithm, at the ith iteration, the first i elements of the original array are sorted. They may not be in their final locations, however, because smaller values may be located later in the array.

The sorting is performed by the for statement in lines 24–39 that loops over the elements of the array. In each iteration, line 26 temporarily stores in variable insert (declared in line 14) the value of the element that will be inserted into the sorted portion of the array. Line 28 declares and initializes the variable moveItem, which keeps track of where to insert the element. Lines 31–36 loop to locate the correct position where the element should be inserted. The loop terminates either when the program reaches the front of the array or when it reaches an element that is less than the value to be inserted. Line 34 moves an element to the right, and line 35 decrements the position at which to insert the next element. After the while loop ends, line 38 inserts the element into place. When the for statement in lines 24–39 terminates, the elements of the array are sorted.

The chief virtue of the insertion sort is that it is easy to program; however, it runs slowly. This becomes apparent when sorting large arrays. In the exercises, we'll investigate some alternate algorithms for sorting an array. We investigate sorting and searching in greater depth in Chapter 20.

8.9 Multidimensional Arrays

Arrays with two or more dimensions are known as *multidimensional arrays*. Arrays with two dimensions often represent *tables of values* consisting of information arranged in *rows* and *columns*. To identify a particular table element, we must specify two subscripts. By convention, the first identifies the element's row and the second identifies the element's column. Arrays that require two subscripts to identify a particular element are called *two-dimensional arrays* or *2-D arrays*. Note that multidimensional arrays can have more than two dimensions (i.e., subscripts). Figure 8.20 illustrates a two-dimensional array, a. The array contains three rows and four columns, so it is said to be a 3-by-4 array. In general, an array with *m* rows and *n* columns is called an *m-by-n array*.

Every element in array a is identified in Fig. 8.20 by an element name of the form a[i][j], where a is the name of the array, and i and j are the subscripts that uniquely identify each element in a. Notice that the names of the elements in row 0 all have a first subscript of 0; the names of the elements in column 3 all have a second subscript of 3.

Common Programming Error 8.11

In native C++ referencing a two-dimensional array element a[x][y] incorrectly as a[x, y] is an error. Actually, a[x, y] is treated as a[y], because C++ evaluates the expression x, y (containing a comma operator) simply as y (the last of the comma-separated expressions).

A multidimensional array can be initialized in its declaration much like a one-dimensional array. For example, a two-dimensional array b with values 1 and 2 in its row-0 elements and values 3 and 4 in its row-1 elements could be declared and initialized with

```
int b[ 2 ][ 2 ] = { { 1, 2 }, { 3, 4 } };
```

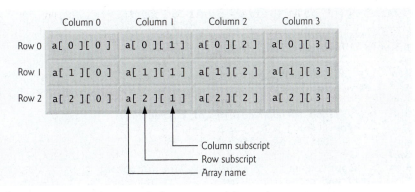

Fig. 8.20 | Two-dimensional array with three rows and four columns.

The values are grouped by row in braces. So, 1 and 2 initialize b[0][0] and b[0][1], respectively, and 3 and 4 initialize b[1][0] and b[1][1], respectively. If there are not enough initializers for a given row, the remaining elements of that row are initialized to 0. Thus, the declaration

> **int** b[2][2] = { { 1 }, { 3, 4 } };

initializes b[0][0] to 1, b[0][1] to 0, b[1][0] to 3 and b[1][1] to 4.

Figure 8.21 demonstrates initializing two-dimensional arrays in declarations. Lines 11–13 declare three arrays, each with two rows and three columns.

```cpp
1   // Fig. 8.21: MultidimensionalArray.cpp
2   // Initializing multidimensional arrays.
3   #include <iostream>
4   using std::cout;
5   using std::endl;
6
7   void printArray( const int [][ 3 ] ); // prototype
8
9   int main()
10  {
11      int array1[ 2 ][ 3 ] = { { 1, 2, 3 }, { 4, 5, 6 } };
12      int array2[ 2 ][ 3 ] = { 1, 2, 3, 4, 5 };
13      int array3[ 2 ][ 3 ] = { { 1, 2 }, { 4 } };
14
15      cout << "Values in array1 by row are:" << endl;
16      printArray( array1 );
17
18      cout << "\nValues in array2 by row are:" << endl;
19      printArray( array2 );
20
21      cout << "\nValues in array3 by row are:" << endl;
22      printArray( array3 );
23      return 0; // indicates successful termination
24  } // end main
```

Fig. 8.21 | Initializing multidimensional arrays. (Part 1 of 2.)

```
25
26   // output array with two rows and three columns
27   void printArray( const int a[][ 3 ] )
28   {
29      // loop through array's rows
30      for ( int i = 0; i < 2; i++ )
31      {
32         // loop through columns of current row
33         for ( int j = 0; j < 3; j++ )
34            cout << a[ i ][ j ] << ' ';
35
36         cout << endl; // start new line of output
37      } // end outer for
38   } // end function printArray
```

```
Values in array1 by row are:
1 2 3
4 5 6

Values in array2 by row are:
1 2 3
4 5 0

Values in array3 by row are:
1 2 0
4 0 0
```

Fig. 8.21 | Initializing multidimensional arrays. (Part 2 of 2.)

The declaration of array1 (line 11) provides six initializers in two sublists. The first sublist initializes row 0 of the array to the values 1, 2 and 3; and the second sublist initializes row 1 of the array to the values 4, 5 and 6. If the braces around each sublist are removed from the array1 initializer list, the compiler initializes the elements of row 0 followed by the elements of row 1, yielding the same result.

The declaration of array2 (line 12) provides only five initializers. The initializers are assigned to row 0, then row 1. Any elements that do not have an explicit initializer are initialized to zero, so array2[1][2] is initialized to zero.

The declaration of array3 (line 13) provides three initializers in two sublists. The sublist for row 0 explicitly initializes the first two elements of row 0 to 1 and 2; the third element is implicitly initialized to zero. The sublist for row 1 explicitly initializes the first element to 4 and implicitly initializes the last two elements to zero.

The program calls function printArray to output each array's elements. Notice that the function definition (lines 27–38) specifies the parameter const int a[][3]. When a function receives a one-dimensional array as an argument, the array brackets are empty in the function's parameter list. The size of the first dimension (i.e., the number of rows) of a two-dimensional array is not required either, but all subsequent dimension sizes are required. The compiler uses these sizes to determine the locations in memory of elements in multidimensional arrays. All array elements are stored consecutively in memory, regardless of the number of dimensions. In a two-dimensional array, row 0 is stored in memory followed by row 1. In a two-dimensional array, each row is a one-dimensional array. To locate an element in a particular row, the function must know exactly how many elements are in each row so it can skip the proper number of memory locations when accessing the array. Thus, when accessing a[1][2], the function knows to skip row 0's three elements in memory to get to row 1. Then, the function accesses element 2 of that row.

Many common array manipulations use for repetition statements. For example, the following for statement sets all the elements in row 2 of array a in Fig. 8.20 to zero:

```
for ( column = 0; column < 4; column++ )
    a[ 2 ][ column ] = 0;
```

The for statement varies only the second subscript (i.e., the column subscript). The preceding for statement is equivalent to the following assignment statements:

```
a[ 2 ][ 0 ] = 0;
a[ 2 ][ 1 ] = 0;
a[ 2 ][ 2 ] = 0;
a[ 2 ][ 3 ] = 0;
```

The following nested for statement determines the total of all the elements in array a:

```
total = 0;

for ( row = 0; row < 3; row++ )

    for ( column = 0; column < 4; column++ )
        total += a[ row ][ column ];
```

The for statement totals the elements of the array one row at a time. The outer for statement begins by setting row (i.e., the row subscript) to 0, so the elements of row 0 may be totaled by the inner for statement. The outer for statement then increments row to 1, so the elements of row 1 can be totaled. Then, the outer for statement increments row to 2, so the elements of row 2 can be totaled. When the nested for statement terminates, total contains the sum of all the array elements.

8.10 Case Study: Class GradeBook Using a Two-Dimensional Array

In Section 8.6, we presented class GradeBook (Figs. 8.15–8.16), which used a one-dimensional array to store student grades on a single exam. In most semesters, students take several exams. Professors are likely to want to analyze grades across the entire semester, both for a single student and for the class as a whole.

Storing Student Grades in a Two-Dimensional Array in Class GradeBook

Figures 8.22–8.23 contain a version of class GradeBook that uses a two-dimensional array grades to store the grades of a number of students on multiple exams. Each row of the array represents a single student's grades for the entire course, and each column represents all the grades the students earned for one particular exam. A client program, such as GradeBookTest.cpp, passes the array as an argument to the GradeBook constructor. In this example, we use a ten-by-three array containing ten students' grades on three exams.

```
1   // Fig. 8.22: GradeBook.h
2   // Definition of class GradeBook that uses a
3   // two-dimensional array to store test grades.
4   // Member functions are defined in GradeBook.cpp
5   #include <string> // program uses C++ Standard Library string class
6   using std::string;
7
8   // GradeBook class definition
9   class GradeBook
10  {
11  public:
12     // constants
13     const static int students = 10; // number of students
14     const static int tests = 3; // number of tests
15
16     // constructor initializes course name and array of grades
17     GradeBook( string, const int [][ tests ] );
18
19     void setCourseName( string ); // function to set the course name
20     string getCourseName(); // function to retrieve the course name
21     void displayMessage(); // display a welcome message
22     void processGrades(); // perform various operations on the grade data
23     int getMinimum(); // find the minimum grade in the grade book
24     int getMaximum(); // find the maximum grade in the grade book
25     double getAverage( const int [], const int ); // get student's average
26     void outputBarChart(); // output bar chart of grade distribution
27     void outputGrades(); // output the contents of the grades array
28  private:
29     string courseName; // course name for this grade book
30     int grades[ students ][ tests ]; // two-dimensional array of grades
31  }; // end class GradeBook
```

Fig. 8.22 | Definition of class `GradeBook` with a two-dimensional array to store grades.

```
1   // Fig. 8.23: GradeBook.cpp
2   // Member-function definitions for class GradeBook that
3   // uses a two-dimensional array to store grades.
4   #include <iostream>
5   using std::cout;
6   using std::cin;
7   using std::endl;
8   using std::fixed;
9
10  #include <iomanip> // parameterized stream manipulators
11  using std::setprecision; // sets numeric output precision
12  using std::setw; // sets field width
13
14  // include definition of class GradeBook from GradeBook.h
15  #include "GradeBook.h"
16
```

Fig. 8.23 | GradeBook class member-function definitions manipulating a two-dimensional array of grades. (Part 1 of 5.)

```
17   // two-argument constructor initializes courseName and grades array
18   GradeBook::GradeBook( string name, const int gradesArray[][ tests ] )
19   {
20      setCourseName( name ); // initialize courseName
21
22      // copy grades from gradeArray to grades
23      for ( int student = 0; student < students; student++ )
24
25         for ( int test = 0; test < tests; test++ )
26            grades[ student ][ test ] = gradesArray[ student ][ test ];
27   } // end two-argument GradeBook constructor
28
29   // function to set the course name
30   void GradeBook::setCourseName( string name )
31   {
32      courseName = name; // store the course name
33   } // end function setCourseName
34
35   // function to retrieve the course name
36   string GradeBook::getCourseName()
37   {
38      return courseName;
39   } // end function getCourseName
40
41   // display a welcome message to the GradeBook user
42   void GradeBook::displayMessage()
43   {
44      // this statement calls getCourseName to get the
45      // name of the course this GradeBook represents
46      cout << "Welcome to the grade book for\n" << getCourseName() << "!"
47         << endl;
48   } // end function displayMessage
49
50   // perform various operations on the data
51   void GradeBook::processGrades()
52   {
53      // output grades array
54      outputGrades();
55
56      // call functions getMinimum and getMaximum
57      cout << "\nLowest grade in the grade book is " << getMinimum()
58         << "\nHighest grade in the grade book is " << getMaximum() << endl;
59
60      // output grade distribution chart of all grades on all tests
61      outputBarChart();
62   } // end function processGrades
63
64   // find minimum grade in the entire gradebook
65   int GradeBook::getMinimum()
66   {
67      int lowGrade = 100; // assume lowest grade is 100
```

Fig. 8.23 | GradeBook class member-function definitions manipulating a two-dimensional array of grades. (Part 2 of 5.)

```
68
69        // loop through rows of grades array
70        for ( int student = 0; student < students; student++ )
71        {
72           // loop through columns of current row
73           for ( int test = 0; test < tests; test++ )
74           {
75              // if current grade less than lowGrade, assign it to lowGrade
76              if ( grades[ student ][ test ] < lowGrade )
77                 lowGrade = grades[ student ][ test ]; // new lowest grade
78           } // end inner for
79        } // end outer for
80
81        return lowGrade; // return lowest grade
82     } // end function getMinimum
83
84     // find maximum grade in the entire gradebook
85     int GradeBook::getMaximum()
86     {
87        int highGrade = 0; // assume highest grade is 0
88
89        // loop through rows of grades array
90        for ( int student = 0; student < students; student++ )
91        {
92           // loop through columns of current row
93           for ( int test = 0; test < tests; test++ )
94           {
95              // if current grade greater than lowGrade, assign it to highGrade
96              if ( grades[ student ][ test ] > highGrade )
97                 highGrade = grades[ student ][ test ]; // new highest grade
98           } // end inner for
99        } // end outer for
100
101       return highGrade; // return highest grade
102    } // end function getMaximum
103
104    // determine average grade for particular set of grades
105    double GradeBook::getAverage( const int setOfGrades[], const int grades )
106    {
107       int total = 0; // initialize total
108
109       // sum grades in array
110       for ( int grade = 0; grade < grades; grade++ )
111          total += setOfGrades[ grade ];
112
113       // return average of grades
114       return static_cast< double >( total ) / grades;
115    } // end function getAverage
116
117    // output bar chart displaying grade distribution
118    void GradeBook::outputBarChart()
119    {
```

Fig. 8.23 | GradeBook class member-function definitions manipulating a two-dimensional array of grades. (Part 3 of 5.)

```
120        cout << "\nOverall grade distribution:" << endl;
121
122        // stores frequency of grades in each range of 10 grades
123        const int frequencySize = 11;
124        int frequency[ frequencySize ] = {}; // initialize elements to 0
125
126        // for each grade, increment the appropriate frequency
127        for ( int student = 0; student < students; student++ )
128
129            for ( int test = 0; test < tests; test++ )
130                ++frequency[ grades[ student ][ test ] / 10 ];
131
132        // for each grade frequency, print bar in chart
133        for ( int count = 0; count < frequencySize; count++ )
134        {
135            // output bar label ("0-9:", ..., "90-99:", "100:" )
136            if ( count == 0 )
137                cout << "  0-9: ";
138            else if ( count == 10 )
139                cout << "  100: ";
140            else
141                cout << count * 10 << "-" << ( count * 10 ) + 9 << ": ";
142
143            // print bar of asterisks
144            for ( int stars = 0; stars < frequency[ count ]; stars++ )
145                cout << '*';
146
147            cout << endl; // start a new line of output
148        } // end outer for
149    } // end function outputBarChart
150
151    // output the contents of the grades array
152    void GradeBook::outputGrades()
153    {
154        cout << "\nThe grades are:\n\n";
155        cout << "              "; // align column heads
156
157        // create a column heading for each of the tests
158        for ( int test = 0; test < tests; test++ )
159            cout << "Test " << test + 1 << "  ";
160
161        cout << "Average" << endl; // student average column heading
162
163        // create rows/columns of text representing array grades
164        for ( int student = 0; student < students; student++ )
165        {
166            cout << "Student " << setw( 2 ) << student + 1;
167
168            // output student's grades
169            for ( int test = 0; test < tests; test++ )
170                cout << setw( 8 ) << grades[ student ][ test ];
```

Fig. 8.23 | GradeBook class member-function definitions manipulating a two-dimensional array of grades. (Part 4 of 5.)

```
171
172            // call member function getAverage to calculate student's average;
173            // pass row of grades and the value of tests as the arguments
174            double average = getAverage( grades[ student ], tests );
175            cout << setw( 9 ) << setprecision( 2 ) << fixed << average << endl;
176        } // end outer for
177    } // end function outputGrades
```

Fig. 8.23 | GradeBook class member-function definitions manipulating a two-dimensional array of grades. (Part 5 of 5.)

Five member functions (declared in lines 23–27 of Fig. 8.22) perform array manipulations to process the grades. Each of these member functions is similar to its counterpart in the earlier one-dimensional array version of class GradeBook (Figs. 8.15–8.16). Member function getMinimum (defined in lines 65–82 of Fig. 8.23) determines the lowest grade of any student for the semester. Member function getMaximum (defined in lines 85–102 of Fig. 8.23) determines the highest grade of any student for the semester. Member function getAverage (lines 105–115 of Fig. 8.23) determines a particular student's semester average. Member function outputBarChart (lines 118–149 of Fig. 8.23) outputs a bar chart of the distribution of all student grades for the semester. Member function output-Grades (lines 152–177 of Fig. 8.23) outputs the two-dimensional array in a tabular format, along with each student's semester average.

Member functions getMinimum, getMaximum, outputBarChart and outputGrades each loop through array grades by using nested for statements. For example, consider the nested for statement in member function getMinimum (lines 70–79). The outer for statement begins by setting student (i.e., the row subscript) to 0, so the elements of row 0 can be compared with variable lowGrade in the body of the inner for statement. The inner for statement loops through the grades of a particular row and compares each grade with lowGrade. If a grade is less than lowGrade, lowGrade is set to that grade. The outer for statement then increments the row subscript to 1. The elements of row 1 are compared with variable lowGrade. The outer for statement then increments the row subscript to 2, and the elements of row 2 are compared with variable lowGrade. This repeats until all rows of grades have been traversed. When execution of the nested statement is complete, low-Grade contains the smallest grade in the two-dimensional array. Member function get-Maximum works similarly to member function getMinimum.

Member function outputBarChart in Fig. 8.23 is nearly identical to the one in Fig. 8.16. However, to output the overall grade distribution for a whole semester, the member function uses a nested for statement (lines 127–130) to create the one-dimensional array frequency based on all the grades in the two-dimensional array. The rest of the code in each of the two outputBarChart member functions that displays the chart is identical.

Member function outputGrades (lines 152–177) also uses nested for statements to output values of the array grades, in addition to each student's semester average. The output in Fig. 8.24 shows the result, which resembles the tabular format of a professor's physical grade book. Lines 158–159 print the column headings for each test. We use a counter-controlled for statement so that we can identify each test with a number. Similarly, the for statement in lines 164–176 first outputs a row label using a counter variable to identify each student (line 166). Although array indices start at 0, note that lines 159 and 166 output test + 1 and student + 1, respectively, to produce test and student numbers starting at 1 (see Fig. 8.24). The inner for statement in lines 169–170 uses the outer for statement's counter variable student to loop through a specific row of array grades and output each student's test grade. Finally, line 174 obtains each student's semester average by passing the current row of grades (i.e., grades[student]) to member function getAverage.

Member function getAverage (lines 105–115) takes two arguments—a one-dimensional array of test results for a particular student and the number of test results in the array. When line 174 calls getAverage, the first argument is grades[student], which specifies that a particular row of the two-dimensional array grades should be passed to getAverage. For example, based on the array created in Fig. 8.24, the argument grades[1] represents the three values (a one-dimensional array of grades) stored in row 1 of the two-dimensional array grades. A two-dimensional array can be considered an array whose elements are one-dimensional arrays. Member function getAverage calculates the sum of the array elements, divides the total by the number of test results and returns the floating-point result as a double value (line 114).

Testing Class GradeBook

The program in Fig. 8.24 creates an object of class GradeBook (Figs. 8.22–8.23) using the two-dimensional array of ints named gradesArray (declared and initialized in lines 10–20). Note that line 10 accesses class GradeBook's static constants students and tests to indicate the size of each dimension of array gradesArray. Lines 22–23 pass a course name and gradesArray to the GradeBook constructor. Lines 24–25 then invoke myGradeBook's displayMessage and processGrades member functions to display a welcome message and obtain a report summarizing the students' grades for the semester, respectively.

```cpp
1   // Fig. 8.24: GradeBookTest.cpp
2   // Creates GradeBook object using a two-dimensional array of grades.
3
4   #include "GradeBook.h" // GradeBook class definition
5
6   // function main begins program execution
7   int main()
8   {
9      // two-dimensional array of student grades
10     int gradesArray[ GradeBook::students ][ GradeBook::tests ] =
11        { { 87, 96, 70 },
12          { 68, 87, 90 },
13          { 94, 100, 90 },
14          { 100, 81, 82 },
15          { 83, 65, 85 },
16          { 78, 87, 65 },
17          { 85, 75, 83 },
18          { 91, 94, 100 },
19          { 76, 72, 84 },
20          { 87, 93, 73 } };
```

Fig. 8.24 | Creating a GradeBook object using a two-dimensional array of grades, then invoking member function processGrades to analyze them. (Part 1 of 2.)

```
21
22       GradeBook myGradeBook(
23          "CS101 Introduction to Visual C++ Programming", gradesArray );
24       myGradeBook.displayMessage();
25       myGradeBook.processGrades();
26       return 0; // indicates successful termination
27    } // end main
```

```
Welcome to the grade book for
CS101 Introduction to Visual C++ Programming!

The grades are:

            Test 1  Test 2  Test 3   Average
Student  1      87      96      70     84.33
Student  2      68      87      90     81.67
Student  3      94     100      90     94.67
Student  4     100      81      82     87.67
Student  5      83      65      85     77.67
Student  6      78      87      65     76.67
Student  7      85      75      83     81.00
Student  8      91      94     100     95.00
Student  9      76      72      84     77.33
Student 10      87      93      73     84.33

Lowest grade in the grade book is 65
Highest grade in the grade book is 100

Overall grade distribution:
  0-9:
 10-19:
 20-29:
 30-39:
 40-49:
 50-59:
 60-69: ***
 70-79: ******
 80-89: ************
 90-99: *******
   100: ***
```

Fig. 8.24 | Creating a GradeBook object using a two-dimensional array of grades, then invoking member function processGrades to analyze them. (Part 2 of 2.)

8.11 Introduction to C++ Standard Library Class Template vector

We now introduce C++ Standard Library class template *vector*, which represents a more robust type of array featuring many additional capabilities. As you'll see in later chapters, C-style pointer-based arrays (i.e., the type of arrays presented thus far) have great potential for errors. For example, as mentioned earlier, a program can easily "walk off" either end of an array, because Visual C++ does not check whether subscripts fall outside the range of an array. Two arrays cannot be meaningfully compared with equality operators or relational operators. As you'll learn in Chapter 9, pointer variables (known more commonly as pointers) contain memory addresses as their values. Array names are simply pointers to where the arrays begin in memory, and, of course, two arrays will always be at different memory locations. When an array is passed to a general-purpose function designed to handle arrays of any size, the size of the array must be passed as an additional argument. Furthermore, one array cannot be assigned to another with the assignment operator(s)—array names are const pointers, and, as you'll learn in Chapter 9, a constant pointer cannot be used on the left side of an assignment operator. These and other capabilities certainly seem like "naturals" for dealing with arrays, but Visual C++ does not provide such capabilities. However, the C++ Standard Library provides class template vector to allow programmers to create a more powerful and less error-prone alternative to arrays. In Chapter 12, we present the means to implement such array capabilities as those provided by vector. You'll learn how to customize operators for use with your own classes (a technique known as operator overloading).

The vector class template is available to anyone building applications with Visual C++. The notations that the vector example uses might be unfamiliar to you, because vectors use template notation. Recall that Section 7.18 discussed function templates. In Chapter 15, Templates and Generics, we discuss class templates. For now, you should feel comfortable using class template vector by mimicking the syntax we use in this section's example. You'll deepen your understanding as we study class templates in Chapter 15. Chapter 23 presents class template vector (and several other standard Visual C++ container classes) in detail.

The program of Fig. 8.25 demonstrates capabilities provided by C++ Standard Library class template vector that are not available for C-style pointer-based arrays. Standard class template vector provides many of the same features as the Array class that we construct in Chapter 12, Operator Overloading; String and Array Objects. Standard class template vector is defined in header <vector> (line 11) and belongs to namespace std (line 12). Chapter 23 discusses the full functionality of standard class template vector.

Lines 19–20 create two vector objects that store values of type int—integers1 contains seven elements, and integers2 contains 10 elements. By default, all the elements of each vector object are set to 0. Note that vectors can be defined to store any data type, by replacing int in vector< int > with the appropriate data type. This notation, which specifies the type stored in the vector, is similar to the template notation that Section 7.18 introduced with function templates. Again, Chapter 15 discusses this syntax in detail.

Line 23 uses vector member function *size* to obtain the size (i.e., the number of elements) of integers1. Line 25 passes integers1 to function outputVector (lines 88–102), which uses square brackets, [] (line 94), to obtain the value in each element of the vector for output. Note the resemblance of this notation to that used to access the value of an array element. Lines 28 and 30 perform the same tasks for integers2.

Member function size of class template vector returns the number of elements in a vector as a value of type size_t (which represents the type unsigned int on many systems). As a result, line 90 declares the control variable i to be of type size_t, too. On some compilers, declaring i as an int causes the compiler to issue a warning message, since the loop-continuation condition (line 92) would compare a signed value (i.e., int i) and an unsigned value (i.e., a value of type size_t returned by function size).

```
1   // Fig. 8.25: Vector.cpp
2   // Demonstrating C++ Standard Library class template vector.
3   #include <iostream>
4   using std::cout;
5   using std::cin;
6   using std::endl;
7
8   #include <iomanip>
9   using std::setw;
10
11  #include <vector>
12  using std::vector;
13
14  void outputVector( const vector< int > & ); // display the vector
15  void inputVector( vector< int > & ); // input values into the vector
16
17  int main()
18  {
19     vector< int > integers1( 7 ); // 7-element vector< int >
20     vector< int > integers2( 10 ); // 10-element vector< int >
21
22     // print integers1 size and contents
23     cout << "Size of vector integers1 is " << integers1.size()
24        << "\nvector after initialization:" << endl;
25     outputVector( integers1 );
26
27     // print integers2 size and contents
28     cout << "\nSize of vector integers2 is " << integers2.size()
29        << "\nvector after initialization:" << endl;
30     outputVector( integers2 );
31
32     // input and print integers1 and integers2
33     cout << "\nEnter 17 integers:" << endl;
34     inputVector( integers1 );
35     inputVector( integers2 );
36
37     cout << "\nAfter input, the vectors contain:\n"
38        << "integers1:" << endl;
39     outputVector( integers1 );
40     cout << "integers2:" << endl;
41     outputVector( integers2 );
42
43     // use inequality (!=) operator with vector objects
44     cout << "\nEvaluating: integers1 != integers2" << endl;
45
46     if ( integers1 != integers2 )
47        cout << "integers1 and integers2 are not equal" << endl;
48
49     // create vector integers3 using integers1 as an
50     // initializer; print size and contents
51     vector< int > integers3( integers1 ); // copy constructor
52
53     cout << "\nSize of vector integers3 is " << integers3.size()
```

Fig. 8.25 | C++ Standard Library class template vector. (Part 1 of 3.)

```
54              << "\nvector after initialization:" << endl;
55      outputVector( integers3 );
56
57      // use overloaded assignment (=) operator
58      cout << "\nAssigning integers2 to integers1:" << endl;
59      integers1 = integers2; // assign integers2 to integers1
60
61      cout << "integers1:" << endl;
62      outputVector( integers1 );
63      cout << "integers2:" << endl;
64      outputVector( integers2 );
65
66      // use equality (==) operator with vector objects
67      cout << "\nEvaluating: integers1 == integers2" << endl;
68
69      if ( integers1 == integers2 )
70          cout << "integers1 and integers2 are equal" << endl;
71
72      // use square brackets to create rvalue
73      cout << "\nintegers1[5] is " << integers1[ 5 ];
74
75      // use square brackets to create lvalue
76      cout << "\n\nAssigning 1000 to integers1[5]" << endl;
77      integers1[ 5 ] = 1000;
78      cout << "integers1:" << endl;
79      outputVector( integers1 );
80
81      // attempt to use out-of-range subscript
82      cout << "\nAttempt to assign 1000 to integers1.at( 15 )" << endl;
83      integers1.at( 15 ) = 1000; // ERROR: out of range
84      return 0;
85  } // end main
86
87  // output vector contents
88  void outputVector( const vector< int > &array )
89  {
90      size_t i; // declare control variable
91
92      for ( i = 0; i < array.size(); i++ )
93      {
94          cout << setw( 12 ) << array[ i ];
95
96          if ( ( i + 1 ) % 4 == 0 ) // 4 numbers per row of output
97              cout << endl;
98      } // end for
99
100     if ( i % 4 != 0 )
101         cout << endl;
102 } // end function outputVector
103
104 // input vector contents
105 void inputVector( vector< int > &array )
106 {
```

Fig. 8.25 | C++ Standard Library class template `vector`. (Part 2 of 3.)

```
107        for ( size_t i = 0; i < array.size(); i++ )
108            cin >> array[ i ];
109    } // end function inputVector
```

```
Size of vector integers1 is 7
vector after initialization:
            0               0               0               0
            0               0               0

Size of vector integers2 is 10
vector after initialization:
            0               0               0               0
            0               0               0               0
            0               0

Enter 17 integers:
1 2 3 4 5 6 7 8 9 10 11 12 13 14 15 16 17

After input, the vectors contain:
integers1:
            1               2               3               4
            5               6               7
integers2:
            8               9              10              11
           12              13              14              15
           16              17

Evaluating: integers1 != integers2
integers1 and integers2 are not equal

Size of vector integers3 is 7
vector after initialization:
            1               2               3               4
            5               6               7

Assigning integers2 to integers1:
integers1:
            8               9              10              11
           12              13              14              15
           16              17
integers2:
            8               9              10              11
           12              13              14              15
           16              17

Evaluating: integers1 == integers2
integers1 and integers2 are equal

integers1[5] is 13

Assigning 1000 to integers1[5]
integers1:
            8               9              10              11
           12            1000              14              15
           16              17

Attempt to assign 1000 to integers1.at( 15 )
```

Fig. 8.25 | C++ Standard Library class template vector. (Part 3 of 3.)

Lines 34–35 pass integers1 and integers2 to function inputVector (lines 105–109) to read values for each vector's elements from the user. The function uses square brackets ([]) to form *lvalues* that are used to store the input values in each vector element.

Line 46 demonstrates that vector objects can be compared with one another using the != operator. If the contents of two vectors are not equal, the operator returns true; otherwise, it returns false.

The C++ Standard Library class template vector allows you to create a new vector object that is initialized with the contents of an existing vector. Line 51 creates a vector object integers3 and initializes it with a copy of integers1. This invokes vector's so-called copy constructor to perform the copy operation. You'll learn about copy constructors in detail in Chapter 12. Lines 53–55 output the size and contents of integers3 to demonstrate that it was initialized correctly.

Line 59 assigns integers2 to integers1, demonstrating that the assignment (=) operator can be used with vector objects. Lines 61–64 output the contents of both objects to show that they now contain identical values. Line 69 then compares integers1 to integers2 with the equality (==) operator to determine whether the contents of the two objects are equal after the assignment in line 59 (which they are).

Lines 73 and 77 demonstrate that a program can use square brackets ([]) to obtain a vector element as an *rvalue* and as an *lvalue*, respectively. Recall from Section 6.9 that an *rvalue* cannot be modified, but an *lvalue* can. As is the case with C-style pointer-based arrays, Visual C++ does not perform any bounds checking when vector elements are accessed with square brackets. Therefore, you must ensure that operations using [] do not accidentally attempt to manipulate elements outside the bounds of the vector. Standard class template vector does, however, provide bounds checking in its member function *at*, which "throws an exception" (see Chapter 16, Exception Handling) if its argument is an invalid subscript. At this point in execution you will see a dialog with options to **Abort**, **Retry** or **Ignore**. Simply click **Abort** to terminate the program. If the subscript is valid, function at returns the element at the specified location as a modifiable *lvalue* or an unmodifiable *lvalue*, depending on the context (non-const or const) in which the call appears. Line 83 demonstrates a call to function at with an invalid subscript. The resulting output varies by compiler.

In this section, we demonstrated the C++ Standard Library class template vector, a robust, reusable class that can replace C-style pointer-based arrays. In Chapter 12, you'll see that vector achieves many of its capabilities by "overloading" Visual C++'s built-in operators, and you'll learn how to customize operators for use with your own classes in similar ways. For example, we create an Array class that, like class template vector, improves upon basic array capabilities. Our Array class also provides additional features, such as the ability to input and output entire arrays with operators >> and <<, respectively.

8.12 Introduction to Managed Arrays with C++/CLI

We now introduce *managed arrays* with C++/CLI. The syntax for managed arrays might look unfamiliar because they are declared with template notation like class vector in Section 8.11. Despite the different declaration syntax, once created and initialized C++/CLI arrays behave almost exactly like native C++ arrays. For now, you should feel comfortable using managed arrays by mimicking the syntax we use in this section's examples. Chapter 15 will provide more detail when we study class templates in depth.

Declaring Managed Arrays

C++/CLI arrays require a new syntax for declaration. To create a managed array you specify the type and name of the array as part of an *array-creation expression* that uses the C++/CLI keyword **gcnew**. Such an expression returns a reference that can be stored in an array variable. Note that this declaration style also makes *array* a context-sensitive keyword in C++/CLI. A managed array declaration is of the form

> **array**< *type* > ^*name* = **gcnew array**< *type* >(*size*);

Let's take a close look at a managed array declaration for an array of ints:

> **array**< **int** > ^managedArray = **gcnew** array< **int** >(3);

We first declare the array object with keyword `array` followed by the type of the array's elements (`int`) in angle brackets. The ^ declares that `managedArray` is a handle to an array, similar to how we use handles to `String` objects. You must always declare a managed array with the ^ after the type name in angle brackets (handles are explained fully in Chapter 9). Next, we specify the name of the array, `managedArray`. At this point our array needs to be assigned a place in memory where it can put each of its elements. To allocate memory for C++/CLI arrays and other managed types we use the C++/CLI keyword gcnew. This tells the program to create memory for an object, in this case enough memory for three integers. Once a managed array has been created, we can access its elements just as with a native C++ array by using an element's index in square brackets. For example,

```
managedArray[ 0 ] = 5;
Console::WriteLine( "Element 0 is: {0}", managedArray[ 0 ] );
```

sets the first element of `managedArray` equal to the integer 5 and prints the element's value. Note that you can declare a C++/CLI array without gcnew and a size; however, you cannot use the variable until you create the array and specify its size. This is important when using a managed array as a data member for a class. You cannot initialize a non-`static` managed array with gcnew in the class definition. Instead, declare the array's variable name and type in the class definition and allocate space for the desired number of elements using gcnew in the class constructor (which we'll demonstrate in later chapters).

Common Programming Error 8.12

A managed array that is a non-static data member of a class cannot be initialized in the class definition. Allocate space for the array elements with gcnew in the class constructor.

Initializer Lists for Managed Arrays

Using gcnew with a size value is not the only way to initialize managed arrays. Like native C++ arrays, managed arrays can be declared with an initializer list. Sometimes when you declare a managed array you may already know the exact size of the array and the value of each element. In this case you can declare a managed array by directly assigning it an initializer list, much as with native C++ arrays. In the declaration

> **array**< **int** >^ managedArray = { 1, 2, 3 };

the compiler determines the size of the array based on the number of elements in the initializer list without requiring that you specify a size parameter. You can accomplish the same thing as above by declaring the array with gcnew and an initializer list as follows:

```
array< int >^ managedArray = gcnew array< int >{ 1, 2, 3 };
```

Alternatively, you may want to use an initializer list but specify the size of the array explicitly. In this case you can declare the array with gcnew followed by a size parameter in parentheses and an initializer list in curly braces. As with native C++ arrays, the number of elements in the initializer list must not be larger than the size of the array. If the initializer list has fewer elements than the array can hold, then other elements simply hold the default value for their type. For example,

```
array< int >^ managedArray = gcnew array< int >( 5 ){ 1, 2, 3 };
```

allocates memory for five integers. It sets managedArray[0] equal to 1, managedArray[1] to 2, and managedArray[2] to 3. The final two elements, managedArray[3] and managedArray[4], hold the default integer value 0, because there were no corresponding values in the initializer list for those elements. The size and initializer list values could just as easily be variables instead of literals, just as with native C++ arrays. Note that, unlike native C++ arrays, when a managed array is allocated, each of its elements is set to the default value according to its type, even if no initializer list is used. This saves you the trouble of writing a for statement to explicitly assign every element a default value.

A final way to initialize a managed array variable is to assign it to an existing managed array of the same type. However, you must make sure the existing array has used one of the above methods for allocating memory. It is important to note that assigning a managed array to an existing array does not create a copy; instead, both arrays now point at the same set of memory locations. Consequently, changing an element in one array actually changes it for both. You should be careful when using this technique, as it can lead to hard-to-find logic errors. This is explained in more detail in Chapter 9.

 Common Programming Error 8.13

A program must know at compile time how many elements of a managed array to allocate memory for. Before using an array you must allocate memory by using an initializer list, gcnew with a size value and/or an initializer list, or by assigning the array to an existing managed array of the same type which already has had memory allocated for it. Trying to access elements of a managed array without doing one of these things causes the program to crash and indicate an error of NullReferenceException (exceptions are explained in Chapter 16).

Using Managed Arrays

Figure 8.26 demonstrates ways to declare and use managed arrays with each of the above techniques. Note that you can define an array and allocate memory on the same line as we did above or on separate lines as in the following example.

In lines 11 and 17 of Fig. 8.26 you see an example of how to split the declaration of an array into two separate statements. Notice that trying to access an array element before allocating memory for the array (line 14) is a runtime error. The program compiles but crashes at runtime. Removing line 14 allows the program to function correctly. At line 26 we use a new technique for the condition inside the for statement. Managed arrays have a Length property which can be accessed using the -> operator (explained in Chapter 9). This is called the member selection operator and is used just like the . operator but for cases when the variable is a reference (such as those declared with handles). Unlike native C++ arrays, each managed array instance knows its own length and provides access to this information via the Length property. Note that the Length property of an array is read-only. It cannot be changed, because it does not provide a set accessor. Lines 32, 41, and 52 demonstrate the other ways to declare managed arrays. Also note the way intArray and myArr are related. When intArray is assigned to myArr (line 52) it causes both array variables to point to the same region in memory. As a result, when the first element of myArr is changed in line 53, it is also changing the first element of intArray because they are pointing at the same elements. The ability to do this is both powerful and dangerous. Based on Fig. 8.26 you can see how all the previous examples using native C++ can easily be applied to managed arrays by simply changing the declaration syntax of the arrays (and using a **CLR** project rather than **Win32**).

```cpp
1   // Fig. 8.26: ManagedArrays.cpp
2   // This example shows some ways you can declare and use C++/CLI arrays
3
4   #include "stdafx.h"
5
6   using namespace System;
7
8   int main( array< System::String ^ > ^args )
9   {
10      // define a managed array without allocating memory
11      array< int >^ intArray;
12
13      // attempt to access array before allocating memory
14      intArray[ 0 ] = 7; // ERROR: NullReferenceException
15
16      // allocate memory for the array so we can use it
17      intArray = gcnew array< int >( 5 );
18
19      // assign values to the first 3 elements
20      intArray[ 0 ] = 3;
21      intArray[ 1 ] = -100;
22      intArray[ 2 ] = 9814;
23
24      // print out each element of intArray with a for loop
25      Console::WriteLine( "The contents of intArray are:" );
26      for( int i = 0; i < intArray->Length; i++ )
27      {
28         Console::Write( "{0} ", intArray[ i ] );
29      } // end for
30
31      // declaring a managed array using just an initializer list
32      array< double >^ doubleArray = { 1.22313, 41.0, -909.5 };
33
34      Console::WriteLine( "\n\nThe contents of doubleArray are:" );
35      for( int i = 0; i < doubleArray->Length; i++ )
36      {
37         Console::Write( "{0} ", doubleArray[ i ] );
38      } // end for
39
```

Fig. 8.26 | Different ways to declare and use managed arrays. (Part 1 of 2.)

```
40        // declare a managed array with a set size and an initializer list
41        array< float >^ floatArray = gcnew array< float >( 5 )
42           { 45, 1 , -180, 112 };
43
44        // print each element of floatArray with a for loop
45        Console::WriteLine( "\n\nThe contents of floatArray are:" );
46        for ( int i = 0; i < floatArray->Length; i++ )
47        {
48           Console::Write( "{0} ", floatArray[ i ] );
49        } // end for
50
51        // declare a managed array and assign it to an existing one
52        array< int >^ myArr = intArray;
53        myArr[ 0 ] = 100; // change the value of the first element of myArr
54
55        // print out each element of myArr with a for loop
56        Console::WriteLine( "\n\nThe contents of myArr are:" );
57        for( int i = 0; i < myArr->Length; i++ )
58        {
59           Console::Write( "{0} ", myArr[ i ] );
60        } // end for
61
62        // print out each element of intArray again
63        // note that line 52 changed the first element of intArray too
64        Console::WriteLine( "\n\nThe new contents of intArray are:" );
65        for( int i = 0; i < intArray->Length; i++ )
66        {
67           Console::Write( "{0} ", intArray[ i ] );
68        } // end for
69
70        return 0;
71    } // end main
```

```
The contents of intArray are:
3 -100 9814 0 0

The contents of doubleArray are:
1.22313 41 -909.5

The contents of floatArray are:
45 1 -180 112 0

The contents of myArr are:
100 -100 9814 0 0

The new contents of intArray are:
100 -100 9814 0 0
```

Fig. 8.26 | Different ways to declare and use managed arrays. (Part 2 of 2.)

Passing Managed Arrays to Functions

Managed arrays are always passed to a function via a reference just like native C++ arrays. Likewise, when passing an individual element of a managed array to a function, it is passed by value unless the array element is a reference type (explained in Chapter 9 and Chapter 11). The concepts demonstrated by Fig. 8.14 are equally applicable to managed arrays.

One convenient difference from native arrays is that with functions you don't need to pass a managed array as well as an integer representing its length. This is because of the Length property described above and array-bounds checking described below. You can always access a managed array's length with the Length property, whether using the array in the scope it was declared or in a function that received it by reference. Note that a function parameter that is a managed array cannot be declared const as a native C++ array can.

Array-Bounds Checking

There is an important difference to note in the way C++/CLI arrays are accessed compared to native C++ arrays. As mentioned in Section 8.4, in native C++ accessing an array element which doesn't exist is an error; however, the compiler and program do not report it. For example, the native C++ code

```
int nativeArray[ 3 ] = { 1, 2, 3 };
nativeArray[ 4 ] = 999;
```

is a logic error because nativeArray[4] is accessing an element outside the array bounds. However, the native C++ program still compiles and possibly even runs, seemingly correctly, despite this logic error. The program writes the value 999 over whatever was at the memory location where nativeArray[4] would be. This could overwrite critical program or system data and cause the program to crash unexpectedly, produce erroneous output or exhibit other undefined behavior. This is a dangerous part of using native C++ arrays. To combat this problem, C++/CLI performs array-bounds checking on all managed arrays. This means that if you try to do as above with a managed array, the program "throws an exception" (see Chapter 16). For example, the code

```
array< int >^ managedArray = { 1, 2, 3 };
managedArray[ 4 ] = 999;
```

creates a managed array and tries to access an element outside its range. At this point in the program's execution a dialog would appear with options to **Debug** or **Close program**. Had we accessed managedArray[3] the program would have continued executing normally. The important part is that the result of running the program is predictable when an element outside the array bounds is accessed. It isn't possible that the array-access expression will create unknown side effects, causing the program to crash unexpectedly later during execution. This prevents some hard-to-find logic errors that can occur if native C++ arrays are misused.

System::Array

In C++/CLI all array objects implicitly inherit from the System::Array class (inheritance is explained in detail in Chapter 14, Object-Oriented Programming: Polymorphism). What this means is that all of the functions available to System::Array objects can be used with managed C++/CLI arrays. Refer to the MSDN documentation for System::Array for a full list of functions available to managed C++/CLI arrays.

8.13 for each Statement

In previous examples, we demonstrated how to use counter-controlled for statements to iterate through the elements in both native and managed arrays. In this section, we introduce a new style of repetition statement using the C++/CLI spaced keyword, *for each*. This is used to iterate through the elements of an entire array or collection. This section discusses how to use the for each statement to loop through an array. We show how to use the for each statement with collections in Chapter 25, Collections. The syntax of a for each statement is:

> **for each** (*type identifier* **in** *arrayName*)
>   *statement*

where *type* and *identifier* are the type and name (e.g., int number) of the *iteration variable*, and *arrayName* is the array through which to iterate. The type of the iteration variable must match the type of the elements in the array. As the next example illustrates, the iteration variable represents successive values in the array on successive iterations of the for each statement. Note that you could just as easily use the for each statement with a native C++ array, vector, or other C++ Standard Library compliant container. It even works without CLR support (turn off the /clr compiler switch in Visual Studio). However, many other compilers and systems don't support the for each statement, so you shouldn't use it in code that runs on non-Windows systems.

Figure 8.27 uses the for each statement (lines 15–16) to calculate the sum of the integers in a managed array of student grades. The type specified is int, because arr contains int values—therefore, the loop selects one int value from the array during each iteration.

```
 1   // Fig. 8.27: ForEachTest.cpp
 2   // Using the for each statement to total integers in an array.
 3
 4   #include "stdafx.h"
 5
 6   using namespace System;
 7
 8   int main( array< System::String ^ > ^args )
 9   {
10      // create a managed array of integers with an initialization list
11      array< int >^ arr = { 87, 68, 94, 100, 83, 78, 85, 91, 76 };
12      int total = 0;
13
14      // add each element's value to total
15      for each ( int number in arr )
16         total += number;
17
18      Console::WriteLine( "Total of array elements: {0}", total );
19
20      return 0;
21   } // end main
```

```
Total of array elements: 762
```

Fig. 8.27 | Using the for each statement to total integers in a managed array.

The for each statement iterates through successive values in the array one-by-one. The for each header can be read concisely as "for each iteration, assign the next element of arr to int variable number, then execute the following statement." Thus, for each iteration, identifier number represents the next int value in the array. Lines 15–16 are equivalent to the following counter-controlled repetition:

```
for ( int counter = 0; counter < arr->Length; counter++ )
   total += arr[ counter ];.
```

The for each statement simplifies the code for iterating through an array. Note, however, that this method won't work if you want to modify array elements. To use a for each statement to modify array elements requires the use of pointers and references which are explained in Chapter 9. For now, use the for each statement only to access array elements, not modify them. If your application needs to modify elements, use the for statement.

The for each statement can be used in place of the for statement whenever code looping through an array does not require access to the counter indicating the index of the current array element. For example, totaling the integers in an array requires access only to the element values—the index of each element is irrelevant. However, if an application must use a counter for some reason other than simply to loop through an array (e.g., to print an index number next to each array element value, as in the examples earlier in this chapter), use the for statement. We show how to use the for each statement with multidimensional arrays in the next section.

8.14 Multidimensional Arrays in C++/CLI

C++/CLI supports two types of multidimensional arrays—*rectangular arrays* and *jagged arrays*. The former is entirely different from native C++, while the latter is quite similar, once you learn the new syntax for declaration.

Rectangular Arrays

In native C++ a multidimensional, rectangular array is actually a single array each of whose elements is an array of the same length. These are called jagged arrays, which we explain shortly. C++/CLI adds support for true multidimensional, rectangular arrays where the data is stored in one contiguous segment. The advantages of rectangular arrays are that the program can sometimes access elements of rectangular arrays faster than elements of jagged arrays and that declaring rectangular arrays is simpler than declaring jagged arrays. On the other hand, rectangular arrays must have the same number of columns in each row, which can lead to wasted space in memory compared to using jagged arrays.

Every element in array a is identified in Fig. 8.28 by an array-access expression of the form a[*row*, *column*]; a is the name of the rectangular array, and *row* and *column* are the indices that uniquely identify each element in array a by row and column number. Notice how this access expression differs from accessing native C++ arrays—both index values are separated by a comma in a single set of square brackets instead of each index being in its own set of square brackets. Also note that the names of the elements in row 0 all have a first index of 0, and the names of the elements in column 3 all have a second index of 3, just like the arrays you've seen previously.

Rectangular array declarations take the general form:

```
array< type, rank >^ arrayName = gcnew array< type, rank >( size );
```

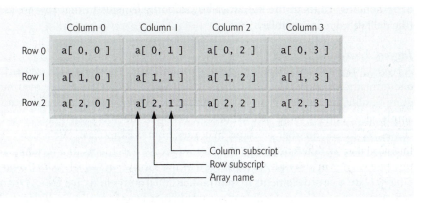

Fig. 8.28 | Rectangular array with three rows and four columns.

In C++/CLI you can declare a rectangular array with three rows and four columns of integers as follows:

```
array< int, 2 >^ rectangular = gcnew array< int, 2 >( 3, 4 );
```

The number in angle brackets after the type name designates the *rank* of the array, or how many dimensions it has. In this case the rank is 2; there is one set of rows and one set of columns. Now we need a size parameter for both dimensions, so we put two numbers inside the parentheses, the first to indicate the number of rows in this array (3), and the second to indicate the number of columns (4). Managed rectangular arrays can also be declared and initialized with *nested array initializers* as follows:

```
array< String^, 2 >^ rectangular = gcnew array< String^, 2 >
   { { "Apple", "Banana" } , { "Cat", "Dog" } };
```

This creates a 2-D rectangular array of String^ objects. The initializer values are grouped by row in braces. So, "Apple" and "Banana" initialize rectangular[0, 0] and rectangular[0, 1], respectively. Likewise, "Cat" and "Dog" initialize rectangular[1, 0] and rectangular[1, 1]. The gcnew array< String^, 2 > on the right-hand side is optional, as the compiler can count the number of nested array initializers (represented by sets of two inner braces within the outer braces) in the array declaration to determine the number of rows in array rectangular. The compiler also counts the initializer values in the nested array initializer for a row to determine the number of columns (two) in that row. Alternatively, you can specify an explicit number of rows and columns in addition to the initializer list, just as with one-dimensional managed arrays. Any rows and columns with values that don't correspond to values in the initializer list are initialized to the default value for their type. For instance,

```
array< double, 2 >^ rectangular = gcnew array< double, 2 > ( 3, 2 )
   { { 1.1, 2.2 } , { 3.3, 4.4 } };
```

creates a 2-D rectangular array of doubles that has three rows and two columns. The two elements in the first row are assigned 1.1 and 2.2, respectively, and the two elements in the second row are assigned 3.3 and 4.4, respectively. The third row does not have any corresponding values in the initializer list, so both elements in that row are assigned 0.0 (the default value for doubles).

Jagged Arrays

A jagged array is maintained as a one-dimensional array in which each element refers to a one-dimensional array. The manner in which jagged arrays are represented makes them quite flexible, because the lengths of the rows in the array need not be the same. For example, jagged arrays could be used to store a single student's exam grades across multiple classes, where the number of exams may vary from class to class. We access the elements in a jagged array differently from the way we accessed elements in a rectangular array. In this case we use an array-access expression of the form *arrayName*[*row*] [*column*]—the same way we accessed elements of multidimensional arrays in native C++. A managed, jagged array in C++/CLI with three rows of different lengths could be declared and initialized with an array-creation expression as follows:

```
array< array< int >^ >^ jagged =
   gcnew array< array< int >^ > ( 3 );
```

Although it looks complicated, if you understand how one-dimensional arrays are declared it's fairly straightforward. Look closely inside the angle brackets of the outermost array declaration, where we declare the type of the array. In this case the type of the array is array< int >^. So, we have created an array with three elements, each a reference to a one-dimensional array of integer values. Declarations of managed, jagged arrays can be made much more readable through the use of the typedef keyword (explained in Chapter 22).

A jagged array cannot be completely created with a single array-creation expression. Each element of jagged is an array which must have its own memory allocated with gcnew before it can be used. We can allocate memory for these arrays by doing the following:

```
jagged[ 0 ] = gcnew array< int >( 4 );
jagged[ 1 ] = gcnew array< int >( 2 );
jagged[ 2 ] = gcnew array< int >( 3 );
```

Now every element of jagged has had memory allocated to hold integer values, and we can use the jagged array however we choose. Alternatively, you can declare a jagged array using an initializer list which contains gcnew declarations. For example,

```
array< array< int >^ >^ jagged = { gcnew array< int > { 1, 2 }
   gcnew array< int > { 3 }
   gcnew array< int > { 4, 5, 6 } };
```

initializes an array of three rows of different lengths and each of the rows. In this statement, 1 and 2 initialize jagged[0][0] and jagged[0][1], respectively; 3 initializes jagged[1][0]; and 4, 5 and 6 initialize jagged[2][0], jagged[2][1] and jagged[2][2], respectively. Therefore, array jagged in the preceding declaration is actually composed of four separate one-dimensional arrays—one that represents the rows, one containing the values in the first row ({ 1, 2 }), one containing the value in the second row ({ 3 }) and one containing the values in the third row ({ 4, 5, 6 }). Thus, array jagged itself is an array of three elements, where each element references a one-dimensional array of int values that is fully initialized. Figure 8.29 illustrates the array reference jagged after it has been declared and initialized.

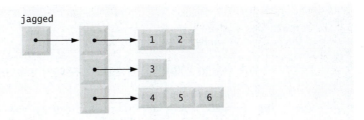

Fig. 8.29 | Jagged array with three rows of different lengths.

 Common Programming Error 8.14

Forgetting to allocate memory for each element of a jagged array is a logic error that causes your program to crash when you try to access those elements.

Two-Dimensional Array Example: Displaying Element Values

Figure 8.30 demonstrates initializing rectangular and jagged arrays with array initializers and using nested for loops to *traverse* the arrays (i.e., visit every element of each array).

```cpp
1   // Fig. 8.30: ManagedMultidimensionalArrays.cpp
2   // Initializing rectangular and jagged arrays
3
4   #include "stdafx.h"
5
6   using namespace System;
7
8   // function prototypes
9   void OutputArray( array< int, 2 >^ );
10  void OutputArray( array< array< int >^ >^ );
11
12  // function main will create and output rectangular and jagged arrays
13  int main( array< System::String ^ > ^args )
14  {
15      // with rectangular arrays,
16      // every column must be the same length
17      array< int, 2 >^ rectangular = { { 1, 2, 3}, {4, 5, 6} };
18
19      // with jagged arrays,
20      // we need to use "gcnew array< int >" for every row,
21      // but every column does not need to be the same length
22      array< array< int >^ >^ jagged ={ gcnew array< int > { 1, 2 },
23          gcnew array< int > { 3 },
24          gcnew array< int > { 4, 5, 6 } };
25
26      OutputArray( rectangular ); // displays array rectangular by row
27      Console::WriteLine(); // output a blank line
28      OutputArray( jagged ); // displays array jagged by row
29
30      return 0;
31  } // end main
```

Fig. 8.30 | Initializing managed jagged and rectangular arrays. (Part 1 of 2.)

```
32
33      // output rows and columns of a rectangular array
34      void OutputArray( array< int, 2 >^ arr )
35      {
36         Console::WriteLine( "Values in the rectangular array by row are" );
37
38         // loop through array's rows
39         for ( int row = 0; row < arr->GetLength( 0 ); row++ )
40         {
41            // loop through columns of current row
42            for ( int column = 0; column < arr->GetLength( 1 ); column++ )
43               Console::Write( "{0} ", arr[ row, column ] );
44
45            Console::WriteLine(); // start new line of output
46         } // end outer for
47      } // end function OutputArray
48
49      void OutputArray( array< array< int >^ >^ arr )
50      {
51         Console::WriteLine( "Values in the jagged array by row are" );
52
53         // loop through array's rows
54         for ( int row = 0; row < arr->Length; row++ )
55         {
56            // loop through columns of current row
57            for ( int column = 0; column < arr[ row ]->Length; column++ )
58               Console::Write( "{0} ", arr[ row ][ column ] );
59
60            Console::WriteLine(); // start new line of output
61         } // end outer for
62      } // end function OutputArray
```

```
Values in the rectangular array by row are
1 2 3
4 5 6

Values in the jagged array by row are
1 2
3
4 5 6
```

Fig. 8.30 | Initializing managed jagged and rectangular arrays. (Part 2 of 2.)

The main function declares two arrays. The declaration of rectangular (line 17) uses nested array initializers to initialize row 0 of the array to the values 1, 2 and 3, and the row 1 to the values 4, 5 and 6. The declaration of jagged (lines 22–24) uses nested initializers of different lengths. In this case, the initializer uses the keyword gcnew to create a one-dimensional array for each row. Row 0 is initialized to have two elements with values 1 and 2, respectively. Row 1 is initialized to have one element with value 3. Row 2 is initialized to have three elements with the values 4, 5 and 6, respectively.

Function OutputArray has been overloaded with two versions. The first version (lines 34–47) specifies the array parameter as array< int, 2>^ arr to indicate that it takes a rectangular array. The second version (lines 49–62) takes a jagged array, because its array parameter is listed as array< array< int >^ >^ arr.

Line 26 invokes function OutputArray with argument rectangular, so the version of OutputArray at lines 34–47 is called. The for statement (lines 39–46) outputs the rows of a rectangular array. The loop-continuation condition of each for statement (lines 39 and 42) uses the rectangular array's GetLength function to obtain the length of each dimension. The dimensions are numbered starting from 0. So the function call GetLength(0) on arr returns the size of the first dimension of the array (the number of rows), and the call GetLength(1) returns the size of the second dimension (the number of columns).

Line 28 invokes function OutputArray with argument jagged, so the version of OutputArray at lines 49–62 is called. The for statement (lines 54–61) outputs the rows of a jagged array. In the loop-continuation condition of the outer for statement (line 54), we use the property arr->Length to determine the number of rows in the array. In the inner for statement (line 57), we use the property array[row]->Length to determine the number of columns in the current row of the array. This condition enables the loop to determine the exact number of columns in each row.

Common Multidimensional-Array Manipulations Performed with for Statements

Many common array manipulations use for statements. As an example, the following for statement sets all the elements in row 2 of rectangular array a in Fig. 8.28 to 0:

```
for ( int column = 0; column < a->GetLength( 1 ); column++)
   a[ 2, column ] = 0;
```

We specified row 2; therefore, we know that the first index is always 2 (0 is the first row, and 1 is the second row). This for loop varies only the second index (i.e., the column index). The preceding for statement is equivalent to the assignment statements

```
a[ 2, 0 ] = 0;
a[ 2, 1 ] = 0;
a[ 2, 2 ] = 0;
a[ 2, 3 ] = 0;
```

The following nested for statement totals the values of all the elements in array a:

```
int total = 0;

for ( int row = 0; row < a->GetLength( 0 ); row++ )
{
   for ( int column = 0; column < a->GetLength( 1 ); column++ )
      total += a[ row, column ];
} // end outer for
```

These nested for statements total the array elements one row at a time. The outer for statement begins by setting the row index to 0 so that row 0's elements can be totaled by the inner for statement. The outer for then increments row to 1 so that row 1's elements can be totaled. Then the outer for increments row to 2 so that row 2's elements can be totaled. The variable total can be displayed when the outer for statement terminates. The for each statement is useful for looping through all the elements of rectangular arrays.

The nested for statements above that total the elements of a could be written with a for each statement as follows

```
int total = 0;

for each( int num in a )
    total += num;
```

As you can see, this is quite concise compared to the nested for statements. Unfortunately, for each statements cannot be used to loop through jagged arrays easily.

8.15 (Optional) Software Engineering Case Study: Collaboration Among Objects in the ATM System

In this section, we concentrate on the collaborations (interactions) among objects in our ATM system. When two objects communicate with each other to accomplish a task, they are said to *collaborate*—they do this by invoking one another's operations. A *collaboration* consists of an object of one class sending a *message* to an object of another class. Messages are sent in Visual C++ via member-function calls.

In Section 7.23, we determined many of the operations of the classes in our system. In this section, we concentrate on the messages that invoke these operations. To identify the collaborations in the system, we return to the requirements specification in Section 3.8. Recall that this document specifies the range of activities that occur during an ATM session (e.g., authenticating a user, performing transactions). The steps used to describe how the system must perform each of these tasks are our first indication of the collaborations in our system. As we proceed through this and the remaining Software Engineering Case Study sections, we may discover additional collaborations.

Identifying the Collaborations in a System

We identify the collaborations in the system by carefully reading the requirements specification sections that specify what the ATM should do to authenticate a user and to perform each transaction type. For each action or step described, we decide which objects in our system must interact to achieve the desired result. We identify one object as the sending object (i.e., the object that sends the message) and another as the receiving object (i.e., the object that offers that operation to clients of the class). We then select one of the receiving object's operations (identified in Section 7.23) that must be invoked by the sending object to produce the proper behavior. For example, the ATM displays a welcome message when idle. We know that an object of class Screen displays a message to the user via its displayMessage operation. Thus, we decide that the system can display a welcome message by employing a collaboration between the ATM and the Screen in which the ATM sends a displayMessage message to the Screen by invoking the displayMessage operation of class Screen. [*Note:* To avoid repeating the phrase "an object of class…," we refer to each object simply by using its class name preceded by an article ("a," "an" or "the")—for example, "the ATM" refers to an object of class ATM.]

Figure 8.31 lists the collaborations that can be derived from the requirements specification. For each sending object, we list the collaborations in the order in which they are discussed in the requirements specification. We list each collaboration involving a unique sender, message and recipient only once, even though the collaboration may occur several times during an ATM session. For example, the first row in Fig. 8.31 indicates that the ATM collaborates with the Screen whenever the ATM needs to display a message to the user.

Let's consider the collaborations in Fig. 8.31. Before allowing a user to perform any transactions, the ATM must prompt the user to enter an account number, then to enter a PIN. It accomplishes each of these tasks by sending a displayMessage message to the Screen. Both of these actions refer to the same collaboration between the ATM and the Screen, which is already listed in Fig. 8.31. The ATM obtains input in response to a prompt by sending a getInput message to the Keypad. Next, the ATM must determine whether the user-specified account number and PIN match those of an account in the database. It does so by sending an authenticateUser message to the BankDatabase. Recall that the BankDatabase cannot authenticate a user directly—only the user's Account (i.e., the Account that contains the account number specified by the user) can access the user's PIN to authenticate the user. Figure 8.31 therefore lists a collaboration in which the BankDatabase sends a validatePIN message to an Account.

An object of class...	sends the message...	to an object of class...
ATM	displayMessage getInput authenticateUser execute execute execute	Screen Keypad BankDatabase BalanceInquiry Withdrawal Deposit
BalanceInquiry	getAvailableBalance getTotalBalance displayMessage	BankDatabase BankDatabase Screen
Withdrawal	displayMessage getInput getAvailableBalance isSufficientCashAvailable debit dispenseCash	Screen Keypad BankDatabase CashDispenser BankDatabase CashDispenser
Deposit	displayMessage getInput isEnvelopeReceived credit	Screen Keypad DepositSlot BankDatabase
BankDatabase	validatePIN getAvailableBalance getTotalBalance debit credit	Account Account Account Account Account

Fig. 8.31 | Collaborations in the ATM system.

After the user is authenticated, the ATM displays the main menu by sending a series of displayMessage messages to the Screen and obtains input containing a menu selection by sending a getInput message to the Keypad. We have already accounted for these collaborations. After the user chooses a type of transaction to perform, the ATM executes the transaction by sending an execute message to an object of the appropriate transaction class (i.e., a BalanceInquiry, a Withdrawal or a Deposit). For example, if the user chooses to perform a balance inquiry, the ATM sends an execute message to a BalanceInquiry.

Further examination of the requirements specification reveals the collaborations involved in executing each transaction type. A BalanceInquiry retrieves the amount of money available in the user's account by sending a getAvailableBalance message to the BankDatabase, which responds by sending a getAvailableBalance message to the user's Account. Similarly, the BalanceInquiry retrieves the amount of money on deposit by sending a getTotalBalance message to the BankDatabase, which sends the same message to the user's Account. To display both measures of the user's balance at the same time, the BalanceInquiry sends a displayMessage message to the Screen.

A Withdrawal sends the Screen several displayMessage messages to display a menu of standard withdrawal amounts (i.e., $20, $40, $60, $100, $200). The Withdrawal sends the Keypad a getInput message to obtain the user's menu selection, then determines whether the requested withdrawal amount is less than or equal to the user's account balance. The Withdrawal can obtain the amount of money available in the account by sending the BankDatabase a getAvailableBalance message. The Withdrawal then tests whether the cash dispenser contains enough cash by sending the CashDispenser an isSufficientCashAvailable message. A Withdrawal sends the BankDatabase a debit message to decrease the user's account balance. The BankDatabase sends the same message to the appropriate Account. Recall that debiting funds from an Account decreases both the totalBalance and the availableBalance. To dispense the requested amount of cash, the Withdrawal sends the CashDispenser a dispenseCash message. Finally, the Withdrawal sends a displayMessage message to the Screen, instructing the user to take the cash.

A Deposit responds to an execute message first by sending a displayMessage message to the Screen to prompt the user for a deposit amount. The Deposit sends a getInput message to the Keypad to obtain the user's input. The Deposit then sends a displayMessage message to the Screen to tell the user to insert a deposit envelope. To determine whether the deposit slot received an incoming deposit envelope, the Deposit sends an isEnvelopeReceived message to the DepositSlot. The Deposit updates the user's account by sending a credit message to the BankDatabase, which subsequently sends a credit message to the user's Account. Recall that crediting funds to an Account increases the totalBalance but not the availableBalance.

Interaction Diagrams

Now that we have identified a set of possible collaborations between the objects in our ATM system, let us graphically model these interactions using the UML. The UML provides several types of *interaction diagrams* that model the behavior of a system by modeling how objects interact with one another. The *communication diagram* emphasizes which objects participate in collaborations. [*Note:* Communication diagrams were called *collaboration diagrams* in earlier versions of the UML.] Like the communication diagram, the *sequence diagram* shows collaborations among objects, but it emphasizes *when* messages are sent between objects *over time*.

Communication Diagrams

Figure 8.32 shows a communication diagram that models the ATM executing a BalanceInquiry. Objects are modeled in the UML as rectangles containing names in the form objectName : ClassName. In this example, which involves only one object of each type, we disregard the object name and list only a colon followed by the class name. [*Note:* Specifying the name of each object in a communication diagram is recommended when modeling multiple objects of the same type.] Communicating objects are connected with solid lines, and messages are passed between objects along these lines in the direction shown by arrows. The name of the message, which appears next to the arrow, is the name of an operation (i.e., a member function) belonging to the receiving object—think of the name as a service that the receiving object provides to sending objects (its "clients").

The solid filled arrow in Fig. 8.32 represents a message—or *synchronous call*—in the UML and a function call in Visual C++. This arrow indicates that the flow of control is from the sending object (the ATM) to the receiving object (a BalanceInquiry). Since this is a synchronous call, the sending object may not send another message, or do anything at all, until the receiving object processes the message and returns control to the sending object—the sender just waits. For example, in Fig. 8.32, the ATM calls member function execute of a BalanceInquiry and may not send another message until execute has finished and returns control to the ATM. [*Note:* If this were an *asynchronous call*, represented by a stick arrowhead, the sending object would not have to wait for the receiving object to return control—it would continue sending additional messages immediately following the asynchronous call. Asynchronous calls often can be implemented in Visual C++ using platform-specific libraries provided with your compiler. Such techniques are beyond the scope of this book.]

Fig. 8.32 | Communication diagram of the ATM executing a balance inquiry.

Sequence of Messages in a Communication Diagram

Figure 8.33 shows a communication diagram that models the interactions among objects in the system when an object of class BalanceInquiry executes. We assume that the object's accountNumber attribute contains the account number of the current user. The collaborations in Fig. 8.33 begin after the ATM sends an execute message to a BalanceInquiry (i.e., the interaction modeled in Fig. 8.32). The number to the left of a message name indicates the order in which the message is passed. The *sequence of messages* in a communication diagram progresses in numerical order from least to greatest. In this diagram, the numbering starts with message 1 and ends with message 3. The BalanceInquiry first sends a getAvailableBalance message to the BankDatabase (message 1), then sends a getTotalBalance message to the BankDatabase (message 2). Within the parentheses following a message name, we can specify a comma-separated list of the names of the parameters sent with the message (i.e., arguments in a Visual C++ function call)—the BalanceInquiry passes attribute accountNumber with its messages to the BankDatabase to indicate which Account's balance information to retrieve. Recall from Fig. 7.36 that operations getAvail-

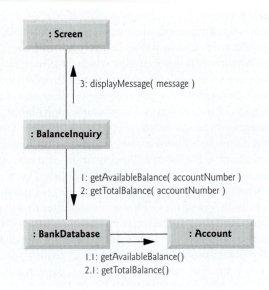

Fig. 8.33 | Communication diagram for executing a balance inquiry.

ableBalance and getTotalBalance of class BankDatabase each require a parameter to identify an account. The BalanceInquiry next displays the availableBalance and the totalBalance to the user by passing a displayMessage message to the Screen (message 3) that includes a parameter indicating the message to be displayed.

Figure 8.33 models two additional messages passing from the BankDatabase to an Account (message 1.1 and message 2.1). To provide the ATM with the two balances of the user's Account (as requested by messages 1 and 2), the BankDatabase must pass a getAvailableBalance and a getTotalBalance message to the user's Account. Messages passed within the handling of another message are called *nested messages*. The UML recommends using a decimal numbering scheme to indicate nested messages. For example, message 1.1 is the first message nested in message 1—the BankDatabase passes a getAvailableBalance message while processing BankDatabase's message of the same name. [*Note:* If the BankDatabase needed to pass a second nested message while processing message 1, the second message would be numbered 1.2.] A message may be passed only when all the nested messages from the previous message have been passed—e.g., the BalanceInquiry passes message 3 only after messages 2 and 2.1 have been passed, in that order.

The nested numbering scheme used in communication diagrams helps clarify precisely when and in what context each message is passed. For example, if we numbered the messages in Fig. 8.33 using a flat numbering scheme (i.e., 1, 2, 3, 4, 5), someone looking at the diagram might not be able to determine that BankDatabase passes the getAvailableBalance message (message 1.1) to an Account *during* the BankDatabase's processing of message 1, as opposed to *after* completing the processing of message 1. The nested decimal numbers make it clear that the second getAvailableBalance message (message 1.1) is passed to an Account within the handling of the first getAvailableBalance message (message 1) by the BankDatabase.

Sequence Diagrams

Communication diagrams emphasize the participants in collaborations but model their timing a bit awkwardly. A sequence diagram helps model the timing of collaborations more clearly. Figure 8.34 shows a sequence diagram modeling the sequence of interactions that occur when a Withdrawal executes. The dotted line extending down from an object's rectangle is that object's *lifeline*, which represents the progression of time. Actions typically occur along an object's lifeline in chronological order from top to bottom—an action near the top typically happens before one near the bottom.

Message passing in sequence diagrams is similar to message passing in communication diagrams. A solid arrow with a filled arrowhead extending from the sending object to

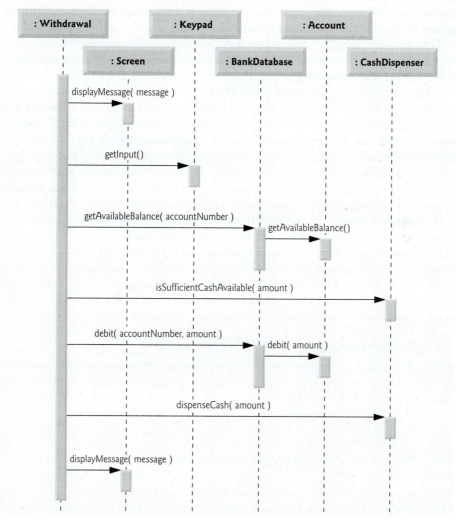

Fig. 8.34 | Sequence diagram that models a Withdrawal executing.

the receiving object represents a message between two objects. The arrowhead points to an activation on the receiving object's lifeline. An ***activation***, shown as a thin vertical rectangle, indicates that an object is executing. When an object returns control, a return message, represented as a dashed line with a stick arrowhead, extends from the activation of the object returning control to the activation of the object that initially sent the message. To eliminate clutter, we omit the return-message arrows—the UML allows this practice to make diagrams more readable. Like communication diagrams, sequence diagrams can indicate message parameters between the parentheses following a message name.

The sequence of messages in Fig. 8.34 begins when a `Withdrawal` prompts the user to choose a withdrawal amount by sending a `displayMessage` message to the `Screen`. The `Withdrawal` then sends a `getInput` message to the `Keypad`, which obtains input from the user. We have already modeled the control logic involved in a `Withdrawal` in the activity diagram of Fig. 6.28, so we do not show this logic in the sequence diagram of Fig. 8.34. Instead, we model the best-case scenario in which the balance of the user's account is greater than or equal to the chosen withdrawal amount, and the cash dispenser contains a sufficient amount of cash to satisfy the request. For information on how to model control logic in a sequence diagram, please refer to the web resources and recommended readings listed at the end of Section 3.8.

After obtaining a withdrawal amount, the `Withdrawal` sends a `getAvailableBalance` message to the `BankDatabase`, which in turn sends a `getAvailableBalance` message to the user's `Account`. Assuming that the user's account has enough money available to permit the transaction, the `Withdrawal` next sends an `isSufficientCashAvailable` message to the `CashDispenser`. Assuming that there is enough cash available, the `Withdrawal` decreases the balance of the user's account (i.e., both the `totalBalance` and the `availableBalance`) by sending a `debit` message to the `BankDatabase`. The `BankDatabase` responds by sending a `debit` message to the user's `Account`. Finally, the `Withdrawal` sends a `dispenseCash` message to the `CashDispenser` and a `displayMessage` message to the `Screen`, telling the user to remove the cash from the machine.

We have identified the collaborations among objects in the ATM system and modeled some of these collaborations using UML interaction diagrams—both communication diagrams and sequence diagrams. In the next Software Engineering Case Study section (Section 10.12), we enhance the structure of our model to complete a preliminary object-oriented design; then we begin implementing the ATM system.

Software Engineering Case Study Self-Review Exercises

8.1 A(n) _____ consists of an object of one class sending a message to an object of another class.
  a) association
  b) aggregation
  c) collaboration
  d) composition

8.2 Which form of interaction diagram emphasizes *what* collaborations occur? Which form emphasizes *when* collaborations occur?

8.3 Create a sequence diagram that models the interactions among objects in the ATM system that occur when a `Deposit` executes successfully, and explain the sequence of messages modeled by the diagram.

Answers to Software Engineering Case Study Self-Review Exercises

8.1   c.

8.2   Communication diagrams emphasize *what* collaborations occur. Sequence diagrams emphasize *when* collaborations occur.

8.3   Figure 8.35 presents a sequence diagram that models the interactions between objects in the ATM system that occur when a Deposit executes successfully. Figure 8.35 indicates that a Deposit first sends a displayMessage message to the Screen to ask the user to enter a deposit amount. Next the Deposit sends a getInput message to the Keypad to receive input from the user. The Deposit then instructs the user to enter a deposit envelope by sending a displayMessage message to the Screen. The Deposit next sends an isEnvelopeReceived message to the DepositSlot to confirm that the deposit envelope has been received by the ATM. Finally, the Deposit increases the total-Balance attribute (but not the availableBalance attribute) of the user's Account by sending a credit message to the BankDatabase. The BankDatabase responds by sending the same message to the user's Account.

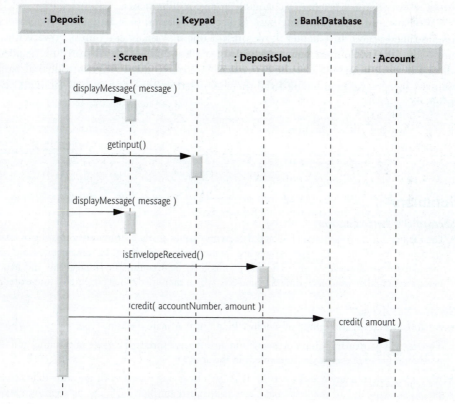

Fig. 8.35 | Sequence diagram that models a Deposit executing.

8.16 Wrap-Up

This chapter began our introduction to data structures, exploring the use of arrays and vectors to store data in and retrieve data from lists and tables of values. The chapter examples demonstrated how to declare an array, initialize an array and refer to individual elements of an array. We also illustrated how to pass arrays to functions and how to use the `const` qualifier to enforce the principle of least privilege. Chapter examples also presented basic searching and sorting techniques. You learned how to declare and manipulate multidimensional arrays. We demonstrated the capabilities of C++ Standard Library class template `vector`, which provides a more robust alternative to arrays. You learned how to use managed arrays with C++/CLI and how to iterate over an array with `for each`. We also demonstrated how to use rectangular and jagged managed multidimensional arrays.

We continue our coverage of data structures in Chapter 15, where we build a stack class template and in Chapter 21, Data Structures, which introduces other dynamic data structures, such as lists, queues, stacks and trees, that can grow and shrink as programs execute. Chapter 23, introduces several of the C++ Standard Library's predefined data structures, which programmers can use instead of building their own. Chapter 23 presents the full functionality of class template `vector` and discusses many additional data-structure classes, including `list` and `deque`, which are arraylike data structures that can grow and shrink in response to a program's changing storage requirements.

We have now introduced the basic concepts of classes, objects, control statements, functions and arrays. In Chapter 9, we present one of Visual C++'s most powerful features—the pointer. Pointers keep track of where data and functions are stored in memory, which allows us to manipulate those items in interesting ways. After introducing basic pointer concepts, we examine in detail the close relationship among arrays, pointers and strings.

Summary

Section 8.1 Introduction
- Data structures are collections of related data items. Arrays are data structures consisting of related data items of the same type. Arrays are "static" entities in that they remain the same size throughout program execution. (They may, of course, be of automatic storage class and hence be created and destroyed each time the blocks in which they are defined are entered and exited.)

Section 8.2 Arrays
- An array is a consecutive group of memory locations that share the same type.
- To refer to a particular location or element in an array, we specify the name of the array and the position number of the particular element in the array.
- A program refers to any one of an array's elements by giving the name of the array followed by the position number of the particular element in square brackets (`[]`). The position number is more formally called a subscript or index (this number specifies the number of elements from the beginning of the array).
- The first element in every array has subscript zero and is sometimes called the zeroth element.
- A subscript must be an integer or integer expression (using any integral type).
- The brackets used to enclose the subscript of an array are an operator in Visual C++. Brackets have the same level of precedence as parentheses.

Section 8.3 Declaring Arrays

• Arrays occupy space in memory. You specify the type of each element and the number of elements required by an array as follows:

> *type arrayName*[*arraySize*] ;

and the compiler reserves the appropriate amount of memory.

• Arrays can be declared to contain any data type. For example, an array of type char can be used to store a character string.

Section 8.4 Examples Using Arrays

• The elements of an array can be initialized in the array declaration by following the array name with an equals sign and an initializer list—a comma-separated list (enclosed in braces) of constant initializers. When initializing an array with an initializer list, if there are fewer initializers than elements in the array, the remaining elements are initialized to zero.

• If the array size is omitted from a declaration with an initializer list, the compiler determines the number of elements in the array by counting the number of elements in the initializer list.

• If the array size and an initializer list are specified in an array declaration, the number of initializers must be less than or equal to the array size. Providing more initializers in an array initializer list than there are elements in the array is a compilation error.

• Constants must be initialized with a constant expression when they are declared and cannot be modified thereafter. Constants can be placed anywhere a constant expression is expected.

• Visual C++ has no array bounds checking to prevent the computer from referring to an element that does not exist. Thus, an executing program can "walk off" either end of an array without warning. You should ensure that all array references remain within the bounds of the array.

• Individual characters in a string can be accessed directly with array subscript notation.

• A static local variable in a function definition exists for the duration of the program but is visible only in the function body.

• A program initializes static local arrays when their declarations are first encountered. If a static array is not initialized explicitly by you, each element of that array is initialized to zero by the compiler when the array is created.

Section 8.5 Passing Arrays to Functions

• To pass an array argument to a function, specify the name of the array without any brackets. To pass an element of an array to a function, use the subscripted name of the array element as an argument in the function call.

• Arrays are passed to functions by reference—the called functions can modify the element values in the callers' original arrays. The value of the name of the array is the address in the computer's memory of the first element of the array. Because the starting address of the array is passed, the called function knows precisely where the array is stored in memory.

• Individual array elements are passed by value exactly as simple variables are. Such simple single pieces of data are called scalars or scalar quantities.

• To receive an array argument, a function's parameter list must specify that the function expects to receive an array. The size of the array is not required between the array brackets.

• C++ provides the type qualifier const that can be used to prevent modification of array values in the caller by code in a called function. When an array parameter is preceded by the const qualifier, the elements of the array become constant in the function body, and any attempt to modify an element of the array in the function body results in a compilation error.

Section 8.6 Case Study: Class GradeBook Using an Array to Store Grades

- Class variables (`static` data members) are shared by all objects of the class in which the variables are declared.

- A `static` data member can be accessed within the class definition and the member-function definitions like any other data member.

- A `public` `static` data member can also be accessed outside of the class, even when no objects of the class exist, using the class name followed by the binary scope resolution operator (`::`) and the name of the data member.

Section 8.7 Searching Arrays with Linear Search

- The linear search compares each element of an array with a search key. Because the array is not in any particular order, it is just as likely that the value will be found in the first element as in the last. On average, therefore, a program must compare the search key with half the elements of the array. To determine that a value is not in the array, the program must compare the search key to every element in the array. The linear searching method works well for small arrays and is acceptable for unsorted arrays.

Section 8.8 Sorting Arrays with Insertion Sort

- An array can be sorted using insertion sort. The first iteration of this algorithm takes the second element and, if it is less than the first element, swaps it with the first element (i.e., the program *inserts* the second element in front of the first element). The second iteration looks at the third element and inserts it into the correct position with respect to the first two elements, so all three elements are in order. At the ith iteration of this algorithm, the first i elements in the original array will be sorted. For small arrays, the insertion sort is acceptable, but for larger arrays it is inefficient compared to other more sophisticated sorting algorithms.

Section 8.9 Multidimensional Arrays

- Multidimensional arrays with two dimensions are often used to represent tables of values consisting of information arranged in rows and columns.

- Arrays that require two subscripts to identify a particular element are called two-dimensional arrays. An array with m rows and n columns is called an m-by-n array.

Section 8.11 Introduction to C++ Standard Library Class Template `vector`

- C++ Standard Library class template vector represents a more robust alternative to arrays featuring many capabilities that are not provided for C-style pointer-based arrays.

- By default, all the elements of an integer vector object are set to 0.

- A vector can be defined to store any data type using a declaration of the form

      vector< *type* > *name*(*size*);

- Member function `size` of class template vector returns the number of elements in the vector on which it is invoked.

- The value of an element of a vector can be accessed or modified using square brackets (`[]`).

- Objects of standard class template vector can be compared directly with the equality (`==`) and inequality (`!=`) operators. The assignment (`=`) operator can also be used with vector objects.

- An unmodifiable *lvalue* is an expression that identifies an object in memory (such as an element in a vector), but cannot be used to modify that object. A modifiable *lvalue* also identifies an object in memory, but can be used to modify the object.

- Standard class template vector provides bounds checking in its member function at, which "throws an exception" if its argument is an invalid subscript. By default, this causes a C++ program to terminate.

Section 8.12 Introduction to Managed Arrays with C++/CLI
- A managed array in C++/CLI can be declared to store any data type using a declaration of the form

    array< *type* >^ *name* = **gcnew array**< *type* >(*size*);

    You can provide an initializer list in curly braces following, or in place of, (*size*).
- By default, all elements of a managed C++/CLI array are initialized to the default value for the elements' type.
- The Length property can be used to access (but not set) the length of a managed array.
- Elements of a managed array can be accessed using square brackets ([]) just like native arrays.
- Managed arrays perform bounds checking whenever an element is accessed. The program "throws an exception" if the element index is an invalid subscript.
- Managed arrays are implicitly of type System::Array, which provides a large number of built-in functions that work with managed arrays.

Section 8.13 for each Statement
- The for each statement iterates through the elements of an entire array or collection. The syntax of a for each statement is:

    for each (*type identifier* **in** *arrayName*)
        statement

    where *type* and *identifier* are the type and name of the iteration variable, and *arrayName* is the array through which to iterate.
- The for each header can be read concisely as "for each iteration, assign the next element of the array to the iteration variable, then execute the following statement."
- The for each statement can be used with native or managed arrays.

Section 8.14 Multidimensional Arrays in C++/CLI
- C++/CLI supports two types of two-dimensional arrays—rectangular arrays and jagged arrays.
- Rectangular arrays are used to represent tables of information in the form of rows and columns, where each row has the same number of columns.
- Elements in rectangular array a are identified by an array-access expression of the form a[row, column].
- A rectangular array can be created with an array-creation expression of the form

    array< *type, rank* >^ *arrayName* = **gcnew array**< *type, rank* >(*size*);

    You can provide an initializer list in curly braces following, or in place of, (*size*).
- A rectangular array could be declared and initialized with array initializers of the form:

    array< *type, rank* >^ *arrayName* = { {*row0 initializer*}, {*row1 initializer*}, ... };

    provided that each row of the rectangular array must have the same length.
- A jagged array is maintained as a one-dimensional array in which each element refers to a one-dimensional array. Each element representing a one-dimensional array must have memory allocated for it.

- The lengths of the rows in a jagged array need not be the same.
- We can access the elements in a jagged array *arrayName* by an array-access expression of the form *arrayName*[*row*][*column*].
- A jagged array can be declared and initialized in the form:

> **array**< *type, rank* >^ *arrayName* = { **gcnew array**< *type* > {*row0 initializer*},
> **gcnew array**< *type* > {*row1 initializer*}, ... };

where *type* is a managed array of the form **array**< *type* >^

Terminology

2-D array	name of an array
a[i]	named constant
a[i][j]	nested
a[i , j]	nested array initializer
array	off-by-one error
array-access expression	one-dimensional array
array-creation expression	pass-by-reference
array initializer list	passing arrays to functions
at member function of vector	position number
bounds checking	rank of an array
column of a two-dimensional array	read-only variables
column subscript	rectangular array
const type qualifier	row of a two-dimensional array
constant variable	row subscript
data structure	scalability
declare an array	scalar
element of an array	scalar quantity
for each statement	search an array
gcnew	search key
index	size member function of vector
index zero	sort an array
initialize an array	square brackets []
initializer	static data member
initializer list	string represented by a character array
insertion sort	subscript
iteration variable	table of values
jagged array	tabular format
key value	traverse an array
Length property	two-dimensional array
linear search of an array	unmodifiable *lvalue*
magic number	value of an element
managed array	vector (C++ Standard Library class template)
m-by-*n* array	"walk off" an array
modifiable *lvalue*	zeroth element
multidimensional array	

Self-Review Exercises

8.1 Answer each of the following:
   a) Lists and tables of values can be stored in _____ or _____.

b) The elements of an array are related by the fact that they have the same _____ and _____.

c) The number used to refer to a particular element of an array is called its _____.

d) A(n) _____ should be used to declare the size of an array, because it makes the program more scalable.

e) The process of placing the elements of an array in order is called _____ the array.

f) The process of determining if an array contains a particular key value is called _____ the array.

g) An array that uses two subscripts is referred to as a(n) _____ array.

8.2 State whether the following are *true* or *false*. If the answer is *false*, explain why.

a) An array can store many different types of values.

b) An array subscript should normally be of data type `float`.

c) If there are fewer initializers in an initializer list than the number of elements in the array, the remaining elements are initialized to the last value in the initializer list.

d) It is an error if an initializer list contains more initializers than there are elements in the array.

e) An individual array element that is passed to a function and modified in that function will contain the modified value when the called function completes execution.

8.3 Write one or more statements that perform the following tasks for an array called `fractions`:

a) Define a constant integer variable `arraySize` initialized to 10.

b) Declare an array with `arraySize` elements of type `double`, and initialize the elements to 0.

c) Name the fourth element of the array.

d) Refer to array element 4.

e) Assign the value `1.667` to array element 9.

f) Assign the value `3.333` to the seventh element of the array.

g) Print array elements 6 and 9 with two digits of precision to the right of the decimal point, and show the output that is actually displayed on the screen.

h) Print all the array elements using a `for` statement. Define the integer variable `i` as a control variable for the loop. Show the output.

8.4 Answer the following questions regarding an array called `table`:

a) Declare the array to be an integer array and to have 3 rows and 3 columns. Assume that the constant variable `arraySize` has been defined to be 3.

b) How many elements does the array contain?

c) Use a `for` statement to initialize each element of the array to the sum of its subscripts. Assume that the integer variables `i` and `j` are declared as control variables.

d) Write a program segment to print the values of each element of array `table` in tabular format with 3 rows and 3 columns. Assume that the array was initialized with the declaration

```
int table[ arraySize ][ arraySize ] = { { 1, 8 }, { 2, 4, 6 }, { 5 } };
```

and the integer variables `i` and `j` are declared as control variables. Show the output.

8.5 Find the error in each of the following program segments and correct the error:

a) `#include <iostream>;`

b) `arraySize = 10; // arraySize was declared const`

c) Assume that `int b[ 10 ] = {};`
```
for ( int i = 0; i <= 10; i++ )
    b[ i ] = 1;
```

d) Assume that *int* a[2][2] = { { 1, 2 }, { 3, 4 } };
   a[1, 1] = 5;

8.6 Answer the following questions regarding a managed array called data:

a) Define a constant integer variable arraySize initialized to 10.

b) Declare the managed array to have arraySize elements.

c) What is the value of data[4]?

d) Use a for statement to initialize each element of the array to the value of its subscript multiplied by 2. Define the integer variable i as a control variable for the loop. Use the Length property of data for the loop condition.

e) What will happen if you run your program with the statement data[11] = 22 after the for statement?

f) Output the value of each element of data using a for each statement and Console::WriteLine.

8.7 Answer the following questions regarding managed, multidimensional arrays:

a) Declare a managed array rect to be a rectangular, integer array with rank 2. Assume constant integer variable rows is initialized to 2 and constant integer variable columns is initialized to 3.

b) Use a for statement to initialize each element of rect to the sum of its subscripts. Assume that the integer variables i and j are declared as control variables.

c) Use Console::WriteLine to print the element in second row and third column of rect.

d) Declare a managed array jag to be a jagged, integer array with 2 rows. The first row should have 3 columns and the second row should have 2 columns.

e) Use a for statement to initialize each element of jag to the sum of its subscripts. Assume that the integer variables i and j are declared as control variables. Use the Length property of jag[i] as the loop condition in the second loop.

f) Use Console::WriteLine to print the element in second row and second column of jag.

Answers to Self-Review Exercises

8.1 a) arrays, vectors. b) array name, type. c) subscript or index. d) constant variable.
e) sorting. f) searching. g) two-dimensional.

8.2 a) False. An array can store only values of the same type.

b) False. An array subscript should be an integer or an integer expression.

c) False. The remaining elements are initialized to zero.

d) True.

e) False. Individual elements of an array are passed by value. If the entire array is passed to a function, then any modifications will be reflected in the original.

8.3 a) *const int* arraySize = 10;

b) *double* fractions[arraySize] = { 0.0 };

c) fractions[3]

d) fractions[4]

e) fractions[9] = 1.667;

f) fractions[6] = 3.333;

g) cout << fixed << setprecision(2);
   cout << fractions[6] << ' ' << fractions[9] << endl;
   Output: 3.33 1.67.

h) *for* (*int* i = 0; i < arraySize; i++)
       cout << "fractions[" << i << "] = " << fractions[i] << endl;
   Output:

```
fractions[ 0 ] = 0.0
fractions[ 1 ] = 0.0
fractions[ 2 ] = 0.0
fractions[ 3 ] = 0.0
fractions[ 4 ] = 0.0
fractions[ 5 ] = 0.0
fractions[ 6 ] = 3.333
fractions[ 7 ] = 0.0
fractions[ 8 ] = 0.0
fractions[ 9 ] = 1.667
```

8.4 a) *int* table[arraySize][arraySize];
  b) Nine.
  c) *for* (i = 0; i < arraySize; i++)

```
        for ( j = 0; j < arraySize; j++ )
           table[ i ][ j ] = i + j;
```
  d) cout << "   [0] [1] [2]" << endl;

```
    for ( int i = 0; i < arraySize; i++ ) {
       cout << '[' << i << "] ";

       for ( int j = 0; j < arraySize; j++ )
          cout << setw( 3 ) << table[ i ][ j ] << "  ";
       cout << endl;
    }
```
  Output:

```
        [0]  [1]  [2]
   [0]   1    8    0
   [1]   2    4    6
   [2]   5    0    0
```

8.5 a) Error: Semicolon at end of #include preprocessor directive.
    Correction: Eliminate semicolon.
  b) Error: Assigning a value to a constant variable using an assignment statement.
    Correction: Initialize the constant variable in a const int arraySize declaration.
  c) Error: Referencing an array element outside the bounds of the array (b[10]).
    Correction: Change the final value of the control variable to 9.
  d) Error: Array subscripting done incorrectly.
    Correction: Change the statement to a[1][1] = 5;

8.6 a) *const int* arraySize = 10;
  b) *array*< *int* >^ data = *gcnew array*< *int* >(arraySize);
  c) 0
  d) *for* (*int* i = 0; i < data->Length; i++)
      data[i] = i * 2;
  e) The program will crash and throw an exception.
  f) *for each* (*int* num *in* data)
      Console::WriteLine(num);

8.7 a) *array*< *int*, 2 >^ rect = *gcnew array*< *int*, 2 >(rows, columns);
  b) *for* (i = 0; i < rows; i++)
      for (j = 0; j < columns; j++)
        rect[i, j] = i + j;

```
  c) Console::WriteLine( rect[ 1, 2 ] );
  d) array< array< int >^ >^ jag = gcnew array< array< int >^ >( 2 );
     jag[ 0 ] = gcnew array< int >( 3 );
     jag[ 1 ] = gcnew array< int >( 2 );
  e) for ( i = 0; i < 2; i++ )
         for ( j = 0; j < jag[ i ]->Length; j++ )
            jag[ i ][ j ] = i + j;
  f) Console::WriteLine( jag[ 1 ][ 1 ] );
```

Exercises

8.8 Fill in the blanks in each of the following:
  a) The names of the four elements of array p (int p[4];) are _____, _____, _____ and _____.
  b) Naming an array, stating its type and specifying the number of elements in the array is called _____ the array.
  c) By convention, the first subscript in a two-dimensional array identifies an element's _____ and the second subscript identifies an element's _____.
  d) An *m*-by-*n* array contains _____ rows, _____ columns and _____ elements.
  e) The name of the element in row 3 and column 5 of array d is _____.

8.9 Determine whether each of the following is *true* or *false*. If *false*, explain why.
  a) To refer to a particular location or element within an array, we specify the name of the array and the value of the particular element.
  b) An array definition reserves space for an array.
  c) To indicate that 100 locations should be reserved for integer array p, you write the declaration

      p[100];

  d) A for statement must be used to initialize the elements of a 15-element array to zero.
  e) Nested for statements must be used to total the elements of a two-dimensional array.

8.10 Write Visual C++ statements to accomplish each of the following:
  a) Display the value of element 6 of character array f.
  b) Input a value into element 4 of one-dimensional floating-point array b.
  c) Initialize each of the 5 elements of one-dimensional integer array g to 8.
  d) Total and print the elements of floating-point array c of 100 elements.
  e) Copy array a into the first portion of array b. Assume double a[11], b[34];.
  f) Determine and print the smallest and largest values contained in 99-element floating-point array w.

8.11 Consider a 2-by-3 integer array t.
  a) Write a declaration for t.
  b) How many rows does t have?
  c) How many columns does t have?
  d) How many elements does t have?
  e) Write the names of all the elements in row 1 of t.
  f) Write the names of all the elements in column 2 of t.
  g) Write a single statement that sets the element of t in the first row and second column to zero.
  h) Write a series of statements that initialize each element of t to zero. Do not use a loop.
  i) Write a nested for statement that initializes each element of t to zero.
  j) Write a statement that inputs the values for the elements of t from the console.

k) Write a series of statements that determine and print the smallest value in array t.

l) Write a statement that displays the elements in row 0 of t.

m) Write a statement that totals the elements in column 3 of t.

n) Write a series of statements that prints the array t in neat, tabular format. List the column subscripts as headings across the top and list the row subscripts at the left of each row.

8.12 Use a one-dimensional array to solve the following problem. A company pays its salespeople on a commission basis. The salespeople each receive $200 per week plus 9 percent of their gross sales for that week. For example, a salesperson who grosses $5000 in sales in a week receives $200 plus 9 percent of $5000, or a total of $650. Write a program (using an array of counters) that determines how many of the salespeople earned salaries in each of the following ranges (assume that each salesperson's salary is truncated to an integer amount):

a) $200–299

b) $300–399

c) $400–499

d) $500–599

e) $600–699

f) $700–799

g) $800–899

h) $900–999

i) $1000 and over

8.13 *(Bubble Sort)* In the ***bubble sort algorithm***, smaller values gradually "bubble" their way upward to the top of the array like air bubbles rising in water, while the larger values sink to the bottom. The bubble sort makes several passes through the array. On each pass, successive pairs of elements are compared. If a pair is in increasing order (or the values are identical), we leave the values as they are. If a pair is in decreasing order, their values are swapped in the array. Write a program that sorts an array of 10 integers using bubble sort.

8.14 The bubble sort described in Exercise 8.13 is inefficient for large arrays. Make the following simple modifications to improve the performance of the bubble sort:

a) After the first pass, the largest number is guaranteed to be in the highest-numbered element of the array; after the second pass, the two highest numbers are "in place," and so on. Instead of making nine comparisons on every pass, modify the bubble sort to make eight comparisons on the second pass, seven on the third pass, and so on.

b) The data in the array may already be in the proper order or near-proper order, so why make nine passes if fewer will suffice? Modify the sort to check at the end of each pass if any swaps have been made. If none have been made, then the data must already be in the proper order, so the program should terminate. If swaps have been made, then at least one more pass is needed.

8.15 Write single statements that perform the following one-dimensional array operations:

a) Initialize the 10 elements of integer array counts to zero.

b) Add 1 to each of the 15 elements of integer array bonus.

c) Read 12 values for double array monthlyTemperatures from the keyboard.

d) Print the 5 values of integer array bestScores in column format.

8.16 Find the error(s) in each of the following statements:

a) Assume that: *int* a[3];

```
cout << a[ 1 ] << " " << a[ 2 ] << " " << a[ 3 ] << endl;
```

b) *double* f[3] = { 1.1, 10.01, 100.001, 1000.0001 };
c) Assume that: *double* d[2][10];

```
d[ 1, 9 ] = 2.345;
```

8.17 Use a one-dimensional array to solve the following problem. Read in 20 numbers, each of which is between 10 and 100, inclusive. As each number is read, validate it and store it in the array only if it is not a duplicate of a number already read. After reading all the values, display only the unique values that the user entered. Provide for the "worst case" in which all 20 numbers are different. Use the smallest possible array to solve this problem.

8.18 Label the elements of a 3-by-5 two-dimensional array sales to indicate the order in which they are set to zero by the following program segment:

```
for ( row = 0; row < 3; row++ )

    for ( column = 0; column < 5; column++ )
        sales[ row ][ column ] = 0;
```

8.19 Write a program that simulates the rolling of two dice. The program should use rand to roll the first die and should use rand again to roll the second die. The sum of the two values should then be calculated. [*Note:* Each die can show an integer value from 1 to 6, so the sum of the two values will vary from 2 to 12, with 7 being the most frequent sum and 2 and 12 being the least frequent sums.] Figure 8.36 shows the 36 possible combinations of the two dice. Your program should roll the two dice 36,000 times. Use a one-dimensional array to tally the numbers of times each possible sum appears. Print the results in a tabular format. Also, determine if the totals are reasonable (i.e., there are six ways to roll a 7, so approximately one-sixth of all the rolls should be 7).

	1	2	3	4	5	6
1	2	3	4	5	6	7
2	3	4	5	6	7	8
3	4	5	6	7	8	9
4	5	6	7	8	9	10
5	6	7	8	9	10	11
6	7	8	9	10	11	12

Fig. 8.36 | The 36 possible outcomes of rolling two dice.

8.20 What does the following program do?

```
1   // Exercise 8.20: Ex08_20.cpp
2   // What does this program do?
3   #include <iostream>
4   using std::cout;
5   using std::endl;
6
7   int whatIsThis( int [], int ); // function prototype
8
```

```
 9   int main()
10   {
11      const int arraySize = 10;
12      int a[ arraySize ] = { 1, 2, 3, 4, 5, 6, 7, 8, 9, 10 };
13
14      int result = whatIsThis( a, arraySize );
15
16      cout << "Result is " << result << endl;
17      return 0; // indicates successful termination
18   } // end main
19
20   // What does this function do?
21   int whatIsThis( int b[], int size )
22   {
23      if ( size == 1 ) // base case
24         return b[ 0 ];
25      else // recursive step
26         return b[ size - 1 ] + whatIsThis( b, size - 1 );
27   } // end function whatIsThis
```

8.21   Modify the program of Fig. 7.11 to play 1000 games of craps. The program should keep track of the statistics and answer the following questions:

    a) How many games are won on the 1st roll, 2nd roll, ..., 20th roll, and after the 20th roll?

    b) How many games are lost on the 1st roll, 2nd roll, ..., 20th roll, and after the 20th roll?

    c) What are the chances of winning at craps? [*Note:* You should discover that craps is one of the fairest casino games. What do you suppose this means?]

    d) What is the average length of a game of craps?

    e) Do the chances of winning improve with the length of the game?

8.22   (*Airline Reservations System*) A small airline has just purchased a computer for its new automated reservations system. You have been asked to program the new system. You are to write a program to assign seats on each flight of the airline's only plane (capacity: 10 seats).

Your program should display the following menu of alternatives—Please type 1 for "First Class" and Please type 2 for "Economy". If the person types 1, your program should assign a seat in the first class section (seats 1–5). If the person types 2, your program should assign a seat in the economy section (seats 6–10). Your program should print a boarding pass indicating the person's seat number and whether it is in the first class or economy section of the plane.

Use a one-dimensional array to represent the seating chart of the plane. Initialize all the elements of the array to 0 to indicate that all seats are empty. As each seat is assigned, set the corresponding elements of the array to 1 to indicate that the seat is no longer available.

Your program should, of course, never assign a seat that has already been assigned. When the first class section is full, your program should ask the person if it is acceptable to be placed in the economy section (and vice versa). If yes, then make the appropriate seat assignment. If no, then print the message "Next flight leaves in 3 hours."

8.23   What does the following program do?

```
1   // Exercise 8.23: Ex08_23.cpp
2   // What does this program do?
3   #include <iostream>
4   using std::cout;
5   using std::endl;
```

```
6
7    void someFunction( int [], int, int ); // function prototype
8
9    int main()
10   {
11      const int arraySize = 10;
12      int a[ arraySize ] = { 1, 2, 3, 4, 5, 6, 7, 8, 9, 10 };
13
14      cout << "The values in the array are:" << endl;
15      someFunction( a, 0, arraySize );
16      cout << endl;
17      return 0; // indicates successful termination
18   } // end main
19
20   // What does this function do?
21   void someFunction( int b[], int current, int size )
22   {
23      if ( current < size )
24      {
25         someFunction( b, current + 1, size );
26         cout << b[ current ] << " ";
27      } // end if
28   } // end function someFunction
```

8.24 Use a two-dimensional array to solve the following problem. A company has four salespeople (1 to 4) who sell five different products (1 to 5). Once a day, each salesperson passes in a slip for each different type of product sold. Each slip contains the following:
  a) The salesperson number
  b) The product number
  c) The total dollar value of that product sold that day

Thus, each salesperson passes in between 0 and 5 sales slips per day. Assume that the information from all of the slips for last month is available. Write a program that will read all this information for last month's sales and summarize the total sales by salesperson by product. All totals should be stored in the two-dimensional array sales. After processing all the information for last month, print the results in tabular format with each of the columns representing a particular salesperson and each of the rows representing a particular product. Cross total each row to get the total sales of each product for last month; cross total each column to get the total sales by salesperson for last month. Your tabular printout should include these cross totals to the right of the totaled rows and to the bottom of the totaled columns.

8.25 (*Turtle Graphics*) The Logo language, which is popular among elementary-school children, made the concept of *turtle graphics* famous. Imagine a mechanical turtle that walks around the room under the control of a Visual C++ program. The turtle holds a pen in one of two positions, up or down. While the pen is down, the turtle traces out shapes as it moves; while the pen is up, the turtle moves about freely without writing anything. In this problem, you'll simulate the operation of the turtle and create a computerized sketchpad as well.

Use a 20-by-20 array floor that is initialized to zeros. Read commands from an array that contains them. Keep track of the current position of the turtle at all times and whether the pen is currently up or down. Assume that the turtle always starts facing upwards at position (0, 0) of the floor with its pen up. The set of turtle commands your program must process are shown in Fig. 8.37.

Suppose that the turtle is somewhere near the center of the floor. The following "program" would draw and print a 12-by-12 square and end with the pen in the up position:

Command	Meaning
1	Pen up
2	Pen down
3	Turn right
4	Turn left
5, 10	Move forward 10 spaces (or a number other than 10)
6	Print the 20-by-20 array
9	End of data (sentinel)

Fig. 8.37 | Turtle graphics commands.

```
2
5,12
3
5,12
3
5,12
3
5,12
1
6
9
```

As the turtle moves with the pen down, set the appropriate elements of array floor to 1s. When the 6 command (print) is given, wherever there is a 1 in the array, display an asterisk or some other character you choose. Wherever there is a zero, display a blank. Write a program to implement the turtle graphics capabilities discussed here. Write several turtle graphics programs to draw interesting shapes. Add other commands to increase the power of your turtle graphics language.

8.26 (*Knight's Tour*) One of the more interesting puzzlers for chess buffs is the Knight's Tour problem. The question is this: Can the chess piece called the knight move around an empty chessboard and touch each of the 64 squares once and only once? We study this intriguing problem in depth in this exercise.

The knight makes L-shaped moves (over two in one direction and then over one in a perpendicular direction). Thus, from a square in the middle of an empty chessboard, the knight can make eight different moves (numbered 0 through 7) as shown in Fig. 8.38.

    a) Draw an 8-by-8 chessboard on a sheet of paper and attempt a Knight's Tour by hand. Put a 1 in the first square you move to, a 2 in the second square, a 3 in the third, etc. Before starting the tour, estimate how far you think you'll get, remembering that a full tour consists of 64 moves. How far did you get? Was this close to your estimate?

    b) Now let us develop a program that will move the knight around a chessboard. The board is represented by an 8-by-8 two-dimensional array board. Each of the squares is initialized to zero. We describe each of the eight possible moves in terms of both its horizontal and vertical components. For example, a move of type 0, as shown in Fig. 8.38, consists of moving two squares horizontally to the right and one square vertically upward. Move 2 consists of moving one square horizontally to the left and two squares vertically upward. Horizontal moves to the left and vertical moves upward are indicated

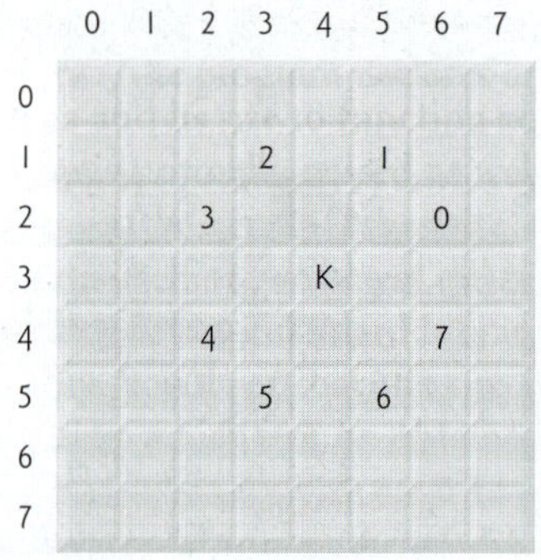

Fig. 8.38 | The eight possible moves of the knight.

with negative numbers. The eight moves may be described by two one-dimensional arrays, horizontal and vertical, as follows:

```
horizontal[ 0 ] = 2      vertical[ 0 ] = -1
horizontal[ 1 ] = 1      vertical[ 1 ] = -2
horizontal[ 2 ] = -1     vertical[ 2 ] = -2
horizontal[ 3 ] = -2     vertical[ 3 ] = -1
horizontal[ 4 ] = -2     vertical[ 4 ] = 1
horizontal[ 5 ] = -1     vertical[ 5 ] = 2
horizontal[ 6 ] = 1      vertical[ 6 ] = 2
horizontal[ 7 ] = 2      vertical[ 7 ] = 1
```

Let the variables currentRow and currentColumn indicate the row and column of the knight's current position. To make a move of type moveNumber, where moveNumber is between 0 and 7, your program uses the statements

```
currentRow += vertical[ moveNumber ];
currentColumn += horizontal[ moveNumber ];
```

Keep a counter that varies from 1 to 64. Record the latest count in each square the knight moves to. Remember to test each potential move to see if the knight has already visited that square, and, of course, test every potential move to make sure that the knight does not land off the chessboard. Now write a program to move the knight around the chessboard. Run the program. How many moves did the knight make?

c) After attempting to write and run a Knight's Tour program, you have probably developed some valuable insights. We'll use these to develop a *heuristic* (or strategy) for moving the knight. Heuristics do not guarantee success, but a carefully developed heuristic greatly improves the chance of success. You may have observed that the outer squares are more troublesome than the squares nearer the center of the board. In fact, the most troublesome, or inaccessible, squares are the four corners.

Intuition may suggest that you should attempt to move the knight to the most troublesome squares first and leave open those that are easiest to get to, so when the board gets congested near the end of the tour, there will be a greater chance of success.

We may develop an "accessibility heuristic" by classifying each square according to how accessible it is and then always moving the knight to the square (within the knight's L-shaped moves, of course) that is most inaccessible. We label a two-dimensional array accessibility with numbers indicating from how many squares each particular square is accessible. On a blank chessboard, each center square is rated as 8, each corner square is rated as 2 and the other squares have accessibility numbers of 3, 4 or 6 as follows:

```
2 3 4 4 4 4 3 2
3 4 6 6 6 6 4 3
4 6 8 8 8 8 6 4
4 6 8 8 8 8 6 4
4 6 8 8 8 8 6 4
4 6 8 8 8 8 6 4
3 4 6 6 6 6 4 3
2 3 4 4 4 4 3 2
```

Now write a version of the Knight's Tour program using the accessibility heuristic. At any time, the knight should move to the square with the lowest accessibility number. In case of a tie, the knight may move to any of the tied squares. Therefore, the tour may begin in any of the four corners. [*Note:* As the knight moves around the chessboard, your program should reduce the accessibility numbers as more and more squares become occupied. In this way, at any given time during the tour, each available square's accessibility number will remain equal to precisely the number of squares from which that square may be reached.] Run this version of your program. Did you get a full tour? Now modify the program to run 64 tours, one starting from each square of the chessboard. How many full tours did you get?

d) Write a version of the Knight's Tour program which, when encountering a tie between two or more squares, decides what square to choose by looking ahead to those squares reachable from the "tied" squares. Your program should move to the square for which the next move would arrive at a square with the lowest accessibility number.

8.27 (*Knight's Tour: Brute Force Approaches*) In Exercise 8.26, we developed a solution to the Knight's Tour problem. The approach used, called the "accessibility heuristic," generates many solutions and executes efficiently.

As computers continue increasing in power, we'll be able to solve more problems with sheer computer power and relatively unsophisticated algorithms. This is the "brute force" approach to problem solving.

a) Use random number generation to enable the knight to walk around the chessboard (in its legitimate L-shaped moves, of course) at random. Your program should run one tour and print the final chessboard. How far did the knight get?

b) Most likely, the preceding program produced a relatively short tour. Now modify your program to attempt 1000 tours. Use a one-dimensional array to keep track of the number of tours of each length. When your program finishes attempting the 1000 tours, it should print this information in neat tabular format. What was the best result?

c) Most likely, the preceding program gave you some "respectable" tours, but no full tours. Now "pull all the stops out" and simply let your program run until it produces a full tour. [*Caution:* This version of the program could run for hours on a powerful computer.] Once again, keep a table of the number of tours of each length, and print this table when the first full tour is found. How many tours did your program attempt before producing a full tour? How much time did it take?

d) Compare the brute force version of the Knight's Tour with the accessibility heuristic version. Which required a more careful study of the problem? Which algorithm was more difficult to develop? Which required more computer power? Could we be certain (in advance) of obtaining a full tour with the accessibility heuristic approach? Could we be certain (in advance) of obtaining a full tour with the brute force approach? Argue the pros and cons of brute force problem solving in general.

8.28 (*Eight Queens*) Another puzzler for chess buffs is the Eight Queens problem. Simply stated: Is it possible to place eight queens on an empty chessboard so that no queen is "attacking" any other, i.e., no two queens are in the same row, the same column, or along the same diagonal? Use the thinking developed in Exercise 8.26 to formulate a heuristic for solving the Eight Queens problem. Run your program. [*Hint:* It is possible to assign a value to each square of the chessboard indicating how many squares of an empty chessboard are "eliminated" if a queen is placed in that square. Each of the corners would be assigned the value 22, as in Fig. 8.39.] Once these "elimination numbers" are placed in all 64 squares, an appropriate heuristic might be: Place the next queen in the square with the smallest elimination number. Why is this strategy intuitively appealing?

8.29 (*Eight Queens: Brute Force Approaches*) In this exercise, you'll develop several brute-force approaches to solving the Eight Queens problem introduced in Exercise 8.28.
  a) Solve the Eight Queens exercise, using the random brute force technique developed in Exercise 8.27.
  b) Use an exhaustive technique, i.e., try all possible combinations of eight queens on the chessboard.
  c) Why do you suppose the exhaustive brute force approach may not be appropriate for solving the Knight's Tour problem?
  d) Compare and contrast the random brute force and exhaustive brute force approaches in general.

8.30 (*Knight's Tour: Closed-Tour Test*) In the Knight's Tour, a full tour occurs when the knight makes 64 moves touching each square of the chess board once and only once. A closed tour occurs when the 64th move is one move away from the location in which the knight started the tour. Modify the Knight's Tour program you wrote in Exercise 8.26 to test for a closed tour if a full tour has occurred.

8.31 (*The Sieve of Eratosthenes*) A prime integer is any integer that is evenly divisible only by itself and 1. The Sieve of Eratosthenes is a method of finding prime numbers. It operates as follows:
  a) Create an array with all elements initialized to 1 (true). Array elements with prime subscripts will remain 1. All other array elements will eventually be set to zero. You'll ignore elements 0 and 1 in this exercise.
  b) Starting with array subscript 2, every time an array element is found whose value is 1, loop through the remainder of the array and set to zero every element whose subscript is a multiple of the subscript for the element with value 1. For array subscript 2, all elements beyond 2 in the array that are multiples of 2 will be set to zero (subscripts 4, 6, 8, 10, etc.); for array subscript 3, all elements beyond 3 in the array that are multiples of 3 will be set to zero (subscripts 6, 9, 12, 15, etc.); and so on.

Fig. 8.39 | The 22 squares eliminated by placing a queen in the upper-left corner.

When this process is complete, the array elements that are still set to one indicate that the subscript is a prime number. These subscripts can then be printed. Write a program that uses an array of 1000 elements to determine and print the prime numbers between 2 and 999. Ignore element 0 of the array.

8.32 (*Bucket Sort*) A **bucket sort** begins with a one-dimensional array of positive integers to be sorted and a two-dimensional array of integers with rows subscripted from 0 to 9 and columns subscripted from 0 to $n - 1$, where n is the number of values in the array to be sorted. Each row of the two-dimensional array is referred to as a bucket. Write a function bucketSort that takes an integer array and the array size as arguments and performs as follows:

    a) Place each value of the one-dimensional array into a row of the bucket array based on the value's ones digit. For example, 97 is placed in row 7, 3 is placed in row 3 and 100 is placed in row 0. This is called a "distribution pass."

    b) Loop through the bucket array row by row, and copy the values back to the original array. This is called a "gathering pass." The new order of the preceding values in the one-dimensional array is 100, 3 and 97.

    c) Repeat this process for each subsequent digit position (tens, hundreds, thousands, etc.).

On the second pass, 100 is placed in row 0, 3 is placed in row 0 (because 3 has no tens digit) and 97 is placed in row 9. After the gathering pass, the order of the values in the one-dimensional array is 100, 3 and 97. On the third pass, 100 is placed in row 1, 3 is placed in row zero and 97 is placed in row zero (after the 3). After the last gathering pass, the original array is now in sorted order.

Note that the two-dimensional array of buckets is 10 times the size of the integer array being sorted. This sorting technique provides better performance than an insertion sort, but requires much more memory. The insertion sort requires space for only one additional element of data. This is an example of the space/time trade-off: The bucket sort uses more memory than the insertion sort, but performs better. This version of the bucket sort requires copying all the data back to the original array on each pass. Another possibility is to create a second two-dimensional bucket array and repeatedly swap the data between the two bucket arrays.

Recursion Exercises

8.33 (*Selection Sort*) A **selection sort** searches an array looking for the smallest element. Then, the smallest element is swapped with the first element of the array. The process is repeated for the subarray beginning with the second element of the array. Each pass of the array results in one element being placed in its proper location. This sort performs comparably to the insertion sort—for an array of n elements, $n - 1$ passes must be made, and for each subarray, $n - 1$ comparisons must be made to find the smallest value. When the subarray being processed contains one element, the array is sorted. Write recursive function selectionSort to perform this algorithm.

8.34 (*Palindromes*) A palindrome is a string that is spelled the same way forward and backward. Some examples of palindromes are "radar," "able was i ere i saw elba" and (if blanks are ignored) "a man a plan a canal panama." Write a recursive function testPalindrome that returns true if the string stored in the array is a palindrome, and false otherwise. The function should ignore spaces and punctuation in the string.

8.35 (*Linear Search*) Modify the program in Fig. 8.18 to use recursive function linearSearch to perform a linear search of the array. The function should receive an integer array and the size of the array as arguments. If the search key is found, return the array subscript; otherwise, return −1.

8.36 (*Eight Queens*) Modify the Eight Queens program you created in Exercise 8.28 to solve the problem recursively.

8.37 (*Print an Array*) Write a recursive function printArray that takes an array, a starting subscript and an ending subscript as arguments and returns nothing. The function should stop processing and return when the starting subscript equals the ending subscript.

8.38 (*Print a String Backward*) Write a recursive function stringReverse that takes a character array containing a string and a starting subscript as arguments, prints the string backward and returns nothing. The function should stop processing and return when the terminating null character is encountered.

8.39 (*Find the Minimum Value in an Array*) Write a recursive function recursiveMinimum that takes an integer array, a starting subscript and an ending subscript as arguments, and returns the smallest element of the array. The function should stop processing and return when the starting subscript equals the ending subscript.

vector Exercises

8.40 Use a vector of integers to solve the problem described in Exercise 8.12.

8.41 Modify the dice-rolling program you created in Exercise 8.19 to use a vector to store the numbers of times each possible sum of the two dice appears.

8.42 (*Find the Minimum Value in a vector*) Modify your solution to Exercise 8.39 to find the minimum value in a vector instead of an array.

Managed Array Exercises

8.43 Use a managed array to solve the problem in Exercise 8.12. Use Double::Parse(String^) to convert user input into a double.

8.44 Use a managed array to solve the problem in Exercise 8.17.

8.45 Use a managed array to solve the problem in Exercise 8.32. Use a single-dimensional managed array and a two-dimensional jagged array.

9

Pointers and Pointer-Based Strings

Addresses are given to us to conceal our whereabouts.
—Saki (H. H. Munro)

By indirection find direction out.
—William Shakespeare

Many things, having full reference
To one consent, may work contrariously.
—William Shakespeare

You will find it a very good practice always to verify your references, sir!
—Dr. Routh

OBJECTIVES

In this chapter you'll learn:

- What pointers are.

- The similarities and differences between pointers and references, and when to use each.

- To use pointers to pass arguments to functions by reference.

- To use pointer-based C-style strings.

- The close relationships among pointers, arrays and C-style strings.

- To use pointers to functions.

- To declare and use arrays of C-style strings.

- What handles and tracking references are.

- To use handles to pass managed objects to functions by reference.

9.1 Introduction

This chapter discusses one of the most powerful features of the Visual C++ programming language, the pointer. In Chapter 7, we saw that references can be used to perform pass-by-reference. Pointers also enable pass-by-reference and can be used to create and manipulate dynamic data structures (i.e., data structures that can grow and shrink), such as linked lists, queues, stacks and trees. This chapter explains basic pointer concepts and reinforces the intimate relationship between arrays and pointers. The view of arrays as pointers derives from the C programming language. As we saw in Chapter 8, C++ Standard Library class `vector` provides an implementation of arrays as full-fledged objects.

Similarly, Visual C++ actually offers two types of strings in native C++—`string` class objects (which we have been using since Chapter 4) and C-style, `char *` pointer-based strings. This chapter on pointers discusses `char *` strings to deepen your knowledge of pointers. This chapter also includes a substantial collection of string-processing exercises that use `char *` strings. C-style, `char *` pointer-based strings are widely used in legacy C and C++ systems. So, if you work with legacy C or C++ systems, you may be required to manipulate these `char *` pointer-based strings.

We'll examine the use of pointers with classes in Chapter 14, Object-Oriented Programming: Polymorphism, where we'll see that the so-called "polymorphic processing" of object-oriented programming is performed with pointers and references. Chapter 21, Data Structures, presents examples of creating and using dynamic data structures that are implemented with pointers.

Finally, we introduce the basics of managed memory and garbage collection for managed objects with C++/CLI. We demonstrate how to use handles and tracking references to create references to managed objects analogous to the way pointers are used with native objects.

9.2 Pointer Variable Declarations and Initialization

Pointer variables contain memory addresses as their values. Normally, a variable directly contains a specific value. However, a pointer contains the memory address of a variable that, in turn, contains a specific value. In this sense, a variable name *directly references a value*, and a pointer *indirectly references a value* (Fig. 9.1). Referencing a value through a pointer is often called *indirection*. Note that diagrams typically represent a pointer as an arrow from the variable that contains an address to the variable located at that address in memory.

Pointers, like any other variables, must be declared before they can be used. For example, for the pointer in Fig. 9.1, the declaration

```
int *countPtr, count;
```

declares the variable countPtr to be of type int * (i.e., a pointer to an int value) and is read, "countPtr is a pointer to int" or "countPtr points to an object of type int." Also, variable count in the preceding declaration is declared to be an int, not a pointer to an int. The * in the declaration applies only to countPtr. Each variable being declared as a pointer must be preceded by an asterisk (*). For example, the declaration

```
double *xPtr, *yPtr;
```

indicates that both xPtr and yPtr are pointers to double values. When * appears in a declaration, it is not an operator; rather, it indicates that the variable being declared is a pointer. Pointers can be declared to point to objects of any data type.

Common Programming Error 9.1

*Assuming that the * used to declare a pointer distributes to all variable names in a declaration's comma-separated list of variables can lead to errors. Each pointer must be declared with the * prefixed to the name (either with or without a space in between—the compiler ignores the space). Declaring only one variable per declaration helps avoid these types of errors and improves program readability.*

Good Programming Practice 9.1

Although it is not a requirement, including the letters Ptr in pointer variable names makes it clear that these variables are pointers and that they must be handled accordingly.

Pointers should be initialized either when they are declared or in an assignment. A pointer may be initialized to 0, NULL or an address of the corresponding type. A pointer

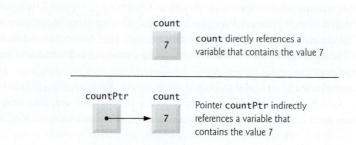

Fig. 9.1 | Directly and indirectly referencing a variable.

with the value 0 or NULL points to nothing and is known as a ***null pointer***. Symbolic constant NULL is defined in header file <iostream> (and in several other standard library header files) to represent the value 0. Initializing a pointer to NULL is equivalent to initializing a pointer to 0, but in Visual C++, 0 is used by convention. When 0 is assigned, it is converted to a pointer of the appropriate type. The value 0 is the only integer value that can be assigned directly to a pointer variable without first casting the integer to a pointer type. Assigning a variable's numeric address to a pointer is discussed in Section 9.3.

Error-Prevention Tip 9.1

Initialize pointers to prevent pointing to unknown or uninitialized areas of memory.

9.3 Pointer Operators

The ***address operator (&)*** is a unary operator that obtains the memory address of its operand. For example, assuming the declarations

```
int y = 5; // declare variable y
int *yPtr; // declare pointer variable yPtr
```

the statement

```
yPtr = &y; // assign address of y to yPtr
```

assigns the address of the variable y to pointer variable yPtr. Then variable yPtr is said to "point to" y. Now, yPtr indirectly references variable y's value. Note that the use of the & in the preceding statement is not the same as the use of the & in a reference variable declaration, which is always preceded by a data-type name. When declaring a reference, the & is part of the type. In an expression like &y, the & is an operator.

Figure 9.2 shows a schematic representation of memory after the preceding assignment. The "pointing relationship" is indicated by drawing an arrow from the box that represents the pointer yPtr in memory to the box that represents the variable y in memory.

Figure 9.3 shows another representation of the pointer in memory, assuming that integer variable y is stored at memory location 600000 and that pointer variable yPtr is stored at memory location 500000. The address operator's operand must be an *lvalue* (i.e., something to which a value can be assigned, such as a variable or a reference); the address operator cannot be applied to constants or to expressions that do not result in references.

Fig. 9.2 | Graphical representation of a pointer pointing to a variable in memory.

	yPtr		y
location 500000	600000	location 600000	5

Fig. 9.3 | Representation of y and yPtr in memory.

The ** operator*, commonly referred to as the ***indirection operator*** or ***dereferencing operator***, returns a synonym (i.e., an alias or a nickname) for the object to which its pointer operand points. For example (referring again to Fig. 9.2), the statement

```
cout << *yPtr << endl;
```

prints the value of variable y, namely, 5, just as the statement

```
cout << y << endl;
```

would. Using * in this manner is called ***dereferencing a pointer***. Note that a dereferenced pointer may also be used on the left side of an assignment statement, as in

```
*yPtr = 9;
```

which would assign 9 to y in Fig. 9.3. The dereferenced pointer may also be used to receive an input value as in

```
cin >> *yPtr;
```

which places the input value in y. The dereferenced pointer is an *lvalue*.

Common Programming Error 9.2

Dereferencing a pointer that has not been properly initialized or that has not been assigned to point to a specific location in memory could cause a fatal execution-time error, or it could accidentally modify important data and allow the program to run to completion, possibly with incorrect results.

Common Programming Error 9.3

An attempt to dereference a variable that is not a pointer is a compilation error.

Common Programming Error 9.4

Dereferencing a null pointer is often a fatal execution-time error.

The program in Fig. 9.4 demonstrates the & and * pointer operators. Memory locations are output by << in this example as hexadecimal (i.e., base-16) integers. (See Chapter D, Number Systems, for more information on hexadecimal integers.) Note that the hexadecimal memory addresses output by this program are compiler and operating-system dependent, so you may get different results when you run the program.

Portability Tip 9.1

The format in which a pointer is output is compiler dependent—some use hexadecimal integers, some use decimal integers and some use other formats.

Notice that the address of a (line 15) and the value of aPtr (line 16) are identical in the output, confirming that the address of a is indeed assigned to the pointer variable aPtr. The & and * operators are inverses of one another—when they are both applied consecutively to aPtr in either order, they "cancel one another out" and the same result (the value in aPtr) is printed.

```cpp
1   // Fig. 9.4: PointerOperators.cpp
2   // Pointer operators & and *.
3   #include <iostream>
4   using std::cout;
5   using std::endl;
6
7   int main()
8   {
9      int a; // a is an integer
10     int *aPtr; // aPtr is an int * -- pointer to an integer
11
12     a = 7; // assigned 7 to a
13     aPtr = &a; // assign the address of a to aPtr
14
15     cout << "The address of a is " << &a
16          << "\nThe value of aPtr is " << aPtr;
17     cout << "\n\nThe value of a is " << a
18          << "\nThe value of *aPtr is " << *aPtr;
19     cout << "\n\nShowing that * and & are inverses of "
20          << "each other.\n&*aPtr = " << &*aPtr
21          << "\n*&aPtr = " << *&aPtr << endl;
22     return 0; // indicates successful termination
23  } // end main
```

```
The address of a is 0012F580
The value of aPtr is 0012F580

The value of a is 7
The value of *aPtr is 7

Showing that * and & are inverses of each other.
&*aPtr = 0012F580
*&aPtr = 0012F580
```

Fig. 9.4 | Pointer operators & and *.

Figure 9.5 lists the precedence and associativity of the operators introduced to this point. Note that the address operator (&) and the dereferencing operator (*) are unary operators on the third level of precedence in the chart.

Operators							Associativity	Type
() []							left to right	highest
++	--	*static_cast*< *type* >(*operand*)					left to right	unary (postfix)
++	--	+	-	!	&	*	right to left	unary (prefix)
*	/	%					left to right	multiplicative
+	-						left to right	additive
<<	>>						left to right	insertion/extraction
<	<=	>	>=				left to right	relational
==	!=						left to right	equality
&&							left to right	logical AND
||							left to right	logical OR
?:							right to left	conditional
=	+=	-=	*=	/=	%=		right to left	assignment
,							left to right	comma

Fig. 9.5 | Operator precedence and associativity.

9.4 Passing Arguments to Functions by Reference with Pointers

There are three ways in Visual C++ to pass arguments to a function—pass-by-value, *pass-by-reference with reference arguments* and *pass-by-reference with pointer arguments*. Chapter 7 compared and contrasted pass-by-value and pass-by-reference with reference arguments. In this section, we explain pass-by-reference with pointer arguments.

As we saw in Chapter 7, return can be used to return one value from a called function to a caller (or to return control from a called function without passing back a value). We also saw that arguments can be passed to a function using reference arguments. Such arguments enable the called function to modify the original values of the arguments in the caller. Reference arguments also enable programs to pass large data objects to a function and avoid the overhead of passing the objects by value (which, of course, requires making a copy of the object). Pointers, like references, also can be used to modify one or more variables in the caller or to pass pointers to large data objects to avoid the overhead of passing the objects by value.

In Visual C++, programmers can use pointers and the indirection operator (*) to accomplish pass-by-reference (exactly as pass-by-reference is done in C programs—C does not have references). When calling a function with an argument that should be modified, the address of the argument is passed. This is normally accomplished by applying the address operator (&) to the name of the variable whose value will be modified.

As we saw in Chapter 8, arrays are not passed using operator &, because the name of the array is the starting location in memory of the array (i.e., an array name is already a pointer). The name of an array, arrayName, is equivalent to &arrayName[0]. When the address of a variable is passed to a function, the indirection operator (*) can be used in the function to form a synonym for the name of the variable—this in turn can be used to modify the value of the variable at that location in the caller's memory.

Figure 9.6 and Fig. 9.7 present two versions of a function that cubes an integer—cubeByValue and cubeByReference. Figure 9.6 passes variable number by value to function cubeByValue (line 15). Function cubeByValue (lines 21–24) cubes its argument and passes the new value back to main using a return statement (line 23). The new value is assigned to number (line 15) in main. Note that the calling function has the opportunity to examine the result of the function call before modifying variable number's value. For example, in this program, we could have stored the result of cubeByValue in another variable, examined its value and assigned the result to number only after determining that the returned value was reasonable.

Figure 9.7 passes the variable number to function cubeByReference using pass-by-reference with a pointer argument (line 16)—the address of number is passed to the function. Function cubeByReference (lines 23–26) specifies parameter nPtr (a pointer to int) to receive its argument. The function dereferences the pointer and cubes the value to which nPtr points (line 25). This directly changes the value of number in main.

```cpp
1   // Fig. 9.6: PassByValue.cpp
2   // Pass-by-value used to cube a variable's value.
3   #include <iostream>
4   using std::cout;
5   using std::endl;
6
7   int cubeByValue( int ); // prototype
8
9   int main()
10  {
11     int number = 5;
12
13     cout << "The original value of number is " << number;
14
15     number = cubeByValue( number ); // pass number by value to cubeByValue
16     cout << "\nThe new value of number is " << number << endl;
17     return 0; // indicates successful termination
18  } // end main
19
20  // calculate and return cube of integer argument
21  int cubeByValue( int n )
22  {
23     return n * n * n; // cube local variable n and return result
24  } // end function cubeByValue
```

Fig. 9.6 | Pass-by-value used to cube a variable's value. (Part I of 2.)

```
The original value of number is 5
The new value of number is 125
```

Fig. 9.6 | Pass-by-value used to cube a variable's value. (Part 2 of 2.)

```
 1   // Fig. 9.7: PassByReference.cpp
 2   // Pass-by-reference with a pointer argument used to cube a
 3   // variable's value.
 4   #include <iostream>
 5   using std::cout;
 6   using std::endl;
 7
 8   void cubeByReference( int * ); // prototype
 9
10   int main()
11   {
12      int number = 5;
13
14      cout << "The original value of number is " << number;
15
16      cubeByReference( &number ); // pass number address to cubeByReference
17
18      cout << "\nThe new value of number is " << number << endl;
19      return 0; // indicates successful termination
20   } // end main
21
22   // calculate cube of *nPtr; modifies variable number in main
23   void cubeByReference( int *nPtr )
24   {
25      *nPtr = *nPtr * *nPtr * *nPtr; // cube *nPtr
26   } // end function cubeByReference
```

```
The original value of number is 5
The new value of number is 125
```

Fig. 9.7 | Pass-by-reference with a pointer argument used to cube a variable's value.

Common Programming Error 9.5

Not dereferencing a pointer when it is necessary to do so to obtain the value to which the pointer points is an error.

A function receiving an address as an argument must define a pointer parameter to receive the address. For example, the header for function cubeByReference (line 23) specifies that cubeByReference receives the address of an int variable (i.e., a pointer to an int) as an argument, stores the address locally in nPtr and does not return a value.

The function prototype for cubeByReference (line 8) contains int * in parentheses. As with other variable types, it is not necessary to include names of pointer parameters in function prototypes. Parameter names included for documentation purposes are ignored by the compiler.

Figures 9.8 and 9.9 analyze graphically the execution of the programs in Figs. 9.6 and 9.7, respectively.

Step 1: Before `main` calls `cubeByValue`:

```
int main()                      number        int cubeByValue( int n )
{                                               {
   int number = 5;                5                 return n * n * n;
                                                }
   number = cubeByValue( number );                               n
}
                                                               undefined
```

Step 2: After `cubeByValue` receives the call:

```
int main()                      number        int cubeByValue( int n )
{                                               {
   int number = 5;                5                 return n * n * n;
                                                }
   number = cubeByValue( number );                               n
}
                                                                  5
```

Step 3: After `cubeByValue` cubes parameter `n` and before `cubeByValue` returns to `main`:

```
int main()                      number        int cubeByValue( int n )
{                                               {             125
   int number = 5;                5                 return n * n * n;
                                                }
   number = cubeByValue( number );                               n
}
                                                                  5
```
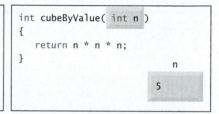

Step 4: After `cubeByValue` returns to `main` and before assigning the result to `number`:

```
int main()                      number        int cubeByValue( int n )
{                                               {
   int number = 5;                5                 return n * n * n;
             125                                }
   number = cubeByValue( number );                             n
}
                                                            undefined
```
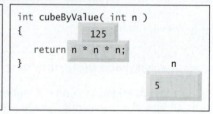

Step 5: After `main` completes the assignment to `number`:

```
int main()                      number        int cubeByValue( int n )
{                                125            {
   int number = 5;                                  return n * n * n;
      125              125                       }
   number = cubeByValue( number );                             n
}
                                                            undefined
```
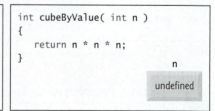

Fig. 9.8 | Pass-by-value analysis of the program of Fig. 9.6.

Step 1: Before `main` calls `cubeByReference`:

```
int main()                                          void cubeByReference( int *nPtr )
{                                number                  {
    int number = 5;                 5                       *nPtr = *nPtr * *nPtr * *nPtr;
                                                        }
    cubeByReference( &number );                                                      nPtr
}
                                                                                  undefined
```

Step 2: After `cubeByReference` receives the call and before `*nPtr` is cubed:

```
int main()                                          void cubeByReference( int *nPtr )
{                                number                  {
    int number = 5;                 5                       *nPtr = *nPtr * *nPtr * *nPtr;
                                                        }
    cubeByReference( &number );                                                      nPtr
}                                call establishes this pointer
```

Step 3: After `*nPtr` is cubed and before program control returns to `main`:

```
int main()                                          void cubeByReference( int *nPtr )
{                                number                                      125
    int number = 5;                125                     *nPtr = *nPtr * *nPtr * *nPtr;
                                                        }
    cubeByReference( &number );    called function modifies caller's          nPtr
}                                 variable
```

Fig. 9.9 | Pass-by-reference analysis (with a pointer argument) of the program of Fig. 9.7.

Software Engineering Observation 9.1

Use pass-by-value to pass arguments to a function unless the caller explicitly requires that the called function directly modify the value of the argument variable in the caller. This is another example of the principle of least privilege.

In the function header and in the prototype for a function that expects a one-dimensional array as an argument, the pointer notation in the parameter list of `cubeByReference` may be used. The compiler does not differentiate between a function that receives a pointer and a function that receives a one-dimensional array. This, of course, means that the function must "know" when it is receiving an array or simply a single variable which is being passed by reference. When the compiler encounters a function parameter for a one-dimensional array of the form `int b[]`, the compiler converts the parameter to the pointer notation `int *b` (pronounced "b is a pointer to an integer"). Both forms of declaring a function parameter as a one-dimensional array are interchangeable.

9.5 Using `const` with Pointers

Recall that the `const` qualifier enables you to inform the compiler that the value of a particular variable should not be modified.

Over the years, a large base of legacy code was written in early versions of C that did not use `const`, because it was not available. For this reason, there are great opportunities for improvement in the software engineering of legacy C code. Also, many programmers currently using ANSI C and C++ do not use `const` in their programs, because they began programming in early versions of C. These programmers are missing many opportunities for good software engineering.

Many possibilities exist for using (or not using) `const` with function parameters. How do you choose the most appropriate of these possibilities? Let the principle of least privilege be your guide. Always award a function enough access to the data in its parameters to accomplish its specified task, but no more. This section discusses how to combine `const` with pointer declarations to enforce the principle of least privilege.

Chapter 7 explained that when a function is called using pass-by-value, a copy of the argument (or arguments) in the function call is made and passed to the function. If the copy is modified in the function, the original value is maintained in the caller without change. In many cases, a value passed to a function is modified so that the function can accomplish its task. However, in some instances, the value should not be altered in the called function, even though the called function manipulates only a copy of the original value.

For example, consider a function that takes a one-dimensional array and its size as arguments and subsequently prints the array. Such a function should loop through the array and output each array element individually. The size of the array is used in the function body to determine the highest subscript of the array so the loop can terminate when the printing completes. The size of the array does not change in the function body, so it should be declared `const`. Of course, because the array is only being printed, it, too, should be declared `const`. This is especially important because an entire array is *always* passed by reference and could easily be changed in the called function.

Software Engineering Observation 9.2

If a value does not (or should not) change in the body of a function to which it is passed, the parameter should be declared `const` to ensure that it is not accidentally modified.

If an attempt is made to modify a `const` value, a warning or an error is issued, depending on the particular compiler.

Error-Prevention Tip 9.2

Before using a function, check its function prototype to determine the parameters that it can modify.

There are four ways to pass a pointer to a function: a nonconstant pointer to nonconstant data (Fig. 9.10), a nonconstant pointer to constant data (Fig. 9.11 and Fig. 9.12), a constant pointer to nonconstant data (Fig. 9.13) and a constant pointer to constant data (Fig. 9.14). Each combination provides a different level of access privileges.

Nonconstant Pointer to Nonconstant Data

The highest access is granted by a ***nonconstant pointer to nonconstant data***—the data can be modified through the dereferenced pointer, and the pointer can be modified to point to other data. The declaration for such a pointer does not include `const`. Such a pointer can be used to receive a null-terminated string in a function that changes the pointer value to process (and possibly modify) each character in the string. A null-terminated string can be placed in a character array that contains the characters of the string and a null character indicating where the string ends.

In Fig. 9.10, function convertToUppercase (lines 25–34) declares parameter sPtr (line 25) to be a nonconstant pointer to nonconstant data (again, const is not used). The function processes one character at a time from the null-terminated string stored in character array phrase (lines 27–33). Keep in mind that a character array's name is really equivalent to a const pointer to the first character of the array, so passing phrase as an argument to convertToUppercase is possible. Function islower (line 29) takes a character argument and returns true if the character is a lowercase letter and false otherwise. Characters in the range 'a' through 'z' are converted to their corresponding uppercase

```cpp
1   // Fig. 9.10: NonconstantPointer.cpp
2   // Converting lowercase letters to uppercase letters
3   // using a nonconstant pointer to nonconstant data.
4   #include <iostream>
5   using std::cout;
6   using std::endl;
7
8   #include <cctype> // prototypes for islower and toupper
9   using std::islower;
10  using std::toupper;
11
12  void convertToUppercase( char * );
13
14  int main()
15  {
16     char phrase[] = "characters and $32.98";
17
18     cout << "The phrase before conversion is: " << phrase;
19     convertToUppercase( phrase );
20     cout << "\nThe phrase after conversion is:  " << phrase << endl;
21     return 0; // indicates successful termination
22  } // end main
23
24  // convert string to uppercase letters
25  void convertToUppercase( char *sPtr )
26  {
27     while ( *sPtr != '\0' ) // loop while current character is not '\0'
28     {
29        if ( islower( *sPtr ) ) // if character is lowercase,
30           *sPtr = toupper( *sPtr ); // convert to uppercase
31
32        sPtr++; // move sPtr to next character in string
33     } // end while
34  } // end function convertToUppercase
```

```
The phrase before conversion is: characters and $32.98
The phrase after conversion is:  CHARACTERS AND $32.98
```

Fig. 9.10 | Converting a string to uppercase letters using a nonconstant pointer to nonconstant data.

letters by function `toupper` (line 30); others remain unchanged—function `toupper` takes one character as an argument. If the character is a lowercase letter, the corresponding uppercase letter is returned; otherwise, the original character is returned. Function `toupper` and function `islower` are part of the character-handling library `<cctype>` (see Chapter 22, Bits, Characters, C Strings and `struct`s). After processing one character, line 32 increments `sPtr` by 1 (this would not be possible if `sPtr` were declared `const`). When operator `++` is applied to a pointer that points to an array, the memory address stored in the pointer is modified to point to the next element of the array (in this case, the next character in the string). Adding 1 to a pointer is one valid operation in **pointer arithmetic**, which is covered in detail in Sections 9.8–9.9.

Nonconstant Pointer to Constant Data

A **nonconstant pointer to constant data** is a pointer that can be modified to point to any data item of the appropriate type, but the data to which it points cannot be modified through that pointer. Such a pointer might be used to receive an array argument to a function that will process each element of the array, but should not be allowed to modify the data. For example, function `printCharacters` (lines 22–26 of Fig. 9.11) declares parameter `sPtr` (line 22) to be of type `const char *`, so that it can receive a null-terminated pointer-based string. The declaration is read from right to left as "`sPtr` is a pointer to a character constant." The body of the function uses a `for` statement (lines 24–25) to output each character in the string until the null character is encountered. After each character is printed, pointer `sPtr` is incremented to point to the next character in the string (this works because the pointer is not `const`). Function `main` creates `char` array `phrase` to be passed to `printCharacters`. Again, we can pass the array `phrase` to `printCharacters` because the name of the array is really a pointer to the first character in the array.

```cpp
1   // Fig. 9.11: PointerToConstantData.cpp
2   // Printing a string one character at a time using
3   // a nonconstant pointer to constant data.
4   #include <iostream>
5   using std::cout;
6   using std::endl;
7
8   void printCharacters( const char * ); // print using pointer to const data
9
10  int main()
11  {
12     const char phrase[] = "print characters of a string";
13
14     cout << "The string is:\n";
15     printCharacters( phrase ); // print characters in phrase
16     cout << endl;
17     return 0; // indicates successful termination
18  } // end main
19
```

Fig. 9.11 | Printing a string one character at a time using a nonconstant pointer to constant data. (Part 1 of 2.)

```
20    // sPtr can be modified, but it cannot modify the character to which
21    // it points, i.e., sPtr is a "read-only" pointer
22    void printCharacters( const char *sPtr )
23    {
24        for ( ; *sPtr != '\0'; sPtr++ ) // no initialization
25            cout << *sPtr; // display character without modification
26    } // end function printCharacters
```

```
The string is:
print characters of a string
```

Fig. 9.11 | Printing a string one character at a time using a nonconstant pointer to constant data. (Part 2 of 2.)

Figure 9.12 demonstrates the compilation error messages produced when attempting to compile a function that receives a nonconstant pointer to constant data, then tries to use that pointer to modify the data. [*Note:* Recall that compiler error messages may vary among compilers.]

As we know, arrays are aggregate data types that store related data items of the same type under one name. When a function is called with an array as an argument, the array is passed to the function by reference. However, objects are always passed by value—a copy of the entire object is passed. This requires the execution-time overhead of making a copy of each data item in the object and storing it on the function call stack. When an object must be passed to a function, we can use a pointer to constant data (or a reference to con-

```
 1    // Fig. 9.12: NonconstantPointer.cpp
 2    // Attempting to modify data through a
 3    // nonconstant pointer to constant data.
 4
 5    void f( const int * ); // prototype
 6
 7    int main()
 8    {
 9        int y;
10
11        f( &y ); // f attempts illegal modification
12        return 0; // indicates successful termination
13    } // end main
14
15    // xPtr cannot modify the value of constant variable to which it points
16    void f( const int *xPtr )
17    {
18        *xPtr = 100; // error: cannot modify a const object
19    } // end function f
```

```
c:\examples\ch09\Fig09_12\NonconstantPointer.cpp(18) :
    error C3892: 'xPtr' : you cannot assign to a variable that is const
```

Fig. 9.12 | Attempting to modify data through a nonconstant pointer to constant data.

stant data) to get the performance of pass-by-reference and the protection of pass-by-value. When a pointer to an object is passed, only a copy of the address of the object must be made—the object itself is not copied. On a machine with four-byte addresses, a copy of four bytes of memory is made rather than a copy of a possibly large object.

Performance Tip 9.1

If they do not need to be modified by the called function, pass large objects using pointers to constant data or references to constant data, to obtain the performance benefits of pass-by-reference.

Software Engineering Observation 9.3

Pass large objects using pointers to constant data, or references to constant data, to obtain the security of pass-by-value.

Constant Pointer to Nonconstant Data

A *constant pointer to nonconstant data* is a pointer that always points to the same memory location; the data at that location can be modified through the pointer. An example of such a pointer is an array name, which is a constant pointer to the beginning of the array. All data in the array can be accessed and changed by using the array name and array subscripting. A constant pointer to nonconstant data can be used to receive an array as an argument to a function that accesses array elements using array subscript notation. Pointers that are declared const must be initialized when they are declared. (If the pointer is a function parameter, it is initialized with a pointer that is passed to the function.) The program of Fig. 9.13 attempts to modify a constant pointer. Line 11 declares pointer ptr to be of type int * const. The declaration in the figure is read from right to left as "ptr is a constant pointer to a nonconstant integer." The pointer is initialized with the address of integer variable x. Line 14 attempts to assign the address of y to ptr, but the compiler generates an error message. Note that no error occurs when line 13 assigns the value 7 to *ptr—the nonconstant value to which ptr points can be modified using the dereferenced ptr, even though ptr itself has been declared const.

```
 1   // Fig. 9.13: ConstantPointer.cpp
 2   // Attempting to modify a constant pointer to nonconstant data.
 3
 4   int main()
 5   {
 6      int x, y;
 7
 8      // ptr is a constant pointer to an integer that can
 9      // be modified through ptr, but ptr always points to the
10      // same memory location.
11      int * const ptr = &x; // const pointer must be initialized
12
13      *ptr = 7; // allowed: *ptr is not const
14      ptr = &y; // error: ptr is const; cannot assign to it a new address
15      return 0; // indicates successful termination
16   } // end main
```

Fig. 9.13 | Attempting to modify a constant pointer to nonconstant data. (Part 1 of 2.)

```
c:\examples\ch09\Fig09_13\ConstantPointer.cpp(14) : error C3892: 'ptr' :
   you cannot assign to a variable that is const
```

Fig. 9.13 | Attempting to modify a constant pointer to nonconstant data. (Part 2 of 2.)

Common Programming Error 9.6

Not initializing a pointer that is declared const is a compilation error.

Constant Pointer to Constant Data

The least amount of access privilege is granted by a ***constant pointer to constant data***. Such a pointer always points to the same memory location, and the data at that memory location cannot be modified using the pointer. This is how an array should be passed to a function that only reads the array, using array subscript notation, and does not modify the array. The program of Fig. 9.14 declares pointer variable ptr to be of type const int * const (line 14). This declaration is read from right to left as "ptr is a constant pointer to an integer constant." The figure shows the error messages generated when an attempt is made to modify the data to which ptr points (line 18) and when an attempt is made to modify the address stored in the pointer variable (line 19). Note that no errors occur when the program attempts to dereference ptr, or when the program attempts to output the val-

```
 1   // Fig. 9.14: ConstantPointer.cpp
 2   // Attempting to modify a constant pointer to constant data.
 3   #include <iostream>
 4   using std::cout;
 5   using std::endl;
 6
 7   int main()
 8   {
 9      int x = 5, y;
10
11      // ptr is a constant pointer to a constant integer.
12      // ptr always points to the same location; the integer
13      // at that location cannot be modified.
14      const int *const ptr = &x;
15
16      cout << *ptr << endl;
17
18      *ptr = 7; // error: *ptr is const; cannot assign new value
19      ptr = &y; // error: ptr is const; cannot assign new address
20      return 0; // indicates successful termination
21   } // end main
```

```
c:\examples\ch09\Fig09_14\ConstantPointer.cpp(18) : error C3892: 'ptr' :
   you cannot assign to a variable that is const
c:\examples\ch09\Fig09_14\ConstantPointer.cpp(19) : error C3892: 'ptr' :
   you cannot assign to a variable that is const
```

Fig. 9.14 | Attempting to modify a constant pointer to constant data.

ue to which `ptr` points (line 16), because neither the pointer nor the data it points to is being modified in this statement.

9.6 Selection Sort Using Pass-by-Reference

In this section, we define a sorting program to demonstrate passing arrays and individual array elements by reference. We use the *selection sort* algorithm, which is an easy-to-program, but unfortunately inefficient, sorting algorithm. The first iteration of the algorithm selects the smallest element in the array and swaps it with the first element. The second iteration selects the second-smallest element (which is the smallest element of the remaining elements) and swaps it with the second element. The algorithm continues until the last iteration selects the second-largest element and swaps it with the second-to-last index, leaving the largest element in the last index. After the ith iteration, the smallest i items of the array will be sorted into increasing order in the first i elements of the array.

As an example, consider the array

| 34 | 56 | 4 | 10 | 77 | 51 | 93 | 30 | 5 | 52 |

A program that implements the selection sort first determines the smallest value (4) in the array, which is contained in element 2. The program swaps the 4 with the value in element 0 (34), resulting in

| **4** | 56 | **34** | 10 | 77 | 51 | 93 | 30 | 5 | 52 |

[*Note:* We use bold to highlight the values that were swapped.] The program then determines the smallest value of the remaining elements (all elements except 4), which is 5, contained in element 8. The program swaps the 5 with the 56 in element 1, resulting in

| 4 | **5** | 34 | 10 | 77 | 51 | 93 | 30 | **56** | 52 |

On the third iteration, the program determines the next smallest value, 10, and swaps it with the value in element 2 (34).

| 4 | 5 | **10** | **34** | 77 | 51 | 93 | 30 | 56 | 52 |

The process continues until the array is fully sorted.

| 4 | 5 | 10 | 30 | 34 | 51 | 52 | 56 | 77 | 93 |

Note that after the first iteration, the smallest element is in the first position. After the second iteration, the two smallest elements are in order in the first two positions. After the third iteration, the three smallest elements are in order in the first three positions.

Figure 9.15 implements selection sort using two functions—`selectionSort` and `swap`. Function `selectionSort` (lines 36–53) sorts the array. Line 38 declares the variable `smallest`, which will store the index of the smallest element in the remaining array. Lines 41–52 loop `size - 1` times. Line 43 sets the index of the smallest element to the current index. Lines 46–49 loop over the remaining elements in the array. For each of these elements, line 48 compares its value to the value of the smallest element. If the current element is smaller than the smallest element, line 49 assigns the current element's index to `smallest`. When this loop finishes, `smallest` will contain the index of the smallest ele-

```
 1   // Fig. 9.15: SelectionSort.cpp
 2   // Selection sort with pass-by-reference. This program puts values into an
 3   // array, sorts them into ascending order and prints the resulting array.
 4   #include <iostream>
 5   using std::cout;
 6   using std::endl;
 7
 8   #include <iomanip>
 9   using std::setw;
10
11   void selectionSort( int * const, const int ); // prototype
12   void swap( int * const, int * const ); // prototype
13
14   int main()
15   {
16      const int arraySize = 10;
17      int a[ arraySize ] = { 2, 6, 4, 8, 10, 12, 89, 68, 45, 37 };
18
19      cout << "Data items in original order\n";
20
21      for ( int i = 0; i < arraySize; i++ )
22         cout << setw( 4 ) << a[ i ];
23
24      selectionSort( a, arraySize ); // sort the array
25
26      cout << "\nData items in ascending order\n";
27
28      for ( int j = 0; j < arraySize; j++ )
29         cout << setw( 4 ) << a[ j ];
30
31      cout << endl;
32      return 0; // indicates successful termination
33   } // end main
34
35   // function to sort an array
36   void selectionSort( int * const array, const int size )
37   {
38      int smallest; // index of smallest element
39
40      // loop over size - 1 elements
41      for ( int i = 0; i < size - 1; i++ )
42      {
43         smallest = i; // first index of remaining array
44
45         // loop to find index of smallest element
46         for ( int index = i + 1; index < size; index++ )
47
48            if ( array[ index ] < array[ smallest ] )
49               smallest = index;
50
51         swap( &array[ i ], &array[ smallest ] );
52      } // end if
53   } // end function selectionSort
```

Fig. 9.15 | Selection sort with pass-by-reference. (Part 1 of 2.)

```
54
55   // swap values at memory locations to which
56   // element1Ptr and element2Ptr point
57   void swap( int * const element1Ptr, int * const element2Ptr )
58   {
59      int hold = *element1Ptr;
60      *element1Ptr = *element2Ptr;
61      *element2Ptr = hold;
62   } // end function swap
```

```
Data items in original order
   2   6   4   8  10  12  89  68  45  37
Data items in ascending order
   2   4   6   8  10  12  37  45  68  89
```

Fig. 9.15 | Selection sort with pass-by-reference. (Part 2 of 2.)

ment in the remaining array. Line 51 calls function swap (lines 57–62) to place the smallest remaining element in the next spot in the array (i.e., exchange the array elements array[i] and array[smallest]).

Let us now look more closely at function swap. Remember that Visual C++ enforces information hiding between functions, so swap does not have access to individual array elements in selectionSort. Because selectionSort *wants* swap to have access to the array elements to be swapped, selectionSort passes each of these elements to swap by reference—the address of each array element is passed explicitly. Although entire arrays are passed by reference, individual array elements are scalars and are ordinarily passed by value. Therefore, selectionSort uses the address operator (&) on each array element in the swap call (line 51) to effect pass-by-reference. Function swap (lines 57–62) receives &array[i] in pointer variable element1Ptr. Information hiding prevents swap from "knowing" the name array[i], but swap can use *element1Ptr as a synonym for array[i]. Thus, when swap references *element1Ptr, it is actually referencing array[i] in selectionSort. Similarly, when swap references *element2Ptr, it is actually referencing array[smallest] in selectionSort.

Even though swap is not allowed to use the statements

```
hold = array[ i ];
array[ i ] = array[ smallest ];
array[ smallest ] = hold;
```

precisely the same effect is achieved by

```
int hold = *element1Ptr;
*element1Ptr = *element2Ptr;
*element2Ptr = hold;
```

in the swap function of Fig. 9.15.

Several features of function selectionSort should be noted. The function header (line 36) declares array as int * const array, rather than int array[], to indicate that the function receives a one-dimensional array as an argument. Both parameter array's pointer and parameter size are declared const to enforce the principle of least privilege.

Although parameter size receives a copy of a value in main and modifying the copy cannot change the value in main, selectionSort does not need to alter size to accomplish its task—the array size remains fixed during the execution of selectionSort. Therefore, size is declared const to ensure that it is not modified. If the size of the array were to be modified during the sorting process, the sorting algorithm would not run correctly.

Note that function selectionSort receives the size of the array as a parameter, because the function must have that information to sort the array. When an array is passed to a function, only the memory address of the first element of the array is received by the function; the array size must be passed separately to the function.

By defining function selectionSort to receive the array size as a parameter, we enable the function to be used by any program that sorts one-dimensional int arrays of arbitrary size. The size of the array could have been programmed directly into the function, but this would restrict the function to processing an array of a specific size and reduce the function's reusability—only programs processing one-dimensional int arrays of the specific size "hard coded" into the function could use the function.

Software Engineering Observation 9.4

When passing an array to a function, also pass the size of the array (rather than building into the function knowledge of the array size)—this makes the function more reusable.

9.7 sizeof Operator

Visual C++ provides the unary operator sizeof to determine the size of an array (or of any other data type, variable or constant) in bytes during program compilation. When applied to the name of an array, as in Fig. 9.16 (line 14), the sizeof operator returns the total number of bytes in the array as a value of type size_t (an unsigned integer type that is at least as big as unsigned int). Note that this is different from the size of a vector< int >, for example, which is the number of integer elements in the vector. The computer we used to compile this program stores variables of type double in 8 bytes of memory, and array is declared to have 20 elements (line 12), so array uses 160 bytes in memory. When applied to a pointer parameter (line 24) in a function that receives an array as an argument, the sizeof operator returns the size of the pointer in bytes (4 on the system we used)—not the size of the array.

Common Programming Error 9.7

Using the sizeof operator in a function to find the size in bytes of an array parameter results in the size in bytes of a pointer, not the size in bytes of the array.

```
 1   // Fig. 9.16: Sizeof.cpp
 2   // Sizeof operator when used on an array name
 3   // returns the number of bytes in the array.
 4   #include <iostream>
 5   using std::cout;
 6   using std::endl;
```

Fig. 9.16 | sizeof operator when applied to an array name returns the number of bytes in the array. (Part 1 of 2.)

```
 7
 8   size_t getSize( double * ); // prototype
 9
10   int main()
11   {
12      double array[ 20 ]; // 20 doubles; occupies 160 bytes on our system
13
14      cout << "The number of bytes in the array is " << sizeof( array );
15
16      cout << "\nThe number of bytes returned by getSize is "
17         << getSize( array ) << endl;
18      return 0; // indicates successful termination
19   } // end main
20
21   // return size of ptr
22   size_t getSize( double *ptr )
23   {
24      return sizeof( ptr );
25   } // end function getSize
```

```
The number of bytes in the array is 160
The number of bytes returned by getSize is 4
```

Fig. 9.16 | sizeof operator when applied to an array name returns the number of bytes in the array. (Part 2 of 2.)

The number of elements in an array also can be determined using the results of two sizeof operations. For example, consider the following array declaration:

> `double realArray[ 22 ];`

If variables of data type double are stored in eight bytes of memory, array realArray contains a total of 176 bytes. To determine the number of elements in the array, the following expression (which is evaluated at compile time) can be used:

> `sizeof realArray / sizeof( double ) // calculate number of elements`

The expression determines the number of bytes in array realArray (176) and divides that value by the number of bytes used in memory to store a double value (8)—the result is the number of elements in realArray (22).

Determining the Sizes of the Fundamental Types, an Array and a Pointer
Figure 9.17 uses sizeof to calculate the number of bytes used to store most of the standard data types. Notice that, in the output, the types double and long double have the same size. Types may have different sizes based on the platform running the program. On another system, for example, double and long double may be of different sizes.

 Portability Tip 9.2

The number of bytes used to store a particular data type may vary among systems. When writing programs that depend on data type sizes, and that will run on several computer systems, use sizeof to determine the number of bytes used to store the data types.

Operator sizeof can be applied to any expression or type name. When sizeof is applied to a variable name (which is not an array name) or other expression, the number of bytes used to store the specific type of the expression's value is returned. Note that the parentheses used with sizeof are required only if a type name (e.g., int) is supplied as its

```cpp
1   // Fig. 9.17: Sizeof.cpp
2   // Demonstrating the sizeof operator.
3   #include <iostream>
4   using std::cout;
5   using std::endl;
6
7   int main()
8   {
9       char c; // variable of type char
10      short s; // variable of type short
11      int i; // variable of type int
12      long l; // variable of type long
13      float f; // variable of type float
14      double d; // variable of type double
15      long double ld; // variable of type long double
16      int array[ 20 ]; // array of int
17      int *ptr = array; // variable of type int *
18
19      cout << "sizeof c = " << sizeof c
20          << "\tsizeof(char) = " << sizeof( char )
21          << "\nsizeof s = " << sizeof s
22          << "\tsizeof(short) = " << sizeof( short )
23          << "\nsizeof i = " << sizeof i
24          << "\tsizeof(int) = " << sizeof( int )
25          << "\nsizeof l = " << sizeof l
26          << "\tsizeof(long) = " << sizeof( long )
27          << "\nsizeof f = " << sizeof f
28          << "\tsizeof(float) = " << sizeof( float )
29          << "\nsizeof d = " << sizeof d
30          << "\tsizeof(double) = " << sizeof( double )
31          << "\nsizeof ld = " << sizeof ld
32          << "\tsizeof(long double) = " << sizeof( long double )
33          << "\nsizeof array = " << sizeof array
34          << "\nsizeof ptr = " << sizeof ptr << endl;
35      return 0; // indicates successful termination
36  } // end main
```

```
sizeof c = 1     sizeof(char) = 1
sizeof s = 2     sizeof(short) = 2
sizeof i = 4     sizeof(int) = 4
sizeof l = 4     sizeof(long) = 4
sizeof f = 4     sizeof(float) = 4
sizeof d = 8     sizeof(double) = 8
sizeof ld = 8    sizeof(long double) = 8
sizeof array = 80
sizeof ptr = 4
```

Fig. 9.17 | sizeof operator used to determine standard data type sizes.

operand. The parentheses used with `sizeof` are not required when `sizeof`'s operand is an expression. Remember that `sizeof` is an operator, not a function, and that it has its effect at compile time, not execution time.

Common Programming Error 9.8

Omitting the parentheses in a `sizeof` operation when the operand is a type name is a compilation error.

Performance Tip 9.2

Because `sizeof` is a compile-time unary operator, not an execution-time operator, using `sizeof` does not negatively impact execution performance.

Error-Prevention Tip 9.3

To avoid errors associated with omitting the parentheses around the operand of operator `sizeof`, many programmers include parentheses around every `sizeof` operand.

9.8 Pointer Expressions and Pointer Arithmetic

Pointers are valid operands in arithmetic expressions, assignment expressions and comparison expressions. However, not all the operators normally used in these expressions are valid with pointer variables. This section describes the operators that can have pointers as operands and how these operators are used with pointers.

Several arithmetic operations may be performed on pointers. A pointer may be incremented (++) or decremented (--), an integer may be added to a pointer (+ or +=), an integer may be subtracted from a pointer (- or -=) or one pointer may be subtracted from another of the same type.

Assume that array `int v[ 5 ]` has been declared and that its first element is at memory location 3000. Assume that pointer `vPtr` has been initialized to point to `v[ 0 ]` (i.e., the value of `vPtr` is 3000). Figure 9.18 diagrams this situation for a machine with four-byte integers. Note that `vPtr` can be initialized to point to array `v` with either of the following statements (because the name of an array is equivalent to the address of its first element):

```
int *vPtr = v;
int *vPtr = &v[ 0 ];
```

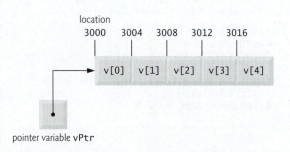

Fig. 9.18 | Array v and a pointer variable `int *vPtr` that points to v.

Portability Tip 9.3

Most computers today have two-byte or four-byte integers. Some of the newer machines use eight-byte integers. Because the results of pointer arithmetic depend on the size of the objects a pointer points to, pointer arithmetic is machine dependent.

In conventional arithmetic, the addition 3000 + 2 yields the value 3002. This is normally not the case with pointer arithmetic. When an integer is added to, or subtracted from, a pointer, the pointer is not simply incremented or decremented by that integer, but by that integer times the size of the object to which the pointer refers. The number of bytes depends on the object's data type. For example, the statement

```
vPtr += 2;
```

would produce 3008 (3000 + 2 * 4), assuming that an int is stored in four bytes of memory. In the array v, vPtr would now point to v[2] (Fig. 9.19). If an integer is stored in two bytes of memory, then the preceding calculation would result in memory location 3004 (3000 + 2 * 2). If the array elements were of a different data type, the preceding statement would increment the pointer by twice the number of bytes it takes to store an object of that data type. When performing pointer arithmetic on a character array, the results will be consistent with regular arithmetic, because each character is one byte long.

If vPtr had been incremented to 3016, which points to v[4], the statement

```
vPtr -= 4;
```

would set vPtr back to 3000—the beginning of the array. If a pointer is being incremented or decremented by one, the increment (++) and decrement (--) operators can be used. Each of the statements

```
++vPtr;
vPtr++;
```

increments the pointer to point to the next element of the array. Each of the statements

```
--vPtr;
vPtr--;
```

decrements the pointer to point to the previous element of the array.

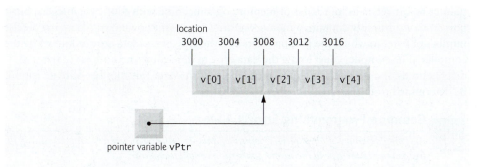

Fig. 9.19 | Pointer vPtr after pointer arithmetic.

Pointer variables that point to the same array may be subtracted from one another. For example, if vPtr contains the address 3000 and v2Ptr contains the address 3008, the statement

```
x = v2Ptr - vPtr;
```

would assign to x the number of array elements from vPtr to v2Ptr—in this case, 2. Pointer arithmetic is meaningless unless performed on a pointer that points to an array. We cannot assume that two variables of the same type are stored contiguously in memory unless they are adjacent elements of an array.

Common Programming Error 9.9

Using pointer arithmetic on a pointer that does not refer to an array of values is a logic error.

Common Programming Error 9.10

Subtracting or comparing two pointers that do not refer to elements of the same array is a logic error.

Common Programming Error 9.11

Using pointer arithmetic to increment or decrement a pointer such that the pointer refers to an element outside the bounds of the array is normally a logic error.

A pointer can be assigned to another pointer if both pointers are of the same type. Otherwise, a cast operator must be used to convert the value of the pointer on the right of the assignment to the type of the pointer on the left of the assignment. The exception to this rule is the pointer to void (i.e., void *), which is a generic pointer capable of representing any pointer type. All pointer types can be assigned to a pointer of type void * without casting. However, a pointer of type void * cannot be assigned directly to a pointer of another type—the pointer of type void * must first be cast to the proper pointer type.

Software Engineering Observation 9.5

Nonconstant pointer arguments can be passed to constant pointer parameters. This is helpful when the body of a program uses a nonconstant pointer to access data, but does not want that data to be modified by a function called in the body of the program.

A void * pointer cannot be dereferenced. For example, the compiler "knows" that a pointer to int refers to four bytes of memory on a machine with four-byte integers, but a pointer to void simply contains a memory address for an unknown data type—the precise number of bytes to which the pointer refers and the type of the data are not known by the compiler. The compiler must know the data type to determine the number of bytes to be dereferenced for a particular pointer—for a pointer to void, this number of bytes cannot be determined from the type.

Common Programming Error 9.12

*Assigning a pointer of one type to a pointer of another (other than void *) without casting the first pointer to the type of the second pointer is a compilation error.*

Common Programming Error 9.13

All operations on a void * *pointer are compilation errors, except comparing* void * *pointers with other pointers, casting* void * *pointers to valid pointer types and assigning addresses to* void * *pointers.*

Pointers can be compared using equality and relational operators. Comparisons using relational operators are meaningless unless the pointers point to members of the same array. Pointer comparisons compare the addresses stored in the pointers. A comparison of two pointers pointing to the same array could show, for example, that one pointer points to a higher-numbered element of the array than the other pointer does. A common use of pointer comparison is determining whether a pointer is 0 (i.e., the pointer is a null pointer—it does not point to anything).

9.9 Relationship Between Pointers and Arrays

Arrays and pointers are intimately related in Visual C++ and may be used *almost* interchangeably. An array name can be thought of as a constant pointer. Pointers can be used to do any operation involving array subscripting.

Assume the following declarations:

```
int b[ 5 ]; // create 5-element int array b
int *bPtr; // create int pointer bPtr
```

Because the array name (without a subscript) is a (constant) pointer to the first element of the array, we can set bPtr to the address of the first element in array b with the statement

```
bPtr = b; // assign address of array b to bPtr
```

This is equivalent to assigning the address of the first element of the array as follows:

```
bPtr = &b[ 0 ]; // also assigns address of array b to bPtr
```

Array element b[3] can alternatively be referenced with the pointer expression

```
*( bPtr + 3 )
```

The 3 in the preceding expression is the *offset* to the pointer. When the pointer points to the beginning of an array, the offset indicates which element of the array should be referenced, and the offset value is identical to the array subscript. The preceding notation is referred to as *pointer/offset notation*. The parentheses are necessary, because the precedence of * is higher than the precedence of +. Without the parentheses, the above expression would add 3 to the value of *bPtr (i.e., 3 would be added to b[0], assuming that bPtr points to the beginning of the array). Just as the array element can be referenced with a pointer expression, the address

```
&b[ 3 ]
```

can be written with the pointer expression

```
bPtr + 3
```

The array name (which is implicitly const) can be treated as a pointer and used in pointer arithmetic. For example, the expression

```
*( b + 3 )
```

also refers to the array element b[3]. In general, all subscripted array expressions can be written with a pointer and an offset. In this case, pointer/offset notation was used with the name of the array as a pointer. Note that the preceding expression does not modify the array name in any way; b still points to the first element in the array.

Pointers can be subscripted exactly as arrays can. For example, the expression

```
bPtr[ 1 ]
```

refers to the array element b[1]; this expression uses *pointer/subscript notation*.

Remember that an array name is a constant pointer; it always points to the beginning of the array. Thus, the expression

```
b += 3
```

causes a compilation error, because it attempts to modify the value of the array name (a constant) with pointer arithmetic.

Common Programming Error 9.14

Although array names are pointers to the beginning of the array and pointers can be modified in arithmetic expressions, array names cannot be modified in arithmetic expressions, because array names are constant pointers.

Good Programming Practice 9.2

For clarity, use array notation instead of pointer notation when manipulating arrays.

Figure 9.20 uses the four notations discussed in this section for referring to array elements—array subscript notation, pointer/offset notation with the array name as a pointer, pointer subscript notation and pointer/offset notation with a pointer—to accomplish the same task, namely printing the four elements of the integer array b.

```
1   // Fig. 9.20: PointerArrays.cpp
2   // Using subscripting and pointer notations with arrays.
3   #include <iostream>
4   using std::cout;
5   using std::endl;
6
7   int main()
8   {
9      int b[] = { 10, 20, 30, 40 }; // create 4-element array b
10     int *bPtr = b; // set bPtr to point to array b
11
12     // output array b using array subscript notation
13     cout << "Array b printed with:\n\nArray subscript notation\n";
14
15     for ( int i = 0; i < 4; i++ )
16        cout << "b[" << i << "] = " << b[ i ] << '\n';
17
```

Fig. 9.20 | Referencing array elements with the array name and with pointers. (Part 1 of 2.)

```
18        // output array b using .the array name and pointer/offset notation
19        cout << "\nPointer/offset notation where "
20           << "the pointer is the array name\n";
21
22        for ( int offset1 = 0; offset1 < 4; offset1++ )
23           cout << "*(b + " << offset1 << ") = " << *( b + offset1 ) << '\n';
24
25        // output array b using bPtr and array subscript notation
26        cout << "\nPointer subscript notation\n";
27
28        for ( int j = 0; j < 4; j++ )
29           cout << "bPtr[" << j << "] = " << bPtr[ j ] << '\n';
30
31        cout << "\nPointer/offset notation\n";
32
33        // output array b using bPtr and pointer/offset notation
34        for ( int offset2 = 0; offset2 < 4; offset2++ )
35           cout << "*(bPtr + " << offset2 << ") = "
36              << *( bPtr + offset2 ) << '\n';
37
38        return 0; // indicates successful termination
39     } // end main
```

```
Array b printed with:

Array subscript notation
b[0] = 10
b[1] = 20
b[2] = 30
b[3] = 40

Pointer/offset notation where the pointer is the array name
*(b + 0) = 10
*(b + 1) = 20
*(b + 2) = 30
*(b + 3) = 40

Pointer subscript notation
bPtr[0] = 10
bPtr[1] = 20
bPtr[2] = 30
bPtr[3] = 40

Pointer/offset notation
*(bPtr + 0) = 10
*(bPtr + 1) = 20
*(bPtr + 2) = 30
*(bPtr + 3) = 40
```

Fig. 9.20 | Referencing array elements with the array name and with pointers. (Part 2 of 2.)

To further illustrate the interchangeability of arrays and pointers, let us look at the two string-copying functions—copy1 and copy2—in the program of Fig. 9.21. Both functions copy a string into a character array. After a comparison of the function prototypes for copy1 and copy2, the functions appear identical (because of the interchange-

```
1   // Fig. 9.21: StringPointers.cpp
2   // Copying a string using array notation and pointer notation.
3   #include <iostream>
4   using std::cout;
5   using std::endl;
6
7   void copy1( char *, const char * ); // prototype
8   void copy2( char *, const char * ); // prototype
9
10  int main()
11  {
12     char string1[ 10 ];
13     char *string2 = "Hello";
14     char string3[ 10 ];
15     char string4[] = "Good Bye";
16
17     copy1( string1, string2 ); // copy string2 into string1
18     cout << "string1 = " << string1 << endl;
19
20     copy2( string3, string4 ); // copy string4 into string3
21     cout << "string3 = " << string3 << endl;
22     return 0; // indicates successful termination
23  } // end main
24
25  // copy s2 to s1 using array notation
26  void copy1( char * s1, const char * s2 )
27  {
28     // copying occurs in the for header
29     for ( int i = 0; ( s1[ i ] = s2[ i ] ) != '\0'; i++ )
30        ; // do nothing in body
31  } // end function copy1
32
33  // copy s2 to s1 using pointer notation
34  void copy2( char *s1, const char *s2 )
35  {
36     // copying occurs in the for header
37     for ( ; ( *s1 = *s2 ) != '\0'; s1++, s2++ )
38        ; // do nothing in body
39  } // end function copy2
```

```
string1 = Hello
string3 = Good Bye
```

Fig. 9.21 | String copying using array notation and pointer notation.

ability of arrays and pointers). These functions accomplish the same task, but they are implemented differently.

Function copy1 (lines 26–31) uses array subscript notation to copy the string in s2 to the character array s1. The function declares an integer counter variable i to use as the array subscript. The for statement header (line 29) performs the entire copy operation—its body is the empty statement. The header specifies that i is initialized to zero and incremented by one on each iteration of the loop. The condition in the for, (s1[i] =

s2[i]) != '\0', performs the copy operation character by character from s2 to s1. When the null character is encountered in s2, it is assigned to s1, and the loop terminates, because the null character is equal to '\0'. Remember that the value of an assignment statement is the value assigned to its left operand.

Function copy2 (lines 34–39) uses pointers and pointer arithmetic to copy the string in s2 to the character array s1. Again, the for statement header (line 37) performs the entire copy operation. The header does not include any variable initialization. As in function copy1, the condition (*s1 = *s2) != '\0' performs the copy operation. Pointer s2 is dereferenced, and the resulting character is assigned to the dereferenced pointer s1. After the assignment in the condition, the loop increments both pointers, so they point to the next element of array s1 and the next character of string s2, respectively. When the loop encounters the null character in s2, the null character is assigned to the dereferenced pointer s1 and the loop terminates. Note that the "increment portion" of this for statement has two increment expressions separated by a comma operator.

The first argument to both copy1 and copy2 must be an array large enough to hold the string in the second argument. Otherwise, an error may occur when an attempt is made to write into a memory location beyond the bounds of the array (recall that when using pointer-based arrays, there is no "built-in" bounds checking). Also, note that the second parameter of each function is declared as const char * (a pointer to a character constant—i.e., a constant string). In both functions, the second argument is copied into the first argument—characters are copied from the second argument one at a time, but the characters are never modified. Therefore, the second parameter is declared to point to a constant value to enforce the principle of least privilege—neither function needs to modify the second argument, so neither function is allowed to modify the second argument.

9.10 Arrays of Pointers

Arrays may contain pointers. A common use of such a data structure is to form an array of pointer-based strings, referred to simply as a *string array*. Each entry in the array is a string, but in Visual C++ a string is essentially a pointer to its first character, so each entry in an array of strings is simply a pointer to the first character of a string. Consider the declaration of string array suit that might be useful in representing a deck of cards:

```
const char *suit[ 4 ] =
    { "Hearts", "Diamonds", "Clubs", "Spades" };
```

The suit[4] portion of the declaration indicates an array of four elements. The const char * portion of the declaration indicates that each element of array suit is of type "pointer to char constant data." The four values to be placed in the array are "Hearts", "Diamonds", "Clubs" and "Spades". Each is stored in memory as a null-terminated character string that is one character longer than the number of characters between quotes. The four strings are seven, nine, six and seven characters long (including their terminating null characters), respectively. Although it appears as though these strings are being placed in the suit array, only pointers are actually stored in the array, as shown in Fig. 9.22. Each pointer points to the first character of its corresponding string. Thus, even though the suit array is fixed in size, it provides access to character strings of any length. This flexibility is one example of Visual C++'s powerful data-structuring capabilities.

Fig. 9.22 | Graphical representation of the suit array.

The suit strings could be placed into a two-dimensional array, in which each row represents one suit and each column represents one of the letters of a suit name. Such a data structure must have a fixed number of columns per row, and that number must be as large as the largest string. Therefore, considerable memory is wasted when we store a large number of strings, of which most are shorter than the longest string. We use arrays of strings to help represent a deck of cards in the next section.

String arrays are commonly used with *command-line arguments* that are passed to function main when a program begins execution. Such arguments follow the program name when a program is executed from the command line. A typical use of command-line arguments is to pass options to a program. For example, from the command line on a Windows computer, the user can type

```
dir /p
```

to list the contents of the current directory and pause after each screen of information. When the dir command executes, the option /p is passed to dir as a command-line argument. Such arguments are placed in a string array that main receives as an argument.

9.11 Case Study: Card Shuffling and Dealing Simulation

This section uses random-number generation to develop a card shuffling and dealing simulation program. This program can then be used as a basis for implementing programs that play specific card games. To reveal some subtle performance problems, we have intentionally used suboptimal shuffling and dealing algorithms. In the exercises, we develop more efficient algorithms.

Using the top-down, stepwise-refinement approach, we develop a program that will shuffle a deck of 52 playing cards and then deal each of the 52 cards. The top-down approach is particularly useful in attacking larger, more complex problems than we have seen in the early chapters.

We use a 4-by-13 two-dimensional array deck to represent the deck of playing cards (Fig. 9.23). The rows correspond to the suits—row 0 corresponds to hearts, row 1 to diamonds, row 2 to clubs and row 3 to spades. The columns correspond to the face values of the cards—columns 0 through 9 correspond to the faces ace through 10, respectively, and columns 10 through 12 correspond to the jack, queen and king, respectively. We shall load the string array suit with character strings representing the four suits (as in Fig. 9.22) and the string array face with character strings representing the 13 face values.

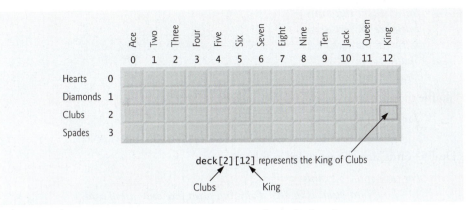

Fig. 9.23 | Two-dimensional array representation of a deck of cards.

This simulated deck of cards may be shuffled as follows. First the 52-element array deck is initialized to zeros. Then, a row (0–3) and a column (0–12) are each chosen at random. The number 1 is inserted in array element deck[row][column] to indicate that this card is going to be the first one dealt from the shuffled deck. This process continues with the numbers 2, 3, …, 52 being randomly inserted in the deck array to indicate which cards are to be placed second, third, …, and 52nd in the shuffled deck. As the deck array begins to fill with card numbers, it is possible that a card will be selected twice (i.e., deck[row][column] will be nonzero when it is selected). This selection is simply ignored, and other row and column combinations are repeatedly chosen at random until an unselected card is found. Eventually, the numbers 1 through 52 will occupy the 52 slots of the deck array. At this point, the deck of cards is fully shuffled.

This shuffling algorithm could execute for an indefinitely long period if cards that have already been shuffled are repeatedly selected at random. This phenomenon is known as ***indefinite postponement*** (also called ***starvation***). In the exercises, we discuss a faster shuffling algorithm that also eliminates the possibility of indefinite postponement.

Performance Tip 9.3

Sometimes algorithms that emerge in a "natural" way can contain subtle performance problems such as indefinite postponement. Seek algorithms that avoid indefinite postponement.

To deal the first card, we search the array for the element deck[row][column] that matches 1. This is accomplished with nested for statements that vary row from 0 to 3 and column from 0 to 12. What card does that slot of the array correspond to? The suit array has been preloaded with the four suits, so to get the suit, we print the character string suit[row]. Similarly, to get the face value of the card, we print the character string face[column]. We also print the character string " of ". Printing this information in the proper order enables us to print each card in the form "King of Clubs", "Ace of Diamonds" and so on.

Let us proceed with the top-down, stepwise-refinement process. The top is simply

Shuffle and deal 52 cards

Our first refinement yields

Initialize the suit array
Initialize the face array
Initialize the deck array
Shuffle the deck
Deal 52 cards

"Shuffle the deck" may be expanded as follows:

For each of the 52 cards
Place card number in randomly selected unoccupied slot of deck

"Deal 52 cards" may be expanded as follows:

For each of the 52 cards
Find card number in deck array and print face and suit of card

Incorporating these expansions yields our complete second refinement:

Initialize the suit array
Initialize the face array
Initialize the deck array

For each of the 52 cards
Place card number in randomly selected unoccupied slot of deck

For each of the 52 cards
Find card number in deck array and print face and suit of card

"Place card number in randomly selected unoccupied slot of deck" may be expanded as follows:

Choose slot of deck randomly

While chosen slot of deck has been previously chosen
Choose slot of deck randomly

Place card number in chosen slot of deck

"Find card number in deck array and print face and suit of card" may be expanded as follows:

For each slot of the deck array
If slot contains card number
Print the face and suit of the card

Incorporating these expansions yields our third refinement (Fig. 9.24).

This completes the refinement process. Figures 9.25–9.27 contain the card shuffling and dealing program and a sample execution. Lines 62–68 of function deal (Fig. 9.26) implement lines 1–2 of Fig. 9.24. The constructor (lines 22–36 of Fig. 9.26) implements lines 1–3 of Fig. 9.24. Function shuffle (lines 39–56 of Fig. 9.26) implements lines 5–11 of Fig. 9.24. Function deal (lines 59–89 of Fig. 9.26) implements lines 13–16 of Fig. 9.24. Note the output formatting used in function deal (lines 82–84 of Fig. 9.26). The output statement outputs the face right justified in a field of five characters and outputs the suit left justified in a field of eight characters (Fig. 9.27). The output is printed in two-column format—if the card being output is in the first column, a tab is output after the card to move to the second column (line 84); otherwise, a newline is output.

```
 1    Initialize the suit array
 2    Initialize the face array
 3    Initialize the deck array
 4
 5    For each of the 52 cards
 6        Choose slot of deck randomly
 7
 8        While slot of deck has been previously chosen
 9            Choose slot of deck randomly
10
11        Place card number in chosen slot of deck
12
13    For each of the 52 cards
14
15        For each slot of deck array
16
17            If slot contains desired card number
18                Print the face and suit of the card
```

Fig. 9.24 | Pseudocode algorithm for card shuffling and dealing program.

```cpp
 1    // Fig. 9.25: DeckOfCards.h
 2    // Definition of class DeckOfCards that
 3    // represents a deck of playing cards.
 4
 5    // DeckOfCards class definition
 6    class DeckOfCards
 7    {
 8    public:
 9        DeckOfCards(); // constructor initializes deck
10        void shuffle(); // shuffles cards in deck
11        void deal(); // deals cards in deck
12    private:
13        int deck[ 4 ][ 13 ]; // represents deck of cards
14    }; // end class DeckOfCards
```

Fig. 9.25 | DeckOfCards header file.

```cpp
 1    // Fig. 9.26: DeckOfCards.cpp
 2    // Member-function definitions for class DeckOfCards that simulates
 3    // the shuffling and dealing of a deck of playing cards.
 4    #include <iostream>
 5    using std::cout;
 6    using std::left;
 7    using std::right;
 8
 9    #include <iomanip>
10    using std::setw;
```

Fig. 9.26 | Definitions of member functions for shuffling and dealing. (Part 1 of 3.)

```
11
12   #include <cstdlib> // prototypes for rand and srand
13   using std::rand;
14   using std::srand;
15
16   #include <ctime> // prototype for time
17   using std::time;
18
19   #include "DeckOfCards.h" // DeckOfCards class definition
20
21   // DeckOfCards default constructor initializes deck
22   DeckOfCards::DeckOfCards()
23   {
24      // loop through rows of deck
25      for ( int row = 0; row <= 3; row++ )
26      {
27         // loop through columns of deck for current row
28         for ( int column = 0; column <= 12; column++ )
29         {
30            deck[ row ][ column ] = 0; // initialize slot of deck to 0
31         } // end inner for
32      } // end outer for
33
34      // seed random number generator
35      srand( static_cast< unsigned >( time( 0 ) ) );
36   } // end DeckOfCards default constructor
37
38   // shuffle cards in deck
39   void DeckOfCards::shuffle()
40   {
41      int row; // represents suit value of card
42      int column; // represents face value of card
43
44      // for each of the 52 cards, choose a slot of the deck randomly
45      for ( int card = 1; card <= 52; card++ )
46      {
47         do // choose a new random location until unoccupied slot is found
48         {
49            row = rand() % 4; // randomly select the row (0 to 3)
50            column = rand() % 13; // randomly select the column (0 to 12)
51         } while( deck[ row ][ column ] != 0 ); // end do...while
52
53         // place card number in chosen slot of deck
54         deck[ row ][ column ] = card;
55      } // end for
56   } // end function shuffle
57
58   // deal cards in deck
59   void DeckOfCards::deal()
60   {
61      // initialize suit array
62      static const char *suit[ 4 ] =
63         { "Hearts", "Diamonds", "Clubs", "Spades" };
```

Fig. 9.26 | Definitions of member functions for shuffling and dealing. (Part 2 of 3.)

```
64
65      // initialize face array
66      static const char *face[ 13 ] =
67         { "Ace", "Deuce", "Three", "Four", "Five", "Six", "Seven",
68           "Eight", "Nine", "Ten", "Jack", "Queen", "King" };
69
70      // for each of the 52 cards
71      for ( int card = 1; card <= 52; card++ )
72      {
73         // loop through rows of deck
74         for ( int row = 0; row <= 3; row++ )
75         {
76            // loop through columns of deck for current row
77            for ( int column = 0; column <= 12; column++ )
78            {
79               // if slot contains current card, display card
80               if ( deck[ row ][ column ] == card )
81               {
82                  cout << setw( 5 ) << right << face[ column ]
83                     << " of " << setw( 8 ) << left << suit[ row ]
84                     << ( card % 2 == 0 ? '\n' : '\t' );
85               } // end if
86            } // end innermost for
87         } // end inner for
88      } // end outer for
89   } // end function deal
```

Fig. 9.26 | Definitions of member functions for shuffling and dealing. (Part 3 of 3.)

There is also a weakness in the dealing algorithm. Once a match is found, even if it is found on the first try, the two inner for statements continue searching the remaining elements of deck for a match. In the exercises, we correct this deficiency.

```
 1   // Fig. 9.27: DeckOfCardsTest.cpp
 2   // Card shuffling and dealing program.
 3   #include "DeckOfCards.h" // DeckOfCards class definition
 4
 5   int main()
 6   {
 7      DeckOfCards deckOfCards; // create DeckOfCards object
 8
 9      deckOfCards.shuffle(); // shuffle the cards in the deck
10      deckOfCards.deal(); // deal the cards in the deck
11      return 0; // indicates successful termination
12   } // end main
```

```
  Nine of Spades        Seven of Clubs
  Five of Spades        Eight of Clubs
Queen of Diamonds       Three of Hearts
  Jack of Spades         Five of Diamonds
  Jack of Diamonds      Three of Diamonds
```

Fig. 9.27 | Card shuffling and dealing program. (Part 1 of 2.)

Three of Clubs	Six of Clubs
Ten of Clubs	Nine of Diamonds
Ace of Hearts	Queen of Hearts
Seven of Spades	Deuce of Spades
Six of Hearts	Deuce of Clubs
Ace of Clubs	Deuce of Diamonds
Nine of Hearts	Seven of Diamonds
Six of Spades	Eight of Diamonds
Ten of Spades	King of Hearts
Four of Clubs	Ace of Spades
Ten of Hearts	Four of Spades
Eight of Hearts	Eight of Spades
Jack of Hearts	Ten of Diamonds
Four of Diamonds	King of Diamonds
Seven of Hearts	King of Spades
Queen of Spades	Four of Hearts
Nine of Clubs	Six of Diamonds
Deuce of Hearts	Jack of Clubs
King of Clubs	Three of Spades
Queen of Clubs	Five of Clubs
Five of Hearts	Ace of Diamonds

Fig. 9.27 | Card shuffling and dealing program. (Part 2 of 2.)

9.12 Function Pointers

A pointer to a function contains the address of the function in memory. In Chapter 8, we saw that the name of an array is actually the address in memory of the first element of the array. Similarly, the name of a function is actually the starting address in memory of the code that performs the function's task. Pointers to functions can be passed to functions, returned from functions, stored in arrays, assigned to other function pointers and used to call the underlying function.

Multipurpose Selection Sort Using Function Pointers

To illustrate the use of pointers to functions, Fig. 9.28 modifies the selection sort program of Fig. 9.15. Figure 9.28 consists of main (lines 17–55) and the functions selectionSort (lines 59–76), swap (lines 80–85), ascending (lines 89–92) and descending (lines 96–99). Function selectionSort receives a pointer to a function—either function ascending or function descending—as an argument in addition to the integer array to sort and the size of the array. Functions ascending and descending determine the sorting order. The program prompts the user to choose whether the array should be sorted in ascending order or in descending order (lines 24–26). If the user enters 1, a pointer to function ascending is passed to function selectionSort (line 37), causing the array to be sorted into increasing order. If the user enters 2, a pointer to function descending is passed to function selectionSort (line 45), causing the array to be sorted into decreasing order.

```
1   // Fig. 9.28: FunctionPointers.cpp
2   // Multipurpose sorting program using function pointers.
3   #include <iostream>
```

Fig. 9.28 | Multipurpose sorting program using function pointers. (Part 1 of 4.)

```
 4    using std::cout;
 5    using std::cin;
 6    using std::endl;
 7
 8    #include <iomanip>
 9    using std::setw;
10
11    // prototypes
12    void selectionSort( int [], const int, bool (*)( int, int ) );
13    void swap( int * const, int * const );
14    bool ascending( int, int ); // implements ascending order
15    bool descending( int, int ); // implements descending order
16
17    int main()
18    {
19       const int arraySize = 10;
20       int order; // 1 = ascending, 2 = descending
21       int counter; // array index
22       int a[ arraySize ] = { 2, 6, 4, 8, 10, 12, 89, 68, 45, 37 };
23
24       cout << "Enter 1 to sort in ascending order,\n"
25          << "Enter 2 to sort in descending order: ";
26       cin >> order;
27       cout << "\nData items in original order\n";
28
29       // output original array
30       for ( counter = 0; counter < arraySize; counter++ )
31          cout << setw( 4 ) << a[ counter ];
32
33       // sort array in ascending order; pass function ascending
34       // as an argument to specify ascending sorting order
35       if ( order == 1 )
36       {
37          selectionSort( a, arraySize, ascending );
38          cout << "\nData items in ascending order\n";
39       } // end if
40
41       // sort array in descending order; pass function descending
42       // as an argument to specify descending sorting order
43       else
44       {
45          selectionSort( a, arraySize, descending );
46          cout << "\nData items in descending order\n";
47       } // end else part of if...else
48
49       // output sorted array
50       for ( counter = 0; counter < arraySize; counter++ )
51          cout << setw( 4 ) << a[ counter ];
52
53       cout << endl;
54       return 0; // indicates successful termination
55    } // end main
56
```

Fig. 9.28 | Multipurpose sorting program using function pointers. (Part 2 of 4.)

```
57   // multipurpose selection sort; the parameter compare is a pointer to
58   // the comparison function that determines the sorting order
59   void selectionSort( int work[], const int size,
60                       bool (*compare)( int, int ) )
61   {
62      int smallestOrLargest; // index of smallest (or largest) element
63
64      // loop over size - 1 elements
65      for ( int i = 0; i < size - 1; i++ )
66      {
67         smallestOrLargest = i; // first index of remaining vector
68
69         // loop to find index of smallest (or largest) element
70         for ( int index = i + 1; index < size; index++ )
71            if ( !(*compare)( work[ smallestOrLargest ], work[ index ] ) )
72               smallestOrLargest = index;
73
74         swap( &work[ smallestOrLargest ], &work[ i ] );
75      } // end if
76   } // end function selectionSort
77
78   // swap values at memory locations to which
79   // element1Ptr and element2Ptr point
80   void swap( int * const element1Ptr, int * const element2Ptr )
81   {
82      int hold = *element1Ptr;
83      *element1Ptr = *element2Ptr;
84      *element2Ptr = hold;
85   } // end function swap
86
87   // determine whether element a is less than
88   // element b for an ascending order sort
89   bool ascending( int a, int b )
90   {
91      return a < b; // returns true if a is less than b
92   } // end function ascending
93
94   // determine whether element a is greater than
95   // element b for a descending order sort
96   bool descending( int a, int b )
97   {
98      return a > b; // returns true if a is greater than b
99   } // end function descending
```

```
Enter 1 to sort in ascending order,
Enter 2 to sort in descending order: 1

Data items in original order
   2   6   4   8  10  12  89  68  45  37
Data items in ascending order
   2   4   6   8  10  12  37  45  68  89
```

Fig. 9.28 | Multipurpose sorting program using function pointers. (Part 3 of 4.)

```
Enter 1 to sort in ascending order,
Enter 2 to sort in descending order: 2

Data items in original order
   2   6   4   8  10  12  89  68  45  37
Data items in descending order
  89  68  45  37  12  10   8   6   4   2
```

Fig. 9.28 | Multipurpose sorting program using function pointers. (Part 4 of 4.)

The following parameter appears in line 60 of selectionSort's function header:

> ***bool*** (*compare)(***int, int***)

This parameter specifies a pointer to a function. The keyword bool indicates that the function being pointed to returns a bool value. The text (*compare) indicates the name of the pointer to the function (the * indicates that parameter compare is a pointer). The text (int, int) indicates that the function pointed to by compare takes two integer arguments. Parentheses are needed around *compare to indicate that compare is a pointer to a function. If we had not included the parentheses, the declaration would have been

> ***bool*** *compare(***int, int***)

which declares a function that receives two integers as parameters and returns a pointer to a bool value.

The corresponding parameter in the function prototype of selectionSort is

> ***bool*** (*)(***int, int***)

Note that only types have been included. As always, for documentation purposes, you can include names that the compiler will ignore.

The function passed to selectionSort is called in line 71 as follows:

> (*compare)(work[smallestOrLargest], work[index])

Just as a pointer to a variable is dereferenced to access the value of the variable, a pointer to a function is dereferenced to execute the function. The parentheses around *compare are necessary—if they were left out, the * operator would attempt to dereference the value returned from the function call. The call to the function could have been made without dereferencing the pointer, as in

> compare(work[smallestOrLargest], work[index])

which uses the pointer directly as the function name. We prefer the first method of calling a function through a pointer, because it explicitly illustrates that compare is a pointer to a function that is dereferenced to call the function. The second method of calling a function through a pointer makes it appear as though compare is the name of an actual function in the program. This may be confusing to a user of the program who would like to see the definition of function compare and finds that it is not defined in the file.

Chapter 23, Standard Template Library (STL), presents many common uses of function pointers.

Arrays of Pointers to Functions

One use of function pointers is in menu-driven systems. For example, a program might prompt a user to select an option from a menu by entering an integer value. The user's choice can be used as a subscript into an array of function pointers, and the pointer in the array can be used to call the function.

Figure 9.29 provides a mechanical example that demonstrates declaring and using an array of pointers to functions. The program defines three functions—function0, function1 and function2—that each take an integer argument and do not return a value. Line 17 stores pointers to these three functions in array f. In this case, all the functions to which the array points must have the same return type and same parameter types. The declaration in line 17 is read beginning in the leftmost set of parentheses as, "f is an array of three pointers to functions that each take an int as an argument and return void." The array is initialized with the names of the three functions (which, again, are pointers). The program prompts the user to enter a number between 0 and 2, or 3 to terminate. When the user enters a value between 0 and 2, the value is used as the subscript into the array of pointers to functions. Line 29 invokes one of the functions in array f. In the call, f[choice] selects the pointer at location choice in the array. The pointer is dereferenced to call the function, and choice is passed as the argument to the function. Each function prints its argument's value and its function name to indicate that the function is called correctly. In the exercises, you'll develop a menu-driven system. We'll see in Chapter 14, Object-Oriented Programming: Polymorphism, that arrays of pointers to functions are used by compiler developers to implement the mechanisms that support virtual functions—the key technology behind polymorphism.

```cpp
1   // Fig. 9.29: ArrayOfFunctionPointers.cpp
2   // Demonstrating an array of pointers to functions.
3   #include <iostream>
4   using std::cout;
5   using std::cin;
6   using std::endl;
7
8   // function prototypes -- each function performs similar actions
9   void function0( int );
10  void function1( int );
11  void function2( int );
12
13  int main()
14  {
15     // initialize array of 3 pointers to functions that each
16     // take an int argument and return void
17     void (*f[ 3 ])( int ) = { function0, function1, function2 };
18
19     int choice;
20
21     cout << "Enter a number between 0 and 2, 3 to end: ";
22     cin >> choice;
23
```

Fig. 9.29 | Array of pointers to functions. (Part 1 of 2.)

```
24       // process user's choice
25       while ( ( choice >= 0 ) && ( choice < 3 ) )
26       {
27          // invoke the function at location choice in
28          // the array f and pass choice as an argument
29          (*f[ choice ])( choice );
30
31          cout << "Enter a number between 0 and 2, 3 to end: ";
32          cin >> choice;
33       } // end while
34
35       cout << "Program execution completed." << endl;
36       return 0; // indicates successful termination
37    } // end main
38
39    void function0( int a )
40    {
41       cout << "You entered " << a << " so function0 was called\n\n";
42    } // end function function0
43
44    void function1( int b )
45    {
46       cout << "You entered " << b << " so function1 was called\n\n";
47    } // end function function1
48
49    void function2( int c )
50    {
51       cout << "You entered " << c << " so function2 was called\n\n";
52    } // end function function2
```

```
Enter a number between 0 and 2, 3 to end: 0
You entered 0 so function0 was called

Enter a number between 0 and 2, 3 to end: 1
You entered 1 so function1 was called

Enter a number between 0 and 2, 3 to end: 2
You entered 2 so function2 was called

Enter a number between 0 and 2, 3 to end: 3
Program execution completed.
```

Fig. 9.29 | Array of pointers to functions. (Part 2 of 2.)

9.13 Introduction to Pointer-Based String Processing

In this section, we introduce some common C++ Standard Library functions that facilitate string processing. The techniques discussed here are appropriate for developing text editors, word processors, page layout software, computerized typesetting systems and other kinds of text-processing software. We have already used the C++ Standard Library string class in several examples to represent strings as full-fledged objects. For example, the GradeBook class case study in Chapters 4–8 represents a course name using a string object. In Chapter 19, Class **string** and String Stream Processing we present class string in detail. Although using `string` objects is usually straightforward, we use null-terminated, pointer-based strings in this section. These are also called C-style strings. Many C++ Standard Library functions operate only on null-terminated, pointer-based strings, which are more complicated to use than `string` objects. Also, if you work with legacy C++ programs, you may be required to manipulate these pointer-based strings.

9.13.1 Fundamentals of Characters and Pointer-Based Strings

Characters are the fundamental building blocks of Visual C++ source programs. Every program is composed of a sequence of characters that—when grouped together meaningfully—is interpreted by the compiler as a series of instructions used to accomplish a task. A program may contain *character constants*. A character constant is an integer value represented as a character in single quotes. The value of a character constant is the integer value of the character in the machine's character set. For example, `'z'` represents the integer value of z (122 in the ASCII character set; see Appendix B), and `'\n'` represents the integer value of newline (10 in the ASCII character set).

A string is a series of characters treated as a single unit. A string may include letters, digits and various *special characters* such as +, -, *, /and $. *String literals*, or *string constants*, in C++ are written in double quotation marks as follows:

```
"John Q. Doe"              (a name)
"9999 Main Street"         (a street address)
"Maynard, Massachusetts"   (a city and state)
"(201) 555-1212"           (a telephone number)
```

A pointer-based string in Visual C++ is an array of characters ending in the null character (`'\0'`), which marks where the string terminates in memory. A string is accessed via a pointer to its first character. The value of a string is the address of its first character, but the `sizeof` a string literal is the length of the string including the terminating null character. In this sense, strings are like arrays, because an array name is also a pointer to its first element.

A string literal may be used as an initializer in the declaration of either a character array or a variable of type char *. The declarations

```
char color[] = "blue";
const char *colorPtr = "blue";
```

each initialize a variable to the string `"blue"`. The first declaration creates a five-element array `color` containing the characters `'b'`, `'l'`, `'u'`, `'e'` and `'\0'`. The second declaration creates pointer variable `colorPtr` that points to the letter b in the string `"blue"` (which ends in `'\0'`) somewhere in memory. String literals have `static` storage class (they exist for the duration of the program) and may or may not be shared if the same string literal is referenced from multiple locations in a program. According to the C++ standard (Section 2.13.4), the effect of attempting to modify a string literal is undefined; thus, you should always declare a pointer to a string literal as `const char *`.

The declaration char color[] = "blue"; could also be written

```
char color[] = { 'b', 'l', 'u', 'e', '\0' };
```

When declaring a character array to contain a string, the array must be large enough to store the string and its terminating null character. The preceding declaration determines the size of the array, based on the number of initializers provided in the initializer list.

Common Programming Error 9.15

Not allocating sufficient space in a character array to store the null character that terminates a string is an error.

Common Programming Error 9.16

Creating or using a C-style string that does not contain a terminating null character can lead to logic errors.

Error-Prevention Tip 9.4

When storing a string of characters in a character array, be sure that the array is large enough to hold the largest string that will be stored. Visual C++ allows strings of any length to be stored. If a string is longer than the character array in which it is to be stored, characters beyond the end of the array will overwrite data in memory following the array, leading to logic errors.

A string can be read into a character array using stream extraction with `cin`. For example, the following statement can be used to read a string into character array `word[ 20 ]`:

```
cin >> word;
```

The string entered by the user is stored in `word`. The preceding statement reads characters until a white-space character or end-of-file indicator is encountered. Note that the string should be no longer than 19 characters to leave room for the terminating null character. The `setw` stream manipulator can be used to ensure that the string read into `word` does not exceed the size of the array. For example, the statement

```
cin >> setw( 20 ) >> word;
```

specifies that `cin` should read a maximum of 19 characters into array `word` and save the 20th location in the array to store the terminating null character for the string. The `setw` stream manipulator applies only to the next value being input. If more than 19 characters are entered, the remaining characters are not saved in `word`, but will be read in and can be stored in another variable.

In some cases, it is desirable to input an entire line of text into an array. For this purpose, Visual C++ provides the function ***cin.getline*** in header file `<iostream>`. In Chapter 4 you were introduced to the similar function `getline` from header file `<string>`, which read input until a newline character was entered, and stored the input (without the newline character) into a `string` specified as an argument. The `cin.getline` function takes three arguments—a character array in which the line of text will be stored, a length and a delimiter character. For example, the program segment

```
char sentence[ 80 ];
cin.getline( sentence, 80, '\n' );
```

declares array `sentence` of 80 characters and reads a line of text from the keyboard into the array. The function stops reading characters when the delimiter character `'\n'` is encountered, when the end-of-file indicator is entered or when the number of characters read so far is one less than the length specified in the second argument. (The last character in the array is reserved for the terminating null character.) If the delimiter character is encountered, it is read and discarded. The third argument to cin.getline has '\n' as a default value, so the preceding function call could have been written as follows:

```
cin.getline( sentence, 80 );
```

Chapter 17, Stream Input/Output and Files, provides a detailed discussion of cin.getline and other input/output functions.

Common Programming Error 9.17

Processing a single character as a char * string can lead to a fatal runtime error. A char * string is a pointer—probably a respectably large integer. However, a character is a small integer (ASCII values range 0–255). On many systems, dereferencing a char value causes an error, because low memory addresses are reserved for special purposes such as operating-system interrupt handlers—so "memory-access violations" occur.

Common Programming Error 9.18

Passing a string as an argument to a function when a character is expected is a compilation error.

9.13.2 String-Manipulation Functions of the String-Handling Library

The string-handling library provides many useful functions for manipulating string data, comparing strings, searching strings for characters and other strings, tokenizing strings (separating strings into logical pieces such as the separate words in a sentence) and determining the length of strings. This section presents some common string-manipulation functions of the string-handling library (from the C++ Standard Library). The functions

Function prototype	Function description
`char *strcpy( char *s1, const char *s2 );`	
	Copies the string s2 into the character array s1. The value of s1 is returned.
`char *strncpy( char *s1, const char *s2, size_t n );`	
	Copies at most n characters of the string s2 into the character array s1. The value of s1 is returned.
`char *strcat( char *s1, const char *s2 );`	
	Appends the string s2 to s1. The first character of s2 overwrites the terminating null character of s1. The value of s1 is returned.
`char *strncat( char *s1, const char *s2, size_t n );`	
	Appends at most n characters of string s2 to string s1. The first character of s2 overwrites the terminating null character of s1. The value of s1 is returned.

Fig. 9.30 | String-manipulation functions of the string-handling library. (Part 1 of 2.)

Function prototype	Function description
`int strcmp( const char *s1, const char *s2 );`	
	Compares the string s1 with the string s2. The function returns a value of zero, less than zero or greater than zero if s1 is equal to, less than or greater than s2, respectively.
`int strncmp( const char *s1, const char *s2, size_t n );`	
	Compares up to n characters of the string s1 with the string s2. The function returns zero, less than zero or greater than zero if the n-character portion of s1 is equal to, less than or greater than the corresponding n-character portion of s2, respectively.
`char *strtok( char *s1, const char *s2 );`	
	A sequence of calls to `strtok` breaks string s1 into "tokens"—logical pieces such as words in a line of text. The string is broken up based on the characters contained in string s2. For instance, if we were to break the string `"this:is:a:string"` into tokens based on the character `':'`, the resulting tokens would be `"this"`, `"is"`, `"a"` and `"string"`. Function `strtok` returns only one token at a time—the first call contains s1 as the first argument, and subsequent calls to continue tokenizing the same string contain NULL as the first argument. A pointer to the current token is returned by each call. If there are no more tokens when the function is called, NULL is returned.
`size_t strlen( const char *s );`	
	Determines the length of string s. The number of characters preceding the terminating null character is returned.

Fig. 9.30 | String-manipulation functions of the string-handling library. (Part 2 of 2.)

are summarized in Fig. 9.30; then each is used in a live-code example. The prototypes for these functions are located in header file `<cstring>`.

Note that several functions in Fig. 9.30 contain parameters with data type `size_t`. This type is defined in the header file `<cstring>` to be an unsigned integral type such as `unsigned int` or `unsigned long`.

Also note that if misused, some of these functions can pose serious security risks in a program. As a result, Microsoft created secure versions of some of these functions (and others in the C Run-Time Library) denoted with `_s`. For instance, function `strtok_s` performs the same task as `strtok`, but ensures that all operations remain inside the array's bounds. We use the original versions of these functions throughout the book, as you will see them most often in existing code. Visual Studio will issue a warning that certain functions (such as `strtok`) are deprecated and recommend that you use the new secure version. Note that these functions are Microsoft specific and will not necessarily work with other compilers or systems.

Common Programming Error 9.19

Forgetting to include the `<cstring>` *header file when using functions from the string-handling library causes compilation errors.*

Copying Strings with `strcpy` and `strncpy`

Function ***strcpy*** copies its second argument—a string—into its first argument—a character array that must be large enough to store the string and its terminating null character, (which is also copied). Function ***strncpy*** is much like `strcpy`, except that `strncpy` specifies the number of characters to be copied from the string into the array. Note that function `strncpy` does not necessarily copy the terminating null character of its second argument—a terminating null character is written only if the number of characters to be copied is at least one more than the length of the string. For example, if `"test"` is the second argument, a terminating null character is written only if the third argument to `strncpy` is at least 5 (four characters in `"test"` plus one terminating null character). If the third argument is larger than 5, null characters are appended to the array until the total number of characters specified by the third argument is written.

Common Programming Error 9.20

When using `strncpy`*, the terminating null character of the second argument (a* char * *string) will not be copied if the number of characters specified by* `strncpy`*'s third argument is not greater than the second argument's length. In that case, a fatal error may occur if you do not manually terminate the resulting* char * *string with a null character.*

Figure 9.31 uses `strcpy` (line 17) to copy the entire string in array x into array y and uses `strncpy` (line 23) to copy the first 14 characters of array x into array z. Line 24 appends a null character (`'\0'`) to array z, because the call to `strncpy` in the program does not write a terminating null character. (The third argument is less than the string length of the second argument plus one.)

```
1   // Fig. 9.31: StringFunctions.cpp
2   // Using strcpy and strncpy.
3   #include <iostream>
4   using std::cout;
5   using std::endl;
6
7   #include <cstring> // prototypes for strcpy and strncpy
8   using std::strcpy;
9   using std::strncpy;
10
11  int main()
12  {
13     char x[] = "Happy Birthday to You"; // string length 21
14     char y[ 25 ];
15     char z[ 15 ];
16
17     strcpy( y, x ); // copy contents of x into y
18
```

Fig. 9.31 | `strcpy` and `strncpy`. (Part 1 of 2.)

```
19      cout << "The string in array x is: " << x
20         << "\nThe string in array y is: " << y << '\n';
21
22      // copy first 14 characters of x into z
23      strncpy( z, x, 14 ); // does not copy null character
24      z[ 14 ] = '\0'; // append '\0' to z's contents
25
26      cout << "The string in array z is: " << z << endl;
27      return 0; // indicates successful termination
28  } // end main
```

```
The string in array x is: Happy Birthday to You
The string in array y is: Happy Birthday to You
The string in array z is: Happy Birthday
```

Fig. 9.31 | strcpy and strncpy. (Part 2 of 2.)

Concatenating Strings with strcat and strncat

Function **strcat** appends its second argument (a string) to its first argument (a character array containing a string). The first character of the second argument replaces the null character ('\0') that terminates the string in the first argument. You must ensure that the array used to store the first string is large enough to store the combination of the first string, the second string and the terminating null character (copied from the second string). Function strncat appends a specified number of characters from the second string to the first string and appends a terminating null character to the result. The program of Fig. 9.32 demonstrates function strcat (lines 19 and 29) and function strncat (line 24).

```
1   // Fig. 9.32: StringFunctions.cpp
2   // Using strcat and strncat.
3   #include <iostream>
4   using std::cout;
5   using std::endl;
6
7   #include <cstring> // prototypes for strcat and strncat
8   using std::strcat;
9   using std::strncat;
10
11  int main()
12  {
13     char s1[ 20 ] = "Happy "; // length 6
14     char s2[] = "New Year "; // length 9
15     char s3[ 40 ] = "";
16
17     cout << "s1 = " << s1 << "\ns2 = " << s2;
18
19     strcat( s1, s2 ); // concatenate s2 to s1 (length 15)
20
21     cout << "\n\nAfter strcat(s1, s2):\ns1 = " << s1 << "\ns2 = " << s2;
22
```

Fig. 9.32 | strcat and strncat. (Part 1 of 2.)

```
23      // concatenate first 6 characters of s1 to s3
24      strncat( s3, s1, 6 ); // places '\0' after last character
25
26      cout << "\n\nAfter strncat(s3, s1, 6):\ns1 = " << s1
27          << "\ns3 = " << s3;
28
29      strcat( s3, s1 ); // concatenate s1 to s3
30      cout << "\n\nAfter strcat(s3, s1):\ns1 = " << s1
31          << "\ns3 = " << s3 << endl;
32      return 0; // indicates successful termination
33  } // end main
```

```
s1 = Happy
s2 = New Year

After strcat(s1, s2):
s1 = Happy New Year
s2 = New Year

After strncat(s3, s1, 6):
s1 = Happy New Year
s3 = Happy

After strcat(s3, s1):
s1 = Happy New Year
s3 = Happy Happy New Year
```

Fig. 9.32 | strcat and strncat. (Part 2 of 2.)

Comparing Strings with strcmp and strncmp

Figure 9.33 compares three strings using strcmp (lines 21, 22 and 23) and strncmp (lines 26, 27 and 28). Function strcmp compares its first string argument with its second string argument character by character. The function returns zero if the strings are equal, a negative value if the first string is less than the second string and a positive value if the first string is greater than the second string. Function strncmp is equivalent to strcmp, except that strncmp compares up to a specified number of characters. Function strncmp stops comparing characters if it reaches the null character in one of its string arguments. The program prints the integer value returned by each function call.

```
1   // Fig. 9.33: StringFunctions.cpp
2   // Using strcmp and strncmp.
3   #include <iostream>
4   using std::cout;
5   using std::endl;
6
7   #include <iomanip>
8   using std::setw;
9
10  #include <cstring> // prototypes for strcmp and strncmp
11  using std::strcmp;
12  using std::strncmp;
```

Fig. 9.33 | strcmp and strncmp. (Part 1 of 2.)

```
13
14   int main()
15   {
16      char *s1 = "Happy New Year";
17      char *s2 = "Happy New Year";
18      char *s3 = "Happy Holidays";
19
20      cout << "s1 = " << s1 << "\ns2 = " << s2 << "\ns3 = " << s3
21         << "\n\nstrcmp(s1, s2) = " << setw( 2 ) << strcmp( s1, s2 )
22         << "\nstrcmp(s1, s3) = " << setw( 2 ) << strcmp( s1, s3 )
23         << "\nstrcmp(s3, s1) = " << setw( 2 ) << strcmp( s3, s1 );
24
25      cout << "\n\nstrncmp(s1, s3, 6) = " << setw( 2 )
26         << strncmp( s1, s3, 6 ) << "\nstrncmp(s1, s3, 7) = " << setw( 2 )
27         << strncmp( s1, s3, 7 ) << "\nstrncmp(s3, s1, 7) = " << setw( 2 )
28         << strncmp( s3, s1, 7 ) << endl;
29      return 0; // indicates successful termination
30   } // end main
```

```
s1 = Happy New Year
s2 = Happy New Year
s3 = Happy Holidays

strcmp(s1, s2) =  0
strcmp(s1, s3) =  1
strcmp(s3, s1) = -1

strncmp(s1, s3, 6) =  0
strncmp(s1, s3, 7) =  6
strncmp(s3, s1, 7) = -6
```

Fig. 9.33 | `strcmp` and `strncmp`. (Part 2 of 2.)

Common Programming Error 9.21

Assuming that `strcmp` and `strncmp` return one (a true value) when their arguments are equal is a logic error. Both functions return zero (Visual C++'s false value) for equality. Therefore, when testing two strings for equality, the result of the `strcmp` or `strncmp` function should be compared with zero to determine whether the strings are equal.

To understand just what it means for one string to be "greater than" or "less than" another string, consider the process of alphabetizing a series of last names. You would, no doubt, place "Jones" before "Smith," because the first letter of "Jones" comes before the first letter of "Smith" in the alphabet. But the alphabet is more than just a list of 26 letters—it is an *ordered* list of characters. Each letter occurs in a specific position within the list. "Z" is more than just a letter of the alphabet; "Z" is specifically the 26th letter of the alphabet.

How does the computer know that one letter comes before another? All characters are represented inside the computer as numeric codes; when the computer compares two strings, it actually compares the numeric codes of the characters in the strings.

In an effort to standardize character representations, most computer manufacturers have designed their machines to utilize one of two popular coding schemes—ASCII or

EBCDIC. Recall that ASCII stands for "American Standard Code for Information Interchange." EBCDIC stands for "Extended Binary Coded Decimal Interchange Code." There are other coding schemes as well.

ASCII and EBCDIC are called *character codes*, or character sets. Most readers of this book will be using desktop or notebook computers that use the ASCII character set. IBM mainframe computers use the EBCDIC character set. As Internet and World Wide Web usage becomes pervasive, the newer Unicode character set is growing in popularity (www.unicode.org). String and character manipulations actually involve the manipulation of the appropriate numeric codes and not the characters themselves. This explains the interchangeability of characters and small integers in Visual C++. Since it is meaningful to say that one numeric code is greater than, less than or equal to another numeric code, it becomes possible to relate various characters or strings to one another by referring to the character codes. Appendix B contains the ASCII character codes.

Portability Tip 9.4

The internal numeric codes used to represent characters may be different on different computers that use different character sets.

Portability Tip 9.5

Do not explicitly test for ASCII codes, as in if (rating == 65); rather, use the corresponding character constant, as in if (rating == 'A').

[*Note:* With some compilers, functions strcmp and strncmp always return -1, 0 or 1. With other compilers, such as Visual C++ 2008, these functions return 0 or the difference between the numeric codes of the first characters that differ in the strings being compared. For example, when s1 and s3 are compared, the first characters that differ between them are the first character of the second word in each string—N (numeric code 78) in s1 and H (numeric code 72) in s3, respectively. In this case, the return value will be 6 (or -6 if s3 is compared to s1).]

Tokenizing a String with strtok

Function *strtok* breaks a string into a series of *tokens*. A token is a sequence of characters separated by *delimiting characters* (usually spaces or punctuation marks). For example, in a line of text, each word can be considered a token, and the spaces separating the words can be considered delimiters.

Multiple calls to strtok are required to break a string into tokens (assuming that the string contains more than one token). The first call to strtok contains two arguments, a string to be tokenized and a string containing characters that separate the tokens (i.e., delimiters). Line 19 in Fig. 9.34 assigns to tokenPtr a pointer to the first token in sentence. The second argument, " ", indicates that tokens in sentence are separated by spaces. Function strtok searches for the first character in sentence that is not a delimiting character (space). This begins the first token. The function then finds the next delimiting character in the string and replaces it with a null ('\0') character. This terminates the current token. Function strtok saves (in a static variable) a pointer to the next character following the token in sentence and returns a pointer to the current token.

Subsequent calls to strtok to continue tokenizing sentence contain NULL as the first argument (line 25). The NULL argument indicates that the call to strtok should continue

```
1   // Fig. 9.34: StringTokenize.cpp
2   // Using strtok to tokenize a string.
3   #include <iostream>
4   using std::cout;
5   using std::endl;
6
7   #include <cstring> // prototype for strtok
8   using std::strtok;
9
10   int main()
11   {
12      char sentence[] = "This is a sentence with 7 tokens";
13      char *tokenPtr;
14
15      cout << "The string to be tokenized is:\n" << sentence
16         << "\n\nThe tokens are:\n\n";
17
18      // begin tokenization of sentence
19      tokenPtr = strtok( sentence, " " );
20
21      // continue tokenizing sentence until tokenPtr becomes NULL
22      while ( tokenPtr != NULL )
23      {
24         cout << tokenPtr << '\n';
25         tokenPtr = strtok( NULL, " " ); // get next token
26      } // end while
27
28      cout << "\nAfter strtok, sentence = " << sentence << endl;
29      return 0; // indicates successful termination
30   } // end main
```

```
The string to be tokenized is:
This is a sentence with 7 tokens

The tokens are:

This
is
a
sentence
with
7
tokens

After strtok, sentence = This
```

Fig. 9.34 | Using strtok to tokenize a string.

tokenizing from the location in sentence saved by the last call to strtok. Note that strtok maintains this saved information in a manner that is not visible to you. If no tokens remain when strtok is called, strtok returns NULL. The program of Fig. 9.34 uses strtok to tokenize the string "This is a sentence with 7 tokens". The program prints each token on a separate line. Line 28 outputs sentence after tokenization. Note that *strtok modifies the input string;* therefore, a copy of the string should be made if the program requires the original after the calls to strtok. When sentence is output after tokenization, note that only the word "This" prints, because strtok replaced each blank in sentence with a null character ('\0') during the tokenization process.

Common Programming Error 9.22

Not realizing that strtok modifies the string being tokenized, then attempting to use that string as if it were the original unmodified string is a logic error.

Determining String Lengths

Function **strlen** takes a string as an argument and returns the number of characters in the string—the terminating null character is not included in the length. The length is also the index of the null character. The program of Fig. 9.35 demonstrates function strlen.

```cpp
1   // Fig. 9.35: Strlen.cpp
2   // Using strlen.
3   #include <iostream>
4   using std::cout;
5   using std::endl;
6
7   #include <cstring> // prototype for strlen
8   using std::strlen;
9
10  int main()
11  {
12     char *string1 = "abcdefghijklmnopqrstuvwxyz";
13     char *string2 = "four";
14     char *string3 = "Boston";
15
16     cout << "The length of \"" << string1 << "\" is " << strlen( string1 )
17        << "\nThe length of \"" << string2 << "\" is " << strlen( string2 )
18        << "\nThe length of \"" << string3 << "\" is " << strlen( string3 )
19        << endl;
20     return 0; // indicates successful termination
21  } // end main
```

```
The length of "abcdefghijklmnopqrstuvwxyz" is 26
The length of "four" is 4
The length of "Boston" is 6
```

Fig. 9.35 | strlen returns the length of a char * string.

9.14 Introduction to C++/CLI Handles

We now demonstrate how to take advantage of the power of pointers with managed code in C++/CLI. Regular pointers like the ones introduced in preceding sections cannot be used with managed objects (such as the managed arrays from Chapter 8). The reason is that managed objects are stored in managed memory, which is subject to the work of the *garbage collector.* We begin this section with an explanation of how these details affect managed code in C++/CLI before introducing the ways to use pointer-like references with managed objects.

In Chapter 11, Classes: A Deeper Look, Part 2, we discuss how to use manual dynamic memory management in native C++ with keywords `new` and `delete`. These keywords allow you to manually create and delete native objects. Though it is powerful, manual memory management often leads to errors in programs. Chapter 11 explains the possible problems. The CLR maintains objects in managed memory. The advantage is that objects in managed memory are subject to automatic memory management via the CLR garbage collector. The garbage collector frees you of the responsibility of having to delete every object you create with `new`. Instead, the garbage collector runs periodically, looks at the objects in managed memory and determines whether they are still needed by the program. If not, the object is considered garbage. When an object is marked as garbage, the garbage collector eventually reclaims the memory occupied by that object. The full details of how garbage collectors work are beyond the scope of this book.

Reclaiming memory isn't all the CLR garbage collector does. After reclaiming all the memory, the garbage collector reorganizes, or "compacts," the remaining pieces as efficiently as possible into a contiguous region of memory. This allows the CLR to maintain a pointer to the next free block of memory. When a new object needs memory allocated, the CLR can use this pointer to allocate memory immediately and quickly. In contrast, unmanaged memory is not compacted. Consequently, the garbage collector makes allocating memory for objects much faster than doing so for objects in unmanaged memory. Using a garbage collector is not a perfect solution, though. A problem with the garbage collector is that you cannot be sure exactly when it will run, or what will be deallocated when it does run (see Chapter 11 for more detail). Another downside of using a garbage collector is that it may cause the program to execute slightly slower than if manual memory management were used. However, this is typically a concern only in large, performance-critical applications. Most programs won't suffer much in terms of speed but will gain the reliability of automatic memory management.

What does this all have to do with pointers? You learned that a pointer holds the address of a variable in memory. Suppose we assign a pointer `ptr` the memory address of an object in managed memory. What happens if the object is moved by the garbage collector when it compacts memory? The address `ptr` points to is unchanged; however, the data at that address is no longer what you originally assigned to `ptr`. Now `ptr` may point to a different object, or perhaps to data that is only part of a different object. If you attempt to use `ptr` after the garbage collector has run, the outcome may be corrupted data, a program crash or other undefined behavior. This is why the garbage collector processes only the CLR's managed memory. If it processed unmanaged memory, then existing native C++ programs would break. This is also why you cannot use native pointers with managed memory. We need a special pointer that can be updated automatically by the garbage collector.

C++/CLI provides exactly this sort of "tracking pointer," formally called a *handle*. A handle is denoted with the ∧ symbol (pronounced "hat") to differentiate it from a normal pointer to unmanaged objects. We have glossed over handles in previous C++/CLI sections but now we describe exactly how to use them. In many cases, a handle performs as you would expect a pointer to, the difference being that a handle can point only to an object in managed memory (which we have been calling managed objects or managed types). Consider a managed `ref class` (introduced in Chapter 4) called `Date`. All objects of this class are created in managed memory. You can create a handle to `Date` as follows:

```
Date ∧dHandle, dateCount;
```

This declares the variable dHandle to be of type Date ^ (i.e., a handle to a Date object) and is read, "dHandle is a handle to Date" or "dHandle points to an object of type Date." Also, just like normal pointers, variable dateCount in the preceding declaration is declared to be a Date object, not a handle to a Date object. The ^ in the declaration applies only to dHandle, exactly as you saw with pointers. While compacting managed memory, if the garbage collector moves the data a handle points to it makes sure to update the handle so that it still points to the correct data. This way, handles continue to point to the data you expect, even though the garbage collector may move the data.

Many of the good programming practices for pointers apply to handles as well. For instance, as with pointers, handles should be initialized either when they are declared or in an assignment. However, we don't assign handles a value of 0 or NULL like native C++ pointers. To assign a null value to a handle always use the C++/CLI keyword ***nullptr***.

Error-Prevention Tip 9.5

Remember to use the nullptr keyword to initialize handles to a null value. Using 0 or NULL may compile but will not set the handle to a null value and may cause hard to find logic errors.

Differences Between Handles and Pointers
There are some things pointers can do that handles cannot. Handles must point to managed objects. Also, you cannot perform pointer arithmetic operations on handles. For instance, if you try to write

```
dHandle++;
```

Visual Studio issues a compilation error. Handles cannot be compared meaningfully with boolean operators (such as ==) the way pointers can. Furthermore, native C++ allows you to create pointers to pointers, a type often used with arrays of C-style strings and with matrices. You cannot do this with handles. Attempting to create a handle to a handle results in a compilation error. You cannot create a handle to a function analogous to what you learned about function pointers in Section 9.12 (see Section 26.11 on using delegates in C++/CLI to accomplish what function pointers do). Finally, handles are "type safe." There is no void ^ analogous to the native pointer void *. While it may appear that handles are significantly less flexible than pointers, C++/CLI does provide other means to overcome these limitations of handles.

Handle Operators
Recall that the unary & operator returns the memory address of its operand (i.e., a pointer). Handles provide an analogous operator, % , for managed types. You can use the % unary operator to return the memory address of a managed object (its operand) to a handle. It is important to note that you can use this operator only for objects in managed memory (and not for handles to those objects). This means you cannot use % on an int value to store its address in a handle. For instance,

```
int ^countPtr = nullptr;
int x = 10;
countPtr = %x; // ERROR
```

results in a compilation error because x is an integer value and thus not in managed memory. Nor could you use the & operator, because that would attempt to assign an int * to countPtr, which is of type "handle to int." However, if we have a managed class, such as Date, we can use the % operator to obtain the address of an object of type Date and assign it to a handle. The following code

```
Date ^dHandle = nullptr;
Date d;
dHandle = %d;
```

creates a managed Date object d and uses the % operator to assign the object's location to handle dHandle. Now we could manipulate the data members of d via dHandle.

 Common Programming Error 9.23

Remember that the & operator returns a pointer. The % returns a handle. Using the & operator on a managed object is a compilation error. Likewise, using the % operator on a native object is also a compilation error.

Handles, like pointers, can be dereferenced with using the * operator, as well as with the -> operator (explained in Chapter 10). Everything you learned in Section 9.3, Pointer Operators, can be applied in an analogous way to handles. You can use a dereferenced handle on the left or right side of an assignment statement just like a dereferenced pointer. Similarly, when dealing with handles, the % and * operators are inverses of one another—when they are both applied consecutively to a handle in either order, they "cancel one another out." We now show a simple example using handles to managed objects (Fig. 9.37). We first define a managed Date class (Fig. 9.36) which has trivial properties Day, Month and Year. Recall that when you declare trivial properties, the compiler generates variables containing the property names that will be used by instances of the class. This is why we do not define three private integer data members for the day, month and year.

```
1   // Fig. 9.36: Data.h
2   // A managed Date class
3
4   #include "stdafx.h"
5
6   using namespace System;
7
8   // managed Date class definition
9   ref class Date
10  {
11  public:
12     Date() {}; // default constructor
13     Date( int d, int m, int y )
14     {
15        Day = d;
16        Month = m;
17        Year = y;
18     }
19     // trivial property declarations
20     // this class does not use any input validation
21     property int Day;
```

Fig. 9.36 | Managed Date class. (Part 1 of 2.)

```
22      property int Month;
23      property int Year;
24
25      void printDate() // function to print the Date
26      {
27         Console::WriteLine( "Day: {0} Month: {1} Year {2}",
28            Day, Month, Year );
29      }
30   }; // end class Date
```

Fig. 9.36 | Managed Date class. (Part 2 of 2.)

```
1    // Fig. 9.37: HandleExample.cpp
2    // Using handles and the % and * operators
3
4    #include "stdafx.h"
5    #include "Date.h" // include the managed date class header file
6
7    using namespace System;
8
9    int main( array< System::String ^ > ^args )
10   {
11      Date d( 10, 5, 2007 ); // d is a Date object
12      Date ^dHandle; // dHandle is a Date ^ -- handle to a Date object
13      dHandle = %d; // assign the address of d to dHandle
14
15      Console::Write( "Start date is " );
16      d.printDate(); // output current date
17
18      (*dHandle).Day = 30; // change the value of Day via dHandle
19
20      Console::Write( "New date is " );
21      d.printDate();
22
23      return 0;
24   } // end main
```

```
Start date is Day: 10 Month: 5 Year: 2007
New date is Day: 30 Month: 5 Year: 2007
```

Fig. 9.37 | Using handle operators * and % with the managed Date class.

The program in Fig. 9.37 uses managed class Date so that we can demonstrate how to use a handle with a managed object type. Line 11 declares a managed object d of type Date and calls the three parameter constructor. Line 12 declares a variable of type "handle to Date" that is assigned the memory address of d at line 13 using the % operator. dHandle is now a reference to d that we can use to access the properties and member functions of d. Line 18 uses the dereference operator (*) to set the value of d.Day using dHandle. As you can see, we have successfully modified the contents of d by using a handle as a reference to d.

Now you understand what we meant in previous chapters when we used ∧ for managed arrays and Strings. Each is declared as a handle to its respective type. For example,

```
String ∧s = "I'm a handle to a String";
```

declares variable s as type "handle to String." Similarly,

```
array< int > ∧managedArray = { 1, 2, 3 };
```

declares variable managedArray as type "handle to a managed array of int." String and managed array objects are always accessed via a reference from a handle. The principle is the same as in native C++. In native C++ every array name is actually a pointer to the first element of the array and strings are arrays of characters. So C++/CLI is providing the same functionality as native C++ by always creating and using strings and arrays with a handle.

Using const with Handles

Handles can be declared const, and the data they point to can be declared const, just as you learned with pointers in Section 9.5. You can declare handles and their data const inside function parameter lists as well. However, there are important differences between the way const is used in native C++ and in C++/CLI, which we explain in Chapter 11. Native C++ puts a heavy emphasis on using const wherever possible to enforce the principle of least privilege. C++/CLI places less emphasis on const use, and outright forbids its use in some places where native C++ emphasizes it.

9.15 Passing Arguments to Functions by Reference with Handles

Handles are used to pass managed types by reference just as pointers do with unmanaged types. You can use handles and the dereference operator (*) on managed objects to accomplish pass-by-reference just as you learned in Section 9.4. We again use the managed Date class from Fig. 9.36 to demonstrate how to use handles with managed objects. In Figure 9.38 we use a handle to pass a managed object by reference, so that changes made to the object in the function are applied to the original object in main.

```
1   // Fig. 9.38: HandleByReference.cpp
2   // Passing handles by reference
3
4   #include "stdafx.h"
5   #include "Date.h"
6
7   using namespace System;
8
9   void doubleDateByReference( Date ∧ ); // function prototype
10
11  int main( array< System::String ∧ > ∧args )
12  {
13      Date d(10, 5, 2007); // create a managed Date object
14      // create a Date handle and assign the memory address of d to it
15      Date ∧dHandle = %d;
```

Fig. 9.38 | Using a handle to pass a managed object by reference (Part 1 of 2.)

```
16
17        Console::Write( "Start date is " );
18        d.printDate(); // print the current date
19
20        doubleDateByReference( dHandle ); // pass a reference to the function
21
22        Console::Write( "New date is ");
23        d.printDate(); // print the date after modification
24
25        return 0;
26   } // end main
27
28   // function which takes a handle to a Date object and doubles the
29   // Day and Month values
30   void doubleDateByReference( Date ^dH )
31   {
32        (*dH).Day *= 2;
33        (*dH).Month *= 2;
34   } // end function doubleDateByReference
```

```
Start date is Day: 10 Month: 5 Year: 2007
New date is Day: 20 Month: 10 Year: 2007
```

Fig. 9.38 | Using a handle to pass a managed object by reference (Part 2 of 2.)

Once again we create a Date object d, a Date handle named dHandle, and assign the memory address of d to dHandle using the % operator (lines 13–15). This time, we pass dHandle as an argument to function doubleDateByReference. You can see in the function prototype (line 9) and definition (line 30) that doubleDateByReference accepts a Date handle argument. When doubleDateByReference executes, dHandle is passed by value, so a copy of dHandle (that points to d) is created locally for the function. Inside doubleDate-ByReference we double the Day and Month values of the referenced object d by dereferencing the function argument (lines 32–33). Now when we call printDate for a second time (line 23) we see that the changes to the Day and Month values were made to the object d in main because the original was passed by reference.

Note that the argument to doubleDateByReference, dH, is a copy of dHandle. dH points to the same object as dHandle, but when the function ends, dH goes out of scope and is destroyed. Like any other variable that is passed by value, changes to the copy in the called function do not affect the original variable in the caller. Section 9.16 explains how to pass a handle by reference.

9.16 Tracking References and References to Handles

In Section 7.14, References and Reference Parameters, you learned about the difference between pass-by-value and pass-by-reference. You were also introduced to reference parameters using & to indicate a reference parameter. Reference parameters suffer from the same problems as native pointers when dealing with objects in managed memory. If the garbage collector moves the data that a reference parameter points to, the reference parameter would continue to point to the same location which now may contain something completely different. Fortunately, C++/CLI provides an analogous type for objects in managed memory, appropriately named *tracking references*. Like handles, tracking references are updated when the data to which they point gets moved by the garbage collector.

You can use a tracking reference as an alias for another variable (of a managed type) in a function just as you did with reference parameters. For example, using the managed class Date defined in Fig. 9.36, the code

```
Date d;
Date %dRef = d;
dRef.Day = 30;
```

sets the Day property of d by using its alias dRef. The declaration of dRef is pronounced as "dRef is a tracking reference to a Date object." Once a tracking reference is declared as an alias for another variable, all operations performed on the alias (i.e., the reference) are actually performed on the original variable. As with reference parameters, a tracking reference must be initialized in its declaration and cannot be reassigned as an alias to a different variable. Attempting to reassign a tracking reference will not make the tracking reference an alias for the new variable. Instead, the initial variable the tracking reference aliased is changed to the value of the newly assigned variable.

Passing a Tracking Reference to a Handle to Functions

Tracking references are often used with function parameters to specify pass-by-reference. You have seen how pointers and reference parameters can be used to pass references to functions that enable changes to argument values in the caller. Handles and tracking references can be used in the same way. Handles are references to an object in managed memory. Passing a handle to a function lets you avoid the cost of copying a large object and allows you to make changes to an existing object that persist after the function ends. However, the handle itself is passed by value. This means a copy is made for the function's own use. We mentioned that this has important implications in Section 9.15. What happens if you pass a function a handle to an object and inside the function attempt to assign a new object to the handle argument? Figure 9.39 demonstrates the need for a tracking reference to a handle in this case.

```
1   // Fig. 9.39: PassHandleByReference.cpp
2   // Using tracking references to pass a handle
3
4   #include "stdafx.h"
5
6   using namespace System;
7
8   void modifyByValue( String ^ ); // function prototype
9   void modifyByReference( String^% ); // function prototype
10
11  int main( array< System::String ^ > ^args )
12  {
13      String ^text = "Original";
14
```

Fig. 9.39 | Using a tracking reference to pass a handle by reference (Part 1 of 2.)

```
15    Console::WriteLine( "String ^text = {0}", text );
16    modifyByValue( text );
17    Console::WriteLine( "String ^text = {0} after modifyByValue", text );
18    modifyByReference( text );
19    Console::WriteLine(
20       "String ^text = {0} after modifyByReference", text );
21
22    return 0;
23 } // end main
24
25 // function which takes a handle to a string and modifies it
26 // the parameter s is a copy of the argument
27 void modifyByValue( String ^s )
28 {
29    s = "Value";
30 } // end function modifyByValue
31
32 // function which takes a reference to a handle to a string
33 // and modifies it
34 // the parameter s is a reference to the argument
35 void modifyByReference( String ^%s )
36 {
37    s = "Reference";
38 } // end function modifyByReference
```

```
String ^text = Original
String ^text = Original after modifyByValue
String ^text = Reference after modifyByReference
```

Fig. 9.39 | Using a tracking reference to pass a handle by reference (Part 2 of 2.)

As you can see in Fig. 9.39, if function modifyByValue is passed a handle (line 16), it makes a copy of the argument for use in the function. In line 27 s is not the handle text that was created in line 13. Instead, s is a new String handle that is a copy of text. It is a local variable of the function modifyByValue. Now there exist two references, text and s, to the memory location where "Original" is stored. At line 29, we assign a new value to s, but s is not an alias for text, it is a reference to the same place in memory as text. Reassigning s to a new memory location doesn't reassign text. When function modify-ByValue ends, s goes out of scope and the object it referenced is marked for reclamation by the garbage collector. Line 17 shows that the intended change to text in modifyBy-Value was not made, because we incorrectly passed the handle by value instead of by reference. If we had only wanted to read the value of text or modify the referenced object (as we did in Fig. 9.38), then passing the handle by value would have worked. To reassign what text references from inside the function, we need a parameter that is a tracking reference to a handle (line 35). Look closely at the argument of function modifyByRefer-ence. It is read right to left, "s is a tracking reference to an object of type handle to String." Now the parameter is not a copy of text but is actually a reference to text. At line 37 we are not performing an operation on s itself, because s is just an alias for the argument passed to the function. Any operations performed on s are actually performed on text, exactly as we wanted. As you can see, lines 19–20 show that we successfully modified text by passing the handle by reference.

The ability to pass a handle as a reference is also useful with the for each control statement you learned about in Section 8.13. We had previously said to use a for each statement only to read the values of an array or collection. However, it is actually possible to modify the values (unlike in other .NET languages like C#) by using a tracking reference to a handle. Figure 9.40 demonstrates how this is done.

Line 11 creates a managed array texts of type handle to String. Lines 15–19 assign objects to texts's elements. Notice that on line 15 the type identifier in the for each statement is a tracking reference to a handle to String. The tracking reference is what allows the loop to make changes to the array elements that persist once the loop ends. In line 17, we use the .NET ToString function to set the current element of texts to the String representation of count. Lines 23–24 loop through texts again to prove that the assignments made in the previous loop (line 17) persisted. Notice that we easily created a managed array of handles much as a native array could contain pointers.

```cpp
 1   // Fig. 9.40: ForEachByReference.cpp
 2   // Example of using tracking reference to a handle with for each
 3
 4   #include "stdafx.h"
 5
 6   using namespace System;
 7
 8   int main( array< System::String ^ > ^args )
 9   {
10      // create a managed array where each element is a handle to a string
11      array< String ^>^ texts = gcnew array< String ^>( 5 );
12      int count = 1;
13
14      // loop through the elements of texts by reference
15      for each( String ^%s in texts )
16      {
17         s = count.ToString();
18         count++; // increment count
19      } // end for each
20
21      Console::WriteLine( "The elements of texts are:" );
22      // loop through the elements of texts again to see the result
23      for each( String ^s in texts )
24         Console::Write( "{0} ",s );
25
26      return 0;
27   } // end main
```

```
The elements of texts are:
1 2 3 4 5
```

Fig. 9.40 | Using a tracking reference to a handle with a for each loop

9.17 Interior Pointers

C++/CLI includes another type of tracking pointer called an *interior pointer*. Just like a handle, if the object an interior pointer references is moved by the garbage collector the interior pointer is updated automatically so that it still points to the data you expect. Interior pointers provide two important features of native pointers that are unavailable with handles. The first is the ability to point directly to the memory address of an object's data member. Handles must point to whole managed objects, but an interior pointer can hold the memory address of an object's data member (even one on the stack or in unmanaged memory). The other use of interior pointers is for pointer arithmetic and comparison, as demonstrated in Section 9.8. Interior pointers are declared with a template-style syntax similar to the way managed arrays are declared. The declaration is of the form

> **interior_ptr**< *type* > ptrName = *memoryAddress*

For example, again using the Date class from Fig. 9.36, the following code

```
Date d;
d.Day = 30;
interior_ptr< int > interiorPointer = &d.value;
```

creates a managed Date object and sets property Day equal to 30. Then it declares an interior pointer of type int called interiorPointer and assigns it the memory address of the integer d.Day. Note that we use & and not % with interior pointers. Alternatively, you could use a handle to int to point to d.Day as follows:

```
int ^dHandle = d.Day;
```

What is the difference between using a handle and an interior pointer to point to d.Day? The interior pointer allows you to perform pointer arithmetic and comparison. Also, remember a handle can only point to objects in managed memory. So, when assigning d.Day to a handle to int, we incur a performance penalty while the CLR creates an object in managed memory to store d.Day (see Section 11.16).

Using the address operator (&) on an interior pointer returns a native pointer. Also, native pointers are implicitly converted to interior pointers (but not vice versa). This allows you to pass native pointers to functions which take interior pointers as parameters—an advanced topic beyond the scope of this book. Note that, unlike handles, interior pointers cannot be used as data members of a class. Also, interior pointers cannot point directly to managed objects, only to handles to managed objects.

9.18 Wrap-Up

In this chapter we provided a detailed introduction to pointers, or variables that contain memory addresses as their values. We began by demonstrating how to declare and initialize pointers. You saw how to use the address operator (&) to assign the address of a variable to a pointer and the indirection operator (*) to access the data stored in the variable indirectly referenced by a pointer. We discussed passing arguments by reference using both pointer arguments and reference arguments.

You learned how to use const with pointers to enforce the principle of least privilege. We demonstrated using nonconstant pointers to nonconstant data, nonconstant pointers to constant data, constant pointers to nonconstant data, and constant pointers to constant data. We then used selection sort to demonstrate passing arrays and individual array elements by reference. We discussed the `sizeof` operator, which can be used to determine the sizes of data types and variables in bytes during program compilation.

We demonstrated how to use pointers in arithmetic and comparison expressions. You saw that pointer arithmetic can be used to jump from one element of an array to another. You learned how to use arrays of pointers, and more specifically string arrays (arrays of strings). We discussed function pointers, which enable programmers to pass functions as parameters. We introduced several Visual C++ functions that manipulate pointer-based strings. You learned string-processing capabilities such as copying strings, tokenizing strings and determining the length of strings.

We introduced the basics of managed memory and the garbage collector. You learned how to use declare and initialize handles and tracking references to managed objects. We demonstrated how to use % and * with handles analogously to using & and * with native pointers. You also learned the nuances of pass-by-value and pass-by-reference with handles and tracking references. Finally, we introduced the basics of interior pointers with managed code that allows for pointer arithmetic and comparison.

In the next chapter, we begin our deeper treatment of classes. You'll learn about the scope of a class's members, and how to keep objects in a consistent state. You'll also learn about using special member functions called constructors and destructors, which execute when an object is created and destroyed, respectively, and we'll discuss when constructors and destructors are called. In addition, we'll demonstrate using default arguments with constructors and using default memberwise assignment to assign one object of a class to another object of the same class. We'll also discuss the danger of returning a reference to a `private` data member of a class.

Summary

Section 9.2 Pointer Variable Declarations and Initialization

- Pointers are variables that contain as their values memory addresses of other variables.

- The declaration

    `int *ptr;`

    declares `ptr` to be a pointer to a variable of type `int` and is read, "`ptr` is a pointer to `int`." The `*` as used here in a declaration indicates that the variable is a pointer.

- There are three values that can be used to initialize a pointer: 0, `NULL` or an address of an object of the same type. Initializing a pointer to 0 and initializing that same pointer to `NULL` are identical—0 is the convention in Visual C++.

- The only integer that can be assigned to a pointer without casting is zero.

Section 9.3 Pointer Operators

- The `&` (address) operator obtains the memory address of its operand.

- The operand of the address operator must be a variable name (or another *lvalue*); the address operator cannot be applied to constants or to expressions that do not return a reference.

- The `*` operator, referred to as the indirection (or dereferencing) operator, returns a synonym, alias or nickname for the name of the object that its operand points to in memory. This is called dereferencing the pointer.

Section 9.4 Passing Arguments to Functions by Reference with Pointers

- When calling a function with an argument that the caller wants the called function to modify, the address of the argument may be passed. The called function then uses the indirection operator (*) to dereference the pointer and modify the value of the argument in the calling function.

- A function receiving an address argument must have a pointer as its corresponding parameter.

Section 9.5 Using const with Pointers

- The const qualifier enables you to inform the compiler that the value of a particular variable cannot be modified through the specified identifier. If an attempt is made to modify a const value, the compiler issues either a warning or an error, depending on the particular compiler.

- There are four ways to pass a pointer to a function—a nonconstant pointer to nonconstant data, a nonconstant pointer to constant data, a constant pointer to nonconstant data, and a constant pointer to constant data.

- The value of the array name is the address of the array's first element.

- To pass a single array element by reference using pointers, pass the address of the array element.

Section 9.6 Selection Sort Using Pass-by-Reference

- The selection sort algorithm is an easy-to-program, but inefficient, sorting algorithm. The first iteration of the algorithm selects the smallest element in the array and swaps it with the first element. The second iteration selects the second-smallest element (which is the smallest element of the remaining elements) and swaps it with the second element. The algorithm continues until the last iteration selects the second-largest element and swaps it with the second-to-last index, leaving the largest element in the last index. After the ith iteration, the smallest i items of the array will be sorted into increasing order in the first i elements of the array.

Section 9.7 sizeof Operator

- Visual C++ provides unary operator sizeof to determine the size of an array (or of any other data type, variable or constant) in bytes at compile time.

- When applied to the name of an array, the sizeof operator returns the total number of bytes in the array as an integer.

Section 9.8 Pointer Expressions and Pointer Arithmetic

- The arithmetic operations that may be performed on pointers are incrementing (++) a pointer, decrementing (--) a pointer, adding (+ or +=) an integer to a pointer, subtracting (- or -=) an integer from a pointer and subtracting one pointer from another.

- When an integer is added or subtracted from a pointer, the pointer is incremented or decremented by that integer times the size of the object to which the pointer refers.

- Pointers can be assigned to one another if both pointers are of the same type. Otherwise, a cast must be used. The exception to this is a void * pointer, which is a generic pointer type that can hold pointer values of any type. Pointers to void can be assigned pointers of other types. A void * pointer can be assigned to a pointer of another type only with an explicit type cast.

- The only valid operations on a void * pointer are comparing void * pointers with other pointers, assigning addresses to void * pointers and casting void * pointers to valid pointer types.

- Pointers can be compared using the equality and relational operators. Comparisons using relational operators are meaningful only if the pointers point to members of the same array.

Section 9.9 Relationship Between Pointers and Arrays

- Pointers that point to arrays can be subscripted exactly as array names can.

- In pointer/offset notation, if the pointer points to the first element of the array, the offset is the same as an array subscript.
- All subscripted array expressions can be written with a pointer and an offset, either using the name of the array as a pointer or using a separate pointer that points to the array.

Section 9.10 Arrays of Pointers
- Arrays may contain pointers.
- Such a data structure can be used to form an array of pointer-based strings. Each entry in the array is a string, but in Visual C++ a string is essentially a pointer to its first character, so each entry in an array of strings is simply a pointer to the first character of a string.
- String arrays are commonly used with command-line arguments that are passed to main when a program begins execution. Such arguments follow the program name when a program is executed from the command line.

Section 9.11 Case Study: Card Shuffling and Dealing Simulation
- Indefinite postponement (also called starvation) occurs when an algorithm can execute for an indefinitely long period of time.

Section 9.12 Function Pointers
- A pointer to a function is the address where the code for the function resides.
- Pointers to functions can be passed to functions, returned from functions, stored in arrays and assigned to other pointers.
- A common use of function pointers is in so-called menu-driven systems. The function pointers are used to select which function to call for a particular menu item.

Section 9.13 Introduction to Pointer-Based String Processing
- Function strcpy copies its second argument—a string—into its first argument—a character array. You must ensure that the target array is large enough to store the string and its terminating null character.
- Function strncpy is equivalent to strcpy, except that a call to strncpy specifies the number of characters to be copied from the string into the array. The terminating null character will be copied only if the number of characters to be copied is at least one more than the length of the string.
- Function strcat appends its second string argument—including the terminating null character—to its first string argument. The first character of the second string replaces the null ('\0') character of the first string. You must ensure that the target array used to store the first string is large enough to store both the first string and the second string.
- Function strncat is equivalent to strcat, except that a call to strncat appends a specified number of characters from the second string to the first string. A terminating null character is appended to the result.
- Function strcmp compares its first string argument with its second string argument character by character. The function returns zero if the strings are equal, a negative value if the first string is less than the second string and a positive value if the first string is greater than the second string.
- Function strncmp is equivalent to strcmp, except that strncmp compares a specified number of characters. If the number of characters in one of the strings is less than the number of characters specified, strncmp compares characters until the null character in the shorter string is encountered.
- A sequence of calls to strtok breaks a string into tokens that are separated by characters contained in a second string argument. The first call specifies the string to be tokenized as the first

argument, and subsequent calls to continue tokenizing the same string specify NULL as the first argument. The function returns a pointer to the current token from each call. If there are no more tokens when strtok is called, NULL is returned.

- Function strlen takes a string as an argument and returns the number of characters in the string—the terminating null character is not included in the length of the string.

Section 9.14 Introduction to C++/CLI Handles
- Managed objects are created in managed memory. Native objects are created in unmanaged memory.

- In managed memory a garbage collector runs periodically to determine when objects are no longer needed and can have the memory they use reclaimed. It also compacts the remaining objects in managed memory.

- The garbage collector does not run on unmanaged memory, because native pointers would have the data they point to moved during compaction but not have the memory locations they reference updated. This would render the data in the pointer useless to the programmer.

- C++/CLI provides handles declared like pointers but with the ∧ symbol instead of *. Handles have the location they point to updated by the garbage collector if that data is moved during compaction. Handles can only point to whole objects in managed memory and cannot be used for pointer arithmetic and comparison. Handles can be dereferenced using the * operator just like native pointers.

- The unary % operator provides analogous function to the & operator but for managed types. Use the % operator on a managed type to return a handle to the object.

- Handles can be declared const and the data they point to can be declared const just like pointers.

Section 9.15 Passing Arguments to Functions by Reference with Handles
- Handles are used to pass managed types by reference analogously to the way pointers are used to pass native types by reference.

Section 9.16 Tracking References and References to Handles
- Use the % symbol to declare a tracking reference analogously to the way & is used to create reference parameters.

- Tracking references are especially useful for passing handles by reference.

Section 9.17 Interior Pointers
- The declaration

```
interior_ptr< int > ptr = memoryAddress;
```

declares ptr to be an interior pointer to a variable of type int. Use & to obtain the memory address to assign to an interior pointer.

- Interior pointers allow you to use pointer arithmetic and comparison, unlike handles.

Terminology

& (address operator)
% (address of a managed type operator)
* (pointer dereference or indirection operator)
'\0' (null character)
address operator (&)

address of a managed type operator (%)
array of pointers to functions
ASCII (American Standard Code for Information Interchange)
calling functions by reference

character code

character constant

command-line arguments

comparing strings

concatenating strings

const with function parameters

constant pointer

constant pointer to constant data

constant pointer to nonconstant data

copying strings

decrement a pointer

delimiter character

dereference a 0 pointer

dereference a handle

dereference a pointer

dereferencing operator (*)

directly reference a value

EBCDIC (Extended Binary Coded Decimal Interchange Code)

function pointer

garbage collector

getline function of cin

handle

increment a pointer

indefinite postponement

indirection

indirection (*) operator

indirectly reference a value

interchangeability of arrays and pointers

interior pointer

islower function (<cctype>)

modify a constant pointer

modify address stored in pointer variable

nonconstant pointer to constant data

nonconstant pointer to nonconstant data

null character ('\0')

null pointer

null-terminated string

nullptr

offset to a pointer

pass-by-reference with pointer arguments

pass-by-reference with reference arguments

pointer arithmetic

pointer-based strings

pointer dereference (*) operator

pointer subtraction

pointer to a function

reference to constant data

referencing array elements

selection sort algorithm

size_t type

sizeof operator

special characters

starvation

strcat function of header file <cstring>

strcmp function of header file <cstring>

strcpy function of header file <cstring>

string array

string being tokenized

string constant

string copying

strlen function of header file <cstring>

strncat function of header file <cstring>

strncmp function of header file <cstring>

strncpy function of header file <cstring>

strtok function of header file <cstring>

terminating null character

token

tokenizing strings

toupper function (<cctype>)

tracking reference

type safe

Unicode character set

Self-Review Exercises

9.1 Answer each of the following:
- a) A pointer is a variable that contains as its value the _____ of another variable.
- b) The three values that can be used to initialize a pointer are _____, _____ and _____.
- c) The only integer that can be assigned directly to a pointer is _____.

9.2 State whether the following are *true* or *false*. If the answer is *false*, explain why.
- a) The address operator & can be applied only to constants and to expressions.
- b) A pointer that is declared to be of type void * can be dereferenced.
- c) Pointers of different types cannot be assigned to one another without a cast operation.

9.3   For each of the following, write Visual C++ statements that perform the specified task. Assume that double-precision, floating-point numbers are stored in eight bytes and that the starting address of the array is at location 1002500 in memory. Each part of the exercise should use the results of previous parts where appropriate.

- a) Declare an array of type `double` called `numbers` with 10 elements, and initialize the elements to the values `0.0, 1.1, 2.2, ..., 9.9`. Assume that the symbolic constant `SIZE` has been defined as `10`.
- b) Declare a pointer `nPtr` that points to a variable of type `double`.
- c) Use a `for` statement to print the elements of array `numbers` using array subscript notation. Print each number with one position of precision to the right of the decimal point.
- d) Write two separate statements that each assign the starting address of array `numbers` to the pointer variable `nPtr`.
- e) Use a `for` statement to print the elements of array `numbers` using pointer/offset notation with pointer `nPtr`.
- f) Use a `for` statement to print the elements of array `numbers` using pointer/offset notation with the array name as the pointer.
- g) Use a `for` statement to print the elements of array `numbers` using pointer/subscript notation with pointer `nPtr`.
- h) Refer to the fourth element of array `numbers` using array subscript notation, pointer/offset notation with the array name as the pointer, pointer subscript notation with `nPtr` and pointer/offset notation with `nPtr`.
- i) Assuming that `nPtr` points to the beginning of array `numbers`, what address is referenced by `nPtr + 8`? What value is stored at that location?
- j) Assuming that `nPtr` points to `numbers[ 5 ]`, what address is referenced by `nPtr` after `nPtr -= 4` is executed? What is the value stored at that location?

9.4   For each of the following, write a single statement that performs the specified task. Assume that floating-point variables `number1` and `number2` have been declared and that `number1` has been initialized to `7.3`. Assume that variable `ptr` is of type `char *`. Assume that arrays `s1` and `s2` are each 100-element char arrays that are initialized with string literals.

- a) Declare the variable `fPtr` to be a pointer to an object of type `double`.
- b) Assign the address of variable `number1` to pointer variable `fPtr`.
- c) Print the value of the object pointed to by `fPtr`.
- d) Assign the value of the object pointed to by `fPtr` to variable `number2`.
- e) Print the value of `number2`.
- f) Print the address of `number1`.
- g) Print the address stored in `fPtr`. Is the value printed the same as the address of `number1`?
- h) Copy the string stored in array `s2` into array `s1`.
- i) Compare the string in `s1` with the string in `s2`, and print the result.
- j) Append the first 10 characters from the string in `s2` to the string in `s1`.
- k) Determine the length of the string in `s1`, and print the result.
- l) Assign to `ptr` the location of the first token in `s2`. The tokens' delimiters are commas (,).

9.5   Perform the task specified by each of the following statements:

- a) Write the function header for a function called `exchange` that takes two pointers to double-precision, floating-point numbers x and y as parameters and does not return a value.
- b) Write the function prototype for the function in part (a).
- c) Write the function header for a function called `evaluate` that returns an integer and that takes as parameters integer x and a pointer to function `poly`. Function `poly` takes an integer parameter and returns an integer.
- d) Write the function prototype for the function in part (c).

e) Write two statements that each initialize character array vowel with the string of vowels, "AEIOU".

9.6   Find the error in each of the following program segments. Assume the following declarations and statements:

```
int *zPtr; // zPtr will reference array z
int *aPtr = 0;
void *sPtr = 0;
int number;
int z[ 5 ] = { 1, 2, 3, 4, 5 };
```

a) ++zPtr;

b) // use pointer to get first value of array
```
number = zPtr;
```

c) // assign array element 2 (the value 3) to number
```
number = *zPtr[ 2 ];
```

d) // print entire array z
```
for ( int i = 0; i <= 5; i++ )
    cout << zPtr[ i ] << endl;
```

e) // assign the value pointed to by sPtr to number
```
number = *sPtr;
```

f) ++z;

g) char s[10];
```
cout << strncpy( s, "hello", 5 ) << endl;
```

h) char s[12];
```
strcpy( s, "Welcome Home" );
```

i) if (strcmp(string1, string2))
```
    cout << "The strings are equal" << endl;
```

9.7   What (if anything) prints when each of the following statements is performed? If the statement contains an error, describe the error and indicate how to correct it. Assume the following variable declarations:

```
char s1[ 50 ] = "jack";
char s2[ 50 ] = "jill";
char s3[ 50 ];
```

a) cout << strcpy(s3, s2) << endl;

b) cout << strcat(strcat(strcpy(s3, s1), " and "), s2)
```
    << endl;
```

c) cout << strlen(s1) + strlen(s2) << endl;

d) cout << strlen(s3) << endl;

9.8   Answer each of the following:

a) A handle is a variable that contains as its value the _____ of a(n) _____ object.

b) Use _____ to initialize a handle to a null value.

c) Use the _____ operator to get the memory address of a managed object that can be assigned to a handle.

9.9   State whether the following are *true* or *false*. If the answer is *false*, explain why.

a) The unary % operator can be applied to constants, native objects, or managed objects.

b) A handle can be declared to be, or cast to, type void ^.

c) Pointers can be used to hold memory addresses of managed objects.

d) You cannot perform pointer arithmetic or comparisons with handles.

Answers to Self-Review Exercises

9.1 a) address. b) 0, NULL, an address. c) 0.

9.2 a) False. The operand of the address operator must be an *lvalue*; the address operator cannot be applied to constants or to expressions that do not result in references.

b) False. A pointer to void cannot be dereferenced. Such a pointer does not have a type that enables the compiler to determine the number of bytes of memory to dereference and the type of the data to which the pointer points.

c) False. Pointers of any type can be assigned to void pointers. Pointers of type void can be assigned to pointers of other types only with an explicit type cast.

9.3 a) *double* numbers[SIZE] = { 0.0, 1.1, 2.2, 3.3, 4.4, 5.5, 6.6, 7.7, 8.8, 9.9 };

b) *double* *nPtr;

c) ```
cout << fixed << showpoint << setprecision(1);
for (int i = 0; i < SIZE; i++)
    cout << numbers[i] << ' ';
```

d) ```
nPtr = numbers;
nPtr = &numbers[ 0 ];
```

e) ```
cout << fixed << showpoint << setprecision(1);
for (int j = 0; j < SIZE; j++)
    cout << *(nPtr + j) << ' ';
```

f) ```
cout << fixed << showpoint << setprecision( 1 );
for ( int k = 0; k < SIZE; k++ )
    cout << *( numbers + k ) << ' ';
```

g) ```
cout << fixed << showpoint << setprecision(1);
for (int m = 0; m < SIZE; m++)
    cout << nPtr[m] << ' ';
```

h) ```
numbers[ 3 ]
*( numbers + 3 )
nPtr[ 3 ]
*( nPtr + 3 )
```

i) The address is 1002500 + 8 * 8 = 1002564. The value is 8.8.

j) The address of numbers[5] is 1002500 + 5 * 8 = 1002540.
The address of nPtr -= 4 is 1002540 - 4 * 8 = 1002508.
The value at that location is 1.1.

9.4 a) *double* *fPtr;

b) fPtr = &number1;

c) cout << "The value of *fPtr is " << *fPtr << endl;

d) number2 = *fPtr;

e) cout << "The value of number2 is " << number2 << endl;

f) cout << "The address of number1 is " << &number1 << endl;

g) cout << "The address stored in fPtr is " << fPtr << endl;
Yes, the value is the same.

h) strcpy(s1, s2);

i) cout << "strcmp(s1, s2) = " << strcmp(s1, s2) << endl;

j) strncat(s1, s2, 10);

k) cout << "strlen(s1) = " << strlen(s1) << endl;

l) ptr = strtok(s2, ",");

9.5 a) *void* exchange(*double* *x, *double* *y)

b) *void* exchange(*double* *, *double* *);

c) `int` evaluate(`int` x, `int` (*poly)(`int`))

d) `int` evaluate(`int`, `int` (*)(`int`));

e) `char` vowel[] = "AEIOU";
   `char` vowel[] = { 'A', 'E', 'I', 'O', 'U', '\0' };

9.6 a) Error: `zPtr` has not been initialized.
Correction: Initialize `zPtr` with `zPtr = z;`

b) Error: The pointer is not dereferenced.
Correction: Change the statement to `number = *zPtr;`

c) Error: `zPtr[ 2 ]` is not a pointer and should not be dereferenced.
Correction: Change `*zPtr[ 2 ]` to `zPtr[ 2 ]`.

d) Error: Referring to an array element outside the array bounds with pointer subscripting.
Correction: To prevent this, change the relational operator in the `for` statement to `<`.

e) Error: Dereferencing a void pointer.
Correction: To dereference the void pointer, it must first be cast to an integer pointer. Change the statement to `number = *static_cast< int * >( sPtr );`

f) Error: Trying to modify an array name with pointer arithmetic.
Correction: Use a pointer variable instead of the array name to accomplish pointer arithmetic, or subscript the array name to refer to a specific element.

g) Error: Function `strncpy` does not write a terminating null character to array `s`, because its third argument is equal to the length of the string `"hello"`.
Correction: Make 6 the third argument of `strncpy` or assign `'\0'` to `s[ 5 ]` to ensure that the terminating null character is added to the string.

h) Error: Character array `s` is not large enough to store the terminating null character.
Correction: Declare the array with more elements.

i) Error: Function `strcmp` will return 0 if the strings are equal; therefore, the condition in the `if` statement will be false, and the output statement will not be executed.
Correction: Explicitly compare the `strcmp` result with 0 in the `if` statement's condition.

9.7 a) `jill`

b) `jack and jill`

c) `8`

d) `13`

9.8 a) address, managed b) `nullptr` c) `%`.

9.9 a) False. A handle can hold only the memory address of a managed object in managed memory. Constants and native objects are not allocated in managed memory.

b) False. Handles are "type safe." Handles of type `void ^` do not exist.

c) False. A pointer can hold only the memory address of a native object or constant. Managed objects can be moved by the garbage collector, so you must use handles to reference them, not pointers. A pointer will not have the address it points to updated by the garbage collector if the data it points to is moved during compaction.

d) True.

Exercises

9.10 State whether the following are *true* or *false*. If *false*, explain why.

a) Two pointers that point to different arrays cannot be compared meaningfully.

b) Because the name of an array is a pointer to the first element of the array, array names can be manipulated in precisely the same manner as pointers.

9.11   For each of the following, write Visual C++ statements that perform the specified task. Assume that unsigned integers are stored in two bytes and that the starting address of the array is at location 1002500 in memory.

a) Declare an array of type unsigned int called values with five elements, and initialize the elements to the even integers from 2 to 10. Assume that the symbolic constant SIZE has been defined as 5.

b) Declare a pointer vPtr that points to an object of type unsigned int.

c) Use a for statement to print the elements of array values using array subscript notation.

d) Write two separate statements that assign the starting address of array values to pointer variable vPtr.

e) Use a for statement to print the elements of array values using pointer/offset notation.

f) Use a for statement to print the elements of array values using pointer/offset notation with the array name as the pointer.

g) Use a for statement to print the elements of array values by subscripting the pointer to the array.

h) Refer to the fifth element of values using array subscript notation, pointer/offset notation with the array name as the pointer, pointer subscript notation and pointer/offset notation.

i) What address is referenced by vPtr + 3? What value is stored at that location?

j) Assuming that vPtr points to values[4], what address is referenced by vPtr -= 4? What value is stored at that location?

9.12   For each of the following, write a single statement that performs the specified task. Assume that long variables value1 and value2 have been declared and value1 has been initialized to 200000.

a) Declare the variable longPtr to be a pointer to an object of type long.

b) Assign the address of variable value1 to pointer variable longPtr.

c) Print the value of the object pointed to by longPtr.

d) Assign the value of the object pointed to by longPtr to variable value2.

e) Print the value of value2.

f) Print the address of value1.

g) Print the address stored in longPtr. Is the value printed the same as value1's address?

9.13   Perform the task specified by each of the following statements:

a) Write the function header for function zero that takes a long integer array parameter bigIntegers and does not return a value.

b) Write the function prototype for the function in part (a).

c) Write the function header for function add1AndSum that takes an integer array parameter oneTooSmall and returns an integer.

d) Write the function prototype for the function described in part (c).

Note: Exercises 9.14–9.17 are reasonably challenging. Once you have solved these problems, you ought to be able to implement many popular card games.

9.14   Modify the program in Fig. 9.27 so that the card dealing function deals a five-card poker hand. Then write functions to accomplish each of the following:

a) Determine whether the hand contains a pair.

b) Determine whether the hand contains two pairs.

c) Determine whether the hand contains three of a kind (e.g., three jacks).

d) Determine whether the hand contains four of a kind (e.g., four aces).

e) Determine whether the hand contains a flush (i.e., all five cards of the same suit).

f) Determine whether the contains a straight (i.e., five cards of consecutive face values).

9.15   Use the functions developed in Exercise 9.14 to write a program that deals two five-card poker hands, evaluates each hand and determines which is the better hand.

9.16   Modify the program developed in Exercise 9.15 so that it can simulate the dealer. The dealer's five-card hand is dealt "face down" so the player cannot see it. The program should then evaluate the dealer's hand, and, based on the quality of the hand, the dealer should draw one, two or three more cards to replace the corresponding number of unneeded cards in the original hand. The program should then reevaluate the dealer's hand. [*Caution:* This is a difficult problem!]

9.17   Modify the program developed in Exercise 9.16 so that it handles the dealer's hand, but the player is allowed to decide which cards of the player's hand to replace. The program should then evaluate both hands and determine who wins. Now use this new program to play 20 games against the computer. Who wins more games, you or the computer? Have one of your friends play 20 games against the computer. Who wins more games? Based on the results of these games, make appropriate modifications to refine your poker-playing program. [*Note:* This, too, is a difficult problem.] Play 20 more games. Does your modified program play a better game?

9.18   In the card shuffling and dealing program of Figs. 9.25–9.27, we intentionally used an inefficient shuffling algorithm that introduced the possibility of indefinite postponement. In this problem, you'll create a high-performance shuffling algorithm that avoids indefinite postponement.

Modify Figs. 9.25–9.27 as follows. Initialize the deck array as shown in Fig. 9.41. Modify the shuffle function to loop row by row and column by column through the array, touching every element once. Each element should be swapped with a randomly selected element of the array. Print the resulting array to determine whether the deck is satisfactorily shuffled (as in Fig. 9.42, for example). You may want your program to call the shuffle function several times to ensure a satisfactory shuffle.

Note that, although the approach in this problem improves the shuffling algorithm, the dealing algorithm still requires searching the deck array for card 1, then card 2, then card 3 and so on. Worse yet, even after the dealing algorithm locates and deals the card, the algorithm continues

Unshuffled deck array

	0	1	2	3	4	5	6	7	8	9	10	11	12
0	1	2	3	4	5	6	7	8	9	10	11	12	13
1	14	15	16	17	18	19	20	21	22	23	24	25	26
2	27	28	29	30	31	32	33	34	35	36	37	38	39
3	40	41	42	43	44	45	46	47	48	49	50	51	52

Fig. 9.41 | Unshuffled deck array.

Sample shuffled deck array

	0	1	2	3	4	5	6	7	8	9	10	11	12
0	19	40	27	25	36	46	10	34	35	41	18	2	44
1	13	28	14	16	21	30	8	11	31	17	24	7	1
2	12	33	15	42	43	23	45	3	29	32	4	47	26
3	50	38	52	39	48	51	9	5	37	49	22	6	20

Fig. 9.42 | Sample shuffled deck array.

searching through the remainder of the deck. Modify the program of Figs. 9.25–9.27 so that once a card is dealt, no further attempts are made to match that card number, and the program immediately proceeds with dealing the next card.

9.19 (*Simulation: The Tortoise and the Hare*) In this exercise, you'll re-create the classic race of the tortoise and the hare. You'll use random number generation to develop a simulation of this memorable event.

Our contenders begin the race at "square 1" of 70 squares. Each square represents a possible position along the race course. The finish line is at square 70. The first contender to reach or pass square 70 is rewarded with a pail of fresh carrots and lettuce. The course weaves its way up the side of a slippery mountain, so occasionally the contenders lose ground.

There is a clock that ticks once per second. With each tick of the clock, your program should adjust the position of the animals according to the rules in Fig. 9.43.

Use variables to keep track of the positions of the animals (i.e., position numbers are 1–70). Start each animal at position 1 (i.e., the "starting gate"). If an animal slips left before square 1, move the animal back to square 1.

Generate the percentages in the preceding table by producing a random integer i in the range $1 \leq i \leq 10$. For the tortoise, perform a "fast plod" when $1 \leq i \leq 5$, a "slip" when $6 \leq i \leq 7$ or a "slow plod" when $8 \leq i \leq 10$. Use a similar technique to move the hare.

Begin the race by printing

```
BANG !!!!!
AND THEY'RE OFF !!!!!
```

For each tick of the clock (i.e., each repetition of a loop), print a 70-position line showing the letter T in the tortoise's position and the letter H in the hare's position. Occasionally, the contenders land on the same square. In this case, the tortoise bites the hare and your program should print OUCH!!! beginning at that position. All print positions other than the T, the H or the OUCH!!! (in case of a tie) should be blank.

After printing each line, test whether either animal has reached or passed square 70. If so, print the winner and terminate the simulation. If the tortoise wins, print TORTOISE WINS!!! YAY!!! If the hare wins, print Hare wins. Yuch. If both animals win on the same clock tick, you may want to favor the tortoise (the "underdog"), or you may want to print It's a tie. If neither animal wins, perform the loop again to simulate the next tick of the clock.

Animal	Move type	Percentage of the time	Actual move
Tortoise	Fast plod	50%	3 squares to the right
	Slip	20%	6 squares to the left
	Slow plod	30%	1 square to the right
Hare	Sleep	20%	No move at all
	Big hop	20%	9 squares to the right
	Big slip	10%	12 squares to the left
	Small hop	30%	1 square to the right
	Small slip	20%	2 squares to the left

Fig. 9.43 | Rules for moving the tortoise and the hare.

Special Section: Building Your Own Computer

In the next several problems, we take a temporary diversion away from the world of high-level-language programming. We "peel open" a computer and look at its internal structure. We introduce machine-language programming and write several machine-language programs. To make this an especially valuable experience, we then build a computer (using software-based *simulation*) on which you can execute your machine-language programs!

9.20   (*Machine-Language Programming*) Let us create a computer we'll call the Simpletron. As its name implies, it is a simple machine, but, as we'll soon see, it is a powerful one as well. The Simpletron runs programs written in the only language it directly understands, that is, Simpletron Machine Language, or SML for short.

The Simpletron contains an *accumulator*—a "special register" in which information is put before the Simpletron uses that information in calculations or examines it in various ways. All information in the Simpletron is handled in terms of *words*. A word is a signed four-digit decimal number, such as +3364, –1293, +0007, –0001, etc. The Simpletron is equipped with a 100-word memory, and these words are referenced by their location numbers 00, 01, …, 99.

Before running an SML program, we must *load,* or place, the program into memory. The first instruction (or statement) of every SML program is always placed in location 00. The simulator will start executing at this location.

Each instruction written in SML occupies one word of the Simpletron's memory; thus, instructions are signed four-digit decimal numbers. Assume that the sign of an SML instruction is always plus, but the sign of a data word may be either plus or minus. Each location in the Simpletron's memory may contain an instruction, a data value used by a program or an unused (and hence undefined) area of memory. The first two digits of each SML instruction are the *operation code* that specifies the operation to be performed. SML operation codes are shown in Fig. 9.44.

Operation code	Meaning
Input/output operations	
`const int READ = 10;`	Read a word from the keyboard into a specific location in memory.
`const int WRITE = 11;`	Write a word from a specific location in memory to the screen.
Load and store operations	
`const int LOAD = 20;`	Load a word from a specific location in memory into the accumulator.
`const int STORE = 21;`	Store a word from the accumulator into a specific location in memory.
Arithmetic operations	
`const int ADD = 30;`	Add a word from a specific location in memory to the word in the accumulator (leave result in accumulator).

Fig. 9.44 | Simpletron Machine Language (SML) operation codes. (Part 1 of 2.)

Operation code	Meaning
`const int SUBTRACT = 31;`	Subtract a word from a specific location in memory from the word in the accumulator (leave result in accumulator).
`const int DIVIDE = 32;`	Divide a word from a specific location in memory into the word in the accumulator (leave result in accumulator).
`const int MULTIPLY = 33;`	Multiply a word from a specific location in memory by the word in the accumulator (leave result in accumulator).
Transfer-of-control operations	
`const int BRANCH = 40;`	Branch to a specific location in memory.
`const int BRANCHNEG = 41;`	Branch to a specific location in memory if the accumulator is negative.
`const int BRANCHZERO = 42;`	Branch to a specific location in memory if the accumulator is zero.
`const int HALT = 43;`	Halt—the program has completed its task.

Fig. 9.44 | Simpletron Machine Language (SML) operation codes. (Part 2 of 2.)

The last two digits of an SML instruction are the *operand*—the address of the memory location containing the word to which the operation applies.

Now let us consider two simple SML programs. The first (Fig. 9.45) reads two numbers from the keyboard and computes and prints their sum. The instruction +1007 reads the first number

Location	Number	Instruction
00	+1007	(Read A)
01	+1008	(Read B)
02	+2007	(Load A)
03	+3008	(Add B)
04	+2109	(Store C)
05	+1109	(Write C)
06	+4300	(Halt)
07	+0000	(Variable A)
08	+0000	(Variable B)
09	+0000	(Result C)

Fig. 9.45 | SML Example I.

Location	Number	Instruction
00	+1009	(Read A)
01	+1010	(Read B)
02	+2009	(Load A)
03	+3110	(Subtract B)
04	+4107	(Branch negative to 07)
05	+1109	(Write A)
06	+4300	(Halt)
07	+1110	(Write B)
08	+4300	(Halt)
09	+0000	(Variable A)
10	+0000	(Variable B)

Fig. 9.46 | SML Example 2.

from the keyboard and places it into location 07 (which has been initialized to zero). Instruction +1008 reads the next number into location 08. The *load* instruction, +2007, places (copies) the first number into the accumulator, and the *add* instruction, +3008, adds the second number to the number in the accumulator. *All SML arithmetic instructions leave their results in the accumulator.* The *store* instruction, +2109, places (copies) the result back into memory location 09. Then the *write* instruction, +1109, takes the number and prints it (as a signed four-digit decimal number). The *halt* instruction, +4300, terminates execution.

The SML program in Fig. 9.46 reads two numbers from the keyboard, then determines and prints the larger value. Note the use of the instruction +4107 as a conditional transfer of control, much the same as Visual C++'s if statement.

Now write SML programs to accomplish each of the following tasks:

a) Use a sentinel-controlled loop to read positive numbers and compute and print their sum. Terminate input when a negative number is entered.

b) Use a counter-controlled loop to read seven numbers, some positive and some negative, and compute and print their average.

c) Read a series of numbers, and determine and print the largest number. The first number read indicates how many numbers should be processed.

9.21   (*Computer Simulator*) It may at first seem outrageous, but in this problem you are going to build your own computer. No, you won't be soldering components together. Rather, you'll use the powerful technique of *software-based simulation* to create a *software model* of the Simpletron. You won't be disappointed. Your Simpletron simulator will turn the computer you are using into a Simpletron, and you actually will be able to run, test and debug the SML programs you wrote in Exercise 9.20.

When you run your Simpletron simulator, it should begin by printing

```
*** Welcome to Simpletron! ***

*** Please enter your program one instruction ***
*** (or data word) at a time. I will type the ***
```

```
*** location number and a question mark (?).  ***
*** You then type the word for that location. ***
*** Type the sentinel -99999 to stop entering ***
*** your program. ***
```

Your program should simulate the Simpletron's memory with a single-subscripted, 100-element array memory. Now assume that the simulator is running, and let us examine the dialog as we enter the program of Example 2 of Exercise 9.20:

```
00 ? +1009
01 ? +1010
02 ? +2009
03 ? +3110
04 ? +4107
05 ? +1109
06 ? +4300
07 ? +1110
08 ? +4300
09 ? +0000
10 ? +0000
11 ? -99999

*** Program loading completed ***
*** Program execution begins  ***
```

Note that the numbers to the right of each ? in the preceding dialog represent the SML program instructions input by the user.

The SML program has now been placed (or loaded) into array memory. Now the Simpletron executes your SML program. Execution begins with the instruction in location 00 and, as in Visual C++, continues sequentially, unless directed to some other part of the program by a transfer of control.

Use variable accumulator to represent the accumulator register. Use variable counter to keep track of the location in memory that contains the instruction being performed. Use variable operationCode to indicate the operation currently being performed (i.e., the left two digits of the instruction word). Use variable operand to indicate the memory location on which the current instruction operates. Thus, operand is the rightmost two digits of the instruction currently being performed. Do not execute instructions directly from memory. Rather, transfer the next instruction to be performed from memory to a variable called instructionRegister. Then "pick off" the left two digits and place them in operationCode, and "pick off" the right two digits and place them in operand. When Simpletron begins execution, the special registers are all initialized to zero.

Now let us "walk through" the execution of the first SML instruction, +1009 in memory location 00. This is called an *instruction execution cycle*.

The counter tells us the location of the next instruction to be performed. We *fetch* the contents of that location from memory by using the Visual C++ statement

```
instructionRegister = memory[ counter ];
```

The operation code and operand are extracted from the instruction register by the statements

```
operationCode = instructionRegister / 100;
operand = instructionRegister % 100;
```

Now, the Simpletron must determine that the operation code is actually a *read* (versus a *write*, a *load*, etc.). A switch differentiates among the 12 operations of SML.

In the switch statement, the behavior of various SML instructions is simulated as shown in Fig. 9.47 (we leave the others to you).

read:	`cin >> memory[ operand ];`
load:	`accumulator = memory[ operand ];`
add:	`accumulator += memory[ operand ];`
branch:	We'll discuss the branch instructions shortly.
halt:	This instruction prints the message `*** Simpletron execution terminated ***`

Fig. 9.47 | Behavior of SML instructions.

The *halt* instruction also causes the Simpletron to print the name and contents of each register, as well as the complete contents of memory. Such a printout is often called a *register and memory dump*. To help you program your dump function, a sample dump format is shown in Fig. 9.48. Note that a dump after executing a Simpletron program would show the actual values of instructions and data values at the moment execution terminated. To format numbers with their sign as shown in the dump, use stream manipulator ***showpos***. To disable the display of the sign, use stream manipulator ***noshowpos***. For numbers that have fewer than four digits, you can format numbers with leading zeros between the sign and the value by using the following statement before outputting the value:

```
cout << setfill( '0' ) << internal;
```

Parameterized stream manipulator ***setfill*** (from header <iomanip>) specifies the fill character that will appear between the sign and the value when a number is displayed with a field width of five characters but does not have four digits. (One position in the field width is reserved for the sign.) Stream manipulator ***internal*** indicates that the fill characters should appear between the sign and the numeric value .

Let us proceed with the execution of our program's first instruction—+1009 in location 00. As we have indicated, the `switch` statement simulates this by performing the Visual C++ statement

```
cin >> memory[ operand ];
```

```
REGISTERS:
accumulator          +0000
counter                 00
instructionRegister  +0000
operationCode           00
operand                 00

MEMORY:
        0     1     2     3     4     5     6     7     8     9
 0  +0000 +0000 +0000 +0000 +0000 +0000 +0000 +0000 +0000 +0000
10  +0000 +0000 +0000 +0000 +0000 +0000 +0000 +0000 +0000 +0000
20  +0000 +0000 +0000 +0000 +0000 +0000 +0000 +0000 +0000 +0000
30  +0000 +0000 +0000 +0000 +0000 +0000 +0000 +0000 +0000 +0000
40  +0000 +0000 +0000 +0000 +0000 +0000 +0000 +0000 +0000 +0000
50  +0000 +0000 +0000 +0000 +0000 +0000 +0000 +0000 +0000 +0000
60  +0000 +0000 +0000 +0000 +0000 +0000 +0000 +0000 +0000 +0000
70  +0000 +0000 +0000 +0000 +0000 +0000 +0000 +0000 +0000 +0000
80  +0000 +0000 +0000 +0000 +0000 +0000 +0000 +0000 +0000 +0000
90  +0000 +0000 +0000 +0000 +0000 +0000 +0000 +0000 +0000 +0000
```

Fig. 9.48 | A sample register and memory dump.

A question mark (?) should be displayed on the screen before the cin statement executes to prompt the user for input. The Simpletron waits for the user to type a value and press the *Enter* key. The value is then read into location 09.

At this point, simulation of the first instruction is complete. All that remains is to prepare the Simpletron to execute the next instruction. The instruction just performed was not a transfer of control, so we need merely increment the instruction counter register as follows:

```
++counter;
```

This completes the simulated execution of the first instruction. The entire process (i.e., the instruction execution cycle) begins anew with the fetch of the next instruction to execute.

Now let us consider how to simulate the branching instructions (i.e., the transfers of control). All we need to do is adjust the value in the instruction counter appropriately. Therefore, the unconditional branch instruction (40) is simulated in the switch as

```
counter = operand;
```

The conditional "branch if accumulator is zero" instruction is simulated as

```
if ( accumulator == 0 )
    counter = operand;
```

At this point, you should implement your Simpletron simulator and run each of the SML programs you wrote in Exercise 9.20. You may embellish SML with additional features and provide for these in your simulator.

Your simulator should check for various types of errors. During the program-loading phase, for example, each number the user types into the Simpletron's memory must be in the range -9999 to +9999. Your simulator should use a while loop to test that each number entered is in this range and, if not, keep prompting the user to reenter the number until the user enters a correct number.

During the execution phase, your simulator should check for various serious errors, such as attempts to divide by zero, attempts to execute invalid operation codes, accumulator overflows (i.e., arithmetic operations resulting in values larger than +9999 or smaller than -9999) and the like. Such serious errors are called *fatal errors*. When a fatal error is detected, your simulator should print an error message such as

```
*** Attempt to divide by zero ***
*** Simpletron execution abnormally terminated ***
```

and should print a full register and memory dump in the format we have discussed previously. This will help the user locate the error in the program.

More Pointer Exercises

9.22 Modify the card shuffling and dealing program of Figs. 9.25–9.27 so the shuffling and dealing operations are performed by the same function (shuffleAndDeal). The function should contain one nested looping statement that is similar to function shuffle in Fig. 9.26.

9.23 What does this program do?

```
1   // Exercise 9.21: ex09_21.cpp
2   // What does this program do?
3   #include <iostream>
4   using std::cout;
5   using std::cin;
6   using std::endl;
7
```

```
8    void mystery1( char *, const char * ); // prototype
9
10   int main()
11   {
12      char string1[ 80 ];
13      char string2[ 80 ];
14
15      cout << "Enter two strings: ";
16      cin >> string1 >> string2;
17      mystery1( string1, string2 );
18      cout << string1 << endl;
19      return 0; // indicates successful termination
20   } // end main
21
22   // What does this function do?
23   void mystery1( char *s1, const char *s2 )
24   {
25      while ( *s1 != '\0' )
26         s1++;
27
28      for ( ; *s1 = *s2; s1++, s2++ )
29         ; // empty statement
30   } // end function mystery1
```

9.24   What does this program do?

```
1    // Exercise 9.22: ex09_22.cpp
2    // What does this program do?
3    #include <iostream>
4    using std::cout;
5    using std::cin;
6    using std::endl;
7
8    int mystery2( const char * ); // prototype
9
10   int main()
11   {
12      char string1[ 80 ];
13
14      cout << "Enter a string: ";
15      cin >> string1;
16      cout << mystery2( string1 ) << endl;
17      return 0; // indicates successful termination
18   } // end main
19
20   // What does this function do?
21   int mystery2( const char *s )
22   {
23      int x;
24
25      for ( x = 0; *s != '\0'; s++ )
26         x++;
27
28      return x;
29   } // end function mystery2
```

9.25   Find the error in each of the following segments. If the error can be corrected, explain how.

a) ***int*** *number;
   cout << number << endl;

b) ***double*** *realPtr;
   long *integerPtr;
   integerPtr = realPtr;

c) ***int*** * x, y;
   x = y;

d) ***char*** s[] = "this is a character array";
   for (; *s != '\0'; s++)
      cout << *s << ' ';

e) ***short*** *numPtr, result;
   void *genericPtr = numPtr;
   result = *genericPtr + 7;

f) ***double*** x = 19.34;
   double xPtr = &x;
   cout << xPtr << endl;

g) ***char*** *s;
   cout << s << endl;

9.26   (*Quicksort*) You have previously seen the sorting techniques of the bucket sort and selection sort. We now present the recursive sorting technique called Quicksort. The basic algorithm for a single-subscripted array of values is as follows:

a) *Partitioning Step:* Take the first element of the unsorted array and determine its final location in the sorted array (i.e., all values to the left of the element in the array are less than the element, and all values to the right of the element in the array are greater than the element). We now have one element in its proper location and two unsorted subarrays.

b) *Recursive Step:* Perform *Step 1* on each unsorted subarray.

Each time *Step 1* is performed on a subarray, another element is placed in its final location of the sorted array, and two unsorted subarrays are created. When a subarray consists of one element, that subarray must be sorted; therefore, that element is in its final location.

The basic algorithm seems simple enough, but how do we determine the final position of the first element of each subarray? As an example, consider the following set of values (the element in bold is the partitioning element—it will be placed in its final location in the sorted array):

37 2 6 4 89 8 10 12 68 45

a) Starting from the rightmost element of the array, compare each element with **37** until an element less than **37** is found. Then swap **37** and that element. The first element less than **37** is 12, so **37** and 12 are swapped. The values now reside in the array as follows:

12 2 6 4 89 8 10 **37** 68 45

Element 12 is in italics to indicate that it was just swapped with **37**.

b) Starting from the left of the array, but beginning with the element after 12, compare each element with **37** until an element greater than **37** is found. Then swap **37** and that element. The first element greater than **37** is 89, so **37** and 89 are swapped. The values now reside in the array as follows:

12 2 6 4 **37** 8 10 *89* 68 45

c) Starting from the right, but beginning with the element before 89, compare each element with **37** until an element less than **37** is found. Then swap **37** and that element.

The first element less than **37** is 10, so **37** and 10 are swapped. The values now reside in the array as follows:

12   2   6   4   *10*   8   **37**   89   68   45

d) Starting from the left, but beginning with the element after 10, compare each element with **37** until an element greater than **37** is found. Then swap **37** and that element. There are no more elements greater than **37**, so when we compare **37** with itself, we know that **37** has been placed in its final location of the sorted array.

Once the partition has been applied to the array, there are two unsorted subarrays. The subarray with values less than 37 contains 12, 2, 6, 4, 10 and 8. The subarray with values greater than 37 contains 89, 68 and 45. The sort continues with both subarrays being partitioned in the same manner as the original array.

Based on the preceding discussion, write recursive function `quickSort` to sort a single-subscripted integer array. The function should receive as arguments an integer array, a starting subscript and an ending subscript. Function `partition` should be called by `quickSort` to perform the partitioning step.

9.27 (*Maze Traversal*) The grid of hashes (#) and dots (.) in Fig. 9.49 is a two-dimensional array representation of a maze. In the two-dimensional array, the hashes represent the walls of the maze and the dots represent squares in the possible paths through the maze. A move can be made only to a location in the array that contains a dot.

There is a simple algorithm for walking through a maze that guarantees finding the exit (assuming that there is an exit). If there is not an exit, you'll arrive at the starting location again. Place your right hand on the wall to your right and begin walking forward. Never remove your hand from the wall. If the maze turns to the right, you follow the wall to the right. As long as you do not remove your hand from the wall, eventually you'll arrive at the exit of the maze. There may be a shorter path than the one you have taken, but you are guaranteed to get out of the maze if you follow the algorithm.

Write recursive function `mazeTraverse` to walk through the maze. The function should receive arguments that include a 12-by-12 character array representing the maze and the starting location of the maze. As `mazeTraverse` attempts to locate the exit from the maze, it should place the character X in each square in the path. The function should display the maze after each move, so the user can watch as the maze is solved.

9.28 (*Generating Mazes Randomly*) Write a function `mazeGenerator` that takes as an argument a two-dimensional 12-by-12 character array and randomly produces a maze. The function should also provide the starting and ending locations of the maze. Try your function `mazeTraverse` from Exercise 9.27, using several randomly generated mazes.

Fig. 9.49 | Two-dimensional array representation of a maze.

9.29 (*Mazes of Any Size*) Generalize functions `mazeTraverse` and `mazeGenerator` of Exercise 9.27 and Exercise 9.28 to process mazes of any width and height.

9.30 (*Modifications to the Simpletron Simulator*) In Exercise 9.21, you wrote a software simulation of a computer that executes programs written in Simpletron Machine Language (SML). In this exercise, we propose several modifications and enhancements to the Simpletron Simulator. In Exercises 21.26–21.27, we propose building a compiler that converts programs written in a high-level programming language (a variation of BASIC) to SML. Some of the following modifications and enhancements may be required to execute the programs produced by the compiler. [*Note:* Some modifications may conflict with others and therefore must be done separately.]

    a) Extend the Simpletron Simulator's memory to contain 1000 memory locations to enable the Simpletron to handle larger programs.

    b) Allow the simulator to perform modulus calculations. This requires an additional Simpletron Machine Language instruction.

    c) Allow the simulator to perform exponentiation calculations. This requires an additional Simpletron Machine Language instruction.

    d) Modify the simulator to use hexadecimal values rather than integer values to represent Simpletron Machine Language instructions.

    e) Modify the simulator to allow output of a newline. This requires an additional Simpletron Machine Language instruction.

    f) Modify the simulator to process floating-point values in addition to integer values.

    g) Modify the simulator to handle string input. [*Hint:* Each Simpletron word can be divided into two groups, each holding a two-digit integer. Each two-digit integer represents the ASCII decimal equivalent of a character. Add a machine-language instruction that inputs a string, and store the string beginning at a specific Simpletron memory location. The first half of the word at that location will be a count of the number of characters in the string (i.e., the length of the string). Each succeeding half-word contains one ASCII character expressed as two decimal digits. The machine-language instruction converts each character into its ASCII equivalent and assigns it to a half-word.]

    h) Modify the simulator to handle output of strings stored in the format of part (g). [*Hint:* Add a machine-language instruction that will print a string beginning at a certain Simpletron memory location. The first half of the word at that location is a count of the number of characters in the string (i.e., the length of the string). Each succeeding half-word contains one ASCII character expressed as two decimal digits. The machine-language instruction checks the length and prints the string by translating each two-digit number into its equivalent character.]

    i) Modify the simulator to include instruction `SML_DEBUG` that prints a memory dump after each instruction executes. Give `SML_DEBUG` an operation code of 44. The word +4401 turns on debug mode, and +4400 turns off debug mode.

9.31 What does this program do?

```
1   // Exercise 9.29: ex09_29.cpp
2   // What does this program do?
3   #include <iostream>
4   using std::cout;
5   using std::cin;
6   using std::endl;
7
8   bool mystery3( const char *, const char * ); // prototype
9
10  int main()
11  {
```

```
12      char string1[ 80 ], string2[ 80 ];
13
14      cout << "Enter two strings: ";
15      cin >> string1 >> string2;
16      cout << "The result is " << mystery3( string1, string2 ) << endl;
17      return 0; // indicates successful termination
18   } // end main
19
20   // What does this function do?
21   bool mystery3( const char *s1, const char *s2 )
22   {
23      for ( ; *s1 != '\0' && *s2 != '\0'; s1++, s2++ )
24
25         if ( *s1 != *s2 )
26            return false;
27
28      return true;
29   } // end function mystery3
```

String-Manipulation Exercises

[*Note:* The following exercises should be implemented using C-style, pointer-based strings.]

9.32 Write a program that uses function strcmp to compare two strings input by the user. The program should state whether the first string is less than, equal to or greater than the second string.

9.33 Write a program that uses function strncmp to compare two strings input by the user. The program should input the number of characters to compare. The program should state whether the first string is less than, equal to or greater than the second string.

9.34 Write a program that uses random number generation to create sentences. The program should use four arrays of pointers to char called article, noun, verb and preposition. The program should create a sentence by selecting a word at random from each array in the following order: article, noun, verb, preposition, article and noun. As each word is picked, it should be concatenated to the previous words in a character array that is large enough to hold the entire sentence. The words should be separated by spaces. When the final sentence is output, it should start with a capital letter and end with a period. The program should generate 20 such sentences.

The arrays should be filled as follows: The article array should contain the articles "the", "a", "one", "some" and "any"; the noun array should contain the nouns "boy", "girl", "dog", "town" and "car"; the verb array should contain the verbs "drove", "jumped", "ran", "walked" and "skipped"; the preposition array should contain the prepositions "to", "from", "over", "under" and "on".

After completing the program, modify it to produce a short story consisting of several of these sentences. (How about a random term-paper writer!)

9.35 *(Limericks)* A limerick is a humorous five-line verse in which the first and second lines rhyme with the fifth, and the third line rhymes with the fourth. Using techniques similar to those developed in Exercise 9.34, write a Visual C++ program that produces random limericks. Polishing this program to produce good limericks is a challenging problem, but the result will be worth the effort!

9.36 Write a program that encodes English language phrases into pig Latin. Pig Latin is a form of coded language often used for amusement. Many variations exist in the methods used to form pig-Latin phrases. For simplicity, use the following algorithm: To form a pig-Latin phrase from an English-language phrase, tokenize the phrase into words with function strtok. To translate each English word into a pig-Latin word, place the first letter of the English word at the end of the English word and add the letters "ay." Thus, the word "jump" becomes "umpjay," the word "the" becomes "hetay" and the word "computer" becomes "omputercay." Blanks between words remain as blanks. Assume that the English phrase consists of words separated by blanks, there are no punctuation marks and all words have two or more letters. Function printLatinWord should display each word. [*Hint:* Each time a token is found in a call to strtok, pass the token pointer to function printLatinWord and print the pig-Latin word.]

9.37 Write a program that inputs a telephone number as a string in the form (555) 555-5555. The program should use function strtok to extract the area code as a token, the first three digits of the phone number as a token, and the last four digits of the phone number as a token. The seven digits of the phone number should be concatenated into one string. Both the area code and the phone number should be printed.

9.38 Write a program that inputs a line of text, tokenizes the line with function strtok and outputs the tokens in reverse order.

9.39 Use the string-comparison functions discussed in Section 9.13.2 and the techniques for sorting arrays developed in Chapter 8 to write a program that alphabetizes a list of strings. Use the names of 10 towns in your area as data for your program.

9.40 Write two versions of each string-copy and string-concatenation function in Fig. 9.30. The first version should use array subscripting, and the second should use pointers and pointer arithmetic.

9.41 Write two versions of each string-comparison function in Fig. 9.30. The first version should use array subscripting, and the second should use pointers and pointer arithmetic.

9.42 Write two versions of function strlen in Fig. 9.30. The first version should use array subscripting, and the second should use pointers and pointer arithmetic.

Special Section: Advanced String-Manipulation Exercises

The preceding exercises are keyed to the text and designed to test your understanding of fundamental string-manipulation concepts. This section includes a collection of intermediate and advanced string-manipulation exercises. You should find these problems challenging, yet enjoyable. The problems vary considerably in difficulty. Some require an hour or two of program writing and implementation. Others are useful for lab assignments that might require two or three weeks of study and implementation. Some are challenging term projects.

9.43 *(Text Analysis)* The availability of computers with string-manipulation capabilities has resulted in some rather interesting approaches to analyzing the writings of great authors. Much attention has been focused on whether William Shakespeare ever lived. Some scholars believe there is substantial evidence that Francis Bacon, Christopher Marlowe or other authors actually penned the masterpieces attributed to Shakespeare. Researchers have used computers to find similarities in the writings of these authors. This exercise examines three methods for analyzing texts with a computer. Note that thousands of texts, including Shakespeare, are available online at www.gutenberg.org.

   a) Write a program that reads several lines of text from the keyboard and prints a table indicating the number of occurrences of each letter of the alphabet in the text. For example, the phrase

      To be, or not to be: that is the question:

   contains one "a," two "b's," no "c's," etc.

   b) Write a program that reads several lines of text and prints a table indicating the number of one-letter words, two-letter words, three-letter words, etc., appearing in the text. For example, the phrase

```
Whether 'tis nobler in the mind to suffer
```

contains the following word lengths and occurrences:

Word length	Occurrences
1	0
2	2
3	1
4	2 (including 'tis)
5	0
6	2
7	1

c) Write a program that reads several lines of text and prints a table indicating the number of occurrences of each different word in the text. The first version of your program should include the words in the table in the same order in which they appear in the text. For example, the lines

```
To be, or not to be: that is the question:
Whether 'tis nobler in the mind to suffer
```

contain the word "to" three times, the word "be" two times, the word "or" once, etc. A more interesting (and useful) printout should then be attempted in which the words are sorted alphabetically.

9.44 *(Word Processing)* One important function in word-processing systems is *type justification*—the alignment of words to both the left and right margins of a page. This generates a professional-looking document that gives the appearance of being set in type rather than prepared on a typewriter. Type justification can be accomplished on computer systems by inserting blank characters between the words in a line so that the rightmost word aligns with the right margin.

Write a program that reads several lines of text and prints the text in type-justified format. Assume that the text is to be printed on paper 8-1/2 inches wide and that one-inch margins are to be allowed on the left and right sides. Assume that the computer prints 10 characters to the horizontal inch. Therefore, your program should print 6-1/2 inches of text, or 65 characters per line.

9.45 *(Printing Dates in Various Formats)* Dates are commonly printed in several different formats in business correspondence. Two of the more common formats are

```
07/21/1955
July 21, 1955
```

Write a program that reads a date in the first format and prints that date in the second format.

9.46 *(Check Protection)* Computers are frequently employed in check-writing systems such as payroll and accounts-payable applications. Many strange stories circulate regarding weekly paychecks being printed (by mistake) for amounts in excess of $1 million. Weird amounts are printed by computerized check-writing systems, because of human error or machine failure. Systems designers build controls into their systems to prevent such erroneous checks from being issued.

Another serious problem is the intentional alteration of a check amount by someone who intends to cash a check fraudulently. To prevent a dollar amount from being altered, most computerized check-writing systems employ a technique called *check protection.*

Checks designed for imprinting by computer contain a fixed number of spaces in which the computer may print an amount. Suppose that a paycheck contains eight blank spaces in which the computer is supposed to print the amount of a weekly paycheck. If the amount is large, then all eight of those spaces will be filled, for example,

```
1,230.60    (check amount)
--------
12345678    (position numbers)
```

On the other hand, if the amount is less than $1000, then several of the spaces would ordinarily be left blank. For example,

```
   99.87
--------
12345678
```

contains three blank spaces. If a check is printed with blank spaces, it is easier for someone to alter the amount of the check. To prevent a check from being altered, many check-writing systems insert *leading asterisks* to protect the amount as follows:

```
***99.87
--------
12345678
```

Write a program that inputs a dollar amount to be printed on a check and then prints the amount in check-protected format with leading asterisks if necessary. Assume that nine spaces are available for printing an amount.

9.47 *(Writing the Word Equivalent of a Check Amount)* Continuing the discussion of the previous example, we reiterate the importance of designing check-writing systems to prevent alteration of check amounts. One common security method requires that the check amount be both written in numbers and "spelled out" in words. Even if someone is able to alter the numerical amount of the check, it is extremely difficult to change the amount in words.

Write a program that inputs a numeric check amount and writes the word equivalent of the amount. Your program should be able to handle check amounts as large as $99.99. For example, the amount 112.43 should be written as

```
ONE HUNDRED TWELVE and 43/100
```

9.48 *(Morse Code)* Perhaps the most famous of all coding schemes is the Morse code, developed by Samuel Morse in 1832 for use with the telegraph system. The Morse code assigns a series of dots and dashes to each letter of the alphabet, each digit and a few special characters (such as period, comma, colon and semicolon). In sound-oriented systems, the dot represents a short sound, and the dash represents a long sound. Other representations of dots and dashes are used with light-oriented systems and signal-flag systems.

Separation between words is indicated by a space, or, quite simply, the absence of a dot or dash. In a sound-oriented system, a space is indicated by a short period of time during which no sound is transmitted. The international version of the Morse code appears in Fig. 9.50.

Write a program that reads an English-language phrase and encodes it into Morse code. Also write a program that reads a phrase in Morse code and converts it into the English-language equivalent. Use one blank between each Morse-coded letter and three blanks between each Morse-coded word.

Character	Code	Character	Code
A	.-	N	-.
B	-...	O	---
C	-.-.	P	.--.
D	-..	Q	--.-
E	.	R	.-.
F	..-.	S	...
G	--.	T	-
H	....	U	..-
I	..	V	...-
J	.---	W	.--
K	-.-	X	-..-
L	.-..	Y	-.--
M	--	Z	--..
Digits			
1	.----	6	-....
2	..---	7	--...
3	...--	8	---..
4	....-	9	----.
5	.....	0	-----

Fig. 9.50 | Morse code alphabet.

9.49 *(A Metric Conversion Program)* Write a program that will assist the user with metric conversions. Your program should allow the user to specify the names of the units as strings (i.e., centimeters, liters, grams, etc., for the metric system and inches, quarts, pounds, etc., for the English system) and should respond to simple questions such as

```
"How many inches are in 2 meters?"
"How many liters are in 10 quarts?"
```

Your program should recognize invalid conversions. For example, the question

```
"How many feet are in 5 kilograms?"
```

is not meaningful, because "feet" are units of length, while "kilograms" are units of weight.

A Challenging String-Manipulation Project

9.50 *(A Crossword Puzzle Generator)* Most people have worked a crossword puzzle, but few have ever attempted to generate one. Generating a crossword puzzle is a difficult problem. It is suggested here as a string-manipulation project requiring substantial sophistication and effort. There are many issues that you must resolve to get even the simplest crossword-puzzle-generator program working. For example, how does one represent the grid of a crossword puzzle inside the computer? Should one use a series of strings, or should two-dimensional arrays be used? You need a source of words (i.e., a computerized dictionary) that can be directly referenced by the program. In what form should these words be stored to facilitate the complex manipulations required by the program? The really ambitious reader will want to generate the "clues" portion of the puzzle, in which the brief hints for each "across" word and each "down" word are printed for the puzzle worker. Merely printing a version of the blank puzzle itself is not a simple problem.

Handle Exercise

9.51 *(Managed GradeBook Class)* Create a managed GradeBook class to store a student's grades. The class should have a String ∧ data member to hold the student's name. The class should also have a managed array data member that holds the student's grades (integers between 0 and 100). Create a function that modifies the student's name by reference. Do likewise for the managed array of grades. Write a test program that creates a GradeBook, initializes its data members, and modifies its values by reference.

10

Classes:
A Deeper Look,
Part 1

My object all sublime
I shall achieve in time.
—W. S. Gilbert

Is it a world to hide virtues
in?
—William Shakespeare

Don't be "consistent," but be
simply true.
—Oliver Wendell Holmes, Jr.

This above all: to thine own
self be true.
—William Shakespeare

OBJECTIVES

In this chapter you'll learn:

- How to use a preprocessor wrapper to prevent multiple definition errors caused by including more than one copy of a header file in a source-code file.

- To understand class scope and accessing class members via the name of an object, a reference to an object or a pointer to an object.

- To define constructors with default arguments.

- How destructors are used to perform "termination housekeeping" on an object before it is destroyed.

- When constructors and destructors are called and the order in which they are called.

- The logic errors that may occur when a `public` member function of a class returns a reference to `private` data.

- To assign the data members of one object to those of another object by default memberwise assignment.

10.1 Introduction

In the preceding chapters, we introduced many basic terms and concepts of Visual C++ object-oriented programming. We also discussed our program development methodology: We selected appropriate attributes and behaviors for each class and specified the manner in which objects of our classes collaborated with objects of C++ Standard Library classes to accomplish each program's overall goals.

In this chapter, we take a deeper look at classes. We use an integrated Time class case study in both this chapter (three examples) and Chapter 11, Classes: A Deeper Look, Part 2 (two examples) to demonstrate several class construction capabilities. We begin with a Time class that reviews several of the features presented in the preceding chapters. The example also demonstrates an important Visual C++ software engineering concept—using a "preprocessor wrapper" in header files to prevent the code in the header from being included into the same source-code file more than once. Since a class can be defined only once, using such preprocessor directives prevents multiple definition errors.

Next, we discuss class scope and the relationships among members of a class. We also demonstrate how client code can access a class's public members via three types of "handles"—the name of an object, a reference to an object or a pointer to an object. Note we use "handles" here as a general term; don't confuse it with C++/CLI handles (denoted with the ∧ character). Outside specific C++/CLI sections we use handles as a general term in this way. As you'll see, object names and references (whether native or managed objects) can be used with the dot (.) member-selection operator to access a public member, and pointers can be used with the arrow (->) member-selection operator.

We discuss access functions that can read or display data in an object. A common use of access functions is to test the truth or falsity of conditions—such functions are known as predicate functions. We also demonstrate the notion of a utility function (also called a helper function)—a private member function that supports the operation of the class's public member functions but is not intended for use by clients of the class.

In the second example of the Time class case study, we demonstrate how to pass arguments to constructors and show how default arguments can be used in a constructor to enable client code to initialize objects of a class using a variety of arguments. Next, we discuss a special member function called a destructor that is part of every class and is used to perform "termination housekeeping" on an object before the object is destroyed. We then demonstrate the order in which constructors and destructors are called, because your programs' correctness depends on using properly initialized objects that have not yet been destroyed.

Our last example of the Time class case study in this chapter shows a dangerous programming practice in which a member function returns a reference to private data. We discuss how this breaks the encapsulation of a class and allows client code to directly access an object's data. This last example shows that objects of the same class can be assigned to one another using default memberwise assignment, which copies the data members in the object on the right side of the assignment into the corresponding data members of the object on the left side of the assignment. The chapter concludes with a discussion of software reusability.

10.2 Time Class Case Study

Our first example (Figs. 10.1–10.3) creates class Time and a driver program that tests the class. You have already created many classes in this book. In this section, we review many of the concepts covered in Chapter 4 and demonstrate an important Visual C++ software

```cpp
1   // Fig. 10.1: Time.h
2   // Declaration of class Time.
3   // Member functions are defined in Time.cpp
4
5   // prevent multiple inclusions of header file
6   #ifndef TIME_H
7   #define TIME_H
8
9   // Time class definition
10  class Time
11  {
12  public:
13     Time(); // constructor
14     void setTime( int, int, int ); // set hour, minute and second
15     void printUniversal(); // print time in universal-time format
16     void printStandard(); // print time in standard-time format
17  private:
18     int hour; // 0 - 23 (24-hour clock format)
19     int minute; // 0 - 59
20     int second; // 0 - 59
21  }; // end class Time
22
23  #endif
```

Fig. 10.1 | Time class definition.

engineering concept—using a "preprocessor wrapper" in header files to prevent the code in the header from being included into the same source code file more than once. Since a class can be defined only once, using such preprocessor directives prevents multiple-definition errors.

Time Class Definition

The class definition (Fig. 10.1) contains prototypes (lines 13–16) for member functions Time, setTime, printUniversal and printStandard. The class includes private integer members hour, minute and second (lines 18–20). Class Time's private data members can be accessed only by its four member functions. Chapter 13 introduces a third access specifier, protected, as we study inheritance and the part it plays in object-oriented programming.

Good Programming Practice 10.1

For clarity and readability, use each access specifier only once in a class definition. Place public members first, where they are easy to locate.

Software Engineering Observation 10.1

Each element of a class should have private visibility unless it can be proven that the element needs public visibility. This is another example of the principle of least privilege.

In Fig. 10.1, note that the class definition is enclosed in the following **preprocessor wrapper** (lines 6, 7 and 23):

```
// prevent multiple inclusions of header file
#ifndef TIME_H
#define TIME_H
   ...
#endif
```

When we build larger programs, other definitions and declarations will also be placed in header files. The preceding preprocessor wrapper prevents the code between **#ifndef** (which means "if not defined") and **#endif** from being included if the name TIME_H has been defined. If the header has not been included previously in a file, the name TIME_H is defined by the **#define** directive and the header file statements are included. If the header has been included previously, TIME_H is defined already and the header file is not included again. Attempts to include a header file multiple times (inadvertently) typically occur in large programs with many header files that may themselves include other header files. [*Note:* The commonly used convention for the symbolic constant name in the preprocessor directives is simply the header file name in upper case with the underscore character replacing the period.]

Error-Prevention Tip 10.1

Use #ifndef, #define and #endif preprocessor directives to form a preprocessor wrapper that prevents header files from being included more than once in a program.

Good Programming Practice 10.2

Use the name of the header file in upper case with the period replaced by an underscore in the #ifndef and #define preprocessor directives of a header file.

Time Class Member Functions

In Fig. 10.2, the `Time` constructor (lines 14–17) initializes the data members to 0 (i.e., the universal-time equivalent of 12 AM). This ensures that the object begins in a consistent state. Invalid values cannot be stored in the data members of a `Time` object, because the constructor is called when the `Time` object is created, and all subsequent attempts by a client to modify the data members are scrutinized by function `setTime` (discussed shortly). Finally, it is important to note that you can define several overloaded constructors for a class.

```cpp
// Fig. 10.2: Time.cpp
// Member-function definitions for class Time.
#include <iostream>
using std::cout;

#include <iomanip>
using std::setfill;
using std::setw;

#include "Time.h" // include definition of class Time from Time.h

// Time constructor initializes each data member to zero.
// Ensures all Time objects start in a consistent state.
Time::Time()
{
    hour = minute = second = 0;
} // end Time constructor

// set new Time value using universal time; ensure that
// the data remains consistent by setting invalid values to zero
void Time::setTime( int h, int m, int s )
{
    hour = ( h >= 0 && h < 24 ) ? h : 0; // validate hour
    minute = ( m >= 0 && m < 60 ) ? m : 0; // validate minute
    second = ( s >= 0 && s < 60 ) ? s : 0; // validate second
} // end function setTime

// print Time in universal-time format (HH:MM:SS)
void Time::printUniversal()
{
    cout << setfill( '0' ) << setw( 2 ) << hour << ":"
        << setw( 2 ) << minute << ":" << setw( 2 ) << second;
} // end function printUniversal

// print Time in standard-time format (HH:MM:SS AM or PM)
void Time::printStandard()
{
    cout << ( ( hour == 0 || hour == 12 ) ? 12 : hour % 12 ) << ":"
        << setfill( '0' ) << setw( 2 ) << minute << ":" << setw( 2 )
        << second << ( hour < 12 ? " AM" : " PM" );
} // end function printStandard
```

Fig. 10.2 | `Time` class member-function definitions.

The data members of a class cannot be initialized where they are declared in the class body. It is strongly recommended that these data members be initialized by the class's constructor (as there is no default initialization for fundamental-type data members). Data members can also be assigned values by Time's *set* functions. [*Note:* Chapter 11 demonstrates that only a class's static const data members of integral or enum types can be initialized in the class's body.]

Common Programming Error 10.1

Attempting to initialize a non-static data member of a class explicitly in the class definition is a syntax error.

Function setTime (lines 21–26) is a public function that declares three int parameters and uses them to set the time. A conditional expression tests each argument to determine whether the value is in a specified range. For example, the hour value (line 23) must be greater than or equal to 0 and less than 24, because the universal-time format represents hours as integers from 0 to 23 (e.g., 1 PM is hour 13 and 11 PM is hour 23; midnight is hour 0 and noon is hour 12). Similarly, both minute and second values (lines 24 and 25) must be greater than or equal to 0 and less than 60. Any values outside these ranges are set to zero to ensure that a Time object always contains consistent data—that is, the object's data values are always kept in range, even if the values provided as arguments to function setTime were incorrect. In this example, zero is a consistent value for hour, minute and second.

A value passed to setTime is a correct value if it is in the allowed range for the member it is initializing. So, any number in the range 0–23 would be a correct value for the hour. A correct value is always a consistent value. However, a consistent value is not necessarily a correct value. If setTime sets hour to 0 because the argument received was out of range, then hour is correct only if the current time is coincidentally midnight.

Function printUniversal (lines 29–33 of Fig. 10.2) takes no arguments and outputs the time in universal-time format, consisting of three colon-separated pairs of digits—for the hour, minute and second, respectively. For example, if the time were 1:30:07 PM, function printUniversal would return 13:30:07. Note that line 31 uses parameterized stream manipulator **setfill** to specify the **fill character** that is displayed when an integer is output in a field wider than the number of digits in the value. By default, the fill characters appear to the left of the digits in the number. In this example, if the minute value is 2, it will be displayed as 02, because the fill character is set to zero ('0'). If the number being output fills the specified field, the fill character will not be displayed. Note that, once the fill character is specified with setfill, it applies for all subsequent values that are displayed in fields wider than the value being displayed (i.e., setfill is a "sticky" setting). This is in contrast to setw, which applies only to the next value displayed (setw is a "non-sticky" setting).

Error-Prevention Tip 10.2

Each sticky setting (such as a fill character or floating-point precision) should be restored to its previous setting when it is no longer needed. Failure to do so may result in incorrectly formatted output later in a program. Chapter 17, Stream Input/Output and Files, discusses how to reset the fill character and precision.

Function printStandard (lines 36–41) takes no arguments and outputs the date in standard-time format, consisting of the hour, minute and second values separated by colons and followed by an AM or PM indicator (e.g., 1:27:06 PM). Like function print-Universal, function printStandard uses setfill('0') to format the minute and second as two digit values with leading zeros if necessary. Line 38 uses the conditional operator (?:) to determine the value of hour to be displayed—if the hour is 0 or 12 (AM or PM), it appears as 12; otherwise, the hour appears as a value from 1 to 11. The conditional operator in line 40 determines whether AM or PM will be displayed.

Defining Member Functions Outside the Class Definition; Class Scope

Even though a member function declared in a class definition may be defined outside that class definition (and "tied" to the class via the binary scope resolution operator), that member function is still within that *class's scope*; i.e., its name is known only to other members of the class unless referred to via an object of the class, a reference to an object of the class, a pointer to an object of the class or the binary scope resolution operator. We'll say more about class scope shortly.

If a member function is defined in the body of a class definition, the compiler attempts to inline calls to the member function. Member functions defined outside a class definition can be inlined by explicitly using keyword inline. Remember that the compiler reserves the right not to inline any function.

Performance Tip 10.1

Defining a member function inside the class definition inlines the member function (if the compiler chooses to do so). This can improve performance.

Software Engineering Observation 10.2

Defining a small member function inside the class definition does not promote the best software engineering, because clients of the class will be able to see the implementation of the function, and the client code must be recompiled if the function definition changes.

Software Engineering Observation 10.3

Only the simplest and most stable member functions (i.e., those whose implementations are unlikely to change) should be defined in the class header.

Member Functions vs. Global Functions

It is interesting that the printUniversal and printStandard member functions take no arguments. This is because these member functions implicitly know that they are to print the data members of the particular Time object for which they are invoked. This can make member function calls more concise than conventional function calls in procedural programming.

Software Engineering Observation 10.4

Using an object-oriented programming approach can often simplify function calls by reducing the number of parameters to be passed. This benefit of object-oriented programming derives from the fact that encapsulating data members and member functions within an object gives the member functions the right to access the data members.

Software Engineering Observation 10.5

Member functions are usually shorter than functions in non-object-oriented programs, because the data stored in data members has ideally been validated by a constructor or by member functions that store new data. Because the data is already in the object, the member-function calls often have no arguments or fewer arguments than typical function calls in non-object-oriented languages. Thus, the calls are shorter, the function definitions are shorter and the function prototypes are shorter. This improves many aspects of program development.

Error-Prevention Tip 10.3

The fact that member function calls generally take either no arguments or substantially fewer arguments than conventional function calls in non-object-oriented languages reduces the likelihood of passing the wrong arguments, the wrong types of arguments or the wrong number of arguments.

Using Class Time

Once class Time has been defined, it can be used as a type in object, array, pointer and reference declarations as follows:

```
Time sunset; // object of type Time
Time arrayOfTimes[ 5 ], // array of 5 Time objects
Time &dinnerTime = sunset; // reference to a Time object
Time *timePtr = &dinnerTime, // pointer to a Time object
```

Figure 10.3 uses class Time. Line 12 instantiates a single object of class Time called t. When the object is instantiated, the Time constructor is called to initialize each private data member to 0. Then, lines 16 and 18 print the time in universal and standard formats, respectively, to confirm that the members were initialized properly. Line 20 sets a new time by calling member function setTime, and lines 24 and 26 print the time again in both formats. Line 28 attempts to use setTime to set the data members to invalid values—function setTime recognizes this and sets the invalid values to 0 to maintain the object in a consistent state. Finally, lines 33 and 35 print the time again in both formats.

Looking Ahead to Composition and Inheritance

Often, classes do not have to be created "from scratch." Rather, they can include objects of other classes as members or they may be **derived** from other classes that provide attributes and behaviors the new classes can use. Such software reuse can greatly enhance programmer productivity and simplify code maintenance. Including class objects as members of other classes is called **composition** (or **aggregation**) and is discussed in Chapter 11. Deriving new classes from existing classes is called **inheritance** and is discussed in Chapter 13.

Object Size

People new to object-oriented programming often suppose that objects must be quite large because they contain data members and member functions. Logically, this is true—you may think of objects as containing data and functions (and our discussion has certainly encouraged this view); physically, however, this is not true.

Performance Tip 10.2

Objects contain only data, so objects are much smaller than if they also contained member functions. Applying operator sizeof to a class name or to an object of that class will report only the size of the class's data members. The compiler creates one copy (only) of the member functions separate from all objects of the class. All objects of the class share this one copy. Each object, of *course, needs its own copy of the class's data, because the data can vary among the objects. The function code is nonmodifiable (also called **reentrant code** or **pure procedure**) and, hence, can be shared among all objects of one class.*

Pragma Directives

Visual C++ includes another sort of preprocessor directive called a *pragma* directive. There are a variety of pragma directives available for use with Visual C++. Note that many are specific to the Visual C++ compiler and should not be used if you expect your C++ program to be used with other compilers. The specific pragma directive we discuss here is used instead of the preprocessor wrapper introduced in Fig. 10.1. Rather than use the three lines in Fig. 10.1 spread across the beginning and end of a header file you can simply place the following at the top of your header file

```
#pragma once
```

This is a simple way to ensure a header file will only be included once during compilation even if its included in many other header files.

10.3 Class Scope and Accessing Class Members

A class's data members (variables declared in the class definition) and member functions (functions declared in the class definition) belong to that class's scope. Nonmember functions are defined at *file scope*.

Within a class's scope, class members are immediately accessible by all of that class's member functions and can be referenced by name. Outside a class's scope, `public` class members are referenced through one of the *handles* on an object—an object name, a reference to an object or a pointer to an object. The type of the object, reference or pointer

```
 1   // Fig. 10.3: TimeTest.cpp
 2   // Program to test class Time.
 3   // NOTE: This file must be compiled with Time.cpp.
 4   #include <iostream>
 5   using std::cout;
 6   using std::endl;
 7
 8   #include "Time.h" // include definition of class Time from Time.h
 9
10   int main()
11   {
12      Time t; // instantiate object t of class Time
13
14      // output Time object t's initial values
15      cout << "The initial universal time is ";
16      t.printUniversal(); // 00:00:00
17      cout << "\nThe initial standard time is ";
18      t.printStandard(); // 12:00:00 AM
19
20      t.setTime( 13, 27, 6 ); // change time
21
```

Fig. 10.3 | Program to test class Time. (Part 1 of 2.)

```
22        // output Time object t's new values
23        cout << "\n\nUniversal time after setTime is ";
24        t.printUniversal(); // 13:27:06
25        cout << "\nStandard time after setTime is ";
26        t.printStandard(); // 1:27:06 PM
27
28        t.setTime( 99, 99, 99 ); // attempt invalid settings
29
30        // output t's values after specifying invalid values
31        cout << "\n\nAfter attempting invalid settings:"
32           << "\nUniversal time: ";
33        t.printUniversal(); // 00:00:00
34        cout << "\nStandard time: ";
35        t.printStandard(); // 12:00:00 AM
36        cout << endl;
37        return 0;
38     } // end main
```

```
The initial universal time is 00:00:00
The initial standard time is 12:00:00 AM

Universal time after setTime is 13:27:06
Standard time after setTime is 1:27:06 PM

After attempting invalid settings:
Universal time: 00:00:00
Standard time: 12:00:00 AM
```

Fig. 10.3 | Program to test class Time. (Part 2 of 2.)

specifies the interface (i.e., the member functions) accessible to the client. [We'll see in Chapter 11 that an implicit handle is inserted by the compiler on every reference to a data member or member function from within an object.]

Member functions of a class can be overloaded, but only by other member functions of that class. To overload a member function, simply provide in the class definition a prototype for each version of the overloaded function, and provide a separate function definition for each version of the function.

Variables declared in a member function have block scope and are known only to that function. If a member function defines a variable with the same name as a variable with class scope, the class-scope variable is hidden by the block-scope variable in the block scope. Such a hidden variable can be accessed by preceding the variable name with the class name followed by the scope resolution operator (::). Hidden global variables can be accessed with the unary scope resolution operator (see Chapter 7).

The dot member-selection operator (.) is preceded by an object's name or with a reference to an object to access the object's members. The arrow member-selection operator (->) is preceded by a pointer to an object (or C++/CLI handle to a managed object) to access the object's members.

Figure 10.4 uses a simple class called Count (lines 8–25) with private data member x of type int (line 24), public member function setX (lines 12–15) and public member function print (lines 18–21) to illustrate accessing the members of a class with the

```cpp
1  // Fig. 10.4: ClassMemberAccess.cpp
2  // Demonstrating the class member access operators . and ->
3  #include <iostream>
4  using std::cout;
5  using std::endl;
6
7  // class Count definition
8  class Count
9  {
10 public: // public data is dangerous
11    // sets the value of private data member x
12    void setX( int value )
13    {
14       x = value;
15    } // end function setX
16
17    // prints the value of private data member x
18    void print()
19    {
20       cout << x << endl;
21    } // end function print
22
23 private:
24    int x;
25 }; // end class Count
26
27 int main()
28 {
29    Count counter; // create counter object
30    Count *counterPtr = &counter; // create pointer to counter
31    Count &counterRef = counter; // create reference to counter
32
33    cout << "Set x to 1 and print using the object's name: ";
34    counter.setX( 1 ); // set data member x to 1
35    counter.print(); // call member function print
36
37    cout << "Set x to 2 and print using a reference to an object: ";
38    counterRef.setX( 2 ); // set data member x to 2
39    counterRef.print(); // call member function print
40
41    cout << "Set x to 3 and print using a pointer to an object: ";
42    counterPtr->setX( 3 ); // set data member x to 3
43    counterPtr->print(); // call member function print
44    return 0;
45 } // end main
```

```
Set x to 1 and print using the object's name: 1
Set x to 2 and print using a reference to an object: 2
Set x to 3 and print using a pointer to an object: 3
```

Fig. 10.4 | Accessing an object's member functions through each type of object handle—the object's name, a reference to the object and a pointer to the object.

member-selection operators. For simplicity, we have included this small class in the same file as the main function that uses it. Lines 29–31 create three variables related to type Count—counter (a Count object), counterPtr (a pointer to a Count object) and counterRef (a reference to a Count object). Variable counterRef refers to counter, and variable counterPtr points to counter. In lines 34–35 and 38–39, note that the program can invoke member functions setX and print by using the dot (.) member selection operator preceded by either the name of the object (counter) or a reference to the object (counterRef, which is an alias for counter). Similarly, lines 42–43 demonstrate that the program can invoke member functions setX and print by using a pointer (countPtr) and the arrow (->) member-selection operator.

10.4 Separating Interface from Implementation

In Chapter 4, we began by including a class's definition and member-function definitions in one file. We then demonstrated separating this code into two files—a header file for the class definition (i.e., the class's interface) and a source code file for the class's member-function definitions (i.e., the class's implementation). Recall that this makes it easier to modify programs—as far as clients of a class are concerned, changes in the class's implementation do not affect the client as long as the class's interface originally provided to the client remains unchanged.

> **Software Engineering Observation 10.6**
>
> *Clients of a class do not need access to the class's source code in order to use the class. The clients do, however, need to be able to link to the class's object code (i.e., the compiled version of the class). This encourages independent software vendors (ISVs) to provide class libraries for sale or license. The ISVs provide in their products only the header files and the object modules. No proprietary information is revealed—as would be the case if source code were provided. The C++ user community benefits by having more ISV-produced class libraries available.*

Actually, things are not quite this rosy. Header files do contain some portions of the implementation and hints about others. Inline member functions, for example, need to be in a header file, so that when the compiler compiles a client, the client can include the inline function definition in place. A class's private members are listed in the class definition in the header file, so these members are visible to clients even though the clients may not access the private members. In Chapter 11, we show how to use a "proxy class" to hide even the private data of a class from clients of the class.

> **Software Engineering Observation 10.7**
>
> *Information important to the interface of a class should be included in the header file. Information that will be used only internally in the class and will not be needed by clients of the class should be included in the unpublished source file. This is yet another example of the principle of least privilege.*

10.5 Access Functions and Utility Functions

Access functions can read or display data. Another common use for access functions is to test the truth or falsity of conditions—such functions are often called *predicate functions.* An example of a predicate function would be an isEmpty function for any container class—a class capable of holding many objects—such as a linked list, a stack or a queue. A program might test isEmpty before attempting to read another item from the container object. An isFull predicate function might test a container-class object to determine whether it has no additional room. Useful predicate functions for our Time class might be isAM and isPM.

The program of Figs. 10.5–10.7 demonstrates the notion of a utility function (also called a *helper function*). A utility function is not part of a class's public interface; rather, it is a private member function that supports the operation of the class's public member functions. Utility functions are not intended to be used by clients of a class (but can be used by friends of a class, as we'll see in Chapter 11).

Class SalesPerson (Fig. 10.5) declares an array of 12 monthly sales figures (line 16) and prototypes for the class's constructor and member functions that manipulate the array.

In Fig. 10.6, the SalesPerson constructor (lines 15–19) initializes array sales to zero. The public member function setSales (lines 36–43) sets the sales figure for one month in array sales. The public member function printAnnualSales (lines 46–51) prints the

```
1   // Fig. 10.5: SalesPerson.h
2   // SalesPerson class definition.
3   // Member functions defined in SalesPerson.cpp.
4   #ifndef SALESP_H
5   #define SALESP_H
6
7   class SalesPerson
8   {
9   public:
10     SalesPerson(); // constructor
11     void getSalesFromUser(); // input sales from keyboard
12     void setSales( int, double ); // set sales for a specific month
13     void printAnnualSales(); // summarize and print sales
14  private:
15     double totalAnnualSales(); // prototype for utility function
16     double sales[ 12 ]; // 12 monthly sales figures
17  }; // end class SalesPerson
18
19  #endif
```

Fig. 10.5 | SalesPerson class definition.

```
1   // Fig. 10.6: SalesPerson.cpp
2   // SalesPerson class member-function definitions.
3   #include <iostream>
4   using std::cout;
5   using std::cin;
6   using std::endl;
7   using std::fixed;
8
9   #include <iomanip>
10  using std::setprecision;
```

Fig. 10.6 | SalesPerson class member-function definitions. (Part 1 of 2.)

```
11
12   #include "SalesPerson.h" // include SalesPerson class definition
13
14   // initialize elements of array sales to 0.0
15   SalesPerson::SalesPerson()
16   {
17      for ( int i = 0; i < 12; i++ )
18         sales[ i ] = 0.0;
19   } // end SalesPerson constructor
20
21   // get 12 sales figures from the user at the keyboard
22   void SalesPerson::getSalesFromUser()
23   {
24      double salesFigure;
25
26      for ( int i = 1; i <= 12; i++ )
27      {
28         cout << "Enter sales amount for month " << i << ": ";
29         cin >> salesFigure;
30         setSales( i, salesFigure );
31      } // end for
32   } // end function getSalesFromUser
33
34   // set one of the 12 monthly sales figures; function subtracts
35   // one from month value for proper subscript in sales array
36   void SalesPerson::setSales( int month, double amount )
37   {
38      // test for valid month and amount values
39      if ( month >= 1 && month <= 12 && amount > 0 )
40         sales[ month - 1 ] = amount; // adjust for subscripts 0-11
41      else // invalid month or amount value
42         cout << "Invalid month or sales figure" << endl;
43   } // end function setSales
44
45   // print total annual sales (with the help of utility function)
46   void SalesPerson::printAnnualSales()
47   {
48      cout << setprecision( 2 ) << fixed
49         << "\nThe total annual sales are: $"
50         << totalAnnualSales() << endl; // call utility function
51   } // end function printAnnualSales
52
53   // private utility function to total annual sales
54   double SalesPerson::totalAnnualSales()
55   {
56      double total = 0.0; // initialize total
57
58      for ( int i = 0; i < 12; i++ ) // summarize sales results
59         total += sales[ i ]; // add month i sales to total
60
61      return total;
62   } // end function totalAnnualSales
```

Fig. 10.6 | SalesPerson class member-function definitions. (Part 2 of 2.)

total sales for the last 12 months. The private utility function totalAnnualSales (lines 54–62) totals the 12 monthly sales figures for the benefit of printAnnualSales. Member function printAnnualSales edits the sales figures into monetary format.

In Fig. 10.7, notice that the main function includes only a simple sequence of member-function calls—there are no control statements. The logic of manipulating the sales array is completely encapsulated in class SalesPerson's member functions.

Software Engineering Observation 10.8

A phenomenon of object-oriented programming is that once a class is defined, creating and manipulating objects of that class often involve issuing only a simple sequence of member-function calls—few, if any, control statements are needed. By contrast, it is common to have control statements in the implementation of a class's member functions.

```cpp
1  // Fig. 10.7: SalesPersonTest.cpp
2  // Utility function demonstration.
3  // Compile this program with SalesPerson.cpp
4
5  // include SalesPerson class definition from SalesPerson.h
6  #include "SalesPerson.h"
7
8  int main()
9  {
10     SalesPerson s; // create SalesPerson object s
11
12     s.getSalesFromUser(); // note simple sequential code; there are
13     s.printAnnualSales(); // no control statements in main
14     return 0;
15  } // end main
```

```
Enter sales amount for month 1: 5314.76
Enter sales amount for month 2: 4292.38
Enter sales amount for month 3: 4589.83
Enter sales amount for month 4: 5534.03
Enter sales amount for month 5: 4376.34
Enter sales amount for month 6: 5698.45
Enter sales amount for month 7: 4439.22
Enter sales amount for month 8: 5893.57
Enter sales amount for month 9: 4909.67
Enter sales amount for month 10: 5123.45
Enter sales amount for month 11: 4024.97
Enter sales amount for month 12: 5923.92

The total annual sales are: $60120.59
```

Fig. 10.7 | Utility function demonstration.

10.6 Time Class Case Study: Constructors with Default Arguments

The program of Figs. 10.8–10.10 enhances class Time to demonstrate how arguments are implicitly passed to a constructor. The constructor defined in Fig. 10.2 initialized hour,

```
 1   // Fig. 10.8: Time.h
 2   // Time class containing a constructor with default arguments.
 3   // Member functions defined in Time.cpp.
 4
 5   // prevent multiple inclusions of header file
 6   #ifndef TIME_H
 7   #define TIME_H
 8
 9   // Time abstract data type definition
10   class Time
11   {
12   public:
13      Time( int = 0, int = 0, int = 0 ); // default constructor
14
15      // set functions
16      void setTime( int, int, int ); // set hour, minute, second
17      void setHour( int ); // set hour (after validation)
18      void setMinute( int ); // set minute (after validation)
19      void setSecond( int ); // set second (after validation)
20
21      // get functions
22      int getHour(); // return hour
23      int getMinute(); // return minute
24      int getSecond(); // return second
25
26      void printUniversal(); // output time in universal-time format
27      void printStandard(); // output time in standard-time format
28   private:
29      int hour; // 0 - 23 (24-hour clock format)
30      int minute; // 0 - 59
31      int second; // 0 - 59
32   }; // end class Time
33
34   #endif
```

Fig. 10.8 | Time class containing a constructor with default arguments.

minute and second to 0 (i.e., midnight in universal time). Like other functions, constructors can specify default arguments. Line 13 of Fig. 10.8 declares the Time constructor to include default arguments, specifying a default value of zero for each argument passed to the constructor. In Fig. 10.9, lines 14–17 define the new version of the Time constructor that receives values for parameters hr, min and sec that will be used to initialize private data members hour, minute and second, respectively. Note that class Time provides *set* and *get* functions for each data member. The Time constructor now calls setTime, which calls the setHour, setMinute and setSecond functions to validate and assign values to the data members. The default arguments to the constructor ensure that, even if no values are provided in a constructor call, the constructor still initializes the data members to maintain the Time object in a consistent state. A constructor that defaults all its arguments is also a default constructor—i.e., a constructor that can be invoked with no arguments. There can be at most one default constructor per class.

```
 1   // Fig. 10.9: Time.cpp
 2   // Member-function definitions for class Time.
 3   #include <iostream>
 4   using std::cout;
 5
 6   #include <iomanip>
 7   using std::setfill;
 8   using std::setw;
 9
10   #include "Time.h" // include definition of class Time from Time.h
11
12   // Time constructor initializes each data member to zero;
13   // ensures that Time objects start in a consistent state
14   Time::Time( int hr, int min, int sec )
15   {
16      setTime( hr, min, sec ); // validate and set time
17   } // end Time constructor
18
19   // set new Time value using universal time; ensure that
20   // the data remains consistent by setting invalid values to zero
21   void Time::setTime( int h, int m, int s )
22   {
23      setHour( h ); // set private field hour
24      setMinute( m ); // set private field minute
25      setSecond( s ); // set private field second
26   } // end function setTime
27
28   // set hour value
29   void Time::setHour( int h )
30   {
31      hour = ( h >= 0 && h < 24 ) ? h : 0; // validate hour
32   } // end function setHour
33
34   // set minute value
35   void Time::setMinute( int m )
36   {
37      minute = ( m >= 0 && m < 60 ) ? m : 0; // validate minute
38   } // end function setMinute
39
40   // set second value
41   void Time::setSecond( int s )
42   {
43      second = ( s >= 0 && s < 60 ) ? s : 0; // validate second
44   } // end function setSecond
45
46   // return hour value
47   int Time::getHour()
48   {
49      return hour;
50   } // end function getHour
51
```

Fig. 10.9 | Time class member-function definitions including a constructor that takes arguments. (Part 1 of 2.)

```
52   // return minute value
53   int Time::getMinute()
54   {
55      return minute;
56   } // end function getMinute
57
58   // return second value
59   int Time::getSecond()
60   {
61      return second;
62   } // end function getSecond
63
64   // print Time in universal-time format (HH:MM:SS)
65   void Time::printUniversal()
66   {
67      cout << setfill( '0' ) << setw( 2 ) << getHour() << ":"
68         << setw( 2 ) << getMinute() << ":" << setw( 2 ) << getSecond();
69   } // end function printUniversal
70
71   // print Time in standard-time format (HH:MM:SS AM or PM)
72   void Time::printStandard()
73   {
74      cout << ( ( getHour() == 0 || getHour() == 12 ) ? 12 : getHour() % 12 )
75         << ":" << setfill( '0' ) << setw( 2 ) << getMinute()
76         << ":" << setw( 2 ) << getSecond() << ( hour < 12 ? " AM" : " PM" );
77   } // end function printStandard
```

Fig. 10.9 | Time class member-function definitions including a constructor that takes arguments. (Part 2 of 2.)

In Fig. 10.9, line 16 of the constructor calls member function setTime with the values passed to the constructor (or the default values). Function setTime calls setHour to ensure that the value supplied for hour is in the range 0–23, then calls setMinute and setSecond to ensure that the values for minute and second are each in the range 0–59. If a value is out of range, that value is set to zero (to ensure that each data member remains in a consistent state). In Chapter 16, Exception Handling, we throw exceptions when a value is out of range, rather than simply assigning a default consistent value.

Note that the Time constructor could be written to include the same statements as member function setTime, or even the individual statements in the setHour, setMinute and setSecond functions. Calling setHour, setMinute and setSecond from the constructor may be slightly more efficient because the extra call to setTime would be eliminated. Similarly, copying the code from lines 31, 37 and 43 into the Time constructor would eliminate the overhead of calling setTime, setHour, setMinute and setSecond. Coding the Time constructor or member function setTime as a copy of the code in lines 31, 37 and 43 would make maintenance of this class more difficult. If the implementations of setHour, setMinute and setSecond were to change, the implementation of any member function that duplicates lines 31, 37 and 43 would have to change accordingly. Having the Time constructor call setTime and having setTime call setHour, setMinute and setSecond enables us to limit the changes to code that validates the hour, minute or second to the corresponding *set* function. This reduces the likelihood of errors when altering the class's implementation. Also, the performance of the Time constructor and setTime can be enhanced by explicitly declaring them inline or by defining them in the class definition (which implicitly inlines the function definition).

Software Engineering Observation 10.9

If a member function of a class already provides all or part of the functionality required by a constructor (or other member function) of the class, call that member function from the constructor (or other member function). This simplifies the maintenance of the code and reduces the likelihood of an error if the implementation of the code is modified. As a general rule: Avoid repeating code.

Software Engineering Observation 10.10

Any change to the default argument values of a function requires the client code to be recompiled (to ensure that the program still functions correctly).

Function main in Fig. 10.10 initializes five Time objects—one with all three arguments defaulted in the implicit constructor call (line 11), one with one argument specified (line 12), one with two arguments specified (line 13), one with three arguments specified (line 14) and one with three invalid arguments specified (line 15). Then the program displays each object in universal-time and standard-time formats.

```cpp
1   // Fig. 10.10: TimeTest.cpp
2   // Demonstrating a default constructor for class Time.
3   #include <iostream>
4   using std::cout;
5   using std::endl;
6
7   #include "Time.h" // include definition of class Time from Time.h
8
9   int main()
10  {
11     Time t1; // all arguments defaulted
12     Time t2( 2 ); // hour specified; minute and second defaulted
13     Time t3( 21, 34 ); // hour and minute specified; second defaulted
14     Time t4( 12, 25, 42 ); // hour, minute and second specified
15     Time t5( 27, 74, 99 ); // all bad values specified
16
17     cout << "Constructed with:\n\nt1: all arguments defaulted\n  ";
18     t1.printUniversal(); // 00:00:00
19     cout << "\n  ";
20     t1.printStandard(); // 12:00:00 AM
21
22     cout << "\n\nt2: hour specified; minute and second defaulted\n  ";
23     t2.printUniversal(); // 02:00:00
24     cout << "\n  ";
25     t2.printStandard(); // 2:00:00 AM
26
27     cout << "\n\nt3: hour and minute specified; second defaulted\n  ";
28     t3.printUniversal(); // 21:34:00
```

Fig. 10.10 | Constructor with default arguments. (Part 1 of 2.)

```
29      cout << "\n  ";
30      t3.printStandard(); // 9:34:00 PM
31
32      cout << "\n\nt4: hour, minute and second specified\n  ";
33      t4.printUniversal(); // 12:25:42
34      cout << "\n  ";
35      t4.printStandard(); // 12:25:42 PM
36
37      cout << "\n\nt5: all invalid values specified\n  ";
38      t5.printUniversal(); // 00:00:00
39      cout << "\n  ";
40      t5.printStandard(); // 12:00:00 AM
41      cout << endl;
42      return 0;
43   } // end main
```

```
Constructed with:

t1: all arguments defaulted
   00:00:00
   12:00:00 AM

t2: hour specified; minute and second defaulted
   02:00:00
   2:00:00 AM

t3: hour and minute specified; second defaulted
   21:34:00
   9:34:00 PM

t4: hour, minute and second specified
   12:25:42
   12:25:42 PM

t5: all invalid values specified
   00:00:00
   12:00:00 AM
```

Fig. 10.10 | Constructor with default arguments. (Part 2 of 2.)

Notes Regarding Class Time's Set *and* Get *Functions and Constructor*

Time's *set* and *get* functions are called throughout the class's body. In particular, function setTime (lines 21–26 of Fig. 10.9) calls functions setHour, setMinute and setSecond, and functions printUniversal and printStandard call functions getHour, getMinute and getSecond in line 67–68 and lines 74–76, respectively. In each case, these functions could have accessed the class's private data directly. However, consider changing the representation of the time from three int values (requiring 12 bytes of memory) to a single int value representing the total number of seconds that have elapsed since midnight (requiring only four bytes of memory). If we made such a change, only the bodies of the functions that access the private data directly would need to change—in particular, the individual *set* and *get* functions for the hour, minute and second. There would be no need to modify the bodies of functions setTime, printUniversal or printStandard, because they do not access the data directly. Designing the class in this manner reduces the likelihood of programming errors when altering the class's implementation.

Similarly, the Time constructor could be written to include a copy of the appropriate statements from function setTime. Doing so may be slightly more efficient, because the extra constructor call and call to setTime are eliminated. However, duplicating statements in multiple functions or constructors makes changing the class's internal data representation more difficult. Having the Time constructor call function setTime directly requires any changes to the implementation of setTime to be made only once.

Common Programming Error 10.2

A constructor can call other member functions of the class, such as set or get functions, but because the constructor is initializing the object, the data members may not yet be in a consistent state. Using data members before they have been properly initialized can cause logic errors.

10.7 Destructors

A *destructor* is another type of special member function. The name of the destructor for a class is the *tilde character (~)* followed by the class name. This naming convention has intuitive appeal because, as we'll see in a later chapter, the tilde operator is the bitwise complement operator, and, in a sense, the destructor is the complement of the constructor. Note that a destructor is often referred to with the abbreviation "dtor" in the literature. We prefer not to use this abbreviation.

A class's destructor is called implicitly when an object is destroyed. This occurs, for example, as an automatic object is destroyed when program execution leaves the scope in which that object was instantiated. *The destructor itself does not actually release the object's memory*—it performs **termination housekeeping** before the object's memory is reclaimed, so the memory may be reused to hold new objects.

A destructor receives no parameters and returns no value. A destructor may not specify a return type—not even void. A class may have only one destructor—destructor overloading is not allowed. A destructor must be public.

Common Programming Error 10.3

It is a syntax error to attempt to pass arguments to a destructor, to specify a return type for a destructor (even void cannot be specified), to return values from a destructor or to overload a destructor.

Even though destructors have not been provided for the classes presented so far, every class has a destructor. If you do not explicitly provide a destructor, the compiler creates an "empty" destructor. [*Note:* We'll see that such an implicitly created destructor does, in fact, perform important operations on objects that are created through composition (Chapter 11) and inheritance (Chapter 13).] In Chapter 12, we'll build destructors appropriate for classes whose objects contain dynamically allocated memory (e.g., for arrays and strings) or use other system resources (e.g., files on disk, which we study in Chapter 17). We discuss how to dynamically allocate and deallocate memory in Chapter 11. Note that while they're syntactically similar, destructors in C++/CLI work quite differently from native C++ destructors (explained in Chapter 11).

Software Engineering Observation 10.11

As we'll see in the remainder of the book, constructors and destructors have much greater prominence in Visual C++ and object-oriented programming than is possible to convey after only our brief introduction here.

10.8 When Constructors and Destructors Are Called

Constructors and destructors are called implicitly by the compiler. The order in which these function calls occur depends on the order in which execution enters and leaves the scopes where the objects are instantiated. Generally, destructor calls are made in the reverse order of the corresponding constructor calls, but as we'll see in Figs. 10.11–10.13, the storage classes of objects can alter the order in which destructors are called.

Constructors are called for objects defined in global scope before any other function (including main) in that file begins execution (although the order of execution of global object constructors between files is not guaranteed). The corresponding destructors are called when main terminates. Function exit forces a program to terminate immediately and does not execute the destructors of automatic objects. The function often is used to terminate a program when an error is detected in the input or if a file to be processed by the program cannot be opened. Function **abort** performs similarly to function exit but forces the program to terminate immediately, without allowing the destructors of any objects to be called. Function abort is usually used to indicate an abnormal termination of the program.

The constructor for an automatic local object is called when execution reaches the point where that object is defined—the corresponding destructor is called when execution leaves the object's scope (i.e., the block in which that object is defined has finished executing). Constructors and destructors for automatic objects are called each time execution enters and leaves the scope of the object. Destructors are not called for automatic objects if the program terminates with a call to function exit or function abort.

The constructor for a static local object is called only once, when execution first reaches the point where the object is defined—the corresponding destructor is called when main terminates or the program calls function exit. Global and static objects are destroyed in the reverse order of their creation. Destructors are not called for static objects if the program terminates with a call to function abort.

The program of Figs. 10.11–10.13 demonstrates the order in which constructors and destructors are called for objects of class CreateAndDestroy (Fig. 10.11 and Fig. 10.12) of various storage classes in several scopes. Each object of class CreateAndDestroy contains an integer (objectID) and a string (message) that are used in the program's output to identify the object (Fig. 10.11 lines 16–17). This mechanical example is purely for pedagogic purposes. For this reason, line 23 of the destructor in Fig. 10.12 determines whether the object being destroyed has an objectID value 1 or 6 and, if so, outputs a newline character. This line makes the program's output easier to follow.

```
1   // Fig. 10.11: CreateAndDestroy.h
2   // CreateAndDestroy class definition.
3   // Member functions defined in CreateAndDestroy.cpp.
4   #include <string>
5   using std::string;
6
7   #ifndef CREATE_H
8   #define CREATE_H
9
```

Fig. 10.11 | CreateAndDestroy class definition. (Part 1 of 2.)

```
10   class CreateAndDestroy
11   {
12   public:
13      CreateAndDestroy( int, string ); // constructor
14      ~CreateAndDestroy(); // destructor
15   private:
16      int objectID; // ID number for object
17      string message; // message describing object
18   }; // end class CreateAndDestroy
19
20   #endif
```

Fig. 10.11 | CreateAndDestroy class definition. (Part 2 of 2.)

```
1    // Fig. 10.12: CreateAndDestroy.cpp
2    // CreateAndDestroy class member-function definitions.
3    #include <iostream>
4    using std::cout;
5    using std::endl;
6
7    #include "CreateAndDestroy.h"// include CreateAndDestroy class definition
8
9    // constructor
10   CreateAndDestroy::CreateAndDestroy( int ID, string messageString )
11   {
12      objectID = ID; // set object's ID number
13      message = messageString; // set object's descriptive message
14
15      cout << "Object " << objectID << "   constructor runs   "
16         << message << endl;
17   } // end CreateAndDestroy constructor
18
19   // destructor
20   CreateAndDestroy::~CreateAndDestroy()
21   {
22      // output newline for certain objects; helps readability
23      cout << ( objectID == 1 || objectID == 6 ? "\n" : "" );
24
25      cout << "Object " << objectID << "   destructor runs   "
26         << message << endl;
27   } // end ~CreateAndDestroy destructor
```

Fig. 10.12 | CreateAndDestroy class member-function definitions.

Figure 10.13 defines object first (line 12) in global scope. Its constructor is actually called before any statements in main execute and its destructor is called at program termination after the destructors for all other objects have run.

Function main (lines 14–26) declares three objects. Objects second (line 17) and fourth (line 23) are local automatic objects, and object third (line 18) is a static local object. The constructor for each of these objects is called when execution reaches the point where that object is declared. The destructors for objects fourth and then second are called (i.e., the reverse of the order in which their constructors were called) when execution

```
1   // Fig. 10.13: CreateAndDestroyTest.cpp
2   // Demonstrating the order in which constructors and
3   // destructors are called.
4   #include <iostream>
5   using std::cout;
6   using std::endl;
7
8   #include "CreateAndDestroy.h" // include CreateAndDestroy class definition
9
10  void create( void ); // prototype
11
12  CreateAndDestroy first( 1, "(global before main)" ); // global object
13
14  int main()
15  {
16     cout << "\nMAIN FUNCTION: EXECUTION BEGINS" << endl;
17     CreateAndDestroy second( 2, "(local automatic in main)" );
18     static CreateAndDestroy third( 3, "(local static in main)" );
19
20     create(); // call function to create objects
21
22     cout << "\nMAIN FUNCTION: EXECUTION RESUMES" << endl;
23     CreateAndDestroy fourth( 4, "(local automatic in main)" );
24     cout << "\nMAIN FUNCTION: EXECUTION ENDS" << endl;
25     return 0;
26  } // end main
27
28  // function to create objects
29  void create( void )
30  {
31     cout << "\nCREATE FUNCTION: EXECUTION BEGINS" << endl;
32     CreateAndDestroy fifth( 5, "(local automatic in create)" );
33     static CreateAndDestroy sixth( 6, "(local static in create)" );
34     CreateAndDestroy seventh( 7, "(local automatic in create)" );
35     cout << "\nCREATE FUNCTION: EXECUTION ENDS" << endl;
36  } // end function create
```

```
Object 1    constructor runs    (global before main)

MAIN FUNCTION: EXECUTION BEGINS
Object 2    constructor runs    (local automatic in main)
Object 3    constructor runs    (local static in main)

CREATE FUNCTION: EXECUTION BEGINS
Object 5    constructor runs    (local automatic in create)
Object 6    constructor runs    (local static in create)
Object 7    constructor runs    (local automatic in create)

CREATE FUNCTION: EXECUTION ENDS
Object 7    destructor runs     (local automatic in create)
Object 5    destructor runs     (local automatic in create)

MAIN FUNCTION: EXECUTION RESUMES
Object 4    constructor runs    (local automatic in main)
```

Fig. 10.13 | Order in which constructors and destructors are called. (Part 1 of 2.)

```
MAIN FUNCTION: EXECUTION ENDS
Object 4    destructor runs    (local automatic in main)
Object 2    destructor runs    (local automatic in main)

Object 6    destructor runs    (local static in create)
Object 3    destructor runs    (local static in main)

Object 1    destructor runs    (global before main)
```

Fig. 10.13 | Order in which constructors and destructors are called. (Part 2 of 2.)

reaches the end of `main`. Because object `third` is `static`, it exists until program termination. The destructor for object `third` is called before the destructor for global object `first`, but after all other objects are destroyed.

Function `create` (lines 29–36) declares three objects—`fifth` (line 32) and `seventh` (line 34) as local automatic objects, and `sixth` (line 33) as a `static` local object. The destructors for objects `seventh` and then `fifth` are called (i.e., the reverse of the order in which their constructors were called) when `create` terminates. Because `sixth` is `static`, it exists until program termination. The destructor for `sixth` is called before the destructors for `third` and `first`, but after all other objects are destroyed.

10.9 Time Class Case Study: A Subtle Trap—Returning a Reference to a `private` Data Member

A reference to an object is an alias for the name of the object and, hence, may be used on the left side of an assignment statement. In this context, the reference makes a perfectly acceptable *lvalue* that can receive a value. One way to use this capability (unfortunately!) is to have a `public` member function of a class return a reference to a `private` data member of that class. Note that if a function returns a `const` reference, that reference cannot be used as a modifiable *lvalue*.

The program of Figs. 10.14–10.16 uses a simplified `Time` class (Fig. 10.14 and Fig. 10.15) to demonstrate returning a reference to a `private` data member with member function `badSetHour` (declared in Fig. 10.14 in line 15 and defined in Fig. 10.15 in lines 29–33). Such a reference return actually makes a call to member function `badSetHour` an alias for `private` data member `hour`! The function call can be used in any way that the `private` data member can be used, including as an *lvalue* in an assignment statement, thus enabling clients of the class to clobber the class's `private` data at will! Note that the same problem would occur if a pointer to the `private` data were to be returned by the function.

```
1   // Fig. 10.14: Time.h
2   // Time class declaration.
3   // Member functions defined in Time.cpp
4
5   // prevent multiple inclusions of header file
6   #ifndef TIME_H
7   #define TIME_H
```

Fig. 10.14 | Time class declaration. (Part 1 of 2.)

```
 8
 9    class Time
10    {
11    public:
12       Time( int = 0, int = 0, int = 0 );
13       void setTime( int, int, int );
14       int getHour();
15       int &badSetHour( int ); // DANGEROUS reference return
16    private:
17       int hour;
18       int minute;
19       int second;
20    }; // end class Time
21
22    #endif
```

Fig. 10.14 | Time class declaration. (Part 2 of 2.)

```
 1    // Fig. 10.15: Time.cpp
 2    // Time class member-function definitions.
 3    #include "Time.h" // include definition of class Time
 4
 5    // constructor function to initialize private data;
 6    // calls member function setTime to set variables;
 7    // default values are 0 (see class definition)
 8    Time::Time( int hr, int min, int sec )
 9    {
10       setTime( hr, min, sec );
11    } // end Time constructor
12
13    // set values of hour, minute and second
14    void Time::setTime( int h, int m, int s )
15    {
16       hour = ( h >= 0 && h < 24 ) ? h : 0; // validate hour
17       minute = ( m >= 0 && m < 60 ) ? m : 0; // validate minute
18       second = ( s >= 0 && s < 60 ) ? s : 0; // validate second
19    } // end function setTime
20
21    // return hour value
22    int Time::getHour()
23    {
24       return hour;
25    } // end function getHour
26
27    // POOR PROGRAMMING PRACTICE:
28    // Returning a reference to a private data member.
29    int &Time::badSetHour( int hh )
30    {
31       hour = ( hh >= 0 && hh < 24 ) ? hh : 0;
32       return hour; // DANGEROUS reference return
33    } // end function badSetHour
```

Fig. 10.15 | Time class member-function definitions.

Figure 10.16 declares `Time` object `t` (line 12) and reference `hourRef` (line 15), which is initialized with the reference returned by the call `t.badSetHour(20)`. Line 17 displays the value of the alias `hourRef`. This shows how `hourRef` breaks the encapsulation of the class—statements in `main` should not have access to the `private` data of the class. Next, line 18 uses the alias to set the value of `hour` to 30 (an invalid value) and line 19 displays the value returned by function `getHour` to show that assigning a value to `hourRef` actually modifies the `private` data in the `Time` object `t`. Finally, line 23 uses the `badSetHour` function call itself as an *lvalue* and assigns 74 (another invalid value) to the reference returned by the function. Line 28 again displays the value returned by function `getHour` to show that assigning a value to the result of the function call in line 23 modifies the `private` data in the `Time` object `t`.

Error-Prevention Tip 10.4

Returning a reference or a pointer to a `private` data member breaks the encapsulation of the class and makes the client code dependent on the representation of the class's data; this is a dangerous practice that should be avoided.

```
 1    // Fig. 10.16: TimeTest.cpp
 2    // Demonstrating a public member function that
 3    // returns a reference to a private data member.
 4    #include <iostream>
 5    using std::cout;
 6    using std::endl;
 7
 8    #include "Time.h" // include definition of class Time
 9
10    int main()
11    {
12       Time t; // create Time object
13
14       // initialize hourRef with the reference returned by badSetHour
15       int &hourRef = t.badSetHour( 20 ); // 20 is a valid hour
16
17       cout << "Valid hour before modification: " << hourRef;
18       hourRef = 30; // use hourRef to set invalid value in Time object t
19       cout << "\nInvalid hour after modification: " << t.getHour();
20
21       // Dangerous: Function call that returns
22       // a reference can be used as an lvalue!
23       t.badSetHour( 12 ) = 74; // assign another invalid value to hour
24
25       cout << "\n\n*********************************************************\n"
26          << "POOR PROGRAMMING PRACTICE!!!!!!!!\n"
27          << "t.badSetHour( 12 ) as an lvalue, invalid hour: "
28          << t.getHour()
29          << "\n*********************************************************" << endl;
30       return 0;
31    } // end main
```

Fig. 10.16 | Returning a reference to a `private` data member. (Part 1 of 2.)

```
Valid hour before modification: 20
Invalid hour after modification: 30

**************************************************
POOR PROGRAMMING PRACTICE!!!!!!!!
t.badSetHour( 12 ) as an lvalue, invalid hour: 74
**************************************************
```

Fig. 10.16 | Returning a reference to a `private` data member. (Part 2 of 2.)

10.10 Default Memberwise Assignment

The assignment operator (=) can be used to assign an object to another object of the same type. By default, such assignment is performed by *memberwise assignment*—each data member of the object on the right of the assignment operator is assigned individually to the same data member in the object on the left of the assignment operator. Figures 10.17–10.18 define class Date for use in this example. Line 20 of Fig. 10.19 uses default memberwise assignment to assign the data members of Date object date1 to the corresponding data members of Date object date2. In this case, the month member of date1 is assigned to the month member of date2, the day member of date1 is assigned to the day member of date2 and the year member of date1 is assigned to the year member of date2. [*Caution:* Memberwise assignment can cause serious problems when used with a class whose data members contain pointers to dynamically allocated memory; we discuss these problems in Chapter 11 and show how to deal with them.] Notice that the Date constructor does not contain any error checking; we leave this to the exercises.

```cpp
 1  // Fig. 10.17: Date.h
 2  // Date class declaration.
 3  // Member functions are defined in Date.cpp
 4
 5  // prevent multiple inclusions of header file
 6  #ifndef DATE_H
 7  #define DATE_H
 8
 9  // class Date definition
10  class Date
11  {
12  public:
13     Date( int = 1, int = 1, int = 2000 ); // default constructor
14     void print();
15  private:
16     int month;
17     int day;
18     int year;
19  }; // end class Date
20
21  #endif
```

Fig. 10.17 | Date class declaration.

```
1    // Fig. 10.18: Date.cpp
2    // Date class member-function definitions.
3    #include <iostream>
4    using std::cout;
5    using std::endl;
6
7    #include "Date.h" // include definition of class Date from Date.h
8
9    // Date constructor (should do range checking)
10   Date::Date( int m, int d, int y )
11   {
12      month = m;
13      day = d;
14      year = y;
15   } // end constructor Date
16
17   // print Date in the format mm/dd/yyyy
18   void Date::print()
19   {
20      cout << month << '/' << day << '/' << year;
21   } // end function print
```

Fig. 10.18 | Date class member-function definitions.

```
1    // Fig. 10.19: DateTest.cpp
2    // Demonstrating that class objects can be assigned
3    // to each other using default memberwise assignment.
4    #include <iostream>
5    using std::cout;
6    using std::endl;
7
8    #include "Date.h" // include definition of class Date from Date.h
9
10   int main()
11   {
12      Date date1( 7, 4, 2004 );
13      Date date2; // date2 defaults to 1/1/2000
14
15      cout << "date1 = ";
16      date1.print();
17      cout << "\ndate2 = ";
18      date2.print();
19
20      date2 = date1; // default memberwise assignment
21
22      cout << "\n\nAfter default memberwise assignment, date2 = ";
23      date2.print();
24      cout << endl;
25      return 0;
26   } // end main
```

Fig. 10.19 | Default memberwise assignment. (Part 1 of 2.)

```
date1 = 7/4/2004
date2 = 1/1/2000

After default memberwise assignment, date2 = 7/4/2004
```

Fig. 10.19 | Default memberwise assignment. (Part 2 of 2.)

Objects may be passed as function arguments and may be returned from functions. Such passing and returning is performed using pass-by-value by default—a copy of the object is passed or returned. In such cases, Visual C++ creates a new object and uses a *copy constructor* to copy the original object's values into the new object. For each class, the compiler provides a default copy constructor that copies each member of the original object into the corresponding member of the new object. Like memberwise assignment, copy constructors can cause serious problems when used with a class whose data members contain pointers to dynamically allocated memory. Chapter 11 discusses how programmers can define customized copy constructors that properly copy objects containing pointers to dynamically allocated memory.

Performance Tip 10.3

Passing an object by value is good from a security standpoint, because the called function has no access to the original object in the caller, but pass-by-value can degrade performance when making a copy of a large object. An object can be passed by reference by passing either a pointer or a reference to the object. Pass-by-reference offers good performance but is weaker from a security standpoint, because the called function is given access to the original object. Pass-by-const-reference is a safe alternative (this can be implemented with a const *reference parameter or with a pointer-to-*const*-data parameter).*

10.11 Class View and Object Browser

Now that we have introduced key concepts of object-oriented programming, we present two features that Visual Studio provides to facilitate the design of object-oriented applications—*Class View* and *Object Browser*.

Using the Class View *Window*

The **Class View** displays the data members and functions for all classes in a project. To access this feature, select **Class View** from the **View** menu. Figure 10.20 shows the **Class View** for the Time project of Figs. 10.1 and 10.2 (class Time). The view follows a hierarchical structure, positioning the project name (Time) as the root and including a series of nodes that represent the classes, variables and functions in the project. If a plus sign (+) appears to the left of a node, that node can be expanded to show other nodes. If a minus sign (-) appears to the left of a node, that node can be collapsed. According to the **Class View**, project Time contains class Time. When class Time is selected, the class's members appear in the lower half of the window. Class Time contains functions SetTime, printStandard and others (indicated by purple boxes) as well as data members hour, minute and second (indicated by blue boxes). The lock icons, placed to the left of the blue box icons for the data members, specify that the variables are private.

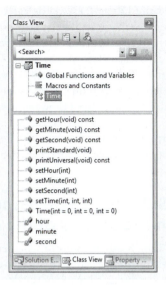

Fig. 10.20 | **Class View** of class Time (Figs. 10.8–10.9)

Using the Object Browser
Visual Studio's **Object Browser** lists all classes in the Framework Class Library. You can use the **Object Browser** to learn about the functionality provided by a specific class. To open the **Object Browser**, select **Object Browser** from the **View** menu. Figure 10.21 depicts the **Object Browser** when the user navigates to the Math class in namespace System in the as-

Fig. 10.21 | **Object Browser** for FCL class Math.

sembly `mscorlib` (Microsoft Core Library). [*Note:* Be careful not to confuse the `System` namespace with the assembly named `System`. The `System` assembly describes other members of the `System` namespace, but class `System::Math` is in `mscorlib`.] The **Object Browser** lists all functions provided by class `Math` in the upper-right frame—this offers you "instant access" to information regarding the functionality of various objects. If you click the name of a member in the upper-right frame, a description of that member appears in the lower-right frame. Note also that the **Object Browser** lists in the left frame all classes of the FCL. The **Object Browser** can be a quick mechanism to learn about a class or a function of a class. Remember that you can also view the complete description of a class or a function in the online documentation available through the **Help** menu in Visual Studio.

10.12 (Optional) Software Engineering Case Study: Starting to Program the Classes of the ATM System

In the Software Engineering Case Study sections in Chapters 1, 3–8, we introduced the fundamentals of object orientation and developed an object-oriented design for our ATM system. Earlier in this chapter, we discussed many of the details of programming with Visual C++ classes. We now begin implementing our object-oriented design in Visual C++. At the end of this section, we show how to convert class diagrams to Visual C++ header files. In the final Software Engineering Case Study section (Section 14.11), we modify the header files to incorporate the object-oriented concept of inheritance. We present the full Visual C++ code implementation in Appendix F, ATM Case Study Code.

Visibility

We now apply access specifiers to the members of our classes. In Chapter 4, we introduced access specifiers `public` and `private`. Access specifiers determine the *visibility* or accessibility of an object's attributes and operations to other objects. Before we can begin implementing our design, we must consider which attributes and operations of our classes should be `public` and which should be `private`.

In Chapter 4, we observed that data members normally should be `private` and that member functions invoked by clients of a given class should be `public`. Member functions that are called only by other member functions of the class as "utility functions," however, normally should be `private`. The UML employs *visibility markers* for modeling the visibility of attributes and operations. Public visibility is indicated by placing a plus sign (+) before an operation or an attribute; a minus sign (–) indicates private visibility. Figure 10.22 shows our updated class diagram with visibility markers included. [*Note:* We do not include any operation parameters in Fig. 10.22. This is perfectly normal. Adding visibility markers does not affect the parameters already modeled in the class diagrams of Figs. 7.35–7.38.]

Navigability

Before we begin implementing our design in Visual C++, we introduce an additional UML notation. The class diagram in Fig. 10.23 further refines the relationships among classes in the ATM system by adding navigability arrows to the association lines. *Navigability arrows* (represented as arrows with stick arrowheads in the class diagram) indicate in which direction an association can be traversed and are based on the collaborations

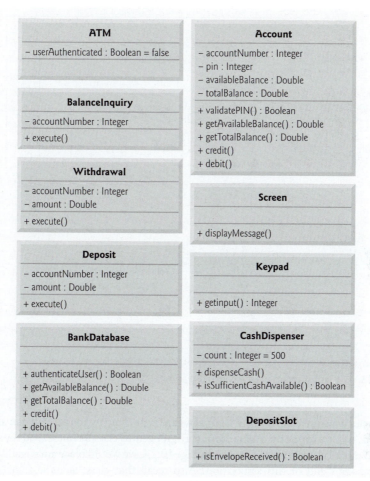

Fig. 10.22 | Class diagram with visibility markers.

modeled in communication and sequence diagrams (see Section 8.15). When implementing a system designed using the UML, programmers use navigability arrows to help determine which objects need references or pointers to other objects. For example, the navigability arrow pointing from class ATM to class BankDatabase indicates that we can navigate from the former to the latter, thereby enabling the ATM to invoke the BankDatabase's operations. However, since Fig. 10.23 does not contain a navigability arrow pointing from class BankDatabase to class ATM, the BankDatabase cannot access the ATM's operations. Note that associations in a class diagram that have navigability arrows at both ends or do not have navigability arrows at all indicate *bidirectional navigability*—navigation can proceed in either direction across the association.

Like the class diagram of Fig. 4.27, the class diagram of Fig. 10.23 omits classes BalanceInquiry and Deposit to keep the diagram simple. The navigability of the associations in which these classes participate closely parallels the navigability of class Withdrawal's associations. Recall from Section 10.12 that BalanceInquiry has an association

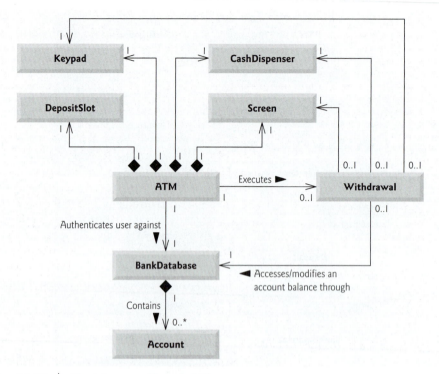

Fig. 10.23 | Class diagram with navigability arrows.

with class Screen. We can navigate from class BalanceInquiry to class Screen along this association, but we cannot navigate from class Screen to class BalanceInquiry. Thus, if we were to model class BalanceInquiry in Fig. 10.23, we would place a navigability arrow at class Screen's end of this association. Also recall that class Deposit associates with classes Screen, Keypad and DepositSlot. We can navigate from class Deposit to each of these classes, but not vice versa. We therefore would place navigability arrows at the Screen, Keypad and DepositSlot ends of these associations. [*Note:* We model these additional classes and associations in our final class diagram in Section 14.11, after we have simplified the structure of our system by incorporating the object-oriented concept of inheritance.]

Implementing the ATM System from Its UML Design

We are now ready to begin implementing the ATM system. We first convert the classes in the diagrams of Fig. 10.22 and Fig. 10.23 into C++ header files. This code will represent the "skeleton" of the system. In Chapter 14, we modify the header files to incorporate the object-oriented concept of inheritance. In Appendix F, we present the complete working Visual C++ code for our model.

As an example, we begin to develop the header file for class Withdrawal from our design of class Withdrawal in Fig. 10.22. We use this figure to determine the attributes and operations of the class. We use the UML model in Fig. 10.23 to determine the associations among classes. We follow the following five guidelines for each class:

1. Use the name located in the first compartment of a class in a class diagram to define the class in a header file (Fig. 10.24). Use #ifndef, #define and #endif preprocessor directives to prevent the header file from being included more than once in a program.

2. Use the attributes located in the class's second compartment to declare the data members. For example, the private attributes accountNumber and amount of class Withdrawal yield the code in Fig. 10.25.

3. Use the associations described in the class diagram to declare references (or pointers, where appropriate) to other objects. For example, according to Fig. 10.23, Withdrawal can access one object of class Screen, one object of class Keypad, one object of class CashDispenser and one object of class BankDatabase. Class Withdrawal must maintain handles on these objects to send messages to them, so lines 19–22 of Fig. 10.26 declare four references as private data members. In the implementation of class Withdrawal in Appendix F, a constructor initializes these data members with references to actual objects. Note that lines 6–9 #include the header files containing the definitions of classes Screen, Keypad, CashDispenser and BankDatabase so that we can declare references to objects of these classes in lines 19–22.

```
1   // Fig. 10.24: Withdrawal.h
2   // Definition of class Withdrawal that represents a withdrawal transaction
3   #ifndef WITHDRAWAL_H
4   #define WITHDRAWAL_H
5
6   class Withdrawal
7   {
8   }; // end class Withdrawal
9
10  #endif // WITHDRAWAL_H
```

Fig. 10.24 | Definition of class Withdrawal enclosed in preprocessor wrappers.

```
1   // Fig. 10.25: Withdrawal.h
2   // Definition of class Withdrawal that represents a withdrawal transaction
3   #ifndef WITHDRAWAL_H
4   #define WITHDRAWAL_H
5
6   class Withdrawal
7   {
8   private:
9      // attributes
10     int accountNumber; // account to withdraw funds from
11     double amount; // amount to withdraw
12  }; // end class Withdrawal
13
14  #endif // WITHDRAWAL_H
```

Fig. 10.25 | Adding attributes to the Withdrawal class header file.

```
1   // Fig. 10.26: Withdrawal.h
2   // Definition of class Withdrawal that represents a withdrawal transaction
3   #ifndef WITHDRAWAL_H
4   #define WITHDRAWAL_H
5
6   #include "Screen.h" // include definition of class Screen
7   #include "Keypad.h" // include definition of class Keypad
8   #include "CashDispenser.h" // include definition of class CashDispenser
9   #include "BankDatabase.h" // include definition of class BankDatabase
10
11  class Withdrawal
12  {
13  private:
14     // attributes
15     int accountNumber; // account to withdraw funds from
16     double amount; // amount to withdraw
17
18     // references to associated objects
19     Screen &screen; // reference to ATM's screen
20     Keypad &keypad; // reference to ATM's keypad
21     CashDispenser &cashDispenser; // reference to ATM's cash dispenser
22     BankDatabase &bankDatabase; // reference to the account info database
23  }; // end class Withdrawal
24
25  #endif // WITHDRAWAL_H
```

Fig. 10.26 | Declaring references to objects associated with class Withdrawal.

4. It turns out that including the header files for classes Screen, Keypad, CashDispenser and BankDatabase in Fig. 10.26 does more than is necessary. Class Withdrawal contains *references* to objects of these classes—it does not contain actual objects—and the amount of information required by the compiler to create a reference differs from that which is required to create an object. Recall that creating an object requires that you provide the compiler with a definition of the class that introduces the name of the class as a new user-defined type and indicates the data members that determine how much memory is required to store the object. Declaring a *reference* (or pointer) to an object, however, requires only that the compiler knows that the object's class exists—it does not need to know the size of the object. Any reference (or pointer), regardless of the class of the object to which it refers, contains only the memory address of the actual object. The amount of memory required to store an address is a physical characteristic of the computer's hardware. The compiler thus knows the size of any reference (or pointer). As a result, including a class's full header file when declaring only a reference to an object of that class is unnecessary—we need to introduce the name of the class, but we do not need to provide the data layout of the object, because the compiler already knows the size of all references. Visual C++ provides a statement called a *forward declaration* that signifies that a header file contains references or pointers to a class, but that the class definition lies outside the header file. We can replace the #includes in the Withdrawal class definition of Fig. 10.26 with forward declarations of classes Screen, Keypad, CashDispenser and BankDatabase (lines 6–

9 in Fig. 10.27). Rather than #include the entire header file for each of these classes, we place only a forward declaration of each class in the header file for class Withdrawal. Note that if class Withdrawal contained actual objects instead of references (i.e., if the ampersands in lines 19–22 were omitted), then we would indeed need to #include the full header files.

Note that using a forward declaration (where possible) instead of including a full header file helps avoid a preprocessor problem called a *circular include*. This problem occurs when the header file for a class A #includes the header file for a class B and vice versa. Some preprocessors are not be able to resolve such #include directives, causing a compilation error. If class A, for example, uses only a reference to an object of class B, then the #include in class A's header file can be replaced by a forward declaration of class B to prevent the circular include.

5. Use the operations located in the third compartment of Fig. 10.22 to write the function prototypes of the class's member functions. If we have not yet specified a return type for an operation, we declare the member function with return type void. Refer to the class diagrams of Figs. 7.34–7.38 to declare any necessary parameters. For example, adding the public operation execute in class Withdrawal, which has an empty parameter list, yields the prototype in line 15 of Fig. 10.28. [*Note:* We code the definitions of member functions in .cpp files when we implement the complete ATM system in Appendix F.]

```cpp
1   // Fig. 10.27: Withdrawal.h
2   // Definition of class Withdrawal that represents a withdrawal transaction
3   #ifndef WITHDRAWAL_H/
4   #define WITHDRAWAL_H
5
6   class Screen; // forward declaration of class Screen
7   class Keypad; // forward declaration of class Keypad
8   class CashDispenser; // forward declaration of class CashDispenser
9   class BankDatabase; // forward declaration of class BankDatabase
10
11  class Withdrawal
12  {
13  private:
14     // attributes
15     int accountNumber; // account to withdraw funds from
16     double amount; // amount to withdraw
17
18     // references to associated objects
19     Screen &screen; // reference to ATM's screen
20     Keypad &keypad; // reference to ATM's keypad
21     CashDispenser &cashDispenser; // reference to ATM's cash dispenser
22     BankDatabase &bankDatabase; // reference to the account info database
23  }; // end class Withdrawal
24
25  #endif // WITHDRAWAL_H
```

Fig. 10.27 | Using forward declarations in place of #include directives.

```
1   // Fig. 10.28: Withdrawal.h
2   // Definition of class Withdrawal that represents a withdrawal transaction
3   #ifndef WITHDRAWAL_H
4   #define WITHDRAWAL_H
5
6   class Screen; // forward declaration of class Screen
7   class Keypad; // forward declaration of class Keypad
8   class CashDispenser; // forward declaration of class CashDispenser
9   class BankDatabase; // forward declaration of class BankDatabase
10
11  class Withdrawal
12  {
13  public:
14     // operations
15     void execute(); // perform the transaction
16  private:
17     // attributes
18     int accountNumber; // account to withdraw funds from
19     double amount; // amount to withdraw
20
21     // references to associated objects
22     Screen &screen; // reference to ATM's screen
23     Keypad &keypad; // reference to ATM's keypad
24     CashDispenser &cashDispenser; // reference to ATM's cash dispenser
25     BankDatabase &bankDatabase; // reference to the account info database
26  }; // end class Withdrawal
27
28  #endif // WITHDRAWAL_H
```

Fig. 10.28 | Adding operations to the `Withdrawal` class header file.

Software Engineering Observation 10.12

Several UML modeling tools can convert UML-based designs into Visual C++ code, considerably speeding the implementation process. For more information on these "automatic" code generators, refer to the Internet and web resources listed at the end of Section 3.8.

This concludes our discussion of the basics of generating class header files from UML diagrams. In the final Software Engineering Case Study section (Section 14.11), we demonstrate how to modify the header files to incorporate the object-oriented concept of inheritance.

Software Engineering Case Study Self-Review Exercises

10.1 State whether the following statement is *true* or *false*, and if *false*, explain why: If an attribute of a class is marked with a minus sign (-) in a class diagram, the attribute is not directly accessible outside of the class.

10.2 In Fig. 10.23, the association between the ATM and the Screen indicates that:
a) we can navigate from the Screen to the ATM
b) we can navigate from the ATM to the Screen
c) Both a and b; the association is bidirectional
d) None of the above

10.3 Write C++ code to begin implementing the design for class Account.

Answers to Software Engineering Case Study Self-Review Exercises

10.1 True. The minus sign (-) indicates private visibility. We've mentioned "friendship" as an exception to private visibility. Friendship is discussed in Chapter 11.

10.2 b.

10.3 The design for class Account yields the header file in Fig. 10.29.

```
1    // Fig. 10.29: Account.h
2    // Account class definition. Represents a bank account.
3    #ifndef ACCOUNT_H
4    #define ACCOUNT_H
5
6    class Account
7    {
8    public:
9       bool validatePIN( int ); // is user-specified PIN correct?
10      double getAvailableBalance(); // returns available balance
11      double getTotalBalance(); // returns total balance
12      void credit( double ); // adds an amount to the Account
13      void debit( double ); // subtracts an amount from the Account
14   private:
15      int accountNumber; // account number
16      int pin; // PIN for authentication
17      double availableBalance; // funds available for withdrawal
18      double totalBalance; // funds available + funds waiting to clear
19   }; // end class Account
20
21   #endif // ACCOUNT_H
```

Fig. 10.29 | Account class header file based on Fig. 10.22 and Fig. 10.23.

10.13 Wrap-Up

This chapter deepened our coverage of classes, using a rich Time class case study to introduce several new features of classes. You saw that member functions are usually shorter than global functions because member functions can directly access an object's data members, so the member functions can receive fewer arguments than functions in procedural programming languages. You learned how to use the arrow operator to access an object's members via a pointer of the object's class type.

You learned that member functions have class scope—i.e., the member function's name is known only to other members of the class unless referred to via an object of the class, a reference to an object of the class, a pointer to an object of the class or the binary scope resolution operator. We also discussed access functions (commonly used to retrieve the values of data members or to test the truth or falsity of conditions) and utility functions (private member functions that support the operation of the class's public member functions).

You learned that a constructor can specify default arguments that enable it to be called in a variety of ways. You also learned that any constructor that can be called with no arguments is a default constructor and that there can be at most one default constructor per class. We discussed destructors and their purpose of performing termination housekeeping on an object of a class before that object is destroyed. We also demonstrated the order in which an object's constructors and destructors are called.

We demonstrated the problems that can occur when a member function returns a reference to a private data member, which breaks the encapsulation of the class. We also showed that objects of the same type can be assigned to one another using default memberwise assignment. Finally, we discussed the benefits of using class libraries to enhance the speed with which code can be created and to increase the quality of software.

Chapter 11 presents additional class features. We'll demonstrate how const can be used to indicate that a member function does not modify an object of a class. You'll learn how to build classes with composition—the capability that allows a class to contain objects of other classes as members. We'll show how a class can allow so-called "friend" functions to access the class's non-public members. We'll also show how a class's non-static member functions can use a special pointer named this to access an object's members. Next, you'll learn how to use Visual C++'s new and delete operators, which enable programmers to obtain and release memory as necessary during a program's execution.

Summary

Section 10.2 Time Class Case Study

- The preprocessor directives #ifndef (which means "if not defined") and #endif are used to prevent multiple inclusions of a header file. If the code between these directives has not previously been included in an application, #define defines a name that can be used to prevent future inclusions, and the code is included in the source-code file.

- Data members of a class cannot be initialized where they are declared in the class body (except for a class's static const data members of integral or enum types, as you'll see in Chapter 11). It is strongly recommended that these data members be initialized by the class's constructor (as there is no default initialization for data members of fundamental types).

- Stream manipulator setfill specifies the fill character that is displayed when an integer is output in a field that is wider than the number of digits in the value.

- By default, the fill characters appear before the digits in the number.

- Stream manipulator setfill is a "sticky" setting, meaning that once the fill character is set, it applies for all subsequent fields being printed.

- Even though a member function declared in a class definition may be defined outside that class definition (and "tied" to the class via the binary scope resolution operator), that member function is still within that class's scope; i.e., its name is known only to other members of the class unless referred to via an object of the class, a reference to an object of the class or a pointer to an object of the class.

- If a member function is defined in the body of a class definition, the Visual C++ compiler attempts to inline calls to the member function.

- Classes do not have to be created "from scratch." Rather, they can include objects of other classes as members or they may be derived from other classes that provide attributes and behaviors the new classes can use. Including class objects as members of other classes is called composition.

- Use the pragma directive #pragma once at the beginning of a header file to prevent multiple inclusions of a header file in an application. This is a convenient alternative to the preprocessor wrapper.

Section 10.3 Class Scope and Accessing Class Members

- A class's data members and member functions belong to that class's scope.

- Nonmember functions are defined at file scope.

- Within a class's scope, class members are immediately accessible by all of that class's member functions and can be referenced by name.

- Outside a class's scope, class members are referenced through one of the handles on an object—an object name, a reference to an object or a pointer to an object. Do not confuse handles in the general sense with the C++/CLI handle denoted by the ∧ character.

- Member functions of a class can be overloaded, but only by other member functions of that class.

- To overload a member function, provide in the class definition a prototype for each version of the overloaded function, and provide a separate definition for each version of the function.

- Variables declared in a member function have block scope and are known only to that function.

- If a member function defines a variable with the same name as a variable with class scope, the class-scope variable is hidden by the block-scope variable in the block scope.

- The dot member-selection operator (.) is preceded by an object's name or by a reference to an object to access the object's `public` members.

- The arrow member-selection operator (->) is preceded by a pointer to an object to access that object's `public` members.

Section 10.4 Separating Interface from Implementation

- Header files do contain some portions of the implementation and hints about others. Inline member functions, for example, need to be in a header file, so that when the compiler compiles a client, the client can include the `inline` function definition in place.

- A class's `private` members that are listed in the class definition in the header file are visible to clients, even though the clients may not access the `private` members.

Section 10.5 Access Functions and Utility Functions

- A utility function (also called a helper function) is a `private` member function that supports the operation of the class's `public` member functions. Utility functions are not intended to be used by clients of a class (but can be used by friends of a class).

Section 10.6 Time Class Case Study: Constructors with Default Arguments

- Like other functions, constructors can specify default arguments.

Section 10.7 Destructors

- A class's destructor is called implicitly when an object of the class is destroyed.

- The name of the destructor for a class is the tilde (~) character followed by the class name.

- A destructor does not release an object's storage—it performs termination housekeeping before the system reclaims an object's memory, so the memory may be reused to hold new objects.

- A destructor receives no parameters and returns no value. A class may have only one destructor.

- If you do not explicitly provide a destructor, the compiler creates an "empty" destructor, so every class has exactly one destructor.

Section 10.8 When Constructors and Destructors Are Called

- The order in which constructors and destructors are called depends on the order in which execution enters and leaves the scopes where the objects are instantiated.

- Generally, destructor calls are made in the reverse order of the corresponding constructor calls, but the storage classes of objects can alter the order in which destructors are called.

Section 10.9 Time Class Case Study: A Subtle Trap—Returning a Reference to a private *Data Member*

- A reference to an object is an alias for the name of the object and, hence, may be used on the left side of an assignment statement. In this context, the reference makes a perfectly acceptable *lvalue* that can receive a value. One way to use this capability (unfortunately!) is to have a public member function of a class return a reference to a private data member of that class. If the function returns a const reference, then the reference cannot be used as a modifiable *lvalue*.

Section 10.10 Default Memberwise Assignment

- The assignment operator (=) can be used to assign an object to another object of the same type. By default, such assignment is performed by memberwise assignment—each member of the object on the right of the assignment operator is assigned individually to the same member in the object on the left of the assignment operator.

- Objects may be passed as function arguments and may be returned from functions. Such passing and returning is performed using pass-by-value by default—a copy of the object is passed or returned. In such cases, Visual C++ creates a new object and uses a copy constructor to copy the original object's values into the new object.

- For each class, the compiler provides a default copy constructor that copies each member of the original object into the corresponding member of the new object.

Section 10.11 Class View *and* Object Browser

- The Class View displays the variables and functions for all classes in a project. The view follows a hierarchical structure, positioning the project name as the root and including a series of nodes that represent the classes, variables and functions in the project.

- The Object Browser lists in the left window all classes of the FCL. The Object Browser can be a quick mechanism to learn about a class or function of a class.

Terminology

abort function	#ifndef preprocessor directive
access function	implicit handle on an object
aggregation	inheritance
arrow member-selection operator (->)	initializer
assigning class objects	memberwise assignment
class libraries	name handle on an object
class scope	object handle
composition	object leaves scope
copy constructor	order in which constructors and destructors are
default arguments with constructors	called
default memberwise assignment	overloaded constructor
#define preprocessor directive	overloaded member function
derive one class from another	pass an object by value
destructor	pointer handle on an object
#endif preprocessor directive	pragma directive
exit function	predicate function
file scope	preprocessor wrapper
fill character	pure procedure
forward declaration	reentrant code
handle on an object	reference handle on an object
helper function	reusable componentry

setfill parameterized stream manipulator   tilde character (~) in a destructor name
termination housekeeping

Self-Review Exercises

10.1   Fill in the blanks in each of the following:
   a) Class members are accessed via the _____ operator in conjunction with the name of
       an object (or reference to an object) of the class or via the _____ operator in conjunc-
       tion with a pointer to an object of the class.
   b) Class members specified as _____ are accessible only to member functions of the
       class and friends of the class.
   c) Class members specified as _____ are accessible anywhere an object of the class is in
       scope.
   d) _____ can be used to assign an object of a class to another object of the same class.

10.2   Find the error(s) in each of the following and explain how to correct it (them):
   a) Assume the following prototype is declared in class Time:

```
void ~Time( int );
```

   b) The following is a partial definition of class Time:

```
class Time
{
public:
    // function prototypes

private:
    int hour = 0;
    int minute = 0;
    int second = 0;
}; // end class Time
```

   c) Assume the following prototype is declared in class Employee:

```
int Employee( const char *, const char * );
```

Answers to Self-Review Exercises

10.1   a) dot (.), arrow (->). b) private. c) public. d) Default memberwise assignment (performed by the assignment operator).

10.2   a) Error: Destructors are not allowed to return values (or even specify a return type) or take
           arguments.
           Correction: Remove the return type void and the parameter int from the declaration.
   b) Error: Members cannot be explicitly initialized in the class definition.
       Correction: Remove the explicit initialization from the class definition and initialize the
       data members in a constructor.
   c) Error: Constructors are not allowed to return values.
       Correction: Remove the return type int from the declaration.

Exercises

10.3   What is the purpose of the scope resolution operator?

10.4   *(Enhancing Class Time)* Provide a constructor that is capable of using the current time from
the time() function—declared in the C++ Standard Library header <ctime>—to initialize an object
of the Time class.

10.5 *(Complex Class)* Create a class called `Complex` for performing arithmetic with complex numbers. Write a program to test your class.

Complex numbers have the form

```
realPart + imaginaryPart * i
```

where *i* is

$$\sqrt{-1}$$

Use `double` variables to represent the `private` data of the class. Provide a constructor that enables an object of this class to be initialized when it is declared. The constructor should contain default values in case no initializers are provided. Provide `public` member functions that perform the following tasks:

a) Adding two `Complex` numbers: The real parts are added together and the imaginary parts are added together.

b) Subtracting two `Complex` numbers: The real part of the right operand is subtracted from the real part of the left operand, and the imaginary part of the right operand is subtracted from the imaginary part of the left operand.

c) Printing `Complex` numbers in the form (a, b), where a is the real part and b is the imaginary part.

10.6 *(Rational Class)* Create a class called `Rational` for performing arithmetic with fractions. Write a program to test your class.

Use integer variables to represent the `private` data of the class—the numerator and the denominator. Provide a constructor that enables an object of this class to be initialized when it is declared. The constructor should contain default values in case no initializers are provided and should store the fraction in reduced form. For example, the fraction

$$\frac{2}{4}$$

would be stored in the object as 1 in the numerator and 2 in the denominator. Provide `public` member functions that perform each of the following tasks:

a) Adding two `Rational` numbers. The result should be stored in reduced form.

b) Subtracting two `Rational` numbers. The result should be stored in reduced form.

c) Multiplying two `Rational` numbers. The result should be stored in reduced form.

d) Dividing two `Rational` numbers. The result should be stored in reduced form.

e) Printing `Rational` numbers in the form a/b, where a is the numerator and b is the denominator.

f) Printing `Rational` numbers in floating-point format.

10.7 *(Enhancing Class Time)* Modify the `Time` class of Figs. 10.8–10.9 to include a `tick` member function that increments the time stored in a `Time` object by one second. The `Time` object should always remain in a consistent state. Write a program that tests the `tick` member function in a loop that prints the time in standard format during each iteration of the loop to illustrate that the `tick` member function works correctly. Be sure to test the following cases:

a) Incrementing into the next minute.

b) Incrementing into the next hour.

c) Incrementing into the next day (i.e., 11:59:59 PM to 12:00:00 AM).

10.8 *(Enhancing Class Date)* Modify the `Date` class of Figs. 10.17–10.18 to perform error checking on the initializer values for data members `month`, `day` and `year`. Also, provide a member function `nextDay` to increment the day by one. The `Date` object should always remain in a consistent state. Write a program that tests function `nextDay` in a loop that prints the date during each iteration to illustrate that `nextDay` works correctly. Be sure to test the following cases:

a) Incrementing into the next month.

b) Incrementing into the next year.

10.9 *(Combining Class* Time *and Class* Date*)* Combine the modified Time class of Exercise 10.7 and the modified Date class of Exercise 10.8 into one class called DateAndTime. (In Chapter 13, we'll discuss inheritance, which will enable us to accomplish this task quickly without modifying the existing class definitions.) Modify the tick function to call the nextDay function if the time increments into the next day. Modify functions printStandard and printUniversal to output the date and time. Write a program to test the new class DateAndTime. Specifically, test incrementing the time into the next day.

10.10 *(Returning Error Indicators from Class* Time*'s set* Functions*)* Modify the *set* functions in the Time class of Figs. 10.8–10.9 to return appropriate error values if an attempt is made to *set* a data member of an object of class Time to an invalid value. Write a program that tests your new version of class Time. Display error messages when *set* functions return error values.

10.11 *(Rectangle Class)* Create a class Rectangle with attributes length and width, each of which defaults to 1. Provide member functions that calculate the perimeter and the area of the rectangle. Also, provide *set* and *get* functions for the length and width attributes. The *set* functions should verify that length and width are each floating-point numbers larger than 0.0 and less than 20.0.

10.12 *(Enhancing Class* Rectangle*)* Create a more sophisticated Rectangle class than the one you created in Exercise 10.11. This class stores only the Cartesian coordinates of the four corners of the rectangle. The constructor calls a *set* function that accepts four sets of coordinates and verifies that each of these is in the first quadrant with no single *x*- or *y*-coordinate larger than 20.0. The *set* function also verifies that the supplied coordinates do, in fact, specify a rectangle. Provide member functions that calculate the length, width, perimeter and area. The length is the larger of the two dimensions. Include a predicate function square that determines whether the rectangle is a square.

10.13 *(Enhancing Class* Rectangle*)* Modify class Rectangle from Exercise 10.12 to include a draw function that displays the rectangle inside a 25-by-25 box enclosing the portion of the first quadrant in which the rectangle resides. Include a setFillCharacter function to specify the character out of which the body of the rectangle will be drawn. Include a setPerimeterCharacter function to specify the character that will be used to draw the border of the rectangle. If you feel ambitious, you might include functions to scale the size of the rectangle, rotate it, and move it around within the designated portion of the first quadrant.

10.14 *(HugeInteger Class)* Create a class HugeInteger that uses a 40-element array of digits to store integers as large as 40 digits each. Provide member functions input, output, add and subtract. For comparing HugeInteger objects, provide functions isEqualTo, isNotEqualTo, isGreaterThan, isLessThan, isGreaterThanOrEqualTo and isLessThanOrEqualTo—each of these is a "predicate" function that simply returns true if the relationship holds between the two HugeIntegers and returns false if the relationship does not hold. Also, provide a predicate function isZero. If you feel ambitious, provide member functions multiply, divide and modulus.

10.15 *(TicTacToe Class)* Create a class TicTacToe that will enable you to write a complete program to play the game of tic-tac-toe. The class contains as private data a 3-by-3 two-dimensional array of integers. The constructor should initialize the empty board to all zeros. Allow two human players. Wherever the first player moves, place a 1 in the specified square. Place a 2 wherever the second player moves. Each move must be to an empty square. After each move, determine whether the game has been won or is a draw. If you feel ambitious, modify your program so that the computer makes the moves for one of the players. Also, allow the player to specify whether he or she wants to go first or second. If you feel exceptionally ambitious, develop a program that will play three-dimensional tic-tac-toe on a 4-by-4-by-4 board. [*Caution:* This is an extremely challenging project that could take many weeks of effort!]

11

Classes: A Deeper Look, Part 2

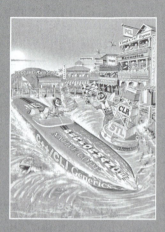

OBJECTIVES

In this chapter you'll learn:

- To specify `const` (constant) objects and `const` member functions.

- To create objects composed of other objects.

- To use `friend` functions and `friend` classes.

- To use the `this` pointer.

- To create and destroy objects dynamically with operators `new` and `delete`, respectively.

- To use `static` data members and member functions.

- The concept of a container class.

- The notion of iterator classes that walk through the elements of container classes.

- To use proxy classes to hide implementation details from a class's clients.

11.1 Introduction

In this chapter, we continue our study of classes and data abstraction with several more advanced topics. We use `const` objects and `const` member functions to prevent modifications of objects and enforce the principle of least privilege. We discuss composition—a form of reuse in which a class can have objects of other classes as members. Next, we introduce friendship, which enables a class designer to specify nonmember functions that can access class's non-`public` members—a technique that is often used in operator overloading (Chapter 12) for performance reasons. We discuss a special pointer (called `this`), which is an implicit argument to each of a class's non-`static` member functions. It allows those member functions to access the correct object's data members and other non-`static` member functions. We then discuss dynamic memory management and show how to create and destroy objects dynamically with the `new` and `delete` operators. Next, we motivate the need for `static` class members and show how to use `static` data members and member functions in your own classes. We show how to create a proxy class to hide the implementation details of a class (including its `private` data members) from clients of the class.

Recall that Chapter 4 introduced C++ Standard Library class `string` to represent strings as full-fledged class objects. In this chapter, however, we use the pointer-based strings we introduced in Chapter 9 to help you master pointers and prepare for the professional world in which you'll see a great deal of C legacy code implemented over the last several decades. Thus, you'll become familiar with the two most prevalent methods of creating and manipulating strings in C++.

The last part of the chapter involves C++/CLI specific rules for using const and the finer details of dynamic memory management with managed code. We also explain the differences between value and reference types in native C++ and C++/CLI. We introduce the concept of finalizers for managed objects and demonstrate how to use indexers to access data members of classes.

11.2 const (Constant) Objects and const Member Functions

We have emphasized the principle of least privilege as one of the most fundamental principles of good software engineering. Let us see how this principle applies to objects.

Some objects need to be modifiable and some do not. You may use keyword const to specify that an object is not modifiable and that any attempt to modify the object should result in a compilation error. The statement

```
const Time noon( 12, 0, 0 );
```

declares a const object noon of class Time and initializes it to 12 noon.

Software Engineering Observation 11.1

Declaring an object as const helps enforce the principle of least privilege. Attempts to modify the object are caught at compile time rather than causing execution-time errors. Using const properly is crucial to proper class design, program design and coding.

Performance Tip 11.1

Declaring variables and objects const can improve performance—today's sophisticated optimizing compilers can perform certain optimizations on constants that cannot be performed on variables.

Visual C++ disallows member function calls for const objects unless the member functions themselves are also declared const. This is true even for *get* member functions that do not modify the object. In addition, the compiler does not allow member functions declared const to modify the object.

A function is specified as const *both* in its prototype (Fig. 11.1; lines 19–24) and in its definition (Fig. 11.2; lines 47, 53, 59 and 65) by inserting the keyword const after the function's parameter list and, in the case of the function definition, before the left brace that begins the function body.

Common Programming Error 11.1

Defining as const a member function that modifies a data member of an object is a compilation error.

Common Programming Error 11.2

Defining as const a member function that calls a non-const member function of the class on the same instance of the class is a compilation error.

Common Programming Error 11.3

Invoking a non-const member function on a `const` object is a compilation error.

Software Engineering Observation 11.2

A const member function can be overloaded with a non-const version. The compiler chooses which overloaded member function to use based on the object on which the function is invoked. If the object is const, the compiler uses the const version. If the object is not const, the compiler uses the non-const version.

An interesting problem arises for constructors and destructors, each of which typically modifies objects. The `const` declaration is not allowed for constructors and destructors. A constructor must be allowed to modify an object so that the object can be initialized properly. A destructor must be able to perform its termination housekeeping chores before an object's memory is reclaimed by the system.

Common Programming Error 11.4

Attempting to declare a constructor or destructor const is a compilation error.

Defining and Using const Member Functions

The program of Figs. 11.1–11.3 modifies class `Time` of Figs. 10.8–10.9 by making its *get* functions and `printUniversal` function `const`. In the header file `Time.h` (Fig. 11.1), lines 19–21 and 24 now include keyword `const` after each function's parameter list. The corresponding definition of each function in Fig. 11.2 (lines 47, 53, 59 and 65, respectively) also specifies keyword `const` after each function's parameter list.

```cpp
1  // Fig. 11.1: Time.h
2  // Time class definition with const member functions.
3  // Member functions defined in Time.cpp.
4  #ifndef TIME_H
5  #define TIME_H
6
7  class Time
8  {
9  public:
10     Time( int = 0, int = 0, int = 0 ); // default constructor
11
12     // set functions
13     void setTime( int, int, int ); // set time
14     void setHour( int ); // set hour
15     void setMinute( int ); // set minute
16     void setSecond( int ); // set second
17
18     // get functions (normally declared const)
19     int getHour() const; // return hour
20     int getMinute() const; // return minute
21     int getSecond() const; // return second
22
```

Fig. 11.1 | `Time` class definition with `const` member functions. (Part 1 of 2.)

```
23      // print functions (normally declared const)
24      void printUniversal() const; // print universal time
25      void printStandard(); // print standard time (should be const)
26  private:
27      int hour; // 0 - 23 (24-hour clock format)
28      int minute; // 0 - 59
29      int second; // 0 - 59
30  }; // end class Time
31
32  #endif
```

Fig. 11.1 | Time class definition with `const` member functions. (Part 2 of 2.)

```
 1   // Fig. 11.2: Time.cpp
 2   // Time class member-function definitions.
 3   #include <iostream>
 4   using std::cout;
 5
 6   #include <iomanip>
 7   using std::setfill;
 8   using std::setw;
 9
10   #include "Time.h" // include definition of class Time
11
12   // constructor function to initialize private data;
13   // calls member function setTime to set variables;
14   // default values are 0 (see class definition)
15   Time::Time( int hour, int minute, int second )
16   {
17       setTime( hour, minute, second );
18   } // end Time constructor
19
20   // set hour, minute and second values
21   void Time::setTime( int hour, int minute, int second )
22   {
23       setHour( hour );
24       setMinute( minute );
25       setSecond( second );
26   } // end function setTime
27
28   // set hour value
29   void Time::setHour( int h )
30   {
31       hour = ( h >= 0 && h < 24 ) ? h : 0; // validate hour
32   } // end function setHour
33
34   // set minute value
35   void Time::setMinute( int m )
36   {
37       minute = ( m >= 0 && m < 60 ) ? m : 0; // validate minute
38   } // end function setMinute
```

Fig. 11.2 | Time class member-function definitions, including `const` member functions. (Part 1 of 2.)

```
39
40    // set second value
41    void Time::setSecond( int s )
42    {
43       second = ( s >= 0 && s < 60 ) ? s : 0; // validate second
44    } // end function setSecond
45
46    // return hour value
47    int Time::getHour() const // get functions should be const
48    {
49       return hour;
50    } // end function getHour
51
52    // return minute value
53    int Time::getMinute() const
54    {
55       return minute;
56    } // end function getMinute
57
58    // return second value
59    int Time::getSecond() const
60    {
61       return second;
62    } // end function getSecond
63
64    // print Time in universal-time format (HH:MM:SS)
65    void Time::printUniversal() const
66    {
67       cout << setfill( '0' ) << setw( 2 ) << hour << ":"
68          << setw( 2 ) << minute << ":" << setw( 2 ) << second;
69    } // end function printUniversal
70
71    // print Time in standard-time format (HH:MM:SS AM or PM)
72    void Time::printStandard() // note lack of const declaration
73    {
74       cout << ( ( hour == 0 || hour == 12 ) ? 12 : hour % 12 )
75          << ":" << setfill( '0' ) << setw( 2 ) << minute
76          << ":" << setw( 2 ) << second << ( hour < 12 ? " AM" : " PM" );
77    } // end function printStandard
```

Fig. 11.2 | Time class member-function definitions, including const member functions. (Part 2 of 2.)

Figure 11.3 instantiates two Time objects—non-const object wakeUp (line 7) and const object noon (line 8). The program attempts to invoke non-const member functions setHour (line 13) and printStandard (line 20) on the const object noon. In each case, the compiler generates an error message. The program also illustrates the three other member-function-call combinations on objects—a non-const member function on a non-const object (line 11), a const member function on a non-const object (line 15) and a const member function on a const object (lines 17–18). The error messages generated for non-const member functions called on a const object are shown in the output window. Notice that, although some current compilers issue only warning messages for

```
 1   // Fig. 11.3: TimeTest.cpp
 2   // Attempting to access a const object with non-const member functions.
 3   #include "Time.h" // include Time class definition
 4
 5   int main()
 6   {
 7      Time wakeUp( 6, 45, 0 ); // non-constant object
 8      const Time noon( 12, 0, 0 ); // constant object
 9
10                                 // OBJECT        MEMBER FUNCTION
11      wakeUp.setHour( 18 );      // non-const     non-const
12
13      noon.setHour( 12 );        // const         non-const
14
15      wakeUp.getHour();          // non-const     const
16
17      noon.getMinute();          // const         const
18      noon.printUniversal();     // const         const
19
20      noon.printStandard();      // const         non-const
21      return 0;
22   } // end main
```

```
C:\examples\ch11\Fig11_01_03\TimeTest.cpp(13) : error C2662:
   'Time::setHour' : cannot convert 'this' pointer from 'const Time' to
   'Time &'
        Conversion loses qualifiers
C:\examples\ch11\Fig11_01_03\TimeTest.cpp(20) : error C2662:
   'Time::printStandard' : cannot convert 'this' pointer from 'const Time' to
   'Time &'
        Conversion loses qualifiers
```

Fig. 11.3 | const objects and const member functions.

lines 13 and 20 (thus allowing this program to be executed), we consider these warnings to be errors—the ISO/IEC C++ standard disallows the invocation of a non-const member function on a const object.

Notice that even though a constructor must be a non-const member function (Fig. 11.2, lines 15–18), it can still be used to initialize a const object (Fig. 11.3, line 8). The definition of the Time constructor (Fig. 11.2, lines 15–18) shows that it calls another non-const member function—setTime (lines 21–26)—to perform the initialization of a Time object. Invoking a non-const member function from the constructor call as part of the initialization of a const object is allowed. The "constness" of a const object is enforced from the time the constructor completes initialization of the object until that object's destructor is called.

Also notice that line 20 in Fig. 11.3 generates a compilation error even though member function printStandard of class Time does not modify the object on which it is invoked. The fact that a member function does not modify an object is not sufficient to indicate that the function is constant function—the function must explicitly be declared const.

Initializing a const Data Member with a Member Initializer

The program of Figs. 11.4–11.6 introduces using *member initializer syntax*. All data members *can* be initialized using member initializer syntax, but const data members and data members that are references *must* be initialized using member initializers. Later in this chapter, we'll see that member objects must be initialized this way as well. In Chapter 13, Object-Oriented Programming: Inheritance, we'll see that base-class portions of derived classes also must be initialized this way.

The constructor definition (Fig. 11.5, lines 11–16) uses a *member initializer list* to initialize class Increment's data members—non-const integer count and const integer increment (declared in lines 19–20 of Fig. 11.4). Member initializers appear between a constructor's parameter list and the left brace that begins the constructor's body. The member initializer list (Fig. 11.5, lines 12–13) is separated from the parameter list with a colon (:). Each member initializer consists of the data member name followed by parentheses containing the member's initial value. In this example, count is initialized with the value of constructor parameter c and increment is initialized with the value of constructor parameter i. Note that multiple member initializers are separated by commas. Also, note that the member initializer list executes before the body of the constructor executes.

Software Engineering Observation 11.3

A const object cannot be modified by assignment, so it must be initialized. When a data member of a class is declared const, a member initializer must be used to provide the constructor with the initial value of the data member for an object of the class. The same is true for references.

```cpp
1   // Fig. 11.4: Increment.h
2   // Definition of class Increment.
3   #ifndef INCREMENT_H
4   #define INCREMENT_H
5
6   class Increment
7   {
8   public:
9      Increment( int c = 0, int i = 1 ); // default constructor
10
11     // function addIncrement definition
12     void addIncrement()
13     {
14        count += increment;
15     } // end function addIncrement
16
17     void print() const; // prints count and increment
18   private:
19      int count;
20      const int increment; // const data member
21   }; // end class Increment
22
23   #endif
```

Fig. 11.4 | Increment class definition containing non-const data member count and const data member increment.

```
1    // Fig. 11.5: Increment.cpp
2    // Member-function definitions for class Increment demonstrate using a
3    // member initializer to initialize a constant of a built-in data type.
4    #include <iostream>
5    using std::cout;
6    using std::endl;
7
8    #include "Increment.h" // include definition of class Increment
9
10   // constructor
11   Increment::Increment( int c, int i )
12      : count( c ), // initializer for non-const member
13        increment( i ) // required initializer for const member
14   {
15      // empty body
16   } // end constructor Increment
17
18   // print count and increment values
19   void Increment::print() const
20   {
21      cout << "count = " << count << ", increment = " << increment << endl;
22   } // end function print
```

Fig. 11.5 | Member initializer used to initialize a constant of a built-in data type.

```
1    // Fig. 11.6: IncrementTest.cpp
2    // Program to test class Increment.
3    #include <iostream>
4    using std::cout;
5
6    #include "Increment.h" // include definition of class Increment
7
8    int main()
9    {
10      Increment value( 10, 5 );
11
12      cout << "Before incrementing: ";
13      value.print();
14
15      for ( int j = 1; j <= 3; j++ )
16      {
17         value.addIncrement();
18         cout << "After increment " << j << ": ";
19         value.print();
20      } // end for
21
22      return 0;
23   } // end main
```

Fig. 11.6 | Invoking an Increment object's print and addIncrement member functions. (Part 1 of 2.)

```
Before incrementing: count = 10, increment = 5
After increment 1: count = 15, increment = 5
After increment 2: count = 20, increment = 5
After increment 3: count = 25, increment = 5
```

Fig. 11.6 | Invoking an Increment object's print and addIncrement member functions. (Part 2 of 2.)

Erroneously Attempting to Initialize a const Data Member with an Assignment
The program of Figs. 11.7–11.9 illustrates the compilation errors caused by attempting to initialize const data member increment with an assignment statement (Fig. 11.8, line 14) in the Increment constructor's body rather than with a member initializer. Note that line 13 of Fig. 11.8 does not generate a compilation error, because count is not declared const.

Common Programming Error 11.5

Not providing a member initializer for a const data member is a compilation error.

Software Engineering Observation 11.4

Constant data members (const objects and const variables) and data members declared as references must be initialized with member initializer syntax; assignments for these types of data in the constructor body are not allowed.

```
1   // Fig. 11.7: Increment.h
2   // Definition of class Increment.
3   #ifndef INCREMENT_H
4   #define INCREMENT_H
5
6   class Increment
7   {
8   public:
9      Increment( int c = 0, int i = 1 ); // default constructor
10
11     // function addIncrement definition
12     void addIncrement()
13     {
14        count += increment;
15     } // end function addIncrement
16
17     void print() const; // prints count and increment
18  private:
19     int count;
20     const int increment; // const data member
21  }; // end class Increment
22
23  #endif
```

Fig. 11.7 | Increment class definition containing non-const data member count and const data member increment.

Note that function `print` (Fig. 11.8, lines 18–21) is declared `const`. It might seem strange to label this function `const`, because a program probably will never have a `const` `Increment` object. However, it is possible that a program will have a `const` reference to an `Increment` object or a pointer to `const` that points to an `Increment` object. Typically, this occurs when objects of class `Increment` are passed to functions or returned from functions. In these cases, only class `Increment`'s `const` member functions can be called through the reference or pointer. Thus, it is reasonable to declare function `print` as `const`—doing so prevents errors in these situations where an `Increment` object is treated as a `const` object.

Error-Prevention Tip 11.1

Declare as const *all of a class's member functions that do not modify the object in which they operate. Occasionally this may seem inappropriate, because you'll have no intention of creating* const *objects of that class or accessing objects of that class through* const *references or pointers to* const. *Declaring such member functions* const *does offer a benefit, though. If the member function is inadvertently written to modify the object, the compiler will issue an error message.*

```
1    // Fig. 11.8: Increment.cpp
2    // Erroneous attempt to initialize a constant of a built-in data
3    // type by assignment.
4    #include <iostream>
5    using std::cout;
6    using std::endl;
7
8    #include "Increment.h" // include definition of class Increment
9
10   // constructor; constant member 'increment' is not initialized
11   Increment::Increment( int c, int i )
12   {
13      count = c; // allowed because count is not constant
14      increment = i; // ERROR: Cannot modify a const object
15   } // end constructor Increment
16
17   // print count and increment values
18   void Increment::print() const
19   {
20      cout << "count = " << count << ", increment = " << increment << endl;
21   } // end function print
```

Fig. 11.8 | Erroneous attempt to initialize a constant of a built-in data type by assignment.

```
1    // Fig. 11.9: IncrementTest.cpp
2    // Program to test class Increment.
3    #include <iostream>
4    using std::cout;
5
6    #include "Increment.h" // include definition of class Increment
7
8    int main()
9    {
```

Fig. 11.9 | Program to test class `Increment` generates compilation errors. (Part 1 of 2.)

```
10      Increment value( 10, 5 );
11
12      cout << "Before incrementing: ";
13      value.print();
14
15      for ( int j = 1; j <= 3; j++ )
16      {
17         value.addIncrement();
18         cout << "After increment " << j << ": ";
19         value.print();
20      } // end for
21
22      return 0;
23   } // end main
```

```
C:\examples\ch11\Fig11_07_09\Increment.cpp(12) : error C2758:
   'Increment::increment' : must be initialized in constructor
   base/member initializer list
         C:\examples\ch11\Fig11_07_09\Increment.h(20) :
            see declaration of 'Increment::increment'
C:\examples\ch11\Fig11_07_09\Increment.cpp(14) : error C2166:
   l-value specifies const object
```

Fig. 11.9 | Program to test class `Increment` generates compilation errors. (Part 2 of 2.)

11.3 Composition: Objects as Members of Classes

An `AlarmClock` object needs to know when it is supposed to sound its alarm, so why not include a `Time` object as a member of the `AlarmClock` class? Such a capability is called *composition* and is sometimes referred to as a *has-a relationship*—a class can have objects of other classes as members.

Software Engineering Observation 11.5

A common form of software reusability is composition, in which a class has objects of other classes as members.

When an object is created, its constructor is called automatically. Previously, we saw how to pass arguments to the constructor of an object we created in `main`. This section shows how an object's constructor can pass arguments to member-object constructors, which is accomplished via member initializers.

Software Engineering Observation 11.6

*Member objects are constructed in the order in which they are declared in the class definition (not in the order they are listed in the constructor's member initializer list) and before their enclosing class objects (sometimes called **host objects**) are constructed.*

The program of Figs. 11.10–11.14 uses class `Date` (Figs. 11.10–11.11) and class `Employee` (Figs. 11.12–11.13) to demonstrate objects as members of other objects. The definition of class `Employee` (Fig. 11.12) contains `private` data members `firstName`, `lastName`, `birthDate` and `hireDate`. Members `birthDate` and `hireDate` are `const` objects of class `Date`, which contains `private` data members `month`, `day` and `year`. The `Employee`

```
1    // Fig. 11.10: Date.h
2    // Date class definition; Member functions defined in Date.cpp
3    #ifndef DATE_H
4    #define DATE_H
5
6    class Date
7    {
8    public:
9       Date( int = 1, int = 1, int = 1900 ); // default constructor
10      void print() const; // print date in month/day/year format
11      ~Date(); // provided to confirm destruction order
12   private:
13      int month; // 1-12 (January-December)
14      int day; // 1-31 based on month
15      int year; // any year
16
17      // utility function to check if day is proper for month and year
18      int checkDay( int ) const;
19   }; // end class Date
20
21   #endif
```

Fig. 11.10 | Date class definition.

```
1    // Fig. 11.11: Date.cpp
2    // Date class member-function definitions.
3    #include <iostream>
4    using std::cout;
5    using std::endl;
6
7    #include "Date.h" // include Date class definition
8
9    // constructor confirms proper value for month; calls
10   // utility function checkDay to confirm proper value for day
11   Date::Date( int mn, int dy, int yr )
12   {
13      if ( mn > 0 && mn <= 12 ) // validate the month
14         month = mn;
15      else
16      {
17         month = 1; // invalid month set to 1
18         cout << "Invalid month (" << mn << ") set to 1.\n";
19      } // end else
20
21      year = yr; // could validate yr
22      day = checkDay( dy ); // validate the day
23
24      // output Date object to show when its constructor is called
25      cout << "Date object constructor for date ";
26      print();
27      cout << endl;
28   } // end Date constructor
```

Fig. 11.11 | Date class member-function definitions. (Part 1 of 2.)

```
29
30  // print Date object in form month/day/year
31  void Date::print() const
32  {
33     cout << month << '/' << day << '/' << year;
34  } // end function print
35
36  // output Date object to show when its destructor is called
37  Date::~Date()
38  {
39     cout << "Date object destructor for date ";
40     print();
41     cout << endl;
42  } // end ~Date destructor
43
44  // utility function to confirm proper day value based on
45  // month and year; handles leap years, too
46  int Date::checkDay( int testDay ) const
47  {
48     static const int daysPerMonth[ 13 ] =
49        { 0, 31, 28, 31, 30, 31, 30, 31, 31, 30, 31, 30, 31 };
50
51     // determine whether testDay is valid for specified month
52     if ( testDay > 0 && testDay <= daysPerMonth[ month ] )
53        return testDay;
54
55     // February 29 check for leap year
56     if ( month == 2 && testDay == 29 && ( year % 400 == 0 ||
57        ( year % 4 == 0 && year % 100 != 0 ) ) )
58        return testDay;
59
60     cout << "Invalid day (" << testDay << ") set to 1.\n";
61     return 1; // leave object in consistent state if bad value
62  } // end function checkDay
```

Fig. 11.11 | Date class member-function definitions. (Part 2 of 2.)

constructor's header (Fig. 11.13, lines 18–21) specifies that the constructor has four parameters (first, last, dateOfBirth and dateOfHire). The first two parameters are used in the constructor's body to initialize the character arrays firstName and lastName. The last two parameters are passed via member initializers to the constructor for class Date. The colon (:) in the header separates the member initializers from the parameter list. The member initializers specify the Employee constructor parameters being passed to the constructors of the member Date objects. Parameter dateOfBirth is passed to object birthDate's constructor (Fig. 11.13, line 20), and parameter dateOfHire is passed to object hireDate's constructor (Fig. 11.13, line 21). Again, member initializers are separated by commas. Note that lines 26 and 32 will generate warnings about strncpy being deprecated. Recall from Section 9.13.2 that this is caused by the Microsoft specific secure versions of the string handling functions which we do not use. As you study class Date (Fig. 11.10), notice that the class does not provide a constructor that receives a parameter of type Date. So, how is the member initializer list in class Employee's constructor able to

```
1   // Fig. 11.12: Employee.h
2   // Employee class definition showing composition.
3   // Member functions defined in Employee.cpp.
4   #ifndef EMPLOYEE_H
5   #define EMPLOYEE_H
6
7   #include "Date.h" // include Date class definition
8
9   class Employee
10  {
11  public:
12     Employee( const char * const, const char * const,
13        const Date &, const Date & );
14     void print() const;
15     ~Employee(); // provided to confirm destruction order
16  private:
17     char firstName[ 25 ];
18     char lastName[ 25 ];
19     const Date birthDate; // composition: member object
20     const Date hireDate; // composition: member object
21  }; // end class Employee
22
23  #endif
```

Fig. 11.12 | Employee class definition showing composition.

```
1   // Fig. 11.13: Employee.cpp
2   // Employee class member-function definitions.
3   #include <iostream>
4   using std::cout;
5   using std::endl;
6
7   #include <cstring> // strlen and strncpy prototypes
8   using std::strlen;
9   using std::strncpy;
10
11  #include "Employee.h" // Employee class definition
12  #include "Date.h" // Date class definition
13
14  // constructor uses member initializer list to pass initializer
15  // values to constructors of member objects birthDate and hireDate
16  // [Note: This invokes the so-called "default copy constructor" which the
17  // C++ compiler provides implicitly.]
18  Employee::Employee( const char * const first, const char * const last,
19     const Date &dateOfBirth, const Date &dateOfHire )
20     : birthDate( dateOfBirth ), // initialize birthDate
21       hireDate( dateOfHire ) // initialize hireDate
22  {
23     // copy first into firstName and be sure that it fits
24     int length = strlen( first );
```

Fig. 11.13 | Employee class member-function definitions, including constructor with a member initializer list. (Part 1 of 2.)

```
25        length = ( length < 25 ? length : 24 );
26        strncpy( firstName, first, length );
27        firstName[ length ] = '\0';
28
29        // copy last into lastName and be sure that it fits
30        length = strlen( last );
31        length = ( length < 25 ? length : 24 );
32        strncpy( lastName, last, length );
33        lastName[ length ] = '\0';
34
35        // output Employee object to show when constructor is called
36        cout << "Employee object constructor: "
37           << firstName << ' ' << lastName << endl;
38     } // end Employee constructor
39
40     // print Employee object
41     void Employee::print() const
42     {
43        cout << lastName << ", " << firstName << "  Hired: ";
44        hireDate.print();
45        cout << "  Birthday: ";
46        birthDate.print();
47        cout << endl;
48     } // end function print
49
50     // output Employee object to show when its destructor is called
51     Employee::~Employee()
52     {
53        cout << "Employee object destructor: "
54           << lastName << ", " << firstName << endl;
55     } // end ~Employee destructor
```

Fig. 11.13 | Employee class member-function definitions, including constructor with a member initializer list. (Part 2 of 2.)

initialize the birthDate and hireDate objects by passing Date object's to their Date constructors? As we mentioned in Chapter 10, the compiler provides each class with a default copy constructor (if the user doesn't define one) that copies each data member of the constructor's argument object into the corresponding member of the object being initialized. Chapter 12 discusses how you can define customized copy constructors.

Figure 11.14 creates two Date objects (lines 11–12) and passes them as arguments to the constructor of the Employee object created in line 13. Line 16 outputs the Employee object's data. When each Date object is created in lines 11–12, the Date constructor defined in lines 11–28 of Fig. 11.11 displays a line of output to show that the constructor was called (see the first two lines of the sample output). [*Note:* Line 13 of Fig. 11.14 causes two additional Date constructor calls that do not appear in the program's output. When each of the Employee's Date member object's is initialized in the Employee constructor's member initializer list (Fig. 11.13, lines 21–21), the default copy constructor for class Date is called. This constructor is defined implicitly by the compiler and does not contain any output statements to demonstrate when it is called. We discuss copy constructors and default copy constructors in detail in Chapter 12.]

```
 1    // Fig. 11.14: EmployeeTest.cpp
 2    // Demonstrating composition--an object with member objects.
 3    #include <iostream>
 4    using std::cout;
 5    using std::endl;
 6
 7    #include "Employee.h" // Employee class definition
 8
 9    int main()
10    {
11       Date birth( 7, 24, 1949 );
12       Date hire( 3, 12, 1988 );
13       Employee manager( "Bob", "Blue", birth, hire );
14
15       cout << endl;
16       manager.print();
17
18       cout << "\nTest Date constructor with invalid values:\n";
19       Date lastDayOff( 14, 35, 1994 ); // invalid month and day
20       cout << endl;
21       return 0;
22    } // end main
```

```
Date object constructor for date 7/24/1949
Date object constructor for date 3/12/1988
Employee object constructor: Bob Blue ───────────   Note that there are actually three
                                                    constructor calls when an
Blue, Bob  Hired: 3/12/1988  Birthday: 7/24/1949    Employee is constructed—two
                                                    calls to the Date class's default
Test Date constructor with invalid values:          copy constructor (called from lines
Invalid month (14) set to 1.                         20–21 of Fig. 11.13) and the call to
Invalid day (35) set to 1.                          the Employee class's constructor.
Date object constructor for date 1/1/1994

Date object destructor for date 1/1/1994
Employee object destructor: Blue, Bob
Date object destructor for date 3/12/1988
Date object destructor for date 7/24/1949
Date object destructor for date 3/12/1988
Date object destructor for date 7/24/1949
```

Fig. 11.14 | Demonstrating composition—an object with member objects.

Class `Date` and class `Employee` each include a destructor (lines 37–42 of Fig. 11.11 and lines 51–55 of Fig. 11.13, respectively) that prints a message when an object of its class is destructed. This enables us to confirm in the program output that objects are constructed from the inside out and destroyed in the reverse order, from the outside in (i.e., the `Date` member objects are destroyed after the `Employee` object that contains them). Notice the last four lines in the output of Fig. 11.14. The last two lines are the outputs of the `Date` destructor running on `Date` objects `hire` (line 12) and `birth` (line 11), respectively. These outputs confirm that the three objects created in `main` are destructed in the reverse of the order in which they were constructed. (The Employee destructor output is five lines from the bottom.) The fourth and third lines from the bottom of the output window show the destructors running for the Employee's member objects hireDate (Fig. 11.12, line 20) and birthDate (Fig. 11.12, line 19). These outputs confirm that the Employee object is destructed from the outside in—i.e., the Employee destructor runs first (output shown five lines from the bottom of the output window), then the member objects are destructed in the reverse order from which they were constructed. Again, the outputs in Fig. 11.14 did not show the constructors running for these member objects, because these were the default copy constructors provided by the C++ compiler.

A member object does not need to be initialized explicitly through a member initializer. If a member initializer is not provided, the member object's default constructor will be called implicitly. Values, if any, established by the default constructor can be overridden by *set* functions. However, for complex initialization, this approach may require significant additional work and time.

Common Programming Error 11.6

A compilation error occurs if a member object is not initialized with a member initializer and the member object's class does not provide a default constructor (i.e., the member object's class defines one or more constructors, but none is a default constructor).

Performance Tip 11.2

Initialize member objects explicitly through member initializers. This eliminates the overhead of "doubly initializing" member objects—once when the member object's default constructor is called and again when set *functions are called in the constructor body (or later) to initialize the member object.*

Software Engineering Observation 11.7

If a class member is an object of another class, making that member object public *does not violate the encapsulation and hiding of that member object's* private *members. However, it does violate the encapsulation and hiding of the containing class's implementation, so member objects of class types should still be* private, *like all other data members.*

In line 26 of Fig. 11.11, notice the call to Date member function print. Many member functions of classes in C++ require no arguments. This is because each member function contains an implicit handle (in the form of a pointer) to the object on which it operates. We discuss the implicit pointer, which is represented by keyword this, in Section 11.5.

Class Employee uses two 25-character arrays (Fig. 11.12, lines 17–18) to represent the first name and last name of the Employee. These arrays may waste space for names shorter than 24 characters. (Remember, one character in each array is for the terminating null character, '\0', of the string.) Also, names longer than 24 characters must be truncated to fit in these fixed-size character arrays. Section 11.7 presents another version of class Employee that dynamically creates the exact amount of space required to hold the first and the last name.

Note that the simplest way to represent an Employee's first and last name using the exact amount of space required is to use two string objects (C++ Standard Library class string was introduced in Chapter 4). If we did this, the Employee constructor would appear as follows:

```
Employee::Employee( const string &first, const string &last,
   const Date &dateOfBirth, const Date &dateOfHire )
   : firstName( first), // initialize firstName
     lastName( last ), // initialize lastName
     birthDate( dateOfBirth ), // initialize birthDate
     hireDate( dateOfHire ) // initialize hireDate
{
   // output Employee object to show when constructor is called
   cout << "Employee object constructor: "
      << firstName << ' ' << lastName << endl;
} // end Employee constructor
```

Notice that data members `firstName` and `lastName` (now `string` objects) are initialized through member initializers. The `Employee` classes presented in Chapters 13–14 use `string` objects in this fashion. In this chapter, we use pointer-based strings to give you additional exposure to pointer manipulation.

11.4 friend Functions and friend Classes

A ***friend function*** of a class is defined outside that class's scope, yet has the right to access the non-`public` (and `public`) members of the class. Standalone functions or entire classes may be declared to be friends of another class.

Using `friend` functions can enhance performance. This section presents a mechanical example of how a `friend` function works. Later in the book, `friend` functions are used to overload operators for use with class objects (Chapter 12) and to create iterator classes (Chapter 21, Data Structures). Objects of an iterator class can successively select items or perform an operation on items in a container class object (see Section 11.9). Objects of container classes can store items. Using friends is often appropriate when a member function cannot be used for certain operations, as we'll see in Chapter 12.

To declare a function as a friend of a class, precede the function prototype in the class definition with keyword `friend`. To declare all member functions of class `ClassTwo` as friends of class `ClassOne`, place a declaration of the form

> ***friend class*** `ClassTwo;`

in the definition of class `ClassOne`.

Software Engineering Observation 11.8

Even though the prototypes for `friend` functions appear in the class definition, friends are not member functions.

Software Engineering Observation 11.9

Member access notions of `private`, `protected` and `public` are not relevant to `friend` declarations, so `friend` declarations can be placed anywhere in a class definition.

Good Programming Practice 11.1

Place all friendship declarations first inside the class definition's body and do not precede them with any access specifier.

Friendship is granted, not taken—i.e., for class B to be a `friend` of class A, class A must explicitly declare that class B is its `friend`. Also, the friendship relation is neither symmetric nor transitive; i.e., if class A is a friend of class B, and class B is a friend of class C, you cannot infer that class B is a friend of class A (again, friendship is not symmetric), that class C is a friend of class B (also because friendship is not symmetric), or that class A is a friend of class C (friendship is not transitive).

Software Engineering Observation 11.10

Some people in the OOP community feel that "friendship" corrupts information hiding and weakens the value of the object-oriented design approach. In this text, we identify several examples of the responsible use of friendship.

Modifying a Class's private Data with a Friend Function

Figure 11.15 is a mechanical example in which we define friend function setX to set the private data member x of class Count. Note that the friend declaration (line 10) appears first (by convention) in the class definition, even before public member functions are declared. Again, this friend declaration can appear anywhere in the class.

```
1   // Fig. 11.15: Friends.cpp
2   // Friends can access private members of a class.
3   #include <iostream>
4   using std::cout;
5   using std::endl;
6
7   // Count class definition
8   class Count
9   {
10     friend void setX( Count &, int ); // friend declaration
11  public:
12     // constructor
13     Count()
14        : x( 0 ) // initialize x to 0
15     {
16        // empty body
17     } // end constructor Count
18
19     // output x
20     void print() const
21     {
22        cout << x << endl;
23     } // end function print
24  private:
25     int x; // data member
26  }; // end class Count
27
28  // function setX can modify private data of Count
29  // because setX is declared as a friend of Count (line 10)
30  void setX( Count &c, int val )
31  {
32     c.x = val; // allowed because setX is a friend of Count
33  } // end function setX
34
```

Fig. 11.15 | Friends can access private members of a class. (Part 1 of 2.)

```
35  int main()
36  {
37     Count counter; // create Count object
38
39     cout << "counter.x after instantiation: ";
40     counter.print();
41
42     setX( counter, 8 ); // set x using a friend function
43     cout << "counter.x after call to setX friend function: ";
44     counter.print();
45     return 0;
46  } // end main
```

```
counter.x after instantiation: 0
counter.x after call to setX friend function: 8
```

Fig. 11.15 | Friends can access `private` members of a class. (Part 2 of 2.)

Function setX (lines 30–33) is a C-style, stand-alone function—it is not a member function of class Count. For this reason, when setX is invoked for object counter, line 42 passes counter as an argument to setX rather than using a handle (such as the name of the object) to call the function, as in

```
counter.setX( 8 );
```

As we mentioned, Fig. 11.15 is a mechanical example of using the friend construct. It would normally be appropriate to define function setX as a member function of class Count. It would also normally be appropriate to separate the program of Fig. 11.15 into three files:

1. A header file (e.g., Count.h) containing the Count class definition, which in turn contains the prototype of friend function setX

2. An implementation file (e.g., Count.cpp) containing the definitions of class Count's member functions and the definition of friend function setX

3. A test program (e.g., CountTest.cpp) with main.

Erroneously Attempting to Modify a `private` Member with a Non-`friend` Function
Figure 11.16 demonstrates the error messages produced by the compiler when non-friend function cannotSetX (lines 29–32) is called to modify private data member x.

```
1   // Fig. 11.16: NonFriends.cpp
2   // Non-friend/non-member functions cannot access private data of a class.
3   #include <iostream>
4   using std::cout;
5   using std::endl;
6
```

Fig. 11.16 | Non-friend/nonmember functions cannot access `private` members. (Part 1 of 2.)

```
7   // Count class definition (note that there is no friendship declaration)
8   class Count
9   {
10  public:
11     // constructor
12     Count()
13        : x( 0 ) // initialize x to 0
14     {
15        // empty body
16     } // end constructor Count
17
18     // output x
19     void print() const
20     {
21        cout << x << endl;
22     } // end function print
23  private:
24     int x; // data member
25  }; // end class Count
26
27  // function cannotSetX tries to modify private data of Count,
28  // but cannot because the function is not a friend of Count
29  void cannotSetX( Count &c, int val )
30  {
31     c.x = val; // ERROR: cannot access private member in Count
32  } // end function cannotSetX
33
34  int main()
35  {
36     Count counter; // create Count object
37
38     cannotSetX( counter, 3 ); // cannotSetX is not a friend
39     return 0;
40  } // end main
```

```
C:\examples\ch11\Fig11_16\NonFriends.cpp(31) : error C2248: 'Count::x'
  : cannot access private member declared in class 'Count'
        C:\examples\ch11\Fig11_16\NonFriends.cpp(24) : see declaration
           of 'Count::x'
        C:\examples\ch11\Fig11_16\NonFriends.cpp(9) : see declaration
           of 'Count'
```

Fig. 11.16 | Non-friend/nonmember functions cannot access private members. (Part 2 of 2.)

It is possible to specify overloaded functions as friends of a class. Each overloaded function intended to be a friend must be explicitly declared in the class definition as a friend of the class.

11.5 Using the this Pointer

We have seen that an object's member functions can manipulate the object's data. How do member functions know *which* object's data members to manipulate? Every object has access to its own address through a pointer called *this* (a Visual C++ keyword). An object's this pointer is *not* part of the object itself—i.e., the size of the memory occupied by the this pointer is not reflected in the result of a sizeof operation on the object. Rather, the this pointer is passed (by the compiler) as an implicit argument to each of the object's non-static member functions. Section 11.7 introduces static class members and explains why the this pointer is *not* implicitly passed to static member functions.

Objects use the this pointer implicitly (as we have done to this point) or explicitly to reference their data members and member functions. The type of the this pointer depends on the type of the object and whether the member function in which this is used is declared const. For example, in a nonconstant member function of class Employee, the this pointer has type Employee * const (a constant pointer to a nonconstant Employee object). In a constant member function of the class Employee, the this pointer has the data type const Employee * const (a constant pointer to a constant Employee object).

The next example shows implicit and explicit use of the this pointer; later in this chapter and in Chapter 12, we show some substantial and subtle examples of using this.

Implicitly and Explicitly Using the this Pointer to Access an Object's Data Members
Figure 11.17 demonstrates the implicit and explicit use of the this pointer to enable a member function of class Test to print the private data x of a Test object.

```cpp
1   // Fig. 11.17: ThisTest.cpp
2   // Using the this pointer to refer to object members.
3   #include <iostream>
4   using std::cout;
5   using std::endl;
6
7   class Test
8   {
9   public:
10     Test( int = 0 ); // default constructor
11     void print() const;
12   private:
13     int x;
14   }; // end class Test
15
16   // constructor
17   Test::Test( int value )
18     : x( value ) // initialize x to value
19   {
20     // empty body
21   } // end constructor Test
22
23   // print x using implicit and explicit this pointers;
24   // the parentheses around *this are required
25   void Test::print() const
26   {
27     // implicitly use the this pointer to access the member x
28     cout << "        x = " << x;
29
```

Fig. 11.17 | this pointer implicitly and explicitly accessing an object's members. (Part 1 of 2.)

```
30        // explicitly use the this pointer and the arrow operator
31        // to access the member x
32        cout << "\n  this->x = " << this->x;
33
34        // explicitly use the dereferenced this pointer and
35        // the dot operator to access the member x
36        cout << "\n(*this).x = " << ( *this ).x << endl;
37     } // end function print
38
39     int main()
40     {
41        Test testObject( 12 ); // instantiate and initialize testObject
42
43        testObject.print();
44        return 0;
45     } // end main
```

```
        x = 12
  this->x = 12
(*this).x = 12
```

Fig. 11.17 | this pointer implicitly and explicitly accessing an object's members. (Part 2 of 2.)

For illustration purposes, member function print (lines 25–37) first prints x by using the this pointer implicitly (line 28)—only the name of the data member is specified. Then print uses two different notations to access x through the this pointer—the arrow operator (->) off the this pointer (line 32) and the dot operator (.) off the dereferenced this pointer (line 36).

Note the parentheses around *this (line 36) when used with the dot member selection operator (.). The parentheses are required because the dot operator has higher precedence than the * operator. Without the parentheses, the expression *this.x would be evaluated as if it were parenthesized as *(this.x), which is a compilation error, because the dot operator cannot be used with a pointer.

Common Programming Error 11.7

Attempting to use the member selection operator (.) with a pointer to an object is a compilation error—the dot member selection operator may be used only with an lvalue such as an object's name, a reference to an object or a dereferenced pointer to an object.

One interesting use of the this pointer is to prevent an object from being assigned to itself. As we'll see in Chapter 12, self-assignment can cause serious errors when the object contains pointers to dynamically allocated storage.

Using the this Pointer to Enable Cascaded Function Calls

Another use of the this pointer is to enable *cascaded member-function calls*—that is, invoking multiple functions in the same statement (as in line 14 of Fig. 11.20). The program of Figs. 11.18–11.20 modifies class Time's *set* functions setTime, setHour, setMinute and setSecond such that each returns a reference to a Time object to enable cascaded member-function calls. Notice in Fig. 11.19 that the last statement in the body of each of these member functions returns *this (lines 26, 33, 40 and 47) into a return type of Time &.

```
 1    // Fig. 11.18: Time.h
 2    // Cascading member function calls.
 3
 4    // Time class definition.
 5    // Member functions defined in Time.cpp.
 6    #ifndef TIME_H
 7    #define TIME_H
 8
 9    class Time
10    {
11    public:
12       Time( int = 0, int = 0, int = 0 ); // default constructor
13
14       // set functions (the Time & return types enable cascading)
15       Time &setTime( int, int, int ); // set hour, minute, second
16       Time &setHour( int ); // set hour
17       Time &setMinute( int ); // set minute
18       Time &setSecond( int ); // set second
19
20       // get functions (normally declared const)
21       int getHour() const; // return hour
22       int getMinute() const; // return minute
23       int getSecond() const; // return second
24
25       // print functions (normally declared const)
26       void printUniversal() const; // print universal time
27       void printStandard() const; // print standard time
28    private:
29       int hour; // 0 - 23 (24-hour clock format)
30       int minute; // 0 - 59
31       int second; // 0 - 59
32    }; // end class Time
33
34    #endif
```

Fig. 11.18 | Time class definition modified to enable cascaded member-function calls.

```
 1    // Fig. 11.19: Time.cpp
 2    // Time class member-function definitions.
 3    #include <iostream>
 4    using std::cout;
 5
 6    #include <iomanip>
 7    using std::setfill;
 8    using std::setw;
 9
10    #include "Time.h" // Time class definition
11
12    // constructor function to initialize private data;
13    // calls member function setTime to set variables;
14    // default values are 0 (see class definition)
```

Fig. 11.19 | Time class member-function definitions modified to enable cascaded member-function calls. (Part 1 of 3.)

```
15    Time::Time( int hr, int min, int sec )
16    {
17       setTime( hr, min, sec );
18    } // end Time constructor
19
20    // set values of hour, minute, and second
21    Time &Time::setTime( int h, int m, int s ) // note Time & return
22    {
23       setHour( h );
24       setMinute( m );
25       setSecond( s );
26       return *this; // enables cascading
27    } // end function setTime
28
29    // set hour value
30    Time &Time::setHour( int h ) // note Time & return
31    {
32       hour = ( h >= 0 && h < 24 ) ? h : 0; // validate hour
33       return *this; // enables cascading
34    } // end function setHour
35
36    // set minute value
37    Time &Time::setMinute( int m ) // note Time & return
38    {
39       minute = ( m >= 0 && m < 60 ) ? m : 0; // validate minute
40       return *this; // enables cascading
41    } // end function setMinute
42
43    // set second value
44    Time &Time::setSecond( int s ) // note Time & return
45    {
46       second = ( s >= 0 && s < 60 ) ? s : 0; // validate second
47       return *this; // enables cascading
48    } // end function setSecond
49
50    // get hour value
51    int Time::getHour() const
52    {
53       return hour;
54    } // end function getHour
55
56    // get minute value
57    int Time::getMinute() const
58    {
59       return minute;
60    } // end function getMinute
61
62    // get second value
63    int Time::getSecond() const
64    {
65       return second;
66    } // end function getSecond
```

Fig. 11.19 | Time class member-function definitions modified to enable cascaded member-function calls. (Part 2 of 3.)

```
67
68   // print Time in universal-time format (HH:MM:SS)
69   void Time::printUniversal() const
70   {
71       cout << setfill( '0' ) << setw( 2 ) << hour << ":"
72           << setw( 2 ) << minute << ":" << setw( 2 ) << second;
73   } // end function printUniversal
74
75   // print Time in standard-time format (HH:MM:SS AM or PM)
76   void Time::printStandard() const
77   {
78       cout << ( ( hour == 0 || hour == 12 ) ? 12 : hour % 12 )
79           << ":" << setfill( '0' ) << setw( 2 ) << minute
80           << ":" << setw( 2 ) << second << ( hour < 12 ? " AM" : " PM" );
81   } // end function printStandard
```

Fig. 11.19 | Time class member-function definitions modified to enable cascaded member-function calls. (Part 3 of 3.)

The program of Fig. 11.20 creates Time object t (line 11), then uses it in cascaded member-function calls (lines 14 and 26). Why does the technique of returning *this as a reference work? The dot operator (.) associates from left to right, so line 14 first evaluates t.setHour(18), then returns a reference to object t as the value of this function call. The remaining expression is then interpreted as

        t.setMinute(30).setSecond(22);

The t.setMinute(30) call executes and returns a reference to the object t. The remaining expression is interpreted as

        t.setSecond(22);

Line 26 also uses cascading. The calls must appear in the order shown in line 26, because printStandard as defined in the class does not return a reference to t. Placing the call to printStandard before the call to setTime in line 26 results in a compilation error. Chapter 12 presents several practical examples of using cascaded function calls. One such example uses multiple << operators with cout to output multiple values in a single statement.

```
1    // Fig. 11.20: CascadingTest.cpp
2    // Cascading member-function calls with the this pointer.
3    #include <iostream>
4    using std::cout;
5    using std::endl;
6
7    #include "Time.h" // Time class definition
8
9    int main()
10   {
11       Time t; // create Time object
12
```

Fig. 11.20 | Cascading member-function calls with the this pointer. (Part 1 of 2.)

```
13        // cascaded function calls
14        t.setHour( 18 ).setMinute( 30 ).setSecond( 22 );
15
16        // output time in universal and standard formats
17        cout << "Universal time: ";
18        t.printUniversal();
19
20        cout << "\nStandard time: ";
21        t.printStandard();
22
23        cout << "\n\nNew standard time: ";
24
25        // cascaded function calls
26        t.setTime( 20, 20, 20 ).printStandard();
27        cout << endl;
28        return 0;
29     } // end main
```

```
Universal time: 18:30:22
Standard time: 6:30:22 PM

New standard time: 8:20:20 PM
```

Fig. 11.20 | Cascading member-function calls with the this pointer. (Part 2 of 2.)

11.6 Dynamic Memory Management with Operators new and delete

Visual C++ enables programmers to control the allocation and deallocation of memory in a program for any built-in or user-defined type. This is known as *dynamic memory management* and is performed with operators *new* and *delete*. Recall that class Employee (Figs. 11.12–11.13) uses two 25-character arrays to represent the first and last name of an Employee. The Employee class definition (Fig. 11.12) must specify the number of elements in each of these arrays when it declares them as data members, because the size of the data members dictates the amount of memory required to store an Employee object. As we discussed earlier, these arrays may waste space for names shorter than 24 characters. Also, names longer than 24 characters must be truncated to fit in these fixed-size arrays.

Wouldn't it be nice if we could use arrays containing exactly the number of elements needed to store an Employee's first and last name? Dynamic memory management allows us to do exactly that. As you'll see in the example of Section 11.7, if we replace array data members firstName and lastName with pointers to char, we can use the new operator to dynamically *allocate* (i.e., reserve) the exact amount of memory required to hold each name at execution time. Dynamically allocating memory in this fashion causes an array (or any other built-in or user-defined type) to be created in the *free store* (also called the *heap*)—a region of memory assigned to each program for storing dynamically allocated objects. Note that we use the term heap (or native heap in C++/CLI sections) rather than free store. Once the memory for an array is allocated on the heap, we can gain access to it by aiming a pointer at the first element of the array. When we no longer need the array, we can return the memory to the heap by using the delete operator to *deallocate* (i.e., release) the memory, which can then be reused by future new operations.

Again, we present the modified `Employee` class as described here in the example of Section 11.7. First, we present the details of using the new and `delete` operators to dynamically allocate memory to store objects, fundamental types and arrays.

Consider the following declaration and statement:

```
Time *timePtr;
timePtr = new Time;
```

The new operator allocates storage of the proper size for an object of type `Time`, calls the default constructor to initialize the object and returns a pointer to the type specified to the right of the new operator (i.e., a `Time *`). Note that new can be used to dynamically allocate any fundamental type (such as `int` or `double`) or class type. If new is unable to find sufficient space in memory for the object, it indicates that an error occurred by "throwing an exception." Chapter 16, Exception Handling, discusses how to deal with new failures in the context of the ISO/IEC C++ standard. In particular, we'll show how to "catch" the exception thrown by new and deal with it. When a program does not "catch" an exception, the program terminates immediately.

Portability Tip 11.1

On failure, the new operator returns a 0 pointer in versions of C++ prior to the ISO/IEC standard. We use the standard version of operator new throughout this book.

To destroy a dynamically allocated object and free the space for the object, use the `delete` operator as follows:

```
delete timePtr;
```

This statement first calls the destructor for the object to which `timePtr` points, then deallocates the memory associated with the object. After the preceding statement, the memory can be reused by the system to allocate other objects.

Common Programming Error 11.8

Not releasing dynamically allocated memory when it is no longer needed can cause the system to run out of memory prematurely. This is sometimes called a "memory leak."

You can provide an *initializer* for a newly created fundamental-type variable, as in

```
double *ptr = new double( 3.14159 );
```

which initializes a newly created `double` to `3.14159` and assigns the resulting pointer to `ptr`. The same syntax can be used to specify a comma-separated list of arguments to the constructor of an object. For example,

```
Time *timePtr = new Time( 12, 45, 0 );
```

initializes a newly created `Time` object to 12:45 PM and assigns the resulting pointer to `timePtr`.

The new operator can be used to allocate arrays dynamically. For example, a 10-element integer array can be allocated and assigned to `gradesArray` as follows:

```
int *gradesArray = new int[ 10 ];
```

which declares int pointer gradesArray and assigns it a pointer to the first element of a dynamically allocated 10-element array of ints. Recall that the size of an array created at compile time must be specified using a constant integral expression. However, the size of a dynamically allocated array can be specified using *any* non-negative integral expression that can be evaluated at execution time. Also note that, when allocating an array of objects dynamically, you cannot pass arguments to each object's constructor. Instead, each object in the array is initialized by its default constructor. To delete the dynamically allocated array to which gradesArray points, use the statement

> *delete* [] gradesArray;

The preceding statement deallocates the array to which gradesArray points. If the pointer in the preceding statement points to an array of objects, the statement first calls the destructor for every object in the array, then deallocates the memory. If the preceding statement did not include the square brackets ([]) and gradesArray pointed to an array of objects, the result is undefined. Some compilers call the destructor only for the first object in the array. Using delete on a null pointer (i.e., a pointer with the value 0) has no effect.

Common Programming Error 11.9

Using delete instead of delete [] for arrays of objects can lead to runtime logic errors. To ensure that every object in the array receives a destructor call, always delete memory allocated as an array with operator delete []. Similarly, always delete memory allocated as an individual element with operator delete; otherwise, the result of the operation is undefined.

11.7 static Class Members

There is an important exception to the rule that each object of a class has its own copy of all the data members of the class. In certain cases, only one copy of a variable should be shared by all objects of a class. A ***static data member*** is used for these and other reasons. Such a variable represents "class-wide" information. In other words, a "property" of the class shared by all instances (don't confuse this with the C++/CLI property keyword). The declaration of a static member begins with keyword static. Recall that the versions of class GradeBook in Chapter 8 use static data members to store constants representing the number of grades that all GradeBook objects can hold.

Let us further motivate the need for static class-wide data with an example. Suppose that we have a video game with Martians and other space creatures. Each Martian tends to be brave and willing to attack other space creatures when the Martian is aware that there are at least five Martians present. If fewer than five are present, each Martian becomes cowardly. So each Martian needs to know the martianCount. We could endow each instance of class Martian with martianCount as a data member. If we do, every Martian will have a separate copy of the data member. Every time we create a new Martian, we'll have to update the data member martianCount in all Martian objects. Doing this would require every Martian object to have, or have access to, handles to all other Martian objects in memory. This wastes space with the redundant copies and wastes time in updating the separate copies. Instead, we declare martianCount to be static. This makes martianCount class-wide data. Every Martian can access martianCount as if it were a data member of the Martian, but only one copy of the static variable martianCount is maintained by

Visual C++. This saves space. We save time by having the `Martian` constructor increment `static` variable `martianCount` and having the `Martian` destructor decrement `martian-Count`. Because there is only one copy, we do not have to increment or decrement separate copies of `martianCount` for each `Martian` object.

Performance Tip 11.3

Use `static` data members to save storage when a single copy of the data for all objects of a class will suffice.

Although they may seem like global variables, a class's `static` data members have class scope. Also, `static` members can be declared `public`, `private` or `protected`. A fundamental-type `static` data member is initialized by default to 0. If you want a different initial value, a `static` data member can be initialized *once* (and only once). A `const static` data member of `int` or `enum` type can be initialized in its declaration in the class definition. However, all other `static` data members must be defined at file scope (i.e., outside the body of the class definition) and can be initialized only in those definitions. Note that `static` data members of class types (i.e., `static` member objects) that have default constructors need not be initialized because their default constructors will be called.

A class's `private` and `protected` `static` members are normally accessed through `public` member functions of the class or through `friend`s of the class. (In Chapter 13, we'll see that a class's `private` and `protected` `static` members can also be accessed through `protected` member functions of the class.) A class's `static` members exist even when no objects of that class exist. To access a `public static` class member when no objects of the class exist, simply prefix the class name and the binary scope resolution operator (`::`) to the name of the data member. For example, if our preceding variable `martian-Count` is `public`, it can be accessed with the expression `Martian::martianCount` when there are no `Martian` objects. (Of course, using `public` data is discouraged.)

A class's `public static` class members can also be accessed through any object of that class using the object's name, the dot operator and the name of the member (e.g., `myMartian.martianCount`). To access a `private` or `protected static` class member when no objects of the class exist, provide a `public static` member function and call the function by prefixing its name with the class name and binary scope resolution operator. (As we'll see in Chapter 13, a `protected static` member function can serve this purpose, too.) A `static` member function is a service of the *class*, not of a specific object of the class.

Software Engineering Observation 11.11

A class's `static` data members and `static` member functions exist and can be used even if no objects of that class have been instantiated.

The program of Figs. 11.21–11.23 demonstrates a `private static` data member called count (Fig. 11.21, line 21) and a `public static` member function called `getCount` (Fig. 11.21, line 15). In Fig. 11.22, line 14 defines and initializes the data member count to zero *at file scope* and lines 18–21 define `static` member function `getCount`. Notice that neither line 14 nor line 18 includes keyword `static`, yet both lines refer to `static` class members. When `static` is applied to an item at file scope, that item becomes known only in that file. The `static` members of the class need to be available from any client code that accesses the file, so we cannot declare them `static` in the `.cpp` file—we declare them

```
1    // Fig. 11.21: Employee.h
2    // Employee class definition.
3    #ifndef EMPLOYEE_H
4    #define EMPLOYEE_H
5
6    class Employee
7    {
8    public:
9       Employee( const char * const, const char * const ); // constructor
10      ~Employee(); // destructor
11      const char *getFirstName() const; // return first name
12      const char *getLastName() const; // return last name
13
14      // static member function
15      static int getCount(); // return number of objects instantiated
16   private:
17      char *firstName;
18      char *lastName;
19
20      // static data
21      static int count; // number of objects instantiated
22   }; // end class Employee
23
24   #endif
```

Fig. 11.21 | Employee class definition with a static data member to track the number of Employee objects in memory.

static only in the .h file. Data member count maintains a count of the number of objects of class Employee that have been instantiated. When objects of class Employee exist, member count can be referenced through any member function of an Employee object—in Fig. 11.22, count is referenced by both line 33 in the constructor and line 48 in the destructor. Also, note that since count is an int, it could have been initialized in the header file in line 21 of Fig. 11.21.

Common Programming Error 11.10

It is a compilation error to include keyword static in the definition of a static data members at file scope.

```
1    // Fig. 11.22: Employee.cpp
2    // Employee class member-function definitions.
3    #include <iostream>
4    using std::cout;
5    using std::endl;
6
7    #include <cstring> // strlen and strcpy prototypes
8    using std::strlen;
9    using std::strcpy;
10
```

Fig. 11.22 | Employee class member-function definitions. (Part 1 of 3.)

```
11  #include "Employee.h" // Employee class definition
12
13  // define and initialize static data member at file scope
14  int Employee::count = 0; // cannot include keyword static
15
16  // define static member function that returns number of
17  // Employee objects instantiated (declared static in Employee.h)
18  int Employee::getCount()
19  {
20     return count;
21  } // end static function getCount
22
23  // constructor dynamically allocates space for first and last name and
24  // uses strcpy to copy first and last names into the object
25  Employee::Employee( const char * const first, const char * const last )
26  {
27     firstName = new char[ strlen( first ) + 1 ]; // create space
28     strcpy( firstName, first ); // copy first into object
29
30     lastName = new char[ strlen( last ) + 1 ]; // create space
31     strcpy( lastName, last ); // copy last into object
32
33     count++; // increment static count of employees
34
35     cout << "Employee constructor for " << firstName
36        << ' ' << lastName << " called." << endl;
37  } // end Employee constructor
38
39  // destructor deallocates dynamically allocated memory
40  Employee::~Employee()
41  {
42     cout << "~Employee() called for " << firstName
43        << ' ' << lastName << endl;
44
45     delete [] firstName; // release memory
46     delete [] lastName; // release memory
47
48     count--; // decrement static count of employees
49  } // end ~Employee destructor
50
51  // return first name of employee
52  const char *Employee::getFirstName() const
53  {
54     // const before return type prevents client from modifying
55     // private data; client should copy returned string before
56     // destructor deletes storage to prevent undefined pointer
57     return firstName;
58  } // end function getFirstName
59
60  // return last name of employee
61  const char *Employee::getLastName() const
62  {
```

Fig. 11.22 | Employee class member-function definitions. (Part 2 of 3.)

```
63      // const before return type prevents client from modifying
64      // private data; client should copy returned string before
65      // destructor deletes storage to prevent undefined pointer
66      return lastName;
67    } // end function getLastName
```

Fig. 11.22 | Employee class member-function definitions. (Part 3 of 3.)

In Fig. 11.22, note the use of the new operator (lines 27 and 30) in the Employee constructor to dynamically allocate the correct amount of memory for members firstName and lastName. If the new operator is unable to fulfill the request for memory for one or both of these character arrays, the program will terminate immediately. In Chapter 16, we'll provide a better mechanism for dealing with cases in which new is unable to allocate memory.

Also note in Fig. 11.22 that the implementations of functions getFirstName (lines 52–58) and getLastName (lines 61–67) return pointers to const character data. In this implementation, if the client wishes to retain a copy of the first name or last name, the client is responsible for copying the dynamically allocated memory in the Employee object after obtaining the pointer to const character data from the object. It is also possible to implement getFirstName and getLastName, so the client is required to pass a character array and the size of the array to each function. Then the functions could copy the first or last name into the character array provided by the client. Once again, note that we could have used class string here to return a copy of a string object to the caller rather than returning a pointer to the private data.

Figure 11.23 uses static member function getCount to determine the number of Employee objects currently instantiated. Note that when no objects are instantiated in the program, the Employee::getCount() function call is issued (lines 14 and 38). However, when objects are instantiated, function getCount can be called through either of the objects, as shown in the statement in lines 22–23, which uses pointer e1Ptr to invoke function getCount. Note that using e2Ptr->getCount() or Employee::getCount() in line 23 would produce the same result, because getCount always accesses the same static member count.

```
 1    // Fig. 11.23: EmployeeTest.cpp
 2    // static data member tracking the number of objects of a class.
 3    #include <iostream>
 4    using std::cout;
 5    using std::endl;
 6
 7    #include "Employee.h" // Employee class definition
 8
 9    int main()
10    {
11       // use class name and binary scope resolution operator to
12       // access static number function getCount
13       cout << "Number of employees before instantiation of any objects is "
14          << Employee::getCount() << endl; // use class name
15
```

Fig. 11.23 | static data member tracking the number of objects of a class. (Part 1 of 2.)

```
16     // use new to dynamically create two new Employees
17     // operator new also calls the object's constructor
18     Employee *e1Ptr = new Employee( "Susan", "Baker" );
19     Employee *e2Ptr = new Employee( "Robert", "Jones" );
20
21     // call getCount on first Employee object
22     cout << "Number of employees after objects are instantiated is "
23        << e1Ptr->getCount();
24
25     cout << "\n\nEmployee 1: "
26        << e1Ptr->getFirstName() << " " << e1Ptr->getLastName()
27        << "\nEmployee 2: "
28        << e2Ptr->getFirstName() << " " << e2Ptr->getLastName() << "\n\n";
29
30     delete e1Ptr; // deallocate memory
31     e1Ptr = 0; // disconnect pointer from free-store space
32     delete e2Ptr; // deallocate memory
33     e2Ptr = 0; // disconnect pointer from free-store space
34
35     // no objects exist, so call static member function getCount again
36     // using the class name and the binary scope resolution operator
37     cout << "Number of employees after objects are deleted is "
38        << Employee::getCount() << endl;
39     return 0;
40  } // end main
```

```
Number of employees before instantiation of any objects is 0
Employee constructor for Susan Baker called.
Employee constructor for Robert Jones called.
Number of employees after objects are instantiated is 2

Employee 1: Susan Baker
Employee 2: Robert Jones

~Employee() called for Susan Baker
~Employee() called for Robert Jones
Number of employees after objects are deleted is 0
```

Fig. 11.23 | static data member tracking the number of objects of a class. (Part 2 of 2.)

Software Engineering Observation 11.12

Some organizations specify in their software engineering standards that all calls to static member functions be made using the class name rather than an object handle.

A member function should be declared static if it does not access non-static data members or non-static member functions of the class. Unlike non-static member functions, a static member function does not have a this pointer, because static data members and static member functions exist independently of any objects of a class. The this pointer must refer to a specific object of the class, and when a static member function is called, there might not be any objects of its class in memory.

Common Programming Error 11.11

Using the this pointer in a static member function is a compilation error.

Common Programming Error 11.12

Declaring a static *member function* const *is a compilation error. The* const *qualifier indicates that a function cannot modify the contents of the object in which it operates, but* static *member functions exist and operate independently of any objects of the class.*

Lines 18–19 of Fig. 11.23 use operator new to dynamically allocate two Employee objects. Remember that the program will terminate immediately if it is unable to allocate one or both of these objects. When each Employee object is allocated, its constructor is called. When delete is used in lines 30 and 32 to deallocate the Employee objects, each object's destructor is called.

Error-Prevention Tip 11.2

After deleting dynamically allocated memory, set the pointer that referred to that memory to 0. This disconnects the pointer from the previously allocated space on the heap. This space in memory could still contain information, despite having been deleted. By setting the pointer to 0, the program loses any access to that free-store space, which, in fact, could have already been reallocated for a different purpose. If you didn't set the pointer to 0, your code could inadvertently access this new information, causing extremely subtle, nonrepeatable logic errors.

Static Constructors

C++/CLI also allows you to define a static constructor. A static constructor for a managed class Date is called before the first use of a Date object. This means the static constructor is called before any instance of Date is created or any reference is made to the class itself, including references to any static data members. The static constructor can be used to initialize static members of the class, but not instance members, as the static constructor is called before any instance of the object type exists. The compiler generates a default static constructor declared as follows

> *static* Date() {};

To use a custom static constructor you simply declare it the same way and initialize static data members to appropriate values inside the body of the constructor. The CLR will automatically call the static constructor before any instances of the class are created. Note that static constructors must always be private (you cannot call the static constructor yourself), cannot take parameters, and cannot return a value.

11.8 Data Abstraction and Information Hiding

A class normally hides its implementation details from its clients. This is called information hiding. As an example of information hiding, let us consider the stack data structure introduced in Section 7.11.

Stacks can be implemented with arrays and with other data structures, such as linked lists. (We discuss stacks and linked lists in Chapter 15, Templates and Generics and Chapter 21, Data Structures.) A client of a stack class need not be concerned with the stack's implementation. The client knows only that when data items are placed in the stack, they will be recalled in last-in, first-out order. The client cares about *what* functionality a stack offers, not about *how* that functionality is implemented. This concept is referred to as *data abstraction*. Although programmers might know the details of a class's implementation, they should not write code that depends on these details. This enables a particular class (such as one that implements a stack and its operations, *push* and *pop*) to be replaced with another version without affecting the rest of the system. As long as the public services of the class do not change (i.e., every original public member function still has the same prototype in the new class definition), the rest of the system is not affected.

Many programming languages emphasize actions. In these languages, data exists to support the actions that programs must take. Data is "less interesting" than actions. Data is "crude." Only a few built-in data types exist, and it is difficult for programmers to create their own types. Visual C++ and the object-oriented style of programming elevate the importance of data. The primary activities of object-oriented programming in Visual C++ are the creation of types (i.e., classes) and the expression of the interactions among objects of those types. To create languages that emphasize data, the programming-languages community needed to formalize some notions about data. The formalization we consider here is the notion of *abstract data types* (*ADTs*), which improve the program development process.

What is an abstract data type? Consider the built-in type int, which most people would associate with an integer in mathematics. Rather, an int is an abstract representation of an integer. Unlike mathematical integers, computer ints are fixed in size. For example, type int on 32-bit machines is typically limited to the range –2,147,483,648 to +2,147,483,647. If the result of a calculation falls outside this range, an "overflow" error occurs and the computer responds in some machine-dependent manner. It might, for example, "quietly" produce an incorrect result, such as a value too large to fit in an int variable (commonly called *arithmetic overflow*). Mathematical integers do not have this problem. Therefore, the notion of a computer int is only an approximation of the notion of a real-world integer. The same is true with double.

Even char is an approximation; char values are normally eight-bit patterns of ones and zeros; these patterns look nothing like the characters they represent, such as a capital Z, a lowercase z, a dollar sign ($), a digit (5), and so on. Values of type char on most computers are quite limited compared with the range of real-world characters. The seven-bit ASCII character set (Appendix B) provides for 128 different character values. This is inadequate for representing languages such as Japanese and Chinese that require thousands of characters. As Internet and World Wide Web usage becomes pervasive, the newer Unicode character set is growing rapidly in popularity, owing to its ability to represent the characters of most languages. For more information on Unicode, visit www.unicode.org.

The point is that even the built-in data types provided with programming languages like C++ are really only approximations or imperfect models of real-world concepts and behaviors. We have taken int for granted until this point, but now you have a new perspective to consider. Types like int, double, char and others are all examples of abstract data types. They are essentially ways of representing real-world notions to some satisfactory level of precision within a computer system.

An abstract data type actually captures two notions—a *data representation* and the *operations* that can be performed on that data. For example, in C++, an int contains an integer value (data) and provides addition, subtraction, multiplication, division and modulus operations (among others)—division by zero is undefined. These allowed operations perform in a manner sensitive to machine parameters, such as the fixed word size of the underlying computer system. Another example is the notion of negative integers, whose operations and data representation are clear, but the operation of taking the square root of a negative integer is undefined. In C++, you can use classes to implement abstract data types and their services. For example, to implement a stack ADT, we create our own stack classes in Chapters 15 and 21, and we study the standard library `stack` class in Chapter 23, Standard Template Library (STL).

11.8.1 Example: Array Abstract Data Type

We discussed arrays in Chapter 8. As described there, an array is not much more than a pointer and some space in memory. This primitive capability is acceptable for performing array operations if you are cautious and undemanding. There are many operations that would be nice to perform with arrays, but that are not built into Visual C++. With Visual C++ classes, you can develop an array ADT that is preferable to "raw" arrays. The array class can provide many helpful new capabilities such as

- subscript range checking
- an arbitrary range of subscripts instead of having to start with 0
- array assignment
- array comparison
- array input/output
- arrays that know their sizes
- arrays that expand dynamically to accommodate more elements
- arrays that can print themselves in neat tabular format.

We create our own array class with many of these capabilities in Chapter 12. Recall that C++ Standard Library class template `vector` (introduced in Chapter 8) provides many of these capabilities as well. Chapter 23 explains class template `vector` in detail. Visual C++ has a small set of built-in types. Classes extend the base programming language with new types.

Software Engineering Observation 11.13

You can create new types through the class mechanism. These new types can be designed to be used as conveniently as the built-in types. Thus, Visual C++ is an extensible *language. Although the language is easy to extend with these new types, the base language itself cannot be changed.*

New classes created in Visual C++ environments can be proprietary to an individual, to small groups or to companies. Classes can also be placed in standard class libraries intended for wide distribution. The C++ Standard includes a standard class library. Once you learn Visual C++ and object-oriented programming, you'll be ready to take advantage of the new kinds of rapid, component-oriented software development made possible with increasingly abundant and rich libraries.

11.8.2 Example: String Abstract Data Type

Visual C++ is an intentionally sparse language that provides programmers with only the raw capabilities needed to build a broad range of systems (consider it a tool for making tools). The language is designed to minimize performance burdens. Visual C++ is appropriate for both applications programming and systems programming—the latter places extraordinary performance demands on programs. Certainly, it would have been possible to include a string data type among Visual C++'s built-in data types. Instead, the language was designed to include mechanisms for creating and implementing string abstract data types through classes. We introduced the C++ Standard Library class string in Chapter 4, and in Chapter 12 we develop our own String ADT. We discuss class string in detail in Chapter 19, Class string and String Stream Processing.

11.8.3 Example: Queue Abstract Data Type

Each of us stands in line from time to time. A waiting line is also called a *queue*. We wait in line at the supermarket to check out, we wait in line to get gasoline, we wait in line to board a bus, we wait in line to pay a highway toll, and students know all too well about waiting in line during registration to get the courses they want. Computer systems use waiting lines internally, so we need to write programs that simulate what queues are and do.

A queue is another example of an abstract data type. Queues offer well-understood behavior to their clients. Clients put things in a queue one at a time—by invoking the queue's *enqueue* operation—and the clients get those things back one at a time on demand—by invoking the queue's *dequeue* operation. Conceptually, a queue can become infinitely long. A real queue, of course, is finite. Items are returned from a queue in *first-in, first-out* (*FIFO*) order—the first item inserted in the queue is the first item removed from the queue.

The queue hides an internal data representation that keeps track of the items currently waiting in line, and it offers a set of operations to its clients, namely, *enqueue* and *dequeue*. The clients are not concerned about the implementation of the queue. Clients merely want the queue to operate "as advertised." When a client enqueues a new item, the queue should accept that item and place it internally in some kind of first-in, first-out data structure. When the client wants the next item from the front of the queue, the queue should remove the item from its internal representation and deliver it to the outside world (i.e., to the client of the queue) in FIFO order (i.e., the item that has been in the queue the longest should be the next one returned by the next *dequeue* operation).

The queue ADT guarantees the integrity of its internal data structure. Clients may not manipulate this data structure directly. Only the queue member functions have access to its internal data. Clients may cause only allowable operations to be performed on the data representation; operations not provided in the ADT's public interface are rejected in some appropriate manner. This could mean issuing an error message, throwing an exception (see Chapter 16), terminating execution or simply ignoring the operation request.

We create our own queue class in Chapter 21, and we study the Standard Library queue class in Chapter 23.

11.9 Container Classes and Iterators

Among the most popular types of classes are *container classes* (also called *collection classes*), i.e., classes designed to hold collections of objects. Container classes commonly provide services such as insertion, deletion, searching, sorting, and testing an item to determine whether it is a member of the collection. Arrays, stacks, queues, trees and linked lists are examples of container classes; we studied arrays in Chapter 8 and will study each of these other data structures in Chapter 21 and Chapter 23.

It is common to associate *iterator objects*—or more simply *iterators*—with container classes. An iterator is an object that "walks through" a collection, returning the next item (or performing some action on the next item). Once an iterator for a class has been written, obtaining the next element from the class can be expressed simply. Just as a book being shared by several people could have several bookmarks in it at once, a container class can have several iterators operating on it at once. Each iterator maintains its own "position" information. We discuss containers and iterators in detail in Chapter 23.

11.10 Proxy Classes

Recall that two of the fundamental principles of good software engineering are separating interface from implementation and hiding implementation details. We strive to achieve these goals by defining a class in a header file and implementing its member functions in a separate implementation file. As we pointed out in Chapter 10, however, header files *do* contain a portion of a class's implementation and hints about others. For example, a class's private members are listed in the class definition in a header file, so these members are visible to clients, even though the clients may not access the private members. Revealing a class's private data in this manner potentially exposes proprietary information to clients of the class. We now introduce the notion of a *proxy class* that allows you to hide even the private data of a class from clients of the class. Providing clients of your class with a proxy class that knows only the public interface to your class enables the clients to use your class's services without giving the clients access to your class's implementation details.

Implementing a proxy class requires several steps, which we demonstrate in Figs. 11.24–11.27. First, we create the class definition for the class that contains the proprietary implementation we would like to hide. Our example class, called Implementation, is shown in Fig. 11.24. The proxy class Interface is shown in Figs. 11.25–11.26. The test program and sample output are shown in Fig. 11.27.

Class Implementation (Fig. 11.24) provides a single private data member called value (the data we would like to hide from the client), a constructor to initialize value and functions setValue and getValue.

```
1   // Fig. 11.24: Implementation.h
2   // Implementation class definition.
3
4   class Implementation
5   {
6   public:
7      // constructor
8      Implementation( int v )
9         : value( v ) // initialize value with v
10     {
11        // empty body
12     } // end constructor Implementation
13
14     // set value to v
15     void setValue( int v )
16     {
```

Fig. 11.24 | Implementation class definition. (Part 1 of 2.)

```
17        value = v; // should validate v
18      } // end function setValue
19
20      // return value
21      int getValue() const
22      {
23          return value;
24      } // end function getValue
25   private:
26      int value; // data that we would like to hide from the client
27   }; // end class Implementation
```

Fig. 11.24 | Implementation class definition. (Part 2 of 2.)

We define a proxy class called Interface (Fig. 11.25) with an identical public interface (except for the constructor and destructor names) to that of class Implementation. The only private member of the proxy class is a pointer to an object of class Implementation. Using a pointer in this manner allows us to hide the implementation details of class Implementation from the client. Notice that the only mentions in class Interface of the proprietary Implementation class are in the pointer declaration (line 17) and in line 6, a *forward class declaration*. When a class definition (such as class Interface) uses only a pointer or reference to an object of another class (such as to an object of class Implementation), the class header file for that other class (which would ordinarily reveal the private data of that class) is not required to be included with #include. This is because the compiler doesn't need to reserve space for an object of the class. The compiler does need to reserve space for the pointer or reference. The sizes of pointers and references are characteristics of the hardware platform on which the compiler runs, so the compiler already knows those sizes. You can simply declare that other class as a data type with a forward class declaration (line 6) before the type is used in the file.

```
1    // Fig. 11.25: Interface.h
2    // Proxy class Interface definition.
3    // Client sees this source code, but the source code does not reveal
4    // the data layout of class Implementation.
5
6    class Implementation; // forward class declaration required by line 17
7
8    class Interface
9    {
10   public:
11      Interface( int ); // constructor
12      void setValue( int ); // same public interface as
13      int getValue() const; // class Implementation has
14      ~Interface(); // destructor
15   private:
16      // requires previous forward declaration (line 6)
17      Implementation *ptr;
18   }; // end class Interface
```

Fig. 11.25 | Proxy class Interface definition.

The member-function implementation file for proxy class `Interface` (Fig. 11.26) is the only file that includes the header file `Implementation.h` (line 5) containing class `Implementation`. The file `Interface.cpp` (Fig. 11.26) is provided to the client as a precompiled object code file along with the header file `Interface.h` that includes the function prototypes of the services provided by the proxy class. Because file `Interface.cpp` is made available to the client only as object code, the client is not able to see the interactions between the proxy class and the proprietary class (lines 9, 17, 23 and 29). Notice that the proxy class imposes an extra "layer" of function calls as the "price to pay" for hiding the `private` data of class Implementation. Given the speed of today's computers and the fact that many compilers can inline simple function calls automatically, the effect of these extra function calls on performance is often negligible.

Figure 11.27 tests class `Interface`. Notice that only the header file for `Interface` is included in the client code (line 7)—there is no mention of the existence of a separate class called `Implementation`. Thus, the client never sees the `private` data of class Implementation, nor can the client code become dependent on the Implementation code.

Software Engineering Observation 11.14

A proxy class insulates client code from implementation changes.

```
1   // Fig. 11.26: Interface.cpp
2   // Implementation of class Interface--client receives this file only
3   // as precompiled object code, keeping the implementation hidden.
4   #include "Interface.h" // Interface class definition
5   #include "Implementation.h" // Implementation class definition
6
7   // constructor
8   Interface::Interface( int v )
9      : ptr ( new Implementation( v ) ) // initialize ptr to point to
10  {                                     // a new Implementation object
11     // empty body
12  } // end Interface constructor
13
14  // call Implementation's setValue function
15  void Interface::setValue( int v )
16  {
17     ptr->setValue( v );
18  } // end function setValue
19
20  // call Implementation's getValue function
21  int Interface::getValue() const
22  {
23     return ptr->getValue();
24  } // end function getValue
25
26  // destructor
27  Interface::~Interface()
28  {
29     delete ptr;
30  } // end ~Interface destructor
```

Fig. 11.26 | `Interface` class member-function definitions.

```
1    // Fig. 11.27: InterfaceTest.cpp
2    // Hiding a class's private data with a proxy class.
3    #include <iostream>
4    using std::cout;
5    using std::endl;
6
7    #include "Interface.h" // Interface class definition
8
9    int main()
10   {
11       Interface i( 5 ); // create Interface object
12
13       cout << "Interface contains: " << i.getValue()
14          << " before setValue" << endl;
15
16       i.setValue( 10 );
17
18       cout << "Interface contains: " << i.getValue()
19          << " after setValue" << endl;
20       return 0;
21   } // end main
```

```
Interface contains: 5 before setValue
Interface contains: 10 after setValue
```

Fig. 11.27 | Implementing a proxy class.

11.11 const and friend in C++/CLI

const in C++/CLI

There is an important difference between the way C++/CLI uses const compared to native C++. In managed code with C++/CLI you cannot declare a function of any type to be const. Recall from Section 11.2 that Visual C++ doesn't allow member function calls for const objects unless the member functions themselves are also declared const. This is true whether writing native or managed code. But we cannot declare functions to be const with managed code in C++/CLI. As a result, although we can declare an object const in C++/CLI there is little we can do with it afterwards without the ability to write const functions. This is an unfortunate limitation of the CLR. The reason for this change is due to C++/CLI's role as a tool to interoperate between languages. Many .NET languages (such as C#) do not include the concept of const that C++ does. Consequently, declaring const functions in C++/CLI would make it impossible for those functions to be used across languages.

Despite this, there are still useful ways to use const to enforce the principle of least privilege in C++/CLI. As mentioned in Chapter 9, you may still use const with handles and function arguments much like const is used with pointers. This is useful whenever you pass a reference to a function but want to limit what modifications can be made to the reference or the data it points to. Note that managed arrays do not support the const modifier. This means you cannot declare or pass managed arrays in C++/CLI with const.

C++/CLI adds two new context-sensitive keywords to use in situations with managed classes where const would be used in native classes. A static const data member in native

C++ should be declared using just the keyword *literal* in C++/CLI. A `literal` data member must be initialized upon declaration to a constant (such as a constant integer or `String` value). Note that a `literal` must be a class data member. It cannot be a global `static` variable. Another new keyword in C++/CLI is *initonly*. Declare a member variable `initonly` to specify that it can only be assigned a value inside a constructor of the class and nowhere else. Note that `initonly` does not mean the variable cannot be reassigned a value, only that it cannot be assigned or reassigned a value outside a constructor. `Literal` and `initonly` are context-sensitive keywords. This means that the Visual Studio 2008 compiler only recognizes them as keywords when placed as the first term in a variable declaration. The compiler will issue a compilation error if they are placed elsewhere in a variable declaration. Outside a variable declaration they can be used as identifier names. However, this capability is provided to ensure compatibility with existing C++ programs that may have used these terms as identifiers. To avoid confusion, when writing a new application we recommend using them only as keywords and not as identifier names.

friend in C++/CLI

C++/CLI managed classes cannot declare `friend` classes or functions. Only native classes can use the `friend` keyword. Note that a native class can declare a managed class a `friend`.

11.12 Dynamic Memory Management in C++/CLI

Recall from Section 8.12 that we introduced the keyword gcnew for creating managed arrays with C++/CLI. We explain gcnew in a broader context now that you have learned about dynamic memory management with new and delete. Just as new is used to allocate memory for objects in native C++, gcnew is used to allocate memory for managed objects in C++/CLI. When the new keyword is used, memory is allocated on the native heap for an object and the operation returns a pointer to the newly allocated memory. Similarly, gcnew allocates memory on the managed heap for managed objects and returns a handle to the newly allocated block of memory. By using a separate keyword for allocating memory on the managed heap C++/CLI makes it clear where an object is being created.

Let's look back at how we create managed arrays now that you have learned about handles and memory management. The statement

```
array< int >^ managedArray = gcnew array< int >{ 1, 2, 3 };
```

declares a handle to a managed array of integers, uses gcnew to allocate memory on the managed heap to store 3 integers, and assigns the resulting handle to managedArray. You could dynamically allocate memory on the managed heap for objects of a managed class Date with the declaration

```
Date ^dHandle = gcnew Date;
```

As you can see, you use gcnew to dynamically allocate memory for managed objects exactly as you would use new to do so in native C++.

To destroy a dynamically allocated object on the managed heap and free space for it you have 2 options. First, C++/CLI supports the use of delete as described in Section 11.6, a concept called *deterministic destruction*. This allows you to perform manual memory management with managed code in a way syntactically similar to native C++. This includes using delete [] to properly deallocate memory for a managed array.

For instance, to deallocate memory on the managed heap for managedArray from above we use the statement

```
delete [] managedArray;
```

just as we would with a native C++ array. Note that delete does not actually deallocate the memory of a managed object. It invokes the class destructor to perform termination housekeeping and the garbage collector is responsible for eventually deallocating and reclaiming the memory. As with pointers in native C++, it is good practice to set a handle to nullptr after using delete. Doing this can also improve performance because it helps the garbage collector more quickly find that the object that was referenced is now garbage.

Good Programming Practice 11.2

Assign a handle the value nullptr after using delete. This ensures no future code can try to call member functions of the deleted object.

As discussed in Section 9.14, C++/CLI uses a garbage collector that will automatically manage memory for you. This means that managed objects that are not deallocated manually with the delete operator will be deallocated automatically when the garbage collector runs. In doing so, the garbage collector ensures that a memory leak isn't caused by forgetting to deallocate a managed object. In fact, you can completely avoid using delete with managed types if you want and the garbage collector will take care of memory deallocation (though this isn't recommended for some types). The way the garbage collector works is called *nondeterministic finalization*. This means you cannot predict exactly when the garbage collector will run. Furthermore, when the garbage collector does run you cannot guarantee which objects will be deallocated. Among those objects that are being deallocated you cannot guarantee the order in which they will be deallocated. This is particularly important when dealing with objects representing resources like files and network connections. It is always best to manually delete objects which represent these sorts of resources so that you can guarantee when memory is deallocated (see Chapter 16 for more detail). Overall, the garbage collector greatly enhances program reliability by freeing the programmer of the responsibility of manual memory deallocation with only a slight cost in performance. Many languages provide either deterministic destruction or nondeterministic finalization, C++/CLI provides the best of both worlds so that you can manually delete objects when speed and determinism are critical and otherwise let the garbage collector deallocate memory as necessary. Note that the CLR garbage collector is highly optimized so you should never explicitly invoke the garbage collector.

It is important to remember that unmanaged objects will never be deallocated by the garbage collector. The garbage collector has no knowledge of objects that are not allocated on the managed heap. Consequently, you must still be careful to properly call delete to release the memory they occupy or else risk causing a memory leak.

11.13 Stack Semantics in C++/CLI

Now that you have learned about dynamic memory management we explain a powerful concept introduced in C++/CLI for managed objects that was not present in its predecessor, Managed Extensions for C++. In previous chapters you have created objects in native C++ without the new operator. When you create a native object without using new, Visual

C++ stores the object (an automatic variable) on the stack instead of the native heap. The stack memory is automatically managed by the runtime so that you are not required to call delete for objects created on the stack. This is extremely useful for avoiding causing memory leaks. For instance, using the Time class from Figure 11.2 the declaration

```
Time t( 10, 30, 45 );
```

initializes a Time object t on the stack with the specified parameters. As you learned in Section 10.8, when this object goes out of scope its destructor is implicitly called and the memory it occupied will be automatically deallocated without requiring the programmer to explicitly call delete. This style of declaration is called *stack semantics*. Alternatively, the programmer could use new and delete to dynamically allocate memory and store the Time object on the heap. The advantage of allocating an object on the stack, besides the automatic memory management, is that it is generally faster than allocating an object on the heap. However, the stack is small and does not allow you to allocate memory dynamically at runtime. For instance, to create an array on the stack you must know its size at compile time, if you do not, then you must use dynamic memory allocation to store the array on the heap.

In Microsoft's first attempt to bind C++ to the CLR it was not possible to use stack semantics with managed objects. C++/CLI remedies this problem and allows the programmer to declare managed objects in a form just like the one above used with the Time class. If we dynamically allocated memory for a managed object d using gcnew as follows:

```
Date ^d = gcnew Date;
```

we would have 2 options for deallocating memory. We could use delete, but occasionally we may forget to do this properly. Even more likely, someone else using our class forgets to properly use delete. If delete isn't used then we let the garbage collector nondeterministically deallocate memory at some point in the future. Using delete is preferable for certain types of objects (discussed later), but always remembering to use delete for every object can be difficult. Using stack semantics we can declare a managed object of a managed class Date as follows:

```
Date d;
```

In many C++/CLI examples earlier in the book you used this style of declaration unaware of the full meaning. Although it looks like d is allocated on the stack this is not the case. C++/CLI does not create this object on the stack because managed types must always be allocated on the managed heap. Behind the scenes the compiler is still allocating d on the managed heap and creating a handle. By declaring the object with stack semantics you are able to access it like a stack-based object. The advantage of this, besides more concise syntax, is that it also ensures deterministic destruction is used when d goes out of scope. Like an automatic variable in native C++, declaring a managed object with stack semantics means its destructor is implicitly called when the object goes out of scope. This gives our code the performance and reliability of deterministic destruction without having to use gcnew and delete with each managed object we create. In Section 16.16 you will see how stack semantics also provides a useful way to avoid having to write explicit exception handling code in certain cases.

Note that unfortunately C++/CLI does not allow you to use stack semantics with three specific managed types: `String` objects, managed arrays, and delegates. Objects of these types must always be defined as handles to their respective type. Any other C++/CLI type, and any custom types you create, can all be declared using stack semantics.

11.14 Finalizers

Managed objects in C++/CLI have constructors and a destructor just like unmanaged objects in native C++. The compiler will automatically create a default constructor and destructor for managed types as with native types. Managed objects can also have, but don't require, a *finalizer*. A finalizer is declared similarly to the destructor but using the *! character* preceding the class name instead of the ~ character. Although the syntax is similar, finalizers do not function like destructors. The compiler will not generate a finalizer for you. In fact, rarely should you ever write an explicit finalizer. The only case where it is necessary is when a managed type includes unmanaged objects as members or references.

Imagine we have created a managed class `ManagedFileHandler`, which we anticipate other programmers using in the future. We have explicitly written a destructor to perform critical termination housekeeping on our `ManagedFileHandler` objects before they are reclaimed by the garbage collector. Unfortunately, we have no guarantee that someone using a `ManagedFileHandler` object will properly call `delete` on it as necessary. Thus the destructor may never be called before the garbage collector runs and reclaims the memory our object used. This isn't a problem if `ManagedFileHandler` consists solely of other managed objects. The garbage collector can figure out how to properly reclaim the memory from any managed objects that were data members. But if a class, such as `ManagedFile-Handler`, has a data member that is an unmanaged object (or a reference to one) then we need to manually clean up the unmanaged object before the garbage collector reclaims the memory of `ManagedFileHandler`. Recall that the garbage collector has no knowledge of objects not allocated on the managed heap, so we cannot rely on it to do this cleanup.

To ensure that the critical termination housekeeping will be performed on unmanaged data members, you can write a finalizer. If it exists, the finalizer is the last member function called on an object before the garbage collector reclaims the object's memory, even if `delete` was never used. If you do write a finalizer you should make sure the class destructor calls the finalizer to perform cleanup on the unmanaged resources.

The garbage collector does an excellent job of cleaning up managed objects. You should never write a finalizer for a class that only involves managed objects because the garbage collector can reclaim the memory from objects of that class without difficulty. In fact, writing a finalizer incurs a significant performance cost both in allocation and deallocation of the object. No examples in this book use managed objects with finalizers. We mention it only because it is an important part of the CLR's memory management capabilities.

11.15 Value Types vs. Reference Types in C++/CLI

In native C++, all types are *value types*—that is, a variable of a native C++ type is allocated on the function-call stack by default, and when such a variable is passed to a function, a copy of the variable's value is passed. As you know, variables can be passed by reference in native C++ by using pointers or references.

C++/CLI Types

In C++/CLI, types are divided into two categories based on how they are defined—value types and *reference types.* A managed class that is defined using the ref class syntax is a reference type (hence the ref part of the keyword) and is always allocated on the managed heap. As you learned in Section 11.13, C++/CLI provides the convenience of stack semantics with managed objects, but such objects are still allocated on the managed heap behind the scenes. In our prior discussions of managed objects, we've dealt only with managed reference types.

C++/CLI also allows managed value types defined with the *value class* keyword. A managed value type object can be allocated on the stack, the native heap, or the managed heap depending on the syntax used to create it. For instance, given the following value class definition:

```
value class Val
{
    // body of class definition
};
```

we could declare a Val object on the stack using stack semantics.

```
Val v;
```

Unlike when we used stack semantics previously with managed objects, a Val object actually is allocated on the stack itself. There is no implicit allocation on the managed heap as there is when creating a ref class object with stack semantics. You can create a Val object on the native heap using a native pointer and the new operator as follows:

```
Val *vPtr = new Val;
```

Now we've allocated a managed value object on the native heap and created a native pointer that holds the memory location where it resides. As you can see, these two declaration styles allow managed classes defined with value class to perform like native C++ classes in terms of memory allocation. Unlike native C++ classes, you can also allocate a managed value type on the managed heap using a handle and gcnew as follows:

```
Val ^vHandle = gcnew Val;
```

Now we are using a handle with a managed object in the same style we explained in Section 11.12. This makes managed value types flexible in where they are stored. Remember that the handle itself is allocated on the stack but points to an object on the managed heap. Note that the C++/CLI enumerations introduced in Section 7.22 using keyword enum class are value types, not reference types.

Using Managed Value Types

There are many limitations of managed value classes not present with managed reference classes. Managed value types are implicitly given the sealed keyword, so they cannot be used as a base class (see Section 14.10). They are passed by value by default. They have a default constructor generated by the compiler that cannot be overridden. They also have a default copy constructor and default assignment operator generated by the compiler. These perform memberwise assignment and they cannot be overridden. Managed value types cannot contain a destructor. They cannot contain a member that is a friend. And although you can create a managed value type on the stack or native heap, they cannot have an object of a native class or native array as data members.

So when should you use a managed value class? You should create a value class rather than a ref class the new type will be used primarily to encapsulate data stored in other value types. Objects of this new type should be small so they don't incur the large performance penalty of pass-by-value. They can provide a convenient way to encapsulate a group of related data. For instance, suppose we are writing a graphics application that has many functions that require pixels with *x* and *y* coordinates. Rather than constantly pass separate integers representing *x* and *y* coordinates of pixels we could create a value type Pixel that has 2 data members to hold the *x* and *y* coordinates. Now we can just pass Pixel objects (by value or via a reference) that encapsulate the data we need. A similar use of managed value classes could be used with complex numbers to encapsulate their real and imaginary components in a single object. Value types are also useful for creating classes of "smart pointers," a topic we cover in later chapters.

Note that we still use the term managed object to refer specifically to C++/CLI classes defined with ref class. In later chapters, we note explicitly when we're describing something specific to managed value types.

11.16 Boxing and Unboxing in C++/CLI

A simple type is defined to be those value types that are built-in types of the language (such as int, bool, float and so on). In C++/CLI all simple types inherit from class *ValueType* in namespace System. Class ValueType inherits from class Object (also in namespace System). Thus, any simple-type value can be assigned to a variable of type "handle to Object"; this is referred to as a ***boxing conversion***. In a boxing conversion, the simple-type value on the stack is copied into a newly created object on the managed heap so that the simple-type value can be manipulated as an Object. Boxing conversions can be performed either explicitly or implicitly as shown in the following statements:

```
int i = 5; // create an int value on the stack

// explicitly box the int value
Object ^object1 = static_cast< Object ^ >( i );
Object ^object2 = i; // implicitly box the int value
```

After executing the preceding code, both object1 and object2 refer to two different Objects that contain a copy of the integer value in int variable i. Each assignment of i to a reference type causes a new Object to be created on the managed heap implicitly. Note that you must use a handle to Object. Attempting to assign i directly to an Object variable results in a compilation error because Object does not define a copy constructor. By using a handle to Object the assignment of i is reassigning the handle to point at a derived type rather than attempting to invoke a non-existent copy constructor.

An ***unboxing conversion*** can be used to explicitly convert an Object reference to a simple value as shown in the following statement:

```
int x = static_cast< int >( object1 );
```

Explicitly attempting to unbox an Object reference that does not refer to the correct simple value type causes an ***InvalidCastException***. Alternatively, if you create a handle to the same type as the simple-type, you can simply dereference the handle as follows:

```
int i = 5; // create an int value on the stack
int ^intObject = i; // implicitly box the int value in an int object
int x = *intObject; // implicitly unbox the int object
```

Here instead of using a handle to Object we used a handle to int. So unboxing can be implicitly performed by dereferencing intObject rather than requiring an explicit cast.

These boxing and unboxing conversions are relevant whenever using simple-types in managed code. They are equally applicable with user defined value types. When defining a value type with value class as explained in Section 11.16 the class automatically inherits from class ValueType. As a result, user-defined value types are boxed and unboxed the same way as simple-types. It is important to be aware of when boxing conversions occur as they can impact performance significantly, especially if placed in a loop or a repeated function call. On the other hand, boxing can be helpful because it allows you to treat value types as objects in certain cases. This is particularly useful with interfaces and polymorphism, topics you will learn about in Chapter 14.

In Chapter 15, Templates and Generics, and Chapter 25, Collections, we discuss C++/CLI's generics and generic collections. As you will see, generics eliminate the overhead of boxing and unboxing conversions by enabling us to create and use collections of specific value types.

11.17 Indexers

Chapter 4 introduced properties as a way to access a managed class's private data in a controlled manner via the properties' get and set accessors. Sometimes a managed class encapsulates lists of data such as arrays. Such a class can define property-like class members called *indexers* (or index properties) that allow array-style indexed access to lists of elements. With "conventional" managed arrays, the index must be an integer value. A benefit of indexers is that you can define both integer indices and non-integer indices. For example, you could allow client code to manipulate data using Strings as indices that represent the data items' names or descriptions. When manipulating "conventional" managed array elements, the array element access operator always returns a value of the same type—i.e., the type of the array. Indexers are more flexible—they can return any type, even one that is different from the type of the underlying data.

Although an indexer's element access operator is used like an array element access operator, indexers are defined like properties in a class. Indexers can be defined with a specific name like normal properties or with context-sensitive keyword *default*. Indexers have the general form:

```
accessModifier returnType indexerName[ IndexType1, IndexType2, ... ]
{
    returnType get( IndexType1 parameter1, IndexType2 parameter2, ... )
    {
        // use parameter1, parameter2, ... here to get data
    }
    void set( IndexType1 parameter1, IndexType2 parameter2, ... )
    {
        // use parameter1, parameter2, ... here to set data
    }
}
```

The *IndexType* parameters specified in the brackets ([]) are accessible to the get and set accessors. These accessors define how to use the index (or indices) to retrieve or modify the appropriate data member. Note that the parameters in the brackets cannot be named or else Visual Studio will issue a compilation error. Assign each parameter a name in the respective parameter list of the get and set accessors. As with properties, the indexer's get accessor must return a value of type *returnType*.

Common Programming Error 11.13

Unlike normal properties, declaring indexers as static is a syntax error.

We demonstrate a class Box with indexers defined in Figure 11.28. In Figure 11.29 we use the indexers to access and set elements of a Box object with array-style access.

Figure 11.28 defines the managed class Box. The 2 private data members of class Box are String^ array names (line 66), which contains the names (i.e., "length", "width" and "height") for the dimensions of a Box, and double array dimensions (line 67), which contains the size of each dimension. Remember that you cannot initialize non-static data members of a ref class so we use gcnew to populate the arrays inside the class constructor (lines 16 and 18). Each element in array names corresponds to an element in array dimensions (e.g., dimensions[2] contains the height of the Box).

```
1   // Fig. 11.28: Box.h
2   // Box class definition represents a box with length, width and height
3   // dimensions with indexers.
4
5   #include "stdafx.h"
6
7   using namespace System;
8
9   ref class Box
10  {
11  public:
12     // constructor
13     Box( double length, double width, double height )
14     {
15        // allocate memory for names array and assign values
16        names = gcnew array< String ^ > { "length", "width", "height" };
17        // allocate memory for dimensions array and assign values
18        dimensions = gcnew array< double >{ length, width, height };
19     }
20
21     // index to access dimensions by integer index number
22     property double default[ int ]
23     {
24        double get( int index )
25        {
26           // validate index to get
27           if ( ( index < 0 ) || ( index > dimensions->Length ) )
28              return -1;
```

Fig. 11.28 | Box class definition represents a box with length, width and height dimensions with indexers. (Part 1 of 2.)

```
29          else
30              return dimensions[ index ];
31      } // end get
32      void set( int index, double value )
33      {
34          // validate index to set
35          if ( ( index >= 0 ) && ( index < dimensions->Length ) )
36              dimensions[ index ] = value;
37      } // end set
38   } // end int indexer
39
40   // indexer to access array elements by their String names
41   property double Name[ String ^ ]
42   {
43      double get( String ^ name )
44      {
45          // locate element to get
46          int i = 0;
47          while ( ( i < names->Length )
48              && ( name->ToLower() != names[ i ] ) )
49              i++;
50
51          return ( i == names->Length ? -1 : dimensions[ i ] );
52      }
53      void set( String ^ name, double value )
54      {
55          // locate element to set
56          int i = 0;
57          while ( ( i < names->Length )
58              && ( name->ToLower() != names[ i ] ) )
59              i++;
60
61          if ( i != names->Length )
62              dimensions[ i ] = value;
63      } // end set
64   } // end String indexer
65 private:
66      array< String ^ > ^names;
67      array< double > ^dimensions;
68 }; // end managed class Box
```

Fig. 11.28 | Box class definition represents a box with length, width and height dimensions with indexers. (Part 2 of 2.)

```
1   // Fig. 11.29: Indexers.cpp
2   // Create a Box object and use indexers to get and set data members
3
4   #include "stdafx.h"
5   #include "Box.h"
6
7   using namespace System;
```

Fig. 11.29 | Indexers provide array-style access to an object's members. (Part 1 of 2.)

```
8
9    int main( array< System::String ^ > ^args )
10   {
11       Box ^box = gcnew Box( 30, 30, 30 ); // create a Box
12
13       // show dimensions with numeric indexers
14       Console::WriteLine( "Created a box with the dimensions:" );
15       Console::WriteLine( "box[ 0 ] = {0}", box[ 0 ] );
16       Console::WriteLine( "box[ 1 ] = {0}", box[ 1 ] );
17       Console::WriteLine( "box[ 2 ] = {0}", box[ 2 ] );
18
19       // set a dimension with the numeric indexer
20       Console::WriteLine( "\nSetting box[ 0 ] to 10...\n" );
21       box[ 0 ] = 10;
22
23       // set a dimension with the String indexer
24       Console::WriteLine( "\nSetting box[ \"width\" ] to 20...\n" );
25       box->Name[ "width" ] = 20;
26
27       // show dimensions with String indexers
28       Console::WriteLine( "Created a box with the dimensions:" );
29       Console::WriteLine(
30          "box[ \"length\" ] = {0}", box->Name[ "length" ] );
31       Console::WriteLine( "box[ \"width\" ] = {0}", box->Name[ "width" ] );
32       Console::WriteLine( "box[ \"height\" ] = {0}", box->Name[ "height" ] );
33
34       return 0;
35   } // end main
```

```
Created a box with the dimensions:
box[ 0 ] = 30
box[ 1 ] = 30
box[ 2 ] = 30

Setting box[ 0 ] to 10...

Setting box[ "width" ] to 20...

Created a box with the dimensions:
box[ "length" ] = 10
box[ "width" ] = 20
box[ "height" ] = 30
```

Fig. 11.29 | Indexers provide array-style access to an object's members. (Part 2 of 2.)

Box defines two indexers (lines 22–38 and lines 41–64) that each return a double value representing the size of the dimension specified by the indexer's parameter. The first indexer (line 22) uses the name default. An indexer that uses this context-sensitive keyword means the indexer is accessed simply by using the object name followed by brackets ([ ]), just like if it were an actual array. The first indexer uses an int index to manipulate an element in the dimensions array. Indexers can be overloaded like functions so we could have named the second indexer default as well. Then the compiler would simply choose which indexer to use based on the index parameter inside the brackets after the object name. Instead, we've chosen to name the String ^ indexer Name to demonstrate the use of *named indexers*. You can see how we access named indexers differently on lines 25 and lines 30-32. We specify the name of the indexer like a member function followed by brackets containing the index parameter. The second indexer uses a String ^ index representing the name of the dimension to manipulate an element in the dimensions array. Each indexer returns -1 if its get accessor encounters an invalid subscript. Each indexer's set accessor assigns index to the appropriate element of dimensions only if the index is valid. Normally, you would have an indexer throw an exception if it receives an invalid index. We discuss how to throw exceptions in Chapter 16, Exception Handling.

Notice that the String ^ indexer Name uses a while structure to search for matching Strings in the names array (lines 47–48 and lines 57–58). We use the .NET function ToLower from the System::String class to convert the String index parameter to all lowercase letters. This ensures the index parameter is correctly matched to one of the dimension names that are defined in all lowercase (line 18). If a match is found, the indexer manipulates the corresponding element in array dimensions (lines 51 and 62).

Figure 11.29 manipulates the private data members of class Box through Box's indexers. Local variable box is declared at line 11, and initialized to a new instance of class Box. We use the Box constructor to initialize box with dimensions of 30, 30, and 30. Lines 15–17 use the indexer declared with parameter int to obtain the three dimensions of box, and display them with WriteLine. The expression box[0] (line 15) implicitly calls the get accessor of the indexer to obtain the value of box's private instance variable dimensions[0]. Similarly, the assignment to box[0] in line 21 implicitly calls the set accessor in lines 32-37 of Fig. 11.28. The set accessor sets the value parameter to 10, then sets dimensions[0] to value (10). Lines 25 and 30-32 in Fig. 11.29 take similar actions, using the named indexer with a String^ parameter to manipulate the same data.

11.18 Wrap-Up

In this chapter, we introduced several advanced topics related to classes and data abstraction. You learned how to specify const objects and const member functions to prevent modifications to objects, thus enforcing the principle of least privilege. You also learned that, through composition, a class can have objects of other classes as members. We introduced the topic of friendship and presented examples that demonstrate how to use friend functions.

You learned that the this pointer is passed as an implicit argument to each of a class's non-static member functions, allowing the functions to access the correct object's data members and other non-static member functions. You also saw explicit use of the this pointer to access the class's members and to enable cascaded member-function calls.

We introduced the concept of dynamic memory management. You learned that you can create and destroy objects dynamically with the new and delete operators, respectively. We motivated the need for static data members and demonstrated how to declare and use static data members and static member functions in your own classes.

You learned about data abstraction and information hiding—two of the fundamental concepts of object-oriented programming. We discussed abstract data types—ways of representing real-world or conceptual notions to some satisfactory level of precision within a computer system. You then learned about three example abstract data types—arrays, strings and queues. We introduced the concept of a container class that holds a collection of objects, as well as the notion of an iterator class that walks through the elements of a container class. Finally, you learned how to create a proxy class to hide the implementation details (including the `private` data members) of a class from clients of the class.

You learned about differences with `const` usage in C++/CLI compared to native C++. We also discussed dynamic memory management in C++/CLI using `gcnew` and the use of stack semantics to enable automatic deterministic destruction. We also explained the differences between value types and reference types in native and managed code. You learned the basics of finalizers of managed objects. Finally, you learned how to use indexers to provide array-style access for lists of elements in a class.

In Chapter 12, we continue our study of classes and objects by showing how to enable Visual C++'s operators to work with objects—a process called operator overloading. For example, you'll see how to "overload" the `<<` operator so it can be used to output a complete array without explicitly using a repetition statement.

Summary

Section 11.2 const (Constant) Objects and const Member Functions
- The keyword `const` can be used to specify that an object is not modifiable and that any attempt to modify the object should result in a compilation error.
- Visual C++ compilers disallow non-const member function calls on `const` objects.
- An attempt by a const member function to modify an object of its class is a compilation error.
- A function is specified as `const` both in its prototype and in its definition.
- A `const` object must be initialized, not assigned to.
- Constructors and destructors cannot be declared `const`.
- const data member and reference data members *must* be initialized using member initializers.

Section 11.3 Composition: Objects as Members of Classes
- A class can have objects of other classes as members—this concept is called composition.
- Member objects are constructed in the order in which they are declared in the class definition and before their enclosing class objects are constructed.
- If a member initializer is not provided for a member object, the member object's default constructor will be called implicitly.

Section 11.4 friend Functions and friend Classes
- A `friend` function of a class is defined outside that class's scope, yet has the right to access the non-public (and `public`) members of the class. Stand-alone functions or entire classes may be declared to be friends of another class.
- A friend declaration can appear anywhere in the class. A friend is essentially a part of the `public` interface of the class.
- The friendship relation is neither symmetric nor transitive.

Section 11.5 Using the this Pointer
- Every object has access to its own address through the `this` pointer.
- An object's `this` pointer is not part of the object itself—i.e., the size of the memory occupied by the `this` pointer is not reflected in the result of a `sizeof` operation on the object.

- The this pointer is passed (by the compiler) as an implicit argument to each of the object's non-static member functions.

- Objects use the this pointer implicitly (as we have done to this point) or explicitly to reference their data members and member functions.

- The this pointer enables cascaded member-function calls in which multiple functions are invoked in the same statement.

Section 11.6 Dynamic Memory Management with Operators *new* and *delete*

- Dynamic memory management enables programmers to control the allocation and deallocation of memory in a program for any built-in or user-defined type.

- The free store (also called the heap) is a region of memory assigned to each program for storing objects dynamically allocated at execution time.

- The new operator allocates storage of the proper size for an object, runs the object's constructor and returns a pointer of the correct type. The new operator can be used to dynamically allocate any fundamental type (such as int or double) or class type. If new is unable to find space in memory for the object, it indicates that an error occurred by "throwing" an "exception." This usually causes the program to terminate immediately, unless the exception is handled.

- To destroy a dynamically allocated object and free the space for the object, use the delete operator.

- An array of objects can be allocated dynamically with new as in

    ```
    int *ptr = new int[ 100 ];
    ```

    which allocates an array of 100 integers and assigns the starting location of the array to ptr. The preceding array of integers is deleted with the statement

    ```
    delete [] ptr;
    ```

Section 11.7 *static* Class Members

- A static data member represents "class-wide" information (i.e., a property of the class shared by all instances, not a property of a specific object of the class).

- static data members have class scope and can be declared public, private or protected.

- A class's static members exist even when no objects of that class exist.

- To access a public static class member when no objects of the class exist, simply prefix the class name and the binary scope resolution operator (::) to the name of the data member.

- A class's public static class members can be accessed through any object of that class.

- A member function should be declared static if it does not access non-static data members or non-static member functions of the class. Unlike non-static member functions, a static member function does not have a this pointer, because static data members and static member functions exist independently of any objects of a class.

Section 11.8 Data Abstraction and Information Hiding

- Abstract data types are ways of representing real-world and conceptual notions to some satisfactory level of precision within a computer system.

- An abstract data type captures two notions: a data representation and the operations that can be performed on that data.

- Visual C++ is an intentionally sparse language that provides programmers with only the raw capabilities needed to build a broad range of systems. Visual C++ is designed to minimize performance burdens.

- Items are returned from a queue in first-in, first-out (FIFO) order—the first item inserted in the queue is the first item removed from the queue.

Section 11.9 Container Classes and Iterators
- Container classes (also called collection classes) are designed to hold collections of objects. Container classes commonly provide services such as insertion, deletion, searching, sorting, and testing an item to determine whether it is a member of the collection.
- It is common to associate iterators with container classes. An iterator is an object that "walks through" a collection, returning the next item (or performing some action on the next item).

Section 11.10 Proxy Classes
- Providing clients of your class with a proxy class that knows only the `public` interface to your class enables the clients to use your class's services without giving the clients access to your class's implementation details, such as its `private` data.
- When a class definition uses only a pointer or reference to an object of another class, the class header file for that other class (which would ordinarily reveal the `private` data of that class) is not required to be included with `#include`. You can simply declare that other class as a data type with a forward class declaration before the type is used in the file.
- The implementation file containing the member functions for a proxy class is the only file that includes the header file for the class whose `private` data we would like to hide.
- The implementation file containing the member functions for the proxy class is provided to the client as a precompiled object code file along with the header file that includes the function prototypes of the services provided by the proxy class.

Section 11.11, `const` and `friend` in C++/CLI
- C++/CLI does not allow functions to be declared `const`. You may declare handles and the data they point to `const`.
- Keyword `literal` should be used to declare data members that would be `static const` in native C++.
- Declare a variable `initonly` to ensure it can only be assigned a value inside a constructor.
- Managed classes cannot declare `friend`s. A managed class may be a `friend` of a native class.

Section 11.12 Dynamic Memory Management in C++/CLI
- Use `gcnew` to dynamically allocate memory on the managed heap for managed objects. The `gcnew` operator returns a handle analogously to the way `new` returns a pointer.
- C++/CLI supports deterministic destruction of managed objects using `delete`. Like native C++, `delete` invokes the class destructor but does not reclaim the memory used by the object. Use `delete []` to delete a managed array, analogously to the way native arrays are deleted.
- The CLR garbage collector will reclaim memory used by managed objects whether `delete` is used or not. However, the garbage collector is nondeterministic. You cannot predict when exactly it will run, which objects it will reclaim when it does run, or in what order those objects will be reclaimed. Write an appropriate destructor and use `delete` when you want to ensure the resources a class uses are cleaned up immediately rather than waiting for the garbage collector.

Section 11.13 Stack Semantics in C++/CLI
- You can declare a managed object without using `gcnew` in a form analogous to the way automatic variables are declared in native C++.

- When declared using stack semantics a managed object is still allocated on the managed heap. However, this declaration style ensures the destructor is called implicitly when the object goes out of scope.

Section 11.14 Finalizers
- The finalizer is the last thing called by the garbage collector before reclaiming the memory used by a managed object.
- Never write an explicit finalizer for a class unless that class contains members or references to unmanaged objects.

Section 11.15 Value Types vs. Reference Types in C++/CLI
- All built-in types and native C++ classes are value types whose instances are allocated on the stack unless created with the new operator.
- C++/CLI classes defined with ref class are reference types and always allocated on the managed heap.
- Define a C++/CLI class with value class to create a managed value type that can be allocated on the stack, native heap, or managed heap depending on the syntax used for object creation.
- There are many restrictions placed on managed value types that are not placed on managed reference classes. Use value types only for classes whose instances will be small and primarily contain other value types to reduce the performance penalty of pass by value.

Section 11.16 Boxing and Unboxing in C++/CLI
- All simple types and user defined value types inherit from class ValueType in namespace System.
- A boxing conversion creates an object on the managed heap that contains a copy of the value of the value-type variable. You must declare and access this new object by reference.
- An unboxing conversion retrieves a value-type value from an object reference.

Section 11.17 Indexers
- A class can use context-sensitive keyword default or another name to define indexers that allow array-style indexed access to lists of elements in a class.
- A benefit of indexers is that you can define both integer and non-integer indices. You can choose to overload indexers or give them separate names.
- Indexers have the general form:

```
accessModifier returnType name[ IndexType1, IndexType2, ... ]
{
    returnType get( IndexType1 parameter1, IndexType2 parameter2, ... )
    {
        // use parameter1, parameter2, ... here to get data
    }
    void set( IndexType1 parameter1, IndexType2 parameter2, ... )
    {
        // use parameter1, parameter2, ... here to set data
    }
}
```

- As with properties, an indexer's get accessor must return a value of type *returnType*. Don't name the parameters in brackets, only name the parameters in the get and accessors themselves.

Terminology

abstract data type (ADT)
allocate memory
arithmetic overflow
cascaded member-function calls
collection class
composition
const member function
const object
context-sensitive keywords
container class
data abstraction
data representation
deallocate memory
default context-sensitive keyword in indexers
delete operator
delete[] operator
dequeue (queue operation)
deterministic destruction
dynamic memory management
dynamic objects
enqueue (queue operation)
exclamation character (!) in a finalizer name
first-in, first-out (FIFO)
finalizer
forward class declaration
free store
friend class

friend function
has-a relationship
heap
host object
index property
indexer
information hiding
initonly
iterator
last-in, first-out (LIFO)
literal
member initializer
member initializer list
member object
member object constructor
memory leak
named indexer
new [] operator
new operator
nondeterministic finalization
operations in an ADT
proxy class
queue abstract data type
stack semantics
static data member
static member function
this pointer

Self-Review Exercises

11.1 Fill in the blanks in each of the following:

a) _____ must be used to initialize constant members of a class.

b) A nonmember function must be declared as a(n) _____ of a class to have access to that class's private data members.

c) The _____ operator dynamically allocates memory for an object of a specified type and returns a _____ to that type.

d) A constant object must be _____; it cannot be modified after it is created.

e) A(n) _____ data member represents class-wide information.

f) An object's non-static member functions have access to a "self pointer" to the object called the _____ pointer.

g) The keyword _____ specifies that an object or variable is not modifiable after it is initialized.

h) If a member initializer is not provided for a member object of a class, the object's _____ is called.

i) A member function should be declared static if it does not access _____ class members.

j) Member objects are constructed _____ their enclosing class object.

k) The _____ operator reclaims memory previously allocated by new.

11.2 Find the errors in the following class and explain how to correct them:

```
class Example
{
public:
   Example( int y = 10 )
      : data( y )
   {
      // empty body
   } // end Example constructor

   int getIncrementedData() const
   {
      return data++;
   } // end function getIncrementedData

   static int getCount()
   {
      cout << "Data is " << data << endl;
      return count;
   } // end function getCount
private:
   int data;
   static int count;
}; // end class Example
```

11.3 Regarding C++/CLI, fill in the blanks in each of the following:
a) _____ cannot be declared const.
b) The _____ operator dynamically allocates memory for a managed object of a specified type and returns a _____ to that type.
c) Use the _____ operator on a managed object to invoke the class' destructor to perform "termination housekeeping." The _____ is responsible for reclaiming the memory of the managed object.
d) Managed objects are always allocated on the _____.
e) Managed objects declared using stack semantics have their _____ called when they _____.
f) Define a managed class with _____ to define a reference class whose instances are always allocated on the managed heap. Use _____ to define a value class whose instances can be allocated on the stack, native heap, or managed heap.
g) Write an _____ to allow array-style access to lists of elements in an object.

Answers to Self-Review Exercises

11.1 a) member initializers. b) friend. c) new, pointer. d) initialized. e) static. f) this. g) const. h) default constructor. i) non-static. j) before. k) delete.

11.2 Error: The class definition for Example has two errors. The first occurs in function get-IncrementedData. The function is declared const, but it modifies the object.
Correction: To correct the first error, remove the const keyword from the definition of getIncrementedData.
Error: The second error occurs in function getCount. This function is declared static, so it is not allowed to access any non-static member (i.e., data) of the class.
Correction: To correct the second error, remove the output line from the getCount definition.

11.3 a) Functions. b) gcnew, handle c) delete, garbage collector d) managed heap e) destructor, go out of scope f) ref class, value class g) indexer

Exercises

11.4 Compare and contrast dynamic memory allocation and deallocation operators new, new [], delete and delete [].

11.5 Explain the notion of friendship. Explain the negative aspects of friendship as described in the text.

11.6 Can a correct Time class definition include both of the following constructors? If not, explain why not.

```
Time( int h = 0, int m = 0, int s = 0 );
Time();
```

11.7 What happens when a return type, even void, is specified for a constructor or destructor?

11.8 Modify class Date in Fig. 11.10 to have the following capabilities:
   a) Output the date in multiple formats such as

```
DDD YYYY
MM/DD/YY
June 14, 1992
```

   b) Use overloaded constructors to create Date objects initialized with dates of the formats in part (a).
   c) Create a Date constructor that reads the system date using the standard library functions of the <ctime> header and sets the Date members. (See your compiler's reference documentation or www.cplusplus.com/ref/ctime/index.html for information on the functions in header <ctime>.)

In Chapter 12, we'll be able to create operators for testing the equality of two dates and for comparing dates to determine whether one date is prior to, or after, another.

11.9 Create a SavingsAccount class. Use a static data member annualInterestRate to store the annual interest rate for each of the savers. Each member of the class contains a private data member savingsBalance indicating the amount the saver currently has on deposit. Provide member function calculateMonthlyInterest that calculates the monthly interest by multiplying the balance by annualInterestRate divided by 12; this interest should be added to savingsBalance. Provide a static member function modifyInterestRate that sets the static annualInterestRate to a new value. Write a driver program to test class SavingsAccount. Instantiate two different objects of class SavingsAccount, saver1 and saver2, with balances of $2000.00 and $3000.00, respectively. Set the annualInterestRate to 3 percent. Then calculate the monthly interest and print the new balances for each of the savers. Then set the annualInterestRate to 4 percent, calculate the next month's interest and print the new balances for each of the savers.

11.10 Create class IntegerSet for which each object can hold integers in the range 0 through 100. A set is represented internally as an array of ones and zeros. Array element a[i] is 1 if integer i is in the set. Array element a[j] is 0 if integer j is not in the set. The default constructor initializes a set to the so-called "empty set," i.e., a set whose array representation contains all zeros.

Provide member functions for the common set operations. For example, provide a unionOfSets member function that creates a third set that is the set-theoretic union of two existing sets (i.e., an element of the third set's array is set to 1 if that element is 1 in either or both of the existing sets, and an element of the third set's array is set to 0 if that element is 0 in each of the existing sets).

Provide an intersectionOfSets member function which creates a third set which is the set-theoretic intersection of two existing sets (i.e., an element of the third set's array is set to 0 if that element is 0 in either or both of the existing sets, and an element of the third set's array is set to 1 if that element is 1 in each of the existing sets).

Provide an insertElement member function that inserts a new integer *k* into a set (by setting a[k] to 1). Provide a deleteElement member function that deletes integer *m* (by setting a[m] to 0).

Provide a printSet member function that prints a set as a list of numbers separated by spaces. Print only those elements that are present in the set (i.e., their position in the array has a value of 1). Print --- for an empty set.

Provide an isEqualTo member function that determines whether two sets are equal.

Provide an additional constructor that receives an array of integers and the size of that array and uses the array to initialize a set object.

Now write a driver program to test your IntegerSet class. Instantiate several IntegerSet objects. Test that all your member functions work properly.

11.11 It would be perfectly reasonable for the Time class of Figs. 11.18–11.19 to represent the time internally as the number of seconds since midnight rather than the three integer values hour, minute and second. Clients could use the same public methods and get the same results. Modify the Time class of Fig. 11.18 to implement the time as the number of seconds since midnight and show that there is no visible change in functionality to the clients of the class. [*Note:* This exercise nicely demonstrates the virtues of implementation hiding.]

11.12 *(Complex Numbers)* Use C++/CLI to create a value class called Complex for performing arithmetic with complex numbers. Complex numbers have the form

   realPart + *imaginaryPart* * *i*

where *i* is

$\sqrt{-1}$

Write an application to test your class. Use floating-point variables to represent the private data of the class. Provide a constructor that enables an object of this class to be initialized when it is declared. Provide a parameterless constructor that sets default values in case no initializers are provided. Provide public methods that perform the following operations:

a) Add two Complex numbers: The real parts are added together and the imaginary parts are added together.

b) Subtract two Complex numbers: The real part of the right operand is subtracted from the real part of the left operand, and the imaginary part of the right operand is subtracted from the imaginary part of the left operand.

c) Printing Complex numbers in the form (a, b), where a is the real part and b is the imaginary part.

d) Why does it make more sense to make Complex a value class rather than a reference class?

12

Operator Overloading; String and Array Objects

OBJECTIVES

In this chapter you'll learn:

- What operator overloading is and how it can make programs more readable and programming more convenient.

- To redefine (overload) operators to work with objects of user-defined classes.

- The differences between overloading unary and binary operators.

- To convert objects from one class to another class.

- When to, and when not to, overload operators.

- To create PhoneNumber, Array, String and Date classes that demonstrate operator overloading.

- To use overloaded operators and other member functions of standard library class string.

- To use keyword explicit to prevent the compiler from using single-argument constructors to perform implicit conversions.

The whole difference between construction and creation is exactly this: that a thing constructed can only be loved after it is constructed; but a thing created is loved before it exists.
—Gilbert Keith Chesterton

The die is cast.
—Julius Caesar

Our doctor would never really operate unless it was necessary. He was just that way. If he didn't need the money, he wouldn't lay a hand on you.
—Herb Shriner

12.1 Introduction

Chapters 10–11 introduced the basics of Visual C++ classes. Services were obtained from objects by sending messages (in the form of member-function calls) to the objects. This function-call notation is cumbersome for certain kinds of classes (such as mathematical classes). Also, many common manipulations are performed with operators (e.g., input and output). We can use Visual C++'s rich set of built-in operators to specify common object manipulations. This chapter shows how to enable Visual C++'s operators to work with objects—a process called *operator overloading*. It is straightforward and natural to extend Visual C++ with these new capabilities, but it must be done cautiously.

One example of an overloaded operator built into Visual C++ is <<, which is used both as the stream insertion operator and as the bitwise left-shift operator (which is discussed in Chapter 22, Bits, Characters, C Strings and `struct`s). Similarly, >> is also overloaded; it is used both as the stream extraction operator and as the bitwise right-shift operator. Both of these operators are overloaded in the C++ Standard Library.

Although operator overloading sounds like an exotic capability, most programmers implicitly use overloaded operators regularly. For example, the Visual C++ language itself overloads the addition operator (+) and the subtraction operator (-). These operators perform differently, depending on their context in integer arithmetic, floating-point arithmetic and pointer arithmetic.

Visual C++ enables you to overload most operators to be sensitive to the context in which they are used—the compiler generates the appropriate code based on the context (in particular, the types of the operands). Some operators are overloaded frequently, especially the assignment, relational and various arithmetic operators such as + and -. The jobs performed by overloaded operators can also be performed by explicit function calls, but operator notation is often clearer and more familiar to programmers.

We discuss when to, and when not to, use operator overloading. We implement user-defined classes `PhoneNumber`, `Array`, `String` and `Date` to demonstrate how to overload operators, including the stream insertion, stream extraction, assignment, equality, relational, subscript, logical negation, parentheses and increment operators. The chapter ends with an example of C++'s Standard Library class `string` and a description of C++/CLI specific details on operator overloading. STL class `string` provides many overloaded operators that are similar to our `String` class that we present earlier in the chapter. In the exercises, we ask you to implement several classes with overloaded operators. The exercises also use classes `Complex` (for complex numbers) and `HugeInt` (for integers larger than a computer can represent with type `long`) to demonstrate overloaded arithmetic operators + and –, and ask you to enhance those classes by overloading other arithmetic operators.

12.2 Fundamentals of Operator Overloading

Visual C++ programming is a type-sensitive and type-focused process. Programmers can use fundamental types and can define new types. The fundamental types can be used with Visual C++'s rich collection of operators. Operators provide programmers with a concise notation for expressing manipulations of data of fundamental types.

Programmers can use operators with user-defined types as well. Although Visual C++ does not allow new operators to be created, it does allow most existing operators to be overloaded so that, when these operators are used with objects, the operators have meaning appropriate to those objects. This is a powerful capability.

Software Engineering Observation 12.1

Operator overloading contributes to Visual C++'s extensibility—one of the language's most appealing attributes.

Good Programming Practice 12.1

Use operator overloading when it makes a program clearer than accomplishing the same operations with function calls.

Good Programming Practice 12.2

Overloaded operators should mimic the functionality of their built-in counterparts—for example, the + operator should be overloaded to perform addition, not subtraction. Avoid excessive or inconsistent use of operator overloading, as this can make a program cryptic and difficult to read.

An operator is overloaded by writing a non-`static` member-function definition or global-function definition as you normally would, except that the function name now becomes the keyword `operator` followed by the symbol for the operator being overloaded. For example, the function name `operator+` would be used to overload the addition operator (+). When operators are overloaded as member functions, they must be non-`static`, because they must be called on an object of the class and operate on that object.

To use an operator on class objects, that operator *must* be overloaded—with three exceptions. The assignment operator (=) may be used with every class to perform memberwise assignment of the data members of the class—each data member is assigned from the "source" object to the "target" object of the assignment. We'll soon see that such default memberwise assignment is dangerous for classes with pointer members; we'll explicitly overload the assignment operator for such classes. The address (&) and comma (,) operators may also be used with objects of any class without overloading. The address operator returns the address of the object in memory. The comma operator evaluates the expression to its left, then the expression to its right. Both of these operators can also be overloaded.

Overloading is especially appropriate for mathematical classes. Often a substantial set of operators must be overloaded to ensure consistency with the way these mathematical classes are handled in the real world. For example, it would be unusual to overload only addition for a complex number class, because other arithmetic operators are also commonly used with complex numbers.

Operator overloading provides the same concise and familiar expressions for user-defined types that Visual C++ provides with its rich collection of operators for fundamental types. Operator overloading is not automatic—you must write operator-overloading functions to perform the desired operations. Sometimes these functions are best made member functions; sometimes they are best as `friend` functions; occasionally they can be made global, non-`friend` functions. We present examples of these possibilities.

12.3 Restrictions on Operator Overloading

Most of Visual C++'s operators can be overloaded. These are shown in Fig. 12.1. Figure 12.2 shows the operators that cannot be overloaded.

 Common Programming Error 12.1

Attempting to overload a nonoverloadable operator is a syntax error.

Operators that can be overloaded							
+	-	*	/	%	^	&	|
~	!	=	<	>	+=	-=	*=
/=	%=	^=	&=	|=	<<	>>	>>=
<<=	==	!=	<=	>=	&&	||	++
--	->*	,	->	[]	()	new	delete
new[]	delete[]						

Fig. 12.1 | Operators that can be overloaded.

Precedence, Associativity and Number of Operands
The precedence of an operator cannot be changed by overloading. This can lead to awkward situations in which an operator is overloaded in a manner for which its fixed precedence is inappropriate. However, parentheses can be used to force the order of evaluation of overloaded operators in an expression.

Operators that cannot be overloaded			
.	.*	::	?:

Fig. 12.2 | Operators that cannot be overloaded.

The associativity of an operator (i.e., whether the operator is applied right-to-left or left-to-right) cannot be changed by overloading.

It is not possible to change the "arity" of an operator (i.e., the number of operands an operator takes): Overloaded unary operators remain unary operators; overloaded binary operators remain binary operators. Visual C++'s only ternary operator (?:) cannot be overloaded. Operators &, *, + and - all have both unary and binary versions, each of which can be overloaded.

Common Programming Error 12.2

Attempting to change the "arity" of an operator via operator overloading is a compilation error.

Creating New Operators

It is not possible to create new operators; only existing operators can be overloaded. Unfortunately, this prevents you from using popular notations like the ** operator used in some other programming languages for exponentiation. [*Note:* You could overload an existing operator to perform exponentiation.]

Common Programming Error 12.3

Attempting to create new operators via operator overloading is a syntax error.

Operators for Fundamental Types

The meaning of how an operator works on objects of fundamental types cannot be changed by operator overloading. You cannot, for example, change the meaning of how + adds two integers. Operator overloading works only with objects of user-defined types or with a mixture of an object of a user-defined type and an object of a fundamental type.

Software Engineering Observation 12.2

At least one argument of an operator function must be an object or reference of a user-defined type. This prevents programmers from changing how operators work on fundamental types.

Common Programming Error 12.4

Attempting to modify how an operator works with objects of fundamental types is a compilation error.

Related Operators

Overloading an assignment operator and an addition operator to allow statements like

    object2 = object2 + object1;

does not imply that the += operator is also overloaded to allow statements such as

    object2 += object1;

Such behavior can be achieved only by explicitly overloading operator += for that class.

Common Programming Error 12.5

Assuming that overloading an operator such as + overloads related operators such as += or that overloading == overloads a related operator like != can lead to errors. Operators can be overloaded only explicitly; there is no implicit overloading.

12.4 Operator Functions as Class Members vs. Global Functions

Operator functions can be member functions or global functions; global functions are often made `friends` for performance reasons. Member functions use the `this` pointer implicitly to obtain one of their class object arguments (the left operand for binary operators). Arguments for both operands of a binary operator must be explicitly listed in a global function call.

Operators That Must Be Overloaded as Member Functions

When overloading (), [], -> or any of the assignment operators, the operator overloading function must be declared as a class member. For the other operators, the operator overloading functions can be class members or global functions.

Operators as Member Functions and Global Functions

Whether an operator function is implemented as a member function or as a global function, the operator is still used the same way in expressions. So which implementation is best?

When an operator function is implemented as a member function, the leftmost (or only) operand must be an object (or a reference to an object) of the operator's class. If the left operand must be an object of a different class or a fundamental type, this operator function must be implemented as a global function (as we'll do in Section 12.5 when overloading << and >> as the stream insertion and stream extraction operators, respectively). A global operator function can be made a `friend` of a class if that function must access `private` or `protected` members of that class directly.

Operator member functions of a specific class are called (implicitly by the compiler) only when the left operand of a binary operator is specifically an object of that class, or when the single operand of a unary operator is an object of that class.

Why Overloaded Stream Insertion and Stream Extraction Operators Are Overloaded as Global Functions

The overloaded stream insertion operator (<<) is used in an expression in which the left operand has type `ostream &`, as in `cout << classObject`. To use the operator in this manner where the *right* operand is an object of a user-defined class, it must be overloaded as a global function. To be a member function, operator << would have to be a member of the `ostream` class. This is not possible for user-defined classes, since we are not allowed to modify C++ Standard Library classes. Similarly, the overloaded stream extraction operator (>>) is used in an expression in which the left operand has type `istream &`, as in `cin >> classObject`, and the *right* operand is an object of a user-defined class, so it, too, must be a global function. Also, each of these overloaded operator functions may require access to the `private` data members of the class object being output or input, so these overloaded operator functions can be made `friend` functions of the class for performance reasons.

Performance Tip 12.1

It is possible to overload an operator as a global, non-`friend` function, but such a function requiring access to a class's `private` or `protected` data would need to use set or get functions provided in that class's `public` interface. The overhead of calling these functions could cause poor performance, so these functions can be inlined to improve performance.

Commutative Operators

Another reason why one might choose a global function to overload an operator is to enable the operator to be commutative. For example, suppose we have an object, number, of type long int, and an object bigInteger1, of class HugeInteger (a class in which integers may be arbitrarily large rather than being limited by the machine word size of the underlying hardware; class HugeInteger is developed in the chapter exercises). The addition operator (+) produces a temporary HugeInteger object as the sum of a HugeInteger and a long int (as in the expression bigInteger1 + number), or as the sum of a long int and a HugeInteger (as in the expression number + bigInteger1). Thus, we require the addition operator to be commutative (exactly as it is with two fundamental-type operands). The problem is that the class object must appear on the *left* of the addition operator if that operator is to be overloaded as a member function. So, we overload the operator as a global function to allow the HugeInteger to appear on the *right* of the addition. The operator+ function, which deals with the HugeInteger on the left, can still be a member function. The global function simply swaps its arguments and calls the member function.

12.5 Overloading Stream Insertion and Stream Extraction Operators

Visual C++ is able to input and output the fundamental types using the stream extraction operator >> and the stream insertion operator <<. The class libraries provided with Visual C++ compilers overload these operators to process each fundamental type, including pointers and C-style char * strings. The stream insertion and stream extraction operators also can be overloaded to perform input and output for user-defined types. The program of Figs. 12.3–12.5 demonstrates overloading these operators to handle data of a user-defined telephone number class called PhoneNumber. This program assumes telephone numbers are input correctly.

```
1   // Fig. 12.3: PhoneNumber.h
2   // PhoneNumber class definition
3   #ifndef PHONENUMBER_H
4   #define PHONENUMBER_H
5
6   #include <iostream>
7   using std::ostream;
8   using std::istream;
9
10  #include <string>
11  using std::string;
12
13  class PhoneNumber
14  {
15     friend ostream &operator<<( ostream &, const PhoneNumber & );
16     friend istream &operator>>( istream &, PhoneNumber & );
17  private:
18     string areaCode; // 3-digit area code
```

Fig. 12.3 | PhoneNumber class with overloaded stream insertion and stream extraction operators as friend functions. (Part 1 of 2.)

```
19        string exchange; // 3-digit exchange
20        string line; // 4-digit line
21    }; // end class PhoneNumber
22
23    #endif
```

Fig. 12.3 | PhoneNumber class with overloaded stream insertion and stream extraction operators as friend functions. (Part 2 of 2.)

```
1    // Fig. 12.4: PhoneNumber.cpp
2    // Overloaded stream insertion and stream extraction operators
3    // for class PhoneNumber.
4    #include <iomanip>
5    using std::setw;
6
7    #include "PhoneNumber.h"
8
9    // overloaded stream insertion operator; cannot be
10   // a member function if we would like to invoke it with
11   // cout << somePhoneNumber;
12   ostream &operator<<( ostream &output, const PhoneNumber &number )
13   {
14      output << "(" << number.areaCode << ") "
15         << number.exchange << "-" << number.line;
16      return output; // enables cout << a << b << c;
17   } // end function operator<<
18
19   // overloaded stream extraction operator; cannot be
20   // a member function if we would like to invoke it with
21   // cin >> somePhoneNumber;
22   istream &operator>>( istream &input, PhoneNumber &number )
23   {
24      input.ignore(); // skip (
25      input >> setw( 3 ) >> number.areaCode; // input area code
26      input.ignore( 2 ); // skip ) and space
27      input >> setw( 3 ) >> number.exchange; // input exchange
28      input.ignore(); // skip dash (-)
29      input >> setw( 4 ) >> number.line; // input line
30      return input; // enables cin >> a >> b >> c;
31   } // end function operator>>
```

Fig. 12.4 | Overloaded stream insertion and stream extraction operators for class PhoneNumber.

```
1    // Fig. 12.5: PhoneNumberTest.cpp
2    // Demonstrating class PhoneNumber's overloaded stream insertion
3    // and stream extraction operators.
4    #include <iostream>
5    using std::cout;
6    using std::cin;
```

Fig. 12.5 | Overloaded stream insertion and stream extraction operators. (Part 1 of 2.)

```
 7   using std::endl;
 8
 9   #include "PhoneNumber.h"
10
11   int main()
12   {
13      PhoneNumber phone; // create object phone
14
15      cout << "Enter phone number in the form (123) 456-7890:" << endl;
16
17      // cin >> phone invokes operator>> by implicitly issuing
18      // the global function call operator>>( cin, phone )
19      cin >> phone;
20
21      cout << "The phone number entered was: ";
22
23      // cout << phone invokes operator<< by implicitly issuing
24      // the global function call operator<<( cout, phone )
25      cout << phone << endl;
26      return 0;
27   } // end main
```

```
Enter phone number in the form (123) 456-7890:
(800) 555-1212
The phone number entered was: (800) 555-1212
```

Fig. 12.5 | Overloaded stream insertion and stream extraction operators. (Part 2 of 2.)

The stream extraction operator function operator>> (Fig. 12.4, lines 22–31) takes istream reference input and PhoneNumber reference num as arguments and returns an istream reference. Operator function operator>> inputs phone numbers of the form

> (800) 555-1212

into objects of class PhoneNumber. When the compiler sees the expression

> cin >> phone

in line 19 of Fig. 12.5, the compiler generates the global function call

> operator>>(cin, phone);

When this call executes, reference parameter input (Fig. 12.4, line 22) becomes an alias for cin and reference parameter number becomes an alias for phone. The operator function reads as strings the three parts of the telephone number into the areaCode (line 25), exchange (line 27) and line (line 29) members of the PhoneNumber object referenced by parameter number. Stream manipulator setw limits the number of characters read into each character array. When used with cin and strings, setw restricts the number of characters read to the number of characters specified by its argument (i.e., setw(3) allows three characters to be read). The parentheses, space and dash characters are skipped by calling istream member function ignore (Fig. 12.4, lines 24, 26 and 28), which discards the specified number of characters in the input stream (one character by default). Function operator>> returns istream reference input (i.e., cin). This enables input operations on

PhoneNumber objects to be cascaded with input operations on other PhoneNumber objects or on objects of other data types. For example, a program can input two PhoneNumber objects in one statement as follows:

```
cin >> phone1 >> phone2;
```

First, the expression cin >> phone1 executes by making the global function call

```
operator>>( cin, phone1 );
```

This call then returns a reference to cin as the value of cin >> phone1, so the remaining portion of the expression is interpreted simply as cin >> phone2. This executes by making the global function call

```
operator>>( cin, phone2 );
```

The stream insertion operator function (Fig. 12.4, lines 12–17) takes an ostream reference (output) and a const PhoneNumber reference (number) as arguments and returns an ostream reference. Function operator<< displays objects of type PhoneNumber. When the compiler sees the expression

```
cout << phone
```

in line 25 of Fig. 12.5, the compiler generates the global function call

```
operator<<( cout, phone );
```

Function operator<< displays the parts of the telephone number as strings, because they are stored as string objects.

Error-Prevention Tip 12.1

Returning a reference from an overloaded << or >> operator function is typically successful because cout, cin and most stream objects are global, or at least long-lived. Returning a reference to an automatic variable or other temporary object is dangerous—this can create "dangling references" to nonexistent objects.

Note that the functions operator>> and operator<< are declared in PhoneNumber as global, friend functions (Fig. 12.3, lines 15–16). They are global functions because the object of class PhoneNumber appears in each case as the right operand of the operator. Remember, overloaded operator functions for binary operators can be member functions only when the left operand is an object of the class in which the function is a member. Overloaded input and output operators are declared as friends if they need to access non-public class members directly for performance reasons or because the class may not offer appropriate *get* functions. Also note that the PhoneNumber reference in function operator<<'s parameter list (Fig. 12.4, line 12) is const, because the PhoneNumber will simply be output, and the PhoneNumber reference in function operator>>'s parameter list (line 22) is non-const, because the PhoneNumber object must be modified to store the input telephone number in the object.

Software Engineering Observation 12.3

New input/output capabilities for user-defined types are added to Visual C++ without modifying standard input/output library classes. This is another example of Visual C++'s extensibility.

12.6 Overloading Unary Operators

A unary operator for a class can be overloaded as a non-static member function with no arguments or as a global function with one argument; that argument must be either an object of the class or a reference to an object of the class. Member functions that implement overloaded operators must be non-static so that they can access the non-static data in each object of the class. Remember that static member functions can access only static members of the class.

Later in this chapter, we'll overload unary operator ! to test whether an object of the String class we create (Section 12.10) is empty and return a bool result. Consider the expression !s, in which s is an object of class String. When a unary operator such as ! is overloaded as a member function with no arguments and the compiler sees the expression !s, the compiler generates the function call s.operator!(). The operand s is the class object for which the String class member function operator! is being invoked. The function is declared in the class definition as follows:

```
class String
{
public:
    bool operator!() const;
    ...
}; // end class String
```

A unary operator such as ! may be overloaded as a global function with one parameter in two different ways—either with a parameter that is an object (this requires a copy of the object, so the side effects of the function are not applied to the original object), or with a parameter that is a reference to an object (no copy of the original object is made, so all side effects of this function are applied to the original object). If s is a String class object (or a reference to a String class object), then !s is treated as if the call operator!(s) had been written, invoking the global operator! function that is declared as follows:

```
bool operator!( const String & );
```

12.7 Overloading Binary Operators

A binary operator can be overloaded as a non-static member function with one parameter or as a global function with two parameters (one of those parameters must be either a class object or a reference to a class object).

Later in this chapter, we'll overload < to compare two String objects. When overloading binary operator < as a non-static member function of a String class with one argument, if y and z are String-class objects, then y < z is treated as if y.operator<(z) had been written, invoking the operator< member function declared below:

```
class String

public:
    bool operator<( const String & ) const;
    ...
}; // end class String
```

If binary operator < is to be overloaded as a global function, it must take two arguments—one of which must be a class object or a reference to a class object. If y and z are

String-class objects or references to String-class objects, then y < z is treated as if the call operator<(y, z) had been written in the program, invoking global function operator< declared as follows:

bool operator<(**const** String &, **const** String &);

12.8 Case Study: Array Class

Pointer-based arrays have a number of problems. For example, a program can easily "walk off" either end of an array, because Visual C++ does not check whether subscripts fall outside the range of an array (you can still do this explicitly, though). Arrays of size n must number their elements $0, \ldots, n-1$; alternate subscript ranges are not allowed. An entire non-char array cannot be input or output at once; each array element must be read or written individually. Two arrays cannot be meaningfully compared with equality operators or relational operators (because the array names are simply pointers to where the arrays begin in memory and, of course, two arrays will always be at different memory locations). When an array is passed to a general-purpose function designed to handle arrays of any size, the size of the array must be passed as an additional argument. One array cannot be assigned to another with the assignment operator(s) (because array names are const pointers and a constant pointer cannot be used on the left side of an assignment operator). These and other capabilities certainly seem like "naturals" for dealing with arrays, but pointer-based arrays don't provide such capabilities. However, Visual C++ does provide the means to implement such array capabilities through the use of classes and operator overloading.

In this example, we create a powerful array class that performs range checking to ensure that subscripts remain within the bounds of the Array. The class allows one array object to be assigned to another with the assignment operator. Objects of the Array class know their size, so the size does not need to be passed separately as an argument when passing an Array to a function. Entire Arrays can be input or output with the stream extraction and stream insertion operators, respectively. Array comparisons can be made with the equality operators == and !=.

This example will sharpen your appreciation of data abstraction. You'll probably want to suggest other enhancements to this Array class. Class development is an interesting, creative and intellectually challenging activity—always with the goal of "crafting valuable classes."

The program of Figs. 12.6–12.8 demonstrates class Array and its overloaded operators. First we walk through main (Fig. 12.8). Then we consider the class definition (Fig. 12.6) and each of the class's member-function and friend-function definitions (Fig. 12.7).

```
1   // Fig. 12.6: Array.h
2   // Array class definition with overloaded operators.
3   #ifndef ARRAY_H
4   #define ARRAY_H
5
```

Fig. 12.6 | Array class definition with overloaded operators. (Part 1 of 2.)

```
 6   #include <iostream>
 7   using std::ostream;
 8   using std::istream;
 9
10   class Array
11   {
12      friend ostream &operator<<( ostream &, const Array & );
13      friend istream &operator>>( istream &, Array & );
14   public:
15      Array( int = 10 ); // default constructor
16      Array( const Array & ); // copy constructor
17      ~Array(); // destructor
18      int getSize() const; // return size
19
20      const Array &operator=( const Array & ); // assignment operator
21      bool operator==( const Array & ) const; // equality operator
22
23      // inequality operator; returns opposite of == operator
24      bool operator!=( const Array &right ) const
25      {
26         return ! ( *this == right ); // invokes Array::operator==
27      } // end function operator!=
28
29      // subscript operator for non-const objects returns modifiable lvalue
30      int &operator[]( int );
31
32      // subscript operator for const objects returns rvalue
33      int operator[]( int ) const;
34   private:
35      int size; // pointer-based array size
36      int *ptr; // pointer to first element of pointer-based array
37   }; // end class Array
38
39   #endif
```

Fig. 12.6 | Array class definition with overloaded operators. (Part 2 of 2.)

```
 1   // Fig. 12.7: Array.cpp
 2   // Array class member- and friend-function definitions.
 3   #include <iostream>
 4   using std::cerr;
 5   using std::cout;
 6   using std::cin;
 7   using std::endl;
 8
 9   #include <iomanip>
10   using std::setw;
11
12   #include <cstdlib> // exit function prototype
13   using std::exit;
14
```

Fig. 12.7 | Array class member- and friend-function definitions. (Part 1 of 4.)

```
15   #include "Array.h" // Array class definition
16
17   // default constructor for class Array (default size 10)
18   Array::Array( int arraySize )
19   {
20      size = ( arraySize > 0 ? arraySize : 10 ); // validate arraySize
21      ptr = new int[ size ]; // create space for pointer-based array
22
23      for ( int i = 0; i < size; i++ )
24         ptr[ i ] = 0; // set pointer-based array element
25   } // end Array default constructor
26
27   // copy constructor for class Array;
28   // must receive a reference to prevent infinite recursion
29   Array::Array( const Array &arrayToCopy )
30      : size( arrayToCopy.size )
31   {
32      ptr = new int[ size ]; // create space for pointer-based array
33
34      for ( int i = 0; i < size; i++ )
35         ptr[ i ] = arrayToCopy.ptr[ i ]; // copy into object
36   } // end Array copy constructor
37
38   // destructor for class Array
39   Array::~Array()
40   {
41      delete [] ptr; // release pointer-based array space
42   } // end destructor
43
44   // return number of elements of Array
45   int Array::getSize() const
46   {
47      return size; // number of elements in Array
48   } // end function getSize
49
50   // overloaded assignment operator;
51   // const return avoids: ( a1 = a2 ) = a3
52   const Array &Array::operator=( const Array &right )
53   {
54      if ( &right != this ) // avoid self-assignment
55      {
56         // for Arrays of different sizes, deallocate original
57         // left-side array, then allocate new left-side array
58         if ( size != right.size )
59         {
60            delete [] ptr; // release space
61            size = right.size; // resize this object
62            ptr = new int[ size ]; // create space for array copy
63         } // end inner if
64
65         for ( int i = 0; i < size; i++ )
66            ptr[ i ] = right.ptr[ i ]; // copy array into object
67      } // end outer if
```

Fig. 12.7 | Array class member- and `friend`-function definitions. (Part 2 of 4.)

```
68
69      return *this; // enables x = y = z, for example
70   } // end function operator=
71
72   // determine if two Arrays are equal and
73   // return true, otherwise return false
74   bool Array::operator==( const Array &right ) const
75   {
76      if ( size != right.size )
77         return false; // arrays of different number of elements
78
79      for ( int i = 0; i < size; i++ )
80         if ( ptr[ i ] != right.ptr[ i ] )
81            return false; // Array contents are not equal
82
83      return true; // Arrays are equal
84   } // end function operator==
85
86   // overloaded subscript operator for non-const Arrays;
87   // reference return creates a modifiable lvalue
88   int &Array::operator[]( int subscript )
89   {
90      // check for subscript out-of-range error
91      if ( subscript < 0 || subscript >= size )
92      {
93         cerr << "\nError: Subscript " << subscript
94            << " out of range" << endl;
95         exit( 1 ); // terminate program; subscript out of range
96      } // end if
97
98      return ptr[ subscript ]; // reference return
99   } // end function operator[]
100
101  // overloaded subscript operator for const Arrays
102  // const reference return creates an rvalue
103  int Array::operator[]( int subscript ) const
104  {
105     // check for subscript out-of-range error
106     if ( subscript < 0 || subscript >= size )
107     {
108        cerr << "\nError: Subscript " << subscript
109           << " out of range" << endl;
110        exit( 1 ); // terminate program; subscript out of range
111     } // end if
112
113     return ptr[ subscript ]; // returns copy of this element
114  } // end function operator[]
115
116  // overloaded input operator for class Array;
117  // inputs values for entire Array
118  istream &operator>>( istream &input, Array &a )
119  {
```

Fig. 12.7 | Array class member- and friend-function definitions. (Part 3 of 4.)

```
120        for ( int i = 0; i < a.size; i++ )
121            input >> a.ptr[ i ];
122
123        return input; // enables cin >> x >> y;
124    } // end function
125
126    // overloaded output operator for class Array
127    ostream &operator<<( ostream &output, const Array &a )
128    {
129        int i;
130
131        // output private ptr-based array
132        for ( i = 0; i < a.size; i++ )
133        {
134            output << setw( 12 ) << a.ptr[ i ];
135
136            if ( ( i + 1 ) % 4 == 0 ) // 4 numbers per row of output
137                output << endl;
138        } // end for
139
140        if ( i % 4 != 0 ) // end last line of output
141            output << endl;
142
143        return output; // enables cout << x << y;
144    } // end function operator<<
```

Fig. 12.7 | Array class member- and `friend`-function definitions. (Part 4 of 4.)

```
 1    // Fig. 12.8: ArrayTest.cpp
 2    // Array class test program.
 3    #include <iostream>
 4    using std::cout;
 5    using std::cin;
 6    using std::endl;
 7
 8    #include "Array.h"
 9
10    int main()
11    {
12        Array integers1( 7 ); // seven-element Array
13        Array integers2; // 10-element Array by default
14
15        // print integers1 size and contents
16        cout << "Size of Array integers1 is "
17            << integers1.getSize()
18            << "\nArray after initialization:\n" << integers1;
19
20        // print integers2 size and contents
21        cout << "\nSize of Array integers2 is "
22            << integers2.getSize()
23            << "\nArray after initialization:\n" << integers2;
```

Fig. 12.8 | Array class test program. (Part 1 of 3.)

```
24
25      // input and print integers1 and integers2
26      cout << "\nEnter 17 integers:" << endl;
27      cin >> integers1 >> integers2;
28
29      cout << "\nAfter input, the Arrays contain:\n"
30          << "integers1:\n" << integers1
31          << "integers2:\n" << integers2;
32
33      // use overloaded inequality (!=) operator
34      cout << "\nEvaluating: integers1 != integers2" << endl;
35
36      if ( integers1 != integers2 )
37          cout << "integers1 and integers2 are not equal" << endl;
38
39      // create Array integers3 using integers1 as an
40      // initializer; print size and contents
41      Array integers3( integers1 ); // invokes copy constructor
42
43      cout << "\nSize of Array integers3 is "
44          << integers3.getSize()
45          << "\nArray after initialization:\n" << integers3;
46
47      // use overloaded assignment (=) operator
48      cout << "\nAssigning integers2 to integers1:" << endl;
49      integers1 = integers2; // note target Array is smaller
50
51      cout << "integers1:\n" << integers1
52          << "integers2:\n" << integers2;
53
54      // use overloaded equality (==) operator
55      cout << "\nEvaluating: integers1 == integers2" << endl;
56
57      if ( integers1 == integers2 )
58          cout << "integers1 and integers2 are equal" << endl;
59
60      // use overloaded subscript operator to create rvalue
61      cout << "\nintegers1[5] is " << integers1[ 5 ];
62
63      // use overloaded subscript operator to create lvalue
64      cout << "\n\nAssigning 1000 to integers1[5]" << endl;
65      integers1[ 5 ] = 1000;
66      cout << "integers1:\n" << integers1;
67
68      // attempt to use out-of-range subscript
69      cout << "\nAttempt to assign 1000 to integers1[15]" << endl;
70      integers1[ 15 ] = 1000; // ERROR: out of range
71      return 0;
72  } // end main
```

Fig. 12.8 | Array class test program. (Part 2 of 3.)

```
Size of Array integers1 is 7
Array after initialization:
            0           0           0           0
            0           0           0

Size of Array integers2 is 10
Array after initialization:
            0           0           0           0
            0           0           0           0
            0           0

Enter 17 integers:
1 2 3 4 5 6 7 8 9 10 11 12 13 14 15 16 17

After input, the Arrays contain:
integers1:
            1           2           3           4
            5           6           7
integers2:
            8           9          10          11
           12          13          14          15
           16          17

Evaluating: integers1 != integers2
integers1 and integers2 are not equal

Size of Array integers3 is 7
Array after initialization:
            1           2           3           4
            5           6           7

Assigning integers2 to integers1:
integers1:
            8           9          10          11
           12          13          14          15
           16          17
integers2:
            8           9          10          11
           12          13          14          15
           16          17

Evaluating: integers1 == integers2
integers1 and integers2 are equal

integers1[5] is 13

Assigning 1000 to integers1[5]
integers1:
            8           9          10          11
           12        1000          14          15
           16          17

Attempt to assign 1000 to integers1[15]

Error: Subscript 15 out of range
```

Fig. 12.8 | Array class test program. (Part 3 of 3.)

Creating Arrays, Outputting Their Size and Displaying Their Contents
The program begins by instantiating two objects of class Array—integers1 (Fig. 12.8, line 12) with seven elements, and integers2 (Fig. 12.8, line 13) with the default Array size—10 elements (specified by the Array default constructor's prototype in Fig. 12.6, line 15). Lines 16–18 use member function getSize to determine the size of integers1 and output integers1, using the Array overloaded stream insertion operator. The sample output confirms that the Array elements were set correctly to zeros by the constructor. Next, lines 21–23 output the size of Array integers2 and output integers2, using the Array overloaded stream insertion operator.

Using the Overloaded Stream Insertion Operator to Fill an Array
Line 26 prompts the user to input 17 integers. Line 27 uses the Array overloaded stream extraction operator to read these values into both arrays. The first seven values are stored in integers1 and the remaining 10 values are stored in integers2. Lines 29–31 output the two arrays with the overloaded Array stream insertion operator to confirm that the input was performed correctly.

Using the Overloaded Inequality Operator
Line 36 tests the overloaded inequality operator by evaluating the condition

```
integers1 != integers2
```

The program output shows that the Arrays are not equal.

Initializing a New Array with a Copy of an Existing Array's Contents
Line 41 instantiates a third Array called integers3 and initializes it with a copy of Array integers1. This invokes the Array *copy constructor* to copy the elements of integers1 into integers3. We discuss the details of the copy constructor shortly. Note that the copy constructor can also be invoked by writing line 41 as follows:

```
Array integers3 = integers1;
```

The equal sign in the preceding statement is *not* the assignment operator. When an equal sign appears in the declaration of an object, it invokes a constructor for that object. This form can be used to pass only a single argument to a constructor.

Lines 43–45 output the size of integers3 and output integers3, using the Array overloaded stream insertion operator to confirm that the Array elements were set correctly by the copy constructor.

Using the Overloaded Assignment Operator
Next, line 49 tests the overloaded assignment operator (=) by assigning integers2 to integers1. Lines 51–52 print both Array objects to confirm that the assignment was successful. Note that integers1 originally held seven integers and was resized to hold a copy of the 10 elements in integers2. As we'll see, the overloaded assignment operator performs this resizing operation in a manner that is transparent to the client code.

Using the Overloaded Equality Operator
Next, line 57 uses the overloaded equality operator (==) to confirm that objects integers1 and integers2 are indeed identical after the assignment.

Using the Overloaded Subscript Operator

Line 61 uses the overloaded subscript operator to refer to integers1[5]—an in-range element of integers1. This subscripted name is used as an *rvalue* to print the value stored in integers1[5]. Line 65 uses integers1[5] as a modifiable *lvalue* on the left side of an assignment statement to assign a new value, 1000, to element 5 of integers1. We'll see that operator[] returns a reference to use as the modifiable *lvalue* after the operator confirms that 5 is a valid subscript for integers1.

Line 70 attempts to assign the value 1000 to integers1[15]—an out-of-range element. In this example, operator[] determines that the subscript is out of range, prints a message and terminates the program. Note that we highlighted line 70 of the program in bold black text to emphasize that it is an error to access an element that is out of range. This is a runtime logic error.

Interestingly, the array subscript operator [] is not restricted for use only with arrays; it also can be used, for example, to select elements from other kinds of container classes, such as linked lists, strings and dictionaries. Also, when operator[] functions are defined, subscripts no longer have to be integers—characters, strings, floats or even objects of user-defined classes also could be used. In Chapter 23, Standard Template Library (STL), we discuss the STL map class that allows noninteger subscripts.

Array Class Definition

Now that we have seen how this program operates, let us walk through the class header (Fig. 12.6). As we refer to each member function in the header, we discuss that function's implementation in Fig. 12.7. In Fig. 12.6, lines 35–36 represent the private data members of class Array. Each Array object consists of a size member indicating the number of elements in the Array and an int pointer—ptr—that points to the dynamically allocated pointer-based array of integers managed by the Array object.

Overloading the Stream Insertion and Stream Extraction Operators as friends

Lines 12–13 of Fig. 12.6 declare the overloaded stream insertion operator and the overloaded stream extraction operator to be friends of class Array. When the compiler sees an expression like cout << arrayObject, it invokes global function operator<< with the call

```
operator<<( cout, arrayObject )
```

When the compiler sees an expression like cin >> arrayObject, it invokes global function operator>> with the call

```
operator>>( cin, arrayObject )
```

We note again that these stream insertion and stream extraction operator functions cannot be members of class Array, because the Array object is always mentioned on the right side of the stream insertion operator and the stream extraction operator. If these operator functions were to be members of class Array, the following awkward statements would have to be used to output and input an Array:

```
arrayObject << cout;
arrayObject >> cin;
```

Such statements would be confusing to most Visual C++ programmers, who are familiar with cout and cin appearing as the left operands of << and >>, respectively.

Function operator<< (defined in Fig. 12.7, lines 127–144) prints the number of elements indicated by size from the integer array to which ptr points. Function operator>> (defined in Fig. 12.7, lines 118–124) inputs directly into the array to which ptr points. Each of these operator functions returns an appropriate reference to enable cascaded output or input statements, respectively. Note that each of these functions has access to an Array's private data because these functions are declared as friends of class Array. Also, note that class Array's getSize and operator[] functions could be used by operator<< and operator>>, in which case these operator functions would not need to be friends of class Array. However, the additional function calls might increase execution-time overhead.

Array Default Constructor

Line 15 of Fig. 12.6 declares the default constructor for the class and specifies a default size of 10 elements. When the compiler sees a declaration like line 13 in Fig. 12.8, it invokes class Array's default constructor (remember that the default constructor in this example actually receives a single int argument that has a default value of 10). The default constructor (defined in Fig. 12.7, lines 18–25) validates and assigns the argument to data member size, uses new to obtain the memory for the internal pointer-based representation of this array and assigns the pointer returned by new to data member ptr. Then the constructor uses a for statement to set all the elements of the array to zero. It is possible to have an Array class that does not initialize its members if, for example, these members are to be read at some later time; but this is considered to be a poor programming practice. Arrays, and objects in general, should be properly initialized and maintained in a consistent state.

Array Copy Constructor

Line 16 of Fig. 12.6 declares a *copy constructor* (defined in Fig. 12.7, lines 29–36) that initializes an Array by making a copy of an existing Array object. Such copying must be done carefully to avoid the pitfall of leaving both Array objects pointing to the same dynamically allocated memory. This is exactly the problem that would occur with default memberwise copying, if the compiler were allowed to define a default copy constructor for this class. Copy constructors are invoked whenever a copy of an object is needed, such as in passing an object by value to a function, returning an object by value from a function or initializing an object with a copy of another object of the same class. The copy constructor is called in a declaration when an object of class Array is instantiated and initialized with another object of class Array, as in the declaration in line 41 of Fig. 12.8.

Software Engineering Observation 12.4

The argument to a copy constructor should be a const reference to allow a const object to be copied.

Common Programming Error 12.6

Note that a copy constructor must receive its argument by reference, not by value. Otherwise, the copy-constructor call results in infinite recursion (a fatal logic error), because receiving an object by value requires the copy constructor to make a copy of the argument object. Recall that any time a copy of an object is required, the class's copy constructor is called. If the copy constructor received its argument by value, the copy constructor would call itself recursively to make a copy of its argument!

The copy constructor for `Array` uses a member initializer (Fig. 12.7, line 30) to copy the `size` of the initializer `Array` into data member `size`, uses `new` (line 32) to obtain the memory for the internal pointer-based representation of this `Array` and assigns the pointer returned by `new` to data member `ptr`.[1] Then the copy constructor uses a `for` statement to copy all the elements of the initializer `Array` into the new `Array` object. Note that an object of a class can look at the `private` data of any other object of that class (using a handle that indicates which object to access).

Common Programming Error 12.7

*If the copy constructor simply copied the pointer in the source object to the target object's pointer, then both objects would point to the same dynamically allocated memory. The first destructor to execute would then delete the dynamically allocated memory, and the other object's ptr would be undefined, a situation called a **dangling pointer**—this would likely result in a serious run-time error (such as early program termination) when the pointer was used.*

Array Destructor
Line 17 of Fig. 12.6 declares the destructor for the class (defined in Fig. 12.7, lines 39–42). The destructor is invoked when an object of class `Array` goes out of scope. The destructor uses `delete []` to release the memory allocated dynamically by `new` in the constructor.

getSize Member Function
Line 18 of Fig. 12.6 declares function `getSize` (defined in Fig. 12.7, lines 45–48) that returns the number of elements in the `Array`.

Overloaded Assignment Operator
Line 20 of Fig. 12.6 declares the overloaded assignment-operator function for the class. When the compiler sees the expression `integers1 = integers2` in line 49 of Fig. 12.8, the compiler invokes member function `operator=` with the call

```
integers1.operator=( integers2 )
```

The implementation of member function `operator=` (Fig. 12.7, lines 52–70) tests for *self-assignment* (line 54) in which an object of class `Array` is being assigned to itself. When `this` is equal to the address of the `right` operand, a self-assignment is being attempted, so the assignment is skipped (i.e., the object already is itself; in a moment we'll see why self-assignment is dangerous). If it is not a self-assignment, then the member function determines whether the sizes of the two arrays are identical (line 58); in that case, the original array of integers in the left-side `Array` object is not reallocated. Otherwise, `operator=` uses `delete` (line 60) to release the memory originally allocated to the target array, copies the `size` of the source array to the `size` of the target array (line 61), uses `new` to allocate memory for the target array and places the pointer returned by `new` into the array's `ptr` member.[2] Then the `for` statement in lines 65–66 copies the array elements from the source array to the target array. Regardless of whether this is a self-assignment, the member func-

---

1. Note that `new` could fail to obtain the needed memory. We deal with `new` failures in Chapter 16, Exception Handling.
2. Once again, `new` could fail.

tion returns the current object (i.e., *this in line 69) as a constant reference; this enables cascaded Array assignments such as x = y = z. If self-assignment occurs, and function operator= did not test for this case, operator= would delete the dynamic memory associated with the Array object before the assignment was complete. This would leave ptr pointing to memory that had been deallocated, which could lead to fatal runtime errors.

Software Engineering Observation 12.5

A copy constructor, a destructor and an overloaded assignment operator are usually provided as a group for any class that uses dynamically allocated memory.

Common Programming Error 12.8

Not providing an overloaded assignment operator and a copy constructor for a class when objects of that class contain pointers to dynamically allocated memory is a logic error.

Software Engineering Observation 12.6

It is possible to prevent one object of a class from being assigned to another. This is done by declaring the assignment operator as a private member of the class.

Software Engineering Observation 12.7

It is possible to prevent class objects from being copied; to do this, simply make both the overloaded assignment operator and the copy constructor of that class private.

Overloaded Equality and Inequality Operators
Line 21 of Fig. 12.6 declares the overloaded equality operator (==) for the class. When the compiler sees the expression integers1 == integers2 in line 57 of Fig. 12.8, the compiler invokes member function operator== with the call

```
integers1.operator==( integers2 )
```

Member function operator== (defined in Fig. 12.7, lines 74–84) immediately returns false if the size members of the arrays are not equal. Otherwise, operator== compares each pair of elements. If they are all equal, the function returns true. The first pair of elements to differ causes the function to return false immediately.

Lines 24–27 of the header file define the overloaded inequality operator (!=) for the class. Member function operator!= uses the overloaded operator== function to determine whether one Array is equal to another, then returns the opposite of that result. Writing operator!= in this manner enables you to reuse operator==, which reduces the amount of code that must be written in the class. Also, note that the full function definition for operator!= is in the Array header file. This allows the compiler to inline the definition of operator!= to eliminate the overhead of the extra function call.

Overloaded Subscript Operators
Lines 30 and 33 of Fig. 12.6 declare two overloaded subscript operators (defined in Fig. 12.7 in lines 88–99 and 103–114, respectively). When the compiler sees the expression integers1[5] (Fig. 12.8, line 61), the compiler invokes the appropriate overloaded operator[] member function by generating the call

```
integers1.operator[]( 5 )
```

The compiler creates a call to the const version of operator[] (Fig. 12.7, lines 103–114) when the subscript operator is used on a const Array object. For example, if const object z is instantiated with the statement

```
const Array z( 5 );
```

then the const version of operator[] is required to execute a statement such as

```
cout << z[ 3 ] << endl;
```

Remember, a program can invoke only the const member functions of a const object.

Each definition of operator[] determines whether the subscript it receives as an argument is in range. If it is not, each function prints an error message and terminates the program with a call to function exit (header <cstdlib>).[3] If the subscript is in range, the non-const version of operator[] returns the appropriate array element as a reference so that it may be used as a modifiable *lvalue* (e.g., on the left side of an assignment statement). If the subscript is in range, the const version of operator[] returns a copy of the appropriate element of the array. The returned character is an *rvalue*.

12.9 Converting between Types

Most programs process information of many types. Sometimes all the operations "stay within a type." For example, adding an int to an int produces an int (as long as the result is not too large to be represented as an int). It is often necessary, however, to convert data of one type to data of another type. This can happen in assignments, in calculations, in passing values to functions and in returning values from functions. The compiler knows how to perform certain conversions among fundamental types (as we discussed in Chapter 7). You can use cast operators to force conversions among fundamental types.

But what about user-defined types? The compiler cannot know in advance how to convert among user-defined types, and between user-defined types and fundamental types, so you must specify how to do this. Such conversions can be performed with *conversion constructors*—single-argument constructors that turn objects of other types (including fundamental types) into objects of a particular class. In Section 12.10, we use a conversion constructor to convert ordinary char * strings into String class objects.

A *conversion operator* (also called a *cast operator*) can be used to convert an object of one class into an object of another class or into an object of a fundamental type. Such a conversion operator must be a non-static member function. The function prototype

```
A::operator char *() const;
```

declares an overloaded cast-operator function for converting an object of user-defined type A into a temporary char * object. The operator function is declared const because it does not modify the original object. An overloaded *cast-operator function* does not specify a return type—the return type is the type to which the object is being converted. If s is a class object, when the compiler sees the expression static_cast< char * >(s), the compiler generates the call

```
s.operator char *()
```

---

3. Note that it is more appropriate when a subscript is out of range to "throw an exception" indicating the out-of-range subscript. Then the program can "catch" that exception, process it and possibly continue execution. See Chapter 16 for more information on exceptions.

The operand s is the class object s for which the member function `operator char *` is being invoked.

Overloaded cast-operator functions can be defined to convert objects of user-defined types into fundamental types or into objects of other user-defined types. The prototypes

```
A::operator int() const;
A::operator OtherClass() const;
```

declare overloaded cast-operator functions that can convert an object of user-defined type A into an integer or into an object of user-defined type OtherClass, respectively.

One of the nice features of cast operators and conversion constructors is that, when necessary, the compiler can call these functions implicitly to create temporary objects. For example, if an object s of a user-defined String class appears in a program at a location where an ordinary char * is expected, such as

```
cout << s;
```

the compiler can call the overloaded cast-operator function `operator char *` to convert the object into a char * and use the resulting char * in the expression. With this cast operator provided for our String class, the stream insertion operator does not have to be overloaded to output a String using cout.

12.10 Case Study: String Class

As a capstone exercise to our study of overloading, we'll build our own String class to handle the creation and manipulation of strings (Figs. 12.9–12.11). The C++ Standard Library provides a similar, more robust class string as well. We present an example of the standard class string in Section 12.13 and study class string in detail in Chapter 19. For now, we'll make extensive use of operator overloading to craft our own class String.

First, we present the header file for class String. We discuss the private data used to represent String objects. Then we walk through the class's public interface, discussing each of the services the class provides. We discuss the member-function definitions for the class String. For each of the overloaded operator functions, we show the code in the program that invokes it, and we provide an explanation of how the overloaded operator function works.

String Class Definition
Now let's walk through the String class header file in Fig. 12.9. We begin with the internal pointer-based representation of a String. Lines 55–56 declare the private data members of the class. Our String class has a length field, which represents the number of characters in the string, not including the null character at the end, and has a pointer sPtr that points to the dynamically allocated memory representing the character string.

```
1   // Fig. 12.9: String.h
2   // String class definition with operator overloading.
3   #ifndef STRING_H
4   #define STRING_H
5
```

Fig. 12.9 | String class definition with operator overloading. (Part 1 of 3.)

```
 6   #include <iostream>
 7   using std::ostream;
 8   using std::istream;
 9
10   class String
11   {
12      friend ostream &operator<<( ostream &, const String & );
13      friend istream &operator>>( istream &, String & );
14   public:
15      String( const char * = "" ); // conversion/default constructor
16      String( const String & ); // copy constructor
17      ~String(); // destructor
18
19      const String &operator=( const String & ); // assignment operator
20      const String &operator+=( const String & ); // concatenation operator
21
22      bool operator!() const; // is String empty?
23      bool operator==( const String & ) const; // test s1 == s2
24      bool operator<( const String & ) const; // test s1 < s2
25
26      // test s1 != s2
27      bool operator!=( const String &right ) const
28      {
29         return !( *this == right );
30      } // end function operator!=
31
32      // test s1 > s2
33      bool operator>( const String &right ) const
34      {
35         return right < *this;
36      } // end function operator>
37
38      // test s1 <= s2
39      bool operator<=( const String &right ) const
40      {
41         return !( right < *this );
42      } // end function operator <=
43
44      // test s1 >= s2
45      bool operator>=( const String &right ) const
46      {
47         return !( *this < right );
48      } // end function operator>=
49
50      char &operator[]( int ); // subscript operator (modifiable lvalue)
51      char operator[]( int ) const; // subscript operator (rvalue)
52      String operator()( int, int = 0 ) const; // return a substring
53      int getLength() const; // return string length
54   private:
55      int length; // string length (not counting null terminator)
56      char *sPtr; // pointer to start of pointer-based string
57
```

Fig. 12.9 | String class definition with operator overloading. (Part 2 of 3.)

```
58      void setString( const char * ); // utility function
59   }; // end class String
60
61   #endif
```

Fig. 12.9 | String class definition with operator overloading. (Part 3 of 3.)

```
1    // Fig. 12.10: String.cpp
2    // String class member-function and friend-function definitions.
3    #include <iostream>
4    using std::cerr;
5    using std::cout;
6    using std::endl;
7
8    #include <iomanip>
9    using std::setw;
10
11   #include <cstring> // strcpy and strcat prototypes
12   using std::strcmp;
13   using std::strcpy;
14   using std::strcat;
15
16   #include <cstdlib> // exit prototype
17   using std::exit;
18
19   #include "String.h" // String class definition
20
21   // conversion (and default) constructor converts char * to String
22   String::String( const char *s )
23      : length( ( s != 0 ) ? strlen( s ) : 0 )
24   {
25      cout << "Conversion (and default) constructor: " << s << endl;
26      setString( s ); // call utility function
27   } // end String conversion constructor
28
29   // copy constructor
30   String::String( const String &copy )
31      : length( copy.length )
32   {
33      cout << "Copy constructor: " << copy.sPtr << endl;
34      setString( copy.sPtr ); // call utility function
35   } // end String copy constructor
36
37   // Destructor
38   String::~String()
39   {
40      cout << "Destructor: " << sPtr << endl;
41      delete [] sPtr; // release pointer-based string memory
42   } // end ~String destructor
43
```

Fig. 12.10 | String class member- and friend-function definitions. (Part 1 of 4.)

```
44   // overloaded = operator; avoids self assignment
45   const String &String::operator=( const String &right )
46   {
47      cout << "operator= called" << endl;
48
49      if ( &right != this ) // avoid self assignment
50      {
51         delete [] sPtr; // prevents memory leak
52         length = right.length; // new String length
53         setString( right.sPtr ); // call utility function
54      } // end if
55      else
56         cout << "Attempted assignment of a String to itself" << endl;
57
58      return *this; // enables cascaded assignments
59   } // end function operator=
60
61   // concatenate right operand to this object and store in this object
62   const String &String::operator+=( const String &right )
63   {
64      size_t newLength = length + right.length; // new length
65      char *tempPtr = new char[ newLength + 1 ]; // create memory
66
67      strcpy( tempPtr, sPtr ); // copy sPtr
68      strcpy( tempPtr + length, right.sPtr ); // copy right.sPtr
69
70      delete [] sPtr; // reclaim old space
71      sPtr = tempPtr; // assign new array to sPtr
72      length = newLength; // assign new length to length
73      return *this; // enables cascaded calls
74   } // end function operator+=
75
76   // is this String empty?
77   bool String::operator!() const
78   {
79      return length == 0;
80   } // end function operator!
81
82   // Is this String equal to right String?
83   bool String::operator==( const String &right ) const
84   {
85      return strcmp( sPtr, right.sPtr ) == 0;
86   } // end function operator==
87
88   // Is this String less than right String?
89   bool String::operator<( const String &right ) const
90   {
91      return strcmp( sPtr, right.sPtr ) < 0;
92   } // end function operator<
93
94   // return reference to character in String as a modifiable lvalue
95   char &String::operator[]( int subscript )
96   {
```

Fig. 12.10 | String class member- and friend-function definitions. (Part 2 of 4.)

```
 97      // test for subscript out of range
 98      if ( subscript < 0 || subscript >= length )
 99      {
100         cerr << "Error: Subscript " << subscript
101            << " out of range" << endl;
102         exit( 1 ); // terminate program
103      } // end if
104
105      return sPtr[ subscript ]; // non-const return; modifiable lvalue
106   } // end function operator[]
107
108   // return reference to character in String as rvalue
109   char String::operator[]( int subscript ) const
110   {
111      // test for subscript out of range
112      if ( subscript < 0 || subscript >= length )
113      {
114         cerr << "Error: Subscript " << subscript
115            << " out of range" << endl;
116         exit( 1 ); // terminate program
117      } // end if
118
119      return sPtr[ subscript ]; // returns copy of this element
120   } // end function operator[]
121
122   // return a substring beginning at index and of length subLength
123   String String::operator()( int index, int subLength ) const
124   {
125      // if index is out of range or substring length < 0,
126      // return an empty String object
127      if ( index < 0 || index >= length || subLength < 0 )
128         return ""; // converted to a String object automatically
129
130      // determine length of substring
131      int len;
132
133      if ( ( subLength == 0 ) || ( index + subLength > length ) )
134         len = length - index;
135      else
136         len = subLength;
137
138      // allocate temporary array for substring and
139      // terminating null character
140      char *tempPtr = new char[ len + 1 ];
141
142      // copy substring into char array and terminate string
143      strncpy( tempPtr, &sPtr[ index ], len );
144      tempPtr[ len ] = '\0';
145
146      // create temporary String object containing the substring
147      String tempString( tempPtr );
148      delete [] tempPtr; // delete temporary array
```

Fig. 12.10 | String class member- and friend-function definitions. (Part 3 of 4.)

```
149       return tempString; // return copy of the temporary String
150    } // end function operator()
151
152    // return string length
153    int String::getLength() const
154    {
155       return length;
156    } // end function getLength
157
158    // utility function called by constructors and operator=
159    void String::setString( const char *string2 )
160    {
161       sPtr = new char[ length + 1 ]; // allocate memory
162
163       if ( string2 != 0 ) // if string2 is not null pointer, copy contents
164          strcpy( sPtr, string2 ); // copy literal to object
165       else // if string2 is a null pointer, make this an empty string
166          sPtr[ 0 ] = '\0'; // empty string
167    } // end function setString
168
169    // overloaded output operator
170    ostream &operator<<( ostream &output, const String &s )
171    {
172       output << s.sPtr;
173       return output; // enables cascading
174    } // end function operator<<
175
176    // overloaded input operator
177    istream &operator>>( istream &input, String &s )
178    {
179       char temp[ 100 ]; // buffer to store input
180       input >> setw( 100 ) >> temp;
181       s = temp; // use String class assignment operator
182       return input; // enables cascading
183    } // end function operator>>
```

Fig. 12.10 | String class member- and friend-function definitions. (Part 4 of 4.)

```
1    // Fig. 12.11: StringTest.cpp
2    // String class test program.
3    #include <iostream>
4    using std::cout;
5    using std::endl;
6    using std::boolalpha;
7
8    #include "String.h"
9
10   int main()
11   {
12      String s1( "happy" );
13      String s2( " birthday" );
14      String s3;
```

Fig. 12.11 | String class test program. (Part 1 of 4.)

```
15
16      // test overloaded equality and relational operators
17      cout << "s1 is \"" << s1 << "\"; s2 is \"" << s2
18          << "\"; s3 is \"" << s3 << '\"'
19          << boolalpha << "\n\nThe results of comparing s2 and s1:"
20          << "\ns2 == s1 yields " << ( s2 == s1 )
21          << "\ns2 != s1 yields " << ( s2 != s1 )
22          << "\ns2 >  s1 yields " << ( s2 > s1 )
23          << "\ns2 <  s1 yields " << ( s2 < s1 )
24          << "\ns2 >= s1 yields " << ( s2 >= s1 )
25          << "\ns2 <= s1 yields " << ( s2 <= s1 );
26
27
28      // test overloaded String empty (!) operator
29      cout << "\n\nTesting !s3:" << endl;
30
31      if ( !s3 )
32      {
33          cout << "s3 is empty; assigning s1 to s3;" << endl;
34          s3 = s1; // test overloaded assignment
35          cout << "s3 is \"" << s3 << "\"";
36      } // end if
37
38      // test overloaded String concatenation operator
39      cout << "\n\ns1 += s2 yields s1 = ";
40      s1 += s2; // test overloaded concatenation
41      cout << s1;
42
43      // test conversion constructor
44      cout << "\n\ns1 += \" to you\" yields" << endl;
45      s1 += " to you"; // test conversion constructor
46      cout << "s1 = " << s1 << "\n\n";
47
48      // test overloaded function call operator () for substring
49      cout << "The substring of s1 starting at\n"
50          << "location 0 for 14 characters, s1(0, 14), is:\n"
51          << s1( 0, 14 ) << "\n\n";
52
53      // test substring "to-end-of-String" option
54      cout << "The substring of s1 starting at\n"
55          << "location 15, s1(15), is: "
56          << s1( 15 ) << "\n\n";
57
58      // test copy constructor
59      String *s4Ptr = new String( s1 );
60      cout << "\n*s4Ptr = " << *s4Ptr << "\n\n";
61
62      // test assignment (=) operator with self-assignment
63      cout << "assigning *s4Ptr to *s4Ptr" << endl;
64      *s4Ptr = *s4Ptr; // test overloaded assignment
65      cout << "*s4Ptr = " << *s4Ptr << endl;
66
```

Fig. 12.11 | String class test program. (Part 2 of 4.)

```
67        // test destructor
68        delete s4Ptr;
69
70        // test using subscript operator to create a modifiable lvalue
71        s1[ 0 ] = 'H';
72        s1[ 6 ] = 'B';
73        cout << "\ns1 after s1[0] = 'H' and s1[6] = 'B' is: "
74           << s1 << "\n\n";
75
76        // test subscript out of range
77        cout << "Attempt to assign 'd' to s1[30] yields:" << endl;
78        s1[ 30 ] = 'd'; // ERROR: subscript out of range
79        return 0;
80    } // end main
```

```
Conversion (and default) constructor: happy
Conversion (and default) constructor:  birthday
Conversion (and default) constructor:
s1 is "happy"; s2 is " birthday"; s3 is ""

The results of comparing s2 and s1:
s2 == s1 yields false
s2 != s1 yields true
s2 >  s1 yields false
s2 <  s1 yields true
s2 >= s1 yields false
s2 <= s1 yields true

Testing !s3:
s3 is empty; assigning s1 to s3;
operator= called
s3 is "happy"

s1 += s2 yields s1 = happy birthday

s1 += " to you" yields
Conversion (and default) constructor:  to you
Destructor:  to you
s1 = happy birthday to you

Conversion (and default) constructor: happy birthday
Copy constructor: happy birthday
Destructor: happy birthday
The substring of s1 starting at
location 0 for 14 characters, s1(0, 14), is:
happy birthday

Destructor: happy birthday
Conversion (and default) constructor: to you
Copy constructor: to you
Destructor: to you
The substring of s1 starting at
location 15, s1(15), is: to you
```

Fig. 12.11 | String class test program. (Part 3 of 4.)

```
Destructor: to you
Copy constructor: happy birthday to you

*s4Ptr = happy birthday to you

assigning *s4Ptr to *s4Ptr
operator= called
Attempted assignment of a String to itself
*s4Ptr = happy birthday to you
Destructor: happy birthday to you

s1 after s1[0] = 'H' and s1[6] = 'B' is: Happy Birthday to you

Attempt to assign 'd' to s1[30] yields:
Error: Subscript 30 out of range
```

Fig. 12.11 | String class test program. (Part 4 of 4.)

Overloading the Stream Insertion and Stream Extraction Operators as friends
Lines 12–13 (Fig. 12.9) declare the overloaded stream insertion operator function oper-
ator<< (defined in Fig. 12.10, lines 170–174) and the overloaded stream extraction operator function operator>> (defined in Fig. 12.10, lines 177–183) as friends of the class.
The implementation of operator<< is straightforward. Note that operator>> restricts the
total number of characters that can be read into array temp to 99 with setw (line 180); the
100th position is reserved for the string's terminating null character. [*Note:* We did not
have this restriction for operator>> in class Array (Figs. 12.6–12.7), because that class's
operator>> read one array element at a time and stopped reading values when the end of
the array was reached. Object cin does not know how to do this by default for input of
character arrays.] Also, note the use of operator= (line 181) to assign the C-style string
temp to the String object to which s refers. This statement invokes the conversion constructor to create a temporary String object containing the C-style string; the temporary
String is then assigned to s. We could eliminate the overhead of creating the temporary
String object here by providing another overloaded assignment operator that receives a
parameter of type const char *.

String Conversion Constructor
Line 15 (Fig. 12.9) declares a conversion constructor. This constructor (defined in
Fig. 12.10, lines 22–27) takes a const char * argument (that defaults to the empty string;
Fig. 12.9, line 15) and initializes a String object containing that same character string.
Any *single-argument constructor* can be thought of as a conversion constructor. As we'll
see, such constructors are helpful when we are doing any String operation using char *
arguments. The conversion constructor can convert a char * string into a String object,
which can then be assigned to the target String object. The availability of this conversion
constructor means that it is not necessary to supply an overloaded assignment operator for
specifically assigning character strings to String objects. The compiler invokes the conversion constructor to create a temporary String object containing the character string;
then the overloaded assignment operator is invoked to assign the temporary String object
to another String object.

Software Engineering Observation 12.8

When a conversion constructor is used to perform an implicit conversion, Visual C++ can apply only one implicit constructor call (i.e., a single user-defined conversion) to try to match the needs of another overloaded operator. The compiler will not match an overloaded operator's needs by performing a series of implicit, user-defined conversions.

The String conversion constructor could be invoked in such a declaration as String s1("happy"). The conversion constructor calculates the length of its character-string argument and assigns it to data member length in the member-initializer list. Then, line 26 calls utility function setString (defined in Fig. 12.10, lines 159–167), which uses new to allocate a sufficient amount of memory to private data member sPtr and uses strcpy to copy the character string into the memory to which sPtr points.[4]

String Copy Constructor

Line 16 in Fig. 12.9 declares a copy constructor (defined in Fig. 12.10, lines 30–35) that initializes a String object by making a copy of an existing String object. As with our class Array (Figs. 12.6–12.7), such copying must be done carefully to avoid the pitfall in which both String objects point to the same dynamically allocated memory. The copy constructor operates similarly to the conversion constructor, except that it simply copies the length member from the source String object to the target String object. Note that the copy constructor calls setString to create new space for the target object's internal character string. If it simply copied the sPtr in the source object to the target object's sPtr, then both objects would point to the same dynamically allocated memory. The first destructor to execute would then delete the dynamically allocated memory, and the other object's sPtr would be undefined (i.e., sPtr would be a dangling pointer), a situation likely to cause a serious runtime error.

String Destructor

Line 17 of Fig. 12.9 declares the String destructor (defined in Fig. 12.10, lines 38–42). The destructor uses delete [] to release the dynamic memory to which sPtr points.

Overloaded Assignment Operator

Line 19 (Fig. 12.9) declares the overloaded assignment-operator function operator= (defined in Fig. 12.10, lines 45–59). When the compiler sees an expression like string1 = string2, it generates the function call

        string1.**operator**=(string2);

The overloaded assignment-operator function operator= tests for self-assignment. If this is a self-assignment, the function does not need to change the object. If this test were omitted, the function would immediately delete the space in the target object and thus lose the character string, such that the pointer would no longer be pointing to valid data—a classic example of a dangling pointer. If there is no self-assignment, the function deletes the mem-

---

4. There is a subtle issue in the implementation of this conversion constructor. As implemented, if a null pointer (i.e., 0) is passed to the constructor, the program will fail. The proper way to implement this constructor would be to detect whether the constructor argument is a null pointer, then "throw an exception." Chapter 16 discusses how we can make classes more robust in this manner. Also, note that a null pointer (0) is not the same as the empty string (""). A null pointer is a pointer that does not point to anything. An empty string is an actual string that contains only a null character ('\0').

ory and copies the length field of the source object to the target object. Then operator= calls setString to create new space for the target object and copy the character string from the source object to the target object. Whether or not this is a self-assignment, operator= returns *this to enable cascaded assignments.

Overloaded Addition Assignment Operator

Line 20 of Fig. 12.9 declares the overloaded string-concatenation operator += (defined in Fig. 12.10, lines 62–74). When the compiler sees the expression s1 += s2 (line 40 of Fig. 12.11), it generates the member-function call

```
s1.operator+=( s2 )
```

Function operator+= calculates the combined length of the concatenated string and stores it in local variable newLength, then creates a temporary pointer (tempPtr) and allocates a new character array in which the concatenated string will be stored. Next, operator+= uses strcpy to copy the original character strings from sPtr and right.sPtr into the memory to which tempPtr points. Note that the location into which strcpy will copy the first character of right.sPtr is determined by the pointer-arithmetic calculation tempPtr + length. This calculation indicates that the first character of right.sPtr should be placed at location length in the array to which tempPtr points. Next, operator+= uses delete [] to release the space occupied by this object's original character string, assigns tempPtr to sPtr so that this String object points to the new character string, assigns newLength to length so that this String object contains the new string length and returns *this as a const String & to enable cascading of += operators.

Do we need a second overloaded concatenation operator to allow concatenation of a String and a char *? No. The const char * conversion constructor converts a C-style string into a temporary String object, which then matches the existing overloaded concatenation operator. This is exactly what the compiler does when it encounters line 45 in Fig. 12.11. Again, Visual C++ can perform such conversions only one level deep to facilitate a match. Visual C++ can also perform an implicit compiler-defined conversion between fundamental types before it performs the conversion between a fundamental type and a class. Note that, when a temporary String object is created in this case, the conversion constructor and the destructor are called (see the output resulting from line 45, s1 += " to you", in Fig. 12.11). This is an example of function-call overhead that is hidden from the client of the class when temporary class objects are created and destroyed during implicit conversions. Similar overhead is generated by copy constructors in call-by-value parameter passing and in returning class objects by value.

Performance Tip 12.2

*Overloading the += concatenation operator with an additional version that takes a single argument of type const char * executes more efficiently than having only a version that takes a String argument. Without the const char * version of the += operator, a const char * argument would first be converted to a String object with class String's conversion constructor, then the += operator that receives a String argument would be called to perform the concatenation.*

Software Engineering Observation 12.9

Using implicit conversions with overloaded operators, rather than overloading operators for many different operand types, often requires less code, which makes a class easier to modify, maintain and debug.

Overloaded Negation Operator

Line 22 of Fig. 12.9 declares the overloaded negation operator (defined in Fig. 12.10, lines 77–80). This operator determines whether an object of our String class is empty. For example, when the compiler sees the expression !string1, it generates the function call

```
string1.operator!()
```

This function simply returns the result of testing whether length is equal to zero.

Overloaded Equality and Relational Operators

Lines 23–24 of Fig. 12.9 declare the overloaded equality operator (defined in Fig. 12.10, lines 83–86) and the overloaded less-than operator (defined in Fig. 12.10, lines 89–92) for class String. These are similar, so let us discuss only one example, namely, overloading the == operator. When the compiler sees the expression string1 == string2, it generates the member-function call

```
string1.operator==( string2 )
```

which returns true if string1 is equal to string2. Each of these operators uses function strcmp (from <cstring>) to compare the character strings in the String objects. Many Visual C++ programmers advocate using some of the overloaded operator functions to implement others. So, the !=, >, <= and >= operators are implemented (Fig. 12.9, lines 27–48) in terms of operator== and operator<. For example, overloaded function operator>= (implemented in lines 45–48 in the header file) uses the overloaded < operator to determine whether one String object is greater than or equal to another. Note that the operator functions for !=, >, <= and >= are defined in the header file. The compiler inlines these definitions to eliminate the overhead of the extra function calls.

Software Engineering Observation 12.10

By implementing member functions using previously defined member functions, you reuse code to reduce the amount of code that must be written and maintained.

Overloaded Subscript Operators

Lines 50–51 in the header file declare two overloaded subscript operators (defined in Fig. 12.10, lines 95–106 and 109–120, respectively)—one for non-const Strings and one for const Strings. When the compiler sees an expression like string1[0], it generates the member-function call

```
string1.operator[]( 0 )
```

(using the appropriate version of operator[] based on whether the String is const). Each implementation of operator[] first validates the subscript to ensure that it is in range. If the subscript is out of range, each function prints an error message and terminates the program with a call to exit.[5] If the subscript is in range, the non-const version of operator[] returns a char & to the appropriate character of the String object; this char & may be used as an *lvalue* to modify the designated character of the String object. The const version of operator[] returns the appropriate character of the String object; this can be used only as an *rvalue* to read the value of the character.

---

5. Again, it is more appropriate when a subscript is out of range to "throw an exception" indicating the out-of-range subscript.

Overloaded Function-Call Operator

Line 52 of Fig. 12.9 declares the *overloaded function-call operator* (defined in Fig. 12.10, lines 123–150). We overload this operator to select a substring from a String. The two integer parameters specify the start location and the length of the substring being selected from the String. If the start location is out of range or the substring length is negative, the operator simply returns an empty String. If the substring length is 0, then the substring is selected to the end of the String object. For example, suppose string1 is a String object containing the string "AEIOU". For the expression string1(2, 2), the compiler generates the member-function call

```
string1.operator()( 2, 2 )
```

When this call executes, it produces a String object containing the string "IO" and returns a copy of that object.

Overloading the function-call operator () is powerful, because functions can take arbitrarily long and complex parameter lists. So we can use this capability for many interesting purposes. One such use of the function-call operator is an alternate array-subscripting notation: Instead of using C's awkward double-square-bracket notation for pointer-based two-dimensional arrays, such as in a[b][c], some programmers prefer to overload the function-call operator to enable the notation a(b, c). The overloaded function-call operator must be a non-static member function. This operator is used only when the "function name" is an object of class String.

String Member Function getLength

Line 53 in Fig. 12.9 declares function getLength (defined in Fig. 12.10, lines 153–156), which returns the length of a String.

Notes on Our String Class

At this point, you should step through the code in main, examine the output window and check each use of an overloaded operator. As you study the output, pay special attention to the implicit constructor calls that are generated to create temporary String objects throughout the program. Many of these calls introduce additional overhead into the program that can be avoided if the class provides overloaded operators that take char * arguments. However, additional operator functions can make the class harder to maintain, modify and debug.

12.11 Overloading ++ and --

The prefix and postfix versions of the increment and decrement operators can all be overloaded. We'll see how the compiler distinguishes between the prefix version and the postfix version of an increment or decrement operator.

To overload the increment operator to allow both prefix and postfix increment usage, each overloaded operator function must have a distinct signature, so that the compiler will be able to determine which version of ++ is intended. The prefix versions are overloaded exactly as any other prefix unary operator would be.

Overloading the Prefix Increment Operator

Suppose, for example, that we want to add 1 to the day in Date object d1. When the compiler sees the preincrementing expression ++d1, it generates the member-function call

```
d1.operator++()
```

The prototype for this operator function would be

```
Date &operator++();
```

If the prefix increment operator is implemented as a global function, then, when the compiler sees the expression ++d1, it generates the function call

```
operator++( d1 )
```

The prototype for this operator function would be declared in the Date class as

```
Date &operator++( Date & );
```

Overloading the Postfix Increment Operator

Overloading the postfix increment operator presents a challenge, because the compiler must be able to distinguish between the signatures of the overloaded prefix and postfix increment operator functions. The convention that has been adopted in Visual C++ is that, when the compiler sees the postincrementing expression d1++, it generates the member-function call

```
d1.operator++( 0 )
```

The prototype for this function is

```
Date operator++( int )
```

The argument 0 is strictly a "dummy value" that enables the compiler to distinguish between the prefix and postfix increment operator functions.

If the postfix increment is implemented as a global function, then, when the compiler sees the expression d1++, it generates the function call

```
operator++( d1, 0 )
```

The prototype for this function would be

```
Date operator++( Date &, int );
```

Once again, the 0 argument is used by the compiler to distinguish between the prefix and postfix increment operators implemented as global functions. Note that the postfix increment operator returns Date objects by value, whereas the prefix increment operator returns Date objects by reference, because the postfix increment operator typically returns a temporary object that contains the original value of the object before the increment occurred. Visual C++ treats such objects as *rvalues*, which cannot be used on the left side of an assignment. The prefix increment operator returns the actual incremented object with its new value. Such an object can be used as an *lvalue* in a continuing expression.

Performance Tip 12.3

The extra object that is created by the postfix increment (or decrement) operator can result in a significant performance problem—especially when the operator is used in a loop. For this reason, you should use the postfix increment (or decrement) operator only when the logic of the program requires postincrementing (or postdecrementing).

Everything stated in this section for overloading prefix and postfix increment operators applies to overloading predecrement and postdecrement operators. Next, we examine a Date class with overloaded prefix and postfix increment operators.

12.12 Case Study: A Date Class

The program of Figs. 12.12–12.14 demonstrates a Date class that uses overloaded prefix and postfix increment operators to add 1 to the day in a Date object, while causing appropriate increments to the month and year if necessary. The Date header file (Fig. 12.12) specifies that Date's public interface includes an overloaded stream insertion operator (line 11), a default constructor (line 13), a setDate function (line 14), an overloaded prefix increment operator (line 15), an overloaded postfix increment operator (line 16), an overloaded += addition assignment operator (line 17), a function to test for leap years (line 18) and a function to determine whether a day is the last day of the month (line 19).

Function main (Fig. 12.14) creates three Date objects (lines 11–13)—d1 is initialized by default to January 1, 1900; d2 is initialized to December 27, 1992; and d3 is initialized to an invalid date. The Date constructor (defined in Fig. 12.13, lines 11–14) calls setDate to validate the month, day and year specified. An invalid month is set to 1, an invalid year is set to 1900 and an invalid day is set to 1.

```
1   // Fig. 12.12: Date.h
2   // Date class definition with overloaded increment operators.
3   #ifndef DATE_H
4   #define DATE_H
5
6   #include <iostream>
7   using std::ostream;
8
9   class Date
10  {
11     friend ostream &operator<<( ostream &, const Date & );
12  public:
13     Date( int m = 1, int d = 1, int y = 1900 ); // default constructor
14     void setDate( int, int, int ); // set month, day, year
15     Date &operator++(); // prefix increment operator
16     Date operator++( int ); // postfix increment operator
17     const Date &operator+=( int ); // add days, modify object
18     bool leapYear( int ) const; // is date in a leap year?
19     bool endOfMonth( int ) const; // is date at the end of month?
20  private:
21     int month;
22     int day;
23     int year;
24
25     static const int days[]; // array of days per month
26     void helpIncrement(); // utility function for incrementing date
27  }; // end class Date
28
29  #endif
```

Fig. 12.12 | Date class definition with overloaded increment operators.

```
 1   // Fig. 12.13: Date.cpp
 2   // Date class member- and friend-function definitions.
 3   #include <iostream>
 4   #include "Date.h"
 5
 6   // initialize static member at file scope; one classwide copy
 7   const int Date::days[] =
 8      { 0, 31, 28, 31, 30, 31, 30, 31, 31, 30, 31, 30, 31 };
 9
10   // Date constructor
11   Date::Date( int m, int d, int y )
12   {
13      setDate( m, d, y );
14   } // end Date constructor
15
16   // set month, day and year
17   void Date::setDate( int mm, int dd, int yy )
18   {
19      month = ( mm >= 1 && mm <= 12 ) ? mm : 1;
20      year = ( yy >= 1900 && yy <= 2100 ) ? yy : 1900;
21
22      // test for a leap year
23      if ( month == 2 && leapYear( year ) )
24         day = ( dd >= 1 && dd <= 29 ) ? dd : 1;
25      else
26         day = ( dd >= 1 && dd <= days[ month ] ) ? dd : 1;
27   } // end function setDate
28
29   // overloaded prefix increment operator
30   Date &Date::operator++()
31   {
32      helpIncrement(); // increment date
33      return *this; // reference return to create an lvalue
34   } // end function operator++
35
36   // overloaded postfix increment operator; note that the
37   // dummy integer parameter does not have a parameter name
38   Date Date::operator++( int )
39   {
40      Date temp = *this; // hold current state of object
41      helpIncrement();
42
43      // return unincremented, saved, temporary object
44      return temp; // value return; not a reference return
45   } // end function operator++
46
47   // add specified number of days to date
48   const Date &Date::operator+=( int additionalDays )
49   {
50      for ( int i = 0; i < additionalDays; i++ )
51         helpIncrement();
52
```

Fig. 12.13 | Date class member- and friend-function definitions. (Part 1 of 2.)

```
53        return *this; // enables cascading
54    } // end function operator+=
55
56    // if the year is a leap year, return true; otherwise, return false
57    bool Date::leapYear( int testYear ) const
58    {
59        if ( testYear % 400 == 0 ||
60            ( testYear % 100 != 0 && testYear % 4 == 0 ) )
61            return true; // a leap year
62        else
63            return false; // not a leap year
64    } // end function leapYear
65
66    // determine whether the day is the last day of the month
67    bool Date::endOfMonth( int testDay ) const
68    {
69        if ( month == 2 && leapYear( year ) )
70            return testDay == 29; // last day of Feb. in leap year
71        else
72            return testDay == days[ month ];
73    } // end function endOfMonth
74
75    // function to help increment the date
76    void Date::helpIncrement()
77    {
78        // day is not end of month
79        if ( !endOfMonth( day ) )
80            day++; // increment day
81        else
82            if ( month < 12 ) // day is end of month and month < 12
83            {
84                month++; // increment month
85                day = 1; // first day of new month
86            } // end if
87            else // last day of year
88            {
89                year++; // increment year
90                month = 1; // first month of new year
91                day = 1; // first day of new month
92            } // end else
93    } // end function helpIncrement
94
95    // overloaded output operator
96    ostream &operator<<( ostream &output, const Date &d )
97    {
98        static char *monthName[ 13 ] = { "", "January", "February",
99            "March", "April", "May", "June", "July", "August",
100            "September", "October", "November", "December" };
101        output << monthName[ d.month ] << ' ' << d.day << ", " << d.year;
102        return output; // enables cascading
103    } // end function operator<<
```

Fig. 12.13 | Date class member- and friend-function definitions. (Part 2 of 2.)

```cpp
1   // Fig. 12.14: DateTest.cpp
2   // Date class test program.
3   #include <iostream>
4   using std::cout;
5   using std::endl;
6
7   #include "Date.h" // Date class definition
8
9   int main()
10  {
11     Date d1; // defaults to January 1, 1900
12     Date d2( 12, 27, 1992 ); // December 27, 1992
13     Date d3( 0, 99, 8045 ); // invalid date
14
15     cout << "d1 is " << d1 << "\nd2 is " << d2 << "\nd3 is " << d3;
16     cout << "\n\nd2 += 7 is " << ( d2 += 7 );
17
18     d3.setDate( 2, 28, 1992 );
19     cout << "\n\n  d3 is " << d3;
20     cout << "\n++d3 is " << ++d3 << " (leap year allows 29th)";
21
22     Date d4( 7, 13, 2002 );
23
24     cout << "\n\nTesting the prefix increment operator:\n"
25        << "  d4 is " << d4 << endl;
26     cout << "++d4 is " << ++d4 << endl;
27     cout << "  d4 is " << d4;
28
29     cout << "\n\nTesting the postfix increment operator:\n"
30        << "  d4 is " << d4 << endl;
31     cout << "d4++ is " << d4++ << endl;
32     cout << "  d4 is " << d4 << endl;
33     return 0;
34  } // end main
```

```
d1 is January 1, 1900
d2 is December 27, 1992
d3 is January 1, 1900

d2 += 7 is January 3, 1993

  d3 is February 28, 1992
++d3 is February 29, 1992 (leap year allows 29th)

Testing the prefix increment operator:
  d4 is July 13, 2002
++d4 is July 14, 2002
  d4 is July 14, 2002

Testing the postfix increment operator:
  d4 is July 14, 2002
d4++ is July 14, 2002
  d4 is July 15, 2002
```

Fig. 12.14 | Date class test program.

Lines 15–16 of main output each of the constructed Date objects, using the overloaded stream insertion operator (defined in Fig. 12.13, lines 96–103). Line 16 of main uses the overloaded operator += to add seven days to d2. Line 18 uses function setDate to set d3 to February 28, 1992, which is a leap year. Then, line 20 preincrements d3 to show that the date increments properly to February 29. Next, line 22 creates a Date object, d4, which is initialized with the date July 13, 2002. Then line 26 increments d4 by 1 with the overloaded prefix increment operator. Lines 24–27 output d4 before and after the preincrement operation to confirm that it worked correctly. Finally, line 31 increments d4 with the overloaded postfix increment operator. Lines 29–32 output d4 before and after the postincrement operation to confirm that it worked correctly.

Overloading the prefix increment operator is straightforward. The prefix increment operator (defined in Fig. 12.13, lines 30–34) calls utility function helpIncrement (defined in Fig. 12.13, lines 76–93) to increment the date. This function deals with "wraparounds" or "carries" that occur when we increment the last day of the month. These carries require incrementing the month. If the month is already 12, then the year must also be incremented and the month must be set to 1. Function helpIncrement uses function endOfMonth to increment the day correctly.

The overloaded prefix increment operator returns a reference to the current Date object (i.e., the one that was just incremented). This occurs because the current object, *this, is returned as a Date &. This enables a preincremented Date object to be used as an *lvalue*, which is how the built-in prefix increment operator works for fundamental types.

Overloading the postfix increment operator (defined in Fig. 12.13, lines 38–45) is trickier. To emulate the effect of the postincrement, we must return an unincremented copy of the Date object. For example, if int variable x has the value 7, the statement

```
cout << x++ << endl;
```

outputs the original value of variable x. So we'd like our postfix increment operator to operate the same way on a Date object. On entry to operator++, we save the current object (*this) in temp (line 40). Next, we call helpIncrement to increment the current Date object. Then, line 44 returns the unincremented copy of the object previously stored in temp. Note that this function cannot return a reference to the local Date object temp, because a local variable is destroyed when the function in which it is declared exits. Thus, declaring the return type to this function as Date & would return a reference to an object that no longer exists. Returning a reference (or a pointer) to a local variable is a common error for which most compilers will issue a warning.

12.13 Standard Library Class string

In this chapter, you learned that you can build a String class (Figs. 12.9–12.11) that is better than the C-style, char * strings that Visual C++ absorbed from C. You also learned that you can build an Array class (Figs. 12.6–12.8) that is better than the C-style, pointer-based arrays that Visual C++ absorbed from C.

Building useful, reusable classes such as String and Array takes work. However, once such classes are tested and debugged, they can be reused by you, your colleagues, your company, many companies, an entire industry or even many industries (if they are placed in public or for-sale libraries). The designers of C++ did exactly that, building class string (which we have been using since Chapter 4) and class template vector (which we introduced in Chapter 8) into standard C++. These classes are available to anyone building applications with Visual C++. As you'll see in Chapter 23, the C++ Standard Library provides several predefined class templates for use in your programs.

We now reimplement the String example (Figs. 12.9–12.11), using the standard C++ string class. We demonstrate the similar functionality provided by standard class string. We also demonstrate three member functions of standard class string—empty, substr and at—that were not part of our String example. Function empty determines whether a string is empty, function substr returns a string that represents a portion of an existing string and function at returns the character at a specific index in a string (after checking that the index is in range). Chapter 19 presents class string in detail.

Standard Library Class *string*

The program of Fig. 12.15 reimplements the program of Fig. 12.11, using standard class string. As you'll see in this example, class string provides all the functionality of our class String presented in Figs. 12.9–12.10. Class string is defined in header <string> (line 7) and belongs to namespace std (line 8).

Lines 12–14 create three string objects—s1 is initialized with the literal "happy", s2 is initialized with the literal " birthday" and s3 uses the default string constructor to create an empty string. Lines 17–18 output these three objects, using cout and operator <<, which the string class designers overloaded to handle string objects. Then lines 19–25 show the results of comparing s2 to s1 by using class string's overloaded equality and relational operators.

```
1   // Fig. 12.15: StringTest.cpp
2   // Standard Library string class test program.
3   #include <iostream>
4   using std::cout;
5   using std::endl;
6
7   #include <string>
8   using std::string;
9
10  int main()
11  {
12     string s1( "happy" );
13     string s2( " birthday" );
14     string s3;
15
16     // test overloaded equality and relational operators
17     cout << "s1 is \"" << s1 << "\"; s2 is \"" << s2
18        << "\"; s3 is \"" << s3 << '\"'
19        << "\n\nThe results of comparing s2 and s1:"
20        << "\ns2 == s1 yields " << ( s2 == s1 ? "true" : "false" )
21        << "\ns2 != s1 yields " << ( s2 != s1 ? "true" : "false" )
22        << "\ns2 >  s1 yields " << ( s2 > s1 ? "true" : "false" )
23        << "\ns2 <  s1 yields " << ( s2 < s1 ? "true" : "false" )
24        << "\ns2 >= s1 yields " << ( s2 >= s1 ? "true" : "false" )
25        << "\ns2 <= s1 yields " << ( s2 <= s1 ? "true" : "false" );
26
```

Fig. 12.15 | Standard Library class string. (Part 1 of 3.)

```
27       // test string member-function empty
28       cout << "\n\nTesting s3.empty():" << endl;
29
30       if ( s3.empty() )
31       {
32          cout << "s3 is empty; assigning s1 to s3;" << endl;
33          s3 = s1; // assign s1 to s3
34          cout << "s3 is \"" << s3 << "\"";
35       } // end if
36
37       // test overloaded string concatenation operator
38       cout << "\n\ns1 += s2 yields s1 = ";
39       s1 += s2; // test overloaded concatenation
40       cout << s1;
41
42       // test overloaded string concatenation operator with C-style string
43       cout << "\n\ns1 += \" to you\" yields" << endl;
44       s1 += " to you";
45       cout << "s1 = " << s1 << "\n\n";
46
47       // test string member function substr
48       cout << "The substring of s1 starting at location 0 for\n"
49          << "14 characters, s1.substr(0, 14), is:\n"
50          << s1.substr( 0, 14 ) << "\n\n";
51
52       // test substr "to-end-of-string" option
53       cout << "The substring of s1 starting at\n"
54          << "location 15, s1.substr(15), is:\n"
55          << s1.substr( 15 ) << endl;
56
57       // test copy constructor
58       string *s4Ptr = new string( s1 );
59       cout << "\n*s4Ptr = " << *s4Ptr << "\n\n";
60
61       // test assignment (=) operator with self-assignment
62       cout << "assigning *s4Ptr to *s4Ptr" << endl;
63       *s4Ptr = *s4Ptr;
64       cout << "*s4Ptr = " << *s4Ptr << endl;
65
66       // test destructor
67       delete s4Ptr;
68
69       // test using subscript operator to create lvalue
70       s1[ 0 ] = 'H';
71       s1[ 6 ] = 'B';
72       cout << "\ns1 after s1[0] = 'H' and s1[6] = 'B' is: "
73          << s1 << "\n\n";
74
75       // test subscript out of range with string member function "at"
76       cout << "Attempt to assign 'd' to s1.at( 30 ) yields:" << endl;
77       s1.at( 30 ) = 'd'; // ERROR: subscript out of range
78       return 0;
79    } // end main
```

Fig. 12.15 | Standard Library class `string`. (Part 2 of 3.)

```
s1 is "happy"; s2 is " birthday"; s3 is ""

The results of comparing s2 and s1:
s2 == s1 yields false
s2 != s1 yields true
s2 >  s1 yields false
s2 <  s1 yields true
s2 >= s1 yields false
s2 <= s1 yields true

Testing s3.empty():
s3 is empty; assigning s1 to s3;
s3 is "happy"

s1 += s2 yields s1 = happy birthday

s1 += " to you" yields
s1 = happy birthday to you

The substring of s1 starting at location 0 for
14 characters, s1.substr(0, 14), is:
happy birthday

The substring of s1 starting at
location 15, s1.substr(15), is:
to you

*s4Ptr = happy birthday to you

assigning *s4Ptr to *s4Ptr
*s4Ptr = happy birthday to you

s1 after s1[0] = 'H' and s1[6] = 'B' is: Happy Birthday to you

Attempt to assign 'd' to s1.at( 30 ) yields:
```

Fig. 12.15 | Standard Library class string. (Part 3 of 3.)

Our class String (Figs. 12.9–12.10) provided an overloaded operator! that tested a String to determine whether it was empty. Standard class string does not provide this functionality as an overloaded operator; instead, it provides member function **empty**, which we demonstrate in line 30. Member function empty returns true if the string is empty; otherwise, it returns false.

Line 33 demonstrates class string's overloaded assignment operator by assigning s1 to s3. Line 34 outputs s3 to demonstrate that the assignment worked correctly.

Line 39 demonstrates class string's overloaded += operator for string concatenation. In this case, the contents of s2 are appended to s1. Then line 40 outputs the resulting string that is stored in s1. Line 44 demonstrates that a C-style string literal can be appended to a string object by using operator +=. Line 45 displays the result.

Our class String (Figs. 12.9–12.10) provided overloaded operator() to obtain substrings. Standard class string does not provide this functionality as an overloaded operator; instead, it provides member function substr (lines 50 and 55). The call to substr in line 50 obtains a 14-character substring (specified by the second argument) of s1 starting at position 0 (specified by the first argument). The call to substr in line 55 obtains a substring starting from position 15 of s1. When the second argument is not specified, substr returns the remainder of the string on which it is called.

Line 58 dynamically allocates a string object and initializes it with a copy of s1. This results in a call to class string's copy constructor. Line 63 uses class string's overloaded = operator to demonstrate that it handles self-assignment properly.

Lines 70–71 used class string's overloaded [] operator to create *lvalues* that enable new characters to replace existing characters in s1. Line 73 outputs the new value of s1. In our class String (Figs. 12.9–12.10), the overloaded [] operator performed bounds checking to determine whether the subscript it received as an argument was a valid subscript in the string. If the subscript was invalid, the operator printed an error message and terminated the program. Standard class string's overloaded [] operator does not perform any bounds checking. Therefore, you must ensure that operations using standard class string's overloaded [] operator do not accidentally manipulate elements outside the bounds of the string. Standard class string does provide bounds checking in its member function at, which "throws an exception" if its argument is an invalid subscript. By default, this causes a C++ program to terminate and produces a dialog with options to **Abort, Retry** or **Ignore** the error (simply click **Abort** in this case).[6] If the subscript is valid, function at returns the character at the specified location as a modifiable *lvalue* or an unmodifiable *lvalue* (i.e., a const reference), depending on the context in which the call appears. Line 77 demonstrates a call to function at with an invalid subscript.

12.14 `explicit` Constructors

In Sections 12.8–12.9, we discussed that any single-argument constructor can be used by the compiler to perform an implicit conversion—the type received by the constructor is converted to an object of the class in which the constructor is defined. The conversion is automatic and you need not use a cast operator. In some situations, implicit conversions are undesirable or error-prone. For example, our Array class in Fig. 12.6 defines a constructor that takes a single int argument. The intent of this constructor is to create an Array object containing the number of elements specified by the int argument. However, this constructor can be misused by the compiler to perform an implicit conversion.

 Common Programming Error 12.9

Unfortunately, the compiler might use implicit conversions in cases that you do not expect, resulting in ambiguous expressions that generate compilation errors or in execution-time logic errors.

Accidentally Using a Single-Argument Constructor as a Conversion Constructor

The program (Fig. 12.16) uses the Array class of Figs. 12.6–12.7 to demonstrate an improper implicit conversion.

Line 13 in main instantiates Array object integers1 and calls the single-argument constructor with the int value 7 to specify the number of elements in the Array. Recall

---

6. Again, Chapter 16, demonstrates how to "catch" and handle such exceptions.

```
 1    // Fig. 12.16: ArrayTest.cpp
 2    // Driver for simple class Array.
 3    #include <iostream>
 4    using std::cout;
 5    using std::endl;
 6
 7    #include "Array.h"
 8
 9    void outputArray( const Array & ); // prototype
10
11    int main()
12    {
13       Array integers1( 7 ); // 7-element array
14       outputArray( integers1 ); // output Array integers1
15       outputArray( 3 ); // convert 3 to an Array and output Array's contents
16       return 0;
17    } // end main
18
19    // print Array contents
20    void outputArray( const Array &arrayToOutput )
21    {
22       cout << "The Array received has " << arrayToOutput.getSize()
23          << " elements. The contents are:\n" << arrayToOutput << endl;
24    } // end outputArray
```

```
The Array received has 7 elements. The contents are:
         0           0          0            0
         0           0          0

The Array received has 3 elements. The contents are:
         0           0          0
```

Fig. 12.16 | Single-argument constructors and implicit conversions.

from Fig. 12.7 that the Array constructor that receives an int argument initializes all the array elements to 0. Line 14 calls function outputArray (defined in lines 20–24), which receives as its argument a const Array & to an Array. The function outputs the number of elements in its Array argument and the contents of the Array. In this case, the size of the Array is 7, so seven 0s are output.

Line 15 calls function outputArray with the int value 3 as an argument. However, this program does not contain a function called outputArray that takes an int argument. So, the compiler determines whether class Array provides a conversion constructor that can convert an int into an Array. Since any constructor that receives a single argument is considered to be a conversion constructor, the compiler assumes the Array constructor that receives a single int is a conversion constructor and uses it to convert the argument 3 into a temporary Array object that contains three elements. Then, the compiler passes the temporary Array object to function outputArray to output the Array's contents. Thus, even though we do not explicitly provide an outputArray function that receives an int argument, the compiler is able to compile line 15. The output shows the contents of the three-element Array containing 0s.

Preventing Accidental Use of a Single-Argument Constructor as a Conversion Constructor
Visual C++ provides the keyword **explicit** to suppress implicit conversions via conversion constructors when such conversions should not be allowed. A constructor that is declared `explicit` cannot be used in an implicit conversion. Figure 12.17 declares an `explicit` constructor in class `Array`. The only modification to `Array.h` was the addition of the keyword `explicit` to the declaration of the single-argument constructor in line 15. No modifications are required to the source-code file containing class `Array`'s member-function definitions.

```cpp
1   // Fig. 12.17: Array.h
2   // Array class for storing arrays of integers.
3   #ifndef ARRAY_H
4   #define ARRAY_H
5
6   #include <iostream>
7   using std::ostream;
8   using std::istream;
9
10  class Array
11  {
12     friend ostream &operator<<( ostream &, const Array & );
13     friend istream &operator>>( istream &, Array & );
14  public:
15     explicit Array( int = 10 ); // default constructor
16     Array( const Array & ); // copy constructor
17     ~Array(); // destructor
18     int getSize() const; // return size
19
20     const Array &operator=( const Array & ); // assignment operator
21     bool operator==( const Array & ) const; // equality operator
22
23     // inequality operator; returns opposite of == operator
24     bool operator!=( const Array &right ) const
25     {
26        return ! ( *this == right ); // invokes Array::operator==
27     } // end function operator!=
28
29     // subscript operator for non-const objects returns lvalue
30     int &operator[]( int );
31
32     // subscript operator for const objects returns rvalue
33     const int &operator[]( int ) const;
34  private:
35     int size; // pointer-based array size
36     int *ptr; // pointer to first element of pointer-based array
37  }; // end class Array
38
39  #endif
```

Fig. 12.17 | Array class definition with `explicit` constructor.

Figure 12.18 presents a slightly modified version of the program in Fig. 12.16. When this program is compiled, the compiler produces an error message indicating that the integer value passed to `outputArray` in line 15 cannot be converted to a `const Array &`. The compiler error message is shown in the output window. Line 16 demonstrates how the explicit constructor can be used to create a temporary `Array` of 3 elements and pass it to function `outputArray`.

Common Programming Error 12.10

Attempting to invoke an explicit *constructor for an implicit conversion is a compilation error.*

Common Programming Error 12.11

Using the explicit *keyword on data members or member functions other than a single-argument constructor is a compilation error.*

Error-Prevention Tip 12.2

Use the explicit *keyword on single-argument constructors that should not be used by the compiler to perform implicit conversions.*

```cpp
1   // Fig. 12.18: ArrayTest.cpp
2   // Driver for simple class Array.
3   #include <iostream>
4   using std::cout;
5   using std::endl;
6
7   #include "Array.h"
8
9   void outputArray( const Array & ); // prototype
10
11  int main()
12  {
13     Array integers1( 7 ); // 7-element array
14     outputArray( integers1 ); // output Array integers1
15     outputArray( 3 ); // convert 3 to an Array and output Array's contents
16     outputArray( Array( 3 ) ); // explicit single-argument constructor call
17     return 0;
18  } // end main
19
20  // print array contents
21  void outputArray( const Array &arrayToOutput )
22  {
23     cout << "The Array received has " << arrayToOutput.getSize()
24        << " elements. The contents are:\n" << arrayToOutput << endl;
25  } // end outputArray
```

```
c:\examples\ch12\Fig12_17_18\ArrayTest.cpp(15) : error C2664:
   'outputArray' : cannot convert parameter 1 from 'int' to 'const Array &'
      Reason: cannot convert from 'int' to 'const Array'
      Constructor for class 'Array' is declared 'explicit'
```

Fig. 12.18 | Demonstrating an `explicit` constructor.

12.15 C++/CLI Operators and Constructors

With respect to operator overloading, C++/CLI works almost exactly like native C++. All the concepts introduced in this chapter translate easily to C++/CLI. Overloading an operator for a managed class (those declared with the ref class keyword) simply requires using handles (^) and tracking references (%) instead of pointers and the address of (&) operator.

In Section 12.8 you learned how to implement a custom class in native C++ by writing a copy constructor and overloading the assignment operator. For native classes the compiler can generate default versions of these two functions for you. However, if your managed class has data members that use dynamic memory allocation, then you should write explicit versions of the copy constructor and assignment operator to ensure that a deep copy of all data members is done correctly. A managed class in C++/CLI doesn't have any form of copy constructor or assignment operator generated by the compiler. When writing managed classes in C++/CLI that require memberwise or deep-copy semantics, be aware that you must explicitly define a copy constructor and assignment operator. Also note that a copy constructor written for a managed class is automatically marked with the explicit modifier by the compiler to avoid any problems caused by implicit conversion. Recall that the compiler generates a default constructor only for a class with no explicit constructors. Consequently, if you write a copy constructor, make sure to also create a default constructor if your class requires one.

Overloaded Arithmetic Assignment Operators
Another nuance of C++/CLI operator overloading involves the use of arithmetic assignment operators. In the following C++/CLI code

```
Date a, b;
a += b;
```

the compiler first looks to see if operator+= is overloaded for managed class Date. If it is, the compiler calls operator+=. If it isn't defined, the compiler expands the code to

```
a = a + b;
```

As you can see, the += operator is calling the addition operator followed by the assignment operator. Unless operator+= is explicitly overloaded, any calls to operator+= use the overloaded version of the addition operator. The same is true for -=, *=, and the other arithmetic assignment operators. The Visual C++ compiler "synthesizes" the arithmetic assignment operators from the existing arithmetic operators and assignment operator. Generally you only need to overload the arithmetic operator and let the compiler synthesize the arithmetic assignment operator for you. Defining an arithmetic assignment operator to perform differently than applying operator+ and operator= in succession makes the behavior of a class unintuitive. This can make your code difficult to understand. In a native C++ class you must explicitly define operator+= and call the overloaded operator+ function inside it. The compiler won't synthesize arithmetic assignment operators for you.

12.16 Wrap-Up

In this chapter, you learned how to build more robust classes by defining overloaded operators that enable programmers to treat objects of your classes as if they were fundamental

Visual C++ data types. We presented basic operator overloading concepts, as well as several restrictions that the C++ standard places on overloaded operators. You learned reasons for implementing overloaded operators as member functions or as global functions. We discussed the differences between overloading unary and binary operators as member functions and global functions. With global functions, we showed how to input and output objects of our classes using the overloaded stream extraction and stream insertion operators, respectively. We showed a special syntax that is required to differentiate between the prefix and postfix versions of the increment (++) operator. We also demonstrated standard C++ class `string`, which makes extensive use of overloaded operators to create a robust, reusable class that can replace C-style, pointer-based strings. Finally, you learned how to use keyword `explicit` to prevent the compiler from using a single-argument constructor to perform implicit conversions. In the next chapter, we continue our discussion of classes by introducing a form of software reuse called inheritance. We'll see that when classes share common attributes and behaviors, it is possible to define those attributes and behaviors in a common "base" class and "inherit" those capabilities into new class definitions.

Summary

Section 12.1 Introduction
- Visual C++ enables you to overload most operators to be sensitive to the context in which they are used—the compiler generates the appropriate code based on the context (in particular, the types of the operands).
- Many of Visual C++'s operators can be overloaded to work with user-defined types.
- One example of an overloaded operator built into Visual C++ is operator <<, which is used both as the stream insertion operator and as the bitwise left-shift operator. Similarly, >> is also overloaded; it is used both as the stream extraction operator and as the bitwise right-shift operator. Both of these operators are overloaded in the C++ Standard Library.
- The C++ language itself overloads + and -. These operators perform differently, depending on their context in integer arithmetic, floating-point arithmetic and pointer arithmetic.
- The jobs performed by overloaded operators can also be performed by function calls, but operator notation is often clearer and more familiar to programmers.

Section 12.2 Fundamentals of Operator Overloading
- An operator is overloaded by writing a non-`static` member-function definition or global function definition in which the function name is the keyword `operator` followed by the symbol for the operator being overloaded.
- When operators are overloaded as member functions, they must be non-`static`, because they must be called on an object of the class and operate on that object.
- To use an operator on class objects, that operator *must* be overloaded, with three exceptions— the assignment operator (=), the address operator (&) and the comma operator (,).

Section 12.3 Restrictions on Operator Overloading
- You cannot change the precedence and associativity of an operator by overloading.
- You cannot change the "arity" of an operator (i.e., the number of operands an operator takes).
- You cannot create new operators—only existing operators can be overloaded.
- You cannot change the meaning of how an operator works on objects of fundamental types.

- Overloading an assignment operator and an addition operator for a class does not imply that the += operator is also overloaded. Such behavior can be achieved only by explicitly overloading operator += for that class.

Section 12.4 Operator Functions as Class Members vs. Global Functions

- Operator functions can be member functions or global functions—global functions are often made friends for performance reasons. Member functions use the this pointer implicitly to obtain one of their class object arguments (the left operand for binary operators). Arguments for both operands of a binary operator must be explicitly listed in a global function call.

- When overloading (), [], -> or any of the assignment operators, the operator overloading function must be declared as a class member. For the other operators, the operator overloading functions can be class members or global functions.

- When an operator function is implemented as a member function, the leftmost (or only) operand must be an object (or a reference to an object) of the operator's class.

- If the left operand must be an object of a different class or a fundamental type, this operator function must be implemented as a global function.

- A global operator function can be made a friend of a class if that function must access private or protected members of that class directly.

Section 12.5 Overloading Stream Insertion and Stream Extraction Operators

- The overloaded stream insertion operator (<<) is used in an expression in which the left operand has type ostream &. For this reason, it must be overloaded as a global function. To be a member function, operator << would have to be a member of the ostream class, but this is not possible, since we are not allowed to modify C++ Standard Library classes. Similarly, the overloaded stream extraction operator (>>) must be a global function.

- Another reason to choose a global function to overload an operator is to enable the operator to be commutative.

- When used with cin and strings, setw restricts the number of characters read to the number of characters specified by its argument.

- istream member function ignore discards the specified number of characters in the input stream (one character by default).

- Overloaded input and output operators are declared as friends if they need to access non-public class members directly for performance reasons.

Section 12.6 Overloading Unary Operators

- A unary operator for a class can be overloaded as a non-static member function with no arguments or as a global function with one argument; that argument must be either an object of the class or a reference to an object of the class.

- Member functions that implement overloaded operators must be non-static so that they can access the non-static data in each object of the class.

Section 12.7 Overloading Binary Operators

- A binary operator can be overloaded as a non-static member function with one argument or as a global function with two arguments (one of those arguments must be either a class object or a reference to a class object).

Section 12.8 Case Study: Array Class

- A copy constructor initializes a new object of a class by copying the members of an existing object of that class. When objects of a class contain dynamically allocated memory, the class should provide a copy constructor to ensure that each copy of an object has its own separate copy of the dynamically allocated memory. Typically, such a class would also provide a destructor and an overloaded assignment operator.

• The implementation of member function `operator=` should test for self-assignment, in which an object is being assigned to itself.

• The `const` version of `operator[]` is called when the subscript operator is used on a `const` object and the non-`const` version is called when it is used on a non-`const` object.

• The array subscript operator (`[]`) is not restricted for use with arrays. It can be used to select elements from other types of container classes. Also, with overloading, the index values no longer need to be integers—characters or strings could be used, for example.

Section 12.9 Converting between Types

• The compiler cannot know in advance how to convert among user-defined types, and between user-defined types and fundamental types, so you must specify how to do this. Such conversions can be performed with conversion constructors—single-argument constructors that turn objects of other types (including fundamental types) into objects of a particular class.

• A conversion operator (also called a cast operator) can be used to convert an object of one class into an object of another class or into an object of a fundamental type. Such a conversion operator must be a non-`static` member function. Overloaded cast-operator functions can be defined for converting objects of user-defined types into fundamental types or into objects of other user-defined types.

• An overloaded cast-operator function does not specify a return type—the return type is the type to which the object is being converted.

• One of the nice features of cast operators and conversion constructors is that, when necessary, the compiler can call these functions implicitly to create temporary objects.

Section 12.10 Case Study: `String` Class

• Any single-argument constructor can be thought of as a conversion constructor.

• Overloading the function-call operator `()` is powerful, because functions can take arbitrarily long and complex parameter lists.

Section 12.11 Overloading ++ and --

• The prefix and postfix increment and decrement operator can all be overloaded.

• To overload the increment operator to allow both preincrement and postincrement usage, each overloaded operator function must have a distinct signature, so that the compiler will be able to determine which version of ++ is intended. The prefix versions are overloaded exactly as any other prefix unary operator would be. Providing a unique signature to the postfix increment operator is accomplished by providing a second argument, which must be of type `int`. This argument is not supplied in the client code. It is used implicitly by the compiler to distinguish between the prefix and postfix versions of the increment operator.

Section 12.13 Standard Library Class `string`

• Standard class `string` is defined in header `<string>` and belongs to namespace `std`.

• Class `string` provides many overloaded operators, including equality, relational, assignment, addition assignment (for concatenation) and subscript operators.

• Class `string` provides member function `empty`, which returns `true` if the `string` is empty; otherwise, it returns `false`.

- Standard class `string` member function `substr` obtains a substring of a length specified by the second argument, starting at the position specified by the first argument. When the second argument is not specified, `substr` returns the remainder of the `string` on which it is called.

- Class `string`'s overloaded `[]` operator does not perform any bounds checking. Therefore, you must ensure that operations using standard class `string`'s overloaded `[]` operator do not accidentally manipulate elements outside the bounds of the `string`.

- Standard class `string` provides bounds checking with member function `at`, which "throws an exception" if its argument is an invalid subscript. By default, this causes the program to terminate. If the subscript is valid, function `at` returns the character at the specified location as an *lvalue* or an *rvalue*, depending on the context in which the call appears.

Section 12.14 `explicit` Constructors
- Visual C++ provides the keyword `explicit` to suppress implicit conversions via conversion constructors when such conversions should not be allowed. A constructor that is declared `explicit` cannot be used in an implicit conversion.

Section 12.15 C++/CLI Operators and Constructors
- Operator overloading in C++/CLI is done analogously to native C++ but with handles and managed address operator (%) instead of pointers and the native address operator (&).

- Managed classes in C++/CLI will not have a copy constructor or overloaded assignment operator generated by the compiler. Write these functions yourself if your class requires the functionality they provide.

- Arithmetic assignment operators can be explicitly overloaded in C++/CLI. If they are not, then they call their respective arithmetic operator followed by the assignment operator. As a result, any overloaded arithmetic or assignment operators you write will be "synthesized" when an arithmetic assignment operator is called, unless you specifically overload the arithmetic assignment operator to do otherwise.

Terminology

"arity" of an operator
Array class
assignment-operator functions
associativity not changed by overloading
cast-operator function
commutative operation
const version of operator[]
conversion between fundamental and class types
conversion constructor
conversion operator
copy constructor
empty member function of string
explicit constructor
function-call operator ()
global function to overload an operator
ignore member function of istream
implicit user-defined conversions
lvalue ("left value")
operator function
operator keyword

operator overloading
operator!
operator!=
operator()
operator+
operator++
operator++(int)
operator<
operator<<
operator=
operator==
operator>=
operator>>
operator[]
overloadable operators
overloaded ! operator
overloaded != operator
overloaded () operator
overloaded + operator
overloaded ++ operator

overloaded ++(int) operator
overloaded += operator
overloaded < operator
overloaded << operator
overloaded <= operator
overloaded == operator
overloaded > operator
overloaded >= operator
overloaded >> operator
overloaded assignment (=) operator
overloaded [] operator
overloaded stream insertion operator

overloaded stream extraction operators
overloading a binary operator
overloading a unary operator
self-assignment
static constructor
string (standard C++ class)
string concatenation
substr member function of string
substring
user-defined conversion
user-defined type

Self-Review Exercises

12.1   Fill in the blanks in each of the following:
   a) Suppose a and b are integer variables and we form the sum a + b. Now suppose c and
      d are floating-point variables and we form the sum c + d. The two + operators here are
      clearly being used for different purposes. This is an example of _____.
   b) Keyword _____ introduces an overloaded operator function definition.
   c) To use operators on class objects, they must be overloaded, with the exception of oper-
      ators _____, _____ and _____.
   d) The _____, _____ and _____ of an operator cannot be changed by overload-
      ing the operator.

12.2   Explain the multiple meanings of the operators << and >>.

12.3   In what context might the name operator/ be used?

12.4   (True/False) Only existing operators can be overloaded.

12.5   How does the precedence of an overloaded operator compare with the precedence of the
original operator?

Answers to Self-Review Exercises

12.1   a) operator overloading.   b) operator.   c) assignment (=),   address (&),   comma (,).
d) precedence, associativity, "arity."

12.2   Operator >> is both the right-shift operator and the stream extraction operator, depending
on its context. Operator << is both the left-shift operator and the stream insertion operator, depending on its context.

12.3   For operator overloading: It would be the name of a function that would provide an overloaded version of the / operator for a specific class.

12.4   True.

12.5   The precedence is identical.

Exercises

12.6   Give as many examples as you can of operator overloading implicit in Visual C++. Give a
reasonable example of a situation in which you might want to overload an operator explicitly in Visual C++.

12.7   The operators that cannot be overloaded are _____, _____, _____ and _____.

12.8 String concatenation requires two operands—the two strings that are to be concatenated. In the text, we showed how to implement an overloaded concatenation operator that concatenates the second `String` object to the right of the first `String` object, thus modifying the first `String` object. In some applications, it is desirable to produce a concatenated `String` object without modifying the `String` arguments. Implement `operator+` to allow operations such as

```
string1 = string2 + string3;
```

12.9 *(Ultimate Operator-Overloading Exercise)* To appreciate the care that should go into selecting operators for overloading, list each of the overloadable operators, and for each, list a possible meaning (or several, if appropriate) for each of several classes you have studied in this text. We suggest you try:
   a) Array
   b) Stack
   c) String

After doing this, comment on which operators seem to have meaning for a wide variety of classes. Which operators seem to be of little value for overloading? Which operators seem ambiguous?

12.10 Now work the process described in Exercise 12.9 in reverse. List each of Visual C++'s overloadable operators. For each, list what you feel is perhaps the "ultimate operation" the operator should be used to represent. If there are several excellent operations, list them all.

12.11 One nice example of overloading the function-call operator () is to allow another form of double-array subscripting popular in some programming languages. Instead of saying

```
chessBoard[ row ][ column ]
```

for an array of objects, overload the function-call operator to allow the alternate form

```
chessBoard( row, column )
```

   Create a class `DoubleSubscriptedArray` that has similar features to class `Array` in Figs. 12.6–12.7. At construction time, the class should be able to create an array of any number of rows and any number of columns. The class should supply `operator()` to perform double-subscripting operations. For example, in a 3-by-5 `DoubleSubscriptedArray` called a, the user could write a(1, 3) to access the element at row 1 and column 3. Remember that `operator()` can receive any number of arguments (see class `String` in Figs. 12.9–12.10 for an example of `operator()`). The underlying representation of the double-subscripted array should be a single-subscripted array of integers with *rows* * *columns* number of elements. Function `operator()` should perform the proper pointer arithmetic to access each element of the array. There should be two versions of `operator()`—one that returns int & (so that an element of a `DoubleSubscriptedArray` can be used as an *lvalue*) and one that returns const int & (so that an element of a const `DoubleSubscriptedArray` can be used only as an *rvalue*). The class should also provide the following operators: ==, !=, =, << (for outputting the array in row-and-column format) and >> (for inputting the entire array contents).

12.12 Overload the subscript operator to return the largest element of a collection, the second largest, the third largest, and so on.

12.13 Consider class `Complex` shown in Figs. 12.19–12.21. The class enables operations on socalled *complex numbers*. These are numbers of the form realPart + imaginaryPart * *i*, where *i* has the value

$$\sqrt{-1}$$

   a) Modify the class to enable input and output of complex numbers through the overloaded >> and << operators, respectively (you should remove the print function from the class).

b) Overload the multiplication operator to enable multiplication of two complex numbers as in algebra.

c) Overload the `==` and `!=` operators to allow comparisons of complex numbers.

```cpp
1   // Fig. 12.19: Complex.h
2   // Complex class definition.
3   #ifndef COMPLEX_H
4   #define COMPLEX_H
5
6   class Complex
7   {
8   public:
9      Complex( double = 0.0, double = 0.0 ); // constructor
10     Complex operator+( const Complex & ) const; // addition
11     Complex operator-( const Complex & ) const; // subtraction
12     void print() const; // output
13  private:
14     double real; // real part
15     double imaginary; // imaginary part
16  }; // end class Complex
17
18  #endif
```

Fig. 12.19 | Complex class definition.

```cpp
1   // Fig. 12.20: Complex.cpp
2   // Complex class member-function definitions.
3   #include <iostream>
4   using std::cout;
5
6   #include "Complex.h" // Complex class definition
7
8   // Constructor
9   Complex::Complex( double realPart, double imaginaryPart )
10     : real( realPart ),
11     imaginary( imaginaryPart )
12  {
13     // empty body
14  } // end Complex constructor
15
16  // addition operator
17  Complex Complex::operator+( const Complex &operand2 ) const
18  {
19     return Complex( real + operand2.real,
20        imaginary + operand2.imaginary );
21  } // end function operator+
22
23  // subtraction operator
24  Complex Complex::operator-( const Complex &operand2 ) const
25  {
26     return Complex( real - operand2.real,
27        imaginary - operand2.imaginary );
28  } // end function operator-
29
30  // display a Complex object in the form: (a, b)
31  void Complex::print() const
32  {
```

Fig. 12.20 | Complex class member-function definitions. (Part 1 of 2.)

```
33        cout << '(' << real << ", " << imaginary << ')';
34    } // end function print
```

Fig. 12.20 | Complex class member-function definitions. (Part 2 of 2.)

```
1    // Fig. 12.21: ComplexTest.cpp
2    // Complex class test program.
3    #include <iostream>
4    using std::cout;
5    using std::endl;
6
7    #include "Complex.h"
8
9    int main()
10   {
11       Complex x;
12       Complex y( 4.3, 8.2 );
13       Complex z( 3.3, 1.1 );
14
15       cout << "x: ";
16       x.print();
17       cout << "\ny: ";
18       y.print();
19       cout << "\nz: ";
20       z.print();
21
22       x = y + z;
23       cout << "\n\nx = y + z:" << endl;
24       x.print();
25       cout << " = ";
26       y.print();
27       cout << " + ";
28       z.print();
29
30       x = y - z;
31       cout << "\n\nx = y - z:" << endl;
32       x.print();
33       cout << " = ";
34       y.print();
35       cout << " - ";
36       z.print();
37       cout << endl;
38       return 0;
39   } // end main
```

```
x: (0, 0)
y: (4.3, 8.2)
z: (3.3, 1.1)

x = y + z:
(7.6, 9.3) = (4.3, 8.2) + (3.3, 1.1)

x = y - z:
(1, 7.1) = (4.3, 8.2) - (3.3, 1.1)
```

Fig. 12.21 | Complex numbers.

12.14 A machine with 32-bit integers can represent integers in the range of approximately –2 billion to +2 billion. This fixed-size restriction is rarely troublesome, but there are applications in which we would like to be able to use a much wider range of integers. This is what Visual C++ was built to do—namely, create powerful new data types. Consider class HugeInt of Figs. 12.22–12.24. Study the class carefully, then answer the following:

    a) Describe precisely how it operates.

    b) What restrictions does the class have?

    c) Overload the * multiplication operator.

    d) Overload the / division operator.

    e) Overload all the relational and equality operators.

[*Note:* We do not show an assignment operator or copy constructor for class HugeInteger, because the assignment operator and copy constructor provided by the compiler are capable of copying the entire array data member properly.]

```cpp
1   // Fig. 12.22: Hugeint.h
2   // HugeInt class definition.
3   #ifndef HUGEINT_H
4   #define HUGEINT_H
5
6   #include <iostream>
7   using std::ostream;
8
9   class HugeInt
10  {
11      friend ostream &operator<<( ostream &, const HugeInt & );
12  public:
13      HugeInt( long = 0 ); // conversion/default constructor
14      HugeInt( const char * ); // conversion constructor
15
16      // addition operator; HugeInt + HugeInt
17      HugeInt operator+( const HugeInt & ) const;
18
19      // addition operator; HugeInt + int
20      HugeInt operator+( int ) const;
21
22      // addition operator;
23      // HugeInt + string that represents large integer value
24      HugeInt operator+( const char * ) const;
25  private:
26      short integer[ 30 ];
27  }; // end class HugetInt
28
29  #endif
```

Fig. 12.22 | HugeInt class definition.

```cpp
1   // Fig. 12.23: Hugeint.cpp
2   // HugeInt member-function and friend-function definitions.
3   #include <cctype> // isdigit function prototype
4   #include <cstring> // strlen function prototype
5   #include "Hugeint.h" // HugeInt class definition
6
7   // default constructor; conversion constructor that converts
8   // a long integer into a HugeInt object
9   HugeInt::HugeInt( long value )
10  {
```

Fig. 12.23 | HugeInt class member- and friend-function definitions. (Part 1 of 3.)

```
11      // initialize array to zero
12      for ( int i = 0; i <= 29; i++ )
13         integer[ i ] = 0;
14
15      // place digits of argument into array
16      for ( int j = 29; value != 0 && j >= 0; j-- )
17      {
18         integer[ j ] = value % 10;
19         value /= 10;
20      } // end for
21   } // end HugeInt default/conversion constructor
22
23   // conversion constructor that converts a character string
24   // representing a large integer into a HugeInt object
25   HugeInt::HugeInt( const char *string )
26   {
27      // initialize array to zero
28      for ( int i = 0; i <= 29; i++ )
29         integer[ i ] = 0;
30
31      // place digits of argument into array
32      int length = strlen( string );
33
34      for ( int j = 30 - length, k = 0; j <= 29; j++, k++ )
35
36         if ( isdigit( string[ k ] ) )
37            integer[ j ] = string[ k ] - '0';
38   } // end HugeInt conversion constructor
39
40   // addition operator; HugeInt + HugeInt
41   HugeInt HugeInt::operator+( const HugeInt &op2 ) const
42   {
43      HugeInt temp; // temporary result
44      int carry = 0;
45
46      for ( int i = 29; i >= 0; i-- )
47      {
48         temp.integer[ i ] =
49            integer[ i ] + op2.integer[ i ] + carry;
50
51         // determine whether to carry a 1
52         if ( temp.integer[ i ] > 9 )
53         {
54            temp.integer[ i ] %= 10;  // reduce to 0-9
55            carry = 1;
56         } // end if
57         else // no carry
58            carry = 0;
59      } // end for
60
61      return temp; // return copy of temporary object
62   } // end function operator+
63
64   // addition operator; HugeInt + int
65   HugeInt HugeInt::operator+( int op2 ) const
66   {
67      // convert op2 to a HugeInt, then invoke
68      // operator+ for two HugeInt objects
```

Fig. 12.23 | HugeInt class member- and friend-function definitions. (Part 2 of 3.)

```
69        return *this + HugeInt( op2 );
70     } // end function operator+
71
72     // addition operator;
73     // HugeInt + string that represents large integer value
74     HugeInt HugeInt::operator+( const char *op2 ) const
75     {
76        // convert op2 to a HugeInt, then invoke
77        // operator+ for two HugeInt objects
78        return *this + HugeInt( op2 );
79     } // end operator+
80
81     // overloaded output operator
82     ostream& operator<<( ostream &output, const HugeInt &num )
83     {
84        int i;
85
86        for ( i = 0; ( num.integer[ i ] == 0 ) && ( i <= 29 ); i++ )
87           ; // skip leading zeros
88
89        if ( i == 30 )
90           output << 0;
91        else
92
93           for ( ; i <= 29; i++ )
94              output << num.integer[ i ];
95
96        return output;
97     } // end function operator<<
```

Fig. 12.23 | `HugeInt` class member- and `friend`-function definitions. (Part 3 of 3.)

```
1     // Fig. 12.24: HugeIntTest.cpp
2     // HugeInt test program.
3     #include <iostream>
4     using std::cout;
5     using std::endl;
6
7     #include "Hugeint.h"
8
9     int main()
10    {
11       HugeInt n1( 7654321 );
12       HugeInt n2( 7891234 );
13       HugeInt n3( "99999999999999999999999999999" );
14       HugeInt n4( "1" );
15       HugeInt n5;
16
17       cout << "n1 is " << n1 << "\nn2 is " << n2
18          << "\nn3 is " << n3 << "\nn4 is " << n4
19          << "\nn5 is " << n5 << "\n\n";
20
21       n5 = n1 + n2;
22       cout << n1 << " + " << n2 << " = " << n5 << "\n\n";
23
24       cout << n3 << " + " << n4 << "\n= " << ( n3 + n4 ) << "\n\n";
25
```

Fig. 12.24 | Huge integers. (Part 1 of 2.)

```
26        n5 = n1 + 9;
27        cout << n1 << " + " << 9 << " = " << n5 << "\n\n";
28
29        n5 = n2 + "10000";
30        cout << n2 << " + " << "10000" << " = " << n5 << endl;
31        return 0;
32    } // end main
```

```
n1 is 7654321
n2 is 7891234
n3 is 99999999999999999999999999999999
n4 is 1
n5 is 0

7654321 + 7891234 = 15545555

99999999999999999999999999999999 + 1
= 100000000000000000000000000000000

7654321 + 9 = 7654330

7891234 + 10000 = 7901234
```

Fig. 12.24 | Huge integers. (Part 2 of 2.)

12.15 Create a class `RationalNumber` (fractions) with the following capabilities:
  a) Create a constructor that prevents a 0 denominator in a fraction, reduces or simplifies fractions that are not in reduced form and avoids negative denominators.
  b) Overload the addition, subtraction, multiplication and division operators for this class.
  c) Overload the relational and equality operators for this class.

12.16 Study the C string-handling library functions (www.cplusplus.com/reference/clibrary/cstring/) and implement each as part of class `String` (Figs. 12.9–12.10). Then, use these functions to perform text manipulations.

12.17 Develop class `Polynomial`. The internal representation of a `Polynomial` is an array of terms. Each term contains a coefficient and an exponent, e.g., the term

$$2x^4$$

has the coefficient 2 and the exponent 4. Develop a complete class containing proper constructor and destructor functions as well as *set* and *get* functions. The class should also provide the following overloaded operator capabilities:
  a) Overload the addition operator (+) to add two `Polynomial`s.
  b) Overload the subtraction operator (-) to subtract two `Polynomial`s.
  c) Overload the assignment operator to assign one `Polynomial` to another.
  d) Overload the multiplication operator (*) to multiply two `Polynomial`s.
  e) Overload the addition assignment operator (+=), subtraction assignment operator (-=), and multiplication assignment operator (*=).

12.18 In the program of Figs. 12.3–12.5, Fig. 12.4 contains the comment "overloaded stream insertion operator; cannot be a member function if we would like to invoke it with cout << somePhoneNumber;." Actually, the stream insertion operator could be a `PhoneNumber` class member function if we were willing to invoke it either as somePhoneNumber.operator<<(cout); or as some-PhoneNumber << cout;. Rewrite the program of Fig. 12.5 with the overloaded stream insertion operator<< as a member function and try the two preceding statements in the program to demonstrate that they work.

13

Object-Oriented Programming: Inheritance

OBJECTIVES

In this chapter you'll learn:

- To create classes by inheriting from existing classes.

- How inheritance promotes software reuse.

- The notions of base classes and derived classes and the relationships between them.

- The **protected** member-access specifier.

- The use of constructors and destructors in inheritance hierarchies.

- The order in which constructors and destructors are called in inheritance hierarchies.

- The differences between **public**, **protected** and **private** inheritance.

- The use of inheritance to customize existing software.

13.1 Introduction

This chapter continues our discussion of object-oriented programming (OOP) by introducing another of its key features—*inheritance.* Inheritance is a form of software reuse in which you create a class that absorbs an existing class's data and behaviors and enhances them with new capabilities. Software reusability saves time during program development. It also encourages the reuse of proven, debugged, high-quality software, which increases the likelihood that a system will be implemented effectively.

When creating a class, instead of writing completely new data members and member functions, you can designate that the new class should *inherit* the members of an existing class. This existing class is called the *base class*, and the new class is called the *derived class.* (Other programming languages, such as Java, refer to the base class as the *superclass* and the derived class as the *subclass.*) A derived class represents a more specialized group of objects. Typically, a derived class contains behaviors inherited from its base class plus additional behaviors. As we'll see, a derived class can also customize behaviors inherited from the base class. A *direct base class* is the base class from which a derived class explicitly inherits. An *indirect base class* is inherited from two or more levels up in the *class hierarchy.* In the case of *single inheritance*, a class is derived from one base class. Visual C++ also supports *multiple inheritance*, in which a derived class inherits from multiple (possibly unrelated) base classes. Single inheritance is straightforward—we show several examples that should enable you to become proficient quickly. Multiple inheritance can be complex and error prone. We discuss multiple inheritance in Chapter 26, Other Topics.

Visual C++ offers public, protected and private inheritance. In this chapter, we concentrate on public inheritance and briefly explain the other two. In Chapter 21, Data

Structures, we show how `private` inheritance can be used as an alternative to composition. The third form, `protected` inheritance, is rarely used. With `public` inheritance, every object of a derived class is also an object of that derived class's base class. However, base-class objects are not objects of their derived classes. For example, if we have vehicle as a base class and car as a derived class, then all cars are vehicles, but not all vehicles are cars. As we continue our study of object-oriented programming in this chapter and Chapter 14, we take advantage of this relationship to perform some interesting manipulations.

Experience in building software systems indicates that significant amounts of code deal with closely related special cases. When you are preoccupied with special cases, the details can obscure the big picture. With object-oriented programming, you focus on the commonalities among objects in the system rather than on the special cases.

We distinguish between the *is-a relationship* and the *has-a* relationship. The *is-a* relationship represents inheritance. In an *is-a* relationship, an object of a derived class also can be treated as an object of its base class—for example, a car *is a* vehicle, so any attributes and behaviors of a vehicle are also attributes and behaviors of a car. By contrast, the *has-a* relationship represents composition. (Composition was discussed in Chapter 11.) In a *has-a* relationship, an object contains one or more objects of other classes as members. For example, a car includes many components—it *has a* steering wheel, *has a* brake pedal, *has a* transmission and *has* many other components.

Derived-class member functions might require access to base-class data members and member functions. A derived class can access the non-`private` members of its base class. Base-class members that should not be accessible to the member functions of derived classes should be declared `private` in the base class. A derived class *can* effect state changes in `private` base-class members, but only through non-`private` member functions provided in the base class and inherited into the derived class.

Software Engineering Observation 13.1

Member functions of a derived class cannot directly access `private` members of the base class.

Software Engineering Observation 13.2

If a derived class could access its base class's `private` members, classes that inherit from that derived class could access that data as well. This would propagate access to what should be `private` data, and the benefits of information hiding would be lost.

One problem with inheritance is that a derived class can inherit data members and member functions it does not need or should not have. It is the class designer's responsibility to ensure that the capabilities provided by a class are appropriate for future derived classes. Even when a base-class member function is appropriate for a derived class, the derived class often requires that the member function behave in a manner specific to the derived class. In such cases, the base-class member function can be redefined in the derived class with an appropriate implementation.

13.2 Base Classes and Derived Classes

Often, an object of one class *is an* object of another class, as well. For example, in geometry, a rectangle *is a* quadrilateral (as are squares, parallelograms and trapezoids). Thus, in C++, class `Rectangle` can be said to *inherit* from class `Quadrilateral`. In this context, class `Quadrilateral` is a base class, and class `Rectangle` is a derived class. A rectangle *is a* specific type of quadrilateral, but it is incorrect to claim that a quadrilateral *is a* rectangle—the quadrilateral could be a parallelogram or some other shape. Figure 13.1 lists several simple examples of base classes and derived classes.

Because every derived-class object *is an* object of its base class, and one base class can have many derived classes, the set of objects represented by a base class typically is larger than the set of objects represented by any of its derived classes. For example, the base class `Vehicle` represents all vehicles, including cars, trucks, boats, airplanes, bicycles and so on. By contrast, derived class `Car` represents a smaller, more specific subset of all vehicles.

Inheritance relationships form treelike hierarchical structures. A base class exists in a hierarchical relationship with its derived classes. Although classes can exist independently, once they are employed in inheritance relationships, they become affiliated with other classes. A class becomes either a base class—supplying members to other classes, a derived class—inheriting its members from other classes, or both.

Let us develop a simple inheritance hierarchy with five levels (represented by the UML class diagram in Fig. 13.2).

Base class	Derived classes
Student	GraduateStudent, UndergraduateStudent
Shape	Circle, Triangle, Rectangle, Sphere, Cube
Loan	CarLoan, HomeImprovementLoan, MortgageLoan
Employee	Faculty, Staff
Account	CheckingAccount, SavingsAccount

Fig. 13.1 | Inheritance examples.

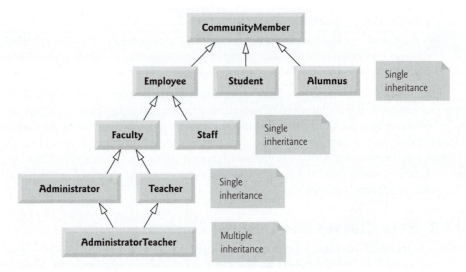

Fig. 13.2 | Inheritance hierarchy for university `CommunityMember`s.

A university community has thousands of members. These members consist of employees, students and alumni. Employees are either faculty members or staff members. Faculty members are either administrators (such as deans and department chairpersons) or teachers. Some administrators, however, also teach classes. Note that we have used multiple inheritance to form class AdministratorTeacher. Also note that this inheritance hierarchy could contain many other classes. For example, students can be graduate or undergraduate students. Undergraduate students can be freshmen, sophomores, juniors and seniors.

Each arrow in the hierarchy (Fig. 13.2) represents an *is-a* relationship. For example, as we follow the arrows in this class hierarchy, we can state "an Employee *is a* Community-Member" and "a Teacher *is a* Faculty member." CommunityMember is the direct base class of Employee, Student and Alumnus. In addition, CommunityMember is an indirect base class of all the other classes in the diagram. Starting from the bottom of the diagram, you can follow the arrows and apply the *is-a* relationship to the topmost base class. For example, an AdministratorTeacher *is an* Administrator, *is a* Faculty member, *is an* Employee and *is a* CommunityMember.

Now consider the Shape inheritance hierarchy in Fig. 13.3. This hierarchy begins with base class Shape. Classes TwoDimensionalShape and ThreeDimensionalShape derive from base class Shape—Shapes are either TwoDimensionalShapes or ThreeDimensional-Shapes. The third level of this hierarchy contains some more specific types of TwoDimen-sionalShapes and ThreeDimensionalShapes. As in Fig. 13.2, we can follow the arrows from the bottom of the diagram to the topmost base class in this class hierarchy to identify several *is-a* relationships. For instance, a Triangle *is a* TwoDimensionalShape and *is a* Shape, while a Sphere *is a* ThreeDimensionalShape and *is a* Shape. Note that this hierarchy could contain many other classes, such as Rectangles, Ellipses and Trapezoids, which are all TwoDimensionalShapes.

To specify that class TwoDimensionalShape (Fig. 13.3) is derived from (or inherits from) class Shape, class TwoDimensionalShape's definition could begin as follows:

> *class* TwoDimensionalShape : *public* Shape

This is an example of **public inheritance**, the most commonly used form. We also will discuss **private inheritance** and **protected inheritance** (Section 13.6). With all forms of inheritance, private members of a base class are not accessible directly from that class's derived classes, but these private base-class members are still inherited (i.e., they are still considered parts of the derived classes). With public inheritance, all other base-class mem-

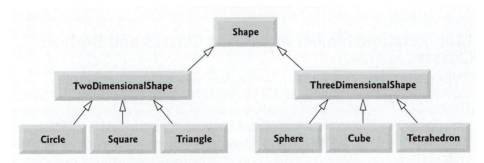

Fig. 13.3 | Inheritance hierarchy for Shapes.

bers retain their original member access when they become members of the derived class (e.g., `public` members of the base class become `public` members of the derived class, and, as we'll soon see, `protected` members of the base class become `protected` members of the derived class). Through these inherited base-class members, the derived class can manipulate `private` members of the base class (if these inherited members provide such functionality in the base class). Note that `friend` functions are not inherited.

Inheritance is not appropriate for every class relationship. In Chapter 11, we discussed the *has-a* relationship, in which classes have members that are objects of other classes. Such relationships create classes by composition of existing classes. For example, given the classes `Employee`, `BirthDate` and `TelephoneNumber`, it is improper to say that an `Employee` *is a* `BirthDate` or that an `Employee` *is a* `TelephoneNumber`. However, it is appropriate to say that an `Employee` *has a* `BirthDate` and that an `Employee` *has a* `TelephoneNumber`.

It is possible to treat base-class objects and derived-class objects similarly; their commonalities are expressed in the members of the base class. Objects of all classes derived from a common base class can be treated as objects of that base class (i.e., such objects have an *is-a* relationship with the base class). In Chapter 14, we consider many examples that take advantage of this relationship.

13.3 protected Members

Chapter 4 introduced access specifiers `public` and `private`. A base class's `public` members are accessible within the body of that base class and anywhere that the program has a handle (i.e., a name, reference or pointer) to an object of that base class or one of its derived classes. A base class's `private` members are accessible only within the body of that base class and the `friend`s of that base class. In this section, we introduce an additional access specifier: *protected*.

Using `protected` access offers an intermediate level of protection between `public` and `private` access. A base class's `protected` members can be accessed within the body of that base class, by members and `friend`s of that base class, and by members and `friend`s of any classes derived from that base class.

Derived-class member functions can refer to `public` and `protected` members of the base class simply by using the member names. When a derived-class member function redefines a base-class member function, the base-class member can be accessed from the derived class by preceding the base-class member name with the base-class name and the binary scope resolution operator (`::`). We discuss accessing redefined members of the base class in Section 13.4 and using `protected` data in Section 13.4.4.

13.4 Relationship between Base Classes and Derived Classes

In this section, we use an inheritance hierarchy containing types of employees in a company's payroll application to discuss the relationship between a base class and a derived class. Commission employees (who will be represented as objects of a base class) are paid a percentage of their sales, while base-salaried commission employees (who will be represented as objects of a derived class) receive a base salary plus a percentage of their sales. We divide our discussion of the relationship between commission employees and base-salaried commission employees into a carefully paced series of five examples:

1. In the first example, we create class CommissionEmployee, which contains as private data members a first name, last name, social security number, commission rate (percentage) and gross (i.e., total) sales amount.

2. The second example defines class BasePlusCommissionEmployee, which contains as private data members a first name, last name, social security number, commission rate, gross sales amount and base salary. We create the latter class by writing every line of code the class requires—we'll soon see that it is much more efficient to create this class simply by inheriting from class CommissionEmployee.

3. The third example defines a class BasePlusCommissionEmployee class that inherits directly from class CommissionEmployee (i.e., a BasePlusCommissionEmployee *is a* CommissionEmployee who also has a base salary) and attempts to access class CommissionEmployee's private members—this results in compilation errors, because the derived class does not have access to the base class's private data.

4. The fourth example shows that if CommissionEmployee's data is declared as protected, a new version of class BasePlusCommissionEmployee that inherits from class CommissionEmployee *can* access that data directly. For this purpose, we define a new version of class CommissionEmployee with protected data. Both the inherited and noninherited BasePlusCommissionEmployee classes contain identical functionality, but we show how the version of BasePlusCommissionEmployee that inherits from class CommissionEmployee is easier to create and manage.

5. After we discuss the convenience of using protected data, we create the fifth example, which sets the CommissionEmployee data members back to private to enforce good software engineering. This example demonstrates that derived class BasePlusCommissionEmployee can use base class CommissionEmployee's public member functions to manipulate CommissionEmployee's private data.

13.4.1 Creating and Using a CommissionEmployee Class

Let's examine CommissionEmployee's class definition (Figs. 13.4–13.5). The CommissionEmployee header file (Fig. 13.4) specifies class CommissionEmployee's public services, which include a constructor (lines 12–13) and member functions earnings (line 30) and print (line 31). Lines 15–28 declare public *get* and *set* functions that manipulate the class's data members (declared in lines 33–37) firstName, lastName, socialSecurityNumber, grossSales and commissionRate. The CommissionEmployee header file specifies that these data members are private, so objects of other classes cannot directly access this data. Declaring data members as private and providing non-private *get* and *set* functions to manipulate and validate the data members helps enforce good software engineering. Member functions setGrossSales (defined in lines 57–60 of Fig. 13.5) and setCommissionRate (defined in lines 69–72 of Fig. 13.5), for example, validate their arguments before assigning the values to data members grossSales and commissionRate, respectively.

The CommissionEmployee constructor definition purposely does not use member-initializer syntax in the first several examples of this section, so that we can demonstrate how private and protected specifiers affect member access in derived classes. As shown in Fig. 13.5, lines 13–15, we assign values to data members firstName, lastName and socialSecurityNumber in the constructor body. Later in this section, we'll return to using member-initializer lists in the constructors.

```
1   // Fig. 13.4: CommissionEmployee.h
2   // CommissionEmployee class definition represents a commission employee.
3   #ifndef COMMISSION_H
4   #define COMMISSION_H
5
6   #include <string> // C++ standard string class
7   using std::string;
8
9   class CommissionEmployee
10  {
11  public:
12     CommissionEmployee( const string &, const string &, const string &,
13        double = 0.0, double = 0.0 );
14
15     void setFirstName( const string & ); // set first name
16     string getFirstName() const; // return first name
17
18     void setLastName( const string & ); // set last name
19     string getLastName() const; // return last name
20
21     void setSocialSecurityNumber( const string & ); // set SSN
22     string getSocialSecurityNumber() const; // return SSN
23
24     void setGrossSales( double ); // set gross sales amount
25     double getGrossSales() const; // return gross sales amount
26
27     void setCommissionRate( double ); // set commission rate (percentage)
28     double getCommissionRate() const; // return commission rate
29
30     double earnings() const; // calculate earnings
31     void print() const; // print CommissionEmployee object
32  private:
33     string firstName;
34     string lastName;
35     string socialSecurityNumber;
36     double grossSales; // gross weekly sales
37     double commissionRate; // commission percentage
38  }; // end class CommissionEmployee
39
40  #endif
```

Fig. 13.4 | CommissionEmployee class header file.

```
1   // Fig. 13.5: CommissionEmployee.cpp
2   // Class CommissionEmployee member-function definitions.
3   #include <iostream>
4   using std::cout;
5
6   #include "CommissionEmployee.h" // CommissionEmployee class definition
7
```

Fig. 13.5 | Implementation file for CommissionEmployee class that represents an employee who is paid a percentage of gross sales. (Part 1 of 3.)

```
 8   // constructor
 9   CommissionEmployee::CommissionEmployee(
10      const string &first, const string &last, const string &ssn,
11      double sales, double rate )
12   {
13      firstName = first; // should validate
14      lastName = last;   // should validate
15      socialSecurityNumber = ssn; // should validate
16      setGrossSales( sales ); // validate and store gross sales
17      setCommissionRate( rate ); // validate and store commission rate
18   } // end CommissionEmployee constructor
19
20   // set first name
21   void CommissionEmployee::setFirstName( const string &first )
22   {
23      firstName = first; // should validate
24   } // end function setFirstName
25
26   // return first name
27   string CommissionEmployee::getFirstName() const
28   {
29      return firstName;
30   } // end function getFirstName
31
32   // set last name
33   void CommissionEmployee::setLastName( const string &last )
34   {
35      lastName = last; // should validate
36   } // end function setLastName
37
38   // return last name
39   string CommissionEmployee::getLastName() const
40   {
41      return lastName;
42   } // end function getLastName
43
44   // set social security number
45   void CommissionEmployee::setSocialSecurityNumber( const string &ssn )
46   {
47      socialSecurityNumber = ssn; // should validate
48   } // end function setSocialSecurityNumber
49
50   // return social security number
51   string CommissionEmployee::getSocialSecurityNumber() const
52   {
53      return socialSecurityNumber;
54   } // end function getSocialSecurityNumber
55
56   // set gross sales amount
57   void CommissionEmployee::setGrossSales( double sales )
58   {
```

Fig. 13.5 | Implementation file for CommissionEmployee class that represents an employee who is paid a percentage of gross sales. (Part 2 of 3.)

```
59       grossSales = ( sales < 0.0 ) ? 0.0 : sales;
60    } // end function setGrossSales
61
62    // return gross sales amount
63    double CommissionEmployee::getGrossSales() const
64    {
65       return grossSales;
66    } // end function getGrossSales
67
68    // set commission rate
69    void CommissionEmployee::setCommissionRate( double rate )
70    {
71       commissionRate = ( rate > 0.0 && rate < 1.0 ) ? rate : 0.0;
72    } // end function setCommissionRate
73
74    // return commission rate
75    double CommissionEmployee::getCommissionRate() const
76    {
77       return commissionRate;
78    } // end function getCommissionRate
79
80    // calculate earnings
81    double CommissionEmployee::earnings() const
82    {
83       return commissionRate * grossSales;
84    } // end function earnings
85
86    // print CommissionEmployee object
87    void CommissionEmployee::print() const
88    {
89       cout << "commission employee: " << firstName << ' ' << lastName
90          << "\nsocial security number: " << socialSecurityNumber
91          << "\ngross sales: " << grossSales
92          << "\ncommission rate: " << commissionRate;
93    } // end function print
```

Fig. 13.5 | Implementation file for CommissionEmployee class that represents an employee who is paid a percentage of gross sales. (Part 3 of 3.)

Note that we do not validate the values of the constructor's arguments first, last and ssn before assigning them to the corresponding data members. We certainly could validate the first and last names—perhaps by ensuring that they are of a reasonable length. Similarly, a social security number could be validated to ensure that it contains nine digits, with or without dashes (e.g., 123-45-6789 or 123456789).

Member function earnings (lines 81–84) calculates a CommissionEmployee's earnings. Line 83 multiplies the commissionRate by the grossSales and returns the result. Member function print (lines 87–93) displays the values of a CommissionEmployee object's data members.

Figure 13.6 tests class CommissionEmployee. Lines 16–17 instantiate object employee of class CommissionEmployee and invoke CommissionEmployee's constructor to initialize the object with "Sue" as the first name, "Jones" as the last name, "222-22-2222" as the social security number, 10000 as the gross sales amount and .06 as the commission rate.

Lines 23–29 use employee's *get* functions to display the values of its data members. Lines 31–32 invoke the object's member functions setGrossSales and setCommissionRate to change the values of data members grossSales and commissionRate, respectively. Line 36 then calls employee's print member function to output the updated CommissionEmployee information. Finally, line 39 displays the CommissionEmployee's earnings, calculated by the object's earnings member function using the updated values of data members gross-Sales and commissionRate.

```cpp
1   // Fig. 13.6: CommissionEmployeeTest.cpp
2   // Testing class CommissionEmployee.
3   #include <iostream>
4   using std::cout;
5   using std::endl;
6   using std::fixed;
7
8   #include <iomanip>
9   using std::setprecision;
10
11  #include "CommissionEmployee.h" // CommissionEmployee class definition
12
13  int main()
14  {
15      // instantiate a CommissionEmployee object
16      CommissionEmployee employee(
17          "Sue", "Jones", "222-22-2222", 10000, .06 );
18
19      // set floating-point output formatting
20      cout << fixed << setprecision( 2 );
21
22      // get commission employee data
23      cout << "Employee information obtained by get functions: \n"
24          << "\nFirst name is " << employee.getFirstName()
25          << "\nLast name is " << employee.getLastName()
26          << "\nSocial security number is "
27          << employee.getSocialSecurityNumber()
28          << "\nGross sales is " << employee.getGrossSales()
29          << "\nCommission rate is " << employee.getCommissionRate() << endl;
30
31      employee.setGrossSales( 8000 ); // set gross sales
32      employee.setCommissionRate( .1 ); // set commission rate
33
34      cout << "\nUpdated employee information output by print function: \n"
35          << endl;
36      employee.print(); // display the new employee information
37
38      // display the employee's earnings
39      cout << "\n\nEmployee's earnings: $" << employee.earnings() << endl;
40
41      return 0;
42  } // end main
```

Fig. 13.6 | CommissionEmployee class test program. (Part 1 of 2.)

```
Employee information obtained by get functions:

First name is Sue
Last name is Jones
Social security number is 222-22-2222
Gross sales is 10000.00
Commission rate is 0.06

Updated employee information output by print function:

commission employee: Sue Jones
social security number: 222-22-2222
gross sales: 8000.00
commission rate: 0.10

Employee's earnings: $800.00
```

Fig. 13.6 | CommissionEmployee class test program. (Part 2 of 2.)

13.4.2 Creating a BasePlusCommissionEmployee Class Without Using Inheritance

We now discuss the second part of our introduction to inheritance by creating and testing (a completely new and independent) class BasePlusCommissionEmployee (Figs. 13.7–13.8), which contains a first name, last name, social security number, gross sales amount, commission rate *and* base salary.

Defining Class BasePlusCommissionEmployee

The BasePlusCommissionEmployee header file (Fig. 13.7) specifies class BasePlusCommissionEmployee's public services, which include the BasePlusCommissionEmployee constructor (lines 13–14) and member functions earnings (line 34) and print (line 35). Lines 16–32 declare public *get* and *set* functions for the class's private data members (declared in lines 37–42) firstName, lastName, socialSecurityNumber, grossSales, commissionRate and baseSalary. These variables and member functions encapsulate all the necessary features of a base-salaried commission employee. Note the similarity between this class and class CommissionEmployee (Figs. 13.4–13.5)—in this example, we will not yet exploit that similarity.

```
1   // Fig. 13.7: BasePlusCommissionEmployee.h
2   // BasePlusCommissionEmployee class definition represents an employee
3   // that receives a base salary in addition to commission.
4   #ifndef BASEPLUS_H
5   #define BASEPLUS_H
6
7   #include <string> // C++ standard string class
8   using std::string;
9
10  class BasePlusCommissionEmployee
11  {
```

Fig. 13.7 | BasePlusCommissionEmployee class header file. (Part 1 of 2.)

```
12   public:
13      BasePlusCommissionEmployee( const string &, const string &,
14        const string &, double = 0.0, double = 0.0, double = 0.0 );
15
16      void setFirstName( const string & ); // set first name
17      string getFirstName() const; // return first name
18
19      void setLastName( const string & ); // set last name
20      string getLastName() const; // return last name
21
22      void setSocialSecurityNumber( const string & ); // set SSN
23      string getSocialSecurityNumber() const; // return SSN
24
25      void setGrossSales( double ); // set gross sales amount
26      double getGrossSales() const; // return gross sales amount
27
28      void setCommissionRate( double ); // set commission rate
29      double getCommissionRate() const; // return commission rate
30
31      void setBaseSalary( double ); // set base salary
32      double getBaseSalary() const; // return base salary
33
34      double earnings() const; // calculate earnings
35      void print() const; // print BasePlusCommissionEmployee object
36   private:
37      string firstName;
38      string lastName;
39      string socialSecurityNumber;
40      double grossSales; // gross weekly sales
41      double commissionRate; // commission percentage
42      double baseSalary; // base salary
43   }; // end class BasePlusCommissionEmployee
44
45   #endif
```

Fig. 13.7 | BasePlusCommissionEmployee class header file. (Part 2 of 2.)

Class BasePlusCommissionEmployee's earnings member function (defined in lines 96–99 of Fig. 13.8) computes the earnings of a base-salaried commission employee. Line 98 returns the result of adding the employee's base salary to the product of the commission rate and the employee's gross sales.

```
1    // Fig. 13.8: BasePlusCommissionEmployee.cpp
2    // Class BasePlusCommissionEmployee member-function definitions.
3    #include <iostream>
4    using std::cout;
5
6    // BasePlusCommissionEmployee class definition
7    #include "BasePlusCommissionEmployee.h"
```

Fig. 13.8 | BasePlusCommissionEmployee class represents an employee who receives a base salary in addition to a commission. (Part 1 of 3.)

```
8
9   // constructor
10  BasePlusCommissionEmployee::BasePlusCommissionEmployee(
11     const string &first, const string &last, const string &ssn,
12     double sales, double rate, double salary )
13  {
14     firstName = first; // should validate
15     lastName = last; // should validate
16     socialSecurityNumber = ssn; // should validate
17     setGrossSales( sales ); // validate and store gross sales
18     setCommissionRate( rate ); // validate and store commission rate
19     setBaseSalary( salary ); // validate and store base salary
20  } // end BasePlusCommissionEmployee constructor
21
22  // set first name
23  void BasePlusCommissionEmployee::setFirstName( const string &first )
24  {
25     firstName = first; // should validate
26  } // end function setFirstName
27
28  // return first name
29  string BasePlusCommissionEmployee::getFirstName() const
30  {
31     return firstName;
32  } // end function getFirstName
33
34  // set last name
35  void BasePlusCommissionEmployee::setLastName( const string &last )
36  {
37     lastName = last; // should validate
38  } // end function setLastName
39
40  // return last name
41  string BasePlusCommissionEmployee::getLastName() const
42  {
43     return lastName;
44  } // end function getLastName
45
46  // set social security number
47  void BasePlusCommissionEmployee::setSocialSecurityNumber(
48     const string &ssn )
49  {
50     socialSecurityNumber = ssn; // should validate
51  } // end function setSocialSecurityNumber
52
53  // return social security number
54  string BasePlusCommissionEmployee::getSocialSecurityNumber() const
55  {
56     return socialSecurityNumber;
57  } // end function getSocialSecurityNumber
58
```

Fig. 13.8 | BasePlusCommissionEmployee class represents an employee who receives a base salary in addition to a commission. (Part 2 of 3.)

```
59   // set gross sales amount
60   void BasePlusCommissionEmployee::setGrossSales( double sales )
61   {
62      grossSales = ( sales < 0.0 ) ? 0.0 : sales;
63   } // end function setGrossSales
64
65   // return gross sales amount
66   double BasePlusCommissionEmployee::getGrossSales() const
67   {
68      return grossSales;
69   } // end function getGrossSales
70
71   // set commission rate
72   void BasePlusCommissionEmployee::setCommissionRate( double rate )
73   {
74      commissionRate = ( rate > 0.0 && rate < 1.0 ) ? rate : 0.0;
75   } // end function setCommissionRate
76
77   // return commission rate
78   double BasePlusCommissionEmployee::getCommissionRate() const
79   {
80      return commissionRate;
81   } // end function getCommissionRate
82
83   // set base salary
84   void BasePlusCommissionEmployee::setBaseSalary( double salary )
85   {
86      baseSalary = ( salary < 0.0 ) ? 0.0 : salary;
87   } // end function setBaseSalary
88
89   // return base salary
90   double BasePlusCommissionEmployee::getBaseSalary() const
91   {
92      return baseSalary;
93   } // end function getBaseSalary
94
95   // calculate earnings
96   double BasePlusCommissionEmployee::earnings() const
97   {
98      return baseSalary + ( commissionRate * grossSales );
99   } // end function earnings
100
101  // print BasePlusCommissionEmployee object
102  void BasePlusCommissionEmployee::print() const
103  {
104     cout << "base-salaried commission employee: " << firstName << ' '
105        << lastName << "\nsocial security number: " << socialSecurityNumber
106        << "\ngross sales: " << grossSales
107        << "\ncommission rate: " << commissionRate
108        << "\nbase salary: " << baseSalary;
109  } // end function print
```

Fig. 13.8 | BasePlusCommissionEmployee class represents an employee who receives a base salary in addition to a commission. (Part 3 of 3.)

Testing Class *BasePlusCommissionEmployee*

Figure 13.9 tests class BasePlusCommissionEmployee. Lines 17–18 instantiate object employee of class BasePlusCommissionEmployee, passing "Bob", "Lewis", "333-33-3333", 5000, .04 and 300 to the constructor as the first name, last name, social security number, gross sales, commission rate and base salary, respectively. Lines 24–31 use BasePlusCommissionEmployee's *get* functions to retrieve the values of the object's data members for output. Line 33 invokes the object's setBaseSalary member function to change the base salary. Member function setBaseSalary (Fig. 13.8, lines 84–87) ensures that data member baseSalary is not assigned a negative value, because an employee's base salary cannot be negative. Line 37 of Fig. 13.9 invokes the object's print member function to output the updated BasePlusCommissionEmployee's information, and line 40 calls member function earnings to display the BasePlusCommissionEmployee's earnings.

```cpp
1   // Fig. 13.9: BasePlusCommissionEmployeeTest.cpp
2   // Testing class BasePlusCommissionEmployee.
3   #include <iostream>
4   using std::cout;
5   using std::endl;
6   using std::fixed;
7
8   #include <iomanip>
9   using std::setprecision;
10
11  // BasePlusCommissionEmployee class definition
12  #include "BasePlusCommissionEmployee.h"
13
14  int main()
15  {
16     // instantiate BasePlusCommissionEmployee object
17     BasePlusCommissionEmployee
18        employee( "Bob", "Lewis", "333-33-3333", 5000, .04, 300 );
19
20     // set floating-point output formatting
21     cout << fixed << setprecision( 2 );
22
23     // get commission employee data
24     cout << "Employee information obtained by get functions: \n"
25        << "\nFirst name is " << employee.getFirstName()
26        << "\nLast name is " << employee.getLastName()
27        << "\nSocial security number is "
28        << employee.getSocialSecurityNumber()
29        << "\nGross sales is " << employee.getGrossSales()
30        << "\nCommission rate is " << employee.getCommissionRate()
31        << "\nBase salary is " << employee.getBaseSalary() << endl;
32
33     employee.setBaseSalary( 1000 ); // set base salary
34
35     cout << "\nUpdated employee information output by print function: \n"
36        << endl;
37     employee.print(); // display the new employee information
```

Fig. 13.9 | BasePlusCommissionEmployee class test program. (Part 1 of 2.)

```
38
39      // display the employee's earnings
40      cout << "\n\nEmployee's earnings: $" << employee.earnings() << endl;
41
42      return 0;
43   } // end main
```

```
Employee information obtained by get functions:

First name is Bob
Last name is Lewis
Social security number is 333-33-3333
Gross sales is 5000.00
Commission rate is 0.04
Base salary is 300.00

Updated employee information output by print function:

base-salaried commission employee: Bob Lewis
social security number: 333-33-3333
gross sales: 5000.00
commission rate: 0.04
base salary: 1000.00

Employee's earnings: $1200.00
```

Fig. 13.9 | BasePlusCommissionEmployee class test program. (Part 2 of 2.)

Exploring the Similarities Between Class BasePlusCommissionEmployee and Class CommissionEmployee

Note that most of the code for class BasePlusCommissionEmployee (Figs. 13.7–13.8) is similar, if not identical, to the code for class CommissionEmployee (Figs. 13.4–13.5). For example, in class BasePlusCommissionEmployee, private data members firstName and lastName and member functions setFirstName, getFirstName, setLastName and get-LastName are identical to those of class CommissionEmployee. Classes CommissionEmployee and BasePlusCommissionEmployee also both contain private data members socialSecurityNumber, commissionRate and grossSales, as well as *get* and *set* functions to manipulate these members. In addition, the BasePlusCommissionEmployee constructor is almost identical to that of class CommissionEmployee, except that BasePlusCommissionEmployee's constructor also sets the baseSalary. The other additions to class BasePlusCommissionEmployee are private data member baseSalary and member functions setBaseSalary and getBaseSalary. Class BasePlusCommissionEmployee's print member function is nearly identical to that of class CommissionEmployee, except that BasePlusCommissionEmployee's print also outputs the value of data member baseSalary.

We literally copied code from class CommissionEmployee and pasted it into class BasePlusCommissionEmployee, then modified class BasePlusCommissionEmployee to include a base salary and member functions that manipulate the base salary. This "copy-and-paste" approach is error prone and time consuming. Worse yet, it can spread many physical copies of the same code throughout a system, creating a code-maintenance nightmare. Is there a way to "absorb" the data members and member functions of a class in a way that makes them part of another class without duplicating code? In the next several examples, we do exactly this, using inheritance.

Software Engineering Observation 13.3

Copying and pasting code from one class to another can spread errors across multiple source-code files. To avoid duplicating code (and possibly errors), use inheritance, rather than the "copy-and-paste" approach, in situations where you want one class to "absorb" the data members and member functions of another class.

Software Engineering Observation 13.4

With inheritance, the common data members and member functions of all the classes in the hierarchy are declared in a base class. When changes are required for these common features, you need to make the changes only in the base class—derived classes then inherit the changes. Without inheritance, changes would need to be made to all the source-code files that contain a copy of the code in question.

13.4.3 Creating a CommissionEmployee– BasePlusCommissionEmployee Inheritance Hierarchy

Now we create and test a new BasePlusCommissionEmployee class (Figs. 13.10–13.11) that derives from class CommissionEmployee (Figs. 13.4–13.5). In this example, a BasePlusCommissionEmployee object *is a* CommissionEmployee (because inheritance passes on the capabilities of class CommissionEmployee), but class BasePlusCommissionEmployee also has data member baseSalary (Fig. 13.10, line 24). The colon (:) in line 12 of the class definition indicates inheritance. Keyword public indicates the type of inheritance. As a derived class (formed with public inheritance), BasePlusCommissionEmployee inherits all the members of class CommissionEmployee, except for the constructor— each class provides its own constructors that are specific to the class. [Note that destructors, too, are not inherited.] Thus, the public services of BasePlusCommissionEmployee include its constructor (lines 15–16) and the public member functions inherited from class CommissionEmployee. Although we cannot see these inherited member functions in BasePlusCommissionEmployee's source code, they are nevertheless a part of derived class BasePlusCommissionEmployee. The derived class's public services also include member functions setBaseSalary, getBaseSalary, earnings and print (lines 18–22).

```
1    // Fig. 13.10: BasePlusCommissionEmployee.h
2    // BasePlusCommissionEmployee class derived from class
3    // CommissionEmployee.
4    #ifndef BASEPLUS_H
5    #define BASEPLUS_H
6
7    #include <string> // C++ standard string class
8    using std::string;
9
10   #include "CommissionEmployee.h" // CommissionEmployee class declaration
11
```

Fig. 13.10 | BasePlusCommissionEmployee class definition indicating inheritance relationship with class CommissionEmployee. (Part 1 of 2.)

```
12   class BasePlusCommissionEmployee : public CommissionEmployee
13   {
14   public:
15      BasePlusCommissionEmployee( const string &, const string &,
16         const string &, double = 0.0, double = 0.0, double = 0.0 );
17
18      void setBaseSalary( double ); // set base salary
19      double getBaseSalary() const; // return base salary
20
21      double earnings() const; // calculate earnings
22      void print() const; // print BasePlusCommissionEmployee object
23   private:
24      double baseSalary; // base salary
25   }; // end class BasePlusCommissionEmployee
26
27   #endif
```

Fig. 13.10 | BasePlusCommissionEmployee class definition indicating inheritance relationship with class CommissionEmployee. (Part 2 of 2.)

Figure 13.11 shows BasePlusCommissionEmployee's member-function implementations. The constructor (lines 10–17) introduces *base-class initializer syntax* (line 14), which uses a member initializer to pass arguments to the base-class (CommissionEmployee) constructor. Visual C++ requires that a derived-class constructor call its base-class constructor to initialize the base-class data members that are inherited into the derived class. Line 14 accomplishes this task by invoking the CommissionEmployee constructor by name, passing the constructor's parameters first, last, ssn, sales and rate as arguments to initialize base-class data members firstName, lastName, socialSecurityNumber, grossSales and commissionRate. If BasePlusCommissionEmployee's constructor did not invoke class CommissionEmployee's constructor explicitly, Visual C++ would attempt to invoke class CommissionEmployee's default constructor—but the class does not have such a constructor, so the compiler would issue an error. Recall from Chapter 4 that the compiler provides a default constructor with no parameters in any class that does not explicitly include a constructor. However, CommissionEmployee *does* explicitly include a constructor, so a default constructor is not provided, and any attempts to implicitly call CommissionEmployee's default constructor would result in compilation errors.

Common Programming Error 13.1

A compilation error occurs if a derived-class constructor calls one of its base-class constructors with arguments that are inconsistent with the number and types of parameters specified in one of the base-class constructor definitions.

Performance Tip 13.1

In a derived-class constructor, initializing member objects and invoking base-class constructors explicitly in the member initializer list prevents duplicate initialization in which a default constructor is called, then data members are modified again in the derived-class constructor's body.

The compiler generates errors for line 35 of Fig. 13.11 because base class CommissionEmployee's data members commissionRate and grossSales are private—derived class

BasePlusCommissionEmployee's member functions are not allowed to access base class CommissionEmployee's private data. Note that we used bold black text in Fig. 13.11 to indicate erroneous code. The compiler issues additional errors in lines 42–45 of BasePlusCommissionEmployee's print member function for the same reason. As you can see, Visual C++ rigidly enforces restrictions on accessing private data members, so that even a derived class (which is intimately related to its base class) cannot access the base class's private data. [*Note:* To save space, we show only the error messages from Visual C++ 2008 in this example. The error messages produced by your compiler may differ from those shown here. Also notice that we highlight key portions of the lengthy error messages in bold.]

```cpp
1   // Fig. 13.11: BasePlusCommissionEmployee.cpp
2   // Class BasePlusCommissionEmployee member-function definitions.
3   #include <iostream>
4   using std::cout;
5
6   // BasePlusCommissionEmployee class definition
7   #include "BasePlusCommissionEmployee.h"
8
9   // constructor
10  BasePlusCommissionEmployee::BasePlusCommissionEmployee(
11     const string &first, const string &last, const string &ssn,
12     double sales, double rate, double salary )
13     // explicitly call base-class constructor
14     : CommissionEmployee( first, last, ssn, sales, rate )
15  {
16     setBaseSalary( salary ); // validate and store base salary
17  } // end BasePlusCommissionEmployee constructor
18
19  // set base salary
20  void BasePlusCommissionEmployee::setBaseSalary( double salary )
21  {
22     baseSalary = ( salary < 0.0 ) ? 0.0 : salary;
23  } // end function setBaseSalary
24
25  // return base salary
26  double BasePlusCommissionEmployee::getBaseSalary() const
27  {
28     return baseSalary;
29  } // end function getBaseSalary
30
31  // calculate earnings
32  double BasePlusCommissionEmployee::earnings() const
33  {
34     // derived class cannot access the base class's private data
35     return baseSalary + ( commissionRate * grossSales );
36  } // end function earnings
37
```

Fig. 13.11 | BasePlusCommissionEmployee implementation file: private base-class data cannot be accessed from derived class. (Part 1 of 3.)

```
38   // print BasePlusCommissionEmployee object
39   void BasePlusCommissionEmployee::print() const
40   {
41      // derived class cannot access the base class's private data
42      cout << "base-salaried commission employee: " << firstName << ' '
43         << lastName << "\nsocial security number: " << socialSecurityNumber
44         << "\ngross sales: " << grossSales
45         << "\ncommission rate: " << commissionRate
46         << "\nbase salary: " << baseSalary;
47   } // end function print
```

```
C:\examples\ch13\Fig13_10_11\BasePlusCommissionEmployee.cpp(35) :
   error C2248: 'CommissionEmployee::commissionRate' :
   cannot access private member declared in class 'CommissionEmployee'
      C:\examples\ch13\Fig13_10_11\CommissionEmployee.h(37) :
      see declaration of 'CommissionEmployee::commissionRate'
      C:\examples\ch13\Fig13_10_11\CommissionEmployee.h(10) :
      see declaration of 'CommissionEmployee'

C:\examples\ch13\Fig13_10_11\BasePlusCommissionEmployee.cpp(35) :
   error C2248: 'CommissionEmployee::grossSales' :
   cannot access private member declared in class 'CommissionEmployee'
      C:\examples\ch13\Fig13_10_11\CommissionEmployee.h(36) :
      see declaration of 'CommissionEmployee::grossSales'
      C:\examples\ch13\Fig13_10_11\CommissionEmployee.h(10) :
      see declaration of 'CommissionEmployee'

C:\examples\ch13\Fig13_10_11\BasePlusCommissionEmployee.cpp(42) :
   error C2248: 'CommissionEmployee::firstName' :
   cannot access private member declared in class 'CommissionEmployee'
      C:\examples\ch13\Fig13_10_11\CommissionEmployee.h(33) :
      see declaration of 'CommissionEmployee::firstName'
      C:\examples\ch13\Fig13_10_11\CommissionEmployee.h(10) :
      see declaration of 'CommissionEmployee'

C:\examples\ch13\Fig13_10_11\BasePlusCommissionEmployee.cpp(43) :
   error C2248: 'CommissionEmployee::lastName' :
   cannot access private member declared in class 'CommissionEmployee'
      C:\examples\ch13\Fig13_10_11\CommissionEmployee.h(34) :
      see declaration of 'CommissionEmployee::lastName'
      C:\examples\ch13\Fig13_10_11\CommissionEmployee.h(10) :
      see declaration of 'CommissionEmployee'

C:\examples\ch13\Fig13_10_11\BasePlusCommissionEmployee.cpp(43) :
   error C2248: 'CommissionEmployee::socialSecurityNumber' :
   cannot access private member declared in class 'CommissionEmployee'
      C:\examples\ch13\Fig13_10_11\CommissionEmployee.h(35) :
      see declaration of 'CommissionEmployee::socialSecurityNumber'
      C:\examples\ch13\Fig13_10_11\CommissionEmployee.h(10) :
      see declaration of 'CommissionEmployee'
```

Fig. 13.11 | BasePlusCommissionEmployee implementation file: private base-class data cannot be accessed from derived class. (Part 2 of 3.)

```
C:examples\ch13\Fig13_10_11\BasePlusCommissionEmployee.cpp(44) :
   error C2248: 'CommissionEmployee::grossSales' :
   cannot access private member declared in class 'CommissionEmployee'
      C:\examples\ch13\Fig13_10_11\CommissionEmployee.h(36) :
         see declaration of 'CommissionEmployee::grossSales'
      C:\examples\ch13\Fig13_10_11\CommissionEmployee.h(10) :
         see declaration of 'CommissionEmployee'

C:\examples\ch13\Fig13_10_11\BasePlusCommissionEmployee.cpp(45) :
   error C2248: 'CommissionEmployee::commissionRate' :
   cannot access private member declared in class 'CommissionEmployee'
      C:\examples\ch13\Fig13_10_11\CommissionEmployee.h(37) :
         see declaration of 'CommissionEmployee::commissionRate'
      C:\examples\ch13\Fig13_10_11\CommissionEmployee.h(10) :
         see declaration of 'CommissionEmployee'
```

Fig. 13.11 | BasePlusCommissionEmployee implementation file: private base-class data cannot be accessed from derived class. (Part 3 of 3.)

We purposely included the erroneous code in Fig. 13.11 to emphasize that a derived class's member functions cannot access its base class's private data. The errors in Base-PlusCommissionEmployee could have been prevented by using the *get* member functions inherited from class CommissionEmployee. For example, line 35 could have invoked get-CommissionRate and getGrossSales to access CommissionEmployee's private data members commissionRate and grossSales, respectively. Similarly, lines 42–45 could have used appropriate *get* member functions to retrieve the values of the base class's data members. In the next example, we show how using protected data also allows us to avoid the errors encountered in this example.

Including the Base-Class Header File in the Derived-Class Header File with #include
Notice that we #include the base class's header file in the derived class's header file (line 10 of Fig. 13.10). This is necessary for three reasons. First, for the derived class to use the base class's name in line 12, we must tell the compiler that the base class exists—the class definition in CommissionEmployee.h does exactly that.

The second reason is that the compiler uses a class definition to determine the size of an object of that class (as we discussed in Section 4.8). A client program that creates an object of a class must #include the class definition to enable the compiler to reserve the proper amount of memory for the object. When using inheritance, a derived-class object's size depends on the data members declared explicitly in its class definition *and* the data members inherited from its direct and indirect base classes. Including the base class's definition in line 10 allows the compiler to determine the memory requirements for the base class's data members that become part of a derived-class object and thus contribute to the total size of the derived-class object.

The last reason for line 10 is to allow the compiler to determine whether the derived class uses the base class's inherited members properly. For example, in the program of Figs. 13.10–13.11, the compiler uses the base-class header file to determine that the data members being accessed by the derived class are private in the base class. Since these are inaccessible to the derived class, the compiler generates errors. The compiler also uses the base class's function prototypes to validate function calls made by the derived class to the inherited base-class functions—you'll see an example of such a function call in Fig. 13.16.

Linking Process in an Inheritance Hierarchy

In Section 4.9, we discussed the linking process for creating an executable GradeBook application. In that example, you saw that the client's object code was linked with the object code for class GradeBook, as well as the object code for any C++ Standard Library classes used in either the client code or in class GradeBook.

The linking process is similar for a program that uses classes in an inheritance hierarchy. The process requires the object code for all classes used in the program and the object code for the direct and indirect base classes of any derived classes used by the program. Suppose a client wants to create an application that uses class BasePlusCommission-Employee, which is a derived class of CommissionEmployee (we'll see an example of this in Section 13.4.4). When compiling the client application, the client's object code must be linked with the object code for classes BasePlusCommissionEmployee and CommissionEmployee, because BasePlusCommissionEmployee inherits member functions from its base class CommissionEmployee. The code is also linked with the object code for any C++ Standard Library classes used in class CommissionEmployee, class BasePlusCommissionEmployee or the client code. This provides the program with access to the implementations of all of the functionality that the program may use.

13.4.4 CommissionEmployee–BasePlusCommissionEmployee Inheritance Hierarchy Using protected Data

To enable class BasePlusCommissionEmployee to directly access CommissionEmployee data members firstName, lastName, socialSecurityNumber, grossSales and commissionRate, we can declare those members as protected in the base class. As we discussed in Section 13.3, a base class's protected members can be accessed by members and friends of the base class and by members and friends of any classes derived from that base class.

Good Programming Practice 13.1

Declare public members first, protected members second and private members last.

Defining Base Class CommissionEmployee with protected Data

Class CommissionEmployee (Figs. 13.12–13.13) now declares data members firstName, lastName, socialSecurityNumber, grossSales and commissionRate as protected (Fig. 13.12, lines 33–37) rather than private. The member-function implementations in Fig. 13.13 are identical to those in Fig. 13.5.

```
1   // Fig. 13.12: CommissionEmployee.h
2   // CommissionEmployee class definition with protected data.
3   #ifndef COMMISSION_H
4   #define COMMISSION_H
```

Fig. 13.12 | CommissionEmployee class definition that declares protected data to allow access by derived classes. (Part 1 of 2.)

```
 5
 6   #include <string> // C++ standard string class
 7   using std::string;
 8
 9   class CommissionEmployee
10   {
11   public:
12      CommissionEmployee( const string &, const string &, const string &,
13         double = 0.0, double = 0.0 );
14
15      void setFirstName( const string & ); // set first name
16      string getFirstName() const; // return first name
17
18      void setLastName( const string & ); // set last name
19      string getLastName() const; // return last name
20
21      void setSocialSecurityNumber( const string & ); // set SSN
22      string getSocialSecurityNumber() const; // return SSN
23
24      void setGrossSales( double ); // set gross sales amount
25      double getGrossSales() const; // return gross sales amount
26
27      void setCommissionRate( double ); // set commission rate
28      double getCommissionRate() const; // return commission rate
29
30      double earnings() const; // calculate earnings
31      void print() const; // print CommissionEmployee object
32   protected:
33      string firstName;
34      string lastName;
35      string socialSecurityNumber;
36      double grossSales; // gross weekly sales
37      double commissionRate; // commission percentage
38   }; // end class CommissionEmployee
39
40   #endif
```

Fig. 13.12 | CommissionEmployee class definition that declares protected data to allow access by derived classes. (Part 2 of 2.)

```
 1   // Fig. 13.13: CommissionEmployee.cpp
 2   // Class CommissionEmployee member-function definitions.
 3   #include <iostream>
 4   using std::cout;
 5
 6   #include "CommissionEmployee.h" // CommissionEmployee class definition
 7
 8   // constructor
 9   CommissionEmployee::CommissionEmployee(
10      const string &first, const string &last, const string &ssn,
11      double sales, double rate )
12   {
```

Fig. 13.13 | CommissionEmployee class with protected data. (Part 1 of 3.)

```
13        firstName = first; // should validate
14        lastName = last; // should validate
15        socialSecurityNumber = ssn; // should validate
16        setGrossSales( sales ); // validate and store gross sales
17        setCommissionRate( rate ); // validate and store commission rate
18     } // end CommissionEmployee constructor
19
20     // set first name
21     void CommissionEmployee::setFirstName( const string &first )
22     {
23        firstName = first; // should validate
24     } // end function setFirstName
25
26     // return first name
27     string CommissionEmployee::getFirstName() const
28     {
29        return firstName;
30     } // end function getFirstName
31
32     // set last name
33     void CommissionEmployee::setLastName( const string &last )
34     {
35        lastName = last; // should validate
36     } // end function setLastName
37
38     // return last name
39     string CommissionEmployee::getLastName() const
40     {
41        return lastName;
42     } // end function getLastName
43
44     // set social security number
45     void CommissionEmployee::setSocialSecurityNumber( const string &ssn )
46     {
47        socialSecurityNumber = ssn; // should validate
48     } // end function setSocialSecurityNumber
49
50     // return social security number
51     string CommissionEmployee::getSocialSecurityNumber() const
52     {
53        return socialSecurityNumber;
54     } // end function getSocialSecurityNumber
55
56     // set gross sales amount
57     void CommissionEmployee::setGrossSales( double sales )
58     {
59        grossSales = ( sales < 0.0 ) ? 0.0 : sales;
60     } // end function setGrossSales
61
62     // return gross sales amount
63     double CommissionEmployee::getGrossSales() const
64     {
```

Fig. 13.13 | CommissionEmployee class with protected data. (Part 2 of 3.)

```
65        return grossSales;
66     } // end function getGrossSales
67
68     // set commission rate
69     void CommissionEmployee::setCommissionRate( double rate )
70     {
71        commissionRate = ( rate > 0.0 && rate < 1.0 ) ? rate : 0.0;
72     } // end function setCommissionRate
73
74     // return commission rate
75     double CommissionEmployee::getCommissionRate() const
76     {
77        return commissionRate;
78     } // end function getCommissionRate
79
80     // calculate earnings
81     double CommissionEmployee::earnings() const
82     {
83        return commissionRate * grossSales;
84     } // end function earnings
85
86     // print CommissionEmployee object
87     void CommissionEmployee::print() const
88     {
89        cout << "commission employee: " << firstName << ' ' << lastName
90           << "\nsocial security number: " << socialSecurityNumber
91           << "\ngross sales: " << grossSales
92           << "\ncommission rate: " << commissionRate;
93     } // end function print
```

Fig. 13.13 | CommissionEmployee class with protected data. (Part 3 of 3.)

Modifying Derived Class *BasePlusCommissionEmployee*

We now modify class BasePlusCommissionEmployee (Figs. 13.14–13.15) so that it inherits from the class CommissionEmployee in Figs. 13.12–13.13. Because class BasePlusCommissionEmployee inherits from this version of class CommissionEmployee, objects of class BasePlusCommissionEmployee can access inherited data members that are declared protected in class CommissionEmployee (i.e., data members firstName, lastName, socialSecurityNumber, grossSales and commissionRate). As a result, the compiler does not generate errors when compiling the BasePlusCommissionEmployee earnings and print member-function definitions in Fig. 13.15 (lines 32–36 and 39–47, respectively). This shows the special privileges that a derived class is granted to access protected base-class data members. Objects of a derived class also can access protected members in any of that derived class's indirect base classes.

Class BasePlusCommissionEmployee does not inherit class CommissionEmployee's constructor. However, class BasePlusCommissionEmployee's constructor (Fig. 13.15, lines 10–17) calls class CommissionEmployee's constructor explicitly with member initializer syntax (line 14). Recall that BasePlusCommissionEmployee's constructor must explicitly call the constructor of class CommissionEmployee, because CommissionEmployee does not contain a default constructor that could be invoked implicitly.

```
1   // Fig. 13.14: BasePlusCommissionEmployee.h
2   // BasePlusCommissionEmployee class derived from class
3   // CommissionEmployee.
4   #ifndef BASEPLUS_H
5   #define BASEPLUS_H
6
7   #include <string> // C++ standard string class
8   using std::string;
9
10  #include "CommissionEmployee.h" // CommissionEmployee class declaration
11
12  class BasePlusCommissionEmployee : public CommissionEmployee
13  {
14  public:
15     BasePlusCommissionEmployee( const string &, const string &,
16        const string &, double = 0.0, double = 0.0, double = 0.0 );
17
18     void setBaseSalary( double ); // set base salary
19     double getBaseSalary() const; // return base salary
20
21     double earnings() const; // calculate earnings
22     void print() const; // print BasePlusCommissionEmployee object
23  private:
24     double baseSalary; // base salary
25  }; // end class BasePlusCommissionEmployee
26
27  #endif
```

Fig. 13.14 | BasePlusCommissionEmployee class header file.

```
1   // Fig. 13.15: BasePlusCommissionEmployee.cpp
2   // Class BasePlusCommissionEmployee member-function definitions.
3   #include <iostream>
4   using std::cout;
5
6   // BasePlusCommissionEmployee class definition
7   #include "BasePlusCommissionEmployee.h"
8
9   // constructor
10  BasePlusCommissionEmployee::BasePlusCommissionEmployee(
11     const string &first, const string &last, const string &ssn,
12     double sales, double rate, double salary )
13     // explicitly call base-class constructor
14     : CommissionEmployee( first, last, ssn, sales, rate )
15  {
16     setBaseSalary( salary ); // validate and store base salary
17  } // end BasePlusCommissionEmployee constructor
18
```

Fig. 13.15 | BasePlusCommissionEmployee implementation file for
BasePlusCommissionEmployee class that inherits protected data from CommissionEmployee.
(Part 1 of 2.)

```
19   // set base salary
20   void BasePlusCommissionEmployee::setBaseSalary( double salary )
21   {
22      baseSalary = ( salary < 0.0 ) ? 0.0 : salary;
23   } // end function setBaseSalary
24
25   // return base salary
26   double BasePlusCommissionEmployee::getBaseSalary() const
27   {
28      return baseSalary;
29   } // end function getBaseSalary
30
31   // calculate earnings
32   double BasePlusCommissionEmployee::earnings() const
33   {
34      // can access protected data of base class
35      return baseSalary + ( commissionRate * grossSales );
36   } // end function earnings
37
38   // print BasePlusCommissionEmployee object
39   void BasePlusCommissionEmployee::print() const
40   {
41      // can access protected data of base class
42      cout << "base-salaried commission employee: " << firstName << ' '
43         << lastName << "\nsocial security number: " << socialSecurityNumber
44         << "\ngross sales: " << grossSales
45         << "\ncommission rate: " << commissionRate
46         << "\nbase salary: " << baseSalary;
47   } // end function print
```

Fig. 13.15 | BasePlusCommissionEmployee implementation file for
BasePlusCommissionEmployee class that inherits protected data from CommissionEmployee.
(Part 2 of 2.)

Testing the Modified *BasePlusCommissionEmployee* Class

Figure 13.16 uses a BasePlusCommissionEmployee object to perform the same tasks that
Fig. 13.9 performed on an object of the first version of class BasePlusCommissionEmployee (Figs. 13.7–13.8). Note that the outputs of the two programs are identical. We created

```
1    // Fig. 13.16: BasePlusCommissionEmployeeTest.cpp
2    // Testing class BasePlusCommissionEmployee.
3    #include <iostream>
4    using std::cout;
5    using std::endl;
6    using std::fixed;
7
8    #include <iomanip>
9    using std::setprecision;
10
```

Fig. 13.16 | protected base-class data can be accessed from derived class. (Part 1 of 2.)

```
11  // BasePlusCommissionEmployee class definition
12  #include "BasePlusCommissionEmployee.h"
13
14  int main()
15  {
16     // instantiate BasePlusCommissionEmployee object
17     BasePlusCommissionEmployee
18        employee( "Bob", "Lewis", "333-33-3333", 5000, .04, 300 );
19
20     // set floating-point output formatting
21     cout << fixed << setprecision( 2 );
22
23     // get commission employee data
24     cout << "Employee information obtained by get functions: \n"
25        << "\nFirst name is " << employee.getFirstName()
26        << "\nLast name is " << employee.getLastName()
27        << "\nSocial security number is "
28        << employee.getSocialSecurityNumber()
29        << "\nGross sales is " << employee.getGrossSales()
30        << "\nCommission rate is " << employee.getCommissionRate()
31        << "\nBase salary is " << employee.getBaseSalary() << endl;
32
33     employee.setBaseSalary( 1000 ); // set base salary
34
35     cout << "\nUpdated employee information output by print function: \n"
36        << endl;
37     employee.print(); // display the new employee information
38
39     // display the employee's earnings
40     cout << "\n\nEmployee's earnings: $" << employee.earnings() << endl;
41
42     return 0;
43  } // end main
```

```
Employee information obtained by get functions:

First name is Bob
Last name is Lewis
Social security number is 333-33-3333
Gross sales is 5000.00
Commission rate is 0.04
Base salary is 300.00

Updated employee information output by print function:

base-salaried commission employee: Bob Lewis
social security number: 333-33-3333
gross sales: 5000.00
commission rate: 0.04
base salary: 1000.00

Employee's earnings: $1200.00
```

Fig. 13.16 | protected base-class data can be accessed from derived class. (Part 2 of 2.)

the first class `BasePlusCommissionEmployee` without using inheritance and created this version of `BasePlusCommissionEmployee` using inheritance; however, both classes provide the same functionality. Note that the code for class `BasePlusCommissionEmployee` (i.e., the header and implementation files), which is 74 lines, is considerably shorter than the code for the noninherited version of the class, which is 154 lines, because the inherited version absorbs part of its functionality from `CommissionEmployee`, whereas the noninherited version does not absorb any functionality. Also, there is now only one copy of the `CommissionEmployee` functionality declared and defined in class `CommissionEmployee`. This makes the source code easier to maintain, modify and debug, because the source code related to a `CommissionEmployee` exists only in the files of Figs. 13.12–13.13.

Notes on Using protected Data

In this example, we declared base-class data members as `protected`, so derived classes can modify the data directly. Inheriting `protected` data members slightly increases performance, because we can directly access the members without incurring the overhead of calls to *set* or *get* member functions. In most cases, however, it is better to use `private` data members to encourage proper software engineering, and leave code-optimization issues to the compiler. Your code will be easier to maintain, modify and debug.

Using `protected` data members creates two serious problems. First, the derived-class object does not have to use a member function to set the value of the base class's `protected` data member. Therefore, a derived-class object easily can assign an invalid value to the `protected` data member, thus leaving the object in an inconsistent state. For example, with `CommissionEmployee`'s data member grossSales declared as `protected`, a derived-class (e.g., `BasePlusCommissionEmployee`) object can assign a negative value to grossSales. The second problem with using `protected` data members is that derived-class member functions are more likely to be written so that they depend on the base-class implementation. In practice, derived classes should depend only on the base-class services (i.e., non-`private` member functions) and not on the base-class implementation. With `protected` data members in the base class, if the base-class implementation changes, we may need to modify all derived classes of that base class. For example, if for some reason we were to change the names of data members firstName and lastName to first and last, then we would have to do so for all occurrences in which a derived class references these base-class data members directly. In such a case, the software is said to be *fragile* or *brittle*, because a small change in the base class can "break" derived-class implementation. You should be able to change the base-class implementation while still providing the same services to derived classes. (Of course, if the base-class services change, we must reimplement our derived classes—good object-oriented design attempts to prevent this.)

Software Engineering Observation 13.5

It is appropriate to use the protected *access specifier when a base class should provide a service (i.e., a member function) only to its derived classes (and* friends*), not to other clients.*

Software Engineering Observation 13.6

Declaring base-class data members private *(as opposed to declaring them* protected*) enables programmers to change the base-class implementation without having to change derived-class implementations.*

Error-Prevention Tip 13.1

When possible, avoid including protected *data members in a base class. Rather, include non-private member functions that access* private *data members, ensuring that the object maintains a consistent state.*

13.4.5 CommissionEmployee–BasePlusCommissionEmployee Inheritance Hierarchy Using private Data

We now reexamine our hierarchy once more, this time using the best software engineering practices. Class CommissionEmployee (Figs. 13.17–13.18) now declares data members firstName, lastName, socialSecurityNumber, grossSales and commissionRate as private (Fig. 13.17, lines 33–37) and provides public member functions setFirstName, getFirstName, setLastName, getLastName, setSocialSecurityNumber, getSocialSecurityNumber, setGrossSales, getGrossSales, setCommissionRate, getCommissionRate, earnings and print for manipulating these values. If we decide to change the data member names, the earnings and print definitions will not require modification—only the definitions of the *get* and *set* member functions that directly manipulate the data members will need to change. Note that these changes occur solely within the base class—no changes to the derived class are needed. Localizing the effects of changes like this is a good software engineering practice. Derived class BasePlusCommissionEmployee (Figs. 13.19–13.20) inherits CommissionEmployee's non-private member functions and can access the private base-class members via those member functions.

```
1   // Fig. 13.17: CommissionEmployee.h
2   // CommissionEmployee class definition with good software engineering.
3   #ifndef COMMISSION_H
4   #define COMMISSION_H
5
6   #include <string> // C++ standard string class
7   using std::string;
8
9   class CommissionEmployee
10  {
11  public:
12     CommissionEmployee( const string &, const string &, const string &,
13        double = 0.0, double = 0.0 );
14
15     void setFirstName( const string & ); // set first name
16     string getFirstName() const; // return first name
17
18     void setLastName( const string & ); // set last name
19     string getLastName() const; // return last name
20
21     void setSocialSecurityNumber( const string & ); // set SSN
22     string getSocialSecurityNumber() const; // return SSN
23
24     void setGrossSales( double ); // set gross sales amount
25     double getGrossSales() const; // return gross sales amount
```

Fig. 13.17 | CommissionEmployee class defined using good software engineering practices. (Part 1 of 2.)

```
26
27      void setCommissionRate( double ); // set commission rate
28      double getCommissionRate() const; // return commission rate
29
30      double earnings() const; // calculate earnings
31      void print() const; // print CommissionEmployee object
32   private:
33      string firstName;
34      string lastName;
35      string socialSecurityNumber;
36      double grossSales; // gross weekly sales
37      double commissionRate; // commission percentage
38   }; // end class CommissionEmployee
39
40   #endif
```

Fig. 13.17 | CommissionEmployee class defined using good software engineering practices. (Part 2 of 2.)

```
1    // Fig. Fig. 13.18: CommissionEmployee.cpp
2    // Class CommissionEmployee member-function definitions.
3    #include <iostream>
4    using std::cout;
5
6    #include "CommissionEmployee.h" // CommissionEmployee class definition
7
8    // constructor
9    CommissionEmployee::CommissionEmployee(
10      const string &first, const string &last, const string &ssn,
11      double sales, double rate )
12      : firstName( first ), lastName( last ), socialSecurityNumber( ssn )
13   {
14      setGrossSales( sales ); // validate and store gross sales
15      setCommissionRate( rate ); // validate and store commission rate
16   } // end CommissionEmployee constructor
17
18   // set first name
19   void CommissionEmployee::setFirstName( const string &first )
20   {
21      firstName = first; // should validate
22   } // end function setFirstName
23
24   // return first name
25   string CommissionEmployee::getFirstName() const
26   {
27      return firstName;
28   } // end function getFirstName
29
```

Fig. 13.18 | CommissionEmployee class implementation file: CommissionEmployee class uses member functions to manipulate its private data. (Part 1 of 3.)

```
30   // set last name
31   void CommissionEmployee::setLastName( const string &last )
32   {
33      lastName = last; // should validate
34   } // end function setLastName
35
36   // return last name
37   string CommissionEmployee::getLastName() const
38   {
39      return lastName;
40   } // end function getLastName
41
42   // set social security number
43   void CommissionEmployee::setSocialSecurityNumber( const string &ssn )
44   {
45      socialSecurityNumber = ssn; // should validate
46   } // end function setSocialSecurityNumber
47
48   // return social security number
49   string CommissionEmployee::getSocialSecurityNumber() const
50   {
51      return socialSecurityNumber;
52   } // end function getSocialSecurityNumber
53
54   // set gross sales amount
55   void CommissionEmployee::setGrossSales( double sales )
56   {
57      grossSales = ( sales < 0.0 ) ? 0.0 : sales;
58   } // end function setGrossSales
59
60   // return gross sales amount
61   double CommissionEmployee::getGrossSales() const
62   {
63      return grossSales;
64   } // end function getGrossSales
65
66   // set commission rate
67   void CommissionEmployee::setCommissionRate( double rate )
68   {
69      commissionRate = ( rate > 0.0 && rate < 1.0 ) ? rate : 0.0;
70   } // end function setCommissionRate
71
72   // return commission rate
73   double CommissionEmployee::getCommissionRate() const
74   {
75      return commissionRate;
76   } // end function getCommissionRate
77
78   // calculate earnings
79   double CommissionEmployee::earnings() const
80   {
```

Fig. 13.18 | CommissionEmployee class implementation file: CommissionEmployee class uses member functions to manipulate its private data. (Part 2 of 3.)

```
81        return getCommissionRate() * getGrossSales();
82   } // end function earnings
83
84   // print CommissionEmployee object
85   void CommissionEmployee::print() const
86   {
87        cout << "commission employee: "
88             << getFirstName() << ' ' << getLastName()
89             << "\nsocial security number: " << getSocialSecurityNumber()
90             << "\ngross sales: " << getGrossSales()
91             << "\ncommission rate: " << getCommissionRate();
92   } // end function print
```

Fig. 13.18 | CommissionEmployee class implementation file: CommissionEmployee class uses member functions to manipulate its private data. (Part 3 of 3.)

In the CommissionEmployee constructor implementation (Fig. 13.18, lines 9–16), note that we use member initializers (line 12) to set the values of members firstName, lastName and socialSecurityNumber. We show how derived-class BasePlusCommissionEmployee (Figs. 13.19–13.20) can invoke non-private base-class member functions (setFirstName, getFirstName, setLastName, getLastName, setSocialSecurityNumber and getSocialSecurityNumber) to manipulate these data members.

Performance Tip 13.2

Using a member function to access a data member's value can be slightly slower than accessing the data directly. However, today's optimizing compilers are carefully designed to perform many optimizations implicitly (such as inlining set and get member-function calls). As a result, programmers should write code that adheres to proper software engineering principles, and leave optimization issues to the compiler. A good rule is "Do not second-guess the compiler."

Class BasePlusCommissionEmployee (Figs. 13.19–13.20) has several changes to its member-function implementations (Fig. 13.20) that distinguish it from the previous version of the class (Figs. 13.14–13.15). Member functions earnings (Fig. 13.20, lines 32–35) and print (lines 38–46) each invoke member function getBaseSalary to obtain the base salary value, rather than accessing baseSalary directly. This insulates earnings and print from potential changes to the implementation of data member baseSalary. For example, if we decide to rename data member baseSalary or change its type, only member functions setBaseSalary and getBaseSalary will need to change.

```
1   // Fig. 13.19: BasePlusCommissionEmployee.h
2   // BasePlusCommissionEmployee class derived from class
3   // CommissionEmployee.
4   #ifndef BASEPLUS_H
5   #define BASEPLUS_H
6
7   #include <string> // C++ standard string class
8   using std::string;
9
```

Fig. 13.19 | BasePlusCommissionEmployee class header file. (Part 1 of 2.)

```
10   #include "CommissionEmployee.h" // CommissionEmployee class declaration
11
12   class BasePlusCommissionEmployee : public CommissionEmployee
13   {
14   public:
15      BasePlusCommissionEmployee( const string &, const string &,
16         const string &, double = 0.0, double = 0.0, double = 0.0 );
17
18      void setBaseSalary( double ); // set base salary
19      double getBaseSalary() const; // return base salary
20
21      double earnings() const; // calculate earnings
22      void print() const; // print BasePlusCommissionEmployee object
23   private:
24      double baseSalary; // base salary
25   }; // end class BasePlusCommissionEmployee
26
27   #endif
```

Fig. 13.19 | BasePlusCommissionEmployee class header file. (Part 2 of 2.)

```
1    // Fig. 13.20: BasePlusCommissionEmployee.cpp
2    // Class BasePlusCommissionEmployee member-function definitions.
3    #include <iostream>
4    using std::cout;
5
6    // BasePlusCommissionEmployee class definition
7    #include "BasePlusCommissionEmployee.h"
8
9    // constructor
10   BasePlusCommissionEmployee::BasePlusCommissionEmployee(
11      const string &first, const string &last, const string &ssn,
12      double sales, double rate, double salary )
13      // explicitly call base-class constructor
14      : CommissionEmployee( first, last, ssn, sales, rate )
15   {
16      setBaseSalary( salary ); // validate and store base salary
17   } // end BasePlusCommissionEmployee constructor
18
19   // set base salary
20   void BasePlusCommissionEmployee::setBaseSalary( double salary )
21   {
22      baseSalary = ( salary < 0.0 ) ? 0.0 : salary;
23   } // end function setBaseSalary
24
25   // return base salary
26   double BasePlusCommissionEmployee::getBaseSalary() const
27   {
28      return baseSalary;
29   } // end function getBaseSalary
```

Fig. 13.20 | BasePlusCommissionEmployee class that inherits from class
CommissionEmployee but cannot directly access the class's private data. (Part 1 of 2.)

```
30
31   // calculate earnings
32   double BasePlusCommissionEmployee::earnings() const
33   {
34      return getBaseSalary() + CommissionEmployee::earnings();
35   } // end function earnings
36
37   // print BasePlusCommissionEmployee object
38   void BasePlusCommissionEmployee::print() const
39   {
40      cout << "base-salaried ";
41
42      // invoke CommissionEmployee's print function
43      CommissionEmployee::print();
44
45      cout << "\nbase salary: " << getBaseSalary();
46   } // end function print
```

Fig. 13.20 | BasePlusCommissionEmployee class that inherits from class CommissionEmployee but cannot directly access the class's private data. (Part 2 of 2.)

Class BasePlusCommissionEmployee's earnings function (Fig. 13.20, lines 32–35) redefines class CommissionEmployee's earnings member function (Fig. 13.18, lines 79–82) to calculate the earnings of a base-salaried commission employee. Class BasePlusCommissionEmployee's version of earnings obtains the portion of the employee's earnings based on commission alone by calling base class CommissionEmployee's earnings function with the expression CommissionEmployee::earnings() (Fig. 13.20, line 34). BasePlusCommissionEmployee's earnings function then adds the base salary to this value to calculate the total earnings of the employee. Note the syntax used to invoke a redefined base-class member function from a derived class—place the base-class name and the binary scope resolution operator (::) before the base-class member-function name. This member-function invocation is a good software engineering practice: Recall from *Software Engineering Observation 10.9* that, if an object's member function performs the actions needed by another object, we should call that member function rather than duplicating its code body. By having BasePlusCommissionEmployee's earnings function invoke CommissionEmployee's earnings function to calculate part of a BasePlusCommissionEmployee object's earnings, we avoid duplicating the code and reduce code-maintenance problems.

Common Programming Error 13.2

When a base-class member function is redefined in a derived class, the derived-class version often calls the base-class version to do additional work. Failure to use the :: operator prefixed with the name of the base class when referencing the base class's member function causes infinite recursion, because the derived-class member function would then call itself.

Common Programming Error 13.3

Including a base-class member function with a different signature in the derived class hides the base-class version of the function. Attempts to call the base-class version through the public interface of a derived-class object result in compilation errors.

Similarly, BasePlusCommissionEmployee's print function (Fig. 13.20, lines 38–46) redefines class CommissionEmployee's print member function (Fig. 13.18, lines 85–92) to output information that is appropriate for a base-salaried commission employee. Class BasePlusCommissionEmployee's version displays part of a BasePlusCommissionEmployee object's information (i.e., the string "commission employee" and the values of class CommissionEmployee's private data members) by calling CommissionEmployee's print member function with the qualified name CommissionEmployee::print() (Fig. 13.20, line 43). BasePlusCommissionEmployee's print function then outputs the remainder of a BasePlusCommissionEmployee object's information (i.e., the value of class BasePlusCommissionEmployee's base salary).

Figure 13.21 performs the same manipulations on a BasePlusCommissionEmployee object as did Fig. 13.9 and Fig. 13.16 on objects of classes CommissionEmployee and BasePlusCommissionEmployee, respectively. Although each "base-salaried commission employee" class behaves identically, class BasePlusCommissionEmployee is the best engineered. By using inheritance and by calling member functions that hide the data and ensure consistency, we have efficiently and effectively constructed a well-engineered class.

In this section, you saw an evolutionary set of examples that was carefully designed to teach key capabilities for good software engineering with inheritance. You learned how to create a derived class using inheritance, how to use protected base-class members to enable a derived class to access inherited base-class data members and how to redefine base-class functions to provide versions that are more appropriate for derived-class objects. In addition, you learned how to apply software engineering techniques from Chapters 10–11 and this chapter to create classes that are easy to maintain, modify and debug.

```cpp
1   // Fig. 13.21: BasePlusCommissionEmployeeTest.cpp
2   // Testing class BasePlusCommissionEmployee.
3   #include <iostream>
4   using std::cout;
5   using std::endl;
6   using std::fixed;
7
8   #include <iomanip>
9   using std::setprecision;
10
11  // BasePlusCommissionEmployee class definition
12  #include "BasePlusCommissionEmployee.h"
13
14  int main()
15  {
16     // instantiate BasePlusCommissionEmployee object
17     BasePlusCommissionEmployee
18        employee( "Bob", "Lewis", "333-33-3333", 5000, .04, 300 );
19
20     // set floating-point output formatting
21     cout << fixed << setprecision( 2 );
22
```

Fig. 13.21 | Base-class private data is accessible to a derived class via public or protected member function inherited by the derived class. (Part 1 of 2.)

```
23        // get commission employee data
24        cout << "Employee information obtained by get functions: \n"
25           << "\nFirst name is " << employee.getFirstName()
26           << "\nLast name is " << employee.getLastName()
27           << "\nSocial security number is "
28           << employee.getSocialSecurityNumber()
29           << "\nGross sales is " << employee.getGrossSales()
30           << "\nCommission rate is " << employee.getCommissionRate()
31           << "\nBase salary is " << employee.getBaseSalary() << endl;
32
33        employee.setBaseSalary( 1000 ); // set base salary
34
35        cout << "\nUpdated employee information output by print function: \n"
36           << endl;
37        employee.print(); // display the new employee information
38
39        // display the employee's earnings
40        cout << "\n\nEmployee's earnings: $" << employee.earnings() << endl;
41
42        return 0;
43   } // end main
```

```
Employee information obtained by get functions:

First name is Bob
Last name is Lewis
Social security number is 333-33-3333
Gross sales is 5000.00
Commission rate is 0.04
Base salary is 300.00

Updated employee information output by print function:

base-salaried commission employee: Bob Lewis
social security number: 333-33-3333
gross sales: 5000.00
commission rate: 0.04
base salary: 1000.00

Employee's earnings: $1200.00
```

Fig. 13.21 | Base-class `private` data is accessible to a derived class via `public` or `protected` member function inherited by the derived class. (Part 2 of 2.)

13.5 Constructors and Destructors in Derived Classes

As we explained in the preceding section, instantiating a derived-class object begins a chain of constructor calls in which the derived-class constructor, before performing its own tasks, invokes its direct base class's constructor either explicitly (via a base-class member initializer) or implicitly (calling the base class's default constructor). Similarly, if the base class is derived from another class, the base-class constructor is required to invoke the constructor of the next class up in the hierarchy, and so on. The last constructor called in this chain is the constructor of the class at the base of the hierarchy, whose body actually finishes executing first. The original derived-class constructor's body finishes executing last. Each base-class constructor initializes the base-class data members that the derived-class object inherits. For example, consider the CommissionEmployee/BasePlusCommissionEmployee hierarchy from Figs. 13.17–13.20. When a program creates an object of class BasePlusCommissionEmployee, the CommissionEmployee constructor is called. Since class CommissionEmployee is at the base of the hierarchy, its constructor executes, initializing the private data members of CommissionEmployee that are part of the BasePlusCommissionEmployee object. When CommissionEmployee's constructor completes execution, it returns control to BasePlusCommissionEmployee's constructor, which initializes the BasePlusCommissionEmployee object's baseSalary.

Software Engineering Observation 13.7

When a program creates a derived-class object, the derived-class constructor immediately calls the base-class constructor, the base-class constructor's body executes, then the derived class's member initializers execute and finally the derived-class constructor's body executes. This process cascades up the hierarchy if it contains more than two levels.

When a derived-class object is destroyed, the program calls that object's destructor. This begins a chain (or cascade) of destructor calls in which the derived-class destructor and the destructors of the direct and indirect base classes and the classes' members execute in reverse of the order in which the constructors executed. When a derived-class object's destructor is called, the destructor performs its task, then invokes the destructor of the next base class up the hierarchy. This process repeats until the destructor of the final base class at the top of the hierarchy is called. Then the object is removed from memory.

Software Engineering Observation 13.8

Suppose that we create an object of a derived class where both the base class and the derived class contain (via composition) objects of other classes. When an object of that derived class is created, first the constructors for the base class's member objects execute, then the base-class constructor executes, then the constructors for the derived class's member objects execute, then the derived class's constructor executes. Destructors for derived-class objects are called in the reverse of the order in which their corresponding constructors are called.

Base-class constructors, destructors and overloaded assignment operators (see Chapter 12, Operator Overloading; String and Array Objects) are not inherited by derived classes. Derived-class constructors, destructors and overloaded assignment operators, however, can call base-class constructors, destructors and overloaded assignment operators.

Our next example defines class CommissionEmployee (Figs. 13.22–13.23) and class BasePlusCommissionEmployee (Figs. 13.24–13.25) with constructors and destructors that each print a message when invoked. As you'll see in the output in Fig. 13.26, these messages demonstrate the order in which the constructors and destructors are called for objects in an inheritance hierarchy.

In this example, we modified the CommissionEmployee constructor (lines 10–21 of Fig. 13.23) and included a CommissionEmployee destructor (lines 24–29), each of which outputs a line of text upon its invocation. We also modified the BasePlusCommissionEmployee constructor (lines 11–22 of Fig. 13.25) and included a BasePlusCommissionEmployee destructor (lines 25–30), each of which outputs a line of text upon its invocation.

```
 1   // Fig. 13.22: CommissionEmployee.h
 2   // CommissionEmployee class definition represents a commission employee.
 3   #ifndef COMMISSION_H
 4   #define COMMISSION_H
 5
 6   #include <string> // C++ standard string class
 7   using std::string;
 8
 9   class CommissionEmployee
10   {
11   public:
12      CommissionEmployee( const string &, const string &, const string &,
13         double = 0.0, double = 0.0 );
14      ~CommissionEmployee(); // destructor
15
16      void setFirstName( const string & ); // set first name
17      string getFirstName() const; // return first name
18
19      void setLastName( const string & ); // set last name
20      string getLastName() const; // return last name
21
22      void setSocialSecurityNumber( const string & ); // set SSN
23      string getSocialSecurityNumber() const; // return SSN
24
25      void setGrossSales( double ); // set gross sales amount
26      double getGrossSales() const; // return gross sales amount
27
28      void setCommissionRate( double ); // set commission rate
29      double getCommissionRate() const; // return commission rate
30
31      double earnings() const; // calculate earnings
32      void print() const; // print CommissionEmployee object
33   private:
34      string firstName;
35      string lastName;
36      string socialSecurityNumber;
37      double grossSales; // gross weekly sales
38      double commissionRate; // commission percentage
39   }; // end class CommissionEmployee
40
41   #endif
```

Fig. 13.22 | CommissionEmployee class header file.

```
 1   // Fig. 13.23: CommissionEmployee.cpp
 2   // Class CommissionEmployee member-function definitions.
 3   #include <iostream>
 4   using std::cout;
 5   using std::endl;
 6
 7   #include "CommissionEmployee.h" // CommissionEmployee class definition
```

Fig. 13.23 | CommissionEmployee's constructor outputs text. (Part 1 of 3.)

```cpp
 8
 9   // constructor
10   CommissionEmployee::CommissionEmployee(
11      const string &first, const string &last, const string &ssn,
12      double sales, double rate )
13      : firstName( first ), lastName( last ), socialSecurityNumber( ssn )
14   {
15      setGrossSales( sales ); // validate and store gross sales
16      setCommissionRate( rate ); // validate and store commission rate
17
18      cout << "CommissionEmployee constructor: " << endl;
19      print();
20      cout << "\n\n";
21   } // end CommissionEmployee constructor
22
23   // destructor
24   CommissionEmployee::~CommissionEmployee()
25   {
26      cout << "CommissionEmployee destructor: " << endl;
27      print();
28      cout << "\n\n";
29   } // end CommissionEmployee destructor
30
31   // set first name
32   void CommissionEmployee::setFirstName( const string &first )
33   {
34      firstName = first; // should validate
35   } // end function setFirstName
36
37   // return first name
38   string CommissionEmployee::getFirstName() const
39   {
40      return firstName;
41   } // end function getFirstName
42
43   // set last name
44   void CommissionEmployee::setLastName( const string &last )
45   {
46      lastName = last; // should validate
47   } // end function setLastName
48
49   // return last name
50   string CommissionEmployee::getLastName() const
51   {
52      return lastName;
53   } // end function getLastName
54
55   // set social security number
56   void CommissionEmployee::setSocialSecurityNumber( const string &ssn )
57   {
58      socialSecurityNumber = ssn; // should validate
59   } // end function setSocialSecurityNumber
60
```

Fig. 13.23 | CommissionEmployee's constructor outputs text. (Part 2 of 3.)

```
61   // return social security number
62   string CommissionEmployee::getSocialSecurityNumber() const
63   {
64      return socialSecurityNumber;
65   } // end function getSocialSecurityNumber
66
67   // set gross sales amount
68   void CommissionEmployee::setGrossSales( double sales )
69   {
70      grossSales = ( sales < 0.0 ) ? 0.0 : sales;
71   } // end function setGrossSales
72
73   // return gross sales amount
74   double CommissionEmployee::getGrossSales() const
75   {
76      return grossSales;
77   } // end function getGrossSales
78
79   // set commission rate
80   void CommissionEmployee::setCommissionRate( double rate )
81   {
82      commissionRate = ( rate > 0.0 && rate < 1.0 ) ? rate : 0.0;
83   } // end function setCommissionRate
84
85   // return commission rate
86   double CommissionEmployee::getCommissionRate() const
87   {
88      return commissionRate;
89   } // end function getCommissionRate
90
91   // calculate earnings
92   double CommissionEmployee::earnings() const
93   {
94      return getCommissionRate() * getGrossSales();
95   } // end function earnings
96
97   // print CommissionEmployee object
98   void CommissionEmployee::print() const
99   {
100     cout << "commission employee: "
101        << getFirstName() << ' ' << getLastName()
102        << "\nsocial security number: " << getSocialSecurityNumber()
103        << "\ngross sales: " << getGrossSales()
104        << "\ncommission rate: " << getCommissionRate();
105  } // end function print
```

Fig. 13.23 | CommissionEmployee's constructor outputs text. (Part 3 of 3.)

```
1   // Fig. 13.24: BasePlusCommissionEmployee.h
2   // BasePlusCommissionEmployee class derived from class
3   // CommissionEmployee.
```

Fig. 13.24 | BasePlusCommissionEmployee class header file. (Part 1 of 2.)

```
 4   #ifndef BASEPLUS_H
 5   #define BASEPLUS_H
 6
 7   #include <string> // C++ standard string class
 8   using std::string;
 9
10   #include "CommissionEmployee.h" // CommissionEmployee class declaration
11
12   class BasePlusCommissionEmployee : public CommissionEmployee
13   {
14   public:
15      BasePlusCommissionEmployee( const string &, const string &,
16         const string &, double = 0.0, double = 0.0, double = 0.0 );
17      ~BasePlusCommissionEmployee(); // destructor
18
19      void setBaseSalary( double ); // set base salary
20      double getBaseSalary() const; // return base salary
21
22      double earnings() const; // calculate earnings
23      void print() const; // print BasePlusCommissionEmployee object
24   private:
25      double baseSalary; // base salary
26   }; // end class BasePlusCommissionEmployee
27
28   #endif
```

Fig. 13.24 | BasePlusCommissionEmployee class header file. (Part 2 of 2.)

```
 1   // Fig. 13.25: BasePlusCommissionEmployee.cpp
 2   // Class BasePlusCommissionEmployee member-function definitions.
 3   #include <iostream>
 4   using std::cout;
 5   using std::endl;
 6
 7   // BasePlusCommissionEmployee class definition
 8   #include "BasePlusCommissionEmployee.h"
 9
10   // constructor
11   BasePlusCommissionEmployee::BasePlusCommissionEmployee(
12      const string &first, const string &last, const string &ssn,
13      double sales, double rate, double salary )
14      // explicitly call base-class constructor
15      : CommissionEmployee( first, last, ssn, sales, rate )
16   {
17      setBaseSalary( salary ); // validate and store base salary
18
19      cout << "BasePlusCommissionEmployee constructor: " << endl;
20      print();
21      cout << "\n\n";
22   } // end BasePlusCommissionEmployee constructor
23
```

Fig. 13.25 | BasePlusCommissionEmployee's constructor outputs text. (Part 1 of 2.)

```
24   // destructor
25   BasePlusCommissionEmployee::~BasePlusCommissionEmployee()
26   {
27      cout << "BasePlusCommissionEmployee destructor: " << endl;
28      print();
29      cout << "\n\n";
30   } // end BasePlusCommissionEmployee destructor
31
32   // set base salary
33   void BasePlusCommissionEmployee::setBaseSalary( double salary )
34   {
35      baseSalary = ( salary < 0.0 ) ? 0.0 : salary;
36   } // end function setBaseSalary
37
38   // return base salary
39   double BasePlusCommissionEmployee::getBaseSalary() const
40   {
41      return baseSalary;
42   } // end function getBaseSalary
43
44   // calculate earnings
45   double BasePlusCommissionEmployee::earnings() const
46   {
47      return getBaseSalary() + CommissionEmployee::earnings();
48   } // end function earnings
49
50   // print BasePlusCommissionEmployee object
51   void BasePlusCommissionEmployee::print() const
52   {
53      cout << "base-salaried ";
54
55      // invoke CommissionEmployee's print function
56      CommissionEmployee::print();
57
58      cout << "\nbase salary: " << getBaseSalary();
59   } // end function print
```

Fig. 13.25 | BasePlusCommissionEmployee's constructor outputs text. (Part 2 of 2.)

Figure 13.26 demonstrates the order in which constructors and destructors are called for objects of classes that are part of an inheritance hierarchy. Function main (lines 15–34) begins by instantiating CommissionEmployee object employee1 (lines 21–22) in a separate block inside main (lines 20–23). The object goes in and out of scope immediately (the end of the block is reached immediately after the object is created), so both the Commission-Employee constructor and destructor are called. Next, lines 26–27 instantiate BasePlus-CommissionEmployee object employee2. This invokes the CommissionEmployee constructor to display outputs with values passed from the BasePlusCommissionEmployee constructor; then the output specified in the BasePlusCommissionEmployee constructor is performed. Lines 30–31 then instantiate BasePlusCommissionEmployee object employee3. Again, the CommissionEmployee and BasePlusCommissionEmployee constructors are both called. Note that, in each case, the body of the CommissionEmployee constructor is executed before the body of the BasePlusCommissionEmployee constructor executes. When the end of `main` is reached, the destructors are called for objects `employee2` and `employee3`. But, because destructors are called in the reverse order of their corresponding constructors, the `BasePlusCommissionEmployee` destructor and `CommissionEmployee` destructor are called (in that order) for object `employee3`, then the `BasePlusCommissionEmployee` and `CommissionEmployee` destructors are called (in that order) for object `employee2`.

```cpp
1   // Fig. 13.26: ConstructorDestructorTest.cpp
2   // Display order in which base-class and derived-class constructors
3   // and destructors are called.
4   #include <iostream>
5   using std::cout;
6   using std::endl;
7   using std::fixed;
8
9   #include <iomanip>
10  using std::setprecision;
11
12  // BasePlusCommissionEmployee class definition
13  #include "BasePlusCommissionEmployee.h"
14
15  int main()
16  {
17     // set floating-point output formatting
18     cout << fixed << setprecision( 2 );
19
20     { // begin new scope
21        CommissionEmployee employee1(
22           "Bob", "Lewis", "333-33-3333", 5000, .04 );
23     } // end scope
24
25     cout << endl;
26     BasePlusCommissionEmployee
27        employee2( "Lisa", "Jones", "555-55-5555", 2000, .06, 800 );
28
29     cout << endl;
30     BasePlusCommissionEmployee
31        employee3( "Mark", "Sands", "888-88-8888", 8000, .15, 2000 );
32     cout << endl;
33     return 0;
34  } // end main
```

```
CommissionEmployee constructor:
commission employee: Bob Lewis
social security number: 333-33-3333
gross sales: 5000.00
commission rate: 0.04

CommissionEmployee destructor:
commission employee: Bob Lewis
social security number: 333-33-3333
```

Fig. 13.26 | Constructor and destructor call order. (Part 1 of 2.)

```
gross sales: 5000.00
commission rate: 0.04


CommissionEmployee constructor:
commission employee: Lisa Jones
social security number: 555-55-5555
gross sales: 2000.00
commission rate: 0.06

BasePlusCommissionEmployee constructor:
base-salaried commission employee: Lisa Jones
social security number: 555-55-5555
gross sales: 2000.00
commission rate: 0.06
base salary: 800.00


CommissionEmployee constructor:
commission employee: Mark Sands
social security number: 888-88-8888
gross sales: 8000.00
commission rate: 0.15

BasePlusCommissionEmployee constructor:
base-salaried commission employee: Mark Sands
social security number: 888-88-8888
gross sales: 8000.00
commission rate: 0.15
base salary: 2000.00


BasePlusCommissionEmployee destructor:
base-salaried commission employee: Mark Sands
social security number: 888-88-8888
gross sales: 8000.00
commission rate: 0.15
base salary: 2000.00

CommissionEmployee destructor:
commission employee: Mark Sands
social security number: 888-88-8888
gross sales: 8000.00
commission rate: 0.15

BasePlusCommissionEmployee destructor:
base-salaried commission employee: Lisa Jones
social security number: 555-55-5555
gross sales: 2000.00
commission rate: 0.06
base salary: 800.00

CommissionEmployee destructor:
commission employee: Lisa Jones
social security number: 555-55-5555
gross sales: 2000.00
commission rate: 0.06
```

Fig. 13.26 | Constructor and destructor call order. (Part 2 of 2.)

13.6 public, protected and private Inheritance

When deriving a class from a base class, the base class may be inherited through public, protected or private inheritance. Use of protected and private inheritance is rare, and each should be used only with great care; we normally use public inheritance in this book. (Chapter 21 demonstrates private inheritance as an alternative to composition.) Figure 13.27 summarizes for each type of inheritance the accessibility of base-class members in a derived class. The first column contains the base-class access specifiers.

When deriving a class from a public base class, public members of the base class become public members of the derived class, and protected members of the base class become protected members of the derived class. A base class's private members are never accessible directly from a derived class, but can be accessed through calls to the public and protected members of the base class.

When deriving from a protected base class, public and protected members of the base class become protected members of the derived class. When deriving from a private base class, public and protected members of the base class become private members (e.g., the functions become utility functions) of the derived class. Private and protected inheritance are not *is-a* relationships.

Base-class member-access specifier	Type of inheritance		
	public inheritance	protected inheritance	private inheritance
public	public in derived class. Can be accessed directly by member functions, friend functions and nonmember functions.	protected in derived class. Can be accessed directly by member functions and friend functions.	private in derived class. Can be accessed directly by member functions and friend functions.
protected	protected in derived class. Can be accessed directly by member functions and friend functions.	protected in derived class. Can be accessed directly by member functions and friend functions.	private in derived class. Can be accessed directly by member functions and friend functions.
private	Hidden in derived class. Can be accessed by member functions and friend functions through public or protected member functions of the base class.	Hidden in derived class. Can be accessed by member functions and friend functions through public or protected member functions of the base class.	Hidden in derived class. Can be accessed by member functions and friend functions through public or protected member functions of the base class.

Fig. 13.27 | Summary of base-class member accessibility in a derived class.

13.7 Software Engineering with Inheritance

In this section, we discuss the use of inheritance to customize existing software. When we use inheritance to create a new class from an existing one, the new class inherits the data members and member functions of the existing class, as described in Fig. 13.27. We can customize the new class to meet our needs by including additional members and by redefining base-class members. The derived-class programmer does this in Visual C++ without accessing the base class's source code. The derived class must be able to link to the base class's object code. This powerful capability is attractive to independent software vendors (ISVs). ISVs can develop proprietary classes for sale or license and make these classes available to users in object-code format. Users then can derive new classes from these library classes rapidly and without accessing the ISVs' proprietary source code. All the ISVs need to supply with the object code are the header files.

Sometimes it is difficult for students to appreciate the scope of problems faced by designers who work on large-scale software projects in industry. People experienced with such projects say that effective software reuse improves the software development process. Object-oriented programming facilitates software reuse, thus shortening development times and enhancing software quality.

The availability of substantial and useful class libraries delivers the maximum benefits of software reuse through inheritance. Just as shrink-wrapped software produced by independent software vendors became an explosive-growth industry with the arrival of the personal computer, interest in the creation and sale of class libraries is growing exponentially. Application designers build their applications with these libraries, and library designers are rewarded by having their libraries included with the applications. The standard C++ libraries that are shipped with C++ compilers tend to be rather general purpose and limited in scope. However, there is massive worldwide commitment to the development of class libraries for a huge variety of applications arenas.

Software Engineering Observation 13.9

At the design stage in an object-oriented system, the designer often determines that certain classes are closely related. The designer should "factor out" common attributes and behaviors and place these in a base class, then use inheritance to form derived classes, endowing them with capabilities beyond those inherited from the base class.

Software Engineering Observation 13.10

The creation of a derived class does not affect its base class's source code. Inheritance preserves the integrity of a base class.

Software Engineering Observation 13.11

Just as designers of non-object-oriented systems should avoid proliferation of functions, designers of object-oriented systems should avoid proliferation of classes. Proliferation of classes creates management problems and can hinder software reusability, because it becomes difficult for a client to locate the most appropriate class of a huge class library. The alternative is to create fewer classes that provide more substantial functionality, but such classes might provide too much functionality.

> ### Performance Tip 13.3
>
> *If classes produced through inheritance are larger than they need to be (i.e., contain too much functionality), memory and processing resources might be wasted. Inherit from the class whose functionality is "closest" to what is needed.*

Reading derived-class definitions can be confusing, because inherited members are not shown physically in the derived classes, but nevertheless are present. A similar problem exists when documenting derived-class members.

13.8 Inheritance in C++/CLI

In general, inheritance in C++/CLI functions exactly as it does in native C++. There are a few differences, though. Although we did not discuss multiple inheritance in detail in this chapter, you should be aware that C++/CLI doesn't support it. A managed class may directly inherit only from a single base class, which must also be a managed class. A managed class, however, can inherit from multiple interfaces. Interfaces are discussed in Section 14.10. Managed classes in C++/CLI also support only `public` inheritance. Attempting to declare a managed class with `private` or `protected` inheritance causes a compilation error. As a result, explicitly specifying `public` inheritance in C++/CLI is redundant, since it is the only option.

Another difference in C++/CLI is the order in which constructors are called in an inheritance hierarchy. In native C++, when a class constructor is called, the compiler first calls the base class constructor (if it exists). Then the compiler executes the initialization list of the class constructor and the body of the class constructor afterward. When using managed classes defined with the `ref class` keyword, this order is slightly different. The initialization list of the class constructor is evaluated first. Then the base-class constructor is called (if it exists). Once the base-class constructor call finishes, the body of the class constructor is executed.

13.9 Wrap-Up

This chapter introduced inheritance—the ability to create a class by absorbing an existing class's data members and member functions and embellishing them with new capabilities. Through a series of examples using an employee inheritance hierarchy, you learned the notions of base classes and derived classes and used `public` inheritance to create a derived class that inherits members from a base class. The chapter introduced the access specifier `protected`—derived-class member functions can access `protected` base-class members. You learned how to access redefined base-class members by qualifying their names with the base-class name and binary scope resolution operator (`::`). You also saw the order in which constructors and destructors are called for objects of classes that are part of an inheritance hierarchy. Finally, we explained the three types of inheritance—`public`, `protected` and `private`—and the accessibility of base-class members in a derived class when using each type.

In Chapter 14, Object-Oriented Programming: Polymorphism, we build on our discussion of inheritance by introducing polymorphism—an object-oriented concept that enables us to write programs that handle, in a more general manner, objects of a wide variety of classes related by inheritance. After studying Chapter 14, you'll be familiar with classes, objects, encapsulation, inheritance and polymorphism—the essential concepts of object-oriented programming.

Summary

Section 13.1 Introduction
- Software reuse reduces program development time and cost.

Section 13.2 Base Classes and Derived Classes
- Inheritance is a form of software reuse in which you create a class that absorbs an existing class's data and behaviors and enhances them with new capabilities. The existing class is called the base class, and the new class is referred to as the derived class.

- A direct base class is the one from which a derived class explicitly inherits (specified by the class name to the right of the : in the first line of a class definition). An indirect base class is inherited from two or more levels up the class hierarchy.

- With single inheritance, a class is derived from one base class. With multiple inheritance, a class inherits from multiple (possibly unrelated) base classes.

- A derived class represents a more specialized group of objects. Typically, a derived class contains behaviors inherited from its base class plus additional behaviors. A derived class can also customize behaviors inherited from the base class.

- Every object of a derived class is also an object of that class's base class. However, a base-class object is not an object of that class's derived classes.

- The *is-a* relationship represents inheritance. In an *is-a* relationship, an object of a derived class also can be treated as an object of its base class.

- The *has-a* relationship represents composition—an object contains one or more objects of other classes as members, but does not disclose their behavior directly in its interface.

- A derived class cannot access the `private` members of its base class directly; allowing this would violate the encapsulation of the base class. A derived class can, however, access the `public` and `protected` members of its base class directly.

- A derived class can effect state changes in `private` base-class members, but only through non-`private` member functions provided in the base class and inherited into the derived class.

- When a base-class member function is inappropriate for a derived class, that member function can be redefined in the derived class with an appropriate implementation.

- Single-inheritance relationships form treelike hierarchical structures—a base class exists in a hierarchical relationship with its derived classes.

- It is possible to treat base-class objects and derived-class objects similarly; the commonality shared between the object types is expressed in the data members and member functions of the base class.

Section 13.3 protected Members
- A base class's `public` members are accessible anywhere that the program has a handle to an object of that base class or to an object of one of that base class's derived classes—or, when using the binary scope resolution operator, whenever the class's name is in scope.

- A base class's `private` members are accessible only within the definition of that base class or from friends of that class.

- A base class's `protected` members have an intermediate level of protection between `public` and `private` access. A base class's `protected` members can be accessed by members and `friends` of that base class and by members and `friends` of any classes derived from that base class.

- Unfortunately, `protected` data members often present two major problems. First, the derived-class object does not have to use a *set* function to change the value of the base-class's `protected` data. Second, derived-class member functions are more likely to depend on base-class implementation details.

- When a derived-class member function redefines a base-class member function, the base-class member function can be accessed from the derived class by qualifying the base-class member-function name with the base-class name and the binary scope resolution operator (`::`).

Section 13.5 Constructors and Destructors in Derived Classes

- When an object of a derived class is instantiated, the base class's constructor is called immediately (either explicitly or implicitly) to initialize the base-class data members in the derived-class object (before the derived-class data members are initialized).

- When a derived-class object is destroyed, the destructors are called in the reverse order of the constructors—first the derived-class destructor is called, then the base-class destructor is called.

Section 13.6 `public`, `protected` and `private` Inheritance

- Declaring data members `private`, while providing non-`private` member functions to manipulate and perform validity checking on this data, enforces good software engineering.

- When deriving a class from a base class, the base class may be declared as either `public`, `protected` or `private`.

- When deriving a class from a `public` base class, `public` members of the base class become `public` members of the derived class, and `protected` members of the base class become `protected` members of the derived class.

- When deriving a class from a `protected` base class, `public` and `protected` members of the base class become `protected` members of the derived class.

- When deriving a class from a `private` base class, `public` and `protected` members of the base class become `private` members of the derived class.

Section 13.8 Inheritance in C++/CLI

- C++/CLI doesn't support multiple inheritance. A managed class may have only a single base class, and that class must also be a managed class.

- Managed classes in C++/CLI use `public` inheritance by default; `private` and `protected` inheritance are not supported.

Terminology

base class	composition
base-class constructor	customize software
base-class default constructor	derived class
base-class destructor	derived-class constructor
base-class initializer	derived-class destructor
brittle software	direct base class
class hierarchy	fragile software

friend of a base class
friend of a derived class
has-a relationship
hierarchical relationship
indirect base class
inherit the members of an existing class
inheritance
is-a relationship
multiple inheritance
private base class
private inheritance

protected base class
protected inheritance
protected keyword
protected member of a class
public base class
public inheritance
qualified name
redefine a base-class member function
single inheritance
subclass
superclass

Self-Review Exercises

13.1 Fill in the blanks in each of the following statements:

a) _____ is a form of software reuse in which new classes absorb the data and behaviors of existing classes and embellish these classes with new capabilities.

b) A base class's _____ members can be accessed only in the base-class definition or in derived-class definitions.

c) In a(n) _____ relationship, an object of a derived class also can be treated as an object of its base class.

d) In a(n) _____ relationship, a class object has one or more objects of other classes as members.

e) In single inheritance, a class exists in a(n) _____ relationship with its derived classes.

f) A base class's _____ members are accessible within that base class and anywhere that the program has a handle to an object of that base class or to an object of one of its derived classes.

g) A base class's `protected` access members have a level of protection between those of `public` and _____ access.

h) Visual C++ provides for _____, which allows a derived class to inherit from many base classes, even if the base classes are unrelated.

i) When an object of a derived class is instantiated, the base class's _____ is called implicitly or explicitly to do any necessary initialization of the base-class data members in the derived-class object.

j) When deriving a class from a base class with `public` inheritance, `public` members of the base class become _____ members of the derived class, and `protected` members of the base class become _____ members of the derived class.

k) When deriving a class from a base class with `protected` inheritance, `public` members of the base class become _____ members of the derived class, and `protected` members of the base class become _____ members of the derived class.

13.2 State whether each of the following is *true* or *false*. If *false*, explain why.

a) Base-class constructors are not inherited by derived classes.

b) A *has-a* relationship is implemented via inheritance.

c) A `Car` class has an *is-a* relationship with the `SteeringWheel` and `Brakes` classes.

d) Inheritance encourages the reuse of proven high-quality software.

e) When a derived-class object is destroyed, the destructors are called in the reverse order of the constructors.

Answers to Self-Review Exercises

13.1   a) Inheritance. b) protected. c) *is-a* or inheritance. d) *has-a* or composition or aggregation. e) hierarchical. f) public. g) private. h) multiple inheritance. i) constructor. j) public, protected. k) protected, protected.

13.2   a) True. b) False. A *has-a* relationship is implemented via composition. An *is-a* relationship is implemented via inheritance. c) False. This is an example of a *has-a* relationship. Class Car has an *is-a* relationship with class Vehicle. d) True. e) True.

Exercises

13.3   Many programs written with inheritance could be written with composition instead, and vice versa. Rewrite class BasePlusCommissionEmployee of the CommissionEmployee–BasePlusCommissionEmployee hierarchy to use composition rather than inheritance. After you do this, assess the relative merits of the two approaches for designing classes CommissionEmployee and BasePlusCommissionEmployee, as well as for object-oriented programs in general. Which approach is more natural? Why?

13.4   Discuss the ways in which inheritance promotes software reuse, saves time during program development and helps prevent errors.

13.5   Some programmers prefer not to use protected access because they believe it breaks the encapsulation of the base class. Discuss the relative merits of using protected access vs. using private access in base classes.

13.6   Draw an inheritance hierarchy for students at a university similar to the hierarchy shown in Fig. 13.2. Use Student as the base class of the hierarchy, then include classes UndergraduateStudent and GraduateStudent that derive from Student. Continue to extend the hierarchy as deep (i.e., as many levels) as possible. For example, Freshman, Sophomore, Junior and Senior might derive from UndergraduateStudent, and DoctoralStudent and MastersStudent might derive from GraduateStudent. After drawing the hierarchy, discuss the relationships that exist between the classes. [*Note:* You do not need to write any code for this exercise.]

13.7   The world of shapes is much richer than the shapes included in the inheritance hierarchy of Fig. 13.3. Write down all the shapes you can think of—both two-dimensional and three-dimensional—and form them into a more complete Shape hierarchy with as many levels as possible. Your hierarchy should have the base class Shape from which class TwoDimensionalShape and class ThreeDimensionalShape are derived. [*Note:* You do not need to write any code for this exercise.] We'll use this hierarchy in the exercises of Chapter 14 to process a set of distinct shapes as objects of base-class Shape. (This technique, called polymorphism, is the subject of Chapter 14.)

13.8   Draw an inheritance hierarchy for classes Quadrilateral, Trapezoid, Parallelogram, Rectangle and Square. Use Quadrilateral as the base class of the hierarchy. Make the hierarchy as deep as possible.

13.9   (*Package Inheritance Hierarchy*) Package-delivery services, such as FedEx®, DHL® and UPS®, offer a number of different shipping options, each with specific costs associated. Create an inheritance hierarchy to represent various types of packages. Use Package as the base class of the hierarchy, then include classes TwoDayPackage and OvernightPackage that derive from Package. Base class Package should include data members representing the name, address, city, state and ZIP code for both the sender and the recipient of the package, in addition to data members that store the weight (in ounces) and cost per ounce to ship the package. Package's constructor should initialize these data members. Ensure that the weight and cost per ounce contain positive values. Package should provide a public member function calculateCost that returns a double indicating the cost associated with shipping the package. Package's calculateCost function should determine the cost by multiplying the weight by the cost per ounce. Derived class TwoDayPackage should inherit the functionality of base class Package but also include a data member that represents a flat fee that the shipping company charges for two-day-delivery service. TwoDayPackage's constructor should receive a value to initialize this data member. TwoDayPackage should redefine member function calculate-Cost so that it computes the shipping cost by adding the flat fee to the weight-based cost calculated by base class Package's calculateCost function. Class OvernightPackage should inherit directly from class Package and contain an additional data member representing an additional fee per ounce charged for overnight-delivery service. OvernightPackage should redefine member function calculateCost so that it adds the additional fee per ounce to the standard cost per ounce before calculating the shipping cost. Write a test program that creates objects of each type of Package and tests member function calculateCost.

13.10 *(Account Inheritance Hierarchy)* Create an inheritance hierarchy that a bank might use to represent customers' bank accounts. All customers at this bank can deposit (i.e., credit) money into their accounts and withdraw (i.e., debit) money from their accounts. More specific types of accounts also exist. Savings accounts, for instance, earn interest on the money they hold. Checking accounts, on the other hand, charge a fee per transaction (i.e., credit or debit).

Create an inheritance hierarchy containing base class Account and derived classes Savings-Account and CheckingAccount that inherit from class Account. Base class Account should include one data member of type double to represent the account balance. The class should provide a constructor that receives an initial balance and uses it to initialize the data member. The constructor should validate the initial balance to ensure that it is greater than or equal to 0.0. If not, the balance should be set to 0.0 and the constructor should display an error message, indicating that the initial balance was invalid. The class should provide three member functions. Member function credit should add an amount to the current balance. Member function debit should withdraw money from the Account and ensure that the debit amount does not exceed the Account's balance. If it does, the balance should be left unchanged and the function should print the message "Debit amount exceeded account balance." Member function getBalance should return the current balance.

Derived class SavingsAccount should inherit the functionality of an Account, but also include a data member of type double indicating the interest rate (percentage) assigned to the Account. SavingsAccount's constructor should receive the initial balance, as well as an initial value for the SavingsAccount's interest rate. SavingsAccount should provide a public member function calculateInterest that returns a double indicating the amount of interest earned by an account. Member function calculateInterest should determine this amount by multiplying the interest rate by the account balance. [*Note:* SavingsAccount should inherit member functions credit and debit as is without redefining them.]

Derived class CheckingAccount should inherit from base class Account and include an additional data member of type double that represents the fee charged per transaction. Checking-Account's constructor should receive the initial balance, as well as a parameter indicating a fee amount. Class CheckingAccount should redefine member functions credit and debit so that they subtract the fee from the account balance whenever either transaction is performed successfully. CheckingAccount's versions of these functions should invoke the base-class Account version to perform the updates to an account balance. CheckingAccount's debit function should charge a fee only if money is actually withdrawn (i.e., the debit amount does not exceed the account balance). [*Hint:* Define Account's debit function so that it returns a bool indicating whether money was withdrawn. Then use the return value to determine whether a fee should be charged.]

After defining the classes in this hierarchy, write a program that creates objects of each class and tests their member functions. Add interest to the SavingsAccount object by first invoking its calculateInterest function, then passing the returned interest amount to the object's credit function.

14

Object-Oriented Programming: Polymorphism

One Ring to rule them all,
One Ring to find them,
One Ring to bring them all
and in the darkness bind
them.
—John Ronald Reuel Tolkien

The silence often of pure
innocence
Persuades when speaking
fails.
—William Shakespeare

General propositions do not
decide concrete cases.
—Oliver Wendell Holmes

A philosopher of imposing
stature doesn't think in a
vacuum. Even his most
abstract ideas are, to some
extent, conditioned by what
is or is not known in the time
when he lives.
—Alfred North Whitehead

OBJECTIVES

In this chapter you'll learn:

- What polymorphism is, how it makes programming more convenient and how it makes systems more extensible and maintainable.

- To declare and use `virtual` functions to effect polymorphism.

- The distinction between abstract and concrete classes.

- To declare pure `virtual` functions to create abstract classes.

- How to use runtime type information (RTTI) with downcasting, `dynamic_cast`, `typeid` and `type_info`.

- How C++ implements `virtual` functions and dynamic binding "under the hood."

- How to use `virtual` destructors to ensure that all appropriate destructors run on an object.

14.1 Introduction

In Chapters 10–13, we discussed key object-oriented programming technologies including classes, objects, encapsulation, operator overloading and inheritance. We now continue our study of OOP by explaining and demonstrating *polymorphism* with inheritance hierarchies. Polymorphism enables us to "program in the general" rather than "program in the specific." In particular, polymorphism enables us to write programs that process objects of classes that are part of the same class hierarchy as if they were all objects of the hierarchy's base class. As we'll soon see, polymorphism works off base-class pointer handles and base-class reference handles, but not off name handles. Remember that we use handles as a general term here, not to be confused with C++/CLI handles denoted with ^.

Consider the following example of polymorphism. Suppose we create a program that simulates the movement of several types of animals for a biological study. Classes Fish,

Frog and Bird represent the three types of animals under investigation. Imagine that each of these classes inherits from base class Animal, which contains a function move and maintains an animal's current location. Each derived class implements function move. Our program maintains a vector of pointers to objects of the various Animal derived classes. To simulate the animals' movements, the program sends each object the same message once per second—namely, move. However, each specific type of Animal responds to a move message in its own unique way—a Fish might swim two feet, a Frog might jump three feet and a Bird might fly ten feet. The program issues the same message (i.e., move) to each animal object generically, but each object knows how to modify its location appropriately for its specific type of movement. Relying on each object to know how to "do the right thing" (i.e., do what is appropriate for that type of object) in response to the same function call is the key concept of polymorphism. The same message (in this case, move) sent to a variety of objects has "many forms" of results—hence the term polymorphism.

With polymorphism, we can design and implement systems that are easily extensible—new classes can be added with little or no modification to the general portions of the program, as long as the new classes are part of the inheritance hierarchy that the program processes generically. The only parts of a program that must be altered to accommodate new classes are those that require direct knowledge of the new classes that you add to the hierarchy. For example, if we create class Tortoise that inherits from class Animal (which might respond to a move message by crawling one inch), we need to write only the Tortoise class and the part of the simulation that instantiates a Tortoise object. The portions of the simulation that process each Animal generically can remain the same.

We begin with a sequence of small, focused examples that lead up to an understanding of virtual functions and dynamic binding—polymorphism's two underlying technologies. We then present a case study that revisits Chapter 13's Employee hierarchy. In the case study, we define a common "interface" (i.e., set of functionality) for all the classes in the hierarchy. This common functionality among employees is defined in a so-called abstract base class, Employee, from which classes SalariedEmployee, HourlyEmployee and CommissionEmployee inherit directly and class BaseCommissionEmployee inherits indirectly. We'll soon see what makes a class "abstract" or its opposite—"concrete."

In this hierarchy, every employee has an earnings function to calculate the employee's weekly pay. These earnings functions vary by employee type—for instance, SalariedEmployees are paid a fixed weekly salary regardless of the number of hours worked, while HourlyEmployees are paid by the hour and receive overtime pay. We show how to process each employee "in the general"—that is, using base-class pointers to call the earnings function of several derived-class objects. This way, you need to be concerned with only one type of function call, which can be used to execute several different functions based on the objects referred to by the base-class pointers.

A key feature of this chapter is its (optional) detailed discussion of polymorphism, virtual functions and dynamic binding "under the hood," which uses a detailed diagram to explain how polymorphism can be implemented in Visual C++.

Occasionally, when performing polymorphic processing, we need to program "in the specific," meaning that operations need to be performed on a specific type of object in a hierarchy—the operation cannot be generally applied to several types of objects. We reuse our Employee hierarchy to demonstrate the powerful capabilities of *runtime type information (RTTI)* and *dynamic casting*, which enable a program to determine the type of an object at execution time and act on that object accordingly. We use these capabilities to determine whether a particular employee object is a `BasePlusCommissionEmployee`, then give that employee a 10 percent bonus on his or her base salary.

14.2 Polymorphism Examples

In this section, we discuss several polymorphism examples. With polymorphism, one function can cause different actions to occur, depending on the type of the object on which the function is invoked. This gives you tremendous expressive capability. If class `Rectangle` is derived from class `Quadrilateral`, then a `Rectangle` object is a more specific version of a `Quadrilateral` object. Therefore, any operation (such as calculating the perimeter or the area) that can be performed on an object of class `Quadrilateral` also can be performed on an object of class `Rectangle`. Such operations also can be performed on other kinds of `Quadrilateral`s, such as `Squares`, `Parallelograms` and `Trapezoids`. The polymorphism occurs when a program invokes a `virtual` function through a base-class (i.e., `Quadrilateral`) pointer or reference—Visual C++ dynamically (i.e., at execution time) chooses the correct function for the class from which the object was instantiated. You'll see a code example that illustrates this process in Section 14.3.

As another example, suppose that we design a video game that manipulates objects of many different types, including objects of classes `Martian`, `Venutian`, `Plutonian`, `SpaceShip` and `LaserBeam`. Imagine that each of these classes inherits from the common base class `SpaceObject`, which contains member function `draw`. Each derived class implements this function in a manner appropriate for that class. A screen-manager program maintains a container (e.g., a `vector`) that holds `SpaceObject` pointers to objects of the various classes. To refresh the screen, the screen manager periodically sends each object the same message—namely, `draw`. Each type of object responds in a unique way. For example, a `Martian` object might draw itself in red with the appropriate number of antennae. A `SpaceShip` object might draw itself as a silver flying saucer. A `LaserBeam` object might draw itself as a bright red beam across the screen. Again, the same message (in this case, `draw`) sent to a variety of objects has "many forms" of results.

A polymorphic screen manager facilitates adding new classes to a system with minimal modifications to its code. Suppose that we want to add objects of class `Mercurian` to our video game. To do so, we must build a class `Mercurian` that inherits from `SpaceObject` but provides its own definition of member function `draw`. Then, when pointers to objects of class `Mercurian` appear in the container, you do not need to modify the code for the screen manager. The screen manager invokes member function `draw` on every object in the container, regardless of the object's type, so the new `Mercurian` objects simply "plug right in." Thus, without modifying the system (other than to build and include the classes themselves), programmers can use polymorphism to accommodate additional classes, including ones that were not even envisioned when the system was created.

Software Engineering Observation 14.1

With `virtual` functions and polymorphism, you can deal in generalities and let the execution-time environment concern itself with the specifics. You can direct a variety of objects to behave in manners appropriate to those objects without even knowing their types (as long as those objects belong to the same inheritance hierarchy and are being accessed off a common base-class pointer).

> **Software Engineering Observation 14.2**
>
> *Polymorphism promotes extensibility: Software written to invoke polymorphic behavior is written independently of the types of the objects to which messages are sent. Thus, new types of objects that can respond to existing messages can be incorporated into such a system without modifying the base system. Only client code that instantiates new objects must be modified to accommodate new types.*

14.3 Relationships Among Objects in an Inheritance Hierarchy

Section 13.4 created an employee class hierarchy, in which class `BasePlusCommission-Employee` inherited from class `CommissionEmployee`. The Chapter 13 examples manipulated `CommissionEmployee` and `BasePlusCommissionEmployee` objects by using the objects' names to invoke their member functions. We now examine the relationships among classes in a hierarchy more closely. The next several sections present a series of examples that demonstrate how base-class and derived-class pointers can be aimed at base-class and derived-class objects, and how those pointers can be used to invoke member functions that manipulate those objects. In Section 14.3.4, we demonstrate how to get polymorphic behavior from base-class pointers aimed at derived-class objects.

In Section 14.3.1, we assign the address of a derived-class object to a base-class pointer, then show that invoking a function via the base-class pointer invokes the base-class functionality—i.e., the type of the handle determines which function is called. In Section 14.3.2, we assign the address of a base-class object to a derived-class pointer, which results in a compilation error. We discuss the error message and investigate why the compiler does not allow such an assignment. In Section 14.3.3, we assign the address of a derived-class object to a base-class pointer, then examine how the base-class pointer can be used to invoke only the base-class functionality—when we attempt to invoke derived-class member functions through the base-class pointer, compilation errors occur. Finally, in Section 14.3.4, we introduce `virtual` functions and polymorphism by declaring a base-class function as `virtual`. We then assign the address of a derived-class object to the base-class pointer and use that pointer to invoke derived-class functionality—precisely the capability we need to achieve polymorphic behavior.

A key concept in these examples is to demonstrate that an object of a derived class can be treated as an object of its base class. This enables various interesting manipulations. For example, a program can create an array of base-class pointers that point to objects of many derived-class types. Despite the fact that the derived-class objects are of different types, the compiler allows this because each derived-class object *is an* object of its base class. However, we cannot treat a base-class object as an object of any of its derived classes. For example, a `CommissionEmployee` is not a `BasePlusCommissionEmployee` in the hierarchy defined in Chapter 13—a `CommissionEmployee` does not have a `baseSalary` data member and does not have member functions `setBaseSalary` and `getBaseSalary`. The *is-a* relationship applies only from a derived class to its direct and indirect base classes.

14.3.1 Invoking Base-Class Functions from Derived-Class Objects

The example in Figs. 14.1–14.5 demonstrates three ways to aim base-class pointers and derived-class pointers at base-class objects and derived-class objects. The first two are straightforward—we aim a base-class pointer at a base-class object (and invoke base-class functionality), and we aim a derived-class pointer at a derived-class object (and invoke derived-class functionality). Then, we demonstrate the relationship between derived classes and base classes (i.e., the *is-a* relationship of inheritance) by aiming a base-class pointer at a derived-class object (and showing that the base-class functionality is indeed available in the derived-class object).

Class CommissionEmployee (Figs. 14.1–14.2), which we discussed in Chapter 13, is used to represent employees who are paid a percentage of their sales. Class BasePlusCommissionEmployee (Figs. 14.3–14.4), which we also discussed in Chapter 13, is used to represent employees who receive a base salary plus a percentage of their sales. Each BasePlusCommissionEmployee object *is a* CommissionEmployee that also has a base salary. Class BasePlusCommissionEmployee's earnings member function (lines 32–35 of Fig. 14.4) redefines class CommissionEmployee's earnings member function (lines 79–82 of Fig. 14.2) to include the object's base salary. Class BasePlusCommissionEmployee's print member function (lines 38–46 of Fig. 14.4) redefines class CommissionEmployee's print member function (lines 85–92 of Fig. 14.2) to display the same information as the print function in class CommissionEmployee, as well as the employee's base salary.

```cpp
1   // Fig. 14.1: CommissionEmployee.h
2   // CommissionEmployee class definition represents a commission employee.
3   #ifndef COMMISSION_H
4   #define COMMISSION_H
5
6   #include <string> // C++ standard string class
7   using std::string;
8
9   class CommissionEmployee
10  {
11  public:
12     CommissionEmployee( const string &, const string &, const string &,
13        double = 0.0, double = 0.0 );
14
15     void setFirstName( const string & ); // set first name
16     string getFirstName() const; // return first name
17
18     void setLastName( const string & ); // set last name
19     string getLastName() const; // return last name
20
21     void setSocialSecurityNumber( const string & ); // set SSN
22     string getSocialSecurityNumber() const; // return SSN
23
24     void setGrossSales( double ); // set gross sales amount
25     double getGrossSales() const; // return gross sales amount
26
27     void setCommissionRate( double ); // set commission rate
28     double getCommissionRate() const; // return commission rate
29
30     double earnings() const; // calculate earnings
31     void print() const; // print CommissionEmployee object
```

Fig. 14.1 | CommissionEmployee class header file. (Part 1 of 2.)

```
32   private:
33      string firstName;
34      string lastName;
35      string socialSecurityNumber;
36      double grossSales; // gross weekly sales
37      double commissionRate; // commission percentage
38   }; // end class CommissionEmployee
39
40   #endif
```

Fig. 14.1 | CommissionEmployee class header file. (Part 2 of 2.)

```
1    // Fig. 14.2: CommissionEmployee.cpp
2    // Class CommissionEmployee member-function definitions.
3    #include <iostream>
4    using std::cout;
5
6    #include "CommissionEmployee.h" // CommissionEmployee class definition
7
8    // constructor
9    CommissionEmployee::CommissionEmployee(
10      const string &first, const string &last, const string &ssn,
11      double sales, double rate )
12      : firstName( first ), lastName( last ), socialSecurityNumber( ssn )
13   {
14      setGrossSales( sales ); // validate and store gross sales
15      setCommissionRate( rate ); // validate and store commission rate
16   } // end CommissionEmployee constructor
17
18   // set first name
19   void CommissionEmployee::setFirstName( const string &first )
20   {
21      firstName = first; // should validate
22   } // end function setFirstName
23
24   // return first name
25   string CommissionEmployee::getFirstName() const
26   {
27      return firstName;
28   } // end function getFirstName
29
30   // set last name
31   void CommissionEmployee::setLastName( const string &last )
32   {
33      lastName = last;  // should validate
34   } // end function setLastName
35
36   // return last name
37   string CommissionEmployee::getLastName() const
38   {
39      return lastName;
40   } // end function getLastNam
```

Fig. 14.2 | CommissionEmployee class implementation file. (Part 1 of 2.)

```
41
42   // set social security number
43   void CommissionEmployee::setSocialSecurityNumber( const string &ssn )
44   {
45      socialSecurityNumber = ssn; // should validate
46   } // end function setSocialSecurityNumber
47
48   // return social security number
49   string CommissionEmployee::getSocialSecurityNumber() const
50   {
51      return socialSecurityNumber;
52   } // end function getSocialSecurityNumber
53
54   // set gross sales amount
55   void CommissionEmployee::setGrossSales( double sales )
56   {
57      grossSales = ( sales < 0.0 ) ? 0.0 : sales;
58   } // end function setGrossSales
59
60   // return gross sales amount
61   double CommissionEmployee::getGrossSales() const
62   {
63      return grossSales;
64   } // end function getGrossSales
65
66   // set commission rate
67   void CommissionEmployee::setCommissionRate( double rate )
68   {
69      commissionRate = ( rate > 0.0 && rate < 1.0 ) ? rate : 0.0;
70   } // end function setCommissionRate
71
72   // return commission rate
73   double CommissionEmployee::getCommissionRate() const
74   {
75      return commissionRate;
76   } // end function getCommissionRate
77
78   // calculate earnings
79   double CommissionEmployee::earnings() const
80   {
81      return getCommissionRate() * getGrossSales();
82   } // end function earnings
83
84   // print CommissionEmployee object
85   void CommissionEmployee::print() const
86   {
87      cout << "commission employee: "
88         << getFirstName() << ' ' << getLastName()
89         << "\nsocial security number: " << getSocialSecurityNumber()
90         << "\ngross sales: " << getGrossSales()
91         << "\ncommission rate: " << getCommissionRate();
92   } // end function print
```

Fig. 14.2 | CommissionEmployee class implementation file. (Part 2 of 2.)

```
1   // Fig. 14.3: BasePlusCommissionEmployee.h
2   // BasePlusCommissionEmployee class derived from class
3   // CommissionEmployee.
4   #ifndef BASEPLUS_H
5   #define BASEPLUS_H
6
7   #include <string> // C++ standard string class
8   using std::string;
9
10  #include "CommissionEmployee.h" // CommissionEmployee class declaration
11
12  class BasePlusCommissionEmployee : public CommissionEmployee
13  {
14  public:
15     BasePlusCommissionEmployee( const string &, const string &,
16        const string &, double = 0.0, double = 0.0, double = 0.0 );
17
18     void setBaseSalary( double ); // set base salary
19     double getBaseSalary() const; // return base salary
20
21     double earnings() const; // calculate earnings
22     void print() const; // print BasePlusCommissionEmployee object
23  private:
24     double baseSalary; // base salary
25  }; // end class BasePlusCommissionEmployee
26
27  #endif
```

Fig. 14.3 | BasePlusCommissionEmployee class header file.

```
1   // Fig. 14.4: BasePlusCommissionEmployee.cpp
2   // Class BasePlusCommissionEmployee member-function definitions.
3   #include <iostream>
4   using std::cout;
5
6   // BasePlusCommissionEmployee class definition
7   #include "BasePlusCommissionEmployee.h"
8
9   // constructor
10  BasePlusCommissionEmployee::BasePlusCommissionEmployee(
11     const string &first, const string &last, const string &ssn,
12     double sales, double rate, double salary )
13     // explicitly call base-class constructor
14     : CommissionEmployee( first, last, ssn, sales, rate )
15  {
16     setBaseSalary( salary ); // validate and store base salary
17  } // end BasePlusCommissionEmployee constructor
18
19  // set base salary
20  void BasePlusCommissionEmployee::setBaseSalary( double salary )
21  {
```

Fig. 14.4 | BasePlusCommissionEmployee class implementation file. (Part 1 of 2.)

```
22        baseSalary = ( salary < 0.0 ) ? 0.0 : salary;
23    } // end function setBaseSalary
24
25    // return base salary
26    double BasePlusCommissionEmployee::getBaseSalary() const
27    {
28        return baseSalary;
29    } // end function getBaseSalary
30
31    // calculate earnings
32    double BasePlusCommissionEmployee::earnings() const
33    {
34        return getBaseSalary() + CommissionEmployee::earnings();
35    } // end function earnings
36
37    // print BasePlusCommissionEmployee object
38    void BasePlusCommissionEmployee::print() const
39    {
40        cout << "base-salaried ";
41
42        // invoke CommissionEmployee's print function
43        CommissionEmployee::print();
44
45        cout << "\nbase salary: " << getBaseSalary();
46    } // end function print
```

Fig. 14.4 │ BasePlusCommissionEmployee class implementation file. (Part 2 of 2.)

In Fig. 14.5, lines 19–20 create a CommissionEmployee object and line 23 creates a pointer to a CommissionEmployee object; lines 26–27 create a BasePlusCommission-Employee object and line 30 creates a pointer to a BasePlusCommissionEmployee object. Lines 37 and 39 use each object's name (commissionEmployee and basePlusCommission-Employee, respectively) to invoke each object's print member function. Line 42 assigns the address of base-class object commissionEmployee to base-class pointer commission-EmployeePtr, which line 45 uses to invoke member function print on that Commission-Employee object. This invokes the version of print defined in base class CommissionEmployee. Similarly, line 48 assigns the address of derived-class object base-PlusCommissionEmployee to derived-class pointer basePlusCommissionEmployeePtr, which line 52 uses to invoke member function print on that BasePlusCommissionEm-ployee object. This invokes the version of print defined in derived class BasePlusCom-missionEmployee. Line 55 then assigns the address of derived-class object basePlusCommissionEmployee to base-class pointer commissionEmployeePtr, which line 59 uses to invoke member function print. This "crossover" is allowed because an object of a derived class *is an* object of its base class. Note that despite the fact that the base-class CommissionEmployee pointer points to a derived-class BasePlusCommissionEmployee object, the base-class CommissionEmployee's print member function is invoked (rather than BasePlusCommissionEmployee's print function). The output of each print member-function invocation in this program reveals that *the invoked functionality depends on the type of the handle (i.e., the pointer or reference type) used to invoke the function, not the type of the object to which the handle points*. In Section 14.3.4, when we introduce virtual

```
 1    // Fig. 14.5: PolymorphismTest.cpp
 2    // Aiming base-class and derived-class pointers at base-class
 3    // and derived-class objects, respectively.
 4    #include <iostream>
 5    using std::cout;
 6    using std::endl;
 7    using std::fixed;
 8
 9    #include <iomanip>
10    using std::setprecision;
11
12    // include class definitions
13    #include "CommissionEmployee.h"
14    #include "BasePlusCommissionEmployee.h"
15
16    int main()
17    {
18       // create base-class object
19       CommissionEmployee commissionEmployee(
20          "Sue", "Jones", "222-22-2222", 10000, .06 );
21
22       // create base-class pointer
23       CommissionEmployee *commissionEmployeePtr = 0;
24
25       // create derived-class object
26       BasePlusCommissionEmployee basePlusCommissionEmployee(
27          "Bob", "Lewis", "333-33-3333", 5000, .04, 300 );
28
29       // create derived-class pointer
30       BasePlusCommissionEmployee *basePlusCommissionEmployeePtr = 0;
31
32       // set floating-point output formatting
33       cout << fixed << setprecision( 2 );
34
35       // output objects commissionEmployee and basePlusCommissionEmployee
36       cout << "Print base-class and derived-class objects:\n\n";
37       commissionEmployee.print(); // invokes base-class print
38       cout << "\n\n";
39       basePlusCommissionEmployee.print(); // invokes derived-class print
40
41       // aim base-class pointer at base-class object and print
42       commissionEmployeePtr = &commissionEmployee; // perfectly natural
43       cout << "\n\n\nCalling print with base-class pointer to "
44          << "\nbase-class object invokes base-class print function:\n\n";
45       commissionEmployeePtr->print(); // invokes base-class print
46
47       // aim derived-class pointer at derived-class object and print
48       basePlusCommissionEmployeePtr = &basePlusCommissionEmployee; // natural
49       cout << "\n\n\nCalling print with derived-class pointer to "
50          << "\nderived-class object invokes derived-class "
51          << "print function:\n\n";
```

Fig. 14.5 | Aiming base-class and derived-class pointers at base-class and derived-class objects. (Part 1 of 2.)

```
52      basePlusCommissionEmployeePtr->print(); // invokes derived-class print
53
54      // aim base-class pointer at derived-class object and print
55      commissionEmployeePtr = &basePlusCommissionEmployee;
56      cout << "\n\n\nCalling print with base-class pointer to "
57         << "derived-class object\ninvokes base-class print "
58         << "function on that derived-class object:\n\n";
59      commissionEmployeePtr->print(); // invokes base-class print
60      cout << endl;
61      return 0;
62   } // end main
```

```
Print base-class and derived-class objects:

commission employee: Sue Jones
social security number: 222-22-2222
gross sales: 10000.00
commission rate: 0.06

base-salaried commission employee: Bob Lewis
social security number: 333-33-3333
gross sales: 5000.00
commission rate: 0.04
base salary: 300.00


Calling print with base-class pointer to
base-class object invokes base-class print function:

commission employee: Sue Jones
social security number: 222-22-2222
gross sales: 10000.00
commission rate: 0.06


Calling print with derived-class pointer to
derived-class object invokes derived-class print function:

base-salaried commission employee: Bob Lewis
social security number: 333-33-3333
gross sales: 5000.00
commission rate: 0.04
base salary: 300.00


Calling print with base-class pointer to derived-class object
invokes base-class print function on that derived-class object:

commission employee: Bob Lewis
social security number: 333-33-3333
gross sales: 5000.00
commission rate: 0.04
```

Fig. 14.5 | Aiming base-class and derived-class pointers at base-class and derived-class objects. (Part 2 of 2.)

functions, we demonstrate that it is possible to invoke the object type's functionality, rather than invoke the handle type's functionality. We'll see that this is crucial to implementing polymorphic behavior—the key topic of this chapter.

14.3.2 Aiming Derived-Class Pointers at Base-Class Objects

In Section 14.3.1, we assigned the address of a derived-class object to a base-class pointer and explained that the Visual C++ compiler allows this assignment, because a derived-class object *is a* base-class object. We take the opposite approach in Fig. 14.6, as we aim a derived-class pointer at a base-class object. [*Note:* This program uses classes CommissionEmployee and BasePlusCommissionEmployee of Figs. 14.1–14.4.] Lines 8–9 of Fig. 14.6 create a CommissionEmployee object, and line 10 creates a BasePlusCommissionEmployee pointer. Line 14 attempts to assign the address of base-class object commissionEmployee to derived-class pointer basePlusCommissionEmployeePtr, but the Visual C++ compiler generates an error. The compiler prevents this assignment, because a CommissionEmployee is not a BasePlusCommissionEmployee. Consider the consequences if the compiler were to allow this assignment. Through a BasePlusCommissionEmployee pointer, we can invoke every BasePlusCommissionEmployee member function, including setBaseSalary, for the object to which the pointer points (i.e., the base-class object commissionEmployee). However, the CommissionEmployee object does not provide a setBaseSalary member function, nor does it provide a baseSalary data member to set. This could lead to problems, because member function setBaseSalary would assume that there is a baseSalary data member to set at its "usual location" in a BasePlusCommissionEmployee object. This memory does not belong to the CommissionEmployee object, so member function setBaseSalary might overwrite other important data in memory, possibly data that belongs to a different object.

```
1   // Fig. 14.6: PolymorphismTest.cpp
2   // Aiming a derived-class pointer at a base-class object.
3   #include "CommissionEmployee.h"
4   #include "BasePlusCommissionEmployee.h"
5
6   int main()
7   {
8      CommissionEmployee commissionEmployee(
9         "Sue", "Jones", "222-22-2222", 10000, .06 );
10     BasePlusCommissionEmployee *basePlusCommissionEmployeePtr = 0;
11
12     // aim derived-class pointer at base-class object
13     // Error: a CommissionEmployee is not a BasePlusCommissionEmployee
14     basePlusCommissionEmployeePtr = &commissionEmployee;
15     return 0;
16  } // end main
```

```
C:\examples\ch14\Fig14_06\PolymorphismTest.cpp(14) : error C2440:
   '=' : cannot convert from 'CommissionEmployee *' to
'BasePlusCommissionEmployee *'
      Cast from base to derived requires dynamic_cast or static_cast
```

Fig. 14.6 | Aiming a derived-class pointer at a base-class object.

14.3.3 Derived-Class Member-Function Calls via Base-Class Pointers

Off a base-class pointer, the compiler allows us to invoke only base-class member functions. Thus, if a base-class pointer is aimed at a derived-class object, and an attempt is made to access a *derived-class-only member function*, a compilation error will occur.

Figure 14.7 shows the consequences of attempting to invoke a derived-class member function off a base-class pointer. [*Note:* We are again using classes CommissionEmployee and BasePlusCommissionEmployee of Figs. 14.1–14.4.] Line 9 creates commissionEmployeePtr—a pointer to a CommissionEmployee object—and lines 10–11 create a BasePlusCommissionEmployee object. Line 14 aims commissionEmployeePtr at derived-class object basePlusCommissionEmployee. Recall from Section 14.3.1 that this is allowed,

```cpp
 1   // Fig. 14.7: PolymorphismTest.cpp
 2   // Attempting to invoke derived-class-only member functions
 3   // through a base-class pointer.
 4   #include "CommissionEmployee.h"
 5   #include "BasePlusCommissionEmployee.h"
 6
 7   int main()
 8   {
 9      CommissionEmployee *commissionEmployeePtr = 0; // base class
10      BasePlusCommissionEmployee basePlusCommissionEmployee(
11         "Bob", "Lewis", "333-33-3333", 5000, .04, 300 ); // derived class
12
13      // aim base-class pointer at derived-class object
14      commissionEmployeePtr = &basePlusCommissionEmployee;
15
16      // invoke base-class member functions on derived-class
17      // object through base-class pointer (allowed)
18      string firstName = commissionEmployeePtr->getFirstName();
19      string lastName = commissionEmployeePtr->getLastName();
20      string ssn = commissionEmployeePtr->getSocialSecurityNumber();
21      double grossSales = commissionEmployeePtr->getGrossSales();
22      double commissionRate = commissionEmployeePtr->getCommissionRate();
23
24      // attempt to invoke derived-class-only member functions
25      // on derived-class object through base-class pointer (disallowed)
26      double baseSalary = commissionEmployeePtr->getBaseSalary();
27      commissionEmployeePtr->setBaseSalary( 500 );
28      return 0;
29   } // end main
```

```
C:\examples\ch14\Fig14_07\CommissionEmployee.cpp(26) : error C2039:
   'getBaseSalary' : is not a member of 'CommissionEmployee'
      C:\examples\ch14\Fig14_07\CommissionEmployee.h(10) :
         see declaration of 'CommissionEmployee'
C:\examples\ch14\Fig14_07\fig14_07.cpp(27) : error C2039:
   'setBaseSalary' : is not a member of 'CommissionEmployee'
      C:\examples\ch14\Fig14_07\CommissionEmployee.h(10) :
         see declaration of 'CommissionEmployee'
```

Fig. 14.7 | Attempting to invoke derived-class-only functions via a base-class pointer.

because a `BasePlusCommissionEmployee` *is a* `CommissionEmployee` (in the sense that a `BasePlusCommissionEmployee` object contains all the functionality of a `CommissionEmployee` object). Lines 18–22 invoke base-class member functions `getFirstName`, `getLastName`, `getSocialSecurityNumber`, `getGrossSales` and `getCommissionRate` off the base-class pointer. All of these calls are legitimate, because `BasePlusCommissionEmployee` inherits these member functions from `CommissionEmployee`. We know that `commissionEmployeePtr` is aimed at a `BasePlusCommissionEmployee` object, so in lines 26–27 we attempt to invoke `BasePlusCommissionEmployee` member functions `getBaseSalary` and `setBaseSalary`. The compiler generates errors on both of these calls, because they are not made to member functions of base-class `CommissionEmployee`. The handle can be used to invoke only those functions that are members of that handle's associated class type. (In this case, off a `CommissionEmployee *`, we can invoke only `CommissionEmployee` member functions `setFirstName`, `getFirstName`, `setLastName`, `getLastName`, `setSocialSecurityNumber`, `getSocialSecurityNumber`, `setGrossSales`, `getGrossSales`, `setCommissionRate`, `getCommissionRate`, `earnings` and `print`.)

The compiler does allow access to derived-class-only members from a base-class pointer that is aimed at a derived-class object if we explicitly cast the base-class pointer to a derived-class pointer—a technique known as ***downcasting***. As you learned in Section 14.3.1, it is possible to aim a base-class pointer at a derived-class object. However, as we demonstrated in Fig. 14.7, a base-class pointer can be used to invoke only the functions declared in the base class. Downcasting allows a derived-class-specific operation on a derived-class object pointed to by a base-class pointer. After a downcast, the program can invoke derived-class functions that are not in the base class. We'll show you a concrete example of downcasting in Section 14.8.

Software Engineering Observation 14.3

If the address of a derived-class object has been assigned to a pointer of one of its direct or indirect base classes, it is acceptable to cast that base-class pointer back to a pointer of the derived-class type. In fact, this must be done to send that derived-class object messages that do not appear in the base class.

14.3.4 Virtual Functions

In Section 14.3.1, we aimed a base-class `CommissionEmployee` pointer at a derived-class `BasePlusCommissionEmployee` object, then invoked member function `print` through that pointer. Recall that the type of the handle determines which class's functionality to invoke. In that case, the `CommissionEmployee` pointer invoked the `CommissionEmployee` member function `print` on the `BasePlusCommissionEmployee` object, even though the pointer was aimed at a `BasePlusCommissionEmployee` object that has its own customized `print` function. *With* `virtual` *functions, the type of the object being pointed to, not the type of the handle, determines which version of a* `virtual` *function to invoke.*

First, we consider why `virtual` functions are useful. Suppose that a set of shape classes such as `Circle`, `Triangle`, `Rectangle` and `Square` are all derived from base class `Shape`. Each of these classes might be endowed with the ability to draw itself via a member function `draw`. Although each class has its own `draw` function, the function for each shape is quite different. In a program that draws a set of shapes, it would be useful to be able to treat all the shapes generically as objects of the base class `Shape`. Then, to draw any shape, we could simply use a base-class Shape pointer to invoke function draw and let the program determine *dynamically* (i.e., at runtime) which derived-class draw function to use, based on the type of the object to which the base-class Shape pointer points at any given time.

To enable this kind of behavior, we declare draw in the base class as a ***virtual function***, and we ***override*** draw in each of the derived classes to draw the appropriate shape. From an implementation perspective, overriding a function is no different than redefining one (which is the approach we have been using until now). An overridden function in a derived class has the same signature and return type (i.e., prototype) as the function it overrides in its base class. If we do not declare the base-class function as virtual, we can redefine that function. By contrast, if we declare the base-class function as virtual, we can override that function to enable polymorphic behavior. We declare a virtual function by preceding the function's prototype with the keyword virtual in the base class. For example,

```
virtual void draw() const;
```

would appear in base class Shape. The preceding prototype declares that function draw is a virtual function that takes no arguments and returns nothing. This function is declared const because a draw function typically would not make changes to the Shape object on which it is invoked—virtual functions do not have to be const functions.

Software Engineering Observation 14.4

Once a function is declared virtual, it remains virtual all the way down the inheritance hierarchy from that point, even if that function is not explicitly declared virtual when a derived class overrides it.

Good Programming Practice 14.1

Even though certain functions are implicitly virtual because of a declaration made higher in the class hierarchy, explicitly declare these functions virtual at every level of the hierarchy to promote program clarity.

Error-Prevention Tip 14.1

When a programmer browses a class hierarchy to locate a class to reuse, it is possible that a function in that class will exhibit virtual function behavior even though it is not explicitly declared virtual. This happens when the class inherits a virtual function from its base class, and it can lead to subtle logic errors. Such errors can be avoided by explicitly declaring all virtual functions virtual throughout the inheritance hierarchy.

Software Engineering Observation 14.5

When a derived class chooses not to override a virtual function from its base class, the derived class simply inherits its base class's virtual function implementation.

If a program invokes a virtual function through a base-class pointer to a derived-class object (e.g., shapePtr->draw()), the program will choose the correct derived-class draw function dynamically (i.e., at execution time) based on the object type—not the pointer type. Choosing the appropriate function to call at execution time (rather than at compile time) is known as ***dynamic binding*** or ***late binding***.

When a `virtual` function is called by referencing a specific object by name and using the dot member-selection operator (e.g., `squareObject.draw()`), the function invocation is resolved at compile time (this is called *static binding*) and the `virtual` function that is called is the one defined for (or inherited by) the class of that particular object—this is not polymorphic behavior. Thus, dynamic binding with `virtual` functions occurs only off pointer (and, as we'll soon see, reference) handles.

Now let's see how `virtual` functions can enable polymorphic behavior in our employee hierarchy. Figures 14.8–14.9 are the header files for classes `CommissionEmployee` and `BasePlusCommissionEmployee`, respectively. Note that the only difference between these files and those of Fig. 14.1 and Fig. 14.3 is that we specify each class's `earnings` and `print` member functions as `virtual` (lines 30–31 of Fig. 14.8 and lines 21–22 of Fig. 14.9). Because functions `earnings` and `print` are `virtual` in class `CommissionEmployee`, class `BasePlusCommissionEmployee`'s `earnings` and `print` functions override class `CommissionEmployee`'s. Now, if we aim a base-class `CommissionEmployee` pointer at a derived-class `BasePlusCommissionEmployee` object, and the program uses that pointer to call either function `earnings` or `print`, the `BasePlusCommissionEmployee` object's corresponding function will be invoked. There were no changes to the member-function implementations of classes `CommissionEmployee` and `BasePlusCommissionEmployee`, so we reuse the versions of Fig. 14.2 and Fig. 14.4.

```cpp
1   // Fig. 14.8: CommissionEmployee.h
2   // CommissionEmployee class definition represents a commission employee.
3   #ifndef COMMISSION_H
4   #define COMMISSION_H
5
6   #include <string> // C++ standard string class
7   using std::string;
8
9   class CommissionEmployee
10  {
11  public:
12     CommissionEmployee( const string &, const string &, const string &,
13        double = 0.0, double = 0.0 );
14
15     void setFirstName( const string & ); // set first name
16     string getFirstName() const; // return first name
17
18     void setLastName( const string & ); // set last name
19     string getLastName() const; // return last name
20
21     void setSocialSecurityNumber( const string & ); // set SSN
22     string getSocialSecurityNumber() const; // return SSN
23
24     void setGrossSales( double ); // set gross sales amount
25     double getGrossSales() const; // return gross sales amount
26
27     void setCommissionRate( double ); // set commission rate
28     double getCommissionRate() const; // return commission rate
```

Fig. 14.8 | `CommissionEmployee` class header file declares `earnings` and `print` functions as `virtual`. (Part 1 of 2.)

```
29
30      virtual double earnings() const; // calculate earnings
31      virtual void print() const; // print CommissionEmployee object
32  private:
33      string firstName;
34      string lastName;
35      string socialSecurityNumber;
36      double grossSales; // gross weekly sales
37      double commissionRate; // commission percentage
38  }; // end class CommissionEmployee
39
40  #endif
```

Fig. 14.8 | CommissionEmployee class header file declares earnings and print functions as virtual. (Part 2 of 2.)

```
1   // Fig. 14.9: BasePlusCommissionEmployee.h
2   // BasePlusCommissionEmployee class derived from class
3   // CommissionEmployee.
4   #ifndef BASEPLUS_H
5   #define BASEPLUS_H
6
7   #include <string> // C++ standard string class
8   using std::string;
9
10  #include "CommissionEmployee.h" // CommissionEmployee class declaration
11
12  class BasePlusCommissionEmployee : public CommissionEmployee
13  {
14  public:
15      BasePlusCommissionEmployee( const string &, const string &,
16          const string &, double = 0.0, double = 0.0, double = 0.0 );
17
18      void setBaseSalary( double ); // set base salary
19      double getBaseSalary() const; // return base salary
20
21      virtual double earnings() const; // calculate earnings
22      virtual void print() const; // print BasePlusCommissionEmployee object
23  private:
24      double baseSalary; // base salary
25  }; // end class BasePlusCommissionEmployee
26
27  #endif
```

Fig. 14.9 | BasePlusCommissionEmployee class header file declares earnings and print functions as virtual.

We modified Fig. 14.5 to create the program of Fig. 14.10. Lines 46–57 demonstrate again that a CommissionEmployee pointer aimed at a CommissionEmployee object can be used to invoke CommissionEmployee functionality, and a BasePlusCommissionEmployee pointer aimed at a BasePlusCommissionEmployee object can be used to invoke Base-PlusCommissionEmployee functionality. Line 60 aims base-class pointer commission-

EmployeePtr at derived-class object basePlusCommissionEmployee. Note that when line 67 invokes member function print off the base-class pointer, the derived-class BasePlus CommissionEmployee's print member function is invoked, so line 67 outputs different text than line 59 does in Fig. 14.5 (when member function print was not declared virtual). We see that declaring a member function virtual causes the program to dynamically determine which function to invoke based on the type of object to which the handle points, rather than on the type of the handle. Note again that when commissionEmployeePtr points to a CommissionEmployee object (line 46), class CommissionEmployee's print function is invoked, and when CommissionEmployeePtr points to a BasePlusCommissionEmployee object, class BasePlusCommissionEmployee's print function is invoked. Thus, the same message—print, in this case—sent (off a base-class pointer) to a variety of objects related by inheritance to that base class, takes on many forms; this is polymorphic behavior.

```cpp
1   // Fig. 14.10: VirtualTest.cpp
2   // Introducing polymorphism, virtual functions and dynamic binding.
3   #include <iostream>
4   using std::cout;
5   using std::endl;
6   using std::fixed;
7
8   #include <iomanip>
9   using std::setprecision;
10
11  // include class definitions
12  #include "CommissionEmployee.h"
13  #include "BasePlusCommissionEmployee.h"
14
15  int main()
16  {
17     // create base-class object
18     CommissionEmployee commissionEmployee(
19        "Sue", "Jones", "222-22-2222", 10000, .06 );
20
21     // create base-class pointer
22     CommissionEmployee *commissionEmployeePtr = 0;
23
24     // create derived-class object
25     BasePlusCommissionEmployee basePlusCommissionEmployee(
26        "Bob", "Lewis", "333-33-3333", 5000, .04, 300 );
27
28     // create derived-class pointer
29     BasePlusCommissionEmployee *basePlusCommissionEmployeePtr = 0;
30
31     // set floating-point output formatting
32     cout << fixed << setprecision( 2 );
33
```

Fig. 14.10 | Demonstrating polymorphism by invoking a derived-class virtual function via a base-class pointer to a derived-class object. (Part 1 of 3.)

```
34       // output objects using static binding
35       cout << "Invoking print function on base-class and derived-class "
36          << "\nobjects with static binding\n\n";
37       commissionEmployee.print(); // static binding
38       cout << "\n\n";
39       basePlusCommissionEmployee.print(); // static binding
40
41       // output objects using dynamic binding
42       cout << "\n\n\nInvoking print function on base-class and "
43          << "derived-class \nobjects with dynamic binding";
44
45       // aim base-class pointer at base-class object and print
46       commissionEmployeePtr = &commissionEmployee;
47       cout << "\n\nCalling virtual function print with base-class pointer"
48          << "\nto base-class object invokes base-class "
49          << "print function:\n\n";
50       commissionEmployeePtr->print(); // invokes base-class print
51
52       // aim derived-class pointer at derived-class object and print
53       basePlusCommissionEmployeePtr = &basePlusCommissionEmployee;
54       cout << "\n\nCalling virtual function print with derived-class "
55          << "pointer\nto derived-class object invokes derived-class "
56          << "print function:\n\n";
57       basePlusCommissionEmployeePtr->print(); // invokes derived-class print
58
59       // aim base-class pointer at derived-class object and print
60       commissionEmployeePtr = &basePlusCommissionEmployee;
61       cout << "\n\nCalling virtual function print with base-class pointer"
62          << "\nto derived-class object invokes derived-class "
63          << "print function:\n\n";
64
65       // polymorphism; invokes BasePlusCommissionEmployee's print;
66       // base-class pointer to derived-class object
67       commissionEmployeePtr->print();
68       cout << endl;
69       return 0;
70    } // end main
```

```
Invoking print function on base-class and derived-class
objects with static binding

commission employee: Sue Jones
social security number: 222-22-2222
gross sales: 10000.00
commission rate: 0.06

base-salaried commission employee: Bob Lewis
social security number: 333-33-3333
gross sales: 5000.00
commission rate: 0.04
base salary: 300.00
```

Fig. 14.10 | Demonstrating polymorphism by invoking a derived-class `virtual` function via a base-class pointer to a derived-class object. (Part 2 of 3.)

```
Invoking print function on base-class and derived-class
objects with dynamic binding

Calling virtual function print with base-class pointer
to base-class object invokes base-class print function:

commission employee: Sue Jones
social security number: 222-22-2222
gross sales: 10000.00
commission rate: 0.06

Calling virtual function print with derived-class pointer
to derived-class object invokes derived-class print function:

base-salaried commission employee: Bob Lewis
social security number: 333-33-3333
gross sales: 5000.00
commission rate: 0.04
base salary: 300.00

Calling virtual function print with base-class pointer
to derived-class object invokes derived-class print function:

base-salaried commission employee: Bob Lewis
social security number: 333-33-3333
gross sales: 5000.00
commission rate: 0.04
base salary: 300.00
```

Fig. 14.10 | Demonstrating polymorphism by invoking a derived-class `virtual` function via a base-class pointer to a derived-class object. (Part 3 of 3.)

14.3.5 Summary of the Allowed Assignments Between Base-Class and Derived-Class Objects and Pointers

Now that you have seen a complete application that processes diverse objects polymorphically, we summarize what you can and cannot do with base-class and derived-class objects and pointers. Although a derived-class object also *is a* base-class object, the two objects are nevertheless different. As discussed previously, derived-class objects can be treated as if they were base-class objects. This is a logical relationship, because the derived class contains all the members of the base class. However, base-class objects cannot be treated as if they were derived-class objects—the derived class can have additional derived-class-only members. For this reason, aiming a derived-class pointer at a base-class object is not allowed without an explicit cast—such an assignment would leave the derived-class-only members undefined on the base-class object. The cast relieves the compiler of the responsibility of issuing an error message. In a sense, by using the cast you are saying, "I know that what I'm doing is dangerous and I take full responsibility for my actions."

In the current section and in Chapter 13, we have discussed four ways to aim base-class pointers and derived-class pointers at base-class objects and derived-class objects:

1. Aiming a base-class pointer at a base-class object is straightforward—calls made off the base-class pointer simply invoke base-class functionality.

2. Aiming a derived-class pointer at a derived-class object is straightforward—calls made off the derived-class pointer simply invoke derived-class functionality.

3. Aiming a base-class pointer at a derived-class object is safe, because the derived-class object *is an* object of its base class. However, this pointer can be used to invoke only base-class member functions. If you attempt to refer to a derived-class-only member through the base-class pointer, the compiler reports an error. To avoid this error, you must cast the base-class pointer to a derived-class pointer. The derived-class pointer can then be used to invoke the derived-class object's complete functionality. This technique, called downcasting, is a potentially dangerous operation—Section 14.8 demonstrates how to safely use downcasting. If a virtual function is defined in the base and derived classes (either by inheritance or overriding), and if that function is invoked on a derived-class object via a base-class pointer, then the derived-class version of that function is called. This is an example of the polymorphic behavior that occurs only with virtual functions.

4. Aiming a derived-class pointer at a base-class object generates a compilation error. The *is-a* relationship applies only from a derived class to its direct and indirect base classes, and not vice versa. A base-class object does not contain the derived-class-only members that can be invoked off a derived-class pointer.

Common Programming Error 14.1

After aiming a base-class pointer at a derived-class object, attempting to reference derived-class-only members with the base-class pointer is a compilation error.

Common Programming Error 14.2

Treating a base-class object as a derived-class object can cause errors.

14.4 Type Fields and switch Statements

One way to determine the type of an object that is incorporated in a larger program is to use a switch statement. This allows us to distinguish among object types, then invoke an appropriate action for a particular object. For example, in a hierarchy of shapes in which each shape object has a shapeType attribute, a switch statement could check the object's shapeType to determine which print function to call.

Using switch logic exposes programs to a variety of potential problems. For example, you might forget to include a type test when one is warranted, or might forget to test all possible cases in a switch statement. When modifying a switch-based system by adding new types, you might forget to insert the new cases in all relevant switch statements. Every addition or deletion of a class requires the modification of every switch statement in the system; tracking these statements down can be time consuming and error prone.

Software Engineering Observation 14.6

Polymorphic programming can eliminate the need for switch logic. By using the polymorphism mechanism to perform the equivalent logic, programmers can avoid the kinds of errors typically associated with switch logic.

Software Engineering Observation 14.7

An interesting consequence of using polymorphism is that programs take on a simplified appearance. They contain less branching logic and simpler sequential code. This simplification facilitates testing, debugging and program maintenance.

14.5 Abstract Classes and Pure `virtual` Functions

When we think of a class as a type, we assume that programs will create objects of that type. However, there are cases in which it is useful to define classes from which you never intend to instantiate any objects. Such classes are called *abstract classes*. Because these classes normally are used as base classes in inheritance hierarchies, we refer to them as *abstract base classes*. These classes cannot be used to instantiate objects, because, as we'll soon see, abstract classes are incomplete—derived classes must define the "missing pieces." We build programs with abstract classes in Section 14.6.

The purpose of an abstract class is to provide an appropriate base class from which other classes can inherit. Classes that can be used to instantiate objects are called *concrete classes*. Such classes provide implementations of every member function they define. We could have an abstract base class TwoDimensionalShape and derive such concrete classes as Square, Circle and Triangle. We could also have an abstract base class ThreeDimensionalShape and derive such concrete classes as Cube, Sphere and Cylinder. Abstract base classes are too generic to define real objects; we need to be more specific before we can think of instantiating objects. For example, if someone tells you to "draw the two-dimensional shape," what shape would you draw? Concrete classes provide the specifics that make it reasonable to instantiate objects.

An inheritance hierarchy does not need to contain any abstract classes, but, as we'll see, many object-oriented systems have class hierarchies headed by abstract base classes. In some cases, abstract classes constitute the top few levels of the hierarchy. A good example of this is the shape hierarchy in Fig. 13.3, which begins with abstract base class Shape. On the next level of the hierarchy we have two more abstract base classes, namely, TwoDimensionalShape and ThreeDimensionalShape. The next level of the hierarchy defines concrete classes for two-dimensional shapes (namely, Circle, Square and Triangle) and for three-dimensional shapes (namely, Sphere, Cube and Tetrahedron).

A class is made abstract by declaring one or more of its `virtual` functions to be "pure." A *pure `virtual` function* is specified by placing "= 0" in its declaration, as in

```
virtual void draw() const = 0; // pure virtual function
```

The "= 0" is known as a *pure specifier*. Pure `virtual` functions do not provide implementations. Every concrete derived class *must* override all base-class pure `virtual` functions with concrete implementations of those functions. The difference between a `virtual` function and a pure `virtual` function is that a `virtual` function has an implementation and gives the derived class the *option* of overriding the function; by contrast, a pure `virtual` function does not provide an implementation and *requires* the derived class to override the function for that derived class to be concrete; otherwise the derived class remains abstract.

Pure `virtual` functions are used when it does not make sense for the base class to have an implementation of a function, but you want all concrete derived classes to implement the function. Returning to our earlier example of space objects, it does not make sense for the base class SpaceObject to have an implementation for function draw (as there is no way to draw a generic space object without having more information about what type of space object is being drawn). An example of a function that would be defined as `virtual` (and not pure `virtual`) would be one that returns a name for the object. We can name a generic SpaceObject (for instance, as "space object"), so a default implementation for this function can be provided, and the function does not need to be pure virtual. The function is still declared virtual, however, because it is expected that derived classes will override this function to provide more specific names for the derived-class objects.

Software Engineering Observation 14.8

An abstract class defines a common public interface for the various classes in a class hierarchy. An abstract class contains one or more pure virtual functions that concrete derived classes must override.

Common Programming Error 14.3

Attempting to instantiate an object of an abstract class causes a compilation error.

Common Programming Error 14.4

Failure to override a pure virtual function in a derived class, then attempting to instantiate objects of that class, is a compilation error.

Software Engineering Observation 14.9

An abstract class has at least one pure virtual function. An abstract class also can have data members and concrete functions (including constructors and destructors), which are subject to the normal rules of inheritance by derived classes.

Although we cannot instantiate objects of an abstract base class, we *can* use the abstract base class to declare pointers and references that can refer to objects of any concrete classes derived from the abstract class. Programs typically use such pointers and references to manipulate derived-class objects polymorphically.

Consider another application of polymorphism. A screen manager needs to display a variety of objects, including new types of objects that you'll add to the system after writing the screen manager. The system might need to display various shapes, such as Circles, Triangles or Rectangles, which are derived from abstract base class Shape. The screen manager uses Shape pointers to manage the objects that are displayed. To draw any object (regardless of the level at which that object's class appears in the inheritance hierarchy), the screen manager uses a base-class pointer to the object to invoke the object's draw function, which is a pure virtual function in base class Shape; therefore, each concrete derived class must implement function draw. Each Shape object in the inheritance hierarchy knows how to draw itself. The screen manager does not have to worry about the type of each object or whether the screen manager has ever encountered objects of that type.

Polymorphism is particularly effective for implementing layered software systems. In operating systems, for example, each type of physical device could operate quite differently from the others. Even so, commands to *read* or *write* data from and to devices may have a certain uniformity. The *write* message sent to a device-driver object needs to be interpreted specifically in the context of that device driver and how that device driver manipulates devices of a specific type. However, the *write* call itself really is no different from the *write* to any other device in the system—place some number of bytes from memory onto that device. An object-oriented operating system might use an abstract base class to provide an interface appropriate for all device drivers. Then, through inheritance from that abstract base class, derived classes are formed that all operate similarly. The capabilities (i.e., the public functions) offered by the device drivers are provided as pure virtual functions in the abstract base class. The implementations of these pure virtual functions are provided in the derived classes that correspond to the specific types of device drivers. This architecture also allows new devices to be added to a system easily, even after the operating system has been defined. The user can just plug in the device and install its new device driver. The operating system "talks" to this new device through its device driver, which has the same public member functions as all other device drivers—those defined in the device-driver abstract base class.

It is common in object-oriented programming to define an *iterator class* that can traverse all the objects in a container (such as an array). For example, a program can print a list of objects in a vector by creating an iterator object, then using the iterator to obtain the next element of the list each time the iterator is called. Iterators often are used in polymorphic programming to traverse an array or a linked list of pointers to objects from various levels of a hierarchy. The pointers in such a list are all base-class pointers. (Chapter 23, Standard Template Library (STL), presents a thorough treatment of iterators.) A list of pointers to objects of base class TwoDimensionalShape could contain pointers to objects of classes Square, Circle, Triangle and so on. Using polymorphism to send a draw message, off a TwoDimensionalShape * pointer, to each object in the list would draw each object correctly on the screen.

14.6 Case Study: Payroll System Using Polymorphism

This section reexamines the CommissionEmployee-BasePlusCommissionEmployee hierarchy that we explored throughout Section 13.4. In this example, we use an abstract class and polymorphism to perform payroll calculations based on the type of employee. We create an enhanced employee hierarchy to solve the following problem:

> *A company pays its employees weekly. The employees are of four types: Salaried employees are paid a fixed weekly salary regardless of the number of hours worked, hourly employees are paid by the hour and receive overtime pay for all hours worked in excess of 40 hours, commission employees are paid a percentage of their sales and base-salary-plus-commission employees receive a base salary plus a percentage of their sales. For the current pay period, the company has decided to reward base-salary-plus-commission employees by adding 10 percent to their base salaries. The company wants to implement a Visual C++ program that performs its payroll calculations polymorphically.*

We use abstract class Employee to represent the general concept of an employee. The classes that derive directly from Employee are SalariedEmployee, CommissionEmployee and HourlyEmployee. Class BasePlusCommissionEmployee—derived from CommissionEmployee—represents the last employee type. The UML class diagram in Fig. 14.11 shows the inheritance hierarchy for our polymorphic employee payroll application. Note that the abstract class name Employee is italicized, as per the convention of the UML.

Abstract base class Employee declares the "interface" to the hierarchy—that is, the set of member functions that a program can invoke on all Employee objects. Each employee, regardless of the way his or her earnings are calculated, has a first name, a last name and a social security number, so private data members firstName, lastName and socialSecurityNumber appear in abstract base class Employee.

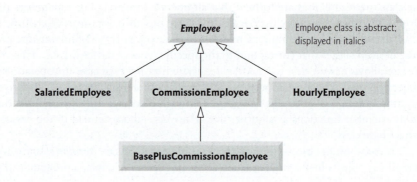

Fig. 14.11 | `Employee` hierarchy UML class diagram.

Software Engineering Observation 14.10

*A derived class can inherit interface or implementation from a base class. Hierarchies designed for **implementation inheritance** tend to have their functionality high in the hierarchy—each new derived class inherits one or more member functions that were defined in a base class, and the derived class uses the base-class definitions. Hierarchies designed for **interface inheritance** tend to have their functionality lower in the hierarchy—a base class specifies one or more functions that should be defined for each class in the hierarchy (i.e., they have the same prototype), but the individual derived classes provide their own implementations of the function(s).*

The following sections implement the `Employee` class hierarchy. The first five each implement one of the abstract or concrete classes. The last section implements a test program that builds objects of all these classes and processes the objects polymorphically.

14.6.1 Creating Abstract Base Class Employee

Class `Employee` (Figs. 14.13–14.14, discussed in further detail shortly) provides functions `earnings` and `print`, in addition to various *get* and *set* functions that manipulate Employee's data members. An `earnings` function certainly applies generically to all employees, but each earnings calculation depends on the employee's class. So we declare `earnings` as pure `virtual` in base class `Employee` because a default implementation does not make sense for that function—there is not enough information to determine what amount `earnings` should return. Each derived class overrides `earnings` with an appropriate implementation. To calculate an employee's earnings, the program assigns the address of an employee's object to a base-class `Employee` pointer, then invokes the `earnings` function on that object. We maintain a `vector` of `Employee` pointers, each of which points to an `Employee` object (of course, there cannot be `Employee` objects, because `Employee` is an abstract class—because of inheritance, however, all objects of all derived classes of `Employee` may nevertheless be thought of as `Employee` objects). The program iterates through the `vector` and calls function `earnings` for each `Employee` object. Visual C++ processes these function calls polymorphically. Including `earnings` as a pure `virtual` function in `Employee` forces every direct derived class of `Employee` that wishes to be a concrete class to override `earnings`. This enables the designer of the class hierarchy to demand that each derived class provide an appropriate pay calculation, if indeed that derived class is to be concrete.

Function print in class Employee displays the first name, last name and social security number of the employee. As we'll see, each derived class of Employee overrides function print to output the employee's type (e.g., "salaried employee:") followed by the rest of the employee's information.

The diagram in Fig. 14.12 shows each of the five classes in the hierarchy down the left side and functions earnings and print across the top. For each class, the diagram shows the desired results of each function. Note that class Employee specifies "= 0" for function earnings to indicate that this is a pure virtual function. Each derived class overrides this function to provide an appropriate implementation. We do not list base-class Employee's *get* and *set* functions because they are not overridden in any of the derived classes—each of these functions is inherited and used "as is" by each of the derived classes.

Let us consider class Employee's header file (Fig. 14.13). The public member functions include a constructor that takes the first name, last name and social security number as arguments (line 12); *set* functions that set the first name, last name and social security number (lines 14, 17 and 20, respectively); *get* functions that return the first name, last name and social security number (lines 15, 18 and 21, respectively); pure virtual function earnings (line 24) and virtual function print (line 25).

Recall that we declared earnings as a pure virtual function because first we must know the specific Employee type to determine the appropriate earnings calculations.

	earnings	print
Employee	= 0	*firstName lastName* social security number: *SSN*
Salaried- Employee	weeklySalary	salaried employee: *firstName lastName* social security number: *SSN* weekly salary: *weeklysalary*

Hourly-
Employee
	If hours <= 40
	  wage * hours
	If hours > 40
	  (40 * wage) +
	  ((hours - 40)
	  * wage * 1.5)
		hourly employee: *firstName lastName*
		social security number: *SSN*
		hourly wage: *wage*; hours worked: *hours*

Commission- Employee	commissionRate * grossSales	commission employee: *firstName lastName* social security number: *SSN* gross sales: *grossSales*; commission rate: *commissionRate*
BasePlus- Commission- Employee	baseSalary + (commissionRate * grossSales)	base salaried commission employee: *firstName lastName* social security number: *SSN* gross sales: *grossSales*; commission rate: *commissionRate*; base salary: *baseSalary*

Fig. 14.12 | Polymorphic interface for the Employee hierarchy classes.

```
 1   // Fig. 14.13: Employee.h
 2   // Employee abstract base class.
 3   #ifndef EMPLOYEE_H
 4   #define EMPLOYEE_H
 5
 6   #include <string> // C++ standard string class
 7   using std::string;
 8
 9   class Employee
10   {
11   public:
12      Employee( const string &, const string &, const string & );
13
14      void setFirstName( const string & ); // set first name
15      string getFirstName() const; // return first name
16
17      void setLastName( const string & ); // set last name
18      string getLastName() const; // return last name
19
20      void setSocialSecurityNumber( const string & ); // set SSN
21      string getSocialSecurityNumber() const; // return SSN
22
23      // pure virtual function makes Employee abstract base class
24      virtual double earnings() const = 0; // pure virtual
25      virtual void print() const; // virtual
26   private:
27      string firstName;
28      string lastName;
29      string socialSecurityNumber;
30   }; // end class Employee
31
32   #endif // EMPLOYEE_H
```

Fig. 14.13 | Employee class header file.

Declaring this function as pure virtual indicates that each concrete derived class *must* provide an appropriate earnings implementation and that a program can use base-class Employee pointers to invoke function earnings polymorphically for any type of Employee.

Figure 14.14 contains the member-function implementations for class Employee. No implementation is provided for virtual function earnings. Note that the Employee constructor (lines 10–15) does not validate the social security number. Normally, such validation should be provided. An exercise in Chapter 13 asks you to validate a social security number to ensure that it is in the form ###-##-####, where each # represents a digit.

```
 1   // Fig. 14.14: Employee.cpp
 2   // Abstract-base-class Employee member-function definitions.
 3   // Note: No definitions are given for pure virtual functions.
 4   #include <iostream>
 5   using std::cout;
```

Fig. 14.14 | Employee class implementation file. (Part 1 of 2.)

```
6
7    #include "Employee.h" // Employee class definition
8
9    // constructor
10   Employee::Employee( const string &first, const string &last,
11      const string &ssn )
12      : firstName( first ), lastName( last ), socialSecurityNumber( ssn )
13   {
14      // empty body
15   } // end Employee constructor
16
17   // set first name
18   void Employee::setFirstName( const string &first )
19   {
20      firstName = first;
21   } // end function setFirstName
22
23   // return first name
24   string Employee::getFirstName() const
25   {
26      return firstName;
27   } // end function getFirstName
28
29   // set last name
30   void Employee::setLastName( const string &last )
31   {
32      lastName = last;
33   } // end function setLastName
34
35   // return last name
36   string Employee::getLastName() const
37   {
38      return lastName;
39   } // end function getLastName
40
41   // set social security number
42   void Employee::setSocialSecurityNumber( const string &ssn )
43   {
44      socialSecurityNumber = ssn; // should validate
45   } // end function setSocialSecurityNumber
46
47   // return social security number
48   string Employee::getSocialSecurityNumber() const
49   {
50      return socialSecurityNumber;
51   } // end function getSocialSecurityNumber
52
53   // print Employee's information (virtual, but not pure virtual)
54   void Employee::print() const
55   {
56      cout << getFirstName() << ' ' << getLastName()
57         << "\nsocial security number: " << getSocialSecurityNumber();
58   } // end function print
```

Fig. 14.14 | Employee class implementation file. (Part 2 of 2.)

Note that `virtual` function `print` (Fig. 14.14, lines 54–58) provides an implementation that will be overridden in each of the derived classes. Each of these functions will, however, use the abstract class's version of `print` to print information common to all classes in the `Employee` hierarchy.

14.6.2 Creating Concrete Derived Class `SalariedEmployee`

Class `SalariedEmployee` (Figs. 14.15–14.16) derives from class `Employee` (line 8 of Fig. 14.15). The `public` member functions include a constructor that takes a first name, a last name, a social security number and a weekly salary as arguments (lines 11–12); a *set* function to assign a new nonnegative value to data member `weeklySalary` (lines 14); a *get* function to return `weeklySalary`'s value (line 15); a `virtual` function `earnings` that calculates a `SalariedEmployee`'s earnings (line 18) and a `virtual` function `print` (line 19) that outputs the employee's type, namely, `"salaried employee: "`, followed by employee-specific information produced by base-class `Employee`'s `print` function and `SalariedEmployee`'s `getWeeklySalary` function.

Figure 14.16 contains the member-function implementations for `SalariedEmployee`. The class's constructor passes the first name, last name and social security number to the `Employee` constructor (line 11) to initialize the `private` data members that are inherited from the base class, but not accessible in the derived class. Function `earnings` (line 30–33) overrides pure `virtual` function `earnings` in `Employee` to provide a concrete implementation that returns the `SalariedEmployee`'s weekly salary. If we did not implement `earnings`, class `SalariedEmployee` would be an abstract class, and any attempt to

```
1   // Fig. 14.15: SalariedEmployee.h
2   // SalariedEmployee class derived from Employee.
3   #ifndef SALARIED_H
4   #define SALARIED_H
5
6   #include "Employee.h" // Employee class definition
7
8   class SalariedEmployee : public Employee
9   {
10  public:
11     SalariedEmployee( const string &, const string &,
12        const string &, double = 0.0 );
13
14     void setWeeklySalary( double ); // set weekly salary
15     double getWeeklySalary() const; // return weekly salary
16
17     // keyword virtual signals intent to override
18     virtual double earnings() const; // calculate earnings
19     virtual void print() const; // print SalariedEmployee object
20  private:
21     double weeklySalary; // salary per week
22  }; // end class SalariedEmployee
23
24  #endif // SALARIED_H
```

Fig. 14.15 | SalariedEmployee class header file.

```
1   // Fig. 14.16: SalariedEmployee.cpp
2   // SalariedEmployee class member-function definitions.
3   #include <iostream>
4   using std::cout;
5
6   #include "SalariedEmployee.h" // SalariedEmployee class definition
7
8   // constructor
9   SalariedEmployee::SalariedEmployee( const string &first,
10     const string &last, const string &ssn, double salary )
11     : Employee( first, last, ssn )
12  {
13     setWeeklySalary( salary );
14  } // end SalariedEmployee constructor
15
16  // set salary
17  void SalariedEmployee::setWeeklySalary( double salary )
18  {
19     weeklySalary = ( salary < 0.0 ) ? 0.0 : salary;
20  } // end function setWeeklySalary
21
22  // return salary
23  double SalariedEmployee::getWeeklySalary() const
24  {
25     return weeklySalary;
26  } // end function getWeeklySalary
27
28  // calculate earnings;
29  // override pure virtual function earnings in Employee
30  double SalariedEmployee::earnings() const
31  {
32     return getWeeklySalary();
33  } // end function earnings
34
35  // print SalariedEmployee's information
36  void SalariedEmployee::print() const
37  {
38     cout << "salaried employee: ";
39     Employee::print(); // reuse abstract base-class print function
40     cout << "\nweekly salary: " << getWeeklySalary();
41  } // end function print
```

Fig. 14.16 | SalariedEmployee class implementation file.

instantiate an object of the class would result in a compilation error (and, of course, we want SalariedEmployee here to be a concrete class). Note that in class SalariedEmployee's header file, we declared member functions earnings and print as virtual (lines 18–19 of Fig. 14.15)—actually, placing the virtual keyword before these member functions is redundant. We defined them as virtual in base class Employee, so they remain virtual functions throughout the class hierarchy. Recall from Good Programming Practice 14.1 that explicitly declaring such functions virtual at every level of the hierarchy can promote program clarity.

Function print of class `SalariedEmployee` (lines 36–41 of Fig. 14.16) overrides `Employee` function print. If class `SalariedEmployee` did not override print, `SalariedEmployee` would inherit the `Employee` version of print. In that case, `SalariedEmployee`'s print function would simply return the employee's full name and social security number, which does not adequately represent a `SalariedEmployee`. To print a `SalariedEmployee`'s complete information, the derived class's print function outputs `"salaried employee: "` followed by the base-class `Employee`-specific information (i.e., first name, last name and social security number) printed by invoking the base class's print function using the scope resolution operator (line 39)—this is a nice example of code reuse. The output produced by `SalariedEmployee`'s print function contains the employee's weekly salary obtained by invoking the class's `getWeeklySalary` function.

14.6.3 Creating Concrete Derived Class HourlyEmployee

Class `HourlyEmployee` (Figs. 14.17–14.18) also derives from class `Employee` (line 8 of Fig. 14.17). The `public` member functions include a constructor (lines 11–12) that takes as arguments a first name, a last name, a social security number, an hourly wage and the number of hours worked; *set* functions that assign new values to data members wage and hours, respectively (lines 14 and 17); *get* functions to return the values of wage and hours, respectively (lines 15 and 18); a `virtual` function earnings that calculates an `HourlyEmployee`'s earnings (line 21) and a `virtual` function print that outputs the employee's type, namely, `"hourly employee: "`, and employee-specific information (line 22).

```
1   // Fig. 14.17: HourlyEmployee.h
2   // HourlyEmployee class definition.
3   #ifndef HOURLY_H
4   #define HOURLY_H
5
6   #include "Employee.h" // Employee class definition
7
8   class HourlyEmployee : public Employee
9   {
10  public:
11     HourlyEmployee( const string &, const string &,
12        const string &, double = 0.0, double = 0.0 );
13
14     void setWage( double ); // set hourly wage
15     double getWage() const; // return hourly wage
16
17     void setHours( double ); // set hours worked
18     double getHours() const; // return hours worked
19
20     // keyword virtual signals intent to override
21     virtual double earnings() const; // calculate earnings
22     virtual void print() const; // print HourlyEmployee object
23  private:
24     double wage; // wage per hour
25     double hours; // hours worked for week
26  }; // end class HourlyEmployee
```

Fig. 14.17 | HourlyEmployee class header file. (Part 1 of 2.)

```
27
28   #endif // HOURLY_H
```

Fig. 14.17 | HourlyEmployee class header file. (Part 2 of 2.)

```
 1   // Fig. 14.18: HourlyEmployee.cpp
 2   // HourlyEmployee class member-function definitions.
 3   #include <iostream>
 4   using std::cout;
 5
 6   #include "HourlyEmployee.h" // HourlyEmployee class definition
 7
 8   // constructor
 9   HourlyEmployee::HourlyEmployee( const string &first, const string &last,
10      const string &ssn, double hourlyWage, double hoursWorked )
11      : Employee( first, last, ssn )
12   {
13      setWage( hourlyWage ); // validate hourly wage
14      setHours( hoursWorked ); // validate hours worked
15   } // end HourlyEmployee constructor
16
17   // set wage
18   void HourlyEmployee::setWage( double hourlyWage )
19   {
20      wage = ( hourlyWage < 0.0 ? 0.0 : hourlyWage );
21   } // end function setWage
22
23   // return wage
24   double HourlyEmployee::getWage() const
25   {
26      return wage;
27   } // end function getWage
28
29   // set hours worked
30   void HourlyEmployee::setHours( double hoursWorked )
31   {
32      hours = ( ( ( hoursWorked >= 0.0 ) && ( hoursWorked <= 168.0 ) ) ?
33         hoursWorked : 0.0 );
34   } // end function setHours
35
36   // return hours worked
37   double HourlyEmployee::getHours() const
38   {
39      return hours;
40   } // end function getHours
41
42   // calculate earnings;
43   // override pure virtual function earnings in Employee
44   double HourlyEmployee::earnings() const
45   {
46      if ( getHours() <= 40 ) // no overtime
47         return getWage() * getHours();
```

Fig. 14.18 | HourlyEmployee class implementation file. (Part 1 of 2.)

```
48        else
49            return 40 * getWage() + ( ( getHours() - 40 ) * getWage() * 1.5 );
50    } // end function earnings
51
52    // print HourlyEmployee's information
53    void HourlyEmployee::print() const
54    {
55        cout << "hourly employee: ";
56        Employee::print(); // code reuse
57        cout << "\nhourly wage: " << getWage() <<
58            "; hours worked: " << getHours();
59    } // end function print
```

Fig. 14.18 | HourlyEmployee class implementation file. (Part 2 of 2.)

Figure 14.18 contains the member-function implementations for class HourlyEm-ployee. Lines 18–21 and 30–34 define *set* functions that assign new values to data members wage and hours, respectively. Function setWage (lines 18–21) ensures that wage is non-negative, and function setHours (lines 30–34) ensures that data member hours is between 0 and 168 (the total number of hours in a week). Class HourlyEmployee's *get* functions are implemented in lines 24–27 and 37–40. We do not declare these functions virtual, so classes derived from class HourlyEmployee cannot override them (although derived classes certainly can redefine them). Note that the HourlyEmployee constructor, like the Sala-riedEmployee constructor, passes the first name, last name and social security number to the base class Employee constructor (line 11) to initialize the inherited private data members declared in the base class. In addition, HourlyEmployee's print function calls base-class function print (line 56) to output the Employee-specific information (i.e., first name, last name and social security number)—this is another nice example of code reuse.

14.6.4 Creating Concrete Derived Class CommissionEmployee

Class CommissionEmployee (Figs. 14.19–14.20) derives from class Employee (line 8 of Fig. 14.19). The member-function implementations (Fig. 14.20) include a constructor (lines 9–15) that takes a first name, a last name, a social security number, a sales amount and a commission rate; *set* functions (lines 18–21 and 30–33) to assign new values to data members commissionRate and grossSales, respectively; *get* functions (lines 24–27 and 36–39) that retrieve the values of these data members; function earnings (lines 43–46) to calculate a CommissionEmployee's earnings; and function print (lines 49–55), which outputs the employee's type, namely, "commission employee: ", and employee-specific information. The CommissionEmployee's constructor also passes the first name, last name and social security number to the Employee constructor (line 11) to initialize Employee's private data members. Function print calls base-class function print (line 52) to display the Employee-specific information (i.e., first name, last name and social security number).

```
1    // Fig. 14.19: CommissionEmployee.h
2    // CommissionEmployee class derived from Employee.
3    #ifndef COMMISSION_H
```

Fig. 14.19 | CommissionEmployee class header file. (Part 1 of 2.)

```
4   #define COMMISSION_H
5
6   #include "Employee.h" // Employee class definition
7
8   class CommissionEmployee : public Employee
9   {
10  public:
11     CommissionEmployee( const string &, const string &,
12        const string &, double = 0.0, double = 0.0 );
13
14     void setCommissionRate( double ); // set commission rate
15     double getCommissionRate() const; // return commission rate
16
17     void setGrossSales( double ); // set gross sales amount
18     double getGrossSales() const; // return gross sales amount
19
20     // keyword virtual signals intent to override
21     virtual double earnings() const; // calculate earnings
22     virtual void print() const; // print CommissionEmployee object
23  private:
24     double grossSales; // gross weekly sales
25     double commissionRate; // commission percentage
26  }; // end class CommissionEmployee
27
28  #endif // COMMISSION_H
```

Fig. 14.19 | CommissionEmployee class header file. (Part 2 of 2.)

```
1   // Fig. 14.20: CommissionEmployee.cpp
2   // CommissionEmployee class member-function definitions.
3   #include <iostream>
4   using std::cout;
5
6   #include "CommissionEmployee.h" // CommissionEmployee class definition
7
8   // constructor
9   CommissionEmployee::CommissionEmployee( const string &first,
10     const string &last, const string &ssn, double sales, double rate )
11     : Employee( first, last, ssn )
12  {
13     setGrossSales( sales );
14     setCommissionRate( rate );
15  } // end CommissionEmployee constructor
16
17  // set commission rate
18  void CommissionEmployee::setCommissionRate( double rate )
19  {
20     commissionRate = ( ( rate > 0.0 && rate < 1.0 ) ? rate : 0.0 );
21  } // end function setCommissionRate
22
```

Fig. 14.20 | CommissionEmployee class implementation file. (Part 1 of 2.)

```
23  // return commission rate
24  double CommissionEmployee::getCommissionRate() const
25  {
26      return commissionRate;
27  } // end function getCommissionRate
28
29  // set gross sales amount
30  void CommissionEmployee::setGrossSales( double sales )
31  {
32      grossSales = ( ( sales < 0.0 ) ? 0.0 : sales );
33  } // end function setGrossSales
34
35  // return gross sales amount
36  double CommissionEmployee::getGrossSales() const
37  {
38      return grossSales;
39  } // end function getGrossSales
40
41  // calculate earnings;
42  // override pure virtual function earnings in Employee
43  double CommissionEmployee::earnings() const
44  {
45      return getCommissionRate() * getGrossSales();
46  } // end function earnings
47
48  // print CommissionEmployee's information
49  void CommissionEmployee::print() const
50  {
51      cout << "commission employee: ";
52      Employee::print(); // code reuse
53      cout << "\ngross sales: " << getGrossSales()
54          << "; commission rate: " << getCommissionRate();
55  } // end function print
```

Fig. 14.20 | CommissionEmployee class implementation file. (Part 2 of 2.)

14.6.5 Creating Indirect Concrete Derived Class BasePlusCommissionEmployee

Class BasePlusCommissionEmployee (Figs. 14.21–14.22) directly inherits from class CommissionEmployee (line 8 of Fig. 14.21) and therefore is an *indirect* derived class of class Employee. Class BasePlusCommissionEmployee's member-function implementations include a constructor (lines 10–16 of Fig. 14.22) that takes as arguments a first name, a last name, a social security number, a sales amount, a commission rate and a base salary. It then passes the first name, last name, social security number, sales amount and commission rate to the CommissionEmployee constructor (line 13) to initialize the inherited members. BasePlusCommissionEmployee also contains a *set* function (lines 19–22) to assign a new value to data member baseSalary and a *get* function (lines 25–28) to return baseSalary's value. Function earnings (lines 32–35) calculates a BasePlusCommissionEmployee's earnings. Note that line 34 in function earnings calls base-class CommissionEmployee's earnings function to calculate the commission-based portion of the employee's earnings. This is a nice example of code reuse. BasePlusCommissionEmployee's print function (lines 38–

```
 1   // Fig. 14.21: BasePlusCommissionEmployee.h
 2   // BasePlusCommissionEmployee class derived from Employee.
 3   #ifndef BASEPLUS_H
 4   #define BASEPLUS_H
 5
 6   #include "CommissionEmployee.h" // CommissionEmployee class definition
 7
 8   class BasePlusCommissionEmployee : public CommissionEmployee
 9   {
10   public:
11      BasePlusCommissionEmployee( const string &, const string &,
12         const string &, double = 0.0, double = 0.0, double = 0.0 );
13
14      void setBaseSalary( double ); // set base salary
15      double getBaseSalary() const; // return base salary
16
17      // keyword virtual signals intent to override
18      virtual double earnings() const; // calculate earnings
19      virtual void print() const; // print BasePlusCommissionEmployee object
20   private:
21      double baseSalary; // base salary per week
22   }; // end class BasePlusCommissionEmployee
23
24   #endif // BASEPLUS_H
```

Fig. 14.21 | BasePlusCommissionEmployee class header file.

```
 1   // Fig. 14.22: BasePlusCommissionEmployee.cpp
 2   // BasePlusCommissionEmployee member-function definitions.
 3   #include <iostream>
 4   using std::cout;
 5
 6   // BasePlusCommissionEmployee class definition
 7   #include "BasePlusCommissionEmployee.h"
 8
 9   // constructor
10   BasePlusCommissionEmployee::BasePlusCommissionEmployee(
11      const string &first, const string &last, const string &ssn,
12      double sales, double rate, double salary )
13      : CommissionEmployee( first, last, ssn, sales, rate )
14   {
15      setBaseSalary( salary ); // validate and store base salary
16   } // end BasePlusCommissionEmployee constructor
17
18   // set base salary
19   void BasePlusCommissionEmployee::setBaseSalary( double salary )
20   {
21      baseSalary = ( ( salary < 0.0 ) ? 0.0 : salary );
22   } // end function setBaseSalary
23
```

Fig. 14.22 | BasePlusCommissionEmployee class implementation file. (Part 1 of 2.)

```
24   // return base salary
25   double BasePlusCommissionEmployee::getBaseSalary() const
26   {
27      return baseSalary;
28   } // end function getBaseSalary
29
30   // calculate earnings;
31   // override pure virtual function earnings in Employee
32   double BasePlusCommissionEmployee::earnings() const
33   {
34      return getBaseSalary() + CommissionEmployee::earnings();
35   } // end function earnings
36
37   // print BasePlusCommissionEmployee's information
38   void BasePlusCommissionEmployee::print() const
39   {
40      cout << "base-salaried ";
41      CommissionEmployee::print(); // code reuse
42      cout << "; base salary: " << getBaseSalary();
43   } // end function print
```

Fig. 14.22 | `BasePlusCommissionEmployee` class implementation file. (Part 2 of 2.)

43) outputs "base-salaried", followed by the output of base-class `CommissionEmployee`'s print function (another example of code reuse), then the base salary. The resulting output begins with "base-salaried commission employee: " followed by the rest of the Base-PlusCommissionEmployee's information. Recall that `CommissionEmployee`'s print displays the employee's first name, last name and social security number by invoking the print function of its base class (i.e., `Employee`)—yet another example of code reuse. Note that `BasePlusCommissionEmployee`'s print initiates a chain of functions calls that spans all three levels of the `Employee` hierarchy.

14.6.6 Demonstrating Polymorphic Processing

To test our `Employee` hierarchy, the program in Fig. 14.23 creates an object of each of the four concrete classes `SalariedEmployee`, `HourlyEmployee`, `CommissionEmployee` and `BasePlusCommissionEmployee`. The program manipulates these objects, first with static binding, then polymorphically, using a vector of `Employee` pointers. Lines 31–38 create objects of each of the four concrete `Employee` derived classes. Lines 43–51 output each Employee's information and earnings. Each member-function invocation in lines 43–51 is an example of static binding—at compile time, because we are using name handles (not pointers or references that could be set at execution time), the compiler can identify each object's type to determine which print and earnings functions are called.

Line 54 allocates vector employees, which contains four `Employee` pointers. Line 57 aims employees[0] at object salariedEmployee. Line 58 aims employees[1] at object hourlyEmployee. Line 59 aims employees[2] at object commissionEmployee. Line 60 aims employee[3] at object basePlusCommissionEmployee. The compiler allows these assignments, because a `SalariedEmployee` *is an* Employee, an `HourlyEmployee` *is an* Employee, a `CommissionEmployee` *is an* Employee and a `BasePlusCommissionEmployee` *is an* Employee. Therefore, we can assign the addresses of SalariedEmployee, HourlyEmployee, CommissionEmployee and BasePlusCommissionEmployee objects to base-class Employee pointers (even though Employee is an abstract class).

The loop in lines 68–69 traverses vector employees and invokes function virtual-ViaPointer (lines 83–87) for each element in employees. Function virtualViaPointer receives in parameter baseClassPtr (of type const Employee * const) the address stored in an employees element. Each call to virtualViaPointer uses baseClassPtr to invoke virtual functions print (line 85) and earnings (line 86). Note that function virtual-

```cpp
1   // Fig. 14.23: EmployeeTest.cpp
2   // Processing Employee derived-class objects individually
3   // and polymorphically using dynamic binding.
4   #include <iostream>
5   using std::cout;
6   using std::endl;
7   using std::fixed;
8
9   #include <iomanip>
10  using std::setprecision;
11
12  #include <vector>
13  using std::vector;
14
15  // include definitions of classes in Employee hierarchy
16  #include "Employee.h"
17  #include "SalariedEmployee.h"
18  #include "HourlyEmployee.h"
19  #include "CommissionEmployee.h"
20  #include "BasePlusCommissionEmployee.h"
21
22  void virtualViaPointer( const Employee * const ); // prototype
23  void virtualViaReference( const Employee & ); // prototype
24
25  int main()
26  {
27     // set floating-point output formatting
28     cout << fixed << setprecision( 2 );
29
30     // create derived-class objects
31     SalariedEmployee salariedEmployee(
32        "John", "Smith", "111-11-1111", 800 );
33     HourlyEmployee hourlyEmployee(
34        "Karen", "Price", "222-22-2222", 16.75, 40 );
35     CommissionEmployee commissionEmployee(
36        "Sue", "Jones", "333-33-3333", 10000, .06 );
37     BasePlusCommissionEmployee basePlusCommissionEmployee(
38        "Bob", "Lewis", "444-44-4444", 5000, .04, 300 );
39
40     cout << "Employees processed individually using static binding:\n\n";
41
42     // output each Employee's information and earnings using static binding
43     salariedEmployee.print();
```

Fig. 14.23 | Employee class hierarchy driver program. (Part 1 of 4.)

```
44         cout << "\nearned $" << salariedEmployee.earnings() << "\n\n";
45         hourlyEmployee.print();
46         cout << "\nearned $" << hourlyEmployee.earnings() << "\n\n";
47         commissionEmployee.print();
48         cout << "\nearned $" << commissionEmployee.earnings() << "\n\n";
49         basePlusCommissionEmployee.print();
50         cout << "\nearned $" << basePlusCommissionEmployee.earnings()
51            << "\n\n";
52
53         // create vector of four base-class pointers
54         vector < Employee * > employees( 4 );
55
56         // initialize vector with Employees
57         employees[ 0 ] = &salariedEmployee;
58         employees[ 1 ] = &hourlyEmployee;
59         employees[ 2 ] = &commissionEmployee;
60         employees[ 3 ] = &basePlusCommissionEmployee;
61
62         cout << "Employees processed polymorphically via dynamic binding:\n\n";
63
64         // call virtualViaPointer to print each Employee's information
65         // and earnings using dynamic binding
66         cout << "Virtual function calls made off base-class pointers:\n\n";
67
68         for ( size_t i = 0; i < employees.size(); i++ )
69            virtualViaPointer( employees[ i ] );
70
71         // call virtualViaReference to print each Employee's information
72         // and earnings using dynamic binding
73         cout << "Virtual function calls made off base-class references:\n\n";
74
75         for ( size_t i = 0; i < employees.size(); i++ )
76            virtualViaReference( *employees[ i ] ); // note dereferencing
77
78         return 0;
79      } // end main
80
81      // call Employee virtual functions print and earnings off a
82      // base-class pointer using dynamic binding
83      void virtualViaPointer( const Employee * const baseClassPtr )
84      {
85         baseClassPtr->print();
86         cout << "\nearned $" << baseClassPtr->earnings() << "\n\n";
87      } // end function virtualViaPointer
88
89      // call Employee virtual functions print and earnings off a
90      // base-class reference using dynamic binding
91      void virtualViaReference( const Employee &baseClassRef )
92      {
93         baseClassRef.print();
94         cout << "\nearned $" << baseClassRef.earnings() << "\n\n";
95      } // end function virtualViaReference
```

Fig. 14.23 | Employee class hierarchy driver program. (Part 2 of 4.)

```
Employees processed individually using static binding:

salaried employee: John Smith
social security number: 111-11-1111
weekly salary: 800.00
earned $800.00

hourly employee: Karen Price
social security number: 222-22-2222
hourly wage: 16.75; hours worked: 40.00
earned $670.00

commission employee: Sue Jones
social security number: 333-33-3333
gross sales: 10000.00; commission rate: 0.06
earned $600.00

base-salaried commission employee: Bob Lewis
social security number: 444-44-4444
gross sales: 5000.00; commission rate: 0.04; base salary: 300.00
earned $500.00

Employees processed polymorphically using dynamic binding:

Virtual function calls made off base-class pointers:

salaried employee: John Smith
social security number: 111-11-1111
weekly salary: 800.00
earned $800.00

hourly employee: Karen Price
social security number: 222-22-2222
hourly wage: 16.75; hours worked: 40.00
earned $670.00

commission employee: Sue Jones
social security number: 333-33-3333
gross sales: 10000.00; commission rate: 0.06
earned $600.00

base-salaried commission employee: Bob Lewis
social security number: 444-44-4444
gross sales: 5000.00; commission rate: 0.04; base salary: 300.00
earned $500.00

Virtual function calls made off base-class references:

salaried employee: John Smith
social security number: 111-11-1111
weekly salary: 800.00
earned $800.00

hourly employee: Karen Price
social security number: 222-22-2222
hourly wage: 16.75; hours worked: 40.00
earned $670.00
```

Fig. 14.23 | Employee class hierarchy driver program. (Part 3 of 4.)

```
commission employee: Sue Jones
social security number: 333-33-3333
gross sales: 10000.00; commission rate: 0.06
earned $600.00

base-salaried commission employee: Bob Lewis
social security number: 444-44-4444
gross sales: 5000.00; commission rate: 0.04; base salary: 300.00
earned $500.00
```

Fig. 14.23 | Employee class hierarchy driver program. (Part 4 of 4.)

ViaPointer does not contain any SalariedEmployee, HourlyEmployee, CommissionEmployee or BasePlusCommissionEmployee type information. The function knows only about base-class type Employee. Therefore, at compile time, the compiler cannot know which concrete class's functions to call through baseClassPtr. Yet at execution time, each virtual-function invocation calls the function on the object to which baseClassPtr points at that moment. The output illustrates that the appropriate functions for each class are indeed invoked and that each object's proper information is displayed. For instance, the weekly salary is displayed for the SalariedEmployee, and the gross sales are displayed for the CommissionEmployee and BasePlusCommissionEmployee. Also note that obtaining the earnings of each Employee polymorphically in line 86 produces the same results as obtaining these employees' earnings via static binding in lines 44, 46, 48 and 50. All virtual function calls to print and earnings are resolved at runtime with dynamic binding.

Finally, another for statement (lines 75–76) traverses employees and invokes function virtualViaReference (lines 91–95) for each element in the vector. Function virtualViaReference receives in its parameter baseClassRef (of type const Employee &) a reference formed by dereferencing the pointer stored in each employees element (line 76). Each call to virtualViaReference invokes virtual functions print (line 93) and earnings (line 94) via reference baseClassRef to demonstrate that polymorphic processing occurs with base-class references as well. Each virtual-function invocation calls the function on the object to which baseClassRef refers at runtime. This is another example of dynamic binding. The output produced using base-class references is identical to the output produced using base-class pointers.

14.7 (Optional) Polymorphism, Virtual Functions and Dynamic Binding "Under the Hood"

Visual C++ makes polymorphism easy to program. It is certainly possible to program for polymorphism in non-object-oriented languages such as C, but doing so requires complex and potentially dangerous pointer manipulations. This section discusses how Visual C++ can implement polymorphism, virtual functions and dynamic binding internally. This will give you a solid understanding of how these capabilities really work. More importantly, it will help you appreciate the overhead of polymorphism—in terms of additional memory consumption and processor time. This will help you determine when to use polymorphism and when to avoid it. As you'll see in Chapter 23, the STL components were implemented without polymorphism and virtual functions—this was done to avoid the associated execution-time overhead and achieve optimal performance to meet the unique requirements of the STL.

First, we'll explain the data structures that the Visual C++ compiler builds at compile time to support polymorphism at execution time. You'll see that polymorphism is accomplished through three levels of pointers (i.e., "triple indirection"). Then we'll show how an executing program uses these data structures to execute virtual functions and achieve the dynamic binding associated with polymorphism. Note that our discussion explains one possible implementation; this is not a language requirement.

When Visual C++ compiles a class that has one or more virtual functions, it builds a *virtual function table (vtable)* for that class. An executing program uses the *vtable* to select the proper function implementation each time a virtual function of that class is called. The leftmost column of Fig. 14.24 illustrates the *vtables* for classes Employee, SalariedEmployee, HourlyEmployee, CommissionEmployee and BasePlusCommissionEmployee.

In the *vtable* for class Employee, the first function pointer is set to 0 (i.e., the null pointer). This is done because function earnings is a pure virtual function and therefore lacks an implementation. The second function pointer points to function print, which displays the employee's full name and social security number. [*Note:* We have abbreviated the output of each print function in this figure to conserve space.] Any class that has one or more null pointers in its *vtable* is an abstract class. Classes without any null *vtable* pointers (such as SalariedEmployee, HourlyEmployee, CommissionEmployee and BasePlusCommissionEmployee) are concrete classes.

Class SalariedEmployee overrides function earnings to return the employee's weekly salary, so the function pointer points to the earnings function of class SalariedEmployee. SalariedEmployee also overrides print, so the corresponding function pointer points to the SalariedEmployee member function that prints "salaried employee: " followed by the employee's name, social security number and weekly salary.

The earnings function pointer in the *vtable* for class HourlyEmployee points to the HourlyEmployee's earnings function that returns the employee's wage multiplied by the number of hours worked. Note that to conserve space, we have omitted the fact that hourly employees receive time-and-a-half pay for overtime hours worked. The print function pointer points to the HourlyEmployee version of the function, which prints "hourly employee: ", the employee's name, social security number, hourly wage and hours worked. Both functions override the functions in class Employee.

The earnings function pointer in the *vtable* for class CommissionEmployee points to CommissionEmployee's earnings function that returns the employee's gross sales multiplied by the commission rate. The print function pointer points to the CommissionEmployee version of the function, which prints the employee's type, name, social security number, commission rate and gross sales. As in class HourlyEmployee, both functions override the functions in class Employee.

The earnings function pointer in the *vtable* for class BasePlusCommissionEmployee points to the BasePlusCommissionEmployee's earnings function, which returns the employee's base salary plus gross sales multiplied by commission rate. The print function pointer points to the BasePlusCommissionEmployee version of the function, which prints the employee's base salary plus the type, name, social security number, commission rate and gross sales. Both functions override the functions in class CommissionEmployee.

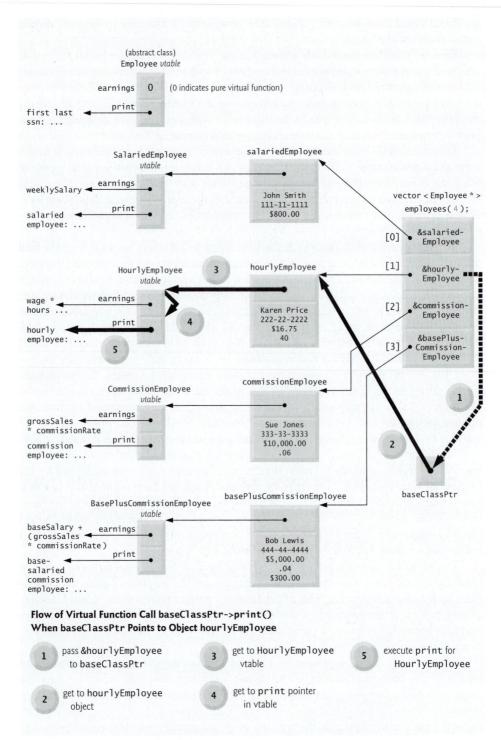

Flow of Virtual Function Call baseClassPtr->print()
When baseClassPtr Points to Object hourlyEmployee

1 pass &hourlyEmployee to baseClassPtr

2 get to hourlyEmployee object

3 get to HourlyEmployee vtable

4 get to print pointer in vtable

5 execute print for HourlyEmployee

Fig. 14.24 | How virtual function calls work.

Notice that in our `Employee` case study, each concrete class provides its own implementation for virtual functions `earnings` and `print`. You've learned that each class which inherits directly from abstract base class `Employee` must implement `earnings` in order to be a concrete class, because `earnings` is a pure virtual function. These classes do not need to implement function `print`, however, to be considered concrete—`print` is not a pure virtual function and derived classes can inherit class `Employee`'s implementation of `print`. Furthermore, class `BasePlusCommissionEmployee` does not have to implement either function `print` or `earnings`—both function implementations can be inherited from class `CommissionEmployee`. If a class in our hierarchy were to inherit function implementations in this manner, the *vtable* pointers for these functions would simply point to the function implementation that was being inherited. For example, if `BasePlusCommissionEmployee` did not override `earnings`, the `earnings` function pointer in the *vtable* for class `BasePlusCommissionEmployee` would point to the same `earnings` function that the *vtable* for class `CommissionEmployee` points to.

Polymorphism is accomplished through an elegant data structure involving three levels of pointers. We have discussed one level—the function pointers in the *vtable*. These point to the actual functions that execute when a virtual function is invoked.

Now we consider the second level of pointers. Whenever an object of a class with one or more virtual functions is instantiated, the compiler attaches to the object a pointer to the *vtable* for that class. This pointer is normally at the front of the object, but it is not required to be implemented that way. In Fig. 14.24, these pointers are associated with the objects created in Fig. 14.23 (one object for each of the types `SalariedEmployee`, `HourlyEmployee`, `CommissionEmployee` and `BasePlusCommissionEmployee`). Notice that the diagram displays each of the object's data-member values. For example, the `salariedEmployee` object contains a pointer to the `SalariedEmployee` *vtable*; the object also contains the values `John Smith`, `111-11-1111` and `$800.00`.

The third level of pointers simply contains the handles to the objects that receive the virtual function calls. The handles in this level may also be references. Note that Fig. 14.24 depicts the `vector` `employees` that contains `Employee` pointers.

Now let us see how a typical virtual function call executes. Consider the call `baseClassPtr->print()` in function `virtualViaPointer` (line 85 of Fig. 14.23). Assume that `baseClassPtr` contains `employees[ 1 ]` (i.e., the address of object `hourlyEmployee` in `employees`). When the compiler compiles this statement, it determines that the call is indeed being made via a base-class pointer and that `print` is a virtual function.

The compiler determines that `print` is the *second* entry in each of the *vtables*. To locate this entry, the compiler notes that it will need to skip the first entry. Thus, the compiler compiles an ***offset*** or ***displacement*** of four bytes (four bytes for each pointer on today's popular 32-bit machines, and only one pointer needs to be skipped) into the table of machine-language object-code pointers to find the code that will execute the virtual function call.

The compiler generates code that performs the following operations [*Note:* The numbers in the list correspond to the circled numbers in Fig. 14.24]:

1. Select the *i*th entry of `employees` (in this case, the address of object `hourlyEmployee`), and pass it as an argument to function `virtualViaPointer`. This sets parameter `baseClassPtr` to point to `hourlyEmployee`.

2. Dereference that pointer to get to the `hourlyEmployee` object—which, as you recall, begins with a pointer to the `HourlyEmployee` *vtable*.

3. Dereference `hourlyEmployee`'s *vtable* pointer to get to the `HourlyEmployee` *vtable*.

4. Skip the offset of four bytes to select the `print` function pointer.

5. Dereference the `print` function pointer to form the "name" of the actual function to execute, and use the function-call operator () to execute the appropriate `print` function, which in this case prints the employee's type, name, social security number, hourly wage and hours worked.

The data structures of Fig. 14.24 may appear to be complex, but this complexity is managed by the compiler and hidden from you, making polymorphic programming straightforward. The pointer dereferencing operations and memory accesses that occur on every `virtual` function call require some additional execution time. The *vtables* and the *vtable* pointers added to the objects require some additional memory. You now have enough information to determine whether `virtual` functions are appropriate for your programs.

Performance Tip 14.1

Polymorphism, as typically implemented with `virtual` *functions and dynamic binding in Visual C++, is efficient. Programmers may use these capabilities with nominal impact on performance.*

Performance Tip 14.2

Virtual functions and dynamic binding enable polymorphic programming as an alternative to `switch` *logic programming. Optimizing compilers normally generate polymorphic code that runs as efficiently as hand-coded* `switch`*-based logic. The overhead of polymorphism is acceptable for most applications. But in some situations—real-time applications with stringent performance requirements, for example—the overhead of polymorphism may be too high.*

Software Engineering Observation 14.11

Dynamic binding enables independent software vendors (ISVs) to distribute software without revealing proprietary secrets. Software distributions can consist of only header files and object files—no source code needs to be revealed. Software developers can then use inheritance to derive new classes from those provided by the ISVs. Other software that worked with the classes the ISVs provided will still work with the derived classes and will use the overridden `virtual` *functions provided in these classes (via dynamic binding).*

14.8 Case Study: Payroll System Using Polymorphism and Runtime Type Information with Downcasting, `dynamic_cast`, `typeid` and `type_info`

Recall from the problem statement at the beginning of Section 14.6 that, for the current pay period, our fictitious company has decided to reward `BasePlusCommissionEmployees` by adding 10 percent to their base salaries. When processing `Employee` objects polymorphically in Section 14.6.6, we did not need to worry about the "specifics." Now, however, to adjust the base salaries of `BasePlusCommissionEmployees`, we have to determine the specific type of each `Employee` object at execution time, then act appropriately. This section demonstrates the powerful capabilities of runtime type information (RTTI) and dynamic casting, which enable a program to determine the type of an object at execution time and act on that object accordingly.

[*Note:* Some compilers require that RTTI be enabled before it can be used in a program. Consult your compiler's documentation to determine whether your compiler has similar requirements. In Visual C++ 2008, this option is enabled by default.]

Figure 14.25 uses the `Employee` hierarchy developed in Section 14.6 and increases by 10 percent the base salary of each `BasePlusCommissionEmployee`. Line 31 declares four-element `vector` `employees` that stores pointers to `Employee` objects. Lines 34–41 populate the `vector` with the addresses of dynamically allocated objects of classes `SalariedEmployee` (Figs. 14.15–14.16), `HourlyEmployee` (Figs. 14.17–14.18), `CommissionEmployee` (Figs. 14.19–14.20) and `BasePlusCommissionEmployee` (Figs. 14.21–14.22).

The `for` statement in lines 44–66 iterates through the `employees` `vector` and displays each `Employee`'s information by invoking member function `print` (line 46). Recall that because `print` is declared `virtual` in base class `Employee`, the system invokes the appropriate derived-class object's `print` function.

In this example, as we encounter `BasePlusCommissionEmployee` objects, we wish to increase their base salary by 10 percent. Since we process the employees generically (i.e., polymorphically), we cannot (with the techniques we've learned) be certain as to which

```cpp
1   // Fig. 14.25: Downcasting.cpp
2   // Demonstrating downcasting and runtime type information.
3   // NOTE: You may need to enable RTTI on your compiler
4   // before you can execute this application.
5   #include <iostream>
6   using std::cout;
7   using std::endl;
8   using std::fixed;
9
10  #include <iomanip>
11  using std::setprecision;
12
13  #include <vector>
14  using std::vector;
15
16  #include <typeinfo>
17
18  // include definitions of classes in Employee hierarchy
19  #include "Employee.h"
20  #include "SalariedEmployee.h"
21  #include "HourlyEmployee.h"
22  #include "CommissionEmployee.h"
23  #include "BasePlusCommissionEmployee.h"
24
25  int main()
26  {
27     // set floating-point output formatting
28     cout << fixed << setprecision( 2 );
```

Fig. 14.25 | Demonstrating downcasting and runtime type information. (Part 1 of 3.)

```
29
30      // create vector of four base-class pointers
31      vector < Employee * > employees( 4 );
32
33      // initialize vector with various kinds of Employees
34      employees[ 0 ] = new SalariedEmployee(
35         "John", "Smith", "111-11-1111", 800 );
36      employees[ 1 ] = new HourlyEmployee(
37         "Karen", "Price", "222-22-2222", 16.75, 40 );
38      employees[ 2 ] = new CommissionEmployee(
39         "Sue", "Jones", "333-33-3333", 10000, .06 );
40      employees[ 3 ] = new BasePlusCommissionEmployee(
41         "Bob", "Lewis", "444-44-4444", 5000, .04, 300 );
42
43      // polymorphically process each element in vector employees
44      for ( size_t i = 0; i < employees.size(); i++ )
45      {
46         employees[ i ]->print(); // output employee information
47         cout << endl;
48
49         // downcast pointer
50         BasePlusCommissionEmployee *derivedPtr =
51            dynamic_cast < BasePlusCommissionEmployee * >
52               ( employees[ i ] );
53
54         // determine whether element points to base-salaried
55         // commission employee
56         if ( derivedPtr != 0 ) // 0 if not a BasePlusCommissionEmployee
57         {
58            double oldBaseSalary = derivedPtr->getBaseSalary();
59            cout << "old base salary: $" << oldBaseSalary << endl;
60            derivedPtr->setBaseSalary( 1.10 * oldBaseSalary );
61            cout << "new base salary with 10% increase is: $"
62               << derivedPtr->getBaseSalary() << endl;
63         } // end if
64
65         cout << "earned $" << employees[ i ]->earnings() << "\n\n";
66      } // end for
67
68      // release objects pointed to by vector's elements
69      for ( size_t j = 0; j < employees.size(); j++ )
70      {
71         // output class name
72         cout << "deleting object of "
73            << typeid( *employees[ j ] ).name() << endl;
74
75         delete employees[ j ];
76      } // end for
77
78      return 0;
79   } // end main
```

Fig. 14.25 | Demonstrating downcasting and runtime type information. (Part 2 of 3.)

```
salaried employee: John Smith
social security number: 111-11-1111
weekly salary: 800.00
earned $800.00

hourly employee: Karen Price
social security number: 222-22-2222
hourly wage: 16.75; hours worked: 40.00
earned $670.00

commission employee: Sue Jones
social security number: 333-33-3333
gross sales: 10000.00; commission rate: 0.06
earned $600.00

base-salaried commission employee: Bob Lewis
social security number: 444-44-4444
gross sales: 5000.00; commission rate: 0.04; base salary: 300.00
old base salary: $300.00
new base salary with 10% increase is: $330.00
earned $530.00

deleting object of class SalariedEmployee
deleting object of class HourlyEmployee
deleting object of class CommissionEmployee
deleting object of class BasePlusCommissionEmployee
```

Fig. 14.25 | Demonstrating downcasting and runtime type information. (Part 3 of 3.)

type of Employee is being manipulated at any given time. This creates a problem, because BasePlusCommissionEmployee employees must be identified when we encounter them so they can receive the 10 percent salary increase. To accomplish this, we use operator ***dynamic_cast*** (line 51) to determine whether the type of each object is BasePlusCommissionEmployee. This is the downcast operation we referred to in Section 14.3.3. Lines 50–52 dynamically downcast employees[i] from type Employee * to type BasePlusCommissionEmployee *. If the vector element points to an object that *is a* BasePlusCommissionEmployee object, then that object's address is assigned to commissionPtr; otherwise, 0 is assigned to derived-class pointer derivedPtr. If dynamic_cast fails then it throws a bad_cast exception (see Chapter 16). Note that the dynamic_cast operator should only be used on polymorphic types.

If the value returned by the dynamic_cast operator in lines 50–52 is not 0, the object is the correct type, and the if statement (lines 56–63) performs the special processing required for the BasePlusCommissionEmployee object. Lines 58, 60 and 62 invoke BasePlusCommissionEmployee functions getBaseSalary and setBaseSalary to retrieve and update the employee's salary.

Line 65 invokes member function earnings on the object to which employees[i] points. Recall that earnings is declared virtual in the base class, so the program invokes the derived-class object's earnings function—another example of dynamic binding.

Lines 69–76 display each employee's object type and use the delete operator to deallocate the dynamic memory to which each vector element points. Operator ***typeid*** (line 73) returns a reference to an object of class ***type_info*** that contains the information about the type of its operand, including the name of that type. When invoked, type_info member function *name* (line 73) returns a pointer-based string that contains the type name (e.g., "class BasePlusCommissionEmployee") of the argument passed to typeid. To use typeid, the program must include header file *<typeinfo>* (line 16).

Portability Tip 14.1

The string returned by type_info member function name may vary by compiler.

Note that we avoid several compilation errors in this example by downcasting an Employee pointer to a BasePlusCommissionEmployee pointer (lines 50–52). If we remove the dynamic_cast from line 51 and attempt to assign the current Employee pointer directly to BasePlusCommissionEmployee pointer derivedPtr, we'll receive a compilation error. Visual C++ does not allow a program to assign a base-class pointer to a derived-class pointer because the *is-a* relationship does not apply—a CommissionEmployee is *not* a BasePlusCommissionEmployee. The *is-a* relationship applies only between the derived class and its base classes, not vice versa.

Similarly, if lines 58, 60 and 62 used the current base-class pointer from employees, rather than derived-class pointer derivedPtr, to invoke derived-class-only functions get-BaseSalary and setBaseSalary, we would receive a compilation error at each of these lines. As you learned in Section 14.3.3, attempting to invoke derived-class-only functions through a base-class pointer is not allowed. Although lines 58, 60 and 62 execute only if commissionPtr is not 0 (i.e., if the cast can be performed), we cannot attempt to invoke derived-class BasePlusCommissionEmployee functions getBaseSalary and setBase-Salary on the base-class Employee pointer. Recall that, using a base class Employee pointer, we can invoke only functions found in base class Employee—earnings, print and Employee's *get* and *set* functions.

14.9 Virtual Destructors

A problem can occur when using polymorphism to process dynamically allocated objects of a class hierarchy. So far you have seen *nonvirtual destructors*—destructors that are not declared with keyword virtual. If a derived-class object with a nonvirtual destructor is destroyed explicitly by applying the delete operator to a base-class pointer to the object, the Visual C++ standard specifies that the behavior is undefined.

The simple solution to this problem is to create a *virtual destructor* (i.e., a destructor that is declared with keyword virtual) in the base class. This makes all derived-class destructors virtual *even though they do not have the same name as the base-class destructor*. Now, if an object in the hierarchy is destroyed explicitly by applying the delete operator to a base-class pointer, the destructor for the appropriate class is called based on the object to which the base-class pointer points. Remember, when a derived-class object is destroyed, the base-class part of the derived-class object is also destroyed, so it is important for the destructors of both the derived class and base class to execute. The base-class destructor automatically executes after the derived-class destructor.

Error-Prevention Tip 14.2

If a class has virtual functions, provide a virtual destructor, even if one is not required for the class. This ensures that a custom derived-class destructor (if there is one) will be invoked when a derived-class object is deleted via a base class pointer.

Common Programming Error 14.5

Constructors cannot be virtual. *Declaring a constructor* virtual *is a compilation error.*

14.10 Polymorphism in C++/CLI

Conceptually, polymorphism in C++/CLI is implemented the same way as native C++, as described previously. Syntactically, C++/CLI requires more explicit declarations of virtual functions and abstract classes to ensure program clarity.

Virtual *Functions in C++/CLI*

Recall that in native C++, when a function of a class is declared virtual, all derived classes inherit that virtual function. If the derived class provides its own implementation of the virtual function, then the base-class version of the function is implicitly overridden. The derived-class function is also marked virtual implicitly, though for clarity you should explicitly declare it as such. In contrast, C++/CLI requires that any virtual functions be declared explicitly virtual in all derived classes and overridden explicitly. For example, imagine a version of the Shape class from above declared as a managed type with ref class. This managed class would declare the following function (remember C++/CLI functions cannot be declared const):

```
ref class Shape
{
public:
   virtual void draw();
   // rest of Shape class definition
};
```

Now all managed classes that derive from Shape will inherit this virtual function.

If we want to override the draw function in a derived class, then C++/CLI requires that we declare it virtual and explicitly declare that it is overriding a base-class function with context-sensitive keyword *override*. This new keyword specifies that a function is overriding a virtual function inherited from a base class. If we create a managed Circle class that derives from Shape, we override the draw function with the following declaration

```
ref class Circle : Shape
{
public:
   virtual void draw() override;
   // rest of Circle class definition
};
```

In native C++ we wouldn't use keyword override and we could optionally leave off the explicit virtual declaration. C++/CLI requires both keywords when overriding inherited virtual functions. By requiring that inherited functions be explicitly declared as virtual and override, users of the derived class can immediately understand the intent and purpose of the functions. As in native C++, the overriding version of the function must have the same function prototype.

The override keyword specifies that a function is explicitly overriding a base class version of the function. Alternatively, the context-sensitive *new* keyword specifies that the derived-class function is not overriding a base-class version, even though it has the function prototype. Note that this version of new is context sensitive, so it performs this role only in a function declaration of a managed type. Outside of this setting it performs dynamic memory allocation for native types as normal. For example, if we declare the draw function of Circle as follows:

```
virtual void draw() new;
```

then Circle's version of draw is a new function that hides, not overrides, the draw function of Shape. As a result, the following statements

```
Shape ^s = gcnew Circle();
s->draw();
```

call the draw function of Shape. In native C++, or C++/CLI when using the override keyword, the above statements would call the draw function of Circle. Now to call the draw function of the Circle class, you must do so directly from a Circle reference or object rather than calling draw from a base-class reference. You won't need to use new like this often, but it can be useful in some class hierarchies.

Keyword *sealed*

A class or function in C++/CLI can be declared with the context-sensitive keyword *sealed* to specify that it cannot be overridden in a derived class. For example, if we declared draw in managed class Shape as follows:

```
void draw() sealed;
```

then no derived class of Shape would be allowed to override the draw function. This is useful when you want to ensure a function has common functionality across all derived classes. Using sealed ensures that no one extending your class hierarchy will ever break the functionality provided by the base class.

A sealed function's declaration can never change, so all derived classes use the same function implementation, and calls to sealed functions are resolved at compile time (recall that this is known as static binding). Since the compiler knows that sealed functions cannot be overridden, it can often optimize code by removing calls to sealed functions and replacing them with the expanded code of their declarations at each function-call location—a technique known as *inlining the code*.

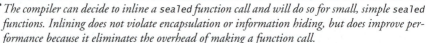

Performance Tip 14.3

The compiler can decide to inline a sealed function call and will do so for small, simple sealed functions. Inlining does not violate encapsulation or information hiding, but does improve performance because it eliminates the overhead of making a function call.

A class that is declared sealed cannot be a base class (i.e., a class cannot extend a sealed class). All functions in a sealed class are implicitly sealed. You can declare a class with sealed as follows:

```
ref class Shape sealed {
    // body of class definition
};
```

This means no class can inherit from Shape. The Visual Studio 2008 compiler issues an error if any class attempts to inherit from Shape. Class String and all C++/CLI value types (declared with value class) are sealed classes.

Common Programming Error 14.6

Attempting to declare a derived class of a sealed class is a compilation error.

Software Engineering Observation 14.12

In the FCL, the vast majority of classes are not declared sealed. This enables inheritance and polymorphism—the fundamental capabilities of object-oriented programming.

Keyword Abstract
Recall that declaring a virtual function with "= 0" marks it as pure. Such functions have no implementation provided by the base class and must be overridden by every derived class. C++/CLI supports this style of declaration for pure virtual functions but also adds a new context-sensitive keyword *abstract* that can be used as an alternative. For instance, the declarations

```
virtual void draw() abstract;
virtual void draw() = 0;
```

are equivalent. Both declarations implicitly make their containing class an abstract class. Some people find that the abstract keyword makes this clearer.

You can also define a class to be abstract. The following class declaration

```
ref class Shape abstract {
    // body of class definition
};
```

defines the Shape class to be abstract. By marking a managed class abstract you clearly communicate that objects of this class cannot be instantiated. However, an abstract managed class is slightly different from a native C++ class that includes a pure virtual function. Declaring a managed class abstract doesn't implicitly make any of the class functions abstract. Unlike native C++, a managed abstract class doesn't have to contain a pure virtual function. Although the class can never be instantiated, you can define a default implementation of every function in an abstract class for any derived classes to use. Consequently, pure virtual functions in an abstract class must be explicitly declared as such with abstract or "= 0". This provides a flexible way to create base classes that won't be instantiated themselves. You can choose which functions, if any, have base-class implementations.

Both sealed and abstract are context-sensitive keywords. They can be used in function declarations only in the places specified above. Elsewhere in a function declaration will result in a compilation error. Outside a function declaration (or class definition) they can be used as normal identifier names to ensure that existing C++ applications continue to function. To avoid confusion, we recommend that you do not use them as identifier names in new applications.

Keyword Interface Class
In addition to sealed and abstract, C++/CLI provides another context-sensitive keyword for use in class definitions. You can declare a class with the *interface class* context-

sensitive keyword. This specifies that every function in the class is a pure virtual function and must be overridden in any derived class. Attempting to define a member function of a class declared with `interface class` will result in a compilation error. The following class declaration

```
interface class IShape {
    // body of class definition
};
```

defines the `IShape` class to be an interface. All functions in this class are implicitly declared with `abstract`. Any class inheriting from `IShape` would be required to override the `draw` function and any other functions declared in `IShape`.

Interfaces are useful for creating a "contract" which all derived classes must follow. You can be sure all classes implementing an interface have some minimum set of functions available without needing to know the exact details of how each is implemented. Also, because C++/CLI doesn't support multiple inheritance, a class will often implement multiple `interface class`es to achieve similar functionality.

Named Overriding

C++/CLI also provides support for *named overriding*. This allows a derived class to override an inherited `virtual` function and provide a new name for the function. The newly named function must still have the same parameter list and return type as the base-class function. For instance, with the managed `Circle` class from above, we could instead override the `draw` function with a newly named function, `display`, as follows:

```
ref class Circle::Shape
{
public:
    virtual void display() = Shape::draw;
// rest of Circle class definition
};
```

Now when we execute the following two lines of code:

```
Shape ^s = gcnew Circle();
s->draw();
```

it will actually call the `display` function of class `Circle`. Inside `Circle` we have mapped `draw` to a newly named `display` function that will be called appropriately. Though we won't discuss it, you can even use named overriding to override multiple functions higher in the class hierarchy. Named overriding is not a technique you will need to use often, but it can come in handy when adding new classes to complex class hierarchies that rely on polymorphism.

14.11 (Optional) Software Engineering Case Study: Incorporating Inheritance into the ATM System

We now revisit our ATM system design to see how it might benefit from inheritance. To apply inheritance, we first look for commonality among classes in the system. We create an inheritance hierarchy to model similar (yet not identical) classes in a more efficient and elegant manner that enables us to process objects of these classes polymorphically. We then modify our class diagram to incorporate the new inheritance relationships. Finally, we demonstrate how our updated design is translated into Visual C++ header files.

In Section 4.13, we encountered the problem of representing a financial transaction in the system. Rather than create one class to represent all transaction types, we decided to create three individual transaction classes—BalanceInquiry, Withdrawal and Deposit— to represent the transactions that the ATM system can perform. Figure 14.26 shows the attributes and operations of these classes. Note that they have one attribute (account-Number) and one operation (execute) in common. Each class requires attribute account-Number to specify the account to which the transaction applies. Each class contains operation execute, which the ATM invokes to perform the transaction. Clearly, Balance Inquiry, Withdrawal and Deposit represent *types of* transactions. Figure 14.26 reveals commonality among the transaction classes, so using inheritance to factor out the common features seems appropriate for designing these classes. We place the common functionality in base class Transaction and derive classes BalanceInquiry, Withdrawal and Deposit from Transaction (Fig. 14.27).

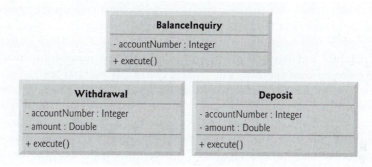

Fig. 14.26 | Attributes and operations of classes BalanceInquiry, Withdrawal and Deposit.

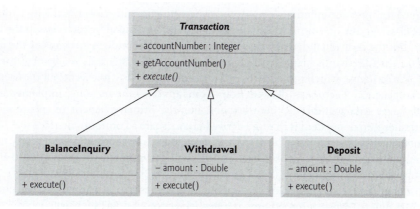

Fig. 14.27 | Class diagram modeling generalization relationship between base class Transaction and derived classes BalanceInquiry, Withdrawal and Deposit.

The UML specifies a relationship called a *generalization* to model inheritance. Figure 14.27 is the class diagram that models the inheritance relationship between base class Transaction and its three derived classes. The arrows with triangular hollow arrowheads indicate that classes BalanceInquiry, Withdrawal and Deposit are derived from class Transaction. Class Transaction is said to be a generalization of its derived classes. The derived classes are said to be *specializations* of class Transaction.

Classes BalanceInquiry, Withdrawal and Deposit share attribute accountNumber, so we factor it out and place it in base class Transaction. We no longer list accountNumber in the second compartment of each derived class, because the three derived classes inherit this attribute from Transaction. Recall, however, that derived classes cannot access private attributes of a base class. So, we include public member function getAccountNumber in class Transaction. Each derived class inherits this member function, enabling the derived class to access its accountNumber as needed to execute a transaction.

According to Fig. 14.26, classes BalanceInquiry, Withdrawal and Deposit also share operation execute, so base class Transaction should contain public member function execute. However, it does not make sense to implement execute in class Transaction, because the functionality that this member function provides depends on the specific type of the actual transaction. We therefore declare member function execute as a pure virtual function in base class Transaction. This makes Transaction an abstract class and forces any class derived from Transaction that must be a concrete class (i.e., BalanceInquiry, Withdrawal and Deposit) to implement pure virtual member function execute to make the derived class concrete. The UML requires that we place abstract class names (and pure virtual functions—*abstract operations* in the UML) in italics, so Transaction and its member function execute appear in italics in Fig. 14.27. Note that operation execute is not italicized in derived classes BalanceInquiry, Withdrawal and Deposit. Each derived class overrides base-class Transaction's execute member function with an appropriate implementation. Note that Fig. 14.27 includes operation execute in the third compartment of classes BalanceInquiry, Withdrawal and Deposit, because each class has a different concrete implementation of the overridden member function.

As you learned in this chapter, a derived class can inherit interface or implementation from a base class. Compared to a hierarchy designed for implementation inheritance, one designed for interface inheritance tends to have its functionality lower in the hierarchy— a base class signifies one or more functions that should be defined by each class in the hierarchy, but the individual derived classes provide their own implementations of the function(s). The inheritance hierarchy designed for the ATM system takes advantage of this type of inheritance, which provides the ATM with an elegant way to execute all transactions "in the general." Each class derived from Transaction inherits some implementation details (e.g., data member accountNumber), but the primary benefit of incorporating inheritance into our system is that the derived classes share a common interface (e.g., pure virtual member function execute). The ATM can aim a Transaction pointer at any transaction, and when the ATM invokes execute through this pointer, the version of execute appropriate to that transaction (i.e., the version implemented in that derived class's .cpp file) runs automatically. For example, suppose a user chooses to perform a balance inquiry. The ATM aims a Transaction pointer at a new object of class BalanceInquiry; the compiler allows this because a BalanceInquiry *is a* Transaction. When the ATM uses this pointer to invoke execute, BalanceInquiry's version of execute is called.

This polymorphic approach also makes the system easily extensible. Should we wish to create a new transaction type (e.g., funds transfer or bill payment), we would just create an additional Transaction derived class that overrides the execute member function with a version appropriate for the new transaction type. We would need to make only minimal changes to the system code to allow users to choose the new transaction type from the main menu and for the ATM to instantiate and execute objects of the new derived class. The ATM could execute transactions of the new type using the current code, because it executes all transactions identically.

As you learned earlier in the chapter, an abstract class like Transaction is one for which you never intend to instantiate objects. An abstract class simply declares common attributes and behaviors for its derived classes in an inheritance hierarchy. Class Transaction defines the concept of what it means to be a transaction that has an account number and executes. You may wonder why we bother to include pure virtual member function execute in class Transaction if execute lacks a concrete implementation. Conceptually, we include this member function because it is the defining behavior of all transactions—executing. Technically, we must include member function execute in base class Transaction so that the ATM (or any other class) can polymorphically invoke each derived class's overridden version of this function through a Transaction pointer or reference.

Derived classes BalanceInquiry, Withdrawal and Deposit inherit attribute account-Number from base class Transaction, but classes Withdrawal and Deposit contain the additional attribute amount that distinguishes them from class BalanceInquiry. Classes Withdrawal and Deposit require this additional attribute to store the amount of money that the user wishes to withdraw or deposit. Class BalanceInquiry has no need for such an attribute and requires only an account number to execute. Even though two of the three Transaction derived classes share this attribute, we do not place it in base class Transaction—we place only features common to *all* the derived classes in the base class, so derived classes do not inherit unnecessary attributes (and operations).

Figure 14.28 updates our model's class diagram to incorporate inheritance and introduce class Transaction. We model an association between class ATM and class Transaction to show that the ATM, at any given moment, either is executing a transaction or is not (i.e., zero or one objects of type Transaction exist in the system at a time). Because a Withdrawal is a type of Transaction, we no longer draw an association line directly between class ATM and class Withdrawal—derived class Withdrawal inherits base-class Transaction's association with class ATM. Derived classes BalanceInquiry and Deposit also inherit this association, which replaces the previously omitted associations between classes BalanceInquiry and Deposit and class ATM. Note again the use of triangular hollow arrowheads to indicate the specializations of class Transaction, as indicated in Fig. 14.27.

We also add an association between class Transaction and the BankDatabase (Fig. 14.28). All Transactions require a reference to the BankDatabase so they can access and modify account information. Each Transaction derived class inherits this reference, so we no longer model the association between class Withdrawal and the BankDatabase. Note that the association between class Transaction and the BankDatabase replaces the previously omitted associations between classes BalanceInquiry and Deposit and the BankDatabase.

We include an association between class Transaction and the Screen because all Transactions display output to the user via the Screen. Each derived class inherits this

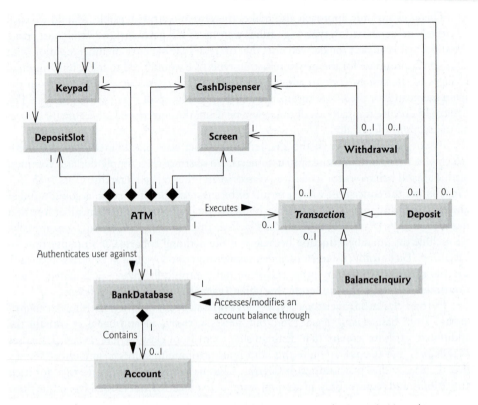

Fig. 14.28 | Class diagram of the ATM system (incorporating inheritance). Note that abstract class name `Transaction` appears in italics.

association. Therefore, we no longer include the association previously modeled between `Withdrawal` and the `Screen`. Class `Withdrawal` still participates in associations with the `CashDispenser` and the `Keypad`. We do not move these associations to base class `Transaction`, because the association with the `Keypad` applies only to classes `Withdrawal` and `Deposit`, and the association with the `CashDispenser` applies only to class `Withdrawal`.

Our class diagram incorporating inheritance (Fig. 14.28) also models `Deposit` and `BalanceInquiry`. We show associations between `Deposit` and both the `DepositSlot` and the `Keypad`. Note that class `BalanceInquiry` takes part in no associations other than those inherited from class `Transaction`—a `BalanceInquiry` interacts only with the `BankDatabase` and the `Screen`.

The class diagram of Fig. 10.20 showed attributes and operations with visibility markers. Now we present a modified class diagram in Fig. 14.29 that includes abstract base class `Transaction`. This abbreviated diagram does not show inheritance relationships (these appear in Fig. 14.28), but instead shows the attributes and operations after we have employed inheritance in our system. Note that abstract class name `Transaction` and abstract operation name `execute` in class `Transaction` appear in italics. To save space, as we did in Fig. 5.24, we do not include those attributes shown by associations in Fig. 14.28—we do, however, include them in the Visual C++ implementation in

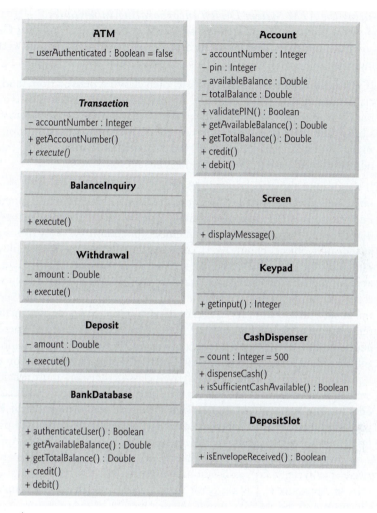

Fig. 14.29 | Class diagram after incorporating inheritance into the system.

Appendix F. We also omit all operation parameters, as we did in Fig. 10.20— incorporating inheritance does not affect the parameters already modeled in Figs. 7.35–7.38.

Software Engineering Observation 14.13

A complete class diagram shows all the associations among classes and all the attributes and operations for each class. When the number of class attributes, operations and associations is substantial (as in Figs. 14.28 and 14.29), a good practice that promotes readability is to divide this information between two class diagrams—one focusing on associations and the other on attributes and operations. However, when examining classes modeled in this fashion, it is crucial to consider both class diagrams to get a complete view of the classes. For example, one must refer to Fig. 14.28 to observe the inheritance relationship between Transaction and its derived classes that is omitted from Fig. 14.29.

Implementing the ATM System Design Incorporating Inheritance

In Section 10.12, we began implementing the ATM system design in Visual C++ code. We now modify our implementation to incorporate inheritance, using class `Withdrawal` as an example.

1. If a class A is a generalization of class B, then class B is derived from (and is a specialization of) class A. For example, abstract base class `Transaction` is a generalization of class `Withdrawal`. Thus, class `Withdrawal` is derived from (and is a specialization of) class `Transaction`. Figure 14.30 contains a portion of class `Withdrawal`'s header file, in which the class definition indicates the inheritance relationship between `Withdrawal` and `Transaction` (line 9).

2. If class A is an abstract class and class B is derived from class A, then class B must implement the pure `virtual` functions of class A if class B is to be a concrete class. For example, class `Transaction` contains pure `virtual` function execute, so class `Withdrawal` must implement this member function if we want to instantiate a `Withdrawal` object. Figure 14.31 contains the Visual C++ header file for class `Withdrawal` from Figs. 14.28 and 14.29. Class `Withdrawal` inherits data member `accountNumber` from base class `Transaction`, so `Withdrawal` does not declare this data member. Class `Withdrawal` also inherits references to the `Screen` and the `BankDatabase` from its base class `Transaction`, so we do not include these references in our code. Figure 14.29 specifies attribute amount and operation execute for class `Withdrawal`. Line 19 of Fig. 14.31 declares a data member for attribute amount. Line 16 contains the function prototype for operation execute. Recall that, to be a concrete class, derived class `Withdrawal` must provide a concrete implementation of the pure `virtual` function execute in base class `Transaction`. The prototype in line 16 signals your intent to override the base class pure `virtual` function. You must provide this prototype if you will provide an implementation in the `.cpp` file. We present this implementation in Appendix F. The keypad and cashDispenser references (lines 20–21) are data members derived from `Withdrawal`'s associations in Fig. 14.28. In the implementation of this class in Appendix F, a constructor initializes these references to actual objects. Once again, to be able to compile the declarations of the references in lines 20–21, we include the forward declarations in lines 8–9.

```
1   // Fig. 14.30: Withdrawal.h
2   // Definition of class Withdrawal that represents a withdrawal transaction
3   #ifndef WITHDRAWAL_H
4   #define WITHDRAWAL_H
5
6   #include "Transaction.h" // Transaction class definition
7
8   // class Withdrawal derives from base class Transaction
9   class Withdrawal : public Transaction
10  {
11  }; // end class Withdrawal
12
13  #endif // WITHDRAWAL_H
```

Fig. 14.30 | `Withdrawal` class definition that derives from `Transaction`.

```
 1   // Fig. 14.31: Withdrawal.h
 2   // Definition of class Withdrawal that represents a withdrawal transaction
 3   #ifndef WITHDRAWAL_H
 4   #define WITHDRAWAL_H
 5
 6   #include "Transaction.h" // Transaction class definition
 7
 8   class Keypad; // forward declaration of class Keypad
 9   class CashDispenser; // forward declaration of class CashDispenser
10
11   // class Withdrawal derives from base class Transaction
12   class Withdrawal : public Transaction
13   {
14   public:
15      // member function overriding execute in base class Transaction
16      virtual void execute(); // perform the transaction
17   private:
18      // attributes
19      double amount; // amount to withdraw
20      Keypad &keypad; // reference to ATM's keypad
21      CashDispenser &cashDispenser; // reference to ATM's cash dispenser
22   }; // end class Withdrawal
23
24   #endif // WITHDRAWAL_H
```

Fig. 14.31 | `Withdrawal` class header file based on Fig. 14.28 and Fig. 14.29.

ATM Case Study Wrap-Up

This concludes our object-oriented design of the ATM system. A complete Visual C++ implementation of the ATM system in 877 lines of code appears in Appendix F. This working implementation uses key programming notions, including classes, objects, encapsulation, visibility, composition, inheritance and polymorphism. The code is abundantly commented and conforms to the coding practices you've learned. Mastering this code is a wonderful capstone experience for you after studying Chapters 1, 3–8, 10, 14.

Software Engineering Case Study Self-Review Exercises

14.1   The UML uses an arrow with a _____ to indicate a generalization relationship.
   a) solid filled arrowhead
   b) triangular hollow arrowhead
   c) diamond-shaped hollow arrowhead
   d) stick arrowhead

14.2   State whether the following statement is *true* or *false*, and if *false*, explain why: The UML requires that we underline abstract class names and operation names.

14.3   Write a Visual C++ header file to begin implementing the design for class `Transaction` specified in Fig. 14.28 and Fig. 14.29. Be sure to include `private` references based on class `Transaction`'s associations. Also be sure to include `public` *get* functions for any of the `private` data members that the derived classes must access to perform their tasks.

Answers to Software Engineering Case Study Self-Review Exercises

14.1   b.

14.2 False. The UML requires that we italicize abstract class names and operation names.

14.3 The design for class Transaction yields the header file in Fig. 14.32. In the implementation in Appendix F, a constructor initializes private reference attributes screen and bankDatabase to actual objects, and member functions getScreen and getBankDatabase access these attributes. These member functions allow classes derived from Transaction to access the ATM's screen and interact with the bank's database.

```cpp
1   // Fig. 14.32: Transaction.h
2   // Transaction abstract base class definition.
3   #ifndef TRANSACTION_H
4   #define TRANSACTION_H
5
6   class Screen; // forward declaration of class Screen
7   class BankDatabase; // forward declaration of class BankDatabase
8
9   class Transaction
10  {
11  public:
12     int getAccountNumber(); // return account number
13     Screen &getScreen(); // return reference to screen
14     BankDatabase &getBankDatabase(); // return reference to bank database
15
16     // pure virtual function to perform the transaction
17     virtual void execute() = 0; // overridden in derived classes
18  private:
19     int accountNumber; // indicates account involved
20     Screen &screen; // reference to the screen of the ATM
21     BankDatabase &bankDatabase; // reference to the account info database
22  }; // end class Transaction
23
24  #endif // TRANSACTION_H
```

Fig. 14.32 | Transaction class header file based on Fig. 14.28 and Fig. 14.29.

14.12 Wrap-Up

In this chapter we discussed polymorphism, which enables us to "program in the general" rather than "program in the specific," and we showed how this makes programs more extensible. We began with an example of how polymorphism would allow a screen manager to display several "space" objects. We then demonstrated how base-class and derived-class pointers can be aimed at base-class and derived-class objects. We said that aiming base-class pointers at base-class objects is natural, as is aiming derived-class pointers at derived-class objects. Aiming base-class pointers at derived-class objects is also natural because a derived-class object *is an* object of its base class. You learned why aiming derived-class pointers at base-class objects is dangerous and why the compiler disallows such assignments. We introduced virtual functions, which enable the proper functions to be called when objects at various levels of an inheritance hierarchy are referenced (at execution time) via base-class pointers. This is known as dynamic or late binding. We then discussed pure virtual functions (virtual functions that do not provide an implementation) and abstract classes (classes with one or more pure virtual functions). You learned that abstract classes cannot be used to instantiate objects, while concrete classes can. We then demonstrated using abstract classes in an inheritance hierarchy. You learned how polymorphism works "under the hood" with *vtables* that are created by the compiler. We discussed downcasting base-class pointers to derived-class pointers to enable a program to call derived-class-only member functions. The chapter discussed the use of `virtual` destructors, and how they ensure that all appropriate destructors in an inheritance hierarchy run on a derived-class object when that object is deleted via a base-class pointer. Finally, we introduced the C++/CLI specific syntax and keywords for taking advantage of polymorphism with managed code.

In the next chapter, we discuss templates, a sophisticated feature of Visual C++ that enables programmers to define a family of related classes or functions with a single code segment.

Summary

Section 14.1 Introduction
- Polymorphism enables us to "program in the general" rather than "program in the specific."
- Polymorphism enables us to write programs that process objects of classes that are part of the same class hierarchy as if they were all objects of the hierarchy's base class.
- With polymorphism, we can design and implement systems that are easily extensible—new classes can be added with little or no modification to the general portions of the program, as long as the new classes are part of the inheritance hierarchy that the program processes generically. The only parts of a program that must be altered to accommodate new classes are those that require direct knowledge of the new classes that you add to the hierarchy.
- Runtime type information (RTTI) and dynamic casting enable a program to determine the type of an object at execution time and act on that object accordingly.

Section 14.2 Polymorphism Examples
- With polymorphism, one function can cause different actions to occur, depending on the type of the object on which the function is invoked.
- With `virtual` functions and polymorphism, it becomes possible to design and implement systems that are more easily extensible. Programs can be written to process objects of types that may not exist when the program is under development.

Section 14.3 Relationships Among Objects in an Inheritance Hierarchy
- Visual C++ enables polymorphism—the ability for objects of different classes related by inheritance to respond differently to the same member-function call.
- Polymorphism is implemented via `virtual` functions and dynamic binding.
- When a request is made through a base-class pointer or reference to use a `virtual` function, Visual C++ chooses the correct overridden function in the appropriate derived class associated with the object.
- If a `virtual` function is called by referencing a specific object by name and using the dot member-selection operator, the reference is resolved at compile time (this is called static binding); the `virtual` function that is called is the one defined for the class of that particular object.
- Derived classes can provide their own implementations of a base-class `virtual` function if necessary, but if they do not, the base class's implementation is used.

Section 14.4 Type Fields and switch Statements

- Polymorphic programming with virtual functions can eliminate the need for switch logic. You can use the virtual function mechanism to perform the equivalent logic automatically, thus avoiding the kinds of errors typically associated with switch logic.

Section 14.5 Abstract Classes and Pure virtual Functions

- In many situations it is useful to define abstract classes for which you never intend to create objects. Because these are used only as base classes, we refer to them as abstract base classes. No objects of an abstract class may be instantiated.

- Classes from which objects can be instantiated are called concrete classes.

- A class is made abstract by declaring one or more of its virtual functions to be pure. A pure virtual function is one with a pure specifier (= 0) in its declaration.

- If a class is derived from a class with a pure virtual function and that derived class does not supply a definition for that pure virtual function, then that virtual function remains pure in the derived class. Consequently, the derived class is also an abstract class.

- Although we cannot instantiate objects of abstract base classes, we can declare pointers and references to objects of abstract base classes. Such pointers and references can be used to enable polymorphic manipulations of derived-class objects instantiated from concrete derived classes.

Section 14.7 (Optional) Polymorphism, Virtual Functions and Dynamic Binding "Under the Hood"

- Dynamic binding requires that at runtime, the call to a virtual member function be routed to the virtual function version appropriate for the class. A virtual function table called the *vtable* is implemented as an array containing function pointers. Each class with virtual functions has a *vtable*. For each virtual function in the class, the *vtable* has an entry containing a function pointer to the version of the virtual function to use for an object of that class. The virtual function to use for a particular class could be the function defined in that class, or it could be a function inherited either directly or indirectly from a base class higher in the hierarchy.

- When a base class provides a virtual member function, derived classes can override the virtual function, but they do not have to override it. Thus, a derived class can use a base class's version of a virtual function.

- Each object of a class with virtual functions contains a pointer to the *vtable* for that class. When a function call is made from a base-class pointer to a derived-class object, the appropriate function pointer in the *vtable* is obtained and dereferenced to complete the call at execution time. This *vtable* lookup and pointer dereferencing require nominal runtime overhead.

- Any class that has one or more 0 pointers in its *vtable* is an abstract class. Classes without any 0 *vtable* pointers are concrete classes.

- New kinds of classes are regularly added to systems. New classes are accommodated by dynamic binding (also called late binding). The type of an object need not be known at compile time for a virtual-function call to be compiled. At runtime, the appropriate member function will be called for the object to which the pointer points.

Section 14.8 Case Study: Payroll System Using Polymorphism and Runtime Type Information with Downcasting, dynamic_cast, typeid and type_info

- Operator dynamic_cast checks the type of the object to which the pointer points, then determines whether this type has an *is-a* relationship with the type to which the pointer is being converted. If there is an *is-a* relationship, dynamic_cast returns the object's address. If not, dynamic_cast returns 0.

- Operator `typeid` returns a reference to an object of class `type_info` that contains information about the type of its operand, including the name of the type. To use `typeid`, the program must include header file `<typeinfo>`.

- When invoked, `type_info` member function `name` returns a pointer-based string that contains the name of the type that the `type_info` object represents.

- Operators `dynamic_cast` and `typeid` are part of Visual C++'s runtime type information (RTTI) feature, which allows a program to determine an object's type at runtime.

Section 14.9 Virtual Destructors

- Declare the base-class destructor `virtual` if the class contains `virtual` functions. This makes all derived-class destructors virtual, even though they do not have the same name as the base-class destructor. If an object in the hierarchy is destroyed explicitly by applying the `delete` operator to a base-class pointer to a derived-class object, the destructor for the appropriate class is called. After a derived-class destructor runs, the destructors for all of that class's base classes run all the way up the hierarchy—the root class's destructor runs last.

Section 14.10 Polymorphism in C++/CLI

- A managed class inheriting `virtual` functions from another managed class must explicitly declare each overloaded function with `virtual` and `override`. Use `new` in place of `override` to stop the derived-class function from overriding the base-class function and instead make a new *vtable* entry.

- Declare a function `abstract` to force any derived classes to provide an implementation. An abstract function cannot be defined in the base class. Declare a function `sealed` to not allow a derived class to override the function.

- Declaring a class `abstract` means you cannot instantiate objects of that type, use it as a parameter type, use it as a return type, or cast to that type.

- Interfaces are declared using `interface class` preceding the class name. This implicitly makes all the class functions pure `virtual` functions and requires that any derived class override them. You cannot create objects of an `interface class`.

Terminology

abstract
abstract base class
abstract class
base-class pointer to a base-class object
base-class pointer to a derived-class object
concrete class
dangerous pointer manipulation
derived-class pointer to a base-class object
derived-class pointer to a derived-class object
downcasting
dynamic binding
dynamic casting
dynamic_cast
dynamically determine function to execute
flow of control of a `virtual` function call
implementation inheritance
interface class declaration
interface inheritance

iterator class
late binding
named overriding
name function of class `type_info`
new in function declarations
nonvirtual destructor
object's *vtable* pointer
offset into a *vtable*
override
override a function
polymorphic programming
polymorphism
polymorphism as an alternative to `switch` logic
programming in the general
programming in the specific
pure specifier (with virtual functions)
pure `virtual` function
RTTI (runtime type information)

sealed	virtual destructor
static binding	virtual function
switch logic	virtual function table (*vtable*)
type_info class	virtual keyword
typeid operator	*vtable*
<typeinfo> header file	*vtable* pointer

Self-Review Exercises

14.1 Fill in the blanks in each of the following statements:

a) Treating a base-class object as a(n) _____ can cause errors.

b) Polymorphism helps eliminate _____ logic.

c) If a class contains at least one pure virtual function, it is a(n) _____ class.

d) Classes from which objects can be instantiated are called _____ classes.

e) Operator _____ can be used to downcast base-class pointers safely.

f) Operator typeid returns a reference to a(n) _____ object.

g) _____ involves using a base-class pointer or reference to invoke virtual functions on base-class and derived-class objects.

h) Overridable functions are declared using keyword _____.

i) Casting a base-class pointer to a derived-class pointer is called _____.

14.2 State whether each of the following is *true* or *false*. If *false*, explain why.

a) All virtual functions in an abstract base class must be declared as pure virtual functions.

b) Referring to a derived-class object with a base-class handle is dangerous.

c) A class is made abstract by declaring that class virtual.

d) If a base class declares a pure virtual function, a derived class must implement that function to become a concrete class.

e) Polymorphic programming can eliminate the need for switch logic.

14.3 Regarding C++/CLI, state whether each of the following is *true* or *false*. If *false*, explain why.

a) When overriding a base-class virtual function you don't need to use any explicit overriding syntax; the compiler will implicitly override the base-class virtual function.

b) Classes declared abstract cannot be instantiated but may provide implementations for functions in the abstract class.

c) There is no way to define a class or function in a way that ensures no class will derive from it or override it.

d) Assume we have defined a base class I that is declared with interface class. We also have defined a ref class D derived from I. D must override every function of I in order for D to be a concrete class.

Answers to Self-Review Exercises

14.1   a) derived-class object. b) switch. c) abstract. d) concrete. e) dynamic_cast. f) type_info. g) Polymorphism. h) virtual. i) downcasting.

14.2   a) False. An abstract base class can include virtual functions with implementations. b) False. Referring to a base-class object with a derived-class handle is dangerous. c) False. Classes are never declared virtual. Rather, a class is made abstract by including at least one pure virtual function in the class. d) True. e) True.

14.3   a) False. C++/CLI requires explicit overriding. You must declare an overriding function with virtual and either override or new. b) True. c) False. Declare a class sealed to ensure no class derives from it. Declare a function sealed to ensure no derived class overrides it. d) True.

Exercises

14.4 How is it that polymorphism enables you to program "in the general" rather than "in the specific"? Discuss the key advantages of programming "in the general."

14.5 Discuss the problems of programming with switch logic. Explain why polymorphism can be an effective alternative to using switch logic.

14.6 Distinguish between inheriting interface and inheriting implementation. How do inheritance hierarchies designed for inheriting interface differ from those designed for inheriting implementation?

14.7 What are virtual functions? Describe a circumstance in which virtual functions would be appropriate.

14.8 Distinguish between static binding and dynamic binding. Explain the use of virtual functions and the *vtable* in dynamic binding.

14.9 Distinguish between virtual functions and pure virtual functions.

14.10 Suggest one or more levels of abstract base classes for the Shape hierarchy discussed in this chapter and shown in Fig. 13.3. (The first level is Shape, and the second level consists of the classes TwoDimensionalShape and ThreeDimensionalShape.)

14.11 How does polymorphism promote extensibility?

14.12 You have been asked to develop a flight simulator that will have elaborate graphical outputs. Explain why polymorphic programming could be especially effective for a problem of this nature.

14.13 *(Payroll System Modification)* Modify the payroll system of Figs. 14.13–14.23 to include private data member birthDate in class Employee. Use class Date from Figs. 12.12–12.13 to represent an employee's birthday. Assume that payroll is processed once per month. Create a vector of Employee references to store the various employee objects. In a loop, calculate the payroll for each Employee (polymorphically), and add a $100.00 bonus to the person's payroll amount if the current month is the month in which the Employee's birthday occurs.

14.14 *(Shape Hierarchy)* Implement the Shape hierarchy designed in Exercise 13.7 (which is based on the hierarchy in Fig. 13.3). Each TwoDimensionalShape should contain function getArea to calculate the area of the two-dimensional shape. Each ThreeDimensionalShape should have member functions getArea and getVolume to calculate the surface area and volume, respectively, of the three-dimensional shape. Create a program that uses a vector of Shape pointers to objects of each concrete class in the hierarchy. The program should print the object to which each vector element points. Also, in the loop that processes all the shapes in the vector, determine whether each shape is a TwoDimensionalShape or a ThreeDimensionalShape. If a shape is a TwoDimensionalShape, display its area. If a shape is a ThreeDimensionalShape, display its area and volume.

14.15 *(Polymorphic Screen Manager Using Shape Hierarchy)* Develop a basic graphics package. Use the Shape hierarchy implemented in Exercise 14.14. Limit yourself to two-dimensional shapes such as squares, rectangles, triangles and circles. Interact with the user. Let the user specify the position, size, shape and fill characters to be used in drawing each shape. The user can specify more than one of the same shape. As you create each shape, place a Shape * pointer to each new Shape object into an array. Each Shape class should now have its own draw member function. Write a polymorphic screen manager that walks through the array, sending draw messages to each object in the array to form a screen image. Redraw the screen image each time the user specifies an additional shape.

14.16 *(Package Inheritance Hierarchy)* Use the Package inheritance hierarchy created in Exercise 13.9 to create a program that displays the address information and calculates the shipping costs for several Packages. The program should contain a vector of Package pointers to objects of classes `TwoDayPackage` and `OvernightPackage`. Loop through the vector to process the `Package`s polymorphically. For each `Package`, invoke *get* functions to obtain the address information of the sender and the recipient, then print the two addresses as they would appear on mailing labels. Also, call each `Package`'s `calculateCost` member function and print the result. Keep track of the total shipping cost for all `Package`s in the vector, and display this total when the loop terminates.

14.17 *(Polymorphic Banking Program Using `Account` Hierarchy)* Develop a polymorphic banking program using the `Account` hierarchy created in Exercise 13.10. Create a vector of `Account` pointers to `SavingsAccount` and `CheckingAccount` objects. For each `Account` in the vector, allow the user to specify an amount of money to withdraw from the `Account` using member function `debit` and an amount of money to deposit into the `Account` using member function `credit`. As you process each `Account`, determine its type. If an `Account` is a `SavingsAccount`, calculate the amount of interest owed to the `Account` using member function `calculateInterest`, then add the interest to the account balance using member function `credit`. After processing an `Account`, print the updated account balance obtained by invoking base-class member function `getBalance`.

14.18 *(Shape Hierarchy)* Implement the `Shape` hierarchy designed in Exercise 13.7 (which is based on the hierarchy in Fig. 13.3) using C++/CLI. Each `TwoDimensionalShape` should contain function `getArea` to calculate the area of the two-dimensional shape. Each `ThreeDimensionalShape` should have member functions `getArea` and `getVolume` to calculate the surface area and volume, respectively, of the three-dimensional shape. Create a program that uses a managed array of `Shape` handles to objects of each concrete class in the hierarchy. The program should print the object to which each array element points. Also, in the loop that processes all the shapes in the array, determine whether each shape is a `TwoDimensionalShape` or a `ThreeDimensionalShape`. If a shape is a `TwoDimensionalShape`, display its area. If a shape is a `ThreeDimensionalShape`, display its area and volume. Override the .NET `ToString` function using `String::Format` to enable printing of each object type.

Templates and Generics

*Behind that outside pattern
the dim shapes get clearer
every day.
It is always the same shape,
only very numerous.*
—Charlotte Perkins Gilman

*Every man of genius sees the
world at a different angle
from his fellows.*
—Havelock Ellis

*…our special individuality,
as distinguished from our
generic humanity.*
—Oliver Wendell Holmes, Sr

OBJECTIVES

In this chapter you'll learn:

- To use function templates to conveniently create a group of related (overloaded) functions.

- To distinguish between function templates and function-template specializations.

- To use class templates to create a group of related types.

- To distinguish between class templates and class-template specializations.

- To overload function templates.

- To understand the relationships among templates, friends, inheritance and static members.

- To use generic managed classes to create a group of related types.

- To use generic type constraints to restrict the types that may be used in generic code.

15.1 Introduction

In this chapter, we discuss one of Visual C++'s more powerful software-reuse features, namely *templates*. *Function templates* and *class templates* enable programmers to specify, with a single code segment, an entire range of related (overloaded) functions—called *function-template specializations*—or an entire range of related classes—called *class-template specializations*. This technique is called *generic programming*.

We might write a single function template for an array-sort function, then have Visual C++ generate separate function-template specializations that will sort `int` arrays, `float` arrays, `string` arrays and so on. We introduced function templates in Chapter 7. We present an additional discussion and example in this chapter.

We might write a single class template for a stack class, then have Visual C++ generate separate class-template specializations, such as a stack-of-`int` class, a stack-of-`float` class, a stack-of-`string` class and so on.

Note the distinction between templates and template specializations: Function templates and class templates are like stencils out of which we trace shapes; function-template specializations and class-template specializations are like the separate tracings that all have the same shape, but could, for example, be drawn in different colors.

In this chapter, we present a function template and a class template. We also consider the relationships between templates and other Visual C++ features, such as overloading, inheritance, friends and `static` members. The design and details of the template mechanisms discussed here are based on the work of Bjarne Stroustrup as presented in his paper, *Parameterized Types for C++*, and as published in the *Proceedings of the USENIX C++ Conference* held in Denver, Colorado, in October 1988.

This chapter provides an introduction to templates. Chapter 23, Standard Template Library (STL), presents an in-depth treatment of the template container classes, iterators and algorithms of the STL, including dozens of live-code template-based examples illustrating more sophisticated template-programming techniques than those used here.

Software Engineering Observation 15.1

Most C++ compilers require the complete definition of a template to appear in the client source-code file that uses the template. For this reason and for reusability, templates are often defined in header files, which are then #included into the appropriate client source-code files. For class templates, this means that the member functions are also defined in the header file.

This chapter also introduces .NET *generics* in C++/CLI—the managed implementation of generic programming, which is similar to native C++ templates. Generics may be used only with managed classes. To illustrate the similarities and differences between templates and generics, we reimplement our Stack class template using C++/CLI generics.

15.2 Function Templates

Overloaded functions normally perform *similar* or *identical* operations on different types of data. If the operations are *identical* for each type, they can be expressed more compactly and conveniently using function templates. Initially, you write a single function-template definition. Based on the argument types provided explicitly or inferred from calls to this function, the compiler generates separate source-code functions (i.e., function-template specializations) to handle each function call appropriately. In C, this task can be performed using *macros* created with the preprocessor directive #define (see Appendix E, Preprocessor). However, macros can have serious side effects and do not enable the compiler to perform type checking. Function templates provide a compact solution, like macros, but enable full type checking.

Error-Prevention Tip 15.1

Function templates, like macros, enable software reuse. Unlike macros, function templates help eliminate many types of errors through the scrutiny of full Visual C++ type checking.

All *function-template definitions* begin with keyword **template** followed by a list of *template parameters* to the function template enclosed in *angle brackets* (< and >); each template parameter that represents a type must be preceded by either of the interchangeable keywords class or **typename**, as in

> **template**< **typename** T >

or

> **template**< **class** ElementType >

or

> **template**< **typename** BorderType, **typename** FillType >

The type template parameters of a function-template definition are used to specify the types of the arguments to the function, to specify the return type of the function and to declare variables within the function. The function definition follows and appears like any other function definition. Note that keywords typename and class used to specify function-template parameters actually mean "any built-in type or user-defined type."

Common Programming Error 15.1

Not placing keyword class or keyword typename before each type template parameter of a function template is a syntax error.

Example: Function Template `printArray`

Let us examine function template `printArray` in Fig. 15.1, lines 8–15. Function template `printArray` declares (line 8) a single template parameter T (T can be any valid identifier) for the type of the array to be printed by function `printArray`; T is referred to as a *type template parameter*, or type parameter. You'll see nontype template parameters in Section 15.5.

```cpp
1   // Fig. 15.1: TemplateFunctions.cpp
2   // Using template functions.
3   #include <iostream>
4   using std::cout;
5   using std::endl;
6
7   // function template printArray definition
8   template< typename T >
9   void printArray( const T * const array, const int count )
10  {
11     for ( int i = 0; i < count; i++ )
12        cout << array[ i ] << " ";
13
14     cout << endl;
15  } // end function template printArray
16
17  int main()
18  {
19     const int ACOUNT = 5; // size of array a
20     const int BCOUNT = 7; // size of array b
21     const int CCOUNT = 6; // size of array c
22
23     int a[ ACOUNT ] = { 1, 2, 3, 4, 5 };
24     double b[ BCOUNT ] = { 1.1, 2.2, 3.3, 4.4, 5.5, 6.6, 7.7 };
25     char c[ CCOUNT ] = "HELLO"; // 6th position for null
26
27     cout << "Array a contains:" << endl;
28
29     // call integer function-template specialization
30     printArray( a, ACOUNT );
31
32     cout << "Array b contains:" << endl;
33
34     // call double function-template specialization
35     printArray( b, BCOUNT );
36
37     cout << "Array c contains:" << endl;
38
39     // call character function-template specialization
40     printArray( c, CCOUNT );
41     return 0;
42  } // end main
```

Fig. 15.1 | Function-template specializations of function template `printArray`. (Part 1 of 2.)

```
Array a contains:
1 2 3 4 5
Array b contains:
1.1 2.2 3.3 4.4 5.5 6.6 7.7
Array c contains:
H E L L O
```

Fig. 15.1 | Function-template specializations of function template `printArray`. (Part 2 of 2.)

When the compiler detects a `printArray` function invocation in the client program (e.g., lines 30, 35 and 40), the compiler uses its overload-resolution capabilities to find a definition of function `printArray` that best matches the function call. In this case, the only `printArray` function with the appropriate number of parameters is the `printArray` function template (lines 8–15). Consider the function call at line 30. The compiler compares the type of `printArray`'s first argument (`int * const` at line 30) to the `printArray` function template's first parameter (`const T * const` at line 9) and deduces that replacing the type parameter `T` with `int` would make the argument consistent with the parameter. Then, the compiler substitutes `int` for `T` throughout the template definition and compiles a `printArray` specialization that can display an array of `int` values. In Fig. 15.1, the compiler creates three `printArray` specializations—one that expects an `int` array, one that expects a `double` array and one that expects a `char` array. For example, the function-template specialization for type `int` is

```
void printArray( const int * const array, const int count )
{
   for ( int i = 0; i < count; i++ )
      cout << array[ i ] << " ";

   cout << endl;
} // end function printArray
```

The name of a template parameter can be declared only once in the template parameter list of a template header but can be used repeatedly in the function's header and body. Template parameter names among function templates need not be unique.

Figure 15.1 demonstrates function template `printArray` (lines 8–15). The program begins by declaring five-element `int` array a, seven-element `double` array b and six-element `char` array c (lines 23–25, respectively). Then, the program outputs each array by calling `printArray`—once with a first argument a of type `int * const` (line 30), once with a first argument b of type `double * const` (line 35) and once with a first argument c of type `char * const` (line 40). The call in line 30, for example, causes the compiler to infer that `T` is `int` and to instantiate a `printArray` function-template specialization, for which type parameter `T` is `int`. The call in line 35 causes the compiler to infer that `T` is `double` and to instantiate a second `printArray` function-template specialization, for which type parameter `T` is `double`. The call in line 40 causes the compiler to infer that `T` is `char` and to instantiate a third `printArray` function-template specialization, for which type parameter `T` is `char`. It is important to note that if `T` (line 8) represents a user-defined type (which it does not in Fig. 15.1), there must be an overloaded stream insertion operator for that type; otherwise, the first stream insertion operator in line 12 will not compile.

Common Programming Error 15.2

If a template is invoked with a user-defined type, and if that template uses functions or operators (e.g., ==, +, <=) with objects of that class type, then those functions or operators must be overloaded for the user-defined type. Forgetting to define the functions or overload such operators causes compilation errors.

In this example, the template mechanism saves you from having to write three separate overloaded functions with prototypes

```
void printArray( const int * const, int );
void printArray( const double * const, int );
void printArray( const char * const, int );
```

that all use the same code, except for type T (as used in line 9).

Performance Tip 15.1

Although templates offer software-reusability benefits, remember that multiple function-template specializations and class-template specializations are instantiated in a program (at compile time), despite the fact that the templates are written only once. These copies can consume considerable memory. This is not normally an issue, though, because the code generated by the template is the same size as the code you would have written to produce the separate overloaded functions.

15.3 Overloading Function Templates

Function templates and overloading are intimately related. The function-template specializations generated from a function template all have the same name, so the compiler uses overloading resolution to invoke the proper function.

A function template may be overloaded in several ways. We can provide other function templates that specify the same function name but different function parameters. For example, function template printArray of Fig. 15.1 could be overloaded with another printArray function template with additional parameters lowSubscript and highSubscript to specify the portion of the array to output (see Exercise 15.6).

A function template also can be overloaded by providing nontemplate functions with the same function name but different function parameters. For example, function template printArray of Fig. 15.1 could be overloaded with a nontemplate version that specifically prints an array of character strings in neat, tabular format (see Exercise 15.7).

The compiler performs a matching process to determine what function to call when a function is invoked. First, the compiler finds all function templates that match the function named in the function call and creates specializations based on the arguments in the function call. Then, the compiler finds all the ordinary functions that match the function named in the function call. If one of the ordinary functions or function-template specializations is the best match for the function call, that ordinary function or specialization is used. If an ordinary function and a specialization are equally good matches for the function call, then the ordinary function is used. Otherwise, if there are multiple matches for the function call, the compiler considers the call to be ambiguous, and the compiler generates an error message.

Common Programming Error 15.3

A compilation error occurs if no matching function definition can be found for a particular function call or if there are multiple matches that the compiler considers ambiguous.

15.4 Class Templates

It is possible to understand the concept of a "stack" (a data structure into which we insert items at the top and retrieve those items in last-in, first-out order) independent of the type of the items being placed in the stack. However, to instantiate a stack, a data type must be specified. This creates a wonderful opportunity for software reusability. We need the means for describing the notion of a stack generically and instantiating classes that are type-specific versions of this generalized stack class. Visual C++ provides this capability through class templates.

Software Engineering Observation 15.2

Class templates encourage software reusability by enabling type-specific versions of parameterized types to be instantiated.

Class templates are called ***parameterized types***, because they require one or more type parameters to specify how to customize a "generic class" template to form a class-template specialization.

To produce a variety of class-template specializations you write only one class-template definition. Each time an additional class-template specialization is needed, you use a concise, simple notation, and the compiler writes the source code for the specialization you require. One Stack class template, for example, could thus become the basis for creating many Stack classes (such as "Stack of double," "Stack of int," "Stack of char," "Stack of Employee," etc.) used in a program.

Creating Class Template Stack< T >

Note the Stack class-template definition in Fig. 15.2. It looks like a conventional class definition, except that it is preceded by the header (line 6)

```
template< typename T >
```

to specify a class-template definition with type parameter T which acts as a placeholder for the type of the Stack class to be created. You need not specifically use identifier T—any valid identifier can be used. The type of element to be stored on this Stack is mentioned generically as T throughout the Stack class header and member-function definitions. In a moment, we show how T becomes associated with a specific type, such as double or int. Due to the way this class template is designed, there are two constraints for nonfundamental data types used with this Stack—they must have a default constructor (for use in line 44 to create the array that stores the stack elements), and they must support the assignment operator (lines 56 and 70).

```
1   // Fig. 15.2: Stack.h
2   // Stack class template.
3   #ifndef STACK_H
4   #define STACK_H
5
6   template< typename T >
7   class Stack
8   {
```

Fig. 15.2 | Class template Stack. (Part 1 of 3.)

```
 9    public:
10       Stack( int = 10 ); // default constructor (Stack size 10)
11
12       // destructor
13       ~Stack()
14       {
15          delete [] stackPtr; // deallocate internal space for Stack
16       } // end ~Stack destructor
17
18       bool push( const T & ); // push an element onto the Stack
19       bool pop( T & ); // pop an element off the Stack
20
21       // determine whether Stack is empty
22       bool isEmpty() const
23       {
24          return top == -1;
25       } // end function isEmpty
26
27       // determine whether Stack is full
28       bool isFull() const
29       {
30          return top == size - 1;
31       } // end function isFull
32
33    private:
34       int size; // # of elements in the Stack
35       int top; // location of the top element (-1 means empty)
36       T *stackPtr; // pointer to internal representation of the Stack
37    }; // end class template Stack
38
39    // constructor template
40    template< typename T >
41    Stack< T >::Stack( int s )
42       : size( s > 0 ? s : 10 ), // validate size
43         top( -1 ), // Stack initially empty
44         stackPtr( new T[ size ] ) // allocate memory for elements
45    {
46       // empty body
47    } // end Stack constructor template
48
49    // push element onto Stack;
50    // if successful, return true; otherwise, return false
51    template< typename T >
52    bool Stack< T >::push( const T &pushValue )
53    {
54       if ( !isFull() )
55       {
56          stackPtr[ ++top ] = pushValue; // place item on Stack
57          return true; // push successful
58       } // end if
59
60       return false; // push unsuccessful
61    } // end function template push
```

Fig. 15.2 | Class template Stack. (Part 2 of 3.)

```
62
63    // pop element off Stack;
64    // if successful, return true; otherwise, return false
65    template< typename T >
66    bool Stack< T >::pop( T &popValue )
67    {
68       if ( !isEmpty() )
69       {
70          popValue = stackPtr[ top-- ]; // remove item from Stack
71          return true; // pop successful
72       } // end if
73
74       return false; // pop unsuccessful
75    } // end function template pop
76
77    #endif
```

Fig. 15.2 | Class template Stack. (Part 3 of 3.)

The member-function definitions that appear outside the class-template definition each begin with the header

> **template< typename** T >

(lines 40, 51 and 65). Thus, each definition resembles a conventional function definition, except that the Stack element type always is listed generically as type parameter T. The binary scope resolution operator is used with the class-template name Stack< T > (lines 41, 52 and 66) to tie each member-function definition to the class template's scope. In this case, the generic class name is Stack< T >. When doubleStack is instantiated as type Stack< double >, the Stack constructor function-template specialization uses new to create an array of elements of type double to represent the stack (line 44). The statement

> stackPtr = **new** T[size];

in the Stack class-template definition is generated by the compiler in the class-template specialization Stack< double > as

> stackPtr = **new double**[size];

Creating a Driver to Test Class Template Stack< T >

Now, let us consider the driver (Fig. 15.3) that exercises the Stack class template. The driver begins by instantiating object doubleStack of size 5 (line 11). This object is declared to be of class Stack< double > (pronounced "Stack of double"). The compiler associates type double with type parameter T in the class template to produce the source code for a Stack class of type double. Although templates offer software-reusability benefits, remember that multiple class-template specializations are instantiated in a program (at compile time), even though the template is written only once.

Lines 17–21 invoke push to place the double values 1.1, 2.2, 3.3, 4.4 and 5.5 onto doubleStack. The while loop terminates when the driver attempts to push a sixth value

```cpp
1   // Fig. 15.3: StackTest.cpp
2   // Stack class template test program.
3   #include <iostream>
4   using std::cout;
5   using std::endl;
6
7   #include "Stack.h" // Stack class template definition
8
9   int main()
10  {
11     Stack< double > doubleStack( 5 ); // size 5
12     double doubleValue = 1.1;
13
14     cout << "Pushing elements onto doubleStack\n";
15
16     // push 5 doubles onto doubleStack
17     while ( doubleStack.push( doubleValue ) )
18     {
19        cout << doubleValue << ' ';
20        doubleValue += 1.1;
21     } // end while
22
23     cout << "\nStack is full. Cannot push " << doubleValue
24        << "\n\nPopping elements from doubleStack\n";
25
26     // pop elements from doubleStack
27     while ( doubleStack.pop( doubleValue ) )
28        cout << doubleValue << ' ';
29
30     cout << "\nStack is empty. Cannot pop\n";
31
32     Stack< int > intStack; // default size 10
33     int intValue = 1;
34     cout << "\nPushing elements onto intStack\n";
35
36     // push 10 integers onto intStack
37     while ( intStack.push( intValue ) )
38     {
39        cout << intValue++ << ' ';
40     } // end while
41
42     cout << "\nStack is full. Cannot push " << intValue
43        << "\n\nPopping elements from intStack\n";
44
45     // pop elements from intStack
46     while ( intStack.pop( intValue ) )
47        cout << intValue << ' ';
48
49     cout << "\nStack is empty. Cannot pop" << endl;
50     return 0;
51  } // end main
```

Fig. 15.3 | Class template Stack test program. (Part 1 of 2.)

```
Pushing elements onto doubleStack
1.1 2.2 3.3 4.4 5.5
Stack is full. Cannot push 6.6

Popping elements from doubleStack
5.5 4.4 3.3 2.2 1.1
Stack is empty. Cannot pop

Pushing elements onto intStack
1 2 3 4 5 6 7 8 9 10
Stack is full. Cannot push 11

Popping elements from intStack
10 9 8 7 6 5 4 3 2 1
Stack is empty. Cannot pop
```

Fig. 15.3 | Class template Stack `test` program. (Part 2 of 2.)

onto doubleStack (which is full, because it holds a maximum of five elements). Note that function push returns false when it is unable to push a value onto the stack.[1]

Lines 27–28 invoke pop in a while loop to remove the five values from the stack (note, in the output of Fig. 15.3, that the values do pop off in last-in, first-out order). When the driver attempts to pop a sixth value, the doubleStack is empty, so the pop loop terminates.

Line 32 instantiates integer stack intStack with the declaration

```
Stack< int > intStack;
```

(pronounced "intStack is a Stack of int"). Because no size is specified, the size defaults to 10 as specified in the default constructor (Fig. 15.2, line 10). Lines 37–40 loop and invoke push to place values onto intStack until it is full, then lines 46–47 loop and invoke pop to remove values from intStack until it is empty. Once again, notice in the output that the values pop off in last-in, first-out order.

Creating Function Templates to Test Class Template Stack< T >

Notice that the code in function main of Fig. 15.3 is almost identical for both the doubleStack manipulations in lines 11–30 and the intStack manipulations in lines 32–49. This presents another opportunity to use a function template. Figure 15.4 defines function template testStack (lines 14–38) to perform the same tasks as main in Fig. 15.3—push a series of values onto a Stack< T > and pop the values off a Stack< T >. Function template testStack uses template parameter T (specified at line 14) to represent the data type stored in the Stack< T >. The function template takes four arguments (lines 16–19)—a reference to an object of type Stack< T >, a value of type T that will be the first value pushed onto the Stack< T >, a value of type T used to increment the values pushed onto the Stack< T >

---

1. Class Stack (Fig. 15.2) provides the function isFull, which you can use to determine whether the stack is full before attempting a push operation. This would avoid the potential error of pushing onto a full stack. In Chapter 16, Exception Handling, if the operation cannot be completed, function push would "throw an exception." You can write code to "catch" that exception, then decide how to handle it appropriately for the application. The same technique can be used with function pop when an attempt is made to pop an element from an empty stack.

and a `string` that represents the name of the Stack< T > object for output purposes. Function `main` (lines 40–49) instantiates an object of type `Stack< double >` called `doubleStack`

```cpp
1   // Fig. 15.4: StackTest.cpp
2   // Stack class template test program. Function main uses a
3   // function template to manipulate objects of type Stack< T >.
4   #include <iostream>
5   using std::cout;
6   using std::endl;
7
8   #include <string>
9   using std::string;
10
11  #include "Stack.h" // Stack class template definition
12
13  // function template to manipulate Stack< T >
14  template< typename T >
15  void testStack(
16     Stack< T > &theStack, // reference to Stack< T >
17     T value, // initial value to push
18     T increment, // increment for subsequent values
19     const string stackName ) // name of the Stack< T > object
20  {
21     cout << "\nPushing elements onto " << stackName << '\n';
22
23     // push element onto Stack
24     while ( theStack.push( value ) )
25     {
26        cout << value << ' ';
27        value += increment;
28     } // end while
29
30     cout << "\nStack is full. Cannot push " << value
31        << "\n\nPopping elements from " << stackName << '\n';
32
33     // pop elements from Stack
34     while ( theStack.pop( value ) )
35        cout << value << ' ';
36
37     cout << "\nStack is empty. Cannot pop" << endl;
38  } // end function template testStack
39
40  int main()
41  {
42     Stack< double > doubleStack( 5 ); // size 5
43     Stack< int > intStack; // default size 10
44
45     testStack( doubleStack, 1.1, 1.1, "doubleStack" );
46     testStack( intStack, 1, 1, "intStack" );
47
48     return 0;
49  } // end main
```

Fig. 15.4 | Passing a `Stack` template object to a function template. (Part 1 of 2.)

```
Pushing elements onto doubleStack
1.1 2.2 3.3 4.4 5.5
Stack is full. Cannot push 6.6

Popping elements from doubleStack
5.5 4.4 3.3 2.2 1.1
Stack is empty. Cannot pop

Pushing elements onto intStack
1 2 3 4 5 6 7 8 9 10
Stack is full. Cannot push 11

Popping elements from intStack
10 9 8 7 6 5 4 3 2 1
Stack is empty. Cannot pop
```

Fig. 15.4 | Passing a Stack template object to a function template. (Part 2 of 2.)

(line 42) and an object of type Stack< int > called intStack (line 43) and uses these objects in lines 45–46. The compiler infers the type of T for testStack from the type used to instantiate the function's first argument (i.e., the type used to instantiate doubleStack or intStack). The output of Fig. 15.4 precisely matches the output of Fig. 15.3.

15.5 Nontype Parameters and Default Types for Class Templates

Class template Stack of Section 15.4 used only a type parameter in the template header (Fig. 15.2, line 6). It is also possible to use *nontype template parameters* or *nontype parameters*, which can have default arguments and are treated as consts. For example, the template header could be modified to take an int elements parameter as follows:

> *template*< *typename* T, *int* elements > // nontype parameter elements

Then, a declaration such as

> Stack< *double*, 100 > mostRecentSalesFigures;

could be used to instantiate (at compile time) a 100-element Stack class-template specialization of double values named mostRecentSalesFigures; this class-template specialization would be of type Stack< double, 100 >. The class header then might contain a private data member with an array declaration such as

> T stackHolder[elements]; // array to hold Stack contents

In addition, a type parameter can specify a default type. For example,

> *template*< *typename* T = string > // defaults to type string

might specify that a Stack contains string objects by default. Then, a declaration such as

> Stack<> jobDescriptions;

could be used to instantiate a Stack class-template specialization of strings named jobDescriptions; this class-template specialization would be of type Stack< string >. Default type parameters must be the rightmost (trailing) parameters in a template's type-parameter list. When one is instantiating a class with two or more default types, if an omitted type is not the rightmost type parameter in the type-parameter list, then all type parameters to the right of that type also must be omitted.

Performance Tip 15.2

When appropriate, specify the size of a container class (such as an array class or a stack class) at compile time (possibly through a nontype template parameter). This eliminates the execution-time overhead of using new to create the space dynamically.

Software Engineering Observation 15.3

Specifying the size of a container at compile time avoids the potentially fatal execution-time error if new is unable to obtain the needed memory.

In the exercises, you'll be asked to use a nontype parameter to create a template for our class Array developed in Chapter 12. This template will enable Array objects to be instantiated with a specified number of elements of a specified type at compile time, rather than creating space for the Array objects at execution time.

In some cases, it may not be possible to use a particular type with a class template. For example, the Stack template of Fig. 15.2 requires that user-defined types that will be stored in a Stack must provide a default constructor and an assignment operator. If a particular user-defined type will not work with our Stack template or requires customized processing, you can define an *explicit specialization* of the class template for a particular type. Let's assume we want to create an explicit specialization Stack for Employee objects. To do this, form a new class with the name Stack< Employee > as follows:

```
template<>
class Stack< Employee >
{
    // body of class definition
};
```

Note that the Stack< Employee > explicit specialization is a complete replacement for the Stack class template that is specific to type Employee—it does not use anything from the original class template and can even have different members.

15.6 Notes on Templates and Inheritance

Templates and inheritance relate in several ways:

- A class template can be derived from a class-template specialization.
- A class template can be derived from a nontemplate class.
- A class-template specialization can be derived from a class-template specialization.
- A nontemplate class can be derived from a class-template specialization.

15.7 Notes on Templates and Friends

We have seen that functions and entire classes can be declared as friends of nontemplate classes. With class templates, friendship can be established between a class template and a global function, a member function of another class (possibly a class-template specialization), or even an entire class (possibly a class-template specialization).

Throughout this section, we assume that we have defined a class template for a class named X with a single type parameter T, as in:

> *template*< *typename* T > *class* X

Under this assumption, it is possible to make a function f1 a friend of every class-template specialization instantiated from the class template for class X. To do so, use a friendship declaration of the form

> *friend void* f1();

For example, function f1 is a friend of X< double >, X< string > and X< Employee >, etc.

It is also possible to make a function f2 a friend of only a class-template specialization with the same type argument. To do so, use a friendship declaration of the form

> *friend void* f2(X< T > &);

For example, if T is a float, function f2(X< float > &) is a friend of class-template specialization X< float > but not a friend of class-template specification X< string >.

You can declare that a member function of another class is a friend of any class-template specialization generated from the class template. To do so, the friend declaration must qualify the name of the other class's member function using the class name and the binary scope resolution operator, as in:

> *friend void* A::f3();

The declaration makes member function f3 of class A a friend of every class-template specialization instantiated from the preceding class template. For example, function f3 of class A is a friend of X< double >, X< string > and X< Employee >, etc.

As with a global function, another template class's member function can be a friend of only a class-template specialization with the same type argument. A friendship declaration of the form

> *friend void* C< T >::f4(X< T > &);

for a particular type T such as float makes member function

> C< *float* >::f4(X< *float* > &)

a friend function of *only* class-template specialization X< float >.

In some cases, it is desirable to make an entire class's set of member functions friends of a class template. In this case, a friend declaration of the form

> *friend class* Y;

makes every member function of class Y a friend of every class-template specialization produced from the class template X.

Finally, it is possible to make all member functions of one class-template specialization friends of another class-template specialization with the same type argument. For example, a friend declaration of the form:

> *friend class* Z< T >;

indicates that when a class-template specialization is instantiated with a particular type for T (such as float), all members of class Z< float > become friends of class-template specialization X< float >. We use this particular relationship in several examples of Chapter 21, Data Structures.

15.8 Notes on Templates and static Members

What about static data members? Recall that, with a nontemplate class, one copy of each static data member is shared among all objects of the class, and the static data member must be initialized at file scope.

Each class-template specialization instantiated from a class template has its own copy of each static data member of the class template; all objects of that specialization share that one static data member. In addition, as with static data members of nontemplate classes, static data members of class-template specializations must be defined and, if necessary, initialized at file scope. Each class-template specialization gets its own copy of the class template's static member functions.

15.9 Templates in C++/CLI

In C++/CLI you can create and use a managed class template or function template just as you would with native C++. For example, the Stack class in Fig. 15.2 can be declared in managed code as follows:

```
template< typename T >
ref class ManagedStack
{
    // body of class definition
};
```

This managed class template can be used to create a ManagedStack of any managed type. Managed class templates fully support all the features of native class templates such as non-type parameters and explicit specialization. As mentioned in Section 11.11, managed classes, including managed class templates, cannot declare other classes or functions as friends but can be declared as friends of native classes.

15.10 .NET Generics in C++/CLI

In C++/CLI, generics provide software-reuse capabilities much like those provided by templates in native C++. Generics are defined by the Common Language Runtime (CLR). The syntax for defining managed *generic classes* is similar to creating managed class templates. A generic class definition begins with the keyword *generic* followed by a list of type parameters enclosed in angle brackets. Although the syntax is nearly identical, generics and templates have many differences.

Generics Example

We now show an example of using a generic class with generic member functions. We've rewritten the Stack class template of Fig. 15.2 using C++/CLI generics. Figure 15.5 defines the generic reference class Stack. There are few differences between this generic class definition and the class template definition in Fig. 15.2. We've replaced the keyword

```
1   // Fig. 15.5: Stack.h
2   // Generic class Stack.
3   #ifndef STACK_H
4   #define STACK_H
5
6   #include "stdafx.h"
7
8   generic< typename T >
9   ref class Stack
10  {
11  public:
12     Stack( int stackSize ); // constructor
13
14     bool push( T% ); // push an element onto the Stack
15     bool pop( T% ); // pop an element off the Stack
16
17     // determine whether Stack is empty
18     bool isEmpty()
19     {
20        return top == -1;
21     } // end function isEmpty
22
23     // determine whether Stack is full
24     bool isFull()
25     {
26        return top == size - 1;
27     } // end function isFull
28
29  private:
30     int size; // # of elements in the Stack
31     int top; // location of the top element (-1 means empty)
32     array< T > ^elements; // internal representation of the Stack
33  }; // end generic class Stack
34
35  #endif
```

Fig. 15.5 | Generic class `Stack`.

`template` with the keyword `generic` throughout. We've also replaced the keyword `class` with the spaced keyword `ref class`. The constructor (line 12) no longer declares a default value, because default values are not supported in C++/CLI. We've replaced & in the function signatures for push and pop (lines 14–15) with % (the syntax for pass-by-reference in C++/CLI). All occurrences of the keyword `const` have been removed, as C++/CLI doesn't support `const` in these situations. We also replaced the `stackPtr` data member with a managed array named `elements` (line 32).

Figure 15.6 defines the implementation of generic class `Stack`. Again, the implementation is similar to that of the `Stack` class template. The keyword `template` has been replaced with keyword `generic`, occurrences of & have been replaced with % and occurrences of keyword `const` have been removed. We also initialize the `elements` data member to a managed array of type `T` (line 12). Other than these minor differences, the implementation is identical to the `Stack` class template.

```
1   // Fig. 15.6: Stack.cpp
2   // Generic class Stack implementation.
3   #include "stdafx.h"
4
5   #include "Stack.h"
6
7   // generic constructor
8   generic< typename T >
9   Stack< T >::Stack( int s )
10     : size( s > 0 ? s : 10 ), // validate size
11       top( -1 ), // Stack initially empty
12       elements( gcnew array< T >( size ) )// allocate memory for elements
13   {
14     // empty body
15   } // end generic Stack constructor
16
17   // push element onto Stack
18   // if successful, return true; otherwise, return false
19   generic< typename T >
20   bool Stack< T >::push( T %pushValue )
21   {
22     if ( !isFull() )
23     {
24         elements[ ++top ] = pushValue; // place item on Stack
25         return true; // push successful
26     } // end if
27
28     return false; // push unsuccessful
29   } // end generic function push
30
31   // pop element off Stack
32   // if successful, return true; otherwise, return false
33   generic< typename T >
34   bool Stack< T >::pop( T %popValue )
35   {
36     if ( !isEmpty() )
37     {
38         popValue = elements[ top-- ]; // remove item from Stack
39         return true; // pop successful
40     } // end if
41
42     return false; // pop unsuccessful
43   } // end generic function pop
```

Fig. 15.6 | Generic class Stack implementation.

Notice that the class definition and implementation are separated into a header file and source file, as per our normal convention for class definitions. This separation is possible because in C++/CLI the specialization of a generic class occurs at runtime—one of the major differences between C++ templates (in native and managed code) and C++/CLI generics. Templates are specialized at compile time, so the Visual C++ compiler requires the complete definition of a template to appear in the client source-code file that uses the template. Had we split the Stack class template into two files (.h and .cpp), including the header file wouldn't provide all the necessary code to generate class-template specializations. By placing all the code in the header file, we ensure that the compiler has all the necessary code to generate a template specialization. Generics are specialized at runtime—the compiler generates one copy of the generic class, and each specialization references that copy at runtime. Because only one copy of the generic class needs to be compiled, we can separate the definition from the implementation and include the Stack.h header when compiling the implementation code.

The code for the Stack generic class test program (Fig. 15.7) performs the same tests as the code in Fig. 15.4. Function testStack (lines 11–38) takes three arguments—a handle to a Stack< T > object, a handle to a managed array< T > containing values to push onto the Stack< T >, and a handle to a String that represents the name of the Stack< T > object for output purposes. The for each statement (lines 18–27) pushes the values in the managed array< T > onto the Stack< T > object. If the Stack< T > is full (i.e., push returns false), we break out of the for each statement (line 25). Next we pop all the values off the Stack< T >. The while statement (lines 34–35) continues to pop values off the Stack< T > until it is empty (i.e., pop returns false). Function main (lines 40–52) first initializes two managed arrays—one containing double values and the other containing int values. It then instantiates one object of type Stack< double > (line 45) and one of type Stack< int > (line 46). Finally it calls function testStack twice to test both the Stack< double > object doubleStack and the Stack< int > object intStack.

```cpp
1   // Fig. 15.7: StackTest.cpp
2   // Generic class Stack test program. Function main uses a generic function
3   // to manipulate objects of type Stack< T >
4   #include "stdafx.h"
5
6   #include "Stack.h"
7
8   using namespace System;
9
10  // generic function to manipulate Stack< T >
11  generic< typename T >
12  void testStack( Stack< T > ^theStack, array< T > ^values,
13     String ^stackName )
14  {
15     Console::WriteLine( "Pushing elements onto {0}", stackName );
16
17     // push elements onto Stack
18     for each ( T value in values )
19     {
20        if ( theStack->push( value ) )
21           Console::Write( "{0} ", value );
22        else
23        {
24           Console::WriteLine( "\nStack is full. Cannot push {0}", value );
25           break;
26        } // end else
27     } // end for each
28
```

Fig. 15.7 | Generic class Stack test program. (Part 1 of 2.)

```
29          Console::WriteLine( "\nPopping elements from {0}", stackName );
30
31          T poppedValue; // holds the value popped from the Stack
32
33          // pop elements from Stack
34          while ( theStack->pop( poppedValue ) )
35             Console::Write( "{0} ", poppedValue );
36
37          Console::WriteLine( "\nStack is empty. Cannot pop" );
38       } // end function testStack
39
40       int main( array< System::String^ > ^args )
41       {
42          array< double > ^doubleValues = { 1.1, 2.2, 3.3, 4.4, 5.5, 6.6 };
43          array< int > ^intValues = { 1, 2, 3, 4, 5, 6, 7, 8, 9, 10, 11 };
44
45          Stack< double > ^doubleStack = gcnew Stack< double >( 5 ); // size 5
46          Stack< int > ^intStack = gcnew Stack< int > ( 10 ); // size 10
47
48          testStack( doubleStack, doubleValues, "doubleStack" );
49          testStack( intStack, intValues, "intStack" );
50
51          return 0;
52       } // end main
```

```
Pushing elements onto doubleStack
1.1 2.2 3.3 4.4 5.5
Stack is full. Cannot push 6.6

Popping elements from doubleStack
5.5 4.4 3.3 2.2 1.1
Stack is empty. Cannot pop

Pushing elements onto intStack
1 2 3 4 5 6 7 8 9 10
Stack is full. Cannot push 11

Popping elements from intStack
10 9 8 7 6 5 4 3 2 1
Stack is empty. Cannot pop
```

Fig. 15.7 | Generic class Stack test program. (Part 2 of 2.)

In Fig. 15.4, the function template testStack populated the Stack< T > object by using a starting value of type T and an increment of type T. The while statement (lines 24–28) pushed the value onto the Stack< T >, then incremented the value using the += operator. In C++/CLI generics, the actual type represented by T isn't known until runtime. To ensure type safety, generic code is restricted to performing operations that are guaranteed to work for every possible type that could replace T. Since not every type overloads the += operator, it can't be used in the generic function testStack (Fig. 15.7, lines 11–38). You can require that types used in generic code support certain operations by declaring generic type constraints, which we discuss in the next section.

15.11 Generic Type Constraints

In this section, we present a generic maximum function that determines and returns the largest of its three arguments (all of the same type). This function uses the type parameter to declare both the function's return type and its parameters. Normally, when comparing values to determine which one is greater, you would use the > operator. However, this operator is not overloaded for use with every type that is built into the FCL or that might be defined by the user. Generic code is restricted to performing operations that are guaranteed to work for every possible type that could be used as a type argument. This is because generic classes and functions are specialized at runtime—the compiler doesn't know what types will used as type arguments. Templates don't have this restriction, because they are specialized at compile time—the compiler knows all the types that are used as type arguments and can check if they support all functions and operators used in the template. Thus, an expression like variable1 < variable2 is allowed in templates if the types used overload operator <, but is *not* allowed in generics unless the compiler can ensure that operator < is provided for every type that could ever be used in the generic code. Similarly, you cannot call a function on a generic type variable unless the compiler can ensure that all types that could ever be used in the generic code support that function.

IComparable< T > Interface

It is possible to compare two objects of the same type if that type implements the generic interface *IComparable< T >* (of namespace System). A benefit of implementing interface IComparable< T > is that IComparable< T > objects can be used with the sorting and searching member functions of classes in the System::Collections namespace—we discuss those functions in Chapter 25, Collections. The structures in the FCL that correspond to the primitive types all implement this interface. For example, the structure for primitive type double is Double and the structure for primitive type int is Int32—both Double and Int32 implement the IComparable< T > interface. Types that implement IComparable< T > must define a CompareTo member function for comparing objects of the same type. For example, if we have two ints, int1 and int2, they can be compared with the expression:

```
int1.CompareTo( int2 )
```

Member function CompareTo must return 0 if the objects are equal, a negative integer if int1 is less than int2 or a positive integer if int1 is greater than int2. It's the responsibility of the programmer who defines a type that implements IComparable< T > to define member function CompareTo such that it compares the contents of two objects of that type and returns the appropriate result.

Specifying Type Constraints

Even though IComparable< T > objects can be compared, they cannot be used with generic code by default, because not all types implement interface IComparable< T >. However, we can restrict the types that can be used in a generic function or class to ensure that they meet certain requirements. This feature—known as a *type constraint*—restricts the type of the argument supplied to a particular type parameter. Figure 15.8 declares function maximum (lines 8–22) with a type constraint that requires each of the function's arguments to be of type IComparable< T >. This restriction is important, because not all objects can be compared. However, all IComparable< T > objects are guaranteed to have a CompareTo member

```
1   // Fig. 15.8: TypeConstraints.cpp
2   // Demonstrating generic type constraints.
3   #include "stdafx.h"
4
5   using namespace System;
6
7   // generic function determines the largest of three IComparable objects
8   generic< typename T > where T : IComparable < T >
9   T maximum( T x, T y, T z )
10  {
11     T max = x; // assume x is initially the largest
12
13     // compare y with max
14     if ( y->CompareTo( max ) > 0 )
15        max = y;
16
17     // compare z with max
18     if ( z->CompareTo( max ) > 0 )
19        max = z;
20
21     return max;
22  } // end function maximum
23
24  int main( array< System::String^ > ^args )
25  {
26     Console::WriteLine( "Maximum of {0}, {1} and {2} is {3}\n",
27        3, 4, 5, maximum( 3, 4, 5 ) );
28     Console::WriteLine( "Maximum of {0}, {1} and {2} is {3}\n",
29        6.6, 8.8, 7.7, maximum( 6.6, 8.8, 7.7 ) );
30     Console::WriteLine( "Maximum of {0}, {1} and {2} is {3}\n",
31        "pear", "apple", "orange", maximum( "pear", "apple", "orange" ) );
32
33     return 0;
34  } // end main
```

```
Maximum of 3, 4 and 5 is 5
Maximum of 6.6, 8.8 and 7.7 is 8.8
Maximum of pear, apple and orange is pear
```

Fig. 15.8 | Demonstrating the use of generic type constraints.

function that can be used in function maximum to determine the largest of its three arguments.

Generic function maximum uses type parameter T as the return type of the function (line 9), as the type of function parameters x, y and z (line 9), and as the type of local variable max (line 11). Generic function maximum's *where* clause (after the type-parameter list in line 8) specifies the type constraint for type parameter T. In this case, the clause

```
where T : IComparable< T >
```

indicates that this function requires the type arguments to implement interface IComparable< T >. Attempting to use a type argument which does not meet the defined type constraint will cause a compilation error. If no type constraint is specified, the default type constraint is Object.

C++/CLI provides several kinds of type constraints. A *class constraint* indicates that the type argument must be an object of a specific base class or one of its subclasses. An *interface constraint* indicates that the type argument must implement a specific interface. The type constraint in line 8 is an interface constraint, because IComparable< T > is an interface. You can specify that the type argument must be a reference type or a value type by using the *reference type constraint* (**ref class**) or the *value type constraint* (**value class**), respectively. Finally, you can specify a *constructor constraint—* **gcnew()**—to indicate that the generic code can use operator gcnew to create new objects of the type represented by the type parameter. If a type parameter is specified with a constructor constraint, the type argument's class must provide a public parameterless or default constructor to ensure that objects of the class can be created without passing constructor arguments; otherwise, a compilation error occurs.

It is possible to apply *multiple constraints* to a type parameter. To do so, simply provide a comma-separated list of constraints in the where clause.

Analyzing the Code

Function maximum assumes that its first argument (x) is the largest and assigns it to local variable max (line 11). Next, the if statement at lines 14–15 determines whether y is greater than max. The condition invokes y's CompareTo member function with the expression y->CompareTo(max). If y is greater than max, then y is assigned to variable max (line 15). Similarly, the statement at lines 18–19 determines whether z is greater than max. If so, line 19 assigns z to max. Then, line 21 returns max to the caller.

In main (lines 24–34), line 27 calls maximum with the integers 3, 4 and 5. Generic function maximum is a match for this call, but its arguments must implement interface IComparable< T > to ensure that they can be compared. Type int is a synonym for struct Int32, which implements interface IComparable< int >. (This is true of all the structs for the primitive types.) Thus, ints (and other primitive types) are valid arguments to function maximum.

Line 29 passes three double arguments to maximum. Again, this is allowed because double is a synonym for the Double struct, which implements IComparable< double >. Line 31 passes maximum three Strings, which are also IComparable< String > objects. Note that we intentionally placed the largest value in a different position in each function call (lines 27, 29 and 31) to show that the generic function always finds the maximum value, regardless of its position in the argument list and regardless of the inferred type argument.

15.12 Contrasting Templates and Generics

Templates and generics may seem redundant at first glance, but there are substantial differences. We've discussed some of the most relevant differences in the preceding sections. Here we provide a brief outline of the key differences:

- Generics are specialized at runtime while templates are specialized at compile time.

- Generic types can't be used as a template type parameter, but a template type may be used as a generic type parameter.

- Generics use type constraints to restrict types that may be used in generic code.

- Generics don't support nontype parameters or default values.

- Generics don't support explicit specialization nor do they support partial specialization.

- Generic type parameters must be a handle to a reference type, an interface-type handle, or a value type.

Generics are also cross assembly, a significant distinction from templates. Recall from Chapter 1 that in C++/CLI, an assembly is a file containing compiled code. The compiled code for all the classes in the .NET Framework Class Library is contained in various assemblies. We use these classes, such as `System::Console`, by referencing those assemblies, which is done automatically by Visual Studio for commonly used .NET classes. When you define a generic class or function in a C++/CLI project, the compiled code is placed in the project's assembly. Because the type parameters are replaced at runtime, other projects can create specializations of your generic class or function by referencing the appropriate assembly. This is how the classes in namespace `System::Collections::Generic` work (see Chapter 25, Collections). With templates, the code for each template specialization is created at compile time and the template itself doesn't exist in the compiled code. Since the assembly doesn't have the template definition, a new template specialization can't be created in another project. Generic classes and functions (declared `public`) can also be used by code written in other .NET languages, such as C# or Visual Basic, again by referencing the assembly containing the compiled generic code.

Notes on Generics and Inheritance
Generics and inheritance relate in several ways:

- Generic classes (as with all managed classes) support only `public`, single inheritance. Attempting to use `private` or `protected` inheritance, or to inherit from multiple classes, results in compilation errors.

- A generic class can be derived from another generic class.

- A generic class can be derived from a nongeneric class.

- A nongeneric class can be derived from a generic class.

Friends and static Members
As with all managed classes in C++/CLI, generic classes can be declared `friends` of native classes, but can't themselves declare `friends`. Declaring a generic class or function as a `friend` follows the same rules as declaring a native class or function as a `friend`.

Generic classes treat `static` data members in the same way templates do. Each new specialization of the generic type has its own copy of each `static` data member; all objects of that specialization share that one `static` data member.

Why Both Have Generics and Templates
Generics may seem like a replacement for templates, but having both is valuable. Each provides unique functionality not available using the other. The fact that templates are specialized at compile time enables advanced programming techniques that are not possible with generics. Templates are also more flexible. Because templates are specialized at com-

pile time, the code needs to be valid only for the types actually used in template specializations. On the other hand, because generics are specialized at runtime, generic code must
be valid for any type that could possibly be used in a specialization. Because generics are
specialized at runtime, generic classes and functions can be specialized by other programs
that reference the appropriate assembly. Together, generics and templates are a powerful
programming tool. The STL/CLR (see Chapter 23) uses both in its implementation.

15.13 Wrap-Up

This chapter introduced two of Visual C++'s most powerful features—templates and generics. You learned how to use function templates to enable the compiler to produce a set
of function-template specializations that represent a group of related overloaded functions.
We also discussed how to overload a function template to create a specialized version of a
function that handles a particular data type's processing in a different manner than the
other function-template specializations. Next, you learned about class templates and class-
template specializations. You saw examples of how to use a class template to create a group
of related types that each perform identical processing on different data types. You also
learned about some of the relationships among templates, friends, inheritance and static members. Next, we discussed .NET generics, a C++/CLI feature similar to templates.
You learned how to create generic classes and functions. We also demonstrated how to use
generic type constraints to ensure that types used in generic code provide certain functionality. Finally, we highlighted the differences between templates and generics.

In the next chapter, we introduce exception handling, which allows you to deal with
certain problems that may occur during a program's execution. We demonstrate basic
exception-handling techniques that often permit a program to continue executing as if no
problem had been encountered. We also present several exception-handling classes provided by the C++ Standard Library and .NET Framework Class Library.

Summary

Section 15.1 Introduction
- Templates enable us to specify a range of related (overloaded) functions—called function-template specializations—or a range of related classes—called class-template specializations.
- Generics offer software-reuse capabilities similar to those of templates, but may be used only with
managed classes.

Section 15.2 Function Templates
- To use function-template specializations, you write a single function-template definition. Based
on the argument types provided in calls to this function, C++ generates separate specializations
to handle each type of call appropriately. These are compiled along with the rest of a program's
source code.
- All function-template definitions begin with the keyword template followed by template parameters to the function template enclosed in angle brackets (< and >); each template parameter that
represents a type must be preceded by keyword class or typename. Keywords typename and
class used to specify function-template parameters mean "any built-in type or user-defined
type."

- Template-definition template parameters are used to specify the kinds of arguments to the function, specify the return type of the function and declare variables in the function.

- The name of a template parameter can be declared only once in the type-parameter list of a template header. Formal type-parameter names among function templates need not be unique.

Section 15.3 Overloading Function Templates

- A function template may be overloaded in several ways. We can provide other function templates that specify the same function name but different function parameters. A function template can also be overloaded by providing other nontemplate functions with the same function name, but different function parameters.

Section 15.4 Class Templates

- Class templates provide the means for describing a class generically and for instantiating classes that are type-specific versions of this generic class.

- Class templates are called parameterized types; they require type parameters to specify how to customize a generic class template to form a specific class-template specialization.

- To use class-template specializations you write one class template. When you need a new type-specific class, you use a concise notation, and the compiler writes the source code for the class-template specialization.

- A class-template definition looks like a conventional class definition, except that it is preceded by `template< typename T >` (or `template< class T >`) to indicate this is a class-template definition with type parameter `T` which acts as a placeholder for the type of the class to create. The type `T` is mentioned throughout the class header and member-function definitions as a generic type name.

- Member-function definitions outside a class template each begin with `template< typename T >` (or `template< class T >`). Then, each function definition resembles a conventional function definition, except that the generic data in the class always is listed generically as type parameter `T`. The binary scope-resolution operator is used with the class-template name to tie each member-function definition to the class template's scope.

Section 15.5 Nontype Parameters and Default Types for Class Templates

- It is possible to use nontype parameters in the header of a class or function template.

- An explicit specialization of a class template can be provided to override a class template for a specific type.

Section 15.6 Notes on Templates and Inheritance

- A class template can be derived from a class-template specialization. A class template can be derived from a nontemplate class. A class-template specialization can be derived from a class-template specialization. A nontemplate class can be derived from a class-template specialization.

Section 15.7 Notes on Templates and Friends

- Functions and entire classes can be declared as friends of nontemplate classes. With class templates, friendship arrangements can be declared. Friendship can be established between a class template and a global function, a member function of another class (possibly a class-template specialization) or even an entire class (possibly a class-template specialization).

Section 15.8 Notes on Templates and **static** Members

- Each class-template specialization instantiated from a class template has its own copy of each `static` data member of the class template; all objects of that specialization share that `static` data member. And as with `static` data members of nontemplate classes, `static` data members of class-template specializations must be defined and, if necessary, initialized at file scope.

- Each class-template specialization gets a copy of the class template's `static` member functions.

Section 15.9 Templates in C++/CLI

- You can declare a managed class template with a standard managed class definition preceded by `template< typename T >` (or `template< class T >`).
- Managed templates support all the features of native templates.
- Managed class templates cannot declare `friends`, but can be declared `friends` of native classes.

Section 15.10 .NET Generics in C++/CLI

- Generics are defined by the Common Language Runtime. As such, generics are usable only with managed code in C++/CLI and not with native C++.
- The syntax for defining managed generic classes is similar to creating managed template classes.
- A generic class definition begins with the keyword `generic` followed by a list of type parameters enclosed in angle brackets.
- Default values are not supported in C++/CLI generics.
- Generics are specialized at runtime—the compiler generates one copy of the generic class, and each specialization references that copy at runtime.

Section 15.11 Generic Type Constraints

- Generic code is restricted to performing operations that are guaranteed to work for every possible type that could be used.
- You cannot call a function on a generic-type variable unless the compiler can ensure that all types that will ever be used in the generic code support that function.
- It is possible to compare two objects of the same type if that type implements the generic interface `IComparable< T >` (of namespace `System`). Types that implement `IComparable< T >` must declare a `CompareTo` member function for comparing objects of the same type. Member function `CompareTo` must return `0` if the objects are equal, a negative integer if the calling object is less than the object passed as an argument or a positive integer if the calling object is greater than the object passed as an argument.
- Type constraints restrict the type of the argument supplied to a particular type parameter.
- The `where` clause (after the type parameter list) specifies the type constraint(s) for the type parameter(s). The clause `where T : IComparable< T >` requires the type arguments to implement interface `IComparable< T >`. If no type constraint is specified, the default type constraint is `Object`.
- A class constraint indicates that the type argument must be an object of a specific base class or one of its subclasses.
- An interface constraint indicates that the type argument's class must implement a specific interface.
- You can specify that the type argument must be a reference type or a value type by using the reference type constraint (`ref class`) or the value type constraint (`value class`), respectively.
- You can specify a constructor constraint—`gcnew()`—to indicate that the generic code can use operator `gcnew` to create new objects of the type represented by the type parameter. The type argument's class must provide `public` a parameterless or default constructor to ensure that objects of the class can be created without passing constructor arguments.
- To apply multiple constraints to a type parameter, provide a comma-separated list of constraints in the `where` clause.

Section 15.12 Contrasting Templates and Generics

- Generics are specialized at runtime while templates are specialized at compile time.
- Generics use type constraints to restrict the types that may be used in generic code.
- Generics are cross assembly and cross language.
- Generics don't support nontype parameters or default values.
- Generics don't support explicit specialization.
- Generic classes support only `public` single inheritance.
- A generic class can be derived from another generic class.
- A generic class can be derived from a nongeneric class.
- A nongeneric class can be derived from a generic class.
- As with all managed classes in C++/CLI, generic classes can be declared `friends` of native classes, but can't themselves declare `friends`.
- Each new specialization of the generic type has its own copy of each `static` data member; all objects of that specialization share that one `static` data member

Terminology

angle brackets (< and >)
assembly
class constraint
class template
class-template definition
class-template specialization
`CompareTo` member function of
    `IComparable< T >`
constructor constraint (`gcnew()`)
explicit specialization
`friend` of a template
function template
function-template definition
function-template specialization
generics
generic class
generic function
generic programming
`generic< class T >`
`generic< typename T >`
`IComparable< T >` interface
interface constraint
keyword `class` in a template type parameter
keyword `class` in a generic type parameter
keyword `generic`
keyword `template`

keyword `typename`
macro
member function of a class-template
    specialization
nontype parameter
nontype template parameter
overloading a function template
parameterized type
reference type constraint (`ref class`)
static data member of a class template
static data member of a class-template
    specialization
static data member of a generic class
static member function of a class template
static member function of a class-template
    specialization
static member function of a generic class
template parameter
`template< class T >`
`template< typename T >`
type constraint
type parameter
type template parameter
value type constraint (`value class`)
`where` clause

Self-Review Exercises

15.1   State which of the following statements are *true* and which are *false*. If a statement is *false*, explain why.

a) The type parameters of a function-template definition or generic function definition are used to specify the types of the arguments to the function, to specify the return type of the function and to declare variables within the function, among other things.

b) Keywords typename and class as used with a type parameter specifically mean "any user-defined class type."

c) A function template can be overloaded by another function template with the same function name.

d) Template parameter names among template definitions must be unique.

e) Type parameter names among generic class and function definitions need not be unique.

f) Each member-function definition outside a class template must begin with a template header.

g) A friend function of a class template must be a function-template specialization.

h) If several class-template specializations are generated from a single class template with a single static data member, each of the class-template specializations shares a single copy of the class template's static data member.

i) A generic class may declare other classes and functions as friends.

j) A generic class may inherit from multiple base classes.

k) A class template or managed class template may declare type constraints.

15.2 Fill in the blanks in each of the following:

a) Templates enable us to specify, with a single code segment, an entire range of related functions called _____, or an entire range of related classes called _____.

b) All function-template definitions begin with the keyword _____, followed by a list of template parameters to the function template enclosed in _____.

c) The related functions generated from a function template all have the same name, so the compiler uses _____ resolution to invoke the proper function.

d) Class templates and generic classes also are called _____ types.

e) The _____ operator is used with a class-template name to tie each member-function definition to the class template's scope.

f) As with static data members of nontemplate classes, static data members of class-template specializations must also be defined and, if necessary, initialized at _____ scope.

g) Generic classes and functions may use _____ to restrict the types that may be used as type arguments.

h) Class-template specializations are instantiated at _____ and generic class specializations are instantiated at _____.

15.3 Find the error in each of the following:

a) ```
generic< typename T, int >
ref class Example
```

b) ```
generic< class T > where T : BaseClass1, BaseClass2
ref class Example
```

c) ```
template< typename T > where T : IComparable< T >
class Example
```

# Answers to Self-Review Exercises

**15.1** a) True. b) False. Keywords typename and class in this context also allow for a type parameter of a fundamental type. c) True. d) False. Template parameter names among function templates need not be unique. e) True. f) True. g) False. It could be a nontemplate function. h) False. Each class-template specialization will have its own copy of the static data member. i) False. Man-
```

aged classes may not declare friends. j) False. Managed classes only support single inheritance. k) False. Generic classes and functions may declare type constraints.

15.2 a) function-template specializations, class-template specializations. b) `template`, angle brackets (< and >). c) overloaded. d) parameterized. e) binary scope resolution. f) file. g) type constraints. h) compile time, runtime.

15.3 a) Generic type parameter lists may not contain nontype parameters. b) Managed classes support only single inheritance. c) Templates do not support type constraints.

Exercises

15.4 Write a function template `selectionSort` based on the sort program of Fig. 9.15. Write a driver program that inputs, sorts and outputs an `int` array and a `float` array.

15.5 Rewrite the solution to Exercise 15.4 using C++/CLI generics.

15.6 Overload function template `printArray` of Fig. 15.1 so that it takes two additional integer arguments, namely `int lowSubscript` and `int highSubscript`. A call to this function will print only the designated portion of the array. Validate `lowSubscript` and `highSubscript`; if either is out of range or if `highSubscript` is less than or equal to `lowSubscript`, the overloaded `printArray` function should return 0; otherwise, `printArray` should return the number of elements printed. Then modify `main` to exercise both versions of `printArray` on arrays a, b and c (lines 23–25 of Fig. 15.1). Be sure to test all capabilities of both versions of `printArray`.

15.7 Overload function template `printArray` of Fig. 15.1 with a nontemplate version that specifically prints an array of character strings in neat, tabular, column format.

15.8 Rewrite the solution to Exercise 15.6 using C++/CLI generics. Write generic versions of both the original `printArray` function and the overloaded version. The functions should have the same output and return values as the function templates. Be sure to test the all the capabilities of both versions of `printArray`.

15.9 Write a simple function template for predicate function `isEqualTo` that compares its two arguments of the same type with the equality operator (`==`) and returns `true` if they are equal and `false` if they are not equal. Use this function template in a program that calls `isEqualTo` only with a variety of built-in types. Now write a separate version of the program that calls `isEqualTo` with a user-defined class type, but does not overload the equality operator. What happens when you attempt to run this program? Now overload the equality operator (with the operator function) `operator==`. Now what happens when you attempt to run this program?

15.10 Use an `int` template nontype parameter `numberOfElements` and a type parameter `elementType` to help create a template for the `Array` class (Figs. 12.6–12.7) we developed in Chapter 12. This template will enable `Array` objects to be instantiated with a specified number of elements of a specified element type at compile time.

15.11 Distinguish between the terms "function template" and "function-template specialization."

15.12 Which is more like a stencil—a class template or a class-template specialization? Explain your answer.

15.13 What is the relationship between function templates and overloading?

15.14 What is the relationship between generic classes and inheritance?

15.15 Why might you choose to use a function template instead of a macro?

15.16 What performance problem can result from using function templates and class templates?

15.17 The compiler performs a matching process to determine which function-template specialization to call when a function is invoked. Under what circumstances does an attempt to make a match result in a compile error?

15.18 Why is it appropriate to refer to a class template or a generic class as a parameterized type?

15.19 Why are type constraints useful in generic classes and functions?

15.20 Explain why a Visual C++ program would use the statement

```
Array< Employee > workerList( 100 );
```

15.21 Review your answer to Exercise 15.20. Why might a Visual C++ program use the statement

```
Array< Employee > workerList;
```

15.22 Explain the use of the following notation in a Visual C++ program:

```
template< typename T > Array< T >::Array( int s )
```

15.23 Why might you use a nontype parameter with a class template for a container such as an array or stack?

15.24 Suppose that a class template has the header

```
template< typename T > class Ct1
```

Describe the friendship relationships established by placing each of the following friend declarations inside this class template. Identifiers beginning with "f" are functions, identifiers beginning with "C" are classes, identifiers beginning with "Ct" are class templates and T is a template type parameter (i.e., T can represent any fundamental or class type).
   a) friend void f1();
   b) friend void f2(Ct1< T > &);
   c) friend void C2::f3();
   d) friend void Ct3< T >::f4(Ct1< T > &);
   e) friend class C4;
   f) friend class Ct5< T >;

15.25 Suppose that class template Employee has a static data member count. Suppose that three class-template specializations are instantiated from the class template. How many copies of the static data member will exist? How will the use of each be constrained (if at all)?

16

Exception Handling

It is common sense to take a method and try it. If it fails, admit it frankly and try another. But above all, try something.

—Franklin Delano Roosevelt

O! throw away the worser part of it, And live the purer with the other half.

—William Shakespeare

If they're running and they don't look where they're going I have to come out from somewhere and catch them.

—Jerome David Salinger

O infinite virtue! com'st thou smiling from the world's great snare uncaught?

—William Shakespeare

I never forget a face, but in your case I'll make an exception.

—Groucho Marx

OBJECTIVES

In this chapter you'll learn:

- What exceptions are and when to use them.

- To use `try`, `catch` and `throw` to detect, handle and indicate exceptions, respectively.

- To process uncaught and unexpected exceptions.

- To declare new exception classes.

- How stack unwinding enables exceptions not caught in one scope to be caught in another scope.

- To handle `new` failures.

- To use `auto_ptr` to prevent memory leaks.

- To understand the standard exception hierarchy.

- To use `finally` with C++/CLI exception handling.

16.1 Introduction

In this chapter, we introduce *exception handling*. An *exception* is an indication of a problem that occurs during a program's execution. The name "exception" implies that the problem occurs infrequently—if the "rule" is that a statement normally executes correctly, then the "exception to the rule" is that a problem occurs. Exception handling enables programmers to create applications that can resolve (or handle) exceptions. In many cases, handling an exception allows a program to continue executing as if no problem had been encountered. A more severe problem could prevent a program from continuing normal execution, instead requiring the program to notify the user of the problem before terminating in a controlled manner. The features presented in this chapter enable programmers to write *robust* and *fault-tolerant programs* that are able to deal with problems that may arise and continue executing or terminate gracefully. The style and details of Visual C++ exception handling are based in part on the work of Andrew Koenig and Bjarne Stroustrup, as presented in their paper, "Exception Handling for C++ (revised)."[1]

---

1. Koenig, A., and B. Stroustrup, "Exception Handling for C++ (revised)," *Proceedings of the Usenix C++ Conference*, pp. 149–176, San Francisco, April 1990.

Error-Prevention Tip 16.1

Exception handling helps improve a program's fault tolerance.

Software Engineering Observation 16.1

Exception handling provides a standard mechanism for processing errors. This is especially important when working on a project with a large team of programmers.

The chapter begins with an overview of exception-handling concepts, then demonstrates basic exception-handling techniques. We show these techniques via an example that demonstrates handling an exception that occurs when a function attempts to divide by zero. We then discuss additional exception-handling issues, such as how to handle exceptions that occur in a constructor or destructor and how to handle exceptions that occur if operator new fails to allocate memory for an object. We also introduce several classes that the C++ Standard Library provides for handling exceptions. We conclude the chapter with a demonstration of exception handling in C++/CLI and how to use the finally keyword with managed code.

16.2 Exception-Handling Overview

Program logic frequently tests conditions that determine how program execution proceeds. Consider the following pseudocode:

> *Perform a task*
>
> *If the preceding task did not execute correctly*
>   *Perform error processing*
>
> *Perform next task*
>
> *If the preceding task did not execute correctly*
>   *Perform error processing*
>
> *...*

In this pseudocode, we begin by performing a task. We then test whether that task executed correctly. If not, we perform error processing. Otherwise, we continue with the next task. Although this form of error handling works, intermixing program logic with error-handling logic can make the program difficult to read, modify, maintain and debug—especially in large applications.

Performance Tip 16.1

If the potential problems occur infrequently, intermixing program logic and error-handling logic can degrade a program's performance, because the program must (potentially frequently) perform tests to determine whether the task executed correctly and the next task can be performed.

Exception handling enables you to remove error-handling code from the "main line" of the program's execution, which improves program clarity and enhances modifiability. Programmers can decide to handle any exceptions they choose—all exceptions, all exceptions of a certain type or all exceptions of a group of related types (e.g., exception types that belong to an inheritance hierarchy). Such flexibility reduces the likelihood that errors will be overlooked and thereby makes a program more robust.

With programming languages that do not support exception handling, programmers often delay writing error-processing code or sometimes forget to include it. This results in less robust software products. Visual C++ enables you to deal with exception handling easily from the inception of a project.

16.3 Example: Divide by Zero Without Exception Handling

First we demonstrate what happens when errors arise in a Visual C++ Console Application that does not use exception handling. Figure 16.1 inputs two integers from the user, then divides the first integer by the second using integer division to obtain an int result. In this example, we will see that an exception is *thrown* (i.e., an exception occurs) when a function detects a problem and is unable to handle it.

```cpp
 1   // Fig. 16.1: DivideByZeroTest.cpp
 2   // A simple program that attempts to divide by zero
 3   #include <iostream>
 4   using std::cin;
 5   using std::cout;
 6   using std::endl;
 7
 8   int main()
 9   {
10      int numerator; // user-specified numerator
11      int denominator; // user-specified denominator
12      double result; // result of division
13
14      cout << "Enter two integers (end-of-file to end): ";
15
16      // get numerator and denominator
17      cin >> numerator >> denominator;
18
19      // divide the two integers, then display the result
20      result = numerator / denominator;
21
22      cout << "\nResult: " << numerator << " / " << denominator
23         << " = " << result << endl;
24
25      return 0; // terminate normally
26   } // end main
```

```
Enter two integers (end-of-file to end): 100 7

Result: 100 / 7 = 14
```

```
Enter two integers (end-of-file to end): 100 0
```

Fig. 16.1 | Integer division without exception handling.

Running the Application

In most of the examples we have created so far, the application appears to run the same with or without debugging. As we discuss shortly, some examples might cause errors, depending on the user's input. The first sample execution in Figure 16.1 shows a successful division. In the second sample execution, the user enters 0 as the denominator. A dialog is displayed indicating the application has stopped working. If you run this application using the **Debug > Start Debugging** menu option, the program pauses at the line where an exception occurs, allowing you to analyze the current state of the program and debug it (Fig. 16.2). We discuss debugging in detail in Appendix H.

In the following examples, we do not wish to debug the application; we simply want to see what happens when errors arise. For this reason, we execute this application from a Command Prompt window. Select **Start > All Programs > Accessories > Command Prompt** to open a Command Prompt window, then use the `cd` command to change to the application's debug directory. For example, if the application resides in the directory `C:\examples\ch16\Fig16_03_04\DivideByZeroException` on your system, you would type

```
cd /d C:\examples\ch16\Fig16_03_04\DivideByZeroException\debug
```

in the Command Prompt, then press *Enter* to change to the application's debug directory. To execute the application, type

```
DivideByZeroException.exe
```

in the Command Prompt, then press *Enter*. If an error arises during execution, a dialog is displayed indicating that the application has encountered a problem and needs to close. The dialog also asks whether you'd like to send information about this error to Microsoft. Since we are creating this error for demonstration purposes, you should click **Don't Send**. [*Note:* On some systems a **Just-In-Time Debugging** dialog is displayed instead. If this oc-

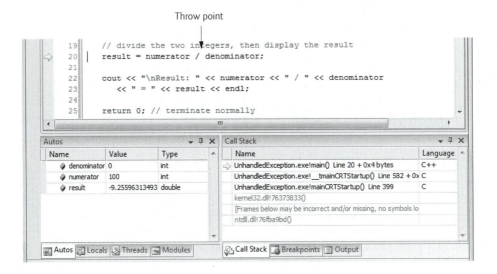

Fig. 16.2 | Visual Studio exception handler.

curs, simply click the **No** button to dismiss the dialog.] At this point, an error message describing the problem may be displayed in the Command Prompt if possible. We formatted the error messages in some examples for readability. [*Note:* Selecting **Debug > Start Without Debugging** (or *<Ctrl> F5*) to run the application from Visual Studio executes the application's so-called release version. The error messages produced by this version of the application may differ from those shown in examples due to optimizations that the compiler performs to create an application's release version.]

16.4 Example: Handling an Attempt to Divide by Zero

Let us consider a simple example of exception handling (Figs. 16.3–16.4). The purpose of this example is to show how to prevent a common arithmetic problem—division by zero. In Visual C++, division by zero using integer arithmetic typically causes a program to terminate prematurely as you saw in Figure 16.1. In floating-point arithmetic, some C++ implementations allow division by zero, in which case positive or negative infinity is displayed as INF or -INF, respectively.

In this example, we define a function named quotient that receives two integers input by the user and divides its first int parameter by its second int parameter. Before performing the division, the function casts the first int parameter's value to type double. Then, the second int parameter's value is promoted to type double for the calculation. So function quotient actually performs the division using two double values and returns a double result.

Although division by zero is allowed in floating-point arithmetic, for the purpose of this example we treat any attempt to divide by zero as an error. Thus, function quotient tests its second parameter to ensure that it is not zero before allowing the division to proceed. If the second parameter is zero, the function uses an exception to indicate to the caller that a problem occurred. The caller (main in this example) can then process the exception and allow the user to type two new values before calling function quotient again. In this way, the program can continue to execute even after an improper value is entered, thus making the program more robust.

The example consists of two files. DivideByZeroException.h (Fig. 16.3) defines an exception class that represents the type of the problem that might occur in the example, and DivideByZeroTest.cpp (Fig. 16.4) defines the quotient function and the main function that calls it. Function main contains the code that demonstrates exception handling.

Defining an Exception Class to Represent the Type of Problem That Might Occur
Figure 16.3 defines class DivideByZeroException as a derived class of Standard Library class ***runtime_error*** (defined in header file ***<stdexcept>***). Class runtime_error—a derived class of Standard Library class ***exception*** (defined in header file ***<exception>***)—is the Visual C++ standard base class for representing runtime errors. Class exception is the standard Visual C++ base class for all exceptions. (Section 16.13 discusses class exception and its derived classes in detail.) A typical exception class that derives from the runtime_error class defines only a constructor (e.g., lines 12–13) that passes an error-message string to the base-class runtime_error constructor. Every exception class that derives directly or indirectly from exception contains the virtual function ***what***, which returns an exception object's error message. Note that you are not required to derive a custom exception class, such as DivideByZeroException, from the standard exception classes provided by Visual

```
 1    // Fig. 16.3: DivideByZeroException.h
 2    // Class DivideByZeroException definition.
 3    #include <stdexcept> // stdexcept header file contains runtime_error
 4    using std::runtime_error; // standard C++ library class runtime_error
 5
 6    // DivideByZeroException objects should be thrown by functions
 7    // upon detecting division-by-zero exceptions
 8    class DivideByZeroException : public runtime_error
 9    {
10    public:
11       // constructor specifies default error message
12       DivideByZeroException()
13          : runtime_error( "attempted to divide by zero" ) {}
14    }; // end class DivideByZeroException
```

Fig. 16.3 | Class DivideByZeroException definition.

C++. However, doing so allows programmers to use the virtual function what to obtain an appropriate error message. We use an object of this DivideByZeroException class in Fig. 16.4 to indicate when an attempt is made to divide by zero.

Demonstrating Exception Handling
The program in Fig. 16.4 uses exception handling to wrap code that might throw a "divide-by-zero" exception and to handle that exception, should one occur. The application enables the user to enter two integers, which are passed as arguments to function quotient (lines 13–21). This function divides its first parameter (numerator) by its second parameter (denominator). Assuming that the user does not specify 0 as the denominator for the division, function quotient returns the division result. However, if the user inputs 0 for the denominator, function quotient throws an exception. In the sample output, the first two lines show a successful calculation, and the next two lines show a failed calculation due to an attempt to divide by zero. When the exception occurs, the program informs the user of the mistake and prompts the user to input two new integers. After we discuss the code, we'll consider the user inputs and flow of program control that yield these outputs.

```
 1    // Fig. 16.4: DivideByZeroTest.cpp
 2    // A simple exception-handling example that checks for
 3    // divide-by-zero exceptions.
 4    #include <iostream>
 5    using std::cin‘;
 6    using std::cout;
 7    using std::endl;
 8
 9    #include "DivideByZeroException.h" // DivideByZeroException class
10
11    // perform division and throw DivideByZeroException object if
12    // divide-by-zero exception occurs
13    double quotient( int numerator, int denominator )
14    {
```

Fig. 16.4 | Exception-handling example that throws exceptions on attempts to divide by zero. (Part 1 of 2.)

```
15      // throw DivideByZeroException if trying to divide by zero
16      if ( denominator == 0 )
17          throw DivideByZeroException(); // terminate function
18
19      // return division result
20      return static_cast< double >( numerator ) / denominator;
21   } // end function quotient
22
23   int main()
24   {
25      int number1; // user-specified numerator
26      int number2; // user-specified denominator
27      double result; // result of division
28
29      cout << "Enter two integers (end-of-file to end): ";
30
31      // enable user to enter two integers to divide
32      while ( cin >> number1 >> number2 )
33      {
34          // try block contains code that might throw exception
35          // and code that should not execute if an exception occurs
36          try
37          {
38              result = quotient( number1, number2 );
39              cout << "The quotient is: " << result << endl;
40          } // end try
41
42          // exception handler handles a divide-by-zero exception
43          catch ( DivideByZeroException &divideByZeroException )
44          {
45              cout << "Exception occurred: "
46                  << divideByZeroException.what() << endl;
47          } // end catch
48
49          cout << "\nEnter two integers (end-of-file to end): ";
50      } // end while
51
52      cout << endl;
53      return 0; // terminate normally
54   } // end main
```

```
Enter two integers (end-of-file to end): 100 7
The quotient is: 14.2857

Enter two integers (end-of-file to end): 100 0
Exception occurred: attempted to divide by zero

Enter two integers (end-of-file to end): ^Z
```

Fig. 16.4 | Exception-handling example that throws exceptions on attempts to divide by zero. (Part 2 of 2.)

Enclosing Code in a try Block

The program begins by prompting the user to enter two integers. The integers are input in the condition of the while loop (line 32). After the user inputs values that represent the numerator and denominator, program control proceeds into the loop's body (lines 33–50). Line 38 passes these values to function `quotient` (lines 13–21), which either divides the integers and returns a result, or throws an exception on an attempt to divide by zero. Exception handling is geared to situations in which the function that detects an error is unable to handle it.

Visual C++ provides ***try blocks*** to enable exception handling. A try block consists of keyword ***try*** followed by braces (`{}`) that define a block of code in which exceptions might occur. The `try` block encloses statements that might cause exceptions and statements that should be skipped if an exception occurs.

Note that a `try` block (lines 36–40) encloses the invocation of function `quotient` and the statement that displays the division result. In this example, because the invocation of function `quotient` (line 38) can throw an exception, we enclose this function invocation in a `try` block. Enclosing the output statement (line 39) in the `try` block ensures that the output will occur only if function `quotient` returns a result.

Software Engineering Observation 16.2

Exceptions may surface through explicitly mentioned code in a try block, through calls to other functions and through deeply nested function calls initiated by code in a try block.

Defining a `catch` Handler to Process a `DivideByZeroException`

Exceptions are processed by ***catch handlers*** (also called *exception handlers*), which catch and handle exceptions. At least one `catch` handler (lines 43–47) must immediately follow each `try` block. Each `catch` handler begins with the keyword ***catch*** and specifies in parentheses an *exception parameter* that represents the type of exception the `catch` handler can process (`DivideByZeroException` in this case). When an exception occurs in a `try` block, the `catch` handler that executes is the one whose type matches the type of the exception that occurred (i.e., the type in the `catch` block matches the thrown exception type exactly or is a base class of it). If an exception parameter includes an optional parameter name, the `catch` handler can use that parameter name to interact with the caught exception in the body of the `catch` handler, which is delimited by braces (`{` and `}`). A `catch` handler typically reports the error to the user, logs it to a file, terminates the program gracefully or tries an alternate strategy to accomplish the failed task. In this example, the `catch` handler simply reports that the user attempted to divide by zero. Then the program prompts the user to enter two new integer values.

Common Programming Error 16.1

It is a syntax error to place code between a try block and its corresponding catch handlers or between its catch handlers.

Common Programming Error 16.2

Each catch handler can have only a single parameter—specifying a comma-separated list of exception parameters is a syntax error.

Common Programming Error 16.3

It is a logic error to catch the same type in two different catch handlers following a single try block.

Termination Model of Exception Handling

If an exception occurs as the result of a statement in a try block, the try block expires (i.e., terminates immediately). Next, the program searches for the first catch handler that can process the type of exception that occurred. The program locates the matching catch by comparing the thrown exception's type to each catch's exception-parameter type until the program finds a match. A match occurs if the types are identical or if the thrown exception's type is a derived class of the exception-parameter type. When a match occurs, the code contained in the matching catch handler executes. When a catch handler finishes processing by reaching its closing right brace (}), the exception is considered handled and the local variables defined within the catch handler (including the catch parameter) go out of scope. Program control does not return to the point at which the exception occurred (known as the ***throw point***), because the try block has expired. Rather, control resumes with the first statement (line 49) after the last catch handler following the try block. This is known as the ***termination model of exception handling***. [*Note:* Some languages use the ***resumption model of exception handling***, in which, after an exception is handled, control resumes just after the throw point.] As with any other block of code, when a try block terminates, local variables defined in the block go out of scope.

Common Programming Error 16.4

Logic errors can occur if you assume that after an exception is handled, control will return to the first statement after the throw point.

Error-Prevention Tip 16.2

With exception handling, a program can continue executing (rather than terminating) after dealing with a problem. This helps ensure the kind of robust applications that contribute to what is called mission-critical computing or business-critical computing.

If the try block completes its execution successfully (i.e., no exceptions occur in the try block), then the program ignores the catch handlers and program control continues with the first statement after the last catch following that try block. If no exceptions occur in a try block, the program ignores the catch handler(s) for that block.

If an exception that occurs in a try block has no matching catch handler, or if an exception occurs in a statement outside a try block, the function containing the statement terminates immediately, and the program attempts to locate an enclosing try block in the calling function. This process is called ***stack unwinding*** and is discussed in Section 16.8.

Flow of Program Control When the User Enters a Nonzero Denominator

Consider the flow of control when the user inputs the numerator 100 and the denominator 7 (as shown in Fig. 16.4). In line 16, function quotient determines that the denominator does not equal zero, so line 20 performs the division and returns the result (14.2857) to line 38 as a double (the static_cast< double > in line 20 ensures the proper return-value type). Program control then continues sequentially from line 38, so line 39 displays the division result—line 40 ends the try block. Because the try block completed successfully and did not throw an exception, the program does not execute the statements contained in the catch handler (lines 43–47), and control continues to line 49 (the first line of code after the catch handler), which prompts the user to enter two more integers.

Flow of Program Control When the User Enters a Denominator of Zero

Now let us consider a more interesting case in which the user inputs the numerator 100 and the denominator 0 (i.e., the third and fourth lines of output in Fig. 16.4). In line 16, quotient determines that the denominator equals zero, which indicates an attempt to divide by zero. Line 17 throws an exception, which we represent as an object of class DivideByZeroException (Fig. 16.3).

To throw an exception, line 17 uses keyword ***throw*** followed by an operand that represents the type of exception to throw. Normally, a throw statement specifies one operand. (In Section 16.6, we discuss how to use a throw statement with no operand.) The operand of a throw can be of any type. If the operand is an object, we call it an *exception object*—in this example, the exception object is an object of type DivideByZeroException. However, a throw operand also can assume other values, such as the value of an expression that does not result in an object (e.g., throw x > 5) or the value of an int (e.g., throw 5). The examples in this chapter focus exclusively on throwing exception objects.

Common Programming Error 16.5

Use caution when throwing the result of a conditional expression (?:)—promotion rules could cause the value to be of a type different from the one expected. For example, when throwing an int or a double from the same conditional expression, the int is promoted to a double. So, a catch handler that catches an int would never execute based on such a conditional expression.

As part of throwing an exception, the throw operand is created and used to initialize the parameter in the catch handler, which we discuss momentarily. In this example, the throw statement in line 17 creates an object of class DivideByZeroException. When line 17 throws the exception, function quotient exits immediately. Therefore, line 17 throws the exception before function quotient can perform the division in line 20. This is a central characteristic of exception handling: A function should throw an exception *before* the error has an opportunity to occur.

We enclosed the invocation of function quotient (line 38) in a try block, so program control enters the catch handler (lines 43–47) that immediately follows the try block. This catch handler serves as the exception handler for the divide-by-zero exception. In general, when an exception is thrown within a try block, the exception is caught by a catch handler that specifies the type matching the thrown exception. In this program, the catch handler specifies that it catches DivideByZeroException objects—this type matches the object type thrown in function quotient. Actually, the catch handler catches a reference to the DivideByZeroException object created by function quotient's throw statement (line 17). The exception object is maintained by the exception-handling mechanism.

Performance Tip 16.2

Catching an exception object by reference eliminates the overhead of copying the object that represents the thrown exception.

Good Programming Practice 16.1

Associating each type of runtime error with an appropriately named exception object improves program clarity.

The catch handler's body (lines 45–46) prints the associated error message returned by calling function what of base class runtime_error. This function returns the string that the `DivideByZeroException` constructor (lines 12–13 in Fig. 16.3) passed to the `runtime_error` base-class constructor.

Uncaught Exceptions

An *uncaught exception* is an exception for which there is no matching `catch` block. The result of an uncaught exception depends on how you execute the program. If you run the application from Visual Studio with debugging and the runtime environment detects an uncaught exception, the application pauses, and windows displaying the type of the exception and helpful information appear. Figure 16.2 shows an example of this.

16.5 When to Use Exception Handling

Exception handling is designed to process *synchronous errors*, which occur when a statement executes. Common examples of these errors are out-of-range array subscripts, arithmetic overflow (i.e., a value outside the representable range of values), division by zero, invalid function parameters and unsuccessful memory allocation (due to lack of memory). Exception handling is not designed to process errors associated with *asynchronous* events (e.g., disk I/O completions, network message arrivals, mouse clicks and keystrokes), which occur in parallel with, and independent of, the program's flow of control.

Software Engineering Observation 16.3

Incorporate your exception-handling strategy into your system from the design process's inception. Including effective exception handling after a system has been implemented can be difficult.

Software Engineering Observation 16.4

Exception handling provides a single, uniform technique for processing problems. This helps programmers working on large projects understand each other's error-processing code.

Software Engineering Observation 16.5

Avoid using exception handling as an alternate form of flow of control. These "additional" exceptions can "get in the way" of genuine error-type exceptions.

Software Engineering Observation 16.6

Exception handling simplifies combining software components and enables them to work together effectively by enabling predefined components to communicate problems to application-specific components, which can then process the problems in an application-specific manner.

The exception-handling mechanism also is useful for processing problems that occur when a program interacts with software elements, such as member functions, constructors, destructors and classes. Rather than handling problems internally, such software elements often use exceptions to notify programs when problems occur. This enables programmers to implement customized error handling for each application.

Performance Tip 16.3

When no exceptions occur, exception-handling code incurs little or no performance penalty. Thus, programs that implement exception handling operate more efficiently than do programs that intermix error-handling code with program logic.

Software Engineering Observation 16.7

Functions with common error conditions should return 0 or NULL (or other appropriate values) rather than throw exceptions. A program calling such a function can check the return value to determine success or failure of the function call.

Complex applications normally consist of predefined software components and application-specific components that use the predefined components. When a predefined component encounters a problem, that component needs a mechanism to communicate the problem to the application-specific component—the predefined component cannot know in advance how each application processes a problem that occurs.

16.6 Rethrowing an Exception

It is possible that an exception handler, upon receiving an exception, might decide either that it cannot process that exception or that it can process the exception only partially. In such cases, the exception handler can defer the exception handling (or perhaps a portion of it) to another exception handler. In either case, you achieve this by *rethrowing the exception* via the statement

   throw;

Regardless of whether a handler can process (even partially) an exception, the handler can rethrow the exception for further processing outside the handler. The next enclosing try block detects the rethrown exception, which a catch handler listed after that enclosing try block attempts to handle.

Common Programming Error 16.6

*Executing an empty throw statement that is situated outside a catch handler causes a call to function **terminate**, which abandons exception processing and terminates the program immediately.*

The program of Fig. 16.5 demonstrates rethrowing an exception. In main's try block (lines 32–37), line 35 calls function throwException (lines 11–27). The throwException function also contains a try block (lines 14–18), from which the throw statement in line 17 throws an instance of standard-library-class exception. Function throwException's catch handler (lines 19–24) catches this exception, prints an error message (lines 21–22) and rethrows the exception (line 23). This terminates function throwException and returns control to line 35 in the try...catch block in main. The try block terminates (so line 36 does not execute), and the catch handler in main (lines 38–41) catches this exception and prints an error message (line 40). [*Note:* Since we do not use the exception parameters in the catch handlers of this example, we omit the exception parameter names and specify only the type of exception to catch (lines 19 and 38).]

```
1   // Fig. 16.5: ExceptionRethrowing.cpp
2   // Demonstrating exception rethrowing.
3   #include <iostream>
4   using std::cout;
5   using std::endl;
```

Fig. 16.5 | Rethrowing an exception. (Part 1 of 2.)

```
6
7    #include <exception>
8    using std::exception;
9
10   // throw, catch and rethrow exception
11   void throwException()
12   {
13      // throw exception and catch it immediately
14      try
15      {
16         cout << "  Function throwException throws an exception\n";
17         throw exception(); // generate exception
18      } // end try
19      catch ( exception & ) // handle exception
20      {
21         cout << "  Exception handled in function throwException"
22            << "\n  Function throwException rethrows exception";
23         throw; // rethrow exception for further processing
24      } // end catch
25
26      cout << "This also should not print\n";
27   } // end function throwException
28
29   int main()
30   {
31      // throw exception
32      try
33      {
34         cout << "\nmain invokes function throwException\n";
35         throwException();
36         cout << "This should not print\n";
37      } // end try
38      catch ( exception & ) // handle exception
39      {
40         cout << "\n\nException handled in main\n";
41      } // end catch
42
43      cout << "Program control continues after catch in main\n";
44      return 0;
45   } // end main
```

```
main invokes function throwException
  Function throwException throws an exception
  Exception handled in function throwException
  Function throwException rethrows exception

Exception handled in main
Program control continues after catch in main
```

Fig. 16.5 | Rethrowing an exception. (Part 2 of 2.)

16.7 Processing Unexpected Exceptions

If a function throws an exception without a matching catch handler, then function unexpected is invoked by the exception-handling mechanism. Function unexpected calls the function registered with function `set_unexpected` (defined in header file `<exception>`). If no function has been registered in this manner, function `terminate` is called by default. Cases in which function `terminate` is called include:

1. the exception mechanism cannot find a matching `catch` for a thrown exception

2. a destructor attempts to `throw` an exception during stack unwinding

3. an attempt is made to rethrow an exception when there is no exception currently being handled

4. a call to function `unexpected` defaults to calling function `terminate`

(Section 15.5.1 of the C++ Standard Document discusses several additional cases.) Function **set_terminate** can specify the function to invoke when `terminate` is called. Otherwise, `terminate` calls **abort**, which terminates the program without calling the destructors of any remaining objects of automatic or static storage class. This could lead to resource leaks when a program terminates prematurely.

Function `set_terminate` and function `set_unexpected` each return a pointer to the last function called by `terminate` and `unexpected`, respectively (0, the first time each is called). This enables you to save the function pointer so it can be restored later. Functions `set_terminate` and `set_unexpected` take as arguments pointers to functions with `void` return types and no arguments.

If the last action of a programmer-defined termination function is not to exit a program, function `abort` will be called to end program execution after the other statements of the programmer-defined termination function are executed.

16.8 Stack Unwinding

When an exception is thrown but not caught in a particular scope, the *function-call stack* is "unwound," and an attempt is made to `catch` the exception in the next outer `try...catch` block. Unwinding the function-call stack means that the function in which the exception was not caught terminates, all local variables in that function are destroyed and control returns to the statement that originally invoked that function. If a `try` block encloses that statement, an attempt is made to `catch` the exception. If a `try` block does not enclose that statement, stack unwinding occurs again. If no `catch` handler ever catches this exception, function `terminate` is called to terminate the program. The program of Fig. 16.6 demonstrates stack unwinding.

```
1   // Fig. 16.6: StackUnwinding.cpp
2   // Demonstrating stack unwinding.
3   #include <iostream>
4   using std::cout;
5   using std::endl;
6
7   #include <stdexcept>
8   using std::runtime_error;
9
```

Fig. 16.6 | Stack unwinding. (Part 1 of 2.)

```
10    // function3 throws runtime error
11    void function3()
12    {
13       cout << "In function 3" << endl;
14
15       // no try block, stack unwinding occurs, return control to function2
16       throw runtime_error( "runtime_error in function3" ); // no print
17    } // end function3
18
19    // function2 invokes function3
20    void function2()
21    {
22       cout << "function3 is called inside function2" << endl;
23       function3(); // stack unwinding occurs, return control to function1
24    } // end function2
25
26    // function1 invokes function2
27    void function1()
28    {
29       cout << "function2 is called inside function1" << endl;
30       function2(); // stack unwinding occurs, return control to main
31    } // end function1
32
33    // demonstrate stack unwinding
34    int main()
35    {
36       // invoke function1
37       try
38       {
39          cout << "function1 is called inside main" << endl;
40          function1(); // call function1 which throws runtime_error
41       } // end try
42       catch ( runtime_error &error ) // handle runtime error
43       {
44          cout << "Exception occurred: " << error.what() << endl;
45          cout << "Exception handled in main" << endl;
46       } // end catch
47
48       return 0;
49    } // end main
```

```
function1 is called inside main
function2 is called inside function1
function3 is called inside function2
In function 3
Exception occurred: runtime_error in function3
Exception handled in main
```

Fig. 16.6 | Stack unwinding. (Part 2 of 2.)

In main, the try block (lines 37–41) calls function1 (lines 27–31). Next, function1 calls function2 (lines 20–24), which in turn calls function3 (lines 11–17). Line 16 of function3 throws a runtime_error object. However, because no try block encloses the throw statement in line 16, stack unwinding occurs—function3 terminates in line 16, then returns control to the statement in function2 that invoked function3 (i.e., line 23). Because no try block encloses line 23, stack unwinding occurs again—function2 terminates in line 23 and returns control to the statement in function1 that invoked function2 (i.e., line 30). Because no try block encloses line 30, stack unwinding occurs one more time—function1 terminates in line 30 and returns control to the statement in main that invoked function1 (i.e., line 40). The try block of lines 37–41 encloses this statement, so the first matching catch handler located after this try block (line 42–46) catches and processes the exception. Line 44 uses function what to display the exception message. Recall that function what is a virtual function of class exception that can be overridden by a derived class to return an appropriate error message.

16.9 Constructors, Destructors and Exception Handling

First, let's discuss an issue that we have mentioned but not yet resolved satisfactorily: What happens when an error is detected in a constructor? For example, how should an object's constructor respond when new fails because it was unable to allocate required memory for storing that object's internal representation? Because the constructor cannot return a value to indicate an error, we must choose an alternative means of indicating that the object has not been constructed properly. One scheme is to return the improperly constructed object and hope that anyone using it would make appropriate tests to determine that it is in an inconsistent state. Another scheme is to set some variable outside the constructor. The preferred alternative is to require the constructor to throw an exception that contains the error information, thus offering an opportunity for the program to handle the failure.

Before an exception is thrown by a constructor, destructors are called for any member objects built as part of the object being constructed. Destructors are called for every automatic object constructed in a try block before an exception is thrown. Stack unwinding is guaranteed to have been completed at the point that an exception handler begins executing. If a destructor invoked as a result of stack unwinding throws an exception, terminate is called.

If an object has member objects, and if an exception is thrown before the outer object is fully constructed, then destructors will be executed for the member objects that have been constructed prior to the occurrence of the exception. If an array of objects has been partially constructed when an exception occurs, only the destructors for the constructed objects in the array will be called.

An exception could preclude the operation of code that would normally release a resource, thus causing a resource leak. One technique to resolve this problem is to initialize a local object to acquire the resource. When an exception occurs, the destructor for that object will be invoked and can free the resource.

 Error-Prevention Tip 16.3

When an exception is thrown from the constructor for an object that is created in a new expression, the dynamically allocated memory for that object is released.

16.10 Exceptions and Inheritance

Various exception classes can be derived from a common base class, as we discussed in Section 16.4, when we created class DivideByZeroException as a derived class of class exception. If a catch handler catches a pointer or reference to an exception object of a base-class type, it also can catch a pointer or reference to all objects of classes publicly derived from that base class—this allows for polymorphic processing of related errors.

Error-Prevention Tip 16.4

Using inheritance with exceptions enables an exception handler to catch related errors with concise notation. One approach is to catch each type of pointer or reference to a derived-class exception object individually, but a more concise approach is to catch pointers or references to base-class exception objects instead. Also, catching pointers or references to derived-class exception objects individually is error prone, especially if you forget to test explicitly for one or more of the derived-class pointer or reference types.

16.11 Processing new Failures

The C++ standard specifies that, when operator new fails, it throws a *bad_alloc* exception (defined in header file <new>). However, some compilers are not compliant with the C++ standard and therefore use the version of new that returns 0 on failure. For example, Visual Studio 2008 throws a bad_alloc exception when new fails, while Visual C++ 6.0 returns 0 on new failure.

Compilers vary in their support for new-failure handling. Many older C++ compilers return 0 by default when new fails. Some compilers support new, throwing an exception if header file <new> (or <new.h>) is included. Other compilers throw bad_alloc by default, regardless of whether header file <new> is included. Consult the compiler documentation to determine the compiler's support for new-failure handling.

This section presents two examples of new failing. The first uses the version of new that throws a bad_alloc exception when new fails. The second uses function *set_new_handler* to handle new failures. [*Note:* The examples in Figs. 16.7–16.8 allocate large amounts of dynamic memory, which could cause your computer to become sluggish.]

new *Throwing bad_alloc on Failure*

Figure 16.7 demonstrates new throwing bad_alloc on failure to allocate the requested memory. The for statement (lines 20–24) inside the try block should loop 50 times and, on each pass, allocate an array of 50,000,000 double values. If new fails and throws a bad_alloc exception, the loop terminates, and the program continues in line 28, where the catch handler catches and processes the exception. Lines 30–31 print the message "Exception occurred:" followed by the message returned from the base-class-exception version of function what (i.e., an implementation-defined exception-specific message, such as "Bad Allocation" in Visual Studio 2008). The output shows that the program performed only three iterations of the loop before new failed and threw the bad_alloc exception. Your output might differ based on the physical memory and disk space available for virtual memory on your system.

```
1   // Fig. 16.7: NewFailing.cpp
2   // Demonstrating standard new throwing bad_alloc when memory
3   // cannot be allocated.
4   #include <iostream>
```

Fig. 16.7 | new throwing bad_alloc on failure. (Part 1 of 2.)

```
 5   using std::cerr;
 6   using std::cout;
 7   using std::endl;
 8
 9   #include <new> // standard operator new
10   using std::bad_alloc;
11
12   int main()
13   {
14      double *ptr[ 50 ];
15
16      // aim each ptr[i] at a big block of memory
17      try
18      {
19         // allocate memory for ptr[ i ]; new throws bad_alloc on failure
20         for ( int i = 0; i < 50; i++ )
21         {
22            ptr[ i ] = new double[ 50000000 ]; // may throw exception
23            cout << "ptr[" << i << "] points to 50,000,000 new doubles\n";
24         } // end for
25      } // end try
26
27      // handle bad_alloc exception
28      catch ( bad_alloc &memoryAllocationException )
29      {
30         cerr << "Exception occurred: "
31            << memoryAllocationException.what() << endl;
32      } // end catch
33
34      return 0;
35   } // end main
```

```
ptr[0] points to 50,000,000 new doubles
ptr[1] points to 50,000,000 new doubles
ptr[2] points to 50,000,000 new doubles
Exception occurred: bad allocation
```

Fig. 16.7 | new throwing bad_alloc on failure. (Part 2 of 2.)

The C++ standard specifies that standard-compliant compilers can continue to use a version of new that returns 0 upon failure. For this purpose, header file <new> defines object **nothrow** (of type nothrow_t), which is used as follows:

> **double** *ptr = **new**(nothrow) **double**[50000000];

The preceding statement uses the version of new that does not throw bad_alloc exceptions (i.e., nothrow) to allocate an array of 50,000,000 doubles.

Software Engineering Observation 16.8

To make programs more robust, use the version of new that throws bad_alloc exceptions on failure.

Handling new Failures Using Function *set_new_handler*

An additional feature for handling new failures is function set_new_handler (prototyped in standard header file <new>). This function takes as its argument a pointer to a function that takes no arguments and returns void. This pointer points to the function that will be called if new fails. This provides you with a uniform approach to handling all new failures, regardless of where a failure occurs in the program. Once set_new_handler registers a *new handler* in the program, operator new does not throw bad_alloc on failure; rather, it defers the error handling to the new-handler function.

If new allocates memory successfully, it returns a pointer to that memory. If new fails to allocate memory and set_new_handler did not register a new-handler function, new throws a bad_alloc exception. If new fails to allocate memory and a new-handler function has been registered, the new-handler function is called. The C++ standard specifies that the new-handler function should perform one of the following tasks:

1. Make more memory available by deleting other dynamically allocated memory (or telling the user to close other applications) and return to operator new to attempt to allocate memory again.

2. Throw an exception of type bad_alloc.

3. Call function abort or exit (both found in header file <cstdlib>) to terminate the program.

Figure 16.8 demonstrates set_new_handler. Function customNewHandler (lines 14–18) prints an error message (line 16), then terminates the program via a call to abort (line 17). The output shows that the program performed only three iterations of the loop before new failed and invoked function customNewHandler. Your output might differ based on the physical memory and disk space available for virtual memory on your system.

```cpp
1  // Fig. 16.8: SetNewHandler.cpp
2  // Demonstrating set_new_handler.
3  #include <iostream>
4  using std::cerr;
5  using std::cout;
6
7  #include <new> // standard operator new and set_new_handler
8  using std::set_new_handler;
9
10 #include <cstdlib> // abort function prototype
11 using std::abort;
12
13 // handle memory allocation failure
14 void customNewHandler()
15 {
16    cerr << "customNewHandler was called";
17    abort();
18 } // end function customNewHandler
19
20 // using set_new_handler to handle failed memory allocation
21 int main()
22 {
```

Fig. 16.8 | set_new_handler specifying the function to call when new fails. (Part 1 of 2.)

```
23      double *ptr[ 50 ];
24
25      // specify that customNewHandler should be called on
26      // memory allocation failure
27      set_new_handler( customNewHandler );
28
29      // aim each ptr[i] at a big block of memory; customNewHandler will be
30      // called on failed memory allocation
31      for ( int i = 0; i < 50; i++ )
32      {
33         ptr[ i ] = new double[ 50000000 ]; // may throw exception
34         cout << "ptr[" << i << "] points to 50,000,000 new doubles\n";
35      } // end for
36
37      return 0;
38   }  // end main
```

```
ptr[0] points to 50,000,000 new doubles
ptr[1] points to 50,000,000 new doubles
ptr[2] points to 50,000,000 new doubles
customNewHandler was called
```

Fig. 16.8 | set_new_handler specifying the function to call when new fails. (Part 2 of 2.)

16.12 Class auto_ptr and Dynamic Memory Allocation

A common programming practice is to allocate dynamic memory, assign the address of that memory to a pointer, use the pointer to manipulate the memory and deallocate the memory with delete when the memory is no longer needed. If an exception occurs after successful memory allocation but before the delete statement executes, a memory leak could occur. The C++ standard provides class template *auto_ptr* in header file *<memory>* to deal with this situation.

An object of class auto_ptr maintains a pointer to dynamically allocated memory. When an auto_ptr object destructor is called (for example, when an auto_ptr object goes out of scope), it performs a delete operation on its pointer data member. Class template auto_ptr provides overloaded operators * and -> so that an auto_ptr object can be used just as a regular pointer variable is. Figure 16.11 demonstrates an auto_ptr object that points to a dynamically allocated object of class Integer (Figs. 16.9–16.10).

```
1    // Fig. 16.9: Integer.h
2    // Integer class definition.
3
4    class Integer
5    {
6    public:
7       Integer( int i = 0 ); // Integer default constructor
8       ~Integer(); // Integer destructor
9       void setInteger( int i ); // functions to set Integer
```

Fig. 16.9 | Integer class definition. (Part 1 of 2.)

```
10       int getInteger() const; // function to return Integer
11   private:
12       int value;
13   }; // end class Integer
```

Fig. 16.9 | Integer class definition. (Part 2 of 2.)

```
1    // Fig. 16.10: Integer.cpp
2    // Integer member function definitions.
3    #include <iostream>
4    using std::cout;
5    using std::endl;
6
7    #include "Integer.h"
8
9    // Integer default constructor
10   Integer::Integer( int i )
11      : value( i )
12   {
13      cout << "Constructor for Integer " << value << endl;
14   } // end Integer constructor
15
16   // Integer destructor
17   Integer::~Integer()
18   {
19      cout << "Destructor for Integer " << value << endl;
20   } // end Integer destructor
21
22   // set Integer value
23   void Integer::setInteger( int i )
24   {
25      value = i;
26   } // end function setInteger
27
28   // return Integer value
29   int Integer::getInteger() const
30   {
31      return value;
32   } // end function getInteger
```

Fig. 16.10 | Member-function definitions of class Integer.

Line 18 of Fig. 16.11 creates `auto_ptr` object `ptrToInteger` and initializes it with a pointer to a dynamically allocated `Integer` object that contains the value 7. Line 21 uses the `auto_ptr` overloaded -> operator to invoke function `setInteger` on the `Integer` object that `ptrToInteger` manages. Line 24 uses the `auto_ptr` overloaded * operator to dereference `ptrToInteger`, then uses the dot (.) operator to invoke function `getInteger` on the `Integer` object. Like a regular pointer, an `auto_ptr`'s -> and * overloaded operators can be used to access the object to which the `auto_ptr` points.

Because `ptrToInteger` is a local automatic variable in `main`, `ptrToInteger` is destroyed when `main` terminates. The `auto_ptr` destructor forces a `delete` of the `Integer` object pointed to by `ptrToInteger`, which in turn calls the `Integer` class destructor. The

```
1   // Fig. 16.11: AutoPtrTest.cpp
2   // Demonstrating auto_ptr.
3   #include <iostream>
4   using std::cout;
5   using std::endl;
6
7   #include <memory>
8   using std::auto_ptr; // auto_ptr class definition
9
10  #include "Integer.h"
11
12  // use auto_ptr to manipulate Integer object
13  int main()
14  {
15     cout << "Creating an auto_ptr object that points to an Integer\n";
16
17     // "aim" auto_ptr at Integer object
18     auto_ptr< Integer > ptrToInteger( new Integer( 7 ) );
19
20     cout << "\nUsing the auto_ptr to manipulate the Integer\n";
21     ptrToInteger->setInteger( 99 ); // use auto_ptr to set Integer value
22
23     // use auto_ptr to get Integer value
24     cout << "Integer after setInteger: " << ( *ptrToInteger ).getInteger();
25     return 0;
26  } // end main
```

```
Creating an auto_ptr object that points to an Integer
Constructor for Integer 7

Using the auto_ptr to manipulate the Integer
Integer after setInteger: 99

Destructor for Integer 99
```

Fig. 16.11 | auto_ptr object manages dynamically allocated memory.

memory that Integer occupies is released, regardless of how control leaves the block (e.g., by a return statement or by an exception). Most importantly, using this technique can prevent memory leaks. For example, suppose a function returns a pointer aimed at some object. Unfortunately, the function caller that receives this pointer might not delete the object, thus resulting in a memory leak. However, if the function returns an auto_ptr to the object, the object will be deleted automatically when the auto_ptr object's destructor gets called.

Only one auto_ptr at a time can own a dynamically allocated object, and the object cannot be an array. By using its overloaded assignment operator or copy constructor, an auto_ptr can transfer ownership of the dynamic memory it manages. The last auto_ptr object that maintains the pointer to the dynamic memory will delete the memory. This makes auto_ptr an ideal mechanism for returning dynamically allocated memory to client code. When the auto_ptr goes out of scope in the client code, the auto_ptr's destructor deletes the dynamic memory.

Note that you should not use `auto_ptr` as an element inside a C++ Standard Template Library container (explained in Chapter 23). Doing so can lead to unpredictable behavior and incorrect results. Consequently, `auto_ptr` will be marked deprecated with the new C++ standard, C++0x, and replaced with a better alternative, `shared_ptr`. This will be discussed in more detail in later chapters.

16.13 Standard Library Exception Hierarchy

Experience has shown that exceptions fall nicely into a number of categories. The C++ Standard Library includes a hierarchy of exception classes (Fig. 16.12). As we first discussed in Section 16.4, this hierarchy is headed by base-class `exception` (defined in header file `<exception>`), which contains `virtual` function `what`, which derived classes can override to issue appropriate error messages.

Immediate derived classes of base-class `exception` include `runtime_error` and *`logic_error`* (both defined in header `<stdexcept>`), each of which has several derived classes. Also derived from `exception` are the exceptions thrown by Visual C++ operators— for example, `bad_alloc` is thrown by `new` (Section 16.11), *`bad_cast`* is thrown by `dynamic_cast` (Chapter 14), *`bad_typeid`* is thrown by `typeid` (Chapter 14) and *`bad_exception`* is thrown by function `unexpected`.

Common Programming Error 16.7

Placing a `catch` handler that catches a base-class object before a `catch` that catches an object of a class derived from that base class is a logic error. The base-class `catch` catches all objects of classes derived from that base class, so the derived-class `catch` will never execute.

Class `logic_error` is the base class of several standard exception classes that indicate errors in program logic. For example, class *`invalid_argument`* indicates that an invalid argument was passed to a function. (Proper coding can, of course, prevent invalid arguments from reaching a function.) Class *`length_error`* indicates that a length larger than the maximum size allowed for the object being manipulated was used for that object. Class

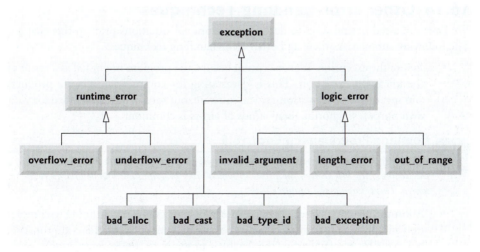

Fig. 16.12 | Standard Library exception classes.

out_of_range indicates that a value, such as a subscript into an array, exceeded its allowed range of values.

Class `runtime_error`, which we used briefly in Section 16.8, is the base class of several other standard exception classes that indicate execution-time errors. For example, class *overflow_error* describes an *arithmetic overflow error* (i.e., the result of an arithmetic operation is larger than the largest number that can be stored in the computer) and class *underflow_error* describes an *arithmetic underflow error* (i.e., the result of an arithmetic operation is smaller than the smallest number that can be stored in the computer).

Common Programming Error 16.8

Programmer-defined exception classes need not be derived from class `exception`. *Thus, writing* `catch( exception anyException )` *is not guaranteed to catch all exceptions a program could encounter.*

Error-Prevention Tip 16.5

To catch all exceptions potentially thrown in a `try` *block, use* `catch(...)`. *One weakness with catching exceptions in this way is that the type of the caught exception is unknown at compile time. Another weakness is that, without a named parameter, there is no way to refer to the exception object inside the exception handler.*

Software Engineering Observation 16.9

The standard `exception` *hierarchy is a good starting point for creating exceptions. Programmers can build programs that can* `throw` *standard exceptions,* `throw` *exceptions derived from the standard exceptions or* `throw` *their own exceptions not derived from the standard exceptions.*

Software Engineering Observation 16.10

Use `catch(...)` *to perform recovery that does not depend on the exception type (e.g., releasing common resources). The exception can be rethrown to alert more specific enclosing* `catch` *handlers.*

16.14 Other Error-Handling Techniques

We have discussed several ways to deal with exceptional situations prior to this chapter. The following summarizes these and other error-handling techniques:

- Ignore the exception. If an exception occurs, the program might fail as a result of the uncaught exception. This is devastating for commercial software products and special-purpose mission-critical software, but for software developed for your own purposes, ignoring many kinds of errors is common.

Common Programming Error 16.9

Aborting a program component due to an uncaught exception could leave a resource—such as a file stream or an I/O device—in a state in which other programs are unable to acquire the resource. This is known as a **resource leak**.

- Abort the program. This, of course, prevents a program from running to completion and producing incorrect results. For many types of errors, this is appropriate, especially for nonfatal errors that enable a program to run to completion (potentially misleading you to think that the program functioned correctly). This strategy is inappropriate for mission-critical applications. Resource issues also are important here—if a program obtains a resource, the program should release that resource before program termination.

- Set error indicators. The problem with this approach is that programs might not check these error indicators at all points at which the errors could be troublesome. Another problem is that the program, after processing the problem, might not clear the error indicators.

- Test for the error condition, issue an error message and call exit (in <cstdlib>) to pass an appropriate error code to the program's environment.

- Use functions setjump and longjump. These <csetjmp> library functions enable you to specify an immediate jump from a deeply nested function call to an error handler. Without using setjump or longjump, a program must execute several returns to exit the deeply nested function calls. Functions setjump and longjump are dangerous, because they unwind the stack without calling destructors for automatic objects. This can lead to serious problems.

- Certain kinds of errors have dedicated capabilities for handling them. For example, when operator new fails to allocate memory, a new_handler function can be called to handle the error. This function can be customized by supplying a function name as the argument to set_new_handler, as we discuss in Section 16.11.

16.15 .NET Exception Hierarchy with C++/CLI

Exception handling in C++/CLI is similar to native C++ in concept. In native C++ you learned how to use class exception from the C++ Standard Library to create new exception classes and catch them during runtime. In managed code with C++/CLI, the exception-handling mechanism allows only objects of class *Exception* (namespace System) and its derived classes to be thrown and caught by reference.

The following sections overview several of the .NET Framework's exception classes and focus exclusively on exceptions in managed code derived from class Exception. In addition, we discuss how to determine whether a particular function throws exceptions.

16.15.1 Classes ApplicationException and SystemException

Class *Exception* of namespace System is the base class of the .NET Framework exception-class hierarchy. Two of the most important classes derived from Exception are *ApplicationException* and *SystemException*. ApplicationException is a base class for nonfatal exceptions that a user application might throw. Programs can recover from most ApplicationExceptions and continue execution.

The CLR generates SystemExceptions, which can occur at any point during program execution. Many of these exceptions can be avoided if applications are coded properly. For example, if a program attempts to access an *out-of-range array index*, the CLR throws an exception of type *IndexOutOfRangeException* (a derived class of SystemException). Similarly, an exception occurs when a program uses an object reference to manipulate an object that does not yet exist (i.e., the reference has a value of nullptr). Attempting to use a nullptr reference causes a *NullReferenceException* (another derived class of System-

Exception). You saw earlier in this chapter how to create a DivideByZeroException class in native C++ derived from C++ Standard Library class exception that handles cases where a program attempts to divide by zero. The .NET Framework already provides a managed class DivideByZeroException that is thrown during integer division when a managed program attempts to divide by zero.

Other SystemException types thrown by the CLR include *OutOfMemoryException*, *StackOverflowException* and *ExecutionEngineException*. These are thrown when something goes wrong that causes the CLR to become unstable. In some cases, such exceptions cannot even be caught. In general, it is best to simply log such exceptions, then terminate your application.

In Section 16.10 you learned the advantages of deriving native exceptions from a common base class. Similarly, a benefit of the .NET Framework exception-class hierarchy is that a catch block can catch managed exceptions of a particular type or—because of the *is-a* relationship of inheritance—can use a base-class type to catch exceptions in a hierarchy of related exception types. A catch block that specifies a parameter of type Exception ^ can catch all exceptions that derive from Exception, because Exception is the base class of all exception classes. This allows a single catch block to catch a whole set of exceptions and access the caught exception's information via the parameter in the catch. We'll say more about accessing exception information in Section 16.17.

Using inheritance with exceptions enables a catch block to catch related exceptions using a concise notation. A set of exception handlers could catch each derived-class exception type individually, but catching the base-class exception type is more concise. However, this technique makes sense only if the handling behavior is the same for a base class and all derived classes. Otherwise, catch each derived-class exception individually. Alternatively, as in native C++ you can catch all exceptions by writing catch(...).

Common Programming Error 16.10

The compiler will issue a warning if you place a catch block that catches a base-class exception before a catch block for any of that class's derived-class types. In this case the base-class catch block would catch all base-class and derived-class exceptions, so the derived-class exception handler would never execute.

16.15.2 Determining Which Exceptions a Function Throws

How do we determine that an exception might occur in a program? For functions contained in the .NET Framework classes, read the detailed descriptions of the functions in the online documentation. If a function throws an exception, its description contains a section called **Exceptions** that specifies the types of exceptions the function throws and briefly describes possible causes for the exceptions. For example, search for "Convert::ToInt32 function" in the **Index** of the Visual Studio online documentation (use the **.NET Framework** filter). (Note that the MSDN documentation uses C# syntax in many cases, replacing the scope resolution operator with a period symbol and the term "function" with "method.") Select the document entitled **Convert.ToInt32 Method (System)**. In the document that describes the function, click the link **Convert.ToInt32(String)**. In the document that appears, the **Exceptions** section (near the bottom of the document) indicates that function Convert.ToInt32 throws two exception types—FormatException and OverflowException—and describes the reason why each might occur.

Software Engineering Observation 16.11

If a function throws exceptions, statements that invoke the function directly or indirectly should be placed in try *blocks, and those exceptions should be caught and handled.*

16.16 finally Block in C++/CLI

Programs frequently request and release resources dynamically (i.e., at execution time). For example, a program that reads a file from disk first makes a file-open request (as we'll see in Chapter 17, Stream Input/Output and Files, and Chapter 18, Files and Streams in .NET). If that request succeeds, the program reads the contents of the file. Operating systems typically prevent more than one program from manipulating a file at once. Therefore, when a program finishes processing a file, the program should close the file (i.e., release the resource) so other programs can use it. If the file is not closed, a resource leak occurs. In such a case, the file resource is not available to other programs, possibly because a program using the file has not closed it.

In native C++, where you are always responsible for dynamic memory management, the most common type of resource leak is a memory leak. Recall that a memory leak occurs when a program allocates memory but does not deallocate the memory when it is no longer needed. Normally, this is not an issue in C++/CLI, because if you do not use delete, the CLR eventually performs garbage collection of memory that is no longer needed by an executing program (Section 9.14). However, other kinds of resource leaks (such as unclosed files) can still occur.

Error-Prevention Tip 16.6

The CLR does not completely eliminate memory leaks. The CLR will not garbage collect an object until the program contains no more references to that object. Thus, memory leaks can occur if programmers inadvertently keep references to unwanted objects.

Moving Resource-Release Code to a finally Block

Typically, exceptions occur when processing resources that require explicit release. For example, a program that processes a file might receive IOExceptions during the processing. For this reason, file-processing code normally appears in a try block. Regardless of whether a program experiences exceptions while processing a file, the program should close the file when it is no longer needed. Suppose a program places all resource-request and resource-release code in a try block. If no exceptions occur, the try block executes normally and releases the resources after using them. However, if an exception occurs, the try block may expire before the resource-release code can execute. We could duplicate all the resource-release code in each of the catch blocks, but this would make the code more difficult to modify and maintain. We could also place the resource-release code after the try statement; however, if the try block terminated due to a return statement, code following the try statement would never execute.

To address these problems, C++/CLI's exception-handling mechanism provides the finally block, which is guaranteed to execute regardless of whether the try block executes successfully or an exception occurs. This makes the finally block an ideal location in which to place resource-release code for resources that are acquired and manipulated in the corresponding try block. If the try block executes successfully, the finally block executes immediately after the try block terminates. If an exception occurs in the try block, the `finally` block executes immediately after a `catch` block completes. If the exception is not caught by a `catch` block associated with the `try` block, or if a `catch` block associated with the `try` block throws an exception itself, the `finally` block executes before the exception is processed by the next enclosing `try` block (if there is one). By placing the resource-release code in a `finally` block, we ensure that even if the program terminates due to an uncaught exception, the resource will be deallocated. Note that local variables in a `try` block cannot be accessed in the corresponding `finally` block. For this reason, variables that must be accessed in both a `try` block and its corresponding `finally` block should be declared before the `try` block.

Error-Prevention Tip 16.7

A `finally` block typically contains code to release resources acquired in the corresponding `try` block, which makes the `finally` block an effective mechanism for eliminating resource leaks.

Performance Tip 16.4

As a rule, resources should be released as soon as they are no longer needed in a program. This makes them available for reuse promptly.

If one or more catch blocks follow a try block, the `finally` block is optional. However, if no catch blocks follow a try block, a `finally` block must appear immediately after the try block. If any catch blocks follow a try block, the `finally` block (if there is one) appears after the last catch block. As with native C++, only white space and comments can separate the blocks in a try statement.

Common Programming Error 16.11

Placing the `finally` block before a catch block is a syntax error.

Demonstrating the `finally` Block

The application in Fig. 16.13 demonstrates that the `finally` block always executes, regardless of whether an exception occurs in the corresponding try block. The program consists of function main (lines 14–55) and four other functions that main invokes to demonstrate finally. These functions are DoesNotThrowException (lines 58–75), ThrowExceptionWithCatch (lines 78–96), ThrowExceptionWithoutCatch (lines 99–114) and ThrowExceptionCatchRethrow (lines 117–141). The try and catch blocks function in exactly the same way as with native C++. Note that we can use throw to explicitly throw or rethrow exceptions just as we did with native C++ exceptions. Since we are creating a managed Exception object, we use gcnew to create the object and then throw it. Also remember that each Exception object is required to be thrown or caught by reference, unlike native C++ exceptions.

```
1   // Fig. 16.13: UsingManagedExceptions.cpp
2   // Using finally blocks. Demonstrate that finally always executes.
3
4   #include "stdafx.h"
```

Fig. 16.13 | `finally` blocks always execute, regardless of whether an exception occurs. (Part 1 of 5.)

```cpp
 5
 6   using namespace System;
 7
 8   // function prototypes
 9   void DoesNotThrowException();
10   void ThrowExceptionWithCatch();
11   void ThrowExceptionWithoutCatch();
12   void ThrowExceptionCatchRethrow();
13
14   int main( array< System::String ^> ^args )
15   {
16      // Case 1: No exceptions occur in called function
17      Console::WriteLine( "Calling DoesNotThrowException" );
18      DoesNotThrowException();
19
20      // Case 2: Exception occurs and is caught in called function
21      Console::WriteLine( "\nCalling ThrowExceptionWithCatch" );
22      ThrowExceptionWithCatch();
23
24      // Case 3: Exception occurs, but is not caught in called function
25      // because there is no catch block.
26      Console::WriteLine( "\nCalling ThrowExceptionWithoutCatch" );
27
28      // call ThrowExceptionWithoutCatch
29      try
30      {
31         ThrowExceptionWithoutCatch();
32      } // end try
33      catch( Exception ^ )
34      {
35         Console::WriteLine(
36            "Caught exception from ThrowExceptionWithoutCatch in main" );
37      } // end catch
38
39      // Case 4: Exception occurs and is caught in called function,
40      // then rethrown to caller.
41      Console::WriteLine( "\nCalling ThrowExceptionCatchRethrow" );
42
43      // call ThrowExceptionCatchRethrow
44      try
45      {
46         ThrowExceptionCatchRethrow();
47      } // end try
48      catch ( Exception ^)
49      {
50         Console::WriteLine(
51            "Caught exception from ThrowExceptionCatchRethrow in main" );
52      } // end catch
53
54      return 0;
55   } // end function main
```

Fig. 16.13 | finally blocks always execute, regardless of whether an exception occurs. (Part 2 of 5.)

```
56
57   // no exceptions thrown
58   static void DoesNotThrowException()
59   {
60      // try block does not throw any exceptions
61      try
62      {
63         Console::WriteLine( "In DoesNotThrowException" );
64      } // end try
65      catch ( Exception ^ )
66      {
67         Console::WriteLine( "This catch never executes" );
68      } // end catch
69      finally
70      {
71         Console::WriteLine( "Finally executed in DoesNotThrowException" );
72      } // end finally
73
74      Console::WriteLine( "End of DoesNotThrowException" );
75   } // end function DoesNotThrowException
76
77   // throws exception and catches it locally
78   static void ThrowExceptionWithCatch()
79   {
80      // try block throws exception
81      try
82      {
83         Console::WriteLine( "In ThrowExceptionWithCatch" );
84         throw gcnew Exception( "Exception in ThrowExceptionWithCatch" );
85      } // end try
86      catch ( Exception ^exceptionParameter )
87      {
88         Console::WriteLine( "Message: " + exceptionParameter->Message );
89      } // end catch
90      finally
91      {
92         Console::WriteLine( "Finally executed in ThrowExceptionWithCatch" );
93      } // end finally
94
95      Console::WriteLine( "End of ThrowExceptionWithCatch" );
96   } // end function ThrowExceptionWithCatch
97
98   // throws exception and does not catch it locally
99   static void ThrowExceptionWithoutCatch()
100  {
101     // throw exception, but do not catch it
102     try
103     {
104        Console::WriteLine( "In ThrowExceptionWithoutCatch" );
105        throw gcnew Exception( "Exception in ThrowExceptionWithoutCatch" );
106     } // end try
```

Fig. 16.13 | finally blocks always execute, regardless of whether an exception occurs. (Part 3 of 5.)

```
107     finally
108     {
109        Console::WriteLine( "Finally executed in ThrowExceptionWithCatch" );
110     } // end finally
111
112     // unreachable code; logic error
113     Console::WriteLine( "End of ThrowExceptionWithoutCatch" );
114  } // end function ThrowExceptionWithoutCatch
115
116  // throws exception, catches it and rethrows it
117  static void ThrowExceptionCatchRethrow()
118  {
119     // try block throws exception
120     try
121     {
122        Console::WriteLine( "In ThrowExceptionCatchRethrow" );
123        throw gcnew Exception( "Exception in ThrowExceptionCatchRethrow" );
124     } // end try
125     catch ( Exception ^exceptionParameter )
126     {
127        Console::WriteLine( "Message: " + exceptionParameter->Message );
128
129        // rethrow exception for further processing
130        throw;
131        // unreachable code; logic error
132     } // end catch
133     finally
134     {
135        Console::WriteLine(
136           "Finally executed in ThrowExceptionCatchRethrow" );
137     } // end finally
138
139     // any code placed here is never reached
140     Console::WriteLine( "End of ThrowExceptionCatchRethrow" );
141  } // end function ThrowExceptionCatchRethrow
```

```
Calling DoesNotThrowException
In DoesNotThrowException
finally executed in DoesNotThrowException
End of DoesNotThrowException

Calling ThrowExceptionWithCatch
In ThrowExceptionWithCatch
Message: Exception in ThrowExceptionWithCatch
finally executed in ThrowExceptionWithCatch
End of ThrowExceptionWithCatch

Calling ThrowExceptionWithoutCatch
In ThrowExceptionWithoutCatch
finally executed in ThrowExceptionWithoutCatch
Caught exception from ThrowExceptionWithoutCatch in main
```

Fig. 16.13 | finally blocks always execute, regardless of whether an exception occurs. (Part 4 of 5.)

```
Calling ThrowExceptionCatchRethrow
In ThrowExceptionCatchRethrow
Message: Exception in ThrowExceptionCatchRethrow
finally executed in ThrowExceptionCatchRethrow
Caught exception from ThrowExceptionCatchRethrow in main
```

Fig. 16.13 | `finally` blocks always execute, regardless of whether an exception occurs. (Part 5 of 5.)

Line 18 of main invokes function `DoesNotThrowException`. The `try` block for this function outputs a message (line 63). Because the `try` block does not throw any exceptions, program control ignores the `catch` block (lines 65–68) and executes the `finally` block (lines 69–72), which outputs a message. At this point, program control continues with the first statement after the close of the `finally` block (line 74), which outputs a message indicating that the end of the function has been reached. Then, program control returns to `main`.

Throwing Managed Exceptions Using the throw Statement

Line 22 of main invokes function `ThrowExceptionWithCatch` (lines 78–96), which begins in its `try` block (lines 81–85) by outputting a message. Next, the `try` block uses gcnew to create an `Exception` object and uses a `throw` statement to throw the exception object (line 84). Executing the `throw` statement indicates that an exception has occurred. A `throw` statement specifies a reference to an object to be thrown. The operand of a `throw` statement can be a reference to type `Exception` or to any type derived from class `Exception`. A throw statement in C++/CLI cannot throw anything other than a reference to an `Exception` object or one of its derived classes. Besides this restriction, the use of `throw` is similar to the way you learned how to throw exceptions in native C++ in Section 16.6, except that native exceptions do not require pass-by-reference.

Common Programming Error 16.12

Objects of class `Exception` or one of its derived classes must be thrown and caught by reference.

The `String` passed to the constructor becomes the exception object's error message. Just as in native C++, when a `throw` statement in a `try` block executes, the `try` block expires immediately, and program control continues with the first matching `catch` block (lines 86–89) following the `try` block. In this example, the type thrown in line 84 (`Exception ^`) matches the type specified in the `catch`, so line 88 outputs a message indicating the exception that occurred (remember, gcnew returns a handle to the object type). Then, the `finally` block (lines 90–94) executes and outputs a message. At this point, program control continues with the first statement after the close of the `finally` block (line 95), which outputs a message indicating that the end of the function has been reached. Program control then returns to `main`. In line 88, note that we use the exception object's `Message` property to retrieve the error message associated with the exception (i.e., the message passed to the `Exception` constructor). Section 16.17 discusses several properties of class `Exception`.

Lines 29–37 of main define a `try` statement in which main invokes function Throw-ExceptionWithoutCatch (lines 99–114). The `try` block enables main to catch any exceptions thrown by ThrowExceptionWithoutCatch. The try block in lines 102–106 of ThrowExceptionWithoutCatch begins by outputting a message. Next, the try block throws an Exception ∧ (line 105) and expires immediately.

Normally, program control would continue at the first catch following this try block. However, this try block does not have any catch blocks. Therefore, the exception is not caught in function ThrowExceptionWithoutCatch. Program control proceeds to the finally block (lines 107–110), which outputs a message. At this point, program control returns to main—any statements appearing after the finally block (e.g., line 113) do not execute. In this example, such statements could cause logic errors, because the exception thrown in line 105 is not caught. In main, the catch block in lines 33–37 catches the exception and displays a message indicating that the exception was caught in main.

Rethrowing Managed Exceptions

Lines 44–52 of main define a try statement in which main invokes function Throw-ExceptionCatchRethrow (lines 117–141). The try statement enables main to catch any exceptions thrown by ThrowExceptionCatchRethrow. The try statement in lines 120–137 of ThrowExceptionCatchRethrow begins by outputting a message. Next, the try block throws an Exception (line 123). The try block expires immediately, and program control continues at the first catch (lines 125–132) following the try block. In this example, the type thrown (Exception ∧) matches the type specified in the catch, so line 127 outputs a message indicating where the exception occurred. Line 130 uses the throw statement to rethrow the exception. This indicates that the catch block performed partial processing of the exception and now is passing the exception back to the calling function (in this case, main) for further processing. This is much like the way you used throw to rethrow native C++ exceptions in Figure 16.5. Remember that the managed exception is always passed by reference.

You can also rethrow an exception with a version of the throw statement which takes an operand that is the reference to the exception that was caught. It is important to note, however, that this form of throw statement resets the throw point, so the original throw point's stack trace information is lost. Section 16.17 demonstrates using a throw statement with an operand from a catch block. In that section, you will see that after an exception is caught, you can create and throw a different type of exception object from the catch block and you can include the original exception as part of the new exception object. Class library designers often do this to customize the exception types thrown from functions in their class libraries or to provide additional debugging information.

The exception handling in function ThrowExceptionCatchRethrow does not complete, because the program cannot run code in the catch block placed after the invocation of the throw statement in line 130. Therefore, function ThrowExceptionCatchRethrow terminates and returns control to main. Once again, the finally block (lines 133–137) executes and outputs a message before control returns to main. When control returns to main, the catch block in lines 48–52 catches the exception and displays a message indicating that the exception was caught. Then the program terminates.

Returning After a finally Block

Note that the next statement to execute after a finally block terminates depends on the exception-handling state. If the try block successfully completes, or if a catch block catches and handles an exception, the program continues its execution with the next statement after the `finally` block. However, if an exception is not caught, or if a `catch` block re-throws an exception, program control continues in the next enclosing `try` block. The enclosing `try` could be in the calling function or in one of its callers. It also is possible to nest a `try` statement in a `try` block; in such a case, the outer `try` statement's `catch` blocks would process any exceptions that were not caught in the inner `try` statement. If a `try` block executes and has a corresponding `finally` block, the `finally` block executes even if the `try` block terminates due to a `return` statement. The `return` occurs after the execution of the `finally` block.

Common Programming Error 16.13

Throwing an exception from a `finally` block can be dangerous. If an uncaught exception is awaiting processing when the `finally` block executes, and the `finally` block throws a new exception that is not caught in the `finally` block, the first exception is lost, and the new exception is passed to the next enclosing `try` block.

Error-Prevention Tip 16.8

When placing code that can throw an exception in a `finally` block, always enclose the code in a `try` statement that catches the appropriate exception types. This prevents the loss of any uncaught and rethrown exceptions that occur before the `finally` block executes.

Software Engineering Observation 16.12

Do not place try blocks around every statement that might throw an exception, because this can make programs difficult to read. It is better to place one `try` block around a significant portion of code, and follow this `try` block with `catch` blocks that handle each of the possible exceptions. Then follow the `catch` blocks with a single `finally` block. Separate `try` blocks should be used when it is important to distinguish between multiple statements that can throw the same exception type.

Using Stack Semantics and Exception Handling

Recall from earlier in this section that resource-release code should be placed in a `finally` block to ensure that a resource is released, regardless of whether there were exceptions when the resource was used in the corresponding `try` block. Placing `try` and `finally` blocks around every resource can make code hard to read. More importantly, you may forget to place a `try` and `finally` block and cause a resource leak. This is where the notion of stack semantics with managed objects (introduced in Section 11.13) is most useful.

For example, we may be writing a program in which we use a `StreamWriter` to write to a file. Don't worry about the details of the `StreamWriter` class and its constructor (explained in Chapter 18); this concept applies to many types of objects and resources. We use `gcnew` to dynamically allocate memory as follows:

```
StreamWriter ^myWriter =
    gcnew StreamWriter( "c:\\testFile.txt", true );
```

This creates a handle to a `StreamWriter` that is encapsulating the file `testFile.txt`. We can now use the handle (`myWriter`) to perform various operations on this file. What happens if an exception is thrown in the block `myWriter` is defined in? Without a `try` and `finally` block `testFile.txt` won't be closed and we have caused a resource leak. Eventually the garbage collector may run and fix this problem for us, but there is no guarantee whether or when this might happen. In the meantime, another line of code (in this program or a different one) may expect `testFile.txt` to be available and try to write to it. Because an exception stopped `myWriter` from closing properly, the other code cannot write to `testFile.txt`.

One solution you've learned is to place the declaration of `myWriter` in a `try` block and make sure to place cleanup code in a `finally` block. This way, when an exception is thrown, we can ensure the stream is closed immediately and the file can be reused by other code. Alternatively, we could declare `myWriter` using stack semantics as follows:

```
StreamWriter myWriter( "c:\\testFile.txt", true );
```

Recall that this object is still created on the managed heap but we are able to manipulate it as if it were on the stack. Most importantly, the compiler ensures the object's destructor is invoked when the object goes out of scope, just like an automatic variable in native C++. The compiler in the MSIL does this behind the scenes by placing the appropriate code in a similar construct to a `try` and `finally` block. Now the compiler can guarantee the destructor of `myWriter` will be called even if an exception is thrown. As long as the class destructor is defined to properly release the resource, we don't have to worry about explicitly placing `myWriter` in a `try` and `finally` block each time we perform some file processing with it. Remember, the garbage collector is still responsible for reclaiming the memory `myWriter` used on the managed heap. But we don't know when the garbage collector will run, and we cannot afford a resource leak that blocks later code from reusing the same resource. By employing stack semantics to create `myWriter`, we have ensured that the resource it encapsulates is immediately released, even if an exception is thrown. Now `testFile.txt` can be reused in other code in our program or another program running at the same time. Thus, whenever you design a class that represents a resource, make sure the class destructor properly releases the resource so that you (or other programmers) can take advantage of stack semantics with that class. Existing .NET classes that encapsulate resources are designed in this way as appropriate.

16.17 Exception Properties in C++/CLI

As we discussed in Section 16.15, managed exception types derive from class `Exception`, which has several properties. These frequently are used to formulate error messages indicating a caught exception. Two important properties are *Message* and *StackTrace*. Property `Message` stores the error message associated with an `Exception` object much like the what member function of native C++ Standard Library class `exception`. This message can be a default message associated with the exception type or a customized message passed to an `Exception` object's constructor when the `Exception` object is thrown. Property `Stack-Trace` contains a `String` that represents the function-call stack. Recall that the runtime environment at all times keeps a list of open function calls that have been made but have not yet returned. The `StackTrace` represents the series of functions that have not finished processing at the time the exception occurs.

 Error-Prevention Tip 16.9

A stack trace shows the complete function-call stack at the time an exception occurred. This enables the programmer to view the series of function calls that led to the exception. Information in the stack trace includes the names of the functions on the call stack at the time of the exception,

the names of the classes in which the functions are defined and the names of the namespaces in which the classes are defined. If the program database (PDB) file that contains the debugging information for the function is available, the stack trace also includes line numbers; the first line number indicates the throw point, and subsequent line numbers indicate the locations from which the functions in the stack trace were called. PDB files are created by the IDE to maintain the debugging information for your projects.

Property `InnerException`

Another property used frequently by class-library programmers is **`InnerException`**. Typically, class-library programmers "wrap" exception objects caught in their code so that they then can throw new exception types that are specific to their libraries. For example, a programmer implementing an accounting system might have some account-number processing code in which account numbers are input as `Strings` but represented as `ints` in the code. A program can convert managed `Strings` to `int` values with `Convert::ToInt32`, which throws a `FormatException` when it encounters an invalid number format. When an invalid account-number format occurs, the accounting-system programmer might wish to employ a different error message than the default message supplied by `FormatException` or might wish to indicate a new exception type, such as `InvalidAccountNumber-FormatException`. In such cases, the programmer would provide code to catch the `FormatException`, then create an appropriate type of `Exception` object in the `catch` block and pass the original exception as one of the constructor arguments. The original exception object becomes the `InnerException` of the new exception object. When an `InvalidAccountNumberFormatException` occurs in code that uses the accounting-system library, the `catch` block that catches the exception can obtain a reference to the original exception via property `InnerException`. Thus the exception indicates both that the user specified an invalid account number and that the problem was an invalid number format. If the `InnerException` property is `nullptr`, this indicates that the exception was not caused by another exception.

Other Exception Properties

Class `Exception` provides other properties, including **`HelpLink`**, **`Source`** and **`TargetSite`**. Property `HelpLink` specifies the location of the help file that describes the problem that occurred. This property is `nullptr` if no such file exists. Property `Source` specifies the name of the application where the exception occurred. Property `TargetSite` specifies the function where the exception originated.

Demonstrating Exception Properties and Stack Unwinding

Our next example (Fig. 16.14) demonstrates properties `Message`, `StackTrace` and `Inner-Exception`, and function `ToString`, of class `Exception`. In addition, the example demonstrates stack unwinding in a managed program. This is similar to what you learned about native C++ exceptions in Section 16.8 but is easily demonstrated via the `StackTrace` property. We can take advantage of the .NET `Exception` class properties to easily output useful information about each exception to help us debug our programs.

We keep track of the functions on the call stack as we discuss property `StackTrace` and the stack-unwinding mechanism. To see the proper stack trace, you should execute this program using steps similar to those presented in Section 16.4. Don't worry about the hexadecimal numbers following the ? symbols; they may differ on your system and aren't important for this example.

```cpp
 1   // Fig. 16.14: ExceptionProperties.cpp
 2   // Stack unwinding and Exception class properties.
 3   // Demonstrates using properties Message, StackTrace and InnerException.
 4
 5   #include "stdafx.h"
 6
 7   using namespace System;
 8
 9   // function prototypes
10   static void Function1();
11   static void Function2();
12   static void Function3();
13
14   int main( array< System::String ^> ^args )
15   {
16      // call Function1; any Exception generated is caught
17      // in the catch block that follows
18      try
19      {
20         Function1();
21      } // end try
22      catch ( Exception ^exceptionParameter )
23      {
24         // output the string representation of the Exception, then output
25         // properties InnerException, Message and StackTrace
26         Console::WriteLine( "exceptionParameter->ToString: \n{0}\n",
27            exceptionParameter->ToString() );
28         Console::WriteLine( "exceptionParameter->Message: \n{0}\n",
29            exceptionParameter->Message );
30         Console::WriteLine( "exceptionParameter->StackTrace: \n{0}\n",
31            exceptionParameter->StackTrace );
32         Console::WriteLine( "exceptionParameter->InnerException: \n{0}\n",
33            exceptionParameter->InnerException );
34      } // end catch
35   } // end function main
36
37   // calls Function2
38   static void Function1()
39   {
40      Function2();
41   } // end function Function1
42
43   // calls Function3
44   static void Function2()
45   {
46      Function3();
47   } // end function Function2
48
49   // throws an Exception containing an InnerException
50   static void Function3()
51   {
```

Fig. 16.14 | Exception properties and stack unwinding. (Part 1 of 2.)

```
52      // attempt to convert String to int
53      try
54      {
55         Convert::ToInt32( "Not an integer" );
56      } // end try
57      catch ( FormatException ^formatExceptionParameter )
58      {
59         // wrap FormatException in new Exception
60         throw gcnew Exception( "Exception occured in Function3",
61            formatExceptionParameter );
62
63      } // end catch
64   } // end function Function1
```

```
exceptionParameter->ToString:
System.Exception: Exception occured in Function3 --->
   System.FormatException: Input string was not in a correct format.
   at System.Number.StringToNumber(String str, NumberStyles options,
      NumberBuffer& number, NumberFormatInfo info, Boolean parseDecimal)
   at System.Number.ParseInt32(String s, NumberStyles style, NumberFormatInfo
      info)
   at System.Convert.ToInt32(String value)
   at ?A0xdc05eeb5.Function3() in c:\examples\ch16\fig16_14\
      exceptionproperties\exceptionproperties\exceptionproperties.cpp:line 55
   --- End of inner exception stack trace ---
   at ?A0xdc05eeb5.Function3() in c:\examples\ch16\fig16_14\
      exceptionproperties\exceptionproperties\exceptionproperties.cpp:line 61
   at ?A0xdc05eeb5.Function2() in c:\examples\ch16\fig16_14\
      exceptionproperties\exceptionproperties\exceptionproperties.cpp:line 46
   at ?A0xdc05eeb5.Function1() in c:\examples\ch16\fig16_14\
      exceptionproperties\exceptionproperties\exceptionproperties.cpp:line 40
   at main(String[] args) in c:\examples\ch16\fig16_14\
      exceptionproperties\exceptionproperties\exceptionproperties.cpp:line 20

exceptionParameter->Message:
Exception occurred in Function3

exceptionParameter->StackTrace:
   at ?A0xdc05eeb5.Function3() in c:\examples\ch16\fig16_14\
      exceptionproperties\exceptionproperties\exceptionproperties.cpp:line 61
   at ?A0xdc05eeb5.Function2() in c:\examples\ch16\fig16_14\
      exceptionproperties\exceptionproperties\exceptionproperties.cpp:line 46
   at ?A0xdc05eeb5.Function1() in c:\examples\ch16\fig16_14\
      exceptionproperties\exceptionproperties\exceptionproperties.cpp:line 40
   at main(String[] args) in c:\examples\ch16\fig16_14\
      exceptionproperties\exceptionproperties\exceptionproperties.cpp:line 20

exceptionParameter->InnerExceptio
System.FormatException: Input string was not in a correct format.
   at System.Number.StringToNumber(String str, NumberStyles options,
      NumberBuffer& number, NumberFormatInfo info, Boolean parseDecimal)
   at System.Number.ParseInt32(String s, NumberStyles style,
      NumberFormatInfo info)
   at System.Convert.ToInt32(String value)
   at ?A0xdc05eeb5.Function3() in c:\examples\ch16\fig16_14\
      exceptionproperties\exceptionproperties\exceptionproperties.cpp:line 55
```

Fig. 16.14 | Exception properties and stack unwinding. (Part 2 of 2.)

Program execution begins with main, which becomes the first function on the function-call stack. Line 20 of the try block in main invokes Function1 (declared in lines 38–41), which becomes the second function on the stack. If Function1 throws an exception, the catch block in lines 22–34 handles the exception and outputs information about the exception that occurred. Line 40 of Function1 invokes Function2 (lines 44–47), which becomes the third function on the stack. Then line 46 of Function2 invokes Function3 (lines 50–64), which becomes the fourth function on the stack.

At this point, the function-call stack (from top to bottom) for the program is:

```
Function3
Function2
Function1
main
```

The function called most recently (Function3) appears at the top of the stack; the first function called (main) appears at the bottom. The try statement (lines 53–63) in Function3 invokes function Convert::ToInt32 (line 55), which attempts to convert a String to an int. At this point, Convert::ToInt32 becomes the fifth and final function on the call stack.

Throwing an *Exception* with an *InnerException*
Because the argument to Convert::ToInt32 is not in int format, line 49 throws a FormatException that is caught in line 57 of Function3. The exception terminates the call to Convert::ToInt32, so the function is removed (or unwound) from the function-call stack. The catch block in Function3 then creates and throws a handle to an Exception object. The first argument to the Exception constructor is the custom error message for our example, "Exception occurred in Function3." The second argument is the InnerException—the FormatException that was caught. The StackTrace for this new exception object reflects the point at which the exception was thrown (lines 60–61). Now Function3 terminates, because the exception thrown in the catch block is not caught in the function body. Thus, control returns to the statement that invoked Function3 in the prior function in the call stack (Function2). This removes, or unwinds, Function3 from the function-call stack.

When control returns to line 46 in Function2, the CLR determines that line 46 is not in a try block. Therefore the exception cannot be caught in Function2, and Function2 terminates. This unwinds Function2 from the call stack and returns control to line 34 in Function1.

Here again, line 34 is not in a try block, so Function1 cannot catch the exception. The function terminates and is unwound from the call stack, returning control to line 20 in main, which *is* located in a try block. The try block in main expires and the catch block (lines 22–34) catches the exception. The catch block uses function ToString and properties Message, StackTrace and InnerException to create the output. Note that stack unwinding continues until a catch block catches the exception or the program terminates.

Displaying Information About the *Exception*
The first block of output (which we reformatted for readability) in Fig. 16.14 contains the exception's String representation, which is returned from function ToString. The String begins with the name of the exception class followed by the Message property val-

ue. The next four items present the stack trace of the InnerException object. The remainder of the block of output shows the StackTrace for the exception thrown in Function3. Note that the StackTrace represents the state of the function-call stack at the throw point of the exception, rather than at the point where the exception eventually is caught. Each StackTrace line that begins with "at" represents a function on the call stack. These lines indicate the function in which the exception occurred, the file in which the function resides and the line number of the throw point in the file. Note that the inner-exception information includes the inner-exception stack trace.

Error-Prevention Tip 16.10

When catching and rethrowing an exception, provide additional debugging information in the rethrown exception. To do so, create an Exception object containing more specific debugging information, then pass the original caught exception to the new exception object's constructor to initialize the InnerException property.

The next block of output (two lines) simply displays the Message property's value (Exception occurred in Function3) of the exception thrown in Function3.

The third block of output displays the StackTrace property of the exception thrown in Function3. Note that this StackTrace property contains the stack trace starting from line 60 in Function3, because that is the point at which the Exception object was created and thrown. The stack trace always begins from the exception's throw point.

Finally, the last block of output displays the String representation of the InnerException property, which includes the namespace and class name of the exception object, as well as its Message and StackTrace properties.

16.18 User-Defined Exception Classes in .NET

In many cases, you can use existing exception classes from the .NET Framework Class Library to indicate exceptions that occur in your programs. However, in some cases, you might wish to create new exception classes specific to the problems that occur in your programs. *User-defined exception classes* should derive directly or indirectly from class Exception of namespace System.

Good Programming Practice 16.2

Associating each type of malfunction with an appropriately named exception class improves program clarity.

Software Engineering Observation 16.13

Before creating a user-defined exception class, investigate the existing exceptions in the .NET Framework Class Library to determine whether an appropriate exception type already exists.

According to "Best Practices for Handling Exceptions [C++/CLI]," user-defined exceptions should extend class Exception, have a class name that ends with "Exception" and define three constructors: a parameterless constructor; a constructor that receives a String ^ argument (the error message); and a constructor that receives a String ^ argument and an Exception ^ argument (the error message and the inner exception object). Defining these three constructors makes your exception class more flexible, allowing other programmers to easily use and extend it. In the past Microsoft recommended that user-defined exception classes extend class `ApplicationException`. This practice has since changed, but you may see old user-defined exceptions that use this style.

16.19 Wrap-Up

In this chapter, you learned how to use exception handling to deal with errors in a program. You learned that exception handling enables programmers to remove error-handling code from the "main line" of the program's execution. We demonstrated exception handling in the context of a divide-by-zero example. We also showed how to use `try` blocks to enclose code that may throw an exception, and how to use `catch` handlers to deal with exceptions that may arise. You learned how to throw and rethrow exceptions, and how to handle the exceptions that occur in constructors. The chapter continued with discussions of processing `new` failures, dynamic memory allocation with class `auto_ptr` and the standard library exception hierarchy.

You learned how the .NET Framework Exception Hierarchy works and how to employ `finally` blocks and stack semantics to properly handle resource release. We also demonstrated how to use some of the properties and member functions of the `Exception` class and the best practices for creating your own managed classes that derive from `Exception`.

The next chapter discusses many of Visual C++'s I/O and file capabilities and demonstrate several stream manipulators that perform various formatting tasks. You'll also learn about file processing, including how persistent data is stored and how to manipulate it.

Summary

Section 16.1 Introduction

- An exception is an indication of a problem that occurs during a program's execution.
- Exception handling enables you to create programs that can resolve problems that occur at execution time—often allowing programs to continue executing as if no problems had been encountered. More severe problems may require a program to notify the user of the problem before terminating in a controlled manner.

Section 16.2 Exception-Handling Overview

- Exception handling enables you to remove error-handling code from the "main line" of the program's execution, which improves program clarity and enhances modifiability.

Section 16.3 Example: Divide by Zero Without Exception Handling

- An uncaught exception is an exception without a matching `catch` block.

Section 16.4 Example: Handling an Attempt to Divide by Zero

- Class `exception` is the standard Visual C++ base class for exceptions. Class `exception` provides virtual function `what` that returns an appropriate error message and can be overridden in derived classes.
- Class `runtime_error` (defined in header `<stdexcept>`) is the Visual C++ standard base class for representing runtime errors.
- Visual C++ uses the termination model of exception handling.

- A try block consists of keyword try followed by braces ({}) that define a block of code in which exceptions might occur. The try block encloses statements that might cause exceptions and statements that should not execute if exceptions occur.

- At least one catch handler must immediately follow a try block. Each catch handler specifies an exception parameter that represents the type of exception the catch handler can process.

- If an exception parameter includes an optional parameter name, the catch handler can use that parameter name to interact with a caught exception object.

- The point in the program at which an exception occurs is called the throw point.

- If an exception occurs in a try block, the try block expires and program control transfers to the first catch in which the exception parameter's type matches that of the thrown exception.

- When a try block terminates, local variables defined in the block go out of scope.

- When a try block terminates due to an exception, the program searches for the first catch handler that can process the type of exception that occurred. The program locates the matching catch by comparing the thrown exception's type to each catch's exception-parameter type until the program finds a match. A match occurs if the types are identical or if the thrown exception's type is a derived class of the exception-parameter type. When a match occurs, the code contained within the matching catch handler executes.

- When a catch handler finishes processing, the catch parameter and local variables defined within the catch handler go out of scope. Any remaining catch handlers that correspond to the try block are ignored, and execution resumes at the first line of code after the try...catch sequence.

- If no exceptions occur in a try block, the program ignores the catch handler(s) for that block. Program execution resumes with the next statement after the try...catch sequence.

- If an exception that occurs in a try block has no matching catch handler, or if an exception occurs in a statement that is not in a try block, the function that contains the statement terminates immediately, and the program attempts to locate an enclosing try block in the calling function. This process is called stack unwinding.

- To throw an exception, use keyword throw followed by an operand that represents the type of exception to throw. The operand of a throw can be of any type.

Section 16.5 When to Use Exception Handling
- Exception handling is for synchronous errors, which occur when a statement executes.

- Exception handling is not designed to process errors associated with asynchronous events, which occur in parallel with, and independent of, the program's flow of control.

Section 16.6 Rethrowing an Exception
- The exception handler can defer the exception handling (or perhaps a portion of it) to another exception handler. In either case, the handler achieves this by rethrowing the exception.

- Common examples of exceptions are out-of-range array subscripts, arithmetic overflow, division by zero, invalid function parameters and unsuccessful memory allocations.

Section 16.7 Processing Unexpected Exceptions
- Function unexpected calls the function registered with function set_unexpected. If no function has been registered in this manner, function terminate is called by default.

- Function set_terminate can specify the function to invoke when terminate is called. Otherwise, terminate calls abort, which terminates the program without calling the destructors of objects that are declared static and auto.

- Functions set_terminate and set_unexpected each return a pointer to the last function called by terminate and unexpected, respectively (0, the first time each is called). This enables you to save the function pointer so it can be restored later.

- Functions set_terminate and set_unexpected take as arguments pointers to functions with void return types and no arguments.

- If a programmer-defined termination function does not exit a program, function abort will be called after the programmer-defined termination function completes execution.

Section 16.8 Stack Unwinding
- Unwinding the function-call stack means that the function in which the exception was not caught terminates, all local variables in that function are destroyed and control returns to the statement that originally invoked that function.

Section 16.9 Constructors, Destructors and Exception Handling
- Exceptions thrown by a constructor cause destructors to be called for any objects built as part of the object being constructed before the exception is thrown.

- Each automatic object constructed in a try block is destructed before an exception is thrown.

- Stack unwinding completes before an exception handler begins executing.

- If a destructor invoked as a result of stack unwinding throws an exception, terminate is called.

- If an object has member objects, and if an exception is thrown before the outer object is fully constructed, then destructors will be executed for the member objects that have been constructed before the exception occurs.

- If an array of objects has been partially constructed when an exception occurs, only the destructors for the constructed array element objects will be called.

- When an exception is thrown from the constructor for an object that is created in a new expression, the dynamically allocated memory for that object is released.

Section 16.10 Exceptions and Inheritance
- If a catch handler catches a pointer or reference to an exception object of a base-class type, it also can catch a pointer or reference to all objects of classes derived publicly from that base class—this allows for polymorphic processing of related errors.

Section 16.11 Processing new Failures
- The C++ standard document specifies that, when operator new fails, it throws a bad_alloc exception (defined in header file <new>).

- Function set_new_handler takes as its argument a pointer to a function that takes no arguments and returns void. This pointer points to the function that will be called if new fails.

- Once set_new_handler registers a new handler in the program, operator new does not throw bad_alloc on failure; rather, it defers the error handling to the new-handler function.

- If new allocates memory successfully, it returns a pointer to that memory.

- If an exception occurs after successful memory allocation but before the delete statement executes, a memory leak could occur.

Section 16.12 Class auto_ptr and Dynamic Memory Allocation
- The C++ Standard Library provides class template auto_ptr to deal with memory leaks.

- An object of class auto_ptr maintains a pointer to dynamically allocated memory. An auto_ptr object's destructor performs a delete operation on the auto_ptr's pointer data member.

- Class template `auto_ptr` provides overloaded operators `*` and `->` so that an `auto_ptr` object can be used just as a regular pointer variable is. An `auto_ptr` also transfers ownership of the dynamic memory it manages via its copy constructor and overloaded assignment operator.

Section 16.13 Standard Library Exception Hierarchy
- The C++ Standard Library includes a hierarchy of exception classes. This hierarchy is headed by base class `exception`.
- Immediate derived classes of base class `exception` include `runtime_error` and `logic_error` (both defined in header `<stdexcept>`), each of which has several derived classes.
- Several operators throw standard exceptions—operator `new` throws `bad_alloc`, operator `dynamic_cast` throws `bad_cast` and operator `typeid` throws `bad_typeid`.
- Including `bad_exception` in the throw list of a function means that, if an unexpected exception occurs, function `unexpected` can throw `bad_exception` rather than terminating the program's execution or calling another function specified by `set_unexpected`.

Section 16.15 .NET Exception Hierarchy with C++/CLI
- The C++/CLI exception-handling mechanism allows references only to objects of class `Exception` and its derived classes to be thrown and caught.
- Class `Exception` of namespace `System` is the base class of the .NET Framework Class Library exception class hierarchy.
- Two of the most important classes derived from `Exception` are `ApplicationException` and `SystemException`.
- The CLR generates `SystemExceptions`, which can occur at any point during the execution of the program. Many of these exceptions can be avoided if applications are coded properly.
- A benefit of using the exception class hierarchy is that a `catch` block can catch exceptions of a particular type or—because of the *is-a* relationship of inheritance—can use a base-class type to catch exceptions in a hierarchy of related exception types.
- A `catch` block that specifies an exception parameter of type `Exception` can catch all exceptions that derive from `Exception`, because `Exception` is the base class of all exception classes.
- Using inheritance with exceptions enables an exception handler to catch related exceptions using a concise notation.

Section 16.16 finally Block in C++/CLI
- C++/CLI's exception-handling mechanism provides the `finally` block, which is guaranteed to execute if program control enters the corresponding `try` block.
- The `finally` block executes regardless of whether the corresponding `try` block executes successfully or an exception occurs. This makes the `finally` block an ideal location in which to place resource-release code for resources acquired and manipulated in the corresponding `try` block.
- If the `try` block executes successfully, the `finally` block executes immediately after the `try` block terminates. If an exception occurs in the `try` block, the `finally` block executes immediately after a `catch` block completes.
- If the exception is not caught by a `catch` block associated with the `try` block, or if a `catch` block associated with the `try` block throws an exception, the `finally` block executes before the exception is processed by the next enclosing `try` block (if there is one).
- The `throw` statement can be used to rethrow an exception, indicating that a `catch` block performed partial processing of the exception and now is passing the exception back to the calling function for further processing.

- If a try block executes and has a corresponding finally block, the finally block always executes—even if the try block terminates due to a return statement. The return occurs after the execution of the finally block.

- Use stack semantics with managed objects to simplify writing code in which you obtain a resource, use the resource in a try block and release the resource in a corresponding finally block.

Section 16.17 Exception Properties in C++/CLI

- Property Message of class Exception stores the error message associated with an Exception object.

- Property StackTrace of class Exception contains a String that represents the function-call stack.

- Another Exception property used frequently by class-library programmers is InnerException. Typically, you use this property to "wrap" exception objects caught in your code so that you then can throw new exception types specific to your libraries.

- As in native C++, when an exception is thrown but not caught in a particular scope, the function-call stack is "unwound," and an attempt is made to catch the exception in the next outer try block—this is known as stack unwinding.

Section 16.18 User-Defined Exception Classes in .NET

- User-defined exception classes should derive directly or indirectly from class Exception of namespace System.

- User-defined exceptions should extend Exception, have a class name that ends with "Exception" and define a parameterless constructor, a constructor that receives a String ^ argument (the error message), and a constructor that receives a String ^ argument and an Exception ^ argument (the error message and the inner exception object).

Terminology

abort function
arithmetic overflow error
arithmetic underflow error
asynchronous event
auto_ptr class template
bad_alloc exception
bad_cast exception
bad_exception exception
bad_typeid exception
catch(...)
catch all exceptions
catch an exception
catch handler
catch keyword
exception
exception class
Exception class
exception handler
exception handling
<exception> header file
exception object
exception parameter
fault-tolerant programs

finally block
handle an exception
InnerException property of Exception class
invalid_argument exception
length_error exception
logic_error exception
<memory> header file
Message property of class Exception
new failure handler
nothrow object
out_of_range exception
overflow_error exception
resumption model of exception handling
rethrow an exception
robust application
runtime_error exception
set_new_handler function
set_terminate function
set_unexpected function
Source property of Exception class
stack unwinding
StackTrace property of Exception class
<stdexcept> header file

synchronous errors	throw without arguments
`TargetSite` property of `Exception` class	throw point
terminate function	try block
termination model of exception handling	try keyword
throw an exception	`underflow_error` exception
throw an unexpected exception	uncaught exception
throw keyword	unexpected function
throw list	`what` virtual function of class `exception`

Self-Review Exercises

16.1 List five common examples of exceptions.

16.2 Give several reasons why exception-handling techniques should not be used for conventional program control.

16.3 Why are exceptions appropriate for dealing with errors produced by library functions?

16.4 What is a "resource leak"?

16.5 If no exceptions are thrown in a try block, where does control proceed to after the try block completes execution?

16.6 What happens if an exception is thrown outside a try block?

16.7 Give a key advantage and a key disadvantage of using catch(...).

16.8 What happens if no catch handler matches the type of a thrown object?

16.9 What happens if several handlers match the type of the thrown object?

16.10 Why would a programmer specify a base-class type as the type of a catch handler, then throw objects of derived-class types?

16.11 Suppose a catch handler with a precise match to an exception object type is available. Under what circumstances might a different handler be executed for exception objects of that type?

16.12 Must throwing an exception cause program termination?

16.13 What happens when a catch handler throws an exception?

16.14 What does the statement throw; do?

16.15 What happens to the automatic objects that have been constructed in a try block when that block throws an exception?

16.16 What are the possible parameters to throw and catch statements in C++/CLI?

16.17 What are two useful techniques to perform resource release in C++/CLI?

Answers to Self-Review Exercises

16.1 Insufficient memory to satisfy a new request, array subscript out of bounds, arithmetic overflow, division by zero, invalid function parameters.

16.2 (a) Exception handling is designed to handle infrequently occurring situations that often result in program termination, so compiler writers are not required to implement exception handling to perform optimally. (b) Flow of control with conventional control structures generally is clearer and more efficient than with exceptions. (c) Problems can occur because the stack is unwound when an exception occurs and resources allocated prior to the exception might not be freed. (d) The "additional" exceptions make it more difficult for you to handle the larger number of exception cases.

16.3 It is unlikely that a library function will perform error processing that will meet the unique needs of all users.

16.4 A program that terminates abruptly could leave a resource in a state in which other programs would not be able to acquire the resource, or the program itself might not be able to reacquire a "leaked" resource.

16.5 The exception handlers (in the `catch` handlers) for that `try` block are skipped, and the program resumes execution after the last `catch` handler.

16.6 An exception thrown outside a `try` block causes a call to `terminate`.

16.7 The form `catch(...)` catches any type of exception thrown in a `try` block. An advantage is that all possible exceptions will be caught. A disadvantage is that the `catch` has no parameter, so it cannot reference information in the thrown object and cannot know the cause of the exception.

16.8 This causes the search for a match to continue in the next enclosing `try` block if there is one. As this process continues, it might eventually be determined that there is no handler in the program that matches the type of the thrown object; in this case, `terminate` is called, which by default calls `abort`. An alternative `terminate` function can be provided as an argument to `set_terminate`.

16.9 The first matching exception handler after the `try` block is executed.

16.10 This is a nice way to `catch` related types of exceptions.

16.11 A base-class handler would catch objects of all derived-class types.

16.12 No, but it does terminate the block in which the exception is thrown.

16.13 The exception will be processed by a `catch` handler (if one exists) associated with the `try` block (if one exists) enclosing the `catch` handler that caused the exception.

16.14 It rethrows the exception if it appears in a `catch` handler; otherwise, function `unexpected` is called.

16.15 The `try` block expires, causing destructors to be called for each of these objects.

16.16 References to object of class `Exception` (from namespace `System`) or one of its derived classes.

16.17 Use a `try` block around code using the resource and a `finally` block to perform resource-release operations. Alternatively, declare the object that encapsulates a resource using stack semantics.

Exercises

16.18 List various exceptional conditions that have occurred throughout this text. List as many additional exceptional conditions as you can. For each of these exceptions, describe briefly how a program typically would handle the exception, using the exception-handling techniques discussed in this chapter. Some typical exceptions are division by zero, arithmetic overflow, array subscript out of bounds, exhaustion of the free store, etc.

16.19 Under what circumstances would you not provide a parameter name when defining the type of the object that will be caught by a handler?

16.20 A program contains the statement

> *throw*;

Where would you normally expect to find such a statement? What if that statement appeared in a different part of the program?

16.21 Compare and contrast exception handling with the various other error-processing schemes discussed in the text.

16.22 Why should exceptions not be used as an alternate form of program control?

16.23 Describe a technique for handling related exceptions.

16.24 Until this chapter, we have found that dealing with errors detected by constructors can be awkward. Exception handling gives us a better means of handling such errors. Consider a constructor for a String class. The constructor uses new to obtain space from the free store. Suppose new fails. Show how you would deal with this without exception handling. Discuss the key issues. Show how you would deal with such memory exhaustion with exception handling. Explain why the exception-handling approach is superior.

16.25 Suppose a program throws an exception and the appropriate exception handler begins executing. Now suppose that the exception handler itself throws the same exception. Does this create infinite recursion? Write a program to check your observation.

16.26 Use inheritance to create various derived classes of runtime_error. Then show that a catch handler specifying the base class can catch derived-class exceptions.

16.27 Write a conditional expression that returns either a double or an int. Provide an int catch handler and a double catch handler. Show that only the double catch handler executes, regardless of whether the int or the double is returned.

16.28 Write a program that generates and handles a memory-exhaustion exception. Your program should loop on a request to create dynamic memory through operator new.

16.29 Write a program illustrating that all destructors for objects constructed in a block are called before an exception is thrown from that block.

16.30 Write a program illustrating that member object destructors are called for only those member objects that were constructed before an exception occurred.

16.31 Write a program that demonstrates several exception types being caught with the catch(...) exception handler.

16.32 Write a program illustrating that the order of exception handlers is important. The first matching handler is the one that executes. Attempt to compile and run your program two different ways to show that two different handlers execute with two different effects.

16.33 Write a program that shows a constructor passing information about constructor failure to an exception handler after a try block.

16.34 Write a program that illustrates rethrowing an exception.

16.35 Write a program that illustrates that a function with its own try block does not have to catch every possible error generated within the try. Some exceptions can slip through to, and be handled in, outer scopes.

16.36 Write a program that throws an exception from a deeply nested function and still has the catch handler following the try block enclosing the call chain catch the exception.

16.37 Write a C++/CLI program that dynamically allocates memory for a managed object in a try block. Write a finally block to delete the object without waiting for the garbage collector to run.

17

Stream Input/Output and Files

Consciousness ... does not appear to itself chopped up in bits ... A "river" or a "stream" are the metaphors by which it is most naturally described.
—William James

All the news that's fit to print.
—Adolph S. Ochs

Remove not the landmark on the boundary of the fields.
—Amenehope

OBJECTIVES

In this chapter you'll learn:

- To use Visual C++ object-oriented stream input/output.
- To format input and output.
- The stream-I/O class hierarchy.
- To use stream manipulators.
- To control justification and padding.
- To determine the success or failure of input/output operations.
- To tie output streams to input streams.
- To create, read, write and update files.
- Sequential file processing.

17.1 Introduction

The C++ Standard Library provides an extensive set of input/output and file stream capabilities. This chapter discusses a range of capabilities sufficient for performing most common I/O and file operations and overviews the remaining capabilities. We discussed some of these features earlier in the text; now we provide a more complete treatment. Many of the I/O and file features that we'll discuss are object oriented. This style of I/O and file processing makes use of other Visual C++ features, such as references, function overloading and operator overloading. We focus on I/O operations in the beginning of this chapter and follow it with a discussion of file processing.

Visual C++ uses *type-safe I/O*. Each I/O operation is executed in a manner sensitive to the data type. If an I/O member function has been defined to handle a particular data type, then that member function is called to handle that data type. If there is no match between the type of the actual data and a function for handling that data type, the compiler generates an error. Thus, improper data cannot "sneak" through the system (as can occur in C, allowing for some subtle and bizarre errors).

Users can specify how to perform I/O for objects of user-defined types by overloading the stream insertion operator (<<) and the stream extraction operator (>>). This *extensibility* is one of Visual C++'s most valuable features.

Software Engineering Observation 17.1

Use the Visual C++-style I/O exclusively in Visual C++ programs, even though C-style I/O is available to Visual C++ programmers.

Error-Prevention Tip 17.1

Visual C++ I/O is type safe.

Software Engineering Observation 17.2

Visual C++ enables a common treatment of I/O for predefined types and user-defined types. This commonality facilitates software development and reuse.

Storage of data in variables and arrays is temporary. *Files* are used for *data persistence*—permanent retention of data. Computers store files on *secondary storage devices,* such as hard disks, CDs, DVDs, flash drives and tapes. Later in this chapter we explain how to build Visual C++ programs that create, update and process data files. We focus on sequential files. We compare formatted-data file processing and raw-data file processing. We examine techniques for input of data from, and output of data to, `string` streams rather than files in Chapter 19, Class `string` and String Stream Processing. Note that this chapter focuses purely on native C++ streams and files. For information on stream and file processing in managed code with C++/CLI, see Chapter 18, Files and Streams in .NET.

17.2 Streams

Visual C++ I/O occurs in *streams*, which are sequences of bytes. In input operations, the bytes flow from a device (e.g., a keyboard, a disk drive, a network connection, etc.) to main memory. In output operations, bytes flow from main memory to a device (e.g., a display screen, a printer, a disk drive, a network connection, etc.).

An application associates meaning with bytes. The bytes could represent characters, raw data, graphics images, digital speech, digital video or any other information an application may require.

The system I/O mechanisms should transfer bytes from devices to memory (and vice versa) consistently and reliably. Such transfers often involve some mechanical motion, such as the rotation of a disk or a tape, or the typing of keystrokes at a keyboard. The time these transfers take is typically much greater than the time the processor requires to manipulate data internally. Thus, I/O operations require careful planning and tuning to ensure optimal performance.

C++ provides both "low-level" and "high-level" I/O capabilities. Low-level I/O capabilities (i.e., *unformatted I/O*) specify that some number of bytes should be transferred device-to-memory or memory-to-device. In such transfers, the individual byte is the item of interest. Such low-level capabilities provide high-speed, high-volume transfers but are not particularly convenient for programmers.

Programmers generally prefer a higher-level view of I/O (i.e., *formatted I/O*), in which bytes are grouped into meaningful units, such as integers, floating-point numbers, characters, strings and user-defined types. These type-oriented capabilities are satisfactory for most I/O other than high-volume file processing.

Performance Tip 17.1

Use unformatted I/O for the best performance in high-volume file processing.

Portability Tip 17.1

Using unformatted I/O can lead to portability problems, because unformatted data is not portable across all platforms.

17.2.1 Classic Streams vs. Standard Streams

In the past, the C++ *classic stream libraries* enabled input and output of chars. Because a char normally occupies one byte, it can represent only a limited set of characters (such as those in the ASCII character set). However, many languages use alphabets that contain more characters than a single-byte char can represent. The ASCII character set does not provide these characters; the *Unicode character set* does. Unicode is an extensive international character set that represents the majority of the world's "commercially viable" languages, mathematical symbols and much more. For more information on Unicode, visit www.unicode.org.

C++ includes the *standard stream libraries*, which enable developers to build systems capable of performing I/O operations with Unicode characters. For this purpose, Visual C++ includes an additional character type called *wchar_t*, which can store two-byte Unicode characters. The C++ Standard also redesigned the classic C++ stream classes, which processed only chars, as class templates with separate specializations for processing characters of types char and wchar_t, respectively. We use the char type of class templates throughout this book.

17.2.2 iostream Library Header Files

The C++ iostream library provides hundreds of I/O capabilities. Several header files contain portions of the library interface.

Most Visual C++ programs include the <iostream> header file, which declares basic services required for all stream-I/O operations. The <iostream> header file defines the cin, cout, cerr and clog objects, which correspond to the standard input stream, the standard output stream, the unbuffered standard error stream and the buffered standard error stream, respectively. (`cerr` and `clog` are discussed in Section 17.2.3.) Both unformatted- and formatted-I/O services are provided.

The `<iomanip>` header declares services useful for performing formatted I/O with so-called *parameterized stream manipulators*, such as `setw` and `setprecision`.

The `<fstream>` header declares services for user-controlled file processing. We use this header in file-processing programs.

C++ implementations generally contain other I/O-related libraries that provide system-specific capabilities, such as the controlling of special-purpose devices for audio and video I/O.

17.2.3 Stream-Input/Output Classes and Objects

The `iostream` library provides many templates for handling common I/O operations. For example, class template `basic_istream` supports stream-input operations, class template `basic_ostream` supports stream-output operations, and class template `basic_iostream` supports both stream-input and stream-output operations. Each template has a predefined template specialization that enables `char` I/O. In addition, the `iostream` library provides a set of `typedef`s that provide aliases for these template specializations. The ***typedef*** specifier declares synonyms (aliases) for previously defined data types. Programmers sometimes use `typedef` to create shorter or more readable type names. For example, the statement

```
typedef Card *CardPtr;
```

defines an additional type name, `CardPtr`, as a synonym for type `Card *`. Note that creating a name using `typedef` does not create a data type; `typedef` creates only a type name that may be used in the program. Section 22.5 discusses `typedef` in detail. The `typedef` ***istream*** represents a specialization of `basic_istream` that enables `char` input. Similarly, the `typedef` ***ostream*** represents a specialization of `basic_ostream` that enables `char` output. Also, the `typedef` ***iostream*** represents a specialization of `basic_iostream` that enables both `char` input and output. We use these `typedef`s throughout this chapter.

Stream-I/O Template Hierarchy and Operator Overloading

Templates `basic_istream` and `basic_ostream` both derive through single inheritance from base template `basic_ios`.[1] Template `basic_iostream` derives through multiple inheritance[2] from templates `basic_istream` and `basic_ostream`. The UML class diagram of Fig. 17.1 summarizes these inheritance relationships.

Operator overloading provides a convenient notation for performing input/output. The left-shift operator (`<<`) is overloaded to designate stream output and is referred to as the stream insertion operator. The right-shift operator (`>>`) is overloaded to designate stream input and is referred to as the stream extraction operator. These operators are used with the standard stream objects `cin`, `cout`, `cerr` and `clog` and, commonly, with user-defined stream objects.

---

1. In this chapter, we discuss templates only in the context of the template specializations that enable char I/O. These specializations are classes and thus can inherit from each other.
2. Multiple inheritance is discussed in Chapter 26, Other Topics.

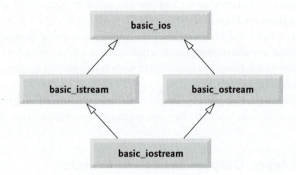

Fig. 17.1 | Stream-I/O template hierarchy portion.

Standard Stream Objects cin, cout, cerr and clog

The predefined object cin is an istream instance and is said to be "connected to" (or attached to) the standard input device, which usually is the keyboard. The stream extraction operator (>>) as used in the following statement causes a value for integer variable grade (assuming that grade has been declared as an int variable) to be input from cin to memory:

```
cin >> grade; // data "flows" in the direction of the arrows
```

Note that the compiler determines the data type of grade and selects the appropriate overloaded stream extraction operator. Assuming that grade has been declared properly, the stream extraction operator does not require additional type information (as is the case, for example, in C-style I/O). The >> operator is overloaded to input data items of built-in types, strings and pointer values.

The predefined object cout is an ostream instance and is said to be "connected to" the standard output device, which usually is the display screen. The stream insertion operator (<<), as used in the following statement, causes the value of variable grade to be output from memory to the standard output device:

```
cout << grade; // data "flows" in the direction of the arrows
```

Note that the compiler also determines the data type of grade (assuming grade has been declared properly) and selects the appropriate stream insertion operator, so the stream insertion operator does not require additional type information. The << operator is overloaded to output data items of built-in types, strings and pointer values.

The predefined object cerr is an ostream instance and is said to be "connected to" the standard error device. Outputs to object cerr are *unbuffered*, implying that each stream insertion to cerr causes its output to appear immediately—this is appropriate for notifying a user promptly about errors.

The predefined object clog is an instance of the ostream class and is said to be "connected to" the standard error device. Outputs to clog are *buffered*. This means that each insertion to clog could cause its output to be held in a buffer until the buffer is filled or until the buffer is flushed. Buffering is an I/O performance-enhancement technique discussed in operating-systems courses.

File-Processing Templates

File processing can be accomplished using class templates *basic_ifstream* (for file input), *basic_ofstream* (for file output) and *basic_fstream* (for file input and output). Each class template has a predefined template specialization that enables char I/O. Visual C++ provides a set of typedefs that provide aliases for these template specializations. For example, the typedef *ifstream* represents a specialization of basic_ifstream that enables char input from a file. Similarly, typedef *ofstream* represents a specialization of basic_ofstream that enables char output to a file. Also, typedef *fstream* represents a specialization of basic_fstream that enables char input from, and output to, a file. Template basic_ifstream inherits from basic_istream, basic_ofstream inherits from basic_ostream and basic_fstream inherits from basic_iostream. The UML class diagram of Fig. 17.2 summarizes the various inheritance relationships of the I/O-related classes. The full stream-I/O class hierarchy provides most of the capabilities that programmers need. Consult the class-library reference for your Visual C++ system for additional file-processing information.

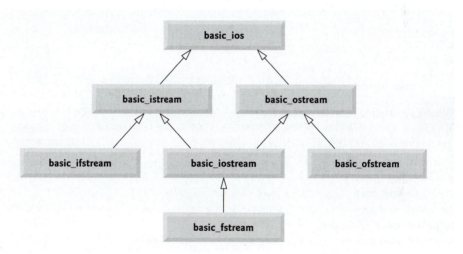

Fig. 17.2 | Stream-I/O template hierarchy portion showing the main file-processing templates.

17.3 Stream Output

Formatted and unformatted output capabilities are provided by ostream. Capabilities for output include output of standard data types with the stream insertion operator (<<); output of characters via the put member function; unformatted output via the write member function (Section 17.5); output of integers in decimal, octal and hexadecimal formats (Section 17.6.1); output of floating-point values with various precision (Section 17.6.2), with forced decimal points (Section 17.7.1), in scientific notation and in fixed notation (Section 17.7.5); output of data justified in fields of designated widths (Section 17.7.2); output of data in fields padded with specified characters (Section 17.7.3); and output of uppercase letters in scientific notation and hexadecimal notation (Section 17.7.6).

17.3.1 Output of char * Variables

Visual C++ determines data types automatically, an improvement over C. This feature sometimes "gets in the way." For example, suppose we want to print the value of a char * to a character string (i.e., the memory address of the first character of that string). However, the << operator has been overloaded to print data of type char * as a null-terminated string. The solution is to cast the char * to a void * (in fact, this should be done to any pointer variable you wish to output as an address). Figure 17.3 demonstrates printing a char * variable in both string and address formats. Note that the address prints as a hexadecimal (base-16) number. [*Note:* To learn more about hexadecimal numbers, read Appendix D, Number Systems.] We say more about controlling the bases of numbers in Section 17.6.1, Section 17.7.4, Section 17.7.5 and Section 17.7.7. [*Note:* The memory address shown in the output of the program in Fig. 17.3 may differ among compilers.]

```cpp
1   // Fig. 17.3: PrintChar.cpp
2   // Printing the address stored in a char * variable.
3   #include <iostream>
4   using std::cout;
5   using std::endl;
6
7   int main()
8   {
9       char *word = "again";
10
11      // display value of char *,
12      // then display value of char * static_cast to void *
13      cout << "Value of word is: " << word << endl
14          << "Value of static_cast< void * >( word ) is: "
15          << static_cast< void * >( word ) << endl;
16      return 0;
17  } // end main
```

```
Value of word is: again
Value of static_cast< void * >( word ) is: 00428300
```

Fig. 17.3 | Printing the address stored in a char * variable.

17.3.2 Character Output Using Member Function put

We can use the put member function to output characters. For example, the statement

```cpp
cout.put( 'A' );
```

displays a single character A. Calls to put may be cascaded, as in the statement

```cpp
cout.put( 'A' ).put( '\n' );
```

which outputs the letter A followed by a newline character. As with <<, the preceding statement executes in this manner, because the dot operator (.) associates from left to right, and the put member function returns a reference to the ostream object (cout) that received the put call. The put function also may be called with a numeric expression that represents an ASCII value, as in the following statement:

```
cout.put( 65 );
```

which also outputs A.

17.4 Stream Input

Now let us consider stream input. Formatted and unformatted input capabilities are provided by istream. The stream extraction operator (i.e., the overloaded >> operator) normally skips *white-space characters* (such as blanks, tabs and newlines) in the input stream; later we'll see how to change this behavior. After each input, the stream extraction operator returns a reference to the stream object that received the extraction message (e.g., cin in the expression cin >> grade). If that reference is used as a condition (e.g., in a while statement's loop-continuation condition), the stream's overloaded void * cast operator function is implicitly invoked to convert the reference into a non-null pointer value or the null pointer based on the success or failure of the last input operation. A non-null pointer converts to the bool value true to indicate success and the null pointer converts to the bool value false to indicate failure. When an attempt is made to read past the end of a stream, the stream's overloaded void * cast operator returns the null pointer to indicate end-of-file.

Each stream object contains a set of *state bits* used to control the state of the stream (i.e., formatting, setting error states, etc.). These bits are used by the stream's overloaded void * cast operator to determine whether to return a non-null pointer or the null pointer. Stream extraction causes the stream's *failbit* to be set if data of the wrong type is input and causes the stream's *badbit* to be set if the operation fails. Section 17.7 and Section 17.8 discuss stream state bits in detail, then show how to test these bits after an I/O operation.

17.4.1 get and getline Member Functions

The *get* member function with no arguments inputs one character from the designated stream (including white-space characters and other nongraphic characters, such as the key sequence that represents end-of-file) and returns it as the value of the function call. This version of get returns EOF when end-of-file is encountered on the stream.

Using Member Functions eof, get and put

Figure 17.4 demonstrates the use of member functions eof and get on input stream cin and member function put on output stream cout. The program first prints the value of cin.eof()—i.e., false (0 on the output)—to show that end-of-file has not occurred on cin. The user enters a line of text and presses *Enter* followed by end-of-file (*<Ctrl> z* on

```
1   // Fig. 17.4: GetAndPut.cpp
2   // Using member functions get, put and eof.
3   #include <iostream>
4   using std::cin;
5   using std::cout;
6   using std::endl;
7
```

Fig. 17.4 | get, put and eof member functions. (Part 1 of 2.)

```
 8    int main()
 9    {
10       int character; // use int, because char cannot represent EOF
11
12       // prompt user to enter line of text
13       cout << "Before input, cin.eof() is " << cin.eof() << endl
14          << "Enter a sentence followed by end-of-file:" << endl;
15
16       // use get to read each character; use put to display it
17       while ( ( character = cin.get() ) != EOF )
18          cout.put( character );
19
20       // display end-of-file character
21       cout << "\nEOF in this system is: " << character << endl;
22       cout << "After input of EOF, cin.eof() is " << cin.eof() << endl;
23       return 0;
24    } // end main
```

```
Before input, cin.eof() is 0
Enter a sentence followed by end-of-file:
Testing the get and put member functions
Testing the get and put member functions
^Z

EOF in this system is: -1
After input of EOF, cin.eof() is 1
```

Fig. 17.4 | get, put and eof member functions. (Part 2 of 2.)

Microsoft Windows systems). Line 17 reads each character, which line 18 outputs to cout using member function put. When end-of-file is encountered, the while statement ends, and line 22 displays the value of cin.eof(), which is now true (1 on the output), to show that end-of-file has been set on cin. Note that this program uses the version of istream member function get that takes no arguments and returns the character being input (line 17). Function eof returns true only after the program attempts to read past the last character in the stream.

The get member function with a character-reference argument inputs the next character from the input stream (even if this is a white-space character) and stores it in the character argument. This version of get returns a reference to the istream object for which the get member function is being invoked.

A third version of get takes three arguments—a character array, a size limit and a delimiter (with default value '\n'). This version reads characters from the input stream. It either reads one fewer than the specified maximum number of characters and terminates or terminates as soon as the delimiter is read. A null character is inserted to terminate the input string in the character array used as a buffer by the program. The delimiter is not placed in the character array but does remain in the input stream (the delimiter will be the next character read). Thus, the result of a second consecutive get is an empty line, unless the delimiter character is removed from the input stream (possibly with cin.ignore()).

Comparing cin and cin.get

Figure 17.5 compares input using stream extraction with cin (which reads characters until a white-space character is encountered) and input using cin.get. Note that the call to cin.get (line 24) does not specify a delimiter, so the default '\n' character is used.

```cpp
 1   // Fig. 17.5: CinGet.cpp
 2   // Contrasting input of a string via cin and cin.get.
 3   #include <iostream>
 4   using std::cin;
 5   using std::cout;
 6   using std::endl;
 7
 8   int main()
 9   {
10      // create two char arrays, each with 80 elements
11      const int SIZE = 80;
12      char buffer1[ SIZE ];
13      char buffer2[ SIZE ];
14
15      // use cin to input characters into buffer1
16      cout << "Enter a sentence:" << endl;
17      cin >> buffer1;
18
19      // display buffer1 contents
20      cout << "\nThe string read with cin was:" << endl
21         << buffer1 << endl << endl;
22
23      // use cin.get to input characters into buffer2
24      cin.get( buffer2, SIZE );
25
26      // display buffer2 contents
27      cout << "The string read with cin.get was:" << endl
28         << buffer2 << endl;
29      return 0;
30   } // end main
```

```
Enter a sentence:
Contrasting string input with cin and cin.get

The string read with cin was:
Contrasting

The string read with cin.get was:
 string input with cin and cin.get
```

Fig. 17.5 | Input of a string using cin with stream extraction contrasted with input using cin.get.

Using Member Function getline

Member function **getline** operates similarly to the third version of the get member function and inserts a null character after the line in the character array. The getline function removes the delimiter from the stream (i.e., reads the character and discards it), but does not store it in the character array. The program of Fig. 17.6 demonstrates the use of the getline member function to input a line of text (line 15).

```cpp
1   // Fig. 17.6: CinGetLine.cpp
2   // Inputting characters using cin member function getline.
3   #include <iostream>
4   using std::cin;
5   using std::cout;
6   using std::endl;
7
8   int main()
9   {
10      const int SIZE = 80;
11      char buffer[ SIZE ]; // create array of 80 characters
12
13      // input characters in buffer via cin function getline
14      cout << "Enter a sentence:" << endl;
15      cin.getline( buffer, SIZE );
16
17      // display buffer contents
18      cout << "\nThe sentence entered is:" << endl << buffer << endl;
19      return 0;
20   } // end main
```

```
Enter a sentence:
Using the getline member function

The sentence entered is:
Using the getline member function
```

Fig. 17.6 | Inputting character data with cin member function getline.

17.4.2 istream Member Functions peek, putback and ignore

The *ignore* member function of istream either reads and discards a designated number of characters (the default is one character) or terminates upon encountering a designated delimiter (the default delimiter is EOF, which causes ignore to skip to the end of the file when reading from a file).

The *putback* member function places the previous character obtained by a get from an input stream back into that stream. This function is useful for applications that scan an input stream looking for a field beginning with a specific character. When that character is input, the application returns the character to the stream, so the character can be included in the input data.

The *peek* member function returns the next character from an input stream but does not remove the character from the stream.

17.4.3 Type-Safe I/O

Visual C++ offers type-safe I/O. The << and >> operators are overloaded to accept data items of specific types. If unexpected data is processed, various error bits are set, which the user may test to determine whether an I/O operation succeeded or failed. If operator <<

has not been overloaded for a user-defined type and you attempt to input into or output the contents of an object of that user-defined type, the compiler reports an error. This enables the program to "stay in control." We discuss these error states in Section 17.8.

17.5 Unformatted I/O Using read, write and gcount

Unformatted input/output is performed using the **read** and **write** member functions of istream and ostream, respectively. Member function read inputs some number of bytes to a character array in memory; member function write outputs bytes from a character array. These bytes are not formatted in any way. They are input or output as raw bytes. For example, the call

```
char buffer[] = "HAPPY BIRTHDAY";
cout.write( buffer, 10 );
```

outputs the first 10 bytes of buffer (including null characters, if any, that would cause output with cout and << to terminate). The call

```
cout.write( "ABCDEFGHIJKLMNOPQRSTUVWXYZ", 10 );
```

displays the first 10 characters of the alphabet.

The read member function inputs a designated number of characters into a character array. If fewer than the designated number of characters are read, failbit is set. Section 17.8 shows how to determine whether failbit has been set. Member function **gcount** reports the number of characters read by the last input operation.

Figure 17.7 demonstrates istream member functions read and gcount, and ostream member function write. The program inputs 20 characters (from a longer input sequence) into the array buffer with read (line 15), determines the number of characters input with gcount (line 19) and outputs the characters in buffer with write (line 19).

```
1   // Fig. 17.7: ReadWriteGcount.cpp
2   // Unformatted I/O using read, gcount and write.
3   #include <iostream>
4   using std::cin;
5   using std::cout;
6   using std::endl;
7
8   int main()
9   {
10      const int SIZE = 80;
11      char buffer[ SIZE ]; // create array of 80 characters
12
13      // use function read to input characters into buffer
14      cout << "Enter a sentence:" << endl;
15      cin.read( buffer, 20 );
16
17      // use functions write and gcount to display buffer characters
18      cout << endl << "The sentence entered was:" << endl;
19      cout.write( buffer, cin.gcount() );
```

Fig. 17.7 | Unformatted I/O using the read, gcount and write member functions. (Part 1 of 2.)

```
20        cout << endl;
21        return 0;
22    } // end main
```

```
Enter a sentence:
Using the read, write, and gcount member functions
The sentence entered was:
Using the read, writ
```

Fig. 17.7 | Unformatted I/O using the read, gcount and write member functions. (Part 2 of 2.)

17.6 Introduction to Stream Manipulators

Visual C++ provides various *stream manipulators* that perform formatting tasks. The stream manipulators provide capabilities such as setting field widths, setting precision, setting and unsetting format state, setting the fill character in fields, flushing streams, inserting a newline into the output stream (and flushing the stream), inserting a null character into the output stream and skipping white space in the input stream. These features are described in the following sections.

17.6.1 Integral Stream Base: dec, oct, hex and setbase

Integers are interpreted normally as decimal (base-10) values. To change the base in which integers are interpreted on a stream, insert the *hex* manipulator to set the base to hexadecimal (base 16) or insert the *oct* manipulator to set the base to octal (base 8). Insert the *dec* manipulator to reset the stream base to decimal. These are all sticky manipulators.

The base of a stream also may be changed by the *setbase* stream manipulator, which takes one integer argument of 10, 8, or 16 to set the base to decimal, octal or hexadecimal, respectively. Because setbase takes an argument, it is called a parameterized stream manipulator. Using setbase (or any other parameterized manipulator) requires the inclusion of the <iomanip> header file. The stream base value remains the same until changed explicitly; setbase settings are "sticky." Figure 17.8 demonstrates stream manipulators hex, oct, dec and setbase.

```
1    // Fig. 17.8: StreamManipulators.cpp
2    // Using stream manipulators hex, oct, dec and setbase.
3    #include <iostream>
4    using std::cin;
5    using std::cout;
6    using std::dec;
7    using std::endl;
8    using std::hex;
9    using std::oct;
10
11   #include <iomanip>
12   using std::setbase;
13
```

Fig. 17.8 | Stream manipulators hex, oct, dec and setbase. (Part 1 of 2.)

```
14   int main()
15   {
16      int number;
17
18      cout << "Enter a decimal number: ";
19      cin >> number; // input number
20
21      // use hex stream manipulator to show hexadecimal number
22      cout << number << " in hexadecimal is: " << hex
23         << number << endl;
24
25      // use oct stream manipulator to show octal number
26      cout << dec << number << " in octal is: "
27         << oct << number << endl;
28
29      // use setbase stream manipulator to show decimal number
30      cout << setbase( 10 ) << number << " in decimal is: "
31         << number << endl;
32      return 0;
33   } // end main
```

```
Enter a decimal number: 20
20 in hexadecimal is: 14
20 in octal is: 24
20 in decimal is: 20
```

Fig. 17.8 | Stream manipulators hex, oct, dec and setbase. (Part 2 of 2.)

17.6.2 Floating-Point Precision (precision, setprecision)

We can control the *precision* of floating-point numbers (i.e., the number of digits to the right of the decimal point) by using either the setprecision stream manipulator or the *precision* member function of ios_base. A call to either of these sets the precision for all subsequent output operations until the next precision-setting call. A call to member function precision with no argument returns the current precision setting (this is what you need to use so that you can restore the original precision eventually after a "sticky" setting is no longer needed). The program of Fig. 17.9 uses both member function precision (line 28) and the setprecision manipulator (line 37) to print a table that shows the square root of 2, with precision varying from 0–9.

```
1    // Fig. 17.9: Precision.cpp
2    // Controlling precision of floating-point values.
3    #include <iostream>
4    using std::cout;
5    using std::endl;
6    using std::fixed;
7
8    #include <iomanip>
9    using std::setprecision;
10
```

Fig. 17.9 | Precision of floating-point values. (Part 1 of 2.)

```
11   #include <cmath>
12   using std::sqrt; // sqrt prototype
13
14   int main()
15   {
16      double root2 = sqrt( 2.0 ); // calculate square root of 2
17      int places; // precision, vary from 0-9
18
19      cout << "Square root of 2 with precisions 0-9." << endl
20         << "Precision set by ios_base member function "
21         << "precision:" << endl;
22
23      cout << fixed; // use fixed-point notation
24
25      // display square root using ios_base function precision
26      for ( places = 0; places <= 9; places++ )
27      {
28         cout.precision( places );
29         cout << root2 << endl;
30      } // end for
31
32      cout << "\nPrecision set by stream manipulator "
33         << "setprecision:" << endl;
34
35      // set precision for each digit, then display square root
36      for ( places = 0; places <= 9; places++ )
37         cout << setprecision( places ) << root2 << endl;
38
39      return 0;
40   } // end main
```

```
Square root of 2 with precisions 0-9.
Precision set by ios_base member function precision:
1
1.4
1.41
1.414
1.4142
1.41421
1.414214
1.4142136
1.41421356
1.414213562

Precision set by stream manipulator setprecision:
1
1.4
1.41
1.414
1.4142
1.41421
1.414214
1.4142136
1.41421356
1.414213562
```

Fig. 17.9 | Precision of floating-point values. (Part 2 of 2.)

17.6.3 Field Width (`width`, `setw`)

The **width** member function (of base class `ios_base`) sets the field width (i.e., the number of character positions in which a value should be output or the maximum number of characters that should be input) and returns the previous width. If values output are narrower than the field width, *fill characters* are inserted as *padding*. A value wider than the designated width will not be truncated—the full number will be printed. The `width` function with no argument returns the current setting.

Common Programming Error 17.1

The width setting applies only for the next insertion or extraction (i.e., the width setting is not "sticky"); afterward, the width is set implicitly to 0 (i.e., input and output will be performed with default settings). Assuming that the width setting applies to all subsequent outputs is a logic error.

Common Programming Error 17.2

When a field is not sufficiently wide to handle outputs, the outputs print as wide as necessary, which can yield confusing outputs.

Figure 17.10 demonstrates the use of the `width` member function on both input and output. Note that, on input into a `char` array, a maximum of one fewer characters than the width will be read, because provision is made for the null character to be placed in the input string. Remember that stream extraction terminates when nonleading white space is encountered. The `setw` stream manipulator also may be used to set the field width.

```cpp
// Fig. 17.10: Width.cpp
// Demonstrating member function width.
#include <iostream>
using std::cin;
using std::cout;
using std::endl;

int main()
{
   int widthValue = 4;
   char sentence[ 10 ];

   cout << "Enter a sentence:" << endl;
   cin.width( 5 ); // input only 5 characters from sentence

   // set field width, then display characters based on that width
   while ( cin >> sentence )
   {
      cout.width( widthValue++ );
      cout << sentence << endl;
      cin.width( 5 ); // input 5 more characters from sentence
   } // end while

   return 0;
} // end main
```

Fig. 17.10 | `width` member function of class `ios_base`. (Part 1 of 2.)

```
Enter a sentence:
This is a test of the width member function
This
   is
      a
   test
      of
      the
      widt
          h
        memb
           er
         func
          tion
```

Fig. 17.10 | `width` member function of class `ios_base`. (Part 2 of 2.)

[*Note:* When prompted for input in Fig. 17.10, the user should enter a line of text and press *Enter* followed by end-of-file (*<Ctrl> z* on Microsoft Windows systems).]

17.6.4 User-Defined Output Stream Manipulators

You can create your own stream manipulators.[3] Figure 17.11 shows the creation and use of new nonparameterized stream manipulators `bell` (lines 10–13), `carriageReturn` (lines 16–19), `tab` (lines 22–25) and `endLine` (lines 29–32). For output stream manipulators, the return type and parameter must be of type `ostream &`. When line 37 inserts the `endLine` manipulator in the output stream, function `endLine` is called and line 31 outputs the escape sequence `\n` and the `flush` manipulator to the standard output stream `cout`. Similarly, when lines 37–46 insert the manipulators `tab`, `bell` and `carriageReturn` in the output stream, their corresponding functions—`tab` (line 22), `bell` (line 10) and `carriageReturn` (line 16)—are called, which in turn output various escape sequences.

```
1    // Fig. 17.11: UserDefinedStreamManipulators.cpp
2    // Creating and testing user-defined, nonparameterized
3    // stream manipulators.
4    #include <iostream>
5    using std::cout;
6    using std::flush;
7    using std::ostream;
8
9    // bell manipulator (using escape sequence \a)
10   ostream& bell( ostream& output )
11   {
12      return output << '\a'; // issue system beep
13   } // end bell manipulator
```

Fig. 17.11 | User-defined, nonparameterized stream manipulators. (Part 1 of 2.)

---

3. You also may create your own parameterized stream manipulators. This concept is beyond the scope of this book.

```
14
15    // carriageReturn manipulator (using escape sequence \r)
16    ostream& carriageReturn( ostream& output )
17    {
18       return output << '\r'; // issue carriage return
19    } // end carriageReturn manipulator
20
21    // tab manipulator (using escape sequence \t)
22    ostream& tab( ostream& output )
23    {
24       return output << '\t'; // issue tab
25    } // end tab manipulator
26
27    // endLine manipulator (using escape sequence \n and member
28    // function flush)
29    ostream& endLine( ostream& output )
30    {
31       return output << '\n' << flush; // issue endl-like end of line
32    } // end endLine manipulator
33
34    int main()
35    {
36       // use tab and endLine manipulators
37       cout << "Testing the tab manipulator:" << endLine
38          << 'a' << tab << 'b' << tab << 'c' << endLine;
39
40       cout << "Testing the carriageReturn and bell manipulators:"
41          << endLine << "..........";
42
43       cout << bell; // use bell manipulator
44
45       // use carriageReturn and endLine manipulators
46       cout << carriageReturn << "-----" << endLine;
47       return 0;
48    } // end main
```

```
Testing the tab manipulator:
a        b        c
Testing the carriageReturn and bell manipulators:
-----.....
```

Fig. 17.11 | User-defined, nonparameterized stream manipulators. (Part 2 of 2.)

17.7 Stream Format States and Stream Manipulators

Various stream manipulators can be used to specify the kinds of formatting to be performed during stream-I/O operations. Stream manipulators control the output's format settings. Figure 17.12 lists each stream manipulator that controls a given stream's format state. All these manipulators belong to class ios_base. We show examples of most of these stream manipulators in the next several sections.

Stream manipulator	Description
skipws	Skip white-space characters on an input stream. This setting is reset with stream manipulator noskipws.
left	Left justify output in a field. Padding characters appear to the right if necessary.
right	Right justify output in a field. Padding characters appear to the left if necessary.
internal	Indicate that a number's sign should be left justified in a field and a number's magnitude should be right justified in that same field (i.e., padding characters appear between the sign and the number).
dec	Specify that integers should be treated as decimal (base 10) values.
oct	Specify that integers should be treated as octal (base 8) values.
hex	Specify that integers should be treated as hexadecimal (base 16) values.
showbase	Specify that the base of a number is to be output ahead of the number (a leading 0 for octals; a leading 0x or 0X for hexadecimals). This setting is reset with stream manipulator noshowbase.
showpoint	Specify that floating-point numbers should be output with a decimal point. This is used normally with fixed to guarantee a certain number of digits to the right of the decimal point, even if they are zeros. This setting is reset with stream manipulator noshowpoint.
uppercase	Specify that uppercase letters (i.e., X and A through F) should be used in a hexadecimal integer and that uppercase E should be used when representing a floating-point value in scientific notation. This setting is reset with stream manipulator nouppercase.
showpos	Specify that positive numbers should be preceded by a plus sign (+). This setting is reset with stream manipulator noshowpos.
scientific	Specify output of a floating-point value in scientific notation.
fixed	Specify output of a floating-point value in fixed-point notation with a specific number of digits to the right of the decimal point.

Fig. 17.12 | Format-state stream manipulators from `<iostream>`.

17.7.1 Trailing Zeros and Decimal Points (showpoint)

Stream manipulator showpoint forces a floating-point number to be output with its decimal point and trailing zeros. For example, the floating-point value 79.0 prints as 79 without using showpoint and prints as 79.000000 (or as many trailing zeros as are specified by the current precision) using showpoint. To reset the showpoint setting, output the stream manipulator *noshowpoint*. The program in Fig. 17.13 shows how to use stream manipulator showpoint to control the printing of trailing zeros and decimal points for floating-point values. Recall that the default precision of a floating-point number is 6. When neither the fixed nor the scientific stream manipulator is used, the precision represents the number of significant digits to display (i.e., the total number of digits to display), not the number of digits to display after decimal point.

```
I    // Fig. 17.13: ShowPoint.cpp
2    // Using showpoint to control the printing of
3    // trailing zeros and decimal points for doubles.
4    #include <iostream>
5    using std::cout;
6    using std::endl;
7    using std::showpoint;
8
9    int main()
10   {
11      // display double values with default stream format
12      cout << "Before using showpoint" << endl
13         << "9.9900 prints as: " << 9.9900 << endl
14         << "9.9000 prints as: " << 9.9000 << endl
15         << "9.0000 prints as: " << 9.0000 << endl << endl;
16
17      // display double value after showpoint
18      cout << showpoint
19         << "After using showpoint" << endl
20         << "9.9900 prints as: " << 9.9900 << endl
21         << "9.9000 prints as: " << 9.9000 << endl
22         << "9.0000 prints as: " << 9.0000 << endl;
23      return 0;
24   } // end main
```

```
Before using showpoint
9.9900 prints as: 9.99
9.9000 prints as: 9.9
9.0000 prints as: 9

After using showpoint
9.9900 prints as: 9.99000
9.9000 prints as: 9.90000
9.0000 prints as: 9.00000
```

Fig. 17.13 | Controlling the printing of trailing zeros and decimal points in floating-point values.

17.7.2 Justification (left, right and internal)

Stream manipulators **left** and **right** enable fields to be left justified with padding characters to the right or right justified with padding characters to the left, respectively. The padding character is specified by the fill member function or the setfill parameterized stream manipulator (which we discuss in Section 17.7.3). Figure 17.14 uses the setw, left and right manipulators to left justify and right justify integer data in a field.

```
I    // Fig. 17.14: Justification.cpp
2    // Demonstrating left justification and right justification.
3    #include <iostream>
```

Fig. 17.14 | Left justification and right justification with stream manipulators left and right. (Part 1 of 2.)

```
 4    using std::cout;
 5    using std::endl;
 6    using std::left;
 7    using std::right;
 8
 9    #include <iomanip>
10    using std::setw;
11
12    int main()
13    {
14       int x = 12345;
15
16       // display x right justified (default)
17       cout << "Default is right justified:" << endl
18          << setw( 10 ) << x;
19
20       // use left manipulator to display x left justified
21       cout << "\n\nUse std::left to left justify x:\n"
22          << left << setw( 10 ) << x;
23
24       // use right manipulator to display x right justified
25       cout << "\n\nUse std::right to right justify x:\n"
26          << right << setw( 10 ) << x << endl;
27       return 0;
28    } // end main
```

```
Default is right justified:
     12345

Use std::left to left justify x:
12345

Use std::right to right justify x:
     12345
```

Fig. 17.14 | Left justification and right justification with stream manipulators `left` and `right`. (Part 2 of 2.)

Stream manipulator ***internal*** indicates that a number's sign (or base when using stream manipulator showbase) should be left justified within a field, that the number's magnitude should be right justified and that intervening spaces should be padded with the fill character. Figure 17.15 shows the `internal` stream manipulator specifying internal spacing (line 15). Note that ***showpos*** forces the plus sign to print (line 15). To reset the showpos setting, output the stream manipulator ***noshowpos***.

```
 1    // Fig. 17.15: Internal.cpp
 2    // Printing an integer with internal spacing and plus sign.
 3    #include <iostream>
 4    using std::cout;
 5    using std::endl;
 6    using std::internal;
```

Fig. 17.15 | Printing an integer with internal spacing and plus sign. (Part 1 of 2.)

```
 7    using std::showpos;
 8
 9    #include <iomanip>
10    using std::setw;
11
12    int main()
13    {
14       // display value with internal spacing and plus sign
15       cout << internal << showpos << setw( 10 ) << 123 << endl;
16       return 0;
17    } // end main
```

```
+         123
```

Fig. 17.15 | Printing an integer with internal spacing and plus sign. (Part 2 of 2.)

17.7.3 Padding (fill, setfill)

The *fill member function* specifies the fill character to be used with justified fields; if no value is specified, spaces are used for padding. The fill function returns the prior padding character. The *setfill manipulator* also sets the padding character. Figure 17.16 demonstrates using member function fill (line 40) and stream manipulator setfill (lines 44 and 47) to set the fill character.

```
 1    // Fig. 17.16: SetFill.cpp
 2    // Using member function fill and stream manipulator setfill to change
 3    // the padding character for fields larger than the printed value.
 4    #include <iostream>
 5    using std::cout;
 6    using std::dec;
 7    using std::endl;
 8    using std::hex;
 9    using std::internal;
10    using std::left;
11    using std::right;
12    using std::showbase;
13
14    #include <iomanip>
15    using std::setfill;
16    using std::setw;
17
18    int main()
19    {
20       int x = 10000;
21
22       // display x
23       cout << x << " printed as int right and left justified\n"
24          << "and as hex with internal justification.\n"
25          << "Using the default pad character (space):" << endl;
```

Fig. 17.16 | Using member function fill and stream manipulator setfill to change the padding character for fields larger than the values being printed. (Part 1 of 2.)

```
26
27      // display x with base
28      cout << showbase << setw( 10 ) << x << endl;
29
30      // display x with left justification
31      cout << left << setw( 10 ) << x << endl;
32
33      // display x as hex with internal justification
34      cout << internal << setw( 10 ) << hex << x << endl << endl;
35
36      cout << "Using various padding characters:" << endl;
37
38      // display x using padded characters (right justification)
39      cout << right;
40      cout.fill( '*' );
41      cout << setw( 10 ) << dec << x << endl;
42
43      // display x using padded characters (left justification)
44      cout << left << setw( 10 ) << setfill( '%' ) << x << endl;
45
46      // display x using padded characters (internal justification)
47      cout << internal << setw( 10 ) << setfill( '^' ) << hex
48          << x << endl;
49      return 0;
50  } // end main
```

```
10000 printed as int right and left justified
and as hex with internal justification.
Using the default pad character (space):
     10000
10000
0x     2710

Using various padding characters:
*****10000
10000%%%%%
0x^^^^2710
```

Fig. 17.16 | Using member function `fill` and stream manipulator `setfill` to change the padding character for fields larger than the values being printed. (Part 2 of 2.)

17.7.4 Integral Stream Base (dec, oct, hex, showbase)

Visual C++ provides stream manipulators dec, hex and oct to specify that integers are to be displayed as decimal, hexadecimal and octal values, respectively. Stream insertions default to decimal if none of these manipulators is used. With stream extraction, integers prefixed with 0 (zero) are treated as octal values, integers prefixed with 0x or 0X are treated as hexadecimal values, and all other integers are treated as decimal values. Once a particular base is specified for a stream, all integers on that stream are processed using that base until a different base is specified or until the program terminates.

Stream manipulator **showbase** forces the base of an integral value to be output. Decimal numbers are output by default, octal numbers are output with a leading 0, and hexadecimal numbers are output with either a leading 0x or a leading 0X. (As we discuss in Section 17.7.6, stream manipulator uppercase determines which option is chosen.) Figure 17.17 demonstrates the use of stream manipulator showbase to force an integer to print in decimal, octal and hexadecimal formats. To reset the showbase setting, output the stream manipulator **noshowbase**.

```cpp
1   // Fig. 17.17: ShowBase.cpp
2   // Using stream manipulator showbase.
3   #include <iostream>
4   using std::cout;
5   using std::endl;
6   using std::hex;
7   using std::oct;
8   using std::showbase;
9
10  int main()
11  {
12     int x = 100;
13
14     // use showbase to show number base
15     cout << "Printing integers preceded by their base:" << endl
16        << showbase;
17
18     cout << x << endl; // print decimal value
19     cout << oct << x << endl; // print octal value
20     cout << hex << x << endl; // print hexadecimal value
21     return 0;
22  } // end main
```

```
Printing integers preceded by their base:
100
0144
0x64
```

Fig. 17.17 | Stream manipulator showbase.

17.7.5 Floating-Point Numbers; Scientific and Fixed Notation (scientific, fixed)

Stream manipulators scientific and fixed control the output format of floating-point numbers. Stream manipulator **scientific** forces the output of a floating-point number to display in scientific format. Stream manipulator **fixed** forces a floating-point number to display a specific number of digits (as specified by member function precision or stream manipulator setprecision) to the right of the decimal point. Without using another manipulator, the floating-point-number value determines the output format.

Figure 17.18 demonstrates displaying floating-point numbers in fixed and scientific formats using stream manipulators scientific (line 21) and fixed (line 25). The exponent format in scientific notation might differ across different compilers.

```
 1   // Fig. 17.18: FloatingPoint.cpp
 2   // Displaying floating-point values in system default,
 3   // scientific and fixed formats.
 4   #include <iostream>
 5   using std::cout;
 6   using std::endl;
 7   using std::fixed;
 8   using std::scientific;
 9
10   int main()
11   {
12      double x = 0.001234567;
13      double y = 1.946e9;
14
15      // display x and y in default format
16      cout << "Displayed in default format:" << endl
17         << x << '\t' << y << endl;
18
19      // display x and y in scientific format
20      cout << "\nDisplayed in scientific format:" << endl
21         << scientific << x << '\t' << y << endl;
22
23      // display x and y in fixed format
24      cout << "\nDisplayed in fixed format:" << endl
25         << fixed << x << '\t' << y << endl;
26      return 0;
27   } // end main
```

```
Displayed in default format:
0.00123457        1.946e+009

Displayed in scientific format:
1.234567e-003     1.946000e+009

Displayed in fixed format:
0.001235          1946000000.000000
```

Fig. 17.18 | Floating-point values displayed in default, scientific and fixed formats.

17.7.6 Uppercase/Lowercase Control (uppercase)

Stream manipulator uppercase outputs an uppercase X or E with hexadecimal-integer values or with scientific notation floating-point values, respectively (Fig. 17.19). Using stream manipulator uppercase also causes all letters in a hexadecimal value to be uppercase. By default, the letters for hexadecimal values and the exponents in scientific notation floating-point values appear in lowercase. To reset the uppercase setting, output the stream manipulator **nouppercase**.

```
 1   // Fig. 17.19: Uppercase.cpp
 2   // Stream manipulator uppercase.
 3   #include <iostream>
```

Fig. 17.19 | Stream manipulator uppercase. (Part 1 of 2.)

```
4    using std::cout;
5    using std::endl;
6    using std::hex;
7    using std::showbase;
8    using std::uppercase;
9
10   int main()
11   {
12      cout << "Printing uppercase letters in scientific" << endl
13         << "notation exponents and hexadecimal values:" << endl;
14
15      // use std::uppercase to display uppercase letters; use std::hex and
16      // std::showbase to display hexadecimal value and its base
17      cout << uppercase << 4.345e10 << endl
18         << hex << showbase << 123456789 << endl;
19      return 0;
20   } // end main
```

```
Printing uppercase letters in scientific
notation exponents and hexadecimal values:
4.345E+010
0X75BCD15
```

Fig. 17.19 | Stream manipulator `uppercase`. (Part 2 of 2.)

17.7.7 Specifying Boolean Format (boolalpha)

Visual C++ provides data type `bool`, whose values may be `false` or `true`, as a preferred alternative to the old style of using 0 to indicate `false` and nonzero to indicate `true`. A `bool` variable outputs as 0 or 1 by default. However, we can use stream manipulator `boolalpha` to set the output stream to display `bool` values as the strings `"true"` and `"false"`. Use stream manipulator **noboolalpha** to set the output stream to display `bool` values as integers (i.e., the default setting). The program of Fig. 17.20 demonstrates these stream manipulators. Line 14 displays the `bool` value, which line 11 sets to `true`, as an integer. Line 18 uses manipulator `boolalpha` to display the `bool` value as a string. Lines 21–22 then change the `bool`'s value and use manipulator `noboolalpha`, so line 25 can display the `bool` value as an integer. Line 29 uses manipulator `boolalpha` to display the `bool` value as a string. Both `boolalpha` and `noboolalpha` are "sticky" settings.

Good Programming Practice 17.1

Displaying `bool` values as `true` or `false`, rather than nonzero or 0, respectively, makes program outputs clearer.

```
1    // Fig. 17.20: BoolAlpha.cpp
2    // Demonstrating stream manipulators boolalpha and noboolalpha.
3    #include <iostream>
4    using std::boolalpha;
5    using std::cout;
```

Fig. 17.20 | Stream manipulators `boolalpha` and `noboolalpha`. (Part 1 of 2.)

```
6   using std::endl;
7   using std::noboolalpha;
8
9   int main()
10  {
11      bool booleanValue = true;
12
13      // display default true booleanValue
14      cout << "booleanValue is " << booleanValue << endl;
15
16      // display booleanValue after using boolalpha
17      cout << "booleanValue (after using boolalpha) is "
18         << boolalpha << booleanValue << endl << endl;
19
20      cout << "switch booleanValue and use noboolalpha" << endl;
21      booleanValue = false; // change booleanValue
22      cout << noboolalpha << endl; // use noboolalpha
23
24      // display default false booleanValue after using noboolalpha
25      cout << "booleanValue is " << booleanValue << endl;
26
27      // display booleanValue after using boolalpha again
28      cout << "booleanValue (after using boolalpha) is "
29         << boolalpha << booleanValue << endl;
30      return 0;
31  } // end main
```

```
booleanValue is 1
booleanValue (after using boolalpha) is true

switch booleanValue and use noboolalpha

booleanValue is 0
booleanValue (after using boolalpha) is false
```

Fig. 17.20 | Stream manipulators `boolalpha` and `noboolalpha`. (Part 2 of 2.)

17.7.8 Setting and Resetting the Format State via Member Function flags

Throughout Section 17.7, we have been using stream manipulators to change output format characteristics. We now discuss how to return an output stream's format to its default state after having applied several manipulations. Member function **flags** without an argument returns the current format settings as a **fmtflags** data type (of class `ios_base`), which represents the *format state*. Member function `flags` with a `fmtflags` argument sets the format state as specified by the argument and returns the prior state settings. The initial settings of the value that `flags` returns might differ across several systems. The program of Fig. 17.21 uses member function `flags` to save the stream's original format state (line 22), then restore the original format settings (line 30).

```cpp
 1   // Fig. 17.21: Flags.cpp
 2   // Demonstrating the flags member function.
 3   #include <iostream>
 4   using std::cout;
 5   using std::endl;
 6   using std::ios_base;
 7   using std::oct;
 8   using std::scientific;
 9   using std::showbase;
10
11   int main()
12   {
13      int integerValue = 1000;
14      double doubleValue = 0.0947628;
15
16      // display flags value, int and double values (original format)
17      cout << "The value of the flags variable is: " << cout.flags()
18         << "\nPrint int and double in original format:\n"
19         << integerValue << '\t' << doubleValue << endl << endl;
20
21      // use cout flags function to save original format
22      ios_base::fmtflags originalFormat = cout.flags();
23      cout << showbase << oct << scientific; // change format
24
25      // display flags value, int and double values (new format)
26      cout << "The value of the flags variable is: " << cout.flags()
27         << "\nPrint int and double in a new format:\n"
28         << integerValue << '\t' << doubleValue << endl << endl;
29
30      cout.flags( originalFormat ); // restore format
31
32      // display flags value, int and double values (original format)
33      cout << "The restored value of the flags variable is: "
34         << cout.flags()
35         << "\nPrint values in original format again:\n"
36         << integerValue << '\t' << doubleValue << endl;
37      return 0;
38   } // end main
```

```
The value of the flags variable is: 513
Print int and double in original format:
1000    0.0947628

The value of the flags variable is: 012011
Print int and double in a new format:
01750   9.476280e-002

The restored value of the flags variable is: 513
Print values in original format again:
1000    0.0947628
```

Fig. 17.21 | flags member function.

17.8 Stream Error States

The state of a stream may be tested through bits in class ios_base. In a moment, we show how to test these bits, in the example of Fig. 17.22.

The *eofbit* is set for an input stream after end-of-file is encountered. A program can use member function eof to determine whether end-of-file has been encountered on a stream after an attempt to extract data beyond the end of the stream. The call

```
cin.eof()
```

returns true if end-of-file has been encountered on cin and false otherwise.

The failbit is set for a stream when a format error occurs on the stream, such as when the program is inputting integers and a nondigit character is encountered in the

```cpp
// Fig. 17.22: ErrorStates.cpp
// Testing error states.
#include <iostream>
using std::cin;
using std::cout;
using std::endl;

int main()
{
    int integerValue;

    // display results of cin functions
    cout << "Before a bad input operation:"
        << "\ncin.rdstate(): " << cin.rdstate()
        << "\n     cin.eof(): " << cin.eof()
        << "\n    cin.fail(): " << cin.fail()
        << "\n     cin.bad(): " << cin.bad()
        << "\n    cin.good(): " << cin.good()
        << "\n\nExpects an integer, but enter a character: ";

    cin >> integerValue; // enter character value
    cout << endl;

    // display results of cin functions after bad input
    cout << "After a bad input operation:"
        << "\ncin.rdstate(): " << cin.rdstate()
        << "\n     cin.eof(): " << cin.eof()
        << "\n    cin.fail(): " << cin.fail()
        << "\n     cin.bad(): " << cin.bad()
        << "\n    cin.good(): " << cin.good() << endl << endl;

    cin.clear(); // clear stream

    // display results of cin functions after clearing cin
    cout << "After cin.clear()" << "\ncin.fail(): " << cin.fail()
        << "\ncin.good(): " << cin.good() << endl;
    return 0;
} // end main
```

Fig. 17.22 | Testing error states. (Part 1 of 2.)

```
Before a bad input operation:
cin.rdstate(): 0
    cin.eof(): 0
   cin.fail(): 0
    cin.bad(): 0
   cin.good(): 1

Expects an integer, but enter a character: A

After a bad input operation:
cin.rdstate(): 2
    cin.eof(): 0
   cin.fail(): 1
    cin.bad(): 0
   cin.good(): 0

After cin.clear()
cin.fail(): 0
cin.good(): 1
```

Fig. 17.22 | Testing error states. (Part 2 of 2.)

input stream. When such an error occurs, the characters are not lost. The ***fail*** member function reports whether a stream operation has failed. Usually, recovering from such errors is possible.

The badbit is set for a stream when an error occurs that results in the loss of data. The ***bad*** member function reports whether a stream operation failed. Generally, such serious failures are nonrecoverable.

The ***goodbit*** is set for a stream if none of the bits eofbit, failbit or badbit is set for the stream.

The ***good*** member function returns true if the bad, fail and eof functions would all return false. I/O operations should be performed only on "good" streams.

Member function ***rdstate*** returns the stream's error state. A call to cout.rdstate, for example, would return the state of the stream, which then could be tested by a switch statement that examines eofbit, badbit, failbit and goodbit. The preferred means of testing the state of a stream is to use member functions eof, bad, fail and good—using these functions does not require you to be familiar with particular status bits.

The ***clear*** member function is used to restore a stream's state to "good," so that I/O may proceed on that stream. The default argument for clear is goodbit, so the statement

    cin.clear();

clears cin and sets goodbit for the stream. The statement

    cin.clear(ios::failbit)

sets the failbit. You might want to do this when performing input on cin with a user-defined type and encountering a problem. The name clear might seem inappropriate in this context, but it is correct. The program of Fig. 17.22 demonstrates member functions rdstate, eof, fail, bad, good and clear.

The operator! member function of basic_ios returns true if the badbit is set, the failbit is set or both are set. The operator void * member function returns false (0) if the `badbit` is set, the `failbit` is set or both are set. These functions are useful in file processing when a `true`/`false` condition is being tested under the control of a selection statement or repetition statement.

17.9 Tying an Output Stream to an Input Stream

Interactive applications generally involve an `istream` for input and an `ostream` for output. When a prompting message appears on the screen, the user responds by entering the appropriate data. Obviously, the prompt needs to appear before the input operation proceeds. With output buffering, outputs appear only when the buffer fills, when outputs are flushed explicitly by the program or automatically at the end of the program. Visual C++ provides member function *tie* to synchronize (i.e., "tie together") the operation of an `istream` and an `ostream` to ensure that outputs appear before their subsequent inputs. The call

```
cin.tie( &cout );
```

ties `cout` (an `ostream`) to `cin` (an `istream`). Actually, this particular call is redundant, because Visual C++ performs this operation automatically to create a user's standard input/output environment. However, the user would tie other `istream`/`ostream` pairs explicitly. To untie an input stream, `inputStream`, from an output stream, use the call

```
inputStream.tie( 0 );
```

17.10 Data Hierarchy

Ultimately, all data items that digital computers process are reduced to combinations of zeros and ones. This occurs because it is simple and economical to build electronic devices that can assume two stable states—one state represents 0 and the other represents 1. It is remarkable that the impressive functions performed by computers ultimately involve only the most fundamental manipulations of 0s and 1s.

The smallest data item that computers support is called a *bit* (short for "*binary digit*"—a digit that can assume one of two values). Each data item, or bit, can assume either the value 0 or the value 1. Computer circuitry performs various simple bit manipulations, such as examining the value of a bit, setting the value of a bit and reversing a bit (from 1 to 0 or from 0 to 1).

Programming with data in the low-level form of bits is cumbersome. It is preferable to program with data in forms such as *decimal digits* (0–9), *letters* (A–Z and a–z) and *special symbols* (e.g., $, @, %, &, * and many others). Digits, letters and special symbols are referred to as *characters*. The set of all characters used to write programs and represent data items on a particular computer is called that computer's *character set*. Because computers can process only 1s and 0s, every character in a computer's character set is represented as a pattern of 1s and 0s. *Bytes* are composed of eight bits. Programmers create programs and data items with characters; computers manipulate and process these characters as patterns of bits. For example, Visual C++ provides data type `char`. Each `char` typically occupies one byte. Visual C++ also provides data type `wchar_t`, which can occupy more than one byte (to support larger character sets, such as the Unicode character set; for more information on Unicode, visit `www.unicode.org`).

Just as characters are composed of bits, *fields* are composed of characters. A field is a group of characters that conveys some meaning. For example, a field consisting of upper-case and lowercase letters can represent a person's name.

Data items processed by computers form a *data hierarchy* (Fig. 17.23), in which data items become larger and more complex in structure as we progress from bits, to characters, to fields and to larger data aggregates.

Typically, a *record* (which can be represented as a `class` in Visual C++) is composed of several fields (called data members in Visual C++). In a payroll system, for example, a record for a particular employee might include the following fields:

1. Employee identification number

2. Name

3. Address

4. Hourly pay rate

5. Number of exemptions claimed

6. Year-to-date earnings

7. Amount of taxes withheld

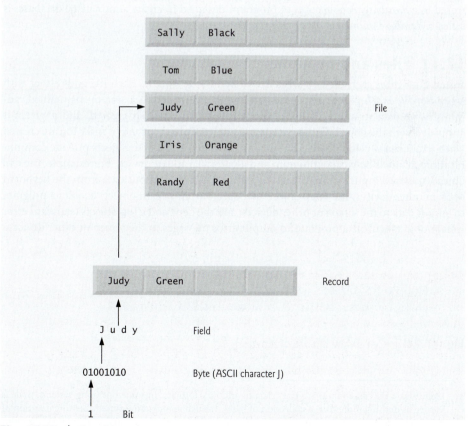

Fig. 17.23 | Data hierarchy.

Thus, a record is a group of related fields. In the preceding example, each field is associated with the same employee. A file is a group of related records.[4] A company's payroll file normally contains one record for each employee. Thus, a payroll file for a small company might contain only 22 records, whereas one for a large company might contain 100,000 records. It is not unusual for a company to have many files, some containing millions, billions, trillions or more characters of information.

To facilitate retrieving specific records from a file, at least one field in each record is chosen as a *record key*. A record key identifies a record as belonging to a particular person or entity and distinguishes that record from all others. In the payroll record described previously, the employee identification number normally would be chosen as the record key.

There are many ways of organizing records in a file. A common type of organization is called a *sequential file,* in which records typically are stored in order by a record-key field. In a payroll file, records usually are placed in order by employee identification number. The first employee record in the file contains the lowest employee identification number, and subsequent records contain increasingly higher ones.

Most businesses use many different files to store data. For example, a company might have payroll files, accounts-receivable files (listing money due from clients), accounts-payable files (listing money due to suppliers), inventory files (listing facts about all the items handled by the business) and many other types of files. A group of related files often are stored in a *database.* A collection of programs designed to create and manage databases is called a *database management system (DBMS).*

17.11 Files and Streams

Visual C++ views each file as a sequence of bytes (Fig. 17.24). Each file ends either with an *end-of-file marker* or at a specific byte number recorded in a system-maintained, administrative data structure. When a file is *opened*, an object is created, and a stream is associated with the object. Earlier we saw that objects cin, cout, cerr and clog are created when <iostream> is included. The streams associated with these objects provide communication channels between a program and a particular file or device. For example, the cin object (standard input stream object) enables a program to input data from the keyboard or from other devices, the cout object (standard output stream object) enables a program to output data to the screen or other devices, and the cerr and clog objects (standard error stream objects) enable a program to output error messages to the screen or other devices.

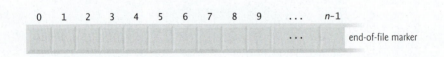

Fig. 17.24 | C++'s view of a file of *n* bytes.

---

4. Generally, a file can contain arbitrary data in arbitrary formats. In some operating systems, a file is viewed as nothing more than a collection of bytes. In such an operating system, any organization of the bytes in a file (such as organizing the data into records) is a view created by the application programmer.

To perform file processing in Visual C++, header files <iostream> and <fstream> must be included. Header <fstream> includes the definitions for the stream class templates basic_ifstream (for file input), basic_ofstream (for file output) and basic_fstream (for file input and output). Each class template has a predefined template specialization that enables char I/O. In addition, the <fstream> library provides typedef aliases for these template specializations. For example, the typedef ifstream represents a specialization of basic_ifstream that enables char input from a file. Similarly, typedef ofstream represents a specialization of basic_ofstream that enables char output to files. Also, typedef fstream represents a specialization of basic_fstream that enables char input from, and output to, files.

Files are opened by creating objects of these stream template specializations. These templates "derive" from class templates basic_istream, basic_ostream and basic_iostream, respectively. Thus, all member functions, operators and manipulators that belong to these templates (described earlier) also can be applied to file streams. Figure 17.2 summarizes the inheritance relationships of the I/O classes that we have discussed to this point.

17.12 Creating a Sequential File

Visual C++ imposes no structure on a file. Thus, a concept like that of a "record" does not exist in a Visual C++ file. Therefore, you must structure files to meet the application's requirements. In the following example, we see how you can impose a simple record structure on a file.

Figure 17.25 creates a sequential file that might be used in an accounts-receivable system to help manage the money owed by a company's credit clients. For each client, the program obtains the client's account number, name and balance (i.e., the amount the client owes the company for goods and services received in the past). The data obtained for each client constitutes a record for that client. The account number serves as the record key; that is, the program creates and maintains the file in account-number order. This program assumes the user enters the records in account-number order. In a comprehensive accounts-receivable system, a sorting capability would be provided for the user to enter records in any order—the records then would be sorted and written to the file.

```
1   // Fig. 17.25: CreateSequentialFile.cpp
2   // Create a sequential file.
3   #include <iostream>
4   using std::cerr;
5   using std::cin;
6   using std::cout;
7   using std::endl;
8   using std::ios;
9
10  #include <fstream> // file stream
11  using std::ofstream; // output file stream
12
13  #include <cstdlib>
14  using std::exit; // exit function prototype
```

Fig. 17.25 | Creating a sequential file. (Part 1 of 2.)

```
15
16   int main()
17   {
18       // ofstream constructor opens file
19       ofstream outClientFile( "clients.dat", ios::out );
20
21       // exit program if unable to create file
22       if ( !outClientFile ) // overloaded ! operator
23       {
24           cerr << "File could not be opened" << endl;
25           exit( 1 );
26       } // end if
27
28       cout << "Enter the account, name, and balance." << endl
29            << "Enter end-of-file to end input.\n? ";
30
31       int account;
32       char name[ 30 ];
33       double balance;
34
35       // read account, name and balance from cin, then place in file
36       while ( cin >> account >> name >> balance )
37       {
38           outClientFile << account << ' ' << name << ' ' << balance << endl;
39           cout << "? ";
40       } // end while
41
42       return 0; // ofstream destructor closes file
43   } // end main
```

```
Enter the account, name, and balance.
Enter end-of-file to end input.
? 100 Jones 24.98
? 200 Doe 345.67
? 300 White 0.00
? 400 Stone -42.16
? 500 Rich 224.62
? ^Z
```

Fig. 17.25 | Creating a sequential file. (Part 2 of 2.)

Let us examine this program. As stated previously, files are opened by creating ifstream, ofstream or fstream objects. In Fig. 17.25, the file is to be opened for output, so an ofstream object is created. Two arguments are passed to the object's constructor—the *filename* and the *file-open mode* (line 19). For an ofstream object, the file-open mode can be either *ios::out* to output data to a file or *ios::app* to append data to the end of a file (without modifying any data already in the file). Existing files opened with mode ios::out are *truncated*—all data in the file is discarded. If the specified file does not yet exist, then the ofstream object creates the file, using that filename. If the file does not contain a full directory path then Visual Studio creates the file in the project directory by default.

Line 19 creates an ofstream object named outClientFile associated with the file clients.dat that is opened for output. The arguments "clients.dat" and ios::out are passed to the ofstream constructor, which opens the file—this establishes a "line of communication" with the file. By default, ofstream objects are opened for output, so line 19 could have used the alternate statement

```
ofstream outClientFile( "clients.dat" );
```

to open clients.dat for output. Figure 17.26 lists the file-open modes.

Common Programming Error 17.3

Use caution when opening an existing file for output (ios::out), especially when you want to preserve the file's contents, which will be discarded without warning.

An ofstream object can be created without opening a specific file—a file can be attached to the object later. For example, the statement

```
ofstream outClientFile;
```

creates an ofstream object named outClientFile. The ofstream member function **open** opens a file and attaches it to an existing ofstream object as follows:

```
outClientFile.open( "clients.dat", ios::out );
```

Common Programming Error 17.4

Not opening a file before attempting to reference it in a program will result in an error.

After creating an ofstream object and attempting to open it, the program tests whether the open operation was successful. The if statement in lines 22–26 uses the overloaded ios operator member function operator! to determine whether the open operation succeeded. The condition returns a true value if either the failbit or the badbit is set for the stream on the open operation. Some possible errors are attempting to open a nonexistent file for reading, attempting to open a file for reading or writing without permission, and opening a file for writing when no disk space is available.

Mode	Description
ios::app	Append all output to the end of the file.
ios::ate	Open a file for output and move to the end of the file (normally used to append data to a file). Data can be written anywhere in the file.
ios::in	Open a file for input.
ios::out	Open a file for output.
ios::trunc	Discard the file's contents if they exist (this also is the default action for ios::out).
ios::binary	Open a file for binary (i.e., nontext) input or output.

Fig. 17.26 | File-open modes.

If the condition indicates an unsuccessful attempt to open the file, line 24 outputs the error message "File could not be opened", and line 25 invokes function exit to terminate the program. The argument to exit is returned to the environment from which the program was invoked. Argument 0 indicates that the program terminated normally; any other value indicates that the program terminated due to an error. The calling environment (most likely the operating system) uses the value returned by exit to respond appropriately to the error.

Another overloaded ios operator member function—operator void *—converts the stream to a pointer, so it can be tested as 0 (i.e., the null pointer) or nonzero (i.e., any other pointer value). When a pointer value is used as a condition, Visual C++ converts a null pointer to the bool value false and converts a non-null pointer to the bool value true. If the failbit or badbit has been set for the stream, 0 (false) is returned. The condition in the while statement of lines 36–40 invokes the operator void * member function on cin implicitly. The condition remains true as long as neither the failbit nor the badbit has been set for cin. Entering the end-of-file indicator sets the failbit for cin. The operator void * function can be used to test an input object for end-of-file instead of calling the eof member function explicitly on the input object.

If line 19 opened the file successfully, the program begins processing data. Lines 28–29 prompt the user to enter either the various fields for each record or the end-of-file indicator (entered with <Ctrl> z on Microsoft Windows) when data entry is complete.

Line 36 extracts each set of data and determines whether end-of-file has been entered. When end-of-file is encountered or bad data is entered, operator void * returns the null pointer (which converts to the bool value false) and the while statement terminates. The user enters end-of-file to inform the program to process no additional data. The end-of-file indicator is set when the user enters the end-of-file key combination. The while statement loops until the end-of-file indicator is set.

Line 38 writes a set of data to the file clients.dat, using the stream insertion operator << and the outClientFile object associated with the file at the beginning of the program. The data may be retrieved by a program designed to read the file (see Section 17.13). Note that, because the file created in Fig. 17.25 is simply a text file, it can be viewed by any text editor.

Once the user enters the end-of-file indicator, main terminates. This implicitly invokes the outClientFile object's destructor function, which closes the clients.dat file. You also can close the ofstream object explicitly, using member function **close** in the statement

```
outClientFile.close();
```

Performance Tip 17.2

Closing files explicitly when the program no longer needs to reference them can reduce resource usage (especially if the program continues execution after closing the files).

In the sample execution for the program of Fig. 17.25, the user enters information for five accounts, then signals that data entry is complete by entering end-of-file (^Z is displayed for Microsoft Windows). This dialog window does not show how the data records appear in the file. To verify that the program created the file successfully, the next section shows how to create a program that reads this file and prints its contents.

17.13 Reading Data from a Sequential File

Files store data so it may be retrieved for processing when needed. The previous section demonstrated how to create a file for sequential access. In this section, we discuss how to read data sequentially from a file.

Figure 17.27 reads records from the clients.dat file created by the program of Fig. 17.25 and displays the records' contents. Because we don't use full path names remember to copy the client.dat file from the the previous example's directory to the current example's directory. Creating an ifstream object opens a file for input. The ifstream constructor can receive the filename and the file-open mode as arguments. Line 31 creates an ifstream object called inClientFile and associates it with the clients.dat file. The arguments in parentheses are passed to the ifstream constructor function, which opens the file and establishes a "line of communication" with the file.

Good Programming Practice 17.2

Open a file for input only (using ios::in) if the file's contents should not be modified. This prevents unintentional modification of the file's contents and is an example of the principle of least privilege.

```
 1    // Fig. 17.27: ReadSequentialFile.cpp
 2    // Reading and printing a sequential file.
 3    #include <iostream>
 4    using std::cerr;
 5    using std::cout;
 6    using std::endl;
 7    using std::fixed;
 8    using std::ios;
 9    using std::left;
10    using std::right;
11    using std::showpoint;
12
13    #include <fstream> // file stream
14    using std::ifstream; // input file stream
15
16    #include <iomanip>
17    using std::setw;
18    using std::setprecision;
19
20    #include <string>
21    using std::string;
22
23    #include <cstdlib>
24    using std::exit; // exit function prototype
25
26    void outputLine( int, const string, double ); // prototype
27
28    int main()
29    {
30       // ifstream constructor opens the file
31       ifstream inClientFile( "clients.dat", ios::in );
```

Fig. 17.27 | Reading and printing a sequential file. (Part 1 of 2.)

```
32
33      // exit program if ifstream could not open file
34      if ( !inClientFile )
35      {
36         cerr << "File could not be opened" << endl;
37         exit( 1 );
38      } // end if
39
40      int account;
41      char name[ 30 ];
42      double balance;
43
44      cout << left << setw( 10 ) << "Account" << setw( 13 )
45         << "Name" << "Balance" << endl << fixed << showpoint;
46
47      // display each record in file
48      while ( inClientFile >> account >> name >> balance )
49         outputLine( account, name, balance );
50
51      return 0; // ifstream destructor closes the file
52   } // end main
53
54   // display single record from file
55   void outputLine( int account, const string name, double balance )
56   {
57      cout << left << setw( 10 ) << account << setw( 13 ) << name
58         << setw( 7 ) << setprecision( 2 ) << right << balance << endl;
59   } // end function outputLine
```

```
Account   Name         Balance
100       Jones          24.98
200       Doe           345.67
300       White           0.00
400       Stone         -42.16
500       Rich          224.62
```

Fig. 17.27 | Reading and printing a sequential file. (Part 2 of 2.)

Objects of class ifstream are opened for input by default. We could have used the statement

```
ifstream inClientFile( "clients.dat" );
```

to open clients.dat for input. Just as with an ofstream object, an ifstream object can be created without opening a specific file, because a file can be attached to it later.

The program uses the condition !inClientFile to determine whether the file was opened successfully before attempting to retrieve data from the file. Line 48 reads a set of data (i.e., a record) from the file. This is possible because we used spaces to delimit the entries in each record. After the preceding line is executed the first time, account has the value 100, name has the value "Jones" and balance has the value 24.98. Each time line 48 executes, it reads another record from the file into the variables account, name and balance. Line 49 displays the records, using function outputLine (lines 55–59), which uses parameterized stream manipulators to format the data for display. When the end-of-file has been reached, the implicit call to operator void * in the while condition returns the null pointer (which converts to the bool value false), the ifstream destructor function closes the file and the program terminates.

To retrieve data sequentially from a file, programs normally start reading from the beginning of the file and read all the data consecutively until the desired data is found. It might be necessary to process the file sequentially several times (from the beginning of the file) during the execution of a program. Both istream and ostream provide member functions for repositioning the *file-position pointer* (the byte number of the next byte in the file to be read or written). These member functions are **seekg** ("seek get") for istream and **seekp** ("seek put") for ostream. Each istream object has a "get pointer," which indicates the byte number in the file from which the next input is to occur, and each ostream object has a "put pointer," which indicates the byte number in the file at which the next output should be placed. The statement

```
inClientFile.seekg( 0 );
```

repositions the file-position pointer to the beginning of the file (location 0) attached to inClientFile. The argument to seekg normally is a long integer. A second argument can be specified to indicate the *seek direction*, which can be **ios::beg** (the default) for positioning relative to the beginning of a stream, **ios::cur** for positioning relative to the current position in a stream or **ios::end** for positioning relative to the end of a stream. The file-position pointer is an integer value that specifies the location in the file as a number of bytes from the file's starting location (this is also referred to as the *offset* from the beginning of the file). Some examples of positioning the "get" file-position pointer are

```
// position to the nth byte of fileObject (assumes ios::beg)
fileObject.seekg( n );

// position n bytes forward in fileObject
fileObject.seekg( n, ios::cur );

// position n bytes back from end of fileObject
fileObject.seekg( n, ios::end );

// position at end of fileObject
fileObject.seekg( 0, ios::end );
```

The same operations can be performed using ostream member function seekp. Member functions **tellg** and **tellp** are provided to return the current locations of the "get" and "put" pointers, respectively. The following statement assigns the "get" file-position pointer value to variable location of type long:

```
location = fileObject.tellg();
```

Figure 17.28 enables a credit manager to display the account information for those customers with zero balances (i.e., customers who do not owe the company any money), credit (negative) balances (i.e., customers to whom the company owes money), and debit (positive) balances (i.e., customers who owe the company money for goods and services received in the past). The program displays a menu and allows the credit manager to enter one of three options to obtain credit information. Option 1 produces a list of accounts with zero balances. Option 2 produces a list of accounts with credit balances. Option 3 produces a list of accounts with debit balances. Option 4 terminates program execution. Entering an invalid option displays the prompt to enter another choice. Again be sure to copy the `clients.dat` file from the previous example's project folder to this example's project folder.

```cpp
1   // Fig. 17.28: CreditInquiry.cpp
2   // Credit inquiry program.
3   #include <iostream>
4   using std::cerr;
5   using std::cin;
6   using std::cout;
7   using std::endl;
8   using std::fixed;
9   using std::ios;
10  using std::left;
11  using std::right;
12  using std::showpoint;
13
14  #include <fstream>
15  using std::ifstream;
16
17  #include <iomanip>
18  using std::setw;
19  using std::setprecision;
20
21  #include <string>
22  using std::string;
23
24  #include <cstdlib>
25  using std::exit; // exit function prototype
26
27  enum RequestType { ZERO_BALANCE = 1, CREDIT_BALANCE, DEBIT_BALANCE, END };
28  int getRequest();
29  bool shouldDisplay( int, double );
30  void outputLine( int, const string, double );
31
32  int main()
33  {
34     // ifstream constructor opens the file
35     ifstream inClientFile( "clients.dat", ios::in );
36
37     // exit program if ifstream could not open file
38     if ( !inClientFile )
39     {
40        cerr << "File could not be opened" << endl;
41        exit( 1 );
42     } // end if
43
44     int request;
45     int account;
46     char name[ 30 ];
```

Fig. 17.28 | Credit inquiry program. (Part 1 of 4.)

```
47        double balance;
48
49        // get user's request (e.g., zero, credit or debit balance)
50        request = getRequest();
51
52        // process user's request
53        while ( request != END )
54        {
55           switch ( request )
56           {
57              case ZERO_BALANCE:
58                 cout << "\nAccounts with zero balances:\n";
59                 break;
60              case CREDIT_BALANCE:
61                 cout << "\nAccounts with credit balances:\n";
62                 break;
63              case DEBIT_BALANCE:
64                 cout << "\nAccounts with debit balances:\n";
65                 break;
66           } // end switch
67
68           // read account, name and balance from file
69           inClientFile >> account >> name >> balance;
70
71           // display file contents (until eof)
72           while ( !inClientFile.eof() )
73           {
74              // display record
75              if ( shouldDisplay( request, balance ) )
76                 outputLine( account, name, balance );
77
78              // read account, name and balance from file
79              inClientFile >> account >> name >> balance;
80           } // end inner while
81
82           inClientFile.clear(); // reset eof for next input
83           inClientFile.seekg( 0 ); // reposition to beginning of file
84           request = getRequest(); // get additional request from user
85        } // end outer while
86
87        cout << "End of run." << endl;
88        return 0; // ifstream destructor closes the file
89     } // end main
90
91     // obtain request from user
92     int getRequest()
93     {
94        int request; // request from user
95
96        // display request options
97        cout << "\nEnter request" << endl
98           << " 1 - List accounts with zero balances" << endl
99           << " 2 - List accounts with credit balances" << endl
```

Fig. 17.28 | Credit inquiry program. (Part 2 of 4.)

```
100              << " 3 - List accounts with debit balances" << endl
101              << " 4 - End of run" << fixed << showpoint;
102
103     do // input user request
104     {
105         cout << "\n? ";
106         cin >> request;
107     } while ( request < ZERO_BALANCE && request > END );
108
109     return request;
110 } // end function getRequest
111
112 // determine whether to display given record
113 bool shouldDisplay( int type, double balance )
114 {
115     bool shouldDisplay = false;
116     // determine whether to display zero balances
117     if ( type == ZERO_BALANCE && balance == 0 )
118         shouldDisplay = true;
119     // determine whether to display credit balances
120     else if ( type == CREDIT_BALANCE && balance < 0 )
121         shouldDisplay = true;
122     // determine whether to display debit balances
123     else if ( type == DEBIT_BALANCE && balance > 0 )
124         shouldDisplay = true;
125
126     return shouldDisplay;
127 } // end function shouldDisplay
128
129 // display single record from file
130 void outputLine( int account, const string name, double balance )
131 {
132     cout << left << setw( 10 ) << account << setw( 13 ) << name
133         << setw( 7 ) << setprecision( 2 ) << right << balance << endl;
134 } // end function outputLine
```

```
Enter request
 1 - List accounts with zero balances
 2 - List accounts with credit balances
 3 - List accounts with debit balances
 4 - End of run
? 1

Accounts with zero balances:
300      White              0.00

Enter request
 1 - List accounts with zero balances
 2 - List accounts with credit balances
 3 - List accounts with debit balances
 4 - End of run
? 2

Accounts with credit balances:
400      Stone             -42.16
```

Fig. 17.28 | Credit inquiry program. (Part 3 of 4.)

```
Enter request
 1 - List accounts with zero balances
 2 - List accounts with credit balances
 3 - List accounts with debit balances
 4 - End of run
? 3

Accounts with debit balances:
100        Jones         24.98
200        Doe          345.67
500        Rich         224.62

Enter request
 1 - List accounts with zero balances
 2 - List accounts with credit balances
 3 - List accounts with debit balances
 4 - End of run
? 4
End of run.
```

Fig. 17.28 | Credit inquiry program. (Part 4 of 4.)

17.14 Updating Sequential Files

Data that is formatted and written to a sequential file as shown in Section 17.12 cannot be modified without the risk of destroying other data in the file. For example, if the name "White" needs to be changed to "Worthington," the old name cannot be overwritten without corrupting the file. The record for White was written to the file as

        300 White 0.00

If this record were rewritten beginning at the same location in the file using the longer name, the record would be

        300 Worthington 0.00

The new record contains six more characters than the original record. Therefore, the characters beyond the second "o" in "Worthington" would overwrite the beginning of the next sequential record in the file. The problem is that, in the formatted input/output model using the stream insertion operator << and the stream extraction operator >>, fields—and hence records—can vary in size. For example, values 7, 14, –117, 2074, and 27383 are all ints, which store the same number of "raw data" bytes internally (typically four bytes on today's popular 32-bit machines). However, these integers become different-sized fields when output as formatted text (character sequences). Therefore, the formatted input/output model usually is not used to update records in place.

Such updating can be done awkwardly. For example, to make the preceding name change, the records before 300 White 0.00 in a sequential file could be copied to a new file, the updated record then written to the new file, and the records after 300 White 0.00 copied to the new file. This requires processing every record in the file to update one record. If many records are being updated in one pass of the file, though, this technique can be acceptable.

17.15 Wrap-Up

This chapter summarized how Visual C++ performs input/output using streams and basic file processing techniques. You learned about the stream-I/O classes and objects, as well as the stream I/O template class hierarchy. We discussed ostream's formatted and unformatted output capabilities performed by the put and write functions. You saw examples using istream's formatted and unformatted input capabilities performed by the eof, get, getline, peek, putback, ignore and read functions. Next, we discussed stream manipulators and member functions that perform formatting tasks—dec, oct, hex and setbase for displaying integers; precision and setprecision for controlling floating-point precision; and width and setw for setting field width. You also learned additional iostream manipulators and member functions for formatting—showpoint for displaying decimal point and trailing zeros; left, right and internal for justification; fill and setfill for padding; scientific and fixed for displaying floating-point numbers in scientific and fixed notation; uppercase for uppercase/lowercase control; boolalpha for specifying boolean format; and flags and fmtflags for resetting the format state.

We presented various file-processing techniques to manipulate persistent data. You learned that data is stored in computers in the form of 0s and 1s, and that combinations of these values form bytes, fields, records and eventually files. You were introduced to the differences between character-based and byte-based streams, and to several file-processing class templates in header file <fstream>. Finally, you learned how to use sequential file processing to manipulate records stored in order, by the record-key field.

In the next chapter, we discuss many of the same stream- and file-processing techniques using managed code in C++/CLI. We explore some of the FCL classes designed for file processing and introduce object serialization.

Summary

Section 17.1 Introduction
- I/O operations are performed in a manner sensitive to the type of the data.

Section 17.2 Streams
- Visual C++ I/O occurs in streams. A stream is a sequence of bytes.
- I/O mechanisms of the system move bytes from devices to memory and vice versa efficiently and reliably.
- Visual C++ provides "low-level" and "high-level" I/O capabilities. Low-level I/O-capabilities specify that some number of bytes should be transferred device-to-memory or memory-to-device. High-level I/O is performed with bytes grouped into such meaningful units as integers, floats, characters, strings and user-defined types.
- Visual C++ provides both unformatted-I/O and formatted-I/O operations. Unformatted-I/O transfers are fast, but they process raw data that is difficult for people to use. Formatted I/O processes data in meaningful units, but requires extra processing time that can degrade the performance of high-volume data transfers.
- The <iostream> header file declares all stream-I/O operations.
- Header <iomanip> declares the parameterized stream manipulators.
- The <fstream> header declares file-processing operations.

- The basic_istream template supports stream-input operations.
- The basic_ostream template supports stream-output operations.
- The basic_iostream template supports both stream-input and stream-output operations.
- The basic_istream template and the basic_ostream template are each derived through single inheritance from the basic_ios template.
- The basic_iostream template is derived through multiple inheritance from both the basic_istream template and the basic_ostream template.
- The left-shift operator (<<) is overloaded to designate stream output and is referred to as the stream insertion operator.
- The right-shift operator (>>) is overloaded to designate stream input and is referred to as the stream extraction operator.
- The istream object cin is tied to the standard input device, normally the keyboard.
- The ostream object cout is tied to the standard output device, normally the screen.
- The ostream object cerr is tied to the standard error device. Outputs to cerr are unbuffered; each insertion to cerr appears immediately.
- The Visual C++ compiler determines data types automatically for input and output.

Section 17.3 Stream Output
- Addresses are displayed in hexadecimal format by default.
- To print the address in a pointer variable, cast the pointer to void *.
- Member function put outputs one character. Calls to put may be cascaded.

Section 17.4 Stream Input
- Stream input is performed with the stream extraction operator >>. This operator automatically skips white-space characters in the input stream.
- The >> operator returns false after end-of-file is encountered on a stream.
- Stream extraction causes failbit to be set for improper input and badbit to be set if the operation fails.
- A series of values can be input using the stream extraction operation in a while-loop header. The extraction returns 0 when end-of-file is encountered.
- The get member function with no arguments inputs one character and returns the character; EOF is returned if end-of-file is encountered on the stream.
- Member function get with a character-reference argument inputs the next character from the input stream and stores it in the character argument. This version of get returns a reference to the istream object for which the get member function is being invoked.
- Member function get with three arguments—a character array, a size limit and a delimiter (with default value newline)—reads characters from the input stream up to a maximum of limit – 1 characters, or until the delimiter is read. The input string is terminated with a null character. The delimiter is not placed in the character array but remains in the input stream.
- The getline member function operates like the three-argument get member function. The getline function removes the delimiter from the input stream but does not store it in the string.
- Member function ignore skips the specified number of characters (the default is 1) in the input stream; it terminates if the specified delimiter is encountered (the default delimiter is EOF).
- The putback member function places the previous character obtained by a get on a stream back onto that stream.

- The peek member function returns the next character from an input stream but does not extract (remove) the character from the stream.
- C++ offers type-safe I/O. If unexpected data is processed by the << and >> operators, various error bits are set, which the user may test to determine whether an I/O operation succeeded or failed. If operator << has not been overloaded for a user-defined type, a compiler error is reported.

Section 17.5 Unformatted I/O Using read, write and gcount

- Unformatted I/O is performed with member functions read and write. These input or output some number of bytes to or from memory, beginning at a designated memory address. They are input or output as raw bytes with no formatting.
- The gcount member function returns the number of characters input by the previous read operation on that stream.
- Member function read inputs a specified number of characters into a character array. failbit is set if fewer than the specified number of characters are read.

Section 17.6 Introduction to Stream Manipulators

- To change the base in which integers output, use the manipulator hex to set the base to hexadecimal (base 16) or oct to set the base to octal (base 8). Use manipulator dec to reset the base to decimal. The base remains the same until changed explicitly.
- The parameterized stream manipulator setbase also sets the base for integer output. setbase takes one integer argument of 10, 8 or 16 to set the base.
- Floating-point precision can be controlled with the setprecision stream manipulator or the precision member function. Both set the precision for all subsequent output operations until the next precision-setting call. The precision member function with no argument returns the current precision value.
- Parameterized manipulators require the inclusion of the <iomanip> header file.
- Member function width sets the field width and returns the previous width. Values narrower than the field are padded with fill characters. This setting applies only for the next insertion or extraction; the field width is set to 0 implicitly. Values wider than a field are printed in their entirety. Function width with no argument returns the current width setting. Manipulator setw also sets the width.
- For input, the setw stream manipulator establishes a maximum string size; if a larger string is entered, the larger line is broken into pieces no larger than the designated size.
- Programmers may create their own stream manipulators.

Section 17.7 Stream Format States and Stream Manipulators

- Stream manipulator showpoint forces a floating-point number to be output with a decimal point and with the number of significant digits specified by the precision.
- Stream manipulators left and right cause fields to be left justified with padding characters to the right or right justified with padding characters to the left.
- Stream manipulator internal indicates that a number's sign (or base when using stream manipulator showbase) should be left justified within a field, its magnitude should be right justified and intervening spaces should be padded with the fill character.
- Member function fill specifies the fill character to be used with stream manipulators left, right and internal (space is the default); the prior padding character is returned. Stream manipulator setfill also sets the fill character.

- Stream manipulators oct, hex and dec specify that integers are to be treated as octal, hexadecimal or decimal values, respectively. Integer output defaults to decimal if none of these bits is set; stream extractions process the data in the form in which the data is supplied.

- Stream manipulator showbase forces the base of an integral value to be output.

- Stream manipulator scientific is used to output a floating-point number in scientific format. Stream manipulator fixed is used to output a floating-point number with the precision specified by the precision member function.

- Stream manipulator uppercase outputs an uppercase X or E for hexadecimal integers and scientific-notation floating-point values, respectively. Hexadecimal values appear in all uppercase.

- Member function flags with no argument returns the long value of the current format state settings. Function flags with a long argument sets the format state specified by the argument.

Section 17.8 Stream Error States

- The state of a stream may be tested through bits in class ios_base.

- The eofbit is set for an input stream after end-of-file is encountered during an input operation. The eof member function reports whether the eofbit has been set.

- A stream's failbit is set when a format error occurs. The fail member function reports whether a stream operation has failed; it is normally possible to recover from such errors.

- A stream's badbit is set when an error occurs that results in data loss. Member function bad reports whether such a stream operation failed. Such serious failures are normally nonrecoverable.

- The good member function returns true if the bad, fail and eof functions would all return false. I/O operations should be performed only on "good" streams.

- The rdstate member function returns the error state of the stream.

- Member function clear restores a stream's state to "good," so that I/O may proceed.

Section 17.9 Tying an Output Stream to an Input Stream

- Visual C++ provides the tie member function to synchronize istream and ostream operations to ensure that outputs appear before subsequent inputs.

Section 17.10 Data Hierarchy

- The smallest data item that computers support is called a bit (short for "binary digit"—a digit that can assume one of two values, 0 or 1).

- Digits, letters and special symbols are referred to as characters.

- The set of all characters used to write programs and represent data items on a particular computer is called that computer's character set.

- Bytes are composed of eight bits.

- Just as characters are composed of bits, fields are composed of characters. A field is a group of characters that conveys some meaning.

- Typically, a record (i.e., a class in Visual C++) is composed of several fields (i.e., data members in C++).

- At least one field in a record is chosen as a record key to identify a record as belonging to a particular person or entity that is distinct from all other records in the file.

- In a sequential file, records typically are stored in order by a record-key field.

- A group of related files often is stored in a database.

- A collection of programs designed to create and manage databases is called a database management system (DBMS).

Section 17.11 Files and Streams

- Visual C++ views each file as a sequence of bytes.
- Each file ends either with an end-of-file marker or at a specific byte number recorded in a system-maintained, administrative data structure.
- When a file is opened, an object is created, and a stream is associated with the object.
- Use header files `<iostream>` and `<fstream>` to access file-processing capabilities.
- Header `<fstream>` includes the definitions for the stream class templates `basic_ifstream` (for file input), `basic_ofstream` (for file output) and `basic_fstream` (for file input and output).
- Each class template has a predefined template specialization that enables char I/O. The `<fstream>` library provides `typedef` aliases for these template specializations. The `typedef` if-stream represents a specialization of `basic_ifstream` that enables char input from a file. The `typedef` ofstream represents a specialization of `basic_ofstream` that enables char output to files. The `typedef` fstream represents a specialization of `basic_fstream` that enables char input from, and output to, files.
- The file-processing templates derive from class templates `basic_istream`, `basic_ostream` and `basic_iostream`, respectively. Thus, all member functions, operators and manipulators that belong to these templates also can be applied to file streams.

Section 17.12 Creating a Sequential File

- Visual C++ imposes no structure on a file, so you must structure files to meet the application's requirements.
- A file can be opened for output when an `ofstream` object is created. Two arguments are passed to the object's constructor—the filename and the file-open mode.
- For an `ofstream` object, the file-open mode can be either `ios::out` to output data to a file or `ios::app` to append data to the end of a file. Existing files opened with mode `ios::out` are truncated—all data in the file is discarded. If the specified file does not yet exist, then the `ofstream` object creates the file, using that filename.
- By default, `ofstream` objects are opened for output, so the second constructor argument is not required.
- An `ofstream` object can be created without opening a specific file—a file can be attached to the object later with member function `open`.
- The `ios` operator member function `operator!` determines whether a stream was opened correctly. This operator can be used in a condition that returns a true value if either the `failbit` or the `badbit` is set for the stream on the open operation. Some possible errors that yield a true result are attempting to open a nonexistent file for reading, attempting to open a file for reading or writing without permission, and opening a file for writing when no disk space is available.
- Another overloaded `ios` operator member function—`operator void *`—converts the stream to a pointer, so it can be tested as 0 or nonzero. When a pointer value is used as a condition, a null pointer represents the `bool` value `false` and a non-null pointer represents the `bool` value `true`. If the `failbit` or `badbit` has been set for the stream, 0 (`false`) is returned.
- Entering the end-of-file indicator sets the `failbit` for `cin`.
- The `operator void *` function can be used to test an input object for end-of-file instead of calling the `eof` member function explicitly on the input object.
- When a stream object's destructor is called, the corresponding stream is closed. You also can close the stream object explicitly, using the stream's `close` member function.
- Closing files explicitly when they are no longer needed can reduce a program's resource usage.

Section 17.13 Reading Data from a Sequential File

- Files store data so it may be retrieved for processing when needed.

- Creating an `ifstream` object opens a file for input. The `ifstream` constructor can receive the file-name and the file-open mode as arguments.

- Open a file for input only (using `ios::in`) if the file's contents should not be modified. This prevents unintentional modification of the file's contents and is an example of the principle of least privilege.

- Objects of class `ifstream` are opened for input by default, so the second constructor argument is not required.

- Just as with an ofstream object, an ifstream object can be created without opening a specific file, because a file can be attached to it later.

- To retrieve data sequentially from a file, programs normally start reading from the beginning of the file and read all the data consecutively until the desired data is found.

- Both `istream` and `ostream` provide member functions for repositioning the file-position pointer (the byte number of the next byte in the file to be read or written). These member functions are `seekg` ("seek get") for `istream` and `seekp` ("seek put") for `ostream`. Each `istream` object has a "get pointer," which indicates the byte number in the file from which the next input is to occur, and each `ostream` object has a "put pointer," which indicates the byte number in the file at which the next output should be placed.

- The argument to `seekg` normally is a long integer. A second argument can be specified to indicate the seek direction, which can be `ios::beg` (the default) for positioning relative to the beginning of a stream, `ios::cur` for positioning relative to the current position in a stream or `ios::end` for positioning relative to the end of a stream.

- The file-position pointer is an integer value that specifies the location in the file as a number of bytes from the file's starting location (i.e., the offset from the beginning of the file).

- Member functions `tellg` and `tellp` are provided to return the current locations of the "get" and "put" pointers, respectively.

Section 17.14 Updating Sequential Files

- Data that is formatted and written to a sequential file cannot be modified without the risk of destroying other data in the file. The problem is that records can vary in size.

- Updating can be done awkwardly. Records before the one to update could be copied to a new file, the updated record then would be written to the new file, then subsequent records after the modified one would be copied to the new file. This requires processing every record in the file to update one record. If many records are being updated in one pass of the file, though, this technique can be acceptable.

Terminology

append data to a file binary digit
bad member function of `basic_ios`
`badbit`
`basic_fstream` class template
`basic_ifstream` class template
`basic_ios` class template
`basic_iostream` class template
`basic_istream` class template
`basic_ofstream` class template

`basic_ostream` class template
bit
byte
`boolalpha` stream manipulator
character field
character set
`clear` member function of `basic_ios`
`clog` (standard error buffered)
`close` member function of `ofstream`

database
database management system (DBMS)
data hierarchy
data persistence
dec stream manipulator
decimal digit
default fill character (space)
default precision
end-of-file
eof member function of basic_ios
eofbit
fail member function of basic_ios
failbit
field
field width
file
filename
file-open modes
file-position pointer
fill character
fill member function of basic_ios
fixed stream manipulator
flags member function of ios_base
fmtflags
format states
formatted I/O
fstream
<fstream> header file
gcount member function of basic_istream
get member function of basic_istream
getline member function of basic_istream
good member function of basic_ios
hex stream manipulator
ifstream
ignore member function of basic_istream
internal stream manipulator
<iomanip> header file
ios_base class
ios::app file-open mode
ios::ate file-open mode
ios::beg seek starting point
ios::cur seek starting point
ios::end seek starting point
ios::in file-open mode
ios::out file-open mode
ios::trunc file-open mode
iostream
istream
leading 0 (octal)
leading 0x or 0X (hexadecimal)

left stream manipulator
noboolalpha stream manipulator
noshowbase stream manipulator
noshowpoint stream manipulator
noshowpos stream manipulator
noskipws stream manipulator
nouppercase stream manipulator
object input/output
oct stream manipulator
offset from the beginning of a file
ofstream
open a file
open member function of ofstream
operator void *
operator! member function of basic_ios
ostream
output buffering
padding
parameterized stream manipulator
peek member function of basic_istream
precision member function of ios_base
predefined streams
put member function of basic_ostream
putback member function of basic_istream
rdstate member function of basic_ios
read member function of basic_istream and
    istream
record
record key
right stream manipulator
scientific stream manipulator
secondary storage device
seek direction
seekg istream member function
seekp ostream member function
setbase stream manipulator
setfill stream manipulator
setprecision stream manipulator
setw stream manipulator
sequential file
showbase stream manipulator
showpoint stream manipulator
showpos stream manipulator
skipws stream manipulator
stream extraction operator (>>)
stream input
stream insertion operator (<<)
stream manipulator
stream output
tellg istream member function

`tellp` ostream member function	unbuffered output
`tie` member function of `basic_ios`	unformatted I/O
truncate an existing file	uppercase stream manipulator
`typedef`	`width` stream manipulator
type-safe I/O	`write` member function of `basic_ostream`

Self-Review Exercises

17.1   Answer each of the following:
   a) Input/output in Visual C++ occurs as _____ of bytes.
   b) The stream manipulators that format justification are _____, _____ and _____.
   c) Member function _____ can be used to set and reset format state.
   d) Most Visual C++ programs that do I/O should include the _____ header file that contains the declarations required for all stream-I/O operations.
   e) When using parameterized manipulators, the header file _____ must be included.
   f) Header file _____ contains the declarations required for file processing.
   g) The `ostream` member function _____ is used to perform unformatted output.
   h) Input operations are supported by class _____.
   i) Standard error stream outputs are directed to the stream objects _____ or _____.
   j) Output operations are supported by class _____.
   k) The symbol for the stream insertion operator is _____.
   l) The four objects that correspond to the standard devices on the system include _____, _____, _____ and _____.
   m) The symbol for the stream extraction operator is _____.
   n) The stream manipulators _____, _____ and _____ specify that integers should be displayed in octal, hexadecimal and decimal formats, respectively.
   o) The _____ stream manipulator causes positive numbers to display with a plus sign.

17.2   State whether the following are *true* or *false*. If the answer is *false*, explain why.
   a) The stream member function `flags` with a `long` argument sets the `flags` state variable to its argument and returns its previous value.
   b) The stream insertion operator `<<` and the stream extraction operator `>>` are overloaded to handle all standard data types—including strings and memory addresses (stream insertion only)—and all user-defined data types.
   c) The stream member function `flags` with no arguments resets the stream's format state.
   d) The stream extraction operator `>>` can be overloaded with an operator function that takes an `istream` reference and a reference to a user-defined type as arguments and returns an `istream` reference.
   e) The stream insertion operator `<<` can be overloaded with an operator function that takes an `istream` reference and a reference to a user-defined type as arguments and returns an `istream` reference.
   f) Input with the stream extraction operator `>>` always skips leading white-space characters in the input stream, by default.
   g) The stream member function `rdstate` returns the current state of the stream.
   h) The `cout` stream normally is connected to the display screen.
   i) The stream member function `good` returns `true` if the bad, `fail` and `eof` member functions all return `false`.
   j) The `cin` stream normally is connected to the display screen.
   k) If a nonrecoverable error occurs during a stream operation, the bad member function will return `true`.
   l) Output to `cerr` is unbuffered and output to `clog` is buffered.

m) Stream manipulator showpoint forces floating-point values to print with the default six digits of precision unless the precision value has been changed, in which case floating-point values print with the specified precision.

n) The ostream member function put outputs the specified number of characters.

o) The stream manipulators dec, oct and hex affect only the next integer output operation.

p) By default, memory addresses are displayed as long integers.

17.3 For each of the following, write a single statement that performs the indicated task.

a) Output the string "Enter your name: ".

b) Use a stream manipulator that causes the exponent in scientific notation and the letters in hexadecimal values to print in capital letters.

c) Output the address of the variable myString of type char *.

d) Use a stream manipulator to ensure that floating-point values print in scientific notation.

e) Output the address in variable integerPtr of type int *.

f) Use a stream manipulator such that, when integer values are output, the integer base for octal and hexadecimal values is displayed.

g) Output the value pointed to by floatPtr of type float *.

h) Use a stream member function to set the fill character to '*' for printing in field widths larger than the values being output. Repeat this statement with a stream manipulator.

i) Output the characters 'O' and 'K' in one statement with ostream function put.

j) Get the value of the next character to input without extracting it from the stream.

k) Input a single character into variable charValue of type char, using the istream member function get in two different ways.

l) Input and discard the next six characters in the input stream.

m) Use istream member function read to input 50 characters into char array line.

n) Read 10 characters into character array name. Stop reading characters if the '.' delimiter is encountered. Do not remove the delimiter from the input stream. Write another statement that performs this task and removes the delimiter from the input.

o) Use the istream member function gcount to determine the number of characters input into character array line by the last call to istream member function read, and output that number of characters, using ostream member function write.

p) Output 124, 18.376, 'Z', 1000000 and "String", separated by spaces.

q) Print the current precision setting, using a member function of object cout.

r) Input an integer value into int variable months and a floating-point value into float variable percentageRate.

s) Print 1.92, 1.925 and 1.9258 separated by tabs and with 3 digits of precision, using a stream manipulator.

t) Print integer 100 in octal, hexadecimal and decimal, using stream manipulators and separated by tabs.

u) Print integer 100 in decimal, octal and hexadecimal separated by tabs, using a stream manipulator to change the base.

v) Print 1234 right justified in a 10-digit field.

w) Read characters into character array line until the character 'z' is encountered, up to a limit of 20 characters (including a terminating null character). Do not extract the delimiter character from the stream.

x) Use integer variables x and y to specify the field width and precision used to display the double value 87.4573, and display the value.

17.4 Identify the error in each of the following statements and explain how to correct it.

a) cout << "Value of x <= y is: " << x <= y;

b) The following statement should print the integer value of 'c'.
cout << 'c';

    c) `cout << ""A string in quotes"";`

17.5 For each of the following, show the output.

    a) `cout << "12345" << endl;`
       `cout.width( 5 );`
       `cout.fill( '*' );`
       `cout << 123 << endl << 123;`

    b) `cout << setw( 10 ) << setfill( '$' ) << 10000;`

    c) `cout << setw( 8 ) << setprecision( 3 ) << fixed << 1024.987654;`

    d) `cout << showbase << oct << 99 << endl << hex << 99;`

    e) `cout << 100000 << endl << showpos << 100000;`

    f) `cout << setw( 10 ) << setprecision( 2 ) << scientific << 444.93738;`

17.6 Fill in the blanks in each of the following:

    a) Ultimately, all data items processed by a computer are reduced to combinations of _____and _____.

    b) The smallest data item a computer can process is called a(n) _____.

    c) A(n) _____ is a group of related records.

    d) Digits, letters and special symbols are referred to as _____.

    e) A group of related files is called a(n) _____.

    f) Member function _____ of the file streams `fstream`, `ifstream` and `ofstream` closes a file.

    g) The `istream` member function _____ reads a character from the specified stream.

    h) Member function _____ of the file streams `fstream`, `ifstream` and `ofstream` opens a file.

    i) Member functions _____ and _____ of `istream` and `ostream` set the file-position pointer to a specific location in an input or output stream, respectively.

17.7 State which of the following are *true* and which are *false*. If *false*, explain why.

    a) Member function `read` cannot be used to read data from the input object `cin`.

    b) You must create the `cin`, `cout`, `cerr` and `clog` objects explicitly.

    c) A program must call function `close` explicitly to close a file associated with an `ifstream`, `ofstream` or `fstream` object.

    d) If the file-position pointer points to a location in a sequential file other than the beginning of the file, the file must be closed and reopened to read from the beginning of the file.

    e) The `ostream` member function `write` can write to standard-output stream `cout`.

    f) Data in sequential files always is updated without overwriting nearby data.

    g) Member functions `seekp` and `seekg` must seek relative to the beginning of a file.

17.8 Assume that each of the following statements applies to the same program.

    a) Write a statement that opens file `oldmast.dat` for input; use an `ifstream` object called `inOldMaster`.

    b) Write a statement that opens file `trans.dat` for input; use an `ifstream` object called `inTransaction`.

    c) Write a statement that opens file `newmast.dat` for output (and creation); use `ofstream` object `outNewMaster`.

    d) Write a statement that reads a record from the file `oldmast.dat`. The record consists of integer `accountNumber`, string `name` and floating-point `currentBalance`; use `ifstream` object `inOldMaster`.

    e) Write a statement that reads a record from the file `trans.dat`. The record consists of integer `accountNum` and floating-point `dollarAmount`; use `ifstream` object `inTransaction`.

f) Write a statement that writes a record to the file `newmast.dat`. The record consists of integer `accountNum`, string `name`, and floating-point `currentBalance`; use `ofstream` object `outNewMaster`.

17.9 Find the error(s) and show how to correct it (them) in each of the following.

a) File `payables.dat` referred to by `ofstream` object `outPayable` has not been opened.

```
outPayable << account << company << amount << endl;
```

b) The following statement should read a record from the file `payables.dat`. The `ifstream` object `inPayable` refers to this file, and `istream` object `inReceivable` refers to the file `receivables.dat`.

```
inReceivable >> account >> company >> amount;
```

c) The file `tools.dat` should be opened to add data to the file without discarding the current data.

```
ofstream outTools( "tools.dat", ios::out );
```

Answers to Self-Review Exercises

17.1 a) streams. b) `left`, `right` and `internal`. c) flags. d) `<iostream>`. e) `<iomanip>`. f) `<fstream>`. g) `write`. h) `istream`. i) `cerr` or `clog`. j) `ostream`. k) `<<`. l) `cin`, `cout`, `cerr` and `clog`. m) `>>`. n) `oct`, `hex` and `dec`. o) `showpos`.

17.2 a) False. The stream member function `flags` with a `fmtflags` argument sets the `flags` state variable to its argument and returns the prior state settings. b) False. The stream insertion and stream extraction operators are not overloaded for all user-defined types. The programmer of a class must specifically provide the overloaded operator functions to overload the stream operators for use with each user-defined type. c) False. The stream member function `flags` with no arguments returns the current format settings as a `fmtflags` data type, which represents the format state. d) True. e) False. To overload the stream insertion operator `<<`, the overloaded operator function must take an `ostream` reference and a reference to a user-defined type as arguments and return an `ostream` reference. f) True. g) True. h) True. i) True. j) False. The `cin` stream is connected to the standard input of the computer, which normally is the keyboard. k) True. l) True. m) True. n) False. The `ostream` member function put outputs its single-character argument. o) False. The stream manipulators `dec`, `oct` and `hex` set the output format state for integers to the specified base until the base is changed again or the program terminates. p) False. Memory addresses are displayed in hexadecimal format by default. To display addresses as `long` integers, the address must be cast to a `long` value.

17.3
a) `cout << "Enter your name: ";`
b) `cout << uppercase;`
c) `cout << static_cast< void * >( myString );`
d) `cout << scientific;`
e) `cout << integerPtr;`
f) `cout << showbase;`
g) `cout << *floatPtr;`
h) `cout.fill( '*' );`
   `cout << setfill( '*' );`
i) `cout.put( 'O' ).put( 'K' );`
j) `cin.peek();`
k) `charValue = cin.get();`
   `cin.get( charValue );`
l) `cin.ignore( 6 );`
m) `cin.read( line, 50 );`

```
      n) cin.get( name, 10, '.' );
         cin.getline( name, 10, '.' );
      o) cout.write( line, cin.gcount() );
      p) cout << 124 << ' ' << 18.376 << ' ' << "Z " << 1000000 << " String";
      q) cout << cout.precision();
      r) cin >> months >> percentageRate;
      s) cout << setprecision( 3 ) << 1.92 << '\t' << 1.925 << '\t' << 1.9258;
      t) cout << oct << 100 << '\t' << hex << 100 << '\t' << dec << 100;
      u) cout << 100 << '\t' << setbase( 8 ) << 100 << '\t' << setbase( 16 ) << 100;
      v) cout << setw( 10 ) << 1234;
      w) cin.get( line, 20, 'z' );
      x) cout << setw( x ) << setprecision( y ) << 87.4573;
```

17.4   a) *Error:* The precedence of the << operator is higher than that of <=, which causes the statement to be evaluated improperly and also causes a compiler error.
Correction: Place parentheses around the expression x <= y.

b) *Error:* In Visual C++, characters are not treated as small integers, as they are in C.
Correction: To print the numerical value for a character in the computer's character set, the character must be cast to an integer value, as in the following:

```
      cout << static_cast< int >( 'c' );
```

c) *Error:* Quote characters cannot be printed in a string unless an escape sequence is used.
Correction: Print the string in one of the following ways:

```
      cout << "\"A string in quotes\"";
```

17.5   a) 12345
```
         **123
         123
```
b) $$$$$10000
c) 1024.988
d) 0143
```
         0x63
```
e) 100000
```
         +100000
```
f)   4.45e+002

17.6   a) 1s, 0s. b) bit. c) file. d) characters. e) database. f) close. g) get. h) open. j) seekg, seekp.

17.7   a) False. Function read can read from any input-stream object derived from istream.

b) False. These four streams are created automatically for you. The <iostream> header must be included in a file to use them. This header includes declarations for each stream object.

c) False. The files will be closed when destructors for ifstream, ofstream or fstream objects execute when the stream objects go out of scope or before program execution terminates, but it is a good programming practice to close all files explicitly with close once they are no longer needed.

d) False. Member function seekp or seekg can be used to reposition the "put" or "get" file-position pointer to the beginning of the file.

e) True.

f) False. In most cases, sequential file records are not of uniform length. Therefore, it is possible that updating a record will cause other data to be overwritten.

g) False. It is possible to seek from the beginning of the file, from the end of the file and from the current position in the file.

17.8 a) `ifstream inOldMaster( "oldmast.dat", ios::in );`
   b) `ifstream inTransaction( "trans.dat", ios::in );`
   c) `ofstream outNewMaster( "newmast.dat", ios::out );`
   d) `inOldMaster >> accountNumber >> name >> currentBalance;`
   e) `inTransaction >> accountNum >> dollarAmount;`
   f) `outNewMaster << accountNum << name << currentBalance;`

17.9 a) *Error:* The file `payables.dat` has not been opened before the attempt is made to output data to the stream.
      Correction: Use ostream function open to open `payables.dat` for output.
   b) *Error:* The incorrect `istream` object is being used to read a record from the file named `payables.dat`.
      Correction: Use `istream` object `inPayable` to refer to `payables.dat`.
   c) *Error:* The file's contents are discarded because the file is opened for output (`ios::out`).
      Correction: To add data to the file, open the file either for updating (`ios::ate`) or for appending (`ios::app`).

Exercises

17.10 Write a statement for each of the following:
   a) Print integer 40000 left justified in a 15-digit field.
   b) Read a string into character array variable `state`.
   c) Print 200 with and without a sign.
   d) Print the decimal value 100 in hexadecimal form preceded by 0x.
   e) Read characters into array `charArray` until the character `'p'` is encountered, up to a limit of 10 characters (including the terminating null character). Extract the delimiter from the input stream, and discard it.
   f) Print 1.234 in a 9-digit field with preceding zeros.

17.11 Write a program to test the inputting of integer values in decimal, octal and hexadecimal formats. Output each integer read by the program in all three formats. Test the program with the following input data: 10, 010, 0x10.

17.12 Write a program that prints pointer values, using casts to all the integer data types. Which ones print strange values? Which ones cause errors?

17.13 Write a program to test the results of printing the integer value 12345 and the floating-point value 1.2345 in various-sized fields. What happens when the values are printed in fields containing fewer digits than the values?

17.14 Write a program that prints the value 100.453627 rounded to the nearest digit, tenth, hundredth, thousandth and ten-thousandth.

17.15 Write a program that inputs a string from the keyboard and determines the length of the string. Print the string in a field width that is twice the length of the string.

17.16 Write a program that converts integer Fahrenheit temperatures from 0 to 212 degrees to floating-point Celsius temperatures with 3 digits of precision. Use the formula

```
celsius = 5.0 / 9.0 * ( fahrenheit - 32 );
```

to perform the calculation. The output should be printed in two right-justified columns and the Celsius temperatures should be preceded by a sign for both positive and negative values.

17.17 In some programming languages, strings are entered surrounded by either single or double quotation marks. Write a program that reads the three strings suzy, "suzy" and 'suzy'. Are the single and double quotes ignored or read as part of the string?

17.18 In Fig. 12.5, the stream extraction and stream insertion operators were overloaded for input and output of objects of the PhoneNumber class. Rewrite the stream extraction operator to perform the following error checking on input. The operator>> function will need to be reimplemented.

    a) Input the entire phone number into an array. Test that the proper number of characters has been entered. There should be a total of 14 characters read for a phone number of the form (800) 555-1212. Use ios_base-member-function clear to set failbit for improper input.

    b) The area code and exchange do not begin with 0 or 1. Test the first digit of the area-code and exchange portions of the phone number to be sure that neither begins with 0 or 1. Use ios_base-member-function clear to set failbit for improper input.

    c) The middle digit of an area code used to be limited to 0 or 1 (although this has changed recently). Test the middle digit for a value of 0 or 1. Use the ios_base-member-function clear to set failbit for improper input. If none of the above operations results in failbit being set for improper input, copy the three parts of the telephone number into the areaCode, exchange and line members of the PhoneNumber object. If failbit has been set on the input, have the program print an error message and end, rather than print the phone number.

17.19 Write a program that accomplishes each of the following:

    a) Create a user-defined class Point that contains the private integer data members xCoordinate and yCoordinate and declares stream insertion and stream extraction overloaded operator functions as friends of the class.

    b) Define the stream insertion and stream extraction operator functions. The stream extraction operator function should determine whether the data entered is valid, and, if not, it should set the failbit to indicate improper input. The stream insertion operator should not be able to display the point after an input error has occurred.

    c) Write a main function that tests input and output of user-defined class Point, using the overloaded stream extraction and stream insertion operators.

17.20 Write a program that accomplishes each of the following:

    a) Create a user-defined class Complex that contains the private integer data members real and imaginary and declares stream insertion and stream extraction overloaded operator functions as friends of the class.

    b) Define the stream insertion and stream extraction operator functions. The stream extraction operator function should determine whether the data entered is valid, and, if not, it should set failbit to indicate improper input. The input should be of the form

        3 + 8i

    c) The values can be negative or positive, and it is possible that one of the two values is not provided, in which case the appropriate data member should be set to 0. The stream insertion operator should not be able to display the point if an input error has occurred. For negative imaginary values, a minus sign should be printed rather than a plus sign.

    d) Write a main function that tests input and output of user-defined class Complex, using the overloaded stream extraction and stream insertion operators.

17.21 Write a program that uses a for statement to print a table of ASCII values for the characters in the ASCII character set from 33 to 126. The program should print the decimal value, octal value, hexadecimal value and character value for each character. Use the stream manipulators dec, oct and hex to print the integer values.

17.22 Write a program to show that the getline and three-argument get istream member functions both end the input string with a string-terminating null character. Also, show that get leaves the delimiter character on the input stream, whereas `getline` extracts the delimiter character and discards it. What happens to the unread characters in the stream?

17.23 Fill in the blanks in each of the following:
a) Computers store large amounts of data on secondary storage devices as _____.
b) A(n) _____ is composed of several fields.
c) To facilitate the retrieval of specific records from a file, one field in each record is chosen as a(n) _____.
d) The vast majority of information stored in computer systems is stored in _____ files.
e) A group of related characters that conveys meaning is called a(n) _____.
f) The standard stream objects declared by header `<iostream>` are _____, _____, _____ and _____.
g) `ostream` member function _____ outputs a character to the specified stream.
h) `istream` member function _____ repositions the file-position pointer in a file.

17.24 State which of the following are *true* and which are *false*. If *false*, explain why.
a) The impressive functions performed by computers essentially involve the manipulation of zeros and ones.
b) People prefer to manipulate bits instead of characters and fields because bits are more compact.
c) People specify programs and data items as characters; computers then manipulate and process these characters as groups of zeros and ones.
d) A person's 5-digit zip code is an example of a numeric field.
e) A person's street address is generally considered to be an alphabetic field in computer applications.
f) Data items represented in computers form a data hierarchy in which data items become larger and more complex as we progress from fields to characters to bits, etc.
g) A record key identifies a record as belonging to a particular field.
h) Most organizations store all information in a single file to facilitate computer processing.
i) When a program creates a file, the file is automatically retained by the computer for future reference; i.e., files are said to be persistent.

17.25 Exercise 17.8 asked you to write a series of single statements. Actually, these statements form the core of an important type of file-processing program, namely, a file-matching program. In commercial data processing, it is common to have several files in each application system. In an accounts-receivable system, for example, there is generally a master file containing detailed information about each customer, such as the customer's name, address, telephone number, outstanding balance, credit limit, discount terms, contract arrangements and, possibly, a condensed history of recent purchases and cash payments.

As transactions occur (e.g., sales are made and cash payments arrive), they are entered into a file. At the end of each business period (a month for some companies, a week for others and a day in some cases), the file of transactions (called `trans.dat` in Exercise 17.8) is applied to the master file (called `oldmast.dat` in Exercise 17.8), thus updating each account's record of purchases and payments. During an updating run, the master file is rewritten as a new file (`newmast.dat`), which is then used at the end of the next business period to begin the updating process again.

File-matching programs must deal with certain problems that do not exist in single-file programs. For example, a match does not always occur. A customer on the master file might not have made any purchases or cash payments in the current business period, and therefore no record for this customer will appear on the transaction file. Similarly, a customer who did make some purchases or cash payments may have just moved to this community, and the company may not have had a chance to create a master record for this customer.

Use the statements from Exercise 17.8 as a basis for writing a complete file-matching accounts-receivable program. Use the account number on each file as the record key for matching purposes. Assume that each file is a sequential file with records stored in increasing order by account number.

When a match occurs (i.e., records with the same account number appear on both the master and transaction files), add the dollar amount on the transaction file to the current balance on the master file, and write the newmast.dat record. (Assume purchases are indicated by positive amounts on the transaction file and payments are indicated by negative amounts.) When there is a master record for a particular account but no corresponding transaction record, merely write the master record to newmast.dat. When there is a transaction record but no corresponding master record, print the error message "Unmatched transaction record for account number ..." (fill in the account number from the transaction record).

17.26 After writing the program of Exercise 17.25, write a simple program to create some test data for checking out the program. Use the following sample account data:

Master file Account number	Name	Balance
100	Alan Jones	348.17
300	Mary Smith	27.19
500	Sam Sharp	0.00
700	Suzy Green	−14.22

Transaction file Account number	Transaction amount
100	27.14
300	62.11
400	100.56
900	82.17

17.27 Run the program of Exercise 17.25, using the files of test data created in Exercise 17.26. Print the new master file. Check that the accounts have been updated correctly.

17.28 It is possible (actually common) to have several transaction records with the same record key. This occurs because a particular customer might make several purchases and cash payments during a business period. Rewrite your accounts-receivable file-matching program of Exercise 17.25 to provide for the possibility of handling several transaction records with the same record key. Modify the test data of Exercise 17.26 to include the following additional transaction records:

Account number	Dollar amount
300	83.89
700	80.78
700	1.53

17.29 (*Telephone-Number Word Generator*) Standard telephone keypads contain the digits 0 through 9. The numbers 2 through 9 each have three letters associated with them, as indicated by the following table:

Digit	Letter
2	A B C
3	D E F
4	G H I
5	J K L
6	M N O
7	P R S
8	T U V
9	W X Y

Many people find it difficult to memorize phone numbers, so they use the correspondence between digits and letters to develop seven-letter words that correspond to their phone numbers. For example, a person whose telephone number is 686-2377 might use the correspondence indicated in the above table to develop the seven-letter word "NUMBERS."

Businesses frequently attempt to get telephone numbers that are easy for their clients to remember. If a business can advertise a simple word for its customers to dial, then no doubt the business will receive a few more calls.

Each seven-letter word corresponds to exactly one seven-digit telephone number. The restaurant wishing to increase its take-home business could surely do so with the number 825-3688 (i.e., "TAKEOUT").

Each seven-digit phone number corresponds to many separate seven-letter words. Unfortunately, most of these represent unrecognizable juxtapositions of letters. It is possible, however, that the owner of a barber shop would be pleased to know that the shop's telephone number, 424-7288, corresponds to "HAIRCUT." A veterinarian with the phone number 738-2273 would be pleased to know that the number corresponds to "PETCARE."

Write a program that, given a seven-digit number, writes to a file every possible seven-letter word corresponding to that number. There are 2187 (3 to the seventh power) such words. Avoid phone numbers with the digits 0 and 1.

17.30 Write a program that uses the `sizeof` operator to determine the sizes in bytes of the various data types on your computer system. Write the results to the file `datasize.dat`, so that you may print the results later. The results should be displayed in two-column format with the type name in the left column and the size of the type in right column, as in:

```
char                1
unsigned char       1
short int           2
unsigned short int  2
int                 4
unsigned int        4
long int            4
unsigned long int   4
float               4
double              8
long double         10
```

[*Note:* The sizes of the built-in data types on your computer might differ from those listed above.]

18

Files and Streams in .NET

OBJECTIVES

In this chapter you will learn:

- To create, read, write and update files using C++/CLI.
- The C++/CLI streams class hierarchy.
- To use classes `File` and `Directory` to obtain information about files and directories on your computer.
- To become familiar with sequential-access file processing with managed code.
- To use classes `FileStream`, `StreamReader` and `StreamWriter` to read text from and write text to files.
- To use classes `FileStream` and `BinaryFormatter` to read objects from and write objects to files.

18.1 Introduction

In this chapter, we explain how to create, update and process data files with managed code in C++/CLI programs. In Chapter 17 you learned how to perform basic I/O and file-processing operations in native C++. With managed code in C++/CLI we instead use the FCL classes that are part of the .NET Framework to manipulate streams and process files. In this chapter we overview some of the FCL's file-processing classes. We present an example that shows how you can determine information about the files and directories on your computer. The remainder of the chapter shows how to write to and read from text files that are human readable and binary files that store entire objects in binary format. You will also learn more about object serialization through examples in managed code.

18.2 Files and Streams

In Section 17.10 we introduced the concepts of the data hierarchy, records, and sequential files in native C++. The concepts are the same in C++/CLI. What changes are the classes and functions we use to interface with files and streams. You learned that each file is viewed as a sequential stream of bytes and ends either with an end-of-file marker or at a specific byte number that is recorded in a system-maintained administrative data structure. Recall that in native C++ when a file is opened, an object is created and a stream such as cin or cout is associated with the object. In C++/CLI the same process takes place but we don't associate streams with cin or cout. Instead, when a managed program executes, the runtime environment creates three stream objects that are accessible via properties ***Console::Out***, ***Console::In*** and ***Console::Error***, respectively. As you may have guessed, these three stream objects are roughly analogous in purpose to cout, cin and cerr, respectively. These objects facilitate communication between a program and a particular file or device. Console::In refers to the *standard input stream object*, which enables a program to input data from the keyboard (like cin). Console::Out refers to the *standard output stream object*, which enables a program to output data to the screen (like cout). Console::Error refers to the *standard error stream object*, which enables a program to output error messages to the screen (like cerr). We have been using Console::Out and Console::In in our previous C++/CLI console applications—Console functions Write and WriteLine use Console::Out to perform output, and Console functions Read and

ReadLine use Console::In to perform input. You have learned to use format specifiers to control the format of output. We discuss more about class String and output in Chapter 19, Class **string** and String Stream Processing.

There are many file-processing classes in the FCL. The System::IO namespace includes stream classes such as *StreamReader* (for text input from a file), *StreamWriter* (for text output to a file) and *FileStream* (for both input from and output to a file). These stream classes inherit from abstract classes *TextReader*, *TextWriter* and Stream, respectively. Actually, properties Console::In and Console::Out are of type TextReader and TextWriter, respectively. The system creates objects of TextReader and TextWriter derived classes to initialize Console properties Console::In and Console::Out.

Abstract class *Stream* provides functionality for representing streams as bytes. Classes FileStream, *MemoryStream* and *BufferedStream* (all from namespace System::IO) inherit from class Stream. Class FileStream can be used to write data to and read data from files. Class MemoryStream enables the transfer of data directly to and from memory— this is much faster than reading from and writing to external devices. Class Buffered-Stream uses buffering to transfer data to or from a stream. Recall that buffering is an I/O performance-enhancement technique, in which each output operation is directed to a region in memory, called a buffer, that is large enough to hold the data from many output operations. In this chapter, we use FCL stream classes to implement file-processing programs in C++/CLI that create and manipulate sequential-access files.

18.3 Classes File and Directory

Information is stored in files, which are organized in directories. FCL classes File and Directory enable programs to manipulate files and directories on disk. Class *File* can determine information about files and can be used to open files for reading or writing. We discuss techniques for writing to and reading from files in subsequent sections.

Figure 18.1 lists several of class File's static functions for manipulating and determining information about files. We demonstrate several of these functions in Fig. 18.3.

static function	Description
AppendText	Returns a StreamWriter that appends text to an existing file or creates a file if one does not exist.
Copy	Copies a file to a new file.
Create	Creates a file and returns its associated FileStream.
CreateText	Creates a text file and returns its associated StreamWriter.
Delete	Deletes the specified file.
Exists	Returns true if the specified file exists and false otherwise.
GetCreationTime	Returns a DateTime object representing when the file was created.

Fig. 18.1 | File class static functions (partial list). (Part 1 of 2.)

static function	Description
GetLastAccessTime	Returns a DateTime object representing when the file was last accessed.
GetLastWriteTime	Returns a DateTime object representing when the file was last modified.
Move	Moves the specified file to a specified location.
Open	Returns a FileStream associated with the specified file and equipped with the specified read/write permissions.
OpenRead	Returns a read-only FileStream associated with the specified file.
OpenText	Returns a StreamReader associated with the specified file.
OpenWrite	Returns a read/write FileStream associated with the specified file.

Fig. 18.1 | File class static functions (partial list). (Part 2 of 2.)

Class **Directory** provides capabilities for manipulating directories. Figure 18.2 lists some of class Directory's static functions for directory manipulation. Figure 18.3 demonstrates several of these functions, as well. The **DirectoryInfo** object returned by function **CreateDirectory** contains information about a directory. Much of the information contained in class DirectoryInfo also can be accessed via the functions of class Directory.

static function	Description
CreateDirectory	Creates a directory and returns its associated DirectoryInfo object.
Delete	Deletes the specified directory.
Exists	Returns true if the specified directory exists and false otherwise.
GetDirectories	Returns a String ^ array containing the names of the subdirectories in the specified directory.
GetFiles	Returns a String ^ array containing the names of the files in the specified directory.
GetCreationTime	Returns a DateTime object representing when the directory was created.
GetLastAccessTime	Returns a DateTime object representing when the directory was last accessed.
GetLastWriteTime	Returns a DateTime object representing when items were last written to the directory.
Move	Moves the specified directory to a specified location.

Fig. 18.2 | Directory class static functions.

Demonstrating Classes File and Directory

The example in Figure 18.3 uses File and Directory functions to access file and directory information. First we prompt the user to enter a file or directory name (line 14). Line 20 uses File function Exists to determine whether the user-specified text is the name of an existing file. If so, line 23 invokes function getInformation (lines 65–85), which calls File functions GetCreationTime (line 74), GetLastWriteTime (line 78) and GetLastAccessTime (line 82) to access file information. When function getInformation returns, line 29 instantiates a StreamReader for reading text from the file. The StreamReader constructor takes as an argument a String containing the name of the file to open. Note that we create the StreamReader using stack semantics. Rather than the declaration in line 29 we could have used gcnew as follows:

```
StreamReader ^stream = gcnew StreamReader( fileName );
```

As you learned in Chapters 11 and 16, by using stack semantics we can ensure the resource is released as soon as it goes out of scope. This frees us of the responsibility of calling delete to manually release the StreamReader when we are done with it. Line 30 calls StreamReader function ReadToEnd to read the entire contents of the file as a String and print it to the console.

```cpp
 1   // Fig. 18.3: FileTest.cpp
 2   // Using classes File and Directory.
 3
 4   #include "stdafx.h";
 5
 6   using namespace System;
 7   using namespace System::IO;
 8
 9   static String^ getInformation( String ^ ); // function prototype
10
11   // displays contents of files and directories
12   int main( array< System::String ^> ^args )
13   {
14      Console::WriteLine( "Enter file or directory name:" );
15
16      String ^fileName; // name of file or directory
17      fileName = Console::ReadLine(); // get user-specified file or directory
18
19      // determine whether fileName is a file
20      if ( File::Exists( fileName ) )
21      {
22         // get file's creation date, modification date, etc.
23         Console::WriteLine( getInformation ( fileName ) );
24
25         // display file contents through StreamReader
26         try
27         {
28            // obtain reader and file contents
29            StreamReader stream( fileName );
```

Fig. 18.3 | Testing classes File and Directory. (Part 1 of 3.)

```
30              Console::WriteLine( stream.ReadToEnd() );
31          } // end try
32          // handle exception if StreamReader is unavailable
33          catch ( IOException ^ )
34          {
35              Console::WriteLine( "Error reading from file" );
36          } // end catch
37      } // end if
38      // determine whether fileName is a directory
39      else if ( Directory::Exists( fileName ) )
40      {
41          array< String^ >^ directoryList // array for directories
42
43          // get directory's creation date, modification date, etc.
44          Console::WriteLine( getInformation( fileName ) );
45
46          // obtain file/directory list of specified directory
47          directoryList = Directory::GetDirectories( fileName );
48
49          Console::WriteLine( "Directory contents:\n" );
50
51          // output directoryList contents
52          for each( String ^directory in directoryList )
53              Console::WriteLine( "{0}", directory );
54      } // end else if
55      else
56      {
57          // notify user that neither file nor directory exists
58          Console::WriteLine( "{0} does not exist ", fileName );
59      } // end else
60
61      return 0;
62  } // end main
63
64  // get information on file or directory
65  static String^ getInformation( String ^fileName )
66  {
67      String ^information;
68
69      // output that file or directory exists
70      information = fileName + " exists\n\n";
71
72      // output when file or directory was created
73      information += "Created: " +
74          File::GetCreationTime( fileName ) + "\n";
75
76      // output when file or directory was last modified
77      information += "Last modified: " +
78          File::GetLastWriteTime( fileName ) + "\n";
79
80      // output when file or directory was last accessed
81      information += "Last accessed: " +
82          File::GetLastAccessTime( fileName ) + "\n\n";
```

Fig. 18.3 | Testing classes `File` and `Directory`. (Part 2 of 3.)

```
83
84      return information;
85  } // end function getInformation
```

```
Enter file or directory name:
c:\
c:\ exists

Created: 11/2/2006 6:18:56 AM
Last modified: 8/3/2007 10:01:50 AM
Last accessed: 8/3/2007 10:01:50 AM


Directory contents:

c:\Books
c:\Boot
c:\deitel.com
c:\dell
c:\doctemp
c:\Documents and Settings
c:\drivers
c:\examples
c:\i386
c:\Inetpub
c:\MSOCache
c:\Program Files
c:\PSFONTS
c:\System Volume Information
c:\temp
c:\Users
c:\Welcome
c:\Windows
```

Fig. 18.3 | Testing classes `File` and `Directory`. (Part 3 of 3.)

If line 20 determines that the user-specified text is not a file, line 39 determines whether it is a directory using `Directory` function **Exists**. If the user specified an existing directory, line 44 invokes function `getInformation` to access the directory information. Function `getInformation` uses the overloaded + operator with `Strings` to concatenate them into one larger `String`. We discuss `String` concatenation in detail in Chapter 19. Line 47 calls `Directory` function **GetDirectories** to obtain a `String^` array containing the names of subdirectories in the specified directory. Lines 52–53 use a `for each` statement to display each element in the `String^` array. Note that, if line 49 determines that the user-specified text is not a directory name, lines 55–59 notify the user that the name the user entered does not exist as a file or directory.

18.4 Creating a Sequential-Access Text File

As with native C++, managed code in C++/CLI imposes no structure on files and has no concept of "records." In the next few examples, we use text and special characters to organize our own concept of a "record."

Class Record

Figure 18.4 contains class Record that Fig. 18.5, Fig. 18.6 and Fig. 18.7 use for maintaining the information in each record that is written to or read from a file. We have created Record not with project template **CLR Console Application** as with our previous projects but instead using the **CLR Class Library** template. We will need to use a class library rather than a normal header file for later examples. When you create a **CLR Class Library**, Visual Studio inserts a namespace declaration automatically. This is to avoid causing naming conflicts with existing libraries. Namespaces are explained in more detail in Chapter 26. When building a **CLR Console Application** the compiler creates an executable file that contains the program logic. When building a **CLR Class Library** the compiler instead creates a file named Record.dll that we can reference from other projects. We explain how to add Record.dll as a reference in another project for Figure 18.5. Note that we put our class only in the .h file for simplicity but Visual Studio creates a .cpp file as well. Both files are required for your class library to function properly.

```cpp
 1   // Fig. 18.4: Record.h
 2   // Serializable class that represents a data record.
 3
 4   #pragma once
 5
 6   using namespace System;
 7
 8   namespace RecordLibrary
 9   {
10      public ref class Record
11      {
12      public:
13         // parameterless constructor sets members to default values
14         Record()
15         {
16            Account = 0;
17            FirstName = "";
18            LastName = "";
19            Balance = Decimal::Parse( "0.0" );
20         } // end constructor
21
22         // overloaded constructor sets members to parameter values
23         Record( int accountValue, String ^firstNameValue,
24            String ^lastNameValue, Decimal balanceValue )
25         {
26            Account = accountValue;
27            FirstName = firstNameValue;
28            LastName = lastNameValue;
29            Balance = balanceValue;
30         } // end constructor
31
32         // trivial property that gets and sets Account
33         property int Account;
34         // trivial property that gets and sets FirstName
35         property String^ FirstName;
```

Fig. 18.4 | Record for sequential-access file-processing applications. (Part 1 of 2.)

```
36          // trivial property that gets and sets LastName
37          property String^ LastName;
38          // trivial property that gets and sets Balance
39          property Decimal Balance;
40      }; // end managed class Record
41  } // end namespace RecordLibrary
```

Fig. 18.4 | Record for sequential-access file-processing applications. (Part 2 of 2.)

Class `Record` contains `public` trivial properties `Account`, `FirstName`, `LastName` and `Balance` (lines 33–39), which collectively represent all the information for a record. Remember that, unlike nontrivial properties, trivial properties generate "backing store" variables automatically. so you don't need to write explicit `private` data members for them. The parameterless constructor (lines 14–20) sets the members (created by the trivial properties) by calling the trivial properties using 0 for the account number, empty strings ("") for the first and last name and 0.0 for the balance. Recall that the `System::Decimal` class provides extra precision useful for dealing with financial calculations. The four-argument constructor (lines 23–30) sets these members to the specified parameter values. Note that, unlike our previous managed classes, `Record` must be explicitly declared as a `public ref class` (line 10). Without the `public` declaration, the examples to follow wouldn't be able to access the necessary parts of our library.

Using a Character Stream to Create an Output File

File `CreateFile.cpp` (Fig. 18.5) uses instances of class `Record` to create a sequential-access file that might be used in an accounts-receivable system—i.e., a program that organizes data regarding money owed by a company's credit clients. For each client, the program obtains an account number and the client's first name, last name and balance (i.e., the amount of money that the client owes to the company for previously received goods and services). The data obtained for each client constitutes a record for that client. In this application, the account number is used as the record key—files are created and maintained in account-number order. This program assumes that the user enters records in account-number order. However, a comprehensive accounts-receivable system would provide a sorting capability, so the user could enter the records in any order.

```
1   // Fig. 18.5: CreateFile.cpp
2   // Using FileStream and StreamWriter to write a sequential file
3
4   #include "stdafx.h"
5
6   using namespace System;
7   using namespace System::IO;
8   using namespace RecordLibrary;
9
10  int main( array< System::String ^ > ^args )
11  {
12     // prompt user for filename
13     Console::WriteLine( "Enter filename to save records to:" );
```

Fig. 18.5 | Creating and writing to a sequential-access file. (Part 1 of 3.)

```
14      String ^fileName = Console::ReadLine();
15
16      // maintains connection to file and opens file with write access
17      FileStream output(
18          fileName, FileMode::OpenOrCreate, FileAccess::Write );
19      // sets file to where data is written
20      StreamWriter fileWriter( %output );
21
22      Console::WriteLine( "Enter information for a record." );
23      Console::WriteLine( "Write account number, first name, last name,"
24          + " and balance on separate lines" );
25
26      String ^line; // first line of input
27      // verify the first entry in a record is not end-of-file
28      while ( ( line = Console::ReadLine() ) != nullptr )
29      {
30          Record record; // record to store input
31          // store the first line of input as the account number
32          record.Account = Int32::Parse( line );
33
34          // ensure Account data member is valid
35          if ( record.Account > 0 )
36          {
37              // store the remaining lines in the record appropriately
38              record.FirstName = Console::ReadLine();
39              record.LastName = Console::ReadLine();
40              record.Balance = Decimal::Parse( Console::ReadLine() );
41
42              // write Record to file, data members separated by commas
43              fileWriter.WriteLine( "{0},{1},{2},{3}", record.Account,
44                  record.FirstName, record.LastName, record.Balance );
45          } // end if
46
47          Console::WriteLine( "Write account number, first name, last name,"
48              + " and balance on separate lines" );
49      } // end while
50
51      // output and FileWriter have their destructors called automatically
52      // ensuring resources they encapsulate are closed as soon as possible
53
54      return 0;
55  } // end main
```

```
Enter filename to save records to:
C:\AccountInfo.txt
Enter information for a record.
Write account number, first name, last name, and balance on separate lines
100
Nancy
Brown
-25.54
```

Fig. 18.5 | Creating and writing to a sequential-access file. (Part 2 of 3.)

```
Write account number, first name, last name, and balance on separate lines
200
Stacey
Dunn
314.33
Write account number, first name, last name, and balance on separate lines
300
Doug
Barker
0.00
Write account number, first name, last name, and balance on separate lines
^Z
```

Fig. 18.5 | Creating and writing to a sequential-access file. (Part 3 of 3.)

This program either creates or opens a file (depending on whether one exists), then allows the user to write records to that file. We first need to tell our program how to access the definition of class `Record` in the `RecordLibrary` class library we created in Figure 18.4. To do this, in Visual Studio we select menu item **Project > CreateFile Properties...** (or press *<Alt> F7*). In the **Framework and References** pane (open by default) click the **Add New Reference...** button. Select the **Browse** tab and browse to the `Record.dll` file located in `C:\examples\ch18\Fig18_04\RecordLibrary\Debug`. Click **OK**. Now we add the `using` directive in line 8 that enables us to use the classes of the `RecordLibrary` namespace; this namespace contains class `Record`.

The program first prompts the user for a filename for the file they would like to create and save records to (line 13). We assume the user enters a valid filename, but a more robust application might use the `File` class to verify proper input before attempting to create the file. At line 14 we store the filename in a `String`.

You can open files to perform text manipulation by creating objects of class `FileStream`. In this example, we want the file to be opened for output, so lines 17–18 create a `FileStream` object. Similar to Fig. 18.3, we could have created a handle to a `FileStream` object and used `gcnew` to dynamically allocate memory. Instead we use stack semantics to create the objects that encapsulate resources to ensure that proper resource release is performed without requiring an explicit `try` and `finally` block. The `FileStream` constructor that we use receives three arguments—a `String` containing the path and name of the file to open, a constant describing how to open the file and a constant describing the file permissions. The constant `FileMode::OpenOrCreate` (line 18) indicates that the `FileStream` object should open the file if the file exists or create the file if it does not exist. Note that even if the file exists already, this `FileMode` specifies that the existing data should be overwritten. There are other `FileMode` constants describing how to open files; we introduce these constants as we use them in examples. The constant `FileAccess::Write` indicates that the program can perform only write operations with the `FileStream` object. There are two other constants for the third constructor parameter—`FileAccess::Read` for read-only access and `FileAccess::ReadWrite` for both read and write access. Line 20 creates a `StreamWriter` using stack semantics. The `StreamWriter` object is constructed with a `FileStream` argument that specifies the file to which the `StreamWriter` will output text. The `StreamWriter` constructor expects a reference to a `FileStream` object, so we pass it the address of `output`. Class `StreamWriter` belongs to the `System::IO` namespace. We could extend this application using `try` and `catch` blocks to handle `IOExceptions` that might occur while using the `StreamWriter`. We omit them in this example so that you can focus on how to use the `StreamWriter` itself.

Good Programming Practice 18.1

When opening files, use the **`FileAccess` enumeration** *to control user access to these files.*

Common Programming Error 18.1

Failure to open a file before attempting to reference it in a program is a logic error.

After prompting the user for information (lines 22–24) the `while` statement (lines 28–49) reads input using `Console::ReadLine` until the user inputs the end-of-file character as the first character of a record. If the user entered a valid account number (i.e., an integer greater than user), lines 32 and 38–40 store the input values in an object of type `Record`. We again assume the user will input valid data. Remember that you should never make this assumption in a real application.

After the four lines of input that constitute a record are read, the program saves the data into the user-specified file. Lines 43–44 write the record to the file by invoking function `WriteLine` of the `StreamWriter` object that was created at line 20. Function `WriteLine` writes a sequence of characters to a file. When the program closes, the `FileStream` and `StreamWriter` have their destructors called as they go out of scope because they were declared with stack semantics. We could have manually closed the `FileStream` using function *`Close`* if we had used a handle to a `FileStream`. Either way, we ensure that the file they encapsulate is immediately available to other code.

Performance Tip 18.1

Close each file explicitly when the program no longer needs to reference it. Do this by declaring variables that encapsulate resources using stack semantics or explicitly calling a cleanup function (such as `delete` *or* `Close`*). This can reduce resource usage in programs that continue executing long after they finish using a specific file. The practice of explicitly closing files also improves program clarity.*

Performance Tip 18.2

Releasing resources explicitly when they are no longer needed makes them immediately available for reuse by other programs, thus improving resource utilization.

Note that the program does not depict how the data records are rendered in the file. To verify that the file has been created successfully, we create a program in the next section to read and display the file. Since this is a text file, you can actually open the file in any text editor to see its contents

18.5 Reading Data from a Sequential-Access Text File

The previous section demonstrated how to create a file for use in sequential-access applications. In this section, we discuss how to read (or retrieve) data sequentially from a file.

The following example (Fig. 18.6) reads records from the file created by the program in Fig. 18.5, then displays the contents of each record. Remember, we must add a reference to `RecordLibrary.dll` as in the previous example.

```
 1   // Fig. 18.6: ReadFile.cpp
 2   // Reading a sequential-access file.
 3
 4   #include "stdafx.h"
 5
 6   using namespace System;
 7   using namespace System::IO;
 8   using namespace RecordLibrary;
 9
10   int main( array< System::String ^ > ^args )
11   {
12      // get filename from user input
13      Console::WriteLine( "Enter filename to read:" );
14      String ^fileName = Console::ReadLine();
15
16      // create FileStream to obtain read access to file
17      FileStream input( fileName, FileMode::Open, FileAccess::Read );
18      // set file from where data is read
19      StreamReader fileReader( %input );
20
21      // get each record available in file
22      String ^inputRecord;
23      while ( ( inputRecord = fileReader.ReadLine() ) != nullptr )
24         Console::WriteLine( inputRecord );
25
26      Console::WriteLine( "No more records in file" );
27
28      return 0;
29   } // end main
```

```
Enter filename to read:
C:\AccountInfo.txt
100,Nancy,Brown,-25.54
200,Stacey,Dunn,314.33
300,Doug,Barker,0.00
```

Fig. 18.6 | Reading sequential-access files.

After the user inputs a filename, line 17 creates a FileStream object input using stack semantics. We pass constant FileMode::Open as the second argument to the FileStream constructor to indicate that the FileStream should open the file if it exists or should throw a FileNotFoundException if the file doesn't exist. (In this example, the FileStream constructor won't throw a FileNotFoundException, because again we assume the user is inputting a valid filename.) In the last example (Fig. 18.5), we wrote text to the file using a FileStream object with write-only access. In this example (Fig. 18.6), we specify read-only access to the file by passing constant FileAccess::Read as the third argument to the FileStream constructor. This FileStream object is used to create a StreamReader object on line 19. We again use stack semantics to simplify resource release. The FileStream object specifies the file from which the StreamReader object will read text.

Error-Prevention Tip 18.1

Open a file with the `FileAccess::Read` file-open mode if the contents of the file should not be modified. This prevents unintentional modification of the contents.

Inside the `while` statement in line 23 we call `StreamReader` function `ReadLine` to read the first record from the file. If an error occurs while reading the file, an `IOException` is thrown. We could improve this program's reliability by adding a `try` and `catch` block to handle this exception. Line 23 determines whether `StreamReader` function `ReadLine` returned `nullptr` (i.e., there is no more text in the file). If not, we output the current line (representing the information in a single `Record`) and the `while` statement gets the next line of the file. If `ReadLine` returns `nullptr`, the program ends after notifying the user there are no more records in the file (line 26). We again avoid having to explicitly release the resources encapsulated by the `FileStream` and `StreamReader` objects because we declared them using stack semantics (lines 17 and 19).

Searching a Sequential-Access File

Recall from Section 17.5 that to retrieve data sequentially from a file, programs normally start from the beginning of the file, reading consecutively until the desired data is found. You learned how to use `seekg` and `seekp` with a native C++ `istream` to process a file sequentially several times during the execution of a program. In managed code we can accomplish the same thing, since a `FileStream` object can reposition its file-position pointer to any position in the file. When a `FileStream` object is opened, its file-position pointer is set to byte position 0 (i.e., the beginning of the file).

We now present a program that builds on the concepts employed in Fig. 18.7 and mirrors the native-code concepts in Fig. 17.28. As in the previous examples, remember we have added a reference to `RecordLibrary.dll`, so we can use the `Record` class from Fig. 18.4.

```
1   // Fig. 18.7: CreditInquiryForm.cpp
2   // Read a file sequentially and display contents based on
3   // account type specified by user ( credit, debit or zero balances ).
4
5   #include "stdafx.h"
6
7   using namespace System;
8   using namespace System::IO;
9   using namespace RecordLibrary;
10
11  int getRequest();
12  bool shouldDisplay( int, Decimal );
13
14  static const int ZERO_BALANCE = 1;
15  static const int CREDIT_BALANCE = 2;
16  static const int DEBIT_BALANCE = 3;
17  static const int END = 4;
18
19  int main( array< System::String ^ > ^args )
20  {
```

Fig. 18.7 | Credit-inquiry program. (Part 1 of 4.)

```cpp
21          // name of file that stores credit, debit and zero balances
22          Console::WriteLine( "Enter file that stores balances" );
23          String ^fileName = Console::ReadLine();
24
25          // get user's request (e.g., zero, credit or debit balance)
26          int request = getRequest();
27
28          // process user's request
29          while ( request != END )
30          {
31             switch ( request )
32             {
33                case ZERO_BALANCE:
34                   Console::WriteLine( "\nAccounts with zero balances:" );
35                   break;
36                case CREDIT_BALANCE:
37                   Console::WriteLine( "\nAccounts with credit balances:" );
38                   break;
39                case DEBIT_BALANCE:
40                   Console::WriteLine( "\nAccounts with debit balances:" );
41                   break;
42             } // end switch
43
44             // create Filestream to obtain read access to file
45             FileStream input( fileName, FileMode::Open, FileAccess::Read );
46             // set file from where data is read
47             StreamReader fileReader( %input );
48
49             // go back to the beginning of the file
50             input.Seek( 0, SeekOrigin::Begin );
51
52             String ^inputRecord;
53             // traverse file until end of file
54             while ( ( inputRecord = fileReader.ReadLine() ) != nullptr )
55             {
56                array< String^ >^ inputFields = gcnew array< String^ >( 4 );
57                inputFields = inputRecord->Split( ',' ); // parse input
58
59                // create record from input
60                Record record( Convert::ToInt32( inputFields[ 0 ] ),
61                   inputFields[ 1 ], inputFields[ 2 ],
62                   Convert::ToDecimal( inputFields[ 3 ] ) );
63
64                // display record
65                if ( shouldDisplay( request, record.Balance ) )
66                   Console::WriteLine( inputRecord );
67             } // end inner while
68
69             request = getRequest(); // get additional request from user
70          } // end outer while
71
72          return 0;
73       } // end main
```

Fig. 18.7 | Credit-inquiry program. (Part 2 of 4.)

```
74
75   // obtain request from user
76   int getRequest()
77   {
78      int request; // request from user
79
80      // display request options
81      Console::WriteLine( "\nEnter request" );
82      Console::WriteLine( " 1 - List accounts with zero balances" );
83      Console::WriteLine( " 2 - List accounts with credit balances" );
84      Console::WriteLine( " 3 - List accounts with debit balances" );
85      Console::WriteLine( " 4 - End of run" );
86
87      do // input user request
88      {
89         Console::Write( "?" );
90         request = Int32::Parse( Console::ReadLine() );
91      } while ( request < ZERO_BALANCE && request > END );
92
93      return request;
94   } // end function getRequest
95
96   // determine whether to display given record
97   bool shouldDisplay( int type, Decimal balance )
98   {
99      bool shouldDisplay = false;
100     // determine whether to display zero balances
101     if ( type == ZERO_BALANCE && balance == 0 )
102        shouldDisplay = true;
103     // determine whether to display credit balances
104     else if ( type == CREDIT_BALANCE && balance < 0 )
105        shouldDisplay = true;
106     // determine whether to display debit balances
107     else if ( type == DEBIT_BALANCE && balance > 0 )
108        shouldDisplay = true;
109
110     return shouldDisplay;
111  } // end function shouldDisplay
```

```
Enter file that stores balances
C:\AccountInfo.txt

Enter request
 1 - List accounts with zero balances
 2 - List accounts with credit balances
 3 - List accounts with debit balances
 4 - End of run
?1

Accounts with zero balances:
300,Doug,Barker,0.00
```

Fig. 18.7 | Credit-inquiry program. (Part 3 of 4.)

```
Enter request
 1 - List accounts with zero balances
 2 - List accounts with credit balances
 3 - List accounts with debit balances
 4 - End of run
?2

Accounts with credit balances:
100,Nancy,Brown,-25.54

Enter request
 1 - List accounts with zero balances
 2 - List accounts with credit balances
 3 - List accounts with debit balances
 4 - End of run
?3

Accounts with debit balances:
200,Stacey,Dunn,314.33

Enter request
 1 - List accounts with zero balances
 2 - List accounts with credit balances
 3 - List accounts with debit balances
 4 - End of run
?4
```

Fig. 18.7 | Credit-inquiry program. (Part 4 of 4.)

This example combines concepts from the previous managed-code examples in this chapter and the native C++ credit-inquiry program from Fig. 17.28. Because of differences in the way C++/CLI enumerations work (see Section 7.22) we've chosen to define four static integer constants to represent the menu options the user will have (lines 14–17). The program prompts the user for a file where credit information is stored, and we store the filename in a String (lines 22–23).

Line 26 uses function getRequest to determine what type of balance the user wants displayed. The while statement in line 29 continues processing the same user-specified file until the user requests it to stop. Lines 45 creates a FileStream object with read-only file access. Line 47 creates a StreamReader object that we use to read text from the FileStream. Line 50 uses FileStream function **Seek** to reset the file-position pointer back to the beginning of the file. FileStream function Seek allows you to reset the file-position pointer by specifying the number of bytes it should be offset from the file's beginning, end or current position. The part of the file you want to be offset from is chosen using constants from the **SeekOrigin** enumeration. In this case, our stream is offset by 0 bytes from the file's beginning (SeekOrigin::Begin). This ensures that when the user enters a new request, the program searches the whole file again.

The while loop obtains each record by repeatedly calling StreamReader function ReadLine (line 54). We create a managed array of String ^ (line 56) to hold the data members of each record. Line 57 uses function Split from class String to separate the stream of characters that was read from the file into Strings that represent the Record's properties (see Chapter 19 for more detail on String functions). These properties are then stored by constructing a Record object using the properties as arguments (lines 60–62). We then use function shouldDisplay much as we did in Fig. 17.28 to determine if the current record should be output for the user.

18.6 Serialization

Section 18.4 demonstrated how to use C++/CLI to write the individual fields of a Record object to a text file, and Section 18.5 demonstrated how to read those fields from a file and place their values in a Record object in memory. In the examples, Record was used to aggregate the information for one record. When the instance variables for a Record were output to a disk file, certain information was lost, such as the type of each value. For instance, if the value "3" is read from a file, there is no way to tell if the value came from an int, a String or a Decimal. We have only data, not type information, on disk. If the program that is going to read this data "knows" what object type the data corresponds to, then the data can be read directly into objects of that type. For example, in Fig. 18.5, we know that we are inputting an int (the account number), followed by two Strings (the first and last name) and a Decimal (the balance). We also know that these values are separated by commas, with only one record on each line. So, we are able to parse the strings and convert the account number to an int and the balance to a Decimal. Sometimes it would be easier to read or write entire objects. The CLR provides such a mechanism built-in, called *object serialization*. A *serialized object* is an object represented as a sequence of bytes that includes the object's data, as well as information about the object's type and the types of data stored in the object. After a serialized object has been written to a file, it can be read from the file and *deserialized*—that is, the type information and bytes that represent the object and its data can be used to recreate the object in memory. Native C++ doesn't provide built-in support for serialization, though it can be added with certain libraries.

Class **BinaryFormatter** (namespace **System::Runtime::Serialization::Formatters::Binary**) enables entire objects to be written to or read from a stream. Its **Serialize** function writes an object's representation to a file. Its **Deserialize** function reads this representation from a file and reconstructs the original object. Both functions throw a **SerializationException** if an error occurs during serialization or deserialization. Both functions require a Stream object (e.g., the FileStream) as a parameter so that the BinaryFormatter can access the correct stream. Note that to perform deserialization a program must know about the objects that were serialized. This is why we created the RecordLibrary.dll that will be used in the examples that follow. If we had only used a RecordSerializable.h file in each project separately, our programs would generate a runtime error. Simply including a RecordSerializable.h file wouldn't be enough for the BinaryFormatter to recognize that the existing file was serialized with that class.

In Sections 18.7–18.8, we create and manipulate sequential-access files using object serialization. Object serialization is performed with byte-based streams, so the sequential files created and manipulated will be binary files. Binary files are not human readable. For this reason, we write a separate application that reads and displays serialized objects.

18.7 Creating a Sequential-Access File Using Object Serialization

We begin by creating and writing serialized objects to a sequential-access file. In this section, we reuse much of the code from Section 18.4, so we focus only on the new features.

Defining the RecordSerializable Class

Let us begin by modifying our Record class (Fig. 18.4) so that objects of this class can be serialized. Class RecordSerializable (Fig. 18.8) is marked with the *[Serializable]* attribute (line 5), which indicates to the CLR that objects of class Record can be serialized. The classes for objects that we wish to write to or read from a stream must include this attribute in their declarations or must implement interface *ISerializable*. Class RecordSerializable provides public trivial properties for accessing the appropriate

```
 1    // Fig. 18.8: RecordSerializable.h
 2    // Serializable class that represents a data record.
 3
 4    #pragma once
 5
 6    using namespace System;
 7
 8    namespace RecordLibrary
 9    {
10       public ref class RecordSerializable
11       {
12       [ Serializable ]
13       public:
14          // parameterless constructor sets members to default values
15          RecordSerializable()
16          {
17             Account = 0;
18             FirstName = "";
19             LastName = "";
20             Balance = Decimal::Parse( "0.0" );
21          } // end constructor
22
23          // overloaded constructor sets members to parameter values
24          RecordSerializable( int accountValue, String ^firstNameValue,
25             String ^lastNameValue, Decimal balanceValue )
26          {
27             Account = accountValue;
28             FirstName = firstNameValue;
29             LastName = lastNameValue;
30             Balance = balanceValue;
31          } // end constructor
32
33          // trivial property that gets and sets Account
34          property int Account;
35          // trivial property that gets and sets FirstName
36          property String^ FirstName;
37          // trivial property that gets and sets LastName
38          property String^ LastName;
39          // trivial property that gets and sets Balance
40          property Decimal Balance;
41       }; // end managed class RecordSerializable
42    } // end namespace RecordLibrary
```

Fig. 18.8 | Record for sequential-access file-processing applications.

"backing store" variables. We have added `RecordSerializable.h` to our `RecordLibrary` project, so it is in the same namespace as the `Record` class from previous examples.

In a class that is marked with the `[Serializable]` attribute or that implements interface `ISerializable`, you must ensure that every instance variable of the class is also serializable. All simple-type variables and `String`s are serializable. For variables of reference types, you must check the class declaration (and possibly its base classes) to ensure that the type is serializable. By default, managed array objects are serializable. However, if the array contains references to other objects, those objects may or may not be serializable.

Using a Serialization Stream to Create an Output File

Now let's create a sequential-access file with serialization (Fig. 18.9). Line 18 creates a `Bi-naryFormatter` for writing serialized objects. Lines 20–21 open the `FileStream` to which this program writes the serialized objects. The `String ^` argument that is passed to the `FileStream`'s constructor represents the name and path of the file to be opened. This specifies the file to which the serialized objects will be written.

```
1   // Fig. 18.9: CreateSequentialFile.cpp
2   // Creating a sequential-access file using serialization
3
4   #include "stdafx.h"
5
6   using namespace System;
7   using namespace System::IO;
8   using namespace RecordLibrary;
9   using namespace System::Runtime::Serialization::Formatters::Binary;
10  using namespace System::Runtime::Serialization;
11
12  int main( array< System::String ^ > ^args )
13  {
14      Console::WriteLine( "Enter a filename to save records to:" );
15      String ^fileName = Console::ReadLine(); // name of file to save data
16
17      // object for serializing Records in binary format
18      BinaryFormatter formatter;
19      // open file with write access
20      FileStream output(
21          fileName, FileMode::OpenOrCreate, FileAccess::Write );
22
23      Console::WriteLine( "Enter information for a record." );
24      Console::WriteLine( "Write account number, first name, last name,"
25          + " and balance on separate lines" );
26
27      String ^line; // first line of input
28      // verify the first entry in a record is not end-of-file
29      while ( ( line = Console::ReadLine() ) != nullptr )
30      {
31          RecordSerializable record; // record to store input
32          // store the first line of input as the account number
33          record.Account = Int32::Parse( line );
34
```

Fig. 18.9 | Sequential file created using serialization. (Part 1 of 2.)

```
35          // ensure Account data member is valid
36          if ( record.Account > 0 )
37          {
38             // store the remaining lines in the record appropriately
39             record.FirstName = Console::ReadLine();
40             record.LastName = Console::ReadLine();
41             record.Balance =
42                Decimal::Parse( Console::ReadLine() );
43
44             // write Record to FileStream( serialize object )
45             formatter.Serialize( %output, %record );
46          } // end if
47
48          Console::WriteLine( "Write account number, first name, last name,"
49             + " and balance on separate lines" );
50       } // end while
51
52       return 0;
53    } // end main
```

```
Enter a filename to save records to:
C:\Balances.txt
Enter information for a record.
Write account number, first name, last name, and balance on separate lines
100
Nancy
Brown
-25.54
Write account number, first name, last name, and balance on separate lines
200
Stacey
Dunn
314.33
Write account number, first name, last name, and balance on separate lines
300
Doug
Barker
0.00
Write account number, first name, last name, and balance on separate lines
^Z
```

Fig. 18.9 | Sequential file created using serialization. (Part 2 of 2.)

Common Programming Error 18.2

It is a logic error to open an existing file for output when the user wishes to preserve the file. The original file's contents will be lost.

This program assumes that data is input correctly and in the proper record-number order. We use a while statement (lines 29–50) to read the information for records that will be written to the file. Line 31 creates a RecordSerializable object, which is assigned values in lines 33 and 39–42. Line 45 calls function Serialize to write the RecordSerializable object to the output file. Function Serialize takes a reference to the FileStream object as the first argument so that the BinaryFormatter can write its second argument to the correct file. Note that only one statement is required to write the entire object.

In the sample execution for the program in Fig. 18.9, we entered information for five accounts. The program does not show how the data records actually appear in the file. Remember that we are using binary files, which are not human readable. To verify that the file was created successfully, the next section presents a program to read the file's contents.

18.8 Reading and Deserializing Data from a Sequential-Access Text File

The preceding section showed how to create a sequential-access file using object serialization. In this section, we discuss how to read serialized objects sequentially from a file.

Figure 18.10 reads and displays the contents of the file created by the program in Figure 18.9. The program opens the file for input by creating a `FileStream` object (line 19). The name of the file to open is specified as the first argument to the `FileStream` constructor. Line 21 creates the `BinaryFormatter` that will be used to read objects.

We use function `Deserialize` (of the `BinaryFormatter` created in line 13) to read the data (lines 25–26 and lines 44–45). Note that we cast the result of `Deserialize` to type `RecordSerializable` (lines 25 and 44)—this cast is necessary, because `Deserialize` returns a reference of type `Object` and we need to access properties that belong to class `RecordSerializable`. If an error occurs during deserialization, a `SerializationException` is thrown, and the `FileStream` object is closed when the `FileStream` and `BinaryFormatter` objects go out of scope.

```cpp
1   // Fig. 18.10: ReadSequentialAccessFile.cpp
2   // Reading a sequential-access file using deserialization.
3
4   #include "stdafx.h"
5
6   using namespace System;
7   using namespace System::IO;
8   using namespace RecordLibrary;
9   using namespace System::Runtime::Serialization::Formatters::Binary;
10  using namespace System::Runtime::Serialization;
11
12  int main( array< System::String ^ > ^args )
13  {
14     // get filename from user input
15     Console::WriteLine( "Enter filename to read:" );
16     String ^fileName = Console::ReadLine(); // name of file containing data
17
18     // create Filestream to obtain read access to file
19     FileStream input( fileName, FileMode::Open, FileAccess::Read );
20     // object for deserializing record in binary format
21     BinaryFormatter reader;
22
23     // get first record available in file
24     // deserialize record and store data
25     RecordSerializable ^record = static_cast< RecordSerializable^ >
26        ( reader.Deserialize( %input ) );
27
```

Fig. 18.10 | Sequential file read using deserialization. (Part 1 of 2.)

```
28        Console::WriteLine( "Records in {0} are: ", fileName );
29        try
30        {
31           // get each record in file until an exception is thrown
32           while( true )
33           {
34              // store record values in temporary string array
35              array< String^ >^ values = {
36                 record->Account.ToString(), record->FirstName->ToString(),
37                 record->LastName->ToString(), record->Balance.ToString() };
38
39              Console::WriteLine( "{0}, {1}, {2}, {3}",
40                 record->Account.ToString(), record->FirstName->ToString(),
41                 record->LastName->ToString(), record->Balance.ToString() );
42
43              // deserialize next record
44              record = static_cast< RecordSerializable^ > (
45                 reader.Deserialize( %input ) );
46           } // end while
47        } // end try
48        catch ( SerializationException ^ )
49        {
50           Console::WriteLine( "No more records in file." );
51           // no need to include resource release code
52           // because we used stack semantics
53        } // end catch
54
55        return 0;
56  } // end main
```

```
Enter filename to read:
C:\Balances.txt
Records in C:\AccountInfo.txt are:
100, Nancy, Brown, -25.54
200, Stacey, Dunn, 314.33
300, Doug, Barker, 0.00
No more records in file.
```

Fig. 18.10 | Sequential file read using deserialization. (Part 2 of 2.)

18.9 Wrap-Up

In this chapter, you learned how to use file processing in C++/CLI to manipulate persistent data. We overviewed the differences between character-based and byte-based streams, as well as several file-processing classes from the System::IO namespace. You used class File to manipulate files and class Directory to manipulate directories. Next, you learned how to use these classes to perform sequential-access file processing to manipulate records in text files with managed code. We then discussed the differences between text-file processing and object serialization, and we used serialization to store entire objects in and retrieve entire objects from files.

In the next chapter, we discuss typical string-manipulation operations provided by class template basic_string. We introduce string stream-processing capabilities that allow strings to be input from and output to memory. We also demonstrate some advanced capabilities of managed `Strings` in C++/CLI.

Summary

Section 18.1 Introduction

- Files are used for long-term retention of large amounts of data, even after the program that created the data terminates.

- Data maintained in files often is called persistent data.

- Computers store files on secondary storage devices, such as magnetic disks, optical disks and magnetic tapes.

- File processing is one of a programming language's most important capabilities, because it enables a language to support commercial applications that typically process massive amounts of persistent data.

Section 18.2 Files and Streams

- C++/CLI views each file as a sequential stream of bytes.

- Like native C++, each file ends either with an end-of-file marker or at a specific byte number that is recorded in a system-maintained administrative data structure.

- Files are opened by creating an object that has a stream associated with it.

- Streams provide communication channels between files and programs.

- To perform file processing in C++/CLI, the `System::IO` namespace must be referenced. This namespace includes definitions for stream classes such as `StreamReader` (for text input from a file), `StreamWriter` (for text output to a file) and `FileStream` (for both input from and output to a file).

- Class `Stream` provides functionality for representing streams as bytes. This class is `abstract`, so objects of this class cannot be instantiated.

- Classes `FileStream`, `MemoryStream` and `BufferedStream` (all from namespace `System::IO`) inherit from class `Stream`.

- Class `FileStream` can be used to read data to and write data from sequential-access files.

- Class `MemoryStream` enables the transfer of data directly to and from memory—this is much faster than other types of data transfer (e.g., to and from disk).

- Class `BufferedStream` uses buffering to transfer data to or from a stream. Buffering is an I/O performance-enhancement technique, in which each output operation is directed to a region in memory, called a buffer, that is large enough to hold the data from many output operations. Then actual transfer to the output device is performed in one large physical output operation each time the buffer fills. The output operations directed to the output buffer in memory often are called logical output operations. Buffering can also be used to speed input operations.

Section 18.3 Classes `File` and `Directory`

- Information on computers is stored in files, which are organized in directories. Classes `File` and `Directory` enable programs to manipulate files and directories on disk.

- Class `File` provides `static` functions determining information about files and can be used to open files for reading or writing.

- Class `Directory` provides `static` functions for manipulating directories.

- The DirectoryInfo object returned by Directory function CreateDirectory contains information about a directory. Much of the information contained in class DirectoryInfo also can be accessed via the functions of class Directory.

- File function Exists determines whether a String is the name of an existing file.

- A StreamReader can be used to read text from a file. The StreamReader constructor takes as an argument a String containing the name of the file to open. StreamReader function ReadToEnd reads the entire contents of a file.

- Directory function Exists determines whether a String is the name of an existing directory.

- Directory function GetDirectories obtains a String ^ array containing the names of subdirectories in the specified directory.

Section 18.4 Creating a Sequential-Access Text File

- C++/CLI imposes no structure on files. Thus, as in native C++, concepts like that of a "record" do not exist in C++/CLI files. This means that you must structure files to meet the requirements of your applications.

- There is a FileStream constructor that receives three arguments—a String containing the name of the file to be opened, a constant describing how to open the file and a constant describing the file permissions.

- The StreamWriter object is constructed with a reference to a FileStream argument that specifies the file to which StreamWriter outputs text.

- Class StreamWriter belongs to the System::IO namespace.

Section 18.5 Reading Data from a Sequential-Access Text File

- To retrieve data sequentially from a file, programs normally start from the beginning of the file, reading data consecutively until the desired data is found. It sometimes is necessary to process a file sequentially several times during the execution of a program.

- FileStream function Seek allows you to reset the file-position pointer by specifying the number of bytes it should be offset from the file's beginning, end or current position. The part of the file you want the pointers to be offset from is chosen using constants from enumeration SeekOrigin.

Section 18.6 Serialization

- A serialized object is represented as a sequence of bytes that includes the object's data, as well as information about the object's type and the types of data stored in the object.

- After a serialized object has been written to a file, it can be read from the file and deserialized (recreated in memory).

- Class BinaryFormatter (namespace System::Runtime::Serialization::Formatters::Binary), which supports the ISerializable interface, enables entire objects to be read from or written to a stream.

- BinaryFormatter functions Serialize and Deserialize write objects to and read objects from streams, respectively.

- Both function Serialize and function Deserialize require a reference to a Stream object (e.g., the FileStream) as a parameter so that the BinaryFormatter can access the correct file.

Section 18.7 Creating a Sequential-Access File Using Object Serialization

- Classes that are marked with the Serializable attribute indicate to the CLR that objects of the class can be serialized. Objects that we wish to write to or read from a stream must include this attribute in their class definitions.

- In a serializable class, you must ensure that every instance variable of the class is also serializable. By default, all simple-type variables are serializable. For reference-type variables, you must check the declaration of the class (and possibly its superclasses) to ensure that the type is serializable.

Section 18.8 Reading and Deserializing Data from a Sequential-Access Text File
- Function Deserialize (of class BinaryFormatter) reads a serialized object from a stream and reforms the object in memory.
- Function Deserialize returns a reference of type Object which must be cast to the appropriate type to manipulate the object.
- If an error occurs during deserialization, a SerializationException is thrown.

Terminology

binary digit (bit)
BinaryFormatter class
BinaryReader class
BinaryWriter class
bit manipulation
buffer
BufferedStream class
buffering
character
character set
Close function of class StreamWriter
closing a file
CLR Class Library project
Console class
Copy function of class File
Create function of class File
CreateDirectory function of class Directory
CreateText function of class File
data hierarchy
database
database management system (DBMS)
Delete function of class Directory
Delete function of class File
Deserialize function of class BinaryFormatter
Directory class
DirectoryInfo class
end-of-file marker
Error property of class Console
Exists function of class Directory
field
file
File class
file-processing programs
FileAccess enumeration
file-position pointer
FileStream class
fixed-length records

GetCreationTime function of class Directory
GetCreationTime function of class File
GetDirectories function of class Directory
GetFiles function of class Directory
GetLastAccessTime function of class Directory
GetLastAccessTime function of class File
GetLastWriteTime function of class Directory
GetLastWriteTime function of class File
In property of class Console
IOException
ISerializable interface
logical output operator
MemoryStream class
Move function of class Directory
Move function of class File
object serialization
Open function of class File
OpenRead function of class File
OpenText function of class File
OpenWrite function of class File
Out property of class Console
physical output operation
Read function of class Console
ReadLine function of class Console
ReadLine function of class StreamReader
record
record key
Seek function of class FileStream
SeekOrigin enumeration
sequential-access file
Serializable attribute
SerializationException
Serialize function of class BinaryFormatter
standard error stream object
standard input stream object
standard output stream object
Stream class

stream of bytes	`TextWriter` class
`StreamReader` class	`Write` function of class `BinaryWriter`
`StreamWriter` class	`Write` function of class `Console`
`System::IO` namespace	`Write` function of class `StreamWriter`
`System::Runtime::Serialization::Format-`	`WriteLine` function of class `Console`
`ters::Binary` namespace	`WriteLine` function of class `StreamWriter`
`TextReader` class	

Self-Review Exercises

18.1   State whether each of the following is *true* or *false*. If *false*, explain why.
   a) Creating instances of classes `File` and `Directory` is impossible.
   b) Typically, a sequential file stores records in order by the record-key field.
   c) Class `StreamReader` inherits from class `Stream`.
   d) Any class can be serialized to a file.
   e) Function `Seek` of class `FileStream` always seeks relative to the beginning of a file.
   f) Classes `StreamReader` and `StreamWriter` are used with sequential-access files.
   g) You cannot instantiate objects of type `Stream`.

18.2   Fill in the blanks in each of the following statements:
   a) Ultimately, all data items processed by a computer are reduced to combinations of _____ and _____.
   b) The smallest data item a computer can process is called a(n) _____.
   c) A(n) _____ is a group of related records.
   d) Digits, letters and special symbols are collectively referred to as _____.
   e) A group of related files is called a(n) _____.
   f) `StreamReader` function _____ reads a line of text from a file.
   g) `StreamWriter` function _____ writes a line of text to a file.
   h) Function `Serialize` of class `BinaryFormatter` takes a(n) _____ and a(n) _____ as arguments.
   i) The _____ namespace contains most of C++/CLI's file-processing classes.
   j) The _____ namespace contains the `BinaryFormatter` class.

Answers to Self-Review Exercises

18.1   a) True. b) True. c) False. Class `StreamReader` inherits from class `TextReader`. d) False. Only classes with the `Serializable` attribute can be serialized. e) False. It seeks relative to the `SeekOrigin` enumeration member that is passed as one of the arguments. f.) True. g) True.

18.2   a) 0s, 1s. b) bit. c) file. d) characters. e) database. f) `ReadLine`. g) `WriteLine`. h) `Stream`, object. i) `System::IO`. j) `System::Runtime::Serialization::Formatters::Binary`.

Exercises

18.3   Create a program that stores student grades in a text file. The file should contain the name, ID number, class taken and grade of every student. Allow the user to load a grade file and display its contents in a read-only `TextBox`. The entries should be displayed in the following format:

```
LastName, FirstName: ID# Class Grade
```

We list some sample data below:

```
Jones, Bob: 1 "Introduction to Computer Science" "A-"
Johnson, Sarah: 2 "Data Structures" "B+"
Smith, Sam: 3 "Data Structures" "C"
```

18.4 Modify the previous program to use objects of a class that can be serialized to and deserialized from a file.

18.5 Extend classes `StreamReader` and `StreamWriter`. Make the class that derives from `StreamReader` have functions `ReadInteger`, `ReadBoolean` and `ReadString`. Make the class that derives from `StreamWriter` have functions `WriteInteger`, `WriteBoolean` and `WriteString`. Think about how to design the writing functions so that the reading functions will be able to read what was written. Design `WriteInteger` and `WriteBoolean` to write `String`s of uniform size so that `ReadInteger` and `ReadBoolean` can read those values accurately. Make sure `ReadString` and `WriteString` use the same character(s) to separate `String`s.

18.6 Create a program that combines the ideas of Fig. 18.5 and Fig. 18.6 to allow a user to write records to and read records from a file. Add an extra field of type `bool` to the record to indicate whether the account has overdraft protection.

18.7 *(Telephone-Number Word Generator)* Standard telephone keypads contain the digits zero through nine. The numbers two through nine each have three letters associated with them (Fig. 18.11). Many people find it difficult to memorize phone numbers, so they use the correspondence between digits and letters to develop seven-letter words that correspond to their phone numbers. For example, a person whose telephone number is 686-2377 might use the correspondence indicated in Fig. 18.11 to develop the seven-letter word "NUMBERS." Every seven-letter word corresponds to exactly one seven-digit telephone number. A restaurant wishing to increase its takeout business could surely do so with the number 825-3688 (i.e., "TAKEOUT").

Every seven-letter phone number corresponds to many different seven-letter words. Unfortunately, most of these words represent unrecognizable juxtapositions of letters. It is possible, however, that the owner of a barbershop would be pleased to know that the shop's telephone number, 424-7288, corresponds to "HAIRCUT." The owner of a liquor store would no doubt be delighted

Digit	Letter
2	A B C
3	D E F
4	G H I
5	J K L
6	M N O
7	P R S
8	T U V
9	W X Y

Fig. 18.11 | Letters that correspond to the numbers on a telephone keypad .

to find that the store's number, 233-7226, corresponds to "BEERCAN." A veterinarian with the phone number 738-2273 would be pleased to know that the number corresponds to the letters "PETCARE." An automotive dealership would be pleased to know that its phone number, 639-2277, corresponds to "NEWCARS."

Write a program that, given a seven-digit number, uses a StreamWriter object to write to a file every possible seven-letter word combination corresponding to that number. There are 2187 (3^7) such combinations. Avoid phone numbers with the digits 0 and 1.

18.8 *(Student Poll)* Suppose we wish to process survey results that are stored in a file. First, create a program that prompts the user for survey responses and outputs each response to a file. Use StreamWriter to create a file called numbers.txt. Each integer should be written using function Write. Then output the frequency of survey responses. The responses should be read from the file by using a StreamReader. Class String's split function should be used to split the input string into separate responses; then each response should be converted to an integer. The program should continue to read responses until it reaches the end of file. The results should be output to the console.

19

Class **string** and String Stream Processing

OBJECTIVES

In this chapter you'll learn:

- To use class **string** from the C++ Standard Library to treat **string**s as full-fledged objects.

- To assign, concatenate, compare, search and swap **string**s.

- To determine **string** characteristics.

- To find, replace and insert characters in **string**s.

- To convert **string**s to C-style strings and vice versa.

- To use **string** iterators.

- To perform input from and output to **string**s in memory.

- To use managed **String**s in C++/CLI and their associated functions and properties.

- To use class **StringBuilder** in C++/CLI.

19.1 Introduction

Previous chapters presented some basic string-processing capabilities, but this chapter provides an in-depth look at strings in native and managed code. The first half of the chapter will focus on native C++ and class `string`. You will learn the fundamentals of strings and the various functions contained in class `string`. The second half of the chapter focuses on the FCL `String` class and other character-processing capabilities.

The class template **`basic_string`** provides typical string-manipulation operations such as copying, searching, etc. The template definition and all support facilities are defined in namespace `std`; these include the `typedef` statement

```
typedef basic_string< char > string;
```

that creates the alias type `string` for ***basic_string< char >***. A typedef also is provided for the ***wchar_t*** type. Type wchar_t[1] stores characters (e.g., two-byte characters, four-byte characters) for supporting other character sets. We use `string` exclusively throughout this chapter for native C++. To use `string`s, include header file <string>.

A `string` object can be initialized with a constructor argument such as

```
string text( "Hello" ); // creates a string from a const char *
```

which creates a `string` containing the characters in "Hello", or with two constructor arguments as in

```
string name( 8, 'x' ); // string of 8 'x' characters
```

which creates a `string` containing eight 'x' characters. Class `string` also provides a default constructor (which creates an empty string) and a copy constructor. An ***empty string*** is a `string` that does not contain any characters.

A `string` also can be initialized via the alternate constructor syntax in the definition of a `string` as in

```
string month = "March"; // same as: string month( "March" );
```

Remember that operator = in the preceding declaration is not an assignment; rather it is an implicit call to the `string` class constructor, which does the conversion.

Note that class `string` provides no conversions from `int` or `char` to `string` in a `string` definition. For example, the definitions

```
string error1 = 'c';
string error2( 'u' );
string error3 = 22;
string error4( 8 );
```

result in syntax errors. Note that assigning a single character to a `string` object is permitted in an assignment statement as in

```
string1 = 'n';
```

Common Programming Error 19.1

Attempting to convert an int or char to a string via an initialization in a declaration or via a constructor argument is a compilation error.

Unlike C-style char * strings, `string`s are not necessarily null terminated. [*Note:* The C++ standard document provides only a description of the interface for class `string`—implementation is platform dependent.] The length of a `string` can be retrieved with member function ***length*** and with member function ***size***. The subscript operator, [], can be used with `string`s to access and modify individual characters. Like C-style strings, `string`s have a first subscript of 0 and a last subscript of length() – 1.

---

1. Type wchar_t commonly is used to represent Unicode, which does have 16-bit characters, but the size of wchar_t is not fixed by the standard. The Unicode Standard outlines a specification to produce consistent encoding of the world's characters and *symbols*. To learn more about the Unicode Standard, visit www.unicode.org.

Most string member functions take as arguments a starting subscript location and the number of characters on which to operate.

The stream extraction operator (>>) is overloaded to support strings. The statements

```
string stringObject;
cin >> stringObject;
```

declare a string object and read a string from the standard input device. Input is delimited by white-space characters. When a delimiter is encountered, the input operation is terminated. Function *getline* also is overloaded for strings. Assuming string1 is a string, the statement

```
getline( cin, string1 );
```

reads a string from the keyboard into string1. Input is delimited by a newline ('\n'), so getLine can read a line of text into a string object.

19.2 string Assignment and Concatenation

Figure 19.1 demonstrates string assignment and concatenation. Line 7 includes header <string> for class string. The strings string1, string2 and string3 are created in lines 12–14. Line 16 assigns the value of string1 to string2. After the assignment takes place, string2 is a copy of string1. Line 17 uses member function *assign* to copy string1 into string3. A separate copy is made (i.e., string1 and string3 are independent objects). Class string also provides an overloaded version of member function assign that copies a specified number of characters, as in

```
targetString.assign( sourceString, start, numberOfCharacters );
```

where sourceString is the string to be copied, start is the starting subscript and numberOfCharacters is the number of characters to copy.

```
1   // Fig. 19.1: AssignmentConcatentation.cpp
2   // Demonstrating string assignment and concatenation.
3   #include <iostream>
4   using std::cout;
5   using std::endl;
6
7   #include <string>
8   using std::string;
9
10  int main()
11  {
12     string string1( "cat" );
13     string string2; // initialized to the empty string
14     string string3; // initialized to the empty string
15
16     string2 = string1; // assign string1 to string2
17     string3.assign( string1 ); // assign string1 to string3
```

Fig. 19.1 | Demonstrating string assignment and concatenation. (Part 1 of 2.)

```
18      cout << "string1: " << string1 << "\nstring2: " << string2
19          << "\nstring3: " << string3 << "\n\n";
20
21      // modify string2 and string3
22      string2[ 0 ] = string3[ 2 ] = 'r';
23
24      cout << "After modification of string2 and string3:\n" << "string1: "
25          << string1 << "\nstring2: " << string2 << "\nstring3: ";
26
27      // demonstrating member function at
28      for ( unsigned int i = 0; i < string3.length(); i++ )
29          cout << string3.at( i );
30
31      // declare string4 and string5
32      string string4( string1 + "apult" ); // concatenation
33      string string5;
34
35      // overloaded +=
36      string3 += "pet"; // create "carpet"
37      string1.append( "acomb" ); // create "catacomb"
38
39      // append subscript locations 4 through end of string1 to
40      // create string "comb" (string5 was initially empty)
41      string5.append( string1, 4, string1.length() - 4 );
42
43      cout << "\n\nAfter concatenation:\nstring1: " << string1
44          << "\nstring2: " << string2 << "\nstring3: " << string3
45          << "\nstring4: " << string4 << "\nstring5: " << string5 << endl;
46      return 0;
47  } // end main
```

```
string1: cat
string2: cat
string3: cat

After modification of string2 and string3:
string1: cat
string2: rat
string3: car

After concatenation:
string1: catacomb
string2: rat
string3: carpet
string4: catapult
string5: comb
```

Fig. 19.1 | Demonstrating string assignment and concatenation. (Part 2 of 2.)

Line 22 uses the subscript operator to assign 'r' to string3[2] (forming "car") and to assign 'r' to string2[0] (forming "rat"). The strings are then output.

Lines 28–29 output the contents of string3 one character at a time using member function **at**. Member function at provides *checked access* (or **range checking**); i.e., going past the end of the string throws an out_of_range exception. (See Chapter 16 for a detailed discussion of exception handling.) Note that the subscript operator, [], does not provide checked access. This is consistent with its use on arrays.

Common Programming Error 19.2

Accessing a string subscript outside the bounds of the string using function at is a logic error that causes an out_of_range exception.

Common Programming Error 19.3

Accessing an element beyond the size of the string using the subscript operator is an unreported logic error.

String string4 is declared (line 32) and initialized to the result of concatenating string1 and "apult" using the overloaded + operator, which for class string denotes concatenation. Line 36 uses the addition assignment operator, +=, to concatenate string3 and "pet". Line 37 uses member function ***append*** to concatenate string1 and "acomb".

Line 41 appends the string "comb" to empty string string5. This member function is passed the string (string1) to retrieve characters from, the starting subscript in the string (4) and the number of characters to append (the value returned by string1.length() - 4).

19.3 Comparing strings

Class string provides member functions for comparing strings. To understand how one string can be "greater than" or "less than" another string, consider the process of alphabetizing a series of last names. The reader would, no doubt, place "Jones" before "Smith", because the first letter of "Jones" comes before the first letter of "Smith" in the alphabet. The alphabet is more than just a set of 26 letters—it is an ordered list of characters in which each letter occurs in a specific position. For example, Z is more than just a letter of the alphabet; Z is specifically the twenty-sixth letter of the alphabet. Figure 19.2 demonstrates class string's comparison capabilities.

The program declares four strings (lines 12–15) and outputs each string (lines 17–18). The condition in line 21 tests string1 against string4 for equality using the overloaded equality operator. If the condition is true, "string1 == string4" is output. If the condition is false, the condition in line 25 is tested. All the string class overloaded operator functions demonstrated here as well as those not demonstrated here (!=, <, >= and <=) return bool values.

```
1   // Fig. 19.2: StringComparison.cpp
2   // Demonstrating string comparison capabilities.
3   #include <iostream>
4   using std::cout;
5   using std::endl;
6
7   #include <string>
8   using std::string;
9
```

Fig. 19.2 | Comparing strings. (Part 1 of 3.)

```
10   int main()
11   {
12      string string1( "Testing the comparison functions." );
13      string string2( "Hello" );
14      string string3( "stinger" );
15      string string4( string2 );
16
17      cout << "string1: " << string1 << "\nstring2: " << string2
18         << "\nstring3: " << string3 << "\nstring4: " << string4 << "\n\n";
19
20      // comparing string1 and string4
21      if ( string1 == string4 )
22         cout << "string1 == string4\n";
23      else // string1 != string4
24      {
25         if ( string1 > string4 )
26            cout << "string1 > string4\n";
27         else // string1 < string4
28            cout << "string1 < string4\n";
29      } // end else
30
31      // comparing string1 and string2
32      int result = string1.compare( string2 );
33
34      if ( result == 0 )
35         cout << "string1.compare( string2 ) == 0\n";
36      else // result != 0
37      {
38         if ( result > 0 )
39            cout << "string1.compare( string2 ) > 0\n";
40         else // result < 0
41            cout << "string1.compare( string2 ) < 0\n";
42      } // end else
43
44      // comparing string1 (elements 2-5) and string3 (elements 0-5)
45      result = string1.compare( 2, 5, string3, 0, 5 );
46
47      if ( result == 0 )
48         cout << "string1.compare( 2, 5, string3, 0, 5 ) == 0\n";
49      else // result != 0
50      {
51         if ( result > 0 )
52            cout << "string1.compare( 2, 5, string3, 0, 5 ) > 0\n";
53         else // result < 0
54            cout << "string1.compare( 2, 5, string3, 0, 5 ) < 0\n";
55      } // end else
56
57      // comparing string2 and string4
58      result = string4.compare( 0, string2.length(), string2 );
59
60      if ( result == 0 )
61         cout << "string4.compare( 0, string2.length(), "
62            << "string2 ) == 0" << endl;
```

Fig. 19.2 | Comparing `string`s. (Part 2 of 3.)

```
63        else // result != 0
64        {
65            if ( result > 0 )
66                cout << "string4.compare( 0, string2.length(), string2 ) > 0"
67                    << endl;
68            else // result < 0
69                cout << "string4.compare( 0, string2.length(), string2 ) < 0"
70                    << endl;
71        } // end else
72
73        // comparing string2 and string4
74        result = string2.compare( 0, 3, string4 );
75
76        if ( result == 0 )
77            cout << "string2.compare( 0, 3, string4 ) == 0" << endl;
78        else // result != 0
79        {
80            if ( result > 0 )
81                cout << "string2.compare( 0, 3, string4 ) > 0" << endl;
82            else // result < 0
83                cout << "string2.compare( 0, 3, string4 ) < 0" << endl;
84        } // end else
85
86        return 0;
87 } // end main
```

```
string1: Testing the comparison functions.
string2: Hello
string3: stinger
string4: Hello

string1 > string4
string1.compare( string2 ) > 0
string1.compare( 2, 5, string3, 0, 5 ) == 0
string4.compare( 0, string2.length(), string2 ) == 0
string2.compare( 0, 3, string4 ) < 0
```

Fig. 19.2 | Comparing strings. (Part 3 of 3.)

Line 32 uses string member function ***compare*** to compare string1 to string2. Variable result is assigned 0 if the strings are equivalent, a positive number if string1 is *lexicographically* greater than string2 or a negative number if string1 is lexicographically less than string2. Because a string starting with 'T' is considered lexicographically greater than a string starting with 'H', result is assigned a value greater than 0, as confirmed by the output. A lexicon is a dictionary. When we say that a string is lexicographically less than another, we mean that the compare function uses the numerical values of the characters (see Appendix B, ASCII Character Set) in each string to determine that the first string is less than the second.

Line 45 uses an overloaded version of member function compare to compare portions of string1 and string3. The first two arguments (2 and 5) specify the starting subscript and length of the portion of string1 ("sting") to compare with string3. The third argument is the comparison string. The last two arguments (0 and 5) are the starting subscript and length of the portion of the `string` being compared (also `"sting"`). The value assigned to `result` is 0 for equality, a positive number if `string1` is lexicographically greater than `string3` or a negative number if `string1` is lexicographically less than `string3`. Because the two pieces being compared here are identical, `result` is assigned 0.

Line 58 uses another overloaded version of function `compare` to compare `string4` and `string2`. The first two arguments are the same—the starting subscript and length. The last argument is the comparison `string`. The value returned is also the same—0 for equality, a positive number if `string4` is lexicographically greater than `string2` or a negative number if `string4` is lexicographically less than `string2`. Because the two pieces of strings being compared here are identical, `result` is assigned 0.

Line 74 calls member function `compare` to compare the first 3 characters in `string2` to `string4`. Because `"Hel"` is less than `"Hello"`, a value less than zero is returned.

19.4 Substrings

Class `string` provides member function ***substr*** for retrieving a substring from a `string`. The result is a new `string` object that is copied from the source `string`. Figure 19.3 demonstrates `substr`.

Line 12 declares and initializes a `string`. Line 16 uses member function `substr` to retrieve a substring from `string1`. The first argument specifies the beginning subscript of the desired substring; the second argument specifies the substring's length.

```
 1    // Fig. 19.3: Substr.cpp
 2    // Demonstrating string member function substr.
 3    #include <iostream>
 4    using std::cout;
 5    using std::endl;
 6
 7    #include <string>
 8    using std::string;
 9
10    int main()
11    {
12       string string1( "The airplane landed on time." );
13
14       // retrieve substring "plane" which
15       // begins at subscript 7 and consists of 5 characters
16       cout << string1.substr( 7, 5 ) << endl;
17       return 0;
18    } // end main
```

```
plane
```

Fig. 19.3 | Demonstrating `string` member function `substr`.

19.5 Swapping strings

Class `string` provides member function ***swap*** for swapping strings. Figure 19.4 swaps two `strings`. Lines 12–13 declare and initialize `strings` `first` and `second`. Each `string` is then output. Line 18 uses `string` member function `swap` to swap the values of `first`

```
 I   // Fig. 19.4: Swap.cpp
 2   // Using the swap function to swap two strings.
 3   #include <iostream>
 4   using std::cout;
 5   using std::endl;
 6
 7   #include <string>
 8   using std::string;
 9
10   int main()
11   {
12      string first( "one" );
13      string second( "two" );
14
15      // output strings
16      cout << "Before swap:\n first: " << first << "\nsecond: " << second;
17
18      first.swap( second ); // swap strings
19
20      cout << "\n\nAfter swap:\n first: " << first
21         << "\nsecond: " << second << endl;
22      return 0;
23   } // end main
```

```
Before swap:
 first: one
second: two

After swap:
 first: two
second: one
```

Fig. 19.4 | Using function swap to swap two strings.

and second. The two strings are printed again to confirm that they were indeed swapped. The string member function swap is useful for implementing programs that sort strings.

19.6 string Characteristics

Class string provides member functions for gathering information about a string's size, length, capacity, maximum length and other characteristics. A string's size or length is the number of characters currently stored in the string. A string's *capacity* is the number of characters that can be stored in the string without allocating more memory. The capacity of a string must be at least equal to the current size of the string, though it can be greater. The exact capacity of a string depends on the implementation. The *maximum size* is the largest possible size a string can have. If this value is exceeded, a length_error exception is thrown. Figure 19.5 demonstrates string class member functions for determining various characteristics of strings.

The program declares empty string string1 (line 16) and passes it to function printStatistics (line 19). Function printStatistics (lines 49–55) takes a reference to a const string as an argument and outputs the capacity (using member function *capacity*), maximum size (using member function *max_size*), size (using member

```cpp
1   // Fig. 19.5: StringCharacteristics.cpp
2   // Demonstrating member functions related to size and capacity.
3   #include <iostream>
4   using std::cout;
5   using std::endl;
6   using std::cin;
7   using std::boolalpha;
8
9   #include <string>
10  using std::string;
11
12  void printStatistics( const string & );
13
14  int main()
15  {
16     string string1; // empty string
17
18     cout << "Statistics before input:\n" << boolalpha;
19     printStatistics( string1 );
20
21     // read in only "tomato" from "tomato soup"
22     cout << "\n\nEnter a string: ";
23     cin >> string1; // delimited by white space
24     cout << "The string entered was: " << string1;
25
26     cout << "\nStatistics after input:\n";
27     printStatistics( string1 );
28
29     // read in "soup"
30     cin >> string1; // delimited by white space
31     cout << "\n\nThe remaining string is: " << string1 << endl;
32     printStatistics( string1 );
33
34     // append 46 characters to string1
35     string1 += "1234567890abcdefghijklmnopqrstuvwxyz1234567890";
36     cout << "\n\nstring1 is now: " << string1 << endl;
37     printStatistics( string1 );
38
39     // add 10 elements to string1
40     string1.resize( string1.length() + 10 );
41     cout << "\n\nStats after resizing by (length + 10):\n";
42     printStatistics( string1 );
43
44     cout << endl;
45     return 0;
46  } // end main
47
48  // display string statistics
49  void printStatistics( const string &stringRef )
50  {
51     cout << "capacity: " << stringRef.capacity() << "\nmax size: "
52        << stringRef.max_size() << "\nsize: " << stringRef.size()
```

Fig. 19.5 | Printing `string` characteristics. (Part 1 of 2.)

```
53            << "\nlength: " << stringRef.length()
54            << "\nempty: " << stringRef.empty();
55    } // end printStatistics
```

```
Statistics before input:
capacity: 15
max size: 4294967294
size: 0
length: 0
empty: true

Enter a string: tomato soup
The string entered was: tomato
Statistics after input:
capacity: 15
max size: 4294967294
size: 6
length: 6
empty: false

The remaining string is: soup
capacity: 15
max size: 4294967294
size: 4
length: 4
empty: false

string1 is now: soup1234567890abcdefghijklmnopqrstuvwxyz1234567890
capacity: 63
max size: 4294967294
size: 50
length: 50
empty: false

Stats after resizing by (length + 10):
capacity: 63
max size: 4294967294
size: 60
length: 60
empty: false
```

Fig. 19.5 | Printing string characteristics. (Part 2 of 2.)

function size), length (using member function length) and whether the string is empty (using member function empty). The initial call to printStatistics indicates that the initial values for the capacity, size and length of string1 are 0.

The size and length of 0 indicate that there are no characters stored in string. Because the initial capacity is 0, when characters are placed in string1, memory is allocated to accommodate the new characters. Recall that the size and length are always identical. In this implementation, the maximum size is 4294967293. Object string1 is an empty string, so function empty returns true.

Line 23 inputs a string. In this example, "tomato soup" is input. Because a space character is a delimiter, only "tomato" is stored in string1; however, "soup" remains in the input buffer. Line 27 calls function printStatistics to output statistics for string1. Notice in the output that the length is 6 and the capacity is 15.

Performance Tip 19.1

To minimize the number of times memory is allocated and deallocated, some `string` class implementations provide a default capacity that is larger than the length of the `string`.

Line 30 reads "soup" from the input buffer and stores it in `string1`, thereby replacing "tomato". Line 32 passes `string1` to `printStatistics`.

Line 35 uses the overloaded += operator to concatenate a 46-character-long string to `string1`. Line 37 passes `string1` to `printStatistics`. Notice that the capacity has increased to 63 elements and the length is now 50.

Line 40 uses member function *resize* to increase the length of `string1` by 10 characters. The additional elements are set to null characters. Notice that in the output the capacity has not changed and the length is now 60.

19.7 Finding Substrings and Characters in a `string`

Class `string` provides const member functions for finding substrings and characters in a string. Figure 19.6 demonstrates the "find" functions.

```
 1   // Fig. 19.6: FindFunctions.cpp
 2   // Demonstrating the string find member functions.
 3   #include <iostream>
 4   using std::cout;
 5   using std::endl;
 6
 7   #include <string>
 8   using std::string;
 9
10   int main()
11   {
12      string string1( "noon is 12 pm; midnight is not." );
13      int location;
14
15      // find "is" at location 5 and 24
16      cout << "Original string:\n" << string1
17         << "\n\n(find) \"is\" was found at: " << string1.find( "is" )
18         << "\n(rfind) \"is\" was found at: " << string1.rfind( "is" );
19
20      // find 'o' at location 1
21      location = string1.find_first_of( "misop" );
22      cout << "\n\n(find_first_of) found '" << string1[ location ]
23         << "' from the group \"misop\" at: " << location;
24
25      // find 'o' at location 29
26      location = string1.find_last_of( "misop" );
27      cout << "\n\n(find_last_of) found '" << string1[ location ]
28         << "' from the group \"misop\" at: " << location;
29
30      // find '1' at location 8
31      location = string1.find_first_not_of( "noi spm" );
```

Fig. 19.6 | Demonstrating the `string` `find` functions. (Part 1 of 2.)

```
32      cout << "\n\n(find_first_not_of) '" << string1[ location ]
33          << "' is not contained in \"noi spm\" and was found at: "
34          << location;
35
36      // find '.' at location 12
37      location = string1.find_first_not_of( "12noi spm" );
38      cout << "\n\n(find_first_not_of) '" << string1[ location ]
39          << "' is not contained in \"12noi spm\" and was "
40          << "found at: " << location << endl;
41
42      // search for characters not in string1
43      location = string1.find_first_not_of(
44          "noon is 12 pm; midnight is not." );
45      cout << "\nfind_first_not_of(\"noon is 12 pm; midnight is not.\")"
46          << " returned: " << location << endl;
47      return 0;
48  } // end main
```

```
Original string:
noon is 12 pm; midnight is not.
(find) "is" was found at: 5
(rfind) "is" was found at: 24
(find_first_of) found 'o' from the group "misop" at: 1
(find_last_of) found 'o' from the group "misop" at: 28
(find_first_not_of) '1' is not contained in "noi spm" and was found at: 8
(find_first_not_of) ';' is not contained in "12noi spm" and was found at: 13
find_first_not_of("noon is 12 pm; midnight is not.") returned: -1
```

Fig. 19.6 | Demonstrating the `string` find functions. (Part 2 of 2.)

String `string1` is declared and initialized in line 12. Line 17 attempts to find `"is"` in `string1` using function **_find_**. If `"is"` is found, the subscript of the starting location of that string is returned. If the `string` is not found, the value **_string::npos_** (a public static constant defined in class `string`) is returned. This value is returned by the `string` find-related functions to indicate that a substring or character was not found in the `string`.

Line 18 uses member function **_rfind_** to search `string1` backward (i.e., right to left). If `"is"` is found, the subscript location is returned. If the string is not found, `string::npos` is returned. [*Note:* The rest of the "find" functions presented in this section return the same type unless otherwise noted.]

Line 21 uses member function **_find_first_of_** to locate the first occurrence in `string1` of any character in `"misop"`. The searching is done from the beginning of `string1`. The character `'o'` is found in element 1.

Line 26 uses member function **_find_last_of_** to find the last occurrence in `string1` of any character in `"misop"`. The searching is done from the end of `string1`. The character `'o'` is found in element 29.

Line 31 uses member function **_find_first_not_of_** to find the first character in `string1` not contained in `"noi spm"`. The character `'1'` is found in element 8. Searching is done from the beginning of `string1`.

Line 37 uses member function `find_first_not_of` to find the first character not contained in `"12noi spm"`. The character `'.'` is found in element 12. Searching is done from the end of `string1`.

Lines 43–44 use member function `find_first_not_of` to find the first character not contained in `"noon is 12 pm; midnight is not."`. In this case, the `string` being searched contains every character specified in the string argument. Because a character was not found, `string::npos` (which has the value –1 in this case) is returned.

19.8 Replacing Characters in a `string`

Figure 19.7 demonstrates `string` member functions for replacing and erasing characters. Lines 13–17 declare and initialize `string string1`. Line 23 uses `string` member function **erase** to erase everything from (and including) the character in position 62 to the end of `string1`. [*Note:* Each newline character occupies one element in the `string`.]

Lines 29–36 use `find` to locate each occurrence of the space character. Each space is then replaced with a period by a call to `string` member function **replace**. Function `replace` takes three arguments: the subscript of the character in the `string` at which replacement should begin, the number of characters to replace and the replacement string. Member function `find` returns `string::npos` when the search character is not found. In line 35, 1 is added to `position` to continue searching at the location of the next character.

Lines 40–48 use function `find` to find every period and another overloaded function `replace` to replace every period and its following character with two semicolons. The arguments passed to this version of `replace` are the subscript of the element where the replace operation begins, the number of characters to replace, a replacement character string from which a substring is selected to use as replacement characters, the element in the character string where the replacement substring begins and the number of characters in the replacement character string to use.

```cpp
1   // Fig. 19.7: EraseReplace.cpp
2   // Demonstrating string member functions erase and replace.
3   #include <iostream>
4   using std::cout;
5   using std::endl;
6
7   #include <string>
8   using std::string;
9
10  int main()
11  {
12     // compiler concatenates all parts into one string
13     string string1( "The values in any left subtree"
14        "\nare less than the value in the"
15        "\nparent node and the values in"
16        "\nany right subtree are greater"
17        "\nthan the value in the parent node" );
18
19     cout << "Original string:\n" << string1 << endl << endl;
```

Fig. 19.7 | Demonstrating functions `erase` and `replace`. (Part 1 of 2.)

```
20
21     // remove all characters from (and including) location 62
22     // through the end of string1
23     string1.erase( 62 );
24
25     // output new string
26     cout << "Original string after erase:\n" << string1
27        << "\n\nAfter first replacement:\n";
28
29     int position = string1.find( " " ); // find first space
30
31     // replace all spaces with period
32     while ( position != string::npos )
33     {
34        string1.replace( position, 1, "." );
35        position = string1.find( " ", position + 1 );
36     } // end while
37
38     cout << string1 << "\n\nAfter second replacement:\n";
39
40     position = string1.find( "." ); // find first period
41
42     // replace all periods with two semicolons
43     // NOTE: this will overwrite characters
44     while ( position != string::npos )
45     {
46        string1.replace( position, 2, "xxxxx;;yyy", 5, 2 );
47        position = string1.find( ".", position + 1 );
48     } // end while
49
50     cout << string1 << endl;
51     return 0;
52  } // end main
```

```
Original string:
The values in any left subtree
are less than the value in the
parent node and the values in
any right subtree are greater
than the value in the parent node

Original string after erase:
The values in any left subtree
are less than the value in the


After first replacement:
The.values.in.any.left.subtree
are.less.than.the.value.in.the


After second replacement:
The;;alues;;n;;ny;;eft;;ubtree
are;;ess;;han;;he;;alue;;n;;he
```

Fig. 19.7 | Demonstrating functions `erase` and `replace`. (Part 2 of 2.)

19.9 Inserting Characters into a `string`

Class `string` provides member functions for inserting characters into a string. Figure 19.8 demonstrates the `string` insert capabilities.

The program declares, initializes and then outputs strings string1, string2, string3 and string4. Line 22 uses `string` member function *insert* to insert string2's content before element 10 of string1.

```cpp
1   // Fig. 19.8: InsertFunction.cpp
2   // Demonstrating class string insert member functions.
3   #include <iostream>
4   using std::cout;
5   using std::endl;
6
7   #include <string>
8   using std::string;
9
10  int main()
11  {
12     string string1( "beginning end" );
13     string string2( "middle " );
14     string string3( "12345678" );
15     string string4( "xx" );
16
17     cout << "Initial strings:\nstring1: " << string1
18        << "\nstring2: " << string2 << "\nstring3: " << string3
19        << "\nstring4: " << string4 << "\n\n";
20
21     // insert "middle" at location 10 in string1
22     string1.insert( 10, string2 );
23
24     // insert "xx" at location 3 in string3
25     string3.insert( 3, string4, 0, string::npos );
26
27     cout << "Strings after insert:\nstring1: " << string1
28        << "\nstring2: " << string2 << "\nstring3: " << string3
29        << "\nstring4: " << string4 << endl;
30     return 0;
31  } // end main
```

```
Initial strings:
string1: beginning end
string2: middle
string3: 12345678
string4: xx

Strings after insert:
string1: beginning middle end
string2: middle
string3: 123xx45678
string4: xx
```

Fig. 19.8 | Demonstrating the `string` insert member functions.

Line 25 uses `insert` to insert `string4` before `string3`'s element 3. The last two arguments specify the starting and last element of `string4` that should be inserted. Using `string::npos` causes the entire `string` to be inserted.

19.10 Conversion to C-Style Pointer-Based char * Strings

Class `string` provides member functions for converting `string` class objects to C-style pointer-based strings. As mentioned earlier, unlike pointer-based strings, `strings` are not necessarily null terminated. These conversion functions are useful when a given function takes a pointer-based string as an argument. Figure 19.9 demonstrates conversion of `strings` to pointer-based strings.

```
 1  // Fig. 19.9: ConvertingStrings.cpp
 2  // Converting to C-style strings.
 3  #include <iostream>
 4  using std::cout;
 5  using std::endl;
 6
 7  #include <string>
 8  using std::string;
 9
10  int main()
11  {
12     string string1( "STRINGS" ); // string constructor with char* arg
13     const char *ptr1 = 0; // initialize *ptr1
14     int length = string1.length();
15     char *ptr2 = new char[ length + 1 ]; // including null
16
17     // copy characters from string1 into allocated memory
18     string1.copy( ptr2, length, 0 ); // copy string1 to ptr2 char*
19     ptr2[ length ] = '\0'; // add null terminator
20
21     cout << "string string1 is " << string1
22        << "\nstring1 converted to a C-Style string is "
23        << string1.c_str()    << "\nptr1 is ";
24
25     // Assign to pointer ptr1 the const char * returned by
26     // function data(). NOTE: this is a potentially dangerous
27     // assignment. If string1 is modified, pointer ptr1 can
28     // become invalid.
29     ptr1 = string1.data();
30
31     // output each character using pointer
32     for ( int i = 0; i < length; i++ )
33        cout << *( ptr1 + i ); // use pointer arithmetic
34
35     cout << "\nptr2 is " << ptr2 << endl;
36     delete [] ptr2; // reclaim dynamically allocated memory
37     return 0;
38  } // end main
```

Fig. 19.9 | Converting `strings` to C-style strings and character arrays. (Part 1 of 2.)

```
string string1 is STRINGS
string1 converted to a C-Style string is STRINGS
ptr1 is STRINGS
ptr2 is STRINGS
```

Fig. 19.9 | Converting `string`s to C-style strings and character arrays. (Part 2 of 2.)

The program declares a `string`, an `int` and two `char` pointers (lines 12–15). The `string` `string1` is initialized to `"STRINGS"`, `ptr1` is initialized to `0` and `length` is initialized to the length of `string1`. Memory of sufficient size to hold a pointer-based string equivalent of `string` `string1` is allocated dynamically and attached to `char` pointer `ptr2`.

Line 18 uses `string` member function *copy* to copy object `string1` into the `char` array pointed to by `ptr2`. Line 19 manually places a terminating null character in the array pointed to by `ptr2`.

Line 23 uses function *c_str* to obtain a `const char *` that points to a null-terminated C-style string with the same content as `string1`. The pointer is passed to the stream insertion operator for output.

Line 29 assigns the `const char *` `ptr1` a pointer returned by class `string` member function *data*. This member function returns a non-null-terminated C-style character array. Note that we do not modify `string` `string1` in this example. If `string1` were to be modified (e.g., the `string`'s dynamic memory changed its address due to a member-function call such as `string1.insert(0, "abcd");`), `ptr1` could become invalid—which could lead to unpredictable results. Lines 32–33 use pointer arithmetic to output the character array pointed to by `ptr1`. We use a loop to print each character because `ptr1` is not null terminated. In lines 35–36, the C-style string pointed to by `ptr2` is output and the memory allocated for `ptr2` is `delete`d to avoid a memory leak.

Common Programming Error 19.4

Not terminating the character array returned by data *with a null character can lead to execution-time errors.*

Good Programming Practice 19.1

Use the more robust string *class objects rather than C-style pointer-based strings.*

19.11 Iterators

Class `string` provides iterators for forward and backward traversal of `string`s. Iterators provide access to individual characters with syntax that is similar to pointer operations. Iterators are not range checked. Note that in this section we provide "mechanical examples" to demonstrate the use of iterators. We discuss more robust uses of iterators in Chapter 23, Standard Template Library (STL). Figure 19.10 demonstrates iterators.

Lines 12–13 declare `string` `string1` and *string::const_iterator* `iterator1`. A `const_iterator` is an iterator that cannot modify the `string`—in this case the `string` through which it is iterating. Iterator `iterator1` is initialized to the beginning of `string1` with the `string` class member function *begin*. Two versions of `begin` exist—one that returns an `iterator` for iterating through a non-const `string` and a const version that returns a `const_iterator` for iterating through a const `string`. Line 15 outputs `string1`.

```
1   // Fig. 19.10: StringIterator.cpp
2   // Using an iterator to output a string.
3   #include <iostream>
4   using std::cout;
5   using std::endl;
6
7   #include <string>
8   using std::string;
9
10  int main()
11  {
12     string string1( "Testing iterators" );
13     string::const_iterator iterator1 = string1.begin();
14
15     cout << "string1 = " << string1
16        << "\n(Using iterator iterator1) string1 is: ";
17
18     // iterate through string
19     while ( iterator1 != string1.end() )
20     {
21        cout << *iterator1; // dereference iterator to get char
22        iterator1++; // advance iterator to next char
23     } // end while
24
25     cout << endl;
26     return 0;
27  } // end main
```

```
string1 = Testing iterators
(Using iterator iterator1) string1 is: Testing iterators
```

Fig. 19.10 | Using an iterator to output a `string`.

Lines 19–23 use iterator `iterator1` to "walk through" `string1`. Class `string` member function **end** returns an `iterator` (or a `const_iterator`) for the position past the last element of `string1`. Each element is printed by dereferencing the iterator much as you would dereference a pointer, and the iterator is advanced one position using operator ++.

Class `string` provides member functions **rend** and **rbegin** for accessing individual `string` characters in reverse from the end of a `string` toward the beginning. Member functions `rend` and `rbegin` return **reverse_iterators** or **const_reverse_iterators** (based on whether the `string` is non-const or const). In the exercises, we ask you to write a program that demonstrates these capabilities. We'll use iterators and reverse iterators more in Chapter 23.

Error-Prevention Tip 19.1

Use `string` member function at (rather than iterators) when you want the benefit of range checking.

Good Programming Practice 19.2

When the operations involving the iterator should not modify the data being processed, use a `const_iterator`. This is another example of employing the principle of least privilege.

19.12 String Stream Processing

In addition to standard stream I/O and file stream I/O, Visual C++ stream I/O includes capabilities for inputting from, and outputting to, `string`s in memory. These capabilities often are referred to as *in-memory I/O* or *string stream processing*.

Input from a `string` is supported by class *istringstream*. Output to a `string` is supported by class *ostringstream*. The class names istringstream and ostringstream are actually aliases defined by the typedefs

```
typedef basic_istringstream< char > istringstream;
typedef basic_ostringstream< char > ostringstream;
```

Class templates `basic_istringstream` and `basic_ostringstream` provide the same functionality as classes `istream` and `ostream` plus other member functions specific to in-memory formatting. Programs that use in-memory formatting must include the *<sstream>* and `<iostream>` header files.

One application of these techniques is data validation. A program can read an entire line at a time from the input stream into a `string`. Next, a validation routine can scrutinize the contents of the `string` and correct (or repair) the data, if necessary. Then the program can proceed to input from the `string`, knowing that the input data is in the proper format.

Outputting to a `string` is a nice way to take advantage of Visual C++'s powerful stream formatting capabilities. Data can be prepared in a `string` to mimic the edited screen format. That `string` could be written to a disk file to preserve the screen image.

An ostringstream object uses a `string` object to store the output data. The **str** member function of class ostringstream returns a copy of that `string`.

Figure 19.11 demonstrates an ostringstream object. The program creates ostringstream object outputString (line 15) and uses the stream insertion operator to output a series of `string`s and numerical values to the object.

Lines 27–28 output string string1, string string2, string string3, double double1, string string4, int integer, string string5 and the address of int integer—all to outputString in memory. Line 31 uses the stream insertion operator and the call outputString.str() to display a copy of the `string` created in lines 27–28. Line 34 demonstrates that more data can be appended to the `string` in memory by simply issuing another stream insertion operation to outputString. Lines 35–36 display string outputString after appending additional characters.

```cpp
1   // Fig. 19.11: OStringStream.cpp
2   // Using a dynamically allocated ostringstream object.
3   #include <iostream>
4   using std::cout;
5   using std::endl;
6
7   #include <string>
8   using std::string;
9
10  #include <sstream> // header file for string stream processing
11  using std::ostringstream; // stream insertion operators
```

Fig. 19.11 | Using a dynamically allocated ostringstream object. (Part 1 of 2.)

```
12
13   int main()
14   {
15      ostringstream outputString; // create ostringstream instance
16
17      string string1( "Output of several data types " );
18      string string2( "to an ostringstream object:" );
19      string string3( "\n          double: " );
20      string string4( "\n             int: " );
21      string string5( "\naddress of int: " );
22
23      double double1 = 123.4567;
24      int integer = 22;
25
26      // output strings, double and int to ostringstream outputString
27      outputString << string1 << string2 << string3 << double1
28         << string4 << integer << string5 << &integer;
29
30      // call str to obtain string contents of the ostringstream
31      cout << "outputString contains:\n" << outputString.str();
32
33      // add additional characters and call str to output string
34      outputString << "\nmore characters added";
35      cout << "\n\nafter additional stream insertions,\n"
36         << "outputString contains:\n" << outputString.str() << endl;
37      return 0;
38   } // end main
```

```
outputString contains:
Output of several data types to an ostringstream object:
        double: 123.457
           int: 22
address of int: 0012F540

after additional stream insertions,
outputString contains:
Output of several data types to an ostringstream object:
        double: 123.457
           int: 22
address of int: 0012F540
more characters added
```

Fig. 19.11 | Using a dynamically allocated ostringstream object. (Part 2 of 2.)

An istringstream object inputs data from a string in memory to program variables. Data is stored in an istringstream object as characters. Input from the istringstream object works identically to input from any file. The end of the string is interpreted by the istringstream object as end-of-file.

Figure 19.12 demonstrates input from an istringstream object. Lines 15–16 create string input containing the data and istringstream object inputString constructed to contain the data in string input. The string input contains the data

```
Input test 123 4.7 A
```

```
 1   // Fig. 19.12: IStringStream.cpp
 2   // Demonstrating input from an istringstream object.
 3   #include <iostream>
 4   using std::cout;
 5   using std::endl;
 6
 7   #include <string>
 8   using std::string;
 9
10   #include <sstream>
11   using std::istringstream;
12
13   int main()
14   {
15      string input( "Input test 123 4.7 A" );
16      istringstream inputString( input );
17      string string1;
18      string string2;
19      int integer;
20      double double1;
21      char character;
22
23      inputString >> string1 >> string2 >> integer >> double1 >> character;
24
25      cout << "The following items were extracted\n"
26         << "from the istringstream object:" << "\nstring: " << string1
27         << "\nstring: " << string2 << "\n   int: " << integer
28         << "\ndouble: " << double1 << "\n  char: " << character;
29
30      // attempt to read from empty stream
31      long value;
32      inputString >> value;
33
34      // test stream results
35      if ( inputString.good() )
36         cout << "\n\nlong value is: " << value << endl;
37      else
38         cout << "\n\ninputString is empty" << endl;
39
40      return 0;
41   } // end main
```

```
The following items were extracted
from the istringstream object:
string: Input
string: test
   int: 123
double: 4.7
  char: A

inputString is empty
```

Fig. 19.12 | Demonstrating input from an `istringstream` object.

which, when read as input to the program, consists of two strings ("Input" and "test"), an int (123), a double (4.7) and a char ('A'). These characters are extracted to variables string1, string2, integer, double1 and character in line 23.

The data is then output in lines 25–28. The program attempts to read from input-String again in line 32. The if condition in line 35 uses function good (Section 17.8) to test if any data remains. Because no data remains, the function returns false and the else part of the if…else statement is executed.

19.13 Fundamentals of Characters and Strings in C++/CLI

A managed String is a series of characters (class Char of namespace System) treated as a unit. Note that Strings are not composed of chars like the native C++ string class. Each Char in a String is a Unicode character occupying two bytes of memory (see Section 19.25 for more information on class Char). These characters can be uppercase letters, lowercase letters, digits and various *special characters:* +, -, *, /, $ and others. A managed string is an object of class String in the System namespace. A declaration can assign a String literal to a String reference. The declaration

```
String ^color = "blue";
```

initializes String handle color to refer to the String literal object "blue". Strings support a number of escape sequences, some of which are listed in Fig. 3.2. Like native C++, Strings in C++/CLI are null terminated. This facilitates easy interoperability with native C++ strings and character arrays.

Performance Tip 19.2

If there are multiple occurrences of the same String literal object in an application, a single copy of the String literal object will be referenced from each location in the program that uses that String literal. It is possible to share the object in this manner, because String literal objects are implicitly constant. Such sharing conserves memory.

19.14 String Constructors

Class String provides eight constructors for initializing Strings in various ways. Figure 19.13 demonstrates the use of three of the constructors.

```
 1    // Fig. 19.13: StringConstructor.cpp
 2    // Demonstrating String class constructors.
 3
 4    #include "stdafx.h"
 5
 6    using namespace System;
 7
 8    int main( array< System::String ^ > ^args )
 9    {
10       String ^originalString, ^string1, ^string2,
11             ^string3, ^string4;
```

Fig. 19.13 | String constructors. (Part 1 of 2.)

```
12      array< Char >^ characterArray =
13          { 'b', 'i', 'r', 't', 'h', ' ', 'd', 'a', 'y' };
14
15      // String initialization
16      originalString = "Welcome to C++/CLI programming!";
17      string1 = originalString;
18      string2 = gcnew String( characterArray );
19      string3 = gcnew String( characterArray, 6, 3 );
20      string4 = gcnew String( 'C', 5 );
21
22      Console::WriteLine( "string1 = \"{0}\"", string1 );
23      Console::WriteLine( "string2 = \"{0}\"", string2 );
24      Console::WriteLine( "string3 = \"{0}\"", string3 );
25      Console::WriteLine( "string4 = \"{0}\"", string4 );
26
27      return 0;
28  } // end function main
```

```
string1 = "Welcome to C++/CLI programming!"
string2 = "birth day"
string3 = "day"
string4 = "CCCCC"
```

Fig. 19.13 | String constructors. (Part 2 of 2.)

Lines 10–11 declare `String` handles `originalString`, `string1`, `string2`, `string3` and `string4`. Lines 12–13 allocate the managed `Char` array `characterArray`, which contains nine characters. Line 16 assigns `String` literal `"Welcome to C++/CLI programming!"` to `String` handle `originalString`. Line 17 sets `string1` to reference the same `String` literal.

Line 18 assigns to `string2` a new `String`, using the `String` constructor that takes a `Char` array as an argument. The new `String` contains a copy of the characters in managed array `characterArray`.

Software Engineering Observation 19.1

In most cases, it is not necessary to make a copy of an existing `String`. All `Strings` are immutable—their character contents cannot be changed after they are created. Also, if there are one or more references to a `String` (or any object for that matter), the object cannot be reclaimed by the garbage collector.

Line 19 assigns to `string3` a new `String`, using the `String` constructor that takes a `Char` array and two `int` arguments. The second argument specifies the starting index position (the *offset*) from which characters in the array are to be copied. The third argument specifies the number of characters (the *count*) to be copied from the specified starting position in the array. The new `String` contains a copy of the specified characters in the array. If the specified offset or count indicates that the program should access an element outside the bounds of the character array, an `ArgumentOutOfRangeException` is thrown.

Line 20 assigns to `string4` a new `String`, using the `String` constructor that takes as arguments a character and an `int` specifying the number of times to repeat that character in the `String`.

19.15 String Indexer, Length Property and CopyTo Function

The application in Fig. 19.14 presents the String indexer (see Section 11.17), which facilitates the retrieval of any character in the String, and the String property Length, which returns the length of the String. The String function CopyTo copies a specified number of characters from a String into a managed Char array.

This application determines the length of a String, displays its characters in reverse order and copies a series of characters from the String to a character array.

Line 21 uses String property Length to determine the number of characters in string1. Like managed arrays, Strings always know their own size.

```cpp
1   // Fig. 19.14: StringFunctions.cpp
2   // Using the indexer, property Length and function CopyTo
3   // of class String.
4
5   #include "stdafx.h"
6
7   using namespace System;
8
9   int main( array< System::String ^ > ^args )
10  {
11     String ^string1;
12     array< Char >^ characterArray;
13
14     string1 = "hello there";
15     characterArray = gcnew array< Char >( 5 );
16
17     // output string1
18     Console::WriteLine( "string1: \"{0}\"", string1 );
19
20     // test Length property
21     Console::WriteLine( "Length of string1: {0}", string1->Length );
22
23     // loop through characters in string1 and display reversed
24     Console::Write( "The string reversed is: " );
25
26     for ( int i = string1->Length - 1; i >= 0; i-- )
27        Console::Write( string1[ i ] );
28
29     // copy characters from string1 into characterArray
30     string1->CopyTo( 0, characterArray, 0, characterArray->Length );
31     Console::Write( "\nThe character array is: " );
32
33     for ( int i = 0; i < characterArray->Length; i++ )
34        Console::Write( characterArray[ i ] );
35
36     Console::WriteLine();
37
38     return 0;
39  } // end function main
```

Fig. 19.14 | String indexer, Length property, and CopyTo function. (Part 1 of 2.)

```
string1: "hello there"
Length of string1: 11
The string reversed is: ereht olleh
The character array is: hello
```

Fig. 19.14 | String indexer, `Length` property, and `CopyTo` function. (Part 2 of 2.)

Lines 26–27 write the characters of `string1` in reverse order using the `String` indexer. The `String` indexer treats a `String` as a managed array of `Char`s and returns the character at a specific position in the `String`. The indexer receives an integer argument as the *position number* and returns the character at that position. As with arrays, the first element of a `String` is considered to be at position 0.

> **Common Programming Error 19.5**
>
> *Attempting to access a character that is outside a `String`'s bounds (i.e., an index less than 0 or an index greater than or equal to the `String`'s length) results in an `IndexOutOfRangeException`.*

Line 30 uses `String` function `CopyTo` to copy the characters of `string1` into a character array (`characterArray`). It is important to use a character array of type `Char` rather than `char`. Class `String` doesn't contain a constructor that takes an array of `char` (see Section 19.25). The first argument given to function `CopyTo` is the index from which the function begins copying characters in the `String`. The second argument is the managed character array into which the characters are copied. The third argument is the index specifying the starting location at which the function begins placing the copied characters into the character array. The last argument is the number of characters that the function will copy from the `String`. Lines 33–34 output the `Char` array contents one character at a time.

19.16 Comparing `Strings`

The next two examples demonstrate various functions for comparing `Strings`. `Strings` are compared in the same way as outlined in Section 19.3 for native C++ class `string`. Computers can order characters alphabetically because the characters are represented internally as Unicode numeric codes. When comparing two `Strings`, C++/CLI simply compares the numeric codes of the characters in the `Strings`.

Class `String` provides several ways to compare `Strings`. The application in Fig. 19.15 demonstrates function `Equals`, function `CompareTo` and the equality operator (`==`).

The condition in the `if` statement (line 22) uses `String` function `Equals` to compare `string1` and literal `String` "`hello`" to determine whether they are equal. Function `Equals` (inherited from `Object` and overridden in `String`) tests any two objects for equality (i.e., checks whether the objects contain identical contents). The function returns `true` if the objects are equal and `false` otherwise. In this instance, the preceding condition returns `true`, because `string1` references `String` literal object "`hello`". Function `Equals` uses a lexicographical comparison—the integer Unicode values that represent each character in each `String` are compared. A comparison of the `String` "`hello`" with the `String` "`HELLO`" would return `false`, because the numeric representations of lowercase letters are different from the numeric representations of corresponding uppercase letters.

```
 1    // Fig. 19.15: StringCompare.cpp
 2    // Comparing strings
 3
 4    #include "stdafx.h"
 5
 6    using namespace System;
 7
 8    int main( array< System::String ^ > ^args )
 9    {
10       String ^string1 = "hello";
11       String ^string2 = "good bye";
12       String ^string3 = "Happy Birthday";
13       String ^string4 = "happy birthday";
14
15       // output values of four strings
16       Console::WriteLine( "string1 = \"{0}\"", string1 );
17       Console::WriteLine( "string2 = \"{0}\"", string2 );
18       Console::WriteLine( "string3 = \"{0}\"", string3 );
19       Console::WriteLine( "string4 = \"{0}\"\n", string4 );
20
21       // test for equality using Equals function
22       if ( string1->Equals( "hello" ) )
23          Console::WriteLine( "string1 equals \"hello\"" );
24       else
25          Console::WriteLine( "string1 does not equal \"hello\"" );
26
27       // test for equality with ==
28       if ( string1 == "hello" )
29          Console::WriteLine( "string1 equals \"hello\"" );
30       else
31          Console::WriteLine( "string1 does not equal \"hello\"" );
32
33       // test for equality comparing case
34       if ( String::Equals( string3, string4 ) ) // static function
35          Console::WriteLine( "string3 equals string4" );
36       else
37          Console::WriteLine( "string3 does not equal string4" );
38
39       // test CompareTo
40       Console::WriteLine( "\nstring1->CompareTo( string2 ) is {0} ",
41          string1->CompareTo( string2 ) );
42       Console::WriteLine( "string2->CompareTo( string1 ) is {0} ",
43          string2->CompareTo( string1 ) );
44       Console::WriteLine( "string1->CompareTo( string1 ) is {0} ",
45          string1->CompareTo( string1 ) );
46       Console::WriteLine( "string3->CompareTo( string4 ) is {0} ",
47          string3->CompareTo( string4 ) );
48       Console::WriteLine( "string4->CompareTo( string3 ) is {0} ",
49          string4->CompareTo( string3 ) );
50
51       return 0;
52    } // end function main
```

Fig. 19.15 | String test to determine equality. (Part 1 of 2.)

```
string1 = "hello"
string2 = "good bye"
string3 = "Happy Birthday"
string4 = "happy birthday"

string1 equals "hello"
string1 equals "hello"
string3 does not equal string4

string1.CompareTo( string2 ) is 1
string2.CompareTo( string1 ) is -1
string1.CompareTo( string1 ) is 0
string3.CompareTo( string4 ) is 1
string4.CompareTo( string3 ) is -1
```

Fig. 19.15 | String test to determine equality. (Part 2 of 2.)

The condition in line 28 uses the equality operator (==) to compare String string1 with the literal String "hello" for equality. In C++/CLI, the equality operator also uses a lexicographical comparison to compare two Strings. Thus, the condition in the if statement evaluates to true, because the values of string1 and "hello" are equal.

We present the test for String equality between string3 and string4 (line 34) to illustrate that comparisons are indeed case sensitive. Here, static function Equals is used to compare the values of two Strings. "Happy Birthday" does not equal "happy birthday", so the condition of the if statement fails, and the message "string3 does not equal string4" is output (line 37).

Lines 40–49 use String function CompareTo to compare Strings. Function CompareTo returns 0 if the Strings are equal, a negative value if the String that invokes CompareTo is less than the String that is passed as an argument and a positive value if the String that invokes CompareTo is greater than the String that is passed as an argument. Function CompareTo uses a lexicographical comparison.

Notice that CompareTo considers string3 to be larger than string4. The only difference between these two Strings is that string3 contains two uppercase letters in positions where string4 contains lowercase letters.

The application in Fig. 19.16 shows how to test whether a String instance begins or ends with a given String. Function StartsWith determines whether a String instance starts with the String text passed to it as an argument. Function EndsWith determines whether a String instance ends with the String text passed to it as an argument. In Figure 19.16 the main function defines a managed array of String ^ (called strings), which contains "started", "starting", "ended" and "ending". The remainder of function main tests the elements of the array to determine whether they start or end with a particular set of characters.

Line 15 uses function StartsWith, which takes a String argument. The condition in the if statement determines whether the String at index i of the array starts with the characters "st". If so, the function returns true, and strings[i] is output.

Line 22 uses function EndsWith, which also takes a String argument. The condition in the if statement determines whether the current String ^ element of the array ends with the characters "ed". If so, the function returns true, and the element is displayed along with a message.

```
1   // Fig. 19.16: StringStartEnd.cpp
2   // Demonstrating StartsWith and EndsWith functions.
3
4   #include "stdafx.h"
5
6   using namespace System;
7
8   int main( array< System::String ^ > ^args )
9   {
10     array< String^ >^ strings =
11        { "started", "starting", "ended", "ending" };
12
13     // test every string to see if it starts with "st"
14     for each ( String ^s in strings )
15        if ( s->StartsWith( "st" ) )
16           Console::WriteLine( "\"{0}\" starts with \"st\"", s );
17
18     Console::WriteLine();
19
20     // test every string to see if it ends with "ed"
21     for each ( String ^s in strings )
22        if ( s->EndsWith( "ed" ) )
23           Console::WriteLine( "\"{0}\" ends with \"ed\"", s );
24
25     Console::WriteLine();
26
27     return 0;
28  } // end function main
```

```
"started" starts with "st"
"starting" starts with "st"

"started" ends with "ed"
"ended" ends with "ed"
```

Fig. 19.16 | StartsWith and EndsWith functions.

19.17 Locating Characters and Substrings in Strings

In many applications, it is necessary to search for a character or set of characters in a String. For example, a programmer creating a word processor would want to provide capabilities for searching through documents. The application in Fig. 19.17 demonstrates some of the many versions of String functions IndexOf, IndexOfAny, LastIndexOf and LastIndexOfAny, which search for a specified character or substring in a String. We perform all searches in this example on the String letters (initialized with "abcdefghijklmabcdefghijklm") located in function main.

```
1   // Fig. 19.17: StringIndexFunctions.cpp
2   // Using string searching functions.
3
4   #include "stdafx.h"
```

Fig. 19.17 | Searching for characters and substrings in Strings. (Part 1 of 3.)

```cpp
5
6   using namespace System;
7
8   int main( array< System::String ^ > ^args )
9   {
10     String ^letters = "abcdefghijklmabcdefghijklm";
11     array< Char >^ searchLetters = { 'c', 'a', '$' };
12
13     // test IndexOf to locate a character in a string
14     Console::WriteLine( "First 'c' is located at index {0}",
15        letters->IndexOf( 'c' ) );
16     Console::WriteLine( "First 'a' starting at 1 is located at index {0}",
17        letters->IndexOf( 'a', 1 ) );
18     Console::WriteLine( "First '$' in the 5 positions starting at 3 "
19        + "is located at index {0}", letters->IndexOf( '$', 3, 5 ) );
20
21     // test LastIndexOf to find a character in a string
22     Console::WriteLine( "\nLast 'c' is located at index {0}",
23        letters->LastIndexOf( 'c' ) );
24     Console::WriteLine( "Last 'a' up to position 25 is located at " +
25        " index {0}", letters->LastIndexOf( 'a', 25 ) );
26     Console::WriteLine( "Last '$' in the 5 positions starting at 15 " +
27        "is located at index {0}", letters->LastIndexOf( '$', 15, 5 ) );
28
29     // test IndexOf to locate a substring in a string
30     Console::WriteLine( "\nFirst \"def\" is located at index {0}",
31        letters->IndexOf( "def" ) );
32     Console::WriteLine( "First \"def\" starting at 7 is located at " +
33        "index {0}", letters->IndexOf( "def", 7 ) );
34     Console::WriteLine( "First \"hello\" in the 15 positions " +
35        "starting at 5 is located at index {0}",
36        letters->IndexOf( "hello", 5, 15 ) );
37
38     // test LastIndexOf to find a substring in a string
39     Console::WriteLine( "\nLast \"def\" is located at index {0}",
40        letters->LastIndexOf( "def" ) );
41     Console::WriteLine( "Last \"def\" up to position 25 is located " +
42        "at index {0}", letters->LastIndexOf( "def", 25 ) );
43     Console::WriteLine( "Last \"hello\" in the 15 positions " +
44        "ending at 20 is located at index {0}",
45        letters->LastIndexOf( "hello", 20, 15 ) );
46
47     // test IndexOfAny to find first occurrence of character in array
48     Console::WriteLine( "\nFirst 'c', 'a' or '$' is " +
49        "located at index {0}", letters->IndexOfAny( searchLetters ) );
50     Console::WriteLine( "First 'c', 'a' or '$' starting at 7 is " +
51        "located at index {0}", letters->IndexOfAny( searchLetters, 7 ) );
52     Console::WriteLine( "First 'c', 'a' or '$' in the 5 positions " +
53        "starting at 7 is located at index {0}",
54        letters->IndexOfAny( searchLetters, 7, 5 ) );
55
56     // test LastIndexOfAny to find last occurrence of character
57     // in array
```

Fig. 19.17 | Searching for characters and substrings in `String`s. (Part 2 of 3.)

```
58      Console::WriteLine( "\nLast 'c', 'a' or '$' is " +
59         "located at index {0}", letters->LastIndexOfAny( searchLetters ) );
60      Console::WriteLine( "Last 'c', 'a' or '$' up to position 1 is " +
61         "located at index {0}",
62         letters->LastIndexOfAny( searchLetters, 1 ) );
63      Console::WriteLine( "Last 'c', 'a' or '$' in the 5 positions " +
64         "ending at 25 is located at index {0}",
65         letters->LastIndexOfAny( searchLetters, 25, 5 ) );
66
67         return 0;
68   } // end function main
```

```
First 'c' is located at index 2
First 'a' starting at 1 is located at index 13
First '$' in the 5 positions starting at 3 is located at index -1

Last 'c' is located at index 15
Last 'a' up to position 25 is located at index 13
Last '$' in the 5 positions starting at 15 is located at index -1

First "def" is located at index 3
First "def" starting at 7 is located at index 16
First "hello" in the 15 positions starting at 5 is located at index -1

Last "def" is located at index 16
Last "def" up to position 25 is located at index 16
Last "hello" in the 15 positions ending at 20 is located at index -1

First 'c', 'a' or '$' is located at index 0
First 'c', 'a' or '$' starting at 7 is located at index 13
First 'c', 'a' or '$' in the 5 positions starting at 7 is located at index -1

Last 'c', 'a' or '$' is located at index 15
Last 'c', 'a' or '$' up to position 1 is located at index 0
Last 'c', 'a' or '$' in the 5 positions ending at 25 is located at index -1
```

Fig. 19.17 | Searching for characters and substrings in Strings. (Part 3 of 3.)

Lines 15, 17 and 19 use function IndexOf to locate the first occurrence of a character or substring in a String. If it finds a character, IndexOf returns the index of the specified character in the String; otherwise, IndexOf returns –1. The expression in line 17 uses a version of function IndexOf that takes two arguments—the character to search for and the starting index at which the search of the String should begin. The function doesn't examine any characters that occur prior to the starting index (in this case, 1). The expression in line 19 uses another version of function IndexOf that takes three arguments—the character to search for, the index at which to start searching and the number of characters to search.

Lines 23, 25 and 27 use function LastIndexOf to locate the last occurrence of a character in a String. Function LastIndexOf performs the search from the end of the String to the beginning of the String. If it finds the character, LastIndexOf returns the index of the specified character in the String; otherwise, LastIndexOf returns –1. There are three versions of LastIndexOf. The expression in line 23 uses the version of function LastIndexOf that takes as an argument the character for which to search. The expression in line 25 uses the version of function `LastIndexOf` that takes two arguments—the character for which to search and the highest index from which to begin searching backward for the character. The expression in line 27 uses a third version of function `LastIndexOf` that takes three arguments—the character for which to search, the starting index from which to start searching backward and the number of characters (the portion of the `String`) to search.

Lines 30–45 use versions of `IndexOf` and `LastIndexOf` that take a `String` instead of a character as the first argument. These versions of the functions perform identically to those described above except that they search for sequences of characters (or substrings) that are specified by their `String` arguments. Lines 48–65 use functions `IndexOfAny` and `LastIndexOfAny`, which take a managed array of characters as the first argument. These versions of the functions also perform identically to those described above except that they return the index of the first occurrence of any of the characters in the character array argument.

Common Programming Error 19.6

In the overloaded functions `LastIndexOf` and `LastIndexOfAny` that take three parameters, the second argument must be greater than or equal to the third. This might seem counterintuitive, but remember that the search moves from the end of the string toward the start of the string.

19.18 Extracting Substrings from `Strings`

Class `String` provides two `Substring` functions, which are used to create a new `String` by copying part of an existing `String`. Each function returns a new `String`. The application in Fig. 19.18 demonstrates the use of both functions.

```
1  // Fig. 19.18: SubString.cpp
2  // Demonstrating the String Substring function.
3
4  #include "stdafx.h"
5
6  using namespace System;
7
8  int main( array< System::String ^ > ^args )
9  {
10     String ^letters = "abcdefghijklmabcdefghijklm";
11
12     // invoke Substring function and pass it one parameter
13     Console::WriteLine( "Substring from index 20 to end is \"{0}\"",
14        letters->Substring( 20 ) );
15
16     // invoke Substring function and pass it two parameters
17     Console::WriteLine( "Substring from index 0 of length 6 is \"{0}\"",
18        letters->Substring( 0, 6 ) );
19
20     return 0;
21  } // end function main
```

Fig. 19.18 | Substrings generated from `Strings`. (Part 1 of 2.)

```
Substring from index 20 to end is "hijklm"
Substring from index 0 of length 6 is "abcdef"
```

Fig. 19.18 | Substrings generated from Strings. (Part 2 of 2.)

The statement in line 14 uses the Substring function that takes one int argument. The argument specifies the starting index from which the function copies characters in the original String. The substring returned contains a copy of the characters from the starting index to the end of the String. If the index specified in the argument is outside the bounds of the String, the program throws an ArgumentOutOfRangeException.

The second version of Substring (line 18) takes two int arguments. The first argument specifies the starting index from which the function copies characters from the original String. The second argument specifies the length of the substring to be copied. The substring returned contains a copy of the specified characters from the original String.

19.19 Concatenating Strings

A few earlier C++/CLI examples showed how the + operator is overloaded for String objects so that you can easily concatenate them together. Remember that Strings are immutable, so concatenating Strings results in a new String object. The + operator is not the only way to perform String concatenation. The static function Concat of class String (Fig. 19.19) concatenates Strings and returns a new String containing the combined characters from both original Strings. Line 17 appends the characters from string2 to the end of a copy of string1, using function Concat. The statement in line 17 does not modify the original Strings.

```cpp
 1   // Fig. 19.19: StringConcatenation.cpp
 2   // Demonstrating String class Concat function.
 3
 4   #include "stdafx.h"
 5
 6   using namespace System;
 7
 8   int main( array< System::String ^ > ^args )
 9   {
10      String ^string1 = "Happy ";
11      String ^string2 = "Birthday";
12
13      Console::WriteLine( "string1 = \"{0}\"", string1 );
14      Console::WriteLine( "string2 = \"{0}\"", string2 );
15      Console::WriteLine(
16         "\nResult of String::Concat( string1, string2 ) = {0}",
17         String::Concat( string1, string2 ) );
18      Console::WriteLine( "string1 after concatenation = \"{0}\"", string1 );
19
20      return 0;
21   } // end function main
```

Fig. 19.19 | Concat static function. (Part 1 of 2.)

```
string1 = "Happy "
string2 = "Birthday"

Result of String::Concat( string1, string2 ) = Happy Birthday
string1 after concatenation = "Happy "
```

Fig. 19.19 | `Concat` static function. (Part 2 of 2.)

In fact, when concatenating `String`s with the + operator the compiler actually calls an overloaded version of `String::Concat` with as many parameters as necessary. For example, if we have declared `String ^` variables `string1`, `string2`, and `string3`, then the statement

> `String ^string4 = string1 + string2 + string3;`

is converted to

> `String ^string4 = String::Concat( string1, string2, string3 );`

by the compiler. This eliminates creating extra copies of `String`s used only for a single statement.

19.20 Miscellaneous `String` Functions

Class `String` provides several functions that return modified copies of `String`s. The application in Fig. 19.20 demonstrates the use of these functions, which include `String` functions `Replace`, `ToLower`, `ToUpper` and `Trim`.

```
1   // Fig. 19.20: StringFunctions2.cpp
2   // Demonstrating String functions Replace, ToLower, ToUpper, Trim,
3   // and ToString.
4
5   #include "stdafx.h"
6
7   using namespace System;
8
9   int main( array< System::String ^ > ^args )
10  {
11      String ^string1 = "cheers!";
12      String ^string2 = "GOOD BYE ";
13      String ^string3 = "   spaces    ";
14
15      Console::WriteLine( "string1 = \"{0}\"", string1 );
16      Console::WriteLine( "string2 = \"}0}\"", string2 );
17      Console::WriteLine( "string3 = \"{0}\"", string3 );
18
19      // call function Replace
20      Console::WriteLine(
21          "\nReplacing \"e\" with \"E\" in string1: \"{0}\"",
22          string1->Replace( 'e', 'E' ) );
```

Fig. 19.20 | `String` functions `Replace`, `ToLower`, `ToUpper` and `Trim`. (Part 1 of 2.)

```
23
24      // call ToLower and ToUpper
25      Console::WriteLine( "\nstring1->ToUpper() = \"{0}\"",
26         string1->ToUpper() );
27      Console::WriteLine( "string2->ToLower() = \"{0}\"",
28         string2->ToLower() );
29
30      // call Trim function
31      Console::WriteLine( "\nstring3 after trim = \"{0}\"",
32         string3->Trim() );
33
34      Console::WriteLine( "\nstring1 = \"{0}\"", string1 );
35
36      return 0;
37   } // end function main
```

```
string1 = "cheers!"
string2 = "GOOD BYE "
string3 = "   spaces   "

Replacing "e" with "E" in string1: "chEErs!"

string1.ToUpper() = "CHEERS!"
string2.ToLower() = "good bye "

string3 after trim = "spaces"

string1 = "cheers!"
```

Fig. 19.20 | String functions Replace, ToLower, ToUpper and Trim. (Part 2 of 2.)

Line 22 uses String function Replace to return a new String, replacing every occurrence in string1 of character 'e' with 'E'. Function Replace takes two arguments—a String for which to search and another String with which to replace all matching occurrences of the first argument. The original String remains unchanged. If there are no occurrences of the first argument in the String, the function returns the original String.

String function ToUpper generates a new String (line 26) that replaces any lowercase letters in string1 with their uppercase equivalents. The function returns a new String containing the converted String; the original String remains unchanged. If there are no characters to convert, a copy of the original String is returned. Line 28 uses String function ToLower to return a new String in which any uppercase letters in string2 are replaced by their lowercase equivalents. The original String is unchanged. As with ToUpper, if there are no characters to convert to lowercase, function ToLower returns a copy of the original String.

Line 32 uses String function Trim to remove all white-space characters that appear at the beginning and end of a String. Without otherwise altering the original String, the function returns a new String that contains the String, but omits leading or trailing white-space characters. Another version of function Trim takes a character array and returns a String that does not contain the characters in the array argument.

19.21   Class **StringBuilder**

The `String` class provides many capabilities for processing `String`s. However a `String`'s contents can never change. Operations that seem to concatenate `String`s are in fact assigning `String` references to newly created `String`s (e.g., the += operator creates a new `String` and assigns the initial `String` reference to the newly created `String`).

The next several sections discuss the features of class `StringBuilder` (namespace `System::Text`), used to create and manipulate dynamic string information—i.e., mutable strings. Every `StringBuilder` can store a certain number of characters that is specified by its capacity. Exceeding the capacity of a `StringBuilder` causes the capacity to expand to accommodate the additional characters. As we will see, members of class `StringBuilder`, such as functions `Append` and `AppendFormat`, can be used for concatenation like the operators + and += for class `String`.

> **Performance Tip 19.3**
>
> *Objects of class `String` are immutable (i.e., constant strings), whereas object of class `String-Builder` are mutable. C++/CLI can perform certain optimizations involving `String`s (such as the sharing of one `String` among multiple references), because it knows these objects will not change.*

Class `StringBuilder` provides six overloaded constructors. The following example (Fig. 19.21) demonstrates three of these overloaded constructors.

```
 1    // Fig. 19.21: StringBuilderConstructor.cpp
 2    // Demonstrating StringBuilder class constructors.
 3
 4    #include "stdafx.h"
 5
 6    using namespace System;
 7    using namespace System::Text;
 8
 9    int main( array< System::String ^ > ^args )
10    {
11        StringBuilder ^buffer1, ^buffer2;
12
13        buffer1 = gcnew StringBuilder();
14        buffer2 = gcnew StringBuilder( 10 );
15        StringBuilder buffer3( "hello" );
16
17        Console::WriteLine( "buffer1 = \"{0}\"", buffer1 );
18        Console::WriteLine( "buffer2 = \"{0}\"", buffer2 );
19        Console::WriteLine( "buffer3 = \"{0}\"", buffer3.ToString() );
20
21        return 0;
22    } // end function main
```

```
buffer1 = ""
buffer2 = ""
buffer3 = "hello"
```

Fig. 19.21 | `StringBuilder` class constructors.

Line 13 employs the no-parameter StringBuilder constructor to create a String-Builder handle that contains no characters and has a default initial capacity of 16 characters. Line 14 uses the StringBuilder constructor that takes an int argument to create a StringBuilder handle that contains no characters and has the initial capacity specified in the int argument (i.e., 10). Line 15 uses stack semantics and the StringBuilder constructor that takes a String argument to create a StringBuilder containing the characters of the String argument. The initial capacity is the smallest power of two greater than or equal to the number of characters in the argument string, with a minimum of 16. Lines 17–18 implicitly use StringBuilder function ToString to obtain String representations of the StringBuilders' contents. Notice that line 19 requires that we explicitly call the ToString function on the StringBuilder we created with stack semantics. Alternatively, we could have used the % operator to return a handle to buffer3. Then ToString would be called implicitly as with buffer1 and buffer2.

19.22 StringBuilder Class Length, Capacity, EnsureCapacity and Indexer

Class StringBuilder provides the Length and Capacity properties to return the number of characters currently in a StringBuilder and the number of characters that a String-Builder can store without allocating more memory, respectively. These properties also can increase or decrease the length or the capacity of the StringBuilder.

Function EnsureCapacity allows you to reduce the number of times that a String-Builder's capacity must be increased. The function doubles the StringBuilder instance's current capacity. If this doubled value is greater than the value that the programmer wishes to ensure, that value becomes the new capacity. Otherwise, EnsureCapacity alters the capacity to make it equal to the requested number. For example, if the current capacity is 17 and we wish to make it 40, 17 multiplied by 2 is not greater than 40, so the call will result in a new capacity of 40. If the current capacity is 23 and we wish to make it 40, 23 will be multiplied by 2 to result in a new capacity of 46. Both 40 and 46 are greater than or equal to 40, so a capacity of 40 is indeed ensured by function EnsureCapacity. The program in Fig. 19.22 demonstrates the use of these functions and properties.

```cpp
1   // Fig. 19.22: StringBuilderFeatures.cpp
2   // Demonstrating some features of class StringBuilder.
3
4   #include "stdafx.h"
5
6   using namespace System;
7   using namespace System::Text;
8
9   int main( array< System::String ^ > ^args )
10  {
11     StringBuilder buffer( "Hello, how are you?" );
12
13     // use Length and Capacity properties
14     Console::WriteLine( "buffer = {0}\nLength = {1}\nCapacity = {2}",
15        buffer.ToString() , buffer.Length, buffer.Capacity );
```

Fig. 19.22 | StringBuilder size manipulation. (Part 1 of 2.)

```
16
17        buffer.EnsureCapacity( 75 ); // ensure a capacity of at least 75
18        Console::WriteLine( "\nNew capacity = {0}", buffer.Capacity );
19
20        // truncate StringBuilder by setting Length property
21        buffer.Length = 10;
22        Console::Write( "\nNew length = {0}\nbuffer = ", buffer.Length );
23
24        // use StringBuilder indexer
25        for ( int i = 0; i < buffer.Length; i++ )
26           Console::Write( buffer[ i ] );
27
28        Console::WriteLine();
29
30        return 0;
31    } // end function main
```

```
buffer = Hello, how are you?
Length = 19
Capacity = 32

New capacity = 75

New length = 10
buffer = Hello, how
```

Fig. 19.22 | `StringBuilder` size manipulation. (Part 2 of 2.)

Line 11 creates a `StringBuilder` called `buffer` using stack semantics and the `StringBuilder` constructor that takes a `String` argument (`"Hello, how are you?"`). Lines 14–15 output the content, length and capacity of the `StringBuilder`. In the output window, notice that the capacity of the `StringBuilder` is initially 32. Remember, the `StringBuilder` constructor that takes a `String` argument creates a `StringBuilder` object with an initial capacity that is the smallest power of two greater than or equal to the number of characters in the `String` passed as an argument.

Line 17 expands the capacity of the `StringBuilder` to a minimum of 75 characters. The current capacity (32) multiplied by two is less than 75, so function `EnsureCapacity` increases the capacity to 75. If new characters are added to a `StringBuilder` so that its length exceeds its capacity, the capacity grows to accommodate the additional characters in the same manner as if function `EnsureCapacity` had been called.

Line 21 uses property `Length` to set the length of the `StringBuilder` to 10. If the specified length is less than the current number of characters in the `StringBuilder`, the contents of the `StringBuilder` are truncated to the specified length. If the specified length is greater than the number of characters currently in the `StringBuilder`, space characters are appended to the `StringBuilder` until the total number of characters in the `StringBuilder` is equal to the specified length.

 Common Programming Error 19.7

Assigning `nullptr` to a `String` reference can lead to logic errors if you attempt to compare `nullptr` to an empty `String`. The keyword `nullptr` is a value that represents a null reference (i.e., a reference that does not refer to an object), not an empty `String` (which is a `String` object that is of length 0 and contains no characters).

19.23 StringBuilder Class Append and AppendFormat Functions

Class StringBuilder provides 19 overloaded Append functions that allow various types of values to be added to the end of a StringBuilder. The FCL provides versions for each of the simple types and for character arrays, Strings and Objects. (Remember that function ToString produces a String representation of any Object.) Each of the functions takes an argument, converts it to a String and appends it to the StringBuilder. Figure 19.23 demonstrates the use of several Append functions.

```cpp
1   // Fig. 19.23: StringBuilderAppend.cpp
2   // Demonstrating StringBuilder Append functions.
3
4   #include "stdafx.h"
5
6   using namespace System;
7   using namespace System::Text;
8
9   int main( array< System::String ^ > ^args )
10  {
11     Object ^objectValue = "hello";
12     String ^stringValue = "good bye";
13     array< Char >^ characterArray = { 'a', 'b', 'c', 'd', 'e', 'f' };
14     bool booleanValue = true;
15     Char characterValue = 'Z';
16     int integerValue = 7;
17     long longValue = 1000000;
18     float floatValue = 2.5F; // F suffix indicates that 2.5 is a float
19     double doubleValue = 33.333;
20     StringBuilder buffer;
21
22     // use function Append to append values to buffer
23     buffer.Append( objectValue );
24     buffer.Append( "  " );
25     buffer.Append( stringValue );
26     buffer.Append( "  " );
27     buffer.Append( characterArray );
28     buffer.Append( "  " );
29     buffer.Append( characterArray, 0, 3 );
30     buffer.Append( "  " );
31     buffer.Append( booleanValue );
32     buffer.Append( "  " );
33     buffer.Append( characterValue );
34     buffer.Append( "  " );
35     buffer.Append( integerValue );
36     buffer.Append( "  " );
37     buffer.Append( longValue );
38     buffer.Append( "  " );
39     buffer.Append( floatValue );
40     buffer.Append( "  " );
41     buffer.Append( doubleValue );
```

Fig. 19.23 | Append functions of StringBuilder. (Part 1 of 2.)

```
42
43          Console::WriteLine( "buffer = {0}", buffer.ToString() );
44
45          return 0;
46      } // end function main
```

```
buffer = hello  good bye  abcdef  abc  True  Z  7  1000000  2.5  33.333
```

Fig. 19.23 | Append functions of `StringBuilder`. (Part 2 of 2.)

Lines 23–41 use 10 different overloaded `Append` functions to attach the string representations of objects created in lines 11–19 to the end of the `StringBuilder`. `Append` behaves similarly to the + operator, which is used to concatenate `String`s.

Class `StringBuilder` also provides function `AppendFormat`, which converts a `String` to a specified format, then appends it to the `StringBuilder`. The example in Fig. 19.24 demonstrates the use of this function.

```
1   // Fig. 19.24: StringBuilderAppendFormat.cpp
2   // Demonstrating function AppendFormat.
3
4   #include "stdafx.h"
5
6   using namespace System;
7   using namespace System::Text;
8
9   int main( array< System::String ^ > ^args )
10  {
11      StringBuilder buffer;
12      String ^string1, ^string2;
13
14      // formatted string
15      string1 = "This {0} costs: {1:C}.\n";
16
17      // string1 argument array
18      array< Object^ >^ objectArray = gcnew array< Object^ >( 2 );
19
20      objectArray[ 0 ] = "car";
21      objectArray[ 1 ] = 1234.56;
22
23      // append to buffer formatted string with argument
24      buffer.AppendFormat( string1, objectArray );
25
26      // formatted string
27      string2 = "Number:{0:d3}.\n" +
28          "Number right aligned with spaces:{0, 4}.\n" +
29          "Number left aligned with spaces:{0, -4}.";
30
31      // append to buffer formatted string with argument
32      buffer.AppendFormat( string2, 5 );
33
```

Fig. 19.24 | `StringBuilder`'s `AppendFormat` function. (Part 1 of 2.)

```
34      // display formatted strings
35      Console::WriteLine( buffer.ToString() );
36
37      return 0;
38  } // end function main
```

```
This car costs: $1,234.56.
Number:005.
Number right aligned with spaces:    5.
Number left aligned with spaces:5    .
```

Fig. 19.24 | StringBuilder's AppendFormat function. (Part 2 of 2.)

Line 15 creates a String that contains formatting information. The information enclosed in braces specifies how to format a specific piece of data. Formats have the form {X[,Y][:FormatString]}, where X is the number of the argument to be formatted, counting from zero. Y is an optional argument, which can be positive or negative, indicating how many characters should be in the result. If the resulting String is less than the number Y, the String will be padded with spaces to make up for the difference. A positive integer aligns the String to the right; a negative integer aligns it to the left. The optional FormatString applies a particular format to the argument—currency, decimal or scientific, among others. In this case, "{0}" means the first argument will be printed out. "{1:C}" specifies that the second argument will be formatted as a currency value.

Line 24 shows a version of AppendFormat that takes two parameters—a String specifying the format and a managed array of objects to serve as the arguments to the format String. The argument referred to by "{0}" is in the object array at index 0.

Lines 27–29 define another String used for formatting. The first format "{0:d3}", specifies that the first argument will be formatted as a three-digit decimal, meaning any number that has fewer than three digits will have leading zeros placed in front to make up the difference. The next format, "{0, 4}", specifies that the formatted String should have four characters and should be right aligned. The third format, "{0, -4}", specifies that the Strings should be aligned to the left. For more formatting options, please refer to the online help documentation.

Line 32 uses a version of AppendFormat that takes two parameters—a String containing a format and an object to which the format is applied. In this case, the object is the number 5. The output of Fig. 19.24 displays the result of applying these two versions of AppendFormat with their respective arguments.

19.24 StringBuilder Class Insert, Remove and Replace Functions

Class StringBuilder provides 18 overloaded Insert functions to allow various types of data to be inserted at any position in a StringBuilder. The class provides versions for each of the simple types and for character arrays, Strings and Objects. Each function takes its second argument, converts it to a String and inserts the String into the StringBuilder in front of the character in the position specified by the first argument. The index specified by the first argument must be greater than or equal to 0 and less than the length of the StringBuilder; otherwise, the program throws an ArgumentOutOfRangeException.

Class `StringBuilder` also provides function `Remove` for deleting any portion of a `StringBuilder`. Function `Remove` takes two arguments—the index at which to begin deletion and the number of characters to delete. The sum of the starting index and the number of characters to be deleted must always be less than the length of the `StringBuilder`; otherwise, the program throws an `ArgumentOutOfRangeException`. The `Insert` and `Remove` functions are demonstrated in Fig. 19.25.

```
 1   // Fig. 19.25: StringBuilderInsertRemove.cpp
 2   // Demonstrating functions Insert and Remove of the StringBuilder class
 3
 4   #include "stdafx.h"
 5
 6   using namespace System;
 7   using namespace System::Text;
 8
 9   int main( array< System::String ^ > ^args )
10   {
11      Object ^objectValue = "hello";
12      String ^stringValue = "good bye";
13      array< Char >^ characterArray = { 'a', 'b', 'c', 'd', 'e', 'f' };
14      bool booleanValue = true;
15      Char characterValue = 'K';
16      int integerValue = 7;
17      long longValue = 10000000;
18      float floatValue = 2.5F; // F suffix indicates that 2.5 is a float
19      double doubleValue = 33.333;
20      StringBuilder buffer;
21
22      // insert values into buffer
23      buffer.Insert( 0, objectValue );
24      buffer.Insert( 0, "  " );
25      buffer.Insert( 0, stringValue );
26      buffer.Insert( 0, "  " );
27      buffer.Insert( 0, characterArray );
28      buffer.Insert( 0, "  " );
29      buffer.Insert( 0, booleanValue );
30      buffer.Insert( 0, "  " );
31      buffer.Insert( 0, characterValue );
32      buffer.Insert( 0, "  " );
33      buffer.Insert( 0, integerValue );
34      buffer.Insert( 0, "  " );
35      buffer.Insert( 0, longValue );
36      buffer.Insert( 0, "  " );
37      buffer.Insert( 0, floatValue );
38      buffer.Insert( 0, "  " );
39      buffer.Insert( 0, doubleValue );
40      buffer.Insert( 0, "  " );
41
42      Console::WriteLine( "buffer after Inserts:\n{0}", buffer );
43
44      buffer.Remove( 10, 1 ); // delete 2 in 2.5
45      buffer.Remove( 4, 4 );  // delete .333 in 33.333
```

Fig. 19.25 | `StringBuilder` text insertion and removal. (Part 1 of 2.)

```
46
47      Console::WriteLine( "buffer after Removes:\n{0}", buffer.ToString() );
48
49      return 0;
50   } // end function main
```

```
buffer after Inserts:
  33.333  2.5  10000000  7  K  True  abcdef  good bye  hello

buffer after Removes:
  33  .5  10000000  7  K  True  abcdef  good bye  hello
```

Fig. 19.25 | `StringBuilder` text insertion and removal. (Part 2 of 2.)

Another useful function included with `StringBuilder` is `Replace`. `Replace` searches for a specified `String` or character and substitutes another `String` or character in its place. Figure 19.26 demonstrates this function.

```
1    // Fig. 19.26: StringBuilderReplace.cpp
2    // Demonstrating function Replace.
3
4    #include "stdafx.h"
5
6    using namespace System;
7    using namespace System::Text;
8
9    int main( array< System::String ^ > ^args )
10   {
11      StringBuilder ^builder1 =
12         gcnew StringBuilder( "Happy Birthday Jane" );
13      StringBuilder builder2( "good bye greg" );
14
15      Console::WriteLine( "Before replacements:\n{0}\n{1}",
16         builder1, builder2.ToString() );
17
18      builder1->Replace( "Jane", "Greg" );
19      builder2.Replace( 'g', 'G', 0, 5 );
20
21      Console::WriteLine( "\nAfter replacements:\n{0}\n{1}",
22         builder1, builder2.ToString() );
23
24      return 0;
25   } // end function main
```

```
Before Replacements:
Happy Birthday Jane
good bye greg

After replacements:
Happy Birthday Greg
Good bye greg
```

Fig. 19.26 | `StringBuilder` text replacement.

Line 18 uses function `Replace` to replace all instances of the `String` "Jane" with the `String` "Greg" in builder1. Another overload of this function takes two characters as parameters and replaces each occurrence of the first character with the second character. Line 19 uses an overload of `Replace` that takes four parameters, of which the first two are characters and the second two are `int`s. The function replaces all instances of the first character with the second character, beginning at the index specified by the first `int` and continuing for a count specified by the second `int`. Thus, in this case, `Replace` looks through only five characters, starting with the character at index 0. As the output illustrates, this version of `Replace` replaces g with G in the word "good", but not in "greg". This is because the gs in "greg" are not in the range indicated by the `int` arguments (i.e., between indexes 0 and 4).

19.25 Char Functions

In C++/CLI, the simple types are actually aliases for FCL value types—an `int` is defined by class `System::Int32`, a `long` by `System::Int64` and so on. Recall that all of these types derive from class **ValueType**, which in turn derives from `Object`. Also, they are all implicitly `sealed` so they do not support `abstract` functions. This means existing value types cannot be used as base classes for user defined value types, though value types can implement interfaces. Remember that instances of value types are created on the stack just as you would expect from simple types in native C++. Until now these aliases in C++/CLI have been transparent and not affected by the way you code C++/CLI compared to native C++.

As you've learned, in native C++ char is a built-in type that holds one signed byte. With one signed byte you can represent integers from −127 to 128. This is useful for representing individual letters, digits, or symbols. However, one signed byte isn't enough to represent every character type, especially when you consider foreign languages. To solve this problem, some languages (including C++/CLI and other .NET languages) make characters a two-byte type. In C++/CLI char isn't an alias to type `System::Char` as you might expect. Class **Char** is a two-byte type designed to represent a wider range of characters. As a result, char is an alias to type `System::SByte` (meaning signed byte). You can use it to represent integers ranging from -127 to 128 just as in native C++. In managed code with C++/CLI you should use class `Char` to create variables that represent characters. Alternatively, in C++/CLI the type `wchar_t` mentioned in Section 19.1 is an alias to type `Char`.

While native C++ strings are composed of one-byte char variables, managed `Strings` are composed of two-byte `Char` objects. You have seen examples earlier in this chapter using managed arrays of type `Char` to build managed strings. Class `String` doesn't provide a constructor that takes an array of type char (which is really type `System::SByte`). `Console::WriteLine` and related functions contain separate overloaded versions for class `Char` and class `SByte`. If you try to use `Console::WriteLine` to print a variable of type char, you see only the integer value of that variable. Using a variable of type `Char`, on the other hand, properly outputs the character value. To print the value of a char with `Console::WriteLine` you need to first cast the char to `Char`.

In this section, we present class Char. Most Char functions are `static`, take at least one character argument and perform either a test or a manipulation on the character. We present several of these functions in the next example. Figure 19.27 demonstrates `static` functions that test characters to determine whether they are of a specific character type and `static` functions that perform case conversions on characters

```
 1    // Fig. 19.27: StaticCharFunctions.cpp
 2    // Demonstrates static character testing functions from class Char
 3
 4    #include "stdafx.h"
 5
 6    using namespace System;
 7
 8    int main( array< System::String ^ > ^args )
 9    {
10       // convert string entered to type Char
11       Console::WriteLine( "Enter a character." );
12       Char character = Convert::ToChar( Console::ReadLine() );
13
14       Console::WriteLine( "is digit: {0}", Char::IsDigit( character ) );
15       Console::WriteLine( "is letter: {0}", Char::IsLetter( character ) );
16       Console::WriteLine( "is letter or digit: {0}",
17          Char::IsLetterOrDigit( character ) );
18       Console::WriteLine( "is lower case: {0}", Char::IsLower( character ) );
19       Console::WriteLine( "is upper case: {0}", Char::IsUpper( character ) );
20       Console::WriteLine( "to lower case: {0}", Char::ToLower( character ) );
21       Console::WriteLine( "to upper case: {0}", Char::ToUpper( character ) );
22       Console::WriteLine( "is punctuation: {0}",
23          Char::IsPunctuation( character ) );
24       Console::WriteLine( "is symbol: {0}", Char::IsSymbol( character ) );
25
26       return 0;
27    } // end function main
```

```
Enter a character.
a
is digit: False
is letter: True
is letter or digit: True
is lower case: True
is upper case: False
to lower case: a
to upper case: A
is punctuation: False
is symbol: False
```

Fig. 19.27 | Char's static character-testing and case-conversion functions.

This program reads a string from the console and converts it to a character using function Convert::ToChar (lines 12). Line 14 uses Char function IsDigit to determine whether character is defined as a digit. If so, the function returns true; otherwise, it returns false (note again that bool values are output capitalized). Line 15 uses Char function IsLetter to determine whether character character is a letter. Line 16 uses Char function IsLetterOrDigit to determine whether character character is a letter or a digit.

Line 18 uses Char function IsLower to determine whether character character is a lowercase letter. Line 19 uses Char function IsUpper to determine whether character character is an uppercase letter. Line 20 uses Char function ToLower to convert character character to its lowercase equivalent. The function returns the converted character if the character has a lowercase equivalent; otherwise, the function returns its original argument. Line 21 uses `Char` function `ToUpper` to convert character `character` to its uppercase equivalent. The function returns the converted character if the character has an uppercase equivalent; otherwise, the function returns its original argument.

Line 23 uses `Char` function `IsPunctuation` to determine whether `character` is a punctuation mark, such as "`!`", "`:`" or "`)`". Line 24 uses `Char` function `IsSymbol` to determine whether character `character` is a symbol, such as "`+`", "`=`" or "`^`".

Class `Char` also contains other functions not shown in this example. Many of the `static` functions are similar—for instance, `IsWhiteSpace` is used to determine whether a certain character is a white-space character (e.g., newline, tab or space). It also contains several `public` instance functions; many of these, such as functions `ToString` and `Equals`, are functions that we have seen before in other classes. This group includes function `CompareTo`, which is used to compare two character values with one another.

19.26 Wrap-Up

This chapter introduced the class `string` from the C++ Standard Library, which allows programs to treat strings as full-fledged objects. We discussed assigning, concatenating, comparing, searching and swapping strings. We also introduced a number of methods to determine string characteristics, to find, replace and insert characters in a string, and to convert strings to C-style strings and vice versa. You also learned about string iterators and performing input from and output to strings in memory.

You also learned about the FCL's `String` class and character-processing capabilities in managed code with C++/CLI. We overviewed the fundamentals of characters and strings. You saw how to determine the length of strings, copy strings, access the individual characters in strings, search strings, obtain substrings from larger strings, compare strings, concatenate strings, replace characters in strings and convert strings to uppercase or lowercase letters.

We showed how to use class `StringBuilder` to build strings dynamically. You learned how to determine and specify the size of a `StringBuilder` object, and how to append, insert, remove and replace characters in a `StringBuilder` object. We then introduced the character-testing functions of type `Char` that enable a program to determine whether a character is a digit, a letter, a lowercase letter, an uppercase letter, a punctuation mark or a symbol other than a punctuation mark, and the functions for converting a character to uppercase or lowercase.

In Chapter 20, Searching and Sorting, we discuss the binary search algorithm and the merge sort algorithm. We also use Big O notation to analyze and compare the efficiency of various searching and sorting algorithms.

Summary

Section 19.1 Introduction
- C++ class template `basic_string` provides typical string-manipulation operations such as copying, searching, etc.
- The `typedef` statement

    typedef basic_string< **char** > string;

creates the alias type string for basic_string< char >. A typedef also is provided for the wchar_t type. Type wchar_t normally stores two-byte (16-bit) characters for supporting other character sets. The size of wchar_t is not fixed by the standard.

- To use strings, include C++ Standard Library header file <string>.
- Class string provides no constructors that convert from int or char to string.
- Assigning a single character to a string object is permitted in an assignment statement.
- strings are not necessarily null terminated.
- Most string member functions take as arguments a starting subscript location and the number of characters on which to operate.

Section 19.2 string Assignment and Concatenation
- Class string provides overloaded operator= and member function assign for string assignments.
- The subscript operator, [], provides read/write access to any element of a string.
- string member function at provides checked access—going past either end of the string throws an out_of_range exception. The subscript operator, [], does not provide checked access.
- Class string provides the overloaded + and += operators and member function append to perform string concatenation.

Section 19.3 Comparing strings
- Class string provides overloaded ==, !=, <, >, <= and >= operators for string comparisons.
- string member function compare compares two strings (or substrings) and returns 0 if the strings are equal, a positive number if the first string is lexicographically greater than the second or a negative number if the first string is lexicographically less than the second.

Section 19.4 Substrings
- string member function substr retrieves a substring from a string.

Section 19.5 Swapping strings
- string member function swap swaps the contents of two strings.

Section 19.6 string Characteristics
- string member functions size and length return the size or length of a string (i.e., the number of characters currently stored in the string).
- string member function capacity returns the total number of characters that can be stored in the string without increasing the amount of memory allocated to the string.
- string member function max_size returns the maximum size a string can have.
- string member function resize changes the length of a string.

Section 19.7 Finding Substrings and Characters in a string
- Class string find functions find, rfind, find_first_of, find_last_of and find_first_not_of locate substrings or characters in a string.

Section 19.8 Replacing Characters in a string
- string member function erase deletes elements of a string.
- string member function replace replaces characters in a string.

Section 19.9 Inserting Characters into a `string`

- `string` member function `insert` inserts characters in a `string`.

Section 19.10 Conversion to C-Style Pointer-Based `char *` Strings

- `string` member function `c_str` returns a `const char *` pointing to a null-terminated C-style character string that contains all the characters in a `string`.

- `string` member function `data` returns a `const char *` pointing to a non-null-terminated C-style character array that contains all the characters in a `string`.

Section 19.11 Iterators

- Class `string` provides member functions `end` and `begin` to iterate through individual elements.

- Class `string` provides member functions `rend` and `rbegin` for accessing individual `string` characters in reverse from the end of a `string` toward the beginning.

Section 19.12 String Stream Processing

- Input from a `string` is supported by type `istringstream`. Output to a `string` is supported by type `ostringstream`.

- `ostringstream` member function `str` returns a `string` copy of a `string`.

Section 19.13 Fundamentals of Characters and Strings in C++/CLI

- Characters are the fundamental building blocks of C++/CLI program code. Every program is composed of a sequence of characters that is interpreted by the compiler as a series of instructions used to accomplish a task.

- A `String` is a series of two-byte characters treated as a single unit. A `String` may include letters, digits and the various special characters: +, -, *, /, $ and others.

Section 19.14 String Constructors

- Class `String` has 8 different constructors to initialize `String` variables with. These include a constructor that takes an array of `Char` and one that takes a single `Char` and an integer specifying the number of copies of that `Char`.

Section 19.15 String Indexer, Length Property, and CopyTo Function

- Class `String`'s indexer allows array-like syntax to access to any character in the `String`.

- Use the `Length` property to access a `String`'s length.

- Function `CopyTo` copies a specified number of characters from a `String` into a `Char` array.

Section 19.16 Comparing Strings

- All characters correspond to numeric codes. When the computer compares two `Strings`, it actually compares the Unicode values of the characters in the `Strings`.

- Function `Equals` uses a lexicographical comparison—if a certain `String` has a higher value than another `String`, it would be found later in a dictionary.

- Function `CompareTo` returns 0 if the `Strings` are equal, a negative number if the `String` that invokes `CompareTo` is less than the `String` passed as an argument and a positive number if the `string` that invokes `CompareTo` is greater than the `String` passed as an argument. Function `CompareTo` uses a lexicographical comparison.

- `String` function `StartsWith` determines whether a `String` starts with the characters specified as an argument. `String` function `EndsWith` determines whether a `String` ends with the characters specified as an argument.

Section 19.17 Locating Characters and Substrings in Strings
- String function IndexOf locates the first occurrence of a character or a substring in a String. Function LastIndexOf locates the last occurrence of a character or a substring in a String.

Section 19.18 Extracting Substrings from Strings
- Class String provides two Substring functions to enable a new String to be created by copying part of an existing String.

Section 19.19 Concatenating Strings
- The static function Concat of class String concatenates two String and returns a new String containing the characters from both original Strings.

Section 19.20 Miscellaneous String Functions
- Functions Replace, ToUpper, ToLower, Trim and Remove are provided for more advanced String manipulation.

Section 19.21 Class StringBuilder
- Once a String is created, its contents can never change. Class StringBuilder is available for creating and manipulating Strings that can change.

Section 19.22 StringBuilder Class Length, Capacity, EnsureCapacity and Indexer
- Class StringBuilder provides Length and Capacity properties to return the number of characters currently in a StringBuilder and the number of characters that can be stored in a StringBuilder without allocating more memory, respectively. These properties also can be used to increase or decrease the length or the capacity of the StringBuilder.

- Function EnsureCapacity allows you to guarantee that a StringBuilder has a minimum capacity. Function EnsureCapacity attempts to double the capacity. If this value is greater than the value that you wish to ensure, this will be the new capacity. Otherwise, EnsureCapacity alters the capacity to make it equal to the requested number.

Section 19.23 StringBuilder Class Append and AppendFormat Functions
- Class StringBuilder provides 19 overloaded Append functions to allow various types of values to be added to the end of a StringBuilder. Versions are provided for each of the simple types and for character arrays, Strings and Objects.

- The braces in a format string specify how to format a specific piece of information. Formats have the form {X[,Y][:FormatString]}, where X is the number of the argument to be formatted, counting from zero. Y is an optional argument, which can be positive or negative. Y indicates how many characters should be in the result of formatting. If the resulting String has fewer characters than this number, it will be padded with spaces to make up for the difference. A positive integer means the String will be right aligned; a negative one means the String will be left aligned. The optional FormatString indicates what kind of formatting should be applied to the argument—currency, decimal, or scientific, among others.

Section 19.24 StringBuilder Class Insert, Remove and Replace Functions
- Class StringBuilder provides 18 overloaded Insert functions to allow various types of values to be inserted at any position in a StringBuilder. Versions are provided for each of the simple types and for character arrays, Strings and Objects.

- Class StringBuilder also provides function Remove for deleting any portion of a StringBuilder.

- StringBuilder function Replace searches for a specified String or character and substitutes another in its place.

Section 19.25 Char Functions

- The simple types in native C++ are actually aliases for FCL `value class` types in C++/CLI.
- All value types derive from class `ValueType`, which in turn derives from `Object`.
- All value types are implicitly `sealed`, so they do not support `abstract` functions.
- `Char` is a class that represents characters with two-bytes of storage.
- Type `char` is an alias for type `System::SByte` in C++/CLI, not `System::Char`.
- Function `Char::Parse` converts `String` data into a character.
- Function `Char::IsDigit` determines whether a character is a defined Unicode digit.
- Function `Char::IsLetter` determines whether a character is a letter.
- Function `Char::IsLetterOrDigit` determines whether a character is a letter or a digit.
- Function `Char::IsLower` determines whether a character is a lowercase letter, if appropriate.
- Function `Char::IsUpper` determines whether a character is an uppercase letter, if appropriate.
- Function `Char::ToUpper` converts a lowercase character to its uppercase equivalent.
- Function `Char::ToLower` converts an uppercase character to its lowercase equivalent.
- Function `Char::IsPunctuation` determines whether a character is a punctuation mark.
- Function `Char::IsSymbol` determines whether a character is a symbol.
- Function `Char::IsWhiteSpace` determines whether a character is a white-space character.
- Function `Char::CompareTo` compares two character values.

Terminology

C++ Terminology

append member function of class string
assign member function of class string
at member function of class string
basic_string class template
begin member function of class string
c_str member function of class string
capacity of a string
capacity member function of class string
checked access
compare member function of class string
concatenation
const_iterator
const_reverse_iterator
copy member function of class string
data member function of class string
empty string
end member function of class string
erase member function of class string
find member function of class string
find_first_not_of member function of class string
find_first_of member function of class string
find_last_of member function of class string
getline member function of class string

in-memory I/O
insert member function of class string
istringstream class
iterator
length member function of class string
length of a string
lexicographical comparison
max_size member function of class string
maximum size of a string
ostringstream class
range checking
rbegin member function of class string
rend member function of class string
replace member function of class string
resize member function of class string
reverse_iterator
rfind member function of class string
size member function of class string
<sstream> header file
str member function of class ostringstream
string::npos constant
string stream processing
substr member function of class string
swap member function of class string
wchar_t type

C++/CLI Terminology

+ operator

+= concatenation operator

== equality operator

alphabetizing

Append function of class StringBuilder

AppendFormat function of class StringBuilder

ArgumentOutOfRangeException

Capacity property of StringBuilder

Char array

Char class

Chars property of class String

character

character constant

CompareTo function of class String

CompareTo function of class Char

Concat function of class String

CopyTo function of class String

EndsWith function of class String

EnsureCapacity function of class
    StringBuilder

Equals function of class String

Equals function of class Char

format string

immutable String

IndexOf function of class String

IndexOfAny function of class String

Insert function of class StringBuilder

IsDigit function of class Char

IsLetter function of class Char

IsLetterOrDigit function of class Char

IsLower function of class Char

IsPunctuation function of class Char

IsSymbol function of class Char

IsUpper function of class Char

IsWhiteSpace function of class Char

LastIndexOf function of class String

LastIndexOfAny function of class String

lazy quantifier

Length property of class String

Length property of class StringBuilder

lexicographical comparison

Remove function of class StringBuilder

Replace function of class String

Replace function of class StringBuilder

special characters

StartsWith function of class String

String class

string literal

String reference

StringBuilder class

Substring function of class String

System namespace

System::Text namespace

ToLower function of class String

ToLower function of class Char

ToString function of class String

ToString function of StringBuilder

ToUpper function of class String

ToUpper function of class Char

trailing white-space characters

Trim function of class String

Unicode character set

ValueType class

verbatim string syntax

white-space character

word character

Self-Review Exercises

19.1 Fill in the blanks in each of the following:

    a) Header _____ must be included for class string.

    b) Class string belongs to the _____ namespace.

    c) Function _____ deletes characters from a string.

    d) Function _____ finds the first occurrence of any character from a string.

19.2 State which of the following statements are *true* and which are *false*. If a statement is *false*, explain why.

    a) Concatenation of string objects can be performed with the addition assignment operator, +=.

    b) Characters within a string begin at index 0.

    c) The assignment operator, =, copies a string.

    d) A C-style string is a string object.

19.3 Find the error(s) in each of the following, and explain how to correct it (them):

a) `string string1( 28 ); // construct string1`
`string string2( 'z' ); // construct string2`

b) `// assume std namespace is known`
`const char *ptr = name.data(); // name is "joe bob"`
`ptr[ 3 ] = '-';`
`cout << ptr << endl;`

19.4 Regarding C++/CLI, state whether each of the following is *true* or *false*. If *false*, explain why.

a) When `Strings` are compared with `==`, the result is `true` if the `Strings` contain the same values.

b) A `String` can be modified after it is created.

c) `StringBuilder` function `EnsureCapacity` sets the `StringBuilder` instance's length to the argument's value.

d) Function `Equals` and the equality operator work the same for `Strings`.

e) Function `Trim` removes all white space at the beginning and the end of a `String`.

f) It is always better to use `Strings`, rather than `StringBuilders`, because `Strings` containing the same value will reference the same object in memory.

g) `String` function `ToUpper` creates a new `String` with the first letter capitalized.

19.5 Regarding C++/CLI, fill in the blanks in each of the following statements:

a) To concatenate `Strings`, use the _____ operator, `StringBuilder` function _____ or `String` function _____.

b) Function `Compare` of class `String` uses a(n) _____ comparison of `Strings`.

c) `StringBuilder` function _____ first formats the specified `String`, then concatenates it to the end of the `StringBuilder`.

d) If the arguments to a `Substring` function call are out of range, a(n) _____ exception is thrown.

e) A C in a format string means to output the number as _____.

Answers to Self-Review Exercises

19.1 a) `<string>`. b) `std`. c) `erase`. d) `find_first_of`.

19.2 a) True.
b) True.
c) True.
d) False. A `string` is an object that provides many different services. A C-style string does not provide any services. C-style strings are null terminated; `strings` are not necessarily null terminated. C-style strings are pointers and `strings` are objects.

19.3 a) Constructors for class `string` do not exist for integer and character arguments. Other valid constructors should be used—converting the arguments to `strings` if need be.
b) Function `data` does not add a null terminator. Also, the code attempts to modify a `const char`. Replace all of the lines with the code:
`cout << name.substr( 0, 3 ) + "-" + name.substr( 4 ) << endl;`

19.4 a) True. b) False. `Strings` are immutable; they cannot be modified after they are created. `StringBuilder` objects can be modified after they are created. c) False. `EnsureCapacity` sets the instance's capacity to either double the current capacity or the value of its argument, whichever is larger. d) True. e) True. f) False. `StringBuilder` should be used if the `String` is to be modified. g) False. `String` function `ToUpper` creates a new `String` with all of its letters capitalized.

19.5 a) `+`, `Append`, `Concat`. b) lexicographical. c) `AppendFormat` d) `ArgumentOutOfRangeException`. e) currency.

Exercises

19.6 Fill in the blanks in each of the following:

    a) Class `string` member functions _____ and _____ convert `string`s to C-style strings.

    b) Class `string` member function _____ is used for assignment.

    c) _____ is the return type of function `rbegin`.

    d) Class `string` member function _____ is used to retrieve a substring.

19.7 State which of the following statements are *true* and which are *false*. If a statement is *false*, explain why.

    a) `string`s are always null terminated.

    b) Class `string` member function `max_size` returns the maximum size for a `string`.

    c) Class `string` member function `at` can throw an `out_of_range` exception.

    d) Class `string` member function `begin` returns an `iterator`.

19.8 Find any errors in the following and explain how to correct them:

    a) `std::cout << s.data() << std::endl; // s is "hello"`

    b) `erase( s.rfind( "x" ), 1 ); // s is "xenon"`

    c)
```
string& foo()
{
    string s( "Hello" );
    ...    // other statements
    return;
} // end function foo
```

19.9 (*Simple Encryption*) Some information on the Internet may be encrypted with a simple algorithm known as "rot13," which rotates each character by 13 positions in the alphabet. Thus, `'a'` corresponds to `'n'`, and `'x'` corresponds to `'k'`. rot13 is an example of *symmetric key encryption*. With symmetric key encryption, both the encrypter and decrypter use the same key.

    a) Write a program that encrypts a message using rot13.

    b) Write a program that decrypts the scrambled message using 13 as the key.

    c) After writing the programs of part (a) and part (b), briefly answer the following question: If you did not know the key for part (b), how difficult do you think it would be to break the code? What if you had access to substantial computing power (e.g., supercomputers)? In Exercise 19.28 we ask you to write a program to accomplish this.

19.10 Write a program using iterators that demonstrates the use of functions `rbegin` and `rend`.

19.11 Write a program that reads in several `string`s and prints only those ending in "r" or "ay". Only lowercase letters should be considered.

19.12 Write a program that demonstrates passing a `string` both by reference and by value.

19.13 Write a program that separately inputs a first name and a last name and concatenates the two into a new `string`.

19.14 Write a program that plays the game of Hangman. The program should pick a word (which is either coded directly into the program or read from a text file) and display the following:

```
Guess the word:    XXXXXX
```

Each X represents a letter. The user tries to guess the letters in the word. The appropriate response yes or no should be displayed after each guess. After each incorrect guess, display the diagram with another body part filled. After seven incorrect guesses, the user should be hanged. The display should look as follows:

```
    0
   /|\
    |
   / \
```

After each guess, display all user guesses. If the user guesses the word correctly, the program should display

```
Congratulations!!! You guessed my word. Play again? yes/no
```

19.15   Write a program that inputs a `string` and prints the `string` backward. Convert all uppercase characters to lowercase and all lowercase characters to uppercase.

19.16   Write a program that uses the comparison capabilities introduced in this chapter to alphabetize a series of animal names. Only uppercase letters should be used for the comparisons.

19.17   Write a program that creates a cryptogram out of a `string`. A cryptogram is a message or word in which each letter is replaced with another letter. For example the `string`

```
The bird was named squawk
```

might be scrambled to form

```
cin vrjs otz ethns zxqtop
```

Note that spaces are not scrambled. In this particular case, 'T' was replaced with 'x', each 'a' was replaced with 'h', etc. Uppercase letters become lowercase letters in the cryptogram. Use techniques similar to those in Exercise 19.9.

19.18   Modify Exercise 19.17 to allow the user to solve the cryptogram. The user should input two characters at a time: The first character specifies a letter in the cryptogram, and the second letter specifies the replacement letter. If the replacement letter is correct, replace the letter in the cryptogram with the replacement letter in uppercase.

19.19   Write a program that inputs a sentence and counts the number of palindromes in it. A palindrome is a word that reads the same backward and forward. For example, "tree" is not a palindrome, but "noon" is.

19.20   Write a program that counts the total number of vowels in a sentence. Output the frequency of each vowel.

19.21   Write a program that inserts the characters "******" in the exact middle of a `string`.

19.22   Write a program that erases the sequences "by" and "BY" from a `string`.

19.23   Write a program that inputs a line of text, replaces all punctuation marks with spaces and uses the C-string library function `strtok` to tokenize the `string` into individual words.

19.24   Write a program that inputs a line of text and prints the text backward. Use iterators in your solution.

19.25   Write a recursive version of Exercise 19.24.

19.26   Write a program that demonstrates the use of the `erase` functions that take `iterator` arguments.

19.27   Write a program that generates the following from the `string` "abcdefghijklmnopqrstu-vwxyz{":

```
            a
           bcb
          cdedc
         defgfed
        efghihgfe
       fghijkjihgf
      ghijklmlkjihg
     hijklmnonmlkjih
    ijklmnopqponmlkji
   jklmnopqrsrqponmlkj
  klmnopqrstutsrqponmlk
 lmnopqrstuvwvutsrqponml
mnopqrstuvwxyxwvutsrqponm
nopqrstuvwxyz{zyxwvutsrqpon
```

19.28 In Exercise 19.9, we asked you to write a simple encryption algorithm. Write a program that will attempt to decrypt a "rot13" message using simple frequency substitution. (Assume that you do not know the key.) The most frequent letters in the encrypted phrase should be replaced with the most commonly used English letters (a, e, i, o, u, s, t, r, etc.). Write the possibilities to a file. What made the code breaking easy? How can the encryption mechanism be improved?

19.29 Write a version of the selection sort routine (Fig. 9.28) that sorts strings. Use function swap in your solution.

19.30 Modify class Employee in Figs. 14.13–14.14 by adding a private utility function called is-ValidSocialSecurityNumber. This member function should validate the format of a social security number (e.g., ###-##-####, where # is a digit). If the format is valid, return true; otherwise return false.

19.31 Write an application that uses String function CompareTo to compare two Strings input by the user. Output whether the first String is less than, equal to or greater than the second.

20

Searching and Sorting

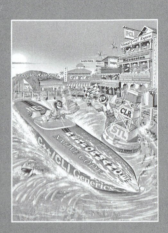

With sobs and tears
he sorted out
Those of the largest size ...
—Lewis Carroll

Attempt the end, and never
stand to doubt;
Nothing's so hard, but search
will find it out.
—Robert Herrick

'Tis in my memory lock'd,
And you yourself shall keep
the key of it.
—William Shakespeare

It is an immutable law in
business that words are
words, explanations are
explanations, promises are
promises — but only
performance is reality.
—Harold S. Green

OBJECTIVES

In this chapter you'll learn:

- To search for a given value in a vector using binary search.

- To use Big O notation to express the efficiency of an algorithm and to compare the performance of algorithms.

- To review the efficiency of the selection sort and insertion sort algorithms.

- To sort a vector using the recursive merge sort algorithm.

- To determine the efficiency of various searching and sorting algorithms.

- To enumerate the searching and sorting algorithms discussed in this text.

- To understand the nature of algorithms of constant, linear and quadratic runtime.

20.1 Introduction

Searching data involves determining whether a value (referred to as the *search key*) is present in the data and, if so, finding the value's location. Two popular search algorithms are the simple linear search (introduced in Section 8.7) and the faster but more complex binary search, which is introduced in this chapter.

    Sorting places data in order, typically ascending or descending, based on one or more *sort keys*. A list of names could be sorted alphabetically, bank accounts could be sorted by account number, employee payroll records could be sorted by social security number, and so on. Previously, you learned about insertion sort (Section 8.8) and selection sort (Section 9.6). This chapter introduces the more efficient, but more complex, merge sort. Figure 20.1 summarizes the searching and sorting algorithms discussed in the examples and exercises of this book. This chapter also introduces *Big O notation*, which is used to estimate the worst-case runtime for an algorithm—that is, how hard an algorithm may have to work to solve a problem. The concepts in this chapter are equally applicable to native and managed code.

Chapter	Algorithm	Location
Searching Algorithms		
8	Linear search	Section 8.7
20	Binary search	Section 20.2.2
	Recursive linear search	Exercise 20.8
	Recursive binary search	Exercise 20.9
21	Binary tree search	Section 21.7
	Linear search of a linked list	Exercise 21.21
23	binary_search standard library function	Section 23.5.6
Sorting Algorithms		
8	Insertion sort	Section 8.8

Fig. 20.1 | Searching and sorting algorithms in this text. (Part 1 of 2.)

Chapter	Algorithm	Location
9	Selection sort	Section 9.6
20	Recursive merge sort	Section 20.3.3
	Bubble sort	Exercise 20.5 and 20.6
	Bucket sort	Exercise 20.7
	Recursive quicksort	Exercise 20.10
21	Binary tree sort	Section 21.7
23	sort standard library function	Section 23.5.6
	Heap sort	Section 23.5.12

Fig. 20.1 | Searching and sorting algorithms in this text. (Part 2 of 2.)

20.2 Searching Algorithms

Looking up a phone number, accessing a website and checking the definition of a word in a dictionary all involve searching large amounts of data. Searching algorithms all accomplish the same goal—finding an element that matches a given search key, if such an element does, in fact, exist. There are, however, a number of things that differentiate search algorithms from one another. The major difference is the amount of effort they require to complete the search. One way to describe this effort is with Big O notation. For searching and sorting algorithms, this is particularly dependent on the number of data elements.

In Chapter 8, we discussed the linear search algorithm, which is a simple and easy-to-implement searching algorithm. We'll now discuss the efficiency of the linear search algorithm as measured by Big O notation. Then, we'll introduce a searching algorithm that is relatively efficient but more complex and difficult to implement.

20.2.1 Efficiency of Linear Search

Suppose an algorithm simply tests whether a vector's first element is equal to its second element. If the vector has 10 elements, this algorithm requires only one comparison. If the vector has 1000 elements, the algorithm still requires only one comparison. In fact, the algorithm is independent of the number of vector elements. This algorithm is said to have a *constant runtime*, which is represented in Big O notation as *O(1)*. An algorithm that is $O(1)$ does not necessarily require only one comparison. $O(1)$ just means that the number of comparisons is *constant*—it does not grow as the size of the vector increases. An algorithm that tests whether the first element of a vector is equal to any of the next three elements will always require three comparisons, but in Big O notation it is still considered $O(1)$. $O(1)$ is often pronounced "on the order of 1" or more simply "*order 1*."

An algorithm that tests whether the first element of a vector is equal to *any* of the other elements of the vector requires at most $n - 1$ comparisons, where n is the number of elements in the vector. If the vector has 10 elements, the algorithm requires up to nine comparisons. If the vector has 1000 elements, the algorithm requires up to 999 comparisons. As n grows larger, the n part of the expression "dominates," and subtracting one becomes inconsequential. Big O is designed to highlight these dominant terms and ignore terms that become unimportant as n grows. For this reason, an algorithm that requires a total of $n - 1$ comparisons (such as the one we described in this paragraph) is said to be $O(n)$. An $O(n)$ algorithm is referred to as having a *linear runtime*. $O(n)$ is often pronounced "on the order of n" or more simply "*order n.*"

Now suppose you have an algorithm that tests whether *any* element of a vector is duplicated elsewhere in the vector. The first element must be compared with every other element in the vector. The second element must be compared with every other element except the first (it was already compared to the first). The third element must be compared with every other element except the first two. In the end, this algorithm will end up making $(n - 1) + (n - 2) + \ldots + 2 + 1$ or $n^2/2 - n/2$ comparisons. As n increases, the n^2 term dominates and the n term becomes inconsequential. Again, Big O notation highlights the n^2 term, leaving $n^2/2$. As we'll soon see, however, constant factors are omitted in Big O notation.

Big O is concerned with how an algorithm's runtime grows in relation to the number of items processed. Suppose an algorithm requires n^2 comparisons. With four elements, the algorithm will require 16 comparisons; with eight elements, 64 comparisons. With this algorithm, doubling the number of elements quadruples the number of comparisons. Consider a similar algorithm requiring $n^2/2$ comparisons. With four elements, the algorithm will require eight comparisons; with eight elements, 32 comparisons. Again, doubling the number of elements quadruples the number of comparisons. Both of these algorithms grow as the square of n, so Big O ignores the constant, and both algorithms are considered to be $O(n^2)$, which is referred to as *quadratic runtime* and pronounced "on the order of n-squared" or more simply "*order n-squared.*"

When n is small, $O(n^2)$ algorithms (running on today's billion-operation-per-second personal computers) will not noticeably affect performance. But as n grows, you'll start to notice the performance degradation. An $O(n^2)$ algorithm running on a million-element vector would require a trillion "operations" (where each could actually require several machine instructions to execute). This could require a few hours to execute. A billion-element vector would require a quintillion operations, a number so large that the algorithm could take decades! $O(n^2)$ algorithms are relatively easy to write. In this chapter, you'll see algorithms with more favorable Big O measures. These efficient algorithms often take a bit more cleverness and effort to create, but their superior performance can be worth the extra effort, especially as n gets large and as algorithms are compounded into larger programs.

The linear search algorithm runs in $O(n)$ time. The worst case in this algorithm is that every element must be checked to determine whether the search key exists in the vector. If the size of the vector is doubled, the number of comparisons that the algorithm must perform is also doubled. Note that linear search can provide outstanding performance if the element matching the search key happens to be at or near the front of the vector. But we seek algorithms that perform well, on average, across all searches, including those where the element matching the search key is near the end of the vector.

Linear search is the easiest search algorithm to implement, but it can be slow compared to other search algorithms. If a program needs to perform many searches on large vectors, it may be better to implement a different, more efficient algorithm, such as the binary search which we present in the next section.

Performance Tip 20.1

Sometimes the simplest algorithms perform poorly. Their virtue is that they are easy to program, test and debug. Sometimes more complex algorithms are required to realize maximum performance.

20.2.2 Binary Search

The *binary search algorithm* is more efficient than the linear search algorithm, but it requires that the vector first be sorted. This is only worthwhile when the vector, once sorted, will be searched a great many times—or when the searching application has stringent performance requirements. The first iteration of this algorithm tests the middle element in the vector. If this matches the search key, the algorithm ends. Assuming the vector is sorted in ascending order, then if the search key is less than the middle element, the search key cannot match any element in the second half of the vector and the algorithm continues with only the first half of the vector (i.e., the first element up to, but not including, the middle element). If the search key is greater than the middle element, the search key cannot match any element in the first half of the vector and the algorithm continues with only the second half of the vector (i.e., the element after the middle element through the last element). Each iteration tests the middle value of the remaining portion of the vector. If the element does not match the search key, the algorithm eliminates half of the remaining elements. The algorithm ends either by finding an element that matches the search key or by reducing the subvector to zero size.

As an example, consider the sorted 15-element vector

2   3   5   10   27   30   34   51   56   65   77   81   82   93   99

and the search key 65. A binary search would first check whether 51 is the search key (because 51 is the middle element of the vector). The search key (65) is larger than 51, so 51 is eliminated from consideration along with the first half of the vector (all elements smaller than 51.) Next, the algorithm checks whether 81 (the middle element of the remainder of the vector) matches the search key. The search key (65) is smaller than 81, so 81 is eliminated from consideration along with the elements larger than 81. After just two tests, the algorithm has narrowed the number of elements to check to three (56, 65 and 77). The algorithm then checks 65 (which matches the search key), and returns the index (9) of the vector element containing 65. In this case, the algorithm required just three comparisons to determine whether a vector element matched the search key. Using a linear search algorithm would have required 10 comparisons. [*Note:* In this example, we have chosen to use a vector with 15 elements, so that there will always be an obvious middle element in the vector. With an even number of elements, the middle of the vector lies between two elements. We implement the algorithm to choose the larger of those two elements.]

Figures 20.2–20.3 define class BinarySearch and its member functions, respectively. Class BinarySearch is similar to LinearSearch (Section 8.7)—it has a constructor, a search function (binarySearch), a displayElements function, two private data members and a private utility function (displaySubElements). Lines 18–28 of Fig. 20.3 define the constructor. After initializing the vector with random ints from 10–99 (lines 24–25), line 27 calls the Standard Library function sort on the vector data. Recall that the binary search algorithm will work only on a sorted vector. Function *sort* requires two arguments that specify the range of elements to sort. These arguments are specified with iterators (discussed briefly in Section 11.9 and in detail in Chapter 23). The vector member functions begin and end return iterators that can be used with function sort to indicate that all the elements from the beginning to the end should be sorted.

```cpp
1   // Fig. 20.1: BinarySearch.h
2   // Class that contains a vector of random integers and a function
3   // that uses binary search to find an integer.
4   #include <vector>
5   using std::vector;
6
7   class BinarySearch
8   {
9   public:
10     BinarySearch( int ); // constructor initializes vector
11     int binarySearch( int ) const; // perform a binary search on vector
12     void displayElements() const; // display vector elements
13  private:
14     int size; // vector size
15     vector< int > data; // vector of ints
16     void displaySubElements( int, int ) const; // display range of values
17  }; // end class BinarySearch
```

Fig. 20.2 | BinarySearch class definition.

```cpp
1   // Fig. 20.3: BinarySearch.cpp
2   // BinarySearch class member-function definition.
3   #include <iostream>
4   using std::cout;
5   using std::endl;
6
7   #include <cstdlib> // prototypes for functions srand and rand
8   using std::rand;
9   using std::srand;
10
11  #include <ctime> // prototype for function time
12  using std::time;
13
14  #include <algorithm> // prototype for sort function
15  #include "BinarySearch.h" // class BinarySearch definition
16
17  // constructor initializes vector with random ints and sorts the vector
18  BinarySearch::BinarySearch( int vectorSize )
19  {
20     size = ( vectorSize > 0 ? vectorSize : 10 ); // validate vectorSize
21     srand( time( 0 ) ); // seed using current time
22
23     // fill vector with random ints in range 10-99
24     for ( int i = 0; i < size; i++ )
25        data.push_back( 10 + rand() % 90 ); // 10-99
26
27     std::sort( data.begin(), data.end() ); // sort the data
28  } // end BinarySearch constructor
```

Fig. 20.3 | BinarySearch class member-function definition. (Part 1 of 2.)

```
29
30   // perform a binary search on the data
31   int BinarySearch::binarySearch( int searchElement ) const
32   {
33      int low = 0; // low end of the search area
34      int high = size - 1; // high end of the search area
35      int middle = ( low + high + 1 ) / 2; // middle element
36      int location = -1; // return value; -1 if not found
37
38      do // loop to search for element
39      {
40         // print remaining elements of vector to be searched
41         displaySubElements( low, high );
42
43         // output spaces for alignment
44         for ( int i = 0; i < middle; i++ )
45            cout << "   ";
46
47         cout << " * " << endl; // indicate current middle
48
49         // if the element is found at the middle
50         if ( searchElement == data[ middle ] )
51            location = middle; // location is the current middle
52         else if ( searchElement < data[ middle ] ) // middle is too high
53            high = middle - 1; // eliminate the higher half
54         else // middle element is too low
55            low = middle + 1; // eliminate the lower half
56
57         middle = ( low + high + 1 ) / 2; // recalculate the middle
58      } while ( ( low <= high ) && ( location == -1 ) );
59
60      return location; // return location of search key
61   } // end function binarySearch
62
63   // display values in vector
64   void BinarySearch::displayElements() const
65   {
66      displaySubElements( 0, size - 1 );
67   } // end function displayElements
68
69   // display certain values in vector
70   void BinarySearch::displaySubElements( int low, int high ) const
71   {
72      for ( int i = 0; i < low; i++ ) // output spaces for alignment
73         cout << "   ";
74
75      for ( int i = low; i <= high; i++ ) // output elements left in vector
76         cout << data[ i ] << " ";
77
78      cout << endl;
79   } // end function displaySubElements
```

Fig. 20.3 | BinarySearch class member-function definition. (Part 2 of 2.)

Lines 31–61 define function binarySearch. The search key is passed into parameter searchElement (line 31). Lines 33–35 calculate the low-end index, high-end index and middle index of the portion of the vector that the program is currently searching. At the beginning of the function, the low end is 0, the high end is the size of the vector minus 1 and the middle is the average of these two values. Line 36 initializes the location of the found element to -1—the value that will be returned if the search key is not found. Lines 38–58 loop until low is greater than high (this occurs when the element is not found) or location does not equal -1 (indicating that the search key was found). Line 50 tests whether the value in the middle element is equal to searchElement. If this is true, line 51 assigns middle to location. Then the loop terminates and location is returned to the caller. Each iteration of the loop tests a single value (line 50) and eliminates half of the remaining values in the vector (line 53 or 55).

Lines 25–41 of Fig. 20.4 loop until the user enters the value -1. For each other number the user enters, the program performs a binary search on the data to determine whether it matches an element in the vector. The first line of output from this program is the vector of ints, in increasing order. When the user instructs the program to search for 38, the program first tests the middle element, which is 67 (as indicated by *). The search key is less than 67, so the program eliminates the second half of the vector and tests the middle element from the first half of the vector. The search key equals 38, so the program returns the index 3.

```cpp
1   // Fig. 20.4:BinarySearchTest.cpp
2   // BinarySearch test program.
3   #include <iostream>
4   using std::cin;
5   using std::cout;
6   using std::endl;
7
8   #include "BinarySearch.h" // class BinarySearch definition
9
10  int main()
11  {
12     int searchInt; // search key
13     int position; // location of search key in vector
14
15     // create vector and output it
16     BinarySearch searchVector ( 15 );
17     searchVector.displayElements();
18
19     // get input from user
20     cout << "\nPlease enter an integer value (-1 to quit): ";
21     cin >> searchInt; // read an int from user
22     cout << endl;
23
24     // repeatedly input an integer; -1 terminates the program
25     while ( searchInt != -1 )
26     {
27        // use binary search to try to find integer
28        position = searchVector.binarySearch( searchInt );'
```

Fig. 20.4 | BinarySearch test program. (Part 1 of 2.)

```
29
30          // return value of -1 indicates integer was not found
31          if ( position == -1 )
32             cout << "The integer " << searchInt << " was not found.\n";
33          else
34             cout << "The integer " << searchInt
35                << " was found in position " << position << ".\n";
36
37          // get input from user
38          cout << "\n\nPlease enter an integer value (-1 to quit): ";
39          cin >> searchInt; // read an int from user
40          cout << endl;
41       } // end while
42
43       return 0;
44    } // end main
```

```
26 31 33 38 47 49 49 67 73 74 82 89 90 91 95

Please enter an integer value (-1 to quit): 38

26 31 33 38 47 49 49 67 73 74 82 89 90 91 95
                  *
26 31 33 38 47 49 49
            *
The integer 38 was found in position 3.


Please enter an integer value (-1 to quit): 91

26 31 33 38 47 49 49 67 73 74 82 89 90 91 95
                  *
                     73 74 82 89 90 91 95
                              *
                                 90 91 95
                                     *
The integer 91 was found in position 13.


Please enter an integer value (-1 to quit): 25

26 31 33 38 47 49 49 67 73 74 82 89 90 91 95
                  *
26 31 33 38 47 49 49
            *
26 31 33
      *
26
*
The integer 25 was not found.


Please enter an integer value (-1 to quit): -1
```

Fig. 20.4 | BinarySearch test program. (Part 2 of 2.)

Efficiency of Binary Search

In the worst-case scenario, searching a sorted vector of 1023 elements will take only 10 comparisons when using a binary search. Repeatedly dividing 1023 by 2 (because, after each comparison, we are able to eliminate from consideration half of the vector) and rounding down (because we also remove the middle element) yields the values 511, 255, 127, 63, 31, 15, 7, 3, 1 and 0. The number 1023 ($2^{10} - 1$) is divided by 2 only 10 times to get the value 0, which indicates that there are no more elements to test. Dividing by 2 is equivalent to one comparison in the binary search algorithm. Thus, a vector of 1,048,575 ($2^{20} - 1$) elements takes a maximum of 20 comparisons to find the key, and a vector of about one billion elements takes a maximum of 30 comparisons to find the key. This is a tremendous improvement in performance over the linear search. For a one-billion-element vector, this is a difference between an average of 500 million comparisons for the linear search and a maximum of only 30 comparisons for the binary search! The maximum number of comparisons needed for the binary search of any sorted vector is the exponent of the first power of 2 greater than the number of elements in the vector, which is represented as $\log_2 n$. All logarithms grow at roughly the same rate, so in Big O notation the base can be omitted. This results in a Big O of *O(log n)* for a binary search, which is also known as ***logarithmic runtime*** and pronounced "on the order of log *n*" or more simply "*order log n.*"

20.3 Sorting Algorithms

Sorting data (i.e., placing the data into some particular order, such as ascending or descending) is one of the most important computing applications. A bank sorts all of its checks by account number so that it can prepare individual bank statements at the end of each month. Telephone companies sort their lists of accounts by last name and, further, by first name to make it easy to find phone numbers. Virtually every organization must sort some data, and often, massive amounts of it. Sorting data is an intriguing, computer-intensive problem that has attracted intense research efforts.

An important point to understand about sorting is that the end result—the sorted vector—will be the same no matter which algorithm you use to sort the vector. The choice of algorithm affects only the runtime and memory use of the program. In previous chapters, we introduced the selection sort and insertion sort—simple algorithms to implement, but inefficient. The next section examines the efficiency of these two algorithms using Big O notation. The last algorithm—merge sort, which we introduce in this chapter—is much faster but is more difficult to implement.

20.3.1 Efficiency of Selection Sort

Selection sort is an easy-to-implement, but inefficient, sorting algorithm. The first iteration of the algorithm selects the smallest element in the vector and swaps it with the first element. The second iteration selects the second-smallest element (which is the smallest element of the remaining elements) and swaps it with the second element. The algorithm continues until the last iteration selects the second-largest element and swaps it with the second-to-last element, leaving the largest element in the last index. After the *i*th iteration, the smallest *i* elements of the vector will be sorted into increasing order in the first *i* elements of the vector.

The selection sort algorithm iterates $n - 1$ times, each time swapping the smallest remaining element into its sorted position. Locating the smallest remaining element requires $n - 1$ comparisons during the first iteration, $n - 2$ during the second iteration, then $n - 3, \ldots, 3, 2, 1$. This results in a total of $n(n - 1)/2$ or $(n^2 - n)/2$ comparisons. In Big O notation, smaller terms drop out and constants are ignored, leaving a final Big O of $O(n^2)$.

20.3.2 Efficiency of Insertion Sort

Insertion sort is another simple, but inefficient, sorting algorithm. The first iteration of this algorithm takes the second element in the vector and, if it is less than the first element, swaps it with the first element. The second iteration looks at the third element and inserts it into the correct position with respect to the first two elements, so all three elements are in order. At the ith iteration of this algorithm, the first i elements in the original vector will be sorted.

Insertion sort iterates $n - 1$ times, inserting an element into the appropriate position in the elements sorted so far. For each iteration, determining where to insert the element can require comparing the element to each of the preceding elements in the vector. In the worst case, this will require $n - 1$ comparisons. Each individual repetition statement runs in $O(n)$ time. For determining Big O notation, nested statements mean that you must multiply the number of comparisons. For each iteration of an outer loop, there will be a certain number of iterations of the inner loop. In this algorithm, for each $O(n)$ iteration of the outer loop, there will be $O(n)$ iterations of the inner loop, resulting in a Big O of $O(n * n)$ or $O(n^2)$.

20.3.3 Merge Sort (A Recursive Implementation)

Merge sort is an efficient sorting algorithm but is conceptually more complex than selection sort and insertion sort. The merge sort algorithm sorts a vector by splitting it into two equal-sized subvectors, sorting each subvector and then merging them into one larger vector. With an odd number of elements, the algorithm creates the two subvectors such that one has one more element than the other.

The implementation of merge sort in this example is recursive. The base case is a vector with one element. A one-element vector is, of course, sorted, so merge sort immediately returns when it is called with a one-element vector. The recursion step splits a vector of two or more elements into two equal-sized subvectors, recursively sorts each subvector, then merges them into one larger, sorted vector. [Again, if there is an odd number of elements, one subvector is one element larger than the other.]

Suppose the algorithm has already merged smaller vectors to create sorted vectors A:

    4   10   34   56   77

and B:

    5   30   51   52   93

Merge sort combines these two vectors into one larger, sorted vector. The smallest value in A is 4 (located in the zeroth element of A). The smallest value in B is 5 (located in the zeroth element of B). In order to determine the smallest element in the larger vector, the algorithm compares 4 and 5. The value from A is smaller, so 4 becomes the value of the first element in the merged vector. The algorithm continues by comparing 10 (the value of the second element in A) to 5 (the value of the first element in B). The value from B is smaller, so 5 becomes the value of the second element in the larger vector. The algorithm continues by comparing 10 to 30, with 10 becoming the value of the third element in the vector, and so on.

Figure 20.5 defines class MergeSort, and lines 31–34 of Fig. 20.6 define the sort function. Line 33 calls function sortSubVector with 0 and size - 1 as the arguments. These arguments correspond to the beginning and ending indices of the vector to be sorted, causing sortSubVector to operate on the entire vector. Function sortSubVector is defined in lines 37–61. Line 40 tests the base case. If the size of the vector is 1, the vector

```cpp
1   // Figure 20.5: MergeSort.h
2   // Class that creates a vector filled with random integers.
3   // Provides a function to sort the vector with merge sort.
4   #include <vector>
5   using std::vector;
6
7   // MergeSort class definition
8   class MergeSort
9   {
10  public:
11     MergeSort( int ); // constructor initializes vector
12     void sort(); // sort vector using merge sort
13     void displayElements() const; // display vector elements
14  private:
15     int size; // vector size
16     vector< int > data; // vector of ints
17     void sortSubVector( int, int ); // sort subvector
18     void merge( int, int, int, int ); // merge two sorted vectors
19     void displaySubVector( int, int ) const; // display subvector
20  }; // end class SelectionSort
```

Fig. 20.5 | MergeSort class definition.

```cpp
1   // Figure 20.6: MergeSort.cpp
2   // Class MergeSort member-function definition.
3   #include <iostream>
4   using std::cout;
5   using std::endl;
6
7   #include <vector>
8   using std::vector;
9
10  #include <cstdlib> // prototypes for functions srand and rand
11  using std::rand;
12  using std::srand;
13
14  #include <ctime> // prototype for function time
15  using std::time;
```

Fig. 20.6 | MergeSort class member-function definition. (Part 1 of 4.)

```
16
17   #include "MergeSort.h" // class MergeSort definition
18
19   // constructor fill vector with random integers
20   MergeSort::MergeSort( int vectorSize )
21   {
22      size = ( vectorSize > 0 ? vectorSize : 10 ); // validate vectorSize
23      srand( static_cast< unsigned >( time( 0 ) ) );
24
25      // fill vector with random ints in range 10-99
26      for ( int i = 0; i < size; i++ )
27         data.push_back( 10 + rand() % 90 );
28   } // end MergeSort constructor
29
30   // split vector, sort subvectors and merge subvectors into sorted vector
31   void MergeSort::sort()
32   {
33      sortSubVector( 0, size - 1 ); // recursively sort entire vector
34   } // end function sort
35
36   // recursive function to sort subvectors
37   void MergeSort::sortSubVector( int low, int high )
38   {
39      // test base case; size of vector equals 1
40      if ( ( high - low ) >= 1 ) // if not base case
41      {
42         int middle1 = ( low + high ) / 2; // calculate middle of vector
43         int middle2 = middle1 + 1; // calculate next element over
44
45         // output split step
46         cout << "split:   ";
47         displaySubVector( low, high );
48         cout << endl << "         ";
49         displaySubVector( low, middle1 );
50         cout << endl << "         ";
51         displaySubVector( middle2, high );
52         cout << endl << endl;
53
54         // split vector in half; sort each half (recursive calls)
55         sortSubVector( low, middle1 ); // first half of vector
56         sortSubVector( middle2, high ); // second half of vector
57
58         // merge two sorted vectors after split calls return
59         merge( low, middle1, middle2, high );
60      } // end if
61   } // end function sortSubVector
62
63   // merge two sorted subvectors into one sorted subvector
64   void MergeSort::merge( int left, int middle1, int middle2, int right )
65   {
66      int leftIndex = left; // index into left subvector
67      int rightIndex = middle2; // index into right subvector
```

Fig. 20.6 | MergeSort class member-function definition. (Part 2 of 4.)

```
68      int combinedIndex = left; // index into temporary working vector
69      vector< int > combined( size ); // working vector
70
71      // output two subvectors before merging
72      cout << "merge:     ";
73      displaySubVector( left, middle1 );
74      cout << endl << "          ";
75      displaySubVector( middle2, right );
76      cout << endl;
77
78      // merge vectors until reaching end of either
79      while ( leftIndex <= middle1 && rightIndex <= right )
80      {
81         // place smaller of two current elements into result
82         // and move to next space in vector
83         if ( data[ leftIndex ] <= data[ rightIndex ] )
84            combined[ combinedIndex++ ] = data[ leftIndex++ ];
85         else
86            combined[ combinedIndex++ ] = data[ rightIndex++ ];
87      } // end while
88
89      if ( leftIndex == middle2 ) // if at end of left vector
90      {
91         while ( rightIndex <= right ) // copy in rest of right vector
92            combined[ combinedIndex++ ] = data[ rightIndex++ ];
93      } // end if
94      else // at end of right vector
95      {
96         while ( leftIndex <= middle1 ) // copy in rest of left vector
97            combined[ combinedIndex++ ] = data[ leftIndex++ ];
98      } // end else
99
100     // copy values back into original vector
101     for ( int i = left; i <= right; i++ )
102        data[ i ] = combined[ i ];
103
104     // output merged vector
105     cout << "          ";
106     displaySubVector( left, right );
107     cout << endl << endl;
108  } // end function merge
109
110  // display elements in vector
111  void MergeSort::displayElements() const
112  {
113     displaySubVector( 0, size - 1 );
114  } // end function displayElements
115
116  // display certain values in vector
117  void MergeSort::displaySubVector( int low, int high ) const
118  {
```

Fig. 20.6 | MergeSort class member-function definition. (Part 3 of 4.)

```
119      // output spaces for alignment
120      for ( int i = 0; i < low; i++ )
121         cout << "   ";
122
123      // output elements left in vector
124      for ( int i = low; i <= high; i++ )
125         cout << " " << data[ i ];
126   } // end function displaySubVector
```

Fig. 20.6 | MergeSort class member-function definition. (Part 4 of 4.)

is already sorted, so the function simply returns immediately. If the size of the vector is greater than 1, the function splits the vector in two, recursively calls function sortSub-Vector to sort the two subvectors, then merges them. Line 55 recursively calls function sortSubVector on the first half of the vector, and line 56 recursively calls function sort-SubVector on the second half of the vector. When these two function calls return, each half of the vector has been sorted. Line 59 calls function merge (lines 64–108) on the two halves of the vector to combine the two sorted vectors into one larger sorted vector.

Lines 79–87 in function merge loop until the program reaches the end of either sub-vector. Line 83 tests which element at the beginning of the vectors is smaller. If the element in the left vector is smaller, line 84 places it in position in the combined vector. If the element in the right vector is smaller, line 86 places it in position in the combined vector. When the while loop has completed (line 87), one entire subvector is placed in the combined vector, but the other subvector still contains data. Line 89 tests whether the left vector has reached the end. If so, lines 91–92 fill the combined vector with the elements of the right vector. If the left vector has not reached the end, then the right vector must have reached the end, and lines 96–97 fill the combined vector with the elements of the left vector. Finally, lines 101–102 copy the combined vector into the original vector. Figure 20.7 creates and uses a MergeSort object. The output from this program displays the splits and merges performed by merge sort, showing the progress of the sort at each step of the algorithm.

Efficiency of Merge Sort

Merge sort is a far more efficient algorithm than either insertion sort or selection sort (although that may be difficult to believe when looking at the rather busy output in Fig. 20.7). Consider the first (nonrecursive) call to function sortSubVector. This results in two recursive calls to function sortSubVector with subvectors each approximately half the size of the original vector, and a single call to function merge. This call to function merge requires, at worst, $n - 1$ comparisons to fill the original vector, which is $O(n)$. (Recall that each vector element is chosen by comparing one element from each of the sub-vectors.) The two calls to function sortSubVector result in four more recursive calls to function sortSubVector—each with a subvector approximately one-quarter the size of the original vector—and two calls to function merge. These two calls to function merge each require, at worst, $n/2 - 1$ comparisons, for a total number of comparisons of $O(n)$. This process continues, each call to sortSubVector generating two additional calls to sortSub-Vector and a call to merge, until the algorithm has split the vector into one-element sub-vectors. At each level, $O(n)$ comparisons are required to merge the subvectors. Each level

```
1    // Figure 20.7: MergeSortTest.cpp
2    // MergeSort test program.
3    #include <iostream>
4    using std::cout;
5    using std::endl;
6
7    #include "MergeSort.h" // class MergeSort definition
8
9    int main()
10   {
11      // create object to perform merge sort
12      MergeSort sortVector( 10 );
13
14      cout << "Unsorted vector:" << endl;
15      sortVector.displayElements(); // print unsorted vector
16      cout << endl << endl;
17
18      sortVector.sort(); // sort vector
19
20      cout << "Sorted vector:" << endl;
21      sortVector.displayElements(); // print sorted vector
22      cout << endl;
23      return 0;
24   } // end main
```

```
Unsorted vector:
 30 47 22 67 79 18 60 78 26 54

split:     30 47 22 67 79 18 60 78 26 54
           30 47 22 67 79
                         18 60 78 26 54

split:     30 47 22 67 79
           30 47 22
                   67 79

split:     30 47 22
           30 47
                 22

split:     30 47
           30
              47

merge:     30
              47
           30 47

merge:     30 47
                 22
           22 30 47

split:              67 79
                    67
                       79
```

Fig. 20.7 | MergeSort test program. (Part 1 of 2.)

```
merge:                    67
                             79
                          67  79

merge:       22  30  47
                          67  79
             22  30  47  67  79

split:                         18  60  78  26  54
                               18  60  78
                                           26  54

split:                         18  60  78
                               18  60
                                       78

split:                         18  60
                               18
                                   60

merge:                         18
                                   60
                               18  60

merge:                         18  60
                                       78
                               18  60  78

split:                                 26  54
                                       26
                                           54

merge:                                 26
                                           54
                                       26  54

merge:                         18  60  78
                                           26  54
                               18  26  54  60  78

merge:       22  30  47  67  79
                               18  26  54  60  78
             18  22  26  30  47  54  60  67  78  79

Sorted vector:
 18  22  26  30  47  54  60  67  78  79
```

Fig. 20.7 | MergeSort test program. (Part 2 of 2.)

splits the size of the vectors in half, so doubling the size of the vector requires one more level. Quadrupling the size of the vector requires two more levels. This pattern is logarithmic and results in $\log_2 n$ levels. This results in a total efficiency of *O(n log n)*. Figure 20.8 summarizes many of the searching and sorting algorithms covered in this book and lists the Big O for each of them. Figure 20.9 lists the Big O values we have covered in this chapter along with a number of values for *n* to highlight the differences in the growth rates.

Algorithm	Location	Big O
Searching Algorithms		
Linear search	Section 8.7	$O(n)$
Binary search	Section 20.2.2	$O(\log n)$
Recursive linear search	Exercise 20.8	$O(n)$
Recursive binary search	Exercise 20.9	$O(\log n)$
Sorting Algorithms		
Insertion sort	Section 8.8	$O(n^2)$
Selection sort	Section 9.6	$O(n^2)$
Merge sort	Section 20.3.3	$O(n \log n)$
Bubble sort	Exercises 8.13– and 8.14	$O(n^2)$
Quicksort	Exercise 20.10	Worst case: $O(n^2)$ Average case: $O(n \log n)$

Fig. 20.8 | Searching and sorting algorithms with Big O values.

n	Approximate decimal value	$O(\log n)$	$O(n)$	$O(n \log n)$	$O(n^2)$
2^{10}	1000	10	2^{10}	$10 \cdot 2^{10}$	2^{20}
2^{20}	1,000,000	20	2^{20}	$20 \cdot 2^{20}$	2^{40}
2^{30}	1,000,000,000	30	2^{30}	$30 \cdot 2^{30}$	2^{60}

Fig. 20.9 | Approximate number of comparisons for common Big O notations.

20.4 Wrap-Up

This chapter discussed searching and sorting data. We discussed the binary search algorithm, which is faster but more complex than linear search (Section 8.7). The binary search algorithm will work only on a sorted array, but each iteration of binary search eliminates from consideration half of the elements in the array. You also learned the merge sort algorithm, which is more efficient than either insertion sort (Section 8.8) or selection sort (Section 9.6). We also introduced Big O notation, which helps you express the efficiency of an algorithm. Big O notation measures the worst-case runtime for an algorithm. The Big O value is useful for comparing algorithms to choose the most efficient one. In the next chapter, you'll learn about dynamic data structures that can grow or shrink at execution time.

Summary

Section 20.1 Introduction
- Searching data involves determining whether a search key is present in the data and, if so, finding its location.

- Sorting involves arranging data into order.
- One way to describe the efficiency of an algorithm is with Big O notation (*O*), which indicates how hard an algorithm may have to work to solve a problem.

Section 20.2 Searching Algorithms
- A major difference among searching algorithms is the amount of effort they require in order to return a result.

Section 20.2.1 Efficiency of Linear Search
- For searching and sorting algorithms, Big O describes how the amount of effort of a particular algorithm varies depending on how many elements are in the data.
- An algorithm that is $O(1)$ is said to have a constant runtime. This does not mean that the algorithm requires only one comparison—it just means that the number of comparisons does not grow as the size of the vector increases.
- An $O(n)$ algorithm is referred to as having a linear runtime.
- Big O highlights dominant factors and ignores terms that are unimportant with high values of *n*.
- Big O notation represents the growth rate of algorithm runtimes, so constants are ignored.
- The linear search algorithm runs in $O(n)$ time.
- In the worst case for linear search every element must be checked to determine whether the search element exists. This occurs if the search key is the last element in the vector or is not present.

Section 20.2.2 Binary Search
- The binary search algorithm is more efficient than the linear search algorithm, but it requires that the vector first be sorted. This is worthwhile only when the vector, once sorted, will be searched a great many times—or when the searching application has stringent performance requirements.
- The first iteration of binary search tests the middle element in the vector. If this is the search key, the algorithm returns its location. If the search key is less than the middle element, binary search continues with the first half of the vector. If the search key is greater than the middle element, binary search continues with the second half of the vector. Each iteration of binary search tests the middle value of the remaining vector and, if the element is not found, eliminates from consideration half of the remaining elements.
- Binary search is more efficient than linear search, because with each comparison it eliminates from consideration half of the elements in the vector.
- Binary search runs in $O(\log n)$ time, because each step removes half of the remaining elements from consideration.
- If the size of the vector is doubled, binary search requires only one extra comparison to complete successfully.

Section 20.3.1 Efficiency of Selection Sort
- Selection sort is a simple, but inefficient, sorting algorithm.
- The first iteration of selection sort selects the smallest element in the vector and swaps it with the first element. The second iteration of selection sort selects the second-smallest element (which is the smallest remaining element) and swaps it with the second element. Selection sort continues until the last iteration selects the second-largest element and swaps it with the second-to-last index, leaving the largest element in the last index. At the *i*th iteration of selection sort, the smallest *i* elements of the whole vector are sorted into the first *i* elements.

Section 20.3.2 Efficiency of Insertion Sort

- The selection sort algorithm runs in $O(n^2)$ time.

- The first iteration of insertion sort takes the second element value in the vector and, if it is less than the first element value, swaps it with the first element value. The second iteration of insertion sort looks at the third element value and inserts it in the correct position with respect to the first two element values. After the ith iteration of insertion sort, the first i element values in the original vector are sorted. Only $n - 1$ iterations are required.

- The insertion sort algorithm runs in $O(n^2)$ time.

Section 20.3.3 Merge Sort (A Recursive Implementation)

- Merge sort is a sorting algorithm that is faster, but more complex to implement, than selection sort and insertion sort.

- The merge sort algorithm sorts a vector by splitting it into two equal-sized subvectors, sorting each and then merging them into one larger vector.

- Merge sort's base case is a vector with one element. A one-element vector is already sorted, so merge sort immediately returns when it is called with a one-element vector. The merge part of merge sort takes two sorted vectors (these could be one-element vectors) and combines them into one larger sorted vector.

- Merge sort performs the merge by looking at the first element in each vector, which is also the smallest element in the vector. Merge sort takes the smallest of these and places it in the first element of the larger, sorted vector. If there are still elements in the subvector, merge sort looks at the second element in that subvector (which is now the smallest element remaining) and compares it to the first element in the other subvector. Merge sort continues this process until the larger vector is filled.

- In the worst case, the first call to merge sort has to make $O(n)$ comparisons to fill the n slots in the final vector.

- The merging portion of the merge sort algorithm is performed on two subvectors, each of approximately size $n/2$. Creating each of these subvectors requires $n/2 - 1$ comparisons for each subvector, or $O(n)$ comparisons total. This pattern continues, as each level works on twice as many vectors, but each is half the size of the previous vector.

- Similar to binary search, this halving results in $\log n$ levels, each level requiring $O(n)$ comparisons, for a total efficiency of $O(n \log n)$.

Terminology

Big O notation	linear search
binary search	logarithmic runtime
bubble sort (exercise)	merge sort (recursive implementation)
constant runtime	merge two vectors
efficiency of binary search	$O(1)$
efficiency of insertion sort	$O(\log n)$
efficiency of linear search	$O(n \log n)$
efficiency of merge sort	$O(n)$
efficiency of selection sort	$O(n^2)$
efficient searching algorithms	order 1
efficient sorting algorithms	order $\log n$
inefficient searching algorithms	order n
inefficient sorting algorithms	order n-squared
linear runtime	quadratic runtime

quick sort	sort key
random-access iterator	sort standard library function
search key	sorting data
searching data	split the vector in merge sort
selection sort	worst-case runtime for an algorithm

Self-Review Exercises

20.1   Fill in the blanks in each of the following statements:
  a) A selection sort application would take approximately _____ times as long to run on a 128-element vector as on a 32-element vector.
  b) The efficiency of merge sort is _____.

20.2   What key aspect of both the binary search and the merge sort accounts for the logarithmic portion of their respective Big Os?

20.3   In what sense is the insertion sort superior to the merge sort? In what sense is the merge sort superior to the insertion sort?

20.4   In the text, we say that after the merge sort splits the vector into two subvectors, it then sorts these two subvectors and merges them. Why might someone be puzzled by our statement that "it then sorts these two subvectors"?

Answers to Self-Review Exercises

20.1   a) 16, because an $O(n^2)$ algorithm takes 16 times as long to sort four times as much information. b) $O(n \log n)$.

20.2   Both of these algorithms incorporate "halving"—somehow reducing something by half. The binary search eliminates from consideration half of the vector after each comparison. The merge sort splits the vector in half each time it is called.

20.3   The insertion sort is easier to understand and to implement than the merge sort. The merge sort is far more efficient ($O(n \log n)$) than the insertion sort ($O(n^2)$).

20.4   In a sense, it does not really sort these two subvectors. It simply keeps splitting the original vector in half until it provides a one-element subvector, which is, of course, sorted. It then builds up the original two subvectors by merging these one-element vectors to form larger subvectors, which are then merged, and so on.

Exercises

[*Note:* Most of the exercises shown here are duplicates of exercises from Chapters 8–9. We include the exercises again here as a convenience for readers studying searching and sorting in this chapter.]

20.5   *(Bubble Sort)* Implement bubble sort—another simple yet inefficient sorting technique. It is called bubble sort or sinking sort because smaller values gradually "bubble" their way to the top of the vector (i.e., toward the first element) like air bubbles rising in water, while the larger values sink to the bottom (end) of the vector. The technique uses nested loops to make several passes through the vector. Each pass compares successive pairs of elements. If a pair is in increasing order (or the values are equal), the bubble sort leaves the values as they are. If a pair is in decreasing order, the bubble sort swaps their values in the vector.

The first pass compares the first two element values of the vector and swaps them if necessary. It then compares the second and third element values in the vector. The end of this pass compares the last two element values in the vector and swaps them if necessary. After one pass, the largest value will be in the last element. After two passes, the largest two values will be in the last two elements. Explain why bubble sort is an $O(n^2)$ algorithm.

20.6 *(Enhanced Bubble Sort)* Make the following simple modifications to improve the performance of the bubble sort you developed in Exercise 20.5:

    a) After the first pass, the largest value is guaranteed to be in the highest-numbered element of the vector; after the second pass, the two highest values are "in place"; and so on. Instead of making nine comparisons (for a 10-element vector) on every pass, modify the bubble sort to make only the eight necessary comparisons on the second pass, seven on the third pass, and so on.

    b) The data in the vector may already be in the proper order or near-proper order, so why make nine passes (of a 10-element vector) if fewer will suffice? Modify the sort to check at the end of each pass whether any swaps have been made. If none have been made, the data must already be in the proper order, so the program should terminate. If swaps have been made, at least one more pass is needed.

20.7 *(Bucket Sort)* A bucket sort begins with a one-dimensional vector of positive integers to be sorted and a two-dimensional vector of integers with rows indexed from 0 to 9 and columns indexed from 0 to $n - 1$, where n is the number of values to be sorted. Each row of the two-dimensional vector is referred to as a *bucket*. Write a class named `BucketSort` containing a function called `sort` that operates as follows:

    a) Place each value of the one-dimensional vector into a row of the bucket vector, based on the value's "ones" (rightmost) digit. For example, 97 is placed in row 7, 3 is placed in row 3 and 100 is placed in row 0. This procedure is called a *distribution pass*.

    b) Loop through the bucket vector row by row, and copy the values back to the original vector. This procedure is called a *gathering pass*. The new order of the preceding values in the one-dimensional vector is 100, 3 and 97.

    c) Repeat this process for each subsequent digit position (tens, hundreds, thousands, etc.).

        On the second (tens digit) pass, 100 is placed in row 0, 3 is placed in row 0 (because 3 has no tens digit) and 97 is placed in row 9. After the gathering pass, the order of the values in the one-dimensional vector is 100, 3 and 97. On the third (hundreds digit) pass, 100 is placed in row 1, 3 is placed in row 0 and 97 is placed in row 0 (after the 3). After this last gathering pass, the original vector is in sorted order.

        Note that the two-dimensional vector of buckets is 10 times the length of the integer vector being sorted. This sorting technique provides better performance than a bubble sort, but requires much more memory—the bubble sort requires space for only one additional element of data. This comparison is an example of the space/time trade-off: The bucket sort uses more memory than the bubble sort, but performs better. This version of the bucket sort requires copying all the data back to the original vector on each pass. Another possibility is to create a second two-dimensional bucket vector and repeatedly swap the data between the two bucket vectors.

20.8 *(Recursive Linear Search)* Modify Fig. 8.18 to use recursive function `recursiveLinearSearch` to perform a linear search of the vector. The function should receive the search key and starting index as arguments. If the search key is found, return its index in the vector; otherwise, return –1. Each call to the recursive function should check one element value in the vector.

20.9 *(Recursive Binary Search)* Modify Fig. 20.3 to use recursive function `recursiveBinarySearch` to perform a binary search of the vector. The function should receive the search key, starting index and ending index as arguments. If the search key is found, return its index in the vector. If the search key is not found, return –1.

20.10 *(Quicksort)* The recursive sorting technique called quicksort uses the following basic algorithm for a one-dimensional vector of values:

    a) *Partitioning Step*: Take the first element of the unsorted vector and determine its final location in the sorted vector (i.e., all values to the left of the element in the vector are less than the element's value, and all values to the right of the element in the vector are greater than the element's value—we show how to do this below). We now have one value in its proper location and two unsorted subvectors.

b) *Recursion Step*: Perform the *Partitioning Step* on each unsorted subvector. Each time the *Partitioning Step* is performed on a subvector, another value is placed in its final location of the sorted vector, and two unsorted subvectors are created. When a subvector consists of one element, that element's value is in its final location (because a one-element vector is already sorted).

The basic algorithm seems simple enough, but how do we determine the final position of the first element value of each subvector? As an example, consider the following set of values (the value in bold is for the partitioning element—it will be placed in its final location in the sorted vector):

37 2 6 4 89 8 10 12 68 45

Starting from the rightmost element of the vector, compare each element value with 37 until an element value less than 37 is found; then swap 37 and that element's value. The first element value less than 37 is 12, so 37 and 12 are swapped. The new vector is

12 2 6 4 89 8 10 **37** 68 45

Element value 12 is in italics to indicate that it was just swapped with 37.

Starting from the left of the vector, but beginning with the element value after 12, compare each element value with 37 until an element value greater than 37 is found—then swap 37 and that element value. The first element value greater than 37 is 89, so 37 and 89 are swapped. The new vector is

12 2 6 4 **37** 8 10 *89* 68 45

Starting from the right, but beginning with the element value before 89, compare each element value with 37 until an element value less than 37 is found—then swap 37 and that element value. The first element value less than 37 is 10, so 37 and 10 are swapped. The new vector is

12 2 6 4 *10* 8 **37** 89 68 45

Starting from the left, but beginning with the element value after 10, compare each element value with 37 until an element value greater than 37 is found—then swap 37 and that element value. There are no more element values greater than 37, so when we compare 37 with itself, we know that 37 has been placed in its final location of the sorted vector. Every value to the left of 37 is smaller than it, and every value to the right of 37 is larger than it.

Once the partition has been applied on the previous vector, there are two unsorted subvectors. The subvector with values less than 37 contains 12, 2, 6, 4, 10 and 8. The subvector with values greater than 37 contains 89, 68 and 45. The sort continues recursively, with both subvectors being partitioned in the same manner as the original vector.

Based on the preceding discussion, write recursive function `quickSortHelper` to sort a one-dimensional integer vector. The function should receive as arguments a starting index and an ending index on the original vector being sorted.

Data Structures

OBJECTIVES

In this chapter you'll learn:

- To form linked data structures using pointers, self-referential classes and recursion.

- To create and manipulate dynamic data structures such as linked lists, queues, stacks and binary trees.

- To use binary search trees for high-speed searching and sorting.

- To understand various important applications of linked data structures.

- To understand how to create reusable data structures with class templates, inheritance and composition.

21.1 Introduction

We've studied fixed-size *data structures* such as one-dimensional arrays and two-dimensional arrays. This chapter introduces *dynamic data structures* that grow and shrink during execution. *Linked lists* are collections of data items logically "lined up in a row"—insertions and removals are made anywhere in a linked list. *Stacks* are important in compilers and operating systems: Insertions and removals are made only at one end of a stack—its *top*. *Queues* represent waiting lines; insertions are made at the back (also referred to as the *tail*) of a queue and removals are made from the front (also referred to as the *head*) of a queue. *Binary trees* facilitate high-speed searching and sorting of data, efficient elimination of duplicate data items and compilation of expressions into machine language. These data structures have many other interesting applications.

We discuss several popular and important data structures and implement programs that create and manipulate them. We use classes, class templates, inheritance and composition to create and package these data structures for reusability and maintainability.

Studying this chapter is solid preparation for Chapter 23, Standard Template Library (STL). The STL is a major portion of the C++ Standard Library. The STL provides containers, iterators for traversing those containers and algorithms for processing the elements of those containers. You'll see that the STL has taken each of the data structures we discuss in this chapter and packaged them into templatized classes. The STL code is carefully written to be portable, efficient and extensible. Once you understand the principles and construction of data structures as presented in this chapter, you'll be able to make the best use of the prepackaged data structures, iterators and algorithms in the STL, a world-class set of reusable components.

The chapter examples are practical programs that you'll be able to use in more advanced courses and in industry applications. The programs employ extensive pointer manipulation. The exercises include a rich collection of useful applications.

We encourage you to attempt the major project described in the special section Building Your Own Compiler. You have been using the Visual Studio 2008 C++ compiler to translate your programs to machine language so that you could execute these programs on your computer. In this project, you'll actually build your own compiler. It will read a file of statements written in a simple, yet powerful, high-level language similar to early versions of the popular language BASIC. Your compiler will translate these statements into a file of Simpletron Machine Language (SML) instructions—SML is the language you learned in the Chapter 9 special section, Building Your Own Computer. Your Simpletron Simulator program will then execute the SML program produced by your compiler! Implementing this project using an object-oriented approach will give you a wonderful opportunity to exercise most of what you have learned in this book. The special section carefully walks you through the specifications of the high-level language and describes the algorithms you'll need to convert each type of high-level language statement into machine-language instructions. If you enjoy being challenged, you might attempt the many enhancements to both the compiler and the Simpletron Simulator suggested in this chapter's exercises. The concepts in this chapter apply equally to native and managed code.

21.2 Self-Referential Classes

A *self-referential class* contains a pointer member that points to a class object of the same class type. For example, the definition

```
class Node
{
public:
    Node( int ); // constructor
    void setData( int ); // set data member
    int getData() const; // get data member
    void setNextPtr( Node * ); // set pointer to next Node
    Node *getNextPtr() const; // get pointer to next Node
private:
    int data; // data stored in this Node
    Node *nextPtr; // pointer to another object of same type
}; // end class Node
```

defines a type, Node. Type Node has two private data members—integer member data and pointer member nextPtr. Member nextPtr points to an object of type Node—another object of the same type as the one being declared here, hence the term "self-referential class." Member nextPtr is referred to as a *link*—i.e., nextPtr can "tie" an object of type Node to another object of the same type. Type Node also has five member functions—a constructor that receives an integer to initialize member data, a setData function to set the value of member data, a getData function to return the value of member data, a setNextPtr function to set the value of member nextPtr and a getNextPtr function to return the value of member nextPtr.

Self-referential class objects can be linked together to form useful data structures such as lists, queues, stacks and trees. Figure 21.1 illustrates two self-referential class objects linked together to form a list. Note that a slash—representing a null (0) pointer—is placed in the link member of the second self-referential class object to indicate that the link does not point to another object. The slash is only for illustration purposes; it does not correspond to the backslash character in Visual C++. A null pointer normally indicates the end of a data structure just as the null character ('\0') indicates the end of a string.

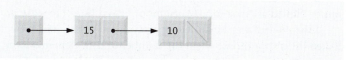

Fig. 21.1 | Two self-referential class objects linked together.

Common Programming Error 21.1

Not setting the link in the last node of a linked data structure to null (0) is a (possibly fatal) logic error.

21.3 Dynamic Memory Allocation and Data Structures

Creating and maintaining dynamic data structures requires dynamic memory allocation, which enables a program to obtain more memory at execution time to hold new nodes. When that memory is no longer needed by the program, the memory can be released so that it can be reused to allocate other objects in the future. The limit for dynamic memory allocation can be as large as the amount of available physical memory in the computer or the amount of available virtual memory in a virtual memory system. Often, the limits are much smaller, because available memory must be shared among many programs.

The new operator takes as an argument the type of the object being dynamically allocated and returns a pointer to an object of that type. For example, the statement

```
Node *newPtr = new Node( 10 ); // create Node with data 10
```

allocates sizeof(Node) bytes, runs the Node constructor and assigns the new Node's address to newPtr. If no memory is available, new throws a bad_alloc exception. The value 10 is passed to the Node constructor, which initializes the Node's data member to 10.

The delete operator runs the Node destructor and deallocates memory allocated with new—the memory is returned to the system so that it can be reallocated in the future. To free memory dynamically allocated by the preceding new, use the statement

```
delete newPtr;
```

Note that newPtr itself is not deleted; rather the space newPtr points to is deleted. If pointer newPtr has the null pointer value 0, the preceding statement has no effect. It is not an error to delete a null pointer.

The following sections discuss lists, stacks, queues and trees. The data structures presented in this chapter are created and maintained with dynamic memory allocation, self-referential classes, class templates and function templates.

21.4 Linked Lists

A linked list is a linear collection of self-referential class objects, called *nodes*, connected by *pointer links*—hence, the term "linked" list. A linked list is accessed via a pointer to the list's first node. Each subsequent node is accessed via the link-pointer member stored in the previous node. By convention, the link pointer in the last node of a list is set to null (0) to mark the end of the list. Data is stored in a linked list dynamically—each node is created as necessary. A node can contain data of any type, including objects of other classes. If nodes contain base-class pointers to base-class and derived-class objects related by inheritance, we can have a linked list of such nodes and process them polymorphically using virtual function calls. Stacks and queues are also *linear data structures* and, as we'll see, can be viewed as constrained versions of linked lists. Trees are *nonlinear data structures*.

Lists of data can be stored in arrays, but linked lists provide several advantages. A linked list is appropriate when the number of data elements to be represented at one time is unpredictable. Linked lists are dynamic, so the length of a list can increase or decrease as necessary. The size of a "conventional" Visual C++ array, however, cannot be altered, because the array size is fixed at compile time. "Conventional" arrays can become full. Linked lists become full only when the system has insufficient memory to satisfy dynamic storage allocation requests.

Performance Tip 21.1

An array can be declared to contain more elements than the number of items expected, but this can waste memory. Linked lists can provide better memory utilization in these situations. Linked lists allow the program to adapt at runtime. Note that class template vector *(introduced in Section 8.11) implements a dynamically resizable array-based data structure.*

Linked lists can be maintained in sorted order by inserting each new element at the proper point in the list. Existing list elements do not need to be moved.

Performance Tip 21.2

Insertion and deletion in a sorted array can be time consuming—all the elements following the inserted or deleted element must be shifted appropriately. A linked list allows efficient insertion operations anywhere in the list.

Performance Tip 21.3

The elements of an array are stored contiguously in memory. This allows immediate access to any array element, because the address of any element can be calculated directly based on its position relative to the beginning of the array. Linked lists do not afford such immediate "direct access" to their elements. So accessing individual elements in a linked list can be considerably more expensive than accessing individual elements in an array. The selection of a data structure is typically based on the performance of specific operations used by a program and the order in which the data items are maintained in the data structure. For example, it is typically more efficient to insert an item in a sorted linked list than a sorted array.

Linked-list nodes are normally not stored contiguously in memory. Logically, however, the nodes of a linked list appear to be contiguous. Figure 21.2 illustrates a linked list with several nodes.

Performance Tip 21.4

Using dynamic memory allocation (instead of fixed-size arrays) for data structures that grow and shrink at execution time can save memory. Keep in mind, however, that pointers occupy space and that dynamic memory allocation incurs the overhead of function calls.

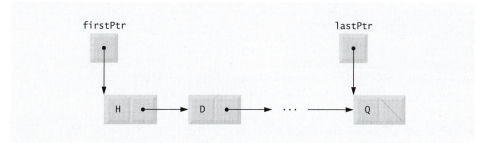

Fig. 21.2 | A graphical representation of a list.

Linked-List Implementation

The program of Figs. 21.3–21.5 uses a List class template (see Chapter 15 for information on class templates) to manipulate a list of integer values and a list of floating-point values. The driver program (Fig. 21.5) provides five options: 1) Insert a value at the beginning of the list, 2) insert a value at the end of the list, 3) delete a value from the beginning of the list, 4) delete a value from the end of the list and 5) end the list processing. A detailed discussion of the program follows. Exercise 21.20 asks you to implement a recursive function that prints a linked list backward, and Exercise 21.21 asks you to implement a recursive function that searches a linked list for a particular data item.

The program uses class templates ListNode (Fig. 21.3) and List (Fig. 21.4). Encapsulated in each List object is a linked list of ListNode objects. Class template ListNode (Fig. 21.3) contains private members data and nextPtr (lines 19–20), a constructor to initialize these members and function getData to return the data in a node. Member data stores a value of type NODETYPE, the type parameter passed to the class template. Member nextPtr stores a pointer to the next ListNode object in the linked list. Note that line 13 of the ListNode class-template definition declares class List< NODETYPE > as a friend. This makes all member functions of a given specialization of class template List friends of the corresponding specialization of class template ListNode, so they can access the private members of ListNode objects of that type. Because the ListNode template parameter

```
1   // Fig. 21.3: ListNode.h
2   // Template ListNode class definition.
3   #ifndef LISTNODE_H
4   #define LISTNODE_H
5
6   // forward declaration of class List required to announce that class
7   // List exists so it can be used in the friend declaration at line 13
8   template< typename NODETYPE > class List;
9
10  template< typename NODETYPE>
11  class ListNode
12  {
13      friend class List< NODETYPE >; // make List a friend
14
15  public:
16      ListNode( const NODETYPE & ); // constructor
17      NODETYPE getData() const; // return data in node
18  private:
19      NODETYPE data; // data
20      ListNode< NODETYPE > *nextPtr; // next node in list
21  }; // end class ListNode
22
23  // constructor
24  template< typename NODETYPE>
25  ListNode< NODETYPE >::ListNode( const NODETYPE &info )
26      : data( info ), nextPtr( 0 )
27  {
28      // empty body
29  } // end ListNode constructor
```

Fig. 21.3 | ListNode class-template definition. (Part 1 of 2.)

```
30
31   // return copy of data in node
32   template< typename NODETYPE >
33   NODETYPE ListNode< NODETYPE >::getData() const
34   {
35      return data;
36   } // end function getData
37
38   #endif
```

Fig. 21.3 | ListNode class-template definition. (Part 2 of 2.)

```
 1   // Fig. 21.4: List.h
 2   // Template List class definition.
 3   #ifndef LIST_H
 4   #define LIST_H
 5
 6   #include <iostream>
 7   using std::cout;
 8
 9   #include "listnode.h" // ListNode class definition
10
11   template< typename NODETYPE >
12   class List
13   {
14   public:
15      List(); // constructor
16      ~List(); // destructor
17      void insertAtFront( const NODETYPE & );
18      void insertAtBack( const NODETYPE & );
19      bool removeFromFront( NODETYPE & );
20      bool removeFromBack( NODETYPE & );
21      bool isEmpty() const;
22      void print() const;
23   private:
24      ListNode< NODETYPE > *firstPtr; // pointer to first node
25      ListNode< NODETYPE > *lastPtr; // pointer to last node
26
27      // utility function to allocate new node
28      ListNode< NODETYPE > *getNewNode( const NODETYPE & );
29   }; // end class List
30
31   // default constructor
32   template< typename NODETYPE >
33   List< NODETYPE >::List()
34      : firstPtr( 0 ), lastPtr( 0 )
35   {
36      // empty body
37   } // end List constructor
38
```

Fig. 21.4 | List class-template definition. (Part 1 of 4.)

```
39   // destructor
40   template< typename NODETYPE >
41   List< NODETYPE >::~List()
42   {
43      if ( !isEmpty() ) // List is not empty
44      {
45         cout << "Destroying nodes ...\n";
46
47         ListNode< NODETYPE > *currentPtr = firstPtr;
48         ListNode< NODETYPE > *tempPtr;
49
50         while ( currentPtr != 0 ) // delete remaining nodes
51         {
52            tempPtr = currentPtr;
53            cout << tempPtr->data << '\n';
54            currentPtr = currentPtr->nextPtr;
55            delete tempPtr;
56         } // end while
57      } // end if
58
59      cout << "All nodes destroyed\n\n";
60   } // end List destructor
61
62   // insert node at front of list
63   template< typename NODETYPE >
64   void List< NODETYPE >::insertAtFront( const NODETYPE &value )
65   {
66      ListNode< NODETYPE > *newPtr = getNewNode( value ); // new node
67
68      if ( isEmpty() ) // List is empty
69         firstPtr = lastPtr = newPtr; // new list has only one node
70      else // List is not empty
71      {
72         newPtr->nextPtr = firstPtr; // point new node to previous 1st node
73         firstPtr = newPtr; // aim firstPtr at new node
74      } // end else
75   } // end function insertAtFront
76
77   // insert node at back of list
78   template< typename NODETYPE >
79   void List< NODETYPE >::insertAtBack( const NODETYPE &value )
80   {
81      ListNode< NODETYPE > *newPtr = getNewNode( value ); // new node
82
83      if ( isEmpty() ) // List is empty
84         firstPtr = lastPtr = newPtr; // new list has only one node
85      else // List is not empty
86      {
87         lastPtr->nextPtr = newPtr; // update previous last node
88         lastPtr = newPtr; // new last node
89      } // end else
90   } // end function insertAtBack
91
```

Fig. 21.4 | List class-template definition. (Part 2 of 4.)

```
 92    // delete node from front of list
 93    template< typename NODETYPE >
 94    bool List< NODETYPE >::removeFromFront( NODETYPE &value )
 95    {
 96       if ( isEmpty() ) // List is empty
 97          return false; // delete unsuccessful
 98       else
 99       {
100          ListNode< NODETYPE > *tempPtr = firstPtr; // hold tempPtr to delete
101
102          if ( firstPtr == lastPtr )
103             firstPtr = lastPtr = 0; // no nodes remain after removal
104          else
105             firstPtr = firstPtr->nextPtr; // point to previous 2nd node
106
107          value = tempPtr->data; // return data being removed
108          delete tempPtr; // reclaim previous front node
109          return true; // delete successful
110       } // end else
111    } // end function removeFromFront
112
113    // delete node from back of list
114    template< typename NODETYPE >
115    bool List< NODETYPE >::removeFromBack( NODETYPE &value )
116    {
117       if ( isEmpty() ) // List is empty
118          return false; // delete unsuccessful
119       else
120       {
121          ListNode< NODETYPE > *tempPtr = lastPtr; // hold tempPtr to delete
122
123          if ( firstPtr == lastPtr ) // List has one element
124             firstPtr = lastPtr = 0; // no nodes remain after removal
125          else
126          {
127             ListNode< NODETYPE > *currentPtr = firstPtr;
128
129             // locate second-to-last element
130             while ( currentPtr->nextPtr != lastPtr )
131                currentPtr = currentPtr->nextPtr; // move to next node
132
133             lastPtr = currentPtr; // remove last node
134             currentPtr->nextPtr = 0; // this is now the last node
135          } // end else
136
137          value = tempPtr->data; // return value from old last node
138          delete tempPtr; // reclaim former last node
139          return true; // delete successful
140       } // end else
141    } // end function removeFromBack
142
```

Fig. 21.4 | List class-template definition. (Part 3 of 4.)

```
143   // is List empty?
144   template< typename NODETYPE >
145   bool List< NODETYPE >::isEmpty() const
146   {
147      return firstPtr == 0;
148   } // end function isEmpty
149
150   // return pointer to newly allocated node
151   template< typename NODETYPE >
152   ListNode< NODETYPE > *List< NODETYPE >::getNewNode(
153      const NODETYPE &value )
154   {
155      return new ListNode< NODETYPE >( value );
156   } // end function getNewNode
157
158   // display contents of List
159   template< typename NODETYPE >
160   void List< NODETYPE >::print() const
161   {
162      if ( isEmpty() ) // List is empty
163      {
164         cout << "The list is empty\n\n";
165         return;
166      } // end if
167
168      ListNode< NODETYPE > *currentPtr = firstPtr;
169
170      cout << "The list is: ";
171
172      while ( currentPtr != 0 ) // get element data
173      {
174         cout << currentPtr->data << ' ';
175         currentPtr = currentPtr->nextPtr;
176      } // end while
177
178      cout << "\n\n";
179   } // end function print
180
181   #endif
```

Fig. 21.4 | List class-template definition. (Part 4 of 4.)

NODETYPE is used as the template argument for List in the friend declaration, ListNodes specialized with a particular type can be processed only by a List specialized with the same type (e.g., a List of int values manages ListNode objects that store int values).

Lines 24–25 of the List class template (Fig. 21.4) declare private data members firstPtr (a pointer to the first ListNode in a List) and lastPtr (a pointer to the last ListNode in a List). The default constructor (lines 32–37) initializes both pointers to 0 (null). The destructor (lines 40–60) ensures that all ListNode objects in a List object are destroyed when that List object is destroyed. The primary List functions are insertAtFront (lines 63–75), insertAtBack (lines 78–90), removeFromFront (lines 93–111) and removeFromBack (lines 114–141).

Function isEmpty (lines 144–148) is called a predicate function—it does not alter the List; rather, it determines whether the List is empty (i.e., the pointer to the first node of the List is null). If the List is empty, true is returned; otherwise, false is returned. Function print (lines 159–179) displays the List's contents. Utility function getNewNode (lines 151–156) returns a dynamically allocated ListNode object. This function is called from functions insertAtFront and insertAtBack.

Error-Prevention Tip 21.1

Assign null (0) to the link member of a new node. Pointers must be initialized before they are used.

The driver program (Fig. 21.5) uses function template testList to enable the user to manipulate objects of class List. Lines 74 and 78 create List objects for types int and double, respectively. Lines 75 and 79 invoke the testList function template with these List objects.

```cpp
1   // Fig. 21.5: ListTest.cpp
2   // List class test program.
3   #include <iostream>
4   using std::cin;
5   using std::cout;
6   using std::endl;
7
8   #include <string>
9   using std::string;
10
11  #include "List.h" // List class definition
12
13  // function to test a List
14  template< typename T >
15  void testList( List< T > &listObject, const string &typeName )
16  {
17     cout << "Testing a List of " << typeName << " values\n";
18     instructions(); // display instructions
19
20     int choice; // store user choice
21     T value; // store input value
22
23     do // perform user-selected actions
24     {
25        cout << "? ";
26        cin >> choice;
27
28        switch ( choice )
29        {
30           case 1: // insert at beginning
31              cout << "Enter " << typeName << ": ";
32              cin >> value;
33              listObject.insertAtFront( value );
34              listObject.print();
35              break;
```

Fig. 21.5 | Manipulating a linked list. (Part 1 of 4.)

```
36                    case 2: // insert at end
37                        cout << "Enter " << typeName << ": ";
38                        cin >> value;
39                        listObject.insertAtBack( value );
40                        listObject.print();
41                        break;
42                    case 3: // remove from beginning
43                        if ( listObject.removeFromFront( value ) )
44                            cout << value << " removed from list\n";
45
46                        listObject.print();
47                        break;
48                    case 4: // remove from end
49                        if ( listObject.removeFromBack( value ) )
50                            cout << value << " removed from list\n";
51
52                        listObject.print();
53                        break;
54                } // end switch
55            } while ( choice != 5 ); // end do...while
56
57            cout << "End list test\n\n";
58        } // end function testList
59
60        // display program instructions to user
61        void instructions()
62        {
63            cout << "Enter one of the following:\n"
64                << "  1 to insert at beginning of list\n"
65                << "  2 to insert at end of list\n"
66                << "  3 to delete from beginning of list\n"
67                << "  4 to delete from end of list\n"
68                << "  5 to end list processing\n";
69        } // end function instructions
70
71        int main()
72        {
73            // test List of int values
74            List< int > integerList;
75            testList( integerList, "integer" );
76
77            // test List of double values
78            List< double > doubleList;
79            testList( doubleList, "double" );
80            return 0;
81        } // end main
```

```
Testing a List of integer values
Enter one of the following:
   1 to insert at beginning of list
   2 to insert at end of list
   3 to delete from beginning of list
```

Fig. 21.5 | Manipulating a linked list. (Part 2 of 4.)

```
     4 to delete from end of list
     5 to end list processing
? 1
Enter integer: 1
The list is: 1

? 1
Enter integer: 2
The list is: 2 1

? 2
Enter integer: 3
The list is: 2 1 3

? 2
Enter integer: 4
The list is: 2 1 3 4

? 3
2 removed from list
The list is: 1 3 4

? 3
1 removed from list
The list is: 3 4

? 4
4 removed from list
The list is: 3

? 4
3 removed from list
The list is empty

? 5
End list test

Testing a List of double values
Enter one of the following:
     1 to insert at beginning of list
     2 to insert at end of list
     3 to delete from beginning of list
     4 to delete from end of list
     5 to end list processing
? 1
Enter double: 1.1
The list is: 1.1

? 1
Enter double: 2.2
The list is: 2.2 1.1

? 2
Enter double: 3.3
The list is: 2.2 1.1 3.3
```

Fig. 21.5 | Manipulating a linked list. (Part 3 of 4.)

```
? 2
Enter double: 4.4
The list is: 2.2 1.1 3.3 4.4

? 3
2.2 removed from list
The list is: 1.1 3.3 4.4

? 3
1.1 removed from list
The list is: 3.3 4.4

? 4
4.4 removed from list
The list is: 3.3

? 4
3.3 removed from list
The list is empty

? 5
End list test

All nodes destroyed

All nodes destroyed
```

Fig. 21.5 | Manipulating a linked list. (Part 4 of 4.)

Member Function insertAtFront

Over the next several pages, we discuss each of the member functions of class List in detail. Function insertAtFront (Fig. 21.4, lines 63–75) places a new node at the front of the list. The function consists of several steps:

1. Call function getNewNode (line 66), passing it value, which is a constant reference to the node value to be inserted.

2. Function getNewNode (lines 151–156) uses operator new to create a new list node and return a pointer to this newly allocated node, which is assigned to newPtr in insertAtFront (line 66).

3. If the list is empty (line 68), then both firstPtr and lastPtr are set to newPtr (line 69).

4. If the list is not empty (line 70), then the node pointed to by newPtr is threaded into the list by copying firstPtr to newPtr->nextPtr (line 72), so that the new node points to what used to be the first node of the list, and copying newPtr to firstPtr (line 73), so that firstPtr now points to the new first node of the list.

Figure 21.6 illustrates function insertAtFront. Part (a) of the figure shows the list and the new node before the insertAtFront operation. The dashed arrows in part (b) illustrate *Step 4* of the insertAtFront operation that enables the node containing 12 to become the new list front.

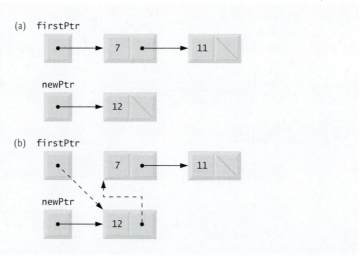

Fig. 21.6 | Operation insertAtFront represented graphically.

Member Function insertAtBack

Function insertAtBack (Fig. 21.4, lines 78–90) places a new node at the back of the list. The function consists of several steps:

1. Call function getNewNode (line 81), passing it value, which is a constant reference to the node value to be inserted.

2. Function getNewNode (lines 151–156) uses operator new to create a new list node and return a pointer to this newly allocated node, which is assigned to newPtr in insertAtBack (line 81).

3. If the list is empty (line 83), then both firstPtr and lastPtr are set to newPtr (line 84).

4. If the list is not empty (line 85), then the node pointed to by newPtr is threaded into the list by copying newPtr into lastPtr->nextPtr (line 87), so that the new node is pointed to by what used to be the last node of the list, and copying newPtr to lastPtr (line 88), so that lastPtr now points to the new last node of the list.

Figure 21.7 illustrates an insertAtBack operation. Part (a) of the figure shows the list and the new node before the operation. The dashed arrows in part (b) illustrate *Step 4* of function insertAtBack that enables a new node to be added to the end of a list that is not empty.

Member Function removeFromFront

Function removeFromFront (Fig. 21.4, lines 93–111) removes the front node of the list and copies the node value to the reference parameter. The function returns false if an attempt is made to remove a node from an empty list (lines 96–97) and returns true if the removal is successful. The function consists of several steps:

1. Assign tempPtr the address to which firstPtr points (line 100). Eventually, tempPtr will be used to delete the node being removed.

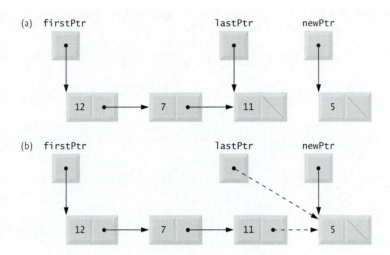

Fig. 21.7 | Operation insertAtBack represented graphically.

2. If firstPtr is equal to lastPtr (line 102), i.e., if the list has only one element prior to the removal attempt, then set firstPtr and lastPtr to zero (line 103) to dethread that node from the list (leaving the list empty).

3. If the list has more than one node prior to removal, then leave lastPtr as is and set firstPtr to firstPtr->nextPtr (line 105); i.e., modify firstPtr to point to what was the second node prior to removal (and is now the new first node).

4. After all these pointer manipulations are complete, copy to reference parameter value the data member of the node being removed (line 107).

5. Now delete the node pointed to by tempPtr (line 108).

6. Return true, indicating successful removal (line 109).

Figure 21.8 illustrates function removeFromFront. Part (a) illustrates the list before the removal operation. Part (b) shows the actual pointer manipulations for removing the front node from a nonempty list.

Member Function removeFromBack
Function removeFromBack (Fig. 21.4, lines 114–141) removes the back node of the list and copies the node value to the reference parameter. The function returns false if an attempt is made to remove a node from an empty list (lines 117–118) and returns true if the removal is successful. The function consists of several steps:

1. Assign to tempPtr the address to which lastPtr points (line 121). Eventually, tempPtr will be used to delete the node being removed.

2. If firstPtr is equal to lastPtr (line 123), i.e., if the list has only one element prior to the removal attempt, then set firstPtr and lastPtr to zero (line 124) to dethread that node from the list (leaving the list empty).

3. If the list has more than one node prior to removal, then assign currentPtr the address to which firstPtr points (line 127) to prepare to "walk the list."

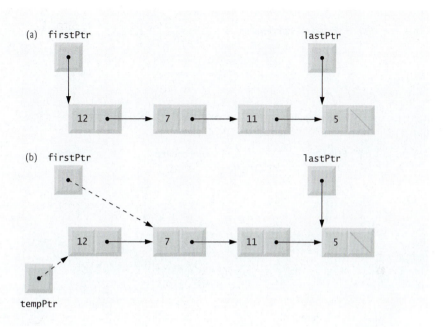

Fig. 21.8 | Operation `removeFromFront` represented graphically.

4. Now "walk the list" with `currentPtr` until it points to the node before the last node. This node will become the last node after the remove operation completes. This is done with a `while` loop (lines 130–131) that keeps replacing `currentPtr` by `currentPtr->nextPtr`, while `currentPtr->nextPtr` is not `lastPtr`.

5. Assign `lastPtr` to the address to which `currentPtr` points (line 133) to dethread the back node from the list.

6. Set `currentPtr->nextPtr` to zero (line 134) in the new last node of the list.

7. After all the pointer manipulations are complete, copy to reference parameter `value` the `data` member of the node being removed (line 137).

8. Now `delete` the node pointed to by `tempPtr` (line 138).

9. Return `true` (line 139), indicating successful removal.

Figure 21.9 illustrates `removeFromBack`. Part (a) of the figure illustrates the list before the removal operation. Part (b) of the figure shows the actual pointer manipulations.

Member Function `print`

Function `print` (lines 159–179) first determines whether the list is empty (line 162). If so, it prints `"The list is empty"` and returns (lines 164–165). Otherwise, it iterates through the list and outputs the value in each node. The function initializes `currentPtr` as a copy of `firstPtr` (line 168), then prints the string `"The list is: "` (line 170). While `currentPtr` is not null (line 172), `currentPtr->data` is printed (line 174) and `current-Ptr` is assigned the value of `currentPtr->nextPtr` (line 175). Note that if the link in the last node of the list is not null, the printing algorithm will erroneously attempt to print

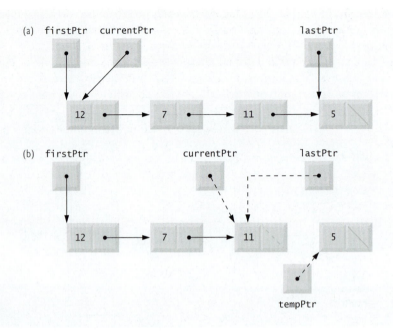

Fig. 21.9 | Operation `removeFromBack` represented graphically.

past the end of the list. The printing algorithm is identical for linked lists, stacks and queues (because we base each of these data structures on the same linked-list infrastructure).

Linear and Circular Singly Linked and Doubly Linked Lists

The kind of linked list we have been discussing is a *singly linked list*—the list begins with a pointer to the first node, and each node contains a pointer to the next node "in sequence." This list terminates with a node whose pointer member has the value 0. A singly linked list may be traversed in only one direction.

A *circular, singly linked list* (Fig. 21.10) begins with a pointer to the first node, and each node contains a pointer to the next node. The "last node" does not contain a 0 pointer; rather, the pointer in the last node points back to the first node, thus closing the "circle."

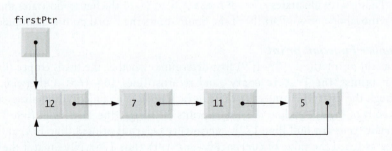

Fig. 21.10 | Circular, singly linked list.

A *doubly linked list* (Fig. 21.11) allows traversals both forward and backward. Such a list is often implemented with two "start pointers"—one that points to the first element of the list to allow front-to-back traversal of the list and one that points to the last element to allow back-to-front traversal. Each node has both a forward pointer to the next node in the list in the forward direction and a backward pointer to the next node in the list in the backward direction. If your list contains an alphabetized telephone directory, for example, a search for someone whose name begins with a letter near the front of the alphabet might begin from the front of the list. Searching for someone whose name begins with a letter near the end of the alphabet might begin from the back of the list.

In a *circular, doubly linked list* (Fig. 21.12), the forward pointer of the last node points to the first node, and the backward pointer of the first node points to the last node, thus closing the "circle."

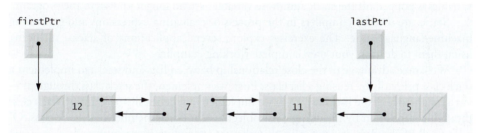

Fig. 21.11 | Doubly linked list.

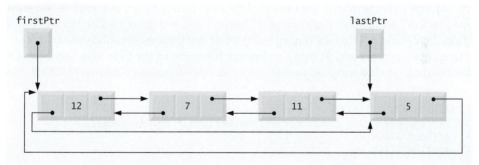

Fig. 21.12 | Circular, doubly linked list.

21.5 Stacks

Chapter 15, explained the notion of a stack class template with an underlying array implementation. In this section, we use an underlying pointer-based linked-list implementation. We also discuss stacks in Chapter 23, Standard Template Library (STL).

A stack data structure allows nodes to be added to the stack and removed from the stack only at the top. For this reason, a stack is referred to as a last-in, first-out (LIFO) data structure. One way to implement a stack is as a constrained version of a linked list. In such an implementation, the link member in the last node of the stack is set to null (zero) to indicate the bottom of the stack.

The primary member functions used to manipulate a stack are push and pop. Function push inserts a new node at the top of the stack. Function pop removes a node from the top of the stack, stores the popped value in a reference variable that is passed to the calling function and returns true if the pop operation was successful (false otherwise).

Stacks have many interesting applications. For example, when a function call is made, the called function must know how to return to its caller, so the return address is pushed onto a stack. If a series of function calls occurs, the successive return values are pushed onto the stack in last-in, first-out order, so that each function can return to its caller. Stacks support recursive function calls in the same manner as conventional nonrecursive calls. Section 7.11 discusses the function-call stack in detail.

Stacks provide the memory for, and store the values of, automatic variables on each invocation of a function. When the function returns to its caller or throws an exception, the destructor (if any) for each local object is called, the space for that function's automatic variables is popped off the stack and those variables are no longer known to the program.

Stacks are used by compilers in the process of evaluating expressions and generating machine-language code. The exercises explore several applications of stacks, including using them to develop your own complete working compiler.

We'll take advantage of the close relationship between lists and stacks to implement a stack class primarily by reusing a list class. First, we implement the stack class through private inheritance of the list class. Then we implement an identically performing stack class through composition by including a list object as a private member of a stack class. Of course, all of the data structures in this chapter, including these two stack classes, are implemented as templates to encourage further reusability.

The program of Figs. 21.13–21.14 creates a Stack class template (Fig. 21.13) primarily through private inheritance (line 9) of the List class template of Fig. 21.4. We want the Stack to have member functions push (lines 13–16), pop (lines 19–22), isStackEmpty (lines 25–28) and printStack (lines 31–34). Note that these are essentially the insertAtFront, removeFromFront, isEmpty and print functions of the List class template. Of course, the List class template contains other member functions (i.e., insertAtBack and

```
1   // Fig. 21.13: Stack.h
2   // Template Stack class definition derived from class List.
3   #ifndef STACK_H
4   #define STACK_H
5
6   #include "List.h" // List class definition
7
8   template< typename STACKTYPE >
9   class Stack : private List< STACKTYPE >
10  {
11  public:
12      // push calls the List function insertAtFront
13      void push( const STACKTYPE &data )
14      {
15          insertAtFront( data );
16      } // end function push
17
```

Fig. 21.13 | Stack class-template definition. (Part 1 of 2.)

```
18      // pop calls the List function removeFromFront
19      bool pop( STACKTYPE &data )
20      {
21          return removeFromFront( data );
22      } // end function pop
23
24      // isStackEmpty calls the List function isEmpty
25      bool isStackEmpty() const
26      {
27          return isEmpty();
28      } // end function isStackEmpty
29
30      // printStack calls the List function print
31      void printStack() const
32      {
33          print();
34      } // end function print
35   }; // end class Stack
36
37   #endif
```

Fig. 21.13 | Stack class-template definition. (Part 2 of 2.)

removeFromBack) that we would not want to make accessible through the public interface to the Stack class. So when we indicate that the Stack class template is to inherit from the List class template, we specify private inheritance. This makes all the List class template's member functions private in the Stack class template. When we implement the Stack's member functions, we then have each of these call the appropriate member function of the List class—push calls insertAtFront (line 15), pop calls removeFromFront (line 21), isStackEmpty calls isEmpty (line 27) and printStack calls print (line 33)—this is referred to as *delegation*.

The stack class template is used in main (Fig. 21.14) to instantiate integer stack int-Stack of type Stack< int > (line 11). Integers 0 through 2 are pushed onto intStack (lines 16–20), then popped off intStack (lines 25–30). The program uses the Stack class template to create doubleStack of type Stack< double > (line 32). Values 1.1, 2.2 and 3.3 are pushed onto doubleStack (lines 38–43), then popped off doubleStack (lines 48–53).

```
1    // Fig. 21.14: StackTest.cpp
2    // Template Stack class test program.
3    #include <iostream>
4    using std::cout;
5    using std::endl;
6
7    #include "Stack.h" // Stack class definition
8
9    int main()
10   {
11       Stack< int > intStack; // create Stack of ints
12
```

Fig. 21.14 | A simple stack program. (Part 1 of 3.)

```
13          cout << "processing an integer stack" << endl;
14
15          // push integers onto intStack
16          for ( int i = 0; i < 3; i++ )
17          {
18             intStack.push( i );
19             intStack.printStack();
20          } // end for
21
22          int popInteger; // store int popped from stack
23
24          // pop integers from intStack
25          while ( !intStack.isStackEmpty() )
26          {
27             intStack.pop( popInteger );
28             cout << popInteger << " popped from stack" << endl;
29             intStack.printStack();
30          } // end while
31
32          Stack< double > doubleStack; // create Stack of doubles
33          double value = 1.1;
34
35          cout << "processing a double stack" << endl;
36
37          // push floating-point values onto doubleStack
38          for ( int j = 0; j < 3; j++ )
39          {
40             doubleStack.push( value );
41             doubleStack.printStack();
42             value += 1.1;
43          } // end for
44
45          double popDouble; // store double popped from stack
46
47          // pop floating-point values from doubleStack
48          while ( !doubleStack.isStackEmpty() )
49          {
50             doubleStack.pop( popDouble );
51             cout << popDouble << " popped from stack" << endl;
52             doubleStack.printStack();
53          } // end while
54
55          return 0;
56       } // end main
```

```
processing an integer stack
The list is: 0

The list is: 1 0

The list is: 2 1 0
```

Fig. 21.14 | A simple stack program. (Part 2 of 3.)

```
2 popped from stack
The list is: 1 0

1 popped from stack
The list is: 0

0 popped from stack
The list is empty

processing a double stack
The list is: 1.1

The list is: 2.2 1.1

The list is: 3.3 2.2 1.1

3.3 popped from stack
The list is: 2.2 1.1

2.2 popped from stack
The list is: 1.1

1.1 popped from stack
The list is empty

All nodes destroyed

All nodes destroyed
```

Fig. 21.14 | A simple stack program. (Part 3 of 3.)

Another way to implement a Stack class template is by reusing the List class template through composition. Figure 21.15 is a new implementation of the Stack class template that contains a List< STACKTYPE > object called stackList (line 38). This version of the Stack class template uses class List from Fig. 21.4. To test this class, use the driver program in Fig. 21.14, but include the new header file—Stackcomposition.h in line 7 of that file. The output of the program is identical for both versions of class Stack.

```
 1   // Fig. 21.15: Stackcomposition.h
 2   // Template Stack class definition with composed List object.
 3   #ifndef STACKCOMPOSITION_H
 4   #define STACKCOMPOSITION_H
 5
 6   #include "List.h" // List class definition
 7
 8   template< typename STACKTYPE >
 9   class Stack
10   {
11   public:
12      // no constructor; List constructor does initialization
```

Fig. 21.15 | Stack class template with a composed List object. (Part 1 of 2.)

```
13
14      // push calls stackList object's insertAtFront member function
15      void push( const STACKTYPE &data )
16      {
17         stackList.insertAtFront( data );
18      } // end function push
19
20      // pop calls stackList object's removeFromFront member function
21      bool pop( STACKTYPE &data )
22      {
23         return stackList.removeFromFront( data );
24      } // end function pop
25
26      // isStackEmpty calls stackList object's isEmpty member function
27      bool isStackEmpty() const
28      {
29         return stackList.isEmpty();
30      } // end function isStackEmpty
31
32      // printStack calls stackList object's print member function
33      void printStack() const
34      {
35         stackList.print();
36      } // end function printStack
37   private:
38      List< STACKTYPE > stackList; // composed List object
39   }; // end class Stack
40
41   #endif
```

Fig. 21.15 | Stack class template with a composed List object. (Part 2 of 2.)

21.6 Queues

A *queue* is similar to a supermarket checkout line—the first person in line is serviced first, and other customers enter the line at the end and wait to be serviced. Queue nodes are removed only from the head of the queue and are inserted only at the tail of the queue. For this reason, a queue is referred to as a first-in, first-out (FIFO) data structure. The insert and remove operations are known as **enqueue** and **dequeue**.

Queues have many applications in computer systems. Computers that have a single processor can service only one user at a time. Entries for the other users are placed in a queue. Each entry gradually advances to the front of the queue as users receive service. The entry at the front of the queue is the next to receive service.

Queues are also used to support *print spooling*. For example, a single printer might be shared by all users of a network. Many users can send print jobs to the printer, even when the printer is already busy. These print jobs are placed in a queue until the printer becomes available. A program called a *spooler* manages the queue to ensure that, as each print job completes, the next print job is sent to the printer.

Information packets also wait in queues in computer networks. Each time a packet arrives at a network node, it must be routed to the next node on the network along the path to the packet's final destination. The routing node routes one packet at a time, so additional packets are enqueued until the router can route them.

A file server in a computer network handles file access requests from many clients throughout the network. Servers have a limited capacity to service requests from clients. When that capacity is exceeded, client requests wait in queues.

The program of Figs. 21.16–21.17 creates a Queue class template (Fig. 21.16) through private inheritance (line 9) of the List class template of Fig. 21.4. We want the Queue to have member functions enqueue (lines 13–16), dequeue (lines 19–22), isQueue-Empty (lines 25–28) and printQueue (lines 31–34). Note that these are essentially the insertAtBack, removeFromFront, isEmpty and print functions of the List class template. Of course, the List class template contains other member functions (i.e., insertAt-Front and removeFromBack) that we would not want to make accessible through the

```cpp
1   // Fig. 21.16: Queue.h
2   // Template Queue class definition derived from class List.
3   #ifndef QUEUE_H
4   #define QUEUE_H
5
6   #include "List.h" // List class definition
7
8   template< typename QUEUETYPE >
9   class Queue : private List< QUEUETYPE >
10  {
11  public:
12     // enqueue calls List member function insertAtBack
13     void enqueue( const QUEUETYPE &data )
14     {
15        insertAtBack( data );
16     } // end function enqueue
17
18     // dequeue calls List member function removeFromFront
19     bool dequeue( QUEUETYPE &data )
20     {
21        return removeFromFront( data );
22     } // end function dequeue
23
24     // isQueueEmpty calls List member function isEmpty
25     bool isQueueEmpty() const
26     {
27        return isEmpty();
28     } // end function isQueueEmpty
29
30     // printQueue calls List member function print
31     void printQueue() const
32     {
33        print();
34     } // end function printQueue
35  }; // end class Queue
36
37  #endif
```

Fig. 21.16 | Queue class-template definition.

public interface to the Queue class. So when we indicate that the Queue class template is to inherit the List class template, we specify private inheritance. This makes all the List class template's member functions private in the Queue class template. When we implement the Queue's member functions, we have each of these call the appropriate member function of the list class—enqueue calls insertAtBack (line 15), dequeue calls remove-FromFront (line 21), isQueueEmpty calls isEmpty (line 27) and printQueue calls print (line 33). Again, this is called delegation.

Figure 21.17 uses the Queue class template to instantiate integer queue intQueue of type Queue< int > (line 11). Integers 0 through 2 are enqueued to intQueue (lines 16–20), then dequeued from intQueue in first-in, first-out order (lines 25–30). Next, the program instantiates queue doubleQueue of type Queue< double > (line 32). Values 1.1, 2.2 and 3.3 are enqueued to doubleQueue (lines 38–43), then dequeued from doubleQueue in first-in, first-out order (lines 48–53).

```cpp
 1   // Fig. 21.17: QueueTest.cpp
 2   // Template Queue class test program.
 3   #include <iostream>
 4   using std::cout;
 5   using std::endl;
 6
 7   #include "Queue.h" // Queue class definition
 8
 9   int main()
10   {
11      Queue< int > intQueue; // create Queue of integers
12
13      cout << "processing an integer Queue" << endl;
14
15      // enqueue integers onto intQueue
16      for ( int i = 0; i < 3; i++ )
17      {
18         intQueue.enqueue( i );
19         intQueue.printQueue();
20      } // end for
21
22      int dequeueInteger; // store dequeued integer
23
24      // dequeue integers from intQueue
25      while ( !intQueue.isQueueEmpty() )
26      {
27         intQueue.dequeue( dequeueInteger );
28         cout << dequeueInteger << " dequeued" << endl;
29         intQueue.printQueue();
30      } // end while
31
32      Queue< double > doubleQueue; // create Queue of doubles
33      double value = 1.1;
34
35      cout << "processing a double Queue" << endl;
36
```

Fig. 21.17 | Queue-processing program. (Part 1 of 2.)

```
37        // enqueue floating-point values onto doubleQueue
38        for ( int j = 0; j < 3; j++ )
39        {
40            doubleQueue.enqueue( value );
41            doubleQueue.printQueue();
42            value += 1.1;
43        } // end for
44
45        double dequeueDouble; // store dequeued double
46
47        // dequeue floating-point values from doubleQueue
48        while ( !doubleQueue.isQueueEmpty() )
49        {
50            doubleQueue.dequeue( dequeueDouble );
51            cout << dequeueDouble << " dequeued" << endl;
52            doubleQueue.printQueue();
53        } // end while
54
55        return 0;
56    } // end main
```

```
processing an integer Queue
The list is: 0

The list is: 0 1

The list is: 0 1 2

0 dequeued
The list is: 1 2

1 dequeued
The list is: 2

2 dequeued
The list is empty

processing a double Queue
The list is: 1.1

The list is: 1.1 2.2

The list is: 1.1 2.2 3.3

1.1 dequeued
The list is: 2.2 3.3

2.2 dequeued
The list is: 3.3

3.3 dequeued
The list is empty

All nodes destroyed

All nodes destroyed
```

Fig. 21.17 | Queue-processing program. (Part 2 of 2.)

21.7 Trees

Linked lists, stacks and queues are linear data structures. A tree is a nonlinear, two-dimensional data structure. Tree nodes contain two or more links. This section discusses *binary trees* (Fig. 21.18)—trees whose nodes all contain two links (none, one or both of which may be null).

Basic Terminology

For this discussion, refer to nodes A, B, C and D in Fig. 21.18. The *root node* (node B) is the first node in a tree. Each link in the root node refers to a *child* (nodes A and D). The *left child* (node A) is the root node of the *left subtree* (which contains only node A), and the *right child* (node D) is the root node of the *right subtree* (which contains nodes D and C). The children of a given node are called *siblings* (e.g., nodes A and D are siblings). A node with no children is a *leaf node* (e.g., nodes A and C are leaf nodes). Computer scientists normally draw trees from the root node down—the opposite of how trees grow in nature.

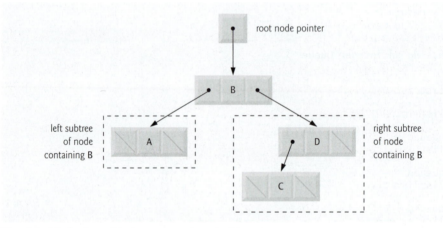

Fig. 21.18 | A graphical representation of a binary tree.

Binary Search Trees

A *binary search tree* (with no duplicate node values) has the characteristic that the values in any left subtree are less than the value in its *parent node*, and the values in any right subtree are greater than the value in its parent node. Figure 21.19 illustrates a binary search tree with 9 values. Note that the shape of the binary search tree that corresponds to a set of data can vary, depending on the order in which the values are inserted into the tree.

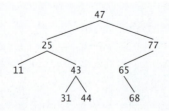

Fig. 21.19 | A binary search tree.

Implementing the Binary Search Tree Program

The program of Figs. 21.20–21.22 creates a binary search tree and traverses it (i.e., walks through all its nodes) three ways—using recursive *inorder*, *preorder* and *postorder traversals*. We explain these traversal algorithms shortly.

We begin our discussion with the driver program (Fig. 21.22), then continue with the implementations of classes TreeNode (Fig. 21.20) and Tree (Fig. 21.21). Function main (Fig. 21.22) begins by instantiating integer tree intTree of type Tree< int > (line 15). The program prompts for 10 integers, each of which is inserted in the binary tree by calling insertNode (line 24). The program then performs preorder, inorder and postorder traversals (these are explained shortly) of intTree (lines 28, 31 and 34, respectively). The program then instantiates floating-point tree doubleTree of type Tree< double > (line 36). The program prompts for 10 double values, each of which is inserted in the binary tree by calling insertNode (line 46). The program then performs preorder, inorder and postorder traversals of doubleTree (lines 50, 53 and 56, respectively).

```cpp
1   // Fig. 21.20: TreeNode.h
2   // Template TreeNode class definition.
3   #ifndef TREENODE_H
4   #define TREENODE_H
5
6   // forward declaration of class Tree
7   template< typename NODETYPE > class Tree;
8
9   // TreeNode class-template definition
10  template< typename NODETYPE >
11  class TreeNode
12  {
13     friend class Tree< NODETYPE >;
14  public:
15     // constructor
16     TreeNode( const NODETYPE &d )
17        : leftPtr( 0 ), // pointer to left subtree
18          data( d ), // tree node data
19          rightPtr( 0 ) // pointer to right subtree
20     {
21        // empty body
22     } // end TreeNode constructor
23
24     // return copy of node's data
25     NODETYPE getData() const
26     {
27        return data;
28     } // end getData function
29  private:
30     TreeNode< NODETYPE > *leftPtr; // pointer to left subtree
31     NODETYPE data;
32     TreeNode< NODETYPE > *rightPtr; // pointer to right subtree
33  }; // end class TreeNode
34
35  #endif
```

Fig. 21.20 | TreeNode class-template definition.

```
 1   // Fig. 21.21: Tree.h
 2   // Template Tree class definition.
 3   #ifndef TREE_H
 4   #define TREE_H
 5
 6   #include <iostream>
 7   using std::cout;
 8   using std::endl;
 9
10   #include "TreeNode.h"
11
12   // Tree class-template definition
13   template< typename NODETYPE > class Tree
14   {
15   public:
16      Tree(); // constructor
17      void insertNode( const NODETYPE & );
18      void preOrderTraversal() const;
19      void inOrderTraversal() const;
20      void postOrderTraversal() const;
21   private:
22      TreeNode< NODETYPE > *rootPtr;
23
24      // utility functions
25      void insertNodeHelper( TreeNode< NODETYPE > **, const NODETYPE & );
26      void preOrderHelper( TreeNode< NODETYPE > * ) const;
27      void inOrderHelper( TreeNode< NODETYPE > * ) const;
28      void postOrderHelper( TreeNode< NODETYPE > * ) const;
29   }; // end class Tree
30
31   // constructor
32   template< typename NODETYPE >
33   Tree< NODETYPE >::Tree()
34   {
35      rootPtr = 0; // indicate tree is initially empty
36   } // end Tree constructor
37
38   // insert node in Tree
39   template< typename NODETYPE >
40   void Tree< NODETYPE >::insertNode( const NODETYPE &value )
41   {
42      insertNodeHelper( &rootPtr, value );
43   } // end function insertNode
44
45   // utility function called by insertNode; receives a pointer
46   // to a pointer so that the function can modify pointer's value
47   template< typename NODETYPE >
48   void Tree< NODETYPE >::insertNodeHelper(
49      TreeNode< NODETYPE > **ptr, const NODETYPE &value )
50   {
51      // subtree is empty; create new TreeNode containing value
52      if ( *ptr == 0 )
53         *ptr = new TreeNode< NODETYPE >( value );
```

Fig. 21.21 | Tree class-template definition. (Part 1 of 3.)

```
54      else // subtree is not empty
55      {
56         // data to insert is less than data in current node
57         if ( value < ( *ptr )->data )
58            insertNodeHelper( &( ( *ptr )->leftPtr ), value );
59         else
60         {
61            // data to insert is greater than data in current node
62            if ( value > ( *ptr )->data )
63               insertNodeHelper( &( ( *ptr )->rightPtr ), value );
64            else // duplicate data value ignored
65               cout << value << " dup" << endl;
66         } // end else
67      } // end else
68   } // end function insertNodeHelper
69
70   // begin preorder traversal of Tree
71   template< typename NODETYPE >
72   void Tree< NODETYPE >::preOrderTraversal() const
73   {
74      preOrderHelper( rootPtr );
75   } // end function preOrderTraversal
76
77   // utility function to perform preorder traversal of Tree
78   template< typename NODETYPE >
79   void Tree< NODETYPE >::preOrderHelper( TreeNode< NODETYPE > *ptr ) const
80   {
81      if ( ptr != 0 )
82      {
83         cout << ptr->data << ' '; // process node
84         preOrderHelper( ptr->leftPtr ); // traverse left subtree
85         preOrderHelper( ptr->rightPtr ); // traverse right subtree
86      } // end if
87   } // end function preOrderHelper
88
89   // begin inorder traversal of Tree
90   template< typename NODETYPE >
91   void Tree< NODETYPE >::inOrderTraversal() const
92   {
93      inOrderHelper( rootPtr );
94   } // end function inOrderTraversal
95
96   // utility function to perform inorder traversal of Tree
97   template< typename NODETYPE >
98   void Tree< NODETYPE >::inOrderHelper( TreeNode< NODETYPE > *ptr ) const
99   {
100     if ( ptr != 0 )
101     {
102        inOrderHelper( ptr->leftPtr ); // traverse left subtree
103        cout << ptr->data << ' '; // process node
104        inOrderHelper( ptr->rightPtr ); // traverse right subtree
105     } // end if
106  } // end function inOrderHelper
```

Fig. 21.21 | Tree class-template definition. (Part 2 of 3.)

```
107
108    // begin postorder traversal of Tree
109    template< typename NODETYPE >
110    void Tree< NODETYPE >::postOrderTraversal() const
111    {
112       postOrderHelper( rootPtr );
113    } // end function postOrderTraversal
114
115    // utility function to perform postorder traversal of Tree
116    template< typename NODETYPE >
117    void Tree< NODETYPE >::postOrderHelper(
118       TreeNode< NODETYPE > *ptr ) const
119    {
120       if ( ptr != 0 )
121       {
122          postOrderHelper( ptr->leftPtr ); // traverse left subtree
123          postOrderHelper( ptr->rightPtr ); // traverse right subtree
124          cout << ptr->data << ' '; // process node
125       } // end if
126    } // end function postOrderHelper
127
128    #endif
```

Fig. 21.21 | Tree class-template definition. (Part 3 of 3.)

Now we discuss the class-template definitions. We begin with the TreeNode class template (Fig. 21.20) definition that declares Tree< NODETYPE > as its friend (line 13). This makes all member functions of a given specialization of class template Tree (Fig. 21.21) friends of the corresponding specialization of class template TreeNode, so they can access the private members of TreeNode objects of that type. Because the TreeNode template parameter NODETYPE is used as the template argument for Tree in the friend declaration, TreeNodes specialized with a particular type can be processed only by a Tree specialized with the same type (e.g., a Tree of int values manages TreeNode objects that store int values).

Lines 30–32 declare a TreeNode's private data—the node's data value, and pointers leftPtr (to the node's left subtree) and rightPtr (to the node's right subtree). The constructor (lines 16–22) sets data to the value supplied as a constructor argument and sets pointers leftPtr and rightPtr to zero (thus initializing this node to be a leaf node). Member function getData (lines 25–28) returns the data value.

```
1    // Fig. 21.22: TreeTest.cpp
2    // Tree class test program.
3    #include <iostream>
4    using std::cout;
5    using std::cin;
6    using std::fixed;
7
8    #include <iomanip>
9    using std::setprecision;
```

Fig. 21.22 | Creating and traversing a binary tree. (Part 1 of 3.)

```
10
11   #include "Tree.h" // Tree class definition
12
13   int main()
14   {
15      Tree< int > intTree; // create Tree of int values
16      int intValue;
17
18      cout << "Enter 10 integer values:\n";
19
20      // insert 10 integers to intTree
21      for ( int i = 0; i < 10; i++ )
22      {
23         cin >> intValue;
24         intTree.insertNode( intValue );
25      } // end for
26
27      cout << "\nPreorder traversal\n";
28      intTree.preOrderTraversal();
29
30      cout << "\nInorder traversal\n";
31      intTree.inOrderTraversal();
32
33      cout << "\nPostorder traversal\n";
34      intTree.postOrderTraversal();
35
36      Tree< double > doubleTree; // create Tree of double values
37      double doubleValue;
38
39      cout << fixed << setprecision( 1 )
40         << "\n\n\nEnter 10 double values:\n";
41
42      // insert 10 doubles to doubleTree
43      for ( int j = 0; j < 10; j++ )
44      {
45         cin >> doubleValue;
46         doubleTree.insertNode( doubleValue );
47      } // end for
48
49      cout << "\nPreorder traversal\n";
50      doubleTree.preOrderTraversal();
51
52      cout << "\nInorder traversal\n";
53      doubleTree.inOrderTraversal();
54
55      cout << "\nPostorder traversal\n";
56      doubleTree.postOrderTraversal();
57
58      cout << endl;
59      return 0;
60   } // end main
```

Fig. 21.22 | Creating and traversing a binary tree. (Part 2 of 3.)

```
Enter 10 integer values:
50 25 75 12 33 67 88 6 13 68

Preorder traversal
50 25 12 6 13 33 75 67 68 88
Inorder traversal
6 12 13 25 33 50 67 68 75 88
Postorder traversal
6 13 12 33 25 68 67 88 75 50


Enter 10 double values:
39.2 16.5 82.7 3.3 65.2 90.8 1.1 4.4 89.5 92.5

Preorder traversal
39.2 16.5 3.3 1.1 4.4 82.7 65.2 90.8 89.5 92.5
Inorder traversal
1.1 3.3 4.4 16.5 39.2 65.2 82.7 89.5 90.8 92.5
Postorder traversal
1.1 4.4 3.3 16.5 65.2 89.5 92.5 90.8 82.7 39.2
```

Fig. 21.22 | Creating and traversing a binary tree. (Part 3 of 3.)

The Tree class template (Fig. 21.21) has as private data rootPtr (line 22), a pointer to the root node of the tree. Lines 17–20 of the class template declare the public member functions insertNode (that inserts a new node in the tree) and preOrderTraversal, inOrderTraversal and postOrderTraversal, each of which walks the tree in the designated manner. Each of these member functions calls its own separate recursive utility function to perform the appropriate operations on the internal representation of the tree, so the program is not required to access the underlying private data to perform these functions. Remember that the recursion requires us to pass in a pointer that represents the next subtree to process. The Tree constructor initializes rootPtr to zero to indicate that the tree is initially empty.

The Tree class's utility function insertNodeHelper (lines 47–68) is called by insert-Node (lines 39–43) to recursively insert a node into the tree. *A node can only be inserted as a leaf node in a binary search tree.* If the tree is empty, a new TreeNode is created, initialized and inserted in the tree (lines 53–54).

If the tree is not empty, the program compares the value to be inserted with the data value in the root node. If the insert value is smaller (line 57), the program recursively calls insertNodeHelper (line 58) to insert the value in the left subtree. If the insert value is larger (line 62), the program recursively calls insertNodeHelper (line 64) to insert the value in the right subtree. If the value to be inserted is identical to the data value in the root node, the program prints the message " dup" (line 65) and returns without inserting the duplicate value into the tree. Note that insertNode passes the address of rootPtr to insertNodeHelper (line 42) so it can modify the value stored in rootPtr (i.e., the address of the root node). To receive a pointer to rootPtr (which is also a pointer), insertNode-Helper's first argument is declared as a pointer to a pointer to a TreeNode.

Each of the member functions inOrderTraversal (lines 90–94), preOrderTraversal (lines 71–75) and postOrderTraversal (lines 109–113) traverses the tree and prints the node values. For the purpose of the following discussion, we use the binary search tree in Fig. 21.23.

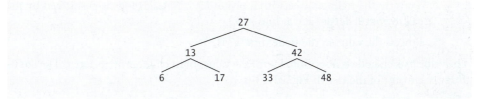

Fig. 21.23 | A binary search tree.

Inorder Traversal Algorithm
Function `inOrderTraversal` invokes utility function `inOrderHelper` to perform the inorder traversal of the binary tree. The steps for an inorder traversal are:

1. Traverse the left subtree with an inorder traversal. (This is performed by the call to `inOrderHelper` at line 102.)

2. Process the value in the node—i.e., print the node value (line 103).

3. Traverse the right subtree with an inorder traversal. (This is performed by the call to `inOrderHelper` at line 104.)

The value in a node is not processed until the values in its left subtree are processed, because each call to `inOrderHelper` immediately calls `inOrderHelper` again with the pointer to the left subtree. The inorder traversal of the tree in Fig. 21.23 is

    6 13 17 27 33 42 48

Note that the inorder traversal of a binary search tree prints the node values in ascending order. The process of creating a binary search tree actually sorts the data—thus, this process is called the *binary tree sort*.

Preorder Traversal Algorithm
Function `preOrderTraversal` invokes utility function `preOrderHelper` to perform the preorder traversal of the binary tree. The steps for a preorder traversal are:

1. Process the value in the node (line 83).

2. Traverse the left subtree with a preorder traversal. (This is performed by the call to `preOrderHelper` at line 84.)

3. Traverse the right subtree with a preorder traversal. (This is performed by the call to `preOrderHelper` at line 85.)

The value in each node is processed as the node is visited. After the value in a given node is processed, the values in the left subtree are processed. Then the values in the right subtree are processed. The preorder traversal of the tree in Fig. 21.23 is

    27 13 6 17 42 33 48

Postorder Traversal Algorithm
Function `postOrderTraversal` invokes utility function `postOrderHelper` to perform the postorder traversal of the binary tree. The steps for a postorder traversal are:

1. Traverse the left subtree with a postorder traversal. (This is performed by the call to `postOrderHelper` at line 122.)

2. Traverse the right subtree with a postorder traversal. (This is performed by the call to `postOrderHelper` at line 123.)

3. Process the value in the node (line 124).

The value in each node is not printed until the values of its children are printed. The `post-OrderTraversal` of the tree in Fig. 21.23 is

```
6  17  13  33  48  42  27
```

Duplicate Elimination

The binary search tree facilitates ***duplicate elimination***. As the tree is being created, an attempt to insert a duplicate value will be recognized, because a duplicate will follow the same "go left" or "go right" decisions on each comparison as the original value did when it was inserted in the tree. Thus, the duplicate will eventually be compared with a node containing the same value. The duplicate value may be discarded at this point.

Searching a binary tree for a value that matches a key value is also fast. If the tree is balanced, then each branch contains about half the number of nodes in the tree. Each comparison of a node to the search key eliminates half the nodes. This is called an $O(\log n)$ algorithm (Big O notation is discussed in Chapter 20). So a binary search tree with n elements would require a maximum of $\log_2 n$ comparisons either to find a match or to determine that no match exists. This means, for example, that when searching a (balanced) 1000-element binary search tree, no more than 10 comparisons need to be made, because $2^{10} > 1000$. When searching a (balanced) 1,000,000-element binary search tree, no more than 20 comparisons need to be made, because $2^{20} > 1,000,000$.

Overview of the Binary Tree Exercises

In the exercises, algorithms are presented for several other binary tree operations such as deleting an item from a binary tree, printing a binary tree in a two-dimensional tree format and performing a level-order traversal of a binary tree. The level-order traversal of a binary tree visits the nodes of the tree row by row, starting at the root node level. On each level of the tree, the nodes are visited from left to right. Other binary tree exercises include allowing a binary search tree to contain duplicate values, inserting string values in a binary tree and determining how many levels are contained in a binary tree.

21.8 Wrap-Up

In this chapter, you learned that linked lists are collections of data items that are "linked up in a chain." You also learned that a program can perform insertions and deletions anywhere in a linked list (though our implementation only performed insertions and deletions at the ends of the list). We demonstrated that the stack and queue data structures are constrained versions of lists. For stacks, you saw that insertions and deletions are made only at the top. For queues that represent waiting lines, you saw that insertions are made at the tail and deletions are made from the head. We also presented the binary tree data structure. You saw a binary search tree that facilitated high-speed searching and sorting of data and efficient duplicate elimination. Throughout the chapter, you learned how to create these data structures for reusability (as templates) and maintainability. In the next chapter, we introduce `struct`s, which are similar to classes, and discuss the manipulation of bits, characters and C-style strings.

Summary

Section 21.1 Introduction
- Dynamic data structures grow and shrink during execution.
- Linked lists are collections of data items "lined up in a row"—insertions and removals are made anywhere in a linked list.
- Stacks are important in compilers and operating systems: Insertions and removals are made only at one end of a stack—its top.
- Queues represent waiting lines; insertions are made at the back (also referred to as the tail) of a queue and removals are made from the front (also referred to as the head).
- Binary trees facilitate high-speed searching and sorting of data, efficient elimination of duplicate data items, representation of file-system directories and compilation of expressions into machine language.

Section 21.2 Self-Referential Classes
- A self-referential class contains a pointer member that points to a class object of the same class type.
- Self-referential class objects can be linked together to form useful data structures such as lists, queues, stacks and trees.

Section 21.3 Dynamic Memory Allocation and Data Structures
- The limit for dynamic memory allocation can be as large as the amount of available physical memory in the computer or the amount of available virtual memory in a virtual memory system.

Section 21.4 Linked Lists
- A linked list is a linear collection of self-referential class objects, called nodes, connected by pointer links—hence, the term "linked" list.
- A linked list is accessed via a pointer to the first node of the list. Each subsequent node is accessed via the link-pointer member stored in the previous node.
- Linked lists, stacks and queues are linear data structures. Trees are nonlinear data structures.
- A linked list is appropriate when the number of data elements to be represented at one time is unpredictable.
- Linked lists are dynamic, so the length of a list can increase or decrease as necessary.
- A singly linked list begins with a pointer to the first node, and each node contains a pointer to the next node "in sequence."
- A circular, singly linked list begins with a pointer to the first node, and each node contains a pointer to the next node. The "last node" does not contain a null pointer; rather, the pointer in the last node points back to the first node, thus closing the "circle."
- A doubly linked list allows traversals both forward and backward.
- A doubly linked list is often implemented with two "start pointers"—one that points to the first element of the list to allow front-to-back traversal of the list and one that points to the last element to allow back-to-front traversal. Each node has both a forward pointer to the next node in the list in the forward direction and a backward pointer to the next node in the backward direction.
- In a circular, doubly linked list, the forward pointer of the last node points to the first node, and the backward pointer of the first node points to the last node, thus closing the "circle."

Section 21.5 Stacks

- A stack data structure allows nodes to be added to and removed from the stack only at the top.

- A stack is referred to as a last-in, first-out (LIFO) data structure.

- The primary member functions used to manipulate a stack are push and pop. Function push inserts a new node at the top of the stack. Function pop removes a node from the top of the stack.

Section 21.6 Queues

- A queue is similar to a supermarket checkout line—the first person in line is serviced first, and other customers enter the line at the end and wait to be serviced.

- Queue nodes are removed only from a queue's head and are inserted only at its tail.

- A queue is referred to as a first-in, first-out (FIFO) data structure. The insert and remove operations are known as enqueue and dequeue.

Section 21.7 Trees

- Binary trees are trees whose nodes all contain two links (none, one or both of which may be null).

- The root node is the first node in a tree.

- Each link in the root node refers to a child. The left child is the root node of the left subtree, and the right child is the root node of the right subtree.

- The children of a single node are called siblings. A node with no children is called a leaf node.

- A binary search tree (with no duplicate node values) has the characteristic that the values in any left subtree are less than the value in its parent node, and the values in any right subtree are greater than the value in its parent node.

- A node can only be inserted as a leaf node in a binary search tree.

- An inorder traversal of a binary tree traverses the left subtree inorder, processes the value in the root node and then traverses the right subtree inorder. The value in a node is not processed until the values in its left subtree are processed.

- A preorder traversal processes the value in the root node, traverses the left subtree preorder, then traverses the right subtree preorder. The value in each node is processed as the node is encountered.

- A postorder traversal traverses the left subtree postorder, traverses the right subtree postorder, then processes the value in the root node. The value in each node is not processed until the values in both its subtrees are processed.

- The binary search tree helps eliminate duplicate data. As the tree is being created, an attempt to insert a duplicate value will be recognized and the duplicate value may be discarded.

- The level-order traversal of a binary tree visits the nodes of the tree row by row, starting at the root node level. On each level of the tree, the nodes are visited from left to right.

Terminology

binary search tree
binary tree
binary tree sort
child node
circular, doubly linked list
circular, singly linked list
data structure
delegation

dequeue
doubly linked list
duplicate elimination
dynamic data structures
enqueue
first-in, first-out (FIFO)
head of a queue
inorder traversal of a binary tree

inserting a node	preorder traversal of a binary tree
last-in, first-out (LIFO)	print spooling
leaf node	push
left child	queue
left subtree	right child
level-order traversal	right subtree
linear data structure	root node
link	self-referential structure
linked list	siblings
node	singly linked list
nonlinear data structure	spooler
parent node	stack
pointer link	tail of a queue
pop	top of a stack
postorder traversal of a binary tree	

Self-Review Exercises

21.1 Fill in the blanks in each of the following:

a) A self-_____ class is used to form dynamic data structures that can grow and shrink at execution time

b) The _____ operator is used to dynamically allocate memory and construct an object; this operator returns a pointer to the object.

c) A(n) _____ is a constrained version of a linked list in which nodes can be inserted and deleted only from the start of the list and node values are returned in last-in, first-out order.

d) A function that does not alter a linked list, but looks at the list to determine whether it is empty, is an example of a(n) _____ function.

e) A queue is referred to as a(n) _____ data structure, because the first nodes inserted are the first nodes removed.

f) The pointer to the next node in a linked list is referred to as a(n) _____.

g) The _____ operator is used to destroy an object and release dynamically allocated memory.

h) A(n) _____ is a constrained version of a linked list in which nodes can be inserted only at the end of the list and deleted only from the start of the list.

i) A(n) _____ is a nonlinear, two-dimensional data structure that contains nodes with two or more links.

j) A stack is referred to as a(n) _____ data structure, because the last node inserted is the first node removed.

k) The nodes of a(n) _____ tree contain two link members.

l) The first node of a tree is the _____ node.

m) Each link in a tree node points to a(n) _____ or _____ of that node.

n) A tree node that has no children is called a(n) _____ node.

o) The four traversal algorithms we mentioned in the text for binary search trees are _____, _____, _____ and _____.

21.2 What are the differences between a linked list and a stack?

21.3 What are the differences between a stack and a queue?

21.4 Perhaps a more appropriate title for this chapter would have been "Reusable Data Structures." Comment on how each of the following entities or concepts contributes to the reusability of data structures:

    a) classes
    b) class templates
    c) inheritance
    d) `private` inheritance
    e) composition

21.5 Manually provide the inorder, preorder and postorder traversals of the binary search tree of Fig. 21.24.

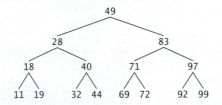

Fig. 21.24 | A 15-node binary search tree.

Answers to Self-Review Exercises

21.1 a) referential. b) `new`. c) stack. d) predicate. e) first-in, first-out (FIFO). f) link. g) `delete`. h) queue. i) tree. j) last-in, first-out (LIFO). k) binary. l) root. m) child or subtree. n) leaf. o) inorder, preorder, postorder and level order.

21.2 It is possible to insert a node anywhere in a linked list and remove a node from anywhere in a linked list. Nodes in a stack may be inserted only at the top of the stack and removed only from the top of a stack.

21.3 A queue data structure allows nodes to be removed only from the head of the queue and inserted only at the tail of the queue. A queue is referred to as a first-in, first-out (FIFO) data structure. A stack data structure allows nodes to be added to the stack and removed from the stack only at the top. A stack is referred to as a last-in, first-out (LIFO) data structure.

21.4 a) Classes allow us to instantiate as many data-structure objects of a certain type (i.e., class) as we wish.

    b) Class templates enable us to instantiate related classes, each based on different type parameters—we can then generate as many objects of each template class as we like.

    c) Inheritance enables us to reuse code from a base class in a derived class, so that the derived-class data structure is also a base-class data structure (with `public` inheritance, that is).

    d) Private inheritance enables us to reuse portions of the code from a base class to form a derived-class data structure; because the inheritance is `private`, all `public` base-class member functions become `private` in the derived class. This enables us to prevent clients of the derived-class data structure from accessing base-class member functions that do not apply to the derived class.

    e) Composition enables us to reuse code by making a class-object data structure a member of a composed class; if we make the class object a `private` member of the composed class, then the class object's `public` member functions are not available through the composed object's interface.

21.5 The inorder traversal is

    11 18 19 28 32 40 44 49 69 71 72 83 92 97 99

The preorder traversal is

    49 28 18 11 19 40 32 44 83 71 69 72 97 92 99

The postorder traversal is

    11 19 18 32 44 40 28 69 72 71 92 99 97 83 49

Exercises

21.6   Write a program that concatenates two linked-list objects of characters. The program should include function `concatenate`, which takes references to both list objects as arguments and concatenates the second list to the first list.

21.7   Write a program that merges two ordered-list objects of integers into a single ordered-list object of integers. Function `merge` should receive references to each of the list objects to be merged and reference to a list object into which the merged elements will be placed.

21.8   Write a program that inserts 25 random integers from 0 to 100 in order in a linked-list object. The program should calculate the sum of the elements and the floating-point average of the elements.

21.9   Write a program that creates a linked-list object of 10 characters and creates a second list object containing a copy of the first list, but in reverse order.

21.10   Write a program that inputs a line of text and uses a stack object to print the line reversed.

21.11   Write a program that uses a stack object to determine if a string is a palindrome (i.e., the string is spelled identically backward and forward). The program should ignore spaces and punctuation.

21.12   Stacks are used by compilers to help in the process of evaluating expressions and generating machine-language code. In this and the next exercise, we investigate how compilers evaluate arithmetic expressions consisting only of constants, operators and parentheses.

Humans generally write expressions like 3 + 4 and 7 / 9 in which the operator (+ or / here) is written between its operands—this is called *infix notation*. Computers "prefer" *postfix notation* in which the operator is written to the right of its two operands. The preceding infix expressions would appear in postfix notation as 3 4 + and 7 9 /, respectively.

To evaluate a complex infix expression, a compiler would first convert the expression to postfix notation and evaluate the postfix version of the expression. Each of these algorithms requires only a single left-to-right pass of the expression. Each algorithm uses a stack object in support of its operation, and in each algorithm the stack is used for a different purpose.

In this exercise, you'll write a Visual C++ version of the infix-to-postfix conversion algorithm. In the next exercise, you'll write a Visual C++ version of the postfix-expression evaluation algorithm. Later in the chapter, you'll discover that code you write in this exercise can help you implement a complete working compiler.

Write a program that converts an ordinary infix arithmetic expression (assume a valid expression is entered) with single-digit integers such as

    (6 + 2) * 5 - 8 / 4

to a postfix expression. The postfix version of the preceding infix expression is

    6 2 + 5 * 8 4 / -

The program should read the expression into character array `infix` and use modified versions of the stack functions implemented in this chapter to help create the postfix expression in character array `postfix`. The algorithm for creating a postfix expression is as follows:

    1) Push a left parenthesis `'('` onto the stack.
    2) Append a right parenthesis `')'` to the end of `infix`.

3) While the stack is not empty, read `infix` from left to right and do the following:

    If the current character in `infix` is a digit, copy it to the next element of `postfix`.

    If the current character in `infix` is a left parenthesis, push it onto the stack.

    If the current character in `infix` is an operator,

        Pop operators (if there are any) at the top of the stack while they have equal or higher precedence than the current operator, and insert the popped operators in `postfix`.

        Push the current character in `infix` onto the stack.

    If the current character in `infix` is a right parenthesis

        Pop operators from the top of the stack and insert them in `postfix` until a left parenthesis is at the top of the stack.

        Pop (and discard) the left parenthesis from the stack.

The following arithmetic operations are allowed in an expression:

- `+`   addition
- `-`   subtraction
- `*`   multiplication
- `/`   division
- `^`   exponentiation
- `%`   modulus

[*Note:* We assume left-to-right associativity for all operators for the purpose of this exercise.] The stack should be maintained with stack nodes, each containing a data member and a pointer to the next stack node.

Some of the functional capabilities you may want to provide are:

a) function `convertToPostfix` that converts the infix expression to postfix notation

b) function `isOperator` that determines whether c is an operator

c) function `precedence` that determines whether the precedence of `operator1` is less than, equal to or greater than the precedence of `operator2` (the function returns −1, 0 and 1, respectively)

d) function `push` that pushes a value onto the stack

e) function `pop` that pops a value off the stack

f) function `stackTop` that returns the top value of the stack without popping the stack

g) function `isEmpty` that determines if the stack is empty

h) function `printStack` that prints the stack

21.13 Write a program that evaluates a postfix expression (assume it is valid) such as

6 2 + 5 * 8 4 / -

The program should read a postfix expression consisting of digits and operators into a character array. Using modified versions of the stack functions implemented earlier in this chapter, the program should scan the expression and evaluate it. The algorithm is as follows:

1) Append the null character (`'\0'`) to the end of the postfix expression. When the null character is encountered, no further processing is necessary.

2) While `'\0'` has not been encountered, read the expression from left to right.

    If the current character is a digit,

        Push its integer value onto the stack (the integer value of a digit character is its value in the computer's character set minus the value of `'0'` in the computer's character set).

    Otherwise, if the current character is an *operator*,

        Pop the two top elements of the stack into variables x and y.

        Calculate y *operator* x.

        Push the result of the calculation onto the stack.

3) When the null character is encountered in the expression, pop the top value of the stack. This is the result of the postfix expression.

[*Note:* In *Step 2* above, if the operator is '/', the top of the stack is 2 and the next element in the stack is 8, then pop 2 into x, pop 8 into y, evaluate 8 / 2 and push the result, 4, back onto the stack. This note also applies to operator '-'.] The arithmetic operations allowed in an expression are

+   addition
–   subtraction
*   multiplication
/   division
∧   exponentiation
%   modulus

[*Note:* We assume left-to-right associativity for all operators for the purpose of this exercise.] The stack should be maintained with stack nodes that contain an int data member and a pointer to the next stack node. You may want to provide the following functional capabilities:

a) function evaluatePostfixExpression that evaluates the postfix expression
b) function calculate that evaluates the expression op1 operator op2
c) function push that pushes a value onto the stack
d) function pop that pops a value off the stack
e) function isEmpty that determines if the stack is empty
f) function printStack that prints the stack

21.14 Modify the postfix evaluator program of Exercise 21.13 so that it can process integer operands larger than 9.

21.15 *(Supermarket Simulation)* Write a program that simulates a checkout line at a supermarket. The line is a queue object. Customers (i.e., customer objects) arrive in random integer intervals of 1–4 minutes. Also, each customer is served in random integer intervals of 1–4 minutes. Obviously, the rates need to be balanced. If the average arrival rate is larger than the average service rate, the queue will grow infinitely. Even with "balanced" rates, randomness can still cause long lines. Run the supermarket simulation for a 12-hour day (720 minutes) using the following algorithm:

1) Choose a random integer between 1 and 4 to determine the minute at which the first customer arrives.
2) At the first customer's arrival time:
   Determine customer's service time (random integer from 1 to 4);
   Begin servicing the customer;
   Schedule arrival time of next customer (random integer 1 to 4 added to the current time).
3) For each minute of the day:
   If the next customer arrives,
       Say so,
       Enqueue the customer;
       Schedule the arrival time of the next customer;
   If service was completed for the last customer;
       Say so
       Dequeue next customer to be serviced
       Determine customer's service completion time
           (random integer from 1 to 4 added to the current time).

Now run your simulation for 720 minutes, and answer each of the following:

a) What is the maximum number of customers in the queue at any time?
b) What is the longest wait any one customer experiences?
c) What happens if the arrival interval is changed from 1–4 minutes to 1–3 minutes?

21.16 Modify the program of Figs. 21.20–21.22 to allow the binary tree object to contain duplicates.

21.17 Write a program based on Figs. 21.20–21.22 that inputs a line of text, tokenizes the sentence into separate words (you may want to use the `strtok` library function), inserts the words in a binary search tree and prints the inorder, preorder and postorder traversals of the tree. Use an OOP approach.

21.18 In this chapter, we saw that duplicate elimination is straightforward when creating a binary search tree. Describe how you would perform duplicate elimination using only a one-dimensional array. Compare the performance of array-based duplicate elimination with the performance of binary-search-tree-based duplicate elimination.

21.19 Write a function `depth` that receives a binary tree and determines how many levels it has.

21.20 (*Recursively Print a List Backward*) Write a member function `printListBackward` that recursively outputs the items in a linked-list object in reverse order. Write a test program that creates a sorted list of integers and prints the list in reverse order.

21.21 (*Recursively Search a List*) Write a member function `searchList` that recursively searches a linked-list object for a specified value. The function should return a pointer to the value if it is found; otherwise, null should be returned. Use your function in a test program that creates a list of integers. The program should prompt the user for a value to locate in the list.

21.22 (*Binary Tree Delete*) In this exercise, we discuss deleting items from binary search trees. The deletion algorithm is not as straightforward as the insertion algorithm. There are three cases that are encountered when deleting an item—the item is contained in a leaf node (i.e., it has no children), the item is contained in a node that has one child or the item is contained in a node that has two children.

If the item to be deleted is contained in a leaf node, the node is deleted and the pointer in the parent node is set to null.

If the item to be deleted is contained in a node with one child, the pointer in the parent node is set to point to the child node and the node containing the data item is deleted. This causes the child node to take the place of the deleted node in the tree.

The last case is the most difficult. When a node with two children is deleted, another node in the tree must take its place. However, the pointer in the parent node cannot be assigned to point to one of the children of the node to be deleted. In most cases, the resulting binary search tree would not adhere to the following characteristic of binary search trees (with no duplicate values): *The values in any left subtree are less than the value in the parent node, and the values in any right subtree are greater than the value in the parent node.*

Which node is used as a *replacement node* to maintain this characteristic? Either the node containing the largest value in the tree less than the value in the node being deleted, or the node containing the smallest value in the tree greater than the value in the node being deleted. Let us consider the node with the smaller value. In a binary search tree, the largest value less than a parent's value is located in the left subtree of the parent node and is guaranteed to be contained in the rightmost node of the subtree. This node is located by walking down the left subtree to the right until the pointer to the right child of the current node is null. We are now pointing to the replacement node, which is either a leaf node or a node with one child to its left. If the replacement node is a leaf node, the steps to perform the deletion are as follows:

1) Store the pointer to the node to be deleted in a temporary pointer variable (this pointer is used to delete the dynamically allocated memory).
2) Set the pointer in the parent of the node being deleted to point to the replacement node.
3) Set the pointer in the parent of the replacement node to null.

4) Set the pointer to the right subtree in the replacement node to point to the right subtree of the node to be deleted.

5) Delete the node to which the temporary pointer variable points.

The deletion steps for a replacement node with a left child are similar to those for a replacement node with no children, but the algorithm also must move the child into the replacement node's position in the tree. If the replacement node is a node with a left child, the steps to perform the deletion are as follows:

1) Store the pointer to the node to be deleted in a temporary pointer variable.

2) Set the pointer in the parent of the node being deleted to point to the replacement node.

3) Set the pointer in the parent of the replacement node to point to the left child of the replacement node.

4) Set the pointer to the right subtree in the replacement node to point to the right subtree of the node to be deleted.

5) Delete the node to which the temporary pointer variable points.

Write member function deleteNode, which takes as its arguments a pointer to the root node of the tree object and the value to be deleted. The function should locate in the tree the node containing the value to be deleted and use the algorithms discussed here to delete the node. The function should print a message that indicates whether the value is deleted. Modify the program of Figs. 21.20–21.22 to use this function. After deleting an item, call the inOrder, preOrder and postOrder traversal functions to confirm that the delete operation was performed correctly.

21.23 (*Binary Tree Search*) Write member function binaryTreeSearch, which attempts to locate a specified value in a binary search tree object. The function should take as arguments a pointer to the root node of the binary tree and a search key to be located. If the node containing the search key is found, the function should return a pointer to that node; otherwise, the function should return a null pointer.

21.24 (*Level-Order Binary Tree Traversal*) The program of Figs. 21.20–21.22 illustrated three recursive methods of traversing a binary tree—inorder, preorder and postorder traversals. This exercise presents the *level-order traversal* of a binary tree, in which the node values are printed level by level, starting at the root node level. The nodes on each level are printed from left to right. The level-order traversal is not a recursive algorithm. It uses a queue object to control the output of the nodes. The algorithm is as follows:

1) Insert the root node in the queue

2) While there are nodes left in the queue,
    Get the next node in the queue
    Print the node's value
    If the pointer to the left child of the node is not null
        Insert the left child node in the queue
    If the pointer to the right child of the node is not null
        Insert the right child node in the queue.

Write member function levelOrder to perform a level-order traversal of a binary tree object. Modify the program of Figs. 21.20–21.22 to use this function. [*Note:* You'll also need to modify and incorporate the queue-processing functions of Fig. 21.16 in this program.]

21.25 (*Printing Trees*) Write a recursive member function outputTree to display a binary tree object on the screen. The function should output the tree row by row, with the top of the tree at the left of the screen and the bottom of the tree toward the right of the screen. Each row is output vertically. For example, the binary tree illustrated in Fig. 21.24 is output as shown in Fig. 21.25. Note that the rightmost leaf node appears at the top of the output in the rightmost column and the root node appears at the left of the output. Each column of output starts five spaces to the right of the previous column. Function outputTree should receive an argument totalSpaces representing the

Fig. 21.25 | Sample level-order traversal.

number of spaces preceding the value to be output (start at zero, so the root node is output at the left of the screen). The function uses a modified inorder traversal to output the tree—it starts at the rightmost node in the tree and works back to the left. The algorithm is as follows:

> While the pointer to the current node is not null
>> Recursively call `outputTree` with the right subtree of the current node and `totalSpaces + 5`
>> Use a for structure to count from 1 to `totalSpaces` and output spaces
>> Output the value in the current node
>> Set the pointer to the current node to point to the left subtree of the current node
>> Increment `totalSpaces` by 5.

Special Section: Building Your Own Compiler

In Exercises 9.20–9.21, we introduced Simpletron Machine Language (SML) and you implemented a Simpletron computer simulator to execute programs written in SML. In this section, we build a compiler that converts programs written in a high-level programming language to SML. This section "ties" together the entire programming process. You'll write programs in this new high-level language, compile these programs on the compiler you build and run them on the simulator you built in Exercise 9.21. You should make every effort to implement your compiler in an object-oriented manner.

21.26 (*The Simple Language*) Before we begin building the compiler, we discuss a simple, yet powerful, high-level language similar to early versions of the popular language BASIC. We call the language *Simple*. Every Simple *statement* consists of a *line number* and a Simple *instruction*. Line numbers must appear in ascending order. Each instruction begins with one of the following Simple *commands*: `rem`, `input`, `let`, `print`, `goto`, `if...goto` and `end` (see Fig. 21.26). All commands except `end` can be used repeatedly. Simple evaluates only integer expressions using the +, -, * and / operators. These operators have the same precedence as in Visual C++. Parentheses can be used to change the order of evaluation of an expression.

Our Simple compiler recognizes only lowercase letters. All characters in a Simple file should be lowercase (uppercase letters result in a syntax error unless they appear in a `rem` statement, in which case they are ignored). A *variable name* is a single letter. Simple does not allow descriptive variable names, so variables should be explained in remarks to indicate their use in a program. Simple uses only integer variables. Simple does not have variable declarations—merely mentioning a variable name in a program causes the variable to be declared and initialized to zero automatically. The syntax of Simple does not allow string manipulation (reading a string, writing a string, comparing strings, etc.). If a string is encountered in a Simple program (after a command other than

Command	Example statement	Description
rem	50 rem this is a remark	Text following rem is for documentation purposes and is ignored by the compiler.
input	30 input x	Display a question mark to prompt the user to enter an integer. Read that integer from the keyboard, and store the integer in x.
let	80 let u = 4 * (j - 56)	Assign u the value of 4 * (j - 56). Note that an arbitrarily complex expression can appear to the right of the equals sign.
print	10 print w	Display the value of w.
goto	70 goto 45	Transfer program control to line 45.
if...goto	35 if i == z goto 80	Compare i and z for equality and transfer control to line 80 if the condition is true; otherwise, continue execution with the next statement.
end	99 end	Terminate program execution.

Fig. 21.26 | Simple commands.

rem), the compiler generates a syntax error. The first version of our compiler will assume that Simple programs are entered correctly. Exercise 21.29 asks the student to modify the compiler to perform syntax error checking.

Simple uses the conditional if...goto statement and the unconditional goto statement to alter the flow of control during program execution. If the condition in the if...goto statement is true, control is transferred to a specific line of the program. The following relational and equality operators are valid in an if...goto statement: <, >, <=, >=, == and !=. The precedence of these operators is the same as in Visual C++.

Let us now consider several programs that demonstrate Simple's features. The first program (Fig. 21.27) reads two integers from the keyboard, stores the values in variables a and b and computes and prints their sum (stored in variable c).

The program of Fig. 21.28 determines and prints the larger of two integers. The integers are input from the keyboard and stored in s and t. The if...goto statement tests the condition s >= t. If the condition is true, control is transferred to line 90 and s is output; otherwise, t is output and control is transferred to the end statement in line 99, where the program terminates.

```
 1    10 rem    determine and print the sum of two integers
 2    15 rem
 3    20 rem    input the two integers
 4    30 input a
 5    40 input b
 6    45 rem
 7    50 rem    add integers and store result in c
 8    60 let c = a + b
 9    65 rem
10    70 rem    print the result
11    80 print c
12    90 rem    terminate program execution
13    99 end
```

Fig. 21.27 | Simple program that determines the sum of two integers.

```
 1    10 rem    determine the larger of two integers
 2    20 input s
 3    30 input t
 4    32 rem
 5    35 rem    test if s >= t
 6    40 if s >= t goto 90
 7    45 rem
 8    50 rem    t is greater than s, so print t
 9    60 print t
10    70 goto 99
11    75 rem
12    80 rem    s is greater than or equal to t, so print s
13    90 print s
14    99 end
```

Fig. 21.28 | Simple program that finds the larger of two integers.

```
 1    10 rem    calculate the squares of several integers
 2    20 input j
 3    23 rem
 4    25 rem    test for sentinel value
 5    30 if j == -9999 goto 99
 6    33 rem
 7    35 rem    calculate square of j and assign result to k
 8    40 let k = j * j
 9    50 print k
10    53 rem
11    55 rem    loop to get next j
12    60 goto 20
13    99 end
```

Fig. 21.29 | Calculate the squares of several integers.

Simple does not provide a repetition statement (such as Visual C++'s for, while or do...while). However, Simple can simulate each of Visual C++'s repetition statements using the if...goto and goto statements. Figure 21.29 uses a sentinel-controlled loop to calculate the squares of several integers. Each integer is input from the keyboard and stored in variable j. If the value entered is the sentinel value -9999, control is transferred to line 99, where the program terminates. Otherwise, k is assigned the square of j, k is output to the screen and control is passed to line 20, where the next integer is input.

Using the sample programs of Fig. 21.27, Fig. 21.28 and Fig. 21.29 as your guide, write a Simple program to accomplish each of the following:

    a) Input three integers, determine their average and print the result.

    b) Use a sentinel-controlled loop to input 10 integers and compute and print their sum.

    c) Use a counter-controlled loop to input seven integers, some positive and some negative, and compute and print their average.

    d) Input a series of integers and determine and print the largest. The first integer input indicates how many numbers should be processed.

    e) Input 10 integers and print the smallest.

    f) Calculate and print the sum of the even integers from 2 to 30.

    g) Calculate and print the product of the odd integers from 1 to 9.

21.27 (*Building a Compiler; Prerequisite: Complete Exercises 8.18, 8.19, 21.12, 21.13 and 21.26*) Now that the Simple language has been presented (Exercise 21.26), we discuss how to build a Simple compiler. First, we consider the process by which a Simple program is converted to SML and executed by the Simpletron simulator (see Fig. 21.30). A file containing a Simple program is read by the compiler and converted to SML code. The SML code is output to a file on disk, in which SML instructions appear one per line. The SML file is then loaded into the Simpletron simulator, and the results are sent to a file on disk and to the screen. Note that the Simpletron program developed in Exercise 9.20 took its input from the keyboard. It must be modified to read from a file so it can run the programs produced by our compiler.

The Simple compiler performs two *passes* of the Simple program to convert it to SML. The first pass constructs a *symbol table* (object) in which every *line number* (object), *variable name* (object) and *constant* (object) of the Simple program is stored with its type and corresponding location in the final SML code (the symbol table is discussed in detail below). The first pass also produces the corresponding SML instruction object(s) for each of the Simple statements (object, etc.). As we'll see, if the Simple program contains statements that transfer control to a line later in the program, the first pass results in an SML program containing some "unfinished" instructions. The second pass of the compiler locates and completes the unfinished instructions, and outputs the SML program to a file.

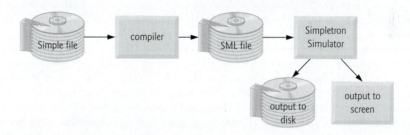

Fig. 21.30 | Writing, compiling and executing a Simple language program.

First Pass

The compiler begins by reading one statement of the Simple program into memory. The line must be separated into its individual *tokens* (i.e., "pieces" of a statement) for processing and compilation (standard library function strtok can be used to facilitate this task). Recall that every statement begins with a line number followed by a command. As the compiler breaks a statement into tokens, if the token is a line number, a variable or a constant, it is placed in the symbol table. A line number is placed in the symbol table only if it is the first token in a statement. The symbolTable object is an array of tableEntry objects representing each symbol in the program. There is no restriction on the number of symbols that can appear in the program. Therefore, the symbolTable for a particular program could be large. Make the symbolTable a 100-element array for now. You can increase or decrease its size once the program is working.

Each tableEntry object contains three members. Member symbol is an integer containing the ASCII representation of a variable (remember that variable names are single characters), a line number or a constant. Member type is one of the following characters indicating the symbol's type: 'C' for constant, 'L' for line number and 'V' for variable. Member location contains the Simpletron memory location (00 to 99) to which the symbol refers. Simpletron memory is an array of 100 integers in which SML instructions and data are stored. For a line number, the location is the element in the Simpletron memory array at which the SML instructions for the Simple statement begin. For a variable or constant, the location is the element in the Simpletron memory array in which the variable or constant is stored. Variables and constants are allocated from the end of Simpletron's memory backward. The first variable or constant is stored in location at 99, the next in location at 98, etc.

The symbol table plays an integral part in converting Simple programs to SML. We learned in Chapter 9 that an SML instruction is a four-digit integer composed of two parts—the *operation code* and the *operand*. The operation code is determined by commands in Simple. For example, the simple command `input` corresponds to SML operation code 10 (read), and the Simple command `print` corresponds to SML operation code 11 (write). The operand is a memory location containing the data on which the operation code performs its task (e.g., operation code 10 reads a value from the keyboard and stores it in the memory location specified by the operand). The compiler searches `symbolTable` to determine the Simpletron memory location for each symbol so the corresponding location can be used to complete the SML instructions.

The compilation of each Simple statement is based on its command. For example, after the line number in a `rem` statement is inserted in the symbol table, the remainder of the statement is ignored by the compiler because a remark is for documentation purposes only. The `input`, `print`, `goto` and `end` statements correspond to the SML *read*, *write*, *branch* (to a specific location) and *halt* instructions. Statements containing these Simple commands are converted directly to SML (note that a `goto` statement may contain an unresolved reference if the specified line number refers to a statement further into the Simple program file; this is sometimes called a forward reference).

When a `goto` statement is compiled with an unresolved reference, the SML instruction must be *flagged* to indicate that the second pass of the compiler must complete the instruction. The flags are stored in 100-element array `flags` of type `int` in which each element is initialized to -1. If the memory location to which a line number in the Simple program refers is not yet known (i.e., it is not in the symbol table), the line number is stored in array `flags` in the element with the same subscript as the incomplete instruction. The operand of the incomplete instruction is set to 00 temporarily. For example, an unconditional branch instruction (making a forward reference) is left as +4000 until the second pass of the compiler. The second pass of the compiler is described shortly.

Compilation of `if...goto` and `let` statements is more complicated than for other statements—they are the only statements that produce more than one SML instruction. For an `if...goto`, the compiler produces code to test the condition and to branch to another line if necessary. The result of the branch could be an unresolved reference. Each of the relational and equality operators can be simulated using SML's *branch zero* or *branch negative* instructions (or a combination of both).

For a `let` statement, the compiler produces code to evaluate an arbitrarily complex arithmetic expression consisting of integer variables and/or constants. Expressions should separate each operand and operator with spaces. Exercise 21.12 and Exercise 21.13 presented the infix-to-postfix conversion algorithm and the postfix evaluation algorithm used by compilers to evaluate expressions. Before proceeding with your compiler, you should complete each of these exercises. When a compiler encounters an expression, it converts the expression from infix notation to postfix notation and then evaluates the postfix expression.

How is it that the compiler produces the machine language to evaluate an expression containing variables? The postfix evaluation algorithm contains a "hook" where the compiler can generate SML instructions rather than actually evaluating the expression. To enable this "hook" in the compiler, the postfix evaluation algorithm must be modified to search the symbol table for each symbol it encounters (and possibly insert it), determine the symbol's corresponding memory location and *push the memory location onto the stack (instead of the symbol)*. When an operator is encountered in the postfix expression, the two memory locations at the top of the stack are popped and machine language for effecting the operation is produced, using the memory locations as operands. The result of each subexpression is stored in a temporary location in memory and pushed back onto the stack so that the evaluation of the postfix expression can continue. When postfix evaluation is complete, the memory location containing the result is the only location left on the stack. This is popped, and SML instructions are generated to assign the result to the variable at the left of the `let` statement.

Second Pass

The second pass of the compiler performs two tasks: Resolve any unresolved references, and output the SML code to a file. Resolution of references occurs as follows:

a) Search the `flags` array for an unresolved reference (i.e., an element with a value other than -1).

b) Locate the object in array `symbolTable`, containing the symbol stored in the `flags` array (be sure that the type of the symbol is 'L' for line number).

c) Insert the memory location from member `location` into the instruction with the unresolved reference (remember that an instruction containing an unresolved reference has operand 00).

d) Repeat *Steps a, b* and *c* until the end of the `flags` array is reached.

After the resolution process is complete, the entire array containing the SML code is output to a disk file with one SML instruction per line. This file can be read by the Simpletron for execution (after the simulator is modified to read its input from a file). Compiling your first Simple program into an SML file and then executing that file should give you a real sense of personal accomplishment.

A Complete Example

The following example illustrates a complete conversion of a Simple program to SML as it will be performed by the Simple compiler. Consider a Simple program that inputs an integer and sums the values from 1 to that integer. The program and the SML instructions produced by the first pass of the Simple compiler are illustrated in Fig. 21.31. The symbol table constructed by the first pass is shown in Fig. 21.32.

Simple program	SML location & instruction		Description
5 rem sum 1 to x	*none*		rem ignored
10 input x	00	+1099	read x into location 99
15 rem check y == x	*none*		rem ignored
20 if y == x goto 60	01	+2098	load y (98) into accumulator
	02	+3199	sub x (99) from accumulator
	03	+4200	branch zero to unresolved location
25 rem increment y	*none*		rem ignored
30 let y = y + 1	04	+2098	load y into accumulator
	05	+3097	add 1 (97) to accumulator
	06	+2196	store in temporary location 96
	07	+2096	load from temporary location 96
	08	+2198	store accumulator in y
35 rem add y to total	*none*		rem ignored
40 let t = t + y	09	+2095	load t (95) into accumulator
	10	+3098	add y to accumulator
	11	+2194	store in temporary location 94

Fig. 21.31 | SML instructions produced after the compiler's first pass. (Part 1 of 2.)

Simple program	SML location & instruction	Description
	12 +2094	load from temporary location 94
	13 +2195	store accumulator in t
45 rem loop y	*none*	rem ignored
50 goto 20	14 +4001	branch to location 01
55 rem output result	*none*	rem ignored
60 print t	15 +1195	output t to screen
99 end	16 +4300	terminate execution

Fig. 21.31 | SML instructions produced after the compiler's first pass. (Part 2 of 2.)

Symbol	Type	Location
5	L	00
10	L	00
'x'	V	99
15	L	01
20	L	01
'y'	V	98
25	L	04
30	L	04
1	C	97
35	L	09
40	L	09
't'	V	95
45	L	14
50	L	14
55	L	15
60	L	15
99	L	16

Fig. 21.32 | Symbol table for program of Fig. 21.31.

Most Simple statements convert directly to single SML instructions. The exceptions in this program are remarks, the if...goto statement in line 20 and the let statements. Remarks don't translate into machine language. However, the line number for a remark is placed in the symbol table in case the line number is referenced in a goto or an if...goto statement. Line 20 of the program specifies that if the condition y == x is true, program control is transferred to line 60. Because line 60 appears later in the program, the first pass of the compiler has not as yet placed 60 in the symbol table (statement line numbers are placed in the symbol table only when they appear as the first token in a statement). Therefore, it is not possible at this time to determine the operand of the

SML *branch zero* instruction at location 03 in the array of SML instructions. The compiler places 60 in location 03 of the `flags` array to indicate that the second pass completes this instruction.

We must keep track of the next instruction location in the SML array, because there is not a one-to-one correspondence between Simple statements and SML instructions. For example, the `if...goto` statement of line 20 compiles into three SML instructions. Each time an instruction is produced, we must increment the *instruction counter* to the next location in the SML array. Note that the size of Simpletron's memory could present a problem for Simple programs with many statements, variables and constants. It is conceivable that the compiler will run out of memory. To test for this case, your program should contain a *data counter* to keep track of the location at which the next variable or constant will be stored in the SML array. If the value of the instruction counter is larger than the value of the data counter, the SML array is full. In this case, the compilation process should terminate and the compiler should print an error message indicating that it ran out of memory during compilation. This serves to emphasize that, although you are freed from the burdens of managing memory by the compiler, the compiler itself must carefully determine the placement of instructions and data in memory, and must check for such errors as memory being exhausted during the compilation process.

A Step-by-Step View of the Compilation Process

Let us now walk through the compilation process for the Simple program in Fig. 21.31. The compiler reads the first line of the program

```
5 rem sum 1 to x
```

into memory. The first token in the statement (the line number) is determined using `strtok` (see Chapter 9 and Chapter 19 for a discussion of Visual C++'s C-style string-manipulation functions). The token returned by `strtok` is converted to an integer using `atoi`, so the symbol 5 can be located in the symbol table. If the symbol is not found, it is inserted in the symbol table. Since we are at the beginning of the program and this is the first line, no symbols are in the table yet. So 5 is inserted into the symbol table as type `L` (line number) and assigned the first location in SML array (00). Although this line is a remark, a space in the symbol table is still allocated for the line number (in case it is referenced by a `goto` or an `if...goto`). No SML instruction is generated for a `rem` statement, so the instruction counter is not incremented.

The statement

```
10 input x
```

is tokenized next. The line number 10 is placed in the symbol table as type `L` and assigned the first location in the SML array (00, because a remark began the program, so the instruction counter is currently 00). The command `input` indicates that the next token is a variable (only a variable can appear in an `input` statement). Because `input` corresponds directly to an SML operation code, the compiler has to determine the location of x in the SML array. Symbol x is not found in the symbol table, so it is inserted into the symbol table as the ASCII representation of x, given type `V`, and assigned location 99 in the SML array (data storage begins at 99 and is allocated backward). SML code can now be generated for this statement. Operation code 10 (the SML read operation code) is multiplied by 100, and the location of x (as determined in the symbol table) is added to complete the instruction. The instruction is then stored in the SML array at location 00. The instruction counter is incremented by 1, because a single SML instruction was produced.

The statement

```
15 rem    check y == x
```

is tokenized next. The symbol table is searched for line number 15 (which is not found). The line number is inserted as type `L` and assigned the next location in the array, 01 (remember that `rem` statements do not produce code, so the instruction counter is not incremented).

The statement

```
20 if y == x goto 60
```

is tokenized next. Line number 20 is inserted in the symbol table and given type L with the next location in the SML array 01. The command if indicates that a condition is to be evaluated. The variable y is not found in the symbol table, so it is inserted and given the type V and the SML location 98. Next, SML instructions are generated to evaluate the condition. Since there is no direct equivalent in SML for the if...goto, it must be simulated by performing a calculation using x and y and branching based on the result. If y is equal to x, the result of subtracting x from y is zero, so the *branch zero* instruction can be used with the result of the calculation to simulate the if...goto statement. The first step requires that y be loaded (from SML location 98) into the accumulator. This produces the instruction 01 +2098. Next, x is subtracted from the accumulator. This produces the instruction 02 +3199. The value in the accumulator may be zero, positive or negative. Since the operator is ==, we want to *branch zero*. First, the symbol table is searched for the branch location (60 in this case), which is not found. So 60 is placed in the flags array at location 03, and the instruction 03 +4200 is generated (we cannot add the branch location, because we have not assigned a location to line 60 in the SML array yet). The instruction counter is incremented to 04.

The compiler proceeds to the statement

```
25 rem   increment y
```

The line number 25 is inserted in the symbol table as type L and assigned SML location 04. The instruction counter is not incremented.

When the statement

```
30 let y = y + 1
```

is tokenized, the line number 30 is inserted in the symbol table as type L and assigned SML location 04. Command let indicates that the line is an assignment statement. First, all the symbols on the line are inserted in the symbol table (if they are not already there). The integer 1 is added to the symbol table as type C and assigned SML location 97. Next, the right side of the assignment is converted from infix to postfix notation. Then the postfix expression (y 1 +) is evaluated. Symbol y is located in the symbol table, and its corresponding memory location is pushed onto the stack. Symbol 1 is also located in the symbol table, and its corresponding memory location is pushed onto the stack. When the operator + is encountered, the postfix evaluator pops the stack into the right operand of the operator, pops the stack again into the left operand of the operator and produces the SML instructions

```
04 +2098    (load y)
05 +3097    (add 1)
```

The result of the expression is stored in a temporary location in memory (96) with instruction

```
06 +2196    (store temporary)
```

and the temporary location is pushed on the stack. Now that the expression has been evaluated, the result must be stored in y (i.e., the variable on the left side of =). So the temporary location is loaded into the accumulator, and the accumulator is stored in y with the instructions

```
07 +2096    (load temporary)
08 +2198    (store y)
```

Notice that SML instructions appear to be redundant. We'll discuss this issue shortly.

When the statement

```
35 rem   add y to total
```

is tokenized, line number 35 is inserted in the symbol table as type L and assigned location 09.

The statement

```
40 let t = t + y
```

is similar to line 30. The variable t is inserted in the symbol table as type V and assigned SML location 95. The instructions follow the same logic and format as line 30, and the instructions 09 +2095, 10 +3098, 11 +2194, 12 +2094 and 13 +2195 are generated. Note that the result of t + y is assigned to temporary location 94 before being assigned to t (95). Once again, note that the instructions in memory locations 11 and 12 appear to be redundant. Again, we'll discuss this shortly.

The statement

```
45 rem    loop y
```

is a remark, so line 45 is added to the symbol table as type L and assigned SML location 14.

The statement

```
50 goto 20
```

transfers control to line 20. Line number 50 is inserted in the symbol table as type L and assigned SML location 14. The equivalent of goto in SML is the *unconditional branch* (40) instruction that transfers control to a specific SML location. The compiler searches the symbol table for line 20 and finds that it corresponds to SML location 01. The operation code (40) is multiplied by 100, and location 01 is added to it to produce the instruction 14 +4001.

The statement

```
55 rem    output result
```

is a remark, so line 55 is inserted in the symbol table as type L and assigned SML location 15.

The statement

```
60 print t
```

is an output statement. Line number 60 is inserted in the symbol table as type L and assigned SML location 15. The equivalent of print in SML is operation code 11 (*write*). The location of t is determined from the symbol table and added to the result of the operation code multiplied by 100.

The statement

```
99 end
```

is the final line of the program. Line number 99 is stored in the symbol table as type L and assigned SML location 16. The end command produces the SML instruction +4300 (43 is *halt* in SML), which is written as the final instruction in the SML memory array.

This completes the first pass of the compiler. We now consider the second pass. The flags array is searched for values other than -1. Location 03 contains 60, so the compiler knows that instruction 03 is incomplete. The compiler completes the instruction by searching the symbol table for 60, determining its location and adding the location to the incomplete instruction. In this case, the search determines that line 60 corresponds to SML location 15, so the completed instruction 03 +4215 is produced, replacing 03 +4200. The Simple program has now been compiled successfully.

To build the compiler, you'll have to perform each of the following tasks:

a) Modify the Simpletron simulator program you wrote in Exercise 9.20 to take its input from a file specified by the user (see Chapter 17). The simulator should output its results to a disk file in the same format as the screen output. Convert the simulator to be an object-oriented program. In particular, make each part of the hardware an object. Arrange the instruction types into a class hierarchy using inheritance. Then execute the program polymorphically by telling each instruction to execute itself with an exe-cuteInstruction message.

b) Modify the infix-to-postfix conversion algorithm of Exercise 21.12 to process multi-digit integer operands and single-letter variable name operands. [*Hint:* C++ Standard

Library function `strtok` can be used to locate each constant and variable in an expression, and constants can be converted from strings to integers using standard library function `atoi` (`<csdtlib>`).] [*Note:* The data representation of the postfix expression must be altered to support variable names and integer constants.]

c) Modify the postfix evaluation algorithm to process multidigit integer operands and variable name operands. Also, the algorithm should now implement the "hook" discussed previously so that SML instructions are produced rather than directly evaluating the expression. [*Hint:* Standard library function `strtok` can be used to locate each constant and variable in an expression, and constants can be converted from strings to integers using standard library function `atoi`.] [*Note:* The data representation of the postfix expression must be altered to support variable names and integer constants.]

d) Build the compiler. Incorporate parts (b) and (c) for evaluating expressions in `let` statements. Your program should contain a function that performs the first pass of the compiler and a function that performs the second pass of the compiler. Both functions can call other functions to accomplish their tasks. Make your compiler as object oriented as possible.

21.28 (*Optimizing the Simple Compiler*) When a program is compiled and converted into SML, a set of instructions is generated. Certain combinations of instructions often repeat themselves, usually in triplets called *productions*. A production normally consists of three instructions such as *load*, *add* and *store*. For example, Fig. 21.33 illustrates five of the SML instructions that were produced in the compilation of the program in Fig. 21.31. The first three instructions are the production that adds 1 to y. Note that instructions 06 and 07 store the accumulator value in temporary location 96 and load the value back into the accumulator so instruction 08 can store the value in location 98. Often a production is followed by a load instruction for the same location that was just stored. This code can be *optimized* by eliminating the store instruction and the subsequent load instruction that operate on the same memory location, thus enabling the Simpletron to execute the program faster. Figure 21.34 illustrates the optimized SML for the program of Fig. 21.31. Note that there are four fewer instructions in the optimized code—a memory-space savings of 25 percent.

1	04	+2098	*(load)*
2	05	+3097	*(add)*
3	06	+2196	*(store)*
4	07	+2096	*(load)*
5	08	+2198	*(store)*

Fig. 21.33 | Nonoptimized code from the program of Fig. 21.31.

Simple program	SML location & instruction		Description
5 rem sum 1 to x	*none*		rem ignored
10 input x	00	+1099	read x into location 99
15 rem check y == x	*none*		rem ignored
20 if y == x goto 60	01	+2098	load y (98) into accumulator
	02	+3199	sub x (99) from accumulator
	03	+4211	branch to location 11 if zero

Fig. 21.34 | Optimized code for the program of Fig. 21.31. (Part 1 of 2.)

Simple program	SML location & instruction	Description
25 rem increment y	*none*	rem ignored
30 let y = y + 1	04 +2098	load y into accumulator
	05 +3097	add 1 (97) to accumulator
	06 +2198	store accumulator in y (98)
35 rem add y to total	*none*	rem ignored
40 let t = t + y	07 +2096	load t from location (96)
	08 +3098	add y (98) accumulator
	09 +2196	store accumulator in t (96)
45 rem loop y	*none*	rem ignored
50 goto 20	10 +4001	branch to location 01
55 rem output result	*none*	rem ignored
60 print t	11 +1196	output t (96) to screen
99 end	12 +4300	terminate execution

Fig. 21.34 | Optimized code for the program of Fig. 21.31. (Part 2 of 2.)

Modify the compiler to provide an option for optimizing the Simpletron Machine Language code it produces. Manually compare the nonoptimized code with the optimized code, and calculate the percentage reduction.

21.29 (*Modifications to the Simple Compiler*) Perform the following modifications to the Simple compiler. Some of these modifications may also require modifications to the Simpletron Simulator program written in Exercise 9.21.

    a) Allow the modulus operator (%) to be used in let statements. Simpletron Machine Language must be modified to include a modulus instruction.

    b) Allow exponentiation in a let statement using ∧ as the exponentiation operator. Simpletron Machine Language must be modified to include an exponentiation instruction.

    c) Allow the compiler to recognize uppercase and lowercase letters in Simple statements (e.g., 'A' is equivalent to 'a'). No modifications to the Simulator are required.

    d) Allow input statements to read values for multiple variables such as input x, y. No modifications to the Simpletron Simulator are required.

    e) Allow the compiler to output multiple values in a single print statement such as print a, b, c. No modifications to the Simpletron Simulator are required.

    f) Add syntax-checking capabilities to the compiler so error messages are output when syntax errors are encountered in a Simple program. No modifications to the Simpletron Simulator are required.

    g) Allow arrays of integers. No modifications to the Simpletron Simulator are required.

    h) Allow subroutines specified by the Simple commands gosub and return. Command gosub passes program control to a subroutine, and command return passes control back to the statement after the gosub. This is similar to a function call in Visual C++. The same subroutine can be called from many gosub commands distributed throughout a program. No modifications to the Simpletron Simulator are required.

    i) Allow repetition statements of the form

```
for x = 2 to 10 step 2
    Simple statements
next
```

This for statement loops from 2 to 10 with an increment of 2. The next line marks the end of the body of the for. No modifications to the Simpletron Simulator are required.

j) Allow repetition statements of the form

```
for x = 2 to 10
    Simple statements
next
```

This for statement loops from 2 to 10 with a default increment of 1. No modifications to the Simpletron Simulator are required.

k) Allow the compiler to process string input and output. This requires the Simpletron Simulator to be modified to process and store string values. [*Hint:* Each Simpletron word can be divided into two groups, each holding a two-digit integer. Each two-digit integer represents the ASCII decimal equivalent of a character. Add a machine-language instruction that will print a string beginning at a certain Simpletron memory location. The first half of the word at that location is a count of the number of characters in the string (i.e., the length of the string). Each succeeding half word contains one ASCII character expressed as two decimal digits. The machine-language instruction checks the length and prints the string by translating each two-digit number into its equivalent character.]

l) Allow the compiler to process floating-point values in addition to integers. The Simpletron Simulator must also be modified to process floating-point values.

21.30 (*A Simple Interpreter*) An interpreter is a program that reads a high-level language program statement, determines the operation to be performed by the statement and executes the operation immediately. The high-level language program is not converted into machine language first. Interpreters execute slowly because each statement encountered in the program must first be deciphered. If statements are contained in a loop, the statements are deciphered each time they are encountered in the loop. Early versions of the BASIC programming language were implemented as interpreters.

Write an interpreter for the Simple language discussed in Exercise 21.26. The program should use the infix-to-postfix converter developed in Exercise 21.12 and the postfix evaluator developed in Exercise 21.13 to evaluate expressions in a let statement. The same restrictions placed on the Simple language in Exercise 21.26 should be adhered to in this program. Test the interpreter with the Simple programs written in Exercise 21.26. Compare the results of running these programs in the interpreter with the results of compiling the Simple programs and running them in the Simpletron Simulator built in Exercise 9.21.

21.31 (*Insert/Delete Anywhere in a Linked List*) Our linked-list class template allowed insertions and deletions at only the front and the back of the linked list. These capabilities were convenient for us when we used private inheritance and composition to produce a stack class template and a queue class template with a minimal amount of code by reusing the list class template. Actually, linked lists are more general than those we provided. Modify the linked-list class template we developed in this chapter to handle insertions and deletions anywhere in the list.

21.32 (*List and Queues without Tail Pointers*) Our implementation of a linked list (Figs. 21.3– 21.5) used both a firstPtr and a lastPtr. The lastPtr was useful for the insertAtBack and removeFromBack member functions of the List class. The insertAtBack function corresponds to the enqueue member function of the Queue class. Rewrite the List class so that it does not use a lastPtr. Thus, any operations on the tail of a list must begin searching the list from the front. Does this affect our implementation of the Queue class (Fig. 21.16)?

21.33 Use the composition version of the stack program (Fig. 21.15) to form a complete working stack program. Modify this program to `inline` the member functions. Compare the two approaches. Summarize the advantages and disadvantages of inlining member functions.

21.34 *(Performance of Binary Tree Sorting and Searching)* One problem with the binary tree sort is that the order in which the data is inserted affects the shape of the tree—for the same collection of data, different orderings can yield binary trees of dramatically different shapes. The performance of the binary tree sorting and searching algorithms is sensitive to the shape of the binary tree. What shape would a binary tree have if its data were inserted in increasing order? in decreasing order? What shape should the tree have to achieve maximal searching performance?

21.35 *(Indexed Lists)* As presented in the text, linked lists must be searched sequentially. For large lists, this can result in poor performance. A common technique for improving list-searching performance is to create and maintain an index to the list. An index is a set of pointers to various key places in the list. For example, an application that searches a large list of names could improve performance by creating an index with 26 entries—one for each letter of the alphabet. A search operation for a last name beginning with "Y" would first search the index to determine where the "Y" entries begin and "jump into" the list at that point and search linearly until the desired name was found. This would be much faster than searching the linked list from the beginning. Use the `List` class of Figs. 21.3–21.5 as the basis of an `IndexedList` class. Write a program that demonstrates the operation of indexed lists. Be sure to include member functions `insertInIndexedList`, `searchIndexedList` and `deleteFromIndexedList`.

22

Bits, Characters, C Strings and **struct**s

OBJECTIVES

In this chapter you'll learn:

- To create and use **struct**s.

- To pass **struct**s to functions by value and by reference.

- To use **typedef** to create aliases for previously defined data types and **struct**s.

- To manipulate data with the bitwise operators and to create bit fields for storing data compactly.

- To use the functions of the character-handling library **<cctype>**.

- To use the string-conversion functions of the general-utilities library **<cstdlib>**.

- To use the string-processing functions of the string-handling library **<cstring>**.

22.1 Introduction

We now discuss structures and the manipulation of bits, characters and C-style strings. Many of the techniques we present here are included for the benefit of the Visual C++ programmer who will work with legacy C and C++ code.

The designers of C++ evolved structures into the notion of a class. Like a class, Visual C++ structures may contain access specifiers, member functions, constructors and destructors. In fact, the only differences between structures and classes in Visual C++ is that structure members default to `public` access and class members default to `private` access when no access specifiers are used, and that structures default to `public` inheritance, whereas classes default to `private` inheritance. Classes have been covered thoroughly in the book, so there is really no need for us to discuss structures in detail. Our presentation of structures in this chapter focuses on their use in C, where structures contain only `public` data members. This use of structures is typical of the legacy C code and early C++ code you'll see in industry.

We discuss how to declare structures, initialize structures and pass structures to functions. Then, we present a high-performance card shuffling and dealing simulation in which we use structure objects and C-style strings to represent the cards. We discuss the bitwise operators that allow programmers to access and manipulate the individual bits in bytes of data. We also present bitfields—special structures that can be used to specify the exact number of bits a variable occupies in memory. These bit-manipulation techniques are common in C and C++ programs that interact directly with hardware devices that have limited memory. The chapter finishes with examples of many character and C-style string-manipulation functions—some of which are designed to process blocks of memory as arrays of bytes.

22.2 Structure Definitions

Structures are *aggregate data types*—that is, they can be built using elements of several types including other `struct`s. Consider the following structure definition:

```
struct Card
{
    char *face;
    char *suit;
}; // end struct Card
```

Keyword *struct* introduces the definition for structure Card. The identifier Card is the *structure name* and is used in Visual C++ to declare variables of the *structure type* (in C, the type name of the preceding structure is struct Card). In this example, the structure type is Card. Data (and possibly functions—just as with classes) declared within the braces of the structure definition are the structure's *members*. Members of the same structure must have unique names, but two different structures may contain members of the same name without conflict. Each structure definition must end with a semicolon.

Common Programming Error 22.1

Forgetting the semicolon that terminates a structure definition is a syntax error.

The definition of Card contains two members of type char *—face and suit. Structure members can be variables of the fundamental data types (e.g., int, double) or aggregates, such as arrays, other structures and or classes. Data members in a single structure definition can be of many data types. For example, an Employee structure might contain character-string members for the first and last names, an int member for the employee's age, a char member containing 'M' or 'F' for the employee's gender, a double member for the employee's hourly salary and so on.

A structure cannot contain an instance of itself. For example, a structure variable Card cannot be declared in the definition for structure Card. A pointer to a Card structure, however, can be included. A structure containing a member that is a pointer to the same structure type is referred to as a *self-referential structure.* We used a similar construct—self-referential classes—in Chapter 21, Data Structures, to build various kinds of linked data structures.

The Card structure definition does not reserve any space in memory; rather, it creates a new data type that is used to declare structure variables. Structure variables are declared like variables of other types. The following declarations

```
Card oneCard;
Card deck[ 52 ];
Card *cardPtr;
```

declare oneCard to be a structure variable of type Card, deck to be an array with 52 elements of type Card and cardPtr to be a pointer to a Card structure. Variables of a given structure type can also be declared by placing a comma-separated list of the variable names between the closing brace of the structure definition and the semicolon that ends the structure definition. For example, the preceding declarations could have been incorporated into the Card structure definition as follows:

```
struct Card
{
    char *face;
    char *suit;
} oneCard, deck[ 52 ], *cardPtr;
```

The structure name is optional. If a structure definition does not contain a structure name, variables of the structure type may be declared only between the closing right brace of the structure definition and the semicolon that terminates the structure definition.

Software Engineering Observation 22.1

Provide a structure name when creating a structure type. The structure name is required for declaring new variables of the structure type later in the program, declaring parameters of the structure type and, if the structure is being used like a Visual C++ class, specifying the name of the constructor and destructor.

The only valid built-in operations that may be performed on structure objects are assigning one structure object to another of the same type, taking the address (&) of a structure object, accessing the members of a structure object (in the same manner as members of a class are accessed) and using the sizeof operator to determine the size of a structure. As with classes, most operators can be overloaded to work with objects of a structure type.

Structure members are not necessarily stored in consecutive bytes of memory. Sometimes there are "holes" in a structure, because some computers store specific data types only on certain memory boundaries, such as half-word, word or double-word boundaries. A word is a standard memory unit used to store data in a computer—usually two bytes or four bytes and typically four bytes on today's popular 32-bit systems. Consider the following structure definition in which structure objects sample1 and sample2 of type Example are declared:

```
struct Example
{
    char c;
    int i;
} sample1, sample2;
```

A computer with two-byte words might require that each of the members of Example be aligned on a word boundary (i.e., at the beginning of a word—this is machine dependent). Figure 22.1 shows a sample storage alignment for an object of type Example that has been assigned the character 'a' and the integer 97 (the bit representations of the values are shown). If the members are stored beginning at word boundaries, there is a one-byte hole (byte 1 in the figure) in the storage for objects of type Example. The value in the one-byte hole is undefined. If the member values of sample1 and sample2 are in fact equal, the structure objects are not necessarily equal, because the undefined one-byte holes are not likely to contain identical values.

Common Programming Error 22.2

Comparing structures is a compilation error.

Byte	0	1	2	3
	01100001		00000000	01100001

Fig. 22.1 | Possible storage alignment for a variable of type Example, showing an undefined area in memory.

22.3 Initializing Structures

Structures can be initialized using initializer lists, as is done with arrays. For example, the declaration

```
Card oneCard = { "Three", "Hearts" };
```

creates `Card` variable `oneCard` and initializes member `face` to `"Three"` and member `suit` to `"Hearts"`. If there are fewer initializers in the list than members in the structure, the remaining members are initialized to their default values. Structure variables declared outside a function definition (i.e., globally) are initialized to their default values if they are not explicitly initialized in the external declaration. Structure variables may also be set in assignment expressions by assigning a structure variable of the same type or by assigning values to the individual data members of the structure.

22.4 Using Structures with Functions

There are two ways to pass the information in structures to functions. You can either pass the entire structure or pass the individual members of a structure. By default, structures are passed by value. Structures and their members can also be passed by reference by passing either references or pointers.

To pass a structure by reference, pass the address of the structure object or a reference to the structure object. Arrays of structures—like all other arrays—are passed by reference.

In Chapter 8, we stated that an array could be passed by value by using a structure. To pass an array by value, create a structure (or a class) with the array as a member, then pass an object of that structure (or class) type to a function by value. Because structure objects are passed by value, the array member, too, is passed by value.

22.5 typedef

Keyword ***typedef*** provides a mechanism for creating synonyms (or aliases) for previously defined data types. Names for structure types are often defined with `typedef` to create shorter, simpler or more readable type names. For example, the statement

```
typedef Card *CardPtr;
```

defines the new type name `CardPtr` as a synonym for type `Card *`.

Creating a new name with `typedef` does not create a new type; `typedef` simply creates a new type name that can then be used in the program as an alias for an existing type name.

Portability Tip 22.2

Synonyms for built-in data types can be created with `typedef` to make programs more portable. For example, a program can use `typedef` to create alias `Integer` for four-byte integers. `Integer` can then be aliased to `int` on systems with four-byte integers and can be aliased to `long int` on systems with two-byte integers where `long int` values occupy four bytes. Then, you simply declare all four-byte integer variables to be of type `Integer`.

22.6 Example: High-Performance Card Shuffling and Dealing Simulation

The program in Figs. 22.2–22.4 is based on the card shuffling and dealing simulation discussed in Chapter 9. The program represents the deck of cards as an array of structures and uses high-performance shuffling and dealing algorithms.

```cpp
1   // Fig. 22.2: DeckOfCards.h
2   // Definition of class DeckOfCards that
3   // represents a deck of playing cards.
4
5   // Card structure definition
6   struct Card
7   {
8      char *face;
9      char *suit;
10  }; // end structure Card
11
12  // DeckOfCards class definition
13  class DeckOfCards
14  {
15  public:
16     DeckOfCards(); // constructor initializes deck
17     void shuffle(); // shuffles cards in deck
18     void deal() const; // deals cards in deck
19
20  private:
21     Card deck[ 52 ]; // represents deck of cards
22  }; // end class DeckOfCards
```

Fig. 22.2 | Header file for `DeckOfCards` class.

```cpp
1   // Fig. 22.3: DeckOfCards.cpp
2   // Member-function definitions for class DeckOfCards that simulates
3   // the shuffling and dealing of a deck of playing cards.
4   #include <iostream>
5   using std::cout;
6   using std::left;
7   using std::right;
```

Fig. 22.3 | Class file for `DeckOfCards`. (Part 1 of 3.)

```
 8
 9   #include <iomanip>
10   using std::setw;
11
12   #include <cstdlib> // prototypes for rand and srand
13   using std::rand;
14   using std::srand;
15
16   #include <ctime> // prototype for time
17   using std::time;
18
19   #include "DeckOfCards.h" // DeckOfCards class definition
20
21   // no-argument DeckOfCards constructor initializes deck
22   DeckOfCards::DeckOfCards()
23   {
24      // initialize suit array
25      static const char *suit[ 4 ] =
26         { "Hearts", "Diamonds", "Clubs", "Spades" };
27
28      // initialize face array
29      static const char *face[ 13 ] =
30         { "Ace", "Deuce", "Three", "Four", "Five", "Six", "Seven",
31           "Eight", "Nine", "Ten", "Jack", "Queen", "King" };
32
33      // set values for deck of 52 Cards
34      for ( int i = 0; i < 52; i++ )
35      {
36         deck[ i ].face = face[ i % 13 ];
37         deck[ i ].suit = suit[ i / 13 ];
38      } // end for
39
40      srand( time( 0 ) ); // seed random number generator
41   } // end no-argument DeckOfCards constructor
42
43   // shuffle cards in deck
44   void DeckOfCards::shuffle()
45   {
46      // shuffle cards randomly
47      for ( int i = 0; i < 52; i++ )
48      {
49         int j = rand() % 52;
50         Card temp = deck[ i ];
51         deck[ i ] = deck[ j ];
52         deck[ j ] = temp;
53      } // end for
54   } // end function shuffle
55
56   // deal cards in deck
57   void DeckOfCards::deal() const
58   {
59      // display each card's face and suit
```

Fig. 22.3 | Class file for `DeckOfCards`. (Part 2 of 3.)

```
60        for ( int i = 0; i < 52; i++ )
61           cout << right << setw( 5 ) << deck[ i ].face << " of "
62              << left << setw( 8 ) << deck[ i ].suit
63              << ( ( i + 1 ) % 2 ? '\t' : '\n' );
64    } // end function deal
```

Fig. 22.3 | Class file for DeckOfCards. (Part 3 of 3.)

```
 1    // Fig. 22.4: DeckTest.cpp
 2    // Card shuffling and dealing program.
 3    #include "DeckOfCards.h" // DeckOfCards class definition
 4
 5    int main()
 6    {
 7       DeckOfCards deckOfCards; // create DeckOfCards object
 8
 9       deckOfCards.shuffle(); // shuffle the cards in the deck
10       deckOfCards.deal(); // deal the cards in the deck
11       return 0; // indicates successful termination
12    } // end main
```

King of Clubs	Ten of Diamonds
Five of Diamonds	Jack of Clubs
Seven of Spades	Five of Clubs
Three of Spades	King of Hearts
Ten of Clubs	Eight of Spades
Eight of Hearts	Six of Hearts
Nine of Diamonds	Nine of Clubs
Three of Diamonds	Queen of Hearts
Six of Clubs	Seven of Hearts
Seven of Diamonds	Jack of Diamonds
Jack of Spades	King of Diamonds
Deuce of Diamonds	Four of Clubs
Three of Clubs	Five of Hearts
Eight of Clubs	Ace of Hearts
Deuce of Spades	Ace of Clubs
Ten of Spades	Eight of Diamonds
Ten of Hearts	Six of Spades
Queen of Diamonds	Nine of Hearts
Seven of Clubs	Queen of Clubs
Deuce of Clubs	Queen of Spades
Three of Hearts	Five of Spades
Deuce of Hearts	Jack of Hearts
Four of Hearts	Ace of Diamonds
Nine of Spades	Four of Diamonds
Ace of Spades	Six of Diamonds
Four of Spades	King of Spades

Fig. 22.4 | High-performance card shuffling and dealing simulation.

The constructor (lines 22–41 of Fig. 22.3) initializes the Card array in order with character strings representing Ace through King of each suit. Function shuffle implements the high-performance shuffling algorithm. The function loops through all 52 cards (array subscripts 0 to 51). For each card, a number between 0 and 51 is picked randomly. Next, the current Card structure and the randomly selected Card structure are swapped in the array. A total of 52 swaps are made in a single pass of the entire array, and the array of Card structures is shuffled! Unlike the shuffling algorithm presented in Chapter 9, this algorithm does not suffer from indefinite postponement. Because the Card structures were swapped in place in the array, the high-performance dealing algorithm implemented in function deal requires only one pass of the array to deal the shuffled cards.

22.7 Bitwise Operators

Visual C++ provides extensive bit-manipulation capabilities for programmers who need to get down to the so-called "bits-and-bytes" level. Operating systems, test-equipment software, networking software and many other kinds of software require that you communicate "directly with the hardware." In this and the next several sections, we discuss Visual C++'s bit-manipulation capabilities. We introduce each of Visual C++'s many bitwise operators, and we discuss how to save memory by using bit fields.

All data is represented internally by computers as sequences of bits. Each bit can assume the value 0 or the value 1. On most systems, a sequence of 8 bits forms a *byte*— the standard storage unit for a variable of type char. Other data types are stored in larger numbers of bytes. Bitwise operators are used to manipulate the bits of integral operands (char, short, int and long; both signed and unsigned). Unsigned integers are normally used with the bitwise operators.

Portability Tip 22.3

Bitwise data manipulations are machine dependent.

Note that the bitwise operator discussions in this section show the binary representations of the integer operands. For a detailed explanation of the binary (also called base-2) number system, see Appendix D, Number Systems. Because of the machine-dependent nature of bitwise manipulations, some of these programs might not work on your system without modification.

The bitwise operators are: *bitwise AND (&), bitwise inclusive OR (|), bitwise exclusive OR (^), left shift (<<), right shift (>>)* and *bitwise complement (~)*—also known as the *one's complement*. (Note that we have been using &, << and >> for other purposes. This is a classic example of operator overloading.) The bitwise AND, bitwise inclusive OR and bitwise exclusive OR operators compare their two operands bit by bit. The bitwise AND operator sets each bit in the result to 1 if the corresponding bit in both operands is 1. The bitwise inclusive OR operator sets each bit in the result to 1 if the corresponding bit in either (or both) operand(s) is 1. The bitwise exclusive OR operator sets each bit in the result to 1 if the corresponding bit in either operand—but not both—is 1. The left-shift operator shifts the bits of its left operand to the left by the number of bits specified in its right operand. The right-shift operator shifts the bits in its left operand to the right by the number of bits specified in its right operand. The bitwise complement operator sets all 0 bits in its operand to 1 in the result and sets all 1 bits in its operand to 0 in the result. Detailed discussions of each bitwise operator appear in the following examples. The bitwise operators are summarized in Fig. 22.5.

Operator	Name	Description
&	bitwise AND	The bits in the result are set to 1 if the corresponding bits in the two operands are both 1.
|	bitwise inclusive OR	The bits in the result are set to 1 if one or both of the corresponding bits in the two operands are 1.
^	bitwise exclusive OR	The bits in the result are set to 1 if exactly one of the corresponding bits in the two operands is 1.
<<	left shift	Shifts the bits of the first operand left by the number of bits specified by the second operand; fill from right with 0 bits.
>>	right shift with sign extension	Shifts the bits of the first operand right by the number of bits specified by the second operand; the method of filling from the left is machine dependent.
~	bitwise complement	All 0 bits are set to 1 and all 1 bits are set to 0.

Fig. 22.5 | Bitwise operators.

Printing a Binary Representation of an Integral Value

When using the bitwise operators, it is useful to illustrate their precise effects by printing values in their binary representation. The program of Fig. 22.6 prints an unsigned integer in its binary representation in groups of eight bits each.

```cpp
 1   // Fig. 22.6: BinaryInteger.cpp
 2   // Printing an unsigned integer in bits.
 3   #include <iostream>
 4   using std::cout;
 5   using std::cin;
 6   using std::endl;
 7
 8   #include <iomanip>
 9   using std::setw;
10
11   void displayBits( unsigned ); // prototype
12
13   int main()
14   {
15      unsigned inputValue; // integral value to print in binary
16
17      cout << "Enter an unsigned integer: ";
18      cin >> inputValue;
19      displayBits( inputValue );
20      return 0;
21   } // end main
22
```

Fig. 22.6 | Printing an unsigned integer in bits. (Part I of 2.)

```
23   // display bits of an unsigned integer value
24   void displayBits( unsigned value )
25   {
26      const int SHIFT = 8 * sizeof( unsigned ) - 1;
27      const unsigned MASK = 1 << SHIFT;
28
29      cout << setw( 10 ) << value << " = ";
30
31      // display bits
32      for ( unsigned i = 1; i <= SHIFT + 1; i++ )
33      {
34         cout << ( value & MASK ? '1' : '0' );
35         value <<= 1; // shift value left by 1
36
37         if ( i % 8 == 0 ) // output a space after 8 bits
38            cout << ' ';
39      } // end for
40
41      cout << endl;
42   } // end function displayBits
```

```
Enter an unsigned integer: 65000
    65000 = 00000000 00000000 11111101 11101000
```

```
Enter an unsigned integer: 29
    29 = 00000000 00000000 00000000 00011101
```

Fig. 22.6 | Printing an unsigned integer in bits. (Part 2 of 2.)

Function `displayBits` (lines 24–42) uses the bitwise AND operator to combine variable `value` with constant `MASK`. Often, the bitwise AND operator is used with an operand called a *mask*—an integer value with specific bits set to 1. Masks are used to hide some bits in a value while selecting other bits. In `displayBits`, line 27 assigns constant `MASK` the value 1 << SHIFT. The value of constant `SHIFT` was calculated in line 26 with the expression

```
8 * sizeof( unsigned ) - 1
```

which multiplies the number of bytes an `unsigned` object requires in memory by 8 (the number of bits in a byte) to get the total number of bits required to store an `unsigned` object, then subtracts 1. The bit representation of 1 << SHIFT on a computer that represents `unsigned` objects in four bytes of memory is

```
10000000 00000000 00000000 00000000
```

The left-shift operator shifts the value 1 from the low-order (rightmost) bit to the high-order (leftmost) bit in `MASK`, and fills in 0 bits from the right. Line 34 determines whether a 1 or a 0 should be printed for the current leftmost bit of variable `value`. Assume that variable `value` contains 65000 (00000000 00000000 11111101 11101000). When `value` and `MASK` are combined using &, all the bits except the high-order bit in variable `value` are "masked off" (hidden), because any bit "ANDed" with 0 yields 0. If the leftmost bit is 1, value & MASK evaluates to

```
00000000 00000000 11111101 11101000      (value)
10000000 00000000 00000000 00000000      (MASK)
-----------------------------------
00000000 00000000 00000000 00000000      (value & MASK)
```

which is interpreted as false, and 0 is printed. Then line 35 shifts variable value left by one bit with the expression value <<= 1 (i.e., value = value << 1). These steps are repeated for each bit variable value. Eventually, a bit with a value of 1 is shifted into the leftmost bit position, and the bit manipulation is as follows:

```
11111101 11101000 00000000 00000000      (value)
10000000 00000000 00000000 00000000      (MASK)
-----------------------------------
10000000 00000000 00000000 00000000      (value & MASK)
```

Because both left bits are 1s, the result of the expression is nonzero (true) and a value of 1 is printed. Figure 22.7 summarizes the results of combining two bits with the bitwise AND operator.

Common Programming Error 22.3

Using the logical AND operator (&&) for the bitwise AND operator (&) and vice versa is a logic error.

The program of Fig. 22.8 demonstrates the bitwise AND operator, the bitwise inclusive OR operator, the bitwise exclusive OR operator and the bitwise complement operator. Function displayBits (lines 57–75) prints the unsigned integer values.

Bit 1	Bit 2	Bit 1 & Bit 2
0	0	0
1	0	0
0	1	0
1	1	1

Fig. 22.7 | Results of combining two bits with the bitwise AND operator (&).

Bitwise AND Operator (&)

In Fig. 22.8, line 21 assigns 2179876355 (10000001 11101110 01000110 00000011) to variable number1, and line 22 assigns 1 (00000000 00000000 00000000 00000001) to variable mask. When mask and number1 are combined using the bitwise AND operator (&) in the expression number1 & mask (line 27), the result is 00000000 00000000 00000000 00000001. All the bits except the low-order bit in variable number1 are "masked off" (hidden) by "ANDing" with constant MASK.

```cpp
1   // Fig. 22.8: BitwiseOperators.cpp
2   // Using the bitwise AND, bitwise inclusive OR, bitwise
3   // exclusive OR and bitwise complement operators.
4   #include <iostream>
5   using std::cout;
6
7   #include <iomanip>
8   using std::endl;
9   using std::setw;
10
11  void displayBits( unsigned ); // prototype
12
13  int main()
14  {
15     unsigned number1;
16     unsigned number2;
17     unsigned mask;
18     unsigned setBits;
19
20     // demonstrate bitwise &
21     number1 = 2179876355;
22     mask = 1;
23     cout << "The result of combining the following\n";
24     displayBits( number1 );
25     displayBits( mask );
26     cout << "using the bitwise AND operator & is\n";
27     displayBits( number1 & mask );
28
29     // demonstrate bitwise |
30     number1 = 15;
31     setBits = 241;
32     cout << "\nThe result of combining the following\n";
33     displayBits( number1 );
34     displayBits( setBits );
35     cout << "using the bitwise inclusive OR operator | is\n";
36     displayBits( number1 | setBits );
37
38     // demonstrate bitwise exclusive OR
39     number1 = 139;
40     number2 = 199;
41     cout << "\nThe result of combining the following\n";
42     displayBits( number1 );
43     displayBits( number2 );
44     cout << "using the bitwise exclusive OR operator ^ is\n";
45     displayBits( number1 ^ number2 );
46
47     // demonstrate bitwise complement
48     number1 = 21845;
49     cout << "\nThe one's complement of\n";
50     displayBits( number1 );
51     cout << "is" << endl;
```

Fig. 22.8 | Bitwise AND, bitwise inclusive OR, bitwise exclusive OR and bitwise complement operators. (Part 1 of 2.)

```
52        displayBits( ~number1 );
53        return 0;
54   } // end main
55
56   // display bits of an unsigned integer value
57   void displayBits( unsigned value )
58   {
59        const int SHIFT = 8 * sizeof( unsigned ) - 1;
60        const unsigned MASK = 1 << SHIFT;
61
62        cout << setw( 10 ) << value << " = ";
63
64        // display bits
65        for ( unsigned i = 1; i <= SHIFT + 1; i++ )
66        {
67           cout << ( value & MASK ? '1' : '0' );
68           value <<= 1; // shift value left by 1
69
70           if ( i % 8 == 0 ) // output a space after 8 bits
71              cout << ' ';
72        } // end for
73
74        cout << endl;
75   } // end function displayBits
```

```
The result of combining the following
2179876355 = 10000001 11101110 01000110 00000011
         1 = 00000000 00000000 00000000 00000001
using the bitwise AND operator & is
         1 = 00000000 00000000 00000000 00000001

The result of combining the following
        15 = 00000000 00000000 00000000 00001111
       241 = 00000000 00000000 00000000 11110001
using the bitwise inclusive OR operator | is
       255 = 00000000 00000000 00000000 11111111

The result of combining the following
       139 = 00000000 00000000 00000000 10001011
       199 = 00000000 00000000 00000000 11000111
using the bitwise exclusive OR operator ^ is
        76 = 00000000 00000000 00000000 01001100

The one's complement of
     21845 = 00000000 00000000 01010101 01010101
is
4294945450 = 11111111 11111111 10101010 10101010
```

Fig. 22.8 | Bitwise AND, bitwise inclusive OR, bitwise exclusive OR and bitwise complement operators. (Part 2 of 2.)

Bitwise Inclusive OR Operator (|)

The bitwise inclusive OR operator is used to set specific bits to 1 in an operand. In Fig. 22.8, line 30 assigns 15 (00000000 00000000 00000000 00001111) to variable `number1`, and line 31 assigns 241 (00000000 00000000 00000000 11110001) to variable `setBits`. When `number1` and `setBits` are combined using the bitwise OR operator in the expression `number1 | setBits` (line 36), the result is 255 (00000000 00000000 00000000 11111111). Figure 22.9 summarizes the results of combining two bits with the bitwise inclusive OR operator.

Common Programming Error 22.4

Using the logical OR operator (||) for the bitwise OR operator (|) and vice versa is a logic error.

Bit 1	Bit 2	Bit 1 | Bit 2
0	0	0
1	0	1
0	1	1
1	1	1

Fig. 22.9 | Combining two bits with the bitwise inclusive OR operator (|).

Bitwise Exclusive OR (∧)

The bitwise exclusive OR operator (∧) sets each bit in the result to 1 if *exactly* one of the corresponding bits in its two operands is 1. In Fig. 22.8, lines 39–40 assign variables `number1` and `number2` the values 139 (00000000 00000000 00000000 10001011) and 199 (00000000 00000000 00000000 11000111), respectively. When these variables are combined with the exclusive OR operator in the expression `number1 ∧ number2` (line 45), the result is 00000000 00000000 00000000 01001100. Figure 22.10 summarizes the results of combining two bits with the bitwise exclusive OR operator.

Bit 1	Bit 2	Bit 1 ∧ Bit 2
0	0	0
1	0	1
0	1	1
1	1	0

Fig. 22.10 | Combining two bits with the bitwise exclusive OR operator (∧).

Bitwise Complement (~)

The bitwise complement operator (~) sets all 1 bits in its operand to 0 in the result and sets all 0 bits to 1 in the result—otherwise referred to as "taking the one's complement of the value." In Fig. 22.8, line 48 assigns variable `number1` the value 21845 (00000000 00000000 01010101 01010101). When the expression `~number1` evaluates, the result is (11111111 11111111 10101010 10101010).

Figure 22.11 demonstrates the left-shift operator (<<) and the right-shift operator (>>). Function displayBits (lines 31–49) prints the unsigned integer values.

```cpp
1   // Fig. 22.11: BitwiseShift.cpp
2   // Using the bitwise shift operators.
3   #include <iostream>
4   using std::cout;
5   using std::endl;
6
7   #include <iomanip>
8   using std::setw;
9
10  void displayBits( unsigned ); // prototype
11
12  int main()
13  {
14     unsigned number1 = 960;
15
16     // demonstrate bitwise left shift
17     cout << "The result of left shifting\n";
18     displayBits( number1 );
19     cout << "8 bit positions using the left-shift operator is\n";
20     displayBits( number1 << 8 );
21
22     // demonstrate bitwise right shift
23     cout << "\nThe result of right shifting\n";
24     displayBits( number1 );
25     cout << "8 bit positions using the right-shift operator is\n";
26     displayBits( number1 >> 8 );
27     return 0;
28  } // end main
29
30  // display bits of an unsigned integer value
31  void displayBits( unsigned value )
32  {
33     const int SHIFT = 8 * sizeof( unsigned ) - 1;
34     const unsigned MASK = 1 << SHIFT;
35
36     cout << setw( 10 ) << value << " = ";
37
38     // display bits
39     for ( unsigned i = 1; i <= SHIFT + 1; i++ )
40     {
41        cout << ( value & MASK ? '1' : '0' );
42        value <<= 1; // shift value left by 1
43
44        if ( i % 8 == 0 ) // output a space after 8 bits
45           cout << ' ';
46     } // end for
47
48     cout << endl;
49  } // end function displayBits
```

Fig. 22.11 | Bitwise shift operators. (Part 1 of 2.)

```
The result of left shifting
        960 = 00000000 00000000 00000011 11000000
8 bit positions using the left-shift operator is
    245760 = 00000000 00000011 11000000 00000000

The result of right shifting
        960 = 00000000 00000000 00000011 11000000
8 bit positions using the right-shift operator is
          3 = 00000000 00000000 00000000 00000011
```

Fig. 22.11 | Bitwise shift operators. (Part 2 of 2.)

Left-Shift Operator

The left-shift operator (<<) shifts the bits of its left operand to the left by the number of bits specified in its right operand. Bits vacated to the right are replaced with 0s; bits shifted off the left are lost. In Fig. 22.11, line 14 assigns variable `number1` the value 960 (00000000 00000000 00000011 11000000). The result of left shifting variable `number1` 8 bits in the expression `number1 << 8` (line 20) is 245760 (00000000 00000011 11000000 00000000).

Right-Shift Operator

The right-shift operator (>>) shifts the bits of its left operand to the right by the number of bits specified in its right operand. Performing a right shift on an `unsigned` integer causes the vacated bits at the left to be replaced by 0s; bits shifted off the right are lost. In the program of Fig. 22.11, the result of right shifting `number1` in the expression `number1 >> 8` (line 26) is 3 (00000000 00000000 00000000 00000011).

Common Programming Error 22.5

The result of shifting a value is undefined if the right operand is negative or if the right operand is greater than or equal to the number of bits in which the left operand is stored.

Portability Tip 22.4

The result of right shifting a signed value is machine dependent. Some machines fill with zeros and others use the sign bit.

Bitwise Assignment Operators

Each bitwise operator (except the bitwise complement operator) has a corresponding assignment operator. These *bitwise assignment operators* are shown in Fig. 22.12; they are used in a similar manner to the arithmetic assignment operators introduced in Chapter 3.

Bitwise assignment operators	
&=	Bitwise AND assignment operator.
|=	Bitwise inclusive OR assignment operator.
^=	Bitwise exclusive OR assignment operator.
<<=	Left-shift assignment operator.
>>=	Right-shift with sign extension assignment operator.

Fig. 22.12 | Bitwise assignment operators.

Figure 22.13 shows the precedence and associativity of the operators introduced up to this point in the text. They are shown top to bottom in decreasing order of precedence.

Operators	Associativity	Type
:: (unary; right to left) :: (binary; left to right)	left to right	highest
() [] . -> ++ -- static_cast< *type* >()	left to right	unary
++ -- + - ! delete sizeof	right to left	unary
* ~ & new		
* / %	left to right	multiplicative
+ -	left to right	additive
<< >>	left to right	shifting
< <= > >=	left to right	relational
== !=	left to right	equality
&	left to right	bitwise AND
^	left to right	bitwise XOR
|	left to right	bitwise OR
&&	left to right	logical AND
||	left to right	logical OR
?:	right to left	conditional
= += -= *= /= %= &= |= ^= <<= >>=	right to left	assignment
,	left to right	comma

Fig. 22.13 | Operator precedence and associativity.

22.8 Bit Fields

Visual C++ provides the ability to specify the number of bits in which an integral type or enum type member of a class or a structure is stored. Such a member is referred to as a ***bit field***. Bit fields enable better memory utilization by storing data in the minimum number of bits required. Bit field members *must* be declared as an integral or enum type.

Performance Tip 22.2

Bit fields help conserve storage.

Consider the following structure definition:

```
struct BitCard
{
    unsigned face : 4;
    unsigned suit : 2;
    unsigned color : 1;
}; // end struct BitCard
```

The definition contains three unsigned bit fields—face, suit and color—used to represent a card from a 52-card deck. A bit field is declared by following an integral type or enum type member with a colon (:) and an integer constant representing the *width of the bit field* (i.e., the number of bits in which the member is stored).

The preceding structure definition indicates that member face is stored in 4 bits, member suit in 2 bits and member color in 1 bit. The number of bits is based on the desired range of values for each structure member. Member face stores values between 0 (Ace) and 12 (King)—4 bits can store a value between 0 and 15. Member suit stores values between 0 and 3 (0 = Diamonds, 1 = Hearts, 2 = Clubs, 3 = Spades)—2 bits can store a value between 0 and 3. Finally, member color stores either 0 (Red) or 1 (Black)—1 bit can store either 0 or 1.

The program in Figs. 22.14–22.16 creates array deck containing 52 BitCard structures (line 21 of Fig. 22.14). The constructor inserts the 52 cards in the deck array, and function deal prints the 52 cards. Notice that bit fields are accessed exactly as any other structure member is (lines 18–20 and 28–33 of Fig. 22.15). The member color is included as a means of indicating the card color on a system that allows color displays.

```
1   // Fig. 22.14: DeckOfCards.h
2   // Definition of class DeckOfCards that
3   // represents a deck of playing cards.
4
5   // BitCard structure definition with bit fields
6   struct BitCard
7   {
8      unsigned face : 4; // 4 bits; 0-15
9      unsigned suit : 2; // 2 bits; 0-3
10     unsigned color : 1; // 1 bit; 0-1
11   }; // end struct BitCard
12
13   // DeckOfCards class definition
14   class DeckOfCards
15   {
16   public:
17      DeckOfCards(); // constructor initializes deck
18      void deal(); // deals cards in deck
19
20   private:
21      BitCard deck[ 52 ]; // represents deck of cards
22   }; // end class DeckOfCards
```

Fig. 22.14 | Header file for class DeckOfCards.

```
1   // Fig. 22.15: DeckOfCards.cpp
2   // Member-function definitions for class DeckOfCards that simulates
3   // the dealing of a deck of playing cards.
4   #include <iostream>
5   using std::cout;
6   using std::endl;
```

Fig. 22.15 | Class file for DeckOfCards. (Part 1 of 2.)

```
 7
 8   #include <iomanip>
 9   using std::setw;
10
11   #include "DeckOfCards.h" // DeckOfCards class definition
12
13   // no-argument DeckOfCards constructor initializes deck
14   DeckOfCards::DeckOfCards()
15   {
16      for ( int i = 0; i <= 51; i++ )
17      {
18         deck[ i ].face = i % 13; // faces in order
19         deck[ i ].suit = i / 13; // suits in order
20         deck[ i ].color = i / 26; // colors in order
21      } // end for
22   } // end no-argument DeckOfCards constructor
23
24   // deal cards in deck
25   void DeckOfCards::deal()
26   {
27      for ( int k1 = 0, k2 = k1 + 26; k1 <= 25; k1++, k2++ )
28         cout << "Card:" << setw( 3 ) << deck[ k1 ].face
29            << "  Suit:" << setw( 2 ) << deck[ k1 ].suit
30            << "  Color:" << setw( 2 ) << deck[ k1 ].color
31            << "     " << "Card:" << setw( 3 ) << deck[ k2 ].face
32            << "  Suit:" << setw( 2 ) << deck[ k2 ].suit
33            << "  Color:" << setw( 2 ) << deck[ k2 ].color << endl;
34   } // end function deal
```

Fig. 22.15 | Class file for DeckOfCards. (Part 2 of 2.)

It is possible to specify an *unnamed bit field*, in which case the field is used as *padding* in the structure. For example, the following structure definition uses an unnamed 3-bit field as padding—nothing can be stored in those 3 bits. Member b is stored in another storage unit.

```
struct Example
{
   unsigned a : 13;
   unsigned   : 3; // align to next storage-unit boundary
   unsigned b : 4;
}; // end struct Example
```

An *unnamed bit field with a zero width* is used to align the next bit field on a new storage-unit boundary. For example, the structure definition

```
struct Example
{
   unsigned a : 13;
   unsigned   : 0; // align to next storage-unit boundary
   unsigned b : 4;
}; // end struct Example
```

uses an unnamed 0-bit field to skip the remaining bits (as many as there are) of the storage unit in which a is stored and align b on the next storage-unit boundary.

```
 1   // Fig. 22.16: DeckTest.cpp
 2   // Card dealing program.
 3   #include "DeckOfCards.h" // DeckOfCards class definition
 4
 5   int main()
 6   {
 7      DeckOfCards deckOfCards; // create DeckOfCards object
 8      deckOfCards.deal(); // deal the cards in the deck
 9      return 0; // indicates successful termination
10   } // end main
```

```
Card:  0  Suit: 0  Color: 0    Card:  0  Suit: 2  Color: 1
Card:  1  Suit: 0  Color: 0    Card:  1  Suit: 2  Color: 1
Card:  2  Suit: 0  Color: 0    Card:  2  Suit: 2  Color: 1
Card:  3  Suit: 0  Color: 0    Card:  3  Suit: 2  Color: 1
Card:  4  Suit: 0  Color: 0    Card:  4  Suit: 2  Color: 1
Card:  5  Suit: 0  Color: 0    Card:  5  Suit: 2  Color: 1
Card:  6  Suit: 0  Color: 0    Card:  6  Suit: 2  Color: 1
Card:  7  Suit: 0  Color: 0    Card:  7  Suit: 2  Color: 1
Card:  8  Suit: 0  Color: 0    Card:  8  Suit: 2  Color: 1
Card:  9  Suit: 0  Color: 0    Card:  9  Suit: 2  Color: 1
Card: 10  Suit: 0  Color: 0    Card: 10  Suit: 2  Color: 1
Card: 11  Suit: 0  Color: 0    Card: 11  Suit: 2  Color: 1
Card: 12  Suit: 0  Color: 0    Card: 12  Suit: 2  Color: 1
Card:  0  Suit: 1  Color: 0    Card:  0  Suit: 3  Color: 1
Card:  1  Suit: 1  Color: 0    Card:  1  Suit: 3  Color: 1
Card:  2  Suit: 1  Color: 0    Card:  2  Suit: 3  Color: 1
Card:  3  Suit: 1  Color: 0    Card:  3  Suit: 3  Color: 1
Card:  4  Suit: 1  Color: 0    Card:  4  Suit: 3  Color: 1
Card:  5  Suit: 1  Color: 0    Card:  5  Suit: 3  Color: 1
Card:  6  Suit: 1  Color: 0    Card:  6  Suit: 3  Color: 1
Card:  7  Suit: 1  Color: 0    Card:  7  Suit: 3  Color: 1
Card:  8  Suit: 1  Color: 0    Card:  8  Suit: 3  Color: 1
Card:  9  Suit: 1  Color: 0    Card:  9  Suit: 3  Color: 1
Card: 10  Suit: 1  Color: 0    Card: 10  Suit: 3  Color: 1
Card: 11  Suit: 1  Color: 0    Card: 11  Suit: 3  Color: 1
Card: 12  Suit: 1  Color: 0    Card: 12  Suit: 3  Color: 1
```

Fig. 22.16 | Bit fields used to store a deck of cards.

Portability Tip 22.5

Bit-field manipulations are machine dependent. For example, some computers allow bit fields to cross word boundaries, whereas others do not.

Common Programming Error 22.6

Attempting to access individual bits of a bit field with subscripting as if they were elements of an array is a compilation error. Bit fields are not "arrays of bits."

Common Programming Error 22.7

Attempting to take the address of a bit field (the & operator may not be used with bit fields because a pointer can designate only a particular byte in memory and bit fields can start in the middle of a byte) is a compilation error.

Performance Tip 22.3

Although bit fields save space, using them can cause the compiler to generate slower-executing machine-language code. This occurs because it takes extra machine-language operations to access only portions of an addressable storage unit. This is one of many examples of the space–time trade-offs that occur in computer science.

22.9 Character-Handling Library Functions

Most data is entered into computers as characters—including letters, digits and various special symbols. In this section, we discuss Visual C++'s capabilities for examining and manipulating individual characters. In the remainder of the chapter, we continue the discussion of character-string manipulation that we began in Chapter 9.

The character-handling poertion of the Standard Library includes several functions that perform useful tests and manipulations of character data. Each function receives a character—represented as an `int`—or `EOF` as an argument. Characters are often manipulated as integers. Remember that `EOF` normally has the value –1 and that some hardware architectures do not allow negative values to be stored in `char` variables. Therefore, the character-handling functions manipulate characters as integers. Figure 22.17 summarizes the functions of the character-handling library. When using functions from the character-handling library, include the `<cctype>` header file.

Prototype	Description
`int isdigit( int c )`	Returns `true` if `c` is a digit and `false` otherwise.
`int isalpha( int c )`	Returns `true` if `c` is a letter and `false` otherwise.
`int isalnum( int c )`	Returns `true` if `c` is a digit or a letter and `false` otherwise.
`int isxdigit( int c )`	Returns `true` if `c` is a hexadecimal digit character and `false` otherwise. (See Appendix D, Number Systems, for a detailed explanation of binary, octal, decimal and hexadecimal numbers.)
`int islower( int c )`	Returns `true` if `c` is a lowercase letter and `false` otherwise.
`int isupper( int c )`	Returns `true` if `c` is an uppercase letter; `false` otherwise.
`int tolower( int c )`	If `c` is an uppercase letter, `tolower` returns `c` as a lowercase letter. Otherwise, `tolower` returns the argument unchanged.
`int toupper( int c )`	If `c` is a lowercase letter, `toupper` returns `c` as an uppercase letter. Otherwise, `toupper` returns the argument unchanged.
`int isspace( int c )`	Returns `true` if `c` is a white-space character—newline (`'\n'`), space (`' '`), form feed (`'\f'`), carriage return (`'\r'`), horizontal tab (`'\t'`), or vertical tab (`'\v'`)—and `false` otherwise.
`int iscntrl( int c )`	Returns `true` if `c` is a control character, such as newline (`'\n'`), form feed (`'\f'`), carriage return (`'\r'`), horizontal tab (`'\t'`), vertical tab (`'\v'`), alert (`'\a'`), or backspace (`'\b'`)—and `false` otherwise.

Fig. 22.17 | Character-handling library functions. (Part 1 of 2.)

Prototype	Description
int ispunct(int c)	Returns true if c is a printing character other than a space, a digit, or a letter and false otherwise.
int isprint(int c)	Returns true value if c is a printing character including space (' ') and false otherwise.
int isgraph(int c)	Returns true if c is a printing character other than space (' ') and false otherwise.

Fig. 22.17 | Character-handling library functions. (Part 2 of 2.)

Figure 22.18 demonstrates functions *isdigit*, *isalpha*, *isalnum* and *isxdigit*. Function isdigit determines whether its argument is a digit (0–9). Function isalpha determines whether its argument is an uppercase letter (A-Z) or a lowercase letter (a–z). Function isalnum determines whether its argument is an uppercase letter, a lowercase letter or a digit. Function isxdigit determines whether its argument is a hexadecimal digit (A–F, a–f, 0–9).

```cpp
1   // Fig. 22.18: charTest.cpp
2   // Using functions isdigit, isalpha, isalnum and isxdigit.
3   #include <iostream>
4   using std::cout;
5   using std::endl;
6
7   #include <cctype> // character-handling function prototypes
8   using std::isalnum;
9   using std::isalpha;
10  using std::isdigit;
11  using std::isxdigit;
12
13  int main()
14  {
15     cout << "According to isdigit:\n"
16        << ( isdigit( '8' ) ? "8 is a" : "8 is not a" ) << " digit\n"
17        << ( isdigit( '#' ) ? "# is a" : "# is not a" ) << " digit\n";
18
19     cout << "\nAccording to isalpha:\n"
20        << ( isalpha( 'A' ) ? "A is a" : "A is not a" ) << " letter\n"
21        << ( isalpha( 'b' ) ? "b is a" : "b is not a" ) << " letter\n"
22        << ( isalpha( '&' ) ? "& is a" : "& is not a" ) << " letter\n"
23        << ( isalpha( '4' ) ? "4 is a" : "4 is not a" ) << " letter\n";
24
25     cout << "\nAccording to isalnum:\n"
26        << ( isalnum( 'A' ) ? "A is a" : "A is not a" )
27        << " digit or a letter\n"
28        << ( isalnum( '8' ) ? "8 is a" : "8 is not a" )
29        << " digit or a letter\n"
```

Fig. 22.18 | Character-handling functions isdigit, isalpha, isalnum and isxdigit. (Part 1 of 2.)

```
30          << ( isalnum( '#' ) ? "# is a" : "# is not a" )
31          << " digit or a letter\n";
32
33     cout << "\nAccording to isxdigit:\n"
34          << ( isxdigit( 'F' ) ? "F is a" : "F is not a" )
35          << " hexadecimal digit\n"
36          << ( isxdigit( 'J' ) ? "J is a" : "J is not a" )
37          << " hexadecimal digit\n"
38          << ( isxdigit( '7' ) ? "7 is a" : "7 is not a" )
39          << " hexadecimal digit\n"
40          << ( isxdigit( '$' ) ? "$ is a" : "$ is not a" )
41          << " hexadecimal digit\n"
42          << ( isxdigit( 'f' ) ? "f is a" : "f is not a" )
43          << " hexadecimal digit" << endl;
44     return 0;
45  } // end main
```

```
According to isdigit:
8 is a digit
# is not a digit

According to isalpha:
A is a letter
b is a letter
& is not a letter
4 is not a letter

According to isalnum:
A is a digit or a letter
8 is a digit or a letter
# is not a digit or a letter

According to isxdigit:
F is a hexadecimal digit
J is not a hexadecimal digit
7 is a hexadecimal digit
$ is not a hexadecimal digit
f is a hexadecimal digit
```

Fig. 22.18 | Character-handling functions isdigit, isalpha, isalnum and isxdigit. (Part 2 of 2.)

Figure 22.18 uses the conditional operator (?:) with each function to determine whether the string " is a " or the string " is not a " should be printed in the output for each character tested. For example, line 16 indicates that if '8' is a digit—i.e., if isdigit returns a true (nonzero) value—the string "8 is a " is printed. If '8' is not a digit (i.e., if isdigit returns 0), the string "8 is not a " is printed.

Figure 22.19 demonstrates functions *islower*, *isupper*, *tolower* and *toupper*. Function islower determines whether its argument is a lowercase letter (a–z). Function isupper determines whether its argument is an uppercase letter (A–Z). Function tolower converts an uppercase letter to lowercase and returns the lowercase letter—if the argument is not an uppercase letter, tolower returns the argument value unchanged. Function toupper converts a lowercase letter to uppercase and returns the uppercase letter—if the argument is not a lowercase letter, toupper returns the argument value unchanged.

```cpp
 1  // Fig. 22.19: charTest2.cpp
 2  // Using functions islower, isupper, tolower and toupper.
 3  #include <iostream>
 4  using std::cout;
 5  using std::endl;
 6
 7  #include <cctype> // character-handling function prototypes
 8  using std::islower;
 9  using std::isupper;
10  using std::tolower;
11  using std::toupper;
12
13  int main()
14  {
15     cout << "According to islower:\n"
16        << ( islower( 'p' ) ? "p is a" : "p is not a" )
17        << " lowercase letter\n"
18        << ( islower( 'P' ) ? "P is a" : "P is not a" )
19        << " lowercase letter\n"
20        << ( islower( '5' ) ? "5 is a" : "5 is not a" )
21        << " lowercase letter\n"
22        << ( islower( '!' ) ? "! is a" : "! is not a" )
23        << " lowercase letter\n";
24
25     cout << "\nAccording to isupper:\n"
26        << ( isupper( 'D' ) ? "D is an" : "D is not an" )
27        << " uppercase letter\n"
28        << ( isupper( 'd' ) ? "d is an" : "d is not an" )
29        << " uppercase letter\n"
30        << ( isupper( '8' ) ? "8 is an" : "8 is not an" )
31        << " uppercase letter\n"
32        << ( isupper( '$' ) ? "$ is an" : "$ is not an" )
33        << " uppercase letter\n";
34
35     cout << "\nu converted to uppercase is "
36        << static_cast< char >( toupper( 'u' ) )
37        << "\n7 converted to uppercase is "
38        << static_cast< char >( toupper( '7' ) )
39        << "\n$ converted to uppercase is "
40        << static_cast< char >( toupper( '$' ) )
41        << "\nL converted to lowercase is "
42        << static_cast< char >( tolower( 'L' ) ) << endl;
43     return 0;
44  } // end main
```

```
According to islower:
p is a lowercase letter
P is not a lowercase letter
5 is not a lowercase letter
! is not a lowercase letter
```

Fig. 22.19 | Character-handling functions `islower`, `isupper`, `tolower` and `toupper`. (Part 1 of 2.)

```
According to isupper:
D is an uppercase letter
d is not an uppercase letter
8 is not an uppercase letter
$ is not an uppercase letter

u converted to uppercase is U
7 converted to uppercase is 7
$ converted to uppercase is $
L converted to lowercase is l
```

Fig. 22.19 | Character-handling functions `islower`, `isupper`, `tolower` and `toupper`. (Part 2 of 2.)

Figure 22.20 demonstrates functions *isspace*, *iscntrl*, *ispunct*, *isprint* and *isgraph*. Function `isspace` determines whether its argument is a white-space character, such as space (' '), form feed ('\f'), newline ('\n'), carriage return ('\r'), horizontal tab ('\t') or vertical tab ('\v'). Function `iscntrl` determines whether its argument is a control character such as horizontal tab ('\t'), vertical tab ('\v'), form feed ('\f'), alert ('\a'), backspace ('\b'), carriage return ('\r') or newline ('\n'). Function `ispunct` determines whether its argument is a printing character other than a space, digit or letter, such as $, #, (,), [,], {, }, ;, : or %. Function `isprint` determines whether its argument is a character that can be displayed on the screen (including the space character). Function `isgraph` tests for the same characters as `isprint`, but the space character is not included.

```
 1    // Fig. 22.20: charTest3.cpp
 2    // Using functions isspace, iscntrl, ispunct, isprint, isgraph.
 3    #include <iostream>
 4    using std::cout;
 5    using std::endl;
 6
 7    #include <cctype> // character-handling function prototypes
 8    using std::iscntrl;
 9    using std::isgraph;
10    using std::isprint;
11    using std::ispunct;
12    using std::isspace;
13
14    int main()
15    {
16       cout << "According to isspace:\nNewline "
17          << ( isspace( '\n' ) ? "is a" : "is not a" )
18          << " whitespace character\nHorizontal tab "
19          << ( isspace( '\t' ) ? "is a" : "is not a" )
20          << " whitespace character\n"
21          << ( isspace( '%' ) ? "% is a" : "% is not a" )
22          << " whitespace character\n";
23
```

Fig. 22.20 | Character-handling functions `isspace`, `iscntrl`, `ispunct`, `isprint` and `isgraph`. (Part 1 of 2.)

```
24      cout << "\nAccording to iscntrl:\nNewline "
25          << ( iscntrl( '\n' ) ? "is a" : "is not a" )
26          << " control character\n"
27          << ( iscntrl( '$' ) ? "$ is a" : "$ is not a" )
28          << " control character\n";
29
30      cout << "\nAccording to ispunct:\n"
31          << ( ispunct( ';' ) ? "; is a" : "; is not a" )
32          << " punctuation character\n"
33          << ( ispunct( 'Y' ) ? "Y is a" : "Y is not a" )
34          << " punctuation character\n"
35          << ( ispunct( '#' ) ? "# is a" : "# is not a" )
36          << " punctuation character\n";
37
38      cout << "\nAccording to isprint:\n"
39          << ( isprint( '$' ) ? "$ is a" : "$ is not a" )
40          << " printing character\nAlert "
41          << ( isprint( '\a' ) ? "is a" : "is not a" )
42          << " printing character\nSpace "
43          << ( isprint( ' ' ) ? "is a" : "is not a" )
44          << " printing character\n";
45
46      cout << "\nAccording to isgraph:\n"
47          << ( isgraph( 'Q' ) ? "Q is a" : "Q is not a" )
48          << " printing character other than a space\nSpace "
49          << ( isgraph( ' ' ) ? "is a" : "is not a" )
50          << " printing character other than a space" << endl;
51      return 0;
52  } // end main
```

```
According to isspace:
Newline is a whitespace character
Horizontal tab is a whitespace character
% is not a whitespace character

According to iscntrl:
Newline is a control character
$ is not a control character

According to ispunct:
; is a punctuation character
Y is not a punctuation character
# is a punctuation character

According to isprint:
$ is a printing character

Alert is not a printing character
Space is a printing character

According to isgraph:
Q is a printing character other than a space
Space is not a printing character other than a space
```

Fig. 22.20 | Character-handling functions `isspace`, `iscntrl`, `ispunct`, `isprint` and `isgraph`. (Part 2 of 2.)

22.10 Pointer-Based String-Conversion Functions

In Chapter 9, we discussed several of Visual C++'s most popular pointer-based string-manipulation functions. In the next several sections, we cover the remaining functions, including functions for converting strings to numeric values, functions for searching strings and functions for manipulating, comparing and searching blocks of memory.

This section presents the pointer-based *string-conversion functions* from the *general-utilities library <cstdlib>*. These functions convert pointer-based strings of characters to integer and floating-point values. Figure 22.21 summarizes the pointer-based string-conversion functions. Note the use of const to declare variable nPtr in the function headers (read from right to left as "nPtr is a pointer to a character constant"). When using functions from the general-utilities library, include the <cstdlib> header file.

Function *atof* (Fig. 22.22, line 12) converts its argument—a string that represents a floating-point number—to a double value. The function returns the double value. If the string cannot be converted—for example, if the first character of the string is not a digit—function atof returns zero.

Prototype	Description
`double atof(` `   const char *nPtr )`	Converts the string nPtr to double. If the string cannot be converted, 0 is returned.
`int atoi( const char *nPtr )`	Converts the string nPtr to int. If the string cannot be converted, 0 is returned.
`long atol( const char *nPtr )`	Converts the string nPtr to long int. If the string cannot be converted, 0 is returned.
`double strtod( const char *nPtr, char **endPtr )`	
	Converts the string nPtr to double. endPtr is the address of a pointer to the rest of the string after the double. If the string cannot be converted, 0 is returned.
`long strtol( const char *nPtr, char **endPtr, int base )`	
	Converts the string nPtr to long. endPtr is the address of a pointer to the rest of the string after the long. If the string cannot be converted, 0 is returned. The base parameter indicates the base of the number to convert (e.g., 8 for octal, 10 for decimal or 16 for hexadecimal). The default is decimal.
`unsigned long strtoul( const char *nPtr, char **endPtr, int base )`	
	Converts the string nPtr to unsigned long. endPtr is the address of a pointer to the rest of the string after the unsigned long. If the string cannot be converted, 0 is returned. The base parameter indicates the base of the number to convert (e.g., 8 for octal, 10 for decimal or 16 for hexadecimal). The default is decimal.

Fig. 22.21 | Pointer-based string-conversion functions of the general-utilities library.

```
 1    // Fig. 22.22: Atof.cpp
 2    // Using atof.
 3    #include <iostream>
 4    using std::cout;
 5    using std::endl;
 6
 7    #include <cstdlib> // atof prototype
 8    using std::atof;
 9
10    int main()
11    {
12       double d = atof( "99.0" ); // convert string to double
13
14       cout << "The string \"99.0\" converted to double is " << d
15          << "\nThe converted value divided by 2 is " << d / 2.0 << endl;
16       return 0;
17    } // end main
```

```
The string "99.0" converted to double is 99
The converted value divided by 2 is 49.5
```

Fig. 22.22 | String-conversion function `atof`.

Function *atoi* (Fig. 22.23, line 12) converts its argument—a string of digits that represents an integer—to an int value. The function returns the int value. If the string cannot be converted, function atoi returns zero.

Function *atol* (Fig. 22.24, line 12) converts its argument—a string of digits representing a long integer—to a long value. The function returns the long value. If the string cannot be converted, function atol returns zero. If int and long are both stored in four bytes, function atoi and function atol work identically.

```
 1    // Fig. 22.23: Atoi.cpp
 2    // Using atoi.
 3    #include <iostream>
 4    using std::cout;
 5    using std::endl;
 6
 7    #include <cstdlib> // atoi prototype
 8    using std::atoi;
 9
10    int main()
11    {
12       int i = atoi( "2593" ); // convert string to int
13
14       cout << "The string \"2593\" converted to int is " << i
15          << "\nThe converted value minus 593 is " << i - 593 << endl;
16       return 0;
17    } // end main
```

Fig. 22.23 | String-conversion function `atoi`. (Part 1 of 2.)

```
The string "2593" converted to int is 2593
The converted value minus 593 is 2000
```

Fig. 22.23 | String-conversion function `atoi`. (Part 2 of 2.)

```
 1   // Fig. 22.24: Atol.cpp
 2   // Using atol.
 3   #include <iostream>
 4   using std::cout;
 5   using std::endl;
 6
 7   #include <cstdlib> // atol prototype
 8   using std::atol;
 9
10   int main()
11   {
12      long x = atol( "1000000" ); // convert string to long
13
14      cout << "The string \"1000000\" converted to long is " << x
15         << "\nThe converted value divided by 2 is " << x / 2 << endl;
16      return 0;
17   } // end main
```

```
The string "1000000" converted to long int is 1000000
The converted value divided by 2 is 500000
```

Fig. 22.24 | String-conversion function `atol`.

Function **strtod** (Fig. 22.25) converts a sequence of characters representing a floating-point value to `double`. Function `strtod` receives two arguments—a string (`char *`) and the address of a `char *` pointer (i.e., a `char **`). The string contains the character sequence to be converted to `double`. The second argument enables `strtod` to modify a `char *` pointer in the calling function, such that the pointer points to the location of the first character after the converted portion of the string. Line 16 indicates that `d` is assigned the `double` value converted from `string` and that `stringPtr` is assigned the location of the first character after the converted value (`51.2`) in `string`.

```
 1   // Fig. 22.25: Strtod.cpp
 2   // Using strtod.
 3   #include <iostream>
 4   using std::cout;
 5   using std::endl;
 6
 7   #include <cstdlib> // strtod prototype
 8   using std::strtod;
 9
10   int main()
11   {
```

Fig. 22.25 | String-conversion function `strtod`. (Part 1 of 2.)

```
12      double d;
13      const char *string1 = "51.2% are admitted";
14      char *stringPtr;
15
16      d = strtod( string1, &stringPtr ); // convert characters to double
17
18      cout << "The string \"" << string1
19          << "\" is converted to the\ndouble value " << d
20          << " and the string \"" << stringPtr << "\"" << endl;
21      return 0;
22   } // end main
```

```
The string "51.2% are admitted" is converted to the
double value 51.2 and the string "% are admitted"
```

Fig. 22.25 | String-conversion function `strtod`. (Part 2 of 2.)

Function **strtol** (Fig. 22.26) converts to long a sequence of characters representing an integer. The function receives three arguments—a string (char *), the address of a char * pointer and an integer. The string contains the character sequence to convert. The second argument is assigned the location of the first character after the converted portion of the string. The integer specifies the *base* of the value being converted. Line 16 indicates that x is assigned the long value converted from `string` and that `remainderPtr` is assigned the location of the first character after the converted value (-1234567) in `string1`. Using a null pointer for the second argument causes the remainder of the string to be ignored. The third argument, 0, indicates that the value to be converted can be in octal (base 8), decimal (base 10) or hexadecimal (base 16). This is determined by the initial characters in the string—0 indicates an octal number, 0x indicates hexadecimal and a number from 1 to 9 indicates decimal.

```
1    // Fig. 22.26: strtol.cpp
2    // Using strtol.
3    #include <iostream>
4    using std::cout;
5    using std::endl;
6
7    #include <cstdlib> // strtol prototype
8    using std::strtol;
9
10   int main()
11   {
12      long x;
13      const char *string1 = "-1234567abc";
14      char *remainderPtr;
15
16      x = strtol( string1, &remainderPtr, 0 ); // convert characters to long
17
18      cout << "The original string is \"" << string1
19          << "\"\nThe converted value is " << x
```

Fig. 22.26 | String-conversion function `strtol`. (Part 1 of 2.)

```
20          << "\nThe remainder of the original string is \"" << remainderPtr
21          << "\"\nThe converted value plus 567 is " << x + 567 << endl;
22      return 0;
23  } // end main
```

```
The original string is "-1234567abc"
The converted value is -1234567
The remainder of the original string is "abc"
The converted value plus 567 is -1234000
```

Fig. 22.26 | String-conversion function strtol. (Part 2 of 2.)

In a call to function strtol, the base can be specified as zero or as any value between 2 and 36. (See Appendix D for a detailed explanation of the octal, decimal, hexadecimal and binary number systems.) Numeric representations of integers from base 11 to base 36 use the characters A–Z to represent the values 10 to 35. For example, hexadecimal values can consist of the digits 0–9 and the characters A–F. A base-11 integer can consist of the digits 0–9 and the character A. A base-24 integer can consist of the digits 0–9 and the characters A–N. A base-36 integer can consist of the digits 0–9 and the characters A–Z. [*Note:* The case of the letter used is ignored.]

Function **strtoul** (Fig. 22.27) converts to unsigned long a sequence of characters representing an unsigned long integer. The function works identically to strtol. Line 17 indicates that x is assigned the unsigned long value converted from string and that remainderPtr is assigned the location of the first character after the converted value (1234567) in string1. The third argument, 0, indicates that the value to be converted can be in octal, decimal or hexadecimal format, depending on the initial characters.

```
 1  // Fig. 22.27: Strtoul.cpp
 2  // Using strtoul.
 3  #include <iostream>
 4  using std::cout;
 5  using std::endl;
 6
 7  #include <cstdlib> // strtoul prototype
 8  using std::strtoul;
 9
10  int main()
11  {
12      unsigned long x;
13      const char *string1 = "1234567abc";
14      char *remainderPtr;
15
16      // convert a sequence of characters to unsigned long
17      x = strtoul( string1, &remainderPtr, 0 );
18
19      cout << "The original string is \"" << string1
20          << "\"\nThe converted value is " << x
21          << "\nThe remainder of the original string is \"" << remainderPtr
```

Fig. 22.27 | String-conversion function strtoul. (Part 1 of 2.)

```
22          << "\"\nThe converted value minus 567 is " << x - 567 << endl;
23      return 0;
24  } // end main
```

```
The original string is "1234567abc"
The converted value is 1234567
The remainder of the original string is "abc"
The converted value minus 567 is 1234000
```

Fig. 22.27 | String-conversion function `strtoul`. (Part 2 of 2.)

22.11 Search Functions of the Pointer-Based String-Handling Library

This section presents the functions of the string-handling library used to search strings for characters and other strings. The functions are summarized in Fig. 22.28. Note that functions `strcspn` and `strspn` specify return type `size_t`. Type `size_t` is a type defined by the standard as the integral type of the value returned by operator `sizeof`.

Prototype	Description
`char *strchr( const char *s, int c )`	
	Locates the first occurrence of character `c` in string `s`. If `c` is found, a pointer to `c` in `s` is returned. Otherwise, a null pointer is returned.
`char *strrchr( const char *s, int c )`	
	Searches from the end of string `s` and locates the last occurrence of character `c` in string `s`. If `c` is found, a pointer to `c` in string `s` is returned. Otherwise, a null pointer is returned.
`size_t strspn( const char *s1, const char *s2 )`	
	Determines and returns the length of the initial segment of string `s1` consisting only of characters contained in string `s2`.
`char *strpbrk( const char *s1, const char *s2 )`	
	Locates the first occurrence in string `s1` of any character in string `s2`. If a character from string `s2` is found, a pointer to the character in string `s1` is returned. Otherwise, a null pointer is returned.
`size_t strcspn( const char *s1, const char *s2 )`	
	Determines and returns the length of the initial segment of string `s1` consisting of characters not contained in string `s2`.
`char *strstr( const char *s1, const char *s2 )`	
	Locates the first occurrence in string `s1` of string `s2`. If the string is found, a pointer to the string in `s1` is returned. Otherwise, a null pointer is returned.

Fig. 22.28 | Search functions of the pointer-based string-handling library.

Function ***strchr*** searches for the first occurrence of a character in a string. If the character is found, strchr returns a pointer to the character in the string; otherwise, strchr returns a null pointer. The program of Fig. 22.29 uses strchr (lines 17 and 25) to search for the first occurrences of 'a' and 'z' in the string "This is a test".

Function ***strcspn*** (Fig. 22.30, line 18) determines the length of the initial part of the string in its first argument that does not contain any characters from the string in its second argument. The function returns the length of the segment.

Function ***strpbrk*** searches for the first occurrence in its first string argument of any character in its second string argument. If a character from the second argument is found, strpbrk returns a pointer to the character in the first argument; otherwise, strpbrk returns a null pointer. Line 16 of Fig. 22.31 locates the first occurrence in string1 of any character from string2.

```cpp
1   // Fig. 22.29: Strchr.cpp
2   // Using strchr.
3   #include <iostream>
4   using std::cout;
5   using std::endl;
6
7   #include <cstring> // strchr prototype
8   using std::strchr;
9
10  int main()
11  {
12     const char *string1 = "This is a test";
13     char character1 = 'a';
14     char character2 = 'z';
15
16     // search for character1 in string1
17     if ( strchr( string1, character1 ) != NULL )
18        cout << '\'' << character1 << "' was found in \""
19           << string1 << "\".\n";
20     else
21        cout << '\'' << character1 << "' was not found in \""
22           << string1 << "\".\n";
23
24     // search for character2 in string1
25     if ( strchr( string1, character2 ) != NULL )
26        cout << '\'' << character2 << "' was found in \""
27           << string1 << "\".\n";
28     else
29        cout << '\'' << character2 << "' was not found in \""
30           << string1 << "\"." << endl;
31
32     return 0;
33  } // end main
```

```
'a' was found in "This is a test".
'z' was not found in "This is a test".
```

Fig. 22.29 | String-search function strchr.

```
1   // Fig. 22.30: Strcspn.cpp
2   // Using strcspn.
3   #include <iostream>
4   using std::cout;
5   using std::endl;
6
7   #include <cstring> // strcspn prototype
8   using std::strcspn;
9
10  int main()
11  {
12     const char *string1 = "The value is 3.14159";
13     const char *string2 = "1234567890";
14
15     cout << "string1 = " << string1 << "\nstring2 = " << string2
16        << "\n\nThe length of the initial segment of string1"
17        << "\ncontaining no characters from string2 = "
18        << strcspn( string1, string2 ) << endl;
19     return 0;
20  } // end main
```

```
string1 = The value is 3.14159
string2 = 1234567890

The length of the initial segment of string1
containing no characters from string2 = 13
```

Fig. 22.30 | String-search function strcspn.

```
1   // Fig. 22.31: strpbrk.cpp
2   // Using strpbrk.
3   #include <iostream>
4   using std::cout;
5   using std::endl;
6
7   #include <cstring> // strpbrk prototype
8   using std::strpbrk;
9
10  int main()
11  {
12     const char *string1 = "This is a test";
13     const char *string2 = "beware";
14
15     cout << "Of the characters in \"" << string2 << "\"\n'"
16        << *strpbrk( string1, string2 ) << "\' is the first character "
17        << "to appear in\n\"" << string1 << '\"' << endl;
18     return 0;
19  } // end main
```

```
Of the characters in "beware"
'a' is the first character to appear in
"This is a test"
```

Fig. 22.31 | String-search function strpbrk.

Function ***strrchr*** searches for the last occurrence of the specified character in a string. If the character is found, strrchr returns a pointer to the character in the string; otherwise, strrchr returns 0. Line 18 of Fig. 22.32 searches for the last occurrence of the character 'z' in the string "A zoo has many animals including zebras".

Function ***strspn*** (Fig. 22.33, line 18) determines the length of the initial part of the string in its first argument that contains only characters from the string in its second argument. The function returns the length of the segment.

```cpp
1   // Fig. 22.32: strrchr.cpp
2   // Using strrchr.
3   #include <iostream>
4   using std::cout;
5   using std::endl;
6
7   #include <cstring> // strrchr prototype
8   using std::strrchr;
9
10  int main()
11  {
12     const char *string1 = "A zoo has many animals including zebras";
13     char c = 'z';
14
15     cout << "string1 = " << string1 << "\n" << endl;
16     cout << "The remainder of string1 beginning with the\n"
17        << "last occurrence of character '"
18        << c << "' is: \"" << strrchr( string1, c ) << '\"' << endl;
19     return 0;
20  } // end main
```

```
string1 = A zoo has many animals including zebras

The remainder of string1 beginning with the
last occurrence of character 'z' is: "zebras"
```

Fig. 22.32 | String-search function strrchr.

```cpp
1   // Fig. 22.33: Strspn.cpp
2   // Using strspn.
3   #include <iostream>
4   using std::cout;
5   using std::endl;
6
7   #include <cstring> // strspn prototype
8   using std::strspn;
9
10  int main()
11  {
12     const char *string1 = "The value is 3.14159";
13     const char *string2 = "aehils Tuv";
```

Fig. 22.33 | String-search function strspn. (Part 1 of 2.)

```
14
15          cout << "string1 = " << string1 << "\nstring2 = " << string2
16             << "\n\nThe length of the initial segment of string1\n"
17             << "containing only characters from string2 = "
18             << strspn( string1, string2 ) << endl;
19          return 0;
20      } // end main
```

```
string1 = The value is 3.14159
string2 = aehils Tuv

The length of the initial segment of string1
containing only characters from string2 = 13
```

Fig. 22.33 | String-search function `strspn`. (Part 2 of 2.)

Function ***strstr*** searches for the first occurrence of its second string argument in its first string argument. If the second string is found in the first string, a pointer to the location of the string in the first argument is returned; otherwise, it returns 0. Line 18 of Fig. 22.34 uses `strstr` to find the string "def" in the string "abcdefabcdef".

```
 1      // Fig. 22.34: Strstr.cpp
 2      // Using strstr.
 3      #include <iostream>
 4      using std::cout;
 5      using std::endl;
 6
 7      #include <cstring> // strstr prototype
 8      using std::strstr;
 9
10      int main()
11      {
12          const char *string1 = "abcdefabcdef";
13          const char *string2 = "def";
14
15          cout << "string1 = " << string1 << "\nstring2 = " << string2
16             << "\n\nThe remainder of string1 beginning with the\n"
17             << "first occurrence of string2 is: "
18             << strstr( string1, string2 ) << endl;
19          return 0;
20      } // end main
```

```
string1 = abcdefabcdef
string2 = def

The remainder of string1 beginning with the
first occurrence of string2 is: defabcdef
```

Fig. 22.34 | String-search function `strstr`.

22.12 Memory Functions of the Pointer-Based String-Handling Library

The string-handling library functions presented in this section facilitate manipulating, comparing and searching blocks of memory. The functions treat blocks of memory as arrays of bytes. These functions can manipulate any block of data. Figure 22.35 summarizes the memory functions of the string-handling library. In the function discussions, "object" refers to a block of data. [*Note:* The string-processing functions in prior sections operate on null-terminated character strings. The functions in this section operate on arrays of bytes. The null-character value (i.e., a byte containing 0) has no significance with the functions in this section.]

The pointer parameters to these functions are declared void *. In Chapter 9, we saw that a pointer to any data type can be assigned directly to a pointer of type void *. For this reason, these functions can receive pointers to any data type. Remember that a pointer of type void * cannot be assigned directly to a pointer of any other data type. Because a void * pointer cannot be dereferenced, each function receives a size argument that specifies the number of characters (bytes) the function will process. For simplicity, the examples in this section manipulate character arrays (blocks of characters).

Prototype	Description
`void *memcpy( void *s1, const void *s2, size_t n )`	
	Copies n characters from the object pointed to by s2 into the object pointed to by s1. A pointer to the resulting object is returned. The area from which characters are copied is not allowed to overlap the area to which characters are copied.
`void *memmove( void *s1, const void *s2, size_t n )`	
	Copies n characters from the object pointed to by s2 into the object pointed to by s1. The copy is performed as if the characters were first copied from the object pointed to by s2 into a temporary array, and then copied from the temporary array into the object pointed to by s1. A pointer to the resulting object is returned. The area from which characters are copied is allowed to overlap the area to which characters are copied.
`int memcmp( const void *s1, const void *s2, size_t n )`	
	Compares the first n characters of the objects pointed to by s1 and s2. The function returns 0, less than 0, or greater than 0 if s1 is equal to, less than or greater than s2, respectively.
`void *memchr( const void *s, int c, size_t n )`	
	Locates the first occurrence of c (converted to unsigned char) in the first n characters of the object pointed to by s. If c is found, a pointer to c in the object is returned. Otherwise, 0 is returned.
`void *memset( void *s, int c, size_t n )`	
	Copies c (converted to unsigned char) into the first n characters of the object pointed to by s. A pointer to the result is returned.

Fig. 22.35 | Memory functions of the string-handling library.

Function ***memcpy*** copies a specified number of characters (bytes) from the object pointed to by its second argument into the object pointed to by its first argument. The function can receive a pointer to any type of object. The result of this function is undefined if the two objects overlap in memory (i.e., are parts of the same object). The program of Fig. 22.36 uses memcpy (line 17) to copy the string in array s2 to array s1.

Function ***memmove***, like memcpy, copies a specified number of bytes from the object pointed to by its second argument into the object pointed to by its first argument. Copying is performed as if the bytes were copied from the second argument to a temporary array of characters, and then copied from the temporary array to the first argument. This allows characters from one part of a string to be copied into another part of the same string.

Common Programming Error 22.8

String-manipulation functions other than memmove *that copy characters have undefined results when copying takes place between parts of the same string.*

The program in Fig. 22.37 uses memmove (line 16) to copy the last 10 bytes of array x into the first 10 bytes of array x.

Function ***memcmp*** (Fig. 22.38, lines 19, 20 and 21) compares the specified number of characters of its first argument with the corresponding characters of its second argument. The function returns a value greater than zero if the first argument is greater than the second argument, zero if the arguments are equal, and a value less than zero if the first argument is less than the second argument. [*Note:* With some compilers, function memcmp

```
1    // Fig. 22.36: Memcpy.cpp
2    // Using memcpy.
3    #include <iostream>
4    using std::cout;
5    using std::endl;
6
7    #include <cstring> // memcpy prototype
8    using std::memcpy;
9
10   int main()
11   {
12      char s1[ 17 ];
13
14      // 17 total characters (includes terminating null)
15      char s2[] = "Copy this string";
16
17      memcpy( s1, s2, 17 ); // copy 17 characters from s2 to s1
18
19      cout << "After s2 is copied into s1 with memcpy,\n"
20         << "s1 contains \"" << s1 << '\"' << endl;
21      return 0;
22   } // end main
```

```
After s2 is copied into s1 with memcpy,
s1 contains "Copy this string"
```

Fig. 22.36 | Memory-handling function `memcpy`.

```
 1    // Fig. 22.37: Memmove.cpp
 2    // Using memmove.
 3    #include <iostream>
 4    using std::cout;
 5    using std::endl;
 6
 7    #include <cstring> // memmove prototype
 8    using std::memmove;
 9
10    int main()
11    {
12       char x[] = "Home Sweet Home";
13
14       cout << "The string in array x before memmove is: " << x;
15       cout << "\nThe string in array x after memmove is:  "
16          << static_cast< char * >( memmove( x, &x[ 5 ], 10 ) ) << endl;
17       return 0;
18    } // end main
```

```
The string in array x before memmove is: Home Sweet Home
The string in array x after memmove is:  Sweet Home Home
```

Fig. 22.37 | Memory-handling function `memmove`.

returns -1, 0 or 1, as in the sample output of Fig. 22.38. With other compilers, this function returns 0 or the difference between the numeric codes of the first characters that differ in the strings being compared. For example, when s1 and s2 are compared, the first character that differs between them is the fifth character of each string—E (numeric code 69) for s1 and X (numeric code 88) for s2. In this case, the return value will be 19 (or -19 when s2 is compared to s1).]

```
 1    // Fig. 22.38: Memcmp.cpp
 2    // Using memcmp.
 3    #include <iostream>
 4    using std::cout;
 5    using std::endl;
 6
 7    #include <iomanip>
 8    using std::setw;
 9
10    #include <cstring> // memcmp prototype
11    using std::memcmp;
12
13    int main()
14    {
15       char s1[] = "ABCDEFG";
16       char s2[] = "ABCDXYZ";
17
18       cout << "s1 = " << s1 << "\ns2 = " << s2 << endl
19          << "\nmemcmp(s1, s2, 4) = " << setw( 3 ) << memcmp( s1, s2, 4 )
```

Fig. 22.38 | Memory-handling function `memcmp`. (Part 1 of 2.)

```
20              << "\nmemcmp(s1, s2, 7) = " << setw( 3 ) << memcmp( s1, s2, 7 )
21              << "\nmemcmp(s2, s1, 7) = " << setw( 3 ) << memcmp( s2, s1, 7 )
22              << endl;
23       return 0;
24    } // end main
```

```
s1 = ABCDEFG
s2 = ABCDXYZ

memcmp(s1, s2, 4) =    0
memcmp(s1, s2, 7) =   -1
memcmp(s2, s1, 7) =    1
```

Fig. 22.38 | Memory-handling function `memcmp`. (Part 2 of 2.)

Function **memchr** searches for the first occurrence of a byte, represented as `unsigned char`, in the specified number of bytes of an object. If the byte is found in the object, a pointer to it is returned; otherwise, the function returns a null pointer. Line 16 of Fig. 22.39 searches for the character (byte) `'r'` in the string `"This is a string"`.

Function **memset** copies the value of the byte in its second argument into a specified number of bytes of the object pointed to by its first argument. Line 16 in Fig. 22.40 uses `memset` to copy `'b'` into the first 7 bytes of `string1`.

```
1    // Fig. 22.39: Memchr.cpp
2    // Using memchr.
3    #include <iostream>
4    using std::cout;
5    using std::endl;
6
7    #include <cstring> // memchr prototype
8    using std::memchr;
9
10   int main()
11   {
12      char s[] = "This is a string";
13
14      cout << "s = " << s << "\n" << endl;
15      cout << "The remainder of s after character 'r' is found is \""
16           << static_cast< char * >( memchr( s, 'r', 16 ) ) << '\"' << endl;
17      return 0;
18   } // end main
```

```
s = This is a string

The remainder of s after character 'r' is found is "ring"
```

Fig. 22.39 | Memory-handling function `memchr`.

```
 1  // Fig. 22.40: Memset.cpp
 2  // Using memset.
 3  #include <iostream>
 4  using std::cout;
 5  using std::endl;
 6
 7  #include <cstring> // memset prototype
 8  using std::memset;
 9
10  int main()
11  {
12     char string1[ 15 ] = "BBBBBBBBBBBBBB";
13
14     cout << "string1 = " << string1 << endl;
15     cout << "string1 after memset = "
16        << static_cast< char * >( memset( string1, 'b', 7 ) ) << endl;
17     return 0;
18  } // end main
```

```
string1 = BBBBBBBBBBBBBB
string1 after memset = bbbbbbbBBBBBBB
```

Fig. 22.40 | Memory-handling function `memset`.

22.13 Wrap-Up

This chapter introduced `struct` definitions, initializing `struct`s and using them with functions. We discussed `typedef`, using it to create aliases to help promote portability. We also introduced bitwise operators to manipulate data and bit fields for storing data compactly. You also learned about the string-conversion functions in `<cstdlib>` and the string-processing functions in `<cstring>`. In the next chapter, we continue our discussion of data structures by discussing containers—data structures defined in the C++ Standard Template Library. We also present the many algorithms defined in the STL as well.

Summary

Section 22.2 Structure Definitions

- Structures are collections of related variables (or aggregates) under one name.
- Structures can contain variables of different data types.
- Keyword `struct` begins every structure definition. Between the braces of the structure definition are the structure member declarations.
- Members of the same structure must have unique names.
- A structure definition creates a new data type that can be used to declare variables.

Section 22.3 Initializing Structures

- A structure can be initialized with an initializer list by following the variable in the declaration with an equal sign and a comma-separated list of initializers enclosed in braces. If there are fewer initializers in the list than members in the structure, the remaining members are initialized to zero (or a null pointer for pointer members).

- Entire structure variables may be assigned to structure variables of the same type.

- A structure variable may be initialized with a structure variable of the same type.

Section 22.4 Using Structures with Functions

- Structure variables and individual structure members are passed to functions by value.

- To pass a structure by reference, pass the address of the structure variable or a reference to the structure variable. An array of structures is passed by reference. To pass an array by value, create a structure with the array as a member.

Section 22.5 `typedef`

- Creating a new type name with `typedef` does not create a new type; it creates a name that is synonymous with a type defined previously.

Section 22.7 Bitwise Operators

- The bitwise AND operator (&) takes two integral operands. A bit in the result is set to one if the corresponding bits in each of the operands are one.

- Masks are used with bitwise AND to hide some bits while preserving others.

- The bitwise inclusive OR operator (|) takes two operands. A bit in the result is set to one if the corresponding bit in either operand is set to one.

- Each of the bitwise operators (except complement) has a corresponding assignment operator.

- The bitwise exclusive OR operator (^) takes two operands. A bit in the result is set to one if exactly one of the corresponding bits in the two operands is set to one.

- The left-shift operator (<<) shifts the bits of its left operand left by the number of bits specified by its right operand. Bits vacated to the right are replaced with zeros.

- The right-shift operator (>>) shifts the bits of its left operand right by the number of bits specified in its right operand. Right shifting an unsigned integer causes bits vacated at the left to be replaced by zeros. Vacated bits in signed integers can be replaced with zeros or ones, depending on the hardware architecture.

- The bitwise complement operator (~) takes one operand and inverts its bits—this produces the one's complement of the operand.

Section 22.8 Bit Fields

- Bit fields reduce storage use by storing data in the minimum number of bits required. Bit-field members must be declared as `int` or `unsigned`.

- A bit field is declared by following an integral type member name with a colon and the width of the bit field.

- The bit-field width must be an integer constant.

- If a bit field is specified without a name, the field is used as padding in the structure.

- An unnamed bit field with width 0 aligns the next bit field on a new machine-word boundary.

Section 22.9 Character-Handling Library Functions

- Function islower determines whether its argument is a lowercase letter (a–z). Function isupper determines whether its argument is an uppercase letter (A–Z).

- Function isdigit determines whether its argument is a digit (0–9).

- Function isalpha determines whether its argument is an uppercase (A–Z) or lowercase letter (a–z).

- Function isalnum determines whether its argument is an uppercase letter (A–Z), a lowercase letter (a–z), or a digit (0–9).

- Function isxdigit determines whether its argument is a hexadecimal digit (A–F, a–f, 0–9).

- Function toupper converts a lowercase letter to an uppercase letter. Function tolower converts an uppercase letter to a lowercase letter.

- Function isspace determines whether its argument is one of the following white-space characters: ' ' (space), '\f', '\n', '\r', '\t' or '\v'.

- Function iscntrl determines whether its argument is a control character, such as '\t', '\v', '\f', '\a', '\b', '\r' or '\n'.

- Function ispunct determines whether its argument is a printing character other than a space, a digit or a letter.

- Function isprint determines whether its argument is any printing character, including space.

- Function isgraph determines whether its argument is a printing character other than space.

Section 22.10 Pointer-Based String-Conversion Functions

- Function atof converts its argument—a string beginning with a series of digits that represents a floating-point number—to a double value.

- Function atoi converts its argument—a string beginning with a series of digits that represents an integer—to an int value.

- Function atol converts its argument—a string beginning with a series of digits that represents a long integer—to a long value.

- Function strtod converts a sequence of characters representing a floating-point value to double. The function receives two arguments—a string (char *) and the address of a char * pointer. The string contains the character sequence to be converted, and the pointer to char * is assigned the remainder of the string after the conversion.

- Function strtol converts a sequence of characters representing an integer to long. The function receives three arguments—a string (char *), the address of a char * pointer and an integer. The string contains the character sequence to be converted, the pointer to char * is assigned the location of the first character after the converted value and the integer specifies the base of the value being converted.

- Function strtoul converts a sequence of characters representing an integer to unsigned long. The function receives three arguments—a string (char *), the address of a char * pointer and an integer. The string contains the character sequence to be converted, the pointer to char * is assigned the location of the first character after the converted value and the integer specifies the base of the value being converted.

Section 22.11 Search Functions of the Pointer-Based String-Handling Library

- Function strchr searches for the first occurrence of a character in a string. If found, strchr returns a pointer to the character in the string; otherwise, strchr returns a null pointer.

- Function `strcspn` determines the length of the initial part of the string in its first argument that does not contain any characters from the string in its second argument. The function returns the length of the segment.

- Function `strpbrk` searches for the first occurrence in its first argument of any character that appears in its second argument. If a character from the second argument is found, `strpbrk` returns a pointer to the character; otherwise, `strpbrk` returns a null pointer.

- Function `strrchr` searches for the last occurrence of a character in a string. If the character is found, `strrchr` returns a pointer to the character in the string; otherwise, it returns a null pointer.

- Function `strspn` determines the length of the initial part of its first argument that contains only characters from the string in its second argument and returns the length of the segment.

- Function `strstr` searches for the first occurrence of its second string argument in its first string argument. If the second string is found in the first string, a pointer to the location of the string in the first argument is returned; otherwise it returns 0.

Section 22.12 Memory Functions of the Pointer-Based String-Handling Library

- Function `memcpy` copies a specified number of characters from the object to which its second argument points into the object to which its first argument points. The function can receive a pointer to any object. The pointers are received as `void` pointers and converted to `char` pointers for use in the function. Function `memcpy` manipulates the bytes of its argument as characters.

- Function `memmove` copies a specified number of bytes from the object pointed to by its second argument to the object pointed to by its first argument. Copying is accomplished as if the bytes were copied from the second argument to a temporary character array, and then copied from the temporary array to the first argument.

- Function `memcmp` compares the specified number of characters of its first and second arguments.

- Function `memchr` searches for the first occurrence of a byte, represented as `unsigned char`, in the specified number of bytes of an object. If the byte is found, a pointer to it is returned; otherwise, a null pointer is returned.

- Function `memset` copies its second argument, treated as an `unsigned char`, to a specified number of bytes of the object pointed to by the first argument.

Terminology

`&` bitwise AND operator	bitwise operators
`&=` bitwise AND assignment operator	`<cstdlib>`
`<<` left-shift operator	general-utilities library
`<<=` left-shift assignment operator	`isalnum`
`>>` right-shift operator	`isalpha`
`>>=` right-shift assignment operator	`iscntrl`
`^` bitwise exclusive OR operator	`isdigit`
`^=` bitwise exclusive OR assignment operator	`isgraph`
`|` bitwise inclusive OR operator	`islower`
`|=` bitwise inclusive OR assignment operator	`isprint`
`~` bitwise complement operator	`ispunct`
aggregate data type	`isspace`
`atof`	`isupper`
`atoi`	`isxdigit`
`atol`	mask
bit field	`memchr`
bitwise assignment operators	`memcmp`

memcpy	strtod
memmove	strtol
memset	strtoul
one's complement	struct
padding	structure name
self-referential structure	structure type
strchr	tolower
strcspn	toupper
string-conversion functions	typedef
strpbrk	unnamed bit field
strrchr	width of a bit field
strspn	zero-width bit field
strstr	

Self-Review Exercises

22.1   Fill in the blanks in each of the following:
a) A(n) _____ is a collection of related variables under one name.
b) The bits in the result of an expression using the _____ operator are set to one if the corresponding bits in each operand are set to one. Otherwise, the bits are set to zero.
c) The variables declared in a structure definition are called its _____.
d) The bits in the result of an expression using the _____ operator are set to one if at least one of the corresponding bits in either operand is set to one. Otherwise, the bits are set to zero.
e) Keyword _____ introduces a structure declaration.
f) Keyword _____ is used to create a synonym for a previously defined data type.
g) Each bit in the result of an expression using the _____ operator is set to one if exactly one of the corresponding bits in either operand is set to one.
h) The bitwise AND operator & is often used to _____ bits (i.e., to select certain bits from a bit string while zeroing others).
i) A structure member is accessed with either operator _____ or _____.
j) The _____ and _____ operators are used to shift the bits of a value to the left or to the right, respectively.

22.2   State whether each of the following is *true* or *false*. If *false*, explain why.
a) Structures may contain only one data type.
b) Members of different structures must have unique names.
c) Keyword typedef is used to define new data types.
d) Structures are always passed to functions by reference.

22.3   Write a single statement or a set of statements to accomplish each of the following:
a) Define a structure called Part containing int variable partNumber and char array partName to store upto a 25 character C-style string.
b) Define PartPtr to be a synonym for the type Part *.
c) Use separate statements to declare variable a to be of type Part, array b[10] to be of type Part and variable ptr to be of type pointer to Part.
d) Read a part number and a part name from the keyboard into the members of variable a.
e) Assign the member values of variable a to element three of array b.
f) Assign the address of array b to the pointer variable ptr.
g) Print the member values of element three of array b, using the variable ptr and the structure pointer operator to refer to the members.

22.4   Find the error in each of the following:

a)   Assume that `struct Card` has been defined as containing two pointers to type char—namely, face and suit. Also, the variable c has been declared to be of type Card, and the variable cPtr has been declared to be of type pointer to Card. Variable cPtr has been assigned the address of c.

```
cout << *cPtr.face << endl;
```

b)   Assume that `struct Card` has been defined as containing two pointers to type char—namely, face and suit. Also, the array hearts[13] has been declared to be of type Card. The following statement should print the member face of element 10 of the array.

```
cout << hearts.face << endl;
```

c)
```
struct Person
{
    char lastName[ 15 ];
    char firstName[ 15 ];
    int age;
}
```

d)   Assume that variable p has been declared as type Person and that variable c has been declared as type Card.

```
p = c;
```

22.5   Write a single statement to accomplish each of the following. Assume that variables c (which stores a character), x, y and z are of type int; variables d, e and f are of type double; variable ptr is of type char * and arrays s1[100] and s2[100] are of type char.

a)   Convert the character stored in variable c to an uppercase letter. Assign the result to variable c.

b)   Determine if the value of variable c is a digit. Use the conditional operator as shown in Figs. 22.18–22.20 to print " is a " or " is not a " when the result is displayed.

c)   Convert the string "1234567" to long, and print the value.

d)   Determine whether the value of variable c is a control character. Use the conditional operator to print " is a " or " is not a " when the result is displayed.

e)   Assign to ptr the location of the last occurrence of c in s1.

f)   Convert the string "8.63582" to double, and print the value.

g)   Determine whether the value of c is a letter. Use the conditional operator to print " is a " or " is not a " when the result is displayed.

h)   Assign to ptr the location of the first occurrence of s2 in s1.

i)   Determine whether the value of variable c is a printing character. Use the conditional operator to print " is a " or " is not a " when the result is displayed.

j)   Assign to ptr the location of the first occurrence in s1 of any character from s2.

k)   Assign to ptr the location of the first occurrence of c in s1.

l)   Convert the string "-21" to int, and print the value.

Answers to Self-Review Exercises

22.1   a) structure. b) bitwise AND (&). c) members. d) bitwise inclusive OR (|). e) `struct`. f) typedef. g) bitwise exclusive OR (^). h) mask. i) structure member (.), structure pointer (->). j) left-shift operator (<<), right-shift operator (>>).

22.2   a)   False. A structure can contain many data types.

b)   False. The members of separate structures can have the same names, but the members of the same structure must have unique names.

c) False. `typedef` is used to define aliases for previously defined data types.

d) False. Structures are passed to functions by value by default and may be passed by reference.

22.3 a) ***struct*** `Part`
```
{
    int partNumber;
    char partName[ 26 ];
};
```
b) ***typedef*** `Part * PartPtr;`

c) `Part a;`
`Part b[ 10 ];`
`Part *ptr;`

d) `cin >> a.partNumber >> a.partName;`

e) `b[ 3 ] = a;`

f) `ptr = b;`

g) `cout << ( ptr + 3 )->partNumber << ' '`
`    << ( ptr + 3 )->partName << endl;`

22.4 a) *Error:* The parentheses that should enclose `*cPtr` have been omitted, causing the order of evaluation of the expression to be incorrect.

b) *Error:* The array subscript has been omitted. The expression should be
`    hearts[ 10 ].face.`

c) *Error:* A semicolon is required to end a structure definition.

d) *Error:* Variables of different structure types cannot be assigned to one another.

22.5 a) `c = toupper( c );`

b) `cout << '\'' << c << "\' "`
`        << ( isdigit( c ) ? "is a" : "is not a" )`
`        << " digit" << endl;`

c) `cout << atol( "1234567" ) << endl;`

d) `cout << '\'' << c << "\' "`
`        << ( iscntrl( c ) ? "is a" : "is not a" )`
`        << " control character" << endl;`

e) `ptr = strrchr( s1, c );`

f) `out << atof( "8.63582" ) << endl;`

g) `cout << '\'' << c << "\' "`
`        << ( isalpha( c ) ? "is a" : "is not a" )`
`        << " letter" << endl;`

h) `ptr = strstr( s1, s2 );`

i) `cout << '\'' << c << "\' "`
`        << ( isprint( c ) ? "is a" : "is not a" )`
`        << " printing character" << endl;`

j) `ptr = strpbrk( s1, s2 );`

k) `ptr = strchr( s1, c );`

l) `cout << atoi( "-21" ) << endl;`

Exercises

22.6 Provide the definition for each of the following structures:

a) Structure `Inventory`, containing character array `partName[ 30 ]`, integer `partNumber`, floating-point `price`, integer `stock` and integer `reorder`.

b) A structure called `Address` that contains character arrays `streetAddress[ 25 ]`, `city[ 20 ]`, `state[ 3 ]` and `zipCode[ 6 ]`.

c) Structure `Student`, containing arrays `firstName[ 15 ]` and `lastName[ 15 ]` and variable `homeAddress` of type `struct Address` from part (b).

d) Structure `Test`, containing 16 bit fields with widths of 1 bit. The names of the bit fields are the letters a to p.

22.7   Consider the following structure definitions and variable declarations:

```
struct Customer {
    char lastName[ 15 ];
    char firstName[ 15 ];
    int customerNumber;

    struct {
        char phoneNumber[ 11 ];
        char address[ 50 ];
        char city[ 15 ];
        char state[ 3 ];
        char zipCode[ 6 ];
    } personal;

} customerRecord, *customerPtr;

customerPtr = &customerRecord;
```

Write a separate expression that accesses the structure members in each of the following parts:

a) Member `lastName` of structure `customerRecord`.

b) Member `lastName` of the structure pointed to by `customerPtr`.

c) Member `firstName` of structure `customerRecord`.

d) Member `firstName` of the structure pointed to by `customerPtr`.

e) Member `customerNumber` of structure `customerRecord`.

f) Member `customerNumber` of the structure pointed to by `customerPtr`.

g) Member `phoneNumber` of member `personal` of structure `customerRecord`.

h) Member `phoneNumber` of member `personal` of the structure pointed to by `customerPtr`.

i) Member `address` of member `personal` of structure `customerRecord`.

j) Member `address` of member `personal` of the structure pointed to by `customerPtr`.

k) Member `city` of member `personal` of structure `customerRecord`.

l) Member `city` of member `personal` of the structure pointed to by `customerPtr`.

m) Member `state` of member `personal` of structure `customerRecord`.

n) Member `state` of member `personal` of the structure pointed to by `customerPtr`.

o) Member `zipCode` of member `personal` of structure `customerRecord`.

p) Member `zipCode` of member `personal` of the structure pointed to by `customerPtr`.

22.8   Modify the program of Fig. 22.14 to shuffle the cards using a high-performance shuffle, as shown in Fig. 22.3. Print the resulting deck in two-column format, as in Fig. 22.4. Precede each card with its color.

22.9   Write a program that right-shifts an integer variable 4 bits. The program should print the integer in bits before and after the shift operation. Does your system place zeros or ones in the vacated bits?

22.10   Left shifting an `unsigned` integer by 1 bit is equivalent to multiplying the value by 2. Write function `power2` that takes two integer arguments, `number` and `pow`, and calculates

$$number * 2^{pow}$$

Use a shift operator to calculate the result. The program should print the values as integers and as bits.

22.11   The left-shift operator can be used to pack two character values into a two-byte unsigned integer variable. Write a program that inputs two characters from the keyboard and passes them to function packCharacters. To pack two characters into an unsigned integer variable, assign the first character to the unsigned variable, shift the unsigned variable left by 8 bit positions and combine the unsigned variable with the second character using the bitwise inclusive OR operator. The program should output the characters in their bit format before and after they are packed into the unsigned integer to prove that they are in fact packed correctly in the unsigned variable.

22.12   Using the right-shift operator, the bitwise AND operator and a mask, write function unpackCharacters that takes the unsigned integer from Exercise 22.11 and unpacks it into two characters. To unpack two characters from an unsigned two-byte integer, combine the unsigned integer with the mask 65280 (11111111 00000000) and right-shift the result 8 bits. Assign the resulting value to a char variable. Then, combine the unsigned integer with the mask 255 (00000000 11111111). Assign the result to another char variable. The program should print the unsigned integer in bits before it is unpacked, then print the characters in bits to confirm that they were unpacked correctly.

22.13   If your system uses four-byte integers, rewrite the program of Exercise 22.11 to pack four characters.

22.14   If your system uses four-byte integers, rewrite the function unpackCharacters of Exercise 22.12 to unpack four characters. Create the masks you need to unpack the four characters by left shifting the value 255 in the mask variable by 8 bits 0, 1, 2 or 3 times (depending on the byte you are unpacking).

22.15   Write a program that reverses the order of the bits in an unsigned integer value. The program should input the value from the user and call function reverseBits to print the bits in reverse order. Print the value in bits both before and after the bits are reversed to confirm that the bits are reversed properly.

22.16   Write a program that demonstrates passing an array by value. [*Hint:* Use a struct.] Prove that a copy was passed by modifying the array copy in the called function.

22.17   Write a program that inputs a character from the keyboard and tests the character with each function in the character-handling library. Print the value returned by each function.

22.18   The following program uses function multiple to determine whether the integer entered from the keyboard is a multiple of some integer. Examine function multiple, then determine the value of that integer.

```
1   // Exercise 22.18: ex22_18.cpp
2   // This program determines if a value is a multiple of X.
3   #include <iostream>
4
5   using std::cout;
6   using std::cin;
7   using std::endl;
8
9   bool multiple( int );
10
11  int main()
12  {
13     int y;
14
15     cout << "Enter an integer between 1 and 32000: ";
16     cin >> y;
17
18     if ( multiple( y ) )
19        cout << y << " is a multiple of X" << endl;
```

```
20      else
21         cout << y << " is not a multiple of X" << endl;
22
23      return 0;
24   } // end main
25
26   // determine if num is a multiple of X
27   bool multiple( int num )
28   {
29      bool mult = true;
30
31      for ( int i = 0, mask = 1; i < 10; i++, mask <<= 1 )
32
33         if ( ( num & mask ) != 0 ) {
34            mult = false;
35            break;
36
37         } // end if
38
39      return mult;
40
41   } // end function multiple
```

22.19 What does the following program do?

```
1    // Exercise 22.19: ex22_19.cpp
2    #include <iostream>
3
4    using std::cout;
5    using std::cin;
6    using std::endl;
7    using std::boolalpha;
8
9    bool mystery( unsigned );
10
11   int main()
12   {
13      unsigned x;
14
15      cout << "Enter an integer: ";
16      cin >> x;
17      cout << boolalpha
18         << "The result is " << mystery( x ) << endl;
19
20      return 0;
21
22   } // end main
23
24   // What does this function do?
25   bool mystery( unsigned bits )
26   {
27      const int SHIFT = 8 * sizeof( unsigned ) - 1;
28      const unsigned MASK = 1 << SHIFT;
29      unsigned total = 0;
30
31      for ( int i = 0; i < SHIFT + 1; i++, bits <<= 1 )
32
33         if ( ( bits & MASK ) == MASK )
34            ++total;
```

```
35
36      return !( total % 2 );
37
38  } // end function mystery
```

22.20 Write a program that inputs a line of text with `istream` member function `getline` (as in Chapter 17) into character array `s[ 100 ]`. Output the line in uppercase letters and lowercase letters.

22.21 Write a program that inputs four strings that represent integers, converts the strings to integers, sums the values and prints the total of the four values. Use only the C-style string-processing techniques shown in this chapter.

22.22 Write a program that inputs four strings that represent floating-point values, converts the strings to double values, sums the values and prints the total of the four values. Use only the C-style string-processing techniques shown in this chapter.

22.23 Write a program that inputs a line of text and a search string from the keyboard. Using function `strstr`, locate the first occurrence of the search string in the line of text, and assign the location to variable `searchPtr` of type char *. If the search string is found, print the remainder of the line of text beginning with the search string. Then use `strstr` again to locate the next occurrence of the search string in the line of text. If a second occurrence is found, print the remainder of the line of text beginning with the second occurrence. [*Hint:* The second call to `strstr` should contain the expression `searchPtr + 1` as its first argument.]

22.24 Write a program based on the program of Exercise 22.23 that inputs several lines of text and a search string, then uses function `strstr` to determine the total number of occurrences of the string in the lines of text. Print the result.

22.25 Write a program that inputs several lines of text and a search character and uses function `strchr` to determine the total number of occurrences of the character in the lines of text.

22.26 Write a program based on the program of Exercise 22.25 that inputs several lines of text and uses function `strchr` to determine the total number of occurrences of each letter of the alphabet in the text. Uppercase and lowercase letters should be counted together. Store the totals for each letter in an array, and print the values in tabular format after the totals have been determined.

22.27 The chart in Appendix B shows the numeric code representations for the characters in the ASCII character set. Study this chart, and then state whether each of the following is *true* or *false*:
  a) The letter "A" comes before the letter "B."
  b) The digit "9" comes before the digit "0."
  c) The commonly used symbols for addition, subtraction, multiplication and division all come before any of the digits.
  d) The digits come before the letters.
  e) If a sort program sorts strings into ascending sequence, then the program will place the symbol for a right parenthesis before the symbol for a left parenthesis.

22.28 Write a program that reads a series of strings and prints only those strings beginning with the letter "b."

22.29 Write a program that reads a series of strings and prints only those strings that end with the letters "ED."

22.30 Write a program that inputs an ASCII code and prints the corresponding character. Modify this program so that it generates all possible three-digit codes in the range 000–255 and attempts to print the corresponding characters. What happens when this program is run?

22.31 Using the ASCII character chart in Appendix B as a guide, write your own versions of the character-handling functions in Fig. 22.17.

22.32 Write your own versions of the functions in Fig. 22.21 for converting strings to numbers.

22.33 Write your own versions of the functions in Fig. 22.28 for searching strings.

22.34 Write your own versions of the functions in Fig. 22.35 for manipulating blocks of memory.

22.35 *(Project: A Spelling Checker)* Many popular word-processing software packages have built-in spell checkers. We used spell-checking capabilities in preparing this book and discovered that, no matter how careful we thought we were in writing a chapter, the software was always able to find a few more spelling errors than we were able to catch manually.

In this project, you are asked to develop your own spell-checker utility. We make suggestions to help get you started. You should then consider adding more capabilities. You might find it helpful to use a computerized dictionary as a source of words.

Why do we type so many words with incorrect spellings? In some cases, it is because we simply do not know the correct spelling, so we make a "best guess." In some cases, it is because we transpose two letters (e.g., "defualt" instead of "default"). Sometimes we double-type a letter accidentally (e.g., "hanndy" instead of "handy"). Sometimes we type a nearby key instead of the one we intended (e.g., "biryhday" instead of "birthday"). And so on.

Design and implement a spell-checker program. Your program maintains an array wordList of character strings. You can either enter these strings or obtain them from a computerized dictionary.

Your program asks a user to enter a word. The program then looks up that word in the wordList array. If the word is present in the array, your program should print "Word is spelled correctly."

If the word is not present in the array, your program should print "Word is not spelled correctly." Then your program should try to locate other words in wordList that might be the word the user intended to type. For example, you can try all possible single transpositions of adjacent letters to discover that the word "default" is a direct match to a word in wordList. Of course, this implies that your program will check all other single transpositions, such as "edfault," "dfeault," "deafult," "defalut" and "defautl." When you find a new word that matches one in wordList, print that word in a message such as "Did you mean "default?"."

Implement other tests, such as the replacing of each double letter with a single letter and any other tests you can develop to improve the value of your spell checker.

Standard Template Library (STL)

The shapes a bright container can contain!
—Theodore Roethke

Journey over all the universe in a map.
—Miguel de Cervantes

O! thou hast damnable iteration, and art indeed able to corrupt a saint.
—William Shakespeare

That great dust heap called "history."
—Augustine Birrell

The historian is a prophet in reverse.
—Friedrich von Schlegel

Attempt the end, and never stand to doubt; Nothing's so hard but search will find it out.
—Robert Herrick

OBJECTIVES

In this chapter you'll learn:

- To be able to use the STL containers, container adapters and "near containers."

- To be able to program with the dozens of STL algorithms.

- To understand how algorithms use iterators to access the elements of STL containers.

- To use STL/CLR with C++/CLI

- To become familiar with the STL resources available on the Internet and the World Wide Web.

23.1 Introduction to the Standard Template Library (STL)

We've repeatedly emphasized the importance of software reuse. Recognizing that many data structures and algorithms commonly are used by C++ programmers, the C++ standard committee added the *Standard Template Library (STL)* to the C++ Standard Library. The STL defines powerful, template-based, reusable components that implement many common data structures and algorithms used to process those data structures. The STL offers proof of concept for generic programming with templates—introduced in Chapter 15, Templates and Generics, and used extensively in Chapter 21, Data Structures. [*Note:* In industry, the features presented in this chapter are often referred to as the Standard Template Library or STL. However, these terms are not used in the C++ standard document, because these features are simply considered to be part of the C++ Standard Library.]

The STL was developed by Alexander Stepanov and Meng Lee at Hewlett-Packard and is based on their research in the field of generic programming, with significant contributions from David Musser. As you'll see, the STL was conceived and designed for performance and flexibility.

This chapter introduces the STL and discusses its three key components—*containers* (popular templatized data structures), *iterators* and *algorithms*. The STL containers are data structures capable of storing objects of almost any data type (there are some restrictions). We'll see that there are three styles of container classes—*first-class containers*, *adapters* and *near containers*.

 Performance Tip 23.1

For any particular application, several different STL containers might be appropriate. Select the most appropriate container that achieves the best performance (i.e., balance of speed and size) for that application. Efficiency was a crucial consideration in the STL's design.

Performance Tip 23.2

Standard Library capabilities are implemented to operate efficiently across many applications. For some applications with unique performance requirements, it might be necessary to write your own customized implementations.

Each STL container has associated member functions. A subset of these member functions is defined in all STL containers. We illustrate most of this common functionality in our examples of STL containers `vector` (a dynamically resizable array which we introduced in Chapter 8), *list* (a doubly linked list) and *deque* (a double-ended queue, pronounced "deck"). We introduce container-specific functionality in examples for each of the other STL containers.

STL iterators, which have properties similar to those of pointers, are used by programs to manipulate the STL-container elements. In fact, standard arrays can be manipulated by STL algorithms, using standard pointers as iterators. We'll see that manipulating containers with iterators is convenient and provides tremendous expressive power when combined with STL algorithms—in some cases, reducing many lines of code to a single statement. There are five categories of iterators, each of which we discuss in Section 23.1.2 and use throughout this chapter.

STL algorithms are functions that perform such common data manipulations as searching, sorting and comparing elements (or entire containers). The STL provides approximately 70 algorithms. Most of them use iterators to access container elements. Each algorithm has minimum requirements for the types of iterators that can be used with it. We'll see that each first-class container supports specific iterator types, some more powerful than others. A container's supported iterator type determines whether the container can be used with a specific algorithm. Iterators encapsulate the mechanism used to access container elements. This encapsulation enables many of the STL algorithms to be applied to several containers without regard for the underlying container implementation. As long as a container's iterators support the minimum requirements of the algorithm, then the algorithm can process that container's elements. This also enables programmers to create new algorithms that can process the elements of multiple container types.

Software Engineering Observation 23.1

The STL approach allows general programs to be written so that the code does not depend on the underlying container. Such a programming style is called generic programming.

In Chapter 21, we studied data structures. We built linked lists, queues, stacks and trees. We carefully wove link objects together with pointers. Pointer-based code is complex, and the slightest omission or oversight can lead to serious memory-access violations and memory-leak errors with no compiler complaints. Implementing additional data structures, such as deques, priority queues, sets and maps, requires substantial extra work. In addition, if many programmers on a large project implement similar containers and algorithms for different tasks, the code becomes difficult to modify, maintain and debug. An advantage of the STL is that programmers can reuse the STL containers, iterators and algorithms to implement common data representations and manipulations. This reuse can save substantial development time, money and effort.

Software Engineering Observation 23.2

Avoid reinventing the wheel; program with the reusable components of the C++ Standard Library. STL includes many of the most popular data structures as containers and provides various popular algorithms to process data in these containers.

Error-Prevention Tip 23.1

When programming pointer-based data structures and algorithms, we must do our own debugging and testing to be sure our data structures, classes and algorithms function properly. It is easy to make errors when manipulating pointers at this low level. Memory leaks and memory-access violations are common in such custom code. For most programmers, and for most of the applications they will need to write, the prepackaged, templatized containers of the STL are sufficient. Using the STL helps programmers reduce testing and debugging time. One caution is that, for large projects, template compile time can be significant.

This chapter introduces the STL. It is by no means complete or comprehensive. However, it is a friendly, accessible chapter that should convince you of the value of the STL in software reuse and encourage further study.

23.1.1 Introduction to Containers

The STL container types are shown in Fig. 23.1. The containers are divided into three major categories—*sequence containers*, *associative containers* and *container adapters*.

Standard Library container class	Description
Sequence containers	
vector	Rapid insertions and deletions at back. Direct access to any element.
deque	Rapid insertions and deletions at front or back. Direct access to any element.
list	Doubly linked list, rapid insertion and deletion anywhere.
Associative containers	
set	Rapid lookup, no duplicates allowed.
multiset	Rapid lookup, duplicates allowed.
map	One-to-one mapping, no duplicates allowed, rapid key-based lookup.
multimap	One-to-many mapping, duplicates allowed, rapid key-based lookup.
Container adapters	
stack	Last-in, first-out (LIFO).
queue	First-in, first-out (FIFO).
priority_queue	Highest-priority element is always the first element out.

Fig. 23.1 | Standard Library container classes.

STL Containers Overview

The sequence containers represent linear data structures, such as vectors and linked lists. Associative containers are nonlinear containers that typically can locate elements stored within them quickly. Such containers can store sets of values or *key/value pairs*. The sequence containers and associative containers are collectively referred to as the first-class containers. As we saw in Chapter 21, stacks and queues actually are constrained versions of sequential containers. For this reason, STL implements stacks and queues as container adapters that enable a program to view a sequential container in a constrained manner. There are other container types that are considered "near containers"—C-like pointer-based arrays (discussed in Chapter 8), bitsets for maintaining sets of flag values and valarrays for performing high-speed mathematical vector operations (this last class is optimized for computation performance and is not as flexible as the first-class containers). These types are considered "near containers" because they exhibit capabilities similar to those of the first-class containers, but do not support all the first-class-container capabilities. Type string (discussed in Chapter 19) supports the same functionality as a sequence container, but stores only character data.

STL Container Common Functions

Most STL containers provide similar functionality. Many generic operations, such as member function size, apply to all containers, and other operations apply to subsets of similar containers. This encourages extensibility of the STL with new classes. Figure 23.2

describes the functions common to all Standard Library containers. [*Note:* Overloaded operators operator<, operator<=, operator>, operator>=, operator== and operator!= are not provided for priority_queues.]

Common member functions for most STL containers	Description
default constructor	A constructor to create an empty container. Normally, each container has several constructors that provide different initialization methods for the container.
copy constructor	A constructor that initializes the container to be a copy of an existing container of the same type.
destructor	Destructor function for cleanup after a container is no longer needed.
empty	Returns true if there are no elements in the container; otherwise, returns false.
insert	Inserts an item in the container.
size	Returns the number of elements currently in the container.
operator=	Assigns one container to another.
operator<	Returns true if the first container is less than the second container; otherwise, returns false.
operator<=	Returns true if the first container is less than or equal to the second container; otherwise, returns false.
operator>	Returns true if the first container is greater than the second container; otherwise, returns false.
operator>=	Returns true if the first container is greater than or equal to the second container; otherwise, returns false.
operator==	Returns true if the first container is equal to the second container; otherwise, returns false.
operator!=	Returns true if the first container is not equal to the second container; otherwise, returns false.
swap	Swaps the elements of two containers.
Functions found only in first-class containers	
max_size	Returns the maximum number of elements for a container.
begin	The two versions of this function return either an iterator or a const_iterator that refers to the first element of the container.
end	The two versions of this function return either an iterator or a const_iterator that refers to the next position after the end of the container.
rbegin	The two versions of this function return either a reverse_iterator or a const_reverse_iterator that refers to the last element of the container.

Fig. 23.2 | STL container common functions. (Part 1 of 2.)

Common member functions for most STL containers	Description
rend	The two versions of this function return either a reverse_iterator or a const_reverse_iterator that refers to the next position after the last element of the reversed container.
erase	Erases one or more elements from the container.
clear	Erases all elements from the container.

Fig. 23.2 | STL container common functions. (Part 2 of 2.)

STL Container Header Files

The header files for each of the Standard Library containers are shown in Fig. 23.3. The contents of these header files are all in namespace std.

Standard Library container header files	
<vector>	
<list>	
<deque>	
<queue>	Contains both queue and priority_queue.
<stack>	
<map>	Contains both map and multimap.
<set>	Contains both set and multiset.
<valarray>	
<bitset>	

Fig. 23.3 | Standard Library container header files.

First-Class Container Common typedefs

Figure 23.4 shows the common typedefs (to create synonyms or aliases for lengthy type names) found in first-class containers. These typedefs are used in generic declarations of variables, parameters to functions and return values from functions. For example, value_type in each container is always a typedef that represents the type of value stored in the container.

typedef	Description
allocator_type	The type of the object used to allocate the container's memory.
value_type	The type of element stored in the container.

Fig. 23.4 | typedefs found in first-class containers. (Part 1 of 2.)

typedef	Description
reference	A reference to the type of element stored in the container.
const_reference	A constant reference to the type of element stored in the container. Such a reference can be used only for *reading* elements in the container and for performing const operations.
pointer	A pointer to the type of element stored in the container.
const_pointer	A pointer to a constant element of the type stored in the container.
iterator	An iterator that points to the type of element stored in the container.
const_iterator	A constant iterator that points to the type of element stored in the container and can be used only to *read* elements.
reverse_iterator	A reverse iterator that points to the type of element stored in the container. This type of iterator is for iterating through a container in reverse.
const_reverse_iterator	A constant reverse iterator that points to the type of element stored in the container and can be used only to *read* elements. This type of iterator is for iterating through a container in reverse.
difference_type	The type of the result of subtracting two iterators that refer to the same container (operator – is not defined for iterators of lists and associative containers).
size_type	The type used to count items in a container and index through a sequence container (cannot index through a list).

Fig. 23.4 | typedefs found in first-class containers. (Part 2 of 2.)

Performance Tip 23.3

STL generally avoids inheritance and virtual functions in favor of using generic programming with templates to achieve better execution-time performance.

Portability Tip 23.1

Programming with STL will enhance the portability of your code.

When preparing to use an STL container, it is important to ensure that the type of element being stored in the container supports a minimum set of functionality. When an element is inserted into a container, a copy of that element is made. For this reason, the element type should provide its own copy constructor and assignment operator. [*Note:* This is required only if default memberwise copy and default memberwise assignment do not perform proper copy and assignment operations for the element type.] Also, the associative containers and many algorithms require elements to be compared. For this reason, the element type should provide an equality operator (==) and a less-than operator (<).

Software Engineering Observation 23.3

The STL containers technically do not require their elements to be comparable with the equality and less-than operators unless a program uses a container member function that must compare the container elements (e.g., the sort function in class list). Unfortunately, some prestandard C++ compilers are not capable of ignoring parts of a template that are not used in a particular program. On compilers with this problem, you may not be able to use the STL containers with objects of classes that do not define overloaded less-than and equality operators.

23.1.2 Introduction to Iterators

Iterators have many features in common with pointers and are used to point to the elements of first-class containers (and for a few other purposes, as we'll see). Iterators hold state information sensitive to the particular containers on which they operate; thus, iterators are implemented appropriately for each type of container. Certain iterator operations are uniform across containers. For example, the dereferencing operator (*) dereferences an iterator so that you can use the element to which it points. The ++ operation on an iterator moves it to the next element of the container (much as incrementing a pointer into an array aims the pointer at the next element of the array).

STL first-class containers provide member functions begin and end. Function **begin** returns an iterator pointing to the first element of the container. Function **end** returns an iterator pointing to the first element past the end of the container (an element that doesn't exist). If iterator i points to a particular element, then ++i points to the "next" element and *i refers to the element pointed to by i. The iterator resulting from end is typically used in an equality or inequality comparison to determine whether the "moving iterator" (i in this case) has reached the end of the container.

We use an object of type iterator to refer to a container element that can be modified. We use an object of type const_iterator to refer to a container element that cannot be modified.

Using *istream_iterator for Input and Using* ostream_iterator *for Output*

We use iterators with *sequences* (also called *ranges*). These sequences can be in containers, or they can be *input sequences* or *output sequences*. The program of Fig. 23.5 demonstrates input from the standard input (a sequence of data for input into a program), using an *istream_iterator*, and output to the standard output (a sequence of data for output from a program), using an *ostream_iterator*. The program inputs two integers from the user at the keyboard and displays the sum of the integers.[1]

Line 15 creates an istream_iterator that is capable of extracting (inputting) int values in a type-safe manner from the standard input object cin. Line 17 dereferences iterator inputInt to read the first integer from cin and assigns that integer to number1. Note that the dereferencing operator * applied to inputInt gets the value from the stream associated with inputInt; this is similar to dereferencing a pointer. Line 18 positions iterator

---

1. The examples in this chapter precede each use of an STL function and each definition of an STL container object with the "std::" prefix rather than placing the using declarations or directives at the beginning of the program, as was shown in most prior examples. Differences in compilers and the complex code generated when using STL make it difficult to construct a proper set of using declarations or directives that enable the programs to compile without errors. To allow these programs to compile on the widest variety of platforms, we chose the "std::" prefix approach.

```
1   // Fig. 23.5: IOIterators.cpp
2   // Demonstrating input and output with iterators.
3   #include <iostream>
4   using std::cout;
5   using std::cin;
6   using std::endl;
7
8   #include <iterator> // ostream_iterator and istream_iterator
9
10  int main()
11  {
12     cout << "Enter two integers: ";
13
14     // create istream_iterator for reading int values from cin
15     std::istream_iterator< int > inputInt( cin );
16
17     int number1 = *inputInt; // read int from standard input
18     ++inputInt; // move iterator to next input value
19     int number2 = *inputInt; // read int from standard input
20
21     // create ostream_iterator for writing int values to cout
22     std::ostream_iterator< int > outputInt( cout );
23
24     cout << "The sum is: ";
25     *outputInt = number1 + number2; // output result to cout
26     cout << endl;
27     return 0;
28  } // end main
```

```
Enter two integers: 12 25
The sum is: 37
```

Fig. 23.5 | Input and output stream iterators.

inputInt to the next value in the input stream. Line 19 inputs the next integer from inputInt and assigns it to number2.

Line 22 creates an ostream_iterator that is capable of inserting (outputting) int values in the standard output object cout. Line 25 outputs an integer to cout by assigning to *outputInt the sum of number1 and number2. Notice the use of the dereferencing operator * to use *outputInt as an *lvalue* in the assignment statement. If you want to output another value using outputInt, the iterator must be incremented with ++ (both the prefix and postfix increment can be used, but the prefix form should be preferred for performance reasons).

Error-Prevention Tip 23.2

*The * (dereferencing) operator of any const iterator returns a const reference to the container element, disallowing the use of non-const member functions.*

Common Programming Error 23.1

Attempting to dereference an iterator positioned outside its container is a runtime logic error. In particular, the iterator returned by end cannot be dereferenced or incremented.

Common Programming Error 23.2

Attempting to create a non-const iterator for a const container results in a compilation error.

Iterator Categories and Iterator Category Hierarchy

Figure 23.6 shows the categories of STL iterators. Each category provides a specific set of functionality. Figure 23.7 illustrates the hierarchy of iterator categories. As you follow the hierarchy from top to bottom, each iterator category supports all the functionality of the categories above it in the figure. Thus the "weakest" iterator types are at the top and the most powerful one is at the bottom. Note that this is not an inheritance hierarchy.

The iterator category that each container supports determines whether that container can be used with specific algorithms in the STL. Containers that support random-access iterators can be used with all algorithms in the STL. As we'll see, pointers into arrays can be used in place of iterators in most STL algorithms, including those that require random-access iterators. Figure 23.8 shows the iterator category of each of the STL containers.

Category	Description
input	Used to read an element from a container. An input iterator can move only in the forward direction (i.e., from the beginning of the container to the end) one element at a time. Input iterators support only one-pass algorithms—the same input iterator cannot be used to pass through a sequence twice.
output	Used to write an element to a container. An output iterator can move only in the forward direction one element at a time. Output iterators support only one-pass algorithms—the same output iterator cannot be used to pass through a sequence twice.
forward	Combines the capabilities of input and output iterators and retains their position in the container (as state information).
bidirectional	Combines the capabilities of a forward iterator with the ability to move in the backward direction (i.e., from the end of the container toward the beginning). Bidirectional iterators support multipass algorithms.
random access	Combines the capabilities of a bidirectional iterator with the ability to directly access any element of the container, i.e., to jump forward or backward by an arbitrary number of elements.

Fig. 23.6 | Iterator categories.

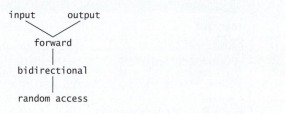

Fig. 23.7 | Iterator category hierarchy.

Note that vectors, deques, lists, sets, multisets, maps, multimaps (i.e., the first-class containers), strings and arrays are traversable with iterators.

Software Engineering Observation 23.4

Using the "weakest iterator" that yields acceptable performance helps produce maximally reusable components. For example, if an algorithm requires only forward iterators, it can be used with any container that supports forward iterators, bidirectional iterators or random-access iterators. However, an algorithm that requires random-access iterators can be used only with containers that have random-access iterators.

Predefined Iterator typedefs

Figure 23.9 shows the predefined iterator typedefs that are found in the class definitions of the STL containers. Not every typedef is defined for every container. We use const versions of the iterators for traversing read-only containers. We use reverse iterators to traverse containers in the reverse direction.

Container	Type of iterator supported
Sequence containers (first class)	
vector	random access
deque	random access
list	bidirectional
Associative containers (first class)	
set	bidirectional
multiset	bidirectional
map	bidirectional
multimap	bidirectional
Container adapters	
stack	no iterators supported
queue	no iterators supported
priority_queue	no iterators supported

Fig. 23.8 | Iterator types supported by each Standard Library container.

Predefined typedefs for iterator types	Direction of ++	Capability
iterator	forward	read/write
const_iterator	forward	read
reverse_iterator	backward	read/write
const_reverse_iterator	backward	read

Fig. 23.9 | Iterator typedefs.

Error-Prevention Tip 23.3

Operations performed on a const_iterator return const references to prevent modification to elements of the container being manipulated. Using const_iterators in preference to iterators where appropriate is another example of the principle of least privilege.

Iterator Operations

Figure 23.10 shows some operations that can be performed on each iterator type. Note that the operations for each iterator type include all operations preceding that type in the figure. Note also that, for input iterators and output iterators, it is not possible to save the iterator and then use the saved value later.

Iterator operation	Description
All iterators	
++p	Preincrement an iterator.
p++	Postincrement an iterator.
Input iterators	
*p	Dereference an iterator.
p = p1	Assign one iterator to another.
p == p1	Compare iterators for equality.
p != p1	Compare iterators for inequality.
Output iterators	
*p	Dereference an iterator.
p = p1	Assign one iterator to another.
Forward iterators	Forward iterators provide all the functionality of both input iterators and output iterators.
Bidirectional iterators	
--p	Predecrement an iterator.
p--	Postdecrement an iterator.
Random-access iterators	
p += i	Increment the iterator p by i positions.
p -= i	Decrement the iterator p by i positions.
p + i *or* i + p	Expression value is an iterator positioned at p incremented by i positions.
p - i	Expression value is an iterator positioned at p decremented by i positions.
p - p1	Expression value is an integer representing the distance between two elements in the same container.
p[i]	Return a reference to the element offset from p by i positions
p < p1	Return true if iterator p is less than iterator p1 (i.e., iterator p is before iterator p1 in the container); otherwise, return false.

Fig. 23.10 | Iterator operations for each type of iterator. (Part 1 of 2.)

Iterator operation	Description
p <= p1	Return true if iterator p is less than or equal to iterator p1 (i.e., iterator p is before iterator p1 or at the same location as iterator p1 in the container); otherwise, return false.
p > p1	Return true if iterator p is greater than iterator p1 (i.e., iterator p is after iterator p1 in the container); otherwise, return false.
p >= p1	Return true if iterator p is greater than or equal to iterator p1 (i.e., iterator p is after iterator p1 or at the same location as iterator p1 in the container); otherwise, return false.

Fig. 23.10 | Iterator operations for each type of iterator. (Part 2 of 2.)

23.1.3 Introduction to Algorithms

STL algorithms can be used generically across a variety of containers. STL provides many algorithms you'll use frequently to manipulate containers. Inserting, deleting, searching, sorting and others are appropriate for some or all of the STL containers.

The STL includes approximately 70 standard algorithms. We provide live-code examples of most of these and summarize the others in tables. The algorithms operate on container elements only indirectly through iterators. Many algorithms operate on sequences of elements defined by pairs of iterators—a first iterator pointing to the first element of the sequence and a second iterator pointing to one element past the last element of the sequence. Also, it is possible to create your own new algorithms that operate in a similar fashion so they can be used with the STL containers and iterators.

Algorithms often return iterators that indicate the results of the algorithms. Algorithm find, for example, locates an element and returns an iterator to that element. If the element is not found, find returns the "one past the end" iterator that was passed in to define the end of the range to be searched, which can be tested to determine whether an element was not found. The find algorithm can be used with any first-class STL container. STL algorithms create yet another opportunity for reuse—using the rich collection of popular algorithms can save programmers much time and effort.

If an algorithm uses less powerful iterators, it can also be used with containers that support more powerful iterators. Some algorithms demand powerful iterators; e.g., sort demands random-access iterators.

Software Engineering Observation 23.5

The STL is implemented concisely. Until now, class designers would have associated the algorithms with the containers by making the algorithms member functions of the containers. The STL takes a different approach. The algorithms are separated from the containers and operate on elements of the containers only indirectly through iterators. This separation makes it easier to write generic algorithms applicable to many container classes.

Software Engineering Observation 23.6

The STL is extensible. It is straightforward to add new algorithms and to do so without changes to STL containers.

Software Engineering Observation 23.7

STL algorithms can operate on STL containers and on pointer-based, C-like arrays.

Portability Tip 23.2

Because STL algorithms process containers only indirectly through iterators, one algorithm can often be used with many different containers.

Figure 23.11 shows many of the ***mutating-sequence algorithms***—i.e., the algorithms that result in modifications of the containers to which the algorithms are applied.

Mutating-sequence algorithms		
copy	remove	reverse_copy
copy_backward	remove_copy	rotate
fill	remove_copy_if	rotate_copy
fill_n	remove_if	stable_partition
generate	replace	swap
generate_n	replace_copy	swap_ranges
iter_swap	replace_copy_if	transform
partition	replace_if	unique
random_shuffle	reverse	unique_copy

Fig. 23.11 | Mutating-sequence algorithms.

Figure 23.12 shows many of the nonmodifying sequence algorithms—i.e., the algorithms that do not result in modifications of the containers to which they are applied. Figure 23.13 shows the numerical algorithms of the header file ***<numeric>***.

Nonmodifying sequence algorithms		
adjacent_find	find	find_if
count	find_each	mismatch
count_if	find_end	search
equal	find_first_of	search_n

Fig. 23.12 | Nonmodifying sequence algorithms.

Numerical algorithms from header file <numeric>	
accumulate	partial_sum
inner_product	adjacent_difference

Fig. 23.13 | Numerical algorithms from header file <numeric>.

23.2 Sequence Containers

The C++ Standard Template Library provides three sequence containers—vector, list and deque. Class template vector and class template deque both are based on arrays. Class template list implements a linked-list data structure similar to our List class presented in Chapter 21, but more robust.

One of the most popular containers in the STL is vector. Recall that we introduced class template vector in Chapter 8 as a more robust type of array. A vector changes size dynamically. Unlike C and C++ "raw" arrays (see Chapter 8), vectors can be assigned to one another. This is not possible with pointer-based, C-like arrays, because those array names are constant pointers and cannot be the targets of assignments. Just as with C arrays, vector subscripting does not perform automatic range checking, but class template vector does provide this capability via member function at (also discussed in Chapter 8).

> **Performance Tip 23.4**
>
> *Insertion at the back of a vector is efficient. The vector simply grows, if necessary, to accommodate the new item. It is expensive to insert (or delete) an element in the middle of a vector—the entire portion of the vector after the insertion (or deletion) point must be moved, because vector elements occupy contiguous cells in memory just as C or C++ "raw" arrays do.*

Figure 23.2 presented the operations common to all the STL containers. Beyond these operations, each container typically provides a variety of other capabilities. Many of these capabilities are common to several containers, but they are not always equally efficient for each container. You must choose the container most appropriate for the application.

> **Performance Tip 23.5**
>
> *Applications that require frequent insertions and deletions at both ends of a container normally use a deque rather than a vector. Although we can insert and delete elements at the front and back of both a vector and a deque, class deque is more efficient than vector for doing insertions and deletions at the front.*

> **Performance Tip 23.6**
>
> *Applications with frequent insertions and deletions in the middle and/or at the extremes of a container normally use a list, due to its efficient implementation of insertion and deletion anywhere in the data structure.*

In addition to the common operations described in Fig. 23.2, the sequence containers have several other common operations—***front*** to return a reference to the first element in a non-empty container, ***back*** to return a reference to the last element in a non-empty container, push_back to insert a new element at the end of the container and pop_back to remove the last element of the container.

23.2.1 vector Sequence Container

Class template vector provides a data structure with contiguous memory locations. This enables efficient, direct access to any element of a vector via the subscript operator [], exactly as with a C or C++ "raw" array. Class template vector is most commonly used when the data in the container must be easily accessible via a subscript or will be sorted. When a vector's memory is exhausted, the vector allocates a larger contiguous area of memory, copies the original elements into the new memory and deallocates the old memory.

Performance Tip 23.7

Choose the vector *container for the best random-access performance.*

Performance Tip 23.8

Objects of class template vector *provide rapid indexed access with the overloaded subscript operator* [] *because they are stored in contiguous memory like a C or C++ raw array.*

Performance Tip 23.9

It is faster to insert many elements at once than one at a time.

An important part of every container is the type of iterator it supports. This determines which algorithms can be applied to the container. A vector supports random-access iterators—i.e., all iterator operations shown in Fig. 23.10 can be applied to a vector iterator. All STL algorithms can operate on a vector. The iterators for a vector are sometimes implemented as pointers to elements of the vector. Each STL algorithm that takes iterator arguments requires those iterators to provide a minimum level of functionality. If an algorithm requires a forward iterator, for example, that algorithm can operate on any container that provides forward iterators, bidirectional iterators or random-access iterators. As long as the container supports the algorithm's minimum iterator functionality, the algorithm can operate on the container.

Using Vector and Iterators

Figure 23.14 illustrates several functions of the vector class template. Many of these functions are available in every first-class container. You must include header file <vector> to use class template vector.

```cpp
 1  // Fig. 23.14: VectorTemplate.cpp
 2  // Demonstrating Standard Library vector class template.
 3  #include <iostream>
 4  using std::cout;
 5  using std::endl;
 6
 7  #include <vector> // vector class-template definition
 8  using std::vector;
 9
10  // prototype for function template printVector
11  template < typename T > void printVector( const vector< T > &integers2 );
12
13  int main()
14  {
15     const int SIZE = 6; // define array size
16     int array[ SIZE ] = { 1, 2, 3, 4, 5, 6 }; // initialize array
17     vector< int > integers; // create vector of ints
18
19     cout << "The initial size of integers is: " << integers.size()
20        << "\nThe initial capacity of integers is: " << integers.capacity();
```

Fig. 23.14 | Standard Library vector class template. (Part 1 of 2.)

```
21
22      // function push_back is in every sequence collection
23      integers.push_back( 2 );
24      integers.push_back( 3 );
25      integers.push_back( 4 );
26
27      cout << "\nThe size of integers is: " << integers.size()
28         << "\nThe capacity of integers is: " << integers.capacity();
29      cout << "\n\nOutput array using pointer notation: ";
30
31      // display array using pointer notation
32      for ( int *ptr = array; ptr != array + SIZE; ptr++ )
33         cout << *ptr << ' ';
34
35      cout << "\nOutput vector using iterator notation: ";
36      printVector( integers );
37      cout << "\nReversed contents of vector integers: ";
38
39      // two const reverse iterators
40      vector< int >::const_reverse_iterator reverseIterator;
41      vector< int >::const_reverse_iterator tempIterator = integers.rend();
42
43      // display vector in reverse order using reverse_iterator
44      for ( reverseIterator = integers.rbegin();
45         reverseIterator!= tempIterator; ++reverseIterator )
46         cout << *reverseIterator << ' ';
47
48      cout << endl;
49      return 0;
50   } // end main
51
52   // function template for outputting vector elements
53   template < typename T > void printVector( const vector< T > &integers2 )
54   {
55      typename vector< T >::const_iterator constIterator; // const_iterator
56
57      // display vector elements using const_iterator
58      for ( constIterator = integers2.begin();
59         constIterator != integers2.end(); ++constIterator )
60         cout << *constIterator << ' ';
61   } // end function printVector
```

```
The initial size of integers is: 0
The initial capacity of integers is: 0
The size of integers is: 3
The capacity of integers is: 3

Output array using pointer notation: 1 2 3 4 5 6
Output vector using iterator notation: 2 3 4
Reversed contents of vector integers: 4 3 2
```

Fig. 23.14 | Standard Library **vector** class template. (Part 2 of 2.)

Line 17 defines an instance called `integers` of class template `vector` that stores `int` values. When this object is instantiated, an empty `vector` is created with size 0 (i.e., the number of elements stored in the `vector`) and capacity 0 (i.e., the number of elements that can be stored without allocating more memory to the `vector`).

Lines 19 and 20 demonstrate the `size` and `capacity` functions; each initially returns 0 for `vector` v in this example. Function `size`—available in every container—returns the number of elements currently stored in the container. Function **capacity** returns the number of elements that can be stored in the `vector` before the `vector` needs to dynamically resize itself to accommodate more elements.

Lines 23–25 use function **push_back**—available in all sequence containers—to add an element to the end of the `vector`. If an element is added to a full `vector`, the `vector` increases its size—some STL implementations have the `vector` double its capacity.

Performance Tip 23.10

It can be wasteful to double a vector's size when more space is needed. For example, a full vector of 1,000,000 elements resizes to accommodate 2,000,000 elements when a new element is added. This leaves 999,999 unused elements. Programmers can use `resize` and `reserve` to control space usage better.

Lines 27 and 28 use `size` and `capacity` to illustrate the new size and capacity of the `vector` after the three `push_back` operations. Function `size` returns 3—the number of elements added to the `vector`. Function `capacity` also returns 3, indicating that the `vector` needs to add more memory before a new item can be added. When we added the first element, the `vector` allocated space for one element, and the size became 1 to indicate that the `vector` contained only one element. When we added the second element, the capacity doubled to 2 and the size became 2 as well. When we added the third element, the capacity doubled again to 4. So we can actually add another element before the `vector` needs to allocation more space. When the `vector` eventually fills its allocated capacity and the program attempts to add one more element to the `vector`, the `vector` will double its capacity to 8 elements.

The manner in which a `vector` grows to accommodate more elements—a time-consuming operation—is not specified by the C++ Standard Document. C++ library implementors use various clever schemes to minimize the overhead of resizing a `vector`. Hence, the output of this program may vary, depending on the version of `vector` that comes with your compiler. Some library implementors allocate a large initial capacity. If a `vector` stores a small number of elements, such capacity may be a waste of space. However, it can greatly improve performance if a program adds many elements to a `vector` and does not have to reallocate memory to accommodate those elements. This is a classic space–time trade-off. Library implementors must balance the amount of memory used against the amount of time required to perform various `vector` operations.

Lines 32–33 demonstrate how to output the contents of an array using pointers and pointer arithmetic. Line 36 calls function `printVector` (defined in lines 53–61) to output the contents of a `vector` using iterators. Function template `printVector` receives a `const` reference to a `vector` (integers2) as its argument. Line 55 defines a `const_iterator` called `constIterator` that iterates through the `vector` and outputs its contents. Notice that the declaration in line 55 is prefixed with the keyword `typename`. Because `printVector` is a function template and `vector< T >` will be specialized differently for each function-template specialization, the compiler cannot tell at compile time whether or not `vector< T >::const_iterator` is a type. In a particular specialization, `const_iterator` could be a `static` variable. The compiler needs this information to compile the program correctly. Therefore, you must tell the compiler that a qualified name, when the qualifier is a dependent type, is expected to be a type in every specialization.

A `const_iterator` enables the program to read the elements of the `vector`, but does not allow the program to modify the elements. The `for` statement in lines 58–60 initializes `constIterator` using `vector` member function `begin`, which returns a `const_iterator` to the first element in the `vector`—there is another version of `begin` that returns an `iterator` that can be used for non-const containers. Note that a `const_iterator` is returned because the identifier `integers2` was declared `const` in the parameter list of function `printVector`. The loop continues as long as `constIterator` has not reached the end of the `vector`. This is determined by comparing `constIterator` to the result of `integers2.end()`, which returns an iterator indicating the location past the last element of the `vector`. If `constIterator` is equal to this value, the end of the `vector` has been reached. Functions `begin` and `end` are available for all first-class containers. The body of the loop dereferences iterator `constIterator` to get the value in the current element of the `vector`. Remember that the iterator acts like a pointer to the element and that operator `*` is overloaded to return a reference to the element. The expression `++constIterator` (line 59) positions the iterator to the next element of the `vector`.

Performance Tip 23.11

Use prefix increment when applied to STL iterators, because the prefix increment operator does not return a value that must be stored in a temporary object.

Error-Prevention Tip 23.4

Only random-access iterators support `<`. *It is better to use* `!=` *and* `end` *to test for the end of a container.*

Line 40 declares a `const_reverse_iterator` that can be used to iterate through a `vector` backward. Line 41 declares a `const_reverse_iterator` variable `tempIterator` and initializes it to the iterator returned by function **rend** (i.e., the iterator for the ending point when iterating through the container in reverse). All first-class containers support this type of iterator. Lines 44–46 use a `for` statement similar to that in function `printVector` to iterate through the `vector`. In this loop, function **rbegin** (i.e., the iterator for the starting point when iterating through the container in reverse) and `tempIterator` delineate the range of elements to output. As with functions `begin` and `end`, `rbegin` and `rend` can return a `const_reverse_iterator` or a `reverse_iterator`, based on whether or not the container is constant.

Performance Tip 23.12

For performance reasons, capture the loop ending value before the loop and compare against that, rather than having a (potentially expensive) function call for each iteration.

Vector Element-Manipulation Functions
Figure 23.15 illustrates functions that enable retrieval and manipulation of the elements of a `vector`. Line 17 uses an overloaded `vector` constructor that takes two iterators as ar-

guments to initialize `integers`. Remember that pointers into an array can be used as iterators. Line 17 initializes `integers` with the contents of `array` from location `array` up to—but not including—location `array + SIZE`.

```cpp
1   // Fig. 23.15: VectorTest.cpp
2   // Testing Standard Library vector class template
3   // element-manipulation functions.
4   #include <iostream>
5   using std::cout;
6   using std::endl;
7
8   #include <vector> // vector class-template definition
9   #include <algorithm> // copy algorithm
10  #include <iterator> // ostream_iterator iterator
11  #include <stdexcept> // out_of_range exception
12
13  int main()
14  {
15     const int SIZE = 6;
16     int array[ SIZE ] = { 1, 2, 3, 4, 5, 6 };
17     std::vector< int > integers( array, array + SIZE );
18     std::ostream_iterator< int > output( cout, " " );
19
20     cout << "Vector integers contains: ";
21     std::copy( integers.begin(), integers.end(), output );
22
23     cout << "\nFirst element of integers: " << integers.front()
24        << "\nLast element of integers: " << integers.back();
25
26     integers[ 0 ] = 7; // set first element to 7
27     integers.at( 2 ) = 10; // set element at position 2 to 10
28
29     // insert 22 as 2nd element
30     integers.insert( integers.begin() + 1, 22 );
31
32     cout << "\n\nContents of vector integers after changes: ";
33     std::copy( integers.begin(), integers.end(), output );
34
35     // access out-of-range element
36     try
37     {
38        integers.at( 100 ) = 777;
39     } // end try
40     catch ( std::out_of_range &outOfRange ) // out_of_range exception
41     {
42        cout << "\n\nException: " << outOfRange.what();
43     } // end catch
44
45     // erase first element
46     integers.erase( integers.begin() );
47     cout << "\n\nVector integers after erasing first element: ";
48     std::copy( integers.begin(), integers.end(), output );
```

Fig. 23.15 | vector-class template element-manipulation functions. (Part 1 of 2.)

```
49
50      // erase remaining elements
51      integers.erase( integers.begin(), integers.end() );
52      cout << "\nAfter erasing all elements, vector integers "
53         << ( integers.empty() ? "is" : "is not" ) << " empty";
54
55      // insert elements from array
56      integers.insert( integers.begin(), array, array + SIZE );
57      cout << "\n\nContents of vector integers before clear: ";
58      std::copy( integers.begin(), integers.end(), output );
59
60      // empty integers; clear calls erase to empty a collection
61      integers.clear();
62      cout << "\nAfter clear, vector integers "
63         << ( integers.empty() ? "is" : "is not" ) << " empty" << endl;
64      return 0;
65   } // end main
```

```
Vector integers contains: 1 2 3 4 5 6
First element of integers: 1
Last element of integers: 6

Contents of vector integers after changes: 7 22 2 10 4 5 6

Exception: invalid vector<T> subscript

Vector integers after erasing first element: 22 2 10 4 5 6
After erasing all elements, vector integers is empty

Contents of vector integers before clear: 1 2 3 4 5 6
After clear, vector integers is empty
```

Fig. 23.15 | vector-class template element-manipulation functions. (Part 2 of 2.)

Line 18 defines an ostream_iterator called output that can be used to output integers separated by single spaces via cout. An ostream_iterator< int > is a type-safe output mechanism that outputs only values of type int or a compatible type. The first argument to the constructor specifies the output stream, and the second argument is a string specifying the separator for the values output—in this case, the string contains a space character. We use the ostream_iterator (defined in header <iterator>) to output the contents of the vector in this example.

Line 21 uses algorithm *copy* from the Standard Library to output the entire contents of vector integers to the standard output. Algorithm copy copies each element in the container starting with the location specified by the iterator in its first argument and continuing up to—but not including—the location specified by the iterator in its second argument. The first and second arguments must satisfy input iterator requirements—they must be iterators through which values can be read from a container. Also, applying ++ to the first iterator must eventually cause it to reach the second iterator argument in the container. The elements are copied to the location specified by the output iterator (i.e., an iterator through which a value can be stored or output) specified as the last argument. In this case, the output iterator is an ostream_iterator (output) that is attached to cout, so the elements are copied to the standard output. To use the algorithms of the Standard Library, you must include the header file *<algorithm>*.

Lines 23–24 use functions front and back (available for all sequence containers) to determine the vector's first and last elements, respectively. Notice the difference between functions front and begin. Function front returns a reference to the first element in the vector, while function begin returns a random-access iterator pointing to the first element in the vector. Also notice the difference between functions back and end. Function back returns a reference to the last element in the vector, while function end returns a random-access iterator pointing to the end of the vector (the location after the last element).

Common Programming Error 23.3

The vector must not be empty; otherwise, results of the front and back functions are undefined.

Lines 26–27 illustrate two ways to subscript through a vector (which also can be used with the deque containers). Line 26 uses the subscript operator that is overloaded to return either a reference to the value at the specified location or a constant reference to that value, depending on whether the container is constant. Function at (line 27) performs the same operation, but with bounds checking. Function at first checks the value supplied as an argument and determines whether it is in the bounds of the vector. If not, function at throws an out_of_bounds exception defined in header <stdexcept> (as demonstrated in lines 36–43). Figure 23.16 shows some of the STL exception types. (The Standard Library exception types are discussed in Chapter 16.)

Line 30 uses one of the three overloaded *insert* functions provided by each sequence container. Line 30 inserts the value 22 before the element at the location specified by the iterator in the first argument. In this example, the iterator is pointing to the second element of the vector, so 22 is inserted as the second element and the original second element becomes the third element of the vector. Other versions of insert allow inserting multiple copies of the same value starting at a particular position in the container, or inserting a range of values from another container (or array) starting at a particular position in the original container.

Lines 46 and 51 use the two *erase* functions that are available in all first-class containers. Line 46 indicates that the element at the location specified by the iterator argument should be removed from the container (in this example, the element at the beginning of the vector). Line 51 specifies that all elements in the range starting with the location of the first argument up to—but not including—the location of the second argument should be erased from the container. In this example, all the elements are erased from the vector. Line 53 uses function *empty* (available for all containers and adapters) to confirm that the vector is empty.

Common Programming Error 23.4

Erasing an element that contains a pointer to a dynamically allocated object does not delete that object; this can lead to a memory leak.

Line 56 demonstrates the version of function insert that uses the second and third arguments to specify the starting location and ending location in a sequence of values (possibly from another container; in this case, from array of integers array) that should be inserted into the vector. Remember that the ending location specifies the position in the

STL exception types	Description
out_of_range	Indicates when subscript is out of range—e.g., when an invalid subscript is specified to vector member function at.
invalid_argument	Indicates an invalid argument was passed to a function.
length_error	Indicates an attempt to create too long a container, string, etc.
bad_alloc	Indicates that an attempt to allocate memory with new (or with an allocator) failed because not enough memory was available.

Fig. 23.16 | Some STL exception types.

sequence after the last element to be inserted; copying is performed up to—but not including—this location.

Finally, line 61 uses function *clear* (found in all first-class containers) to empty the vector. This function calls the version of erase used in line 51 to empty the vector.

[*Note:* Other functions that are common to all containers and common to all sequence containers have not yet been covered. We'll cover most of these in the next few sections. We'll also cover many functions that are specific to each container.]

23.2.2 list Sequence Container

The list sequence container provides an efficient implementation for insertion and deletion operations at any location in the container. If most of the insertions and deletions occur at the ends of the container, the deque data structure (Section 23.2.3) provides a more efficient implementation. Class template list is implemented as a doubly linked list—every node in the list contains a pointer to the previous node in the list and to the next node in the list. This enables class template list to support bidirectional iterators that allow the container to be traversed both forward and backward. Any algorithm that requires input, output, forward or bidirectional iterators can operate on a list. Many list member functions manipulate the elements of the container as an ordered set of elements.

In addition to the member functions of all STL containers in Fig. 23.2 and the common member functions of all sequence containers discussed in Section 23.2, class template list provides nine other member functions—splice, push_front, pop_front, remove, remove_if, unique, merge, reverse and sort. Several of these member functions are list-optimized implementations of STL algorithms presented in Section 23.5. Figure 23.17 demonstrates several features of class list. Remember that many of the functions presented in Figs. 23.14–23.15 can be used with class list. Header file *<list>* must be included to use class list.

```
1   // Fig. 23.17: ListTest.cpp
2   // Standard library list class template test program.
3   #include <iostream>
4   using std::cout;
5   using std::endl;
```

Fig. 23.17 | Standard Library list class template. (Part 1 of 4.)

```
6
7   #include <list> // list class-template definition
8   #include <algorithm> // copy algorithm
9   #include <iterator> // ostream_iterator
10
11  // prototype for function template printList
12  template < typename T > void printList( const std::list< T > &listRef );
13
14  int main()
15  {
16     const int SIZE = 4;
17     int array[ SIZE ] = { 2, 6, 4, 8 };
18     std::list< int > values; // create list of ints
19     std::list< int > otherValues; // create list of ints
20
21     // insert items in values
22     values.push_front( 1 );
23     values.push_front( 2 );
24     values.push_back( 4 );
25     values.push_back( 3 );
26
27     cout << "values contains: ";
28     printList( values );
29
30     values.sort(); // sort values
31     cout << "\nvalues after sorting contains: ";
32     printList( values );
33
34     // insert elements of array into otherValues
35     otherValues.insert( otherValues.begin(), array, array + SIZE );
36     cout << "\nAfter insert, otherValues contains: ";
37     printList( otherValues );
38
39     // remove otherValues elements and insert at end of values
40     values.splice( values.end(), otherValues );
41     cout << "\nAfter splice, values contains: ";
42     printList( values );
43
44     values.sort(); // sort values
45     cout << "\nAfter sort, values contains: ";
46     printList( values );
47
48     // insert elements of array into otherValues
49     otherValues.insert( otherValues.begin(), array, array + SIZE );
50     otherValues.sort();
51     cout << "\nAfter insert and sort, otherValues contains: ";
52     printList( otherValues );
53
54     // remove otherValues elements and insert into values in sorted order
55     values.merge( otherValues );
56     cout << "\nAfter merge:\n   values contains: ";
57     printList( values );
```

Fig. 23.17 | Standard Library `list` class template. (Part 2 of 4.)

```
58        cout << "\n   otherValues contains: ";
59        printList( otherValues );
60
61        values.pop_front(); // remove element from front
62        values.pop_back(); // remove element from back
63        cout << "\nAfter pop_front and pop_back:\n   values contains: "
64        printList( values );
65
66        values.unique(); // remove duplicate elements
67        cout << "\nAfter unique, values contains: ";
68        printList( values );
69
70        // swap elements of values and otherValues
71        values.swap( otherValues );
72        cout << "\nAfter swap:\n   values contains: ";
73        printList( values );
74        cout << "\n   otherValues contains: ";
75        printList( otherValues );
76
77        // replace contents of values with elements of otherValues
78        values.assign( otherValues.begin(), otherValues.end() );
79        cout << "\nAfter assign, values contains: ";
80        printList( values );
81
82        // remove otherValues elements and insert into values in sorted order
83        values.merge( otherValues );
84        cout << "\nAfter merge, values contains: ";
85        printList( values );
86
87        values.remove( 4 ); // remove all 4s
88        cout << "\nAfter remove( 4 ), values contains: ";
89        printList( values );
90        cout << endl;
91        return 0;
92    } // end main
93
94    // printList function template definition; uses
95    // ostream_iterator and copy algorithm to output list elements
96    template < typename T > void printList( const std::list< T > &listRef )
97    {
98        if ( listRef.empty() ) // list is empty
99            cout << "List is empty";
100       else
101       {
102           std::ostream_iterator< T > output( cout, " " );
103           std::copy( listRef.begin(), listRef.end(), output );
104       } // end else
105   } // end function printList
```

```
values contains: 2 1 4 3
values after sorting contains: 1 2 3 4
After insert, otherValues contains: 2 6 4 8
```

Fig. 23.17 | Standard Library list class template. (Part 3 of 4.)

```
After splice, values contains: 1 2 3 4 2 6 4 8
After sort, values contains: 1 2 2 3 4 4 6 8
After insert and sort, otherValues contains: 2 4 6 8
After merge:
   values contains: 1 2 2 2 3 4 4 4 6 6 8 8
   otherValues contains: List is empty
After pop_front and pop_back:
   values contains: 2 2 2 3 4 4 4 6 6 8
After unique, values contains: 2 3 4 6 8
After swap:
   values contains: List is empty
   otherValues contains: 2 3 4 6 8
After assign, values contains: 2 3 4 6 8
After merge, values contains: 2 2 3 3 4 4 6 6 8 8
After remove( 4 ), values contains: 2 2 3 3 6 6 8 8
```

Fig. 23.17 | Standard Library `list` class template. (Part 4 of 4.)

Lines 18–19 instantiate two `list` objects capable of storing integers. Lines 22–23 use function ***push_front*** to insert integers at the beginning of `values`. Function push_front is specific to classes `list` and `deque` (not to `vector`). Lines 24–25 use function push_back to insert integers at the end of `values`. Remember that function push_back is common to all sequence containers.

Line 30 uses `list` member function ***sort*** to arrange the elements in the `list` in ascending order. [*Note:* This is different from the sort in the STL algorithms.] A second version of function sort allows you to supply a binary predicate function that takes two arguments (values in the list), performs a comparison and returns a `bool` value indicating the result. This function determines the order in which the elements of the `list` are sorted. This version could be particularly useful for a `list` that stores pointers rather than values. [*Note:* We demonstrate a unary predicate function in Fig. 23.28. A unary predicate function takes a single argument, performs a comparison using that argument and returns a `bool` value indicating the result.]

Line 40 uses `list` function ***splice*** to remove the elements in otherValues and insert them into `values` before the iterator position specified as the first argument. There are two other versions of this function. Function splice with three arguments allows one element to be removed from the container specified as the second argument from the location specified by the iterator in the third argument. Function splice with four arguments uses the last two arguments to specify a range of locations that should be removed from the container in the second argument and placed at the location specified in the first argument.

After inserting more elements in otherValues and sorting both `values` and other-Values, line 55 uses `list` member function ***merge*** to remove all elements of otherValues and insert them in sorted order into `values`. Both `lists` must be sorted in the same order before this operation is performed. A second version of merge enables you to supply a predicate function that takes two arguments (values in the list) and returns a `bool` value. The predicate function specifies the sorting order used by merge.

Line 61 uses `list` function ***pop_front*** to remove the first element in the `list`. Line 62 uses function ***pop_back*** (available for all sequence containers) to remove the last element in the `list`.

Line 66 uses `list` function ***unique*** to remove duplicate elements in the `list`. The `list` should be in sorted order (so that all duplicates are side by side) before this operation is performed, to guarantee that all duplicates are eliminated. A second version of `unique` enables you to supply a predicate function that takes two arguments (values in the list) and returns a `bool` value specifying whether two elements are equal.

Line 71 uses function ***swap*** (available to all containers) to exchange the contents of `values` with the contents of `otherValues`.

Line 78 uses `list` function ***assign*** to replace the contents of `values` with the contents of `otherValues` in the range specified by the two iterator arguments. A second version of `assign` replaces the original contents with copies of the value specified in the second argument. The first argument of the function specifies the number of copies. Line 87 uses `list` function ***remove*** to delete all copies of the value 4 from the `list`.

23.2.3 deque Sequence Container

Class `deque` provides many of the benefits of a `vector` and a `list` in one container. The term deque is short for "double-ended queue." Class `deque` is implemented to provide efficient indexed access (using subscripting) for reading and modifying its elements, much like a `vector`. Class `deque` is also implemented for efficient insertion and deletion operations at its front and back, much like a `list` (although a `list` is also capable of efficient insertions and deletions in the middle of the `list`). Class `deque` provides support for random-access iterators, so deques can be used with all STL algorithms. One of the most common uses of a deque is to maintain a first-in, first-out queue of elements. In fact, a `deque` is the default underlying implementation for the `queue` adaptor (Section 23.4.2).

Additional storage for a `deque` can be allocated at either end of the `deque` in blocks of memory that are typically maintained as an array of pointers to those blocks.[2] Due to the noncontiguous memory layout of a deque, a deque iterator must be more intelligent than the pointers that are used to iterate through `vectors` or pointer-based arrays.

Performance Tip 23.13

In general, `deque` has higher overhead than `vector`.

Performance Tip 23.14

Insertions and deletions in the middle of a `deque` are optimized to minimize the number of elements copied, so it is more efficient than a `vector` but less efficient than a `list` for this kind of modification.

Class `deque` provides the same basic operations as class `vector`, but adds member functions ***push_front*** and ***pop_front*** to allow insertion and deletion at the beginning of the deque, respectively.

Figure 23.18 demonstrates features of class `deque`. Remember that many of the functions presented in Fig. 23.14, Fig. 23.15 and Fig. 23.17 also can be used with class `deque`. Header file ***<deque>*** must be included to use class deque.

---

2. This is an implementation-specific detail, not a requirement of the C++ standard.

```cpp
 1    // Fig. 23.18: DequeTest.cpp
 2    // Standard Library class deque test program.
 3    #include <iostream>
 4    using std::cout;
 5    using std::endl;
 6
 7    #include <deque> // deque class-template definition
 8    #include <algorithm> // copy algorithm
 9    #include <iterator> // ostream_iterator
10
11    int main()
12    {
13       std::deque< double > values; // create deque of doubles
14       std::ostream_iterator< double > output( cout, " " );
15
16       // insert elements in values
17       values.push_front( 2.2 );
18       values.push_front( 3.5 );
19       values.push_back( 1.1 );
20
21       cout << "values contains: ";
22
23       // use subscript operator to obtain elements of values
24       for ( unsigned int i = 0; i < values.size(); i++ )
25          cout << values[ i ] << ' ';
26
27       values.pop_front(); // remove first element
28       cout << "\nAfter pop_front, values contains: ";
29       std::copy( values.begin(), values.end(), output );
30
31       // use subscript operator to modify element at location 1
32       values[ 1 ] = 5.4;
33       cout << "\nAfter values[ 1 ] = 5.4, values contains: ";
34       std::copy( values.begin(), values.end(), output );
35       cout << endl;
36       return 0;
37    } // end main
```

```
values contains: 3.5 2.2 1.1
After pop_front, values contains: 2.2 1.1
After values[ 1 ] = 5.4, values contains: 2.2 5.4
```

Fig. 23.18 | Standard Library deque class template.

Line 13 instantiates a deque that can store double values. Lines 17–19 use functions push_front and push_back to insert elements at the beginning and end of the deque. Remember that push_back is available for all sequence containers, but push_front is available only for class list and class deque.

The for statement in lines 24–25 uses the subscript operator to retrieve the value in each element of the deque for output. Note that the condition uses function size to ensure that we do not attempt to access an element outside the bounds of the deque.

Line 27 uses function `pop_front` to demonstrate removing the first element of the deque. Remember that `pop_front` is available only for class `list` and class `deque` (not for class `vector`).

Line 32 uses the subscript operator to create an *lvalue*. This enables values to be assigned directly to any element of the deque.

23.3 Associative Containers

The STL's associative containers provide direct access to store and retrieve elements via *keys* (often called *search keys*). The four associative containers are `multiset`, `set`, `multimap` and `map`. Each associative container maintains its keys in sorted order. Iterating through an associative container traverses it in the sort order for that container. Classes *multiset* and *set* provide operations for manipulating sets of values where the values are the keys—there is not a separate value associated with each key. The primary difference between a `multiset` and a `set` is that a `multiset` allows duplicate keys and a `set` does not. Classes *multimap* and *map* provide operations for manipulating values associated with keys (these values are sometimes referred to as *mapped values*). The primary difference between a `multimap` and a `map` is that a `multimap` allows duplicate keys with associated values to be stored and a `map` allows only unique keys with associated values. In addition to the common member functions of all containers presented in Fig. 23.2, all associative containers also support several other member functions, including `find`, `lower_bound`, `upper_bound` and `count`. Examples of each of the associative containers and the common associative-container member functions are presented in the next several subsections.

23.3.1 `multiset` Associative Container

The `multiset` associative container provides fast storage and retrieval of keys and allows duplicate keys. The ordering of the elements is determined by a *comparator function object*. For example, in an integer `multiset`, elements can be sorted in ascending order by ordering the keys with *comparator function object `less< int >`*. We discuss function objects in detail in Section 23.7. The data type of the keys in all associative containers must support comparison properly based on the comparator function object specified—keys sorted with `less< T >` must support comparison with `operator<`. If the keys used in the associative containers are of user-defined data types, those types must supply the appropriate comparison operators. A `multiset` supports bidirectional iterators (but not random-access iterators).

Figure 23.19 demonstrates the `multiset` associative container for a `multiset` of integers sorted in ascending order. Header file `<set>` must be included to use class `multiset`. Containers `multiset` and `set` provide the same basic functionality.

```
1   // Fig. 23.19: MultisetTest.cpp
2   // Testing Standard Library class multiset
3   #include <iostream>
4   using std::cout;
5   using std::endl;
6
```

Fig. 23.19 | Standard Library `multiset` class template. (Part 1 of 3.)

```
7   #include <set> // multiset class-template definition
8
9   // define short name for multiset type used in this program
10  typedef std::multiset< int, std::less< int > > Ims;
11
12  #include <algorithm> // copy algorithm
13  #include <iterator> // ostream_iterator
14
15  int main()
16  {
17     const int SIZE = 10;
18     int a[ SIZE ] = { 7, 22, 9, 1, 18, 30, 100, 22, 85, 13 };
19     Ims intMultiset; // Ims is typedef for "integer multiset"
20     std::ostream_iterator< int > output( cout, " " );
21
22     cout << "There are currently " << intMultiset.count( 15 )
23        << " values of 15 in the multiset\n";
24
25     intMultiset.insert( 15 ); // insert 15 in intMultiset
26     intMultiset.insert( 15 ); // insert 15 in intMultiset
27     cout << "After inserts, there are " << intMultiset.count( 15 )
28        << " values of 15 in the multiset\n\n";
29
30     // iterator that cannot be used to change element values
31     Ims::const_iterator result;
32
33     // find 15 in intMultiset; find returns iterator
34     result = intMultiset.find( 15 );
35
36     if ( result != intMultiset.end() ) // if iterator not at end
37        cout << "Found value 15\n"; // found search value 15
38
39     // find 20 in intMultiset; find returns iterator
40     result = intMultiset.find( 20 );
41
42     if ( result == intMultiset.end() ) // will be true hence
43        cout << "Did not find value 20\n"; // did not find 20
44
45     // insert elements of array a into intMultiset
46     intMultiset.insert( a, a + SIZE );
47     cout << "\nAfter insert, intMultiset contains:\n";
48     std::copy( intMultiset.begin(), intMultiset.end(), output );
49
50     // determine lower and upper bound of 22 in intMultiset
51     cout << "\n\nLower bound of 22: "
52        << *( intMultiset.lower_bound( 22 ) );
53     cout << "\nUpper bound of 22: " << *( intMultiset.upper_bound( 22 ) );
54
55     // p represents pair of const_iterators
56     std::pair< Ims::const_iterator, Ims::const_iterator > p;
57
58     // use equal_range to determine lower and upper bound
59     // of 22 in intMultiset
```

Fig. 23.19 | Standard Library `multiset` class template. (Part 2 of 3.)

```
60        p = intMultiset.equal_range( 22 );
61
62        cout << "\n\nequal_range of 22:" << "\n    Lower bound: "
63           << *( p.first ) << "\n    Upper bound: " << *( p.second );
64        cout << endl;
65        return 0;
66    } // end main
```

```
There are currently 0 values of 15 in the multiset
After inserts, there are 2 values of 15 in the multiset

Found value 15
Did not find value 20

After insert, intMultiset contains:
1 7 9 13 15 15 18 22 22 30 85 100

Lower bound of 22: 22
Upper bound of 22: 30

equal_range of 22:
   Lower bound: 22
   Upper bound: 30
```

Fig. 23.19 | Standard Library multiset class template. (Part 3 of 3.)

Line 10 uses a typedef to create a new type name (alias) for a multiset of integers ordered in ascending order, using the function object less< int >. Ascending order is the default for a multiset, so std::less< int > can be omitted in line 10. This new type (Ims) is then used to instantiate an integer multiset object, intMultiset (line 19).

 Good Programming Practice 23.1

Use typedefs to make code with long type names (such as multisets) easier to read.

The output statement in line 22 uses function **count** (available to all associative containers) to count the number of occurrences of the value 15 currently in the multiset.

Lines 25–26 use one of the three versions of function insert to add the value 15 to the multiset twice. A second version of insert takes an iterator and a value as arguments and begins the search for the insertion point from the iterator position specified. A third version of insert takes two iterators as arguments that specify a range of values to add to the multiset from another container.

Line 34 uses function **find** (available to all associative containers) to locate the value 15 in the multiset. Function find returns an iterator or a const_iterator pointing to the earliest location at which the value is found. If the value is not found, find returns an iterator or a const_iterator equal to the value returned by a call to end. Line 42 demonstrates this case.

Line 46 uses function **insert** to insert the elements of array a into the multiset. In line 48, the copy algorithm copies the elements of the multiset to the standard output. Note that the elements are displayed in ascending order.

Lines 52 and 53 use functions *lower_bound* and *upper_bound* (available in all associative containers) to locate the earliest occurrence of the value 22 in the multiset and the element *after* the last occurrence of the value 22 in the multiset. Both functions return iterators or const_iterators pointing to the appropriate location or the iterator returned by end if the value is not in the multiset.

Line 56 instantiates an instance of class pair called p. Objects of class pair are used to associate pairs of values. In this example, the contents of a pair are two const_iterators for our integer-based multiset. The purpose of p is to store the return value of multiset function *equal_range* that returns a pair containing the results of both a lower_bound and an upper_bound operation. Type pair contains two public data members called *first* and *second*.

Line 60 uses function equal_range to determine the lower_bound and upper_bound of 22 in the multiset. Line 63 uses p.first and p.second, respectively, to access the lower_bound and upper_bound. We dereferenced the iterators to output the values at the locations returned from equal_range.

23.3.2 set Associative Container

The set associative container is used for fast storage and retrieval of unique keys. The implementation of a set is identical to that of a multiset, except that a set must have unique keys. Therefore, if an attempt is made to insert a duplicate key into a set, the duplicate is ignored; because this is the intended mathematical behavior of a set, we do not identify it as a common programming error. A set supports bidirectional iterators (but not random-access iterators). Figure 23.20 demonstrates a set of doubles. Header file <set> must be included to use class set.

```
1   // Fig. 23.20: SetTest.cpp
2   // Standard Library class set test program.
3   #include <iostream>
4   using std::cout;
5   using std::endl;
6
7   #include <set>
8
9   // define short name for set type used in this program
10  typedef std::set< double, std::less< double > > DoubleSet;
11
12  #include <algorithm>
13  #include <iterator> // ostream_iterator
14
15  int main()
16  {
17     const int SIZE = 5;
18     double a[ SIZE ] = { 2.1, 4.2, 9.5, 2.1, 3.7 };
19     DoubleSet doubleSet( a, a + SIZE );
20     std::ostream_iterator< double > output( cout, " " );
21
```

Fig. 23.20 | Standard Library set class template. (Part 1 of 2.)

```
22        cout << "doubleSet contains: ";
23        std::copy( doubleSet.begin(), doubleSet.end(), output );
24
25        // p represents pair containing const_iterator and bool
26        std::pair< DoubleSet::const_iterator, bool > p;
27
28        // insert 13.8 in doubleSet; insert returns pair in which
29        // p.first represents location of 13.8 in doubleSet and
30        // p.second represents whether 13.8 was inserted
31        p = doubleSet.insert( 13.8 ); // value not in set
32        cout << "\n\n" << *( p.first )
33           << ( p.second ? " was" : " was not" ) << " inserted";
34        cout << "\ndoubleSet contains: ";
35        std::copy( doubleSet.begin(), doubleSet.end(), output );
36
37        // insert 9.5 in doubleSet
38        p = doubleSet.insert( 9.5 ); // value already in set
39        cout << "\n\n" << *( p.first )
40           << ( p.second ? " was" : " was not" ) << " inserted";
41        cout << "\ndoubleSet contains: ";
42        std::copy( doubleSet.begin(), doubleSet.end(), output );
43        cout << endl;
44        return 0;
45  } // end main
```

```
doubleSet contains: 2.1 3.7 4.2 9.5

13.8 was inserted
doubleSet contains: 2.1 3.7 4.2 9.5 13.8

9.5 was not inserted
doubleSet contains: 2.1 3.7 4.2 9.5 13.8
```

Fig. 23.20 | Standard Library set class template. (Part 2 of 2.)

Line 10 uses typedef to create a new type name (DoubleSet) for a set of double values ordered in ascending order, using the function object less< double >.

Line 19 uses the new type DoubleSet to instantiate object doubleSet. The constructor call takes the elements in array a between a and a + SIZE (i.e., the entire array) and inserts them into the set. Line 23 uses algorithm copy to output the contents of the set. Notice that the value 2.1—which appeared twice in array a—appears only once in doubleSet. This is because container set does not allow duplicates.

Line 26 defines a pair consisting of a const_iterator for a DoubleSet and a bool value. This object stores the result of a call to set function insert.

Line 31 uses function insert to place the value 13.8 in the set. The returned pair, p, contains an iterator p.first pointing to the value 13.8 in the set and a bool value that is true if the value was inserted and false if the value was not inserted (because it was already in the set). In this case, 13.8 was not in the set, so it was inserted. Line 38 attempts to insert 9.5, which is already in the set. The output of lines 39–40 shows that 9.5 was not inserted.

23.3.3 multimap Associative Container

The multimap associative container is used for fast storage and retrieval of keys and associated values (often called key/value pairs). Many of the functions used with multisets and sets are also used with multimaps and maps. The elements of multimaps and maps are pairs of keys and values instead of individual values. When inserting into a multimap or map, a pair object that contains the key and the value is used. The ordering of the keys is determined by a comparator function object. For example, in a multimap that uses integers as the key type, keys can be sorted in ascending order by ordering them with comparator function object less< int >. Duplicate keys are allowed in a multimap, so multiple values can be associated with a single key. This is often called a one-to-many relationship. For example, in a credit-card transaction-processing system, one credit-card account can have many associated transactions; in a university, one student can take many courses, and one professor can teach many students; in the military, one rank (like "private") has many people. A multimap supports bidirectional iterators, but not random-access iterators. Figure 23.21 demonstrates the multimap associative container. Header file **<map>** must be included to use class multimap.

```cpp
1   // Fig. 23.21: MultimapTest.cpp
2   // Standard Library class multimap test program.
3   #include <iostream>
4   using std::cout;
5   using std::endl;
6
7   #include <map> // map class-template definition
8
9   // define short name for multimap type used in this program
10  typedef std::multimap< int, double, std::less< int > > Mmid;
11
12  int main()
13  {
14     Mmid pairs; // declare the multimap pairs
15
16     cout << "There are currently " << pairs.count( 15 )
17        << " pairs with key 15 in the multimap\n";
18
19     // insert two value_type objects in pairs
20     pairs.insert( Mmid::value_type( 15, 2.7 ) );
21     pairs.insert( Mmid::value_type( 15, 99.3 ) );
22
23     cout << "After inserts, there are " << pairs.count( 15 )
24        << " pairs with key 15\n\n";
25
26     // insert five value_type objects in pairs
27     pairs.insert( Mmid::value_type( 30, 111.11 ) );
28     pairs.insert( Mmid::value_type( 10, 22.22 ) );
29     pairs.insert( Mmid::value_type( 25, 33.333 ) );
30     pairs.insert( Mmid::value_type( 20, 9.345 ) );
31     pairs.insert( Mmid::value_type( 5, 77.54 ) );
32
```

Fig. 23.21 | Standard Library multimap class template. (Part 1 of 2.)

```
33          cout << "Multimap pairs contains:\nKey\tValue\n";
34
35          // use const_iterator to walk through elements of pairs
36          for ( Mmid::const_iterator iter = pairs.begin();
37             iter != pairs.end(); ++iter )
38             cout << iter->first << '\t' << iter->second << '\n';
39
40          cout << endl;
41          return 0;
42       } // end main
```

```
There are currently 0 pairs with key 15 in the multimap
After inserts, there are 2 pairs with key 15

Multimap pairs contains:
Key      Value
5        77.54
10       22.22
15       2.7
15       99.3
20       9.345
25       33.333
30       111.11
```

Fig. 23.21 | Standard Library multimap class template. (Part 2 of 2.)

Performance Tip 23.15

A multimap is implemented to efficiently locate all values paired with a given key.

Line 10 uses typedef to define alias Mmid for a multimap type in which the key type is int, the type of a key's associated value is double and the elements are ordered in ascending order. Line 14 uses the new type to instantiate a multimap called pairs. Line 16 uses function count to determine the number of key/value pairs with a key of 15.

Line 20 uses function insert to add a new key/value pair to the multimap. The expression Mmid::value_type(15, 2.7) creates a pair object in which first is the key (15) of type int and second is the value (2.7) of type double. The type Mmid::value_type is defined as part of the typedef for the multimap. Line 21 inserts another pair object with the key 15 and the value 99.3. Then lines 23–24 output the number of pairs with key 15.

Lines 27–31 insert five additional pairs into the multimap. The for statement in lines 36–38 outputs the contents of the multimap, including both keys and values. Line 38 uses the const_iterator called iter to access the members of the pair in each element of the multimap. Notice in the output that the keys appear in ascending order.

23.3.4 map Associative Container

The map associative container performs fast storage and retrieval of unique keys and associated values. Duplicate keys are not allowed—a single value can be associated with each key. This is called a *one-to-one mapping*. For example, a company that uses unique employee numbers, such as 100, 200 and 300, might have a map that associates employee numbers with their telephone extensions—4321, 4115 and 5217, respectively. With a map you specify the key and get back the associated data quickly. A map is also known as an *associative array*. Providing the key in a map's subscript operator [] locates the value associated with that key in the map. Insertions and deletions can be made anywhere in a map.

Figure 23.22 demonstrates the map associative container and uses the same features as Fig. 23.21 to demonstrate the subscript operator. Header file <map> must be included to use class map. Lines 33–34 use the subscript operator of class map. When the subscript is a key that is already in the map (line 33), the operator returns a reference to the associated value. When the subscript is a key that is not in the map (line 34), the operator inserts the key in the map and returns a reference that can be used to associate a value with that key. Line 33 replaces the value for the key 25 (previously 33.333 as specified in line 21) with a new value, 9999.99. Line 34 inserts a new key/value pair in the map (called *creating an association*).

```
1   // Fig. 23.22: MapTest.cpp
2   // Standard Library class map test program.
3   #include <iostream>
4   using std::cout;
5   using std::endl;
6
7   #include <map> // map class-template definition
8
9   // define short name for map type used in this program
10  typedef std::map< int, double, std::less< int > > Mid;
11
12  int main()
13  {
14     Mid pairs;
15
16     // insert eight value_type objects in pairs
17     pairs.insert( Mid::value_type( 15, 2.7 ) );
18     pairs.insert( Mid::value_type( 30, 111.11 ) );
19     pairs.insert( Mid::value_type( 5, 1010.1 ) );
20     pairs.insert( Mid::value_type( 10, 22.22 ) );
21     pairs.insert( Mid::value_type( 25, 33.333 ) );
22     pairs.insert( Mid::value_type( 5, 77.54 ) ); // dup ignored
23     pairs.insert( Mid::value_type( 20, 9.345 ) );
24     pairs.insert( Mid::value_type( 15, 99.3 ) ); // dup ignored
25
26     cout << "pairs contains:\nKey\tValue\n";
27
28     // use const_iterator to walk through elements of pairs
29     for ( Mid::const_iterator iter = pairs.begin();
30        iter != pairs.end(); ++iter )
31        cout << iter->first << '\t' << iter->second << '\n';
32
33     pairs[ 25 ] = 9999.99; // use subscripting to change value for key 25
34     pairs[ 40 ] = 8765.43; // use subscripting to insert value for key 40
35
36     cout << "\nAfter subscript operations, pairs contains:\nKey\tValue\n";
37
```

Fig. 23.22 | Standard Library map class template. (Part 1 of 2.)

```
38        // use const_iterator to walk through elements of pairs
39        for ( Mid::const_iterator iter2 = pairs.begin();
40           iter2 != pairs.end(); ++iter2 )
41           cout << iter2->first << '\t' << iter2->second << '\n';
42
43        cout << endl;
44        return 0;
45     } // end main
```

```
pairs contains:
Key      Value
5        1010.1
10       22.22
15       2.7
20       9.345
25       33.333
30       111.11

After subscript operations, pairs contains:
Key      Value
5        1010.1
10       22.22
15       2.7
20       9.345
25       9999.99
30       111.11
40       8765.43
```

Fig. 23.22 | Standard Library map class template. (Part 2 of 2.)

23.4 Container Adapters

The STL provides three *container adapters*—stack, queue and priority_queue. Adapters are not first-class containers, because they do not provide the actual data-structure implementation in which elements can be stored and because adapters do not support iterators. The benefit of an adapter class is that you can choose an appropriate underlying data structure. All three adapter classes provide member functions *push* and *pop* that properly insert an element into each adapter data structure and properly remove an element from each adapter data structure. The next several subsections provide examples of the adapter classes.

23.4.1 stack Adapter

Class *stack* enables insertions into and deletions from the underlying data structure at one end (commonly referred to as a last-in, first-out data structure). A stack can be implemented with any of the sequence containers: vector, list and deque. This example creates three integer stacks, using each of the sequence containers of the Standard Library as the underlying data structure to represent the stack. By default, a stack is implemented with a deque. The stack operations are *push* to insert an element at the top of the stack (implemented by calling function push_back of the underlying container), *pop* to remove the top element of the stack (implemented by calling function pop_back of the underlying container), *top* to get a reference to the top element of the stack (implemented by calling function back of the underlying container), **empty** to determine whether the stack is empty (implemented by calling function empty of the underlying container) and **size** to get the number of elements in the stack (implemented by calling function size of the underlying container).

Performance Tip 23.16

Each of the common operations of a stack is implemented as an inline function that calls the appropriate function of the underlying container. This avoids the overhead of a second function call.

Performance Tip 23.17

For the best performance, use class vector as the underlying container for a stack.

Figure 23.23 demonstrates the stack adapter class. Header file **<stack>** must be included to use class stack.

```cpp
1   // Fig. 23.23: StackTest.cpp
2   // Standard Library adapter stack test program.
3   #include <iostream>
4   using std::cout;
5   using std::endl;
6
7   #include <stack> // stack adapter definition
8   #include <vector> // vector class-template definition
9   #include <list> // list class-template definition
10
11  // pushElements function-template prototype
12  template< typename T > void pushElements( T &stackRef );
13
14  // popElements function-template prototype
15  template< typename T > void popElements( T &stackRef );
16
17  int main()
18  {
19     // stack with default underlying deque
20     std::stack< int > intDequeStack;
21
22     // stack with underlying vector
23     std::stack< int, std::vector< int > > intVectorStack;
24
25     // stack with underlying list
26     std::stack< int, std::list< int > > intListStack;
27
28     // push the values 0-9 onto each stack
29     cout << "Pushing onto intDequeStack: ";
30     pushElements( intDequeStack );
31     cout << "\nPushing onto intVectorStack: ";
32     pushElements( intVectorStack );
33     cout << "\nPushing onto intListStack: ";
```

Fig. 23.23 | Standard Library stack adapter class. (Part 1 of 2.)

```
34        pushElements( intListStack );
35        cout << endl << endl;
36
37        // display and remove elements from each stack
38        cout << "Popping from intDequeStack: ";
39        popElements( intDequeStack );
40        cout << "\nPopping from intVectorStack: ";
41        popElements( intVectorStack );
42        cout << "\nPopping from intListStack: ";
43        popElements( intListStack );
44        cout << endl;
45        return 0;
46    } // end main
47
48    // push elements onto stack object to which stackRef refers
49    template< typename T > void pushElements( T &stackRef )
50    {
51        for ( int i = 0; i < 10; i++ )
52        {
53            stackRef.push( i ); // push element onto stack
54            cout << stackRef.top() << ' '; // view (and display) top element
55        } // end for
56    } // end function pushElements
57
58    // pop elements from stack object to which stackRef refers
59    template< typename T > void popElements( T &stackRef )
60    {
61        while ( !stackRef.empty() )
62        {
63            cout << stackRef.top() << ' '; // view (and display) top element
64            stackRef.pop(); // remove top element
65        } // end while
66    } // end function popElements
```

```
Pushing onto intDequeStack: 0 1 2 3 4 5 6 7 8 9
Pushing onto intVectorStack: 0 1 2 3 4 5 6 7 8 9
Pushing onto intListStack: 0 1 2 3 4 5 6 7 8 9

Popping from intDequeStack: 9 8 7 6 5 4 3 2 1 0
Popping from intVectorStack: 9 8 7 6 5 4 3 2 1 0
Popping from intListStack: 9 8 7 6 5 4 3 2 1 0
```

Fig. 23.23 | Standard Library stack adapter class. (Part 2 of 2.)

Lines 20, 23 and 26 instantiate three integer stacks. Line 20 specifies a stack of integers that uses the default deque container as its underlying data structure. Line 23 specifies a stack of integers that uses a vector of integers as its underlying data structure. Line 26 specifies a stack of integers that uses a list of integers as its underlying data structure.

Function pushElements (lines 49–56) pushes the elements onto each stack. Line 53 uses function push (available in each adapter class) to place an integer on top of the stack. Line 54 uses stack function top to retrieve the top element of the stack for output. Function top does not remove the top element.

Function popElements (lines 59–66) pops the elements off each stack. Line 63 uses stack function top to retrieve the top element of the stack for output. Line 64 uses function pop (available in each adapter class) to remove the top element of the stack. Function pop does not return a value.

23.4.2 queue Adapter

Class *queue* enables insertions at the back of the underlying data structure and deletions from the front (commonly referred to as a first-in, first-out data structure). A queue can be implemented with STL data structure list or deque. By default, a queue is implemented with a deque. The common queue operations are *push* to insert an element at the back of the queue (implemented by calling function push_back of the underlying container), *pop* to remove the element at the front of the queue (implemented by calling function pop_front of the underlying container), *front* to get a reference to the first element in the queue (implemented by calling function front of the underlying container), *back* to get a reference to the last element in the queue (implemented by calling function back of the underlying container), *empty* to determine whether the queue is empty (implemented by calling function empty of the underlying container) and *size* to get the number of elements in the queue (implemented by calling function size of the underlying container).

Performance Tip 23.18

Each of the common operations of a queue is implemented as an inline function that calls the appropriate function of the underlying container. This avoids the overhead of a second function call.

Performance Tip 23.19

For the best performance, use class deque *as the underlying container for a queue.*

Figure 23.24 demonstrates the queue adapter class. Header file *<queue>* must be included to use a queue.

```
1   // Fig. 23.24: QueueTest.cpp
2   // Standard Library adapter queue test program.
3   #include <iostream>
4   using std::cout;
5   using std::endl;
6
7   #include <queue> // queue adapter definition
8
9   int main()
10  {
11     std::queue< double > values; // queue with doubles
12
13     // push elements onto queue values
14     values.push( 3.2 );
15     values.push( 9.8 );
16     values.push( 5.4 );
```

Fig. 23.24 | Standard Library queue adapter class templates. (Part 1 of 2.)

```
17
18      cout << "Popping from values: ";
19
20      // pop elements from queue
21      while ( !values.empty() )
22      {
23         cout << values.front() << ' '; // view front element
24         values.pop(); // remove element
25      } // end while
26
27      cout << endl;
28      return 0;
29   } // end main
```

```
Popping from values: 3.2 9.8 5.4
```

Fig. 23.24 | Standard Library **queue** adapter class templates. (Part 2 of 2.)

Line 11 instantiates a queue that stores double values. Lines 14–16 use function push to add elements to the queue. The while statement in lines 21–25 uses function empty (available in all containers) to determine whether the queue is empty (line 21). While there are more elements in the queue, line 23 uses queue function front to read (but not remove) the first element in the queue for output. Line 24 removes the first element in the queue with function pop (available in all adapter classes).

23.4.3 priority_queue Adapter

Class **priority_queue** provides functionality that enables insertions in sorted order into the underlying data structure and deletions from the front of the underlying data structure. A priority_queue can be implemented with STL sequence containers vector or deque. By default, a priority_queue is implemented with a vector as the underlying container. When elements are added to a priority_queue, they are inserted in priority order, such that the highest-priority element (i.e., the largest value) will be the first element removed from the priority_queue. This is usually accomplished via a sorting technique called *heapsort* that always maintains the largest value (i.e., highest-priority element) at the front of the data structure—such a data structure is called a *heap*. The comparison of elements is performed with comparator function object less< T > by default, but you can supply a different comparator.

There are several common priority_queue operations. *push* inserts an element at the appropriate location based on priority order of the priority_queue (implemented by calling function push_back of the underlying container, then reordering the elements using heapsort). *pop* removes the highest-priority element of the priority_queue (implemented by calling function pop_back of the underlying container after removing the top element of the heap). *top* gets a reference to the top element of the priority_queue (implemented by calling function front of the underlying container). *empty* determines whether the priority_queue is empty (implemented by calling function empty of the underlying container). *size* gets the number of elements in the priority_queue (implemented by calling function size of the underlying container).

Performance Tip 23.20

Each of the common operations of a priority_queue *is implemented as an inline function that calls the appropriate function of the underlying container. This avoids the overhead of a second function call.*

Performance Tip 23.21

For the best performance, use class vector *as the underlying container for a* priority_queue.

Figure 23.25 demonstrates the priority_queue adapter class. Header file **<queue>** must be included to use class priority_queue.

Line 11 instantiates a priority_queue that stores double values and uses a vector as the underlying data structure. Lines 14–16 use function push to add elements to the priority_queue. The while statement in lines 21–25 uses function empty (available in all containers) to determine whether the priority_queue is empty (line 21). While there are more elements, line 23 uses priority_queue function top to retrieve the highest-priority element in the priority_queue for output. Line 24 removes the highest-priority element in the priority_queue with function pop (available in all adapter classes).

```cpp
1   // Fig. 23.25: PriorityQueueTest.cpp
2   // Standard Library adapter priority_queue test program.
3   #include <iostream>
4   using std::cout;
5   using std::endl;
6
7   #include <queue> // priority_queue adapter definition
8
9   int main()
10  {
11     std::priority_queue< double > priorities; // create priority_queue
12
13     // push elements onto priorities
14     priorities.push( 3.2 );
15     priorities.push( 9.8 );
16     priorities.push( 5.4 );
17
18     cout << "Popping from priorities: ";
19
20     // pop element from priority_queue
21     while ( !priorities.empty() )
22     {
23        cout << priorities.top() << ' '; // view top element
24        priorities.pop(); // remove top element
25     } // end while
26
27     cout << endl;
28     return 0;
29  } // end main
```

Fig. 23.25 | Standard Library priority_queue adapter class. (Part 1 of 2.)

```
Popping from priorities: 9.8 5.4 3.2
```

Fig. 23.25 | Standard Library `priority_queue` adapter class. (Part 2 of 2.)

23.5 Algorithms

Until the STL, class libraries of containers and algorithms were essentially incompatible among vendors. Early container libraries generally used inheritance and polymorphism, with the associated overhead of `virtual` function calls. Early libraries built the algorithms into the container classes as class behaviors. The STL separates the algorithms from the containers. This makes it much easier to add new algorithms. With the STL, the elements of containers are accessed through iterators. The next several subsections demonstrate many of the STL algorithms.

Performance Tip 23.22

The STL is implemented for efficiency. It avoids the overhead of virtual function calls.

Software Engineering Observation 23.8

STL algorithms do not depend on the implementation details of the containers on which they operate. As long as the container's (or array's) iterators satisfy the requirements of the algorithm, STL algorithms can work on C-style, pointer-based arrays, on STL containers and on user-defined data structures.

Software Engineering Observation 23.9

Algorithms can be added easily to the STL without modifying the container classes.

23.5.1 `fill`, `fill_n`, `generate` and `generate_n`

Figure 23.26 demonstrates algorithms `fill`, `fill_n`, `generate` and `generate_n`. Functions *fill* and *fill_n* set every element in a range of container elements to a specific value. Functions *generate* and *generate_n* use a *generator function* to create values for every element in a range of container elements. The generator function takes no arguments and returns a value that can be placed in an element of the container.

```cpp
 1   // Fig. 23.26: AlgorithmTest.cpp
 2   // Standard Library algorithms fill, fill_n, generate and generate_n.
 3   #include <iostream>
 4   using std::cout;
 5   using std::endl;
 6
 7   #include <algorithm> // algorithm definitions
 8   #include <vector> // vector class-template definition
 9   #include <iterator> // ostream_iterator
10
11   char nextLetter(); // prototype of generator function
```

Fig. 23.26 | Algorithms `fill`, `fill_n`, `generate` and `generate_n`. (Part 1 of 2.)

```
12
13    int main()
14    {
15       std::vector< char > chars( 10 );
16       std::ostream_iterator< char > output( cout, " " );
17       std::fill( chars.begin(), chars.end(), '5' ); // fill chars with 5s
18
19       cout << "Vector chars after filling with 5s:\n";
20       std::copy( chars.begin(), chars.end(), output );
21
22       // fill first five elements of chars with As
23       std::fill_n( chars.begin(), 5, 'A' );
24
25       cout << "\n\nVector chars after filling five elements with As:\n";
26       std::copy( chars.begin(), chars.end(), output );
27
28       // generate values for all elements of chars with nextLetter
29       std::generate( chars.begin(), chars.end(), nextLetter );
30
31       cout << "\n\nVector chars after generating letters A-J:\n";
32       std::copy( chars.begin(), chars.end(), output );
33
34       // generate values for first five elements of chars with nextLetter
35       std::generate_n( chars.begin(), 5, nextLetter );
36
37       cout << "\n\nVector chars after generating K-O for the"
38          << " first five elements:\n";
39       std::copy( chars.begin(), chars.end(), output );
40       cout << endl;
41       return 0;
42    } // end main
43
44    // generator function returns next letter (starts with A)
45    char nextLetter()
46    {
47       static char letter = 'A';
48       return letter++;
49    } // end function nextLetter
```

```
Vector chars after filling with 5s:
5 5 5 5 5 5 5 5 5 5

Vector chars after filling five elements with As:
A A A A A 5 5 5 5 5

Vector chars after generating letters A-J:
A B C D E F G H I J

Vector chars after generating K-O for the first five elements:
K L M N O F G H I J
```

Fig. 23.26 | Algorithms fill, fill_n, generate and generate_n. (Part 2 of 2.)

Line 15 defines a 10-element `vector` that stores `char` values. Line 17 uses function `fill` to place the character `'5'` in every element of `vector chars` from `chars.begin()` up to, but not including, `chars.end()`. Note that the iterators supplied as the first and second argument must be at least forward iterators (i.e., they can be used for both input from a container and output to a container in the forward direction).

Line 23 uses function `fill_n` to place the character `'A'` in the first five elements of `vector chars`. The iterator supplied as the first argument must be at least an output iterator (i.e., it can be used for output to a container in the forward direction). The second argument specifies the number of elements to fill. The third argument specifies the value to place in each element.

Line 29 uses function `generate` to place the result of a call to generator function `nextLetter` in every element of `vector chars` from `chars.begin()` up to, but not including, `chars.end()`. The iterators supplied as the first and second arguments must be at least forward iterators. Function `nextLetter` (lines 45–49) begins with the character `'A'` maintained in a `static` local variable. The statement in line 48 postincrements the value of `letter` and returns the old value of `letter` each time `nextLetter` is called.

Line 35 uses function `generate_n` to place the result of a call to generator function `nextLetter` in five elements of `vector chars`, starting from `chars.begin()`. The iterator supplied as the first argument must be at least an output iterator.

23.5.2 equal, mismatch and lexicographical_compare

Figure 23.27 demonstrates comparing sequences of values for equality using algorithms `equal`, `mismatch` and `lexicographical_compare`.

```
1    // Fig. 23.27: AlgorithmTest2.cpp
2    // Standard Library functions equal, mismatch and lexicographical_compare.
3    #include <iostream>
4    using std::cout;
5    using std::endl;
6
7    #include <algorithm> // algorithm definitions
8    #include <vector> // vector class-template definition
9    #include <iterator> // ostream_iterator
10
11   int main()
12   {
13      const int SIZE = 10;
14      int a1[ SIZE ] = { 1, 2, 3, 4, 5, 6, 7, 8, 9, 10 };
15      int a2[ SIZE ] = { 1, 2, 3, 4, 1000, 6, 7, 8, 9, 10 };
16      std::vector< int > v1( a1, a1 + SIZE ); // copy of a1
17      std::vector< int > v2( a1, a1 + SIZE ); // copy of a1
18      std::vector< int > v3( a2, a2 + SIZE ); // copy of a2
19      std::ostream_iterator< int > output( cout, " " );
20
21      cout << "Vector v1 contains: ";
22      std::copy( v1.begin(), v1.end(), output );
23      cout << "\nVector v2 contains: ";
24      std::copy( v2.begin(), v2.end(), output );
```

Fig. 23.27 | Algorithms `equal`, `mismatch` and `lexicographical_compare`. (Part 1 of 2.)

```
25        cout << "\nVector v3 contains: ";
26        std::copy( v3.begin(), v3.end(), output );
27
28        // compare vectors v1 and v2 for equality
29        bool result = std::equal( v1.begin(), v1.end(), v2.begin() );
30        cout << "\n\nVector v1 " << ( result ? "is" : "is not" )
31           << " equal to vector v2.\n";
32
33        // compare vectors v1 and v3 for equality
34        result = std::equal( v1.begin(), v1.end(), v3.begin() );
35        cout << "Vector v1 " << ( result ? "is" : "is not" )
36           << " equal to vector v3.\n";
37
38        // location represents pair of vector iterators
39        std::pair< std::vector< int >::iterator,
40           std::vector< int >::iterator > location;
41
42        // check for mismatch between v1 and v3
43        location = std::mismatch( v1.begin(), v1.end(), v3.begin() );
44        cout << "\nThere is a mismatch between v1 and v3 at location "
45           << ( location.first - v1.begin() ) << "\nwhere v1 contains "
46           << *location.first << " and v3 contains " << *location.second
47           << "\n\n";
48
49        char c1[ SIZE ] = "HELLO";
50        char c2[ SIZE ] = "BYE BYE";
51
52        // perform lexicographical comparison of c1 and c2
53        result = std::lexicographical_compare( c1, c1 + SIZE, c2, c2 + SIZE );
54        cout << c1 << ( result ? " is less than " :
55           " is greater than or equal to " ) << c2 << endl;
56        return 0;
57     } // end main
```

```
Vector v1 contains: 1 2 3 4 5 6 7 8 9 10
Vector v2 contains: 1 2 3 4 5 6 7 8 9 10
Vector v3 contains: 1 2 3 4 1000 6 7 8 9 10

Vector v1 is equal to vector v2.
Vector v1 is not equal to vector v3.

There is a mismatch between v1 and v3 at location 4
where v1 contains 5 and v3 contains 1000

HELLO is greater than or equal to BYE BYE
```

Fig. 23.27 | Algorithms `equal`, `mismatch` and `lexicographical_compare`. (Part 2 of 2.)

Line 29 uses function *equal* to compare two sequences of values for equality. Each sequence need not necessarily contain the same number of elements—equal returns false if the sequences are not of the same length. The == operator (whether built-in or overloaded) performs the comparison of the elements. In this example, the elements in vector v1 from v1.begin() up to, but not including, v1.end() are compared to the elements in vector v2 starting from v2.begin(). In this example, v1 and v2 are equal. The three iterator arguments must be at least input iterators (i.e., they can be used for input from a sequence in the forward direction). Line 34 uses function equal to compare vectors v1 and v3, which are not equal.

There is another version of function equal that takes a binary predicate function as a fourth parameter. The binary predicate function receives the two elements being compared and returns a bool value indicating whether the elements are equal. This can be useful in sequences that store objects or pointers to values rather than actual values, because you can define one or more comparisons. For example, you can compare Employee objects for age, social security number, or location rather than comparing entire objects. You can compare what pointers refer to rather than comparing the pointer values (i.e., the addresses stored in the pointers).

Lines 39–43 begin by instantiating a pair of iterators called location for a vector of integers. This object stores the result of the call to mismatch (line 43). Function *mismatch* compares two sequences of values and returns a pair of iterators indicating the location in each sequence of the mismatched elements. If all the elements match, the two iterators in the pair are equal to the last iterator for each sequence. The three iterator arguments must be at least input iterators. Line 45 determines the actual location of the mismatch in the vectors with the expression location.first - v1.begin(). The result of this calculation is the number of elements between the iterators (this is analogous to pointer arithmetic, which we studied in Chapter 9). This corresponds to the element number in this example, because the comparison is performed from the beginning of each vector. As with function equal, there is another version of function mismatch that takes a binary predicate function as a fourth parameter.

Line 53 uses function *lexicographical_compare* to compare the contents of two character arrays. This function's four iterator arguments must be at least input iterators. As you know, pointers into arrays are random-access iterators. The first two iterator arguments specify the range of locations in the first sequence. The last two specify the range of locations in the second sequence. While iterating through the sequences, the lexicographical_compare checks if the element in the first sequence is less than the corresponding element in the second sequence. If so, the function returns true. If the element in the first sequence is greater than or equal to the element in the second sequence, the function returns false. This function can be used to arrange sequences lexicographically. Typically, such sequences contain strings.

23.5.3 remove, remove_if, remove_copy and remove_copy_if

Figure 23.28 demonstrates removing values from a sequence with algorithms remove, remove_if, remove_copy and remove_copy_if.

Line 26 uses function *remove* to eliminate all elements with the value 10 in the range from v.begin() up to, but not including, v.end() from v. The first two iterator arguments must be forward iterators so that the algorithm can modify the elements in the sequence. This function does not modify the number of elements in the vector or destroy the eliminated elements, but it does move all elements that are not eliminated toward the beginning of the vector. The function returns an iterator positioned after the last vector element that was not deleted. Elements from the iterator position to the end of the vector have undefined values (in this example, each "undefined" position has value 0).

```
1   // Fig. 23.28: AlgorithmTest3.cpp
2   // Standard Library functions remove, remove_if,
3   // remove_copy and remove_copy_if.
4   #include <iostream>
5   using std::cout;
6   using std::endl;
7
8   #include <algorithm> // algorithm definitions
9   #include <vector> // vector class-template definition
10  #include <iterator> // ostream_iterator
11
12  bool greater9( int ); // prototype
13
14  int main()
15  {
16     const int SIZE = 10;
17     int a[ SIZE ] = { 10, 2, 10, 4, 16, 6, 14, 8, 12, 10 };
18     std::ostream_iterator< int > output( cout, " " );
19     std::vector< int > v( a, a + SIZE ); // copy of a
20     std::vector< int >::iterator newLastElement;
21
22     cout << "Vector v before removing all 10s:\n   ";
23     std::copy( v.begin(), v.end(), output );
24
25     // remove all 10s from v
26     newLastElement = std::remove( v.begin(), v.end(), 10 );
27     cout << "\nVector v after removing all 10s:\n   ";
28     std::copy( v.begin(), newLastElement, output );
29
30     std::vector< int > v2( a, a + SIZE ); // copy of a
31     std::vector< int > c( SIZE, 0 ); // instantiate vector c
32     cout << "\n\nVector v2 before removing all 10s and copying:\n   ";
33     std::copy( v2.begin(), v2.end(), output );
34
35     // copy from v2 to c, removing 10s in the process
36     std::remove_copy( v2.begin(), v2.end(), c.begin(), 10 );
37     cout << "\nVector c after removing all 10s from v2:\n   ";
38     std::copy( c.begin(), c.end(), output );
39
40     std::vector< int > v3( a, a + SIZE ); // copy of a
41     cout << "\n\nVector v3 before removing all elements"
42        << "\ngreater than 9:\n   ";
43     std::copy( v3.begin(), v3.end(), output );
44
45     // remove elements greater than 9 from v3
46     newLastElement = std::remove_if( v3.begin(), v3.end(), greater9 );
47     cout << "\nVector v3 after removing all elements"
48        << "\ngreater than 9:\n   ";
49     std::copy( v3.begin(), newLastElement, output );
50
51     std::vector< int > v4( a, a + SIZE ); // copy of a
52     std::vector< int > c2( SIZE, 0 ); // instantiate vector c2
```

Fig. 23.28 | Algorithms remove, remove_if, remove_copy and remove_copy_if. (Part 1 of 2.)

```
53        cout << "\n\nVector v4 before removing all elements"
54           << "\ngreater than 9 and copying:\n    ";
55        std::copy( v4.begin(), v4.end(), output );
56
57        // copy elements from v4 to c2, removing elements greater
58        // than 9 in the process
59        std::remove_copy_if( v4.begin(), v4.end(), c2.begin(), greater9 );
60        cout << "\nVector c2 after removing all elements"
61           << "\ngreater than 9 from v4:\n    ";
62        std::copy( c2.begin(), c2.end(), output );
63        cout << endl;
64        return 0;
65   } // end main
66
67   // determine whether argument is greater than 9
68   bool greater9( int x )
69   {
70        return x > 9;
71   } // end function greater9
```

```
Vector v before removing all 10s:
   10 2 10 4 16 6 14 8 12 10
Vector v after removing all 10s:
   2 4 16 6 14 8 12

Vector v2 before removing all 10s and copying:
   10 2 10 4 16 6 14 8 12 10
Vector c after removing all 10s from v2:
   2 4 16 6 14 8 12 0 0 0

Vector v3 before removing all elements
greater than 9:
   10 2 10 4 16 6 14 8 12 10
Vector v3 after removing all elements
greater than 9:
   2 4 6 8

Vector v4 before removing all elements
greater than 9 and copying:
   10 2 10 4 16 6 14 8 12 10
Vector c2 after removing all elements
greater than 9 from v4:
   2 4 6 8 0 0 0 0 0 0
```

Fig. 23.28 | Algorithms remove, remove_if, remove_copy and remove_copy_if. (Part 2 of 2.)

Line 36 uses function **remove_copy** to copy all elements that do not have the value 10 in the range from v2.begin() up to, but not including, v2.end() from v2. The elements are placed in c, starting at position c.begin(). The iterators supplied as the first two arguments must be input iterators. The iterator supplied as the third argument must be an output iterator so that the element being copied can be inserted into the copy location. This function returns an iterator positioned after the last element copied into vector c. Note, in line 31, the use of the vector constructor that receives the number of elements in the vector and the initial values of those elements.

Line 46 uses function ***remove_if*** to delete all those elements in the range from v3.begin() up to, but not including, v3.end() from v3 for which our user-defined unary predicate function greater9 returns true. Function greater9 (defined in lines 68–71) returns true if the value passed to it is greater than 9; otherwise, it returns false. The iterators supplied as the first two arguments must be forward iterators so that the algorithm can modify the elements in the sequence. This function does not modify the number of elements in the vector, but it does move to the beginning of the vector all elements that are not eliminated. This function returns an iterator positioned after the last element in the vector that was not deleted. All elements from the iterator position to the end of the vector have undefined values.

Line 59 uses function ***remove_copy_if*** to copy all those elements in the range from v4.begin() up to, but not including, v4.end() from v4 for which the unary predicate function greater9 returns true. The elements are placed in c2, starting at position c2.begin(). The iterators supplied as the first two arguments must be input iterators. The iterator supplied as the third argument must be an output iterator so that the element being copied can be inserted into the copy location. This function returns an iterator positioned after the last element copied into c2.

23.5.4 replace, replace_if, replace_copy and replace_copy_if

Figure 23.29 demonstrates replacing values from a sequence using algorithms replace, replace_if, replace_copy and replace_copy_if.

```
1   // Fig. 23.29: AlgorithmTest4.cpp
2   // Standard Library functions replace, replace_if,
3   // replace_copy and replace_copy_if.
4   #include <iostream>
5   using std::cout;
6   using std::endl;
7
8   #include <algorithm>
9   #include <vector>
10  #include <iterator> // ostream_iterator
11
12  bool greater9( int ); // predicate function prototype
13
14  int main()
15  {
16     const int SIZE = 10;
17     int a[ SIZE ] = { 10, 2, 10, 4, 16, 6, 14, 8, 12, 10 };
18     std::ostream_iterator< int > output( cout, " " );
19
20     std::vector< int > v1( a, a + SIZE ); // copy of a
21     cout << "Vector v1 before replacing all 10s:\n    ";
22     std::copy( v1.begin(), v1.end(), output );
23
24     // replace all 10s in v1 with 100
25     std::replace( v1.begin(), v1.end(), 10, 100 );
```

Fig. 23.29 | Algorithms replace, replace_if, replace_copy and replace_copy_if. (Part 1 of 3.)

```
26        cout << "\nVector v1 after replacing 10s with 100s:\n    ";
27        std::copy( v1.begin(), v1.end(), output );
28
29        std::vector< int > v2( a, a + SIZE ); // copy of a
30        std::vector< int > c1( SIZE ); // instantiate vector c1
31        cout << "\n\nVector v2 before replacing all 10s and copying:\n    ";
32        std::copy( v2.begin(), v2.end(), output );
33
34        // copy from v2 to c1, replacing 10s with 100s
35        std::replace_copy( v2.begin(), v2.end(), c1.begin(), 10, 100 );
36        cout << "\nVector c1 after replacing all 10s in v2:\n    ";
37        std::copy( c1.begin(), c1.end(), output );
38
39        std::vector< int > v3( a, a + SIZE ); // copy of a
40        cout << "\n\nVector v3 before replacing values greater than 9:\n    ";
41        std::copy( v3.begin(), v3.end(), output );
42
43        // replace values greater than 9 in v3 with 100
44        std::replace_if( v3.begin(), v3.end(), greater9, 100 );
45        cout << "\nVector v3 after replacing all values greater"
46           << "\nthan 9 with 100s:\n    ";
47        std::copy( v3.begin(), v3.end(), output );
48
49        std::vector< int > v4( a, a + SIZE ); // copy of a
50        std::vector< int > c2( SIZE ); // instantiate vector c2'
51        cout << "\n\nVector v4 before replacing all values greater "
52           << "than 9 and copying:\n    ";
53        std::copy( v4.begin(), v4.end(), output );
54
55        // copy v4 to c2, replacing elements greater than 9 with 100
56        std::replace_copy_if(
57           v4.begin(), v4.end(), c2.begin(), greater9, 100 );
58        cout << "\nVector c2 after replacing all values greater "
59           << "than 9 in v4:\n    ";
60        std::copy( c2.begin(), c2.end(), output );
61        cout << endl;
62        return 0;
63     } // end main
64
65     // determine whether argument is greater than 9
66     bool greater9( int x )
67     {
68        return x > 9;
69     } // end function greater9
```

```
Vector v1 before replacing all 10s:
   10 2 10 4 16 6 14 8 12 10
Vector v1 after replacing 10s with 100s:
   100 2 100 4 16 6 14 8 12 100
```

Fig. 23.29 | Algorithms replace, replace_if, replace_copy and replace_copy_if. (Part 2 of 3.)

```
Vector v2 before replacing all 10s and copying:
   10 2 10 4 16 6 14 8 12 10
Vector c1 after replacing all 10s in v2:
   100 2 100 4 16 6 14 8 12 100

Vector v3 before replacing values greater than 9:
   10 2 10 4 16 6 14 8 12 10
Vector v3 after replacing all values greater
than 9 with 100s:
   100 2 100 4 100 6 100 8 100 100

Vector v4 before replacing all values greater than 9 and copying:
   10 2 10 4 16 6 14 8 12 10
Vector c2 after replacing all values greater than 9 in v4:
   100 2 100 4 100 6 100 8 100 100
```

Fig. 23.29 | Algorithms `replace`, `replace_if`, `replace_copy` and `replace_copy_if`. (Part 3 of 3.)

Line 25 uses function ***replace*** to replace all elements with the value 10 in the range from `v1.begin()` up to, but not including, `v1.end()` in v1 with the new value 100. The iterators supplied as the first two arguments must be forward iterators so that the algorithm can modify the elements in the sequence.

Line 35 uses function ***replace_copy*** to copy all elements in the range from `v2.begin()` up to, but not including, `v2.end()` from v2, replacing all elements with the value 10 with the new value 100. The elements are copied into c1, starting at position `c1.begin()`. The iterators supplied as the first two arguments must be input iterators. The iterator supplied as the third argument must be an output iterator so that the element being copied can be inserted into the copy location. This function returns an iterator positioned after the last element copied into c1.

Line 44 uses function ***replace_if*** to replace all those elements in the range from `v3.begin()` up to, but not including, `v3.end()` in v3 for which the unary predicate function greater9 returns `true`. Function greater9 (defined in lines 66–69) returns `true` if the value passed to it is greater than 9; otherwise, it returns `false`. The value 100 replaces each value greater than 9. The iterators supplied as the first two arguments must be forward iterators so that the algorithm can modify the elements in the sequence.

Lines 56–57 use function ***replace_copy_if*** to copy all elements in the range from `v4.begin()` up to, but not including, `v4.end()` from v4. Elements for which the unary predicate function greater9 returns `true` are replaced with the value 100. The elements are placed in c2, starting at position `c2.begin()`. The iterators supplied as the first two arguments must be input iterators. The iterator supplied as the third argument must be an output iterator so that the element being copied can be inserted into the copy location. This function returns an iterator positioned after the last element copied into c2.

23.5.5 Mathematical Algorithms

Figure 23.30 demonstrates several common mathematical algorithms from the STL, including `random_shuffle`, `count`, `count_if`, `min_element`, `max_element`, `accumulate`, `for_each` and `transform`.

```cpp
 1   // Fig. 23.30: NumericAlgorithms.cpp
 2   // Mathematical algorithms of the Standard Library.
 3   #include <iostream>
 4   using std::cout;
 5   using std::endl;
 6
 7   #include <algorithm> // algorithm definitions
 8   #include <numeric> // accumulate is defined here
 9   #include <vector>
10   #include <iterator>
11
12   bool greater9( int ); // predicate function prototype
13   void outputSquare( int ); // output square of a value
14   int calculateCube( int ); // calculate cube of a value
15
16   int main()
17   {
18      const int SIZE = 10;
19      int a1[ SIZE ] = { 1, 2, 3, 4, 5, 6, 7, 8, 9, 10 };
20      std::vector< int > v( a1, a1 + SIZE ); // copy of a1
21      std::ostream_iterator< int > output( cout, " " );
22
23      cout << "Vector v before random_shuffle: ";
24      std::copy( v.begin(), v.end(), output );
25
26      std::random_shuffle( v.begin(), v.end() ); // shuffle elements of v
27      cout << "\nVector v after random_shuffle: ";
28      std::copy( v.begin(), v.end(), output );
29
30      int a2[ SIZE ] = { 100, 2, 8, 1, 50, 3, 8, 8, 9, 10 };
31      std::vector< int > v2( a2, a2 + SIZE ); // copy of a2
32      cout << "\n\nVector v2 contains: ";
33      std::copy( v2.begin(), v2.end(), output );
34
35      // count number of elements in v2 with value 8
36      int result = std::count( v2.begin(), v2.end(), 8 );
37      cout << "\nNumber of elements matching 8: " << result;
38
39      // count number of elements in v2 that are greater than 9
40      result = std::count_if( v2.begin(), v2.end(), greater9 );
41      cout << "\nNumber of elements greater than 9: " << result;
42
43      // locate minimum element in v2
44      cout << "\n\nMinimum element in Vector v2 is: "
45         << *( std::min_element( v2.begin(), v2.end() ) );
46
47      // locate maximum element in v2
48      cout << "\nMaximum element in Vector v2 is: "
49         << *( std::max_element( v2.begin(), v2.end() ) );
50
51      // calculate sum of elements in v
52      cout << "\n\nThe total of the elements in Vector v is: "
53         << std::accumulate( v.begin(), v.end(), 0 );
```

Fig. 23.30 | Mathematical algorithms of the Standard Library. (Part 1 of 2.)

```
54
55      // output square of every element in v
56      cout << "\n\nThe square of every integer in Vector v is:\n";
57      std::for_each( v.begin(), v.end(), outputSquare );
58
59      std::vector< int > cubes( SIZE ); // instantiate vector cubes
60
61      // calculate cube of each element in v; place results in cubes
62      std::transform( v.begin(), v.end(), cubes.begin(), calculateCube );
63      cout << "\n\nThe cube of every integer in Vector v is:\n";
64      std::copy( cubes.begin(), cubes.end(), output );
65      cout << endl;
66      return 0;
67   } // end main
68
69   // determine whether argument is greater than 9
70   bool greater9( int value )
71   {
72      return value > 9;
73   } // end function greater9
74
75   // output square of argument
76   void outputSquare( int value )
77   {
78      cout << value * value << ' ';
79   } // end function outputSquare
80
81   // return cube of argument
82   int calculateCube( int value )
83   {
84      return value * value * value;
85   } // end function calculateCube
```

```
Vector v before random_shuffle: 1 2 3 4 5 6 7 8 9 10
Vector v after random_shuffle: 5 4 1 3 7 8 9 10 6 2

Vector v2 contains: 100 2 8 1 50 3 8 8 9 10
Number of elements matching 8: 3
Number of elements greater than 9: 3

Minimum element in Vector v2 is: 1
Maximum element in Vector v2 is: 100

The total of the elements in Vector v is: 55

The square of every integer in Vector v is:
25 16 1 9 49 64 81 100 36 4

The cube of every integer in Vector v is:
125 64 1 27 343 512 729 1000 216 8
```

Fig. 23.30 | Mathematical algorithms of the Standard Library. (Part 2 of 2.)

Line 26 uses function ***random_shuffle*** to reorder randomly the elements in the range from v.begin() up to, but not including, v.end() in v. This function takes two random-access iterator arguments.

Line 36 uses function ***count*** to count the elements with the value 8 in the range from v2.begin() up to, but not including, v2.end() in v2. This function requires its two iterator arguments to be at least input iterators.

Line 40 uses function ***count_if*** to count elements in the range from v2.begin() up to, but not including, v2.end() in v2 for which the predicate function greater9 returns true. Function count_if requires its two iterator arguments to be at least input iterators.

Line 45 uses function ***min_element*** to locate the smallest element in the range from v2.begin() up to, but not including, v2.end(). The function returns a forward iterator located at the smallest element, or v2.end() if the range is empty. The function's two iterator arguments must be at least input iterators. A second version of this function takes as its third argument a binary function that compares two elements in the sequence. This function returns the bool value true if the first argument is less than the second.

Good Programming Practice 23.2

It is a good practice to check that the range specified in a call to min_element is not empty and that the return value is not the "past the end" iterator.

Line 49 uses function ***max_element*** to locate the largest element in the range from v2.begin() up to, but not including, v2.end() in v2. The function returns an input iterator located at the largest element. The function's two iterator arguments must be at least input iterators. A second version of this function takes as its third argument a binary predicate function that compares the elements in the sequence. The binary function takes two arguments and returns the bool value true if the first argument is less than the second.

Line 53 uses function ***accumulate*** (the template of which is in header file <numeric>) to sum the values in the range from v.begin() up to, but not including, v.end() in v. The function's two iterator arguments must be at least input iterators and its third argument represents the initial value of the total. A second version of this function takes as its fourth argument a general function that determines how elements are accumulated. The general function must take two arguments and return a result. The first argument to this function is the current value of the accumulation. The second argument is the value of the current element in the sequence being accumulated.

Line 57 uses function ***for_each*** to apply a general function to every element in the range from v.begin() up to, but not including, v.end(). The general function takes the current element as an argument and may modify that element (if it is received by reference). Function for_each requires its two iterator arguments to be at least input iterators.

Line 62 uses function ***transform*** to apply a general function to every element in the range from v.begin() up to, but not including, v.end() in v. The general function (the fourth argument) should take the current element as an argument, should not modify the element and should return the transformed value. Function transform requires its first two iterator arguments to be at least input iterators and its third argument to be at least an output iterator. The third argument specifies where the transformed values should be placed. Note that the third argument can equal the first. Another version of transform accepts five arguments—the first two arguments are input iterators that specify a range of elements from one source container, the third argument is an input iterator that specifies the first element in another source container, the fourth argument is an output iterator that specifies where the transformed values should be placed and the last argument is a general function that takes two arguments. This version of transform takes one element from each of the two input sources and applies the general function to that pair of elements, then places the transformed value at the location specified by the fourth argument.

23.5.6 Basic Searching and Sorting Algorithms

Figure 23.31 demonstrates some basic searching and sorting capabilities of the Standard Library, including find, find_if, sort and binary_search.

```cpp
1    // Fig. 23.31: SearchSortAlgorithms.cpp
2    // Standard Library search and sort algorithms.
3    #include <iostream>
4    using std::cout;
5    using std::endl;
6
7    #include <algorithm> // algorithm definitions
8    #include <vector> // vector class-template definition
9    #include <iterator>
10
11   bool greater10( int value ); // predicate function prototype
12
13   int main()
14   {
15      const int SIZE = 10;
16      int a[ SIZE ] = { 10, 2, 17, 5, 16, 8, 13, 11, 20, 7 };
17      std::vector< int > v( a, a + SIZE ); // copy of a
18      std::ostream_iterator< int > output( cout, " " );
19
20      cout << "Vector v contains: ";
21      std::copy( v.begin(), v.end(), output ); // display output vector
22
23      // locate first occurrence of 16 in v
24      std::vector< int >::iterator location;
25      location = std::find( v.begin(), v.end(), 16 );
26
27      if ( location != v.end() ) // found 16
28         cout << "\n\nFound 16 at location " << ( location - v.begin() );
29      else // 16 not found
30         cout << "\n\n16 not found";
31
32      // locate first occurrence of 100 in v
33      location = std::find( v.begin(), v.end(), 100 );
34
35      if ( location != v.end() ) // found 100
36         cout << "\nFound 100 at location " << ( location - v.begin() );
37      else // 100 not found
38         cout << "\n100 not found";
39
```

Fig. 23.31 | Basic searching and sorting algorithms of the Standard Library. (Part 1 of 2.)

```
40    // locate first occurrence of value greater than 10 in v
41    location = std::find_if( v.begin(), v.end(), greater10 );
42
43    if ( location != v.end() ) // found value greater than 10
44       cout << "\n\nThe first value greater than 10 is " << *location
45          << "\nfound at location " << ( location - v.begin() );
46    else // value greater than 10 not found
47       cout << "\n\nNo values greater than 10 were found";
48
49    // sort elements of v
50    std::sort( v.begin(), v.end() );
51    cout << "\n\nVector v after sort: ";
52    std::copy( v.begin(), v.end(), output );
53
54    // use binary_search to locate 13 in v
55    if ( std::binary_search( v.begin(), v.end(), 13 ) )
56       cout << "\n\n13 was found in v";
57    else
58       cout << "\n\n13 was not found in v";
59
60    // use binary_search to locate 100 in v
61    if ( std::binary_search( v.begin(), v.end(), 100 ) )
62       cout << "\n100 was found in v";
63    else
64       cout << "\n100 was not found in v";
65
66    cout << endl;
67    return 0;
68 } // end main
69
70 // determine whether argument is greater than 10
71 bool greater10( int value )
72 {
73    return value > 10;
74 } // end function greater10
```

```
Vector v contains: 10 2 17 5 16 8 13 11 20 7

Found 16 at location 4
100 not found

The first value greater than 10 is 17
found at location 2

Vector v after sort: 2 5 7 8 10 11 13 16 17 20

13 was found in v
100 was not found in v
```

Fig. 23.31 | Basic searching and sorting algorithms of the Standard Library. (Part 2 of 2.)

Line 25 uses function *find* to locate the value 16 in the range from v.begin() up to, but not including, v.end() in v. The function requires its two iterator arguments to be at least input iterators and returns an input iterator that either is positioned at the first element containing the value or indicates the end of the sequence (as is the case in line 33).

Line 41 uses function ***find_if*** to locate the first value in the range from v.begin() up to, but not including, v.end() in v for which the unary predicate function greater10 returns true. Function greater10 (defined in lines 71–74) takes an integer and returns a bool value indicating whether the integer argument is greater than 10. Function find_if requires its two iterator arguments to be at least input iterators. The function returns an input iterator that either is positioned at the first element containing a value for which the predicate function returns true or indicates the end of the sequence.

Line 50 uses function ***sort*** to arrange the elements in the range from v.begin() up to, but not including, v.end() in v in ascending order. The function requires its two iterator arguments to be random-access iterators. A second version of this function takes a third argument that is a binary predicate function taking two arguments that are values in the sequence and returning a bool indicating the sorting order—if the return value is true, the two elements being compared are in sorted order.

Common Programming Error 23.5

Attempting to sort a container by using an iterator other than a random-access iterator is a compilation error. Function sort requires a random-access iterator.

Line 55 uses function ***binary_search*** to determine whether the value 13 is in the range from v.begin() up to, but not including, v.end() in v. The sequence of values must be sorted in ascending order first. Function binary_search requires its two iterator arguments to be at least forward iterators. The function returns a bool indicating whether the value was found in the sequence. Line 61 demonstrates a call to function binary_search in which the value is not found. A second version of this function takes a fourth argument that is a binary predicate function taking two arguments that are values in the sequence and returning a bool. The predicate function returns true if the two elements being compared are in sorted order. To obtain the location of the search key in the container, use the lower_bound or find algorithms.

23.5.7 swap, iter_swap and swap_ranges

Figure 23.32 demonstrates algorithms swap, iter_swap and swap_ranges for swapping elements. Line 20 uses function ***swap*** to exchange two values. In this example, the first and second elements of array a are exchanged. The function takes as arguments references to the two values being exchanged.

```
 1   // Fig. 23.32: AlgorithmTest5.cpp
 2   // Standard Library algorithms iter_swap, swap and swap_ranges.
 3   #include <iostream>
 4   using std::cout;
 5   using std::endl;
 6
 7   #include <algorithm> // algorithm definitions
 8   #include <iterator>
 9
10   int main()
11   {
```

Fig. 23.32 | Demonstrating swap, iter_swap and swap_ranges. (Part 1 of 2.)

```
12       const int SIZE = 10;
13       int a[ SIZE ] = { 1, 2, 3, 4, 5, 6, 7, 8, 9, 10 };
14       std::ostream_iterator< int > output( cout, " " );
15
16       cout << "Array a contains:\n   ";
17       std::copy( a, a + SIZE, output ); // display array a
18
19       // swap elements at locations 0 and 1 of array a
20       std::swap( a[ 0 ], a[ 1 ] );
21
22       cout << "\nArray a after swapping a[0] and a[1] using swap:\n   ";
23       std::copy( a, a + SIZE, output ); // display array a
24
25       // use iterators to swap elements at locations 0 and 1 of array a
26       std::iter_swap( &a[ 0 ], &a[ 1 ] ); // swap with iterators
27       cout << "\nArray a after swapping a[0] and a[1] using iter_swap:\n   ";
28       std::copy( a, a + SIZE, output );
29
30       // swap elements in first five elements of array a with
31       // elements in last five elements of array a
32       std::swap_ranges( a, a + 5, a + 5 );
33
34       cout << "\nArray a after swapping the first five elements\n"
35            << "with the last five elements:\n   ";
36       std::copy( a, a + SIZE, output );
37       cout << endl;
38       return 0;
39  } // end main
```

```
Array a contains:
   1 2 3 4 5 6 7 8 9 10
Array a after swapping a[0] and a[1] using swap:
   2 1 3 4 5 6 7 8 9 10
Array a after swapping a[0] and a[1] using iter_swap:
   1 2 3 4 5 6 7 8 9 10
Array a after swapping the first five elements
with the last five elements:
   6 7 8 9 10 1 2 3 4 5
```

Fig. 23.32 | Demonstrating swap, iter_swap and swap_ranges. (Part 2 of 2.)

Line 26 uses function *iter_swap* to exchange the two elements. The function takes two forward iterator arguments (in this case, pointers to elements of an array) and exchanges the values in the elements to which the iterators refer.

Line 32 uses function *swap_ranges* to exchange the elements from a up to, but not including, a + 5 with the elements beginning at position a + 5. The function requires three forward iterator arguments. The first two arguments specify the range of elements in the first sequence that will be exchanged with the elements in the second sequence starting from the iterator in the third argument. In this example, the two sequences of values are in the same array, but the sequences can be from different arrays or containers.

23.5.8 copy_backward, merge, unique and reverse

Figure 23.33 demonstrates STL algorithms copy_backward, merge, unique and reverse. Line 28 uses function **copy_backward** to copy elements in the range from v1.begin() up to, but not including, v1.end(), placing the elements in results by starting from the element before results.end() and working toward the beginning of the vector. The function returns an iterator positioned at the last element copied into the results (i.e., the beginning of results, because of the backward copy). The elements are placed in results in the same order as v1. This function requires three bidirectional iterator arguments (iterators that can be incremented and decremented to iterate forward and backward through a sequence, respectively). One difference between copy_backward and copy is that the iterator returned from copy is positioned *after* the last element copied and the one returned from copy_backward is positioned *at* the last element copied (i.e., the first element in the sequence). Also, copy_backward can manipulate overlapping ranges of elements in a container as long as the first element to copy is not in the destination range of elements.

```cpp
1   // Fig. 23.33: AlgorithmTest6.cpp
2   // Standard Library functions copy_backward, merge, unique and reverse.
3   #include <iostream>
4   using std::cout;
5   using std::endl;
6
7   #include <algorithm> // algorithm definitions
8   #include <vector> // vector class-template definition
9   #include <iterator> // ostream_iterator
10
11  int main()
12  {
13     const int SIZE = 5;
14     int a1[ SIZE ] = { 1, 3, 5, 7, 9 };
15     int a2[ SIZE ] = { 2, 4, 5, 7, 9 };
16     std::vector< int > v1( a1, a1 + SIZE ); // copy of a1
17     std::vector< int > v2( a2, a2 + SIZE ); // copy of a2
18     std::ostream_iterator< int > output( cout, " " );
19
20     cout << "Vector v1 contains: ";
21     std::copy( v1.begin(), v1.end(), output ); // display vector output
22     cout << "\nVector v2 contains: ";
23     std::copy( v2.begin(), v2.end(), output ); // display vector output
24
25     std::vector< int > results( v1.size() );
26
27     // place elements of v1 into results in reverse order
28     std::copy_backward( v1.begin(), v1.end(), results.end() );
29     cout << "\n\nAfter copy_backward, results contains: ";
30     std::copy( results.begin(), results.end(), output );
31
32     std::vector< int > results2( v1.size() + v2.size() );
33
34     // merge elements of v1 and v2 into results2 in sorted order
35     std::merge( v1.begin(), v1.end(), v2.begin(), v2.end(),
```

Fig. 23.33 | Demonstrating copy_backward, merge, unique and reverse. (Part 1 of 2.)

```
36             results2.begin() );
37
38     cout << "\n\nAfter merge of v1 and v2 results2 contains:\n";
39     std::copy( results2.begin(), results2.end(), output );
40
41     // eliminate duplicate values from results2
42     std::vector< int >::iterator endLocation;
43     endLocation = std::unique( results2.begin(), results2.end() );
44
45     cout << "\n\nAfter unique results2 contains:\n";
46     std::copy( results2.begin(), endLocation, output );
47
48     cout << "\n\nVector v1 after reverse: ";
49     std::reverse( v1.begin(), v1.end() ); // reverse elements of v1
50     std::copy( v1.begin(), v1.end(), output );
51     cout << endl;
52     return 0;
53  } // end main
```

```
Vector v1 contains: 1 3 5 7 9
Vector v2 contains: 2 4 5 7 9

After copy_backward, results contains: 1 3 5 7 9

After merge of v1 and v2 results2 contains:
1 2 3 4 5 5 7 7 9 9

After unique results2 contains:
1 2 3 4 5 7 9

Vector v1 after reverse: 9 7 5 3 1
```

Fig. 23.33 | Demonstrating copy_backward, merge, unique and reverse. (Part 2 of 2.)

Lines 35–36 use function **merge** to combine two sorted ascending sequences of values into a third sorted ascending sequence. The function requires five iterator arguments. The first four must be at least input iterators and the last must be at least an output iterator. The first two arguments specify the range of elements in the first sorted sequence (v1), the second two arguments specify the range of elements in the second sorted sequence (v2) and the last argument specifies the starting location in the third sequence (results2) where the elements will be merged. A second version of this function takes as its sixth argument a binary predicate function that specifies the sorting order.

Note that line 32 creates vector results2 with the number of elements v1.size() + v2.size(). Using the merge function as shown here requires that the sequence where the results are stored be at least the size of the two sequences being merged. If you do not want to allocate the number of elements for the resulting sequence before the merge operation, you can use the following statements:

```
std::vector< int > results2;
std::merge ( v1.begin(), v1.end(), v2.begin(), v2.end(),
   std::back_inserter( results2 ) );
```

The argument std::back_inserter(results2) uses function template ***back_inserter*** (header file <iterator>) for the container results2. A back_inserter calls the container's default push_back function to insert an element at the end of the container. More importantly, if an element is inserted into a container that has no more space available, the container grows in size. Thus, the number of elements in the container does not have to be known in advance. There are two other inserters—***front_inserter*** (to insert an element at the beginning of a container specified as its argument) and ***inserter*** (to insert an element before the iterator supplied as its second argument in the container supplied as its first argument).

Line 43 uses function ***unique*** on the sorted sequence of elements in the range from results2.begin() up to, but not including, results2.end() in results2. After this function is applied to a sorted sequence with duplicate values, only a single copy of each value remains in the sequence. The function takes two arguments that must be at least forward iterators. The function returns an iterator positioned after the last element in the sequence of unique values. The values of all elements in the container after the last unique value are undefined. A second version of this function takes as a third argument a binary predicate function specifying how to compare two elements for equality.

Line 49 uses function ***reverse*** to reverse all the elements in the range from v1.begin() up to, but not including, v1.end() in v1. The function takes two arguments that must be at least bidirectional iterators.

23.5.9 inplace_merge, unique_copy and reverse_copy

Figure 23.34 demonstrates STL algorithms inplace_merge, unique_copy and reverse_copy. Line 24 uses function ***inplace_merge*** to merge two sorted sequences of elements in the same container. In this example, the elements from v1.begin() up to, but not including, v1.begin() + 5 are merged with the elements from v1.begin() + 5 up to, but not including, v1.end(). This function requires its three iterator arguments to be at least bidirectional iterators. A second version of this function takes as a fourth argument a binary predicate function for comparing elements in the two sequences.

```
1   // Fig. 23.34: AlgorithmTest7.cpp
2   // Standard Library algorithms inplace_merge,
3   // reverse_copy and unique_copy.
4   #include <iostream>
5   using std::cout;
6   using std::endl;
7
8   #include <algorithm> // algorithm definitions
9   #include <vector> // vector class-template definition
10  #include <iterator> // back_inserter definition
11
12  int main()
13  {
14     const int SIZE = 10;
15     int a1[ SIZE ] = { 1, 3, 5, 7, 9, 1, 3, 5, 7, 9 };
16     std::vector< int > v1( a1, a1 + SIZE ); // copy of a
```

Fig. 23.34 | Demonstrating inplace_merge, unique_copy and reverse_copy. (Part 1 of 2.)

```
17       std::ostream_iterator< int > output( cout, " " );
18
19       cout << "Vector v1 contains: ";
20       std::copy( v1.begin(), v1.end(), output );
21
22       // merge first half of v1 with second half of v1 such that
23       // v1 contains sorted set of elements after merge
24       std::inplace_merge( v1.begin(), v1.begin() + 5, v1.end() );
25
26       cout << "\nAfter inplace_merge, v1 contains: ";
27       std::copy( v1.begin(), v1.end(), output );
28
29       std::vector< int > results1;
30
31       // copy only unique elements of v1 into results1
32       std::unique_copy(
33          v1.begin(), v1.end(), std::back_inserter( results1 ) );
34       cout << "\nAfter unique_copy results1 contains: ";
35       std::copy( results1.begin(), results1.end(), output );
36
37       std::vector< int > results2;
38
39       // copy elements of v1 into results2 in reverse order
40       std::reverse_copy(
41          v1.begin(), v1.end(), std::back_inserter( results2 ) );
42       cout << "\nAfter reverse_copy, results2 contains: ";
43       std::copy( results2.begin(), results2.end(), output );
44       cout << endl;
45       return 0;
46  } // end main
```

```
Vector v1 contains: 1 3 5 7 9 1 3 5 7 9
After inplace_merge, v1 contains: 1 1 3 3 5 5 7 7 9 9
After unique_copy results1 contains: 1 3 5 7 9
After reverse_copy, results2 contains: 9 9 7 7 5 5 3 3 1 1
```

Fig. 23.34 | Demonstrating `inplace_merge`, `unique_copy` and `reverse_copy`. (Part 2 of 2.)

Lines 32–33 use function ***unique_copy*** to make a copy of all the unique elements in the sorted sequence of values from `v1.begin()` up to, but not including, `v1.end()`. The copied elements are placed into `vector` `results1`. The first two arguments must be at least input iterators and the last must be at least an output iterator. In this example, we did not preallocate enough elements in `results1` to store all the elements copied from `v1`. Instead, we use function `back_inserter` (defined in header file `<iterator>`) to add elements to the end of `v1`. The `back_inserter` uses class `vector`'s capability to insert elements at the end of the `vector`. Because the `back_inserter` inserts an element rather than replacing an existing element's value, the `vector` is able to grow to accommodate additional elements. A second version of the `unique_copy` function takes as a fourth argument a binary predicate function for comparing elements for equality.

Lines 40–41 use function ***reverse_copy*** to make a reversed copy of the elements in the range from `v1.begin()` up to, but not including, `v1.end()`. The copied elements are inserted into `results2` using a `back_inserter` object to ensure that the `vector` can grow to accommodate the appropriate number of elements copied. Function `reverse_copy` requires its first two iterator arguments to be at least bidirectional iterators and its third to be at least an output iterator.

23.5.10 Set Operations

Figure 23.35 demonstrates Standard Library functions `includes`, `set_difference`, `set_intersection`, `set_symmetric_difference` and `set_union` for manipulating sets of sorted values. To demonstrate that Standard Library functions can be applied to arrays and containers, this example uses only arrays (remember, a pointer into an array is a random-access iterator).

```cpp
 1  // Fig. 23.35: AlgorithmTest8.cpp
 2  // Standard Library algorithms includes, set_difference,
 3  // set_intersection, set_symmetric_difference and set_union.
 4  #include <iostream>
 5  using std::cout;
 6  using std::endl;
 7
 8  #include <algorithm> // algorithm definitions
 9  #include <iterator> // ostream_iterator
10
11  int main()
12  {
13     const int SIZE1 = 10, SIZE2 = 5, SIZE3 = 20;
14     int a1[ SIZE1 ] = { 1, 2, 3, 4, 5, 6, 7, 8, 9, 10 };
15     int a2[ SIZE2 ] = { 4, 5, 6, 7, 8 };
16     int a3[ SIZE2 ] = { 4, 5, 6, 11, 15 };
17     std::ostream_iterator< int > output( cout, " " );
18
19     cout << "a1 contains: ";
20     std::copy( a1, a1 + SIZE1, output ); // display array a1
21     cout << "\na2 contains: ";
22     std::copy( a2, a2 + SIZE2, output ); // display array a2
23     cout << "\na3 contains: ";
24     std::copy( a3, a3 + SIZE2, output ); // display array a3
25
26     // determine whether set a2 is completely contained in a1
27     if ( std::includes( a1, a1 + SIZE1, a2, a2 + SIZE2 ) )
28        cout << "\n\na1 includes a2";
29     else
30        cout << "\n\na1 does not include a2";
31
32     // determine whether set a3 is completely contained in a1
33     if ( std::includes( a1, a1 + SIZE1, a3, a3 + SIZE2 ) )
34        cout << "\na1 includes a3";
35     else
36        cout << "\na1 does not include a3";
37
```

Fig. 23.35 | set operations of the Standard Library. (Part 1 of 2.)

```
38        int difference[ SIZE1 ];
39
40        // determine elements of a1 not in a2
41        int *ptr = std::set_difference( a1, a1 + SIZE1,
42           a2, a2 + SIZE2, difference );
43        cout << "\n\nset_difference of a1 and a2 is: ";
44        std::copy( difference, ptr, output );
45
46        int intersection[ SIZE1 ];
47
48        // determine elements in both a1 and a2
49        ptr = std::set_intersection( a1, a1 + SIZE1,
50           a2, a2 + SIZE2, intersection );
51        cout << "\n\nset_intersection of a1 and a2 is: ";
52        std::copy( intersection, ptr, output );
53
54        int symmetric_difference[ SIZE1 + SIZE2 ];
55
56        // determine elements of a1 that are not in a2 and
57        // elements of a2 that are not in a1
58        ptr = std::set_symmetric_difference( a1, a1 + SIZE1,
59           a3, a3 + SIZE2, symmetric_difference );
60        cout << "\n\nset_symmetric_difference of a1 and a3 is: ";
61        std::copy( symmetric_difference, ptr, output );
62
63        int unionSet[ SIZE3 ];
64
65        // determine elements that are in either or both sets
66        ptr = std::set_union( a1, a1 + SIZE1, a3, a3 + SIZE2, unionSet );
67        cout << "\n\nset_union of a1 and a3 is: ";
68        std::copy( unionSet, ptr, output );
69        cout << endl;
70        return 0;
71    } // end main
```

```
a1 contains: 1 2 3 4 5 6 7 8 9 10
a2 contains: 4 5 6 7 8
a3 contains: 4 5 6 11 15

a1 includes a2
a1 does not include a3

set_difference of a1 and a2 is: 1 2 3 9 10

set_intersection of a1 and a2 is: 4 5 6 7 8

set_symmetric_difference of a1 and a3 is: 1 2 3 7 8 9 10 11 15

set_union of a1 and a3 is: 1 2 3 4 5 6 7 8 9 10 11 15
```

Fig. 23.35 | set operations of the Standard Library. (Part 2 of 2.)

Lines 27 and 33 call function ***includes*** in the conditions of if statements. Function includes compares two sets of sorted values to determine whether every element of the second set is in the first set. If so, `includes` returns `true`; otherwise, it returns `false`. The first two iterator arguments must be at least input iterators and must describe the first set of values. In line 27, the first set consists of the elements from a1 up to, but not including, a1 + SIZE1. The last two iterator arguments must be at least input iterators and must describe the second set of values. In this example, the second set consists of the elements from a2 up to, but not including, a2 + SIZE2. A second version of function `includes` takes a fifth argument that is a binary predicate function for comparing elements for equality.

Lines 41–42 use function ***set_difference*** to find the elements from the first set of sorted values that are not in the second set of sorted values (both sets of values must be in ascending order). The elements that are different are copied into the fifth argument (in this case, the array `difference`). The first two iterator arguments must be at least input iterators for the first set of values. The next two iterator arguments must be at least input iterators for the second set of values. The fifth argument must be at least an output iterator indicating where to store a copy of the values that are different. The function returns an output iterator positioned immediately after the last value copied into the set to which the fifth argument points. A second version of function `set_difference` takes a sixth argument that is a binary predicate function indicating the order in which the elements were originally sorted. The two sequences must be sorted using the same comparison function.

Lines 49–50 use function ***set_intersection*** to determine the elements from the first set of sorted values that are in the second set of sorted values (both sets of values must be in ascending order). The elements common to both sets are copied into the fifth argument (in this case, array `intersection`). The first two iterator arguments must be at least input iterators for the first set of values. The next two iterator arguments must be at least input iterators for the second set of values. The fifth argument must be at least an output iterator indicating where to store a copy of the values that are the same. The function returns an output iterator positioned immediately after the last value copied into the set to which the fifth argument points. A second version of function `set_intersection` takes a sixth argument that is a binary predicate function indicating the order in which the elements were originally sorted. The two sequences must be sorted using the same comparison function.

Lines 58–59 use function ***set_symmetric_difference*** to determine the elements in the first set that are not in the second set and the elements in the second set that are not in the first set (both sets must be in ascending order). The elements that are different are copied from both sets into the fifth argument (the array `symmetric_difference`). The first two iterator arguments must be at least input iterators for the first set of values. The next two iterator arguments must be at least input iterators for the second set of values. The fifth argument must be at least an output iterator indicating where to store a copy of the values that are different. The function returns an output iterator positioned immediately after the last value copied into the set to which the fifth argument points. A second version of function `set_symmetric_difference` takes a sixth argument that is a binary predicate function indicating the order in which the elements were originally sorted. The two sequences must be sorted using the same comparison function.

Line 66 uses function ***set_union*** to create a set of all the elements that are in either or both of the two sorted sets (both sets of values must be in ascending order). The elements are copied from both sets into the fifth argument (in this case the array `unionSet`). Elements that appear in both sets are copied only from the first set. The first two iterator arguments must be at least input iterators for the first set of values. The next two iterator arguments must be at least input iterators for the second set of values. The fifth argument must be at least an output iterator indicating where to store the copied elements. The function returns an output iterator positioned immediately after the last value copied into the set to which the fifth argument points. A second version of set_union takes a sixth argument that is a binary predicate function indicating the order in which the elements were originally sorted. The two sequences must be sorted using the same comparison function.

23.5.11 lower_bound, upper_bound and equal_range

Figure 23.36 demonstrates functions lower_bound, upper_bound and equal_range. Line 24 uses function *lower_bound* to find the first location in a sorted sequence of values at which the third argument could be inserted in the sequence such that the sequence would still be sorted in ascending order. The first two iterator arguments must be at least forward iterators. The third argument is the value for which to determine the lower bound. The function returns a forward iterator pointing to the position at which the insert can occur. A second version of function lower_bound takes as a fourth argument a binary predicate function indicating the order in which the elements were originally sorted.

```
1   // Fig. 23.36: AlgorithmTest9.cpp
2   // Standard Library functions lower_bound, upper_bound and
3   // equal_range for a sorted sequence of values.
4   #include <iostream>
5   using std::cout;
6   using std::endl;
7
8   #include <algorithm> // algorithm definitions
9   #include <vector> // vector class-template definition
10  #include <iterator> // ostream_iterator
11
12  int main()
13  {
14     const int SIZE = 10;
15     int a1[ SIZE ] = { 2, 2, 4, 4, 4, 6, 6, 6, 6, 8 };
16     std::vector< int > v( a1, a1 + SIZE ); // copy of a1
17     std::ostream_iterator< int > output( cout, " " );
18
19     cout << "Vector v contains:\n";
20     std::copy( v.begin(), v.end(), output );
21
22     // determine lower-bound insertion point for 6 in v
23     std::vector< int >::iterator lower;
24     lower = std::lower_bound( v.begin(), v.end(), 6 );
25     cout << "\n\nLower bound of 6 is element "
26        << ( lower - v.begin() ) << " of vector v";
27
28     // determine upper-bound insertion point for 6 in v
29     std::vector< int >::iterator upper;
30     upper = std::upper_bound( v.begin(), v.end(), 6 );
31     cout << "\nUpper bound of 6 is element "
32        << ( upper - v.begin() ) << " of vector v";
```

Fig. 23.36 | Algorithms lower_bound, upper_bound and equal_range. (Part 1 of 3.)

```
33
34     // use equal_range to determine both the lower- and
35     // upper-bound insertion points for 6
36     std::pair< std::vector< int >::iterator,
37                std::vector< int >::iterator > eq;
38     eq = std::equal_range( v.begin(), v.end(), 6 );
39     cout << "\nUsing equal_range:\n   Lower bound of 6 is element "
40          << ( eq.first - v.begin() ) << " of vector v";
41     cout << "\n   Upper bound of 6 is element "
42          << ( eq.second - v.begin() ) << " of vector v";
43     cout << "\n\nUse lower_bound to locate the first point\n"
44          << "at which 5 can be inserted in order";
45
46     // determine lower-bound insertion point for 5 in v
47     lower = std::lower_bound( v.begin(), v.end(), 5 );
48     cout << "\n   Lower bound of 5 is element "
49          << ( lower - v.begin() ) << " of vector v";
50     cout << "\n\nUse upper_bound to locate the last point\n"
51          << "at which 7 can be inserted in order";
52
53     // determine upper-bound insertion point for 7 in v
54     upper = std::upper_bound( v.begin(), v.end(), 7 );
55     cout << "\n   Upper bound of 7 is element "
56          << ( upper - v.begin() ) << " of vector v";
57     cout << "\n\nUse equal_range to locate the first and\n"
58          << "last point at which 5 can be inserted in order";
59
60     // use equal_range to determine both the lower- and
61     // upper-bound insertion points for 5
62     eq = std::equal_range( v.begin(), v.end(), 5 );
63     cout << "\n   Lower bound of 5 is element "
64          << ( eq.first - v.begin() ) << " of vector v";
65     cout << "\n   Upper bound of 5 is element "
66          << ( eq.second - v.begin() ) << " of vector v" << endl;
67     return 0;
68  } // end main
```

```
Vector v contains:
2 2 4 4 4 6 6 6 6 8

Lower bound of 6 is element 5 of vector v
Upper bound of 6 is element 9 of vector v
Using equal_range:
   Lower bound of 6 is element 5 of vector v
   Upper bound of 6 is element 9 of vector v

Use lower_bound to locate the first point
at which 5 can be inserted in order
   Lower bound of 5 is element 5 of vector v

Use upper_bound to locate the last point
at which 7 can be inserted in order
   Upper bound of 7 is element 9 of vector v
```

Fig. 23.36 | Algorithms `lower_bound`, `upper_bound` and `equal_range`. (Part 2 of 3.)

```
Use equal_range to locate the first and
last point at which 5 can be inserted in order
   Lower bound of 5 is element 5 of vector v
   Upper bound of 5 is element 5 of vector v
```

Fig. 23.36 | Algorithms `lower_bound`, `upper_bound` and `equal_range`. (Part 3 of 3.)

Line 30 uses function **upper_bound** to find the last location in a sorted sequence of values at which the third argument could be inserted in the sequence such that the sequence would still be sorted in ascending order. The first two iterator arguments must be at least forward iterators. The third argument is the value for which to determine the upper bound. The function returns a forward iterator pointing to the position at which the insert can occur. A second version of `upper_bound` takes as a fourth argument a binary predicate function indicating the order in which the elements were originally sorted.

Line 38 uses function **equal_range** to return a `pair` of forward iterators containing the combined results of performing both a `lower_bound` and an `upper_bound` operation. The first two iterator arguments must be at least forward iterators. The third argument is the value for which to locate the equal range. The function returns a `pair` of forward iterators for the lower bound (`eq.first`) and upper bound (`eq.second`), respectively.

Functions `lower_bound`, `upper_bound` and `equal_range` are often used to locate insertion points in sorted sequences. Line 47 uses `lower_bound` to locate the first point at which 5 can be inserted in order in v. Line 54 uses `upper_bound` to locate the last point at which 7 can be inserted in order in v. Line 62 uses `equal_range` to locate the first and last points at which 5 can be inserted in order in v.

23.5.12 Heapsort

Figure 23.37 demonstrates the Standard Library functions for performing the *heapsort sorting algorithm*. *Heapsort* is a sorting algorithm in which an array of elements is arranged into special binary tree called a *heap*. The key features of a heap are that the largest element is always at the top of the heap and the values of the children of any node in the binary tree are always less than or equal to that node's value. A heap arranged in this manner is often called a *maxheap*. Heapsort is discussed in detail in computer science courses called "Data Structures" and "Algorithms."

Line 23 uses function **make_heap** to take a sequence of values in the range from `v.begin()` up to, but not including, `v.end()` and create a heap that can be used to produce a sorted sequence. The two iterator arguments must be random-access iterators, so this function will work only with arrays, `vectors` and `deques`. A second version of this function takes as a third argument a binary predicate function for comparing values.

```
1   // Fig. 23.37: Heapsort.cpp
2   // Standard Library algorithms push_heap, pop_heap,
3   // make_heap and sort_heap.
4   #include <iostream>
5   using std::cout;
```

Fig. 23.37 | Using Standard Library functions to perform a heapsort. (Part 1 of 3.)

```
 6   using std::endl;
 7
 8   #include <algorithm>
 9   #include <vector>
10   #include <iterator>
11
12   int main()
13   {
14      const int SIZE = 10;
15      int a[ SIZE ] = { 3, 100, 52, 77, 22, 31, 1, 98, 13, 40 };
16      std::vector< int > v( a, a + SIZE ); // copy of a
17      std::vector< int > v2;
18      std::ostream_iterator< int > output( cout, " " );
19
20      cout << "Vector v before make_heap:\n";
21      std::copy( v.begin(), v.end(), output );
22
23      std::make_heap( v.begin(), v.end() ); // create heap from vector v
24      cout << "\nVector v after make_heap:\n";
25      std::copy( v.begin(), v.end(), output );
26
27      std::sort_heap( v.begin(), v.end() ); // sort elements with sort_heap
28      cout << "\nVector v after sort_heap:\n";
29      std::copy( v.begin(), v.end(), output );
30
31      // perform the heapsort with push_heap and pop_heap
32      cout << "\n\nArray a contains: ";
33      std::copy( a, a + SIZE, output ); // display array a
34      cout << endl;
35
36      // place elements of array a into v2 and
37      // maintain elements of v2 in heap
38      for ( int i = 0; i < SIZE; i++ )
39      {
40         v2.push_back( a[ i ] );
41         std::push_heap( v2.begin(), v2.end() );
42         cout << "\nv2 after push_heap(a[" << i << "]): ";
43         std::copy( v2.begin(), v2.end(), output );
44      } // end for
45
46      cout << endl;
47
48      // remove elements from heap in sorted order
49      for ( unsigned int j = 0; j < v2.size(); j++ )
50      {
51         cout << "\nv2 after " << v2[ 0 ] << " popped from heap\n";
52         std::pop_heap( v2.begin(), v2.end() - j );
53         std::copy( v2.begin(), v2.end(), output );
54      } // end for
55
56      cout << endl;
57      return 0;
58   } // end main
```

Fig. 23.37 | Using Standard Library functions to perform a heapsort. (Part 2 of 3.)

```
Vector v before make_heap:
3 100 52 77 22 31 1 98 13 40
Vector v after make_heap:
100 98 52 77 40 31 1 3 13 22
Vector v after sort_heap:
1 3 13 22 31 40 52 77 98 100

Array a contains: 3 100 52 77 22 31 1 98 13 40

v2 after push_heap(a[0]): 3
v2 after push_heap(a[1]): 100 3
v2 after push_heap(a[2]): 100 3 52
v2 after push_heap(a[3]): 100 77 52 3
v2 after push_heap(a[4]): 100 77 52 3 22
v2 after push_heap(a[5]): 100 77 52 3 22 31
v2 after push_heap(a[6]): 100 77 52 3 22 31 1
v2 after push_heap(a[7]): 100 98 52 77 22 31 1 3
v2 after push_heap(a[8]): 100 98 52 77 22 31 1 3 13
v2 after push_heap(a[9]): 100 98 52 77 40 31 1 3 13 22

v2 after 100 popped from heap
98 77 52 22 40 31 1 3 13 100
v2 after 98 popped from heap
77 40 52 22 13 31 1 3 98 100
v2 after 77 popped from heap
52 40 31 22 13 3 1 77 98 100
v2 after 52 popped from heap
40 22 31 1 13 3 52 77 98 100
v2 after 40 popped from heap
31 22 3 1 13 40 52 77 98 100
v2 after 31 popped from heap
22 13 3 1 31 40 52 77 98 100
v2 after 22 popped from heap
13 1 3 22 31 40 52 77 98 100
v2 after 13 popped from heap
3 1 13 22 31 40 52 77 98 100
v2 after 3 popped from heap
1 3 13 22 31 40 52 77 98 100
v2 after 1 popped from heap
1 3 13 22 31 40 52 77 98 100
```

Fig. 23.37 | Using Standard Library functions to perform a heapsort. (Part 3 of 3.)

Line 27 uses function **sort_heap** to sort a sequence of values in the range from v.begin() up to, but not including, v.end() that are already arranged in a heap. The two iterator arguments must be random-access iterators. A second version of this function takes as a third argument a binary predicate function for comparing values.

Line 41 uses function **push_heap** to add a new value into a heap. We take one element of array a at a time, append that element to the end of vector v2 and perform the push_heap operation. If the appended element is the only element in the vector, the vector is already a heap. Otherwise, function push_heap rearranges the elements of the vector into a heap. Each time push_heap is called, it assumes that the last element currently in the vector (i.e., the one that is appended before the push_heap function call) is the element being added to the heap and that all other elements in the vector are already arranged as a heap. The two iterator arguments to push_heap must be random-access iterators. A second version of this function takes as a third argument a binary predicate function for comparing values.

Line 52 uses ***pop_heap*** to remove the top heap element. This function assumes that the elements in the range specified by its two random-access iterator arguments are already a heap. Repeatedly removing the top heap element results in a sorted sequence of values. Function pop_heap swaps the first heap element (v2.begin()) with the last heap element (the element before v2.end() - i), then ensures that the elements up to, but not including, the last element still form a heap. Notice in the output that, after the pop_heap operations, the vector is sorted in ascending order. A second version of this function takes as a third argument a binary predicate function for comparing values.

23.5.13 min and max

Algorithms ***min*** and ***max*** determine the minimum and the maximum of two elements, respectively. Figure 23.38 demonstrates min and max for int and char values.

```
1   // Fig. 23.38: MinMaxTest.cpp
2   // Standard Library algorithms min and max.
3   #include <iostream>
4   using std::cout;
5   using std::endl;
6
7   #include <algorithm>
8
9   int main()
10  {
11      cout << "The minimum of 12 and 7 is: " << std::min( 12, 7 );
12      cout << "\nThe maximum of 12 and 7 is: " << std::max( 12, 7 );
13      cout << "\nThe minimum of 'G' and 'Z' is: " << std::min( 'G', 'Z' );
14      cout << "\nThe maximum of 'G' and 'Z' is: " << std::max( 'G', 'Z' );
15      cout << endl;
16      return 0;
17  } // end main
```

```
The minimum of 12 and 7 is: 7
The maximum of 12 and 7 is: 12
The minimum of 'G' and 'Z' is: G
The maximum of 'G' and 'Z' is: Z
```

Fig. 23.38 | Algorithms min and max.

23.5.14 STL Algorithms Not Covered in This Chapter

Figure 23.39 summarizes the STL algorithms that are not covered in this chapter.

Algorithm	Description
inner_product	Calculate the sum of the products of two sequences by taking corresponding elements in each sequence, multiplying those elements and adding the result to a total.

Fig. 23.39 | Algorithms not covered in this chapter. (Part 1 of 3.)

Algorithm	Description
adjacent_difference	Beginning with the second element in a sequence, calculate the difference (using operator –) between the current and previous elements, and store the result. The first two input iterator arguments indicate the range of elements in the container and the third indicates where the results should be stored. A second version of this algorithm takes as a fourth argument a binary function to perform a calculation between the current element and the previous element.
partial_sum	Calculate a running total (using operator +) of the values in a sequence. The first two input iterator arguments indicate the range of elements in the container and the third indicates where the results should be stored. A second version of this algorithm takes as a fourth argument a binary function that performs a calculation between the current value in the sequence and the running total.
nth_element	Use three random-access iterators to partition a range of elements. The first and last arguments represent the range of elements. The second argument is the partitioning element's location. After this algorithm executes, all elements before the partitioning element are less than that element and all elements after the partitioning element are greater than or equal to that element. A second version of this algorithm takes as a fourth argument a binary comparison function.
partition	This algorithm is similar to nth_element, but it requires less powerful bidirectional iterators, making it more flexible than nth_element. Algorithm partition requires two bidirectional iterators indicating the range of elements to partition. The third element is a unary predicate function that helps partition the elements so that all elements in the sequence for which the predicate is true are to the left (toward the beginning of the sequence) of all elements for which the predicate is false. A bidirectional iterator is returned indicating the first element in the sequence for which the predicate returns false.
stable_partition	This algorithm is similar to partition except that this algorithm guarantees that equivalent elements will be maintained in their original order.
next_permutation	Next lexicographical permutation of a sequence.
prev_permutation	Previous lexicographical permutation of a sequence.
rotate	Use three forward iterator arguments to rotate the sequence indicated by the first and last argument by the number of positions indicated by subtracting the first argument from the second argument. For example, the sequence 1, 2, 3, 4, 5 rotated by two positions would be 4, 5, 1, 2, 3.

Fig. 23.39 | Algorithms not covered in this chapter. (Part 2 of 3.)

Algorithm	Description
rotate_copy	This algorithm is identical to rotate except that the results are stored in a separate sequence indicated by the fourth argument—an output iterator. The two sequences must have the same number of elements.
adjacent_find	This algorithm returns an input iterator indicating the first of two identical adjacent elements in a sequence. If there are no identical adjacent elements, the iterator is positioned at the **end** of the sequence.
search	This algorithm searches for a subsequence of elements within a sequence of elements and, if such a subsequence is found, returns a forward iterator that indicates the first element of that subsequence. If there are no matches, the iterator is positioned at the end of the sequence to be searched.
search_n	This algorithm searches a sequence of elements looking for a subsequence in which the values of a specified number of elements have a particular value and, if such a subsequence is found, returns a forward iterator that indicates the first element of that subsequence. If there are no matches, the iterator is positioned at the end of the sequence to be searched.
partial_sort	Use three random-access iterators to sort part of a sequence. The first and last arguments indicate the sequence of elements. The second argument indicates the ending location for the sorted part of the sequence. By default, elements are ordered using operator < (a binary predicate function can also be supplied). The elements from the second argument iterator to the end of the sequence are in an undefined order.
partial_sort_copy	Use two input iterators and two random-access iterators to sort part of the sequence indicated by the two input iterator arguments. The results are stored in the sequence indicated by the two random-access iterator arguments. By default, elements are ordered using operator < (a binary predicate function can also be supplied). The number of elements sorted is the smaller of the number of elements in the result and the number of elements in the original sequence.
stable_sort	The algorithm is similar to sort except that all equivalent elements are maintained in their original order. This sort is $O(n \log n)$ if enough memory is available; otherwise, it is $O(n(\log n)^2)$.

Fig. 23.39 | Algorithms not covered in this chapter. (Part 3 of 3.)

23.6 Class bitset

Class *bitset* makes it easy to create and manipulate *bit sets*, which are useful for representing a set of bit flags. bitsets are fixed in size at compile time. Class bitset is an alternate tool for bit manipulation, discussed in Chapter 22. The declaration

```
bitset< size > b;
```

creates bitset b, in which every bit is initially 0. The statement

```
b.set( bitNumber );
```

sets bit bitNumber of bitset b "on." The expression b.set() sets all bits in b "on."
The statement

```
b.reset( bitNumber );
```

sets bit bitNumber of bitset b "off." The expression b.reset() sets all bits in b "off." The
statement

```
b.flip( bitNumber );
```

"flips" bit bitNumber of bitset b (e.g., if the bit is on, flip sets it off). The expression
b.flip() flips all bits in b. The statement

```
b[ bitNumber ];
```

returns a reference to the bit bitNumber of bitset b. Similarly,

```
b.at( bitNumber );
```

performs range checking on bitNumber first. Then, if bitNumber is in range, at returns a
reference to the bit. Otherwise, at throws an out_of_range exception. The statement

```
b.test( bitNumber );
```

performs range checking on bitNumber first. Then, if bitNumber is in range, test returns
true if the bit is on, false if the bit is off. Otherwise, test throws an out_of_range exception. The expression

```
b.size()
```

returns the number of bits in bitset b. The expression

```
b.count()
```

returns the number of bits that are set in bitset b. The expression

```
b.any()
```

returns true if any bit is set in bitset b. The expression

```
b.none()
```

returns true if none of the bits is set in bitset b. The expressions

```
b == b1
b != b1
```

compare the two bitsets for equality and inequality, respectively.

Each of the bitwise assignment operators &=, |= and ^= can be used to combine bitsets. For example,

```
b &= b1;
```

performs a bit-by-bit logical AND between bitsets b and b1. The result is stored in b. Bitwise logical OR and bitwise logical XOR are performed by

```
b |= b1;
b ^= b2;
```

The expression

```
b >>= n;
```

shifts the bits in bitset b right by n positions. The expression

```
b <<= n;
```

shifts the bits in bitset b left by n positions. The expressions

```
b.to_string()
b.to_ulong()
```

convert bitset b to a string and an unsigned long, respectively.

Sieve of Eratosthenes with bitset

Figure 23.40 revisits the Sieve of Eratosthenes for finding prime numbers that we discussed in Exercise 8.31. A bitset is used instead of an array to implement the algorithm. The program displays all the prime numbers from 2 to 1023, then allows the user to enter a number to determine whether that number is prime.

```cpp
1   // Fig. 23.40: BitsetSieve.cpp
2   // Using a bitset to demonstrate the Sieve of Eratosthenes.
3   #include <iostream>
4   using std::cin;
5   using std::cout;
6   using std::endl;
7
8   #include <iomanip>
9   using std::setw;
10
11  #include <cmath>
12  using std::sqrt; // sqrt prototype
13
14  #include <bitset> // bitset class definition
15
16  int main()
17  {
18     const int SIZE = 1024;
19     int value;
```

Fig. 23.40 | Class bitset and the Sieve of Eratosthenes. (Part 1 of 3.)

```
20      std::bitset< SIZE > sieve; // create bitset of 1024 bits
21      sieve.flip(); // flip all bits in bitset sieve
22      sieve.reset( 0 ); // reset first bit (number 0)
23      sieve.reset( 1 ); // reset second bit (number 1)
24
25      // perform Sieve of Eratosthenes
26      int finalBit = sqrt( static_cast< double > ( sieve.size() ) ) + 1;
27
28      // determine all prime numbers from 2 to 1024
29      for ( int i = 2; i < finalBit; i++ )
30      {
31         if ( sieve.test( i ) ) // bit i is on
32         {
33            for ( int j = 2 * i; j < SIZE; j += i )
34               sieve.reset( j ); // set bit j off
35         } // end if
36      } // end for
37
38      cout << "The prime numbers in the range 2 to 1023 are:\n";
39
40      // display prime numbers in range 2-1023
41      for ( int k = 2, counter = 1; k < SIZE; k++ )
42      {
43         if ( sieve.test( k ) ) // bit k is on
44         {
45            cout << setw( 5 ) << k;
46
47            if ( counter++ % 12 == 0 ) // counter is a multiple of 12
48               cout << '\n';
49         } // end if
50      } // end for
51
52      cout << endl;
53
54      // get value from user to determine whether value is prime
55      cout << "\nEnter a value from 2 to 1023 (-1 to end): ";
56      cin >> value;
57
58      // determine whether user input is prime
59      while ( value != -1 )
60      {
61         if ( sieve[ value ] ) // prime number
62            cout << value << " is a prime number\n";
63         else // not a prime number
64            cout << value << " is not a prime number\n";
65
66         cout << "\nEnter a value from 2 to 1023 (-1 to end): ";
67         cin >> value;
68      } // end while
69
70      return 0;
71   } // end main
```

Fig. 23.40 | Class `bitset` and the Sieve of Eratosthenes. (Part 2 of 3.)

```
The prime numbers in the range 2 to 1023 are:
    2    3    5    7   11   13   17   19   23   29   31   37
   41   43   47   53   59   61   67   71   73   79   83   89
   97  101  103  107  109  113  127  131  137  139  149  151
  157  163  167  173  179  181  191  193  197  199  211  223
  227  229  233  239  241  251  257  263  269  271  277  281
  283  293  307  311  313  317  331  337  347  349  353  359
  367  373  379  383  389  397  401  409  419  421  431  433
  439  443  449  457  461  463  467  479  487  491  499  503
  509  521  523  541  547  557  563  569  571  577  587  593
  599  601  607  613  617  619  631  641  643  647  653  659
  661  673  677  683  691  701  709  719  727  733  739  743
  751  757  761  769  773  787  797  809  811  821  823  827
  829  839  853  857  859  863  877  881  883  887  907  911
  919  929  937  941  947  953  967  971  977  983  991  997
 1009 1013 1019 1021

Enter a value from 2 to 1023 (-1 to end): 389
389 is a prime number

Enter a value from 2 to 1023 (-1 to end): 88
88 is not a prime number

Enter a value from 2 to 1023 (-1 to end): -1
```

Fig. 23.40 | Class bitset and the Sieve of Eratosthenes. (Part 3 of 3.)

Line 20 creates a bitset of size bits (size is 1024 in this example). By default, all the bits in the bitset are set "off." Line 21 calls function *flip* to set all bits "on." Numbers 0 and 1 are not prime numbers, so lines 22–23 call function *reset* to set bits 0 and 1 "off." Lines 29–36 determine all the prime numbers from 2 to 1023. The integer finalBit (line 26) is used to determine when the algorithm is complete. The basic algorithm is that a number is prime if it has no divisors other than 1 and itself. Starting with the number 2, we can eliminate all multiples of that number. The number 2 is divisible only by 1 and itself, so it is prime. Therefore, we can eliminate 4, 6, 8 and so on. The number 3 is divisible only by 1 and itself. Therefore, we can eliminate all multiples of 3 (keep in mind that all even numbers have already been eliminated).

23.7 Function Objects

Many STL algorithms allow you to pass a function pointer into the algorithm to help the algorithm perform its task. For example, the binary_search algorithm that we discussed in Section 23.5.6 is overloaded with a version that requires as its fourth parameter a pointer to a function that takes two arguments and returns a bool value. The binary_search algorithm uses this function to compare the search key to an element in the collection. The function returns true if the search key and element being compared are equal; otherwise, the function returns false. This enables binary_search to search a collection of elements for which the element type does not provide an overloaded equality == operator.

STL's designers made the algorithms more flexible by allowing any algorithm that can receive a function pointer to receive an object of a class that overloads the parentheses operator with a function named operator(), provided that the overloaded operator meets the requirements of the algorithm—in the case of `binary_search`, it must receive two arguments and return a `bool`. An object of such a class is known as a *function object* and can be used syntactically and semantically like a function or function pointer—the overloaded parentheses operator is invoked by using a function object's name followed by parentheses containing the arguments to the function. Together, function objects and functions used are known as *functors*. Most algorithms can use function objects and functions interchangeably.

Function objects provide several advantages over function pointers. Since function objects are commonly implemented as class templates that are included into each source-code file that uses them, the compiler can inline an overloaded `operator()` to improve performance. Also, since they are objects of classes, function objects can have data members that `operator()` can use to perform its task.

Predefined Function Objects of the Standard Template Library

Many predefined function objects can be found in the header *<functional>*. Figure 23.41 lists several of the STL function objects, which are all implemented as class templates. We used the function object `less< T >` in the `set`, `multiset` and `priority_queue` examples, to specify the sorting order for elements in a container.

STL function objects	Type	STL function objects	Type
`divides< T >`	arithmetic	`logical_or< T >`	logical
`equal_to< T >`	relational	`minus< T >`	arithmetic
`greater< T >`	relational	`modulus< T >`	arithmetic
`greater_equal< T >`	relational	`negate< T >`	arithmetic
`less< T >`	relational	`not_equal_to< T >`	relational
`less_equal< T >`	relational	`plus< T >`	arithmetic
`logical_and< T >`	logical	`multiplies< T >`	arithmetic
`logical_not< T >`	logical		

Fig. 23.41 | Function objects in the Standard Library.

Using the STL Accumulate Algorithm

Figure 23.42 demonstrates the `accumulate` numeric algorithm (discussed in Fig. 23.30) to calculate the sum of the squares of the elements in a `vector`. The fourth argument to `accumulate` is a *binary function object* (that is, a function object for which `operator()` takes two arguments) or a function pointer to a *binary function* (that is, a function that takes two arguments). Function `accumulate` is demonstrated twice—once with a function pointer and once with a function object.

Lines 15–18 define a function `sumSquares` that squares its second argument `value`, adds that square and its first argument `total` and returns the sum. Function `accumulate` will pass each of the elements of the sequence over which it iterates as the second argument to `sumSquares` in the example. On the first call to `sumSquares`, the first argument will be the initial value of the `total` (which is supplied as the third argument to `accumulate`; 0 in this program). All subsequent calls to sumSquares receive as the first argument the running sum returned by the previous call to sumSquares. When accumulate completes, it returns the sum of the squares of all the elements in the sequence.

```cpp
// Fig. 23.42: FunctionObjects.cpp
// Demonstrating function objects.
#include <iostream>
using std::cout;
using std::endl;

#include <vector> // vector class-template definition
#include <algorithm> // copy algorithm
#include <numeric> // accumulate algorithm
#include <functional> // binary_function definition
#include <iterator> // ostream_iterator

// binary function adds square of its second argument and the
// running total in its first argument, then returns the sum
int sumSquares( int total, int value )
{
   return total + value * value;
} // end function sumSquares

// binary function class template defines overloaded operator()
// that adds the square of its second argument and running
// total in its first argument, then returns sum
template< typename T >
class SumSquaresClass : public std::binary_function< T, T, T >
{
public:
   // add square of value to total and return result
   T operator()( const T &total, const T &value )
   {
      return total + value * value;
   } // end function operator()
}; // end class SumSquaresClass

int main()
{
   const int SIZE = 10;
   int array[ SIZE ] = { 1, 2, 3, 4, 5, 6, 7, 8, 9, 10 };
   std::vector< int > integers( array, array + SIZE ); // copy of array
   std::ostream_iterator< int > output( cout, " " );
   int result;

   cout << "vector integers contains:\n";
   std::copy( integers.begin(), integers.end(), output );

   // calculate sum of squares of elements of vector integers
   // using binary function sumSquares
   result = std::accumulate( integers.begin(), integers.end(),
      0, sumSquares );
```

Fig. 23.42 | Binary function object. (Part I of 2.)

```
49
50        cout << "\n\nSum of squares of elements in integers using "
51           << "binary\nfunction sumSquares: " << result;
52
53        // calculate sum of squares of elements of vector integers
54        // using binary function object
55        result = std::accumulate( integers.begin(), integers.end(),
56           0, SumSquaresClass< int >() );
57
58        cout << "\n\nSum of squares of elements in integers using "
59           << "binary\nfunction object of type "
60           << "SumSquaresClass< int >: " << result << endl;
61        return 0;
62   } // end main
```

```
vector integers contains:
1 2 3 4 5 6 7 8 9 10

Sum of squares of elements in integers using binary
function sumSquares: 385

Sum of squares of elements in integers using binary
function object of type SumSquaresClass< int >: 385
```

Fig. 23.42 | Binary function object. (Part 2 of 2.)

Lines 23–32 define a class SumSquaresClass that inherits from the class template *binary_function* (in header file <functional>)—an empty base class for creating function objects in which operator receives two parameters and returns a value. Class binary_function accepts three type parameters that represent the types of the first argument, second argument and return value of operator, respectively. In this example, the type of these parameters is T (line 24). On the first call to the function object, the first argument will be the initial value of the total (which is supplied as the third argument to accumulate: 0 in this program) and the second argument will be the first element in vector integers. All subsequent calls to operator receive as the first argument the result returned by the previous call to the function object, and the second argument will be the next element in the vector. When accumulate completes, it returns the sum of the squares of all the elements in the vector.

Lines 47–48 call function accumulate with a pointer to function sumSquares as its last argument.

The statement in lines 55–56 calls function accumulate with an object of class SumSquaresClass as the last argument. The expression SumSquaresClass< int >() creates an instance of class SumSquaresClass (a function object) that is passed to accumulate, which sends the object the message (invokes the function) operator. The statement could be written as two separate statements, as follows:

```
SumSquaresClass< int > sumSquaresObject;
result = std::accumulate( integers.begin(), integers.end(),
   0, sumSquaresObject );
```

The first line defines an object of class SumSquaresClass. That object is then passed to function accumulate.

23.8 Introduction to STL/CLR

The original STL is usable only with native C++. Before Visual Studio 2008 was released, when writing managed code targeting the .NET Framework C++/CLI developers needed to use the `System::Collections::Generic` namespace (discussed in detail in Chapters 15 and 25) for using data structures like those in the STL. While there is nothing wrong with this .NET library, it required native C++ developers to learn a new set of functions rather than use their existing knowledge of the STL. Also, the `System::Collections::Generic` library uses a more conventional container model than the STL. It doesn't separate the algorithms from the containers like the STL, requiring further specialized knowledge of each container type in the library.

To remedy these problems, in Visual Studio 2008 Microsoft has included a new library named STL/CLR. STL/CLR was developed to mimic the STL as closely as possible in both application and performance to provide the power of the STL to managed code in C++/CLI programs. STL/CLR separates the containers from the algorithms and focuses on using iterators over collections, just like the original STL. This allows native C++ developers who have spent significant time learning the STL to apply that knowledge to managed code in C++/CLI. To use an STL/CLR container you must include the appropriate header file. For example, to use the STL/CLR `vector` class and the STL/CLR `deque` class put the following `include` statements at the top of your program:

```
#include <cliext/vector>
#include <cliext/deque>
```

Each STL/CLR container is in a similarly named header. To include STL/CLR algorithms and functions for use with STL/CLR containers you can use the following declarations:

```
#include <cliext/algorithms>
#include <cliext/numeric>
```

STL/CLR containers and functions are contained in namespace `cliext`. So, where in previous examples in the chapter we used `std::vector` for a native C++ STL `vector`, we would use `cliext::vector` for its STL/CLR counterpart. The STL/CLR algorithms are designed to use the same function prototypes as the original STL versions. Further, they were developed to operate the same way and in the same time complexity as the original STL versions. STL/CLR containers do provide some functions that their STL counterparts do not, most of which are related to interoperating with .NET FCL collections.

STL/CLR containers can have elements that are reference types (classes defined with `ref class`), handles to reference types, value types (those defined with `value class`), or built-in types. Recall from Section 23.1 that, when inserting an element into an STL container, you must ensure the element type has a copy constructor and assignment operator. The same holds true for STL/CLR containers. Native C++ types have default versions of these generated by the compiler. However, as you learned in Section 11.15, unlike native types, managed reference types don't have copy constructors or assignment operators generated by the compiler. Therefore, ensure that the type being inserted into the STL/CLR container has defined these functions even if the type requires only memberwise copy and assignment. This is particularly important in user-defined types. You can avoid this issue by inserting handles to reference types into STL/CLR containers. Similarly, certain containers support operator==, operator>, and others. Any types inserted into such STL/CLR containers must support the associated operators the container requires.

As with all managed objects in C++/CLI, STL/CLR container objects are allocated on the managed heap. And as with all managed objects, STL/CLR container objects are subject to automatic memory management by the CLR garbage collector. Note that just as the original STL cannot contain managed types or handles, the STL/CLR cannot contain native types or pointers. Also be aware that you cannot use STL/CLR with native C++ streams such as the ostream_iterator used throughout this chapter. Instead, you should use CLR based streams (such as the Console class).

STL/CLR containers and algorithms are generally faster than their managed counterparts in the .NET FCL classes from the System::Collections::Generic namespace. STL/CLR containers do implement certain interfaces to interoperate easily with .NET container classes (a topic beyond the scope of this book).

23.9 Wrap-Up

In this chapter, we introduced the Standard Template Library and discussed its three key components—containers, iterators and algorithms. You learned the STL sequence containers, vector, deque and list, which represent linear data structures. We discussed associative containers, set, multiset, map and multimap, which represent nonlinear data structures. You also saw that the container adapters stack, queue and priority_queue can be used to restrict the operations of the sequence containers for the purpose of implementing the specialized data structures represented by the container adapters. We then demonstrated many of the STL algorithms, including mathematical algorithms, basic searching and sorting algorithms and set operations. You learned the types of iterators each algorithm requires and that each algorithm can be used with any container that supports the minimum iterator functionality the algorithm requires. You also learned class bitset, which makes it easy to create and manipulate bit sets as a container. We introduced function objects that work syntactically and semantically like ordinary functions, but offer advantages such as performance and the ability to store data. Finally, we discussed the new STL/CLR that allows developers to use their existing STL knowledge with managed code.

In the chapters that follow, we explore advanced Visual C++ topics in managed code. Chapter 24 introduces databases, which organize data in such a way that the data can be selected and updated quickly. We introduce Structured Query Language (SQL) for writing simple database queries(i.e., searches) and ADO.NET for manipulating information in a database through C++/CLI.

23.10 STL Web Resources

Our C++ Resource Center (www.deitel.com/cplusplus/) focuses on the enormous amount of free C++ content available online. Start your search here for resources, downloads, tutorials, documentation, books, e-books, journals, articles, blogs, RSS feeds and more that will help you develop C++ applications. The C++ Resource Center includes links to many STL resources and tutorials.

Summary

Section 23.1 Introduction to the Standard Template Library (STL)
- The Standard Template Library defines powerful, template-based, reusable components that implement many common data structures, and algorithms used to process those data structures.
- The STL has three key components—containers, iterators and algorithms.
- The STL containers are data structures capable of storing objects of any data type. There are three styles of container classes—first-class containers, container adapters and near containers.
- STL algorithms are functions that perform such common data manipulations as searching, sorting and comparing elements or entire containers.

Section 23.1.1 Introduction to Containers
- The containers are divided into sequence containers, associative containers and container adapters.
- The sequence containers represent linear data structures, such as vectors and linked lists.
- Associative containers are nonlinear containers that quickly locate elements stored in them, such as sets of values or key/value pairs.
- Sequence containers and associative containers are collectively referred to as first-class containers.

Section 23.1.2 Introduction to Iterators
- First-class container function `begin` returns an iterator pointing to the first element of a container. Function `end` returns an iterator pointing to the first element past the end of the container (an element that doesn't exist and is typically used in a loop to indicate when to terminate processing of the container's elements).
- An `istream_iterator` is capable of extracting values in a type-safe manner from an input stream. An `ostream_iterator` is capable of inserting values in an output stream.
- Input and output iterators can move only in the forward direction (i.e., from the beginning of the container to the end) one element at a time.
- A forward iterator combines the capabilities of input and output iterators.
- A bidirectional iterator has the capabilities of a forward iterator and the ability to move in the backward direction (i.e., from the end of the container toward the beginning).
- A random-access iterator has the capabilities of a bidirectional iterator and the ability to directly access any element of the container.

Section 23.1.3 Introduction to Algorithms
- Containers that support random-access iterators, such as `vector`, can be used with all algorithms in the STL.

Section 23.2 Sequence Containers
- The STL provides sequence containers `vector`, `list` and `deque`. Class templates `vector` and `deque` both are based on arrays. Class template `list` implements a linked-list data structure.

Section 23.2.1 `vector` Sequence Container
- Function `capacity` returns the number of elements that can be stored in a vector before the vector dynamically resizes itself to accommodate more elements.
- Sequence container function `push_back` adds an element to the end of a container.
- To use the algorithms of the STL, you must include the header file `<algorithm>`.

- Algorithm copy copies each element in a container starting with the location specified by the iterator in its first argument and up to—but not including—the location specified by the iterator in its second argument.
- Function front returns a reference to the first element in a sequence container. Function begin returns an iterator pointing to the beginning of a sequence container.
- Function back returns a reference to the last element in a sequence container. Function end returns an iterator pointing to the element one past the end of a sequence container.
- Sequence container function insert inserts value(s) before the element at a specific location.
- Function erase (in all first-class containers) removes specific element(s) from the container.
- Function empty (in all containers and adapters) returns true if the container is empty.
- Function clear (in all first-class containers) empties the container.

Section 23.2.2 list Sequence Container
- The list sequence container provides an efficient implementation for insertion and deletion operations at any location in the container. Header file <list> must be included to use class template list.
- The list member function push_front inserts values at the beginning of a list.
- The list member function sort arranges the elements in the list in ascending order.
- The list member function splice removes elements in one list and inserts them into another list at a specific position.
- The list member function unique removes duplicate elements in a list.
- The list member function assign replaces the contents of one list with the contents of another.
- The list member function remove deletes all copies of a specified value from a list.

Section 23.2.3 deque Sequence Container
- Class template deque provides the same operations as vector, but adds member functions push_front and pop_front to allow insertion and deletion at the beginning of a deque, respectively. Header file <deque> must be included to use class template deque.

Section 23.3 Associative Containers
- The STL's associative containers provide direct access to store and retrieve elements via keys.
- The four associative containers are multiset, set, multimap and map.
- Class templates multiset and set provide operations for manipulating sets of values where the values are the keys—there is not a separate value associated with each key. Header file <set> must be included to use class templates set and multiset.
- The primary difference between a multiset and a set is that a multiset allows duplicate keys and a set does not.

Section 23.3.1 multiset Associative Container
- The multiset associative container provides fast storage and retrieval of keys and allows duplicate keys. The ordering of the elements is determined by a comparator function object.
- A multiset's keys can be sorted in ascending order by ordering the keys with comparator function object less<T>.
- The type of the keys in all associative containers must support comparison properly based on the comparator function object specified—e.g., keys sorted with less<T> must support comparison with operator<.

- A `multiset` supports bidirectional iterators.
- Header file `<set>` must be included to use class `multiset`.

Section 23.3.2 `set` Associative Container
- The `set` associative container is used for fast storage and retrieval of unique keys.
- If an attempt is made to insert a duplicate key into a `set`, the duplicate is ignored.
- A `set` supports bidirectional iterators.
- Header file `<set>` must be included to use class set.

Section 23.3.3 `multimap` Associative Container
- Class templates `multimap` and `map` provide operations for manipulating values associated with keys.
- The primary difference between a `multimap` and a `map` is that a `multimap` allows duplicate keys with associated values to be stored and a map allows only unique keys with associated values.
- Function `count` (available to all associative containers) counts the number of occurrences of the specified value currently in a container.
- Function `find` (available to all associative containers) locates a specified value in a container.
- Functions `lower_bound` and `upper_bound` (available in all associative containers) locate the earliest occurrence of the specified value in a container and the element after the last occurrence of the specified value in a container, respectively.
- Function `equal_range` (available in all associative containers) returns a `pair` containing the results of both a `lower_bound` and an `upper_bound` operation.
- The `multimap` associative container is used for fast storage and retrieval of keys and associated values (often called key/value pairs).
- Duplicate keys are allowed in a `multimap`, so multiple values can be associated with a single key. This is called a one-to-many relationship.
- Header file `<map>` must be included to use class templates `map` and `multimap`.

Section 23.3.4 `map` Associative Container
- Duplicate keys are not allowed in a `map`, so only a single value can be associated with each key. This is called a one-to-one mapping.
- A map is commonly called an associative array.

Section 23.4 Container Adapters
- The STL provides three container adapters—`stack`, `queue` and `priority_queue`.
- Adapters are not first-class containers, because they do not provide the actual data structure implementation in which elements can be stored and they do not support iterators.
- All three adapter class templates provide member functions `push` and `pop` that properly insert an element into and remove an element from each adapter data structure, respectively.

Section 23.4.1 `stack` Adapter
- Class template `stack` is a last-in, first-out data structure. Header file `<stack>` must be included to use class template `stack`.
- The `stack` member function `top` returns a reference to the top element of the `stack` (implemented by calling function `back` of the underlying container).
- The `stack` member function `empty` determines whether the `stack` is empty (implemented by calling function `empty` of the underlying container).

- The stack member function size returns the number of elements in the stack (implemented by calling function size of the underlying container).

Section 23.4.2 queue *Adapter*
- Class template queue enables insertions at the back of the underlying data structure and deletions from the front of the underlying data structure (commonly referred to as a first-in, first-out data structure). Header file <queue> must be included to use a queue or a priority_queue.
- The queue member function front returns a reference to the first element in the queue (implemented by calling function front of the underlying container).
- The queue member function back returns a reference to the last element in the queue (implemented by calling function back of the underlying container).
- The queue member function empty determines whether the queue is empty (implemented by calling function empty of the underlying container).
- The queue member function size returns the number of elements in the queue (implemented by calling function size of the underlying container).

Section 23.4.3 priority_queue *Adapter*
- Class template priority_queue provides functionality that enables insertions in sorted order into the underlying data structure and deletions from the front of the underlying data structure.
- The common priority_queue operations are push, pop, top, empty and size.

Section 23.5.1 fill, fill_n, generate *and* generate_n
- Algorithms fill and fill_n set every element in a range of container elements to a specific value.
- Algorithms generate and generate_n use a generator function or function object to create values for every element in a range of container elements.

Section 23.5.2 equal, mismatch *and* lexicographical_compare
- Algorithm equal compares two sequences of values for equality.
- Algorithm mismatch compares two sequences of values and returns a pair of iterators indicating the location in each sequence of the mismatched elements.
- Algorithm lexicographical_compare compares the contents of two sequences.

Section 23.5.3 remove, remove_if, remove_copy *and* remove_copy_if
- Algorithm remove eliminates all elements with a specific value in a certain range.
- Algorithm remove_copy copies all elements that do not have a specific value in a certain range.
- Algorithm remove_if deletes all elements that satisfy the if condition in a certain range.
- Algorithm remove_copy_if copies all elements that satisfy the if condition in a certain range.

Section 23.5.4 replace, replace_if, replace_copy *and* replace_copy_if
- Algorithm replace replaces all elements with a specific value in certain range.
- Algorithm replace_copy copies all elements with a specific value in a certain range.
- Algorithm replace_if replaces all elements that satisfy the if condition in a certain range.
- Algorithm replace_copy_if copies all elements that satisfy the if condition in a certain range.

Section 23.5.5 *Mathematical Algorithms*
- Algorithm random_shuffle reorders randomly the elements in a certain range.
- Algorithm count counts the elements with a specific value in a certain range.

- Algorithm `count_if` counts the elements that satisfy the `if` condition in a certain range.
- Algorithm `min_element` locates the smallest element in a certain range.
- Algorithm `max_element` locates the largest element in a certain range.
- Algorithm `accumulate` sums the values in a certain range.
- Algorithm `for_each` applies a general function or function object to every element in a range.
- Algorithm `transform` applies a general function or function object to every element in a range and replaces each element with the result of the function.

Section 23.5.6 Basic Searching and Sorting Algorithms
- Algorithm `find` locates a specific value in a certain range.
- Algorithm `find_if` locates the first value in a certain range that satisfies the `if` condition.
- Algorithm `sort` arranges the elements in a certain range in ascending order or an order specified by a predicate.
- Algorithm `binary_search` determines whether a specific value is in a sorted range of elements.

Section 23.5.7 `swap`, `iter_swap` and `swap_ranges`
- Algorithm `swap` exchanges two values.
- Algorithm `iter_swap` exchanges the two elements.
- Algorithm `swap_ranges` exchanges the elements in a certain range.

Section 23.5.8 `copy_backward`, `merge`, `unique` and `reverse`
- Algorithm `copy_backward` copies elements in a range and places the elements into a container starting from the end and working toward the front.
- Algorithm `merge` combines two sorted ascending sequences of values into a third sorted ascending sequence.
- Algorithm `unique` removes duplicated elements in a sorted sequence of elements in a certain range.
- Algorithm `reverse` reverses all the elements in a certain range.

Section 23.5.9 `inplace_merge`, `unique_copy` and `reverse_copy`
- Algorithm `inplace_merge` merges two sorted sequences of elements in the same container.
- Algorithm `unique_copy` makes a copy of all the unique elements in the sorted sequence of values in a certain range.
- Algorithm `reverse_copy` makes a reversed copy of the elements in a certain range.

Section 23.5.10 Set Operations
- The set function `includes` compares two sets of sorted values to determine whether every element of the second set is in the first set.
- The set function `set_difference` finds the elements from the first set of sorted values that are not in the second set of sorted values (both sets of values must be in ascending order).
- The set function `set_intersection` determines the elements from the first set of sorted values that are in the second set of sorted values (both sets of values must be in ascending order).
- The set function `set_symmetric_difference` determines the elements in the first set that are not in the second set and the elements in the second set that are not in the first set (both sets of values must be in ascending order).

- The set function set_union creates a set of all the elements that are in either or both of the two sorted sets (both sets of values must be in ascending order).

Section 23.5.11 lower_bound, upper_bound and equal_range

- Algorithm lower_bound finds the first location in a sorted sequence of values at which the third argument could be inserted in the sequence such that the sequence would still be sorted in ascending order.

- Algorithm upper_bound finds the last location in a sorted sequence of values at which the third argument could be inserted in the sequence such that the sequence would still be sorted in ascending order.

- Algorithm equal_range performs returns the lower bound and upper bound as a pair.

Section 23.5.12 Heapsort

- Algorithm make_heap takes a sequence of values in a certain range and creates a heap that can be used to produce a sorted sequence.

- Algorithm sort_heap sorts a sequence of values in a certain range that are already arranged in a heap.

- Algorithm pop_heap removes the top heap element.

Section 23.5.13 min and max

- Algorithms min and max determine the minimum of two elements and the maximum of two elements, respectively.

Section 23.6 Class bitset

- Class template bitset makes it easy to create and manipulate bit sets, which are useful for representing a set of bit flags.

Section 23.7 Function Objects

- A function object is an instance of a class that overloads operator().

- STL provides many predefined function objects, which can be found in header <functional>.

- Binary function objects are function objects that take two arguments and return a value. Class template binary_function is an empty base class for creating binary function objects that provides standard type names for the function's parameters and result.

Section 23.8 Introduction to STL/CLR

- STL containers and algorithms cannot be used with managed code in C++/CLI.

- STL/CLR is an implementation of the STL that uses STL-like containers and algorithms to provide functionality similar to the STL but with managed code in C++/CLI.

- Include STL/CLR containers with include declarations of the form:

      #include <cliext/*ContainerName*>

  where *ContainerName* is the same name as the STL counterpart (such as vector, deque, etc). STL/CLR algorithms are in cliext/algorithm and cliext/numeric.

- STL/CLR containers are in namespace cliext.

- STL/CLR containers are just like normal managed objects. They can be created with gcnew or stack semantics and are subject to automatic memory management by the CLR garbage collector.

- STL/CLR containers and algorithms cannot be used with native objects or native pointers.

Terminology

accumulate algorithm
adapter
algorithm
<algorithm> header file
assign member function of list
associative array
associative container
back member function of sequence containers
back_inserter function template
begin member function of first-class containers
bidirectional iterator
binary function
binary function object
binary_function class template
binary_search algorithm
capacity member function of vector
comparator function object
const_iterator
const_reverse_iterator
container
container adapter
copy_backward algorithm
count algorithm
count_if algorithm
<deque> header file
deque sequence container
empty member function of containers
end member function of containers
equal algorithm
equal_range algorithm
equal_range function of associative container
erase member function of containers
fill algorithm
fill_n algorithm
find algorithm
find function of associative container
find_if algorithm
first data member of pair
first-class container
flip function of bitset
for_each algorithm
forward iterator
front_inserter function template
front member function of sequence container
function object
functor
<functional> header file
generate algorithm
generate_n algorithm

heap
heapsort sorting algorithm
includes algorithm
inplace_merge algorithm
input iterator
input sequence
insert member function of containers
inserter function template
istream_iterator
iterator
iter_swap algorithm
key/value pair
less< int >
lexicographical_compare algorithm
<list> header file
list sequence container
lower_bound algorithm
lower_bound function of associative container
make_heap algorithm
<map> header file
map associative container
max algorithm
max_element algorithm
merge algorithm
min algorithm
min_element algorithm
mismatch algorithm
multimap associative container
multiset associative container
mutating-sequence algorithm
near container
<numeric> header file
one-to-one mapping
ostream_iterator
output iterator
output sequence
pop_back function
pop_front function
pop_heap algorithm
pop member function of container adapters
priority_queue adapter class template
push_heap algorithm
push member function of container adapters
queue adapter class template
<queue> header file
random-access iterator
random_shuffle algorithm
range
rbegin member function of vector

remove algorithm
remove member function of list
remove_copy algorithm
remove_copy_if algorithm
remove_if algorithm
rend member function of containers
replace algorithm
replace_copy algorithm
replace_copy_if algorithm
replace_if algorithm
reset function of bitset
reverse algorithm
reverse_copy algorithm
reverse_iterator
search key
second data member of pair
sequence
sequence container
set associative container
set_difference algorithm
<set> header file

set_intersection algorithm
set_symmetric_difference algorithm
set_union algorithm
size member function of containers
sort algorithm
sort_heap algorithm
sort member function of list
splice member function of list
stack adapter class template
<stack> header file
Standard Template Library (STL)
swap algorithm
swap member function of list
swap_ranges algorithm
top member function of container adapters
unique algorithm
unique_copy algorithm
unique member function of list
upper_bound algorithm

Self-Review Exercises

23.1   State whether the following are *true* or *false* or fill in the blanks. For the true/false questions, if the answer is *false*, explain why.

23.2   (T/F) The STL makes abundant use of inheritance and virtual functions.

23.3   The two types of first-class STL containers are sequence containers and _____ containers.

23.4   The five main iterator types are _____, _____, _____, _____ and _____.

23.5   (T/F) An iterator acts like a pointer to an element.

23.6   (T/F) STL algorithms can operate on C-like pointer-based arrays.

23.7   (T/F) STL algorithms are encapsulated as member functions within each container class.

23.8   (T/F) When the remove algorithm is used on a vector, the algorithm does not decrease the size of the vector from which elements are being removed.

23.9   The three STL container adapters are _____, _____ and _____.

23.10   (T/F) Container member function end yields the position of the container's last element.

23.11   STL algorithms operate on container elements indirectly, using _____.

23.12   The sort algorithm requires a(n) _____ iterator.

Answers to Self-Review Exercises

23.1   False. These were avoided for performance reasons.

23.2   Associative.

23.3   Input, output, forward, bidirectional, random access.

23.4   False. It is actually vice versa.

23.5   True.

23.6   False. STL algorithms are not member functions. They operate indirectly on containers, through iterators.

23.7   True.

23.8   `stack`, `queue`, `priority_queue`.

23.9   False. It actually yields the position just after the end of the container.

23.10   Iterators.

23.11   Random-access.

Exercises

23.13   Write a function template `palindrome` that takes a `vector` parameter and returns `true` or `false` according to whether the `vector` does or does not read the same forward as backward (e.g., a `vector` containing 1, 2, 3, 2, 1 is a palindrome, but a `vector` containing 1, 2, 3, 4 is not).

23.14   Modify Fig. 23.40, the Sieve of Eratosthenes, so that, if the number the user inputs into the program is not prime, the program displays the prime factors of the number. Remember that a prime number's factors are only 1 and the prime number itself. Every nonprime number has a unique prime factorization. For example, the factors of 54 are 2, 3, 3 and 3. When these values are multiplied together, the result is 54. For the number 54, the prime factors output should be 2 and 3.

23.15   Modify Exercise 23.14 so that, if the number the user inputs into the program is not prime, the program displays the prime factors of the number and the number of times each prime factor appears in the unique prime factorization. For example, the output for the number 54 should be

```
The unique prime factorization of 54 is: 2 * 3 * 3 * 3
```

Recommended Reading

Ammeraal, L. *STL for C++ Programmers*. New York: John Wiley, 1997.

Austern, M. H. *Generic Programming and the STL: Using and Extending the C++ Standard Template Library*. Reading, MA: Addison-Wesley, 1998.

Glass, G., and B. Schuchert. *The STL <Primer>*. Upper Saddle River, NJ: Prentice Hall PTR, 1995.

Henricson, M., and E. Nyquist. *Industrial Strength C++: Rules and Recommendations*. Upper Saddle River, NJ: Prentice Hall, 1997.

Josuttis, N. *The C++ Standard Library: A Tutorial and Handbook*. Reading, MA: Addison-Wesley, 1999.

Koenig, A., and B. Moo. *Ruminations on C++*. Reading, MA: Addison-Wesley, 1997.

Meyers, S. *Effective STL: 50 Specific Ways to Improve Your Use of the Standard Template Library*. Reading, MA: Addison-Wesley, 2001.

Musser, D. R., and A. Saini. *STL Tutorial and Reference Guide: C++ Programming with the Standard Template Library*. Reading, MA: Addison-Wesley, 1996.

Musser, D. R., and A. A. Stepanov. "Algorithm-Oriented Generic Libraries," *Software Practice and Experience,* Vol. 24, No. 7, July 1994.

Nelson, M. *C++ Programmer's Guide to the Standard Template Library*. Foster City, CA: Programmer's Press, 1995.

Pohl, I. *C++ Distilled: A Concise ANSI/ISO Reference and Style Guide.* Reading, MA: Addison-Wesley, 1997.

Pohl, I. *Object-Oriented Programming Using C++, Second Edition.* Reading, MA: Addison-Wesley, 1997.

Robson, R. *Using the STL: The C++ Standard Template Library.* New York: Springer Verlag, 2000.

Schildt, H. *STL Programming from the Ground Up*, New York: Osborne McGraw-Hill, 1999.

Stepanov, A., and M. Lee. "The Standard Template Library," *Internet Distribution* 31 October 1995 <www.cs.rpi.edu/~musser/doc.ps>.

Stroustrup, B. "Making a vector Fit for a Standard," *The C++ Report,* October 1994.

Stroustrup, B. *The Design and Evolution of C++.* Reading, MA: Addison-Wesley, 1994.

Stroustrup, B. *The C++ Programming Language, Third Edition.* Reading, MA: Addison-Wesley, 1997.

Vilot, M. J. "An Introduction to the Standard Template Library," *The C++ Report,* Vol. 6, No. 8, October 1994.

24

Regular Expressions

OBJECTIVES

In this chapter you will learn:

- What regular expressions are and when they are useful.
- To use regular expressions in conjunction with classes **Regex** and **Match**.
- To iterate over matches to a regular expression.
- To use character classes to match any character from a set of characters.
- To use quantifiers to match a pattern multiple times.
- To search for complex patterns in text using regular expressions.
- To validate data using regular expressions.
- To modify **String**s using regular expressions and class **Regex**.

24.1 Introduction

This chapter introduces *regular expressions*—specially formatted strings that are used to find patterns in text. They can be used to ensure that data is in a particular format. For example, a U.S. ZIP code must consist of five digits, or five digits followed by a dash followed by four more digits. Compilers use regular expressions to validate program syntax. If the program code does not match the regular expression, the compiler indicates that there is a syntax error. We discuss classes Regex and Match from the System::Text:: RegularExpressions namespace as well as the symbols used to form regular expressions. We then demonstrate how to find patterns in a string, match entire strings to patterns, replace characters in a string that match a pattern and split strings at delimiters specified as a pattern in a regular expression.

24.2 Simple Regular Expressions and Class Regex

The .NET Framework provides several classes to help developers manipulate regular expressions. Figure 24.1 demonstrates the basic regular expression classes. To use these classes, add a using directive for the namespace System::Text::RegularExpressions. Class Regex represents a regular expression. We create a Regex object named expression (line 16) to represent the regular expression "e". This regular expression matches the literal character "e" anywhere in an arbitrary String. Regex *member function* Match returns an object of *class* Match that represents a single regular expression match. Class Match's ToString member function returns the substring that matched the regular expression. The call to member function Match (line 17) matches the leftmost occurrence of the character "e". Regex also provides member function Matches (line 21), which finds all matches of

```
I    // Fig. 24.1: BasicRegularExpressions.cpp
2    // Demonstrate basic regular expressions.
3    #include "stdafx.h"
4
5    using namespace System;
6    using namespace System::Text::RegularExpressions;
7
8    int main( array< System::String^ > ^args )
9    {
10       String ^testString =
11          "regular expressions are sometimes called regex or regexp";
```

Fig. 24.1 | Demonstrating basic regular expressions. (Part I of 2.)

```
12      Console::WriteLine( "The test string is:\n  \"{0}\"", testString );
13      Console::WriteLine( "\nMatch 'e' in the test string" );
14
15      // match an 'e' in the test string
16      Regex ^expression = gcnew Regex( "e" );
17      Console::WriteLine( expression->Match( testString ) );
18      Console::WriteLine( "\nMatch every 'e' in the test string" );
19
20      // match 'e' multiple times in the string
21      for each ( Match ^match in expression->Matches( testString ) )
22         Console::Write( "{0} ", match );
23
24      Console::WriteLine( "\n\nMatch \"regex\" in the test string" );
25
26      // match 'regex' in the string
27      for each ( Match ^match in Regex::Matches( testString, "regex" ) )
28         Console::Write( "{0} ", match );
29
30      Console::WriteLine(
31         "\n\nMatch \"regex\" or \"regexp\" using an optional 'p'" );
32
33      // use the ? quantifier to include an optional 'p'
34      for each ( Match ^match in Regex::Matches( testString, "regexp?" ) )
35         Console::Write( "{0} ", match );
36
37      Console::WriteLine( "\n\nMatch \"cat\" or \"hat\"" );
38
39      // use alternation to match either cat or hat
40      expression = gcnew Regex( "(c|h)at" );
41      Console::WriteLine( expression->Match( "hat cat" ) ); // matches hat
42      Console::WriteLine( expression->Match( "cat hat" ) ); // matches cat
43
44      return 0;
45   } // end main
```

```
The test string is:
  "regular expressions are sometimes called regex or regexp"

Match 'e' in the test string
e

Match every 'e' in the test string
e e e e e e e e e e

Match "regex" in the test string
regex regex

Match "regex" or "regexp" using an optional 'p'
regex regexp

Match "cat" or "hat"
hat
cat
```

Fig. 24.1 | Demonstrating basic regular expressions. (Part 2 of 2.)

the regular expression in an arbitrary String and returns a MatchCollection object containing all the Matches. A collection is a data structure, similar to an array, and can be used with a for each statement to iterate through the collection's elements. We discuss collections in more detail in Chapter 25, Collections. We use a for each statement (lines 21–22) to print all the matches to expression in testString. The elements in the Match-Collection are Match objects, so the for each statement declares variable match to be of type Match ∧. For each Match, line 22 outputs the text that matched the regular expression.

Regular expressions can also be used to match a sequence of literal characters anywhere in a String. Lines 27–28 print all the occurrences of the character sequence "regex" in testString. Here we use the static Regex member function Matches. Class Regex provides static versions of both member functions Match and Matches. The static versions take a regular expression as an argument in addition to the String to be searched. This is useful when you want to use a regular expression only once. The call to member function Matches (line 27) returns two matches to the regular expression "regex". Notice that "regexp" matches the regular expression "regex", but the "p" is excluded. We use the regular expression "regexp?" (line 34) to match occurrences of both "regex" and "regexp". The question mark (?) is a *metacharacter*—a character with special meaning in a regular expression. More specifically, the question mark is a quantifier. A *quantifier* is a metacharacter that describes how many times a part of the pattern may occur in a match. The *? quantifier* matches zero or one occurrences of the pattern to its left. In line 34, we apply the ? quantifier to the character "p". This means that a match to the regular expression contains the sequence of characters "regex", and may be followed by a "p". Notice that the for each statement (lines 34–35) prints both "regex" and "regexp".

Metacharacters allow you to create more complex patterns. The *"|" (alternation)* metacharacter matches the expression to its left or to its right. We use alternation in the regular expression "(c|h)at" (line 40) to match either "cat" or "hat". Parentheses, (and), are used to group parts of a regular expression, much like you group parts of a mathematic expression. The "|" causes the pattern to match a sequence of characters starting with either "c" or "h", followed by "at". Note that the "|" character will match the entire expression to its left or to its right. If we didn't use the parentheses around "c|h", the regular expression would match either the single character "c" or the sequence of characters "hat". Lines 41–42 use the regular expression (line 40) to search the strings "hat cat" and "cat hat", respectively. Notice in the output that the first match in "hat cat" is "hat", while the first match in "cat hat" is "cat". Alternation chooses the leftmost match in the string for either of the alternating expressions—the order of the expressions in the alternation doesn't matter.

Regular Expression Character Classes and Quantifiers

The table in Fig. 24.2 lists some character classes that can be used with regular expressions. A *character class* represents a group of characters that might appear in a String. For example, a *word character (\w)* is any alphanumeric character (a-z, A-Z and 0-9) or underscore. A *white-space character (\s)* is a space, a tab, a carriage return, a newline or a form feed. A *digit (\d)* is any numeric character.

Figure 24.3 uses character classes in regular expressions. For this example, we use function displayMatches (lines 56–62) to display all of a regular expression's matches. Function displayMatches takes two handles to String objects representing the string to

Character class	Matches	Character class	Matches
\d	any digit	\D	any non-digit
\w	any word character	\W	any non-word character
\s	any whitespace	\S	any non-whitespace

Fig. 24.2 | Character classes.

search and the regular expression to match. The function uses a for each statement to print each Match in the MatchCollection object returned by the static member function Matches of class Regex.

```
 1   // Fig. 24.3: CharacterClasses.cpp
 2   // Demonstrate using character classes and quantifiers.
 3   #include "stdafx.h"
 4
 5   using namespace System;
 6   using namespace System::Text::RegularExpressions;
 7
 8   void displayMatches( String^, String^ );
 9
10   int main( array< System::String^ > ^args )
11   {
12      String ^testString = "abc, DEF, 123";
13      Console::WriteLine( "The test string is: \"{0}\"", testString );
14
15      // find the digits in the test string
16      Console::WriteLine( "Match any digit" );
17      displayMatches( testString, "\\d" );
18
19      // find anything that isn't a digit
20      Console::WriteLine( "\nMatch any non-digit" );
21      displayMatches( testString, "\\D" );
22
23      // find the word characters in the test string
24      Console::WriteLine( "\nMatch any word character" );
25      displayMatches( testString, "\\w" );
26
27      // find sequences of word characters
28      Console::WriteLine( "\nMatch a group of at least one word character" );
29      displayMatches( testString, "\\w+" );
30
31      // use a lazy quantifier
32      Console::WriteLine(
33         "\nMatch a group of at least one word character (lazy)" );
34      displayMatches( testString, "\\w+?" );
35
```

Fig. 24.3 | Demonstrating character classes and quantifiers. (Part 1 of 2.)

```
36        // match characters from 'a' to 'f'
37        Console::WriteLine( "\nMatch anything from 'a' - 'f'" );
38        displayMatches( testString, "[a-f]" );
39
40        // match anything that isn't in the range 'a' to 'f'
41        Console::WriteLine( "\nMatch anything not from 'a' - 'f'" );
42        displayMatches( testString, "[^a-f]" );
43
44        // match any letter in any case
45        Console::WriteLine( "\nMatch a group of at least one letter" );
46        displayMatches( testString, "[a-zA-Z]+" );
47
48        // use the . (dot) metacharacter to match any character
49        Console::WriteLine( "\nMatch a group of any type of characters" );
50        displayMatches( testString, ".*" );
51
52        return 0;
53     } // end main
54
55     // display the matches to a regular expression
56     void displayMatches( String ^input, String ^expression )
57     {
58        for each ( Match ^myMatch in Regex::Matches( input, expression ) )
59           Console::Write( "{0} ", myMatch );
60
61        Console::WriteLine();
62     } // end function displayMatches
```

```
The test string is: "abc, DEF, 123"
Match any digit
1 2 3

Match any non-digit
a b c ,     D E F ,

Match any word character
a b c D E F 1 2 3

Match a group of at least one word character
abc DEF 123

Match a group of at least one word character (lazy)
a b c D E F 1 2 3

Match anything from 'a' - 'f'
a b c

Match anything not from 'a' - 'f'
,     D E F ,     1 2 3

Match a group of at least one letter
abc DEF

Match a group of any type of characters
abc, DEF, 123
```

Fig. 24.3 | Demonstrating character classes and quantifiers. (Part 2 of 2.)

The first regular expression (line 17) matches digits in the testString. We use the digit character class (\d) to match any digit (0-9). Notice that we use an extra backslash in the regular expression "\\d". Normally, a backslash is the beginning of an escape sequence. To insert a literal backslash in a string, you must escape the backslash character with another backslash. The output shows that the regular expression matches each of 1, 2, and 3 in the testString. You can also match anything that *isn't* a member of a particular character class using an uppercase letter instead of a lower case letter. For example, the regular expression "\\D" (line 21) matches any character that isn't a digit. Notice in the output that this includes punctuation and whitespace. Negating a character class matches *everything* that *isn't* a member of the character class.

The next regular expression (line 25) uses the character class \w to match any word character in the testString. Notice that each match consists of a single character. It would be useful to match a sequence of word characters rather than a single character. The regular expression in line 29 uses the + quantifier to match a sequence of word characters. The *+ quantifier* matches one or more occurrences of the pattern to its left. There are only three matches for this expression, each three characters long. Quantifiers are *greedy*—they will match as many occurrences of the pattern as possible. You can follow a quantifier with a question mark (?) to make it *lazy*—it will match as *few* occurrences of the pattern as possible. The regular expression "\\w+?" (line 34) uses a lazy + quantifier to match the shortest sequence of word characters possible. This produces nine matches of length one instead of three matches of length three. Figure 24.4 lists other quantifiers that you can place after a pattern in a regular expression, and the purpose of each quantifier.

Regular expressions are not limited to the character classes in Fig. 24.2. You can create your own character class by listing the members of the character class between square brackets, [and]. [*Note:* Metacharacters in square brackets are treated as literal characters.] You can include a range of characters using the "-" character. The regular expression in line 38 of Fig. 24.3 creates a character class to match any lowercase letter from a to f. These custom character classes match a single character that is a member of the class. The output shows three matches, a, b and c. Notice that D, E and F don't match the character class [a-f] because they are uppercase. You can negate a custom character class by placing a "^" character after the opening square bracket. The regular expression in line 42 matches any character that *isn't* in the range a-f. As with the predefined character classes, negating

Quantifier	Matches
*	Matches zero or more occurrences of the preceding pattern.
+	Matches one or more occurrences of the preceding pattern.
?	Matches zero or one occurrences of the preceding pattern.
.	Matches any single character.
{n}	Matches exactly n occurrences of the preceding pattern.
{n,}	Matches at least n occurrences of the preceding pattern.
{n,m}	Matches between n and m (inclusive) occurrences of the preceding pattern.

Fig. 24.4 | Quantifiers used in regular expressions.

a custom character class matches *everything* that isn't a member, including punctuation and whitespace. You can use quantifiers with custom character classes. The regular expression in line 46 uses a character class with two ranges of characters, a-z and A-Z, and the + quantifier to match a sequence of lowercase or uppercase letters. You can also use the "." (dot) character to match any character other than a newline (\n). The regular expression ".*" (line 50) matches any sequence of characters. The * quantifier matches zero or more occurrences of the pattern to its left. Unlike the + quantifier, the * quantifier can be used to match an empty string.

24.3 Complex Regular Expressions

The program of Fig. 24.5 tries to match birthdays to a regular expression. For demonstration purposes, the expression matches only birthdays that do not occur in April and that belong to people whose names begin with "J". We can do this by combining the basic regular expression techniques we've already covered.

Lines 11–12 create a Regex object and pass a regular expression pattern string to the Regex constructor. The first character in the regular expression, "J", is a literal character. Any String matching this regular expression is required to start with "J". The next part of the regular expression (".*") matches any number of unspecified characters except newlines (\n). The pattern "J.*" matches a person's name that starts with J and any characters that may come after that.

```cpp
1   // Fig. 24.5: RegexMatches.cpp
2   // A more complex regular expression.
3   #include "stdafx.h"
4
5   using namespace System;
6   using namespace System::Text::RegularExpressions;
7
8   int main( array< System::String^ > ^args )
9   {
10      // create a regular expression
11      Regex ^expression =
12         gcnew Regex( "J.*\\d[\\d-[4]]-\\d\\d-\\d\\d" );
13
14      String ^string1 = "Jane's Birthday is 05-12-75\n" +
15         "Dave's Birthday is 11-04-68\n" +
16         "John's Birthday is 04-28-73\n" +
17         "Joe's Birthday is 12-17-77";
18
19      // match the regular expression to a string and
20      // print out all the matches
21      for each ( Match ^myMatch in expression->Matches( string1 ) )
22         Console::WriteLine( myMatch );
23   } // end main
```

```
Jane's Birthday is 05-12-75
Joe's Birthday is 12-17-77
```

Fig. 24.5 | A more complex regular expression.

Next we match the person's birthday. We use the \d character class to match the first digit of the month. Since the birthday must not occur in April, the second digit in the month can't be 4. We could use the character class "[0-35-9]" to match any digit other than 4. However, .NET regular expressions allow you to subtract members from a character class, called *character class subtraction*. In line 12, we use the pattern "[\\d-[4]]" to match any digit other than 4. When the "-" character in a character class is followed by a character class instead of a literal character, the "-" is interpreted as subtraction instead of a range of characters. The members of the character class following the "-" are subtracted from the character class preceding the "-". When using character class subtraction, the class being subtracted must be the last item in the enclosing square brackets. This notation allows you to write shorter, easier-to-read regular expressions.

Although the "-" character indicates a range or character class subtraction when it is enclosed in square brackets, instances of the "-" character outside a character class are treated as literal characters. Thus, the regular expression in line 12 searches for a String that starts with the letter "J", followed by any number of characters, followed by a two-digit number (of which the second digit cannot be 4), followed by a dash, another two-digit number, a dash and another two-digit number.

Lines 21–22 use a for each statement to iterate through the MatchCollection object returned by the expression object's member function Matches, which received string1 as an argument. For each Match, line 22 outputs the text that matched the regular expression. The output in Fig. 24.5 indicates the two matches that were found in string1. Notice that both matches conform to the pattern specified by the regular expression.

24.4 Validating User Input with Regular Expressions

The program in Fig. 24.6 presents a more involved example that uses regular expressions to validate name, address and telephone number information input by a user. The program first asks the user to input a last name (line 13) by calling function inputData. The inputData function (lines 52–67) takes two String ∧ arguments, the name of the data being input and a regular expression that it must match. The function prompts the user (line 55) to input the specified data. Then inputData checks whether the input is in the correct format by matching it to the regular expression. The while statement (lines 59–64) calls the static member function Match of class Regex, then inspects the Success property of the Match object returned. The *Success* property of class Match is a bool indicating whether the string matched the regular expression. If the input doesn't match the given pattern, inputData prompts the user to enter the information again. Once the user enters a valid input, the data is returned as a String ∧. The program repeats that process until all the data fields have been validated (lines 16–35). Then we display the validated information (lines 38–46).

In the previous example, we searched a String for substrings that matched a regular expression. In this example, we want to ensure that the entire String for each input conforms to a particular regular expression. For example, we want to accept "Smith" as a last name, but not "9@Smith#". In a regular expression that begins with a "∧" character and ends with a "$" character, the characters "∧" and "$" represent the beginning and end of a String, respectively. These characters force a regular expression to return a match only if the entire String being processed matches the regular expression.

```cpp
1   // Fig. 24.6: Validate.cpp
2   // Validating user input with regular expressions.
3   #include "stdafx.h"
4
5   using namespace System;
6   using namespace System::Text::RegularExpressions;
7
8   String^ inputData( String^, String^ );
9
10  int main( array< System::String^ > ^args )
11  {
12     // enter the last name
13     String ^lastName = inputData( "last name", "^[A-Z][a-zA-Z]*$" );
14
15     // enter the first name
16     String ^firstName = inputData( "first name", "^[A-Z][a-zA-Z]*$" );
17
18     // enter the address
19     String ^address = inputData( "address",
20        "^[0-9]+\\s([a-zA-Z]+|[a-zA-Z]+\\s[a-zA-Z]+)$" );
21
22     // enter the city
23     String ^city =
24        inputData( "city", "^([a-zA-Z]+|[a-zA-Z]+\\s[a-zA-Z]+)$" );
25
26     // enter the state
27     String ^state = inputData( "state",
28        "^([a-zA-Z]+|[a-zA-Z]+\\s[a-zA-Z]+)$" );
29
30     // enter the zip code
31     String ^zipCode = inputData( "zip code", "^\\d{5}$" );
32
33     // enter the phone number
34     String ^phoneNumber = inputData( "phone number",
35        "^[1-9]\\d{2}-[1-9]\\d{2}-\\d{4}$" );
36
37     // display the validated data
38     Console::WriteLine( "\nValidated Data\n\n" +
39        "Last name: {0}\n" +
40        "First name: {1}\n" +
41        "Address: {2}\n" +
42        "City: {3}\n" +
43        "State: {4}\n" +
44        "Zip code: {5}\n" +
45        "Phone number: {6}\n",
46        lastName, firstName, address, city, state, zipCode, phoneNumber );
47
48     return 0;
49  } // end main
50
51  // collect input from the user
52  String^ inputData( String ^fieldName, String ^expression )
53  {
```

Fig. 24.6 | Validating user input with regular expressions. (Part 1 of 2.)

```
54      // request the data from the user
55      Console::Write( "Enter {0}:", fieldName );
56      String ^data = Console::ReadLine();
57
58      // validate the data
59      while ( !( Regex::Match( data, expression )->Success ) )
60      {
61          Console::WriteLine( "Invalid {0}.", fieldName );
62          Console::Write( "Enter {0}:", fieldName );
63          data = Console::ReadLine();
64      } // end while
65
66      return data;
67  } // end of function inputData
```

```
Enter last name: Doe
Enter first name: Jane
Enter address: 123 Some Street
Enter city: Some City
Enter state: Some State
Enter zip code: 12345
Enter phone number: 123-456-7890

Validated Data

Last name: Doe
First name: Jane
Address: 123 Some Street
City: Some City
State: Some State
Zip code: 12345
Phone number: 123-456-7890
```

Fig. 24.6 | Validating user input with regular expressions. (Part 2 of 2.)

The regular expression in line 13 uses a character class to match an uppercase first letter followed by letters of any case—a-z matches any lowercase letter, and A-Z matches any uppercase letter. The * quantifier signifies that the second range of characters may occur zero or more times in the String. Thus, this expression matches any String consisting of one uppercase letter, followed by zero or more additional letters.

The \s character class matches a single white-space character (lines 20, 24 and 28). In the expression "\\d{5}", used for the zipCode String (line 31), {5} is a quantifier (see Fig. 24.2). The pattern to the left of {n} must occur exactly n times. Thus "\\d{5}" matches any five digits. Recall that the character "|" (lines 20, 24 and 28) matches the expression to its left *or* the expression to its right. In line 20, we use the character "|" to indicate that the address can contain a word of one or more characters *or* a word of one or more characters followed by a space and another word of one or more characters. Note the use of parentheses to group parts of the regular expression. This ensures that "|" is applied to the correct parts of the pattern.

The lastName and firstName variables (lines 13 and 16) both accept Strings of any length that begin with an uppercase letter. The regular expression for the address String (line 20) matches a number of at least one digit, followed by a space and then either one or more letters or else one or more letters followed by a space and another series of one or more letters. Therefore, "10 Broadway" and "10 Main Street" are both valid addresses. As currently formed, the regular expression in line 20 doesn't match an address that does not start with a number, or that has more than two words. The regular expressions for the city (line 24) and state (line 28) Strings match any word of at least one character or, alternatively, any two words of at least one character if the words are separated by a single space. This means both Waltham and West Newton would match. Again, these regular expressions would not accept names that have more than two words. The regular expression for the zipCode String (line 31) ensures that the zip code is a five-digit number. The regular expression for the phoneNumber String (line 35) indicates that the phone number must be of the form xxx-yyy-yyyy, where the xs represent the area code and the ys the number. The first x and the first y cannot be zero, as specified by the range [1–9] in each case.

24.5 Regex Member Functions `Replace` and `Split`

Sometimes it is useful to replace parts of one String with another or to split a String according to a regular expression. For this purpose, class Regex provides static and instance versions of member functions Replace and Split, which are demonstrated in Fig. 24.7.

```
 1   // Fig. 24.7: RegexSubstitution.cpp
 2   // Using Regex member functions Replace and Split.
 3   #include "stdafx.h"
 4
 5   using namespace System;
 6   using namespace System::Text::RegularExpressions;
 7
 8   int main( array< System::String^ > ^args )
 9   {
10      String ^testString1 =
11         "This sentence ends in 5 stars *****";
12      String ^output = "";
13      String ^testString2 = "1, 2, 3, 4, 5, 6, 7, 8";
14      Regex ^testRegex1 = gcnew Regex( "\\d" );
15      array< String^ > ^result;
16
17      Console::WriteLine( "Original string: {0}", testString1 );
18      testString1 = Regex::Replace( testString1, "\\*", "^" );
19      Console::WriteLine( "^ substituted for *: {0}", testString1 );
20      testString1 = Regex::Replace( testString1, "stars",
21         "carets" );
22      Console::WriteLine( "\"carets\" substituted for \"stars\": {0}",
23         testString1 );
24      Console::WriteLine( "Every word replaced by \"word\": {0}",
25         Regex::Replace( testString1, "\\w+", "word" ) );
26      Console::WriteLine( "\nOriginal string: {0}", testString2 );
27      Console::WriteLine( "Replace first 3 digits by \"digit\": {0}",
28         testRegex1->Replace( testString2, "digit", 3 ) );
29      Console::Write( "string split at commas [" );
30      result = Regex::Split( testString2, ",\\s" );
```

Fig. 24.7 | Using Regex member functions Replace and Split. (Part 1 of 2.)

```
31
32      for each ( String ^resultString in result )
33         output += "\"" + resultString + "\", ";
34
35      // Delete ", " at the end of output string
36      Console::WriteLine( output->Substring( 0, output->Length - 2 ) + "]" );
37
38      return 0;
39   } // end main
```

```
Original string: This sentence ends in 5 stars *****
^ substituted for *: This sentence ends in 5 stars ^^^^^
"carets" substituted for "stars": This sentence ends in 5 carets ^^^^^
Every word replaced by "word": word word word word word word ^^^^^

Original string: 1, 2, 3, 4, 5, 6, 7, 8
Replace first 3 digits by "digit": digit, digit, digit, 4, 5, 6, 7, 8
string split at commas ["1", "2", "3", "4", "5", "6", "7", "8"]
```

Fig. 24.7 | Using Regex member functions Replace and Split. (Part 2 of 2.)

Regex member function **Replace** replaces text in a String with new text wherever the original String matches a regular expression. We use two versions of this member function in Fig. 24.7. The first version (line 18) is static and takes three parameters—the String to modify, the String containing the regular expression to match and the replacement String. Here, Replace replaces every instance of "*" in testString1 with "^". Notice that the regular expression ("*") precedes character * with two backslashes, \\. Normally, * is a quantifier indicating that a regular expression should match any number of occurrences of a preceding pattern. However, in line 18, we want to find all occurrences of the literal character *; to do this, we must escape character * with character \ (recall that we must also escape the \ with another \). By escaping a special regular expression character, we tell the regular-expression matching engine to find the actual character * rather than use it as a quantifier.

The second version of member function Replace (line 28) is an instance member function that uses the regular expression passed to the constructor for testRegex1 (line 14) to perform the replacement operation. Line 14 instantiates testRegex1 with argument "\\d". The call to instance member function Replace in line 28 takes three arguments—a String to modify, a String containing the replacement text and an int specifying the number of replacements to make. In this case, line 28 replaces the first three instances of a digit ("\\d") in testString2 with the text "digit".

Member function **Split** divides a String into several substrings. The original String is broken at delimiters that match a specified regular expression. Member function Split returns an array containing the substrings. In line 30, we use the static version of member function Split to separate a String of comma-separated integers. The first argument is the String to split; the second argument is the regular expression that represents the delimiter. The regular expression ",\\s" separates the substrings at each comma. By matching a white-space character (\\s in the regular expression), we eliminate the extra spaces from the resulting substrings.

24.6 Wrap-Up

In this chapter we discussed classes `Regex`, `Match` and `MatchCollection` from the `System::Text::RegularExpressions` namespace and the symbols that are used to form regular expressions. You learned how to find patterns in a string and match entire strings to patterns with `Regex` member functions `Match` and `Matches`, how to replace characters in a string with `Regex` member function `Replace` and how to split strings at delimiters with `Regex` member function `Split`.

Summary

Section 24.2 Regular Expressions and Class Regex

- The .NET Framework provides several classes to help developers manipulate regular expressions. To use these classes, add a using directive for the `System::Text::RegularExpressions` namespace.

- Class `Regex` represents a regular expression.

- `Regex` *member function* `Match` returns an object of *class* `Match` that represents a single regular expression match. Member function `Match` matches the leftmost occurrence of the pattern.

- Class `Regex` member function `Matches` finds all matches of the regular expression in an arbitrary `String` and returns an object of the class `MatchCollection` containing all the matches. The elements in the `MatchCollection` are `Match` objects.

- Class `Regex` provides `static` versions of both member functions `Match` and `Matches`. The `static` versions take a regular expression as an argument in addition to the `String` to be searched. This is useful when you want to use a regular expression only once.

- A quantifier is a metacharacter that describes how many times a part of the pattern may occur.

- The `?` quantifier matches zero or one occurrences of the pattern to its left.

- The `"|"` (alternation) metacharacter matches the expression to its left or to its right. Alternation chooses the leftmost match in the string for either of the alternating expressions—the order of the expressions in the alternation doesn't matter.

- Parentheses, (and), are used to group parts of the regular expression, much like you group parts of a mathematic expression.

- A character class represents a group of characters that might appear in a `String`.

- A word character is any alphanumeric character (a-z, A-Z and 0-9) or underscore.

- A white-space character is a space, a tab, a carriage return, a newline or a form feed.

- A digit is any numeric character.

- Normally, a backslash is the beginning of an escape sequence. To insert a literal backslash in a string, you must escape the backslash character with another backslash.

- You can match anything that isn't a member of a particular predefined character class using an uppercase letter instead of a lower case letter. Negating a character class matches everything that isn't a member of the character class.

- The `+` quantifier matches one or more occurrences of the pattern to its left.

- Quantifiers are greedy—they match as many occurrences of the pattern as possible. A quantifier followed by a question mark (`?`) is lazy—it matches as few occurrences of the pattern as possible.

- You can create your own character class by listing the members of the character class between square brackets, [and]. You can include a range of characters using the "-" character. You can negate a custom character class by placing a "^" character at the beginning.

- The "." (dot) character matches any character other than a newline (\n).

- The * quantifier matches zero or more occurrences of the pattern to its left. The * quantifier can be used to match an empty String.

Section 24.3 Complex Regular Expressions

- When the "-" character in a character class is followed by a character class instead of a literal character, the "-" represents character class subtraction. The members of the character class following the "-" are subtracted from the character class preceding the "-". When using character class subtraction, the class being subtracted must be the last item in the enclosing square brackets.

- Instances of the "-" character outside square brackets are treated as literal characters.

Section 24.4 Validating User Input with Regular Expressions

- The Success property of class Match is a bool indicating whether the String matched a regular expression.

- In a regular expression that begins with a "^" character and ends with a "$" character, "^" and "$" represent the beginning and end of a String, respectively. These characters force a regular expression to return a match only if the entire String being processed matches the regular expression.

- The {n} quantifier matches the pattern to its left exactly n times.

Section 24.5 Regex Member Functions Replace and Split

- Regex member function Replace replaces text in a String with new text wherever the original String matches a regular expression. By default, Replace replaces every instance of the pattern found in the String.

- By escaping a special regular expression character, we tell the regular-expression matching engine to find the actual character rather than use its special meaning.

- Regex member function Split divides a String into several substrings. The original String is broken at delimiters that match a specified regular expression. Member function Split returns an array containing the substrings.

Terminology

\d (digit)	character class subtraction
\w (word character)	escape sequence
\s (whitespace)	greedy quantifier
\D (non-digit)	lazy quantifier
\W (non-word character)	literal character
\S (non-whitespace)	Match class
$, end of String anchor	MatchCollection class
^, beginning of String anchor	Match member function of class Regex
+ quantifier	Matches member function of class Regex
* quantifier	metacharacter
{n} quantifier	page-layout software
|, alternation	pattern
character	quantifier, in regular expressions
character class, in regular expressions	Regex class for regular expressions

regular expression	`System::Text::RegularExpressions`
`Replace` member function of class `Regex`	namespace
special characters	text editor
`Split` member function of class `Regex`	trailing white-space characters
`Success` property of class `Match`	white-space character
`System` namespace	word character

Self-Review Exercises

24.1 State whether each of the following is *true* or *false*. If *false*, explain why.
   a) A regular expression matches a `String` to a pattern.
   b) The expression \d in a regular expression denotes all letters.

24.2 Fill in the blanks in each of the following statements:
   a) Class _____ represents a regular expression.
   b) `Regex` member function _____ changes all occurrences of a pattern in a `String` to a specified `String`.
   c) Class `Regex` is located in namespace _____.
   d) Regular expression quantifier _____ matches zero or more occurrences of an expression.
   e) Regular expression operator _____ inside square brackets will not match any of the characters in that set of brackets.

24.3 Write statements to accomplish each of the following tasks:
   a) Create a regular expression to match either a five-letter word or five-digit number.
   b) Create a regular expression to match a phone number in the form of (123) 456-7890.

Answers to Self-Review Exercises

24.1 a) True. b) False. The expression \d in a regular expression denotes all digits.

24.2 a) `Regex`. b) `Replace`. c) `System::Text::RegularExpressions`. d) *. e) ^.

24.3
   a) `Regex ^regex = gcnew Regex( "\\w{5}|\\d{5}" );`
   b) `Regex ^regex = gcnew Regex( "\\([1-9]\\d{2}\\)\\s[1-9]\\d{2}-\\d{4}" );`

Exercises

24.4 (*Pig Latin*) Write a program that encodes English language phrases into pig Latin. Pig Latin is a form of coded language often used for amusement. Many variations exist in the methods used to form pig Latin phrases. For simplicity, use the following algorithm:

   To translate each English word into a pig Latin word, place the first letter of the English word at the end of the word and add the letters "ay." Thus, the word "jump" becomes "umpjay," the word "the" becomes "hetay" and the word "computer" becomes "omputercay." Blanks between words remain blanks. Assume the following: The English phrase consists of words separated by blanks, there are no punctuation marks and all words have two or more letters. Have the user input a sentence. Use techniques discussed in this chapter to divide the sentence into separate words. Function `getPigLatin` should translate a single word into pig Latin.

24.5 Write a program that uses regular expressions to convert the first letter of all words to uppercase. Have it do this for an arbitrary string input by the user.

24.6 Use a regular expression to count the number of digits, characters and white-space characters in a string. [*Hint:* `Regex` function `Matches` returns an `IEnumerable`, which has a `Count` property.]

24.7   Write a regular expression that will search a string and match a valid number. A number can have any number of digits, but it can have only digits and a decimal point. The decimal point is optional, but if it appears in the number, there must be only one, and it must have digits on its left and its right. There should be whitespace or a beginning- or end-of-line character on either side of a valid number. Negative numbers are preceded by a minus sign.

24.8   Write a program that will take HTML as input and will output the number of HTML tags in the string. The program should use regular expressions to count the number of elements nested at each level. For example, the HTML:

```
<p><strong>hi</strong></p>
```

has a p element (nesting level 0—i.e., not nested in another tag) and a strong element (nesting level 1). For simplicity, use HTML in which none of the elements contain nested elements of the same type—for example, a table element should not contain another table element.

This solution requires a regular expression concept called a *back reference* to determine the start and end tags of an HTML element. To find these tags, the same word must appear in the start and end tags. A back reference allows you to use a previous match in the expression in another part of the regular expression. When you enclose a portion of a regular expression in parentheses, the match for that subexpression is stored for you. You can then access the result of that expression using the syntax *digit*, where *digit* is a number in the range 1–9. For example, the regular expression

```
^(7+).*\1$
```

matches an entire string that starts and ends with one or more 7s. The strings "777abcd777" and "7abcdef7" both match this regular expression. The \1 in the preceding regular expression is a back reference indicating that whatever matched the subexpression (7+) should also appear at the end of the string. The first parenthesized subexpression is back referenced with \1, the second is back referenced with \2, etc.

You'll need a recursive function so that you can process the nested HTML elements. In each recursive call, you'll need to pass the contents of an element as the string to be processed in that call—for example, the contents of the p element in this example's HTML would be

```
<strong>hi</strong>
```

Use parentheses to store the content that appears between the start and end tags of a string that matches your regular expression. This value is stored in the Groups property of the Match object and can be accessed using the [] operator on that property. As with back references, the subexpression matches are indexed from 1–9.

24.9   Write a program that asks the user to enter a sentence and uses a regular expression to check whether the sentence contains more than one space between words. If so, the program should remove the extra spaces. For example, "Hello   World" should be "Hello World".

25

Collections

OBJECTIVES

In this chapter you will learn:

- The nongeneric and generic collections that are provided by the .NET Framework.

- To use class **Array**'s **static** member functions to manipulate managed arrays.

- To use enumerators to "walk through" a collection.

- To use the **for each** statement with the .NET collections.

- To use nongeneric collection classes **ArrayList**, **Stack**, and **Hashtable**.

- To use generic collection classes **SortedDictionary** and **LinkedList**.

The shapes a bright container can contain!
—Theodore Roethke

Not by age but by capacity is wisdom acquired.
—Titus Maccius Plautus

It is a riddle wrapped in a mystery inside an enigma.
—Winston Churchill

I think this is the most extraordinary collection of talent, of human knowledge, that has ever been gathered together at the White House—with the possible exception of when Thomas Jefferson dined alone.
—John F. Kennedy

25.1 Introduction

In Chapter 21, we showed you how to build your own data structures. In Chapter 23, we discussed the reusable data structures in the Standard Template Library. In this chapter, we consider the prepackaged data-structure classes provided by the .NET Framework Class Library known as ***collection classes***. Each instance of one of these classes is a ***collection*** of items. Collections provide functionality similar to the STL. In the STL, the algorithms that operate on the data structures are implemented separately from the data structures themselves. In .NET, each collection class provides the implementations for the algorithms supported by that data structure. We discuss the collection interfaces that list the capabilities of each collection type, the classes that implement these interfaces and the ***enumerators*** (analogous to iterators) that "walk through" collections.

The .NET Framework provides three namespaces dedicated to collections. The `System::Collections` namespace contains collection classes that store references to `Objects`. The **`System::Collections::Generic`** namespace contains generic classes to store collections of specified types. The **`System::Collections::Specialized`** namespace contains collections that support specific types, such as `Strings` and bits. You can learn more about this namespace at `msdn2.microsoft.com/en-us/library/system.collections.specialized.aspx`. The collections in these namespaces provide standardized, reusable components; you do not need to write your own collection classes. These collections are written for broad reuse. They are tuned for rapid execution and efficient use of memory.

25.2 Collections Overview

All collection classes in the .NET Framework implement some combination of the collection interfaces. These interfaces declare the operations to be performed on various types of collections. Figure 25.1 lists some of these interfaces, all of which are declared in namespace `System::Collections` and have generic analogs in namespace `System::Collections::Generic`. Implementations of these interfaces are provided within the framework. You may also provide implementations specific to your own requirements.

Interface	Description
ICollection	The root interface in the collections hierarchy from which interfaces IList and IDictionary inherit. Contains a Count property to determine the size of a collection and a CopyTo member function for copying a collection's contents into a managed array.
IList	An ordered collection that can be manipulated like an array. Provides an indexer for accessing elements with an int index. Also has member functions for searching and modifying a collection, including Add, Remove, Contains and IndexOf.
IDictionary	A collection of values, indexed by an arbitrary "key" object. Provides an indexer for accessing elements with an Object index and member functions for modifying the collection (e.g. Add, Remove). IDictionary property Keys contains the Objects used as indices, and property Values contains all the stored Objects.
IEnumerable	An object that can be enumerated. This interface contains exactly one member function, GetEnumerator, which returns an IEnumerator object (discussed in Section 25.3). ICollection implements IEnumerable, so all collection classes implement IEnumerable directly or indirectly.

Fig. 25.1 | Some common collection interfaces.

In earlier versions, the .NET Framework provided the collection classes in the System::Collections. These classes store and manipulate Object references. You can store any Object in a collection. One inconvenient aspect of storing Object references occurs when retrieving them from a collection. An application normally needs to process *specific* types of objects. As a result, the Object references obtained from a collection typically need to be downcast to an appropriate type to allow the application to process the objects correctly.

The classes and interfaces of the System::Collections::Generic namespace use the generics capabilities we introduced in Chapter 15, Templates and Generics. Many of these are simply generic counterparts of the classes and interfaces in namespace System::Collections that enable you to specify the exact type that will be stored in a collection. You also receive the benefits of compile-time type checking—the compiler ensures that you are using appropriate types with your collection and, if not, issues compile-time error messages. This eliminates the need for explicit type casts that can throw InvalidCastExceptions at execution time if the referenced object is not of the appropriate type. It also eliminates the overhead of explicit casting, improving efficiency.

In this chapter, we demonstrate six collection classes—Array, ArrayList, Stack, Hashtable, generic SortedDictionary, and generic LinkedList—plus built-in array capabilities. Namespace System::Collections provides several other data structures, including *BitArray* (a collection of true/false values), Queue, and SortedList (a collection of key–value pairs that are sorted by key and can be accessed either by key or by index). Figure 25.2 summarizes many of the collection classes. We also discuss the IEnumerator interface. Collection classes can create enumerators for iterating over collection elements.

Although these enumerators have different implementations, they all implement the
IEnumerator interface so that they can be processed polymorphically. As we will soon see,
the for each statement is simply a convenient notation for using an enumerator. In the
next section, we begin our discussion by examining enumerators and the collections capabilities for array manipulation.

Class	Implements	Description
System namespace:		
Array	IList	The base class of all managed arrays. See Section 25.3.
System::Collections namespace:		
ArrayList	IList	Mimics conventional managed arrays, but will grow or shrink as needed to accommodate the number of elements. See Section 25.4.1.
BitArray	ICollection	A memory-efficient array of bools.
Hashtable	IDictionary	An unordered collection of key–value pairs that can be accessed by key. See Section 25.4.3.
Queue	ICollection	A first-in first-out collection. See Section 23.4.2.
SortedList	IDictionary	A Hashtable that sorts data by keys and can be accessed either by key or by index.
Stack	ICollection	A last-in, first-out collection. See Section 25.4.2.
System::Collections::Generic namespace:		
Dictionary< K, E >	IDictionary< K, E >	A generic, unordered collection of key–value pairs that can be accessed by key.
LinkedList< E >	ICollection< E >	A doubly linked list. See Section 25.5.2.
List< E >	IList< E >	A generic ArrayList.
Queue< E >	ICollection< E >	A generic Queue.
SortedDictionary < K, E >	IDictionary< K, E >	A Dictionary that sorts the data by the keys in a binary tree. See Section 25.5.1.
SortedList< K, E >	IDictionary< K, E >	A generic SortedList.
Stack< E >	ICollection< E >	A generic Stack.

[Note: *All collection classes directly or indirectly implement ICollection and IEnumerable (or the
equivalent generic interfaces ICollection< E > and IEnumerable< E > for generic collections).*]

Fig. 25.2 | Some collection classes of the .NET Framework.

25.3 Class Array and Enumerators

Chapter 8 presented basic array-processing capabilities. Managed arrays implicitly inherit from abstract class Array (namespace System), which defines property Length that specifies the number of elements in the array. In addition, class Array provides static member functions that implement algorithms for processing arrays. Typically, class Array overloads these member functions—for example, Array member function Reverse can reverse the order of the elements in an entire array or can reverse the elements in a specified range of elements in an array. For a complete list of class Array's static member functions visit:

> msdn2.microsoft.com/en-us/library/system.array.aspx

Figure 25.3 demonstrates several static member functions of class Array.

The using directive in line 6 includes the System::Collections namespace (for interface IEnumerator, which we discuss shortly). Our test program declares three managed array variables (lines 12–16). The first two lines initialize intValues and doubleValues as an int and double array, respectively. Line 16 initializes intValuesCopy to an int array with the same length as array intValues. Line 21 calls function printArray (lines 56–82) to output the initial contents of these arrays. We discuss this function shortly. Notice that each element of array intValuesCopy is initialized to 0 by default. Line 24 uses static Array member function **Sort** to sort array doubleValues into ascending order.

```
1   // Fig. 25.3: UsingArray.cpp
2   // Array class static member functions for common array manipulations.
3   #include "stdafx.h"
4
5   using namespace System;
6   using namespace System::Collections;
7
8   void printArrays( array< double >^, array< int >^, array< int >^ );
9
10  int main( array< System::String^ > ^args )
11  {
12      array< int > ^intValues = { 1, 2, 3, 4, 5, 6 };
13      array< double > ^doubleValues = { 8.4, 9.3, 0.2, 7.9, 3.4 };
14
15      // elements default to zero
16      array< int > ^intValuesCopy = gcnew array< int >( intValues->Length );
17
18      Console::WriteLine( "Initial array values:\n" );
19
20      // output initial array contents
21      printArrays( doubleValues, intValues, intValuesCopy );
22
23      // sort doubleValues
24      Array::Sort( doubleValues );
25
26      // copy intValues into intValuesCopy
27      Array::Copy( intValues, intValuesCopy, intValues->Length );
28
29      Console::WriteLine( "\nArray values after Sort and Copy:\n" );
```

Fig. 25.3 | Array class static member functions for common array manipulations. (Part 1 of 3.)

```
30
31      // output array contents
32      printArrays( doubleValues, intValues, intValuesCopy );
33      Console::WriteLine();
34
35      // search for 5 in intValues
36      int result = Array::BinarySearch( intValues, 5 );
37
38      if ( result >= 0 )
39         Console::WriteLine( "5 found at element {0} in intValues", result );
40      else
41         Console::WriteLine( "5 not found in intValues" );
42
43      // search for 8763 in intValues
44      result = Array::BinarySearch( intValues, 8763 );
45
46      if ( result >= 0 )
47         Console::WriteLine( "8763 found at element {0} in intValues",
48            result );
49      else
50         Console::WriteLine( "8763 not found in intValues" );
51
52      return 0;
53   } // end main
54
55   // output array contents using enumerators
56   void printArrays( array< double > ^doubleArray, array< int > ^intArray,
57      array< int > ^intArrayCopy )
58   {
59      Console::Write( "doubleValues: " );
60
61      // iterate through the double array with an enumerator
62      IEnumerator ^enumerator = doubleArray->GetEnumerator();
63
64      while ( enumerator->MoveNext() )
65         Console::Write( enumerator->Current + " " );
66
67      Console::Write( "\nintValues: " );
68
69      // iterate through the int array with an enumerator
70      enumerator = intArray->GetEnumerator();
71
72      while ( enumerator->MoveNext() )
73         Console::Write( enumerator->Current + " " );
74
75      Console::Write( "\nintValuesCopy: " );
76
77      // iterate through the second int array with a for each statement
78      for each ( int element in intArrayCopy )
79         Console::Write( element + " " );
80
81      Console::WriteLine();
82   } // end function printArrays
```

Fig. 25.3 | Array class static member functions for common array manipulations. (Part 2 of 3.)

```
Initial array values:

doubleValues: 8.4 9.3 0.2 7.9 3.4
intValues: 1 2 3 4 5 6
intValuesCopy: 0 0 0 0 0 0

Array values after Sort and Copy:

doubleValues: 0.2 3.4 7.9 8.4 9.3
intValues: 1 2 3 4 5 6
intValuesCopy: 1 2 3 4 5 6

5 found at element 4 in intValues
8763 not found in intValues
```

Fig. 25.3 | Array class `static` member functions for common array manipulations. (Part 3 of 3.)

Line 27 uses `static` Array member function ***Copy*** to copy elements from array `intValues` to array `intValuesCopy`. The first argument is the array to copy (`intValues`), the second argument is the destination array (`intValuesCopy`) and the third argument is an `int` representing the number of elements to copy (in this case, `intValues->Length` specifies all elements).

Lines 36 and 44 invoke `static` Array member function ***BinarySearch*** to perform binary searches on array `intValues`. Member function `BinarySearch` receives the *sorted* array in which to search and the key for which to search. The function returns the index in the array at which it finds the key (or a negative number if the key was not found). `BinarySearch` assumes that it receives a sorted array. Chapter 20 discussed binary searching in detail.

Common Programming Error 25.1

Passing an unsorted array to BinarySearch is a logic error—the value returned is undefined.

The `printArrays` function uses class Array's member functions to output the contents of each array. In line 62, the GetEnumerator member function obtains an enumerator for array doubleValues. Recall that class Array implements the ***IEnumerable*** interface. All managed arrays implicitly inherit from Array, so both the array< int > and array< double > array types implement the IEnumerable interface member function ***GetEnumerator***, which returns an enumerator that can iterate over the collection. Interface ***IEnumerator*** (which all enumerators implement) defines member functions MoveNext and Reset and property Current. ***MoveNext*** moves the enumerator to the next element in the collection. The first call to MoveNext positions the enumerator at the first element of the collection. MoveNext returns true if there is at least one more element in the collection; otherwise, the member function returns false. Member function ***Reset*** positions the enumerator *before* the first element of the collection. Member functions MoveNext and Reset throw an ***InvalidOperationException*** if the contents of the collection are modified in any way after the enumerator is created. Property ***Current*** returns the object at the current location in the collection.

Common Programming Error 25.2

If a collection is modified after an enumerator is created for that collection, the enumerator immediately becomes invalid—any member functions called with the enumerator after this point throw InvalidOperationExceptions. For this reason, enumerators are said to be "fail fast."

When an enumerator is returned by the GetEnumerator member function in line 62, it is initially positioned *before* the first element in Array doubleValues. When line 64 calls MoveNext, the enumerator advances to the first element in doubleValues. The while statement in lines 64–65 iterates over each element until MoveNext returns false to indicate that the end of the array has been reached. In each iteration, we use the enumerator's Current property to obtain and output the current array element. Lines 70–73 perform the same operations for array intValues.

Notice that printArrays is called twice (lines 21 and 32), so GetEnumerator is called twice on doubleValues. The GetEnumerator member function (lines 62 and 70) always returns an enumerator positioned before the first element. Also note that the IEnumerator property Current is read-only. Enumerators cannot be used to modify the contents of collections.

Lines 78–79 use a for each statement to iterate over the collection's elements like an enumerator. In fact, the for each statement uses an enumerator. The for each statement implicitly obtains an enumerator via the GetEnumerator member function and uses the enumerator's MoveNext member function and Current property to traverse the collection, just as we did explicitly in lines 62–65. For this reason, we can use the for each statement to iterate over *any* collection that implements the IEnumerable interface—not just arrays. We demonstrate this functionality in the next section when we discuss class ArrayList. [*Note:* In C++/CLI, if the control variable in the for each statement is a tracking reference to a handle, you can modify the elements of a managed array (but not other types of collections). You cannot add or remove elements. See Section 9.16, Tracking References and References to Handles.]

Other static Array member functions include ***Clear*** (to set a range of elements to 0 or nullptr), ***CreateInstance*** (to create a new array of a specified type), ***IndexOf*** (to locate the first occurrence of an object in an array or portion of an array), ***LastIndexOf*** (to locate the last occurrence of an object in an array or portion of an array) and ***Reverse*** (to reverse the contents of an array or portion of an array).

25.4 Nongeneric Collections

The System::Collections namespace in the .NET Framework is the primary source for nongeneric collections. These classes provide standard implementations of many of the data structures discussed in Chapter 21 with collections that store references of type Object. In this section, we demonstrate classes ArrayList, Stack and Hashtable.

25.4.1 Class ArrayList

In most programming languages, conventional arrays have a fixed size—they cannot be changed dynamically to conform to an application's execution-time memory requirements. In some applications, this fixed-size limitation presents a problem for programmers. They must choose between using fixed-size arrays that are large enough to store the maximum number of elements the application may require and using dynamic data structures that can grow and shrink the amount of memory used to store data in response to an application's changing requirements at execution time.

The .NET Framework's *ArrayList* collection class mimics the functionality of managed arrays and provides dynamic resizing of the collection through the class's member functions much like the STL's std::vector (discussed in Chapter 8). At any time, an ArrayList contains a number of elements less than or equal to its *capacity*—the number of elements currently reserved for the ArrayList. An application can manipulate the capacity with ArrayList property Capacity. If an ArrayList needs to grow, it doubles its Capacity by default.

Performance Tip 25.1

It is a slow operation to insert an element into an ArrayList that needs to grow larger to accommodate a new element. An ArrayList that is at its capacity must have its memory reallocated and the existing values copied into the new memory.

Performance Tip 25.2

If storage is at a premium, use member function TrimToSize of class ArrayList to trim an ArrayList to its exact size. This will optimize an ArrayList's memory use. Be careful—if the application needs to insert additional elements, the process will be slower because the ArrayList must grow dynamically (trimming leaves no room for growth).

Performance Tip 25.3

The default capacity increment (doubling the size of the ArrayList) may seem to waste storage, but doubling is an efficient way for an ArrayList to grow quickly to "about the right size."

ArrayLists store references to Objects. All managed classes derive from class Object, so an ArrayList can contain objects of any managed type. Figure 25.4 lists some useful member functions and properties of class ArrayList.

Member function or property	Description
Add	Adds an Object to the ArrayList and returns an int specifying the index at which the Object was added.
Capacity	Property that gets and sets the number of elements for which space is currently reserved in the ArrayList.
Clear	Removes all the elements from the ArrayList.
Contains	Returns true if the specified Object is in the ArrayList; otherwise, returns false.
Count	Read-only property that gets the number of elements stored in the ArrayList.

Fig. 25.4 | Some member functions and properties of class ArrayList. (Part 1 of 2.)

Member function or property	Description
IndexOf	Returns the index of the first occurrence of the specified Object in the ArrayList.
Insert	Inserts an Object at the specified index.
Remove	Removes the first occurrence of the specified Object.
RemoveAt	Removes the Object at the specified index.
RemoveRange	Removes a specified number of elements starting at a specified index in the ArrayList.
Sort	Sorts the ArrayList.
TrimToSize	Sets the Capacity of the ArrayList to the number of elements the ArrayList currently contains (Count).

Fig. 25.4 | Some member functions and properties of class ArrayList. (Part 2 of 2.)

Figure 25.5 demonstrates class ArrayList and several of its member functions. Class ArrayList belongs to the System::Collections namespace (line 6). Lines 13–15 declare two managed arrays of String^ (colors and colorsToRemove) that we use to fill two ArrayList objects. We create an ArrayList with an initial capacity of one element and assign it to variable list (line 17). Note that we create the ArrayList by using gcnew to dynamically allocate memory. Recall from Chapters 11 and 16 that using stack semantics to declare objects ensures the class destructor is invoked as soon as the object goes out of scope. Rather than the declaration at line 17 we could have used stack semantics as follows:

```
ArrayList list(1);
```

Remember that if we use this style of declaration we must access data members and member functions of list via the . operator and not the -> operator. In the examples throughout this chapter we create objects using gcnew but we could just as easily use stack semantics with any of the .NET collection classes. The for each statement in lines 20–21 adds the five elements of array colors to list via ArrayList's **Add** member function, so list grows to accommodate these new elements. Line 25 uses ArrayList's overloaded constructor to create a new ArrayList initialized with the contents of array colorsToRemove, then assigns it to variable removeList. This constructor can initialize the contents of an ArrayList with the elements of any ICollection passed to it. Many of the collection classes have such a constructor. The constructor call in line 25 performs the same basic task of lines 20–21.

```
1    // Fig. 25.5: ArrayListTest.cpp
2    // Using class ArrayList.
3    #include "stdafx.h"
4
```

Fig. 25.5 | Using class ArrayList. (Part 1 of 3.)

```
 5   using namespace System;
 6   using namespace System::Collections;
 7
 8   void displayInformation( ArrayList^ ); // function prototype
 9   void removeColors( ArrayList^, ArrayList^ ); // function prototype
10
11   int main( array< System::String^ > ^args )
12   {
13      array< String^ > ^colors =
14         { "MAGENTA", "RED", "WHITE", "BLUE", "CYAN" };
15      array< String^ > ^colorsToRemove = { "RED", "WHITE", "BLUE" };
16
17      ArrayList ^list = gcnew ArrayList( 1 ); // initial capacity of 1
18
19      // add the elements of the colors array to the ArrayList list
20      for each ( String^ color in colors )
21         list->Add( color ); // add color to the ArrayList list
22
23      // add elements in the colorsToRemove array to the
24      // ArrayList removeList with the ArrayList constructor
25      ArrayList ^removeList = gcnew ArrayList( colorsToRemove );
26
27      Console::WriteLine( "ArrayList: " );
28      displayInformation( list ); // output the list
29
30      // remove from ArrayList list the colors in removeList
31      removeColors( list, removeList );
32
33      Console::WriteLine( "\nArrayList after calling removeColors: " );
34      displayInformation( list );
35
36      return 0;
37   } // end main
38
39   // displays information on the contents of an ArrayList
40   void displayInformation( ArrayList ^arrayList )
41   {
42      // iterate through ArrayList with a for each statement
43      for each ( Object ^element in arrayList )
44         Console::Write( "{0} ", element ); // invokes ToString
45
46      // display the size and capacity
47      Console::WriteLine( "\nSize = {0}; Capacity = {1}",
48         arrayList->Count, arrayList->Capacity );
49
50      int index = arrayList->IndexOf( "BLUE" );
51
52      if ( index != -1 )
53         Console::WriteLine( "The array list contains BLUE at index {0}.",
54            index );
55      else
56         Console::WriteLine( "The array list does not contain BLUE." );
57   } // end function displayInformation
```

Fig. 25.5 | Using class ArrayList. (Part 2 of 3.)

```
58
59    // remove colors specified in secondList from firstList
60    void removeColors( ArrayList ^firstList, ArrayList ^secondList )
61    {
62       // iterate through second ArrayList like an array
63       for ( int count = 0; count < secondList->Count; count++ )
64          firstList->Remove( secondList[ count ] );
65    } // end function removeColors
```

```
ArrayList:
MAGENTA RED WHITE BLUE CYAN
Size = 5; Capacity = 8
The array list contains BLUE at index 3.

ArrayList after calling removeColors:
MAGENTA CYAN
Size = 2; Capacity = 8
The array list does not contain BLUE.
```

Fig. 25.5 | Using class ArrayList. (Part 3 of 3.)

Line 28 calls function displayInformation (lines 40–57) to output the contents of the list. This function uses a for each statement to traverse the elements of an Array-List. As we discussed in Section 25.3, the for each statement is a convenient shorthand for calling ArrayList's GetEnumerator member function and using an enumerator to traverse the elements of the collection. Also, we must use a control variable of type Object^ because class ArrayList is nongeneric and stores references to Objects.

We use the **Count** and **Capacity** properties in line 48 to display the current number of elements and the maximum number of elements that can be stored without allocating more memory to the ArrayList. The output of Fig. 25.5 indicates that the ArrayList has capacity 8—recall that an ArrayList doubles its capacity whenever it needs more space.

Line 50 invokes member function **IndexOf** to determine the position of the String "BLUE" in arrayList and store the result in local variable index. IndexOf returns -1 if the element is not found. If arrayList contains "BLUE", lines 53–54 output its index. Array-List also provides member function **Contains**, which simply returns true if an object is in the ArrayList, and false otherwise. Member function Contains is preferred if we do not need the index of the element.

Performance Tip 25.4

ArrayList member functions IndexOf and Contains each perform a linear search, which is a costly operation for large ArrayLists. If the ArrayList is sorted, use ArrayList member function BinarySearch to perform a more efficient search. Member function BinarySearch returns the index of the element, or a negative number if the element is not found.

After function displayInformation returns, we call function removeColors (lines 60–65) with the two ArrayLists. Lines 63–64 iterate over ArrayList secondList. Line 64 uses an indexer to access an ArrayList element—by following the ArrayList reference name with square brackets ([]) containing the desired index of the element. An ArgumentOutOfRangeException occurs if the specified index is not greater than or equal to 0 and less than the number of elements currently stored in the ArrayList (specified by the ArrayList's Count property).

We use the indexer to obtain each of secondList's elements, then remove each one from firstList with the *Remove* member function. This member function deletes a specified item from an ArrayList by performing a linear search and removing the first occurrence of the specified object. All subsequent elements shift toward the beginning of the ArrayList to fill the emptied position. After the call to removeColors, line 34 again outputs the contents of list, confirming that the elements of removeList were, indeed, removed from list.

25.4.2 Class Stack

The Stack class implements a stack data structure and provides much of the functionality that we defined in our own implementation in Section 21.5. Refer to that section for a discussion of stack data-structure concepts. We created a test application in Fig. 21.14 to demonstrate the Stack data structure that we developed. In Fig. 25.6 we adapt Fig. 21.14 to demonstrate the .NET Framework collection class Stack.

The using directive in line 6 allows us to use the Stack class with its unqualified name from the System::Collections namespace. Line 12 creates a Stack with the default initial capacity (10 elements). As one might expect, class Stack has member functions Push and Pop to perform the basic stack operations.

Member function Push takes an Object as an argument and inserts it at the top of the Stack. If the number of items on the Stack (the Count property) is equal to the capacity at the time of the Push operation, the Stack grows to accommodate more Objects. Lines 21–28 use member function Push to add four elements (a bool, a Char, an int and a String^) to the stack and invoke function printStack (lines 54–68) after each Push to output the contents of the stack. We used the CLI value type Char rather than the native char for output purposes. Notice that this nongeneric Stack class can store only references to Objects, so each of the value-type items—the bool, the Char and the int—is implicitly boxed before it is added to the Stack. (Namespace System::Collections:: Generic provides a generic Stack class that has many of the same member functions and properties used in Fig. 25.6.)

```
1   // Fig. 25.6: StackTest.cpp
2   // Demonstrating class Stack.
3   #include "stdafx.h"
4
5   using namespace System;
6   using namespace System::Collections;
7
8   void printStack( Stack^ ); // function prototype
9
10  int main( array< System::String^ > ^args )
11  {
12      Stack ^stack = gcnew Stack(); // default capacity of 10
13
```

Fig. 25.6 | Demonstrating class Stack. (Part 1 of 3.)

```
14      // create objects to store in the stack
15      bool aBoolean = true;
16      Char aCharacter = '$';
17      int anInteger = 34567;
18      String ^aString = "hello";
19
20      // use member function Push to add items to (the top of) the stack
21      stack->Push( aBoolean );
22      printStack( stack );
23      stack->Push( aCharacter );
24      printStack( stack );
25      stack->Push( anInteger );
26      printStack( stack );
27      stack->Push( aString );
28      printStack( stack );
29
30      // check the top element of the stack
31      Console::WriteLine( "The top element of the stack is {0}\n",
32         stack->Peek() );
33
34      // remove items from stack
35      try
36      {
37         while ( true )
38         {
39            Object ^removedObject = stack->Pop();
40            Console::WriteLine( removedObject + " popped" );
41            printStack( stack );
42         } // end while
43      } // end try
44      catch ( InvalidOperationException ^exception )
45      {
46         // if exception occurs, print stack trace
47         Console::WriteLine( exception );
48      } // end catch
49
50      return 0;
51   } // end main
52
53   // print the contents of a stack
54   void printStack( Stack ^stack )
55   {
56      if ( stack->Count == 0 )
57         Console::WriteLine( "stack is empty\n" ); // the stack is empty
58      else
59      {
60         Console::Write( "The stack is: " );
61
62         // iterate through the stack with a for each statement
63         for each ( Object ^element in stack )
64            Console::Write( "{0} ", element ); // invokes ToString
65
```

Fig. 25.6 | Demonstrating class Stack. (Part 2 of 3.)

```
66          Console::WriteLine( "\n" );
67      } // end else
68   } // end function printStack
```

```
The stack is: True

The stack is: $ True

The stack is: 34567 $ True

The stack is: hello 34567 $ True

The top element of the stack is hello

hello popped
The stack is: 34567 $ True

34567 popped
The stack is: $ True

$ popped
The stack is: True

True popped
stack is empty

System.InvalidOperationException: Stack empty.
   at System.Collections.Stack.Pop()
   at main(String[] args) in c:\examples\ch26\fig26_06\stacktest\stack
test.cpp:line 39
```

Fig. 25.6 | Demonstrating class Stack. (Part 3 of 3.)

Function printStack uses Stack property Count to obtain the number of elements in stack. If the stack is not empty (i.e., Count is not equal to 0), we use a for each statement to iterate over the stack and output its contents by implicitly invoking the ToString member function of each element.

Member function **Peek** returns the value of the top stack element, but does not remove the element from the Stack. We use Peek at line 32 to obtain the top object of the Stack, then output that object, implicitly invoking the object's ToString member function. An InvalidOperationException occurs if the Stack is empty when the application calls Peek. (We do not need an exception-handling block because we know the stack is not empty here.)

Member function Pop takes no arguments—it removes and returns the object currently on top of the Stack. An infinite loop (lines 37–42) pops objects off the stack and outputs them until the stack is empty. When the application calls Pop on the empty stack, an InvalidOperationException is thrown. The catch block (lines 44–48) outputs the exception, implicitly invoking the InvalidOperationException's ToString member function to obtain its error message and stack trace.

Common Programming Error 25.3

Attempting to Peek or Pop an empty Stack (a Stack whose Count property is 0) causes an InvalidOperationException.

Although Fig. 25.6 does not demonstrate it, class Stack also has member function Contains, which returns true if the Stack contains the specified object, and returns false otherwise.

25.4.3 Class Hashtable

When an application creates objects of new or existing types, it needs to manage those objects efficiently. This includes sorting and retrieving objects. Sorting and retrieving information with arrays is efficient if some aspect of your data directly matches the key value and if those keys are unique and tightly packed. If you have 100 employees with nine-digit social security numbers and you want to store and retrieve employee data by using the social security number as a key, it would nominally require an array with 999,999,999 elements, because there are 999,999,999 unique nine-digit numbers. If you have an array that large, you could get very high performance storing and retrieving employee records by simply using the social security number as the array index, but it would be a large waste of memory. Many applications have this problem—either the keys are of the wrong type (i.e., not positive integers), or they are of the right type, but they are sparsely spread over a large range.

What is needed is a high-speed scheme for converting keys such as social security numbers and inventory part numbers to unique array indices. Then, when an application needs to store something, the scheme could convert the application key rapidly to an index, and the record of information could be stored at that location in the array. Retrieval occurs the same way—once the application has a key for which it wants to retrieve the data record, the application simply applies the conversion to the key, which produces the array subscript where the data resides in the array and retrieves the data.

The scheme we describe here is the basis of a technique called *hashing*, in which we store data in a data structure called a *hash table*. Why the name? Because, when we convert a key into an array subscript, we literally scramble the bits, making a "hash" of the number. The number actually has no real significance beyond its usefulness in storing and retrieving this particular data record.

A glitch in the scheme becomes apparent when *collisions* occur (i.e., two different keys "hash into" the same cell, or element, in the array). Since we cannot store two different data records to the same space, we need to find an alternative home for all records beyond the first that hash to a particular array subscript. One scheme for doing this is to "hash again" (i.e., to reapply the hashing transformation to the key to provide a next candidate cell in the array). The hashing process is designed to be random, so the assumption is that with just a few hashes, an available cell will be found.

Another scheme uses one hash to locate the first candidate cell. If the cell is occupied, successive cells are searched linearly until an available cell is found. Retrieval works the same way—the key is hashed once, the resulting cell is checked to determine whether it contains the desired data. If it does, the search is complete. If it does not, successive cells are searched linearly until the desired data is found.

The most popular solution to hash-table collisions is to have each cell of the table be a hash "bucket"—typically, a linked list of all the key–value pairs that hash to that cell. This is the solution that the .NET Framework's *Hashtable* class implements.

The *load factor* affects the performance of hashing schemes. The load factor is the ratio of the number of objects stored in the hash table to the total number of cells in the hash table. As this ratio gets higher, the chance of collisions tends to increase.

Performance Tip 25.5

*The load factor in a hash table is a classic example of a **space/time trade-off**. By increasing the load factor, we get better memory utilization, but the application runs slower due to increased hashing collisions. By decreasing the load factor, we get better application speed because of reduced hashing collisions, but we get poorer memory utilization because a larger portion of the hash table remains empty.*

Computer science students study hashing schemes in courses called "Data Structures" and "Algorithms." Recognizing the value of hashing, the .NET Framework provides class Hashtable to enable programmers to easily employ hashing in applications.

This concept is profoundly important in our study of object-oriented programming. Classes encapsulate and hide complexity (i.e., implementation details) and offer user-friendly interfaces. Crafting classes to do this properly is one of the most valued skills in the field of object-oriented programming.

A *hash function* performs a calculation that determines where to place data in the hash table. The hash function is applied to the key in a key–value pair of objects. Class Hashtable can accept any Object as a key. For this reason, class Object defines member function GetHashCode, which all objects inherit. Most classes that are candidates to be used as keys in a hash table override this member function to provide one that performs efficient hash-code calculations for a specific type. For example, a String has a hash-code calculation that is based on the contents of the String. Figure 25.7 uses a Hashtable to count the number of occurrences of each word in a String.

Lines 6–8 contain using directives for namespaces System (for classes Console and String), System::Collections (for class Hashtable) and System::Text::RegularExpressions (for class Regex, discussed in Chapter 25). Figure 25.7 declares three functions. Function collectWords (lines 25–49) takes a String as input from the user and returns a Hashtable in which each value stores the number of times that word appears in the String and the word is used for the key. Function displayHashtable (lines 52–63) displays the Hashtable passed to it in column format. The main function (lines 13–22) simply invokes collectWords (line 16), then passes the Hashtable returned by collectWords to displayHashtable (line 19).

```
1   // Fig. 25.7: HashtableTest.cpp
2   // Application counts the number of occurrences of each word in a string
3   // and stores them in a hash table.
4   #include "stdafx.h"
5
6   using namespace System;
7   using namespace System::Collections;
8   using namespace System::Text::RegularExpressions;
9
10  Hashtable^ collectWords(); // function prototype
11  void displayHashtable( Hashtable^ ); // function prototype
12
13  int main( array< System::String^ > ^args )
14  {
```

Fig. 25.7 | Application counts the number of occurrences of each word in a String and stores them in a hash table. (Part 1 of 3.)

```cpp
15       // create hash table based on user input
16       Hashtable ^table = collectWords();
17
18       // display hash table content
19       displayHashtable( table );
20
21       return 0;
22    } // end main
23
24    // create hash table from user input
25    Hashtable^ collectWords()
26    {
27       Hashtable ^table = gcnew Hashtable(); // create a new hash table
28
29       Console::WriteLine( "Enter a string: " );
30       String ^input = Console::ReadLine(); // get input
31
32       // split input text into tokens
33       array< String^ > ^words = Regex::Split( input, "\\s+" );
34
35       // processing input words
36       for each ( String ^word in words )
37       {
38          String ^wordKey = word->ToLower(); // get word in lowercase
39
40          // if the hash table contains the word
41          if ( table->ContainsKey( wordKey ) )
42             table[ wordKey ] = static_cast< int >( table[ wordKey ] ) + 1;
43          else
44             // add new word with a count of 1 to the hash table
45             table->Add( wordKey, 1 );
46       } // end for each
47
48       return table;
49    } // end function collectWords
50
51    // display hash table content
52    void displayHashtable( Hashtable ^table )
53    {
54       Console::WriteLine( "\nHashtable contains:\n{0,-12}{1,-12}",
55          "Key:", "Value:" );
56
57       // generate output for each key in hash table by iterating through
58       // the Keys property with a for each statement
59       for each ( Object ^key in table->Keys )
60          Console::WriteLine( "{0,-12}{1,-12}", key, table[ key ] );
61
62       Console::WriteLine( "\nsize: {0}", table->Count );
63    } // end function displayHashtable
```

Fig. 25.7 | Application counts the number of occurrences of each word in a `String` and stores them in a hash table. (Part 2 of 3.)

```
Enter a string:
To be or not to be: that is the question Whether 'tis nobler to suffer

Hashtable contains:
Key:          Value:
that          1
nobler        1
or            1
not           1
is            1
be:           1
suffer        1
whether       1
question      1
be            1
to            3
'tis          1
the           1

size: 13
```

Fig. 25.7 | Application counts the number of occurrences of each word in a `String` and stores them in a hash table. (Part 3 of 3.)

Function `collectWords` begins by initializing local variable `table` with a new `Hashtable` (line 27) that has a default initial capacity of 0 elements and a default maximum load factor of 1.0. When the number of items in the `Hashtable` becomes greater than the number of cells times the load factor, the capacity is increased automatically. (This implementation detail is invisible to clients of the class.) Lines 29–30 prompt the user for input and store it in a `String`. We use `static` member function `Split` of class `Regex` in line 33 to break the `String` into tokens that are separated by white-space characters. This creates an array of "words," which we then store in local array variable `words`.

Lines 36–46 iterate over the elements of array `words`. Each word is converted to lowercase with `String` member function ***ToLower***, then stored in variable `wordKey` (line 38). Then line 41 calls `Hashtable` member function ***ContainsKey*** to determine whether the word is in the hash table (and thus has occurred previously in the `String`). If the `Hashtable` does not contain an entry for the word, line 45 uses `Hashtable` member function `Add` to create a new entry in the hash table, with the lowercase word as the key and an object containing 1 as the value. Note that implicit boxing occurs when the application passes integer 1 to member function `Add`, because the hash table stores both the key and value as `Object` references.

Common Programming Error 25.4

Using the `Add` member function to add a key that already exists in the hash table causes an `ArgumentException`.

If the word is already a key in the hash table, line 42 uses the `Hashtable`'s indexer to obtain and set the key's associated value (the word count) in the hash table. We first downcast the value obtained by the `get` accessor from an `Object` to an `int`. This unboxes the value so that we can increment it by 1. Then, when we use the indexer's `set` accessor to assign the key's associated value, the incremented value is implicitly reboxed so that it can be stored in the hash table.

Notice that invoking the get accessor of a Hashtable indexer with a key that does not exist in the hash table obtains a nullptr reference. Using the set accessor with a key that does not exist in the hash table creates a new entry, as if you had used the Add member function.

Line 48 returns the hash table to the main function, which then passes it to function displayHashtable (lines 52–63), which displays all the entries. This function uses read-only property **Keys** (line 59) to get an ICollection that contains all the keys. Because ICollection extends IEnumerable, we can use this collection in the for each statement in lines 59–60 to iterate over the keys of the hash table. This loop accesses and outputs each key and its value in the hash table using the iteration variable and table's get accessor. Each key together with its value is displayed in a field width of -12. The negative field width indicates that the output is left justified. Note that a hash table is not sorted, so the key–value pairs are not displayed in any particular order. Line 62 uses Hashtable property **Count** to get the number of key–value pairs in the Hashtable.

Lines 59–60 could have also used the for each statement with the Hashtable object itself, instead of using the Keys property. If you use a for each statement with a Hashtable object, the iteration variable will be of type **DictionaryEntry**. The enumerator of a Hashtable (or any other class that implements **IDictionary**) uses the DictionaryEntry structure to store key–value pairs. This structure provides properties Key and Value for retrieving the key and value of the current element. If you do not need the key, class Hashtable also provides a read-only **Values** property that gets an ICollection of all the values stored in the Hashtable.

Problems with Nongeneric Collections

In the word-counting application of Fig. 25.7, our Hashtable stores its keys and data as Object references, even though we store only String^ keys and int values by convention. This results in some awkward code. For example, in line 42 we were forced to unbox and box the int data stored in the Hashtable every time it incremented the count for a particular key. This is inefficient. A similar problem occurs in line 59—the iteration variable of the for each statement is an Object reference. If we need to use any of its String-specific member functions, we need an explicit downcast.

This can cause subtle bugs. Suppose we decide to improve the readability of Fig. 25.7 by using the indexer's set accessor instead of the Add member function to add a key–value pair in line 45, but accidentally type:

```
table[ wordKey ] = wordKey; // initialize to 1
```

This statement will create a new entry with a String^ key and String^ value instead of an int value of 1. Although the application will compile correctly, this is clearly incorrect. If a word appears twice, line 42 will try to downcast this String^ to an int, causing an InvalidCastException at execution time. The error that appears at execution time will indicate that the problem is at line 42, where the exception occurred, *not* at line 45. This makes the error more difficult to find and debug, especially in large software applications where the exception may occur in a different file—and even in a different assembly. In Chapter 15, we introduced generics, which help eliminate the problem described here. The next two sections demonstrate how to use generic collections.

25.5 Generic Collections

The System::Collections::Generic namespace in the FCL contains generic classes that allow us to create collections of specific types. As you saw in Fig. 25.2, many of the classes are simply generic versions of non-generic collections. A few classes implement new data structures. In this section, we demonstrate generic collections SortedDictionary and LinkedList.

25.5.1 Generic Class SortedDictionary

A *dictionary* is the general term for a collection of key–value pairs. A hash table is one way to implement a dictionary. The .NET Framework provides several implementations of dictionaries, both generic and non-generic (all of which implement the IDictionary interface in Fig. 25.1). The application in Fig. 25.8 is a modification of Fig. 25.7 that uses the generic class **SortedDictionary**. Generic class SortedDictionary does not use a hash table, but instead stores its key–value pairs in a binary search tree. (We discuss binary trees in depth in Section 21.7.) As the class name suggests, the entries in a SortedDictionary are sorted in the tree by key. When the key implements generic interface IComparable, the SortedDictionary uses the results of IComparable member function CompareTo to sort the keys. Notice that despite these implementation details, we use the same public member functions, properties and indexers with classes Hashtable and SortedDictionary in the same ways. In fact, except for the generic-specific syntax, Fig. 25.8 looks remarkably similar to Fig. 25.7. This is the beauty of object-oriented programming.

Line 7 contains a using directive for the System::Collections::Generic namespace, which contains class SortedDictionary. The generic class SortedDictionary takes two type arguments—the first specifies the type of key (i.e., String^), and the second specifies the type of value (i.e., int). We have simply replaced the word Hashtable in line 18 and lines 30–31 with SortedDictionary< String^, int > to create a dictionary of key-value pairs consisting of String references and int values. Now, the compiler can check and notify us if we attempt to store an object of the wrong type in the dictionary. Also, because the compiler now knows that the data structure contains int values, there is no longer any need to use a downcast in line 46. This allows line 46 to use the more concise prefix increment (++) notation. These are the only changes made to functions main and collectWords.

```
1    // Fig. 25.8 SortedDictionaryTest.cpp
2    // Application counts the number of occurrences of each word in a string
3    // and stores them in a generic sorted dictionary.
4    #include "stdafx.h"
5
6    using namespace System;
7    using namespace System::Collections::Generic;
8    using namespace System::Text::RegularExpressions;
9
10   SortedDictionary< String^, int >^ collectWords(); // function prototype
11
```

Fig. 25.8 | Application counts the number of occurrences of each word in a String and stores them in a generic sorted dictionary. (Part 1 of 3.)

```
12    generic< typename K, typename V >
13    void displayDictionary( SortedDictionary< K, V >^ ); // function prototype
14
15    int main( array< System::String^ > ^args )
16    {
17       // create sorted dictionary based on user input
18       SortedDictionary< String^, int > ^dictionary = collectWords();
19
20       // display sorted dictionary content
21       displayDictionary( dictionary );
22
23       return 0;
24    } // end main
25
26    // create sorted dictionary from user input
27    SortedDictionary< String^, int >^ collectWords()
28    {
29       // create a new sorted dictionary
30       SortedDictionary< String^, int > ^dictionary =
31          gcnew SortedDictionary< String^, int >();
32
33       Console::WriteLine( "Enter a string: " ); // prompt user for input
34       String ^input = Console::ReadLine(); // get input
35
36       // split input text into tokens
37       array< String^ > ^words = Regex::Split( input, "\\s+" );
38
39       // processing input words
40       for each ( String ^word in words )
41       {
42          String ^wordKey = word->ToLower(); // get word in lowercase
43
44          // if the sorted dictionary contains the word
45          if ( dictionary->ContainsKey( wordKey ) )
46             ++dictionary[ wordKey ];
47          else
48             // add new word with a count of 1 to the sorted dictionary
49             dictionary->Add( wordKey, 1 );
50       } // end for each
51
52       return dictionary;
53    } // end function collectWords
54
55    // display sorted dictionary content
56    generic< typename K, typename V >
57    void displayDictionary( SortedDictionary< K, V > ^dictionary )
58    {
59       Console::WriteLine( "\nSorted dictionary contains:\n{0,-12}{1,-12}",
60          "Key:", "Value:" );
61
```

Fig. 25.8 | Application counts the number of occurrences of each word in a `String` and stores them in a generic sorted dictionary. (Part 2 of 3.)

```
62        // generate output for each key in the sorted dictionary by iterating
63        // through the Keys property with a for each statement
64        for each ( K key in dictionary->Keys )
65           Console::WriteLine( "{0,-12}{1,-12}", key, dictionary[ key ] );
66
67        Console::WriteLine( "\nsize: {0}", dictionary->Count );
68     } // end function displayDictionary
```

```
Enter a string:
To be or not to be: that is the question Whether 'tis nobler to suffer

Sorted dictionary contains:
Key:         Value:
be           1
be:          1
is           1
nobler       1
not          1
or           1
question     1
suffer       1
that         1
the          1
'tis         1
to           3
whether      1

size: 13
```

Fig. 25.8 | Application counts the number of occurrences of each word in a `String` and stores them in a generic sorted dictionary. (Part 3 of 3.)

Function `displayDictionary` (lines 56–68) is now a generic function with type parameters K and V. These parameters are used in line 57 to indicate that `display-Dictionary` takes a `SortedDictionary` with keys of type K and values of type V. We use type parameter K again in line 64 as the type of the control variable. This use of generics is a marvelous example of code reuse. If we decide to change the application to count the number of times each character appears in a string, function `displayDictionary` could receive an argument of type `SortedDictionary< Char, int >` without modification. This is precisely what you will do in Exercise 25.12.

Performance Tip 25.6

Because class `SortedDictionary` keeps its elements sorted in a binary tree, obtaining or inserting a key–value pair takes O(log n) time.

Common Programming Error 25.5

Invoking the get accessor of a `SortedDictionary` indexer with a key that does not exist in the collection causes a `KeyNotFoundException`. This behavior is different from that of the `Hash-table` indexer's get accessor, which would return `nullptr`.

25.5.2 Generic Class LinkedList

Chapter 21 began our discussion of dynamic data structures with the concept of a linked list. We end our discussion with the .NET Framework's generic *LinkedList* class. The LinkedList class is a doubly linked list—we can navigate the list both backward and forward with nodes of generic class *LinkedListNode*. Each node contains property *Value* and read-only properties *Previous* and *Next*. The Value property's type matches LinkedList's single type parameter because it contains the data stored in the node. The Previous property gets a reference to the preceding node in the linked list (or nullptr if the node is the first of the list). Similarly, the Next property gets a reference to the subsequent reference in the linked list (or nullptr if the node is the last of the list). We demonstrate a few linked-list manipulations in Fig. 25.9.

```cpp
1   // Fig. 25.9: LinkedListTest.cpp
2   // Using LinkedLists.
3   #include "stdafx.h"
4
5   using namespace System;
6   using namespace System::Collections::Generic;
7
8   generic< typename E >
9   void printList( LinkedList< E >^ ); // function prototype
10
11  generic< typename E >
12  void concatenate( LinkedList< E >^, LinkedList< E >^ ); // prototype
13
14  generic< typename E >
15  void removeItemsBetween( LinkedList< E >^, E, E ); // function prototype
16
17  generic< typename E >
18  void printReversedList( LinkedList< E >^ ); // function prototype
19
20  void toUppercaseStrings( LinkedList< String^ >^ ); // function prototype
21
22  int main( array< System::String^ > ^args )
23  {
24     array< String^ > ^colors = { "black", "yellow",
25        "green", "blue", "violet", "silver" };
26     array< String^ > ^colors2 = { "gold", "white",
27        "brown", "blue", "gray" };
28
29     LinkedList< String^ > ^list1 = gcnew LinkedList< String^ >();
30
31     // add elements to the first linked list
32     for each ( String ^color in colors )
33        list1->AddLast( color );
34
35     // add elements to the second linked list via constructor
36     LinkedList< String^ > ^list2 = gcnew LinkedList< String^ >( colors2 );
37
38     concatenate( list1, list2 ); // concatenate list2 onto list1
```

Fig. 25.9 | Using LinkedLists. (Part 1 of 3.)

```
39        printList( list1 ); // print list1 elements
40
41        Console::WriteLine( "\nConverting strings in list1 to uppercase\n" );
42        toUppercaseStrings( list1 ); // convert to uppercase strings
43        printList( list1 ); // print list1 elements
44
45        Console::WriteLine( "\nDeleting strings between BLACK and BROWN\n" );
46        removeItemsBetween( list1, "BLACK", "BROWN" );
47
48        printList( list1 ); // print list1 elements
49        printReversedList( list1 ); // print the list in reverse order
50
51        return 0;
52   } // end main
53
54   // output list contents
55   generic< typename E >
56   void printList( LinkedList< E > ^list )
57   {
58        Console::WriteLine( "Linked list: " );
59
60        for each ( E value in list )
61            Console::Write( "{0} ", value );
62
63        Console::WriteLine();
64   } // end function printList
65
66   // concatenate the second list on the end of the first list
67   generic< typename E >
68   void concatenate( LinkedList< E > ^list1, LinkedList< E > ^list2 )
69   {
70        // concatenate lists by copying element values
71        // in order from the second list to the first list
72        for each ( E value in list2 )
73            list1->AddLast( value ); // add new node
74   } // end function concatenate
75
76   // locate string objects and convert to uppercase
77   void toUppercaseStrings( LinkedList< String^ > ^list )
78   {
79        // iterate over the list by using the nodes
80        LinkedListNode< String^ > ^currentNode = list->First;
81
82        while ( currentNode != nullptr )
83        {
84            String ^color = currentNode->Value; // get value in node
85            currentNode->Value = color->ToUpper(); // convert to uppercase
86            currentNode = currentNode->Next; // get next node
87        } // end while
88   } // end function toUppercaseStrings
89
```

Fig. 25.9 | Using LinkedLists. (Part 2 of 3.)

```
90    // delete list items between two given items
91    generic< typename E >
92    void removeItemsBetween( LinkedList< E > ^list,
93        E startItem, E endItem )
94    {
95        // get the nodes corresponding to the start and end item
96        LinkedListNode< E > ^currentNode = list->Find( startItem );
97        LinkedListNode< E > ^endNode = list->Find( endItem );
98
99        // remove items after the start item until we find
100       // the end item or the end of the linked list
101       while ( ( currentNode->Next != nullptr ) &&
102           ( currentNode->Next != endNode ) )
103       {
104           list->Remove( currentNode->Next ); // remove the next node
105       } // end while
106   } // end function removeItemsBetween
107
108   // print reversed list
109   generic< typename E >
110   void printReversedList( LinkedList< E > ^list )
111   {
112       Console::WriteLine( "Reversed List:" );
113
114       // iterate over the list by using the nodes
115       LinkedListNode< E > ^currentNode = list->Last;
116
117       while ( currentNode != nullptr )
118       {
119           Console::Write( "{0} ", currentNode->Value );
120           currentNode = currentNode->Previous; // get previous node
121       } // end while
122
123       Console::WriteLine();
124   } // end function printReversedList
```

```
Linked list:
black yellow green blue violet silver gold white brown blue gray

Converting strings in list1 to uppercase

Linked list:
BLACK YELLOW GREEN BLUE VIOLET SILVER GOLD WHITE BROWN BLUE GRAY

Deleting strings between BLACK and BROWN

Linked list:
BLACK BROWN BLUE GRAY
Reversed List:
GRAY BLUE BROWN BLACK
```

Fig. 25.9 | Using LinkedLists. (Part 3 of 3.)

The using directive in line 6 allows us to use the LinkedList class. Lines 29–36 create LinkedLists list1 and list2 of String handles and fill them with the contents of arrays colors and colors2, respectively. Note that LinkedList is a generic class that has one type parameter for which we specify the type argument String^ in this example (lines 29 and 36). We demonstrate two ways to fill the lists. In lines 32–33, we use the for each statement and member function *AddLast* to fill list1. The AddLast member function creates a new LinkedListNode (with the given value available via the Value property) and appends this node to the end of the list. There is also an AddFirst member function that inserts a node at the beginning of the list. Line 36 invokes the constructor that takes an IEnumerable< String^ > parameter. All managed arrays implicitly inherit from the generic interfaces IList< T > and IEnumerable< T > with the type of the array as the type argument, so the String^ array colors2 implements IEnumerable< String^ >. The type parameter of this generic IEnumerable matches the type parameter of the generic LinkedList object. This constructor call copies the contents of the array colors2 to list2.

Line 38 calls generic function concatenate (lines 67–74) to append all elements of list2 to the end of list1. Line 39 calls function printList (lines 55–64) to output list1's contents. Line 42 calls function toUppercaseStrings (lines 77–88) to convert each String^ element to uppercase, then line 43 displays the modified Strings. Line 46 calls function removeItemsBetween (lines 91–106) to remove the elements between "BLACK" and "BROWN", but not including either. Line 48 outputs the list again, then line 49 invokes function printReversedList (lines 109–124) to print the list in reverse order.

Generic function concatenate (lines 67–74) iterates over list2 with a for each statement and calls member function AddLast to append each value to the end of list1. The LinkedList class's enumerator loops over the values of the nodes, not the nodes themselves, so the iteration variable has type E. Notice that this creates a new node in list1 for each node in list2. One LinkedListNode cannot be a member of more than one LinkedList. Any attempt to add a node from one LinkedList to another generates an InvalidOperationException. If you want the same data to belong to more than one LinkedList, you must make a copy of the node for each list.

Generic function printList (lines 55–64) similarly uses a for each statement to iterate over the values in a LinkedList and output them. Function toUppercaseStrings (lines 77–88) takes a linked list of String^ objects and converts each String value to uppercase. This function replaces the String references stored in the list, so we cannot use an enumerator (via a for each statement) as in the previous two functions. Instead, we obtain the first LinkedListNode via the First property (line 80), and use a while statement to loop through the list (lines 82–87). Each iteration of the while statement obtains and updates the contents of currentNode via property Value, using String member function *ToUpper* to create an uppercase version of String color. At the end of each iteration, we move the current node to the next node in the list by assigning currentNode to the node obtained by its own Next property (line 86). The Next property of the last node of the list gets nullptr, so when the while statement iterates past the end of the list, the loop exits.

Notice that it does not make sense to declare toUppercaseStrings as a generic function, because it uses the String-specific member functions of the node values. Functions printList and concatenate do not need to use any String-specific member functions, so they can be declared with generic type parameters to promote maximal code reuse.

Generic function removeItemsBetween (lines 91–106) removes a range of items between two nodes. Lines 96–97 obtain the two "boundary" nodes of the range by using member function **Find**. This member function performs a linear search on the list and returns the first node that contains a value equal to the passed argument. Member function Find returns nullptr if the value is not found. We store the node preceding the range in local variable currentNode and the node following the range in endNode.

The while statement in lines 101–105 removes all the elements between current-Node and endNode. On each iteration of the loop, we remove the node following current-Node by invoking member function **Remove** (line 104). Member function Remove takes a LinkedListNode, splices that node out of the LinkedList, and fixes the references of the surrounding nodes. After the Remove call, currentNode's Next property now gets the node *following* the node just removed, and that node's Previous property now gets current-Node. The while statement continues to loop until there are no nodes left between currentNode and endNode, or until currentNode is the last node in the list. (Note that there is also an overloaded version of member function Remove that performs a linear search for the specified value and removes the first node in the list that contains it.)

Function printReversedList (lines 109–124) prints the list backward by navigating the nodes manually. Line 115 obtains the last element of the list via the **Last** property and stores it in currentNode. The while statement in lines 117–121 iterates through the list backward by moving the currentNode reference to the previous node at the end of each iteration, then exiting when we move past the beginning of the list. Note how similar this code is to lines 80–87, which iterated through the list from the beginning to the end.

25.6 Wrap-Up

This chapter introduced the .NET Framework collection classes. You learned about the hierarchy of interfaces that many of the collection classes implement. You saw how to use class Array to perform array manipulations. You learned that the System::Collections and System::Collections::Generic namespaces contain many nongeneric and generic collection classes, respectively. We presented the nongeneric classes ArrayList, Stack and Hashtable as well as generic classes SortedDictionary and LinkedList. In doing so, we discussed data structures in greater depth. We discussed dynamically expanding collections, hashing schemes, and two implementations of a dictionary. You saw the advantages of generic collections over their nongeneric counterparts.

You also used enumerators to traverse these data structures and obtain their contents. We demonstrated the for each statement with FCL classes, and explained that this works by using enumerators "behind the scenes" to traverse the collections.

In the next chapter, we discuss several more advanced Visual C++ features, including cast operators, namespaces, operator keywords, pointer-to-class-member operators, multiple inheritance, virtual base classes, variable-length argument lists and delegates and events in C++/CLI.

Summary

Section 25.1 Introduction
- The prepackaged data-structure classes provided by the .NET Framework are known as collection classes—they store collections of data.
- With collection classes, instead of creating data structures to store sets of items, the programmer simply uses existing data structures, without concern for how they are implemented.

Section 25.2 Collections Overview

- The .NET Framework collections provide high-performance, high-quality implementations of common data structures and enable effective software reuse.

- In earlier versions, the .NET Framework primarily provided the collection classes in the `System::Collections` namespace to store and manipulate object references.

- The .NET Framework includes the `System::Collections::Generic` namespace, which contains classes that take advantage of .NET's generics capabilities.

Section 25.3 Class Array and Enumerators

- All arrays implicitly inherit from abstract base class `Array` (namespace `System`).

- The `static` `Array` member function `Sort` sorts an array.

- The `static` `Array` member function `Copy` copies elements from one array to another.

- The `static` `Array` member function `BinarySearch` performs binary searches on an array. This member function assumes that it receives a sorted array.

- A collection's `GetEnumerator` member function returns an enumerator that can iterate over the collection.

- All enumerators have member functions `MoveNext` and `Reset` and property `Current`.

- `MoveNext` moves the enumerator to the next element in the collection and returns `true` if there is at least one more element in the collection; otherwise, the member function returns `false`.

- Member function `Reset` positions the enumerator *before* the first element of the collection.

- Read-only property `Current` returns the object at the current location in the collection.

- If a collection is modified after an enumerator is created for that collection, the enumerator immediately becomes invalid.

- The `for each` statement implicitly obtains an enumerator via the `GetEnumerator` member function and uses the enumerator's `MoveNext` member function and `Current` property to traverse the collection. This can be done with any collection that implements the `IEnumerable` interface—not just arrays.

Section 25.4.1 Class ArrayList

- In most programming languages, including Visual C++, conventional arrays have a fixed size.

- The .NET Framework's `ArrayList` collection class mimics the functionality of conventional arrays and provides dynamic resizing of the collection.

- If an `ArrayList` needs to grow, it doubles its current `Capacity` by default.

- `ArrayList`s store references to `Object`s.

- `ArrayList` has a constructor that can initialize the contents of an `ArrayList` with the elements of any `ICollection` passed to it. Many of the collection classes have such a constructor.

- The `Count` and `Capacity` properties correspond, respectively, to the current number of elements in the `ArrayList` and the maximum number of elements that can be stored without allocating more memory to the `ArrayList`.

- Member function `IndexOf` returns the position of a value in an `ArrayList`. `IndexOf` returns `-1` if the element is not found.

- We can access an element of an `ArrayList` by following the `ArrayList` variable name with square brackets (`[]`) containing the desired index of the element.

- The `Remove` member function removes the first occurrence of the specified object. All subsequent elements shift toward the beginning of the `ArrayList` to fill the emptied position.

Section 25.4.2 Class `Stack`

- Class `Stack` has member functions `Push` and `Pop` to perform the basic stack operations.

- The nongeneric `Stack` class can store only references to `Object`, so value-type items are implicitly boxed before they are added to the `Stack`.

- Member function `Peek` returns the value of the top stack element, but does not remove the element from the `Stack`.

- Attempting to `Peek` or `Pop` an empty `Stack` causes an `InvalidOperationException`.

Section 25.4.3 Class `Hashtable`

- Many applications need a high-speed scheme for converting keys to unique array indices. One such scheme is called hashing, in which we store data in a data structure called a hash table. The .NET Framework provides class `Hashtable` to enable programmers to employ hashing.

- Class `Hashtable` can accept any `Object` as a key.

- Member function `ContainsKey` determines whether a key is in the hash table.

- `Hashtable` member function `Add` creates a new entry in the hash table, with the first argument as the key and the second argument as the value.

- We can use the `Hashtable`'s indexer to obtain and set the key's associated value in the hash table.

- `Hashtable` property `Keys` gets an `ICollection` that contains all the keys.

- If you use a `for each` statement with a `Hashtable`, the iteration variable is of type `Dictionary-Entry`, which has properties `Key` and `Value` for retrieving the key and value of the current element.

Section 25.5.1 Generic Class `SortedDictionary`

- A dictionary is the general term for a collection of key–value pairs. A hash table is one way to implement a dictionary.

- Generic class `SortedDictionary` does not use a hash table, but instead stores its key–value pairs in a binary search tree.

- Generic class `SortedDictionary` takes two type arguments—the first specifies the type of key, and the second specifies the type of value.

- When the compiler knows the type that the data structure contains, there is no need to downcast when we need to use the type-specific member functions.

- Invoking the `get` accessor of a `SortedDictionary` indexer with a key that does not exist in the collection causes a `KeyNotFoundException`. This behavior is different from that of the `Hashtable` indexer's get accessor, which would return `nullptr`.

Section 25.5.2 Generic Class `LinkedList`

- The `LinkedList` class is a doubly linked list—we can navigate the list both backward and forward with nodes of generic class `LinkedListNode`.

- Each node contains property `Value` and read-only properties `Previous` and `Next`.

- The `LinkedList` class's enumerator loops over the values of the nodes, not the nodes themselves.

- One `LinkedListNode` cannot be a member of more than one `LinkedList`. Any attempt to add a node from one `LinkedList` to another generates an `InvalidOperationException`.

- Member function `Find` performs a linear search on the list, and returns the first node that contains a value equal to the passed argument.

- Member function `Remove` splices a node out of a `LinkedList`, then fixes the references of the surrounding nodes.

Terminology

Add member function of class `ArrayList`
Add member function of class `Hashtable`
AddLast member function of class `LinkedList`
`ArgumentException`
`Array` class
`ArrayList` class
BinarySearch member function of class `Array`
`BitArray` class
capacity
Capacity property of class `ArrayList`
Clear member function of class `Array`
Clear member function of class `ArrayList`
collection
collection class
collision
Contains member function of class `ArrayList`
Contains member function of class `Stack`
ContainsKey member function of `Hashtable`
Copy member function of interface `ICollection`
Count property of interface `ICollection`
CreateInstance member function of `Array`
Current property of interface `IEnumerator`
dictionary
DictionaryEntry structure of interface
    `IDictionary`
enumerator
Find member function of class `LinkedList`
First property of class `LinkedList`
GetEnumerator member function of interface
    `IEnumerable`
GetHashCode member function of class `Object`
hash function
hash table
hashing
`Hashtable` class
`ICollection` interface
`IDictionary` interface
`IEnumerable` interface
`IEnumerator` interface
`IList` interface

IndexOf member function of class `Array`
IndexOf member function of class `ArrayList`
int indexer of class `ArrayList`
`InvalidOperationException`
`KeyNotFoundException`
Keys property of interface `IDictionary`
Last property of class `LinkedList`
LastIndexOf member function of class `Array`
`LinkedList` generic class
`LinkedListNode` generic class
load factor
MoveNext member function of interface
    `IEnumerator`
Next property of class `LinkedListNode`
Object indexer of class `Hashtable`
Peek member function of class `Stack`
Pop member function of class `Stack`
Previous property of class `LinkedListNode`
Push member function of class `Stack`
`Queue` class
Remove member function of class `ArrayList`
Remove member function of class `LinkedList`
RemoveAt member function of class `ArrayList`
RemoveRange member function of `ArrayList`
Reset member function ofs `IEnumerator`
Reverse member function of class `Array`
Sort member function of class `Array`
Sort member function of class `ArrayList`
`SortedDictionary` generic class
`SortedList` class
space/time trade-off
`Stack` class
`System::Collections` namespace
`System::Collections::Generic` namespace
ToLower member function of class `String`
ToUpper member function of class `String`
TrimToSize member function of class
    `ArrayList`
Value property of class `LinkedListNode`
Values property of interface `IDictionary`

Self-Review Exercises

25.1 Fill in the blanks in each of the following statements:

a) A(n) _____ is used to walk through a collection but cannot remove elements from the collection during the iteration.

b) Class _____ provides the capabilities of an arraylike data structure that can resize itself dynamically.

c) An element in an `ArrayList` can be accessed by using the `ArrayList`'s _____.

d) If you do not specify a capacity increment, an `ArrayList` will (by default) _____ its size each time additional capacity is needed.

e) `IEnumerator` member function _____ advances the enumerator to the next item.

f) If the collection it references has been altered since the enumerator's creation, calling member function `Reset` will cause a(n) _____.

25.2 State whether each of the following is *true* or *false*. If *false*, explain why.
a) Class `Stack` is in the `System::Collections` namespace.
b) A class implementing interface `IEnumerator` must define only member functions `MoveNext` and `Reset`, and no properties.
c) A `Hashtable` stores key–value pairs.
d) Values of simple types may be stored directly in an `ArrayList`.
e) An `ArrayList` can contain duplicate values.
f) A `Hashtable` can contain duplicate keys.
g) A `LinkedList` can contain duplicate values.
h) `Dictionary` is an interface.
i) With hashing, as the load factor increases, the chance of collisions decreases.

Answers to Self-Review Exercises

25.1 a) enumerator (or for each statement). b) `ArrayList`. c) indexer. d) double. e) `MoveNext`. f) `InvalidOperationException`.

25.2 a) True. b) False. The class must also implement property `Current`. c) True. d) False. An `ArrayList` stores `Object`s. Implicit boxing occurs when adding a value type to the `ArrayList`. You can prevent boxing by using generic class `List` with a value type. e) True. f) False. A `Hashtable` cannot contain duplicate keys. g) True. h) False. `Dictionary` is a class; `IDictionary` is an interface. i) False. With hashing, as the load factor increases, there are fewer available slots, so the chance of selecting an occupied slot (a collision) with a hashing operation increases.

Exercises

25.3 Define each of the following terms:
a) `ICollection`
b) `Array`
c) `IList`
d) load factor
e) collision
f) space/time trade-off in hashing
g) `Hashtable`

25.4 Explain briefly the operation of each of the following members of class `ArrayList`:
a) `Add`
b) `Insert`
c) `Remove`
d) `Clear`
e) `RemoveAt`
f) `Contains`
g) `IndexOf`
h) `Count`
i) `Capacity`

25.5 Explain why appending additional elements onto an `ArrayList` object whose current size is less than its capacity is a relatively efficient operation and why appending additional elements into an `ArrayList` object whose current size is at capacity is a relatively slow operation.

25.6 In our implementation of a stack in Fig. 21.13, we were able to quickly extend a linked list to create class Stack. The .NET Framework designers chose not to use inheritance to create their Stack class. What are the negative aspects of inheritance, particularly for class Stack?

25.7 Briefly answer the following questions:
   a) What happens when you add a simple type (e.g., double) value to a nongeneric collection?
   b) Can you print all the elements in an IEnumerable object without explicitly using an enumerator? If yes, how?

25.8 Explain briefly the operation of each of the following enumerator-related members:
   a) GetEnumerator
   b) Current
   c) MoveNext

25.9 Explain briefly the operation of each of the following member functions and properties of class Hashtable:
   a) Add
   b) Keys
   c) Values
   d) ContainsKey

25.10 Determine whether each of the following statements is *true* or *false*. If *false*, explain why.
   a) Elements in an array must be sorted in ascending order before a BinarySearch may be performed.
   b) Member First gets the first node in a LinkedList.
   c) Class Array provides static member function Sort for sorting array elements.

25.11 Write an application that reads in a series of first names and stores them in a LinkedList. Do not store duplicate names. Allow the user to search for a first name.

25.12 Modify the application in Fig. 25.8 to count the number of occurrences of each letter rather than of each word. For example, the string "HELLO THERE" contains two Hs, three Es, two Ls, one O, one T and one R. Display the results.

25.13 Write an application that determines and prints the number of duplicate words in a sentence. Treat uppercase and lowercase letters the same. Ignore punctuation.

25.14 Recall from Fig. 25.2 that class List is the generic equivalent of class ArrayList. Write an application that inserts 25 random integers from 0 to 100 in order into an object of class List. The application should calculate the sum of the elements and the floating-point average of the elements.

25.15 Write an application that creates a LinkedList object of 10 characters, then creates a second list object containing a copy of the first list, but in reverse order.

25.16 Write an application that takes a whole-number input from a user and determines whether it is prime. If the number is not prime, display the unique prime factors of the number. Remember that a prime number's factors are only 1 and the prime number itself. Every number that is not prime has a unique prime factorization. For example, consider the number 54. The prime factors of 54 are 2, 3, 3 and 3. When the values are multiplied together, the result is 54. For the number 54, the prime factors output should be 2 and 3. Use generic SortedDictionarys as part of your solution by recording the factors as the keys and using the Keys property to enumerate the factors.

25.17 In Exercise 20.7, you performed a bucket sort of ints by using a two-dimensional array, where each row of the array represented a bucket. By instead using a dynamically expanding data structure to represent each bucket, you do not have to write code that keeps track of the number of ints in each bucket. Rewrite your solution to use a one-dimensional array of LinkedList< int > buckets.

26

Other Topics

What's in a name? that which we call a rose By any other name would smell as sweet.
—William Shakespeare

O Diamond! Diamond! thou little knowest the mischief done!
—Sir Isaac Newton

OBJECTIVES

In this chapter you'll learn:

- To use `const_cast` to temporarily treat a `const` object as a non-`const` object.
- To use `namespace`s.
- To use operator keywords.
- To use `mutable` members in `const` objects.
- To use class-member pointer operators `.*` and `->*`.
- To use multiple inheritance.
- The role of `virtual` base classes in multiple inheritance.
- To use command-line arguments.
- To use variable-length argument lists.
- To use delegates with C++/CLI.

26.1 Introduction

We now consider several advanced Visual C++ features. First, you'll learn about some new cast operators including the const_cast operator, which allows programmers to add or remove the const qualification of a variable. Next, we discuss namespaces, which can be used to ensure that every identifier in a program has a unique name and can help resolve naming conflicts caused by using libraries that have the same variable, function or class names. We then present several operator keywords that are useful for programmers whose keyboards do not support certain characters used in operator symbols, such as !, &, ^, ~ and |. We continue our discussion with the mutable storage-class specifier, which enables a programmer to indicate that a data member should always be modifiable, even when it appears in an object currently being treated as a const object by the program. Next we introduce two special operators that we can use with pointers to class members to access a data member or member function without knowing its name in advance. We introduce multiple inheritance, which enables a derived class to inherit the members of several base classes. As part of this introduction, we discuss potential problems with multiple inheritance and how virtual inheritance can be used to solve those problems. We then discuss command-line arguments and variable-length argument lists in both native and managed code. Finally, we introduce the basics of .NET delegates and events in C++/CLI.

26.2 Other Cast Operators

const_cast
Visual C++ provides the *const_cast* operator for casting away const or volatile qualification. You declare a variable with the *volatile* qualifier when you expect the variable to be modified by hardware or other programs not known to the compiler. Declaring a variable volatile indicates that the compiler should not optimize the use of that variable, because doing so could affect the ability of those other programs to access and modify the volatile variable.

In general, it is dangerous to use the const_cast operator, because it allows a program to modify a variable that was declared const, and thus was not supposed to be modifiable. There are cases in which it is desirable, or even necessary, to cast away const-ness. For example, older C and C++ libraries might provide functions that have non-const parameters and that do not modify their parameters. If you wished to pass const data to such a function, you would need to cast away the data's const-ness; otherwise, the compiler would report error messages.

Similarly, you could pass non-const data to a function that treats the data as if it were constant, then returns that data as a constant. In such cases, you might need to cast away the const-ness of the returned data, as we demonstrate in Fig. 26.1.

In this program, function maximum (lines 11–14) receives two C-style strings as const char * parameters and returns a const char * that points to the larger of the two strings. Function main declares the two C-style strings as non-const char arrays (lines 18–19); thus, these arrays are modifiable. In main, we wish to output the larger of the two C-style strings, then modify that C-style string by converting it to uppercase letters.

Function maximum's two parameters are of type const char *, so the function's return type also must be declared as const char *. If the return type is specified only as char *, the compiler issues an error message indicating that the value being returned cannot be converted from const char * to char *—a dangerous conversion, because it attempts to treat data that the function believes to be const as if it were non-const.

```cpp
1   // Fig. 26.1: ConstCast.cpp
2   // Demonstrating const_cast.
3   #include <iostream>
4   using std::cout;
5   using std::endl;
6
7   #include <cstring> // contains prototypes for functions strcmp and strlen
8   #include <cctype> // contains prototype for function toupper
9
10  // returns the larger of two C-style strings
11  const char *maximum( const char *first, const char *second )
12  {
13     return ( strcmp( first, second ) >= 0 ? first : second );
14  } // end function maximum
15
16  int main()
17  {
18     char s1[] = "hello"; // modifiable array of characters
19     char s2[] = "goodbye"; // modifiable array of characters
20
21     // const_cast required to allow the const char * returned by maximum
22     // to be assigned to the char * variable maxPtr
23     char *maxPtr = const_cast< char * >( maximum( s1, s2 ) );
24
25     cout << "The larger string is: " << maxPtr << endl;
26
27     for ( size_t i = 0; i < strlen( maxPtr ); i++ )
28        maxPtr[ i ] = toupper( maxPtr[ i ] );
```

Fig. 26.1 | Demonstrating operator const_cast. (Part 1 of 2.)

```
29
30      cout << "The larger string capitalized is: " << maxPtr << endl;
31      return 0;
32   } // end main
```

```
The larger string is: hello
The larger string capitalized is: HELLO
```

Fig. 26.1 | Demonstrating operator `const_cast`. (Part 2 of 2.)

Even though function `maximum` believes the data to be constant, we know that the original arrays in `main` do not contain constant data. Therefore, `main` should be able to modify the contents of those arrays as necessary. Since we know these arrays are modifiable, we use `const_cast` (line 23) to cast away the `const`-ness of the pointer returned by `maximum`, so we can then modify the data in the array representing the larger of the two C-style strings. We can then use the pointer as the name of a character array in the `for` statement (lines 27–28) to convert the contents of the larger string to uppercase letters. Without the `const_cast` in line 23, this program will not compile, because we are not allowed to assign a pointer of type `const char *` to a pointer of type `char *`.

Error-Prevention Tip 26.1

In general, a `const_cast` should be used only when it is known in advance that the original data is not constant. Otherwise, unexpected results may occur.

Converting Between Pointer Types with the `reinterpret_cast` Operator

Sometimes we need to pass a pointer of one type to a function with a parameter of another type. Visual C++ provides the ***reinterpret_cast*** operator for cases like this. We can also use this cast operator to convert between pointer and integer types, and vice versa.

A `reinterpret_cast` is performed at compile time and does not change the value of the object to which its operand points. Instead, it requests that the compiler reinterpret the operand as the target type (specified in the angle brackets following the keyword `reinterpret_cast`). This makes `reinterpret_cast` very dangerous if used improperly. You should not use `reinterpret_cast` as a means to downcast in a class hierarchy or to remove `const` or `volatile` qualifiers (that is what `const_cast` is for). A `reinterpret_cast` is rarely necessary, and you should think carefully before using it rather than one of the safer cast operations (such as `static_cast` or `dynamic_cast`).

Error-Prevention Tip 26.2

Beware of using `reinterpret_cast` to perform dangerous manipulations that could lead to serious execution-time errors.

Portability Tip 26.1

The use of `reinterpret_cast` is compiler dependent and can cause programs to behave differently on different platforms. It should be avoided unless absolute necessary.

Portability Tip 26.2

A program that reads unformatted data (written by `write`) must be compiled and executed on a system compatible with the program that wrote the data, because different systems may represent internal data differently.

safe_cast *in* C++/CLI

C++/CLI also provides a new cast operator called **safe_cast**. In most situations a static_cast could be used in the same places as a safe_cast. The main difference is that safe_cast produces verifiable code which may be important in certain situations such as interacting with code written in other .NET languages such as C#. (For more information on verifiable and unverifiable code see msdn2.microsoft.com/en-us/library/ 85344whh(VS.90).aspx.) A safe_cast can be used to cast one type of handle, tracking reference, or value type to another compatible handle, tracking reference, or value type. This includes casting up or down class hierarchies when appropriate. However, unlike static_cast, if you attempt to use a safe_cast between incompatible types, then the program will throw an InvalidCastException at runtime.

26.3 namespaces

A program includes many identifiers defined in different scopes. Sometimes a variable of one scope will "overlap" (i.e., collide) with a variable of the same name in a different scope, possibly creating a naming conflict. Such overlapping can occur at many levels. Identifier overlapping occurs frequently in third-party libraries that happen to use the same names for global identifiers (such as functions). This can cause compiler errors.

Good Programming Practice 26.1

Avoid identifiers that begin with the underscore character, as these can lead to linker errors. Many code libraries use names that begin with underscores.

The Visual C++ standard solves this problem with **namespaces**. You have seen namespace declarations in examples of native C++ and C++/CLI throughout this book. We discuss them in detail here. Each namespace defines a scope in which identifiers and variables are placed. To use a **namespace member**, either the member's name must be qualified with the namespace name and the binary scope resolution operator (::), as in

> *MyNameSpace*::*member*

or a using declaration or using directive must appear before the name is used in the program. Typically, such using statements are placed at the beginning of the file in which members of the namespace are used. For example, placing the following using directive at the beginning of a source-code file

> **using namespace** *MyNameSpace*;

specifies that members of namespace *MyNameSpace* can be used in the file without being preceded by *MyNameSpace* and the scope resolution operator (::).

A using declaration (e.g., using std::cout;) brings one name into the scope where the declaration appears. A using directive (e.g., using namespace std; or using namespace System;) brings all the names from the specified namespace into the scope where the directive appears.

Software Engineering Observation 26.1

Ideally, in large programs, every entity should be declared in a class, function, block or namespace. This helps clarify every entity's role.

Error-Prevention Tip 26.3

Precede a member with its namespace name and the scope resolution operator (::) if the possibility exists of a naming conflict.

Not all namespaces are guaranteed to be unique. Two third-party vendors might inadvertently use the same identifiers for their namespace names. Figure 26.2 demonstrates the use of namespaces.

```cpp
1   // Fig. 26.2: Namespaces.cpp
2   // Demonstrating namespaces.
3   #include <iostream>
4   using namespace std; // use std namespace
5
6   int integer1 = 98; // global variable
7
8   // create namespace Example
9   namespace Example
10  {
11     // declare two constants and one variable
12     const double PI = 3.14159;
13     const double E = 2.71828;
14     int integer1 = 8;
15
16     void printValues(); // prototype
17
18     // nested namespace
19     namespace Inner
20     {
21        // define enumeration
22        enum Years { FISCAL1 = 1990, FISCAL2, FISCAL3 };
23     } // end Inner namespace
24  } // end Example namespace
25
26  // create unnamed namespace
27  namespace
28  {
29     double doubleInUnnamed = 88.22; // declare variable
30  } // end unnamed namespace
31
32  int main()
33  {
34     // output value doubleInUnnamed of unnamed namespace
35     cout << "doubleInUnnamed = " << doubleInUnnamed;
36
37     // output global variable
38     cout << "\n(global) integer1 = " << integer1;
39
40     // output values of Example namespace
41     cout << "\nPI = " << Example::PI << "\nE = " << Example::E
42        << "\ninteger1 = " << Example::integer1 << "\nFISCAL3 = "
43        << Example::Inner::FISCAL3 << endl;
44
```

Fig. 26.2 | Demonstrating the use of namespaces. (Part 1 of 2.)

```
45       Example::printValues(); // invoke printValues function
46       return 0;
47  } // end main
48
49  // display variable and constant values
50  void Example::printValues()
51  {
52      cout << "\nIn printValues:\ninteger1 = " << integer1 << "\nPI = "
53          << PI << "\nE = " << E << "\ndoubleInUnnamed = "
54          << doubleInUnnamed << "\n(global) integer1 = " << ::integer1
55          << "\nFISCAL3 = " << Inner::FISCAL3 << endl;
56  } // end printValues
```

```
doubleInUnnamed = 88.22
(global) integer1 = 98
PI = 3.14159
E = 2.71828
integer1 = 8
FISCAL3 = 1992

In printValues:
integer1 = 8
PI = 3.14159
E = 2.71828
doubleInUnnamed = 88.22
(global) integer1 = 98
FISCAL3 = 1992
```

Fig. 26.2 | Demonstrating the use of `namespaces`. (Part 2 of 2.)

Using the std Namespace

Line 4 informs the compiler that namespace `std` is being used. The contents of header file `<iostream>` are all defined as part of namespace `std`. [*Note:* Most Visual C++ programmers consider it poor practice to write a `using` directive such as line 4 because the entire contents of the namespace are included, thus increasing the likelihood of a naming conflict.]

The `using namespace` directive specifies that the members of a namespace will be used frequently throughout a program. This allows you to access all the members of the namespace and to write more concise statements, such as

```
cout << "double1 = " << double1;
```

rather than

```
std::cout << "double1 = " << double1;
```

Without line 4, either every `cout` and `endl` in Fig. 26.2 would have to be qualified with `std::`, or individual using declarations must be included for `cout` and `endl` as in:

```
using std::cout;
using std::endl;
```

The `using namespace` directive can be used for predefined namespaces (e.g., `std`) or programmer-defined namespaces.

Defining Namespaces

Lines 9–24 use the keyword `namespace` to define namespace `Example`. The body of a namespace is delimited by braces (`{}`). Namespace `Example`'s members consist of two constants (`PI` and `E` in lines 12–13), an `int` (`integer1` in line 14), a function (`printValues` in line 16) and a *nested namespace* (`Inner` in lines 19–23). Notice that member `integer1` has the same name as global variable `integer1` (line 6). Variables that have the same name must have different scopes—otherwise compilation errors occur. A namespace can contain constants, data, classes, nested namespaces, functions, etc. Definitions of namespaces must occupy the global scope or be nested within other namespaces.

Lines 27–30 create an *unnamed namespace* containing the member `doubleInUn-named`. The unnamed namespace has an implicit `using` directive, so its members appear to occupy the *global namespace*, are accessible directly and do not have to be qualified with a namespace name. Global variables are also part of the global namespace and are accessible in all scopes following the declaration in the file.

Software Engineering Observation 26.2

Each separate compilation unit has its own unique unnamed namespace; i.e., the unnamed namespace replaces the `static` *linkage specifier.*

Accessing Namespace Members with Qualified Names

Line 35 outputs the value of variable `doubleInUnnamed`, which is directly accessible as part of the unnamed namespace. Line 38 outputs the value of global variable `integer1`. For both of these variables, the compiler first attempts to locate a local declaration of the variables in `main`. Since there are no local declarations, the compiler assumes those variables are in the global namespace.

Lines 41–43 output the values of `PI`, `E`, `integer1` and `FISCAL3` from namespace `Example`. Notice that each must be qualified with `Example::` because the program does not provide any `using` directive or declarations indicating that it will use members of namespace `Example`. In addition, member `integer1` must be qualified, because a global variable has the same name. Otherwise, the global variable's value is output. Notice that `FISCAL3` is a member of nested namespace `Inner`, so it must be qualified with `Example::Inner::`.

Function `printValues` (defined in lines 50–56) is a member of `Example`, so it can access other members of the `Example` namespace directly without using a namespace qualifier. The output statement in lines 52–55 outputs `integer1`, `PI`, `E`, `doubleInUnnamed`, global variable `integer1` and `FISCAL3`. Notice that `PI` and `E` are not qualified with `Example`. Variable `doubleInUnnamed` is still accessible, because it is in the unnamed namespace and the variable name does not conflict with any other members of namespace `Example`. The global version of `integer1` must be qualified with the unary scope resolution operator (`::`), because its name conflicts with a member of namespace `Example`. Also, `FISCAL3` must be qualified with `Inner::`. When accessing members of a nested namespace, the members must be qualified with the namespace name (unless the member is being used inside the nested namespace).

Common Programming Error 26.1

Placing `main` *in a namespace is a compilation error.*

Aliases for Namespace Names

Namespaces can be aliased. For example, the statement

```
namespace CPPHTP6E = CPlusPlusHowToProgram6E;
```

creates the alias CPPHTP6E for CPlusPlusHowToProgram6E.

26.4 Operator Keywords

The C++ standard provides *operator keywords* (Fig. 26.3) that can be used in place of several Visual C++ operators. Operator keywords are useful for programmers whose keyboards do not support certain characters such as !, &, ^, ~, |, etc.

Figure 26.4 demonstrates the operator keywords. This program was compiled with Visual C++ 2008, which requires the header file <iso646.h> (line 8) to use the operator keywords. Other compilers may require you to include another header file or to use a compiler option to enable support for these keywords.

Operator	Operator keyword	Description
Logical operator keywords		
&&	*and*	logical AND
||	*or*	logical OR
!	*not*	logical NOT
Inequality operator keyword		
!=	*not_eq*	inequality
Bitwise operator keywords		
&	*bitand*	bitwise AND
|	*bitor*	bitwise inclusive OR
^	*xor*	bitwise exclusive OR
~	*compl*	bitwise complement
Bitwise assignment operator keywords		
&=	*and_eq*	bitwise AND assignment
|=	*or_eq*	bitwise inclusive OR assignment
^=	*xor_eq*	bitwise exclusive OR assignment

Fig. 26.3 | Operator keyword alternatives to operator symbols.

```
1   // Fig. 26.4: OperatorKeywords.cpp
2   // Demonstrating operator keywords.
3   #include <iostream>
4   using std::boolalpha;
5   using std::cout;
6   using std::endl;
7
```

Fig. 26.4 | Demonstrating the operator keywords. (Part 1 of 2.)

```
 8   #include <iso646.h> // enables operator keywords in Microsoft Visual C++
 9
10   int main()
11   {
12       bool a = true;
13       bool b = false;
14       int c = 2;
15       int d = 3;
16
17       // sticky setting that causes bool values to display as true or false
18       cout << boolalpha;
19
20       cout << "a = " << a << "; b = " << b
21          << "; c = " << c << "; d = " << d;
22
23       cout << "\n\nLogical operator keywords:";
24       cout << "\n   a and a: " << ( a and a );
25       cout << "\n   a and b: " << ( a and b );
26       cout << "\n    a or a: " << ( a or a );
27       cout << "\n    a or b: " << ( a or b );
28       cout << "\n     not a: " << ( not a );
29       cout << "\n     not b: " << ( not b );
30       cout << "\na not_eq b: " << ( a not_eq b );
31
32       cout << "\n\nBitwise operator keywords:";
33       cout << "\nc bitand d: " << ( c bitand d );
34       cout << "\nc bit_or d: " << ( c bitor d );
35       cout << "\n   c xor d: " << ( c xor d );
36       cout << "\n   compl c: " << ( compl c );
37       cout << "\nc and_eq d: " << ( c and_eq d );
38       cout << "\n c or_eq d: " << ( c or_eq d );
39       cout << "\nc xor_eq d: " << ( c xor_eq d ) << endl;
40       return 0;
41   } // end main
```

```
a = true; b = false; c = 2; d = 3

Logical operator keywords:
   a and a: true
   a and b: false
    a or a: true
    a or b: true
     not a: false
     not b: true
a not_eq b: true

Bitwise operator keywords:
c bitand d: 2
c bit_or d: 3
   c xor d: 1
   compl c: -3
c and_eq d: 2
 c or_eq d: 3
c xor_eq d: 0
```

Fig. 26.4 | Demonstrating the operator keywords. (Part 2 of 2.)

The program declares and initializes two bool variables and two integer variables (lines 12–15). Logical operations (lines 24–30) are performed with bool variables a and b using the various logical operator keywords. Bitwise operations (lines 33–39) are performed with the int variables c and d using the various bitwise operator keywords. The result of each operation is output.

26.5 mutable Class Members

In Section 26.2, we introduced the const_cast operator, which allowed us to remove the "const-ness" of a type. A const_cast operation can also be applied to a data member of a const object from the body of a const member function of that object's class. This enables the const member function to modify the data member, even though the object is considered to be const in the body of that function. Such an operation might be performed when most of an object's data members should be considered const, but a particular data member still needs to be modified.

As an example, consider a linked list that maintains its contents in sorted order. Searching through the linked list does not require modifications to the data of the linked list, so the search function could be a const member function of the linked-list class. However, it is conceivable that a linked-list object, in an effort to make future searches more efficient, might keep track of the location of the last successful match. If the next search operation attempts to locate an item that appears later in the list, the search could begin from the location of the last successful match, rather than from the beginning of the list. To do this, the const member function that performs the search must be able to modify the data member that keeps track of the last successful search.

If a data member such as the one described above should always be modifiable, Visual C++ provides the storage-class specifier *mutable* as an alternative to const_cast. A mutable data member is always modifiable, even in a const member function or const object. This reduces the need to cast away "const-ness."

Portability Tip 26.3

The effect of attempting to modify an object that was defined as constant, regardless of whether that modification was made possible by a const_cast or C-style cast, varies among compilers.

mutable and const_cast are used in different contexts. For a const object with no mutable data members, operator const_cast must be used every time a member is to be modified. This greatly reduces the chance of a member being accidentally modified, because the member is not permanently modifiable. Operations involving const_cast are typically hidden in a member function's implementation. The user of a class might not be aware that a member is being modified.

Software Engineering Observation 26.3

mutable members are useful in classes that have "secret" implementation details that do not contribute to the logical value of an object.

Mechanical Demonstration of a mutable Data Member

Figure 26.5 demonstrates using a mutable member. The program defines class Test-Mutable (lines 8–22), which contains a constructor, function getValue and a private

```
 1   // Fig. 26.5: MutableTest.cpp
 2   // Demonstrating storage-class specifier mutable.
 3   #include <iostream>
 4   using std::cout;
 5   using std::endl;
 6
 7   // class TestMutable definition
 8   class TestMutable
 9   {
10   public:
11      TestMutable( int v = 0 )
12      {
13         value = v;
14      } // end TestMutable constructor
15
16      int getValue() const
17      {
18         return value++; // increments value
19      } // end function getValue
20   private:
21      mutable int value; // mutable member
22   }; // end class TestMutable
23
24   int main()
25   {
26      const TestMutable test( 99 );
27
28      cout << "Initial value: " << test.getValue();
29      cout << "\nModified value: " << test.getValue() << endl;
30      return 0;
31   } // end main
```

```
Initial value: 99
Modified value: 100
```

Fig. 26.5 │ Demonstrating a `mutable` data member.

data member `value` that is declared `mutable`. Lines 16–19 define function `getValue` as a `const` member function that returns a copy of `value`. Notice that the function increments `mutable` data member `value` in the `return` statement. Normally, a `const` member function cannot modify data members unless the object on which the function operates—i.e., the one to which `this` points—is cast (using `const_cast`) to a non-const type. Because `value` is `mutable`, this `const` function is able to modify the data.

Line 26 declares `const TestMutable` object `test` and initializes it to 99. Line 28 calls the `const` member function `getValue`, which adds one to `value` and returns its previous contents. Notice that the compiler allows the call to member function `getValue` on the object `test` because it is a `const` object and `getValue` is a `const` member function. However, `getValue` modifies variable `value`. Thus, when line 29 invokes `getValue` again, the new `value` (100) is output to prove that the `mutable` data member was indeed modified.

26.6 Pointers to Class Members (. * and ->*)

Visual C++ provides the `.*` and `->*` operators for accessing class members via pointers. This capability is used primarily by advanced Visual C++ programmers. We provide only a mechanical example of using pointers to class members here. Figure 26.6 demonstrates the pointer-to-class-member operators.

```
1   // Fig. 26.6: PointerToClassMember.cpp
2   // Demonstrating operators .* and ->*.
3   #include <iostream>
4   using std::cout;
5   using std::endl;
6
7   // class Test definition
8   class Test
9   {
10  public:
11     void test()
12     {
13        cout << "In test function\n";
14     } // end function test
15
16     int value; // public data member
17  }; // end class Test
18
19  void arrowStar( Test * ); // prototype
20  void dotStar( Test * ); // prototype
21
22  int main()
23  {
24     Test test;
25     test.value = 8; // assign value 8
26     arrowStar( &test ); // pass address to arrowStar
27     dotStar( &test ); // pass address to dotStar
28     return 0;
29  } // end main
30
31  // access member function of Test object using ->*
32  void arrowStar( Test *testPtr )
33  {
34     void ( Test::*memPtr )() = &Test::test; // declare function pointer
35     ( testPtr->*memPtr )(); // invoke function indirectly
36  } // end arrowStar
37
38  // access members of Test object data member using .*
39  void dotStar( Test *testPtr2 )
40  {
41     int Test::*vPtr = &Test::value; // declare pointer
42     cout << ( *testPtr2 ).*vPtr << endl; // access value
43  } // end dotStar
```

Fig. 26.6 | Demonstrating the `.*` and `->*` operators. (Part 1 of 2.)

```
In test function
8
```

Fig. 26.6 | Demonstrating the .* and ->* operators. (Part 2 of 2.)

The program declares class Test (lines 8–17), which provides public member function test and public data member value. Lines 19–20 provide prototypes for the functions arrowStar (defined in lines 32–36) and dotStar (defined in lines 39–43), which demonstrate the ->* and .* operators, respectively. Lines 24 creates object test, and line 25 assigns 8 to its data member value. Lines 26–27 call functions arrowStar and dotStar with the address of the object test.

Line 34 in function arrowStar declares and initializes variable memPtr as a pointer to a member function. In this declaration, Test::* indicates that the variable memPtr is a pointer to a member of class Test. To declare a pointer to a function, enclose the pointer name preceded by * in parentheses, as in (Test::*memPtr). A pointer to a function must specify, as part of its type, both the return type of the function it points to and the parameter list of that function. The function's return type appears to the left of the left parenthesis, and the parameter list appears in a separate set of parentheses to the right of the pointer declaration. In this case, the function has a void return type and no parameters. The pointer memPtr is initialized with the address of class Test's member function named test. Note that the header of the function must match the function pointer's declaration—i.e., function test must have a void return type and no parameters. Notice that the right side of the assignment uses the address operator (&) to get the address of the member function test. Also, notice that neither the left side nor the right side of the assignment in line 34 refers to a specific object of class Test. Only the class name is used with the binary scope resolution operator (::). Line 35 invokes the member function stored in memPtr (i.e., test), using the ->* operator. Because memPtr is a pointer to a member of a class, the ->* operator must be used rather than the -> operator to invoke the function.

Line 41 declares and initializes vPtr as a pointer to an int data member of class Test. The right side of the assignment specifies the address of the data member value. Line 42 dereferences the pointer testPtr2, then uses the .* operator to access the member to which vPtr points. Note that the client code can create pointers to class members for only those class members that are accessible to the client code. In this example, both member function test and data member value are publicly accessible.

Common Programming Error 26.2

Declaring a member-function pointer without enclosing the pointer name in parentheses is a syntax error.

Common Programming Error 26.3

Declaring a member-function pointer without preceding the pointer name with a class name followed by the scope resolution operator (::) is a syntax error.

Common Programming Error 26.4

*Attempting to use the -> or * operator with a pointer to a class member generates syntax errors.*

26.7 Multiple Inheritance

Chapters 13 and 14 discussed single inheritance, in which each class is derived from exactly one base class. In native C++, a class may be derived from more than one base class—a technique known as *multiple inheritance* in which a derived class inherits the members of two or more base classes. This powerful capability encourages interesting forms of software reuse but can cause a variety of ambiguity problems. Multiple inheritance is a difficult concept that should be used only by experienced programmers. In fact, some of the problems associated with multiple inheritance are so subtle that newer programming languages, such as Java and C#, do not enable a class to derive from more than one base class. Recall that C++/ CLI disallows multiple inheritance for managed types even though native C++ allows it.

Good Programming Practice 26.2

Multiple inheritance is a powerful capability when used properly. Multiple inheritance should be used when an is-a *relationship exists between a new type and two or more existing types (i.e., type A is a type B and type A is a type C).*

Software Engineering Observation 26.4

Multiple inheritance can introduce complexity into a system. Great care is required in the design of a system to use multiple inheritance properly; it should not be used when single inheritance and/or composition will do the job.

A common problem with multiple inheritance is that each of the base classes might contain data members or member functions that have the same name. This can lead to ambiguity problems when you attempt to compile. Consider the multiple-inheritance example (Figs. 26.7–26.11). Class `Base1` (Fig. 26.7) contains one `protected int` data

```
 1   // Fig. 26.7: Base1.h
 2   // Definition of class Base1
 3   #ifndef BASE1_H
 4   #define BASE1_H
 5
 6   // class Base1 definition
 7   class Base1
 8   {
 9   public:
10      Base1( int parameterValue )
11      {
12         value = parameterValue;
13      } // end Base1 constructor
14
15      int getData() const
16      {
17         return value;
18      } // end function getData
19   protected: // accessible to derived classes
20      int value; // inherited by derived class
21   }; // end class Base1
22
23   #endif // BASE1_H
```

Fig. 26.7 | Demonstrating multiple inheritance—`Base1.h`.

member—value (line 20), a constructor (lines 10–13) that sets value and public member function getData (lines 15–18) that returns value.

Class Base2 (Fig. 26.8) is similar to class Base1, except that its protected data is a char named letter (line 20). Like class Base1, Base2 has a public member function get-Data, but this function returns the value of char data member letter.

Class Derived (Figs. 26.9–26.10) inherits from both class Base1 and class Base2 through multiple inheritance. Class Derived has a private data member of type double named real (line 21), a constructor to initialize all the data of class Derived and a public member function getReal that returns the value of double variable real.

```
1   // Fig. 26.8: Base2.h
2   // Definition of class Base2
3   #ifndef BASE2_H
4   #define BASE2_H
5
6   // class Base2 definition
7   class Base2
8   {
9   public:
10     Base2( char characterData )
11     {
12        letter = characterData;
13     } // end Base2 constructor
14
15     char getData() const
16     {
17        return letter;
18     } // end function getData
19   protected: // accessible to derived classes
20     char letter; // inherited by derived class
21   }; // end class Base2
22
23   #endif // BASE2_H
```

Fig. 26.8 | Demonstrating multiple inheritance—Base2.h.

```
1   // Fig. 26.9: Derived.h
2   // Definition of class Derived which inherits
3   // multiple base classes (Base1 and Base2).
4   #ifndef DERIVED_H
5   #define DERIVED_H
6
7   #include <iostream>
8   using std::ostream;
9
10  #include "Base1.h"
11  #include "Base2.h"
12
13  // class Derived definition
14  class Derived : public Base1, public Base2
15  {
```

Fig. 26.9 | Demonstrating multiple inheritance—Derived.h. (Part 1 of 2.)

```
16        friend ostream &operator<<( ostream &, const Derived & );
17    public:
18        Derived( int, char, double );
19        double getReal() const;
20    private:
21        double real; // derived class's private data
22    }; // end class Derived
23
24    #endif // DERIVED_H
```

Fig. 26.9 | Demonstrating multiple inheritance—`Derived.h`. (Part 2 of 2.)

```
1    // Fig. 26.10: Derived.cpp
2    // Member-function definitions for class Derived
3    #include "Derived.h"
4
5    // constructor for Derived calls constructors for
6    // class Base1 and class Base2.
7    // use member initializers to call base-class constructors
8    Derived::Derived( int integer, char character, double double1 )
9        : Base1( integer ), Base2( character ), real( double1 ) { }
10
11    // return real
12    double Derived::getReal() const
13    {
14        return real;
15    } // end function getReal
16
17    // display all data members of Derived
18    ostream &operator<<( ostream &output, const Derived &derived )
19    {
20        output << "   Integer: " << derived.value << "\n  Character: "
21            << derived.letter << "\nReal number: " << derived.real;
22        return output; // enables cascaded calls
23    } // end operator<<
```

Fig. 26.10 | Demonstrating multiple inheritance—`Derived.cpp`.

To indicate multiple inheritance we follow the colon (:) after class `Derived` with a comma-separated list of base classes (line 14). In Fig. 26.10, notice that constructor `Derived` explicitly calls base-class constructors for each of its base classes—`Base1` and `Base2`—using the member-initializer syntax (line 9). The base-class constructors are called in the order that the inheritance is specified, not in the order in which their constructors are mentioned; also, if the base-class constructors are not explicitly called in the member-initializer list, their default constructors will be called implicitly.

The overloaded stream insertion operator (Fig. 26.10, lines 18–23) uses its second parameter—a reference to a `Derived` object—to display a `Derived` object's data. This operator function is a `friend` of `Derived`, so `operator<<` can directly access all of class `Derived`'s protected and private members, including the protected data member `value` (inherited from class `Base1`), protected data member `letter` (inherited from class `Base2`) and private data member `real` (declared in class `Derived`).

Now let us examine the `main` function (Fig. 26.11) that tests the classes in Figs. 26.7–26.10. Line 13 creates `Base1` object `base1` and initializes it to the `int` value 10, then creates the pointer `base1Ptr` and initializes it to the null pointer (i.e., 0). Line 14 creates `Base2` object `base2` and initializes it to the `char` value `'Z'`, then creates the pointer `base2Ptr` and initializes it to the null pointer. Line 15 creates `Derived` object `derived` and initializes it to contain the `int` value 7, the `char` value `'A'` and the `double` value 3.5.

Lines 18–20 display each object's data values. For objects `base1` and `base2`, we invoke each object's `getData` member function. Even though there are two `getData` functions in this example, the calls are not ambiguous. In line 18, the compiler knows that `base1` is an object of class `Base1`, so class `Base1`'s `getData` is called. In line 19, the compiler knows that `base2` is an object of class `Base2`, so class `Base2`'s `getData` is called. Line 20 displays the contents of object `derived` using the overloaded stream insertion operator.

```cpp
1   // Fig. 26.11: MultipleInheritanceTest.cpp
2   // Driver for multiple-inheritance example.
3   #include <iostream>
4   using std::cout;
5   using std::endl;
6
7   #include "Base1.h"
8   #include "Base2.h"
9   #include "Derived.h"
10
11  int main()
12  {
13     Base1 base1( 10 ), *base1Ptr = 0; // create Base1 object
14     Base2 base2( 'Z' ), *base2Ptr = 0; // create Base2 object
15     Derived derived( 7, 'A', 3.5 ); // create Derived object
16
17     // print data members of base-class objects
18     cout << "Object base1 contains integer " << base1.getData()
19        << "\nObject base2 contains character " << base2.getData()
20        << "\nObject derived contains:\n" << derived << "\n\n";
21
22     // print data members of derived-class object
23     // scope resolution operator resolves getData ambiguity
24     cout << "Data members of Derived can be accessed individually:"
25        << "\n    Integer: " << derived.Base1::getData()
26        << "\n  Character: " << derived.Base2::getData()
27        << "\nReal number: " << derived.getReal() << "\n\n";
28     cout << "Derived can be treated as an object of either base class:\n";
29
30     // treat Derived as a Base1 object
31     base1Ptr = &derived;
32     cout << "base1Ptr->getData() yields " << base1Ptr->getData() << '\n';
33
34     // treat Derived as a Base2 object
35     base2Ptr = &derived;
36     cout << "base2Ptr->getData() yields " << base2Ptr->getData() << endl;
37     return 0;
38  } // end main
```

Fig. 26.11 | Demonstrating multiple inheritance. (Part 1 of 2.)

```
Object base1 contains integer 10
Object base2 contains character Z
Object derived contains:
    Integer: 7
  Character: A
Real number: 3.5

Data members of Derived can be accessed individually:
    Integer: 7
  Character: A
Real number: 3.5

Derived can be treated as an object of either base class:
base1Ptr->getData() yields 7
base2Ptr->getData() yields A
```

Fig. 26.11 | Demonstrating multiple inheritance. (Part 2 of 2.)

Resolving Ambiguity Issues That Arise When a Derived Class Inherits Member Functions of the Same Name from Multiple Base Classes

Lines 24–27 output the contents of object derived again by using the *get* member functions of class Derived. However, there is an ambiguity problem, because this object contains two getData functions, one inherited from class Base1 and one inherited from class Base2. This problem is easy to solve by using the binary scope resolution operator. The expression derived.Base1::getData() gets the value of the variable inherited from class Base1 (i.e., the int variable named value) and derived.Base2::getData() gets the value of the variable inherited from class Base2 (i.e., the char variable named letter). The double value in real is printed without ambiguity with the call derived.getReal()—there are no other member functions with that name in the hierarchy.

Demonstrating the Is-A Relationships in Multiple Inheritance

The *is-a* relationships of single inheritance also apply in multiple-inheritance relationships. To demonstrate this, line 31 assigns the address of object derived to the Base1 pointer base1Ptr. This is allowed because an object of class Derived *is an* object of class Base1. Line 32 invokes Base1 member function getData via base1Ptr to obtain the value of only the Base1 part of the object derived. Line 35 assigns the address of object derived to the Base2 pointer base2Ptr. This is allowed because an object of class Derived *is an* object of class Base2. Line 36 invokes Base2 member function getData via base2Ptr to obtain the value of only the Base2 part of the object derived.

26.8 Multiple Inheritance and virtual Base Classes

In Section 26.7, we discussed multiple inheritance, the process by which one class inherits from two or more classes. Multiple inheritance is used, for example, in the C++ standard library to form class basic_iostream (Fig. 26.12).

Class basic_ios is the base class for both basic_istream and basic_ostream, each of which is formed with single inheritance. Class basic_iostream inherits from both basic_istream and basic_ostream. This enables class basic_iostream objects to provide the functionality of basic_istreams and basic_ostreams. In multiple-inheritance hierarchies, the situation described in Fig. 26.12 is referred to as *diamond inheritance*.

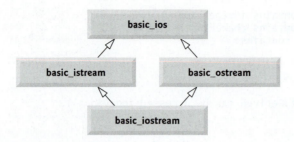

Fig. 26.12 | Multiple inheritance to form class `basic_iostream`.

Because classes `basic_istream` and `basic_ostream` each inherit from `basic_ios`, a potential problem exists for `basic_iostream`. Class `basic_iostream` could contain two copies of the members of class `basic_ios`—one inherited via class `basic_istream` and one inherited via class `basic_ostream`. Such a situation would be ambiguous and would result in a compilation error, because the compiler would not know which version of the members from class `basic_ios` to use. Of course, `basic_iostream` does not really suffer from the problem we mentioned. In this section, you'll see how using `virtual` base classes solves the problem of inheriting duplicate copies of an indirect base class.

Compilation Errors Produced When Ambiguity Arises in Diamond Inheritance
Figure 26.13 demonstrates the ambiguity that can occur in diamond inheritance. The program defines class `Base` (lines 9–13), which contains pure `virtual` function `print` (line 12). Classes `DerivedOne` (lines 16–24) and `DerivedTwo` (lines 27–35) each publicly inherit from class `Base` and override the `print` function. Class `DerivedOne` and class `DerivedTwo` each contain what the C++ standard refers to as a ***base-class subobject***—i.e., the members of class `Base` in this example.

Class `Multiple` (lines 38–46) inherits from both classes `DerivedOne` and `DerivedTwo`. In class `Multiple`, function `print` is overridden to call `DerivedTwo`'s `print` (line 44). Notice that we must qualify the `print` call with the class name `DerivedTwo` to specify which version of `print` to call.

Function `main` (lines 48–64) declares objects of classes `Multiple` (line 50), `DerivedOne` (line 51) and `DerivedTwo` (line 52). Line 53 declares an array of `Base *` pointers. Each array element is initialized with the address of an object (lines 55–57). An error occurs when the address of `both`—an object of class `Multiple`—is assigned to `array[ 0 ]`. The object `both` actually contains two subobjects of type `Base`, so the compiler does not know which subobject the pointer `array[ 0 ]` should point to, and it generates a compilation error indicating an ambiguous conversion.

```
1   // Fig. 26.13: MultipleBaseClasses.cpp
2   // Attempting to polymorphically call a function that is
3   // multiply inherited from two base classes.
4   #include <iostream>
5   using std::cout;
6   using std::endl;
```

Fig. 26.13 | Attempting to call a multiply inherited function polymorphically. (Part 1 of 3.)

```
7
8   // class Base definition
9   class Base
10  {
11  public:
12     virtual void print() const = 0; // pure virtual
13  }; // end class Base
14
15  // class DerivedOne definition
16  class DerivedOne : public Base
17  {
18  public:
19     // override print function
20     void print() const
21     {
22        cout << "DerivedOne\n";
23     } // end function print
24  }; // end class DerivedOne
25
26  // class DerivedTwo definition
27  class DerivedTwo : public Base
28  {
29  public:
30     // override print function
31     void print() const
32     {
33        cout << "DerivedTwo\n";
34     } // end function print
35  }; // end class DerivedTwo
36
37  // class Multiple definition
38  class Multiple : public DerivedOne, public DerivedTwo
39  {
40  public:
41     // qualify which version of function print
42     void print() const
43     {
44        DerivedTwo::print();
45     } // end function print
46  }; // end class Multiple
47
48  int main()
49  {
50     Multiple both; // instantiate Multiple object
51     DerivedOne one; // instantiate DerivedOne object
52     DerivedTwo two; // instantiate DerivedTwo object
53     Base *array[ 3 ]; // create array of base-class pointers
54
55     array[ 0 ] = &both; // ERROR--ambiguous
56     array[ 1 ] = &one;
57     array[ 2 ] = &two;
58
```

Fig. 26.13 | Attempting to call a multiply inherited function polymorphically. (Part 2 of 3.)

```
59        // polymorphically invoke print
60        for ( int i = 0; i < 3; i++ )
61           array[ i ] -> print();
62
63        return 0;
64   } // end main
```

```
C:\Projects\vcpphtp2\examples\ch26\Fig26_13\MultipleBaseClasses.cpp(55):
    error C2594: '=' : ambiguous conversions from 'Multiple *' to 'Base *'
```

Fig. 26.13 | Attempting to call a multiply inherited function polymorphically. (Part 3 of 3.)

Eliminating Duplicate Subobjects with virtual *Base-Class Inheritance*

The problem of duplicate subobjects is resolved with virtual inheritance. When a base class is inherited as virtual, only one subobject will appear in the derived class—a process called *virtual base-class inheritance*. Figure 26.14 revises the program of Fig. 26.13 to use a virtual base class.

The key change in the program is that classes DerivedOne (line 15) and DerivedTwo (line 26) each inherit from class Base by specifying virtual public Base. Since both of these classes inherit from Base, they each contain a Base subobject. The benefit of virtual inheritance is not clear until class Multiple inherits from both DerivedOne and DerivedTwo (line 37). Since each of the base classes used virtual inheritance to inherit class Base's members, the compiler ensures that only one subobject of type Base is inherited into class Multiple. This eliminates the ambiguity error generated by the compiler in Fig. 26.13. The compiler now allows the implicit conversion of the derived-class pointer (&both) to the base-class pointer array[0] in line 56 in main. The for statement in lines 61–62 polymorphically calls print for each object.

```
1    // Fig. 26.14: VirtualBaseClasses.cpp
2    // Using virtual base classes.
3    #include <iostream>
4    using std::cout;
5    using std::endl;
6
7    // class Base definition
8    class Base
9    {
10   public:
11      virtual void print() const = 0; // pure virtual
12   }; // end class Base
13
14   // class DerivedOne definition
15   class DerivedOne : virtual public Base
16   {
17   public:
18      // override print function
19      void print() const
20      {
```

Fig. 26.14 | Using virtual base classes. (Part 1 of 2.)

```
21              cout << "DerivedOne\n";
22          } // end function print
23      }; // end DerivedOne class
24
25      // class DerivedTwo definition
26      class DerivedTwo : virtual public Base
27      {
28      public:
29          // override print function
30          void print() const
31          {
32              cout << "DerivedTwo\n";
33          } // end function print
34      }; // end DerivedTwo class
35
36      // class Multiple definition
37      class Multiple : public DerivedOne, public DerivedTwo
38      {
39      public:
40          // qualify which version of function print
41          void print() const
42          {
43              DerivedTwo::print();
44          } // end function print
45      }; // end Multiple class
46
47      int main()
48      {
49          Multiple both; // instantiate Multiple object
50          DerivedOne one; // instantiate DerivedOne object
51          DerivedTwo two; // instantiate DerivedTwo object
52
53          // declare array of base-class pointers and initialize
54          // each element to a derived-class type
55          Base *array[ 3 ];
56          array[ 0 ] = &both;
57          array[ 1 ] = &one;
58          array[ 2 ] = &two;
59
60          // polymorphically invoke function print
61          for ( int i = 0; i < 3; i++ )
62              array[ i ]->print();
63
64          return 0;
65      } // end main
```

```
DerivedTwo
DerivedOne
DerivedTwo
```

Fig. 26.14 | Using virtual base classes. (Part 2 of 2.)

Constructors in Multiple-Inheritance Hierarchies with `virtual` *Base Classes*

Implementing hierarchies with `virtual` base classes is simpler if default constructors are used for the base classes. The examples in Figs. 26.13 and 26.14 use compiler-generated default constructors. If a `virtual` base class provides a constructor that requires arguments, the implementation of the derived classes becomes more complicated, because the *most derived class* must explicitly invoke the virtual base class's constructor to initialize the members inherited from the `virtual` base class.

> **Software Engineering Observation 26.5**
>
> *Providing a default constructor for* `virtual` *base classes simplifies hierarchy design.*

Additional Information on Multiple Inheritance

Multiple inheritance is a complex topic typically covered in more advanced C++ texts. For more information on multiple inheritance, please visit our C++ Resource Center at

> www.deitel.com/cplusplus/

In the *C++ Multiple Inheritance* category, you'll find links to several articles and resources, including a multiple inheritance FAQ and tips for using multiple inheritance.

26.9 Variable-Length Argument Lists[1]

Native C++

It is possible to create functions that receive an unspecified number of arguments in native C++. An ellipsis (. . .) in a function's prototype indicates that the function receives a variable number of arguments of any type. Note that the ellipsis must always be placed at the end of the parameter list, and there must be at least one argument before the ellipsis. The macros and definitions of the *variable arguments header* <cstdarg> (Fig. 26.15) provide the capabilities necessary to build functions with variable-length argument lists.

Identifier	Description
`va_list`	A type suitable for holding information needed by macros `va_start`, `va_arg` and `va_end`. To access the arguments in a variable-length argument list, an object of type `va_list` must be declared.
`va_start`	A macro that is invoked before the arguments of a variable-length argument list can be accessed. The macro initializes the object declared with `va_list` for use by the `va_arg` and `va_end` macros.
`va_arg`	A macro that expands to an expression of the value and type of the next argument in the variable-length argument list. Each invocation of `va_arg` modifies the object declared with `va_list` so that the object points to the next argument in the list.

Fig. 26.15 | The type and the macros defined in header <cstdarg>. (Part 1 of 2.)

---

1. In native C++, programmers use function overloading to accomplish much of what C programmers accomplish with variable-length argument lists.

Identifier	Description
va_end	A macro that performs termination housekeeping in a function whose variable-length argument list was referred to by the va_start macro.

Fig. 26.15 | The type and the macros defined in header `<cstdarg>`. (Part 2 of 2.)

Figure 26.16 demonstrates function `average` that receives a variable number of arguments. The first argument of `average` is always the number of values to be averaged, and the remainder of the arguments must all be of type `double`.

```
1   // Fig. 26.16: VarLengthArgs.cpp
2   // Using variable-length argument lists.
3   #include <iostream>
4   using std::cout;
5   using std::endl;
6   using std::ios;
7
8   #include <iomanip>
9   using std::setw;
10  using std::setprecision;
11  using std::setiosflags;
12  using std::fixed;
13
14  #include <cstdarg>
15  using std::va_list;
16
17  double average( int, ... );
18
19  int main()
20  {
21     double double1 = 37.5;
22     double double2 = 22.5;
23     double double3 = 1.7;
24     double double4 = 10.2;
25
26     cout << fixed << setprecision( 1 ) << "double1 = "
27        << double1 << "\ndouble2 = " << double2 << "\ndouble3 = "
28        << double3 << "\ndouble4 = " << double4 << endl
29        << setprecision( 3 )
30        << "\nThe average of double1 and double2 is "
31        << average( 2, double1, double2 )
32        << "\nThe average of double1, double2, and double3 is "
33        << average( 3, double1, double2, double3 )
34        << "\nThe average of double1, double2, double3"
35        << " and double4 is "
36        << average( 4, double1, double2, double3, double4 )
37        << endl;
38     return 0;
39  } // end main
```

Fig. 26.16 | Using variable-length argument lists. (Part 1 of 2.)

```
40
41    // calculate average
42    double average( int count, ... )
43    {
44        double total = 0;
45        va_list list;  // for storing information needed by va_start
46
47        va_start( list, count );
48
49        // process variable-length argument list
50        for ( int i = 1; i <= count; i++ )
51            total += va_arg( list, double );
52
53        va_end( list ); // end the va_start
54        return total / count;
55    } // end function average
```

```
double1 = 37.5
double2 = 22.5
double3 = 1.7
double4 = 10.2

The average of double1 and double2 is 30.000
The average of double1, double2, and double3 is 20.567
The average of double1, double2, double3 and double4 is 17.975
```

Fig. 26.16 | Using variable-length argument lists. (Part 2 of 2.)

Function average uses all the definitions and macros of header <cstdarg>. Object list, of type va_list, is used by macros va_start, va_arg and va_end to process the variable-length argument list of function average. The function invokes va_start to initialize object list for use in va_arg and va_end. The macro receives two arguments—object list and the identifier of the rightmost argument in the argument list before the ellipsis—count in this case (va_start uses count here to determine where the variable-length argument list begins).

Next, function average repeatedly adds the arguments in the variable-length argument list to the total. The value to be added to total is retrieved from the argument list by invoking macro va_arg. Macro va_arg receives two arguments—object list and the type of the value expected in the argument list (double in this case)—and returns the value of the argument. Function average invokes macro va_end with object list as an argument before returning. Finally, the average is calculated and returned to main. Note that we used only double arguments for the variable-length portion of the argument list.

Variable-length argument lists promote variables of type float to type double. These argument lists also promote integral variables that are smaller than int to type int (variables of type int, unsigned, long and unsigned long are left alone).

Software Engineering Observation 26.6

Variable-length argument lists can be used only with fundamental-type arguments and with arguments of C-style struct types that do not contain C++ specific features such as virtual functions, constructors, destructors, references, const data members and virtual base classes.

Common Programming Error 26.5

Placing an ellipsis in the middle of a function parameter list is a syntax error. An ellipsis may be placed only at the end of the parameter list.

C++/CLI

Variable-length argument lists that allow you to create functions that receive an arbitrary number of arguments can also be used with managed code in C++/CLI. A one-dimensional managed array-type argument preceded by ... in a function's parameter list indicates that the function receives a variable number of arguments with the type of the array's elements. This use of a ... modifier can occur only in the last entry of the parameter list. While you can use function overloading and array passing to accomplish much of what is accomplished with "varargs"—another name for variable-length argument lists—using the ... modifier is more concise.

Figure 26.17 shows what Figure 26.16 would look like using C++/CLI rather than native C++. Again, we use a function Average (lines 33–42), which receives a variable-length sequence of doubles (line 33). C++/CLI treats the variable-length argument list as a one-dimensional array whose elements are all of the same type. Hence, the function body can manipulate the parameter numbers as an array of doubles. Lines 38–39 use a for each statement to walk through the array and calculate the total of the doubles in the array. Line 41 accesses numbers->Length to obtain the size of the numbers array for use in the averaging calculation. Lines 23, 25 and 27 in main call function Average with two, three and four arguments, respectively. Function Average has a variable-length argument list, so it can average as many double arguments as the caller passes. The output reveals that each call to function Average returns the correct value.

```
1   // Fig. 26.17: VarargsTest.cpp
2   // Using variable-length argument lists.
3
4   #include "stdafx.h"
5
6   using namespace System;
7
8   //function prototype
9   static double Average( ... array< double >^ numbers );
10
11  int main( array< System::String ^ > ^args )
12  {
13     double d1 = 10.0;
14     double d2 = 20.0;
15     double d3 = 30.0;
16     double d4 = 40.0;
17
18     Console::WriteLine(
19        "d1 = {0:F1}\nd2 = {1:F1}\nd3 = {2:F1}\nd4 = {3:F1}\n",
20        d1, d2, d3, d4 );
21
22     Console::WriteLine( "Average of d1 and d2 is {0:F1}",
23        Average( d1, d2 ) );
```

Fig. 26.17 | Using variable-length argument lists. (Part 1 of 2.)

```
24        Console::WriteLine( "Average of d1, d2 and d3 is {0:F1}",
25           Average( d1, d2, d3 ) );
26        Console::WriteLine( "Average of d1, d2, d3 and d4 is {0:F1}",
27           Average( d1, d2, d3, d4 ) );
28
29        return 0;
30     } // end main
31
32     // calculate average
33     static double Average( ... array< double >^ numbers )
34     {
35        double total = 0.0; // initialize total
36
37        // calculate total using the for each statement
38        for each ( double d in numbers )
39           total += d;
40
41        return total / numbers->Length;
42     } // end function Average
```

```
d1 = 10.0
d2 = 20.0
d3 = 30.0
d4 = 40.0

Average of d1 and d2 is 15.0
Average of d1, d2 and d3 is 20.0
Average of d1, d2, d3 and d4 is 25.0
```

Fig. 26.17 | Using variable-length argument lists. (Part 2 of 2.)

Common Programming Error 26.6

Using the ... modifier with a parameter in the middle of a function parameter list is a syntax error. The ... modifier may be used only with the last parameter of the parameter list.

26.10 Using Command-Line Arguments

Native C++

On many systems—Windows, UNIX, Linux and Mac OS X in particular—it is possible to pass arguments to main from a command line by including parameters int argc and char *argv[] in the parameter list of main. Parameter argc receives the number of command-line arguments. Parameter argv is an array of char *'s pointing to strings in which the actual command-line arguments are stored. Common uses of command-line arguments include printing the arguments, passing options to a program and passing filenames to a program.

Figure 26.18 copies a file into another file one character at a time. The executable file for the program is called copyFile (i.e., the executable name for the file). A typical command line for the copyFile program on a Windows system is

    copyFile.exe C:\input.txt C:\output.txt

```
 1    // Fig. 26.18: CmdLineTest.cpp
 2    // Using command-line arguments
 3    #include <iostream>
 4    using std::cout;
 5    using std::endl;
 6    using std::ios;
 7
 8    #include <fstream>
 9    using std::ifstream;
10    using std::ofstream;
11
12    int main( int argc, char *argv[] )1
13    {
14       // check number of command-line arguments
15       if ( argc != 3 )
16          cout << "Usage: copyFile infile_name outfile_name" << endl;
17       else
18       {
19          ifstream inFile( argv[ 1 ], ios::in );
20
21          // input file could not be opened
22          if ( !inFile )
23          {
24             cout << argv[ 1 ] << " could not be opened" << endl;
25             return -1;
26          } // end if
27
28          ofstream outFile( argv[ 2 ], ios::out );
29
30          // output file could not be opened
31          if ( !outFile )
32          {
33             cout << argv[ 2 ] << " could not be opened" << endl;
34             inFile.close();
35             return -2;
36          } // end if
37
38          char c = inFile.get(); // read first character
39
40          while ( inFile )
41          {
42             outFile.put( c );   // output character
43             c = inFile.get();   // read next character
44          } // end while
45       } // end else
46
47       return 0;
48    } // end main
```

Fig. 26.18 | Using command-line arguments.

This command line indicates that file `input.txt` is to be copied to file `output.txt`. When the program executes, if `argc` is not 3 (`copyFile.exe` counts as one of the arguments), the program prints an error message (line 16). Otherwise, array `argv` contains the strings "copyFile.exe", "C:\input.txt" and "C:\output.txt". The second and third arguments on the command line are used as filenames by the program. The files are opened by creating ifstream object inFile and ofstream object outFile (lines 19 and 28). If both files are opened successfully, characters are read from file input with member function get and written to file output with member function put until the end-of-file indicator for file input.txt is set (lines 40–44). Then the program terminates. The result is an exact copy of file input.txt.

C++/CLI

It is possible to pass arguments from the command line to a C++/CLI application by including a parameter of type array< System::String ^> ^args) (i.e., an array of Strings) in the parameter list of main, exactly as we have done in every C++/CLI application in the book. By convention, this parameter is named args. When an application is executed from the **Command Prompt**, the execution environment passes the command-line arguments that appear after the application name to the application's main function as Strings in the one-dimensional array args. Rather than use argc for the number of command-line arguments like native C++, the number of arguments passed from the command line is obtained by accessing the array's Length property. For example, the command "MyApplication a b" passes two command-line arguments to application MyApplication. Note that command-line arguments are separated by white space, not commas. When the preceding command executes, the main function entry point receives the two-element array args (i.e., args->Length is 2) in which args[0] contains the String "a" and args[1] contains the String "b". Note that, unlike native C++, the application's name is not included as the first element of the args array.

Figure 26.19 uses three command-line arguments to initialize a managed array. When the application executes, if args->Length is not 3, the application prints an error message and terminates (lines 11–14). Otherwise, lines 17–34 initialize and display the array based on the values of the command-line arguments.

```
1   // Fig. 26.19: InitArray.cpp
2   // Using command-line arguments to initialize an array
3
4   #include "stdafx.h"
5
6   using namespace System;
7
8   int main( array< System::String ^ > ^args )
9   {
10      // check number of command-line arguments
11      if ( args->Length != 3 )
12          Console::WriteLine(
13          "Error: Please re-enter the entire command, including\n" +
14          "an array size, initial value and increment." );
15      else
16      {
17          // get array size from first command-line argument
18          int arrayLength = Convert::ToInt32( args[ 0 ] );
```

Fig. 26.19 | Using command-line arguments to initialize an array (Part 1 of 2.)

```
19          // create array
20          array< int >^ arr = gcnew array< int >( arrayLength );
21
22          // get initial value and increment from command-line argument
23          int initialValue = Convert::ToInt32( args[ 1 ] );
24          int increment = Convert::ToInt32( args[ 2 ] );
25
26          // calculate value for each array element
27          for ( int counter = 0; counter < arr->Length; counter++ )
28             arr [ counter ] = initialValue + increment * counter;
29
30          Console::WriteLine( "{0}{1,8}", "Index", "Value" );
31
32          //display array index and value
33          for ( int counter = 0; counter < arr->Length; counter++ )
34             Console::WriteLine( "{0,5}{1,8}", counter, arr[ counter ] );
35       } // end else
36
37       return 0;
38    } // end main
```

```
C:\examples\ch26\fig26_19\InitArray\debug>InitArray.exe
Error: Please re-enter the entire command, including
an array size, initial value and increment.
```

```
C:\examples\ch26\fig26_19\InitArray\debug>InitArray.exe 5 0 4
Index    Value
   0         0
   1         4
   2         8
   3        12
   4        16
```

```
C:\examples\ch26\fig26_19\InitArray\debug>InitArray.exe 10 1 2
Index    Value
   0         1
   1         3
   2         5
   3         7
   4         9
   5        11
   6        13
   7        15
   8        17
   9        19
```

Fig. 26.19 | Using command-line arguments to initialize an array (Part 2 of 2.)

The command-line arguments become available to main as Strings in args. Line 18 gets args[0]—a String that specifies the array size—and converts it to an int value, which the application uses to create the array in line 20. The static function ToInt32 of class Convert converts its String argument to an int.

Lines 23–24 convert the args[1] and args[2] command-line arguments to int values and store them in initialValue and increment, respectively. Lines 27–28 calculate the value for each array element.

The output of the first sample execution indicates that the application received an insufficient number of command-line arguments. The second sample execution uses command-line arguments 5, 0 and 4 to specify the size of the array (5), the value of the first element (0) and the increment of each value in the array (4), respectively. The corresponding output indicates that these values create an array containing the integers 0, 4, 8, 12 and 16. The output from the third sample execution illustrates that the command-line arguments 10, 1 and 2 produce an array whose 10 elements are the nonnegative odd integers from 1 to 19.

26.11 Delegates and Events in .NET

At a number of points we have described reasons why managed code in C++/CLI does not allow the use of pointers in the same way as native C++; this includes the use of function pointers (see Section 9.12) and functors (see Section 23.7). What if we need the power of function pointers and functors in managed code? Fortunately, the .NET Framework provides *delegates* to accomplish just that. Delegates have similar functionality to function pointers in some respects, similar functionality to functors in other respects, and some nuances of their own. Delegates are a fairly complicated topic and their full power goes beyond the scope of this book. In this section we give an introduction to the basics of delegates and provide a simple code example.

Delegates are managed objects (subject to the work of the CLR garbage collector) that encapsulate a type-safe reference to a function or functions. For the moment we consider only delegates that encapsulate a single function. Delegates can encapsulate member functions or nonmember functions (whether they are static or not). When you declare a delegate you specify a return type and arguments for the type of functions the delegate can reference. Any function that you attempt to add to the delegate must match the return type and arguments specified in the declaration of the delegate. The syntax for declaring a delegate is as follows:

> *accessSpecifier* **delegate** *returnType delegateName*(*parameter1, parameter2, ...*);

The *accessSpecifier* is private by default and can be omitted if the delegate does not need to be public. Note that this is essentially the delegate keyword preceding a function prototype.

Delegates are not simple types like ints or doubles. Each delegate actually represents a separate class. At runtime the compiler takes any delegates in the program and creates a new class for each one. Each of these classes are derived from **MulticastDelegate** (namespace System) which is derived from class **Delegate** (also in namespace System). The resulting class inherits a number of member functions from System::Delegate including an **Invoke** function. The Invoke function has the return type and parameters that the delegate was declared with. Figure 26.20 demonstrates how to declare a delegate, create an instance of it and give it a specific function to encapsulate.

```
 1   // Fig 26.20: DelegateTest.cpp
 2   // Simple example using a delegate and a class member function
 3
 4   #include "stdafx.h"
 5
 6   using namespace System;
 7
 8   // declare a delegate that encapsulates a function that
 9   // returns a String ^ and takes 2 String ^ parameters
10   public delegate String ^ StringCat( String ^, String ^ );
11
12   // simple managed class with a member function that matches the type of
13   // the delegate
14   ref class StringFormatter
15   {
16   public:
17      String ^ append( String ^a, String ^b)
18      {
19         Console::WriteLine( "Calling StringFormatter::append" );
20         return a + b;
21      } // end function append
22   }; // end managed class StringFormatter
23
24   int main( array< System::String ^ > ^args )
25   {
26      // create an instance of the StringFormatter class
27      StringFormatter ^F = gcnew StringFormatter();
28
29      // create an instance of the StringCat delegate
30      // pass as parameters the address of a class member function
31      // and an instance of that class
32      StringCat ^S = gcnew StringCat( F, &StringFormatter::append );
33
34      // invoke the delegate with 2 parameters
35      String ^result = S( "Hello", " World!" );
36      Console::WriteLine( "Delegate result is: {0}", result );
37
38      return 0;
39   } // end main
```

```
Calling StringFormatter::append
Delegate result is: Hello World!
```

Fig. 26.20 | Using delegates.

At line 10 we declare a delegate named StringCat that can encapsulate functions that return a String ^ and take two String ^ as parameters. Lines 14–22 define a simple managed class StringFormatter. The class has a single member function append that takes two String ^ as parameters, concatenates them and returns the result. Clearly the return type and arguments of append match that of StringCat so we will be able to use them together. Inside main in line 27 we create an instance of the StringFormatter class called F which we will need to pass to the delegate constructor.

The delegate declaration at line 10 actually defines a new managed class called StringCat that we can create instances of just like any other managed type. However, delegates cannot be created with stack semantics; you are required to create a handle to the delegate using gcnew as we did in line 32. This delegate constructor takes two parameters: a reference to an instance of a managed class and a reference to a member function of that managed class. Notice the syntax used to pass a reference to the member function of StringFormatter. You must use & for the address of a function and not % as you would for a reference to a managed object. We pass append based on the class StringFormatter using the scope resolution operator (::), not on a specific instance of the class. Also note we don't pass append with parentheses; doing so would result in a compilation error. Had we attempted to pass a member function which did not match the return type and parameters specified in the delegate declaration at line 10, the compiler would have issued an error. If we wanted to have our delegate encapsulate a nonmember function, we could simply pass the address of the function (using the & operator) without passing an instance of a class.

Common Programming Error 26.7

Attempting to create a delegate using stack semantics results in a compilation error. Attempting to pass a function to the delegate constructor using % rather than & also causes a compilation error.

Once the delegate has been created, we can use it one of two ways. In line 35 we invoke the delegate by calling it as if it were a function, passing two String ^ arguments. This actually calls the delegate's Invoke function that is inherited from System::Delegate. Instead of line 35 we could have chosen to invoke the delegate by explicitly calling this function as follows:

```
String ^result = S->Invoke( "Hello", " World!" );
```

As you can see, we are storing the result of the delegate's invocation in a String ^ because that is the type we declared the delegate would return. At line 36 we print the result and see that by invoking the delegate append was called and the two strings were concatenated. We used a simple example here for demonstration purposes. Obviously using a delegate is unnecessarily complicated for doing simple string concatenation. There are many situations though in which delegates are extremely useful. In particular, because delegates can be passed as arguments to functions, they can be used to pass a function from one class to another class.

MulticastDelegate

Native C++ function pointers can point to only a single function at a time. Delegates do not have this limitation. Class MulticastDelegate allows a delegate to encapsulate multiple functions at once by storing a linked list of delegate instances called the delegate's *invocation list*. When you declare a delegate with the delegate keyword you are actually creating a MulticastDelegate capable of encapsulating one or many functions. To encapsulate multiple functions with a MulticastDelegate you can use the overloaded += operator after the delegate has been created. For example, using the instance S of the StringCat delegate from Fig. 26.20, we could add another delegate encapsulating a nonmember function test (which must return a String ^ and takes two String ^ as parameters) to S's invocation list as follows:

```
S += gcnew StringCat( &test );
```

Now when we invoke S, all the delegates in its invocation list will have the functions they encapsulate called. In this case both StringFormatter::append and test will be called with the arguments passed to S. Using the += operator is a convenient way to add new delegates without having to explicitly call the *Combine* function of class Delegate. A MulticastDelegate can have the same function in its invocation list multiple times if you add a delegate encapsulating that function multiple times. When the delegate is invoked, the function will be called as many times as it was added to the invocation list. You may be wondering what the MulticastDelegate will do with the return result of each of the called functions. The answer is that the return result is undefined. Therefore, you should always declare MulticastDelegates with a return type of void. If you are using a delegate that encapsulates only a single function then you are free to use that function's return result by declaring the delegate with a non-void return type. You can remove functions from a MulticastDelegate's invocation list by using the overloaded -= operator. This avoids having to explicitly call the *Remove* function of class Delegate. For example, using the same instance S of StringCat, we could write:

```
S -= gcnew StringCat( &test );
```

This would remove function test from S's invocation list.

Error-Prevention Tip 26.4

The return result of a MulticastDelegate is undefined if there are multiple delegates in its invocation list. Generally you should declare MulticastDelegates with a return type of void, although it is not a compilation error to do otherwise.

Events

Normally, a user interacts with an application's GUI (graphical user interface) to indicate the tasks that the application should perform. For example, when you write an e-mail in an e-mail application, clicking the **Send** button tells the application to send the e-mail to the specified e-mail addresses. GUIs are *event driven*. When the user interacts with a GUI component, the interaction—known as an *event*—drives the program to perform a task. Common events (user interactions) that might cause an application to perform a task include clicking a Button, typing in a TextBox, selecting an item from a menu, closing a window and moving the mouse. A function that performs a task in response to an event is called an *event handler*, and the overall process of responding to events is known as *event handling*. Note that events aren't used for only GUIs but also for any situation in which a class wants to trigger some function when a certain action occurs on objects of that class.

An event is declared with the following form:

accessSpecifier **event** *delegateType* ^*eventName*;

As you can see, we use an access specifier (usually public), then the event keyword followed by a delegate type (such as StringCat from Fig. 26.20) and finally a name for the event type. Now the event can be accessed like a data member of the class it was declared in. Inside the event handler that you want to trigger the event you would call the event as if it were a function, passing arguments of a type compatible with the delegate type the event was declared with. Finally, to use the event we need to add a new delegate to it of the declared type using the overloaded += operator. The passed delegate specifies what functions will be called when the event is triggered. Unfortunately a full treatment of events and event handlers goes beyond the scope of this book.

26.12 Wrap-Up

In this chapter, you learned how to use the const_cast operator to remove the const qualification of a variable as well as the basics of reinterpret_cast and safe_cast in C++/CLI. We then showed how to use namespaces to ensure that every identifier in a program has a unique name and explained how they can help resolve naming conflicts. You saw several operator keywords for programmers whose keyboards do not support certain characters used in operator symbols, such as !, &, ^, ~ and |. Next, we showed how the mutable storage-class specifier enables a programmer to indicate that a data member should always be modifiable, even when it appears in an object that is currently being treated as a const. We also showed the mechanics of using pointers to class members and the ->* and .* operators. We introduced multiple inheritance and discussed problems associated with allowing a derived class to inherit the members of several base classes. As part of this discussion, we demonstrated how virtual inheritance can be used to solve those problems. We also discussed command-line arguments and how to use variable length arguments in native C++ and C++/CLI. We concluded the chapter with a discussion of delegates and events in C++/CLI.

Summary

Section 26.2 Other Cast Operators

- Visual C++ provides the const_cast operator for casting away const or volatile qualification.

- A program declares a variable with the volatile qualifier when that program expects the variable to be modified by other programs. Declaring a variable volatile indicates that the compiler should not optimize the use of that variable, because doing so could affect the ability of those other programs to access and modify the volatile variable.

- In general, it is dangerous to use the const_cast operator, because it allows a program to modify a variable that was declared const, and thus was not supposed to be modifiable.

- There are cases in which it is desirable, or even necessary, to cast away const-ness. For example, older C and C++ libraries might provide functions that have non-const parameters and that do not modify their parameters. If you wished to pass const data to such a function, you would need to cast away the data's const-ness; otherwise, the compiler would report error messages.

- If you pass non-const data to a function that treats the data as if it were constant, then returns that data as a constant, you might need to cast away the const-ness of the returned data to access and modify that data.

- The reinterpret_cast operator can be used to cast a pointer from one type to another unrelated type. It can also be used to convert pointers to integers and vice versa.

- It is dangerous to use reinterpret_cast because it does not change any of the underlying bytes of the object it is operating on. It simply requests that the compiler reinterpret the object as a different type.

- The C++/CLI specific safe_cast operator is similar in use to static_cast except that it is guaranteed to produce verifiable code. If a safe_cast is used to try to cast between incompatible types, then the program will throw an InvalidCastException at runtime.

Section 26.3 namespaces
- A program includes many identifiers defined in different scopes. Sometimes a variable of one scope will "overlap" with a variable of the same name in a different scope, possibly creating a naming conflict. The C++ standard solves this problem with namespaces.

- Each namespace defines a scope in which identifiers are placed. To use a namespace member, either the member's name must be qualified with the namespace name and the binary scope resolution operator (::), or a using directive or declaration must appear before the name is used in the program.

- Typically, using statements are placed at the beginning of the file in which members of the namespace are used.

- Not all namespaces are guaranteed to be unique. Two third-party vendors might inadvertently use the same identifiers for their namespace names.

- A using namespace directive specifies that the members of a namespace will be used frequently throughout a program. This allows you to access all the members of the namespace.

- A using namespace directive can be used for predefined namespaces (e.g., std) or programmer-defined namespaces.

- A namespace can contain constants, data, classes, nested namespaces, functions, etc. Definitions of namespaces must occupy the global scope or be nested within other namespaces.

- An unnamed namespace has an implicit using directive, so its members appear to occupy the global namespace, are accessible directly and do not have to be qualified with a namespace name. Global variables are also part of the global namespace.

- When accessing members of a nested namespace, the members must be qualified with the namespace name (unless the member is being used inside the nested namespace).

- Namespaces can be aliased.

Section 26.4 Operator Keywords
- The C++ standard provides operator keywords that can be used in place of several Visual C++ operators. Operator keywords are useful for programmers whose keyboards do not support certain characters such as !, &, ^, ~, |, etc.

Section 26.5 mutable Class Members
- If a data member should always be modifiable, Visual C++ provides the storage-class specifier mutable as an alternative to const_cast. A mutable data member is always modifiable, even in a const member function or const object. This reduces the need to cast away "const-ness."

- mutable and const_cast are used in different contexts. For a const object with no mutable data members, operator const_cast must be used every time a member is to be modified. This greatly reduces the chance of a member being accidentally modified, because the member is not permanently modifiable.

- Operations involving const_cast are typically hidden in a member function's implementation. The user of a class might not be aware that a member is being modified.

Section 26.6 Pointers to Class Members (.* and ->*)
- Visual C++ provides the .* and ->* operators for accessing class members via pointers. This is rarely used capability that is used primarily by advanced Visual C++ programmers.

- Declaring a pointer to a function requires that you enclose the pointer name preceded by an * in parentheses. A pointer to a function must specify, as part of its type, both the return type of the function it points to and the parameter list of that function.

Section 26.7 Multiple Inheritance

- In Visual C++, a class may be derived from more than one base class—a technique known as multiple inheritance, in which a derived class inherits the members of two or more base classes. This is only possible in native C++. C++/CLI specifically forbids multiple inheritance.

- A common problem with multiple inheritance is that each of the base classes might contain data members or member functions that have the same name. This can lead to ambiguity problems when you attempt to compile.

- The *is-a* relationships of single inheritance also apply in multiple-inheritance relationships.

- Multiple inheritance is used, for example, in the C++ Standard Library to form class `basic_iostream`. Class `basic_ios` is the base class for both `basic_istream` and `basic_ostream`, each of which is formed with single inheritance. Class `basic_iostream` inherits from both `basic_istream` and `basic_ostream`. This enables objects of class `basic_iostream` to provide the functionality of both `basic_istream`s and `basic_ostream`s. In multiple-inheritance hierarchies, the situation described here is referred to as diamond inheritance.

- Because classes `basic_istream` and `basic_ostream` each inherit from `basic_ios`, a potential problem exists for `basic_iostream`. If not implemented correctly, class `basic_iostream` could contain two copies of the members of class `basic_ios`—one inherited via class `basic_istream` and one inherited via class `basic_ostream`. Such a situation would be ambiguous and would result in a compilation error, because the compiler would not know which version of the members from class `basic_ios` to use.

Section 26.8 Multiple Inheritance and `virtual` Base Classes

- The ambiguity in diamond inheritance occurs when a derived-class object inherits two or more base-class subobjects. The problem of duplicate subobjects is resolved with `virtual` inheritance. When a base class is inherited as `virtual`, only one subobject will appear in the derived class—a process called `virtual` base-class inheritance.

- Implementing hierarchies with `virtual` base classes is simpler if default constructors are used for the base classes. If a `virtual` base class provides a constructor that requires arguments, the implementation of the derived classes becomes more complicated, because the most derived class must explicitly invoke the virtual base class's constructor to initialize the members inherited from the `virtual` base class.

Section 26.9 Variable-Length Argument Lists

- The macros and definitions of the variable arguments header `<cstdarg>` provide the capabilities necessary to build functions with variable-length argument lists.

- An ellipsis (…) in a function prototype indicates that the function receives a variable number of arguments.

- Type `va_list` is suitable for holding information needed by macros `va_start`, `va_arg` and `va_end`. To access the arguments in a variable-length argument list, an object of type `va_list` must be declared.

- Macro `va_start` is invoked before the arguments of a variable-length argument list can be accessed. The macro initializes the object declared with `va_list` for use by macros `va_arg` and `va_end`.

- Macro `va_arg` expands to an expression of the value and type of the next argument in the variable-length argument list. Each invocation of `va_arg` modifies the `va_list` object so that the object points to the next argument in the list.

- Macro `va_end` facilitates a normal return from a function whose variable argument list was referred to by the `va_start` macro.

- A managed one-dimensional array-type argument preceded by the ... modifier in a C++/CLI's function's parameter list indicates that the function receives a variable number of arguments with the type of the array's elements.
- The ... modifier can appear only in the last entry of the parameter list in C++/CLI.
- C++/CLI treats the variable-length argument list as a managed, one-dimensional array whose elements are all of the same type.

Section 26.10 Using Command-Line Arguments
- On many systems—UNIX, Linux, Mac OS X and Windows in particular—it is possible to pass command-line arguments in native C++ to main by including in main's parameter list the parameters int argc and char *argv[]. Parameter argc is the number of command-line arguments. Parameter argv is an array of char *'s containing the command-line arguments.
- When a C++/CLI application is executed from the **Command Prompt**, the execution environment passes the command-line arguments that appear after the application name to the application's main function as Strings in a one-dimensional array. The number of command line arguments can be found using the Length property of this array. The application's name does not count as one of these arguments.

Section 26.11 Delegates and Events in .NET
- Delegates are managed objects that encapsulate type-safe references to a function or functions.
- A delegate declaration includes a return type and parameter list. Only functions with a matching return type and parameter list can be encapsulated by that delegate.
- Calling the Invoke function on a delegate will call every function in its invocation list. Invoke can be called by executing the delegate as if it were a function name.
- The overloaded += operator can be used to add other delegates to a MulticastDelegate's invocation list. The overloaded -= operator can be used to remove them.
- Events drive programs to perform tasks based on certain actions that occur, such as key presses or mouse clicks.
- A function that is called in response to an event is called an event handler.

Terminology

.* operator
->* operator
and operator keyword
and_eq operator keyword
base-class subobject
bitand operator keyword
bitor operator keyword
bitwise assignment operator keywords
bitwise operator keywords
cast away const-ness
comma-separated list of base classes
command-line arguments
compl operator keyword
const_cast operator
delegate
diamond inheritance
event handler

events
global namespace
inequality operator keywords
logical operator keywords
most derived class
multiple inheritance
mutable data member
namespace
namespace alias
namespace keyword
naming conflict
nested namespace
not operator keyword
not_eq operator keyword
operator keyword
or operator keyword
or_eq operator keyword

pointer-to-member operators	variable-length argument lists
reinterpret_cast operator	virtual base class
safe_cast operator	virtual inheritance
unnamed namespace	volatile qualifier
using declaration	xor operator keyword
using namespace declaration	xor_eq operator keyword

Self-Review Exercises

26.1 Fill in the blanks for each of the following:
  a) The _____ operator qualifies a member with its namespace.
  b) The _____ operator allows an object's "const-ness" to be cast away.
  c) Because an unnamed namespace has an implicit using directive, its members appear to occupy the _____, are accessible directly and do not have to be qualified with a namespace name.
  d) Operator _____ is the operator keyword for inequality.
  e) _____ allows a class to be derived from more than one base class.
  f) When a base class is inherited as _____, only one subobject of the base class will appear in the derived class.

26.2 State which of the following are *true* and which are *false*. If a statement is *false*, explain why.
  a) When passing a non-const argument to a const function, the const_cast operator should be used to cast away the "const-ness" of the function.
  b) namespaces are guaranteed to be unique.
  c) Like class bodies, namespace bodies also end in semicolons.
  d) namespaces cannot have namespaces as members.
  e) A mutable data member cannot be modified in a const member function.

26.3 Fill in the blanks for each of the following:
  a) Access command-line arguments in native C++ using the _____ parameter to main.
  b) Use _____ in the parameter list of a function to define a variable-length argument list.
  c) _____ is an unsafe cast operator which should be used carefully.
  d) Delegates are _____ references (unlike function pointers) that can be used to encapsulate multiple _____.

Answers to Self-Review Exercises

26.1 a) binary scope resolution (::). b) const_cast. c) global namespace. d) not_eq. e) multiple inheritance. f) virtual.

26.2 a) False. It is legal to pass a non-const argument to a const function. However, when passing a const reference or pointer to a non-const function, the const_cast operator should be used to cast away the "const-ness" of the reference or pointer
  b) False. Programmers might inadvertently choose the namespace already in use.
  c) False. namespace bodies do not end in semicolons.
  d) False. namespaces can be nested.
  e) False. A mutable data member is always modifiable, even in a const member function.

26.3 a) argv. b) ... . c) reinterpret_cast. d) type-safe, functions.

Exercises

26.4 Fill in the blanks for each of the following:
  a) Keyword _____ specifies that a namespace or namespace member is being used.

b) Operator _____ is the operator keyword for logical OR.

c) Storage specifier _____ allows a member of a const object to be modified.

d) The _____ qualifier specifies that an object can be modified by other programs.

e) Precede a member with its _____ name and the scope resolution operator if the possibility exists of a scoping conflict.

f) The body of a namespace is delimited by _____.

g) For a const object with no _____ data members, operator _____ must be used every time a member is to be modified.

26.5 Write a namespace, Currency, that defines constant members ONE, TWO, FIVE, TEN, TWENTY, FIFTY and HUNDRED. Write two short programs that use Currency. One program should make all constants available and the other should make only FIVE available.

26.6 Given the namespaces in Fig. 26.21, determine whether each statement is *true* or *false*. Explain any *false* answers.

a) Variable kilometers is visible within namespace Data.

b) Object string1 is visible within namespace Data.

c) Constant POLAND is not visible within namespace Data.

d) Constant GERMANY is visible within namespace Data.

e) Function function is visible to namespace Data.

f) Namespace Data is visible to namespace CountryInformation.

g) Object map is visible to namespace CountryInformation.

h) Object string1 is visible within namespace RegionalInformation.

26.7 Compare and contrast mutable and const_cast. Give at least one example of when one might be preferred over the other. [*Note:* This exercise does not require any code to be written.]

26.8 Write a program that uses const_cast to modify a const variable. [*Hint:* Use a pointer in your solution to point to the const identifier.]

26.9 What problem do virtual base classes solve?

26.10 Write a program that uses virtual base classes. The class at the top of the hierarchy should provide a constructor that takes at least one argument (i.e., do not provide a default constructor). What challenges does this present for the inheritance hierarchy?

```
 I   namespace CountryInformation
 2   {
 3      using namespace std;
 4      enum Countries { POLAND, SWITZERLAND, GERMANY,
 5                       AUSTRIA, CZECH_REPUBLIC };
 6      int kilometers;
 7      string string1;
 8
 9      namespace RegionalInformation
10      {
11         short getPopulation(); // assume definition exists
12         MapData map; // assume definition exists
13      } // end RegionalInformation
14   } // end CountryInformation
15
16   namespace Data
17   {
18      using namespace CountryInformation::RegionalInformation;
19      void *function( void *, int );
20   } // end Data
```

Fig. 26.21 | namespaces for Exercise 26.6.

26.11 Find the error(s) in each of the following. When possible, explain how to correct each error.

a) ```
namespace Name {
    int x;
    int y;
    mutable int z;
};
```

b) ```
int integer = const_cast< int >( double );
```

c) ```
namespace PCM(111, "hello");   // construct namespace
```

**26.12** Write a program with a function `option` that has a variable-length argument list (assume each argument is a `double`). Make `option` print its arguments in reverse order if the program is run with a single command line `reverse`. Otherwise `option` should print its arguments in sorted order.

**26.13** Repeat Exercise 26.12 using C++/CLI.
```

Operator Precedence and Associativity Chart

A.1 Operator Precedence

Operators are shown in decreasing order of precedence from top to bottom (Fig. A.1).

Operator	Type	Associativity
:: ::	binary scope resolution unary scope resolution	left to right
() [] . -> ++ -- *typeid* *dynamic_cast* < *type* > *static_cast*< *type* > *reinterpret_cast*< *type* > *const_cast*< *type* > *safe_cast*< *type* >	parentheses array subscript member selection via object member selection via pointer or handle unary postfix increment unary postfix decrement runtime type information runtime type-checked cast compile-time type-checked cast cast for nonstandard conversions cast away const-ness execute optimal cast type for CLR types	left to right

Fig. A.1 | Operator precedence and associativity chart. (Part 1 of 3.)

Operator	Type	Associativity
++	unary prefix increment	right to left
--	unary prefix decrement	
+	unary plus	
-	unary minus	
!	unary logical negation	
~	unary bitwise complement	
sizeof	determine size in bytes	
&	address	
%	address	
new	dereference pointer or handle	
new[]	dynamic memory allocation	
delete	dynamic array allocation	
delete[]	dynamic memory deallocation	
(*type*)	dynamic array deallocation	
	C-style unary cast	
.*	pointer to member via object	left to right
->*	pointer to member via pointer	
*	multiplication	left to right
/	division	
%	modulus	
+	addition	left to right
-	subtraction	
<<	bitwise left shift	left to right
>>	bitwise right shift	
<	relational less than	left to right
<=	relational less than or equal to	
>	relational greater than	
>=	relational greater than or equal to	
==	relational is equal to	left to right
!=	relational is not equal to	
&	bitwise AND	left to right
^	bitwise exclusive OR	left to right
|	bitwise inclusive OR	left to right
&&	logical AND	left to right
||	logical OR	left to right
?:	ternary conditional	right to left

Fig. A.1 | Operator precedence and associativity chart. (Part 2 of 3.)

Operator	Type	Associativity
=	assignment	right to left
+=	addition assignment	
-=	subtraction assignment	
*=	multiplication assignment	
/=	division assignment	
%=	modulus assignment	
&=	bitwise AND assignment	
^=	bitwise exclusive OR assignment	
|=	bitwise inclusive OR assignment	
<<=	bitwise left-shift assignment	
>>=	bitwise right-shift assignment	
,	comma	left to right

Fig. A.1 | Operator precedence and associativity chart. (Part 3 of 3.)

ASCII Character Set

Fig. B.1 | ASCII character set.

The digits at the left of the table are the left digits of the decimal equivalent (0–127) of the character code, and the digits at the top of the table are the right digits of the character code. For example, the character code for "F" is 70, and the character code for "&" is 38.

Fundamental Types

Figure C.1 lists C++'s fundamental types. The C++ Standard Document does not provide the exact number of bytes required to store variables of these types in memory. However, the C++ Standard Document does indicate how the memory requirements for fundamental types relate to one another. By order of increasing memory requirements, the signed integer types are signed char, short int, int and long int. This means that a short int must provide at least as much storage as a signed char; an int must provide at least as much storage as a short int; and a long int must provide at least as much storage as an int. Each signed integer type has a corresponding unsigned integer type that has the same memory requirements. Unsigned types cannot represent negative values, but can represent twice as many positive values as their associated signed types. By order of increasing mem-

Integral types	Floating-point types
bool	float
char	double
signed char	long double
unsigned char	
short int	
unsigned short int	
int	
unsigned int	
long int	
unsigned long int	
wchar_t	

Fig. C.1 | C++ fundamental types.

ory requirements, the floating-point types are `float`, `double` and `long double`. Like integer types, a `double` must provide at least as much storage as a `float` and a `long double` must provide at least as much storage as a `double`.

The exact sizes and ranges of values for the fundamental types are implementation dependent. The header files `<climits>` (for the integral types) and `<cfloat>` (for the floating-point types) specify the ranges of values supported on your system.

The range of values a type supports depends on the number of bytes that are used to represent that type. For example, consider a system with 4 byte (32 bit) `int`s. For the signed `int` type, the nonnegative values are in the range 0 to 2,147,483,647 ($2^{31} - 1$). The negative values are in the range -1 to $-2,147,483,648$ (-2^{31}). This is a total of 2^{32} possible values. An `unsigned` `int` on the same system would use the same number of bits to represent data, but would not represent any negative values. This results in values in the range 0 to 4,294,967,295 ($2^{32} - 1$). On the same system, a `short int` could not use more than 32 bits to represent its data and a `long int` must use at least 32 bits.

C++ provides the data type `bool` for variables that can hold only the values `true` and `false`.

Finally, Visual C++ also provides the keyword `__int64` to represent a 64-bit signed integer in C++/CLI. The underlying type of `__int64` is `System::Int64`.

Number Systems

*Here are only numbers
ratified.*
—William Shakespeare

*Nature has some sort of
arithmetic-geometrical
coordinate system, because
nature has all kinds of
models. What we experience
of nature is in models, and
all of nature's models are so
beautiful.
It struck me that nature's
system must be a real beauty,
because in chemistry we find
that the associations are
always in beautiful whole
numbers—there are no
fractions.*
—Richard Buckminster Fuller

OBJECTIVES

In this appendix you'll learn:

■ To understand basic number systems concepts, such as base, positional value and symbol value.

■ To understand how to work with numbers represented in the binary, octal and hexadecimal number systems.

■ To abbreviate binary numbers as octal numbers or hexadecimal numbers.

■ To convert octal numbers and hexadecimal numbers to binary numbers.

■ To convert back and forth between decimal numbers and their binary, octal and hexadecimal equivalents.

■ To understand binary arithmetic and how negative binary numbers are represented using two's complement notation.

D.1 Introduction

In this appendix, we introduce the key number systems that C++ programmers use, especially when they are working on software projects that require close interaction with machine-level hardware. Projects like this include operating systems, computer networking software, compilers, database systems and applications requiring high performance.

When we write an integer such as 227 or –63 in a C++ program, the number is assumed to be in the decimal (base 10) number system. The digits in the decimal number system are 0, 1, 2, 3, 4, 5, 6, 7, 8 and 9. The lowest digit is 0 and the highest is 9—one less than the base of 10. Internally, computers use the binary (base 2) number system. The binary number system has only two digits, namely 0 and 1. Its lowest digit is 0 and its highest is 1—one less than the base of 2.

As we'll see, binary numbers tend to be much longer than their decimal equivalents. Programmers who work in assembly languages, and in high-level languages like C++ that enable them to reach down to the machine level, find it cumbersome to work with binary numbers. So two other number systems—the octal number system (base 8) and the hexadecimal number system (base 16)—are popular, primarily because they make it convenient to abbreviate binary numbers.

In the octal number system, the digits range from 0 to 7. Because both the binary and the octal number systems have fewer digits than the decimal number system, their digits are the same as the corresponding digits in decimal.

The hexadecimal number system poses a problem because it requires 16 digits—a lowest digit of 0 and a highest digit with a value equivalent to decimal 15 (one less than the base of 16). By convention, we use the letters A through F to represent the hexadecimal digits corresponding to decimal values 10 through 15. Thus in hexadecimal we can have numbers like 876 consisting solely of decimal-like digits, numbers like 8A55F consisting of digits and letters and numbers like FFE consisting solely of letters. Occasionally, a hexadecimal number spells a common word such as FACE or FEED—this can appear strange to programmers accustomed to working with numbers. The digits of the binary, octal, decimal and hexadecimal number systems are summarized in Figs. D.1–D.2.

Each of these number systems uses positional notation—each position in which a digit is written has a different positional value. For example, in the decimal number 937 (the 9, the 3 and the 7 are referred to as symbol values), we say that the 7 is written in the ones position, the 3 is written in the tens position and the 9 is written in the hundreds position. Note that each of these positions is a power of the base (base 10) and that these powers begin at 0 and increase by 1 as we move left in the number (Fig. D.3).

Binary digit	Octal digit	Decimal digit	Hexadecimal digit
0	0	0	0
1	1	1	1
	2	2	2
	3	3	3
	4	4	4
	5	5	5
	6	6	6
	7	7	7
		8	8
		9	9
			A (decimal value of 10)
			B (decimal value of 11)
			C (decimal value of 12)
			D (decimal value of 13)
			E (decimal value of 14)
			F (decimal value of 15)

Fig. D.1 | Digits of the binary, octal, decimal and hexadecimal number systems.

Attribute	Binary	Octal	Decimal	Hexadecimal
Base	2	8	10	16
Lowest digit	0	0	0	0
Highest digit	1	7	9	F

Fig. D.2 | Comparing the binary, octal, decimal and hexadecimal number systems.

Positional values in the decimal number system			
Decimal digit	9	3	7
Position name	Hundreds	Tens	Ones
Positional value	100	10	1
Positional value as a power of the base (10)	10^2	10^1	10^0

Fig. D.3 | Positional values in the decimal number system.

For longer decimal numbers, the next positions to the left would be the thousands position (10 to the 3rd power), the ten-thousands position (10 to the 4th power), the hundred-thousands position (10 to the 5th power), the millions position (10 to the 6th power), the ten-millions position (10 to the 7th power) and so on.

In the binary number 101, the rightmost 1 is written in the ones position, the 0 is written in the twos position and the leftmost 1 is written in the fours position. Note that each position is a power of the base (base 2) and that these powers begin at 0 and increase by 1 as we move left in the number (Fig. D.4). So, $101 = 2^2 + 2^0 = 4 + 1 = 5$.

For longer binary numbers, the next positions to the left would be the eights position (2 to the 3rd power), the sixteens position (2 to the 4th power), the thirty-twos position (2 to the 5th power), the sixty-fours position (2 to the 6th power) and so on.

In the octal number 425, we say that the 5 is written in the ones position, the 2 is written in the eights position and the 4 is written in the sixty-fours position. Note that each of these positions is a power of the base (base 8) and that these powers begin at 0 and increase by 1 as we move left in the number (Fig. D.5).

For longer octal numbers, the next positions to the left would be the five-hundred-and-twelves position (8 to the 3rd power), the four-thousand-and-ninety-sixes position (8 to the 4th power), the thirty-two-thousand-seven-hundred-and-sixty-eights position (8 to the 5th power) and so on.

In the hexadecimal number 3DA, we say that the A is written in the ones position, the D is written in the sixteens position and the 3 is written in the two-hundred-and-fifty-sixes position. Note that each of these positions is a power of the base (base 16) and that these powers begin at 0 and increase by 1 as we move left in the number (Fig. D.6).

For longer hexadecimal numbers, the next positions to the left would be the four-thousand-and-ninety-sixes position (16 to the 3rd power), the sixty-five-thousand-five-hundred-and-thirty-sixes position (16 to the 4th power) and so on.

Positional values in the binary number system			
Binary digit	1	0	1
Position name	Fours	Twos	Ones
Positional value	4	2	1
Positional value as a power of the base (2)	2^2	2^1	2^0

Fig. D.4 | Positional values in the binary number system.

Positional values in the octal number system			
Decimal digit	4	2	5
Position name	Sixty-fours	Eights	Ones
Positional value	64	8	1
Positional value as a power of the base (8)	8^2	8^1	8^0

Fig. D.5 | Positional values in the octal number system.

Positional values in the hexadecimal number system			
Decimal digit	3	D	A
Position name	Two-hundred-and-fifty-sixes	Sixteens	Ones
Positional value	256	16	1
Positional value as a power of the base (16)	16^2	16^1	16^0

Fig. D.6 | Positional values in the hexadecimal number system.

D.2 Abbreviating Binary Numbers as Octal and Hexadecimal Numbers

The main use for octal and hexadecimal numbers in computing is for abbreviating lengthy binary representations. Figure D.7 highlights the fact that lengthy binary numbers can be expressed concisely in number systems with higher bases than the binary number system.

A particularly important relationship that both the octal number system and the hexadecimal number system have to the binary system is that the bases of octal and hexadecimal (8 and 16 respectively) are powers of the base of the binary number system (base 2).

Decimal number	Binary representation	Octal representation	Hexadecimal representation
0	0	0	0
1	1	1	1
2	10	2	2
3	11	3	3
4	100	4	4
5	101	5	5
6	110	6	6
7	111	7	7
8	1000	10	8
9	1001	11	9
10	1010	12	A
11	1011	13	B
12	1100	14	C
13	1101	15	D
14	1110	16	E
15	1111	17	F
16	10000	20	10

Fig. D.7 | Decimal, binary, octal and hexadecimal equivalents.

Consider the following 12-digit binary number and its octal and hexadecimal equivalents. See if you can determine how this relationship makes it convenient to abbreviate binary numbers in octal or hexadecimal. The answers follow the numbers.

Binary number	Octal equivalent	Hexadecimal equivalent
100011010001	4321	8D1

To see how the binary number converts easily to octal, simply break the 12-digit binary number into groups of three consecutive bits each, starting from the right, and write those groups over the corresponding digits of the octal number as follows:

100	011	010	001
4	3	2	1

Note that the octal digit you have written under each group of thee bits corresponds precisely to the octal equivalent of that 3-digit binary number, as shown in Fig. D.7.

The same kind of relationship can be observed in converting from binary to hexadecimal. Break the 12-digit binary number into groups of four consecutive bits each, starting from the right, and write those groups over the corresponding digits of the hexadecimal number as follows:

1000	1101	0001
8	D	1

Notice that the hexadecimal digit you wrote under each group of four bits corresponds precisely to the hexadecimal equivalent of that 4-digit binary number as shown in Fig. D.7.

D.3 Converting Octal and Hexadecimal Numbers to Binary Numbers

In the previous section, we saw how to convert binary numbers to their octal and hexadecimal equivalents by forming groups of binary digits and simply rewriting them as their equivalent octal digit values or hexadecimal digit values. This process may be used in reverse to produce the binary equivalent of a given octal or hexadecimal number.

For example, the octal number 653 is converted to binary simply by writing the 6 as its 3-digit binary equivalent 110, the 5 as its 3-digit binary equivalent 101 and the 3 as its 3-digit binary equivalent 011 to form the 9-digit binary number 110101011.

The hexadecimal number FAD5 is converted to binary simply by writing the F as its 4-digit binary equivalent 1111, the A as its 4-digit binary equivalent 1010, the D as its 4-digit binary equivalent 1101 and the 5 as its 4-digit binary equivalent 0101 to form the 16-digit 1111101011010101.

D.4 Converting from Binary, Octal or Hexadecimal to Decimal

We are accustomed to working in decimal, and therefore it is often convenient to convert a binary, octal, or hexadecimal number to decimal to get a sense of what the number is "really" worth. Our figures in Section D.1 express the positional values in decimal. To convert a number to decimal from another base, multiply the decimal equivalent of each digit by its positional value and sum these products. For example, the binary number 110101 is converted to decimal 53 as shown in Fig. D.8.

To convert octal 7614 to decimal 3980, we use the same technique, this time using appropriate octal positional values, as shown in Fig. D.9.

To convert hexadecimal AD3B to decimal 44347, we use the same technique, this time using appropriate hexadecimal positional values, as shown in Fig. D.10.

D.5 Converting from Decimal to Binary, Octal or Hexadecimal

The conversions in Section D.4 follow naturally from the positional notation conventions. Converting from decimal to binary, octal, or hexadecimal also follows these conventions.

Suppose we wish to convert decimal 57 to binary. We begin by writing the positional values of the columns right to left until we reach a column whose positional value is greater than the decimal number. We do not need that column, so we discard it. Thus, we first write:

Positional values: 64   32   16   8   4   2   1

Then we discard the column with positional value 64, leaving:

Positional values: 32   16   8   4   2   1

Converting a binary number to decimal					
Positional values:	32	16	8	4	2	1
Symbol values:	1	1	0	1	0	1
Products:	1*32=32	1*16=16	0*8=0	1*4=4	0*2=0	1*1=1
Sum:	= 32 + 16 + 0 + 4 + 0s + 1 = 53					

Fig. D.8 | Converting a binary number to decimal.

Converting an octal number to decimal			
Positional values:	512	64	8	1
Symbol values:	7	6	1	4
Products	7*512=3584	6*64=384	1*8=8	4*1=4
Sum:	= 3584 + 384 + 8 + 4 = 3980			

Fig. D.9 | Converting an octal number to decimal.

Converting a hexadecimal number to decimal			
Positional values:	4096	256	16	1
Symbol values:	A	D	3	B
Products	A*4096=40960	D*256=3328	3*16=48	B*1=11
Sum:	= 40960 + 3328 + 48 + 11 = 44347			

Fig. D.10 | Converting a hexadecimal number to decimal.

Next we work from the leftmost column to the right. We divide 32 into 57 and observe that there is one 32 in 57 with a remainder of 25, so we write 1 in the 32 column. We divide 16 into 25 and observe that there is one 16 in 25 with a remainder of 9 and write 1 in the 16 column. We divide 8 into 9 and observe that there is one 8 in 9 with a remainder of 1. The next two columns each produce quotients of 0 when their positional values are divided into 1, so we write 0s in the 4 and 2 columns. Finally, 1 into 1 is 1, so we write 1 in the 1 column. This yields:

Positional values:	32	16	8	4	2	1
Symbol values:	1	1	1	0	0	1

and thus decimal 57 is equivalent to binary 111001.

To convert decimal 103 to octal, we begin by writing the positional values of the columns until we reach a column whose positional value is greater than the decimal number. We do not need that column, so we discard it. Thus, we first write:

Positional values:	512	64	8	1

Then we discard the column with positional value 512, yielding:

Positional values:	64	8	1

Next we work from the leftmost column to the right. We divide 64 into 103 and observe that there is one 64 in 103 with a remainder of 39, so we write 1 in the 64 column. We divide 8 into 39 and observe that there are four 8s in 39 with a remainder of 7 and write 4 in the 8 column. Finally, we divide 1 into 7 and observe that there are seven 1s in 7 with no remainder, so we write 7 in the 1 column. This yields:

Positional values:	64	8	1
Symbol values:	1	4	7

and thus decimal 103 is equivalent to octal 147.

To convert decimal 375 to hexadecimal, we begin by writing the positional values of the columns until we reach a column whose positional value is greater than the decimal number. We do not need that column, so we discard it. Thus, we first write:

Positional values:	4096	256	16	1

Then we discard the column with positional value 4096, yielding:

Positional values:	256	16	1

Next we work from the leftmost column to the right. We divide 256 into 375 and observe that there is one 256 in 375 with a remainder of 119, so we write 1 in the 256 column. We divide 16 into 119 and observe that there are seven 16s in 119 with a remainder of 7 and write 7 in the 16 column. Finally, we divide 1 into 7 and observe that there are seven 1s in 7 with no remainder, so we write 7 in the 1 column. This yields:

Positional values:	256	16	1
Symbol values:	1	7	7

and thus decimal 375 is equivalent to hexadecimal 177.

D.6 Negative Binary Numbers: Two's Complement Notation

The discussion so far in this appendix has focused on positive numbers. In this section, we explain how computers represent negative numbers using *two's complement notation*. First we explain how the two's complement of a binary number is formed, then we show why it represents the negative value of the given binary number.

Consider a machine with 32-bit integers. Suppose

```
int value = 13;
```

The 32-bit representation of value is

```
00000000 00000000 00000000 00001101
```

To form the negative of value we first form its *one's complement* by applying C++'s bitwise complement operator (~):

```
onesComplementOfValue = ~value;
```

Internally, ~value is now value with each of its bits reversed—ones become zeros and zeros become ones, as follows:

```
value:
00000000 00000000 00000000 00001101

~value  (i.e., value's one's complement):
11111111 11111111 11111111 11110010
```

To form the two's complement of value, we simply add 1 to value's one's complement. Thus

```
Two's complement of value:
11111111 11111111 11111111 11110011
```

Now if this is in fact equal to –13, we should be able to add it to binary 13 and obtain a result of 0. Let us try this:

```
  00000000 00000000 00000000 00001101
+ 11111111 11111111 11111111 11110011
-------------------------------------
  00000000 00000000 00000000 00000000
```

The carry bit coming out of the leftmost column is discarded and we indeed get 0 as a result. If we add the one's complement of a number to the number, the result will be all 1s. The key to getting a result of all zeros is that the two's complement is one more than the one's complement. The addition of 1 causes each column to add to 0 with a carry of 1. The carry keeps moving leftward until it is discarded from the leftmost bit, and thus the resulting number is all zeros.

Computers actually perform a subtraction, such as

```
x = a - value;
```

by adding the two's complement of value to a, as follows:

```
x = a + (~value + 1);
```

Suppose a is 27 and `value` is 13 as before. If the two's complement of `value` is actually the negative of `value`, then adding the two's complement of value to a should produce the result 14. Let us try this:

```
a (i.e., 27)          00000000 00000000 00000000 00011011
+(~value + 1)        +11111111 11111111 11111111 11110011
                     ------------------------------------
                      00000000 00000000 00000000 00001110
```

which is indeed equal to 14.

Summary

- An integer such as 19 or 227 or –63 in a C++ program is assumed to be in the decimal (base 10) number system. The digits in the decimal number system are 0, 1, 2, 3, 4, 5, 6, 7, 8 and 9. The lowest digit is 0 and the highest is 9—one less than the base of 10.
- Internally, computers use the binary (base 2) number system. The binary number system has only two digits, namely 0 and 1. Its lowest digit is 0 and its highest is 1—one less than the base of 2.
- The octal number system (base 8) and the hexadecimal number system (base 16) are popular primarily because they make it convenient to abbreviate binary numbers.
- The digits of the octal number system range from 0 to 7.
- The hexadecimal number system poses a problem because it requires 16 digits—a lowest digit of 0 and a highest digit with a value equivalent to decimal 15 (one less than the base of 16). By convention, we use the letters A through F to represent the hexadecimal digits corresponding to decimal values 10 through 15.
- Each number system uses positional notation—each position in which a digit is written has a different positional value.
- A particularly important relationship of both the octal and the hexadecimal number systems to the binary system is that their bases (8 and 16 respectively) are powers of the base of the binary number system (base 2).
- To convert an octal to a binary number, replace each octal digit with its three-digit binary equivalent.
- To convert a hexadecimal to a binary number, simply replace each hexadecimal digit with its four-digit binary equivalent.
- Because we are accustomed to working in decimal, it is convenient to convert a binary, octal or hexadecimal number to decimal to get a sense of the number's "real" worth.
- To convert a number to decimal from another base, multiply the decimal equivalent of each digit by its positional value and sum the products.
- Computers represent negative numbers using two's complement notation.
- To form the negative of a value in binary, first form its one's complement by applying C++'s bitwise complement operator (~). This reverses the bits of the value. To form the two's complement of a value, simply add one to the value's one's complement.

Terminology

base	base 8 number system
base 2 number system	base 10 number system

base 16 number system	negative value
binary number system	octal number system
bitwise complement operator (~)	one's complement notation
conversions	positional notation
decimal number system	positional value
digit	symbol value
hexadecimal number system	two's complement notation

Self-Review Exercises

D.1   The bases of the decimal, binary, octal and hexadecimal number systems are _____, _____, _____ and _____ respectively.

D.2   In general, the decimal, octal and hexadecimal representations of a given binary number contain (more/fewer) digits than the binary number contains.

D.3   (*True/False*) A popular reason for using the decimal number system is that it forms a convenient notation for abbreviating binary numbers simply by substituting one decimal digit per group of four binary bits.

D.4   The [octal/hexadecimal/decimal] representation of a large binary value is the most concise (of the given alternatives).

D.5   (*True/False*) The highest digit in any base is one more than the base.

D.6   (*True/False*) The lowest digit in any base is one less than the base.

D.7   The positional value of the rightmost digit of any number in either binary, octal, decimal or hexadecimal is always _____.

D.8   The positional value of the digit to the left of the rightmost digit of any number in binary, octal, decimal or hexadecimal is always equal to _____.

D.9   Fill in the missing values in this chart of positional values for the rightmost four positions in each of the indicated number systems:

decimal	1000	100	10	1
hexadecimal	...	256	...	...
binary	...	...	...	...
octal	512	...	8	...

D.10   Convert binary 110101011000 to octal and to hexadecimal.

D.11   Convert hexadecimal FACE to binary.

D.12   Convert octal 7316 to binary.

D.13   Convert hexadecimal 4FEC to octal. [*Hint:* First convert 4FEC to binary, then convert that binary number to octal.]

D.14   Convert binary 1101110 to decimal.

D.15   Convert octal 317 to decimal.

D.16   Convert hexadecimal EFD4 to decimal.

D.17   Convert decimal 177 to binary, to octal and to hexadecimal.

D.18   Show the binary representation of decimal 417. Then show the one's complement of 417 and the two's complement of 417.

D.19   What is the result when a number and its two's complement are added to each other?

Answers to Self-Review Exercises

D.1   10, 2, 8, 16.

D.2   Fewer.

D.3   False. Hexadecimal does this.

D.4   Hexadecimal.

D.5   False. The highest digit in any base is one less than the base.

D.6   False. The lowest digit in any base is zero.

D.7   1 (the base raised to the zero power).

D.8   The base of the number system.

D.9   Filled in chart shown below:

decimal	1000	100	10	1
hexadecimal	4096	256	16	1
binary	8	4	2	1
octal	512	64	8	1

D.10   Octal 6530; Hexadecimal D58.

D.11   Binary 1111 1010 1100 1110.

D.12   Binary 111 011 001 110.

D.13   Binary 0 100 111 111 101 100; Octal 47754.

D.14   Decimal 2 + 4 + 8 + 32 + 64 = 110.

D.15   Decimal 7 + 1 * 8 + 3 * 64 = 7 + 8 + 192 = 207.

D.16   Decimal 4 + 13 * 16 + 15 * 256 + 14 * 4096 = 61396.

D.17   Decimal 177
to binary:

```
256 128 64 32 16 8 4 2 1
128 64 32 16 8 4 2 1
(1*128)+(0*64)+(1*32)+(1*16)+(0*8)+(0*4)+(0*2)+(1*1)
10110001
```

to octal:

```
512 64 8 1
64 8 1
(2*64)+(6*8)+(1*1)
261
```

to hexadecimal:

```
256 16 1
16 1
(11*16)+(1*1)
(B*16)+(1*1)
B1
```

D.18 Binary:

```
512 256 128 64 32 16 8 4 2 1
256 128 64 32 16 8 4 2 1
(1*256)+(1*128)+(0*64)+(1*32)+(0*16)+(0*8)+(0*4)+(0*2)+(1*1)
110100001
```

One's complement: 001011110
Two's complement: 001011111
Check: Original binary number + its two's complement

```
110100001
001011111
---------
000000000
```

D.19 Zero.

Exercises

D.20 Some people argue that many of our calculations would be easier in the base 12 than in the base 10 (decimal) number system because 12 is divisible by so many more numbers than 10. What is the lowest digit in base 12? What would be the highest symbol for the digit in base 12? What are the positional values of the rightmost four positions of any number in the base 12 number system?

D.21 Complete the following chart of positional values for the rightmost four positions in each of the indicated number systems:

	1000	100	10	1
decimal	1000	100	10	1
base 6	...	...	6	...
base 13	...	169	...	...
base 3	27	...	...	...

D.22 Convert binary 100101111010 to octal and to hexadecimal.

D.23 Convert hexadecimal 3A7D to binary.

D.24 Convert hexadecimal 765F to octal. [*Hint:* First convert 765F to binary, then convert that binary number to octal.]

D.25 Convert binary 1011110 to decimal.

D.26 Convert octal 426 to decimal.

D.27 Convert hexadecimal FFFF to decimal.

D.28 Convert decimal 299 to binary, to octal and to hexadecimal.

D.29 Show the binary representation of decimal 779. Then show the one's complement of 779 and the two's complement of 779.

D.30 Show the two's complement of integer value −1 on a machine with 32-bit integers.

E

Preprocessor

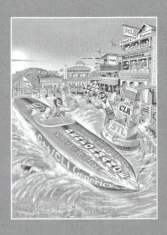

OBJECTIVES

In this appendix you'll learn:

- To use `#include` for developing large programs.
- To use `#define` to create macros and macros with arguments.
- To understand conditional compilation.
- To display error messages during conditional compilation.
- To use assertions to test if the values of expressions are correct.

E.1 Introduction

This chapter introduces the *preprocessor*. Preprocessing occurs before a program is compiled. Some possible actions are inclusion of other files in the file being compiled, definition of *symbolic constants* and *macros*, *conditional compilation* of program code and *conditional execution of preprocessor directives*. All preprocessor directives begin with #, and only white-space characters may appear before a preprocessor directive on a line. Preprocessor directives are not C++ statements, so they do not end in a semicolon (;). Preprocessor directives are processed fully before compilation begins.

Common Programming Error E.1

Placing a semicolon at the end of a preprocessor directive can lead to a variety of errors, depending on the type of preprocessor directive.

Software Engineering Observation E.1

Many preprocessor features (especially macros) are more appropriate for C programmers than for C++ programmers. C++ programmers should familiarize themselves with the preprocessor, because they might need to work with C legacy code.

E.2 The #include Preprocessor Directive

The *#include preprocessor directive* has been used throughout this text. The #include directive causes a copy of a specified file to be included in place of the directive. The two forms of the #include directive are

```
#include <filename>
#include "filename"
```

The difference between these is the location the preprocessor searches for the file to be included. If the filename is enclosed in angle brackets (< and >)—used for standard library header files—the preprocessor searches for the specified file in an implementation-dependent manner, normally through predesignated directories. If the file name is enclosed in quotes, the preprocessor searches first in the same directory as the file being compiled, then in the same implementation-dependent manner as for a file name enclosed in angle brackets. This method is normally used to include programmer-defined header files.

The #include directive is used to include standard header files such as <iostream> and <iomanip>. The #include directive is also used with programs consisting of several source files that are to be compiled together. A header file containing declarations and definitions common to the separate program files is often created and included in the file. Examples of such declarations and definitions are classes, structures, unions, enumerations and function prototypes, constants and stream objects (e.g., cin).

E.3 The #define Preprocessor Directive: Symbolic Constants

The *#define preprocessor directive* creates *symbolic constants*—constants represented as symbols—and macros—operations defined as symbols. The #define preprocessor directive format is

> **#define** *identifier* *replacement-text*

When this line appears in a file, all subsequent occurrences (except those inside a string) of *identifier* in that file will be replaced by *replacement-text* before the program is compiled. For example,

> **#define** PI 3.14159

replaces all subsequent occurrences of the symbolic constant PI with the numeric constant 3.14159. Symbolic constants enable you to create a name for a constant and use the name throughout the program. Later, if the constant needs to be modified throughout the program, it can be modified once in the #define preprocessor directive—and when the program is recompiled, all occurrences of the constant in the program will be modified. [*Note:* Everything to the right of the symbolic constant name replaces the symbolic constant. For example, #define PI = 3.14159 causes the preprocessor to replace every occurrence of PI with = 3.14159. Such replacement is the cause of many subtle logic and syntax errors.] Redefining a symbolic constant with a new value without first undefining it is also an error. Note that const variables in C++ are preferred over symbolic constants. Constant variables have a specific data type and are visible by name to a debugger. Once a symbolic constant is replaced with its replacement text, only the replacement text is visible to a debugger. A disadvantage of const variables is that they might require a memory location of their data type size—symbolic constants do not require any additional memory.

Common Programming Error E.2

Using symbolic constants in a file other than the file in which the symbolic constants are defined is a compilation error (unless they are #included from a header file).

Good Programming Practice E.1

Using meaningful names for symbolic constants makes programs more self-documenting.

E.4 The #define Preprocessor Directive: Macros

[*Note:* This section is included for the benefit of C++ programmers who will need to work with C legacy code. In C++, macros can often be replaced by templates and inline functions.] A macro is an operation defined in a #define preprocessor directive. As with symbolic constants, the ***macro-identifier*** is replaced with the ***replacement-text*** before the program is compiled. Macros may be defined with or without ***arguments***. A macro without arguments is processed like a symbolic constant. In a macro with arguments, the arguments are substituted in the *replacement-text*, then the macro is expanded—i.e., the *replacement-text* replaces the macro-identifier and argument list in the program. There is no data type checking for macro arguments. A macro is used simply for text substitution.

Consider the following macro definition with one argument for the area of a circle:

```
#define CIRCLE_AREA( x ) ( PI * ( x ) * ( x ) )
```

Wherever CIRCLE_AREA(y) appears in the file, the value of y is substituted for x in the replacement text, the symbolic constant PI is replaced by its value (defined previously) and the macro is expanded in the program. For example, the statement

```
area = CIRCLE_AREA( 4 );
```

is expanded to

```
area = ( 3.14159 * ( 4 ) * ( 4 ) );
```

Because the expression consists only of constants, at compile time the value of the expression can be evaluated, and the result is assigned to area at runtime. The parentheses around each x in the replacement text and around the entire expression force the proper order of evaluation when the macro argument is an expression. For example, the statement

```
area = CIRCLE_AREA( c + 2 );
```

is expanded to

```
area = ( 3.14159 * ( c + 2 ) * ( c + 2 ) );
```

which evaluates correctly, because the parentheses force the proper order of evaluation. If the parentheses are omitted, the macro expansion is

```
area = 3.14159 * c + 2 * c + 2;
```

which evaluates incorrectly as

```
area = ( 3.14159 * c ) + ( 2 * c ) + 2;
```

because of the rules of operator precedence.

 Common Programming Error E.3

Forgetting to enclose macro arguments in parentheses in the replacement text is an error.

Macro CIRCLE_AREA could be defined as a function. Function circleArea, as in

```
double circleArea( double x ) { return 3.14159 * x * x; }
```

performs the same calculation as CIRCLE_AREA, but the overhead of a function call is associated with function circleArea. The advantages of CIRCLE_AREA are that macros insert code directly in the program—avoiding function overhead—and the program remains readable because CIRCLE_AREA is defined separately and named meaningfully. A disadvantage is that its argument is evaluated twice. Also, every time a macro appears in a program, the macro is expanded. If the macro is large, this produces an increase in program size. Thus, there is a trade-off between execution speed and program size (if disk space is low).

Note that `inline` functions (see Chapter 7) are preferred to obtain the performance of macros and the software engineering benefits of functions.

Performance Tip E.1

Macros can sometimes be used to replace a function call with `inline` code prior to execution time. This eliminates the overhead of a function call. Inline functions are preferable to macros because they offer the type-checking services of functions.

The following is a macro definition with two arguments for the area of a rectangle:

```
#define RECTANGLE_AREA( x, y )  ( ( x ) * ( y ) )
```

Wherever `RECTANGLE_AREA( a, b )` appears in the program, the values of a and b are substituted in the macro replacement text, and the macro is expanded in place of the macro name. For example, the statement

```
rectArea = RECTANGLE_AREA( a + 4, b + 7 );
```

is expanded to

```
rectArea = ( ( a + 4 ) * ( b + 7 ) );
```

The value of the expression is evaluated and assigned to variable `rectArea`.

The replacement text for a macro or symbolic constant is normally any text on the line after the identifier in the `#define` directive. If the replacement text for a macro or symbolic constant is longer than the remainder of the line, a backslash (\) must be placed at the end of each line of the macro (except the last line), indicating that the replacement text continues on the next line.

Symbolic constants and macros can be discarded using the ***#undef preprocessor directive.*** Directive #undef "undefines" a symbolic constant or macro name. The scope of a symbolic constant or macro is from its definition until it is either undefined with #undef or the end of the file is reached. Once undefined, a name can be redefined with `#define`.

Note that expressions with side effects (e.g., variable values are modified) should not be passed to a macro, because macro arguments may be evaluated more than once.

Common Programming Error E.4

Macros often replace a name that wasn't intended to be a use of the macro but just happened to be spelled the same. This can lead to exceptionally mysterious compilation and syntax errors.

E.5 Conditional Compilation

Conditional compilation enables you to control the execution of preprocessor directives and the compilation of program code. Each of the conditional preprocessor directives evaluates a constant integer expression that will determine whether the code will be compiled. Cast expressions, `sizeof` expressions and enumeration constants cannot be evaluated in preprocessor directives because these are all determined by the compiler and preprocessing happens before compilation.

The conditional preprocessor construct is much like the `if` selection structure. Consider the following preprocessor code:

```
#ifndef NULL
    #define NULL 0
#endif
```

which determines whether the symbolic constant NULL is already defined. The expression #ifndef NULL includes the code up to #endif if NULL is not defined, and skips the code if NULL is defined. Every #if construct ends with #endif. Directives *#ifdef* and *#ifndef* are shorthand for #if defined(*name*) and #if !defined(*name*). A multiple-part conditional preprocessor construct may be tested using the #elif (the equivalent of else if in an if structure) and the #else (the equivalent of else in an if structure) directives.

During program development, programmers often find it helpful to "comment out" large portions of code to prevent it from being compiled. If the code contains C-style comments, /* and */ cannot be used to accomplish this task, because the first */ encountered would terminate the comment. Instead, you can use the following preprocessor construct:

```
#if 0
    code prevented from compiling
#endif
```

To enable the code to be compiled, simply replace the value 0 in the preceding construct with the value 1.

Conditional compilation is commonly used as a debugging aid. Output statements are often used to print variable values and to confirm the flow of control. These output statements can be enclosed in conditional preprocessor directives so that the statements are compiled only until the debugging process is completed. For example,

```
#ifdef DEBUG
    cerr << "Variable x = " << x << endl;
#endif
```

causes the cerr statement to be compiled in the program if the symbolic constant DEBUG has been defined before directive #ifdef DEBUG. This symbolic constant is normally set by a command-line compiler or by settings in the IDE (e.g., Visual Studio) and not by an explicit #define definition. When debugging is completed, the #define directive is removed from the source file, and the output statements inserted for debugging purposes are ignored during compilation. In larger programs, it might be desirable to define several different symbolic constants that control the conditional compilation in separate sections of the source file.

Common Programming Error E.5

Inserting conditionally compiled output statements for debugging purposes in locations where C++ currently expects a single statement can lead to syntax errors and logic errors. In this case, the conditionally compiled statement should be enclosed in a compound statement. Thus, when the program is compiled with debugging statements, the flow of control of the program is not altered.

E.6 The #error and #pragma Preprocessor Directives

The *#error directive*

> *#error* tokens

prints an implementation-dependent message including the *tokens* specified in the directive. The tokens are sequences of characters separated by spaces. For example,

> *#error* 1 - Out of range error

contains six tokens. In one popular C++ compiler, for example, when a #error directive is processed, the tokens in the directive are displayed as an error message, preprocessing stops and the program does not compile.

The ***#pragma*** *directive*

> ***#pragma*** *tokens*

causes an implementation-defined action. A pragma not recognized by the implementation is ignored. A particular C++ compiler, for example, might recognize pragmas that enable you to take advantage of that compiler's specific capabilities. For more information on #error and #pragma, see the documentation for your C++ implementation.

E.7 Operators # and

The ***#*** and ***##*** preprocessor operators are available in C++ and ANSI/ISO C. The ***#*** operator causes a replacement-text token to be converted to a string surrounded by quotes. Consider the following macro definition:

> ***#define*** HELLO(x) cout << "Hello, " #x << endl;

When HELLO(John) appears in a program file, it is expanded to

> cout << "Hello, " "John" << endl;

The string "John" replaces #x in the replacement text. Strings separated by whitespace are concatenated during preprocessing, so the above statement is equivalent to

> cout << "Hello, John" << endl;

Note that the # operator must be used in a macro with arguments, because the operand of # refers to an argument of the macro.

The ## operator concatenates two tokens. Consider the following macro definition:

> ***#define*** TOKENCONCAT(x, y) x ## y

When TOKENCONCAT appears in the program, its arguments are concatenated and used to replace the macro. For example, TOKENCONCAT(O, K) is replaced by OK in the program. The ## operator must have two operands.

E.8 Predefined Symbolic Constants

There are six *predefined symbolic constants* (Fig. E.1). The identifiers for each of these begin and (except for __cplusplus) end with *two* underscores. These identifiers and preprocessor operator defined (Section E.5) cannot be used in #define or #undef directives.

Symbolic constant	Description
__LINE__	The line number of the current source-code line (an integer constant).
__FILE__	The presumed name of the source file (a string).
__DATE__	The date the source file is compiled (a string of the form "Mmm dd yyyy" such as "Aug 19 2002").

Fig. E.1 | The predefined symbolic constants. (Part 1 of 2.)

Symbolic constant	Description
__STDC__	Indicates whether the program conforms to the ANSI/ISO C standard. Contains value 1 if there is full conformance and is undefined otherwise.
__TIME__	The time the source file is compiled (a string literal of the form `"hh:mm:ss"`).
__cplusplus	Contains the value 199711L (the date the ISO C++ standard was approved) if the file is being compiled by a C++ compiler, undefined otherwise. Allows a file to be set up to be compiled as either C or C++.

Fig. E.1 | The predefined symbolic constants. (Part 2 of 2.)

E.9 Assertions

The *assert macro*—defined in the <cassert> header file—tests the value of an expression. If the value of the expression is 0 (false), then assert prints an error message and calls function *abort* (of the general utilities library—<cstdlib>) to terminate program execution. This is a useful debugging tool for testing whether a variable has a correct value. For example, suppose variable x should never be larger than 10 in a program. An assertion may be used to test the value of x and print an error message if the value of x is incorrect. The statement would be

```
assert( x <= 10 );
```

If x is greater than 10 when the preceding statement is encountered in a program, an error message containing the line number and file name is printed, and the program terminates. You may then concentrate on this area of the code to find the error. If the symbolic constant NDEBUG is defined, subsequent assertions will be ignored. Thus, when assertions are no longer needed (i.e., when debugging is complete), we insert the line

```
#define NDEBUG
```

in the program file rather than deleting each assertion manually. As with the DEBUG symbolic constant, NDEBUG is often set by compiler command-line options or through a setting in the IDE.

Most C++ compilers now include exception handling. C++ programmers prefer using exceptions rather than assertions. But assertions are still valuable for C++ programmers who work with C legacy code.

E.10 Wrap-Up

This appendix discussed the #include directive, which is used to develop larger programs. You also learned about the #define directive, which is used to create macros. We introduced conditional compilation, displaying error messages and using assertions. In the next appendix, you'll implement the design of the ATM system from the Software Engineering Case Study found in Chapters 1, 3–8, 10 and 14.

Summary

Section E.2 The #include Preprocessor Directive
- All preprocessor directives begin with # and are processed before the program is compiled.
- Only white-space characters may appear before a preprocessor directive on a line.
- The #include directive includes a copy of the specified file. If the filename is enclosed in quotes, the preprocessor begins searching in the same directory as the file being compiled for the file to be included. If the filename is enclosed in angle brackets (< and >), the search is performed in an implementation-defined manner.

Section E.3 The #define Preprocessor Directive: Symbolic Constants
- The #define preprocessor directive is used to create symbolic constants and macros.
- A symbolic constant is a name for a constant.

Section E.4 The #define Preprocessor Directive: Macros
- A macro is an operation defined in a #define preprocessor directive. Macros may be defined with or without arguments.
- The replacement text for a macro or symbolic constant is any text remaining on the line after the identifier (and, if any, the macro argument list) in the #define directive. If the replacement text for a macro or symbolic constant is too long to fit on one line, a backslash (\) is placed at the end of the line, indicating that the replacement text continues on the next line.
- Symbolic constants and macros can be discarded using the #undef preprocessor directive. Directive #undef "undefines" the symbolic constant or macro name.
- The scope of a symbolic constant or macro is from its definition until it is either undefined with #undef or the end of the file is reached.

Section E.5 Conditional Compilation
- Conditional compilation enables you to control the execution of preprocessor directives and the compilation of program code.
- The conditional preprocessor directives evaluate constant integer expressions. Cast expressions, sizeof expressions and enumeration constants cannot be evaluated in preprocessor directives.
- Every #if construct ends with #endif.
- Directives #ifdef and #ifndef are provided as shorthand for #if defined(*name*) and #if !defined(*name*).
- A multiple-part conditional preprocessor construct is tested with directives #elif and #else.

Section E.6 The #error and #pragma Preprocessor Directives
- The #error directive prints an implementation-dependent message that includes the tokens specified in the directive and terminates preprocessing and compiling.
- The #pragma directive causes an implementation-defined action. If the pragma is not recognized by the implementation, the pragma is ignored.

Section E.7 Operators # and
- The # operator causes the following replacement text token to be converted to a string surrounded by quotes. The # operator must be used in a macro with arguments, because the operand of # must be an argument of the macro.
- The ## operator concatenates two tokens. The ## operator must have two operands.

Section E.8 Predefined Symbolic Constants
* There are six predefined symbolic constants. Constant `__LINE__` is the line number of the current source-code line (an integer). Constant `__FILE__` is the presumed name of the file (a string). Constant `__DATE__` is the date the source file is compiled (a string). Constant `__TIME__` is the time the source file is compiled (a string). Note that each of the predefined symbolic constants begins (and, with the exception of `__cplusplus`, ends) with two underscores.

Section E.9 Assertions
* The assert macro—defined in the `<cassert>` header file—tests the value of an expression. If the value of the expression is 0 (false), then `assert` prints an error message and calls function `abort` to terminate program execution.

Terminology

\ (backslash) continuation character	`__FILE__`
`abort`	header file
argument	`#if`
`assert`	`#ifdef`
`<cassert>`	`#ifndef`
concatenation preprocessor operator ##	`#include "filename"`
conditional compilation	`#include <filename>`
conditional execution of preprocessor	`__LINE__`
convert-to-string preprocessor directive	macro
`__cplusplus`	macro with arguments
`<cstdio>`	operator #
`<cstdlib>`	`#pragma`
`__DATE__`	predefined symbolic constants
debugger	preprocessing directive
`#define`	preprocessor
directives	replacement text
`#elif`	scope of a symbolic constant or macro
`#else`	standard library header files
`#endif`	symbolic constant
`#error`	`__TIME__`
expand a macro	`#undef`

Self-Review Exercises

E.1 Fill in the blanks in each of the following:

a) Every preprocessor directive must begin with _____.

b) The conditional compilation construct may be extended to test for multiple cases by using the _____ and the _____ directives.

c) The _____ directive creates macros and symbolic constants.

d) Only _____ characters may appear before a preprocessor directive on a line.

e) The _____ directive discards symbolic constant and macro names.

f) The _____ and _____ directives are provided as shorthand notation for `#if defined(`*name*`)` and `#if !defined(`*name*`)`.

g) _____ enables you to control the execution of preprocessor directives and the compilation of program code.

h) The _____ macro prints a message and terminates program execution if the value of the expression the macro evaluates is 0.

i) The _____ directive inserts a file in another file.

j) The _____ operator concatenates its two arguments.

k) The _____ operator converts its operand to a string.

l) The character _____ indicates that the replacement text for a symbolic constant or macro continues on the next line.

E.2 Write a program to print the values of the predefined symbolic constants __LINE__, __FILE__, __DATE__ and __TIME__ listed in Fig. E.1.

E.3 Write a preprocessor directive to accomplish each of the following:

a) Define symbolic constant YES to have the value 1.

b) Define symbolic constant NO to have the value 0.

c) Include the header file common.h. The header is found in the same directory as the file being compiled.

d) If symbolic constant TRUE is defined, undefine it, and redefine it as 1. Do not use #ifdef.

e) If symbolic constant TRUE is defined, undefine it, and redefine it as 1. Use the #ifdef preprocessor directive.

f) If symbolic constant ACTIVE is not equal to 0, define symbolic constant INACTIVE as 0. Otherwise, define INACTIVE as 1.

g) Define macro CUBE_VOLUME that computes the volume of a cube (takes one argument).

Answers to Self-Review Exercises

E.1 a) #. b) #elif, #else. c) #define. d) whitespace. e) #undef. f) #ifdef, #ifndef. g) Conditional compilation. h) assert. i) #include. j) ##. k) #. l) \.

E.2 (See below.)

```
1    // exF_02.cpp
2    // Self-Review Exercise F.2 solution.
3    #include <iostream>
4
5    using std::cout;
6    using std::endl;
7
8    int main()
9    {
10       cout << "__LINE__ = " << __LINE__ << endl
11            << "__FILE__ = " << __FILE__ << endl
12            << "__DATE__ = " << __DATE__ << endl
13            << "__TIME__ = " << __TIME__ << endl
14            << "__cplusplus = " << __cplusplus << endl;
15
16       return 0;
17
18   } // end main
```

```
__LINE__ = 9
__FILE__ = c:\cpp4e\ch19\ex19_02.CPP
__DATE__ = Jul 17 2002
__TIME__ = 09:55:58
__cplusplus = 199711L
```

E.3 a) #define YES 1

b) #define NO 0

```
c)  #include "common.h"
d)  #if defined(TRUE)
        #undef TRUE
        #define TRUE 1
    #endif
e)  #ifdef TRUE
        #undef TRUE
        #define TRUE 1
    #endif
f)  #if ACTIVE
        #define INACTIVE 0
    #else
        #define INACTIVE 1
    #endif
g)  #define CUBE_VOLUME( x )  ( ( x ) * ( x ) * ( x ) )
```

Exercises

E.4   Write a program that defines a macro with one argument to compute the volume of a sphere. The program should compute the volume for spheres of radii from 1 to 10 and print the results in tabular format. The formula for the volume of a sphere is

$$(4.0 / 3) * \pi * r^3$$

where π is 3.14159.

E.5   Write a program that produces the following output:

```
The sum of x and y is 13
```

The program should define macro SUM with two arguments, x and y, and use SUM to produce the output.

E.6   Write a program that uses macro MINIMUM2 to determine the smaller of two numeric values. Input the values from the keyboard.

E.7   Write a program that uses macro MINIMUM3 to determine the smallest of three numeric values. Macro MINIMUM3 should use macro MINIMUM2 defined in Exercise E.6 to determine the smallest number. Input the values from the keyboard.

E.8   Write a program that uses macro PRINT to print a string value.

E.9   Write a program that uses macro PRINTARRAY to print an array of integers. The macro should receive the array and the number of elements in the array as arguments.

E.10   Write a program that uses macro SUMARRAY to sum the values in a numeric array. The macro should receive the array and the number of elements in the array as arguments.

E.11   Rewrite the solutions to Exercises E.4–E.10 as inline functions.

E.12   For each of the following macros, identify the possible problems (if any) when the preprocessor expands the macros:

```
a)  #define SQR( x ) x * x
b)  #define SQR( x ) ( x * x )
c)  #define SQR( x ) ( x ) * ( x )
d)  #define SQR( x ) ( ( x ) * ( x ) )
```

ATM Case Study Code

F.1 ATM Case Study Implementation

This appendix contains the complete working implementation of the ATM system that we designed in the Software Engineering Case Study sections found at the ends of Chapters 1, 3–8, 10 and 14. The implementation comprises 877 lines of C++ code. We consider the classes in the order in which we identified them in Section 4.13:

- ATM
- Screen
- Keypad
- CashDispenser
- DepositSlot
- Account
- BankDatabase
- Transaction
- BalanceInquiry
- Withdrawal
- Deposit

We apply the guidelines discussed in Section 10.12 and Section 14.11 to code these classes based on how we modeled them in the UML class diagrams of Fig. 14.28 and Fig. 14.29. To develop the definitions of classes' member functions, we refer to the activity diagrams presented in Section 6.11 and the communication and sequence diagrams presented in Section 8.15. Note that our ATM design does not specify all the program logic and may not specify all the attributes and operations required to complete the ATM implementation. This is a normal part of the object-oriented design process. As we implement the system, we complete the program logic and add attributes and behaviors as necessary to construct the ATM system specified by the requirements specification in Section 3.8.

We conclude the discussion by presenting a C++ program (`ATMCaseStudy.cpp`) that starts the ATM and puts the other classes in the system in use. Recall that we are developing a first version of the ATM system that runs on a personal computer and uses the computer's keyboard and monitor to approximate the ATM's keypad and screen. We also only simulate the actions of the ATM's cash dispenser and deposit slot. We attempt to implement the system, however, so that real hardware versions of these devices could be integrated without significant changes in the code.

F.2 Class ATM

Class ATM (Figs. F.1–F.2) represents the ATM as a whole. Figure F.1 contains the ATM class definition, enclosed in `#ifndef`, `#define` and `#endif` preprocessor directives to ensure that this definition gets included only once in a program. We discuss lines 6–11 shortly. Lines

```
1   // ATM.h
2   // ATM class definition. Represents an automated teller machine.
3   #ifndef ATM_H
4   #define ATM_H
5
6   #include "Screen.h" // Screen class definition
7   #include "Keypad.h" // Keypad class definition
8   #include "CashDispenser.h" // CashDispenser class definition
9   #include "DepositSlot.h" // DepositSlot class definition
10  #include "BankDatabase.h" // BankDatabase class definition
11  class Transaction; // forward declaration of class Transaction
12
13  class ATM
14  {
15  public:
16     ATM(); // constructor initializes data members
17     void run(); // start the ATM
18  private:
19     bool userAuthenticated; // whether user is authenticated
20     int currentAccountNumber; // current user's account number
21     Screen screen; // ATM's screen
22     Keypad keypad; // ATM's keypad
23     CashDispenser cashDispenser; // ATM's cash dispenser
24     DepositSlot depositSlot; // ATM's deposit slot
25     BankDatabase bankDatabase; // account information database
26
27     // private utility functions
28     void authenticateUser(); // attempts to authenticate user
29     void performTransactions(); // performs transactions
30     int displayMainMenu() const; // displays main menu
31
32     // return object of specified Transaction derived class
33     Transaction *createTransaction( int );
34  }; // end class ATM
35
36  #endif // ATM_H
```

Fig. F.1 | Definition of class ATM, which represents the ATM.

16–17 contain the function prototypes for the class's `public` member functions. The class diagram of Fig. 14.29 does not list any operations for class `ATM`, but we now declare a `public` member function `run` (line 17) in class `ATM` that allows an external client of the class (i.e., `ATMCaseStudy.cpp`) to tell the `ATM` to run. We also include a function prototype for a default constructor (line 16), which we discuss shortly.

Lines 19–25 of Fig. F.1 implement the class's attributes as `private` data members. We determine all but one of these attributes from the UML class diagrams of Fig. 14.28 and Fig. 14.29. Note that we implement the UML `Boolean` attribute `userAuthenticated` in Fig. 14.29 as a `bool` data member in C++ (line 19). Line 20 declares a data member not found in our UML design—an `int` data member `currentAccountNumber` that keeps track of the account number of the current authenticated user. We'll soon see how the class uses this data member.

Lines 21–24 create objects to represent the parts of the ATM. Recall from the class diagram of Fig. 14.28 that class `ATM` has composition relationships with classes `Screen`, `Keypad`, `CashDispenser` and `DepositSlot`, so class `ATM` is responsible for their creation. Line 25 creates a `BankDatabase`, with which the `ATM` interacts to access and manipulate bank account information. [*Note:* If this were a real ATM system, the `ATM` class would receive a reference to an existing database object created by the bank. However, in this implementation we are only simulating the bank's database, so class `ATM` creates the `BankDatabase` object with which it interacts.] Note that lines 6–10 `#include` the class definitions of `Screen`, `Keypad`, `CashDispenser`, `DepositSlot` and `BankDatabase` so that the `ATM` can store objects of these classes.

Lines 28–30 and 33 contain function prototypes for `private` utility functions that the class uses to perform its tasks. We'll see how these functions serve the class shortly. Note that member function `createTransaction` (line 33) returns a `Transaction` pointer. To include the class name `Transaction` in this file, we must at least include a forward declaration of class `Transaction` (line 11). Recall that a forward declaration tells the compiler that a class exists, but that the class is defined elsewhere. A forward declaration is sufficient here, as we are using a `Transaction` pointer as a return type—if we were creating or returning an actual `Transaction` object, we would need to `#include` the full `Transaction` header file.

ATM *Class Member-Function Definitions*

Figure F.2 contains the member-function definitions for class `ATM`. Lines 3–7 `#include` the header files required by the implementation file `ATM.cpp`. Note that including the `ATM` header file allows the compiler to ensure that the class's member functions are defined correctly. This also allows the member functions to use the class's data members.

Line 10 declares an enum named `MenuOption` that contains constants corresponding to the four options in the ATM's main menu (i.e., balance inquiry, withdrawal, deposit and

```
1   // ATM.cpp
2   // Member-function definitions for class ATM.
3   #include "ATM.h" // ATM class definition
4   #include "Transaction.h" // Transaction class definition
5   #include "BalanceInquiry.h" // BalanceInquiry class definition
6   #include "Withdrawal.h" // Withdrawal class definition
7   #include "Deposit.h" // Deposit class definition
```

Fig. F.2 | ATM class member-function definitions. (Part 1 of 4.)

```
 8
 9    // enumeration constants represent main menu options
10    enum MenuOption { BALANCE_INQUIRY = 1, WITHDRAWAL, DEPOSIT, EXIT };
11
12    // ATM default constructor initializes data members
13    ATM::ATM()
14       : userAuthenticated ( false ), // user is not authenticated to start
15         currentAccountNumber( 0 ) // no current account number to start
16    {
17       // empty body
18    } // end ATM default constructor
19
20    // start ATM
21    void ATM::run()
22    {
23       // welcome and authenticate user; perform transactions
24       while ( true )
25       {
26          // loop while user is not yet authenticated
27          while ( !userAuthenticated )
28          {
29             screen.displayMessageLine( "\nWelcome!" );
30             authenticateUser(); // authenticate user
31          } // end while
32
33          performTransactions(); // user is now authenticated
34          userAuthenticated = false; // reset before next ATM session
35          currentAccountNumber = 0; // reset before next ATM session
36          screen.displayMessageLine( "\nThank you! Goodbye!" );
37       } // end while
38    } // end function run
39
40    // attempt to authenticate user against database
41    void ATM::authenticateUser()
42    {
43       screen.displayMessage( "\nPlease enter your account number: " );
44       int accountNumber = keypad.getInput(); // input account number
45       screen.displayMessage( "\nEnter your PIN: " ); // prompt for PIN
46       int pin = keypad.getInput(); // input PIN
47
48       // set userAuthenticated to bool value returned by database
49       userAuthenticated =
50          bankDatabase.authenticateUser( accountNumber, pin );
51
52       // check whether authentication succeeded
53       if ( userAuthenticated )
54       {
55          currentAccountNumber = accountNumber; // save user's account #
56       } // end if
57       else
58          screen.displayMessageLine(
59             "Invalid account number or PIN. Please try again." );
60    } // end function authenticateUser
```

Fig. F.2 | ATM class member-function definitions. (Part 2 of 4.)

```
61
62    // display the main menu and perform transactions
63    void ATM::performTransactions()
64    {
65       // local pointer to store transaction currently being processed
66       Transaction *currentTransactionPtr;
67
68       bool userExited = false; // user has not chosen to exit
69
70       // loop while user has not chosen option to exit system
71       while ( !userExited )
72       {
73          // show main menu and get user selection
74          int mainMenuSelection = displayMainMenu();
75
76          // decide how to proceed based on user's menu selection
77          switch ( mainMenuSelection )
78          {
79             // user chose to perform one of three transaction types
80             case BALANCE_INQUIRY:
81             case WITHDRAWAL:
82             case DEPOSIT:
83                // initialize as new object of chosen type
84                currentTransactionPtr =
85                   createTransaction( mainMenuSelection );
86
87                currentTransactionPtr->execute(); // execute transaction
88
89                // free the space for the dynamically allocated Transaction
90                delete currentTransactionPtr;
91
92                break;
93             case EXIT: // user chose to terminate session
94                screen.displayMessageLine( "\nExiting the system..." );
95                userExited = true; // this ATM session should end
96                break;
97             default: // user did not enter an integer from 1-4
98                screen.displayMessageLine(
99                   "\nYou did not enter a valid selection. Try again." );
100                break;
101          } // end switch
102       } // end while
103    } // end function performTransactions
104
105    // display the main menu and return an input selection
106    int ATM::displayMainMenu() const
107    {
108       screen.displayMessageLine( "\nMain menu:" );
109       screen.displayMessageLine( "1 - View my balance" );
110       screen.displayMessageLine( "2 - Withdraw cash" );
111       screen.displayMessageLine( "3 - Deposit funds" );
112       screen.displayMessageLine( "4 - Exit\n" );
```

Fig. F.2 | ATM class member-function definitions. (Part 3 of 4.)

```
113        screen.displayMessage( "Enter a choice: " );
114        return keypad.getInput(); // return user's selection
115    } // end function displayMainMenu
116
117    // return object of specified Transaction derived class
118    Transaction *ATM::createTransaction( int type )
119    {
120        Transaction *tempPtr; // temporary Transaction pointer
121
122        // determine which type of Transaction to create
123        switch ( type )
124        {
125          case BALANCE_INQUIRY: // create new BalanceInquiry transaction
126              tempPtr = new BalanceInquiry(
127                 currentAccountNumber, screen, bankDatabase );
128              break;
129          case WITHDRAWAL: // create new Withdrawal transaction
130              tempPtr = new Withdrawal( currentAccountNumber, screen,
131                 bankDatabase, keypad, cashDispenser );
132              break;
133          case DEPOSIT: // create new Deposit transaction
134              tempPtr = new Deposit( currentAccountNumber, screen,
135                 bankDatabase, keypad, depositSlot );
136              break;
137        } // end switch
138
139        return tempPtr; // return the newly created object
140    } // end function createTransaction
```

Fig. F.2 | ATM class member-function definitions. (Part 4 of 4.)

exit). Note that setting BALANCE_INQUIRY to 1 causes the subsequent enumeration constants to be assigned the values 2, 3 and 4, as enumeration constant values increment by 1.

Lines 13–18 define class ATM's constructor, which initializes the class's data members. When an ATM object is first created, no user is authenticated, so line 14 uses a member initializer to set userAuthenticated to false. Likewise, line 15 initializes currentAccount-Number to 0 because there is no current user yet.

ATM member function run (lines 21–38) uses an infinite loop (lines 24–37) to repeatedly welcome a user, attempt to authenticate the user and, if authentication succeeds, allow the user to perform transactions. After an authenticated user performs the desired transactions and chooses to exit, the ATM resets itself, displays a goodbye message to the user and restarts the process. We use an infinite loop here to simulate the fact that an ATM appears to run continuously until the bank turns it off (an action beyond the user's control). An ATM user has the option to exit the system, but does not have the ability to turn off the ATM completely.

Inside member function run's infinite loop, lines 27–31 cause the ATM to repeatedly welcome and attempt to authenticate the user as long as the user has not been authenticated (i.e., !userAuthenticated is true). Line 29 invokes member function displayMessage-Line of the ATM's screen to display a welcome message. Like Screen member function displayMessage designed in the case study, member function displayMessageLine (declared in line 13 of Fig. F.3 and defined in lines 20–23 of Fig. F.4) displays a message to the user, but this member function also outputs a newline after displaying the message. We have added this member function during implementation to give class Screen's clients more control over the placement of displayed messages. Line 30 of Fig. F.2 invokes class ATM's private utility function authenticateUser (lines 41–60) to attempt to authenticate the user.

We refer to the requirements specification to determine the steps necessary to authenticate the user before allowing transactions to occur. Line 43 of member function authenticateUser invokes member function displayMessage of the ATM's screen to prompt the user to enter an account number. Line 44 invokes member function getInput of the ATM's keypad to obtain the user's input, then stores the integer value entered by the user in a local variable accountNumber. Member function authenticateUser next prompts the user to enter a PIN (line 45), and stores the PIN input by the user in a local variable pin (line 46). Next, lines 49–50 attempt to authenticate the user by passing the accountNumber and pin entered by the user to the bankDatabase's authenticateUser member function. Class ATM sets its userAuthenticated data member to the bool value returned by this function—userAuthenticated becomes true if authentication succeeds (i.e., accountNumber and pin match those of an existing Account in bankDatabase) and remains false otherwise. If userAuthenticated is true, line 55 saves the account number entered by the user (i.e., accountNumber) in the ATM data member currentAccountNumber. The other member functions of class ATM use this variable whenever an ATM session requires access to the user's account number. If userAuthenticated is false, lines 58–59 use the screen's displayMessageLine member function to indicate that an invalid account number and/or PIN was entered and the user must try again. Note that we set currentAccountNumber only after authenticating the user's account number and the associated PIN—if the database could not authenticate the user, currentAccountNumber remains 0.

After member function run attempts to authenticate the user (line 30), if userAuthenticated is still false, the while loop in lines 27–31 executes again. If userAuthenticated is now true, the loop terminates and control continues with line 33, which calls class ATM's utility function performTransactions.

Member function performTransactions (lines 63–103) carries out an ATM session for an authenticated user. Line 66 declares a local Transaction pointer, which we aim at a BalanceInquiry, Withdrawal or Deposit object representing the ATM transaction currently being processed. Note that we use a Transaction pointer here to allow us to take advantage of polymorphism. Also note that we use the role name included in the class diagram of Fig. 4.24—currentTransaction—in naming this pointer. As per our pointer-naming convention, we append "Ptr" to the role name to form the variable name currentTransactionPtr. Line 68 declares another local variable—a bool called userExited that keeps track of whether the user has chosen to exit. This variable controls a while loop (lines 71–102) that allows the user to execute an unlimited number of transactions before choosing to exit. Within this loop, line 74 displays the main menu and obtains the user's menu selection by calling an ATM utility function displayMainMenu (defined in lines 106–115). This member function displays the main menu by invoking member functions of the ATM's screen and returns a menu selection obtained from the user through the ATM's keypad. Note that this member function is const because it does not modify the contents of the object. Line 74 stores the user's selection returned by displayMainMenu in local variable mainMenuSelection.

After obtaining a main menu selection, member function performTransactions uses a switch statement (lines 77–101) to respond to the selection appropriately. If mainMenuSelection is equal to any of the three enumeration constants representing transaction types (i.e., if the user chose to perform a transaction), lines 84–85 call utility function createTransaction (defined in lines 118–140) to return a pointer to a newly instantiated object of the type that corresponds to the selected transaction. Pointer currentTransactionPtr is assigned the pointer returned by createTransaction. Line 87 then uses currentTransactionPtr to invoke the new object's execute member function to execute the transaction. We'll discuss Transaction member function execute and the three Transaction derived classes shortly. Finally, when the Transaction derived class object is no longer needed, line 90 releases the memory dynamically allocated for it.

Note that we aim the Transaction pointer currentTransactionPtr at an object of one of the three Transaction derived classes so that we can execute transactions polymorphically. For example, if the user chooses to perform a balance inquiry, mainMenuSelection equals BALANCE_INQUIRY, leading createTransaction to return a pointer to a BalanceInquiry object. Thus, currentTransactionPtr points to a BalanceInquiry, and invoking currentTransactionPtr->execute() results in BalanceInquiry's version of execute being called.

Member function createTransaction (lines 118–140) uses a switch statement (lines 123–137) to instantiate a new Transaction derived class object of the type indicated by the parameter type. Recall that member function performTransactions passes mainMenuSelection to this member function only when mainMenuSelection contains a value corresponding to one of the three transaction types. Therefore type equals either BALANCE_INQUIRY, WITHDRAWAL or DEPOSIT. Each case in the switch statement aims the temporary pointer tempPtr at a newly created object of the appropriate Transaction derived class. Note that each constructor has a unique parameter list, based on the specific data required to initialize the derived class object. A BalanceInquiry requires only the account number of the current user and references to the ATM's screen and the bankDatabase. In addition to these parameters, a Withdrawal requires references to the ATM's keypad and cashDispenser, and a Deposit requires references to the ATM's keypad and depositSlot. Note that, as you'll soon see, the BalanceInquiry, Withdrawal and Deposit constructors each specify reference parameters to receive the objects representing the required parts of the ATM. Thus, when member function createTransaction passes objects in the ATM (e.g., screen and keypad) to the initializer for each newly created Transaction derived class object, the new object actually receives *references* to the ATM's composite objects. We discuss the transaction classes in more detail in Sections F.9–F.12.

After executing a transaction (line 87 in performTransactions), userExited remains false and the while loop in lines 71–102 repeats, returning the user to the main menu. However, if a user does not perform a transaction and instead selects the main menu option to exit, line 95 sets userExited to true, causing the condition of the while loop (!userExited) to become false. This while is the final statement of member function performTransactions, so control returns to the calling function run. If the user enters an invalid main menu selection (i.e., not an integer from 1–4), lines 98–99 display an appropriate error message, userExited remains false and the user returns to the main menu to try again.

When performTransactions returns control to member function run, the user has chosen to exit the system, so lines 34–35 reset the ATM's data members userAuthenticated and currentAccountNumber to prepare for the next ATM user. Line 36 displays a goodbye message before the ATM starts over and welcomes the next user.

F.3 Class Screen

Class Screen (Figs. F.3–F.4) represents the screen of the ATM and encapsulates all aspects of displaying output to the user. Class Screen approximates a real ATM's screen with a computer monitor and outputs text messages using cout and the stream insertion operator (<<). In this case study, we designed class Screen to have one operation—displayMessage. For greater flexibility in displaying messages to the Screen, we now declare three Screen member functions—displayMessage, displayMessageLine and displayDollarAmount. The prototypes for these member functions appear in lines 12–14 of Fig. F.3.

Screen Class Member-Function Definitions

Figure F.4 contains the member-function definitions for class Screen. Line 11 #includes the Screen class definition. Member function displayMessage (lines 14–17) takes a string as an argument and prints it to the console using cout and the stream insertion operator (<<). The cursor stays on the same line, making this member function appropriate for displaying prompts to the user. Member function displayMessageLine (lines 20–23) also prints a string, but outputs a newline to move the cursor to the next line. Finally, member function displayDollarAmount (lines 26–29) outputs a properly formatted dollar amount (e.g., $123.45). Line 28 uses stream manipulators fixed and setprecision to output a value formatted with two decimal places. See Chapter 17, Stream Input/Output and Files, for more information about formatting output.

```cpp
1   // Screen.h
2   // Screen class definition. Represents the screen of the ATM.
3   #ifndef SCREEN_H
4   #define SCREEN_H
5
6   #include <string>
7   using std::string;
8
9   class Screen
10  {
11  public:
12     void displayMessage( string ) const; // output a message
13     void displayMessageLine( string ) const; // output message with newline
14     void displayDollarAmount( double ) const; // output a dollar amount
15  }; // end class Screen
16
17  #endif // SCREEN_H
```

Fig. F.3 | Screen class definition.

```cpp
1   // Screen.cpp
2   // Member-function definitions for class Screen.
3   #include <iostream>
4   using std::cout;
5   using std::endl;
6   using std::fixed;
7
```

Fig. F.4 | Screen class member-function definitions. (Part 1 of 2.)

```
 8   #include <iomanip>
 9   using std::setprecision;
10
11   #include "Screen.h" // Screen class definition
12
13   // output a message without a newline
14   void Screen::displayMessage( string message ) const
15   {
16      cout << message;
17   } // end function displayMessage
18
19   // output a message with a newline
20   void Screen::displayMessageLine( string message ) const
21   {
22      cout << message << endl;
23   } // end function displayMessageLine
24
25   // output a dollar amount
26   void Screen::displayDollarAmount( double amount ) const
27   {
28      cout << fixed << setprecision( 2 ) << "$" << amount;
29   } // end function displayDollarAmount
```

Fig. F.4 | Screen class member-function definitions. (Part 2 of 2.)

F.4 Class Keypad

Class Keypad (Figs. F.5–F.6) represents the keypad of the ATM and is responsible for receiving all user input. Recall that we are simulating this hardware, so we use the computer's keyboard to approximate the keypad. A computer keyboard contains many keys not found on the ATM's keypad. However, we assume that the user presses only the keys on the computer keyboard that also appear on the keypad—the keys numbered 0–9 and the *Enter* key. Line 9 of Fig. F.5 contains the function prototype for class Keypad's one member function getInput. This member function is declared const because it does not change the object.

```
 1   // Keypad.h
 2   // Keypad class definition. Represents the keypad of the ATM.
 3   #ifndef KEYPAD_H
 4   #define KEYPAD_H
 5
 6   class Keypad
 7   {
 8   public:
 9      int getInput() const; // return an integer value entered by user
10   }; // end class Keypad
11
12   #endif // KEYPAD_H
```

Fig. F.5 | Keypad class definition.

Keypad *Class Member-Function Definition*

In the Keypad implementation file (Fig. F.6), member function getInput (defined in lines 9–14) uses the standard input stream cin and the stream extraction operator (>>) to obtain input from the user. Line 11 declares a local variable to store the user's input. Line 12 reads input into local variable input, then line 13 returns this value. Recall that getInput obtains all the input used by the ATM. Keypad's getInput member function simply returns the integer input by the user. If a client of class Keypad requires input that satisfies some particular criteria (i.e., a number corresponding to a valid menu option), the client must perform the appropriate error checking. [*Note:* Using the standard input stream cin and the stream extraction operator (>>) allows noninteger input to be read from the user. Because the real ATM's keypad permits only integer input, however, we assume that the user enters an integer and do not attempt to fix problems caused by noninteger input.]

```cpp
1   // Keypad.cpp
2   // Member-function definition for class Keypad (the ATM's keypad).
3   #include <iostream>
4   using std::cin;
5
6   #include "Keypad.h" // Keypad class definition
7
8   // return an integer value entered by user
9   int Keypad::getInput() const
10  {
11     int input; // variable to store the input
12     cin >> input; // we assume that user enters an integer
13     return input; // return the value entered by user
14  } // end function getInput
```

Fig. F.6 | Keypad class member-function definition.

F.5 Class CashDispenser

Class CashDispenser (Figs. F.7–F.8) represents the cash dispenser of the ATM. The class definition (Fig. F.7) contains the function prototype for a default constructor (line 9). Class CashDispenser declares two additional public member functions—dispenseCash (line 12) and isSufficientCashAvailable (line 15). The class trusts that a client (i.e., Withdrawal) calls dispenseCash only after establishing that sufficient cash is available by calling isSufficientCashAvailable. Thus, dispenseCash simply simulates dispensing the requested amount without checking whether sufficient cash is available. Line 17 declares private constant INITIAL_COUNT, which indicates the initial count of bills in the cash dispenser when the ATM starts (i.e., 500). Line 18 implements attribute count (modeled in Fig. 14.29), which keeps track of the number of bills remaining in the CashDispenser at any time.

CashDispenser *Class Member-Function Definitions*

Figure F.8 contains the definitions of class CashDispenser's member functions. The constructor (lines 6–9) sets count to the initial count (i.e., 500). Member function dispenseCash (lines 13–17) simulates cash dispensing. If our system were hooked up to a real hardware cash dispenser, this member function would interact with the hardware device

```
 1   // CashDispenser.h
 2   // CashDispenser class definition. Represents the ATM's cash dispenser.
 3   #ifndef CASH_DISPENSER_H
 4   #define CASH_DISPENSER_H
 5
 6   class CashDispenser
 7   {
 8   public:
 9      CashDispenser(); // constructor initializes bill count to 500
10
11      // simulates dispensing of specified amount of cash
12      void dispenseCash( int );
13
14      // indicates whether cash dispenser can dispense desired amount
15      bool isSufficientCashAvailable( int ) const;
16   private:
17      const static int INITIAL_COUNT = 500;
18      int count; // number of $20 bills remaining
19   }; // end class CashDispenser
20
21   #endif // CASH_DISPENSER_H
```

Fig. F.7 | CashDispenser class definition.

```
 1   // CashDispenser.cpp
 2   // Member-function definitions for class CashDispenser.
 3   #include "CashDispenser.h" // CashDispenser class definition
 4
 5   // CashDispenser default constructor initializes count to default
 6   CashDispenser::CashDispenser()
 7   {
 8      count = INITIAL_COUNT; // set count attribute to default
 9   } // end CashDispenser default constructor
10
11   // simulates dispensing of specified amount of cash; assumes enough cash
12   // is available (previous call to isSufficientCashAvailable returned true)
13   void CashDispenser::dispenseCash( int amount )
14   {
15      int billsRequired = amount / 20; // number of $20 bills required
16      count -= billsRequired; // update the count of bills
17   } // end function dispenseCash
18
19   // indicates whether cash dispenser can dispense desired amount
20   bool CashDispenser::isSufficientCashAvailable( int amount ) const
21   {
22      int billsRequired = amount / 20; // number of $20 bills required
23
24      if ( count >= billsRequired )
25         return true; // enough bills are available
26      else
27         return false; // not enough bills are available
28   } // end function isSufficientCashAvailable
```

Fig. F.8 | CashDispenser class member-function definitions.

to physically dispense cash. Our simulated version of the member function simply decreases the count of bills remaining by the number required to dispense the specified amount (line 16). Note that line 15 calculates the number of $20 bills required to dispense the specified amount. The ATM allows the user to choose only withdrawal amounts that are multiples of $20, so we divide amount by 20 to obtain the number of billsRequired. Also note that it is the responsibility of the client of the class (i.e., Withdrawal) to inform the user that cash has been dispensed—CashDispenser cannot interact directly with Screen.

Member function isSufficientCashAvailable (lines 20–28) has a parameter amount that specifies the amount of cash in question. Lines 24–27 return true if the Cash-Dispenser's count is greater than or equal to billsRequired (i.e., enough bills are available) and false otherwise (i.e., not enough bills). For example, if a user wishes to withdraw $80 (i.e., billsRequired is 4), but only three bills remain (i.e., count is 3), the member function returns false.

F.6 Class DepositSlot

Class DepositSlot (Figs. F.9–F.10) represents the deposit slot of the ATM. Like the version of class CashDispenser presented here, this version of class DepositSlot merely simulates the functionality of a real hardware deposit slot. DepositSlot has no data members and only one member function—isEnvelopeReceived (declared in line 9 of Fig. F.9 and defined in lines 7–10 of Fig. F.10)—that indicates whether a deposit envelope was received.

```
1   // DepositSlot.h
2   // DepositSlot class definition. Represents the ATM's deposit slot.
3   #ifndef DEPOSIT_SLOT_H
4   #define DEPOSIT_SLOT_H
5
6   class DepositSlot
7   {
8   public:
9      bool isEnvelopeReceived() const; // tells whether envelope was received
10  }; // end class DepositSlot
11
12  #endif // DEPOSIT_SLOT_H
```

Fig. F.9 | DepositSlot class definition.

```
1   // DepositSlot.cpp
2   // Member-function definition for class DepositSlot.
3   #include "DepositSlot.h" // DepositSlot class definiton
4
5   // indicates whether envelope was received (always returns true,
6   // because this is only a software simulation of a real deposit slot)
7   bool DepositSlot::isEnvelopeReceived() const
8   {
9      return true; // deposit envelope was received
10  } // end function isEnvelopeReceived
```

Fig. F.10 | DepositSlot class member-function definition.

Recall from the requirements specification that the ATM allows the user up to two minutes to insert an envelope. The current version of member function isEnvelope-Received simply returns true immediately (line 9 of Fig. F.10), because this is only a software simulation, and we assume that the user has inserted an envelope within the required time frame. If an actual hardware deposit slot were connected to our system, member function isEnvelopeReceived might be implemented to wait for a maximum of two minutes to receive a signal from the hardware deposit slot indicating that the user has indeed inserted a deposit envelope. If isEnvelopeReceived were to receive such a signal within two minutes, the member function would return true. If two minutes elapsed and the member function still had not received a signal, then the member function would return false.

F.7 Class Account

Class Account (Figs. F.11–F.12) represents a bank account. Lines 9–15 in the class definition (Fig. F.11) contain function prototypes for the class's constructor and six member functions, which we discuss shortly. Each Account has four attributes (modeled in Fig. 14.29)—accountNumber, pin, availableBalance and totalBalance. Lines 17–20 implement these attributes as private data members. Data member availableBalance represents the amount of funds available for withdrawal. Data member totalBalance represents the amount of funds available, plus the amount of deposited funds still pending confirmation or clearance.

Account Class Member-Function Definitions
Figure F.12 presents the definitions of class Account's member functions. The class's constructor (lines 6–14) takes an account number, the PIN established for the account, the

```
 1   // Account.h
 2   // Account class definition. Represents a bank account.
 3   #ifndef ACCOUNT_H
 4   #define ACCOUNT_H
 5
 6   class Account
 7   {
 8   public:
 9      Account( int, int, double, double ); // constructor sets attributes
10      bool validatePIN( int ) const; // is user-specified PIN correct?
11      double getAvailableBalance() const; // returns available balance
12      double getTotalBalance() const; // returns total balance
13      void credit( double ); // adds an amount to the Account balance
14      void debit( double ); // subtracts an amount from the Account balance
15      int getAccountNumber() const; // returns account number
16   private:
17      int accountNumber; // account number
18      int pin; // PIN for authentication
19      double availableBalance; // funds available for withdrawal
20      double totalBalance; // funds available + funds waiting to clear
21   }; // end class Account
22
23   #endif // ACCOUNT_H
```

Fig. F.11 | Account class definition.

initial available balance and the initial total balance as arguments. Lines 8–11 assign these values to the class's data members using member initializers.

Member function validatePIN (lines 17–23) determines whether a user-specified PIN (i.e., parameter userPIN) matches the PIN associated with the account (i.e., data member pin). Recall that we modeled this member function's parameter userPIN in the UML class diagram of Fig. 7.36. If the two PINs match, the member function returns true (line 20); otherwise, it returns false (line 22).

Member functions getAvailableBalance (lines 26–29) and getTotalBalance (lines 32–35) are *get* functions that return the values of double data members availableBalance and totalBalance, respectively.

```cpp
1   // Account.cpp
2   // Member-function definitions for class Account.
3   #include "Account.h" // Account class definition
4
5   // Account constructor initializes attributes
6   Account::Account( int theAccountNumber, int thePIN,
7      double theAvailableBalance, double theTotalBalance )
8      : accountNumber( theAccountNumber ),
9        pin( thePIN ),
10       availableBalance( theAvailableBalance ),
11       totalBalance( theTotalBalance )
12  {
13     // empty body
14  } // end Account constructor
15
16  // determines whether a user-specified PIN matches PIN in Account
17  bool Account::validatePIN( int userPIN ) const
18  {
19     if ( userPIN == pin )
20        return true;
21     else
22        return false;
23  } // end function validatePIN
24
25  // returns available balance
26  double Account::getAvailableBalance() const
27  {
28     return availableBalance;
29  } // end function getAvailableBalance
30
31  // returns the total balance
32  double Account::getTotalBalance() const
33  {
34     return totalBalance;
35  } // end function getTotalBalance
36
37  // credits an amount to the account
38  void Account::credit( double amount )
39  {
40     totalBalance += amount; // add to total balance
41  } // end function credit
```

Fig. F.12 | Account class member-function definitions. (Part 1 of 2.)

```
42
43   // debits an amount from the account
44   void Account::debit( double amount )
45   {
46      availableBalance -= amount; // subtract from available balance
47      totalBalance -= amount; // subtract from total balance
48   } // end function debit
49
50   // returns account number
51   int Account::getAccountNumber() const
52   {
53      return accountNumber;
54   } // end function getAccountNumber
```

Fig. F.12 | Account class member-function definitions. (Part 2 of 2.)

Member function credit (lines 38–41) adds an amount of money (i.e., parameter amount) to an Account as part of a deposit transaction. Note that this member function adds the amount only to data member totalBalance (line 40). The money credited to an account during a deposit does not become available immediately, so we modify only the total balance. We assume that the bank updates the available balance appropriately at a later time. Our implementation of class Account includes only member functions required for carrying out ATM transactions. Therefore, we omit the member functions that some other bank system would invoke to add to data member availableBalance (to confirm a deposit) or subtract from data member totalBalance (to reject a deposit).

Member function debit (lines 44–48) subtracts an amount of money (i.e., parameter amount) from an Account as part of a withdrawal transaction. This member function subtracts the amount from both data member availableBalance (line 46) and data member totalBalance (line 47), because a withdrawal affects both measures of an account balance.

Member function getAccountNumber (lines 51–54) provides access to an Account's accountNumber. We include this member function in our implementation so that a client of the class (i.e., BankDatabase) can identify a particular Account. For example, BankDatabase contains many Account objects, and it can invoke this member function on each of its Account objects to locate the one with a specific account number.

F.8 Class BankDatabase

Class BankDatabase (Figs. F.13–F.14) models the bank's database with which the ATM interacts to access and modify a user's account information. The class definition (Fig. F.13) declares function prototypes for the class's constructor and several member functions. We discuss these momentarily. The class definition also declares the BankDatabase's data members. We determine one data member for class BankDatabase based on its composition relationship with class Account. Recall from Fig. 14.28 that a BankDatabase is composed of zero or more objects of class Account. Line 24 of Fig. F.13 implements data member accounts—a vector of Account objects—to implement this composition relationship. Lines 6–7 allow us to use vector in this file. Line 27 contains the function prototype for a private utility function getAccount that allows the member functions of the class to obtain a pointer to a specific Account in the accounts vector.

```
1   // BankDatabase.h
2   // BankDatabase class definition. Represents the bank's database.
3   #ifndef BANK_DATABASE_H
4   #define BANK_DATABASE_H
5
6   #include <vector> // class uses vector to store Account objects
7   using std::vector;
8
9   #include "Account.h" // Account class definition
10
11  class BankDatabase
12  {
13  public:
14     BankDatabase(); // constructor initializes accounts
15
16     // determine whether account number and PIN match those of an Account
17     bool authenticateUser( int, int ); // returns true if Account authentic
18
19     double getAvailableBalance( int ); // get an available balance
20     double getTotalBalance( int ); // get an Account's total balance
21     void credit( int, double ); // add amount to Account balance
22     void debit( int, double ); // subtract amount from Account balance
23  private:
24     vector< Account > accounts; // vector of the bank's Accounts
25
26     // private utility function
27     Account * getAccount( int ); // get pointer to Account object
28  }; // end class BankDatabase
29
30  #endif // BANK_DATABASE_H
```

Fig. F.13 | BankDatabase class definition.

BankDatabase Class Member-Function Definitions

Figure F.14 contains the member-function definitions for class BankDatabase. We implement the class with a default constructor (lines 6–15) that adds Account objects to data member accounts. For the sake of testing the system, we create two new Account objects with test data (lines 9–10), then add them to the end of the vector (lines 13–14). Note

```
1   // BankDatabase.cpp
2   // Member-function definitions for class BankDatabase.
3   #include "BankDatabase.h" // BankDatabase class definition
4
5   // BankDatabase default constructor initializes accounts
6   BankDatabase::BankDatabase()
7   {
8      // create two Account objects for testing
9      Account account1( 12345, 54321, 1000.0, 1200.0 );
10     Account account2( 98765, 56789, 200.0, 200.0 );
11
```

Fig. F.14 | BankDatabase class member-function definitions. (Part 1 of 3.)

```
12        // add the Account objects to the vector accounts
13        accounts.push_back( account1 ); // add account1 to end of vector
14        accounts.push_back( account2 ); // add account2 to end of vector
15     } // end BankDatabase default constructor
16
17     // retrieve Account object containing specified account number
18     Account * BankDatabase::getAccount( int accountNumber )
19     {
20        // loop through accounts searching for matching account number
21        for ( size_t i = 0; i < accounts.size(); i++ )
22        {
23           // return current account if match found
24           if ( accounts[ i ].getAccountNumber() == accountNumber )
25              return &accounts[ i ];
26        } // end for
27
28        return NULL; // if no matching account was found, return NULL
29     } // end function getAccount
30
31     // determine whether user-specified account number and PIN match
32     // those of an account in the database
33     bool BankDatabase::authenticateUser( int userAccountNumber,
34        int userPIN )
35     {
36        // attempt to retrieve the account with the account number
37        Account * const userAccountPtr = getAccount( userAccountNumber );
38
39        // if account exists, return result of Account function validatePIN
40        if ( userAccountPtr != NULL )
41           return userAccountPtr->validatePIN( userPIN );
42        else
43           return false; // account number not found, so return false
44     } // end function authenticateUser
45
46     // return available balance of Account with specified account number
47     double BankDatabase::getAvailableBalance( int userAccountNumber )
48     {
49        Account * const userAccountPtr = getAccount( userAccountNumber );
50        return userAccountPtr->getAvailableBalance();
51     } // end function getAvailableBalance
52
53     // return total balance of Account with specified account number
54     double BankDatabase::getTotalBalance( int userAccountNumber )
55     {
56        Account * const userAccountPtr = getAccount( userAccountNumber );
57        return userAccountPtr->getTotalBalance();
58     } // end function getTotalBalance
59
60     // credit an amount to Account with specified account number
61     void BankDatabase::credit( int userAccountNumber, double amount )
62     {
```

Fig. F.14 | BankDatabase class member-function definitions. (Part 2 of 3.)

```
63      Account * const userAccountPtr = getAccount( userAccountNumber );
64      userAccountPtr->credit( amount );
65   } // end function credit
66
67   // debit an amount from Account with specified account number
68   void BankDatabase::debit( int userAccountNumber, double amount )
69   {
70      Account * const userAccountPtr = getAccount( userAccountNumber );
71      userAccountPtr->debit( amount );
72   } // end function debit
```

Fig. F.14 | BankDatabase class member-function definitions. (Part 3 of 3.)

that the Account constructor has four parameters—the account number, the PIN assigned to the account, the initial available balance and the initial total balance.

Recall that class BankDatabase serves as an intermediary between class ATM and the actual Account objects that contain users' account information. Thus, the member functions of class BankDatabase do nothing more than invoke the corresponding member functions of the Account object belonging to the current ATM user.

We include private utility function getAccount (lines 18–29) to allow the Bank-Database to obtain a pointer to a particular Account within vector accounts. To locate the user's Account, the BankDatabase compares the value returned by member function getAccountNumber for each element of accounts to a specified account number until it finds a match. Lines 21–26 traverse the accounts vector. If the account number of the current Account (i.e., accounts[i]) equals the value of parameter accountNumber, the member function immediately returns the address of the current Account (i.e., a pointer to the current Account). If no account has the given account number, then line 28 returns NULL. Note that this member function must return a pointer, as opposed to a reference, because there is the possibility that the return value could be NULL—a reference cannot be NULL, but a pointer can.

Note that vector function size (invoked in the loop-continuation condition in line 21) returns the number of elements in a vector as a value of type size_t (which is usually unsigned int). As a result, we declare the control variable i to be of type size_t, too. On some compilers, declaring i as an int would cause the compiler to issue a warning message, because the loop-continuation condition would compare a signed value (i.e., an int) and an unsigned value (i.e., a value of type size_t).

Member function authenticateUser (lines 33–44) proves or disproves the an ATM user's identity. This function takes a user-specified account number and user-specified PIN as arguments and indicates whether they match the account number and PIN of an Account in the database. Line 37 calls utility function getAccount, which returns either a pointer to an Account with userAccountNumber as its account number or NULL to indicate that userAccountNumber is invalid. We declare userAccountPtr to be a const pointer because, once the member function aims this pointer at the user's Account, the pointer should not change. If getAccount returns a pointer to an Account object, line 41 returns the bool value returned by that object's validatePIN member function. Note that Bank-Database's authenticateUser member function does not perform the PIN comparison itself—rather, it forwards userPIN to the Account object's validatePIN member function to do so. The value returned by Account member function validatePIN indicates whether the user-specified PIN matches the PIN of the user's Account, so member function authenticateUser simply returns this value to the client of the class (i.e., ATM).

BankDatabase trusts the ATM to invoke member function authenticateUser and receive a return value of true before allowing the user to perform transactions. BankDatabase also trusts that each Transaction object created by the ATM contains the valid account number of the current authenticated user and that this is the account number passed to the remaining BankDatabase member functions as argument userAccountNumber. Member functions getAvailableBalance (lines 47–51), getTotalBalance (lines 54–58), credit (lines 61–65) and debit (lines 68–72) therefore simply retrieve a pointer to the user's Account object with utility function getAccount, then use this pointer to invoke the appropriate Account member function on the user's Account object. We know that the calls to getAccount within these member functions will never return NULL, because userAccountNumber must refer to an existing Account. Note that getAvailableBalance and getTotalBalance return the values returned by the corresponding Account member functions. Also note that credit and debit simply redirect parameter amount to the Account member functions they invoke.

F.9 Class Transaction

Class Transaction (Figs. F.15–F.16) is an abstract base class that represents the notion of an ATM transaction. It contains the common features of derived classes BalanceInquiry, Withdrawal and Deposit. Figure F.15 expands upon the Transaction header file first developed in Section 14.11. Lines 13, 17–19 and 22 contain function prototypes for the class's constructor and four member functions, which we discuss shortly. Line 15 defines a virtual destructor with an empty body—this makes all derived-class destructors virtual (even those defined implicitly by the compiler) and ensures that dynamically allocated derived-class objects get destroyed properly when they are deleted via a base-class pointer. Lines 24–26 declare the class's private data members. Recall from the class diagram of Fig. 14.29 that class Transaction contains an attribute accountNumber (implemented in line 24) that indicates the account involved in the Transaction. We derive data members screen (line 25) and bankDatabase (line 26) from class Transaction's associations modeled in Fig. 14.28—all transactions require access to the ATM's screen and the bank's database, so we include references to a Screen and a BankDatabase as data members of class Transaction. As you'll soon see, Transaction's constructor initializes these references. Note that the forward declarations in lines 6–7 signify that the header file contains references to objects of classes Screen and BankDatabase, but that the definitions of these classes lie outside the header file.

```
1   // Transaction.h
2   // Transaction abstract base class definition.
3   #ifndef TRANSACTION_H
4   #define TRANSACTION_H
5
6   class Screen; // forward declaration of class Screen
7   class BankDatabase; // forward declaration of class BankDatabase
8
```

Fig. F.15 | Transaction class definition. (Part 1 of 2.)

```
9   class Transaction
10  {
11  public:
12      // constructor initializes common features of all Transactions
13      Transaction( int, Screen &, BankDatabase & );
14
15      virtual ~Transaction() { } // virtual destructor with empty body
16
17      int getAccountNumber() const; // return account number
18      Screen &getScreen() const; // return reference to screen
19      BankDatabase &getBankDatabase() const; // return reference to database
20
21      // pure virtual function to perform the transaction
22      virtual void execute() = 0; // overridden in derived classes
23  private:
24      int accountNumber; // indicates account involved
25      Screen &screen; // reference to the screen of the ATM
26      BankDatabase &bankDatabase; // reference to the account info database
27  }; // end class Transaction
28
29  #endif // TRANSACTION_H
```

Fig. F.15 | Transaction class definition. (Part 2 of 2.)

```
1   // Transaction.cpp
2   // Member-function definitions for class Transaction.
3   #include "Transaction.h" // Transaction class definition
4   #include "Screen.h" // Screen class definition
5   #include "BankDatabase.h" // BankDatabase class definition
6
7   // constructor initializes common features of all Transactions
8   Transaction::Transaction( int userAccountNumber, Screen &atmScreen,
9       BankDatabase &atmBankDatabase )
10      : accountNumber( userAccountNumber ),
11        screen( atmScreen ),
12        bankDatabase( atmBankDatabase )
13  {
14      // empty body
15  } // end Transaction constructor
16
17  // return account number
18  int Transaction::getAccountNumber() const
19  {
20      return accountNumber;
21  } // end function getAccountNumber
22
23  // return reference to screen
24  Screen &Transaction::getScreen() const
25  {
26      return screen;
27  } // end function getScreen
28
```

Fig. F.16 | Transaction class member-function definitions. (Part 1 of 2.)

```
29    // return reference to bank database
30    BankDatabase &Transaction::getBankDatabase() const
31    {
32       return bankDatabase;
33    } // end function getBankDatabase
```

Fig. F.16 | `Transaction` class member-function definitions. (Part 2 of 2.)

Class `Transaction` has a constructor (declared in line 13 of Fig. F.15 and defined in lines 8–15 of Fig. F.16) that takes the current user's account number and references to the ATM's screen and the bank's database as arguments. Because `Transaction` is an abstract class, this constructor will never be called directly to instantiate `Transaction` objects. Instead, the constructors of the `Transaction` derived classes will use base-class initializer syntax to invoke this constructor.

Class `Transaction` has three `public` *get* functions—`getAccountNumber` (declared in line 17 of Fig. F.15 and defined in lines 18–21 of Fig. F.16), `getScreen` (declared in line 18 of Fig. F.15 and defined in lines 24–27 of Fig. F.16) and `getBankDatabase` (declared in line 19 of Fig. F.15 and defined in lines 30–33 of Fig. F.16). `Transaction` derived classes inherit these member functions from `Transaction` and use them to gain access to class `Transaction`'s `private` data members.

Class `Transaction` also declares a pure `virtual` function `execute` (line 22 of Fig. F.15). It does not make sense to provide an implementation for this member function, because a generic transaction cannot be executed. Thus, we declare this member function to be a pure `virtual` function and force each `Transaction` derived class to provide its own concrete implementation that executes that particular type of transaction.

F.10 Class `BalanceInquiry`

Class `BalanceInquiry` (Figs. F.17–F.18) derives from abstract base class `Transaction` and represents a balance-inquiry ATM transaction. `BalanceInquiry` does not have any data members of its own, but it inherits `Transaction` data members `accountNumber`, `screen` and `bankDatabase`, which are accessible through `Transaction`'s `public` *get* functions. Note that line 6 `#include`s the definition of base class `Transaction`. The `BalanceInquiry` constructor (declared in line 11 of Fig. F.17 and defined in lines 8–13 of Fig. F.18) takes arguments corresponding to the `Transaction` data members and simply forwards them to `Transaction`'s constructor, using base-class initializer syntax (line 10 of Fig. F.18). Line 12 of Fig. F.17 contains the function prototype for member function `execute`, which is required to indicate the intention to override the base class's pure `virtual` function of the same name.

Class `BalanceInquiry` overrides `Transaction`'s pure `virtual` function `execute` to provide a concrete implementation (lines 16–37 of Fig. F.18) that performs the steps involved in a balance inquiry. Lines 19–20 get references to the bank database and the ATM's screen by invoking member functions inherited from base class `Transaction`. Lines 23–24 retrieve the available balance of the account involved by invoking member function `getAvailableBalance` of `bankDatabase`. Note that line 24 uses inherited member function `getAccountNumber` to get the account number of the current user, which it then passes to `getAvailableBalance`. Lines 27–28 retrieve the total balance of the current user's account. Lines 31–36 display the balance information on the ATM's

```
 1   // BalanceInquiry.h
 2   // BalanceInquiry class definition. Represents a balance inquiry.
 3   #ifndef BALANCE_INQUIRY_H
 4   #define BALANCE_INQUIRY_H
 5
 6   #include "Transaction.h" // Transaction class definition
 7
 8   class BalanceInquiry : public Transaction
 9   {
10   public:
11      BalanceInquiry( int, Screen &, BankDatabase & ); // constructor
12      virtual void execute(); // perform the transaction
13   }; // end class BalanceInquiry
14
15   #endif // BALANCE_INQUIRY_H
```

Fig. F.17 | BalanceInquiry class definition.

```
 1   // BalanceInquiry.cpp
 2   // Member-function definitions for class BalanceInquiry.
 3   #include "BalanceInquiry.h" // BalanceInquiry class definition
 4   #include "Screen.h" // Screen class definition
 5   #include "BankDatabase.h" // BankDatabase class definition
 6
 7   // BalanceInquiry constructor initializes base-class data members
 8   BalanceInquiry:: BalanceInquiry( int userAccountNumber, Screen &atmScreen,
 9      BankDatabase &atmBankDatabase )
10      : Transaction( userAccountNumber, atmScreen, atmBankDatabase )
11   {
12      // empty body
13   } // end BalanceInquiry constructor
14
15   // performs transaction; overrides Transaction's pure virtual function
16   void BalanceInquiry::execute()
17   {
18      // get references to bank database and screen
19      BankDatabase &bankDatabase = getBankDatabase();
20      Screen &screen = getScreen();
21
22      // get the available balance for the current user's Account
23      double availableBalance =
24         bankDatabase.getAvailableBalance( getAccountNumber() );
25
26      // get the total balance for the current user's Account
27      double totalBalance =
28         bankDatabase.getTotalBalance( getAccountNumber() );
29
30      // display the balance information on the screen
31      screen.displayMessageLine( "\nBalance Information:" );
32      screen.displayMessage( " - Available balance: " );
33      screen.displayDollarAmount( availableBalance );
```

Fig. F.18 | BalanceInquiry class member-function definitions. (Part 1 of 2.)

```
34      screen.displayMessage( "\n - Total balance:      " );
35      screen.displayDollarAmount( totalBalance );
36      screen.displayMessageLine( "" );
37   } // end function execute
```

Fig. F.18 | `BalanceInquiry` class member-function definitions. (Part 2 of 2.)

screen. Recall that `displayDollarAmount` takes a `double` argument and outputs it to the screen formatted as a dollar amount. For example, if a user's `availableBalance` is 700.5, line 33 outputs $700.50. Note that line 36 inserts a blank line of output to separate the balance information from subsequent output (i.e., the main menu repeated by class `ATM` after executing the `BalanceInquiry`).

F.11 Class `Withdrawal`

Class `Withdrawal` (Figs. F.19–F.20) derives from `Transaction` and represents a withdrawal ATM transaction. Figure F.19 expands upon the header file for this class developed in Fig. 14.31. Class `Withdrawal` has a constructor and one member function `execute`, which we discuss shortly. Recall from the class diagram of Fig. 14.29 that class `Withdrawal` has one attribute, `amount`, which line 16 implements as an `int` data member. Fig. 14.28 models associations between class `Withdrawal` and classes `Keypad` and `CashDispenser`, for which lines 17–18 implement references `keypad` and `cashDispenser`, respectively. Line 19 is the function prototype of a `private` utility function that we soon discuss.

```
1   // Withdrawal.h
2   // Withdrawal class definition. Represents a withdrawal transaction.
3   #ifndef WITHDRAWAL_H
4   #define WITHDRAWAL_H
5
6   #include "Transaction.h" // Transaction class definition
7   class Keypad; // forward declaration of class Keypad
8   class CashDispenser; // forward declaration of class CashDispenser
9
10  class Withdrawal : public Transaction
11  {
12  public:
13     Withdrawal( int, Screen &, BankDatabase &, Keypad &, CashDispenser & );
14     virtual void execute(); // perform the transaction
15  private:
16     int amount; // amount to withdraw
17     Keypad &keypad; // reference to ATM's keypad
18     CashDispenser &cashDispenser; // reference to ATM's cash dispenser
19     int displayMenuOfAmounts() const; // display the withdrawal menu
20  }; // end class Withdrawal
21
22  #endif // WITHDRAWAL_H
```

Fig. F.19 | `Withdrawal` class definition.

```cpp
1   // Withdrawal.cpp
2   // Member-function definitions for class Withdrawal.
3   #include "Withdrawal.h" // Withdrawal class definition
4   #include "Screen.h" // Screen class definition
5   #include "BankDatabase.h" // BankDatabase class definition
6   #include "Keypad.h" // Keypad class definition
7   #include "CashDispenser.h" // CashDispenser class definition
8
9   // global constant that corresponds to menu option to cancel
10  const static int CANCELED = 6;
11
12  // Withdrawal constructor initialize class's data members
13  Withdrawal::Withdrawal( int userAccountNumber, Screen &atmScreen,
14     BankDatabase &atmBankDatabase, Keypad &atmKeypad,
15     CashDispenser &atmCashDispenser )
16     : Transaction( userAccountNumber, atmScreen, atmBankDatabase ),
17       keypad( atmKeypad ), cashDispenser( atmCashDispenser )
18  {
19     // empty body
20  } // end Withdrawal constructor
21
22  // perform transaction; overrides Transaction's pure virtual function
23  void Withdrawal::execute()
24  {
25     bool cashDispensed = false; // cash was not dispensed yet
26     bool transactionCanceled = false; // transaction was not canceled yet
27
28     // get references to bank database and screen
29     BankDatabase &bankDatabase = getBankDatabase();
30     Screen &screen = getScreen();
31
32     // loop until cash is dispensed or the user cancels
33     do
34     {
35        // obtain the chosen withdrawal amount from the user
36        int selection = displayMenuOfAmounts();
37
38        // check whether user chose a withdrawal amount or canceled
39        if ( selection != CANCELED )
40        {
41           amount = selection; // set amount to the selected dollar amount
42
43           // get available balance of account involved
44           double availableBalance =
45              bankDatabase.getAvailableBalance( getAccountNumber() );
46
47           // check whether the user has enough money in the account
48           if ( amount <= availableBalance )
49           {
50              // check whether the cash dispenser has enough money
51              if ( cashDispenser.isSufficientCashAvailable( amount ) )
52              {
```

Fig. F.20 | Withdrawal class member-function definitions. (Part 1 of 3.)

```
53              // update the account involved to reflect withdrawal
54              bankDatabase.debit( getAccountNumber(), amount );
55
56              cashDispenser.dispenseCash( amount ); // dispense cash
57              cashDispensed = true; // cash was dispensed
58
59              // instruct user to take cash
60              screen.displayMessageLine(
61                 "\nPlease take your cash from the cash dispenser." );
62           } // end if
63           else // cash dispenser does not have enough cash
64              screen.displayMessageLine(
65                 "\nInsufficient cash available in the ATM."
66                 "\n\nPlease choose a smaller amount." );
67        } // end if
68        else // not enough money available in user's account
69        {
70           screen.displayMessageLine(
71              "\nInsufficient funds in your account."
72              "\n\nPlease choose a smaller amount." );
73        } // end else
74     } // end if
75     else // user chose cancel menu option
76     {
77        screen.displayMessageLine( "\nCanceling transaction..." );
78        transactionCanceled = true; // user canceled the transaction
79     } // end else
80  } while ( !cashDispensed && !transactionCanceled ); // end do...while
81  } // end function execute
82
83  // display a menu of withdrawal amounts and the option to cancel;
84  // return the chosen amount or 0 if the user chooses to cancel
85  int Withdrawal::displayMenuOfAmounts() const
86  {
87     int userChoice = 0; // local variable to store return value
88
89     Screen &screen = getScreen(); // get screen reference
90
91     // array of amounts to correspond to menu numbers
92     int amounts[] = { 0, 20, 40, 60, 100, 200 };
93
94     // loop while no valid choice has been made
95     while ( userChoice == 0 )
96     {
97        // display the menu
98        screen.displayMessageLine( "\nWithdrawal options:" );
99        screen.displayMessageLine( "1 - $20" );
100       screen.displayMessageLine( "2 - $40" );
101       screen.displayMessageLine( "3 - $60" );
102       screen.displayMessageLine( "4 - $100" );
103       screen.displayMessageLine( "5 - $200" );
104       screen.displayMessageLine( "6 - Cancel transaction" );
105       screen.displayMessage( "\nChoose a withdrawal option (1-6): " );
```

Fig. F.20 | Withdrawal class member-function definitions. (Part 2 of 3.)

```
106
107        int input = keypad.getInput(); // get user input through keypad
108
109        // determine how to proceed based on the input value
110        switch ( input )
111        {
112           case 1: // if the user chose a withdrawal amount
113           case 2: // (i.e., chose option 1, 2, 3, 4 or 5), return the
114           case 3: // corresponding amount from amounts array
115           case 4:
116           case 5:
117              userChoice = amounts[ input ]; // save user's choice
118              break;
119           case CANCELED: // the user chose to cancel
120              userChoice = CANCELED; // save user's choice
121              break;
122           default: // the user did not enter a value from 1-6
123              screen.displayMessageLine(
124                 "\nIvalid selection. Try again." );
125        } // end switch
126     } // end while
127
128     return userChoice; // return withdrawal amount or CANCELED
129  } // end function displayMenuOfAmounts
```

Fig. F.20 | Withdrawal class member-function definitions. (Part 3 of 3.)

Withdrawal *Class Member-Function Definitions*

Figure F.20 contains the member-function definitions for class Withdrawal. Line 3 #includes the class's definition, and lines 4–7 #include the definitions of the other classes used in Withdrawal's member functions. Line 11 declares a global constant corresponding to the cancel option on the withdrawal menu. We'll soon discuss how the class uses this constant.

Class Withdrawal's constructor (defined in lines 13–20 of Fig. F.20) has five parameters. It uses a base-class initializer in line 16 to pass parameters userAccountNumber, atmScreen and atmBankDatabase to base class Transaction's constructor to set the data members that Withdrawal inherits from Transaction. The constructor also takes references atmKeypad and atmCashDispenser as parameters and assigns them to reference data members keypad and cashDispenser using member initializers (line 17).

Class Withdrawal overrides Transaction's pure virtual function execute with a concrete implementation (lines 23–81) that performs the steps involved in a withdrawal. Line 25 declares and initializes a local bool variable cashDispensed. This variable indicates whether cash has been dispensed (i.e., whether the transaction has completed successfully) and is initially false. Line 26 declares and initializes to false a bool variable transactionCanceled that indicates whether the transaction has been canceled by the user. Lines 29–30 get references to the bank database and the ATM's screen by invoking member functions inherited from base class Transaction.

Lines 33–80 contain a do...while statement that executes its body until cash is dispensed (i.e., until cashDispensed becomes true) or until the user chooses to cancel (i.e., until transactionCanceled becomes true). This loop continuously returns the user to the start of the transaction if an error occurs (i.e., the requested withdrawal amount is greater than the user's available balance or greater than the amount of cash in the cash dispenser). Line 36 displays a menu of withdrawal amounts and obtains a user selection by calling `private` utility function `displayMenuOfAmounts` (defined in lines 85–129). This function displays the menu of amounts and returns either an `int` withdrawal amount or the `int` constant `CANCELED` to indicate that the user has chosen to cancel the transaction.

Member function `displayMenuOfAmounts` (lines 85–129) first declares local variable `userChoice` (initially 0) to store the value that the member function will return (line 87). Line 89 gets a reference to the screen by calling member function `getScreen` inherited from base class `Transaction`. Line 92 declares an integer array of withdrawal amounts that correspond to the amounts displayed in the withdrawal menu. We ignore the first element in the array (index 0) because the menu has no option 0. The `while` statement in lines 95–126 repeats until `userChoice` takes on a value other than 0. We'll see shortly that this occurs when the user makes a valid selection from the menu. Lines 98–105 display the withdrawal menu on the screen and prompt the user to enter a choice. Line 107 obtains integer `input` through the keypad. The `switch` statement in lines 110–125 determines how to proceed based on the user's input. If the user selects a number between 1 and 5, line 117 sets `userChoice` to the value of the element in `amounts` at index `input`. For example, if the user enters 3 to withdraw $60, line 117 sets `userChoice` to the value of `amounts[ 3 ]` (i.e., 60). Line 118 terminates the `switch`. Variable `userChoice` no longer equals 0, so the `while` in lines 95–126 terminates and line 128 returns `userChoice`. If the user selects the cancel menu option, lines 120–121 execute, setting `userChoice` to CANCELED and causing the member function to return this value. If the user does not enter a valid menu selection, lines 123–124 display an error message and the user is returned to the withdrawal menu.

The `if` statement in line 39 in member function `execute` determines whether the user has selected a withdrawal amount or chosen to cancel. If the user cancels, lines 77–78 execute to display an appropriate message to the user and set `transactionCanceled` to `true`. This causes the loop-continuation test in line 80 to fail and control to return to the calling member function (i.e., `ATM` member function `performTransactions`). If the user has chosen a withdrawal amount, line 41 assigns local variable `selection` to data member `amount`. Lines 44–45 retrieve the available balance of the current user's `Account` and store it in a local `double` variable `availableBalance`. Next, the `if` statement in line 48 determines whether the selected amount is less than or equal to the user's available balance. If it is not, lines 70–72 display an appropriate error message. Control then continues to the end of the `do...while`, and the loop repeats because both `cashDispensed` and `transactionCanceled` are still `false`. If the user's balance is high enough, the `if` statement in line 51 determines whether the cash dispenser has enough money to satisfy the withdrawal request by invoking the `cashDispenser`'s `isSufficientCashAvailable` member function. If this member function returns `false`, lines 64–66 display an appropriate error message and the `do...while` repeats. If sufficient cash is available, then the requirements for the withdrawal are satisfied, and line 54 debits `amount` from the user's account in the database. Lines 56–57 then instruct the cash dispenser to dispense the cash to the user and set `cashDispensed` to `true`. Finally, lines 60–61 display a message to the user that cash has been dispensed. Because `cashDispensed` is now `true`, control continues after the `do...while`. No additional statements appear below the loop, so the member function returns control to class `ATM`.

In the function calls in lines 64–66 and lines 70–72, we divide the argument to Screen member function displayMessageLine into two string literals, each placed on a separate line in the program. We do so because each argument is too long to fit on a single line. C++ concatenates (i.e., combines) string literals adjacent to each other, even if they are on separate lines. For example, if you write "Happy " "Birthday" in a program, C++ will view these two adjacent string literals as the single string literal "Happy Birthday". As a result, when lines 64–66 execute, displayMessageLine receives a single string as a parameter, even though the argument in the function call appears as two string literals.

F.12 Class Deposit

Class Deposit (Figs. F.21–F.22) derives from Transaction and represents a deposit ATM transaction. Figure F.21 contains the Deposit class definition. Like derived classes BalanceInquiry and Withdrawal, Deposit declares a constructor (line 13) and member function execute (line 14)—we discuss these momentarily. Recall from the class diagram of Fig. 14.29 that class Deposit has one attribute amount, which line 16 implements as an int data member. Lines 17–18 create reference data members keypad and depositSlot that implement the associations between class Deposit and classes Keypad and Deposit-Slot modeled in Fig. 14.28. Line 19 contains the function prototype for a private utility function promptForDepositAmount that we'll discuss shortly.

Deposit Class Member-Function Definitions

Figure F.22 presents the Deposit class implementation. Line 3 #includes the Deposit class definition, and lines 4–7 #include the class definitions of the other classes used in Deposit's member functions. Line 9 declares a constant CANCELED that corresponds to the value a user enters to cancel a deposit. We'll soon discuss how the class uses this constant.

```
1   // Deposit.h
2   // Deposit class definition. Represents a deposit transaction.
3   #ifndef DEPOSIT_H
4   #define DEPOSIT_H
5
6   #include "Transaction.h" // Transaction class definition
7   class Keypad; // forward declaration of class Keypad
8   class DepositSlot; // forward declaration of class DepositSlot
9
10  class Deposit : public Transaction
11  {
12  public:
13     Deposit( int, Screen &, BankDatabase &, Keypad &, DepositSlot & );
14     virtual void execute(); // perform the transaction
15  private:
16     double amount; // amount to deposit
17     Keypad &keypad; // reference to ATM's keypad
18     DepositSlot &depositSlot; // reference to ATM's deposit slot
19     double promptForDepositAmount() const; // get deposit amount from user
20  }; // end class Deposit
21
22  #endif // DEPOSIT_H
```

Fig. F.21 | Deposit class definition.

```
1    // Deposit.cpp
2    // Member-function definitions for class Deposit.
3    #include "Deposit.h" // Deposit class definition
4    #include "Screen.h" // Screen class definition
5    #include "BankDatabase.h" // BankDatabase class definition
6    #include "Keypad.h" // Keypad class definition
7    #include "DepositSlot.h" // DepositSlot class definition
8
9    const static int CANCELED = 0; // constant representing cancel option
10
11   // Deposit constructor initializes class's data members
12   Deposit::Deposit( int userAccountNumber, Screen &atmScreen,
13      BankDatabase &atmBankDatabase, Keypad &atmKeypad,
14      DepositSlot &atmDepositSlot )
15      : Transaction( userAccountNumber, atmScreen, atmBankDatabase ),
16        keypad( atmKeypad ), depositSlot( atmDepositSlot )
17   {
18      // empty body
19   } // end Deposit constructor
20
21   // performs transaction; overrides Transaction's pure virtual function
22   void Deposit::execute()
23   {
24      BankDatabase &bankDatabase = getBankDatabase(); // get reference
25      Screen &screen = getScreen(); // get reference
26
27      amount = promptForDepositAmount(); // get deposit amount from user
28
29      // check whether user entered a deposit amount or canceled
30      if ( amount != CANCELED )
31      {
32         // request deposit envelope containing specified amount
33         screen.displayMessage(
34            "\nPlease insert a deposit envelope containing " );
35         screen.displayDollarAmount( amount );
36         screen.displayMessageLine( " in the deposit slot." );
37
38         // receive deposit envelope
39         bool envelopeReceived = depositSlot.isEnvelopeReceived();
40
41         // check whether deposit envelope was received
42         if ( envelopeReceived )
43         {
44            screen.displayMessageLine( "\nYour envelope has been received."
45               "\nNOTE: The money deposited will not be available until we"
46               "\nverify the amount of any enclosed cash, and any enclosed "
47               "checks clear." );
48
49            // credit account to reflect the deposit
50            bankDatabase.credit( getAccountNumber(), amount );
51         } // end if
52         else // deposit envelope not received
53         {
```

Fig. F.22 | Deposit class member-function definitions. (Part 1 of 2.)

```
54              screen.displayMessageLine( "\nYou did not insert an "
55                 "envelope, so the ATM has canceled your transaction." );
56          } // end else
57       } // end if
58       else // user canceled instead of entering amount
59       {
60          screen.displayMessageLine( "\nCanceling transaction..." );
61       } // end else
62    } // end function execute
63
64    // prompt user to enter a deposit amount in cents
65    double Deposit::promptForDepositAmount() const
66    {
67       Screen &screen = getScreen(); // get reference to screen
68
69       // display the prompt and receive input
70       screen.displayMessage( "\nPlease enter a deposit amount in "
71          "CENTS (or 0 to cancel): " );
72       int input = keypad.getInput(); // receive input of deposit amount
73
74       // check whether the user canceled or entered a valid amount
75       if ( input == CANCELED )
76          return CANCELED;
77       else
78       {
79          return static_cast< double >( input ) / 100; // return dollar amount
80       } // end else
81    } // end function promptForDepositAmount
```

Fig. F.22 | Deposit class member-function definitions. (Part 2 of 2.)

Like class Withdrawal, class Deposit contains a constructor (lines 12–19) that passes three parameters to base class Transaction's constructor using a base-class initializer (line 15). The constructor also has parameters atmKeypad and atmDepositSlot, which it assigns to its corresponding data members (line 16).

Member function execute (lines 22–62) overrides pure virtual function execute in base class Transaction with a concrete implementation that performs the steps required in a deposit transaction. Lines 24–25 get references to the database and the screen. Line 27 prompts the user to enter a deposit amount by invoking private utility function promptForDepositAmount (defined in lines 65–81) and sets data member amount to the value returned. Member function promptForDepositAmount asks the user to enter a deposit amount as an integer number of cents (because the ATM's keypad does not contain a decimal point; this is consistent with many real ATMs) and returns the double value representing the dollar amount to be deposited.

Line 67 in member function promptForDepositAmount gets a reference to the ATM's screen. Lines 70–71 display a message on the screen asking the user to input a deposit amount as a number of cents or "0" to cancel the transaction. Line 72 receives the user's input from the keypad. The if statement in lines 75–80 determines whether the user has entered a real deposit amount or chosen to cancel. If the user chooses to cancel, line 76 returns the constant CANCELED. Otherwise, line 79 returns the deposit amount after converting from the number of cents to a dollar amount by casting input to a double, then dividing by 100. For example, if the user enters 125 as the number of cents, line 79 returns 125.0 divided by 100, or 1.25—125 cents is $1.25.

The if statement in lines 30–61 in member function execute determines whether the user has chosen to cancel the transaction instead of entering a deposit amount. If the user cancels, line 60 displays an appropriate message, and the member function returns. If the user enters a deposit amount, lines 33–36 instruct the user to insert a deposit envelope with the correct amount. Recall that Screen member function displayDollarAmount outputs a double formatted as a dollar amount.

Line 39 sets a local bool variable to the value returned by depositSlot's isEnvelope-Received member function, indicating whether a deposit envelope has been received. Recall that we coded isEnvelopeReceived (lines 7–10 of Fig. F.10) to always return true, because we are simulating the functionality of the deposit slot and assume that the user always inserts an envelope. However, we code member function execute of class Deposit to test for the possibility that the user does not insert an envelope—good software engineering demands that programs account for all possible return values. Thus, class Deposit is prepared for future versions of isEnvelopeReceived that could return false. Lines 44–50 execute if the deposit slot receives an envelope. Lines 44–47 display an appropriate message to the user. Line 50 then credits the deposit amount to the user's account in the database. Lines 54–55 will execute if the deposit slot does not receive a deposit envelope. In this case, we display a message to the user stating that the ATM has canceled the transaction. The member function then returns without modifying the user's account.

F.13 Test Program ATMCaseStudy.cpp

ATMCaseStudy.cpp (Fig. F.23) is a simple C++ program that allows us to start, or "turn on," the ATM and test the implementation of our ATM system model. The program's main function (lines 6–11) does nothing more than instantiate a new ATM object named atm (line 8) and invoke its run member function (line 9) to start the ATM.

```
1   // ATMCaseStudy.cpp
2   // Driver program for the ATM case study.
3   #include "ATM.h" // ATM class definition
4
5   // main function creates and runs the ATM
6   int main()
7   {
8      ATM atm; // create an ATM object
9      atm.run(); // tell the ATM to start
10     return 0;
11  } // end main
```

Fig. F.23 | ATMCaseStudy.cpp starts the ATM system.

F.14 Wrap-Up

Congratulations on completing the Software Engineering ATM Case Study! We hope you found this experience to be valuable and that it reinforced many of the concepts that you learned in Chapters 1, 3–8, 10 and 14. We would sincerely appreciate your comments, criticisms and suggestions. You can reach us at deitel@deitel.com. We'll respond promptly.

UML 2: Additional Diagram Types

G.1 Introduction

If you have read the optional Software Engineering Case Study sections in Chapters 1, 3–8, 10 and 14, you should now have a comfortable grasp of the UML diagram types that we use to model our ATM system. The case study is intended for use in first- or second-semester courses, so we limit our discussion to a concise subset of the UML. The UML 2 provides a total of 13 diagram types. The end of Section 3.8 summarizes the six diagram types that we use in the case study. This appendix lists and briefly defines the seven remaining diagram types.

G.2 Additional Diagram Types

The following are the seven diagram types that we have chosen not to use in our Software Engineering Case Study.

- *Object diagrams* model a "snapshot" of the system by modeling a system's objects and their relationships at a specific point in time. Each object represents an instance of a class from a class diagram, and several objects may be created from one class. For our ATM system, an object diagram could show several distinct Account objects side by side, illustrating that they are all part of the bank's account database.

- *Component diagrams* model the *artifacts* and *components*—resources (which include source files)—that make up the system.

- *Deployment diagrams* model the system's runtime requirements (such as the computer or computers on which the system will reside), memory requirements, or other devices the system requires during execution.

- *Package diagrams* model the hierarchical structure of *packages* (which are groups of classes) in the system at compile time and the relationships that exist between the packages.

- *Composite structure diagrams* model the internal structure of a complex object at runtime. New in UML 2, they allow system designers to hierarchically decompose a complex object into smaller parts. Composite structure diagrams are beyond the scope of our case study. They are more appropriate for larger industrial applications, which exhibit complex groupings of objects at execution time.

- *Interaction overview diagrams*, new in UML 2, provide a summary of control flow in the system by combining elements of several types of behavioral diagrams (e.g., activity diagrams, sequence diagrams).

- *Timing diagrams*, also new in UML 2, model the timing constraints imposed on stage changes and interactions between objects in a system.

To learn more about these diagrams and advanced UML topics, please visit www.uml.org and the web resources listed at the ends of Section 1.21 and Section 3.8.

Using the Visual Studio Debugger

OBJECTIVES

In this appendix you'll learn:

- To set breakpoints to debug programs.
- To run a program through the debugger.
- To set, disable and remove a breakpoint.
- To use the **Continue** command to continue execution.
- To use the **Locals** window to view and modify the values of variables.
- To use the **Watch** window to evaluate expressions.
- To use the **Step Into**, **Step Out** and **Step Over** commands to control execution.
- To use the **Autos** window to view variables that are used in the surrounding statements.

H.1 Introduction

In Chapter 3, you learned that there are two types of errors—compilation errors and logic errors—and you learned how to eliminate compilation errors from your code. Logic errors (also called *bugs*) do not prevent a program from compiling successfully, but can cause the program to produce erroneous results when it runs. Most C++ compiler vendors provide software called a *debugger*, which allows you to monitor the execution of your programs to locate and remove logic errors. The debugger will be one of your most important program development tools. This appendix demonstrates key features of the Visual Studio debugger.

H.2 Breakpoints and the Continue Command

We begin our study of the debugger by investigating *breakpoints*, which are markers that can be set at any executable line of code. When program execution reaches a breakpoint, execution pauses, allowing you to examine the values of variables to help determine whether a logic error exists. For example, you can examine the value of a variable that stores the result of a calculation to determine whether the calculation was performed correctly. Note that attempting to set a breakpoint at a line of code that is not executable (such as a comment) will actually set the breakpoint at the next executable line of code in that function.

To illustrate the features of the debugger, we use the program listed in Fig. H.3, which creates and manipulates an object of class Account (Figs. H.1–H.2). Execution begins in main (lines 12–30 of Fig. H.3). Line 14 creates an Account object with an initial balance of $50.00. Account's constructor (lines 10–22 of Fig. H.2) accepts one argument, which specifies the Account's initial balance. Line 17 of Fig. H.3 outputs the initial account balance using Account member function getBalance. Line 19 declares a local variable withdrawalAmount, which stores a withdrawal amount read from the user. Line 21 prompts the user for the withdrawal amount, and line 22 inputs the amount into withdrawalAmount. Line 25 subtracts the withdrawal from the Account's balance using its debit member function. Finally, line 28 displays the new balance.

```
1    // Fig. H.1: Account.h
2    // Definition of Account class.
3
4    class Account
5    {
```

Fig. H.1 | Header file for the Account class. (Part 1 of 2.)

```
6   public:
7       Account( int ); // constructor initializes balance
8       void credit( int ); // add an amount to the account balance
9       void debit( int ); // subtract an amount from the account balance
10      int getBalance(); // return the account balance
11  private:
12      int balance; // data member that stores the balance
13  }; // end class Account
```

Fig. H.1 | Header file for the Account class. (Part 2 of 2.)

```
1   // Fig. H.2: Account.cpp
2   // Member-function definitions for class Account.
3   #include <iostream>
4   using std::cout;
5   using std::endl;
6
7   #include "Account.h" // include definition of class Account
8
9   // Account constructor initializes data member balance
10  Account::Account( int initialBalance )
11  {
12      balance = 0; // assume that the balance begins at 0
13
14      // if initialBalance is greater than 0, set this value as the
15      // balance of the account; otherwise, balance remains 0
16      if ( initialBalance > 0 )
17          balance = initialBalance;
18
19      // if initialBalance is negative, print error message
20      if ( initialBalance < 0 )
21          cout << "Error: Initial balance cannot be negative.\n" << endl;
22  } // end Account constructor
23
24  // credit (add) an amount to the account balance
25  void Account::credit( int amount )
26  {
27      balance = balance + amount; // add amount to balance
28  } // end function credit
29
30  // debit (subtract) an amount from the account balance
31  void Account::debit( int amount )
32  {
33      if ( amount <= balance ) // debit amount does not exceed balance
34          balance = balance - amount;
35
36      else // debit amount exceeds balance
37          cout << "Debit amount exceeded account balance.\n" << endl;
38  } // end function debit
39
```

Fig. H.2 | Definition for the Account class. (Part 1 of 2.)

```
40    // return the account balance
41    int Account::getBalance()
42    {
43        return balance; // gives the value of balance to the calling function
44    } // end function getBalance
```

Fig. H.2 | Definition for the Account class. (Part 2 of 2.)

```
1     // Fig. H.3: figH_03.cpp
2     // Create and manipulate Account objects.
3     #include <iostream>
4     using std::cin;
5     using std::cout;
6     using std::endl;
7
8     // include definition of class Account from Account.h
9     #include "Account.h"
10
11    // function main begins program execution
12    int main()
13    {
14        Account account1( 50 ); // create Account object
15
16        // display initial balance of each object
17        cout << "account1 balance: $" << account1.getBalance() << endl;
18
19        int withdrawalAmount; // stores withdrawal amount read from user
20
21        cout << "\nEnter withdrawal amount for account1: "; // prompt
22        cin >> withdrawalAmount; // obtain user input
23        cout << "\nattempting to subtract " << withdrawalAmount
24            << " from account1 balance\n\n";
25        account1.debit( withdrawalAmount ); // try to subtract from account1
26
27        // display balances
28        cout << "account1 balance: $" << account1.getBalance() << endl;
29        return 0; // indicate successful termination
30    } // end main
```

Fig. H.3 | Test class for debugging.

In the following steps, you'll use breakpoints and various debugger commands to examine the value of the variable withdrawalAmount declared in Fig. H.3.

1. *Enabling the debugger.* The debugger is normally enabled by default. If it is not enabled, you have to change the settings of the *Solution Configurations combo box* (Fig. H.4) in the toolbar. To do this, click the combo box's down arrow, then select **Debug**.

2. *Inserting breakpoints in Visual Studio 2008.* To insert a breakpoint in Visual Studio 2008, click inside the *margin indicator bar* (the gray margin at the left of the code window in Fig. H.5) next to the line of code at which you wish to break or right click that line of code and select **Breakpoint > Insert Breakpoint**. You can

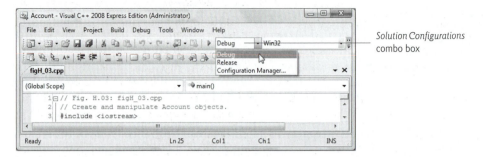

Fig. H.4 | Enabling the debugger.

set as many breakpoints as necessary. Set breakpoints at lines 21 and 25 of your code. A red circle appears in the margin indicator bar where you clicked, indicating that a breakpoint has been set (Fig. H.5). When the program runs, the debugger pauses execution at any line that contains a breakpoint. The program is said to be in *break mode* when the debugger pauses the program. Breakpoints can be set before running a program, in break mode and while a program is running.

3. *Starting to debug.* After setting breakpoints in the code editor, select **Build > Build Solution** to compile the program, then select **Debug > Start Debugging** to begin the debugging process. [*Note:* If you do not compile the program first, it will still be compiled when you select **Debug > Start Debugging**.] When you debug a console application, a **Command Prompt** window appears (Fig. H.6) in which you can specify program input and view program output. The debugger enters break mode when execution reaches the breakpoint at line 21.

4. *Examining program execution.* Upon entering break mode at the first breakpoint (line 21), the IDE becomes the active window (Fig. H.7). The *yellow arrow* to the left of line 21 indicates that this line contains the next statement to execute.

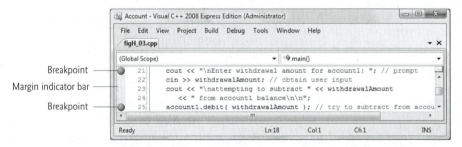

Fig. H.5 | Setting two breakpoints.

Fig. H.6 | **Inventory** program running.

5. *Using the* Continue *command to resume execution.* To resume execution, select **Debug > Continue**. The ***Continue*** *command* resumes program execution until the next breakpoint or the end of main is encountered, whichever comes first. The program continues executing and pauses for input at line 22. Enter 13 as the withdrawal amount. The program executes until it stops at the next breakpoint (line 25). Notice that when you place your mouse pointer over the variable name withdrawalAmount, the value stored in the variable is displayed in a ***Quick Info box*** (Fig. H.8). As you'll see, this can help you spot logic errors in your programs.

6. *Setting a breakpoint at the **return** statement.* Set a breakpoint at line 29 in the source code by clicking in the margin indicator bar to the left of line 29. This will prevent the program from closing immediately after displaying its result. When there are no more breakpoints at which to suspend execution, the program will execute to completion and the **Command Prompt** window will close. If you do not set this breakpoint, you won't be able to view the program's output before the console window closes.

7. *Continuing program execution.* Use the **Debug > Continue** command to execute the code up to the next breakpoint. The program displays the result of its calculation (Fig. H.9).

8. *Disabling a breakpoint.* To *disable a breakpoint*, right click a line of code on which a breakpoint has been set (or the breakpoint itself) and select **Breakpoint > Disable Breakpoint**. The disabled breakpoint is indicated by a hollow circle

Yellow arrow that indicates the next statement to execute

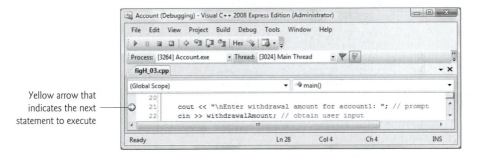

Fig. H.7 | Program execution suspended at the first breakpoint.

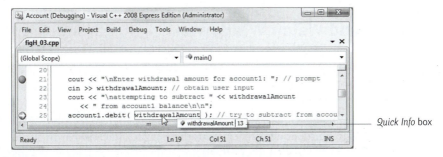

Quick Info box

Fig. H.8 | *Quick Info* box showing the value of a variable.

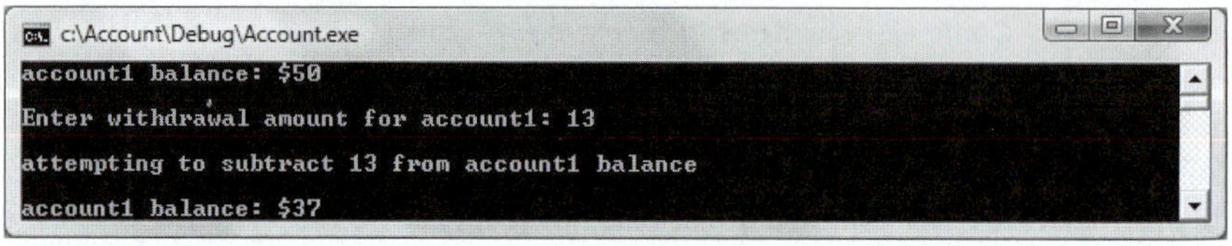

Fig. H.9 | Program output.

(Fig. H.10). Disabling rather than removing a breakpoint allows you to reenable the breakpoint later by clicking the hollow circle or by right-clicking the hollow circle and selecting **Enable Breakpoint**.

9. *Removing a breakpoint.* To remove a breakpoint that you no longer need, right click a line of code on which a breakpoint has been set and select **Breakpoint > Delete Breakpoint**. You also can remove a breakpoint by clicking the breakpoint in the margin indicator bar.

10. *Finishing program execution.* Select **Debug > Continue** to execute the program to completion.

In this section, you learned how to enable the debugger and set breakpoints so that you can examine the results of code while a program is running. You also learned how to continue execution after a program suspends execution at a breakpoint and how to disable and remove breakpoints.

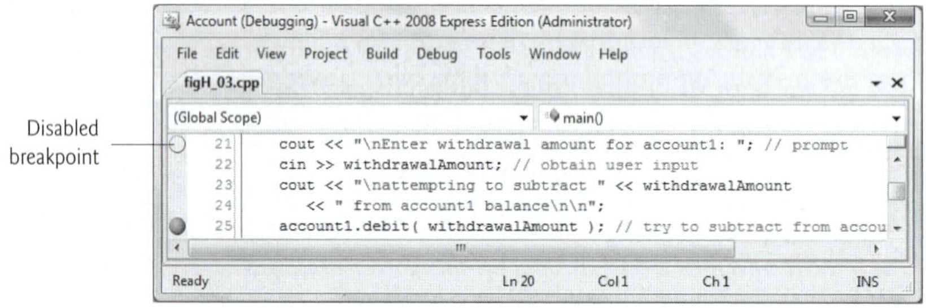

Fig. H.10 | Disabled breakpoint.

H.3 Locals and Watch Windows

In the preceding section, you learned that the *Quick Info* feature allows you to examine a variable's value. In this section, you'll learn to use the **Locals** *window* to assign new values to variables while your program is running. You'll also use the **Watch** *window* to examine the value of more complex expressions.

1. *Inserting breakpoints.* Clear the existing breakpoints. Then, set a breakpoint at line 25 in the source code by clicking in the margin indicator bar to the left of line 25 (Fig. H.11). Set another breakpoint at line 28 by clicking in the margin indicator bar to the left of line 28.

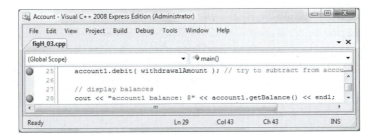

Fig. H.11 | Setting breakpoints at lines 25 and 28.

2. *Starting debugging.* Select **Debug > Start Debugging.** Type 13 at the **Enter withdrawal amount for account1:** prompt and press *Enter* so that your program reads the value you just entered. The program executes until the breakpoint at line 25.

3. *Suspending program execution.* The debugger enters break mode at line 25 (Fig. H.12). At this point, line 22 has input the withdrawalAmount that you entered (13), lines 23–24 have output that the program will attempt to withdraw money and line 25 is the next statement that will execute.

4. *Examining data.* In break mode, you can explore the values of your local variables using the debugger's **Locals** window. To view the **Locals** window, select **Debug > Windows > Locals.** Figure H.13 shows the values for main's local variables account1 and withdrawalAmount (13).

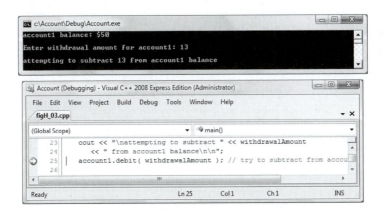

Fig. H.12 | Program execution suspended when debugger reaches the breakpoint at line 25.

Locals		
Name	Value	Type
account1	{balance=50 }	Account
withdrawalAmount	13	int

Fig. H.13 | Examining variable withdrawalAmount.

5. *Evaluating arithmetic and boolean expressions.* You can evaluate arithmetic and boolean expressions using the **Watch** window. You can display up to four **Watch** windows. Select **Debug > Windows > Watch > Watch 1**. In the first row of the **Name** column, type (withdrawalAmount + 3) * 5, then press *Enter*. The value of this expression (80 in this case) is displayed in the **Value** column (Fig. H.14). In the next row of the **Name** column, type withdrawalAmount == 3, then press *Enter*. This expression determines whether the value of withdrawalAmount is 3. Expressions containing the == operator (or any other relational or equality operator) are treated as bool expressions. The value of the expression in this case is false (Fig. H.14), because withdrawalAmount currently contains 13, not 3.

6. *Resuming execution.* Select **Debug > Continue** to resume execution. Line 25 debits the account by the withdrawal amount, and the debugger reenters break mode at line 28. Select **Debug > Windows > Locals** or click the **Locals** tab at the bottom of Visual Studio to redisplay the **Locals** window. The updated balance value in account1 is now displayed in red (Fig. H.15) to indicate that it has been modified since the last breakpoint. Click the plus box to the left of account1 in the **Name** column of the **Locals** window. This allows you to view each of account1's data member values individually—this is particularly useful for objects that have several data members.

7. *Modifying values.* Based on the value input by the user (13), the account balance output by the program should be $37. However, you can use the **Locals** window to change the values of variables during the program's execution. This can be valuable for experimenting with different values and for locating logic errors. In the **Locals** window, click the **Value** field in the balance row to select the value 37. Type 33, then press *Enter*. The debugger changes the value of balance and displays its new value in red (Fig. H.16).

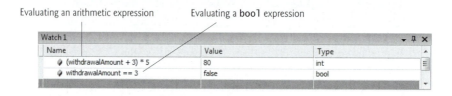

Evaluating an arithmetic expression   Evaluating a bool expression

Name	Value	Type
(withdrawalAmount + 3) * 5	80	int
withdrawalAmount == 3	false	bool

Fig. H.14 | Examining the values of expressions.

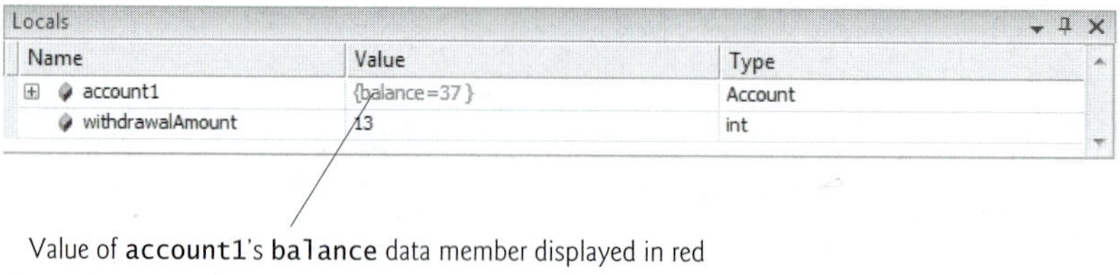

Name	Value	Type
account1	{balance=37}	Account
withdrawalAmount	13	int

Value of account1's balance data member displayed in red

Fig. H.15 | Displaying the value of local variables.

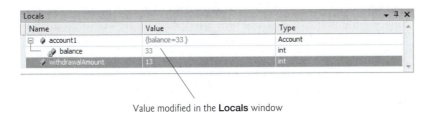

Value modified in the **Locals** window

Fig. H.16 | Modifying the value of a variable.

8. *Setting a breakpoint at the **return** statement.* Set a breakpoint at line 29 in the source code to prevent the program from closing immediately after displaying its result. If you do not set this breakpoint, you won't be able to view the program's output before the console window closes.

9. *Viewing the program result.* Select **Debug > Continue** to continue program execution. Function main executes until the return statement in line 29 and displays the result. Notice that the result is $33 (Fig. H.17). This shows that *Step 7* changed the value of balance from the calculated value (37) to 33.

10. *Stopping the debugging session.* Select **Debug > Stop Debugging**. This will close the **Command Prompt** window. Remove all remaining breakpoints.

In this section, you learned how to use the debugger's **Watch** and **Locals** windows to evaluate arithmetic and boolean expressions. You also learned how to modify the value of a variable during your program's execution.

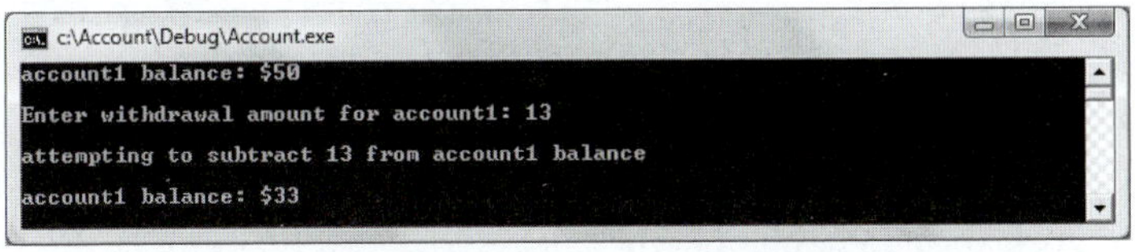

```
c:\Account\Debug\Account.exe
account1 balance: $50

Enter withdrawal amount for account1: 13

attempting to subtract 13 from account1 balance

account1 balance: $33
```

Fig. H.17 | Output displayed after modifying the account1 variable.

H.4 Controlling Execution Using the Step Into, Step Over, Step Out and Continue Commands

Sometimes executing a program line by line can help you verify that a function's code executes correctly, and can help you find and fix logic errors. The commands you learn in this section allow you to execute a function line by line, execute all the statements of a function at once or execute only the remaining statements of a function (if you have already executed some statements within the function).

1. *Setting a breakpoint.* Set a breakpoint at line 25 by clicking in the margin indicator bar to the left of the line.

2. *Starting the debugger.* Select **Debug > Start Debugging**. Enter the value 13 at the **Enter withdrawal amount for account1:** prompt. Execution will halt when the program reaches the breakpoint at line 25.

3. *Using the Step Into command.* The **Step Into** command executes the next statement in the program (the one that the yellow arrow points to in line 25 of Fig. H.18), then immediately halts. If that statement is a function call (as is the case here), control transfers into the called function. This enables you to execute each statement inside the function individually to confirm the function's execution. Select **Debug > Step Into** to enter the debit function. Then, Select **Debug > Step Into** again so the yellow arrow is positioned at line 33, as shown in Fig. H.19.

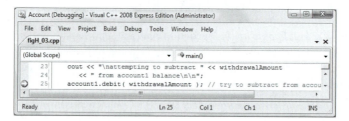

Fig. H.18 | Using the **Step Into** command to execute a statement.

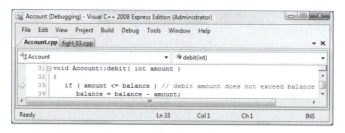

Fig. H.19 | Stepping into the debit function.

4. *Using the Step Over command.* Select **Debug > Step Over** to execute the current statement (line 33 in Fig. H.19) and transfer control to line 34 (Fig. H.20). The **Step Over** *command* behaves like the **Step Into** command when the next statement to execute does not contain a function call. You'll see how the **Step Over** command differs from the **Step Into** command in *Step 10.*

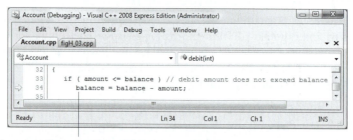

Control transfers to the next statement

Fig. H.20 | Stepping over a statement in the debit function.

5. *Using the Step Out command.* Select **Debug > Step Out** to execute the remaining statements in the function and return control to the next executable statement (line 28 in Fig. H.3). Often, in lengthy functions, you'll want to look at a few key lines of code, then continue debugging the caller's code. The ***Step Out*** *command* enables you to continue program execution in the caller without having to step through the entire called function line by line.

6. *Setting a breakpoint.* Set a breakpoint at the return statement of main at line 29 of Fig. H.3. You'll make use of this breakpoint in the next step.

7. *Using the Continue command.* Select **Debug > Continue** to execute until the next breakpoint is reached at line 29. Using the **Continue** command is useful when you wish to execute all the code up to the next breakpoint.

8. *Stopping the debugger.* Select **Debug > Stop Debugging** to end the debugging session. This will close the **Command Prompt** window.

9. *Starting the debugger.* Before we can demonstrate the next debugger feature, you must start the debugger again. Start it, as you did in *Step 2*, and enter 13 in response to the prompt. The debugger enters break mode at line 25.

10. *Using the Step Over command.* Select **Debug > Step Over** (Fig. H.21) Recall that this command behaves like the **Step Into** command when the next statement to execute does not contain a function call. If the next statement to execute contains a function call, the called function executes in its entirety (without pausing execution at any statement inside the function), and the yellow arrow advances to the next executable line (after the function call) in the current function. In this case, the debugger executes line 25, located in main (Fig. H.3). Line 25 calls the debit function. The debugger then pauses execution at line 28, the next executable line in the current function, main.

11. *Stopping the debugger.* Select **Debug > Stop Debugging**. This will close the **Command Prompt** window. Remove all remaining breakpoints.

In this section, you learned how to use the debugger's **Step Into** command to debug functions called during your program's execution. You saw how the **Step Over** command can be used to step over a function call. You used the **Step Out** command to continue execution until the end of the current function. You also learned that the **Continue** command continues execution until another breakpoint is found or the program exits.

The debit function call executes to completion when the **Step Over** command is selected

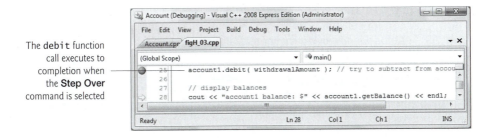

Fig. H.21 | Using the debugger's **Step Over** command.

H.5 Autos Window

The **Autos** *window* displays the variables used in the previous statement executed (including the return value of a function, if there is one) and the variables in the next statement to execute.

1. *Setting breakpoints.* Set breakpoints at lines 14 and 22 in `main` by clicking in the margin indicator bar.

2. *Using the* **Autos** *window.* Start the debugger by selecting **Debug > Start Debugging**. When the debugger enters break mode at line 14, open the **Autos** window (Fig. H.22) by selecting **Debug > Windows > Autos**. Since we are just beginning the program's execution, the **Autos** window lists only the variables in the next statement that will execute—in this case, the `account1` object, its value and its type. Viewing the values stored in an object lets you verify that your program is manipulating these variables correctly. Notice that `account1` contains a large negative value. This value, which may be different each time the program executes, is `account1`'s uninitialized value. This unpredictable (and often undesirable) value demonstrates why it is important to initialize C++ variables before they are used.

3. *Using the* **Step Over** *command.* Select **Debug > Step Over** to execute line 14. The **Autos** window updates the value of `account1`'s `balance` data member (Fig. H.23) after it is initialized. The value of `balance` is displayed in red to indicate that it just changed.

4. *Continuing execution.* Select **Debug > Continue** to execute the program until the second breakpoint at line 22. The **Autos** window displays uninitialized local variable `withdrawalAmount` (Fig. H.24), which has a large negative value.

Fig. H.22 | **Autos** window displaying the state of `account1` object.

Fig. H.23 | **Autos** window displaying the state of `account1` object after initialization.

Fig. H.24 | **Autos** window displaying local variable `withdrawalAmount`.

5. *Entering data.* Select **Debug > Step Over** to execute line 22. At the program's input prompt, enter a value for the withdrawal amount. The **Autos** window updates the value of local variable withdrawalAmount with the value you entered (Fig. H.25).

6. *Stopping the debugger.* Select **Debug > Stop Debugging** to end the debugging session. Remove all remaining breakpoints.

Name	Value	Type
withdrawalAmount	13	int

Fig. H.25 | **Autos** window displaying updated local variable withdrawalAmount.

H.6 Wrap-Up

In this appendix, you learned how to insert, disable and remove breakpoints in the Visual Studio debugger. Breakpoints allow you to pause program execution so you can examine variable values. This capability will help you locate and fix logic errors in your programs. You saw how to use the **Locals** and **Watch** windows to examine the value of an expression and how to change the value of a variable. You also learned debugger commands **Step Into**, **Step Over**, **Step Out** and **Continue** that can be used to determine whether a function is executing correctly. Finally, you learned how to use the **Autos** window to examine variables used specifically in the previous and next commands.

Summary

Section H.1 Introduction
- Most C++ compiler vendors provide software called a debugger, which allows you to monitor the execution of your programs to locate and remove logic errors.
- Breakpoints are markers that can be set at any executable line of code. When program execution reaches a breakpoint, execution pauses.
- The debugger is enabled by default. If it is not enabled, you have to change the settings of the *Solution Configurations* combo box.

Section H.2 Breakpoints and the *Continue* Command
- To insert a breakpoint, either click inside the margin indicator bar next to the line of code or right click that line of code and select **Breakpoint > Insert Breakpoint**. A red circle appears where you clicked, indicating that a breakpoint has been set.
- When the program runs, it suspends execution at any line that contains a breakpoint. It is then said to be in break mode.
- A yellow arrow indicates that this line contains the next statement to execute.
- When you place your mouse pointer over a variable name, the value that the variable stores is displayed in a *Quick Info* box.
- To disable a breakpoint, right click a line of code on which a breakpoint has been set and select **Breakpoint > Disable Breakpoint**. The disabled breakpoint is indicated by a hollow circle.

- To remove a breakpoint that you no longer need, right click a line of code on which a breakpoint has been set and select **Breakpoint > Delete Breakpoint**. You also can remove a breakpoint by clicking the circle in the margin indicator bar.

Section H.3 Locals *and* Watch **Windows**
- Once the program has entered break mode, you can explore the values of your variables using the debugger's **Locals** window. To view the **Locals** window, select **Debug > Windows > Locals**.
- You can evaluate arithmetic and boolean expressions using the **Watch** window.
- Updated variables are displayed in red to indicate that they have been modified since the last breakpoint.
- Clicking the plus box next to an object in the **Name** column of the **Locals** window allows you to view each of object's data member values individually.
- You can click the **Value** field of a variable to change its value in the **Locals** window.

Section H.4 Controlling Execution Using the Using the Step Into, Step Over, Step Out *and* Continue *Commands*
- The **Step Into** command executes the next statement (the yellow highlighted line) in the program. If the next statement is to execute a function call and you select **Step Into**, control is transferred to the called function.
- The **Step Over** command behaves like the **Step Into** command when the next statement to execute does not contain a function call. If the next statement to execute contains a function call, the called function executes in its entirety, and the yellow arrow advances to the next executable line in the current function.
- The **Step Over** command executes the remaining statements in the function and returns control to the function call.
- The **Continue** command will execute any statements between the next executable statement and the next breakpoint or the end of main, whichever comes first.

Section H.5 Autos *Window*
- The **Autos** window allows you to view the contents of the variables used in the last statement that was executed. The **Autos** window also lists the values in the next statement to be executed.

Terminology

Autos window	margin indicator bar
break mode	*Quick Info* box
breakpoint	*Solution Configurations* combo box
bug	**Step Into** command
Continue command	**Step Out** command
debugger	**Step Over** command
disabling a breakpoint	**Watch** window
Locals window	yellow arrow in break mode

Self-Review Exercises

H.1 Fill in the blanks in each of the following statements:
   a) When the debugger suspends program execution at a breakpoint, the program is said to be in _____ mode.

b) The _____ feature in Visual Studio 2008 allows you to look at the value of a variable by positioning the mouse over the variable name in the code.

c) You can examine the value of an expression by using the debugger's _____ window.

d) The _____ command behaves like the **Step Into** command when the next statement to execute does not contain a function call.

H.2 State whether each of the following is *true* or *false*. If *false*, explain why.

a) When program execution suspends at a breakpoint, the next statement to be executed is the statement after the breakpoint.

b) When a variable's value is changed, it becomes yellow in the **Autos** and **Locals** windows.

c) During debugging, the **Step Out** command executes the remaining statements in the current function and returns program control to the place where the function was called.

Answers to Self-Review Exercises

H.1 a) break. b) *Quick Info* box. c) **Watch.** d) **Step Over.**

H.2 a) False. When program execution suspends at a breakpoint, the next statement to be executed is the statement at the breakpoint. b) False. A variable turns red when its value is changed. c) True.

Index

The DEITEL® Suite of Products...

HOW TO PROGRAM BOOKS

C++ How to Program Sixth Edition

BOOK / CD-ROM

©2008, 1400 pp., paper
(0-13-615250-3)

The complete authoritative DEITEL® *LIVE-CODE* introduction to programming with C++!
The Sixth Edition takes an easy-to-follow, carefully developed early classes and objects approach to programming in C++. The text includes comprehensive coverage of the fundamentals of object-oriented programming in C++. It includes an optional automated teller machine (ATM) case study that teaches the fundamentals of software engineering and object-oriented design with the UML 2.0 in Chapters 1-7, 9 and 13. Additional integrated case studies appear throughout the text, including the **Time** class (Chapter 9), the **Employee** class (Chapters 12 and 13) and the **GradeBook** class (Chapters 3-7). This new edition includes a chapter on C++ game programming with the OGRE and OpenAL libraries, and a chapter on the Boost C++ Libraries, Technical Report 1 (TR1) and the forthcoming C++0X standard.

Java™ How to Program Seventh Edition

BOOK / CD-ROM

©2007, 1596 pp., paper
(0-13-222220-5)

The complete authoritative DEITEL® *LIVE-CODE* introduction to programming with the new Java™ Standard Edition 6! *Java How to Program, Seventh Edition* is up-to-date with Java™ SE 6 and includes comprehensive coverage of the fundamentals of object-oriented programming in Java; an early classes and objects approach; and an optional automated teller machine (ATM) case study that teaches the fundamentals of software engineering and object oriented design with the UML 2.0 in Chapters 1-8 and 10. Additional integrated case studies appear throughout the text, including GUI and graphics (Chapters 3-12), the **Time** class (Chapter 8), the **Employee** class (Chapters 9 and 10) and the **GradeBook** class (Chapters 3-8). New topics covered include Java Desktop Integration Components, Ajax Web application development with JavaServer Faces, web services and more.

Small C++ How to Program Fifth Edition

BOOK / CD-ROM

©2005, 773 pp., paper
(0-13-185758-4)

Based on chapters 1-13 (except the optional OOD/UML case study) and appendices of *C++ How to Program, Fifth Edition*, *Small C++* features a new early classes and objects approach and comprehensive coverage of the fundamentals of object-oriented programming in C++. Key topics include applications, variables, memory concepts, data types, control statements, functions, arrays, pointers and strings, inheritance and polymorphism.

📖 Now available for both *C++ How to Program, 6/e* and *Small C++ How to Program, 5/e*: C++ Web-based *Cyber Classroom* included with the purchase of a new textbook. The *Cyber Classroom* includes a complete e-book, audio walkthroughs of the code examples, a Lab Manual and selected student solutions. See the *Cyber Classroom* section of this advertorial for more information.

Small Java™ How to Program Sixth Edition

BOOK / CD-ROM

©2005, 540 pp., paper
(0-13-148660-8)

Based on chapters 1-10 of *Java™ How to Program, Sixth Edition* (not Seventh), *Small Java* is for use with J2SE™ 5.0, features an early classes and objects approach and comprehensive coverage of the fundamentals of object-oriented programming in Java. Key topics include applications, variables, data types, control statements, methods, arrays, object-based programming, inheritance and polymorphism.

📖 Now available for both *Java How to Program, 7/e* and *Small Java How to Program, 6/e*: Java Web-based *Cyber Classroom* included with the purchase of a new textbook. The *Cyber Classroom* includes a complete e-book, audio walkthroughs of the code examples, a Lab Manual and selected student solutions. See the *Cyber Classroom* section of this advertorial for more information.

Sign up now for the FREE DEITEL® *Buzz Online* newsletter at:
www.deitel.com/newsletter/subscribe.html

Visual Basic® 2005 How to Program Third Edition

BOOK / CD-ROM

©2006, 1513 pp., paper
(0-13-186900-0)

The complete authoritative DEITEL® LIVE-CODE introduction to Visual Basic programming. *Visual Basic® 2005 How to Program, Third Edition* is up-to-date with Microsoft's Visual Basic 2005. The text includes comprehensive coverage of the fundamentals of object-oriented programming in Visual Basic including a new early classes and objects approach and a new optional automated teller machine (ATM) case study that teaches the fundamentals of software engineering and object-oriented design with the UML 2.0 in Chapters 1, 3–9 and 11. Additional integrated case studies appear throughout the text, including the Time class (Chapter 9), the Employee class (Chapters 10 and 11) and the Gradebook class (Chapters 4–9). This book also includes discussions of more advanced topics such as XML, ASP.NET, ADO.NET and Web services. New Visual Basic 2005 topics covered include partial classes, generics, the My namespace and Visual Studio's updated debugger features.

Visual C#® 2005 How to Program Second Edition

BOOK / CD-ROM

©2006, 1591 pp., paper
(0-13-152523-9)

The complete authoritative DEITEL® LIVE-CODE introduction to C# programming. *Visual C#® 2005 How to Program, Second Edition* is up-to-date with Microsoft's Visual C# 2005. The text includes comprehensive coverage of the fundamentals of object-oriented programming in C#, including a new early classes and objects approach and a new optional automated teller machine (ATM) case study that teaches the fundamentals of software engineering and object-oriented design with the UML 2.0 in Chapters 1, 3–9 and 11. Additional integrated case studies appear throughout the text, including the Time class (Chapter 9), the Employee class (Chapters 10 and 11) and the Gradebook class (Chapters 4–9). This book also includes discussions of more advanced topics such as XML, ASP.NET, ADO.NET and Web services. New Visual C# 2005 topics covered include partial classes, generics, the My namespace, .NET remoting and Visual Studio's updated debugger features.

Visual C++® 2008 How to Program, Second Edition

BOOK / CD-ROM

©2008, 1500 pp., paper
(0-13-615157-4)

This Second Edition is based on our C++-standard-compliant textbook, *C++ How to Program, Sixth Edition*, and is intended for courses that offer a Microsoft-specific C++ programming focus using Visual C++ 2008. Microsoft has determined that most Visual C++ developers primarily use native C++. As a result, the book now focuses on native C++ and presents examples of .NET managed code programming with C++/CLI, where appropriate. The book takes an easy-to-follow, carefully developed early classes and objects approach, with comprehensive coverage of object-oriented programming. The optional automated teller machine (ATM) case study teaches the fundamentals of software engineering and object-oriented design with the UML 2.0. Additional integrated case studies appear throughout the text. This edition includes new coverage of .NET generics, collections and regular expressions.

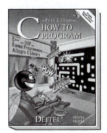

C How to Program Fifth Edition

BOOK / CD-ROM

©2007, 1130 pp., paper
(0-13-240416-8)

C How to Program, Fifth Edition—the world's best-selling C text—is designed for introductory through intermediate courses and programming languages survey courses. This comprehensive text is aimed at readers with little or no programming experience through intermediate audiences. Highly practical in approach, it introduces fundamental notions of structured programming and software engineering and gets up to speed quickly. The Fifth Edition features new chapters on the C99 standard and an introduction to game programming with the Allegro C Library.

Advanced Java™ 2 Platform How to Program

BOOK / CD-ROM

©2002, 1811 pp., paper
(0-13-089560-1)

Expanding on the world's best-selling Java textbook—*Java™ How to Program—Advanced Java™ 2 Platform How To Program* presents advanced Java topics for developing sophisticated, user-friendly GUIs; significant, scalable enterprise applications; wireless applications and distributed systems. Primarily based on Java 2 Enterprise Edition (J2EE) 1.2.1, this textbook integrates technologies such as XML, JavaBeans, security, JDBC™, JavaServer Pages (JSP™), servlets, Remote Method Invocation (RMI), Enterprise JavaBeans™ (EJB), design patterns, Swing, J2ME™, Java 2D and 3D, XML, design patterns, CORBA, Jini™, JavaSpaces™, Jiro™, Java Management Extensions (JMX) and Peer-to-Peer networking with an introduction to JXTA.

Internet & World Wide Web How to Program Fourth Edition

BOOK / CD-ROM

©2008, 1500 pp., paper
(0-13-175242-1)

This book introduces students with little or no programming experience to the exciting world of Web-based applications. It has been substantially reworked to reflect today's Web 2.0 rich Internet application-development methodologies. The book teaches the skills and tools for creating dynamic Web applications. Topics include introductory programming principles, markup languages (XHTML/XML), scripting languages (JavaScript, PHP and Ruby/Ruby on Rails), Ajax, web services, web servers (IIS/Apache), relational databases (MySQL/SQL Server 2005 Express/Apache Derby/Java DB), ASP .NET 2.0 and JavaServer™ Faces (JSF). You'll build Ajax-enabled rich Internet applications (RIAs)—using Ajax frameworks, Adobe® Flex™ and Microsoft® Silverlight—with the look-and-feel of desktop applications. The Dive Into® Web 2.0 chapter exposes readers to many other topics associated with Web 2.0 applications and businesses. After mastering the material in this book, students will be well prepared to build real-world, industrial-strength, Web-based applications.

Python How to Program

BOOK / CD-ROM

©2002, 1376 pp., paper
(0-13-092361-3)

This exciting textbook provides a comprehensive introduction to Python—a powerful object-oriented programming language with clear syntax and the ability to bring together various technologies quickly and easily. This book covers introductory programming techniques and more advanced topics such as graphical user interfaces, databases, wireless Internet programming, networking, security, process management, multithreading, XHTML, CSS, PSP and multimedia. Readers will learn principles that are applicable to both systems development and Web programming.

XML How to Program

BOOK / CD-ROM

©2001, 934 pp., paper
(0-13-028417-3)

This book is a comprehensive guide to programming in XML. It teaches how to use XML to create customized tags and includes chapters that address markup languages for science and technology, multimedia, commerce and many other fields. Concise introductions to Java, JavaServer Pages, VBScript, Active Server Pages and Perl/CGI provide readers with the essentials of these programming languages and server-side development technologies to enable them to work effectively with XML. The book also covers topics such as XSL, DOM™, SAX, a real-world e-commerce case study and a complete chapter on Web accessibility that addresses Voice XML. Other topics covered include XHTML, CSS, DTD, schema, parsers, XPath, XLink, namespaces, XBase, XInclude, XPointer, XSLT, XSL Formatting Objects, JavaServer Pages, XForms, topic maps, X3D, MathML, OpenMath, CML, BML, CDF, RDF, SVG, Cocoon, WML, XBRL and BizTalk™ and SOAP™ Web resources.

Perl How to Program

©2001, 1057 pp., paper (0-13-028418-1)

This comprehensive guide to Perl programming emphasizes the use of the Common Gateway Interface (CGI) with Perl to create powerful, dynamic multi-tier Web-based client/server applications. The book begins with a clear and careful introduction to programming concepts at a level suitable for beginners, and proceeds through advanced topics such as references and complex data structures. Key Perl topics such as regular expressions and string manipulation are covered in detail. The authors address important and topical issues such as object-oriented programming, the Perl database interface (DBI), graphics and security. Also included is a treatment of XML, a bonus chapter introducing the Python programming language, supplemental material on career resources and a complete chapter on Web accessibility.

e-Business & e-Commerce How to Program

BOOK / CD-ROM

©2001, 1254 pp., paper (0-13-028419-X)

This book explores programming technologies for developing Web-based e-business and e-commerce solutions, and covers e-business and e-commerce models and business issues. Readers learn a full range of options, from "build-your-own" to turnkey solutions. The book examines scores of the top e-businesses (examples include Amazon, eBay, Priceline, Travelocity, etc.), explaining the technical details of building successful e-business and e-commerce sites and their underlying business premises. Learn how to implement the dominant e-commerce models—shopping carts, auctions, name-your-own-price, comparison shopping and bots/intelligent agents—by using markup languages (HTML, Dynamic HTML and XML), scripting languages (JavaScript, VBScript and Perl), server-side technologies (Active Server Pages and Perl/CGI) and database (SQL and ADO), security and online payment technologies.

For ordering information,
visit us on the Web at www.prenhall.com.

INTERNATIONAL ORDERING INFORMATION
CANADA:
Pearson Education Canada
26 Prince Andrew Place
PO Box 580
Don Mills, Ontario M3C 2T8 Canada
Tel.: 416-925-2249; Fax: 416-925-0068
e-mail: phcinfo.pubcanada@pearsoned.com

EUROPE, MIDDLE EAST, AND AFRICA:
Pearson Education
Edinburgh Gate
Harlow, Essex CM20 2JE UK
Tel: 01279 623928; Fax: 01279 414130
e-mail: enq.orders@pearsoned-ema.com

BENELUX REGION:
Pearson Education
Concertgebouwplein 25
1071 LM Amsterdam
The Netherlands
Tel: 31 20 5755 800; Fax: 31 20 664 5334
e-mail: amsterdam@pearsoned-ema.com

ASIA:
Pearson Education Asia Pte. Ltd.
23/25 First Lok Yang Road
Jurong, 629733 Singapore
Tel: 65 476 4688; Fax: 65 378 0370

JAPAN:
Pearson Education Japan
Ogikubo TM Bldg. 6F. 5-26-13 Ogikubo
Suginami-ku, Tokyo 167-0051 Japan
Tel: 81 3 3365 9001; Fax: 81 3 3365 9009

INDIA:
Pearson Education
Indian Branch
482 FIE, Patparganj
Delhi – 110092 India
Tel: 91 11 2059850 & 2059851
Fax: 91 11 2059852

AUSTRALIA:
Pearson Education Australia
Unit 4, Level 2, 14 Aquatic Drive
Frenchs Forest, NSW 2086, Australia
Tel: 61 2 9454 2200; Fax: 61 2 9453 0089
e-mail: marketing@pearsoned.com.au

NEW ZEALAND/FIJI:
Pearson Education
46 Hillside Road
Auckland 10, New Zealand
Tel: 649 444 4968; Fax: 649 444 4957
E-mail: sales@pearsoned.co.nz

SOUTH AFRICA:
Maskew Miller Longman
Central Park Block H
16th Street Midrand 1685
South Africa
Tel: 27 21 686 6356; Fax: 27 21 686 4590

LATIN AMERICA:
Pearson Education Latin America
Attn: Tina Sheldon
1 Lake Street
Upper Saddle River, NJ 07458

The SIMPLY SERIES!

The Deitels' *Simply Series* takes an engaging new approach to teaching programming languages from the ground up. The pedagogy of this series combines the DEITEL® signature *LIVE-CODE Approach* with an *APPLICATION-DRIVEN Tutorial Approach* to teach programming with outstanding pedagogical features that help students learn. They have merged the notion of a lab manual with that of a conventional textbook, creating a book in which readers build and execute complete applications from start to finish, while learning the fundamental concepts of programming!

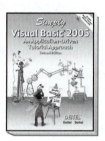

Simply Visual Basic® 2005
An APPLICATION-DRIVEN Tutorial Approach

©2007, 795 pp., paper
(0-13-243862-3)

Simply Visual Basic® 2005 An APPLICATION-DRIVEN Tutorial Approach guides readers through building real-world applications that incorporate Visual Basic 2005 programming fundamentals. Learn GUI design, controls, methods, functions, data types, control statements, procedures, arrays, object-oriented programming, strings and characters, sequential files and more in this comprehensive introduction to Visual Basic 2005. Higher-end topics include ADO .NET 2.0, ASP .NET 2.0, Visual Web Developer 2005 Express, database programming, multimedia and graphics and Web applications development.

Simply Java™ Programming
An APPLICATION-DRIVEN Tutorial Approach

©2004, 971 pp., paper
(0-13-142648-6)

Simply Java™ Programming An APPLICATION-DRIVEN Tutorial Approach guides readers through building real-world applications that incorporate Java programming fundamentals. Learn GUI design, components, methods, event-handling, types, control statements, arrays, object-oriented programming, exception-handling, strings and characters, sequential files and more in this comprehensive introduction to Java. We also include higher-end topics such as database programming, multimedia, graphics and Web applications development.

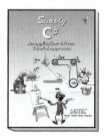

Simply C#
An APPLICATION-DRIVEN Tutorial Approach

©2004, 924 pp., paper
(0-13-142641-9)

Simply C# An APPLICATION-DRIVEN Tutorial Approach guides readers through building real-world applications that incorporate C# programming fundamentals. Learn GUI design, controls, methods, functions, data types, control statements, procedures, arrays, object-oriented programming, strings and characters, sequential files and more in this comprehensive introduction to C#. We also include higher-end topics such as database programming, multimedia and graphics and Web applications development.

Simply C++
An APPLICATION-DRIVEN Tutorial Approach

©2005, 644 pp., paper
(0-13-142660-5)

Simply C++ An APPLICATION-DRIVEN Tutorial Approach guides readers through building real-world applications that incorporate C++ programming fundamentals. Learn methods, functions, data types, control statements, procedures, arrays, object-oriented programming, strings and characters, pointers, references, templates, operator overloading and more in this comprehensive introduction to C++.

MULTIMEDIA CYBER CLASSROOMS

Premium content available with *Java™ How to Program, Seventh Edition* and *C++ How to Program, Sixth Edition!*

Java How to Program, 7/e and *C++ How to Program, 6/e* are now available with 12-month access to the Web-based *Multimedia Cyber Classroom* for students who purchase new copies of these books! The *Cyber Classroom* is an interactive, multimedia, tutorial version of DEITEL textbooks. *Cyber Classrooms* are a great value, giving students additional hands-on experience and study aids.

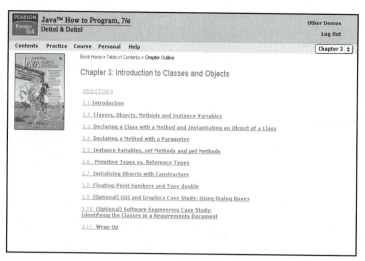

DEITEL® Multimedia Cyber Classrooms *feature an e-book with the complete text of their corresponding* How to Program *titles.*

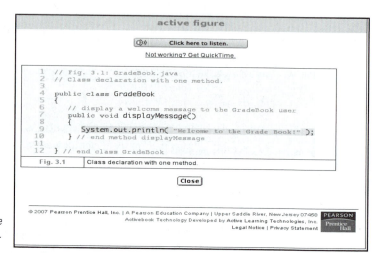

Unique audio "walkthroughs" of code examples reinforce key concepts.

Sign up now for the FREE DEITEL® *Buzz Online* newsletter at:
www.deitel.com/newsletter/subscribe.html

MULTIMEDIA CYBER CLASSROOMS

DEITEL® *Multimedia Cyber Classrooms* include:

- The full text, illustrations and program listings of its corresponding *How to Program* book.

- Hours of detailed, expert audio descriptions of hundreds of lines of code that help to reinforce important concepts.

- An abundance of self-assessment material, including practice exams, hundreds of programming exercises and self-review questions and answers.

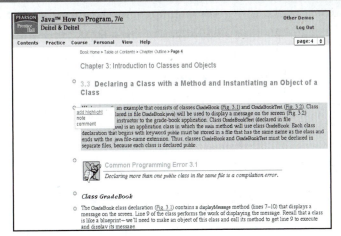

DEITEL® Multimedia Cyber Classrooms *offer a host of interactive features, such as highlighting of key sections of the text...*

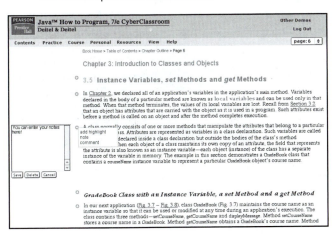

...and the ability to write notes in the margin of a given page for future reference.

- Intuitive browser-based interface designed to be easy and accessible.

- A Lab Manual featuring lab exercises as well as pre- and post-lab activities.

- Student Solutions to approximately one-half of the exercises in the textbook.

Students receive 12-month access to a protected Web site via access code cards packaged with these new textbooks. (Simply tear the strip on the inside of the Cyber Classroom package to reveal access code.)

For more information, please visit:
www.prenhall.com/deitel/cyberclassroom

PearsonChoices

For Instructors and Students using DEITEL® Publications

Today's students have increasing demands on their time and money, and they need to be resourceful about how, when and where they study. Pearson Education has responded to that need by creating PearsonChoices, which allows faculty and students to choose from a variety of formats and prices.

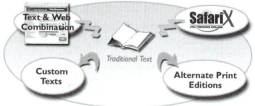

Visit www.pearsonchoices.com for more information.

We are pleased to announce PearsonChoices for our leading DEITEL publications:

- SafariX eTextbooks—We are pleased to offer students ten DEITEL SafariX eTextbooks available at 50% off the print version's price!
  - Internet & World Wide Web, Fourth Edition
  - Java How to Program, Seventh Edition
  - Small Java How to Program, Sixth Edition
  - C++ How to Program, Sixth Edition
  - Small C++ How to Program, Fifth Edition
  - Simply C++: An Application-Driven Tutorial Approach
  - Visual C# 2005 How to Program, Second Edition
  - SafariX for Visual Basic 2005 How to Program, Third Edition
  - SafariX for C How to Program, Fifth Edition
  - SafariX for Simply Visual Basic 2005 How to Program
  - Visual C++® 2008 How to Program, Second Edition

SafariX eTextbooks Online is an exciting new service for college students looking to save money on required or recommended textbooks for academic courses!

This secure eTextbooks platform creates a new option in the higher education market: an additional choice for students alongside conventional textbooks and online learning services. By eliminating the costs relating to printing, manufacturing and retail distribution for the physical textbook, Pearson provides students with an eTextbook at 50% of the cost of its conventional print equivalent. Students can choose to purchase a print edition textbook or subscribe to the same textbook content through SafariX eTextbooks Online.

SafariX eTextbooks are digital versions of print textbooks enhanced with features such as high-speed search, note taking and bookmarking. SafariX eTextbooks are viewed through a Web browser connected to the Internet. SafariX eTextbooks Online requires no special plug-ins and no applications download to your computer. Students just log in, purchase access and begin studying!

With SafariX eTextbooks Online students will be able to search the text, make notes online, print out reading assignments that incorporate your lecture notes and bookmark important passages they want to review later. They can navigate easily to a page number, reading assignment or chapter. The Table of Contents of each eTextbook appears in the left hand column alongside the text.

Visit www.safarix.com for more information!

Sign up now for the FREE DEITEL® Buzz Online newsletter at:
www.deitel.com/newsletter/subscribe.html

DEITEL® BUZZ ONLINE NEWSLETTER

Each issue of our free, e-mail newsletter, the *DEITEL® BUZZ ONLINE*, is now sent to about 50,000 opt-in subscribers. This weekly newsletter provides updates on our publishing program, our instructor-led professional training courses, timely industry topics and the continuing stream of innovations and new Web 2.0 business ventures emerging from Deitel.

The DEITEL® Buzz Online includes:

- Resource centers on programming, Web 2.0 and more.

- Updates on all Deitel publications of interest to students, instructors and professionals.

- Free tutorials and guest articles. (part of the Deitel Free Content Initiative)

- Information on our instructor-led professional training courses taught worldwide.

Recent Deitel Publications

Java™ How to Program, 7/E
ISBN: 0132222205
© 2007, pp. 1596
More Information
Order now at
Amazon.com
Informit.com

C How to Program, 5/e
ISBN: 0132404168
© 2006, pages: 1112
More Information
Order it at:
Amazon.com
Informit.com

C# for Programmers, 2/e
(Professional book; Part of the Deitel Developer Series)
ISBN: 0131345915
© 2006, pages: 1360
More Information
Order it at:
Amazon.com
Informit.com

Simply C++, 1/e
ISBN: 0-13-142660-5
© 2005, pages: 704
More Information
Order it at:
Amazon.com
Informit.com

Simply C#, 1/e
ISBN: 0-13-142641-9
© 2004, pages: 992
More Information
Order it at:
Amazon.com
InformIt.com

Simply Java Programming, 1/e
ISBN: 0-13-142648-6
© 2004, pages: 971
More Information
Order it at:
Amazon.com
Informit.com

Simply Visual Basic 2005, 2/e
ISBN: 0-13-243862-3
© 2007, pages: 800
More Information
Order it at:
Amazon.com
Informit.com

Small C++ How to Program, 5/e
ISBN: 0131857584
© 2005, pages: 848
More Information
Order it at:
Amazon.com
Informit.com

Small Java How to Program, 6/e
ISBN: 0131486608
© 2005, pages: 624
More Information
Order it at:
Amazon.com
Informit.com

Visual Basic 2005 How to Program, 3/e (College Textbook)
ISBN: 0131869000
© 2006, pages: 1513
More Information
Order it at:
Amazon.com
Informit.com

Visual Basic 2005 for Programmers, 2/e (Professional book; Part of the Deitel Developer Series)
ISBN: 013225140X
© 2006, pages: 1300
More Information
Order it at:
Amazon.com
Informit.com

Visual C# 2005 How to Program, 2/e (College Textbook)
ISBN: 0131525239
© 2006, pages: 1591
More Information
Order it at:
Amazon.com
Informit.com

- Detailed ordering information, additional book resources, code downloads and more.

- Available in both HTML or plain-text format.

- Previous issues are archived at: www.deitel.com/newsletter/backissues.html.

- Check out the complete list of Resource Centers at www.deitel.com/ResourceCenters.html.

Turn the page to find out more about Deitel & Associates!

To sign up for the *DEITEL® BUZZ ONLINE* newsletter, visit www.deitel.com/newsletter/subscribe.html.

Deitel & Associates, Inc. provides intensive, lecture-and-laboratory courses to organizations worldwide. The programming courses use our signature *LIVE-CODE Approach*, presenting complete working programs.

Deitel & Associates, Inc. has trained over one million students and professionals worldwide through Dive Into® Series corporate training courses, public seminars, university teaching, *How to Program Series* textbooks, *DEITEL® Developer Series* books, *Simply Series* textbooks, *Cyber Classroom Series* multimedia packages, *Complete Training Course Series* textbook and multimedia packages, broadcast-satellite courses and Web-based training.

Educational Consulting

Deitel & Associates, Inc. offers complete educational consulting services for corporate training programs and professional schools including:

- Curriculum design and development
- Preparation of Instructor Guides
- Customized courses and course materials
- Design and implementation of professional training certificate programs
- Instructor certification
- Train-the-trainers programs
- Delivery of software-related corporate training programs

Visit our Web site for more information on our Dive Into® Series corporate training curriculum and to purchase our training products.

www.deitel.com/training

Would you like to review upcoming publications?

If you are a professor or senior industry professional interested in being a reviewer of our forthcoming publications, please contact us by email at deitel@deitel.com. Insert "Content Reviewer" in the subject heading.

Are you interested in a career in computer education, publishing and training?

We offer a limited number of full-time positions available for college graduates in computer science, information systems, information technology, management information systems, advertising and marketing. Please check our Web site for the latest job postings or contact us by email at deitel@deitel.com. Insert "Full-time Job" in the subject heading.

Are you a Boston-area college student looking for an internship?

We have a limited number of competitive summer positions and 20-hr./week school-year opportunities for computer science, IT/IS, MIS and marketing majors. Students work at our headquarters west of Boston. We also offer full-time internships for students taking a semester off from school. This is an excellent opportunity for students looking to gain industry experience and earn money to pay for school. Please contact us by email at deitel@deitel.com. Insert "Internship" in the subject heading.

Would you like to explore contract training opportunities with us?

Deitel & Associates, Inc. is looking for contract instructors to teach software-related topics at our clients' sites in the United States and worldwide. Applicants should be experienced professional trainers or college professors. For more information, please visit www.deitel.com and send your resume to Abbey Deitel at deitel@deitel.com.

Are you a training company in need of quality course materials?

Corporate training companies worldwide use our *How to Program Series* textbooks, *Complete Training Course Series* book and multimedia packages, *Simply Series* textbooks and our *DEITEL® Developer Series* books in their classes. We have extensive ancillary instructor materials for many of our products. For more details, please visit www.deitel.com or contact us by email at deitel@deitel.com.